Essentials of Sociology

Essentials of Sociology

A Down-to-Earth Approach

Twelfth Edition

James M. Henslin
Southern Illinois University, Edwardsville

Boston   Columbus   Indianapolis   New York   San Francisco   Upper Saddle River
Amsterdam   Cape Town   Dubai   London   Madrid   Milan   Munich   Paris   Montréal   Toronto
Delhi   Mexico City   São Paulo   Sydney   Hong Kong   Seoul   Singapore   Taipei   Tokyo

VP, Product Development: Dickson Musslewhite
Senior Acquisitions Editor: Billy J. Grieco
Editorial Assistant: Amandria Guadalupe
Development Editors: Dusty Friedman/Jennifer Auvil
VP, Director of Marketing: Brandy Dawson
Project Team Lead: Denise Forlow
Project Manager: Marianne Peters-Riordan
Program Team Lead: Maureen Richardson
Program Manager: Joseph Vella
Director of Field Marketing: Jonathan Cottrell
Product Marketer: Tricia Murphy
Field Marketer: Brittany Pogue-Mohammed Acosta
Marketing Assistant, Field Marketing: Andrea Giamis

Marketing Assistant, Product Marketing: Samantha Cilibrasi
Operations Manager: Mary Fischer
Operations Specialist: Mary Ann Gloriande
Director of Design: Blair Brown
Cover Art Director: Maria Lange
Cover Illustration: Alec Doherty
Cover Design: Pentagram
Digital Studio Product Manager: Claudine Bellanton
Digital Studio Project Manager: Rich Barnes
Full-Service Project Management and Composition: Katy Gabel/Lumina Datamatics
Printer/Binder: RR Donnelley/Kendallville
Cover Printer: Phoenix Color/Hagerstown

Acknowledgements of third party content appear on pages CR-1–CR-5, which constitutes an extension of this copyright page. *Cultural Diversity Around the World: Doing Business in the Global Village* box contains art with the following credit: Demashita! Powerpuff Girls Z © 2009 Cartoon Network, Toei Animation & Aniplex. All Rights Reserved. THE POWERPUFF GIRLS and all related characters and elements are trademarks of and © Cartoon Network.

Library of Congress Cataloging-in-Publication Data

Names: Henslin, James M., author.
Title: Essentials of sociology : a down-to-earth approach / James M. Henslin, Southern Illinois University, Edwardsville.
Description: Twelfth edition. | Boston : Pearson Education, [2017]
Identifiers: LCCN 2015043069 | ISBN 9780134205588
Subjects: LCSH: Sociology.
Classification: LCC HM586 .H43 2017 | DDC 301—dc23
LC record available at http://lccn.loc.gov/2015043069

10 9 8 7 6 5 4 3 2 1

Student Edition:
ISBN-10:   0-13-420558-8
ISBN-13: 978-0-13-420558-8

Books A La Carte
ISBN 10:   0-13-420564-2
ISBN 13: 978-0-13-420564-9

To my fellow sociologists,

who do such creative research on social life and who communicate the sociological imagination to generations of students. With my sincere admiration and appreciation,

Jim Henslin

Brief Contents

Contents

Special Features

Down-to-Earth Sociology

Cultural Diversity in the United States

Cultural Diversity around the World

Thinking Critically

Sociology and the New Technology

Mass Media in Social Life

Guide to Social Maps

To the Student ... from the Author

WELCOME TO SOCIOLOGY! I've loved sociology since I was in my teens, and I hope you enjoy it, too. Sociology is fascinating because it is about human behavior, and many of us find that it holds the key to understanding social life.

If you like to watch people and try to figure out why they do what they do, you will like sociology. Sociology pries open the doors of society so you can see what goes on behind them. *Sociology: A Down-to-Earth Approach* stresses how profoundly our society and the groups to which we belong influence us. Social class, for example, sets us on a particular path in life. For some, the path leads to more education, more interesting jobs, higher income, and better health, but for others it leads to dropping out of school, dead-end jobs, poverty, and even a higher risk of illness and disease. These paths are so significant that they affect our chances of making it to our first birthday, as well as of getting in trouble with the police. They even influence our satisfaction in marriage, the number of children we will have—and whether or not we will read this book in the first place.

When I took my first course in sociology, I was "hooked." Seeing how marvelously my life had been affected by these larger social influences opened my eyes to a new world, one that has been fascinating to explore. I hope that you will have this experience, too.

From how people become homeless to how they become presidents, from why people commit suicide to why women are discriminated against in every society around the world—all are part of sociology. This breadth, in fact, is what makes sociology so intriguing. We can place the sociological lens on broad features of society, such as social class, gender, and race–ethnicity, and then immediately turn our focus on the smaller, more intimate level. If we look at two people interacting—whether quarreling or kissing—we see how these broad features of society are being played out in their lives.

We aren't born with instincts. Nor do we come into this world with preconceived notions of what life should be like. At birth, we have no concepts of race–ethnicity, gender, age, or social class. We have no idea, for example, that people "ought" to act in certain ways because they are male or female. Yet we all learn such things as we grow up in our society. Uncovering the "hows" and the "whys" of this process is also part of what makes sociology so fascinating.

One of sociology's many pleasures is that as we study life in groups (which can be taken as a definition of sociology), whether those groups are in some far-off part of the world or in some nearby corner of our own society, we gain new insights into who we are and how we got that way. As we see how *their* customs affect *them*, the effects of our own society on us become more visible.

This book, then, can be part of an intellectual adventure, for it can lead you to a new way of looking at your social world and, in the process, help you to better understand both society and yourself.

I wish you the very best in college—and in your career afterward. It is my sincere desire that *Sociology: A Down-to-Earth Approach* will contribute to that success.

James M. Henslin
Department of Sociology
Southern Illinois University, Edwardsville

P.S. I enjoy communicating with students, so feel free to comment on your experiences with this text. You can write me at henslin@aol.com

To the Instructor ... from the Author

REMEMBER WHEN YOU FIRST GOT "HOOKED" on sociology, how the windows of perception opened as you began to see life-in-society through the sociological perspective? For most of us, this was an eye-opening experience. This text is designed to open those windows onto social life, so students can see clearly the vital effects of group membership on their lives. Although few students will get into what Peter Berger calls "the passion of sociology," we at least can provide them the opportunity.

To study sociology is to embark on a fascinating process of discovery. We can compare sociology to a huge jigsaw puzzle. Only gradually do we see how the smaller pieces fit together. As we begin to see the interconnections, our perspective changes as we shift our eyes from the many small, disjointed pieces to the whole that is being formed. Of all the endeavors we could have entered, we chose sociology because of the ways in which it joins the "pieces" of society together and the challenges it poses to "ordinary" thinking. It is our privilege to share with students this process of awareness and discovery called the sociological perspective.

As instructors of sociology, we have set ambitious goals for ourselves: to teach both social structure and social interaction and to introduce students to the sociological literature—both the classic theorists and contemporary research. As we accomplish this, we would also like to enliven the classroom, encourage critical thinking, and stimulate our students' sociological imagination. Although formidable, these goals *are* attainable. This book is designed to help you reach them. Based on many years of frontline (classroom) experience, its subtitle, *A Down-to-Earth Approach*, was not proposed lightly. My goal is to share the fascination of sociology with students and in doing so to make your teaching more rewarding.

One of the fascinating aspects of the introductory course in sociology is to see students' faces light up as they begin to see how separate pieces of their world fit together. It is a pleasure to watch them gain insight into how their social experiences give shape to even their innermost desires. This is precisely what this text is designed to do—to stimulate your students' sociological imagination so they can better perceive how the "pieces" of society fit together—and what this means for their own lives.

Filled with examples from around the world as well as from our own society, this text helps to make today's multicultural, global society come alive for students. From learning how the international elite carve up global markets to studying the intimacy of friendship and marriage, students can see how sociology is the key to explaining contemporary life—and their own place in it.

In short, this text is designed to make your teaching easier. There simply is no justification for students to have to wade through cumbersome approaches to sociology. I am firmly convinced that the introduction to sociology should be enjoyable and that the introductory textbook can be an essential tool in sharing the discovery of sociology with students.

The Organization of This Text

The text is laid out in five parts. Part I focuses on the sociological perspective, which is introduced in the first chapter. We then look at how culture influences us (Chapter 2), examine socialization (Chapter 3), and compare macrosociology and microsociology (Chapter 4).

Part II, which focuses on groups and social control, adds to the students' understanding of how far-reaching society's influence is—how group membership penetrates even our thinking, attitudes, and orientations to life. We first examine the different types of groups that have such profound influences on us and then look at the fascinating area of group dynamics (Chapter 5). After this, we focus on how groups "keep us in line" and sanction those who violate their norms (Chapter 6).

In Part III, we turn our focus on social inequality, examining how it pervades society and how it has an impact on our own lives. Because social stratification is so significant, I have written two chapters on this topic. The first (Chapter 7), with its global focus, presents an overview of the principles of stratification. The second (Chapter 8), with its emphasis on social class, focuses on stratification in the United States. After establishing this broader context of social stratification, we examine inequalities of race–ethnicity (Chapter 9) and then those of gender and age (Chapter 10).

Part IV helps students to become more aware of how social institutions encompass their lives. We first look at politics and the economy, our overarching social institutions (Chapter 11). After examining the family (Chapter 12), we then turn our focus on education and religion (Chapter 13). One of the emphases in this part of the book is how our social institutions are changing and how their changes, in turn, influence our orientations and decisions.

With its focus on broad social change, Part V provides an appropriate conclusion for the book. Here we examine why our world is changing so rapidly, as well as catch a glimpse of what is yet to come. We first analyze trends in population and urbanization, those sweeping forces that affect our lives so significantly but that ordinarily remain below our level of awareness (Chapter 14). We conclude the book with an analysis of technology, social movements, and the environment (Chapter 15), which takes us to the cutting edge of the vital changes that engulf us all.

Themes and Features

Six central themes run throughout this text: down-to-earth sociology, globalization, cultural diversity, critical thinking, the new technology, and the influence of the mass media on our lives. For each of these themes, except globalization, which is incorporated throughout the text, I have written a series of boxes. These boxed features are one of my favorite components of the book. They are especially useful for introducing the controversial topics that make sociology such a lively activity.

Let's look at these six themes.

Down-to-Earth Sociology

As many years of teaching have shown me, all too often textbooks are written to appeal to the adopters of texts rather than to the students who will learn from them. In writing this book, my central concern has been to present sociology in a way that not only facilitates understanding but also shares its excitement. During the course of writing other texts, I often have been told that my explanations and writing style are "down-to-earth," or accessible and inviting to students—so much so that I chose this phrase as the book's subtitle. The term is also featured in my introductory reader, *Down-to-Earth Sociology: Introductory Readings*, to appear in its 15th edition (New York: The Free Press, 2017).

This first theme is highlighted by a series of boxed features that explore sociological processes that underlie everyday life. The topics that we review in these *Down-to-Earth Sociology* boxes are highly diverse. Here are some of them.

- How a sociologist became a gang leader—for a day (Chapter 1)
- The experiences of W. E. B. Du Bois, an early sociologist, in studying U.S. race relations (Chapter 1)
- How gossip and ridicule enforce adolescent norms (Chapter 3)
- Boot camp as a total institution (Chapter 3)
- How football can help us understand social structure (Chapter 4)
- Beauty and success (Chapter 4)
- The McDonaldization of society (Chapter 5)
- Serial killers (Chapter 6)
- Urban gangs (Chapter 6)

- What life is like after hitting it big in the lottery (Chapter 8)
- How the super-rich live (Chapter 8)
- National research on the American Dream: Actual social mobility (Chapter 8)
- Stealth racism in the rental market (Chapter 9)
- How a man became a live exhibit in a New York zoo (Chapter 9)
- Greedy surgeons and their women victims (Chapter 10)
- Do we need affirmative action for men? (Chapter 10)
- Testing stereotypes by looking at the background of suicide terrorists (Chapter 12)
- Our chances of getting divorced (Chapter 12)
- How tsunamis can help us to understand world population growth (Chapter 14)
- The possible dangers of bio foods (Chapter 14)
- Deception and persuasion in propaganda (Chapter 15)

This first theme is actually a hallmark of the text, as my goal is to make sociology "down to earth." To help students grasp the fascination of sociology, I continuously stress sociology's relevance to their lives. To reinforce this theme, I avoid unnecessary jargon and use concise explanations and clear and simple (but not reductive) language. I also use student-relevant examples to illustrate key concepts, and I base several of the chapters' opening vignettes on my own experiences in exploring social life. That this goal of sharing sociology's fascination is being reached is evident from the many comments I receive from instructors and students alike that the text helps make sociology "come alive."

Globalization

In the second theme, *globalization*, we explore the impact of global issues on our lives and on the lives of people around the world. All of us are feeling the effects of an increasingly powerful and encompassing global economy, one that intertwines the fates of nations. The globalization of capitalism influences the kinds of skills and knowledge we need, the types of work available to us—and whether work is available at all. Globalization also underlies the costs of the goods and services we consume and whether our country is at war or peace—or in some uncharted middle ground between the two. In addition to the strong emphasis on global issues that runs throughout this text, I have written a separate chapter on global stratification (Chapter 7). I also feature global issues in the chapters on social institutions and the final chapters on social change: population, urbanization, social movements, and the environment.

What occurs in Russia, Germany, and China, as well as in much smaller nations, such as Syria and Iraq, has far-reaching consequences on our own lives. Consequently, in addition to the global focus that runs throughout the text, the next theme, cultural diversity, also has a strong global emphasis.

Cultural Diversity around the World and in the United States

The third theme, *cultural diversity*, has two primary emphases. The first is cultural diversity around the world. Gaining an understanding of how social life is "done" in other parts of the world often challenges our taken-for-granted assumptions about social life. At times, when we learn about other cultures, we gain an appreciation for the life of other peoples; at other times, we may be shocked or even disgusted at some aspect of another group's way of life (such as female circumcision) and come away with a renewed appreciation of our own customs.

To highlight this first subtheme, I have written a series of boxes called **Cultural Diversity around the World.** Among the topics with this subtheme are

- food customs that shock people from different cultures (Chapter 2)
- why the dead need money (Chapter 2)
- where virgins become men (Chapter 3)
- human sexuality in Mexico and Kenya (Chapter 6)
- how blaming the rape victim protects India's caste system (Chapter 6)
- female circumcision (Chapter 10)
- the life of child workers (Chapter 11)
- China's new capitalism (Chapter 11)
- love and arranged marriage in India (Chapter 12)
- female infanticide in China and India (Chapter 14)
- urbanization in the Least Industrialized Nations (Chapter 14)
- the destruction of the rain forests and indigenous peoples of Brazil (Chapter 15)

In the second subtheme, **Cultural Diversity in the United States,** we examine groups that make up the fascinating array of people who form the U.S. population. The boxes I have written with this subtheme review such topics as

- how studying job discrimination turned into public sociology (Chapter 1)
- the language of race (Chapter 2)
- the controversy over the use of Spanish or English (Chapter 2)
- how education can cause conflict for immigrants (Chapter 3)
- how the Amish resist social change (Chapter 4)
- how our social networks produce social inequality (Chapter 5)
- how Tiger Woods represents a changing racial–ethnic identity (Chapter 9)
- the author's travels with a Mexican who transports undocumented workers to the U.S. border (Chapter 9)

- human heads, animal sacrifices, and religious freedom (Chapter 13)

Seeing that there are so many ways of "doing" social life can remove some of our cultural smugness, making us more aware of how arbitrary our own customs are—and how our taken-for-granted ways of thinking are rooted in culture. The stimulating contexts of these contrasts can help students develop their sociological imagination. They encourage students to see connections among key sociological concepts, such as culture, socialization, norms, race–ethnicity, gender, and social class. As your students' sociological imagination grows, they can attain a new perspective on their experiences in their own corners of life—and a better understanding of the social structure of U.S. society.

Critical Thinking

In our fourth theme, *critical thinking*, we focus on controversial social issues, inviting students to examine various sides of those issues. In these sections, titled **Thinking Critically,** I present objective, fair portrayals of positions and do not take a side—although occasionally I do play the "devil's advocate" in the questions that close each of the topics. Like the boxed features, these sections can enliven your classroom with a vibrant exchange of ideas. Among the social issues we tackle are

- are we prisoners of our genes? (Chapter 2)
- managing diversity in the workplace (Chapter 5)
- our tendency to conform to evil authority (the Milgram experiments) (Chapter 5)
- labeling in everyday life illustrated by the Saints and the Roughnecks: (Chapter 6)
- bounties paid to kill homeless children in Brazil (Chapter 7)
- *maquiladoras* on the Mexican–U.S. border (Chapter 7)
- the deserving and the undeserving poor (Chapter 8)
- emerging masculinities and femininities (Chapter 10)
- targeted killings (Chapter 11)
- the coming disappearance of some island nations (Chapter 15)
- cyber war and cyber defense (Chapter 15)
- ecosabotage (Chapter 15)

These *Thinking Critically* sections are based on controversial social issues that either affect the student's own life or focus on topics that have intrinsic interest for students. Because of their controversial nature, these sections stimulate both critical thinking and lively class discussions. These sections also provide provocative topics for in-class debates and small discussion groups, effective ways to enliven a class and present sociological ideas. In the Instructor's Manual, I describe the nuts and bolts of using small groups in the classroom.

Sociology and the New Technology

The fifth theme, *sociology and the new technology*, explores an aspect of social life that has come to be central in our lives. We welcome these new technological tools, for they help us to be more efficient at performing our daily tasks, from making a living to communicating with others—whether those people are nearby or on the other side of the globe. The significance of our new technology, however, extends far beyond the tools and the ease and efficiency they bring to our lives. The new technology is better envisioned as a social revolution that will leave few aspects of our lives untouched. Its effects are so profound that it even changes the ways we view life.

This theme is introduced in Chapter 2, where technology is defined and presented as a major aspect of culture. The impact of technology is then discussed throughout the text. Examples include how technology is related to cultural change (Chapter 2), fantasy life (Chapter 4), the control of workers (Chapter 5), and the maintenance of global stratification (Chapter 7). We also examine how technology led to social inequality in early human history and how it now may lead to world peace—and to Big Brother's net thrown over us all (Chapter 11). The final chapter (Chapter 15), "Social Change and the Environment," concludes the book with a focus on the effects of technology.

To highlight this theme, I have written a series of boxes called **Sociology and the New Technology.** In these boxes, we explore how technology affects our lives as it changes society. We examine how technology

- is making our clothing smart (Chapter 2)
- blurs the distinction between reality and fantasy (Chapter 4)
- is changing the way people find mates (Chapter 12)
- is changing the way families handle disagreements (Chapter 12)
- by allowing "designer babies," might change society (Chapter 12)
- is likely to lead to real "star wars" (Chapter 15)

The Mass Media and Social Life

In the sixth theme, we stress how the *mass media* influence our behavior and permeate our thinking. We consider how they penetrate our consciousness to such a degree that they even influence how we perceive our own bodies. As your students consider this theme, they may begin to grasp how the mass media shape their attitudes. If so, they will come to view the mass media in a different light, which should further stimulate their sociological imagination.

To make this theme more prominent for students, I have written a series of boxed features called **Mass Media in Social Life.** Among these are

- the presentation of gender in computer games (Chapter 3)
- the worship of thinness—and how this affects our body images (Chapter 4)
- the reemergence of slavery in today's world (Chapter 7)
- the slowly changing status of women in Iran (Chapter 10)
- how the mass media shape our perceptions of the elderly (Chapter 10)
- the myth of increasing school shootings (Chapter 13)
- God on the Net (Chapter 13)

What's New in This Edition?

It is always a goal—as well as a pleasure and a challenge—to keep *Essentials of Sociology* current with cutting–edge sociological research and to incorporate into the analyses national and global changes that affect our lives. For an indication of the thoroughness of incorporating recent sociological research and current events, look at the chapter-by-chapter listing of this edition's changes in "What's New In The 12th Edition?" on page xxix.

As is discussed in the next section, some of the most interesting—and even fascinating—topics are presented in a visual form.

Visual Presentations of Sociology

SHOWING CHANGES OVER TIME　A hallmark of this text is showing how social change affects your students' lives. Many figures and tables show how social data have changed over time. This allows students to see trends in social life and to make predictions of how these trends, if they continue, might affect their own lives. Examples include Figure 1.5, *U.S. Marriage, U.S. Divorce* (Chapter 1) Figure 8.3, *The More Things Change, the More They Stay the Same: Dividing the Nation's Income* (Chapter 8); Figure 10.2, *Changes in College Enrollment, by Sex* (Chapter 10); Figure 10.17, *Trends in Poverty* (Chapter 10); Figure 12.4, *The Number of Children Americans Think Are Ideal* (Chapter 12), and Figure 12.11, *Cohabitation in the United States* (Chapter 12).

THROUGH THE AUTHOR'S LENS　Using this format, in which I share sociological research by means of photos I have taken, students are able to look over my shoulder as I experience other cultures or explore aspects of this one. These eight photo essays should expand your students' sociological imagination and open their minds to other ways of doing social life, as well as stimulate thought-provoking class discussions.

VIENNA: SOCIAL STRUCTURE AND SOCIAL INTERACTION IN A VIBRANT CITY　appears in Chapter 4. The photos I took in this city illustrate how social structure surrounds us, setting the scene for our interactions, limiting and directing them.

WHEN A TORNADO STRIKES: SOCIAL ORGANIZATION FOLLOWING A NATURAL DISASTER   When a tornado hit a small town just hours from where I lived, I photographed the aftermath of the disaster. The police let me in to view the neighborhood where the tornado had struck, destroying homes and killing several people. I was impressed by how quickly people were putting their lives back together, the topic of this photo essay (Chapter 4).

COMMUNITY IN THE CITY,   in Chapter 5, is also from Vienna. This sequence of four photos focuses on strangers who are helping a man who has just fallen. This event casts doubt on the results of Darley and Latane's laboratory experiments. This short sequence was serendipitous in my research. One of my favorite photos is the last in the series, which portrays the cop coming toward me to question why I was taking photos of the accident. It fits the sequence perfectly.

THE DUMP PEOPLE: WORKING AND LIVING AND PLAYING IN THE CITY DUMP OF PHNOM PENH, CAMBODIA   Among the culture shocks I experienced in Cambodia was not to discover that people scavenge at Phnom Penh's huge city dump—this I knew about—but that they also live there. With the aid of an interpreter, I was able to interview these people, as well as photograph them as they went about their everyday lives. An entire community lives in the city dump, complete with restaurants amid the smoke and piles of garbage. This photo essay reveals not just these people's activities but also their social organization (Chapter 7).

WORK AND GENDER: WOMEN AT WORK IN INDIA   As I traveled in India, I took photos of women at work in public places. The more I traveled in this country and the more photos I took, the more insight I gained into gender relations. Despite the general dominance of men in India, women's worlds are far from limited to family and home. Women are found at work throughout the society. What is even more remarkable is how vastly different "women's work" is in India than it is in the United States. This, too, is an intellectually provocative photo essay (Chapter 10).

SMALL TOWN USA: STRUGGLING TO SURVIVE   To take the photos for this essay, I went off the beaten path. On a road trip from California to Florida, instead of following the interstates, I followed those "little black lines" on the map. They took me to out-of-the-way places that the national transportation system has bypassed. Many of these little towns are putting on a valiant face as they struggle to survive, but, as the photos show, the struggle is apparent, and, in some cases, so are the scars (Chapter 11).

HOLY WEEK IN SPAIN   I was fortunate to be able to photograph religious processions in two cities, Malaga, a provincial capital, and Almuñecar, a smaller city of Granada. Spain has a Roman Catholic heritage so deep that some of its city streets are named Conception, Piety, Humility, Calvary, Crucifixion, The Blessed Virgin, etc. In large and small towns throughout Spain, elaborate processions during Holy Week feature *tronos* that depict the biblical account of Jesus' suffering, death, and resurrection. As these photos make clear, these events have a decidedly Spanish flavor.

I was allowed to photograph the preparations for one of the processions, so this essay also includes "behind-the-scenes" photos.

During the processions in Malaga, the participants walk slowly for one or two minutes; then because of the weight of the *tronos*, they rest for one or two minutes. Except for Saturdays, this process repeats for about six hours each day during Holy Week, with different *tronos* featured and different bands and organizations participating. As you will see, some of the most interesting activities occur during the rest periods (Chapter 13).

A WALK THROUGH EL TIRO IN MEDELLIN, COLOMBIA   One of the most significant social changes in the world is taking place in the Least Industrialized Nations. There, in the search for a better life, people are abandoning rural areas. Fleeing poverty, they are flocking to the cities, only to find even more poverty. Some of these settlements of the new urban poor are dangerous. I was fortunate to be escorted by an insider through a section of Medellin, Colombia, that is controlled by gangs (Chapter 14).

OTHER PHOTOS BY THE AUTHOR   Sprinkled throughout the text are photos that I took in Austria, Cambodia, India, Latvia, Spain, and the United States. These photos illustrate sociological principles and topics better than photos available from commercial sources. As an example, while in the United States, I received a report about a feral child who had been discovered living with monkeys and who had been taken to an orphanage in Cambodia. The possibility of photographing and interviewing that child was one of the reasons that I went to Cambodia. That particular photo is on page 69. Another of my favorites is on page 198.

PHOTO ESSAY ON SUBCULTURES   To help students better understand subcultures, I have produced the photo essay on subcultures in Chapter 2. Because this photo essay consists of photos taken by others, it is not a part of the series, Through the Author's Lens. The variety of subcultures featured in this photo essay, however, should be instructive to your students.

PHOTO COLLAGES   Because sociology lends itself so well to photographic illustrations, this text also includes photo collages. I am very pleased with the one in Chapter 1 that features some of the many women who became sociologists in earlier generations, as these women have largely gone unacknowledged as sociologists.

Other Special Pedagogical Features

In addition to chapter summaries and reviews, key terms, and a comprehensive glossary, I have included several special features to help students learn sociology. **In Sum** sections help students review important points within the chapter before going on to new materials. I have also developed a series of **Social Maps** that illustrate how social conditions vary by geography. These social maps, personally prepared, are unique to my texts.

Learning Objectives To help students, *learning objectives* are woven into the text. This feature enhances your students' mastery of the materials. As students move to a new section, they can understand clearly what they are expected to learn in that section. The learning objectives are introduced at the beginning of each chapter, then repeated in the Summary and Review at the end of the chapter.

CHAPTER-OPENING VIGNETTES These accounts feature down-to-earth illustrations of a major aspect of each chapter's content. Some are based on my research with the homeless, the time I spent with them on the streets and slept in their shelters (Chapters 1 and 8). Others recount my travels in Africa (Chapters 2 and 10) and Mexico (Chapters 12 and 14). I also share my experiences when I spent a night with street people at Dupont Circle in Washington, D.C. (Chapter 4). For other vignettes, I use current and historical events (Chapters 7, 9, 13, and 15), classic studies in the social sciences (Chapters 3 and 6), and even scenes from novels (Chapters 5 and 11). Students have often told me that they find the vignettes compelling, that they stimulate interest in the chapter.

THINKING CRITICALLY ABOUT THE CHAPTERS I close each chapter with critical thinking questions. Each question focuses on a major feature of the chapter, asking students to reflect on and consider some issue. Many of the questions ask the students to apply sociological findings and principles to their own lives.

ON SOURCES Sociological data are found in a wide variety of sources, and this text reflects that variety. Cited throughout this text are standard journals such as the *American Journal of Sociology, Social Problems, American Sociological Review*, and *Journal of Marriage and Family*, as well as more esoteric journals such as the *Bulletin of the History of Medicine, Chronobiology International*, and *Western Journal of Black Studies*. I have also drawn heavily from standard news sources, especially the *New York Times* and the *Wall Street Journal*, as well as more unusual sources such as *El País*. In addition, I cite unpublished research and theoretical papers by sociologists.

Acknowledgments

The gratifying response to this text's earlier editions indicates that my efforts at making sociology down-to-earth have succeeded. The years that have gone into writing this text are a culmination of the many years that preceded its writing—from graduate school to that equally demanding endeavor known as classroom teaching. No text, of course, comes solely from its author. Although I am responsible for the final words on the printed page, I have received excellent feedback from instructors who have taught from the first eleven editions.

Reviewers of the First through Eleventh Editions

Francis O. Adeola, *University of New Orleans*
Brian W. Agnitsch, *Marshalltown Community College*
Sandra L. Albrecht, *The University of Kansas*
Christina Alexander, *Linfield College*
Richard Alman, *Sierra College*
Gabriel C. Alvarez, *Duquesne University*
Kenneth Ambrose, *Marshall University*
Alberto Arroyo, *Baldwin–Wallace College*
Karren Baird-Olsen, *Kansas State University*
Rafael Balderrama, *University of Texas—Pan American*
Linda Barbera-Stein, *The University of Illinois*
Brenda Blackburn, *California State University—Fullerton*
Ronnie J. Booxbaum, *Greenfield Community College*
Cecil D. Bradfield, *James Madison University*
Karen Bradley, *Central Missouri State University*
Francis Broouer, *Worcester State College*
Valerie S. Brown, *Cuyahoga Community College*
Sandi Brunette-Hill, *Carrol College*
Richard Brunk, *Francis Marion University*
Karen Bullock, *Salem State College*
Allison R. Camelot, *California State University—Fullerton*
Paul Ciccantell, *Kansas State University*
John K. Cochran, *The University of Oklahoma*
James M. Cook, *Duke University*
Joan Cook-Zimmern, *College of Saint Mary*
Larry Curiel, *Cypress College*
Russell L. Curtis, *University of Houston*
John Darling, *University of Pittsburgh—Johnstown*
Ray Darville, *Stephen F. Austin State University*
Jim David, *Butler County Community College*
Nanette J. Davis, *Portland State University*
Vincent Davis, *Mt. Hood Community College*
Lynda Dodgen, *North Harris Community College*
Terry Dougherty, *Portland State University*
Marlese Durr, *Wright State University*
Helen R. Ebaugh, *University of Houston*
Obi N. Ebbe, *State University of New York—Brockport*
Cy Edwards, Chair, *Cypress Community College*
John Ehle, *Northern Virginia Community College*

Morten Ender, *U.S. Military Academy*
Rebecca Susan Fahrlander, *Bellevue University*
Louis J. Finkle, *Horry-Georgetown Technical College*
Nicole T. Flynn, *University of South Alabama*
Lorna E. Forster, *Clinton Community College*
David O. Friedrichs, *University of Scranton*
Bruce Friesen, *Kent State University—Stark*
Lada Gibson-Shreve, *Stark State College*
Norman Goodman, *State University of New York—Stony Brook*
Rosalind Gottfried, *San Joaquin Delta College*
G. Kathleen Grant, *The University of Findlay*
Bill Grisby, *University of Northern Colorado*
Ramon Guerra, *University of Texas—Pan American*
Remi Hajjar, *U.S. Military Academy*
Donald W. Hastings, *The University of Tennessee—Knoxville*
Lillian O. Holloman, *Prince George's Community College*
Michael Hoover, *Missouri Western State College*
Howard R. Housen, *Broward Community College*
James H. Huber, *Bloomsburg University*
Erwin Hummel, *Portland State University*
Charles E. Hurst, *The College of Wooster*
Nita Jackson, *Butler County Community College*
Jennifer A. Johnson, *Germanna Community College*
Kathleen R. Johnson, *Keene State College*
Tammy Jolley, *University of Arkansas Community College at Batesville*
David Jones, *Plymouth State College*
Arunas Juska, *East Carolina University*
Ali Kamali, *Missouri Western State College*
Irwin Kantor, *Middlesex County College*
Mark Kassop, *Bergen Community College*
Myles Kelleher, *Bucks County Community College*
Mary E. Kelly, *Central Missouri State University*
Alice Abel Kemp, *University of New Orleans*
Diana Kendall, *Austin Community College*
Gary Kiger, *Utah State University*
Gene W. Kilpatrick, *University of Maine—Presque Isle*
Jerome R. Koch, *Texas Tech University*
Joseph A. Kotarba, *University of Houston*
Michele Lee Kozimor-King, *Pennsylvania State University*
Darina Lepadatu, *Kennesaw State University*
Abraham Levine, *El Camino Community College*
Diane Levy, *The University of North Carolina—Wilmington*
Stephen Mabry, *Cedar Valley College*
David Maines, *Oakland University*
Ron Matson, *Wichita State University*
Armaund L. Mauss, *Washington State University*
Evelyn Mercer, *Southwest Baptist University*
Robert Meyer, *Arkansas State University*
Michael V. Miller, *University of Texas—San Antonio*
John Mitrano, *Central Connecticut State University*

W. Lawrence Neuman, *University of Wisconsin—Whitewater*

Charles Norman, *Indiana State University*

Patricia H. O'Brien, *Elgin Community College*

Robert Ostrow, *Wayne State*

Laura O'Toole, *University of Delaware*

Mike K. Pate, *Western Oklahoma State College*

Lawrence Peck, *Erie Community College*

Ruth Pigott, *University of Nebraska—Kearney*

Phil Piket, *Joliet Junior College*

Trevor Pinch, *Cornell University*

Daniel Polak, *Hudson Valley Community College*

James Pond, *Butler Community College*

Deedy Ramo, *Del Mar College*

Adrian Rapp, *North Harris Community College*

Ray Rich, *Community College of Southern Nevada*

Barbara Richardson, *Eastern Michigan University*

Salvador Rivera, *State University of New York—Cobleskill*

Howard Robboy, *Trenton State College*

Paulina X. Ruf, *University of Tampa*

Michael Samano, *Portland Community College*

Michael L. Sanow, *Community College of Baltimore County*

Mary C. Sengstock, *Wayne State University*

Walt Shirley, *Sinclair Community College*

Marc Silver, *Hofstra University*

Roberto E. Socas, *Essex County College*

Susan Sprecher, *Illinois State University*

Mariella Rose Squire, *University of Maine at Fort Kent*

Rachel Stehle, *Cuyahoga Community College*

Marios Stephanides, *University of Tampa*

Randolph G. Ston, *Oakland Community College*

Vickie Holland Taylor, *Danville Community College*

Maria Jose Tenuto, *College of Lake County*

Gary Tiederman, *Oregon State University*

Kathleen Tiemann, *University of North Dakota*

Judy Turchetta, *Johnson & Wales University*

Stephen L. Vassar, *Minnesota State University—Mankato*

William J. Wattendorf, *Adirondack Community College*

Jay Weinstein, *Eastern Michigan University*

Larry Weiss, *University of Alaska*

Douglas White, *Henry Ford Community College*

Stephen R. Wilson, *Temple University*

Anthony T. Woart, *Middlesex Community College*

Stuart Wright, *Lamar University*

Mary Lou Wylie, *James Madison University*

Diane Kholos Wysocki, *University of Nebraska—Kearney*

Stacey G. H. Yap, *Plymouth State College*

William Yoels, *University of Alabama Birmingham*

I couldn't ask for a more outstanding team than the one that I have the pleasure to work with at Pearson. I want to thank Billy Grieco and Emily Tamburri, who joined the team for this 12th edition, for coordinating the many tasks that were necessary to produce this new edition; Diane Melliot, who provided excellent research, tracking down both standard and esoteric items that made an impact on the book; Jenn Auvil, for for juggling so many tasks; Dusty Friedman, for working with me on yet another edition; and Kate Cebik, for her creativity in photo research and for her willingness to "keep on looking"; and for the many others, unnamed, who worked behind the scenes to help make this text accessible to students.

I appreciate this team. It is difficult to heap too much praise on fine, capable, and creative people. Often going "beyond the call of duty" as we faced nonstop deadlines, their untiring efforts coalesced with mine to produce this text. Students, whom we constantly kept in mind as we prepared this edition and exchanged many hundreds of emails, are the beneficiaries of this intricate teamwork.

I would also like to thank those who prepared the supplements that go with *Essentials of Sociology*. Their efforts, so often unacknowledged, are important in our goal of introducing students to sociology and awakening their sociological imagination. The Instructor's Manual/Test Bank for this edition of *Essentials of Sociology* was prepared by Jessica Herrmeyer.

Since this text is based on the contributions of many, I would count it a privilege if you would share with me your teaching experiences with this book, including suggestions for improving the text. Both positive and negative comments are welcome. This is one way that I continue to learn.

I wish you the very best in your teaching. It is my sincere desire that *Sociology: A Down-to-Earth Approach* contributes to your classroom success.

James M. Henslin
Professor Emeritus
Department of Sociology
Southern Illinois University, Edwardsville

I welcome your correspondence. You can reach me at henslin@aol.com

What's New in the 12th Edition?

Chapter 2 Culture

Cultural Diversity around the World box: Why the Dead Need Money

Sociology and the New Technology box: How Smart Is Your Clothing?

Topic: The coming wearable computers will make Google Glass look like a museum piece

Chapter 3 Socialization

Topic: Transitional adulthood has become so extended that some companies have a "Bring Your Parents to Work Day"

Topic: Research on orphans in Romania, with experimental and control groups shows that personalized care improves not only social skills but also increases brain cells

Topic: A university is offering a varsity sports scholarship in videogames

Chapter 4 Social Structure and Social Interaction

Topic: To apply body language, Homeland Security spends $200 million a year on training" Behavior Detection Officers"

Topic: Attractive people are treated more favorably by judges and juries

Topic: "Image consultants" teach women executives how to display power amidst "soft" femininity

Chapter 5 Social Groups and Formal Organizations

Sociology and the New Technology box: Welcome to the Memory Hole: Enjoy the Security State

Chapter 6 Deviance and Social Control

Down-to-Earth Sociology box: Sexting: Getting On the Phone Isn't What It Used to Be

Figure 6.3 How Fast They Return: Recidivism of U.S. Prisoners

Topic: Differential association in the cyber age

Topic: Mexico moves against the militias that citizens have formed to fight the drug cartels

Topic: GM executives did not take action on the ignition problem that accidently turned off the engine and air bags, even though it caused many deaths.

Chapter 7 Global Stratification

Down-to-Earth Sociology box: Inequality? What Inequality?

Topic: The FBI is pressuring Google and Amazon to stop sales of encrypted mobile devices

Chapter 8 Social Class in the United States

Thinking Critically section: The Frightful Future: The Three-Tier Society

Figure 8.12 How Does Income Influence Births to Single Women?

Topic: The gender gap in social mobility: As adults, women are less likely than men to live in families with higher income than the one in which they grew up

Topic: Larry Ellison has a basketball court on his yacht and a basketball retriever who trails the yacht, scooping up errant balls

Topic: A $39,000 backpack for the ultra-rich by Ashley and Mary-Kate Olsen.

Topic: The Waltons of Wal-Mart fame are worth more than the bottom 40 percent of all Americans

Topic: Callie Rogers, youngest lottery winner in Great Britain, added to the box on lottery winners

Chapter 9 Race and Ethnicity

Topic: Supreme Court upholds states' rights to ban affirmative action in college admissions

Topic: Associate's degree added to Table 9.3

Topic: North Koreans who defile the "sacred Korean race" are tortured, raped, and starved

Topic: Native American tribes clash over casino profits

Topic: Donald Sterling forced to forfeit the ownership of the Los Angeles Clippers, banned from professional basketball for life, and fined $2.5 million

Topic: Social class as the answer to the affirmative action controversy in college admissions

Chapter 10 Gender and Age

Thinking Critically section: New Masculinities and Femininities Are on the Way

Topic: *Swara*, a practice in tribal areas of Pakistan: Unmarried girls, even children, are given as brides to compensate a family for a man's crime

Chapter 11 Politics and the Economy

Topic: New research by Gilens and Page on 1,800 policy decisions by the U.S. government supports the power elite perspective.

Chapter 12 Marriage and Family

Topic: The single father

Topic: Same-sex and heterosexual couples have about the same rate of divorce

Topic: Uber as a parent substitute

Chapter 13 Education and Religion

Down-to-Earth Sociology box: You Want to Get Through College? Let's Apply Sociology

Chapter 14 Population and Urbanization

Topic: To encourage childbirth, officials in Turkey pin a gold medal on women who have their first child

Topic: Since the 1990s, world hunger has dropped 40 percent

Topic: Update on the controversy over biofoods

Topic: Corporate funding and the threat to objective scientific research

Topic: There are 28 megacities; by 2030 there will be 41.

Topic: Edge cities are being changed to give them the look and feel of traditional cities

Topic: Forced urbanization: deciding that urbanization fuels economic growth, China's top leaders are forcing villagers to move to the city

Topic: Some aging suburbs are turning their malls into town centers

Topic: Megaregions have developed.

A Note from the Publisher on the Supplements

Instructor Supplements

Unless otherwise noted, instructor supplements are available at no charge to adopters—in electronic formats through the Instructor's Resource Center (www.pearsonhighered.com/irc).

Instructor's Manual and Test Bank

For each chapter in the text, the Instructor's Manual provides a list of key changes to the new edition, chapter summaries and outlines, learning objectives, key terms and people, discussion topics, classroom activities, recommended films and Web sites, and additional references. The Instructor's Manual also includes sample syllabi and a section by Jim Henslin on how to make your class more interactive and stimulating by using small, in-class discussion groups.

Test Bank

The Test Bank contains approximately 125 questions for each chapter in multiple-choice, true/false, short answer, essay, and matching formats. There is also a set of questions based on the text's figures, tables, and maps. The questions are correlated to each chapter's in-text learning objectives.

MyTest Computerized Test Bank

The printed Test Bank is also available online through Pearson's computerized testing system, MyTest. The user-friendly interface allows you to view, edit, and add questions, transfer questions to tests, and print tests in a variety of fonts. Search and sort features allow you to locate questions quickly and to arrange them in whatever order you prefer. The Test Bank can be accessed anywhere with a free MyTest user account. There is no need to download a program or file to your computer.

PowerPoint Presentation Slides

Lecture PowerPoint Presentations are available for this edition. The lecture slides outline each chapter of the text, while the line art slides provide the charts, graphs, and maps found in the text. PowerPoint software is not required as PowerPoint viewer is included.

REVEL™

Educational technology designed for the way today's students read, think, and learn

When students are engaged deeply, they learn more effectively and perform better in their courses. This simple fact inspired the creation of REVEL: an immersive learning experience designed for the way today's students read, think, and learn. Built in collaboration with educators and students nationwide, REVEL is the newest, fully digital way to deliver respected Pearson content.

REVEL enlivens course content with media interactives and assessments — integrated directly within the authors' narrative — that provide opportunities for students to read about and practice the course material in tandem. This immersive educational technology boosts student engagement, which leads to better understanding of concepts and improved performance throughout the course.

Learn more about REVEL http://www.pearsonhighered.com/revel/

About the Author

Jim Henslin was born in Minnesota, graduated from high school and junior college in California and from college in Indiana. Awarded scholarships, he earned his master's and doctorate degrees in sociology at Washington University in St. Louis, Missouri. After this, he won a postdoctoral fellowship from the National Institute of Mental Health and spent a year studying how people adjust to the suicide of a family member. His primary interests in sociology are the sociology of everyday life, deviance, and international relations. Among his many books are *Down-to-Earth Sociology: Introductory Readings* (Free Press), soon in its 15th edition, and *Social Problems* (Allyn and Bacon), soon to be in its 12th edition. He has also published widely in sociology journals, including *Social Problems* and *American Journal of Sociology*.

While a graduate student, Jim taught at the University of Missouri at St. Louis. After completing his doctorate, he joined the faculty at Southern Illinois University, Edwardsville, where he is Professor Emeritus of Sociology. He says, "I've always found the introductory course enjoyable to teach. I love to see students' faces light up when they first glimpse the sociological perspective and begin to see how society has become an essential part of how they view the world."

Jim enjoys reading and fishing, and he also does a bit of kayaking and weight lifting. His two favorite activities are writing and traveling. He especially enjoys visiting and living in other cultures, for this brings him face to face with behaviors and ways of thinking that challenge his perspectives and "make sociological principles come alive." A special pleasure has been the preparation of *Through the Author's Lens*, the series of photo essays that appear in this text.

Jim moved to Latvia, an Eastern European country formerly dominated by the Soviet Union, where he had the experience of becoming an immigrant. There he observed firsthand how people struggle to adjust to capitalism. While there, he interviewed aged political prisoners who had survived the Soviet gulag. He then moved to Spain, where he was able to observe how people adjust to a declining economy and the immigration of people from contrasting cultures. (Of course, for this he didn't need to leave the United States.) To better round out his cultural experiences, Jim recently visited South Korea, Vietnam, and again India. He plans to travel extensively in South America, where he expects to do more photo essays to reflect their fascinating cultures. He is grateful to be able to live in such exciting social, technological, and geopolitical times—and to have access to portable broadband Internet while he pursues his sociological imagination.

Chapter 1
The Sociological Perspective

Learning Objectives

After you have read this chapter, you should be able to:

1.1 Explain why both history and biography are essential for the sociological perspective. (p. 3)

1.2 Trace the origins of society, from tradition to Max Weber. (p. 4)

1.3 Trace the development of sociology in North America and explain the tension between objective analysis and social reform. (p. 8)

1.4 Explain the basic ideas of symbolic interactionism, functional analysis, and conflict theory. (p. 13)

1.5 Explain why common sense can't replace sociological research. (p. 20)

1.6 Know the eight steps of the research model. (p. 21)

1.7 Know the main elements of the seven research methods: surveys, participant observation, case studies, secondary analysis, analysis of documents, experiments, and unobtrusive measures. (p. 23)

1.8 Explain how gender is significant in sociological research. (p. 32)

1.9 Explain why it's vital for sociologists to protect the people they study; discuss the two cases that are presented. (p. 33)

1.10 Explain how research versus reform and globalization are likely to influence sociology. (p. 35)

I quickly scanned the room filled with 100 or so bunks. I was relieved to see that an upper bunk was still open. I grabbed it, figuring that attacks are more difficult in an upper bunk. Even from the glow of the faded red-and-white exit sign, its faint light barely illuminating this bunk, I could see that the sheet was filthy. Resigned to another night of fitful sleep, I reluctantly crawled into bed.

I kept my clothes on.

The next morning, I joined the long line of disheveled men leaning against the chain-link fence. Their faces were as downcast as their clothes were dirty. Not a glimmer of hope among them.

No one spoke as the line slowly inched forward.

When my turn came, I was handed a cup of coffee, a white plastic spoon, and a bowl of semiliquid that I couldn't identify. It didn't look like any food I had seen before. Nor did it taste like anything I had ever eaten.

> The room was strangely silent. Hundreds of men were eating, each immersed in his own private hell, . . .

My stomach fought the foul taste, every spoonful a battle. But I was determined. "I will experience what they experience," I kept telling myself. My stomach reluctantly gave in and accepted its morning nourishment.

The room was strangely silent. Hundreds of men were eating, each one immersed in his own private hell, his mind awash with disappointment, remorse, bitterness.

As I stared at the Styrofoam cup that held my coffee, grateful for at least this small pleasure, I noticed what looked like teeth marks. I shrugged off the thought, telling myself that my long weeks as a sociological observer of the homeless were finally getting to me. "It must be some sort of crease from handling," I concluded.

I joined the silent ranks of men turning in their bowls and cups. When I saw the man behind the counter swishing out Styrofoam cups in a washtub of murky water, I began to feel sick to my stomach. I knew then that the jagged marks on my cup really had come from another person's mouth.

How much longer did this research have to last? I felt a deep longing to return to my family—to a welcome world of clean sheets, healthy food, and "normal" conversations.

The Sociological Perspective

1.1 **Explain why both history and biography are essential for the sociological perspective.**

Seeing the Broader Social Context

The **sociological perspective** stresses the social contexts in which people live. It examines how these contexts influence people's lives. At the center of the sociological perspective is the question of how groups influence people, especially how people are influenced by their **society**—a group of people who share a culture and a territory.

To find out why people do what they do, sociologists look at **social location**, the corners in life that people occupy because of their place in a society. Sociologists look at how jobs, income, education, gender, race–ethnicity, and age affect people's ideas and behavior. Consider, for example, how being identified with a group called *females* or with a group called *males* when you were growing up has shaped *your* ideas of who you are. Growing up as a female or a male has influenced not only how you feel about yourself but also your ideas of what you should attain in life and how you should relate to others. Even your gestures and the way you laugh come from your identifying with one of these groups.

Sociologist C. Wright Mills (1959) put it this way: "The sociological imagination [perspective] enables us to grasp the connection between history and biography." By *history*, Mills meant that each society is located in a broad stream of events. This gives each society specific characteristics—such as its ideas about what roles are proper for men and women. By *biography*, Mills referred to people's experiences within a specific historical setting, which gives them their orientations to life. In short, you don't do what you do because you inherited some internal mechanism, such as instincts. Rather, *external* influences—your experiences—become part of your thinking and motivation. Or we can put it this way: At the center of what you do and how you think is the society in which you grow up and your particular location in that society.

Consider a newborn baby. As you know, if we were to take the baby away from its U.S. parents and place it with the Yanomamö Indians in the jungles of South America, his or her first words would not be in English. You also know that the child would not think like an American. The child would

sociological perspective
understanding human behavior by placing it within its broader social context

society
people who share a culture and a territory

social location
the group memberships that people have because of their location in history and society

Perhaps from this photo taken in Athens, Greece, you can see why silence is common in homeless shelters. An optimistic view of life and exciting things to talk about are not part of the homeless.

We all learn our basic views of the world from the group in which we grow up. Just as this principle applies to this woman in the Bayaka tribe of the Central African Republic, so it applies to you.

not grow up wanting credit cards, for example, or designer clothes, a car, a smart phone, an iPod, and video games. He or she would take his or her place in Yanomamö society—perhaps as a food gatherer, a hunter, or a warrior—and would not even know about the world left behind at birth. And, whether male or female, the child would grow up assuming that it is natural to want many children, not debating whether to have one, two, or three children.

If you have been thinking along with me—and I hope you have—you should be thinking about how *your* social groups have shaped *your* ideas and desires. Over and over in this text, you will see that the way you look at the world is the result of your exposure to specific human groups. I think you will enjoy the process of self-discovery that sociology offers.

The Global Context—and the Local

As is evident to all of us—from the labels on our clothing that say Hong Kong, Brunei, or Macau to the many other imported products that have become part of our daily lives—our world has become a global village. How life has changed! Our predecessors lived on isolated farms and in small towns. They grew their own food and made their own clothing, buying only sugar, coffee, and a few other items that they couldn't produce. Beyond the borders of their communities lay a world they perceived only dimly.

And how slow communications used to be! In December 1814, the United States and Great Britain signed a peace treaty to end the War of 1812. Yet two weeks *later*, their armies fought a major battle at New Orleans. Neither the American nor the British forces there had heard that the war was over (Volti 1995).

Now we can grab our cell phone or use the Internet to communicate instantly with people anywhere on the planet. News flashes from around the world are part of our everyday life. Although we are engulfed in instantaneous global communications, we also continue to occupy our own little corners of life. Like those of our predecessors, our worlds, too, are marked by differences in family background, religion, job, gender, race–ethnicity, and social class. In these smaller corners of life, we continue to learn distinctive ways of viewing the world.

One of the beautiful—and fascinating—aspects of sociology is that it enables us to look at both parts of our current reality: being part of a global network *and* having unique experiences in our smaller corners of life. This text reflects both of these worlds, each vital in understanding who we are.

Origins of Sociology

1.2   Trace the origins of society, from tradition to Max Weber.

Tradition versus Science

So when did sociology begin? Even ancient peoples tried to figure out how social life works. They, too, asked questions about why war exists, why some people become more powerful than others, and why some are rich but others are poor. However, they often based their answers on superstition, myth, even the positions of the stars. They did not test their assumptions.

Science, in contrast, requires theories that can be tested by research. Measured by this standard, sociology emerged about the middle of the 1800s, when social observers began to use scientific methods to test their ideas.

Sociology was born in social upheaval. The Industrial Revolution had just begun, and masses of people were moving to cities in search of work. This broke their ties to the land—and to a culture that had provided ready answers to the difficult questions of life. The city's greeting was harsh: miserable pay, long hours, and dangerous work. Families lived on the edge of starvation, so children had to work alongside the adults. With their ties to the land broken and their world turned upside down, no longer could people count on tradition to provide the answers to the difficult questions of life.

Tradition suffered further blows. With the success of the American and French revolutions, new ideas swept out the old. As the idea that individuals possess inalienable rights caught fire, many traditional Western monarchies gave way to more democratic forms of government. This stimulated new perspectives.

About this time, the scientific method—using objective, systematic observations to test theories—was being tried out in chemistry and physics. This revealed many secrets that had been concealed in nature. With traditional answers failing, the next step was to apply the scientific method to questions about social life. The result was the birth of sociology.

Let's take a quick overview of some of the main figures in this development.

Upsetting the entire social order, the French Revolution removed the past as a sure guide to the present. This stimulated Auguste Comte to analyze how societies change. Shown here is the king of France, Luis XVI, as he is about to be executed by guillotine in 1793.

Auguste Comte and Positivism

Auguste Comte (1798–1857) suggested that we apply the scientific method to the social world, a process known as **positivism**. With the bloody upheavals of the French Revolution fresh in his mind—and he knew that the crowds had cheered at the public execution of the king and queen of France—Comte started to wonder what holds society together. Why do we have social order instead of anarchy or chaos? And when society becomes set on a particular course, what causes it to change?

These were pressing questions, and Comte decided that the scientific method held the key to answering them. Just as the scientific method had revealed the law of gravity, so, too, it would uncover the laws that underlie society. Comte called this new science **sociology**—"the study of society" (from the Greek *logos*, "study of," and the Latin *socius*, "companion," or "being with others"). The purpose of this new science, he said, would not only be to discover social principles but also to apply them to social reform. Comte developed a grandiose view: Sociologists would reform society, making it a better place to live.

Applying the scientific method to social life meant something quite different to Comte than it does to sociologists today. To Comte, it meant a kind of "armchair philosophy"—drawing conclusions from informal observations of social life. Comte did not do what we today call research, and his conclusions have been abandoned. But because he proposed that we observe and classify human activities to uncover society's fundamental laws and coined the term *sociology* to describe this process, Comte often is credited with being the founder of sociology.

Auguste Comte (1798–1857), who is credited as the founder of sociology, began to analyze the bases of the social order. Although he stressed that the scientific method should be applied to the study of society, he did not apply it himself.

positivism

the application of the scientific approach to the social world

sociology

the scientific study of so... human behavior

Herbert Spencer and Social Darwinism

Herbert Spencer (1820–1903), who grew up in England, is sometimes called the second founder of sociology. Spencer disagreed sharply with Comte. He said that sociologists

Herbert Spencer (1820–1903), sometimes called the second founder of sociology, coined the term "survival of the fittest." Spencer thought that helping the poor was wrong, that this merely helped the "less fit" survive.

Karl Marx (1818–1883) believed that the roots of human misery lay in class conflict, the exploitation of workers by those who own the means of production. Social change, in the form of the workers overthrowing the capitalists was inevitable from Marx's perspective. Although Marx did not consider himself a sociologist, his ideas have influenced many sociologists, particularly conflict theorists.

class conflict

Marx's term for the struggle between capitalists and workers

bourgeoisie

Marx's term for capitalists, those who own the means of production

proletariat

Marx's term for the exploited class, the mass of workers who do not own the means of production

should *not* guide social reform. If they did, he said, it would interfere with a natural process that improves societies. Societies are evolving from a lower form ("barbarian") to higher ("civilized") forms. As generations pass, a society's most capable and intelligent members ("the fittest") survive, while the less capable die out. These fittest members produce a more advanced society—unless misguided do-gooders get in the way and help the less fit (the lower classes) survive.

Spencer called this principle *the survival of the fittest*. Although Spencer coined this phrase, it usually is credited to his contemporary, Charles Darwin. Where Spencer proposed that societies evolve over time as the fittest people adapt to their environment, Darwin applied this idea to organisms. Because Darwin is better known, Spencer's idea is called *social Darwinism*. History is fickle, and if fame had gone the other way, we might be speaking of "biological Spencerism."

Like Comte, Spencer did armchair philosophy instead of conducting scientific research.

Karl Marx and Class Conflict

Karl Marx (1818–1883) not only influenced sociology but also left his mark on world history. Marx's influence has been so great that even the *Wall Street Journal,* that staunch advocate of capitalism, has called him one of the three greatest modern thinkers (the other two being Sigmund Freud and Albert Einstein).

Like Comte, Marx thought that people should try to change society. His proposal for change was radical: revolution. This got him thrown out of Germany, and he settled in England. Marx believed that the engine of human history is **class conflict**. He said that society is made up of two social classes, and they are natural enemies of one another: the **bourgeoisie** (boo-shwa-ZEE) (the *capitalists*, those who own the means of production—the money, land, factories, and machines) and the **proletariat** (the exploited workers, who do not own the means of production). Eventually, the workers will unite and break their chains of bondage. The workers' revolution will be bloody, but it will usher in a classless society, one free of exploitation. People will work according to their abilities and receive goods and services according to their needs (Marx and Engels 1848/1967).

Marxism is not the same as communism. Although Marx proposed revolution as the way for workers to gain control of society, he did not develop the political system called *communism.* This is a later application of his ideas. Marx himself felt disgusted when he heard debates about his insights into social life. After listening to some of the positions attributed to him, he shook his head and said, "I am not a Marxist" (Dobriner 1969:222; Gitlin 1997:89).

Unlike Comte and Spencer, Marx did not think of himself as a sociologist—and with his reputation for communism and revolution, many sociologists wish that no one else did either. Because of his insights into the relationship between the social classes, Marx is generally recognized as a significant early sociologist. He introduced *conflict theory,* one of today's major perspectives in sociology. Later, we will examine this perspective in detail.

Emile Durkheim and Social Integration

Until the time of Emile Durkheim (1858–1917), sociology was viewed as part of history and economics. Durkheim, who grew up in France, wanted to change this, and his major professional goal was to get sociology recognized as a separate academic discipline (Coser 1977). He achieved this goal in 1887 when the University of Bordeaux awarded him the world's first academic appointment in sociology.

Durkheim's second goal was to show how social forces affect people's behavior. To accomplish this, he conducted rigorous research. Comparing the suicide rates of several European countries, Durkheim (1897/1966) found that each country has a different suicide rate—and that these rates remain about the same year after year. He also found that different groups within a country have different suicide rates and that these, too, remain stable from year to year. Males are more likely than females to kill themselves, Protestants more likely than Catholics or Jews, and the unmarried more likely than the married. From these observations, Durkheim concluded that suicide is not what it appears—simply a matter of individuals here and there deciding to take their lives for personal reasons. Instead, *social factors underlie suicide*, which is why a group's rate remains fairly constant year after year.

In his search for the key social factors in suicide, Durkheim identified **social integration**, the degree to which people are tied to their social groups: He found that people who have weaker social ties are more likely to commit suicide. This, he said, explains why Protestants, males, and the unmarried have higher suicide rates. This is how it works: Protestantism encourages greater freedom of thought and action; males are more independent than females; and the unmarried lack the ties and responsibilities that come with marriage. In other words, members of these groups have fewer of the social bonds that keep people from committing suicide. In Durkheim's term, they have less social integration.

Despite the many years that have passed since Durkheim did his research, the principle he uncovered still applies: People who are less socially integrated have higher rates of suicide. Even today, more than a century later, those same groups that Durkheim identified—Protestants, males, and the unmarried—are more likely to kill themselves.

It is important for you to understand the principle that was central in Durkheim's research: *Human behavior cannot be understood only in terms of the individual; we must always examine the social forces that affect people's lives.* Suicide, for example, appears to be such an intensely individual act that psychologists should study it, not sociologists. As Durkheim stressed, however, if we look at human behavior only in reference to the individual, we miss its *social* basis.

APPLYING DURKHEIM   Did you know that 29,000 whites and 2,000 African Americans will commit suicide in the next twelve months? Of course not. And you probably are wondering if anyone can know something like this before it happens. Sociologists can. How? Sociologists look at **patterns of behavior**, recurring characteristics or events.

The patterns of suicide let us be even more specific. Look at Figure 1.1. There you can see the methods by which African Americans and whites commit suicide. These patterns are so consistent that we can predict with high certainty that of the 29,000 whites, about 15,500 will use guns to kill themselves, and that of the 2,000 African Americans, 60 to 70 will jump to their deaths.

The French sociologist Emile Durkheim (1858–1917) contributed many important concepts to sociology. His comparison of the suicide rates of several countries revealed an underlying social factor: People are more likely to commit suicide if their ties to others in their communities are weak. Durkheim's identification of the key role of social integration in social life remains central to sociology today.

patterns of behavior
recurring behaviors or events

Figure 1.1 How Americans Commit Suicide

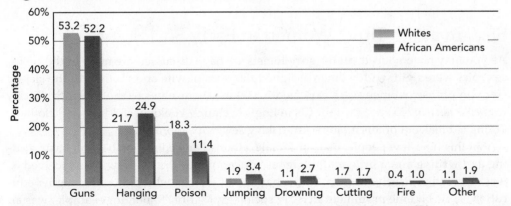

NOTE: These totals are the mean of years 2001–2011. ("Mean" is explained in Table 1.3 on page 25.)

SOURCE: By the author. Based on Centers for Disease Control and Prevention 2012 and earlier years; Center for Injury Prevention and Control 2013.

These patterns—both the numbers and the way people take their lives—recur year after year. This indicates something far beyond the individuals who kill themselves. They reflect conditions in society, such as the popularity and accessibility of guns. They also reflect conditions that we don't understand. I am hoping that one day, this textbook will pique a student's interest enough to investigate these patterns.

Max Weber and the Protestant Ethic

Max Weber (Mahx VAY-ber) (1864–1920), a German sociologist and a contemporary of Durkheim, also held professorships in the new academic discipline of sociology. Like Durkheim and Marx, Weber is one of the most influential of all sociologists, and you will come across his writings and theories in later chapters. For now, let's consider an issue Weber raised that remains controversial today.

RELIGION AND THE ORIGIN OF CAPITALISM   Weber disagreed with Marx's claim that economics is the central force in social change. That role, he said, belongs to religion. Weber (1904/1958) theorized that the Roman Catholic belief system encouraged followers to hold on to their traditional ways of life, while the Protestant belief system encouraged its members to embrace change. Roman Catholics were taught that because they were Church members they were on the road to heaven, but Protestants, those of the Calvinist tradition, were told that they wouldn't know if they were saved until Judgment Day. You can see why this made them uncomfortable. Calvinists began to look for a "sign" that they were in God's will. They found this "sign" in financial success, which they took as a blessing that indicated that God was on their side. To bring about this "sign" and receive spiritual comfort, they began to live frugal lives, saving their money and investing it in order to make even more. This accumulation and investment of capital, said Weber, brought about the birth of capitalism.

Weber called this self-denying approach to life the *Protestant ethic*. He termed the desire to invest capital in order to make more money the *spirit of capitalism*. To test his theory, Weber compared the extent of capitalism in Roman Catholic and Protestant countries. In line with his theory, he found that capitalism was more likely to flourish in Protestant countries. Weber's conclusion that religion was the key factor in the rise of capitalism was controversial when he made it, and it continues to be debated today (Kotz 2015).

Max Weber (1864–1920) was another early sociologist who left a profound impression on sociology. He used cross-cultural and historical materials to trace the causes of social change and to determine how social groups affect people's orientations to life.

Sociology in North America

1.3   Trace the development of sociology in North America and explain the tension between objective analysis and social reform.

Now let's turn to the development of sociology on this side of the Atlantic Ocean.

Sexism at the Time: Women in Early Sociology

As you may have noticed, all the sociologists we have discussed are men. In the 1800s, sex roles were rigid, with women assigned the roles of wife and mother. In the classic German phrase, women were expected to devote themselves to the four K's: *Kirche, Küche, Kinder, und Kleider* (the four C's in English: church, cooking, children, and clothes). Trying to break out of this mold meant risking severe disapproval.

At this time, few people, male or female, attained any education beyond basic reading and writing and a little math. Higher education, for the rare few who received it, was reserved primarily for men. Of the handful of women who did pursue higher education, some became prominent in early sociology. Marion Talbot, for example, was an associate editor of the *American Journal of Sociology* for thirty years, from its founding in 1895 to 1925. The influence of some early female sociologists went far beyond sociology.

Figure 1.2   The Forgotten Sociologists

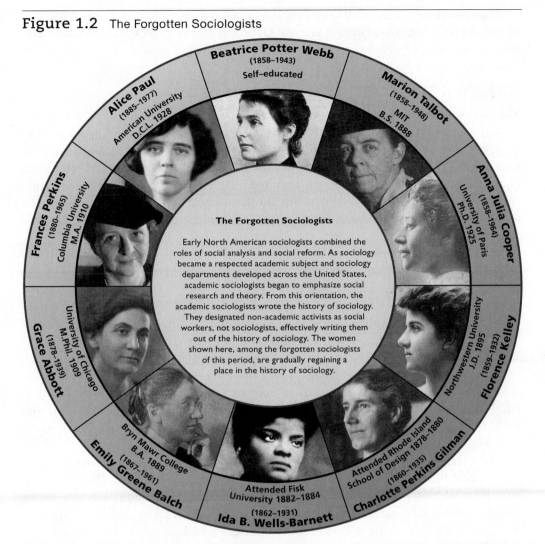

The Forgotten Sociologists

Early North American sociologists combined the roles of social analysis and social reform. As sociology became a respected academic subject and sociology departments developed across the United States, academic sociologists began to emphasize social research and theory. From this orientation, the academic sociologists wrote the history of sociology. They designated non-academic activists as social workers, not sociologists, effectively writing them out of the history of sociology. The women shown here, among the forgotten sociologists of this period, are gradually regaining a place in the history of sociology.

Beatrice Potter Webb (1858–1943) Self–educated

Alice Paul (1885–1977) American University D.C.L. 1928

Marion Talbot (1858–1948) MIT B.S. 1888

Frances Perkins (1880–1965) Columbia University M.A. 1910

Anna Julia Cooper (1858–1964) University of Paris Ph.D. 1925

Grace Abbott (1878–1939) University of Chicago M.Phil. 1909

Florence Kelley (1859–1932) Northwestern University J.D. 1895

Emily Greene Balch (1867–1961) Bryn Mawr College B.A. 1889

Ida B. Wells-Barnett (1862–1931) Attended Fisk University 1882–1884

Charlotte Perkins Gilman (1860–1935) Attended Rhode Island School of Design 1878–1880

SOURCE: Photo wheel copyright 2017 © James M. Henslin.

Grace Abbott became chief of the U.S. government's Children's Bureau, and Frances Perkins was the first woman to hold a cabinet position, serving twelve years as Secretary of Labor under President Franklin Roosevelt. The photo wheel above portrays some of these early sociologists.

Most early female sociologists viewed sociology as a path to social reform. They focused on ways to improve society, such as how to stop lynching, integrate immigrants into society, and improve the conditions of workers. As sociology developed in North America, a debate arose about the purpose of sociology. Should it be to reform society or to do objective research on society? Those who held the university positions won the debate. They feared that advocating for social causes would jeopardize the reputation of sociology—and their own university positions. It was these men who wrote the history of sociology. Distancing themselves from the social reformers, they ignored the early female sociologists (Lengermann and Niebrugge 2007). Now that women have regained their voice in sociology—and have begun to rewrite its history—early female sociologists are again, as here, being acknowledged.

Harriet Martineau (1802–1876) provides an excellent example of how the contributions of early female sociologists were ignored. Although Martineau was from England, she is included here because she did extensive analyses of U.S. social customs. Sexism was so pervasive that when Martineau first began to analyze social life, she would hide her writing beneath her sewing when visitors arrived: Writing was "masculine" and sewing "feminine" (Gilman 1911/1971:88). Despite her extensive and acclaimed research on social life in both Great Britain and the United States, until recently Martineau was known primarily for translating Comte's ideas into English.

Racism at the Time: W. E. B. Du Bois

Not only was sexism assumed to be normal during this early period of sociology but so was racism. This made life difficult for African American professionals such as W. E. B. Du Bois (1868–1963). After earning a bachelor's degree from Fisk University, Du Bois became the first African American to earn a doctorate at Harvard. He then studied at the University of Berlin, where he attended lectures by Max Weber. After teaching Greek and Latin at Wilberforce University, Du Bois moved to Atlanta University in 1897 to teach sociology and do research. He remained there for most of his career (Du Bois 1935/1992).

The Down-to-Earth Sociology box on the next page features Du Bois' description of race relations when he was in college.

It is difficult to grasp how racist society was at this time. As Du Bois passed a butcher shop in Georgia one day, he saw the fingers of a lynching victim displayed in the window (Aptheker 1990). When Du Bois went to national meetings of the American Sociological Society, restaurants and hotels would not allow him to eat or room with the white sociologists. How times have changed. Not only would today's sociologists boycott such businesses but also they would refuse to hold meetings in that state. At that time, however, racism, like sexism, prevailed throughout society, rendering it mostly invisible to white sociologists. Du Bois eventually became such an outspoken critic of racism that the U.S. State Department, fearing he would criticize the United States abroad, refused to issue him a passport (Du Bois 1968).

Each year between 1896 and 1914, Du Bois published a book on relations between African Americans and whites. Not content to collect and interpret data, Du Bois, along with Jane Addams and others from Hull-House (see the next section), was one of the founders of the National Association for the Advancement of Colored People (NAACP) (Deegan 1988). Continuing to battle racism both as a sociologist and as a journalist, Du Bois eventually embraced revolutionary Marxism. At age 93, dismayed that so little improvement had been made in race relations, he moved to Ghana, where he was buried (Stark 1989).

W(illiam) E(dward) B(urghardt) Du Bois (1868–1963) spent his lifetime studying relations between African Americans and whites. Like many early North American sociologists, Du Bois combined the role of academic sociologist with that of social reformer.

Jane Addams: Sociologist and Social Reformer

Of the many early sociologists who combined the role of sociologist with that of social reformer, none was as successful as Jane Addams (1860–1935), who was a member of the American Sociological Society from its founding in 1905. Like Harriet Martineau, Addams, too, came from a background of wealth and privilege. She attended the Women's Medical College of Philadelphia but dropped out because of illness (Addams 1910/1981). On a trip to Europe, Addams saw the work being done to help London's poor. The memory wouldn't leave her, she said, and she decided to work for social justice.

In 1889, Addams co-founded Hull-House with Ellen Gates Starr. Located in Chicago's notorious slums, Hull-House was open to people who needed refuge—to immigrants, the sick, the aged, the poor. Sociologists from the nearby University of Chicago were frequent visitors at Hull-House. With her piercing insights into the exploitation of workers and how rural immigrants adjusted to city life, Addams strove to bridge the gap between the powerful and the powerless. She co-founded the American Civil Liberties Union and campaigned for the eight-hour workday and for laws against child labor. She wrote books on poverty, democracy, and peace. Addams' writings and efforts at social reform were so outstanding that in 1931, she was a co-winner of the Nobel Prize for Peace. She and Emily Greene Balch are the only sociologists to have won this coveted award.

Jane Addams (1860–1935), a recipient of the Nobel Prize for Peace, worked on behalf of poor immigrants. With Ellen G. Starr, she founded Hull-House, a center to help immigrants in Chicago. She was also a leader in women's rights (women's suffrage), as well as the peace movement of World War I.

Down-to-Earth Sociology

W. E. B. Du Bois: The Souls of Black Folk

Du Bois wrote more like an accomplished novelist than a sociologist. The following excerpts are from pages 66–68 of his 1903 book, *The Souls of Black Folk*. In this book, Du Bois analyzes changes that occurred in the social and economic conditions of African Americans during the thirty years following the Civil War.

For two summers, while he was a student at Fisk, Du Bois taught in a segregated school in a little log cabin "way back in the hills" of rural Tennessee. These excerpts help us understand conditions at that time.

It was a hot morning late in July when the school opened. I trembled when I heard the patter of little feet down the dusty road, and saw the growing row of dark solemn faces and bright eager eyes facing me. . . . There they sat, nearly thirty of them, on the rough benches, their faces shading from a pale cream to deep brown, the little feet bare and swinging, the eyes full of expectation, with here and there a twinkle of mischief, and the hands grasping Webster's blue-black spelling-book. I loved my school, and the fine faith the children had in the wisdom of their teacher was truly marvelous. We read and spelled together, wrote a little, picked flowers, sang, and listened to stories of the world beyond the hill. . . .

On Friday nights I often went home with some of the children,—sometimes to Doc Burke's farm. He was a great, loud, thin Black, ever working, and trying to buy these seventy-five acres of hill and dale where he lived; but people said that he would surely fail and the "white folks would get it all." His wife was a magnificent Amazon, with saffron face and shiny hair, uncorseted and barefooted, and the children were strong and barefooted. They lived in a one-and-a-half-room cabin in the hollow of the farm near the spring. . . .

In the 1800s, most people were poor, and formal education beyond the first several grades was a luxury. This photo depicts the conditions of the people Du Bois worked with.

Often, to keep the peace, I must go where life was less lovely; for instance, 'Tildy's mother was incorrigibly dirty, Reuben's larder was limited seriously, and herds of untamed insects wandered over the Eddingses' beds. Best of all I loved to go to Josie's, and sit on the porch, eating peaches, while the mother bustled and talked: how Josie had bought the sewing-machine; how Josie worked at service in winter, but that four dollars a month was "mighty little" wages; how Josie longed to go away to school, but that it "looked like" they never could get far enough ahead to let her; how the crops failed and the well was yet unfinished; and, finally, how mean some of the white folks were.

For two summers I lived in this little world. . . . I have called my tiny community a world, and so its isolation made it; and yet there was among us but a half-awakened common consciousness, sprung from common joy and grief, at burial, birth, or wedding; from common hardship in poverty, poor land, and low wages, and, above all, from the sight of the Veil* that hung between us and Opportunity. All this caused us to think some thoughts together; but these, when ripe for speech, were spoken in various languages. Those whose eyes twenty-five and more years had seen "the glory of the coming of the Lord," saw in every present hindrance or help a dark fatalism bound to bring all things right in His own good time. The mass of those to whom slavery was a dim recollection of childhood found the world a puzzling thing: it asked little of them, and they answered with little, and yet it ridiculed their offering. Such a paradox they could not understand, and therefore sank into listless indifference, or shiftlessness, or reckless bravado.

*"The Veil" is shorthand for the Veil of Race, referring to how race colors all human relations. Du Bois' hope, as he put it, was that "sometime, somewhere, men will judge men by their souls and not by their skins" (p. 261).

Talcott Parsons and C. Wright Mills: Theory versus Reform

Like Du Bois and Addams, many early North American sociologists worked toward the reform of society, but by the 1940s, the emphasis had shifted to social theory. Talcott Parsons (1902–1979), for example, a major sociologist of this period, developed abstract models of society that influenced a generation of sociologists.

C. Wright Mills (1916–1962) was a controversial figure in sociology because of his analysis of the role of the power elite in U.S. society. Today, his analysis is taken for granted by many sociologists and members of the public.

basic (or pure) sociology

sociological research for the purpose of making discoveries about life in human groups, not for making changes in those groups

applied sociology

the use of sociology to solve problems— from the micro level of classroom interaction and family relationships to the macro level of crime and pollution

public sociology

applying sociology for the public good; especially the use of the sociological perspective (how things are related to one another) to guide politicians and policy makers

Another sociologist, C. Wright Mills (1916–1962), deplored such theoretical abstractions. Trying to push the pendulum the other way, he urged sociologists to get back to social reform. In his writings, he warned that the nation faced an imminent threat to freedom—the coalescing of interests of a *power elite*, the top leaders of business, politics, and the military. Shortly after Mills' death came the turbulent late 1960s and the 1970s. This precedent-shaking era sparked interest in social activism, making Mills' ideas popular among a new generation of sociologists.

The Continuing Tension: Basic, Applied, and Public Sociology

BASIC SOCIOLOGY As we have seen, two contradictory goals—analyzing society versus working toward its reform—have run through North American sociology since its founding. This tension is still with us. Some sociologists see their proper role as doing **basic (or pure) sociology**, analyzing some aspect of society with no goal other than gaining knowledge. Others reply, "Knowledge for what?" They argue that gaining knowledge through research is not enough, that sociologists need to use their expertise to help reform society, especially to help bring justice and better conditions to the poor and oppressed.

APPLIED SOCIOLOGY As Figure 1.3 shows, one attempt to go beyond basic sociology is **applied sociology**, using sociology to solve problems. Applied sociology goes back to the roots of sociology: As you have seen, sociologists founded the NAACP. Today's applied sociologists lack the broad vision that the early sociologists had of reforming society, but their application of sociology is wide-ranging. Some work for business firms to solve problems in the workplace, while others investigate social problems such as pornography, rape, pollution, or the spread of AIDS. Sociology is even being applied to find ways to disrupt terrorist groups (Sageman 2008a) and to improve technology for the mentally ill (Kelly and Farahbakhsh 2012).

PUBLIC SOCIOLOGY To encourage sociologists to apply sociology, the American Sociological Association (ASA) is promoting a middle ground between research and reform called **public sociology**. By this term, the ASA refers to harnessing the sociological perspective for the benefit of the public. Of special interest to the ASA is getting politicians and policy makers to apply the sociological understanding of how society works as they develop social policy (American Sociological Association 2004; Gans 2014). Public sociology would incorporate both items 3 and 4 of Figure 1.3.

With roots that go back a century or more, this debate about the purpose and use of sociology is likely to continue for another generation. Making the issue more complicated is this: The lines between basic, applied, and public sociology are not always firm. Basic sociology can even morph into public sociology, as you can see in the Cultural Diversity box on the next page.

At this point, let's consider how theory fits into sociology.

Figure 1.3 Comparing Basic and Applied Sociology

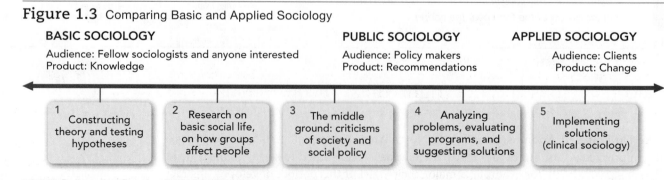

BASIC SOCIOLOGY	PUBLIC SOCIOLOGY	APPLIED SOCIOLOGY
Audience: Fellow sociologists and anyone interested Product: Knowledge	Audience: Policy makers Product: Recommendations	Audience: Clients Product: Change

1. Constructing theory and testing hypotheses
2. Research on basic social life, on how groups affect people
3. The middle ground: criticisms of society and social policy
4. Analyzing problems, evaluating programs, and suggesting solutions
5. Implementing solutions (clinical sociology)

SOURCE: By the author. Based on DeMartini 1982, plus events since then.

Cultural Diversity in the United States

Unanticipated Public Sociology: Studying Job Discrimination

Basic sociology—research aimed at learning more about some behavior—can turn into public sociology. Here is what happened to Devah Pager (2003). When Pager was a graduate student at the University of Wisconsin in Madison, she did volunteer work at a homeless shelter. When some of the men told her how hard it was to find work if they had been in prison, she wondered if the men were exaggerating. Pager decided to find out what difference a prison record makes in getting a job. She sent pairs of college men to apply for 350 entry-level jobs in Milwaukee. One team was African American, and one was white. Pager prepared identical résumés for the teams, but with one difference: On each team, one of the men said he had served eighteen months in prison for possession of cocaine.

Figure 1.4 Call-Back Rates by Race-Ethnicity and Criminal Record

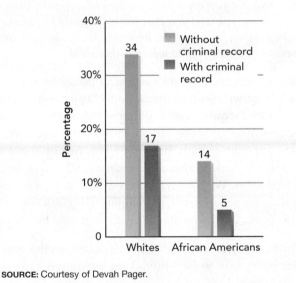

SOURCE: Courtesy of Devah Pager.

Figure 1.4 shows the difference that the prison record made. Men without a prison record were two or three times more likely to be called back.

But Pager came up with another significant finding. Look at the difference that race–ethnicity made. White men with a prison record were more likely to be offered a job than African American men who had a clean record!

Sociological research often remains in obscure journals, read by only a few specialists. But Pager's findings got around, turning basic research into public sociology. Someone told President George W. Bush about the research, and he announced in his State of the Union speech that he wanted Congress to fund a $300 million program to provide mentoring and other support to help former prisoners get jobs (Kroeger 2004).

And it isn't just Wisconsin. When Pager repeated her research in New York City, she found similar results (Pager et al. 2009).

As you can see, sometimes only a thin line separates basic and public sociology.

For Your Consideration

→ What findings would you expect if women had been included in this study?

Theoretical Perspectives in Sociology

1.4   Explain the basic ideas of symbolic interactionism, functional analysis, and conflict theory.

Facts never interpret themselves. To make sense out of life, we use our common sense. That is, to understand our experiences (our "facts"), we place them into a framework of more-or-less related ideas. Sociologists do this, too, but they place their observations into a conceptual framework called a theory. A **theory** is a general statement about how some parts of the world fit together and how they work. It is an explanation of how two or more "facts" are related to one another.

Sociologists use three major theories: symbolic interactionism, functional analysis, and conflict theory. Each theory is like a lens through which we can view social life. Let's first examine the main elements of each theory and then apply each to the U.S. divorce

theory

a general statement about how some parts of the world fit together and how they work; an explanation of how two or more facts are related to one another rate to see why it is so high. As we do this, you will see how each theory, or perspective, provides a distinct interpretation of social life.

Symbolic Interactionism

The central idea of **symbolic interactionism** is that *symbols*—things to which we attach meaning—are the key to understanding how we view the world and communicate with one another. Charles Horton Cooley (1864–1929) and George Herbert Mead (1863–1931) developed this perspective in sociology. Let's look at the main elements of this theory.

SYMBOLS IN EVERYDAY LIFE   Without symbols, our social life would be no more sophisticated than that of animals. For example, without symbols, we would have no aunts or uncles, employers or teachers—or even brothers and sisters. I know that this sounds strange, but it is symbols that define our relationships. There would still be reproduction, of course, but no symbols to tell us how we are related to whom. We would not know to whom we owe respect and obligations, or from whom we can expect privileges—two elements that lie at the essence of human relationships.

I know it is vague to say that symbols tell you how you are related to others and how you should act toward them, so let's make this less abstract:

Suppose that you have fallen head over heels in love. Finally, after what seems forever, it is the night before your wedding. As you are contemplating tomorrow's bliss, your mother comes to you in tears. Sobbing, she tells you that she had a child before she married your father, a child that she gave up for adoption. Breaking down, she says that she has just discovered that the person you are going to marry is this child.

You can see how the symbol will change overnight—and your behavior, too!

The symbols "boyfriend" and "brother"—or "girlfriend" and "sister"—are certainly different, and, as you know, each symbol requires rather different behavior.

Not only do relationships depend on symbols, but so does society itself. Without symbols, we could not coordinate our actions with those of others. We could not make plans for a future day, time, and place. Unable to specify times, materials, sizes, or goals, we could not build bridges and highways. Without symbols, we would have no movies or musical instruments, no hospitals, no government, no religion. The class you are taking could not exist—nor could this book. On the positive side, there would be no war.

IN SUM   Symbolic interactionists analyze how social life depends on the ways we define ourselves and others. They study face-to-face interaction, examining how people make sense out of life and their place in it.

APPLYING SYMBOLIC INTERACTIONISM   Look at Figure 1.5 on the next page, which shows U.S. marriages and divorces over time. Let's see how symbolic interactionists would use changing symbols to explain this figure. For background, you should understand that marriage used to be a *lifelong commitment*. A hundred years ago (and less), getting divorced was viewed as immoral, a flagrant disregard for public opinion, and the abandonment of adult responsibilities. Let's see what changed.

THE MEANING OF MARRIAGE   Marriage had been based mainly on the obligations and duties that a couple vowed to one another. By the 1930s, young Americans were coming to view marriage in a different way, a change that was reported by sociologists of the time. In 1933, William Ogburn observed that people were placing more emphasis on the personality of their potential mates. Then in 1945, Ernest Burgess and Harvey Locke reported that people were expecting more affection, understanding, and compatibility from marriage. As feelings became more important in marriage, duty and obligation became less important. Eventually, marriage came to be viewed as an arrangement that was based mostly on feelings—on attraction and intimacy. Marriage then became an arrangement that could be broken when feelings changed.

George Herbert Mead (1863–1931) is one of the founders of symbolic interactionism, a major theoretical perspective in sociology. He taught at the University of Chicago, where his lectures were popular. Although he wrote little, after his death students compiled his lectures into an influential book, *Mind, Self, and Society*.

symbolic interactionism

a theoretical perspective in which society is viewed as composed of symbols that people use to establish meaning, develop their views of the world, and communicate with one another

Figure 1.5 U.S. Marriage, U.S. Divorce

SOURCE: By the author. Based on *Statistical Abstract of the United States* 1998:Table 92 and 2014:84, 137; earlier editions for earlier years. The broken lines indicate the author's estimates.

THE MEANING OF DIVORCE   As divorce became more common, its meaning also changed. Rather than being a symbol of failure, divorce came to indicate freedom and new beginnings. Removing the stigma from divorce shattered a strong barrier that had prevented husbands and wives from breaking up.

THE MEANING OF PARENTHOOD   Parents used to have little responsibility for their children beyond providing food, clothing, shelter, and moral guidance. And they needed to do this for only a short time, because children began to contribute to the support of the family early in life. Among many people, parenthood is still like this. In Colombia, for example, children of the poor often are expected to support themselves by the age of 8 or 10. In industrial societies, however, we assume that children are vulnerable beings who must depend on their parents for financial and emotional support for many years—often until they are well into their 20s. In some cases, this is now being extended to the 30s. The greater responsibilities that we assign to parenthood place heavier burdens on today's couples and, with them, more strain on marriage.

THE MEANING OF LOVE   And we can't overlook the love symbol. As surprising as it may sound, to have love as the main reason for marriage weakens marriage. In some depth of our being, we expect "true love" to deliver constant emotional highs. This expectation sets people up for crushed hopes, as dissatisfactions in marriage are inevitable. When they come, spouses tend to blame one another for failing to deliver the illusive satisfaction.

IN SUM   Symbolic interactionists look at how changing ideas (or symbols) of marriage, divorce, parenthood, and love put pressure on married couples. No single change is *the* cause of our divorce rate. Taken together, however, these changes provide a strong push toward marriages breaking up.

Functional Analysis

The central idea of **functional analysis** is that society is a whole unit, made up of inter-related parts that work together. Functional analysis (also known as *functionalism* and *structural functionalism*) is rooted in the origins of sociology. Auguste Comte and Herbert

functional analysis
a theoretical framework in which society is viewed as composed of various parts, each with a function that, when fulfilled, contributes to society's equilibrium; also *known as functionalism* and *structural functionalism*

Robert K. Merton (1910–2003), who spent most of his academic career at Columbia University, was a major proponent of functionalism, one of the main theoretical perspectives in sociology.

Spencer viewed society as a kind of living organism, similar to an animal's body. Just as a person or animal has organs that function together, they wrote, so does society. And like an organism, if society is to function smoothly, its parts must work together in harmony.

Emile Durkheim also viewed society as being composed of many parts, each with its own function. He said that when all the parts of society fulfill their functions, society is in a "normal" state. If they do not fulfill their functions, society is in an "abnormal" or "pathological" state. To understand society, then, functionalists say that we need to look at both *structure* (how the parts of a society fit together to make the whole) and *function* (what each part does, how it contributes to society).

ROBERT MERTON AND FUNCTIONALISM   Robert Merton (1910–2003) dismissed the comparison of society to a living organism, but he did maintain the essence of functionalism—the image of society as a whole unit composed of parts that work together. Merton used the term *functions* to refer to the beneficial consequences of people's actions: Functions help keep a group (society, social system) in balance. In contrast, *dysfunctions* are the harmful consequences of people's actions. They undermine a system's equilibrium.

Functions can be either manifest or latent. If an action is *intended* to help some part of a system, it is a *manifest function*. For example, suppose that government officials become concerned that women are having so few children. Congress offers a $10,000 bonus for every child born to a married couple. The intention, or manifest function, of the bonus is to increase childbearing within the family unit. Merton pointed out that people's actions can also have *latent functions*; that is, they can have *unintended* consequences that help a system adjust. Let's suppose that the bonus works. As the birth rate jumps, so does the sale of diapers and baby furniture. Because the benefits to these businesses were not the intended consequences, they are latent functions of the bonus.

Of course, human actions can also hurt a system. Because such consequences usually are unintended, Merton called them *latent dysfunctions*. Let's assume that the government has failed to specify a "stopping point" with regard to its bonus system. To collect more bonuses, some people keep on having children. The more children they have, however, the more they need the next bonus to survive. Large families become common, and poverty increases. As welfare and taxes jump, the nation erupts in protest. Because these results were not intended and because they harmed the social system, they would be latent dysfunctions of the bonus program.

IN SUM   From the perspective of functional analysis, society is a functioning unit, with each part related to the whole. Whenever we examine a smaller part, we need to look for its functions and dysfunctions to see how it is related to the larger unit. This basic approach can be applied to any social group, whether an entire society, a college, or even a group as small as a family.

APPLYING FUNCTIONAL ANALYSIS   Now let's apply functional analysis to the U.S. divorce rate. Functionalists stress that industrialization and urbanization undermined the traditional functions of the family. For example, before industrialization, the family formed an economic team. On the farm, where most people lived, each family member had jobs or "chores" to do. The wife was in charge not only of household tasks but also of raising small animals, such as chickens, milking cows, collecting eggs, and churning butter. She also did the cooking, baking, canning, sewing, darning, washing, and cleaning. The daughters helped her. The husband was responsible for caring for large animals, such as horses and cattle, for planting and harvesting, and for maintaining buildings and tools. The sons helped him.

This certainly doesn't sound like life today! But what does it have to do with divorce? Simply put, there wasn't much divorce because the husband and wife formed an economic unit in which each depended on the other for survival. There weren't many alternatives.

Other functions also bound family members to one another: educating the children, teaching them religion, providing home-based recreation, and caring for the sick and elderly. All these were functions of the family, certainly quite different from today's situation. To further see how sharply family functions have changed, look at this example from the 1800s:

When Phil became sick, he was nursed by Ann, his wife. She cooked for him, fed him, changed the bed linens, bathed him, read to him from the Bible, and gave him his medicine. (She did this in addition to doing the housework and taking care of their six children.) Phil was also surrounded by the children, who shouldered some of his chores while he was sick. When Phil died, the male neighbors and relatives made the casket while Ann, her mother, and female friends washed and dressed the body. Phil was then "laid out" in the front parlor (the formal living room), where friends, neighbors, and relatives paid their last respects. From there, friends moved his body to the church for the final message and then to the grave they themselves had dug.

IN SUM   When the family loses functions, it becomes more fragile, making an increase in divorce inevitable. These changes in economic production illustrate how the family has lost functions. When making a living was a cooperative, home-based effort, husbands and wives depended on one another for their interlocking contributions to a mutual endeavor. With today's individual paychecks, husbands and wives increasingly function as separate components in an impersonal, multinational, and even global system. The fewer functions that family members share, the fewer are their "ties that bind"—and these ties are what help husbands and wives get through the problems they inevitably experience.

Sociologists who use the functionalist perspective stress how industrialization and urbanization undermined the traditional functions of the family. Before industrialization, members of the family worked together as an economic unit, as in this photo of a farm family in Minnesota in the 1890s. As production moved away from the home, it took with it first the father and, more recently, the mother. One consequence is a major dysfunction, the weakening of family ties.

Conflict Theory

Conflict theory provides a third perspective on social life. Unlike the functionalists, who view society as a harmonious whole with its parts working together, conflict theorists stress that society is composed of groups that compete with one another for scarce resources. If you look at the surface, you might see cooperation, but scratch that surface and you will find a struggle for power.

conflict theory

a theoretical framework in which society is viewed as composed of groups that are competing for scarce resources

KARL MARX AND CONFLICT THEORY Karl Marx, the founder of conflict theory, witnessed the Industrial Revolution that transformed Europe. He saw that peasants who had left the land to work in cities earned barely enough to eat. Things were so bad that the average worker died at age 30, the average wealthy person at age 50 (Edgerton 1992:87). Shocked by this suffering and exploitation, Marx began to analyze society and history. As he did so, he developed **conflict theory**. He concluded that the key to human history is *class conflict*. In each society, some small group controls the means of production and exploits those who are not in control. In industrialized societies, the struggle is between the *bourgeoisie*, the small group of capitalists who own the means to produce wealth, and the *proletariat*, the mass of workers who are exploited by the bourgeoisie. The capitalists control the legal and political system: If the workers rebel, the capitalists call on the power of the state to subdue them.

When Marx made his observations, capitalism was in its infancy and workers were at the mercy of their employers. There was none of what many workers take for granted today—minimum wages, eight-hour days, coffee breaks, five-day work weeks, paid vacations and holidays, medical benefits, sick leave, unemployment compensation, Social Security, and, for union workers, the right to strike. Marx's analysis reminds us that these benefits came not from generous hearts but from workers forcing concessions by their employers.

CONFLICT THEORY TODAY Many sociologists extend conflict theory beyond the relationship of capitalists and workers. They examine how opposing interests run through every layer of society—whether in a small group, an organization, a community, or an entire society. For example, when teachers, parents, or the police try to enforce conformity, this creates resentment and resistance. It is the same when a teenager tries to "change the rules" to gain more independence. Throughout society, then, there is a constant struggle to determine who has authority or influence and how far that dominance goes (Turner 1978; Piven 2008; Manza and McCarthy 2011).

Sociologist Lewis Coser (1913–2003) pointed out that conflict is most likely to develop among people who are in close relationships. These people have worked out ways to distribute power and privilege, responsibilities and rewards. Any change in this arrangement can lead to hurt feelings, resentment, and conflict. Even in intimate relationships, then, people are in a constant balancing act, with conflict lying uneasily just beneath the surface.

FEMINISTS AND CONFLICT THEORY Just as Marx examined conflict between capitalists and workers, many feminists analyze conflict between men and women. Their primary focus is the historical, contemporary, and global inequalities of men and women—and how the traditional dominance by men can be overcome to bring about equality of the sexes. Feminists are not united by the conflict perspective, however. They tackle a variety of topics and use whatever theory applies. (Feminism is discussed in Chapter 10.)

APPLYING CONFLICT THEORY To explain why the U.S. divorce rate is high, conflict theorists focus on how men's and women's relationships have changed. For millennia, men dominated women, and women had few alternatives other than to accept that dominance. As industrialization transformed the world, it brought women the ability to meet their basic survival needs without depending on a man. This new ability gave them the power to refuse to bear burdens that earlier generations accepted as inevitable. The result is that today's women are likely to dissolve a marriage that becomes intolerable—or even just unsatisfactory.

IN SUM   The dominance of men over women was once considered natural and right. As women gained education and earnings, however, they first questioned and then rejected this assumption. As wives strove for more power and grew less inclined to put up with relationships that they defined as unfair, the divorce rate increased. From the conflict perspective, then, our high divorce rate does not mean that marriage has weakened but, rather, that women are making headway in their historical struggle with men.

Putting the Theoretical Perspectives Together

Which of these theoretical perspectives is *the* right one? As you have seen, each is a lens that produces a contrasting picture of divorce. The pictures that emerge are quite different from the commonsense understanding that two people are simply "incompatible." Because each theory focuses on different features of social life, each provides a distinct interpretation. Consequently, we need to use all three theoretical lenses to analyze human behavior. By combining the contributions of each, we gain a more comprehensive picture of social life.

Levels of Analysis: Macro and Micro

A major difference between these three theoretical perspectives is their level of analysis. Functionalists and conflict theorists focus on the **macro level**; that is, they examine large-scale patterns of society. In contrast, symbolic interactionists usually focus on the **micro level**, on **social interaction**—what people do when they are in one another's presence. These levels are summarized in Table 1.1.

To make this distinction between micro and macro levels clearer, let's return to the example of the homeless, with which we opened this chapter. To study homeless people, symbolic interactionists would focus on the micro level. They would analyze what homeless people do when they are in shelters and on the streets. They would also analyze their communications, both their talk and their **nonverbal interaction** (gestures, use of space, and so on).

macro-level analysis
an examination of large-scale patterns of society; such as how Wall Street and the political establishment are interrelated

micro-level analysis
an examination of small-scale patterns of society; such as how the members of a group interact

social interaction
one person's actions influencing someone else; usually refers to what people do when they are in one another's presence, but also includes communications at a distance

nonverbal interaction
communication without words through gestures, use of space, silence, and so on

Table 1.1 Three Theoretical Perspectives in Sociology

Theoretical Perspective	Usual Level of Analysis	Focus of Analysis	Key Terms	Applying the Perspective to the U.S. Divorce Rate
Symbolic Interactionism	Microsociological: examines small-scale patterns of social interaction	Face-to-face interaction, how people use symbols to create social life	Symbols Interaction Meanings Definitions	Industrialization and urbanization changed marital roles and led to a redefinition of love, marriage, children, and divorce.
Functional Analysis (also called functionalism and structural functionalism)	Macrosociological: examines large-scale patterns of society	Relationships among the parts of society; how these parts are functional (have beneficial consequences) or dysfunctional (have negative consequences)	Structure Functions (manifest and latent) Dysfunctions Equilibrium	As social change erodes the traditional functions of the family, family ties weaken, and the divorce rate increases.
Conflict Theory	Macrosociological: examines large-scale patterns of society	The struggle for scarce resources by groups in a society; how the elites use their power to control the weaker groups	Inequality Power Conflict Competition Exploitation	When men control economic life, the divorce rate is low because women find few alternatives to a bad marriage. The high divorce rate reflects a shift in the balance of power between men and women.

SOURCE: By the author.

Because sociologists find all human behavior to be valid research topics, their research ranges from the macro level of the globalization of capitalism to the micro level of fads and fashion. Peer pressure can be so strong in fads and fashion that some people are willing to sacrifice their health, as with this woman in 1899.

This micro level would not interest functionalists and conflict theorists. They would focus instead on the macro level, how changes in some parts of society increase homelessness. Functionalists might stress that jobs have dried up—how there is less need for unskilled labor and that millions of jobs have been transferred to workers overseas. Or they might focus on changes in the family, that families are smaller and divorce more common. This means that many people who can't find work end up on the streets because they don't have others to fall back on. For their part, conflict theorists would stress the struggle between social classes. They would be interested in how the decisions of international elites affect not only global production and trade but also the local job market, unemployment, and homelessness.

How Theory and Research Work Together

Theory cannot stand alone. Nor can research. As sociologist C. Wright Mills (1959) argued so forcefully, theory without research is abstract and empty. But research without theory, Mills added, is simply a collection of unrelated "facts."

Theory and research, then, are both essential for sociology. Every theory must be tested, which requires research. And as sociologists do research, often coming up with surprising findings, those results must be explained: For that, we need theory. As sociologists study social life, then, they combine research and theory.

And how do sociologists do research? Let's find out.

Doing Sociological Research

1.5 Explain why common sense can't replace sociological research.

Around the globe, people make assumptions about the way the world "is." Common sense, the things that "everyone knows are true," may or may not be true, however. It takes research to find out. Are you ready to test your own common sense? Take the little quiz below.

As you can see, to understand social life, we need to move beyond "common sense" and learn what is really going on. Let's look at how sociologists do their research.

Down-to-Earth Sociology

Enjoying a Sociology Quiz—Testing Your Common Sense

Some findings of sociology support commonsense understandings of social life, and others contradict them. Can you tell the difference? To enjoy this quiz, complete *all* the questions before turning to page 22 to check your answers.

1. **True/False** More U.S. students are killed in school shootings now than ten or fifteen years ago.

2. **True/False** The earnings of U.S. women have just about caught up with those of U.S. men.

3. **True/False** With life so rushed and more women working for wages, today's parents spend less time with their children than parents of previous generations did.

4. **True/False** It is more dangerous to walk near topless bars than fast-food restaurants.

5. **True/False** Most rapists are mentally ill.

6. **True/False** A large percentage of terrorists are mentally ill.

7. **True/False** Most people on welfare are lazy and looking for a handout. They could work if they wanted to.

8. **True/False** Compared with women, men make more eye contact in face-to-face conversations.

9. **True/False** Because bicyclists are more likely to wear helmets now than a few years ago, their rate of head injuries has dropped.

10. **True/False** As measured by their divorce rate, couples who live together before marriage are usually more satisfied with their marriages than couples who did not live together before marriage.

A Research Model

1.6   Know the eight steps of the research model.

As shown in Figure 1.6 below, scientific research follows eight basic steps. This is an ideal model, however, and in the real world of research, some of these steps may run together. Some may even be omitted.

1. Selecting a Topic

The first step is to select a topic. What do you want to know more about? Many sociologists simply follow their curiosity, their drive to learn more about social life. They become interested in a particular topic and they pursue it, as I did in studying the homeless. Some sociologists choose a topic because funding is available, others because they want to help people better understand a social problem—and perhaps to help solve it. Let's use spouse abuse as our example.

2. Defining the Problem

The second step is to define the problem, to specify what you want to learn about the topic. My interest in the homeless grew until I wanted to learn about homelessness across the nation. Ordinarily, sociologists' interests are much more focused than this; they examine some specific aspect of a topic, such as how homeless people survive on the streets. In the case of spouse abuse, sociologists may want to know whether violent and nonviolent husbands have different work experiences. Or they may want to learn what can be done to reduce spouse abuse.

3. Reviewing the Literature

You must read what has been published on your topic. This helps you to narrow the problem, identify areas that are already known, and learn what areas need to be researched. Reviewing the literature may also help you to pinpoint the questions that you will ask.

Figure 1.6 The Research Model

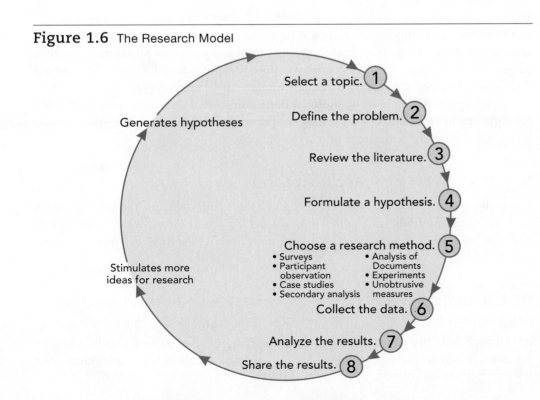

Down-to-Earth Sociology

Testing Your Common Sense—Answers to the Sociology Quiz

1. **False.** More students met violent deaths at U.S. schools in the 1990s than now (National Center for Education Statistics 2014).

2. **False.** Over the years, the wage gap has narrowed, but only slightly. On average, full-time working women earn about 72 percent of what full-time working men earn. This low figure is actually an improvement over earlier years. See Figures 10.7 and 10.8 on pages 317–318.

3. **False.** Today's parents spend more time with their children (Bianchi 2010). To see how this could be, see Figure 12.2 on page 382.

4. **False.** The crime rate outside fast-food restaurants is considerably higher. The likely reason is that topless bars hire private security and parking lot attendants (Linz et al. 2004).

5. **False.** Sociologists compared the psychological profiles of prisoners convicted of rape and prisoners convicted of other crimes. Their profiles were similar. Like robbery, rape is a learned behavior (Scully and Marolla 1984, 2016).

6. **False.** Extensive testing of Islamic terrorists shows that they actually tend to score more "normal" on psychological tests than most "normal" people do. As a group, they are in better mental health than the rest of the population (Sageman 2008b:64).

7. **False.** Most people on welfare are children, young mothers with few skills, or are elderly, sick, mentally challenged, or physically handicapped. Less than 2 percent fit the stereotype of an able-bodied man. See page 249.

8. **False.** Women make considerably more eye contact (Henley et al. 1985).

9. **False.** Bicyclists today are more likely to wear helmets, but their rate of head injuries is higher. Apparently, they take more risks because the helmets make them feel safer (Barnes 2001).

10. **False.** Until recently, the divorce rate of couples who cohabited before marriage was higher than those who did not cohabit. Now the divorce rate seems to be about the same (Kuperberg 2014). Neither divorce rate indicates that couples who previously cohabited are more satisfied with their marriages.

---

hypothesis

a statement of how variables are expected to be related to one another, often according to predictions from a theory

variable

a factor thought to be significant for human behavior, which can vary (or change) from one case to another

operational definition

the way in which a researcher measures a variable

research method (or **research design**)

one of seven procedures that sociologists use to collect data: surveys, participant observation, case studies, secondary analysis, analysis of documents, experiments, and unobtrusive measures

validity

the extent to which an operational definition measures what it is intended to measure

You might even find out that what you are interested in learning has been answered already. You don't want to waste your time rediscovering what is already known.

4. Formulating a Hypothesis

The fourth step is to formulate a **hypothesis**, a statement of what you expect to find according to predictions from a theory. A hypothesis predicts a relationship between or among **variables**, factors that change, or vary, from one person or situation to another. For example, the statement "Men who are more socially isolated are likelier to abuse their wives than men who are more socially integrated" is a hypothesis.

Your hypothesis will need **operational definitions**—that is, precise ways to measure the variables. In this example, you would need operational definitions for three variables: social isolation, social integration, and spouse abuse.

5. Choosing a Research Method

You then need to decide how you are going to collect your data. Sociologists use seven basic **research methods** (or *research designs*), which are outlined in the next section. You will want to choose the research method that will best answer your particular questions.

6. Collecting the Data

When you gather your data, you have to take care to assure their **validity**; that is, your operational definitions must measure what they are intended to measure. In this case, you must be certain that you really are measuring social isolation, social integration, and spouse abuse—and not something else. Spouse abuse, for example, seems to be obvious. Yet what some people consider abusive is not regarded as abuse by others. Which definition will you choose? In other words, you must state your operational definitions so precisely that no one has any question about what you are measuring.

You must also be sure that your data are reliable. **Reliability** means that if other researchers use your operational definitions, their findings will be consistent with yours. If your operational definitions are sloppy, husbands who have committed the same act of violence might be included in some research but excluded from other studies. You would end up with erratic results. If you show a 10 percent rate of spouse abuse, for example, but another researcher using the same operational definitions determines it to be 30 percent, the research is unreliable.

Would we sociologists ruin the fun if we were to gather data at the International Pillow Fight Day in London. Maybe. But look at this photo. Where are the old folks? Why aren't they grabbing pillows and . . .? The sociological blood really gets flowing when we look at events, even something as "non-serious" as this.

7. Analyzing the Results

You will have been trained in a variety of techniques to analyze your data—from those that apply to observations of people in small settings to the analysis of large-scale surveys. If a hypothesis has been part of your research, now is when you will test it. (Some research, especially participant observation and case studies, has no hypothesis. You may know so little about the setting you are going to research that you cannot even specify the variables in advance.)

8. Sharing the Results

To wrap up your research, you will write a report to share your findings with the scientific community. You will review how you did your research and specify your operational definitions. You will also compare your findings with published reports on the topic and examine how they support or disagree with theories that others have applied. As Table 1.2 on the next page illustrates, sociologists often summarize their findings in tables.

Let's look in greater detail at the fifth step to see what research methods sociologists use.

reliability

the extent to which research produces consistent or dependable results

Research Methods (Designs)

1.7 Know the main elements of the seven research methods: surveys, participant observation, case studies, secondary analysis, analysis of documents, experiments, and unobtrusive measures.

As we review the seven research methods (or *research designs*) that sociologists use, we will continue our example of spouse abuse. As you will see, the method you choose will depend on the questions you want to answer. So that you can have a yardstick for comparing the results of your research, you will want to know what "average" is in your research findings. Table 1.3 on page 25 summarizes the three ways that sociologists measure average.

Table 1.2 How to Read a Table

Tables summarize information. Because sociological findings are often presented in tables, it is important to understand how to read them. Tables contain six elements: title, headnote, headings, columns, rows, and source. When you understand how these elements fit together, you will know how to read a table.

① The *title* states the topic. It is located at the top of the table. What is the title of this table? Please determine your answer before looking at the correct answer at the bottom of this page.

② The *headnote* is not always included in a table. When it is present, it is located just below the title. Its purpose is to give more detailed information about how the data were collected or how data are presented in the table. What are the first eight words of the headnote for this table?

③ The *headings* tell what kind of information is contained in the table. There are three headings in this table. What are they? In the second heading, what does *n* = 25 mean?

④ The *columns* present information arranged vertically. What is the fourth number in the second column and the second number in the third column?

⑤ The *rows* present information arranged horizontally. In the fourth row, which husbands are more likely to have less education than their wives?

⑥ The *source* of a table, usually listed at the bottom, provides information on where the data in the table originated. Often, as in this instance, the information is specific enough for you to consult the original source. What is the source for this table?

Comparing Violent and Nonviolent Husbands

Based on interviews with 150 husbands and wives in a Midwestern city who were getting a divorce.

Husband's Achievement and Job Satisfaction	Violent Husbands (*n* = 25)	Nonviolent Husbands (*n* = 125)
He started but failed to complete high school or college.	44%	27%
He is very dissatisfied with his job.	44%	18%
His income is a source of constant conflict.	84%	24%
He has less education than his wife.	56%	14%
His job has less prestige than his father-in-law's.	37%	28%

SOURCE: Modification of Table 1 in O'Brien 1975.

Some tables are much more complicated than this one, but all follow the same basic pattern. To apply these concepts to a table with more information, see page 284.

Answers
1. Comparing Violent and Nonviolent Husbands
2. Based on interviews with 150 husbands and wives
3. Husband's Achievement and Job Satisfaction, Violent Husbands, Nonviolent Husbands. The *n* is an abbreviation for number, and *n* = 25 means that 25 violent husbands were in the sample.
4. 56%, 18%
5. Violent Husbands
6. A 1975 article by O'Brien (listed in the References section of this text).

Table 1.3 Three Ways to Measure "Average"

The Mean	The Median	The Mode
The term *average* seems clear enough. As you learned in grade school, to find the average, you add a group of numbers and then divide the total by the number of cases that you added. Assume that the following numbers represent men convicted of battering their wives.	To compute the second average, the *median*, first arrange the cases in order—either from the highest to the lowest or the lowest to the highest. That arrangement will produce the following distribution.	The third measure of average, the *mode,* is simply the cases that occur the most often. In this instance, the mode is 57, which is way off the mark.

The Mean	The Median	The Mode
Example 321 229 57 289 136 57 1,795	**Example** 57 1,795 57 321 136 289 229 or 229 289 136 321 57 1,795 57	**Example** (57) (57) 136 229 289 321 1,795

The Mean	The Median	The Mode

The total is 2,884. Divided by 7 (the number of cases), the average is 412. Sociologists call this form of average the *mean*.
 	
    The mean can be deceptive because it is strongly influenced by extreme scores, either low or high. Note that six of the seven cases are less than the mean.
 	
    Two other ways to compute averages are the median and the mode.
	Then look for the middle case, the one that falls halfway between the top and the bottom. That number is 229, since three numbers are lower and three numbers are higher. When there is an even numbers of cases, the median is the halfway mark between the two middle cases.	Because the mode is often deceptive, and only by chance comes close to either of the other two averages, sociologists seldom use it. In addition, not every distribution of cases has a mode. And if two or more numbers appear with the same frequency, you can have more than one mode.

SOURCE: By the author.

Surveys

Let's suppose that you want to know how many wives are abused each year. Some husbands also are abused, of course, but let's assume that you are going to focus on wives. An appropriate method for this purpose would be the **survey**, in which you would ask individuals a series of questions. Before you begin your research, however, you must deal with practical matters that face all researchers. Let's look at these issues.

SELECTING A SAMPLE Ideally, you might want to learn about all wives in the world, but obviously you don't have enough resources to do this. You will have to narrow your **population**, the target group that you are going to study.

Let's assume that your resources (money, assistants, time) allow you to investigate spouse abuse only among the students on your campus. Let's also assume that your college enrollment is large, so you won't be able to survey all the married women who are enrolled. Now you must select a **sample**, individuals from among your target population. Not all samples are equal. For example, married women enrolled in introductory sociology and engineering courses might have quite different experiences. If so, surveying just one or the other would produce skewed results.

Remember that your goal is to get findings that apply to your entire school. For this, you need a sample that represents the students. How can you get a *representative* sample?

The best way is to use a **random sample**. This does *not* mean that you stand on some campus corner and ask questions of any woman who happens to walk by. *In a random sample, everyone in your population (the target group) has the same chance of being included in the study.* In this case, because your population is every married woman enrolled in your college, all married women—whether first-year or graduate students, full- or part-time—must have the same chance of being included in your sample.

How can you get a random sample? First, you need a list of all the married women enrolled in your college. Then you assign a number to each name on the list. Using a table

© Robert Weber/The New Yorker Collection/www.cartoonbank.com

"That's the worst set of opinions I've heard in my entire life."

To attain their goal of objectivity and accuracy in their research, sociologists must put away their personal opinions.

survey

the collection of data by having people answer a series of questions

population

a target group to be studied

If sociologists were to study a cock fight, such as this one in India, they would not be interested in which cock won the fight. They would want to know who organized the fight, who trains the cocks, how the cocks are matched, what the betting rules are, how those rules are enforced, and so on. To answer such questions, what research methods do you think sociologists would choose?

sample

the individuals intended to represent the population to be studied

random sample

a sample in which everyone in the target population has the same chance of being included in the study

stratified random sample

a sample from selected subgroups of the target population in which everyone in those subgroups has an equal chance of being included in the research

respondents

people who respond to a survey, either in interviews or by self-administered questionnaires

rapport

(ruh-POUR) a feeling of trust between researchers and the people they are studying

of random numbers, you then determine which of these women will become part of your sample. (Tables of random numbers are available in statistics books and online, or they can be generated by a computer.)

A random sample will represent your target population fairly—in this case, married women enrolled at your college. This means that you will be able to generalize your findings to *all* the married women students on your campus, even if they were not included in your sample.

What if you want to know only about certain subgroups, such as the freshmen and seniors? You could use a **stratified random sample**. You would need a list of the freshmen and senior married women. Then, using random numbers, you would select a sample from each group. This would allow you to generalize to all the freshmen and senior married women at your college, but you would not be able to draw any conclusions about the sophomores or juniors.

ASKING NEUTRAL QUESTIONS   After you have decided on your population and sample, the next task is to make certain that your questions are neutral. The questions must allow **respondents**, the people who answer your questions, to express their own opinions. Otherwise, you will end up with biased answers, which are worthless. For example, if you were to ask, "Don't you think that men who beat their wives should go to prison?" you would be tilting the answer toward agreement with a prison sentence. The *Doonesbury* cartoon below illustrates another blatant example of biased questions. For other examples of flawed research, see the Down-to-Earth Sociology box on the next page.

TYPES OF QUESTIONS   You must also decide whether to use closed- or open-ended questions. Closed-ended questions are followed by a list of possible answers. This format would work for questions about someone's age (possible ages would be listed), but not for many other items. For example, how could you list all the opinions that people hold about what should be done to spouse abusers? The choices provided for closed-ended questions can miss the respondent's opinions.

As Table 1.4 on the next page illustrates, you can use open-ended questions, which allow people to answer in their own words. Although open-ended questions allow you to tap the full range of people's opinions, they make it difficult to compare answers. For example, how would you compare these answers to the question "Why do you think men abuse their wives?"

"They're sick."
"I think they must have had problems with their mother."
"We ought to string them up!"

Improperly worded questions can steer respondents toward answers that are not their own, which produces invalid results.

ESTABLISHING RAPPORT Research on spouse abuse brings up a significant issue. You may have been wondering if women who have been abused will really give honest answers to strangers.

If your method of interviewing consists of walking up to women on the street and asking if their husbands have ever beaten them, there would be little reason to take your findings seriously. Researchers need to establish **rapport** (ruh-POUR), a feeling of trust, with their respondents, especially when it comes to sensitive topics—those that elicit feelings of embarrassment, shame, or other negative emotions.

Once rapport is gained (often by first asking nonsensitive questions), victims will talk about personal, sensitive issues. A good example is rape. To go beyond police statistics, researchers interview a random sample of 100,000 Americans each year. They ask them whether they have been victims of burglary, robbery, or other crimes. After establishing rapport, the researchers ask about rape. This National Crime Victimization Survey shows that rape victims will talk about their experiences (Weiss 2009; *Statistical Abstract* 2014:Tables 328, 329, 330).

Table 1.4 Closed- and Open-Ended Questions

A. Closed-Ended Question	B. Open-Ended Question
Which of the following best fits your idea of what should be done to someone who has been convicted of spouse abuse? 1. Probation 2. Jail time 3. Community service 4. Counseling 5. Divorce 6. Nothing—It's a family matter	What do you think should be done to someone who has been convicted of spouse abuse?

SOURCE: By the author.

Down-to-Earth Sociology

Loading the Dice: How *Not* to Do Research

The methods of science lend themselves to distortion, misrepresentation, and downright fraud. Consider these findings from surveys:

> *Americans overwhelmingly prefer Toyotas to Chryslers.*
> *Americans overwhelmingly prefer Chryslers to Toyotas.*

Obviously, these opposite conclusions cannot both be true. In fact, both sets of findings are misrepresentations, even though the responses came from surveys conducted by so-called independent researchers. It turns out that some researchers load the dice. Hired by firms that have a vested interest in the outcome of the research, they deliver the results their clients are looking for (Armstrong 2007). Here are six ways to load the dice.

1. **Choose a biased sample.** If you want to "prove" that Americans prefer Chryslers over Toyotas, interview unemployed union workers who trace their job loss to Japanese imports. The answer is predictable. You'll get what you're looking for.

2. **Ask biased questions.** Even if you choose an unbiased sample, you can phrase questions in such a way that you direct people to the answer you're looking for. Suppose that you ask this question:

> *We are losing millions of jobs to workers overseas who work for just a few dollars a day. After losing their jobs, some Americans are even homeless and hungry. Do you prefer a car that gives jobs to Americans or one that forces our workers to lose their homes?*

This question is obviously designed to channel people's thinking toward a predetermined answer—quite contrary to the standards of scientific research. Look again at the *Doonesbury* cartoon on page 26.

3. **List biased choices.** Another way to load the dice is to use closed-ended questions that push people into the answers you want. Consider this finding:

> *U.S. college students overwhelmingly prefer Levi's 501 to the jeans of any competitor.*

Sound good? Before you rush out to buy Levis, note what these researchers did: In asking students which jeans would be the most popular in the coming year, their list of choices included no other jeans but Levi's 501!

4. **Discard undesirable results.** Researchers can keep silent about results they don't like, or they can continue to survey samples until they find one that matches what they are looking for.

5. **Misunderstand the subjects' world.** This route can lead to errors every bit as great as those just cited. Even researchers who use an adequate sample and word their questions properly can end up with skewed results. They might, for example, fail to anticipate interviewer bias, that people may be embarrassed to express an opinion that isn't "politically correct." For example, surveys show that 80 percent of Americans are environmentalists. Is this an accurate figure? Most Americans are probably embarrassed to tell a stranger otherwise. This would be like going against the flag, motherhood, and apple pie.

6. **Analyze the data incorrectly.** Even when researchers strive for objectivity, the sample is good, the wording is neutral, and the respondents answer the questions honestly, the results can still be skewed. The researchers may make a mistake in their calculations, such as entering incorrect data into computer programs. This, too, of course, is inexcusable in science.

Of these six sources of bias, the first four demonstrate fraud. The final two reflect sloppiness, which is also not acceptable in science.

As has been stressed in this chapter, research must be objective if it is to be scientific. The underlying problem with the research cited here—and with so many surveys bandied about in the media as fact—is that survey research has become big business. Simply put, the money offered by corporations has corrupted some researchers.

The beginning of the corruption is subtle. Paul Light, dean at the University of Minnesota, put it this way: "A funder will never come to an academic and say, 'I want you to produce finding X, and here's a million dollars to do it.' Rather, the subtext is that if the researchers produce the right finding, more work—and funding—will come their way."

SOURCES: Based on Crossen 1991; Goleman 1993; Barnes 1995; Resnik 2000; Augoustinos et al. 2009.

---

participant observation (or fieldwork)

research in which the researcher participates in a research setting while observing what is happening in that setting

case study

an intensive analysis of a single event, situation, or individual

To gather data on sensitive areas, some researchers use Computer-Assisted Self-Interviewing. In this technique, the interviewer gives the individual a laptop computer or a tablet, then moves aside while he or she answers questions on the computer. In some versions of this method, the individual listens to the questions on headphones and answers on the computer screen. When the individual clicks the "Submit" button, the interviewer has no idea how any question was answered (Kaestle 2012). This technique provides privacy, and many people like it. However, some prefer a live interviewer even for sensitive areas of their lives. They say that they want positive feedback from interviewers (Estes et al. 2010).

Participant Observation (Fieldwork)

In the second method, **participant observation** (or **fieldwork**), the researcher *participates* in a research setting while *observing* what is happening in that setting. But how is it possible to study spouse abuse by participant observation? Obviously, you would not sit around and watch someone being abused.

Let's suppose that you are interested in learning how spouse abuse affects wives. You might want to know how the abuse has changed their relationships with their husbands. Or how has it changed their hopes and dreams? Or their ideas about men? Certainly it has affected their self-concepts as well. But how? By observing people as they live their lives, participant observation could provide insight into such questions.

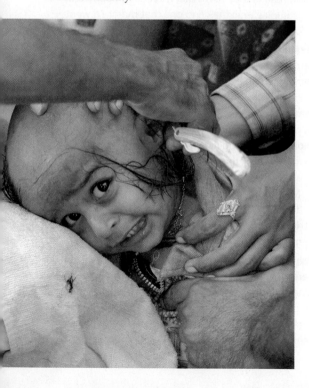

Participant observation, participating and observing in a research setting, is usually supplemented by interviewing, asking questions to better understand why people do what they do. In this instance, the sociologist would want to know what this hair removal ceremony in Gujarat, India, means to the child's family and to the community.

For example, if your campus has a crisis intervention center, you might be able to observe victims of spouse abuse from the time they report the attack through their participation in counseling. With good rapport, you might even be able to spend time with them in other settings, observing further aspects of their lives. What they say and how they interact with others might help you understand how abuse has affected them. This, in turn, could give you insight into how to improve college counseling services.

If you were doing participant observation, you would face this dilemma: How involved should you get in the lives of the people you are observing? Consider this as you read the Down-to-Earth Sociology box on the next page.

Case Studies

To do a **case study**, the researcher focuses on a single event, situation, or individual. The purpose is to understand the dynamics of relationships and power or even the thinking that motivates people. Sociologist Ken Levi (1981/2016, for example, wanted to study hit men. He would have loved having many hit men to interview, but he had access to only one. He interviewed this man over and over, giving us an understanding of how someone can kill others for money. On another level entirely, sociologist Kai Erikson (1978) investigated the bursting of a dam in West Virginia that killed several hundred people. He focused on the events that led up to this disaster and

Down-to-Earth Sociology

Gang Leader for a Day: Adventures of a Rogue Sociologist

Next to the University of Chicago is an area of poverty so dangerous that the professors warn students to avoid it. One graduate student in sociology, Sudhir Venkatesh, the son of immigrants from India, who was working on a research project with William Julius Wilson, ignored the warning.

With clipboard in hand, Sudhir entered "the projects." Ignoring the glares of the young men standing around, he went into the lobby of a high-rise. Seeing a gaping hole where the elevator was supposed to be, he decided to climb the stairs, where he was almost overpowered by the smell of urine. After climbing five flights, Sudhir came upon some young men shooting craps in a dark hallway. One of them jumped up, grabbed Sudhir's clipboard, and demanded to know what he was doing there.

Sudhir blurted, "I'm a student at the university, doing a survey, and I'm looking for some families to interview."

One man took out a knife and began to twirl it. Another pulled out a gun, pointed it at Sudhir's head, and said, "I'll take him."

Then came a series of rapid-fire questions that Sudhir couldn't answer. He had no idea what they meant: "You flip right or left? Five or six? You run with the Kings, right?"

Grabbing Sudhir's bag, two of the men searched it. They could find only questionnaires, pen and paper, and a few sociology books. The man with the gun then told Sudhir to go ahead and ask him a question.

Sweating despite the cold, Sudhir read the first question on his survey, "How does it feel to be black and poor?" Then he read the multiple-choice answers: "Very bad, somewhat bad, neither bad nor good, somewhat good, very good."

As you might surmise, the man's answer was too obscenity-laden to be printed here.

As the men deliberated Sudhir's fate ("If he's here and he don't get back, you know they're going to come looking for him"), a powerfully built man with glittery gold teeth and a sizable diamond earring appeared. The man, known as J. T., who, it turned out, directed the drug trade in the building, asked what was going on. When the younger men mentioned the questionnaire, J. T. said to ask *him* a question.

Amidst an eerie silence, Sudhir asked, "How does it feel to be black and poor?"

"I'm not black," came the reply.

"Well, then, how does it feel to be African American and poor?"

"I'm not African American either. I'm a nigger."

Sudhir was left speechless. Despite his naïveté, he knew better than to ask, "How does it feel to be a nigger and poor?"

As Sudhir stood with his mouth agape, J. T. added, "Niggers are the ones who live in this building. African Americans live in the suburbs. African Americans wear ties to work. Niggers can't find no work."

Not exactly the best start to a research project.

But this weird and frightening beginning turned into several years of fascinating research. Over time, J. T. guided Sudhir into a world that few outsiders ever see. Not only did Sudhir get to know drug dealers, crackheads, squatters, prostitutes, and pimps, but he also was present at beatings by drug crews, drive-by shootings done by rival gangs, and armed robberies by the police.

How Sudhir got out of his predicament in the stairwell, his immersion into a threatening underworld—the daily life for many people in "the projects"—and his moral dilemma at witnessing crimes are part of his fascinating experience in doing participant observation of the Black Kings.

Sudhir, who was reared in a middle-class suburb in California, even took over this Chicago gang for a day. This is one reason that he calls himself a rogue sociologist—the decisions he made that day were violations of law, felonies that could bring years in prison. There are other reasons, too: During the research, he kicked a man in the stomach, and he was present as the gang planned drive-by shootings.

Sudhir Venkatesh, who now teaches at Columbia University, New York City.

Update: Sudhir survived and completed his Ph.D. He teaches at Columbia University, where both fame and controversy have followed. He has appeared on television talk shows, has worked for the FBI, and has been investigated by Columbia University for ethical irregularities.

SOURCES: Based on Venkatesh 2008; Kaminer 2012.

For Your Consideration

→ From Sudhir's experiences, what do you see as the advantages of participant observation? Its disadvantages?

→ Do you think that doing sociological research justifies being present at beatings? At the planning of drive-by shootings?

documents

in its narrow sense, written sources that provide data; in its extended sense, archival material of any sort, including photographs, movies, CDs, DVDs, and so on

experimental group

the group of subjects in an experiment who are exposed to the independent variable

control group

the subjects in an experiment who are not exposed to the independent variable

independent variable

a factor that causes a change in another variable, called the *dependent variable*

dependent variable

a factor in an experiment that is changed by an independent variable

The research methods that sociologists choose depend partially on the questions they want to answer. They might want to learn, for example, which forms of publicity are more effective in increasing awareness of spouse abuse as a social problem.

how people tried to put their lives together after the devastation. For spouse abuse, a case study would focus on a single couple, exploring their history and relationship.

As you can see, the case study reveals a lot of detail about some particular situation, but the question always remains: How much of this detail applies to other situations? This problem of generalizability, which plagues case studies, is the primary reason that few sociologists use this method.

Secondary Analysis

If you were to analyze data that someone else has already collected, you would be doing **secondary analysis**. For example, if you were to examine the original data from a study of women who had been abused by their husbands, you would be doing secondary analysis.

Analysis of Documents

The fifth method that sociologists use is the analysis of **documents**, recorded sources. To investigate social life, they examine such diverse sources as books, newspapers, diaries, bank records, police reports, immigration files, and records kept by organizations. The term *documents* is so broad that it includes video and audio recordings, even *Facebook*, which sociologists have used to study the race–ethnicity of friendships among college students (Wimmer and Lewis 2011).

To study spouse abuse, you might examine police reports to find out how many men in your community have been arrested for abuse. You might also use court records to find out what proportion of those men were charged, convicted, or put on probation. If you wanted to learn about the social and emotional adjustment of the victims, however, these documents would tell you nothing. Other documents, though, might provide those answers. For example, a crisis intervention center might have records that contain key information—but gaining access to them is almost impossible. Perhaps an unusually cooperative center might ask victims to keep diaries for you to study.

Experiments

Do you think abusers need therapy? This sounds like common sense, but no one knows whether therapy would make any difference. Here is where experiments are useful, as they allow us to determine cause and effect. To see the basic requirements of cause and effect, look at Table 1.5 on the next page. Let's suppose that you propose an experiment to a judge and she gives you access to men who have been arrested for spouse abuse. As in Figure 1.7 on page 32, you would divide the men randomly into two groups. This would help ensure that their individual characteristics (attitudes, number of arrests, severity of crimes, education, race–ethnicity, age, and so on) are distributed between the groups. You then would arrange for the men in the **experimental group** to receive some form of therapy that the men in the **control group** would not get.

The therapy would be your **independent variable**, something that causes a change in another variable. Your **dependent variable**, the variable that might change, would be the men's behavior, whether they abuse women after they get out of jail. Unfortunately, your operational definition of the men's behavior will be sloppy: either reports from the wives or records indicating who has been rearrested for abuse. This is sloppy because some of the women will not report the abuse, and some of the men who abuse their wives will not be arrested. Yet it might be the best you can do.

Let's assume that you choose rearrest as your operational definition of the independent variable. If *fewer* of the men who received therapy are rearrested for abuse, you can conclude that the therapy worked. If you find *no difference* in rearrest rates, you

Table 1.5 Cause, Effect, and Spurious Correlations

Causation means that a change in one variable is caused by another variable. Three conditions are necessary for causation: correlation, temporal priority, and no spurious correlation. Let's apply each of these conditions to spouse abuse and alcohol abuse.

1 The first necessary condition is *correlation*

If two variables exist together, they are said to be correlated. If batterers get drunk, battering and alcohol abuse are correlated.

Spouse Abuse + Alcohol Abuse

People sometimes assume that correlation is causation. In this instance, they conclude that alcohol abuse causes spouse abuse.

Alcohol Abuse ⟶ Spouse Abuse

But *correlation never proves causation. Either* variable could be the cause of the other. Perhaps battering upsets men and they then get drunk.

Spouse Abuse ⟶ Alcohol Abuse

2 The second necessary condition is *temporal priority*.

Temporal priority means that one thing happens before something else does. For a variable to be a cause (*the independent variable*), it must precede that which is changed (*the dependent variable*).

          precedes
Alcohol Abuse ⟶ Spouse Abuse

If the men had not drunk alcohol until after they beat their wives, obviously alcohol abuse could not be the cause of the spouse abuse. Although the necessity of temporal priority is obvious, in many studies this is not easy to determine.

3 The third necessary condition is *no spurious correlation*.

This is the necessary condition that really makes things difficult. Even if we identify the correlation of getting drunk and spouse abuse and can determine temporal priority, we still don't know that alcohol abuse is the cause. We could have a *spurious correlation*; that is, the cause may be some underlying third variable. These are usually not easy to identify. Some sociologists think that male culture is that underlying third variable.

Male Culture ⟶ Spouse Abuse

Socialized into dominance, some men learn to view women as objects on which to take out their frustration. In fact, this underlying third variable could be a cause of both spouse abuse and alcohol abuse.

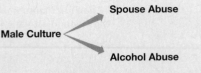

But since only some men beat their wives, while all males are exposed to male culture, other variables must also be involved. Perhaps specific subcultures that promote violence and denigrate women lead to both spouse abuse and alcohol abuse.

If so, this does *not* mean that it is the only causal variable; spouse abuse probably has many causes. Unlike the movement of amoebas or the action of heat on some object, human behavior is infinitely complicated. Especially important are people's *definitions of the situation*, including their views of right and wrong. To explain spouse abuse, then, we need to add such variables as the ways that men view violence and their ideas about the relative rights of women and men. It is precisely to help unravel such complicating factors in human behavior that we need the experiment method.

MORE ON CORRELATIONS

Correlation simply means that two or more variables are present together. The more often that these variables are found together, the stronger their relationship. To indicate their strength, sociologists use a number called a *correlation coefficient*. If two variables are always related, that is, they are always present together, they have what is called a *perfect positive correlation*. The number 1.0 represents this correlation coefficient. Nature has some 1.0's, such as the lack of water and the death of trees; 1.0's also apply to the human physical state, such as the absence of nutrients and the absence of life. But social life is much more complicated than physical conditions, and there are no 1.0's in human behavior.

Two variables can also have a *perfect negative correlation*. This means that when one variable is present, the other is always absent. The number −1.0 represents this correlation coefficient.

Positive correlations of 0.1, 0.2, and 0.3 mean that one variable is associated with another only 1 time out of 10, 2 times out of 10, and 3 times out of 10. In other words, in most instances the first variable is *not* associated with the second, indicating a weak relationship. A strong relationship may indicate causation, but not necessarily. Testing the relationship between variables is the goal of some sociological research.

SOURCE: By the author.

can conclude that the therapy was ineffective. And if you find that the men who received the therapy have a *higher* rearrest rate, you can conclude that the therapy backfired.

Ideally, you would test different types of therapy. Perhaps only some types work. You could even test self-therapy by assigning, articles, books, and videos.

Figure 1.7 The Experiment

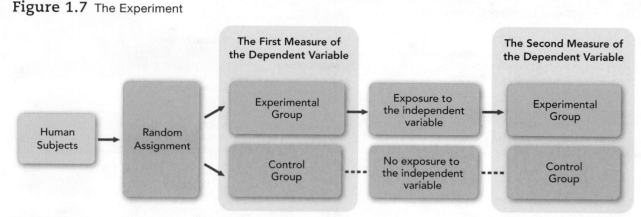

SOURCE: By the author.

The surveillance society is not limited to the United States. This photo was taken as Nice, France, added its 1000th video camera to its surveillance system. How do the unobtrusive measures of sociologists differ from hidden crime surveillance?

unobtrusive measures

ways of observing people so they do not know they are being studied

Unobtrusive Measures

Let's suppose you go to the mall. As you enter, you see a mannequin dressed in the latest fashions. As you glance at it, this bionic mannequin, which looks like a regular one, reports your age, sex, and race–ethnicity (Roberts 2012). Then as you stroll past stores, you are tracked by your smartphone and sent targeted ads (Ramstad 2012; Troianovski 2012). Embedded in the Web coupons you use to make purchases are bar codes that contain your name and Facebook information. Cameras follow you throughout the store, recording each item you touch, as well as every time you pick your nose (Singer 2010).

In our technological society, we are surrounded by **unobtrusive measures**, ways to observe people who are not aware that they are being studied. The face-recognition cameras and tracking devices are part of marketing or law enforcement, not sociological research. In contrast to these technological marvels, the unobtrusive measures used by sociologists are downright primitive. To determine whiskey consumption in a town that was legally "dry," for example, sociologists counted the empty bottles in trashcans (Lee 2000).

How could we use unobtrusive measures to study spouse abuse? As you might surmise, sociologists would consider it unethical to watch someone being abused. If abused or abusing spouses held a public forum on the Internet, however, you could record and analyze their online conversations. Or you could analyze 911 calls. The basic ethical principle is this: To record the behavior of people in public settings, such as a crowd, without announcing that you are doing so is acceptable. To do this in private settings is not.

Gender in Sociological Research

1.8 Explain how gender is significant in sociological research.

You know how significant gender is in your own life, how it affects your orientations and attitudes. Because gender is so influential, researchers take steps to prevent it from biasing their findings (Davis et al. 2010; Rabin 2014). For example, sociologists Diana Scully and Joseph Marolla (1984, 2016) interviewed convicted rapists in prison. They were concerned that gender might lead to *interviewer bias*—that the prisoners might shift their answers, sharing certain experiences or opinions with Marolla but saying something else to Scully. To prevent gender bias, each researcher interviewed half the sample.

Gender certainly can be an impediment in research. In our imagined research on spouse abuse, for example, could a man even do participant observation of women who have been beaten by their husbands? Technically, the answer is yes. But because the women have been victimized by men, they might be less likely to share their experiences and feelings with men. If so, women would be better suited to conduct this research, more likely to achieve valid results. The supposition that these victims will be more open with women than with men, however, is just that—a supposition. Research alone would verify or refute this assumption.

Gender issues can pop up in unexpected ways in sociological research. I vividly recall an incident in San Francisco.

> *The streets were getting dark, and I was still looking for homeless people. When I saw someone lying down, curled up in a doorway, I approached the individual. As I got close, I began my opening research line, "Hi, I'm Dr. Henslin from. . . ." The individual began to scream and started to thrash her arms and legs. Startled by this sudden, high-pitched scream and by the rapid movements, I quickly backed away. When I later analyzed what had happened, I concluded that I had intruded into a woman's bedroom.*

This incident also holds another lesson. Researchers do their best, but they make mistakes. Sometimes these mistakes are minor, even humorous. The woman sleeping in the doorway wasn't frightened. It was only just getting dark, and there were many people on the street. She was just assertively marking her territory and letting me know in no uncertain terms that I was an intruder. If we make a mistake in research, we pick up and go on. As we do so, we take ethical considerations into account, which is the topic of our next section.

Ethics in Sociological Research

1.9   Explain why it's vital for sociologists to protect the people they study; discuss the two cases that are presented.

In addition to choosing an appropriate research method, we must also follow the ethics of sociology (American Sociological Association 1999; Joungtrakul and Allen 2012). Research ethics require honesty, truth, and openness (sharing findings with the scientific community). Ethics clearly forbid the falsification of results, as well as plagiarism—that is, stealing someone else's work. Another ethical guideline states that, generally, people should be informed that they are being studied and that they never should be harmed by the research. Sociologists are also required to protect the anonymity of those who provide information. Sometimes people reveal things that are intimate, potentially embarrassing, or otherwise harmful to themselves or others. Finally, although not all sociologists agree, it generally is considered unethical for researchers to misrepresent themselves.

Sociologists take their ethical standards seriously. To illustrate the extent to which they will go to protect their respondents, consider the research conducted by Mario Brajuha.

Protecting the Subjects: The Brajuha Research

Mario Brajuha, a graduate student at the State University of New York at Stony Brook, was doing participant observation of restaurant workers. He lost his job as a waiter when the restaurant where he was working burned down—a fire of "suspicious origin," as the police said. When detectives learned that Brajuha had taken field notes, they asked to see them (Brajuha and Hallowell 1986). Because he had promised to keep the information confidential, Brajuha refused to hand them over. When the district attorney subpoenaed the notes, Brajuha still refused. The district attorney then threatened to put Brajuha in jail. By this time, Brajuha's notes had become rather famous, and unsavory characters—perhaps those who had set the fire—also wanted to know what was in them. They, too, demanded to see them, accompanying their demands with threats of a different nature. Brajuha found himself between a rock and a hard place.

Ethics in social research are of vital concern to sociologists. As discussed in the text, sociologists may disagree on some of the issue's finer points, but none would approve of slipping LSD to unsuspecting subjects like this Marine. This was done to U.S. soldiers in the 1960s under the guise of legitimate testing—just "to see what would happen."

For two years, Brajuha refused to hand over his notes, even though he grew anxious and had to appear at several court hearings. Finally, the district attorney dropped the subpoena. When the two men under investigation for setting the fire died, the threats to Brajuha, his wife, and their children ended.

Sociologists applaud the way Brajuha protected his respondents and the professional manner in which he handled himself.

Misleading the Subjects: The Humphreys Research

Another ethical problem involves what you tell participants about your research. Although it is considered acceptable for sociologists to do covert participant observation (studying some situation without announcing that they are doing research), to misrepresent oneself is considered unethical. Let's look at the case of Laud Humphreys, whose research forced sociologists to rethink and refine their ethical stance.

Laud Humphreys, a classmate of mine at Washington University in St. Louis, was an Episcopal priest who decided to become a sociologist. For his Ph.D. dissertation, Humphreys (1971, 1975) studied social interaction in "tearooms," public restrooms where some men go for quick, anonymous oral sex with other men.

Humphreys found that some restrooms in Forest Park, just across from our campus, were tearooms. He began a participant observation study by hanging around these restrooms. He found that in addition to the two men having sex, a third man—called a "watch queen"—served as a lookout for police and other unwelcome strangers. Humphreys took on the role of watch queen, not only watching for strangers but also observing what the men did. He wrote field notes after the encounters.

Humphreys decided that he wanted to learn about the regular lives of these men. For example, what was the significance of the wedding rings that many of the men wore? He came up with an ingenious technique: Many of the men parked their cars near the tearooms, and Humphreys recorded their license plate numbers. A friend in the St. Louis police department gave Humphreys each man's address. About a year later, Humphreys arranged for these men to be included in a medical survey conducted by some of the sociologists on our faculty.

Disguising himself with a different hairstyle and clothing, Humphreys visited the men at home, supposedly to interview them for the medical study. He found that they led conventional lives. They voted, mowed their lawns, and took their kids to Little League games. Many reported that their wives were not aroused sexually or were afraid of getting pregnant because their religion did not allow birth control. Humphreys concluded that heterosexual men were also using the tearooms for a form of quick sex.

This research stirred controversy among sociologists and nonsociologists alike. Many sociologists criticized Humphreys, and a national columnist even wrote a scathing denunciation of "sociological snoopers" (Von Hoffman 1970). One of our professors even tried to get Humphreys' Ph.D. revoked. (This professor also hit Humphreys and kicked him after he was down—but that is another story.) As the controversy heated up and a court case loomed, Humphreys feared that his list of respondents might be subpoenaed. He gave me the list to take from Missouri to Illinois, where I had begun teaching. When he called and asked me to destroy it, I burned the list in my backyard.

Was this research ethical? This question is not decided easily. Although many sociologists sided with Humphreys—and his book reporting the research won a highly acclaimed award—the criticisms continued. At first, Humphreys defended his position vigorously, but five years later, in a second edition of his book (1975), he stated that he should have identified himself as a researcher.

Before we close this chapter, I would like to give you a glimpse of two trends that are shaping sociology.

Trends Shaping the Future of Sociology

1.10 **Explain how research versus reform and globalization are likely to influence sociology.**

As we review these changing directions in sociology, let's look first at social reform and then at globalization.

Sociology's Tension: Research versus Reform

THREE STAGES IN SOCIOLOGY As you have seen, a tension between social reform and social analysis runs through the history of sociology. To better understand this tension, we can divide sociology into three time periods (Lazarsfeld and Reitz 1989). During the *first* phase, which lasted until the 1920s, the primary purpose of sociological research was to improve society. During the *second* phase, from the 1920s until the 1960s, the concern switched to developing abstract knowledge. We are still in the *third* phase in which sociologists seek ways to apply their research findings. Many sociology departments offer courses in applied sociology, with some offering internships in applied sociology at both the graduate and undergraduate levels.

DIVERSITY OF ORIENTATIONS I want to stress that sociology is filled with diverse opinions. (From my observations, I would say that when two sociologists meet, they will express three firmly held, contradictory opinions on the same topic.) In any event, to divide sociology into three separate phases overlooks as much as it reveals. During the first phase, for example, some sociologists campaigned against helping the poor, saying that their deaths were good for the progress of society (Stokes 2009). Similarly, during the second phase, many sociologists wanted to reform society. They chafed that knowledge should be the goal of research. And today, many sociologists want the emphasis to remain on basic sociology. Some say that applied sociology is not "real" sociology; it is social work or psychology masquerading as sociology. As you can see, sociologists do not move in lockstep toward a single goal.

Each particular period, however, does have basic emphases, and this division of sociology into three phases pinpoints major trends. The tension that has run through sociology—between gaining knowledge and applying knowledge—will continue. During this current phase, the pendulum is swinging toward applying sociological knowledge.

Globalization

A second major trend, globalization, is also leaving its mark on sociology. **Globalization** is the breaking down of national boundaries because of advances in communications, trade, and travel. Because the United States dominates sociology and we U.S. sociologists tend to concentrate on events and relationships that occur in our own country, most of our findings are based on research in the United States. Globalization is destined to broaden our horizons, directing us to a greater consideration of global issues. This, in turn, is likely to motivate us to try more vigorously to identify universal principles.

APPLICATION OF GLOBALIZATION TO THIS TEXT You are living at a time of major turning point in society, and great historical moments don't make life easy. You are personally experiencing globalization, one of the most significant events in all of world history. This process is shaping your life, your hopes, and your future—sometimes even twisting them. As globalization shrinks the globe, that is, as people around the world become more interconnected within the same global village, your welfare is increasingly tied to that of people in other nations. From time to time in the following pages, you will also explore how the **globalization of capitalism**—capitalism becoming the world's dominant economic system—is having profound effects on your life. You will also confront the developing *new world order,* which, if it can shave off its rough edges, also appears destined to play a significant role in your future.

To help broaden your horizons, in the following chapters you will visit many cultures around the world, looking at what life is like for the people who live in those cultures. Seeing how *their* society affects their behavior and orientations to life should help you understand how *your* society influences what you do and how you feel about life. This, of course, takes you to one of the main goals of this book.

I wish you a fascinating sociological journey, one with new insights around every corner.

globalization of capitalism

capitalism (investing to make profits within a rational system) becoming the globe's dominant economic system

---

Summary and Review

The Sociological Perspective

1.1 Explain why both history and biography are essential for the sociological perspective.

What is the sociological perspective?

The **sociological perspective** stresses that people's social experiences—the groups to which they belong and their experiences within these groups—underlie their behavior. C. Wright Mills referred to this as the intersection of biography (the individual) and history (broad conditions that influence the individual).

Origins of Sociology

1.2 Trace the origins of society, from tradition to Max Weber.

When did sociology first appear as a separate discipline?

Sociology emerged in the mid-1800s in western Europe, during the onset of the Industrial Revolution. Industrialization affected all aspects of human existence—where people lived, the nature of their work, their relationships, and how they viewed life. Early sociologists who focused on these social changes include Auguste Comte, Herbert Spencer, Karl Marx, Emile Durkheim, Max Weber, Harriet Martineau, and W. E. B. Du Bois.

Sociology in North America

1.3 Trace the development of sociology in North America and explain the tension between objective analysis and social reform.

What was the position of women and minorities in early sociology?

The few women who received the education required to become sociologists tended to focus on social reform. The debate between social reform and social analysis was won by male university professors who ignored the contributions of the women. W. E. B. Du Bois faced deep racism in his sociological career.

Why are the positions of Parsons and Mills important?

C. Wright Mills criticized Parsons' abstract analysis of the components of society, saying that it does nothing for social reform, which should be the goal of sociologists. The significance of this position is that the debate about the purpose and use of sociology continues today.

Theoretical Perspectives in Sociology

1.4 Explain the basic ideas of symbolic interactionism, functional analysis, and conflict theory.

What is a theory?

A **theory** is a statement about how facts are related to one another. A theory provides a conceptual framework for interpreting facts.

What are sociology's major theoretical perspectives?

Sociologists use three primary theoretical frameworks to interpret social life. **Symbolic interactionists** examine how people use symbols (meanings) to develop and share their views of the world. Symbolic interactionists usually focus on the **micro level**—on small-scale, face-to-face interaction. **Functional analysts,** in contrast, focus on the macro level—on large-scale patterns of society. Functional theorists stress that a social system is made up of inter-related parts. When working properly, each part contributes to the stability of the whole, fulfilling a function that contributes to the system's equilibrium. **Conflict theorists** also focus on large-scale patterns of society. They stress that society is composed of competing groups that struggle for scarce resources.

With each perspective focusing on select features of social life, and each providing a unique interpretation, no single perspective is adequate. The combined insights of all three yield a more comprehensive picture of social life.

What is the relationship between theory and research?

Theory and research depend on one another. Sociologists use theory to interpret the data they gather. Theory also generates questions that need to be answered by research, while research, in turn, helps to generate theory. Theory without research is not likely to represent real life, while research without theory is merely a collection of empty facts.

Doing Sociological Research

1.5 **Explain why common sense can't replace sociological research.**

Why do we need sociological research when we have common sense?

Common sense is unreliable. Research shows that commonsense ideas are often limited or false.

A Research Model

1.6 **Know the eight steps of the research model.**

What are the eight basic steps in sociological research?

(1) Selecting a topic, (2) Defining the problem, (3) Reviewing the literature, (4) Formulating a **hypothesis**, (5) Choosing a research method, (6) Collecting the data, (7) Analyzing the results, and (8) Sharing the results. These steps are explained on pages 21–23.

Research Methods

1.7 **Know the main elements of the seven research methods: surveys, participant observation, case** studies, secondary analysis, analysis of documents, experiments, and unobtrusive measures.

How do sociologists gather data?

To collect data, sociologists use seven **research methods** (or research designs): **surveys**, **participant observation** (fieldwork), **case studies**, **secondary analysis**, **documents**, **experiments**, and **unobtrusive measures**.

Gender in Sociological Research

1.8 **Explain how gender is significant in sociological research.**

How can gender affect research?

Gender can lead to interviewer bias, with participants shaping their responses based on the gender of the researcher.

Ethics in Sociological Research

1.9 **Explain why it's vital for sociologists to protect the people they study; discuss the two cases that are presented.**

How important are ethics in sociological research?

Ethics are of fundamental concern to sociologists, who are committed to openness, honesty, truth, and protecting their subjects from harm. The Brajuha research on restaurant workers and the Humphreys research on "tearooms" illustrate ethical issues of concern to sociologists.

Trends Shaping the Future of Sociology

1.10 **Explain how research versus reform and globalization are likely to influence sociology.**

What trends are likely to have an impact on sociology?

Sociology has gone through three phases: In the first, the emphasis was on reforming society; in the second, the focus was on basic sociology; the third, today's phase, with its **applied sociology** and **public sociology**, is taking us closer to our roots of applying sociology to social change. Today's **globalization** is likely to broaden sociological horizons, refocusing research and theory away from its concentration on U.S. society.

Thinking Critically about Chapter 1

1. Do you think that sociologists should try to reform society or just study it to gain knowledge?

2. Of the three theoretical perspectives, which one would you prefer to use if you were a sociologist? Why?

3. Considering the macro- and micro-level approaches in sociology, which one do you think better explains social life? Why?

4. What are the differences between good and bad sociological research? How can biases be avoided?

5. What ethics do sociologists follow in their research?

6. Do you think it is okay (or ethical) for sociologists to not identify themselves when they do research? To misrepresent themselves?

Chapter 2
Culture

Learning Objectives

2.1 Explain what culture is, how culture provides orientations to life, and what practicing cultural relativism means. (p. 40)

2.2 Know the components of symbolic culture: gestures, language, values, norms, sanctions, folkways, mores, and taboos; also explain the Sapir-Whorf hypothesis. (p. 46)

2.3 Distinguish between subcultures and countercultures. (p. 53)

2.4 Discuss the major U.S. values and explain value clusters, value contradictions, value clashes, how values are lenses of perception, and ideal versus real culture. (p. 56)

2.5 Explain what cultural universals are and why they do not seem to exist. (p. 60)

2.6 Explain why most sociologists consider genes to be an inadequate explanation of human behavior. (p. 61)

2.7 Explain how technology changes culture and what cultural lag and cultural leveling are. (p. 62)

When I first arrived in Morocco, I found the sights that greeted me exotic—not unlike the scenes in *Casablanca* or *Raiders of the Lost Ark*. The men, women, and even the children really did wear those white robes that reach down to their feet. What was especially striking was that the women were almost totally covered. Despite the heat, they wore not only full-length gowns but also head coverings that reached down over their foreheads with veils that covered their faces from the nose down. You could see nothing but their eyes—and every eye seemed the same shade of brown.

And how short everyone was! The Arab women looked to be, on average, 5 feet, and the men only about 3 or 4 inches taller. As the only blue-eyed, blond, 6-foot-plus person around and the only one who was wearing jeans and a pullover shirt, in a world of white-robed short people I stood out like a creature from another planet. Everyone stared. No matter where I went, they stared. Wherever I looked, I saw people watching me intently. Even staring back had no effect. It was so different from home, where, if you caught someone staring at you, that person would look embarrassed and immediately glance away.

And lines? The concept apparently didn't even exist. Buying a ticket for a bus or train meant pushing and shoving toward the ticket man, always a man—no women were visible in any public position. He took the money from whichever outstretched hand he decided on.

And germs? That notion didn't seem to exist here either. Flies swarmed over the food in the restaurants and the unwrapped loaves of bread in the stores. Shopkeepers would considerately shoo off the flies before handing me a loaf. They also offered home delivery. I watched a bread vendor deliver a loaf to a woman who was standing on a second-floor balcony. She first threw her money to the bread vendor, and he then threw the unwrapped bread up to her. Unfortunately, his throw was off. The bread bounced off the wrought-iron balcony railing

"Everyone stared. No matter where I went, they stared."

and landed in the street, which was filled with people, wandering dogs, and the ever-present urinating and defecating donkeys. The vendor simply picked up the unwrapped loaf and threw it again. This certainly wasn't his day: He missed again. But he made it on his third attempt. The woman smiled as she turned back into her apartment, apparently to prepare the noon meal for her family.

What Is Culture?

2.1 Explain what culture is, how culture provides orientations to life, and what practicing cultural relativism means.

What is culture? The concept is sometimes easier to grasp by description than by definition. For example, suppose you meet a young woman from India who has just arrived in the United States. That her culture is different from yours is immediately evident. You first see it in her clothing, jewelry, makeup, and hairstyle. Next, you hear it in her speech. It then becomes apparent by her gestures. Later, you might hear her express unfamiliar beliefs about relationships or what is valuable in life. All of these characteristics are indicative of **culture**—the language, beliefs, values, norms, behaviors, and even material objects that are passed from one generation to the next.

In northern Africa, I was surrounded by a culture quite different from mine. It was evident in everything I saw and heard. The **material culture**—such things as jewelry, art, buildings, weapons, machines, and even eating utensils, hairstyles, and clothing—provided a sharp contrast to what I was used to seeing. There is nothing inherently "natural" about material culture. That is, it is no more natural (or unnatural) to wear gowns on the street than it is to wear jeans.

I also found myself immersed in an unfamiliar **nonmaterial culture**, that is, a group's ways of thinking (its beliefs, values, and other assumptions about the world) and doing (its common *patterns of behavior*, including language, gestures, and other forms of interaction). North African assumptions that it is acceptable to stare at others in public and to push people aside to buy tickets are examples of nonmaterial culture. So are U.S. assumptions that it is wrong to do either of these things. Like material culture, neither custom is "right." People simply become comfortable with the customs they learn during childhood, and—as happened to me in northern Africa—uncomfortable when their basic assumptions about life are challenged.

Culture and Taken-for-Granted Orientations to Life

"The last thing a fish would ever notice would be water."

Ralph Linton, anthropologist, 1936

To develop a sociological imagination, it is essential to understand how culture affects people's lives. If we meet someone from a different culture, the encounter can make us aware of how culture influences all aspects of someone else's life. Attaining the same level of awareness regarding our own culture, however, is quite another matter. We usually take *our* speech, *our* gestures, *our* beliefs, and *our* customs for granted. We assume that they are "normal" or "natural," and we almost always follow them without question. Ralph Linton made the comment about fish to get this point across: Except in unusual circumstances, most characteristics of our own culture remain imperceptible to us.

Yet culture's significance is profound; it touches almost every aspect of who and what we are. We came into this life without a language; without values and morality; with no ideas about religion, war, money, love, use of space, and so on. We possessed none of these fundamental orientations that are so essential in determining the type of

---

culture

the language, beliefs, values, norms, behaviors, and even material objects that characterize a group and are passed from one generation to the next

material culture

the material objects that distinguish a group of people, such as their art, buildings, weapons, utensils, machines, hairstyles, clothing, and jewelry

nonmaterial culture

a group's ways of thinking (including its beliefs, values, and other assumptions about the world) and doing (its common patterns of behavior, including language and other forms of interaction); also called *symbolic culture* people we become. Yet by this point in our lives, we all have acquired them—and take them for granted. Sociologists call this *culture within us*. These learned and shared ways of believing and of doing (another definition of culture) penetrate our being at an early age and quickly become part of our taken-for-granted assumptions about what normal behavior is. *Culture becomes the lens through which we perceive and evaluate what is going on around us.* Seldom do we question these assumptions: Like water to a fish, the lens through which we view life remains largely beyond our perception.

The rare instances in which these assumptions are challenged, however, can be upsetting. Although as a sociologist I should be able to look at my own culture "from the outside," my trip to Africa quickly revealed how fully I had internalized my own culture. My upbringing in Western culture had given me assumptions about aspects of social life that had become rooted deeply in my being—"appropriate" eye contact, hygiene, and the use of space. But in this part of Africa, these assumptions were useless in helping me navigate everyday life. No longer could I count on people to stare only surreptitiously, to take precautions against invisible microbes, or to stand in line, one behind the other.

As you can tell from the opening vignette, I found these unfamiliar behaviors unsettling—they violated my basic expectations of "the way people *ought* to be"—and I did not even realize how firmly I held these expectations until they were challenged so abruptly. When my nonmaterial culture failed me—when it no longer enabled me to make sense out of the world—I experienced a disorientation known as **culture shock**. In the case of buying tickets, the fact that I was several inches taller than most Moroccans and thus able to outreach others helped me to adjust partially to their different ways of doing things. But I never did get used to the idea that pushing ahead of others was "right," and I always felt guilty when I used my size to receive preferential treatment.

An important consequence of culture within us is **ethnocentrism**, a tendency to use our own group's ways of doing things as a yardstick for judging others. All of us learn that the ways of our own group are good, right, and even superior to other ways of life. As sociologist William Sumner (1906), who developed this concept, said, "One's own group is the center of everything, and all others are scaled and rated with reference to it." Ethnocentrism has both positive and negative consequences. On the positive side, it

culture shock
the disorientation that people experience when they come in contact with a fundamentally different culture and can no longer depend on their taken-for-granted assumptions about life

ethnocentrism
the use of one's own culture as a yardstick for judging the ways of other individuals or societies, generally leading to a negative evaluation of their values, norms, and behaviors

What a tremendous photo for sociologists! Seldom are we treated to such cultural contrasts. Can you see how the cultures of these women have given them not only different orientations concerning the presentation of their bodies but also of gender relations?

creates in-group loyalties. On the negative side, ethnocentrism can lead to discrimination against people whose ways differ from ours.

The many ways in which culture affects our lives fascinate sociologists. In this chapter, we'll examine how profoundly culture influences everything we are and whatever we do. This will serve as a basis from which you can start to analyze your own assumptions of reality. I should give you a warning at this point: You might develop a changed perspective on social life and your role in it. If so, life will never look the same.

IN SUM   To avoid losing track of the ideas under discussion, let's pause for a moment to summarize and, in some instances, clarify the principles we have covered.

1. There is nothing "natural" about material culture. Arabs wear gowns on the street and feel that it is natural to do so. Americans do the same with jeans.

2. There is nothing "natural" about nonmaterial culture. It is just as arbitrary to stand in line as to push and shove.

3. Culture penetrates deeply into our thinking, becoming a taken-for-granted lens through which we see the world and obtain our perception of reality.

4. Culture provides implicit instructions that tell us what we ought to do and how we ought to think. Culture establishes a fundamental basis for our decision making.

5. Culture also provides a "moral imperative"; that is, the culture that we internalize becomes the "right" way of doing things. (I, for example, believed deeply that it was wrong to push and shove to get ahead of others.)

6. Coming into contact with a radically different culture challenges our basic assumptions about life. (I experienced culture shock when I discovered that my deeply ingrained cultural ideas about hygiene and the use of personal space no longer applied.)

7. Although the particulars of culture differ from one group of people to another, culture itself is universal. That is, all people have culture, for a society cannot exist without developing shared, learned ways of dealing with the challenges of life.

8. All people are ethnocentric, which has both positive and negative consequences.

I think you'll enjoy the Cultural Diversity box on the next page. Beyond seeing why sociology is such a pleasure, it will also help you better understand how culture shapes ideas and behavior.

cultural relativism

not judging a culture but trying to understand it on its own terms

Practicing Cultural Relativism

To counter our tendency to use our own culture as the standard by which we judge other cultures, we can practice **cultural relativism**; that is, we can try to understand a culture on its own terms. This means looking at how the elements of a culture fit together, without judging those elements as inferior or superior to our own way of life.

With our own culture embedded so deeply within us, practicing cultural relativism is difficult to do. It is likely that it seems strange to you to think that the dead need money and wrong to you for matadors to stab bulls to death in front of joyful crowds that shout "Olé!" If we practice cultural relativism, however, we will view both giving money to the dead and bullfighting from the perspective of the cultures in which they take place. It will be *their* history, *their* folklore, *their* ideas of mortality and bravery and sex roles that we will use to understand their behavior.

You may still regard bullfighting as wrong, of course, particularly if your culture, which is deeply ingrained in you, has no history of bullfighting. We

Many Americans perceive bullfighting as a cruel activity that should be illegal everywhere. To most Spaniards, bullfighting is a sport that pits matador and bull in a unifying image of power, courage, and glory. Cultural relativism requires that we suspend our own perspectives in order to grasp the perspectives of others, something easier described than attained.

Cultural Diversity around the World

Why the Dead Need Money

Ideas and beliefs about what happens to people after they die vary remarkably among the world's cultures. Common to many cultures are beliefs about ghosts, that the spirits of the dead, especially the recent dead, continue an existence of some sort on the Earth.

Some cultures have built elaborate systems of beliefs about ghosts. One of the most elaborate is that of the traditional Chinese. Their view is that the afterlife closely mirrors the real world (Chen 2013). When people die, their ghosts live in a place just like the one they lived in when they were alive. There, the ghosts have the same needs as living people: food, clothing, houses, and entertainment.

Since these things cost money in the world of the living, they also cost money in the world of the departed. To obtain money, the ghosts depend on the living, and one of the obligations of descendants is to provide that money.

For hundreds of years, traditional Chinese have provided money for their ancestors. Today, they shop in specialized stores that sell ghost money. This money, featuring an image of the Emperor of Hell, looks like an elaborate version of Monopoly money. They get the money to the ghosts by burning it. The ghosts then spend the money on what they need to enjoy life.

As you and I live out our lives, our ideas of what we need keep increasing. This means that we need more and more money. Earlier generations didn't know about cars, televisions, and cell phones, so they had no need of them. These things aren't free for us, so to keep up with our changing needs, we have to keep increasing our incomes.

Like us, those in the ghost world also want to keep up with changing times, so they, too, need computers, iPads, flat-screen televisions, sports cars, and bigger houses. The ghost stores have come up with a solution to these changing needs, and they sell paper replicas of these items. Just as with the ghost money, to send these items to their ancestors, the purchasers burn the replicas.

A woman at a temple in Liuzhou, south China, burning ghost money for her deceased relatives to spend in the afterlife.

Unfortunately, just like in the land of the living, prices in the ghost world also keep increasing. The ghost world has been especially hard hit, though, and it is experiencing hyperinflation. A few years ago, a $100 ghost bill would have gone a long way. Now the ghosts need hundreds of thousands, even millions of dollars. Sometimes they need a billion dollars. Inflation in the ghost world is so out of control that the stores now sell a trillion dollar ghost bill.

As economists do, one Hong Kong economist has come up with a plan to bring ghost inflation to a screaming halt. Citing Milton Friedman that the cause of inflation is an increase in the money supply, he suggests that people burn real money instead of ghost money. This, he says, would immediately reduce the amount of cash flowing into hell.

For Your Consideration

→ How do the traditional Chinese customs regarding the dead differ from your culture's customs?

→ Why do these customs seem strange to Americans and ordinary to traditional Chinese?

→ How has your culture shaped your ideas about death and the relationship of the dead and the living?

all possess culturally specific ideas about how to treat animals, ideas that have evolved slowly and match other elements of our culture. In some areas of the United States, cock fighting, dog fighting, and bear–dog fighting were once common. Only as the culture changed were they gradually eliminated.

Cultural relativism is an attempt to refocus our lens of perception so we can appreciate other ways of life rather than simply asserting, "Our way is right." Although none of us can be entirely successful at practicing cultural relativism, look at the photos on the next page and try to appreciate the cultural differences they illustrate about standards of beauty. I think you will enjoy the Cultural Diversity box below, too, but my best guess is that you will evaluate these "strange" foods through the lens of your own culture.

Cultural Diversity around the World

You Are What You Eat? An Exploration in Cultural Relativity

Here is a chance to test your ethnocentrism and ability to practice cultural relativity. You probably know that the French like to eat snails and that in some Asian cultures, chubby dogs and cats are considered a delicacy ("Ah, lightly browned with a little doggy sauce!"). You might also know that in some cultures, the bull's penis and testicles are prized foods (Jakab 2012). But did you know that cod sperm is a delicacy in Japan (Halpern 2011)? That flies and scorpions are on the menu of restaurants in parts of Thailand (Gampbell 2006)? That on the Italian island of Sardinia, *casu marzi*, a cheese filled with live maggots, is popular (Herz 2012)?

Marston Bates (1967), a zoologist, noted this ethnocentric reaction to food:

> I remember once, in the llanos of Colombia, sharing a dish of toasted ants at a remote farmhouse. . . . My host and I fell into conversation about the general question of what people eat or do not eat, and I remarked that in my country people eat the legs of frogs.
>
> The very thought of this filled my ant-eating friends with horror; it was as though I had mentioned some repulsive sex habit.

Then there is the experience of a friend, Dusty Friedman, who told me:

> When traveling in Sudan, I ate some interesting things that I wouldn't likely eat now that I'm back in our society. Raw baby camel's liver with chopped herbs was a delicacy. So was camel's milk cheese patties that had been cured in dry camel's dung.

What some consider food, even delicacies, can turn the stomach of others. Grilled guinea pigs are served in restaurants in the Peruvian Andes.

You might be able to see yourself eating frog legs and toasted ants, beetles, even flies. (Or maybe not.) Perhaps you could even stomach cod sperm and raw camel liver, maybe even dogs and cats, but here's another test of your ethnocentrism and cultural relativity. Maxine Kingston (1975), an English professor whose parents grew up in China, wrote:

> "Do you know what people in [the Nantou region of] China eat when they have the money?" my mother began. "They buy into a monkey feast. The eaters sit around a thick wood table with a hole in the middle. Boys bring in the monkey at the end of a pole. Its neck is in a collar at the end of the pole, and it is screaming. Its hands are tied behind it. They clamp the monkey into the table; the whole table fits like another collar around its neck. Using a surgeon's saw, the cooks cut a clean line in a circle at the top of its head. To loosen the bone, they tap with a tiny hammer and wedge here and there with a silver pick. Then an old woman reaches out her hand to the monkey's face and up to its scalp, where she tufts some hairs and lifts off the lid of the skull. The eaters spoon out the brains."

For Your Consideration

→ What is your opinion about eating toasted ants? Beetles? Flies? Fried frog legs? Cod sperm? Maggot cheese? About eating puppies and kittens? About eating brains scooped out of a living monkey?

→ If you were reared in U.S. society, more than likely you think that eating frog legs is okay; eating ants or flies is disgusting; and eating cod sperm, maggot cheese, monkey brains, and cats and dogs is downright repugnant. How would you apply the concepts of ethnocentrism and cultural relativism to your perceptions of these customs?

Standards of Beauty

Standards of beauty vary so greatly from one culture to another that what one group finds attractive, another may not. Yet, in its *ethnocentrism,* each group thinks that its standards are the best—that the appearance reflects what beauty "really" is.

As indicated by these photos, around the world men and women aspire to their group's norms of physical attractiveness. To make themselves appealing to others, they try to make their appearance reflect those standards.

Ecuador

USA

Thailand

China

Kenya

Angola

Tibet

New Guinea

ATTACK ON CULTURAL RELATIVISM   Although cultural relativism helps us avoid cultural smugness, this view has come under attack (Mitchum 2013). In a provocative book, *Sick Societies*, anthropologist Robert Edgerton (1992) suggested that we develop a scale for evaluating cultures on their "quality of life," much as we do for U.S. cities. He asks why we should consider cultures that practice genital cutting, gang rape, or wife beating, or cultures that sell little girls into prostitution, as morally equivalent to those that do not. Cultural values that result in exploitation, he says, are inferior to those that enhance people's lives.

The sharp questions and incisive examples of critics bring us to a topic that comes up repeatedly in this text: the disagreements that arise among scholars as they confront contrasting views of reality. It is such questioning of assumptions that keeps sociology interesting.

Components of Symbolic Culture

2.2   Know the components of symbolic culture: gestures, language, values, norms, sanctions, folkways, mores, and taboos; also explain the Sapir-Whorf hypothesis.

Sociologists often refer to nonmaterial culture as **symbolic culture**, because it consists of the symbols that people use. A **symbol** is something to which people attach meaning and that they use to communicate with one another. Symbols include gestures, language, values, norms, sanctions, folkways, and mores. Let's look at each of these components of symbolic culture.

Gestures

Gestures, movements of the body to communicate with others, are shorthand ways to convey messages without using words. Although people in every culture of the world use gestures, a gesture's meaning may change completely from one culture to another. North Americans, for example, communicate a succinct message by raising the middle finger in a short, upward stabbing motion. I wish to stress "North Americans," because this gesture does not convey the same message in most parts of the world.

> *I had internalized this finger gesture to such an extent that I thought everyone knew what it meant, but in Mexico I was surprised to find that it is not universal. When I was comparing gestures with friends in Mexico, this gesture drew a blank look. After I explained its meaning, they laughed and said they would show me their rudest gesture. They placed one hand under an armpit, brought their other hand to the opposite shoulder, and moved their upper arm up and down. To me, they simply looked as if they were imitating a monkey, but to my Mexican hosts the gesture meant "Your mother is a whore"—the worst possible insult in their culture.*

Some gestures are so closely associated with emotional messages that the gestures themselves summon up emotions. For example, my introduction to Mexican gestures took place at a dinner table. It was evident that my husband-and-wife hosts were trying to hide their embarrassment at using their culture's obscene gesture at their dinner table. And I felt the same way—not about *their* gesture, of course, which meant nothing to me—but about the one I was teaching them.

MISUNDERSTANDING AND OFFENSE   Gestures not only facilitate communication, but because they differ around the world they also can lead to misunderstanding, embarrassment, or worse. One time in Mexico, for example, I raised my hand to a certain height to indicate how tall a child was. My hosts began to laugh. It turned out that Mexicans use three hand gestures to indicate height: one for people, a second for animals, and yet another for plants. They were amused because I had used the plant gesture to indicate the child's height. (See Figure 2.1.)

symbolic culture

another term for nonmaterial culture

symbol

something to which people attach meaning and then use to communicate with one another

gestures

the ways in which people use their bodies to communicate with one another

Figure 2.1 Gestures to Indicate Height, Southern Mexico

SOURCE: By the author.

To get along in another culture, then, it is important to learn the gestures of that culture. If you don't, you will fail to achieve the simplicity of communication that gestures allow. You may also overlook or misunderstand much of what is happening, run the risk of appearing foolish, and possibly offend people. In some cultures, for example, you would provoke deep offense if you were to offer food or a gift with your left hand, because the left hand is reserved for dirty tasks, such as wiping after going to the toilet. Left-handed Americans visiting Arabs, please note!

Suppose for a moment that you are visiting southern Italy. After eating one of the best meals in your life, you are so pleased that when you catch the waiter's eye, you smile broadly and use the standard U.S. "A-OK" gesture of putting your thumb and forefinger together and making a large "O." The waiter looks horrified, and you are struck speechless when the manager marches over and angrily asks you to leave. What have you done? Nothing on purpose, of course, but in that culture this gesture refers to a lower part of the human body that is not mentioned in polite company. (Ekman et al. 1984)

UNIVERSAL GESTURES? Is it really true that there are no universal gestures? There is some disagreement on this point. Some anthropologists claim that no gesture is universal. They point out that even nodding the head up and down to indicate "yes" is not universal. In an area of Turkey, nodding the head up and down means "no" (Ekman et al. 1984). However, ethologists, researchers who study the biological bases of behavior, claim that expressions of anger, pouting, fear, and sadness are built into our biological makeup and are universal (Eibl-Eibesfeldt 1970:404; Horwitz and Wakefield 2007). They point out that even infants who are born blind and deaf, who have had no chance to learn these gestures, express themselves in the same way.

Although the details of what is learned and what is inborn is not yet settled, we can note that gestures tend to vary remarkably around the world.

Although most gestures are learned, and therefore vary from culture to culture, some gestures that represent fundamental emotions such as sadness, anger, and fear appear to be inborn. This crying child whom I photographed in India differs little from a crying child in China—or the United States or anywhere else on the globe. In a few years, however, this child will demonstrate a variety of gestures highly specific to his Hindu culture.

Language

The primary way in which people communicate with one another is through **language**—symbols that can be combined in an infinite number of ways for the purpose of communicating abstract thought. Each word is actually a symbol, a sound to

language

a system of symbols that can be combined in an infinite number of ways and can represent not only objects but also abstract thought which we have attached some particular meaning. Although all human groups have language, there is nothing universal about the meanings given to particular sounds. Like gestures, in different cultures the same sound may mean something entirely different—or may have no meaning at all. In German, for example, *gift* means "poison," so if you give a box of chocolates to a non-English-speaking German and say, "Gift, eat,". . . .

Because *language allows culture to exist*, its significance for human life is difficult to overstate. Consider the following effects of language.

LANGUAGE ALLOWS HUMAN EXPERIENCE TO BE CUMULATIVE   By means of language, we pass ideas, knowledge, and even attitudes on to the next generation. This allows others to build on experiences in which they may never directly participate. As a result, humans are able to modify their behavior in light of what earlier generations have learned. This takes us to the central sociological significance of language: *Language allows culture to develop by freeing people to move beyond their immediate experiences.*

Without language, human culture would be little more advanced than that of the lower primates. If we communicated by grunts and gestures, we would be limited to a short time span—to events now taking place, those that have just taken place, or those that will take place immediately—a sort of slightly extended present. You can grunt and gesture, for example, that you are thirsty or hungry, but in the absence of language, how could you share ideas concerning past or future events? There would be little or no way to communicate to others what event you had in mind, much less the greater complexities that humans communicate—ideas and feelings about events.

LANGUAGE PROVIDES A SOCIAL OR SHARED PAST   Without language, we would have few memories, since we associate experiences with words and then use those words to recall the experience. In the absence of language, how would we communicate the few memories we had to others? By attaching words to an event, however, and then using those words to recall it, we are able to discuss the event. This is highly significant: Our talking is far more than "just talk." As we talk about past events, we develop shared understandings about what those events mean. In short, through talk, people develop a shared past.

LANGUAGE PROVIDES A SOCIAL OR SHARED FUTURE   Language also extends our time horizons forward. Because language enables us to agree on times, dates, and places, it allows us to plan activities with one another. Think about it for a moment. Without language, how could you ever plan future events? How could you possibly communicate goals, times, and plans? Whatever planning could exist would be limited to rudimentary communications, perhaps to an agreement to meet at a certain place when the sun is in a certain position. But think of the difficulty, perhaps the impossibility, of conveying just a slight change in this simple arrangement, such as "I can't make it tomorrow, but my neighbor can take my place, if that's all right with you."

LANGUAGE ALLOWS SHARED PERSPECTIVES   Our ability to speak, then, provides us with a social (or shared) past and future. This is vital for humanity. It is a watershed that distinguishes us from animals. But speech does much more than this. When we talk with one another, we are exchanging ideas about events; that is, we are sharing ideas and perspectives. Our words are the embodiment of our experiences, distilled into a readily exchangeable form, one that is mutually understandable to people who have learned that language. *Talking about events allows us to arrive at the shared understandings that form the basis of social life.*

Not sharing a language while living alongside one another, however, invites miscommunication and suspicion. This risk, which comes with a diverse society, is discussed in the following Cultural Diversity box.

Cultural Diversity in the United States

Miami—Continuing Controversy over Language

Immigration from Cuba and other Spanish-speaking countries has been so vast that most residents of Miami are Latinos. Sixty percent of Miamians speak English at home, and half have trouble speaking English. Immigration has so changed Miami that one debate among the candidates for mayor of Miami was held only in Spanish.

English-speaking Miamians were upset. "They need to learn English," they said. Pedro Falcon, an immigrant from Nicaragua, replied, "Miami is the capital of Latin America. The population speaks Spanish." As the English-speakers see it, this pinpoints the problem: Miami, they stress, is in the United States, not in Latin America.

Controversy over immigrants and language isn't new. The millions of Germans who moved to the United States in the 1800s brought their language with them. Not only did they hold religious services in German but they also opened schools where the students were taught in German; published German-language newspapers; and spoke German at home, in the stores, and in the taverns.

Mural from Miami.

Some of their English-speaking neighbors didn't like this one bit. "Why don't those Germans assimilate?" they wondered. "Just whose side would they fight on if we had a war?"

This question was answered with the participation of German Americans in two world wars. It was even a general descended from German immigrants (Eisenhower) who led the armed forces that defeated Hitler.

What happened to all this German language? The first generation of immigrants spoke German almost exclusively. The second generation assimilated, speaking English at home, but also speaking German when visiting their parents.

For the most part, the third generation knew German only as "that language" that their grandparents spoke.

The same thing is happening with the Latino immigrants, but at a slower pace. Spanish is being kept alive longer because Mexico borders the United States, and there is constant traffic between the countries. The continuing migration from Mexico and other Spanish-speaking countries also feeds the language.

If Germany bordered the United States, there would still be a lot of German spoken here.

SOURCES: Based on Kent and Lalasz 2007; Salomon 2008; Costantini 2011; Nelson 2013.

For Your Consideration

→ Do you think that Miami points to the future of the United States?
→ Like the grandchildren of the European immigrants who lost the ability to speak their grandparent's native language, when do you think the grandchildren of Mexican and South American immigrants will be unable to speak Spanish?

LANGUAGE ALLOWS SHARED, GOAL-DIRECTED BEHAVIOR. Common understandings enable us to establish a *purpose* for getting together. Let's suppose you want to go on a picnic. You use speech not only to plan the picnic but also to decide on reasons for having the picnic—which may be anything from "because it's a nice day and it shouldn't be wasted studying" to "because it's my birthday." Language permits you to blend individual activities into an integrated sequence. In other words, as you talk, you decide when and where you will go; who will drive; who will bring the hamburgers, the potato chips, the soda; where and when you will meet. Only because of language can you participate in such a common yet complex event as a picnic—or build roads and bridges or attend college classes.

IN SUM The sociological significance of language is that it takes us beyond the world of apes and allows culture to develop. Language frees us from the present, actually giving us a social past and a social future. That is, language gives us the capacity to share understandings about the past and to develop shared perceptions about the future. Language also allows us to establish underlying purposes for our activities. In short, *language is the basis of culture.*

Language and Perception: The Sapir-Whorf Hypothesis

In the 1930s, two anthropologists, Edward Sapir and Benjamin Whorf, were intrigued when they noticed that the Hopi Indians of the southwestern United States had no words to distinguish the past, the present, and the future. English, in contrast—as well as French, Spanish, Swahili, and other languages—carefully distinguishes these three time frames. From this observation, Sapir and Whorf began to think that words might be more than labels that people attach to things. Eventually, they concluded that *language has embedded within it ways of looking at the world*. In other words, language not only expresses our thoughts and perceptions, but language also *shapes* the way we think and perceive (Sapir 1949; Whorf 1956).

The **Sapir-Whorf hypothesis** challenges common sense: It indicates that rather than objects and events forcing themselves onto our consciousness, it is our language that determines our consciousness and hence our perception of objects and events. Sociologist Eviatar Zerubavel (1991) points out that his native language, Hebrew, does not have separate words for jam and jelly. Both go by the same term, and only when Zerubavel learned English could he "see" this difference, which is "obvious" to native English speakers. Similarly, if you learn to classify students as Jocks, Goths, Stoners, Skaters, Band Geeks, and Preps, you will perceive students in entirely different ways from someone who does not know these classifications.

When I lived in Spain, I was struck by the relevance of the Sapir-Whorf hypothesis. As a native English speaker, I had learned that the term *dried fruits* refers to apricots, apples, and so on. In Spain, I found that *frutos secos* refers not only to such objects but also to things like almonds, walnuts, and pecans. My English makes me see fruits and nuts as very different types of objects. This seems "natural" to me, while combining them into one unit seems "natural" to Spanish speakers. If I had learned Spanish first, my perception of these objects would be different.

Although Sapir and Whorf's observation that the Hopi do not have tenses was wrong (Edgerton 1992:27), they did stumble onto a major truth about social life. Learning a language means not only learning words but also acquiring the perceptions embedded in that language. In other words, language both reflects and shapes our cultural experiences (Boroditsky 2010). The racial–ethnic terms that our culture provides, for example, influence how we see both ourselves and others, a point that is discussed in the Cultural Diversity box on the next page.

Values, Norms, and Sanctions

To learn a culture is to learn people's **values**, their ideas of what is desirable in life. When we uncover people's values, we learn a great deal about them, since values are the standards by which people define what is good and bad, beautiful and ugly. Values underlie our preferences, guide our choices, and indicate what we hold worthwhile in life.

Every group develops expectations concerning the "right" way to reflect its values. Sociologists use the term **norms** to describe those expectations (or rules of behavior) that develop out of a group's values. The term **sanctions** refers to the reactions people receive for following or breaking norms. A **positive sanction** expresses approval for following a norm, and a **negative sanction** reflects disapproval for breaking a norm. Positive sanctions can be material, such as a prize, a trophy, or money, but in everyday life they usually

---

Sapir–Whorf hypothesis

Edward Sapir and Benjamin Whorf's hypothesis that language creates ways of thinking and perceiving

values

the standards by which people define what is desirable or undesirable, superior or inferior, good or bad, beautiful or ugly

norms

expectations of "right" behavior

sanctions

either expressions of approval given to people for following norms or expressions of disapproval for violating them

positive sanction

a reward or positive reaction for following norms, ranging from a smile to a material reward

negative sanction

an expression of disapproval for breaking a norm, ranging from a mild, informal reaction such as a frown to a formal reaction such as a prize or a prison sentence

Cultural Diversity in the United States

Race and Language: Searching for Self-Labels

The groups that dominate society often determine the names that are used to refer to racial–ethnic groups. If those names become associated with oppression, they take on negative meanings. For example, the terms *Negro* and *colored people* came to be associated with submissiveness and low status. To overcome these meanings, those referred to by these terms began to identify themselves as *black* or *African American*. They infused these new terms with respect—a basic source of self-esteem that they felt the old terms denied them.

In a twist, African Americans—and to a lesser extent Latinos, Asian Americans, and Native Americans—have changed the rejected term *colored people* to *people of color*. Those who embrace this modified term are imbuing it with meanings that offer an identity of respect. The term also has political meanings. It implies bonds that cross racial–ethnic lines, mutual ties, and a sense of identity rooted in historical oppression.

There is *always* disagreement about racial–ethnic terms, and *colored people* is no exception. Although most rejected the term, some found in it a sense of respect and claimed it for themselves. The acronym NAACP, for example, stands for the National Association for the Advancement of Colored People. The new term, *people of color*, arouses similar feelings. Some individuals whom this term would include point out that this new label still makes color the primary identifier of people—and it assumes that white people have no color. They stress that humans transcend race–ethnicity, that what we have in

The ethnic terms we choose— or which are given to us—are major self-identifiers. They indicate both membership in some group and a separation from other groups.

common as human beings goes much deeper than what you see on the surface. They stress that we should avoid terms that focus on differences in the pigmentation of our skin.

The language of self-reference in a society that is so conscious of skin color is an ongoing issue. As long as our society continues to emphasize such superficial differences, the search for adequate terms is not likely to ever be "finished." In this quest for terms that strike the right chord, the term *people of color* may become a historical footnote. If it does, the term that replaces it will also indicate changing self-identities within a changing culture.

For Your Consideration

→ What terms do you use to refer to your race–ethnicity? What "bad" terms do you know that others have used to refer to your race–ethnicity? What is the difference in meaning between the terms you use and the "bad" terms? Where does that meaning come from?

---

consist of hugs, smiles, a pat on the back, or even handshakes and "high fives." Negative sanctions can also be material—being fined in court is one example—but negative sanctions, too, are more likely to be symbolic: harsh words, or gestures such as frowns, stares, clenched jaws, or raised fists. Getting a raise at work is a positive sanction, indicating that you have followed the norms clustering around work values. Getting fired, in contrast, is a negative sanction, indicating that you have violated these norms. The North American finger gesture discussed earlier is, of course, a negative sanction.

Because people can find norms stifling, some cultures relieve the pressure through *moral holidays*, specified times when people are allowed to break norms. Moral holidays such as Mardi Gras often center on getting rowdy. Some activities for which people would otherwise be arrested are permitted—and expected—including public drunkenness and

As with Spring Break in Florida, many societies relax their norms during specified occasions. At these times, known as moral holidays, behavior that is ordinarily not permitted is allowed. When a moral holiday is over, the usual enforcement of rules follows.

folkways

norms that are not strictly enforced

mores

norms that are strictly enforced because they are thought essential to core values or the wellbeing of the group

some nudity. The norms are never completely dropped, however—just loosened a bit. Go too far, and the police step in.

Some societies have *moral holiday places*, locations where norms are expected to be broken. The red-light district of a city is one example. There, prostitutes are allowed to work the streets, bothered only when political pressure builds to "clean up" the area. If these same prostitutes attempt to solicit customers in adjacent areas, however, they are promptly arrested. Each year, the hometown of the team that wins the Super Bowl becomes a moral holiday place—for one night.

One of the more interesting examples is "Party Cove" at Lake of the Ozarks in Missouri, a fairly straitlaced area of the country.

During the summer, hundreds of boaters—those operating everything from cabin cruisers to jet skis—moor their vessels together in a highly publicized cove, where many get drunk, take off their clothes, and dance on the boats. In one of the more humorous incidents, boaters complained that a nude woman was riding a jet ski outside of the cove. The water patrol investigated but refused to arrest the woman because she was within the law—she had sprayed shaving cream on certain parts of her body.

The Missouri Water Patrol has even given a green light to Party Cove, announcing in the local newspaper that officers will not enter this cove, supposedly because "there is so much traffic that they might not be able to get out in time to handle an emergency elsewhere."

Folkways, Mores, and Taboos

Norms that are not strictly enforced are called **folkways**. We expect people to follow folkways, but we are likely to shrug our shoulders and not make a big deal about it if they don't. If someone insists on passing you on the right side of the sidewalk, for example, you are unlikely to take corrective action, although if the sidewalk is crowded and you must move out of the way, you might give the person a dirty look.

Other norms, however, are taken much more seriously. We think of them as essential to our core values, and we insist on conformity. These are called **mores** (MORE-rays). A person who steals, rapes, or kills has violated some of society's most important mores. As sociologist Ian Robertson (1987:62) put it:

A man who walks down a street wearing nothing on the upper half of his body is violating a folkway; a man who walks down the street wearing nothing on the lower half of his body is violating one of our most important mores, the requirement that people cover their genitals and buttocks in public.

You can see, then, that one group's folkways can be another group's mores: The man walking down the street with the upper half of his body uncovered is deviating from a folkway, but a woman doing the same thing is violating the mores. In addition, the folkways and mores of a subculture (discussed in the next section) may be the opposite of mainstream culture. For example, to walk down the sidewalk in a nudist camp with the entire body uncovered would conform to that subculture's folkways.

A **taboo** refers to a norm so strongly ingrained that even the thought of its violation is greeted with revulsion. Eating human flesh and parents having sex with their children are examples of such behaviors. When someone breaks a taboo, the individual is usually judged unfit to live in the same society as others. The sanctions are severe and may include prison, banishment, or death.

Many Cultural Worlds

2.3   Distinguish between subcultures and countercultures.

Subcultures

Groups of people who occupy some small corner in life, such as an occupation, tend to develop specialized ways of communicating with one another. To outsiders, their talk, even if it is in English, can sound like a foreign language. Here is one of my favorite quotations by a politician:

The violation of *mores* is a serious matter. In this case, it is serious enough that the security at a football match in Edmonton, Alberta (Canada), have swung into action to protect the public from seeing a "disgraceful" sight, at least one so designated by this group.

> *There are things we know that we know. There are known unknowns; that is to say, there are things that we now know we don't know. But there are also unknown unknowns; there are things we do not know we don't know. (Donald Rumsfeld, quoted in Dickey and Barry 2006:38)*

Whatever Rumsfeld, the former secretary of defense under George W. Bush, meant by his statement probably will remain a known unknown. (Or would it be an unknown unknown?)

We have a similar problem in sociology. Try to figure out what this means:

> *The interaction of world market dynamics and state capacities is shaped by the continued separation of the profit-oriented, market-mediated dimension of accumulation from its crucial extra-economic supports in the legal and political system (among other institutional orders) and, notwithstanding this variable institutional separation, the continued reciprocal interdependence of 'market' and 'state 'as complementary moments of the capital relation. (Jessop 2010)*

As much as possible, I will spare you from such "insider" talk.

Sociologists and politicians form a **subculture**, *a world within the larger world of the dominant culture.* Subcultures are not limited to occupations. They include any corner in life in which people's experiences lead them to have distinctive ways of looking at the world. Even if we cannot understand the quotation from Donald Rumsfeld, it makes us aware that politicians don't view life in quite the same way most of us do.

U.S. society contains *thousands* of subcultures. Some are as broad as the way of life we associate with teenagers, others as narrow as those we associate with bodybuilders— or with politicians. Some U.S. ethnic groups also form subcultures: Their values, norms, and foods set them apart. So might their religion, music, language, and clothing. Even sociologists form a subculture. As you are learning, they also use a unique language in their efforts to understand the world.

For a visual depiction of subcultures, see the photo essay on the next two pages.

taboo

a norm so strong that it brings extreme sanctions, even revulsion, if violated

subculture

the values and related behaviors of a group that distinguish its members from the larger culture; a world within a world

Looking at Subcultures

Each subculture provides its members with values and distinctive ways of viewing the world. What values and perceptions do you think are common among bodybuilders?

Why would anyone decorate herself like this? Among the many reasons, one is to show solidarity (appreciation, shared interest) with the subculture that centers on comic book characters.

With their specialized language and activities, surfers are highly recognized as members of a subculture. This surfer is "in the tube."

Specialized values and interests are two of the characteristics that mark subcultures. What values and interests distinguish the modeling subculture?

Membership in this subculture is not easily awarded. Not only must high-steel ironworkers prove that they are able to work at great heights but also that they fit into the group socially. Newcomers are tested by members of the group, and they must demonstrate that they can take joking without offense.

The cabbies' subculture, centering on their occupational activities and interests, is also broken into smaller subcultures that reflect their experiences of race–ethnicity.

The subculture that centers around tattooing previously existed on the fringes of society, with seamen and circus folk its main participants. It now has entered mainstream society, but not to this extreme.

Even subcultures can have subcultures. The rodeo subculture is a subculture of "western" subculture. The values that unite its members are reflected in their speech, clothing, and specialized activities, such as the one shown here.

Countercultures

Look what a different world this person is living in:

> *If everyone applying for welfare had to supply a doctor's certificate of sterilization, if every-*
> *one who had committed a felony were sterilized, if anyone who had mental illness to any*
> *degree were sterilized—then our economy could easily take care of these people for the rest of*
> *their lives, giving them a decent living standard—but getting them out of the way. That way*
> *there would be no children abused, no surplus population, and, after a while, no pollution. . . .*
>
> *When the . . . present world system collapses, it'll be good people like you who will*
> *be shooting people in the streets to feed their families. (Zellner 1995:58, 65)*

Welcome to the world of the Aryan supremacist survivalists, where the message is much clearer than that of politicians—and much more disturbing.

The values and norms of most subcultures blend in with mainstream society. In some cases, however, as with the survivalists quoted above, some of the group's values and norms place it at odds with the dominant culture. Sociologists use the term **counterculture** to refer to such groups. To better see this distinction, consider motorcycle enthusiasts and motorcycle gangs.

Motorcycle enthusiasts—who emphasize personal freedom and speed *and* affirm cultural values of success through work or education—are members of a subculture. In contrast, the Hell's Angels, Pagans, and Bandidos not only stress freedom and speed but also value dirtiness and contempt toward women, work, and education. This makes them a counterculture.

An assault on core values is always met with resistance. To affirm their own values, members of the mainstream culture may ridicule, isolate, or even attack members of the counterculture. The Mormons, for example, were driven out of several states before they finally settled in Utah, which was at that time a wilderness. Even there, the federal government would not let them practice *polygyny* (one man having more than one wife), and Utah's statehood was made conditional on its acceptance of monogamy (Anderson 1942/1966; Williams 2007).

counterculture

a group whose values, beliefs, norms, and related behaviors place its members in opposition to the broader culture

Why are the Outlaws part of a counterculture and not a subculture? This photo was taken in Mettenheim, Germany, as 1,000 Outlaws attended the burial of their leader, who had just been murdered.

Values in U.S. Society

2.4 Discuss the major U.S. values and explain value clusters, value contradictions, value clashes, how values are lenses of perception, and ideal versus real culture.

An Overview of U.S. Values

As you know, the United States is a **pluralistic society**, made up of many different groups. The United States has numerous religious and racial–ethnic groups, as well as countless interest groups that focus on activities as divergent as hunting deer or collecting Barbie dolls. Within this huge diversity, sociologists have tried to identify the country's **core values**, those that are shared by most of the groups that make up U.S. society. Here are ten core values that sociologist Robin Williams (1965) identified:

pluralistic society

a society made up of many different groups

core values

the values that are central to a group, those around which a group builds a common identity

1. *Achievement and success.* Americans praise personal achievement, especially outdoing others. This value includes getting ahead at work and school and attaining wealth, power, and prestige.

2. *Individualism.* Americans cherish the ideal that an individual can rise from the bottom of society to its very top. If someone fails to "get ahead," Americans generally find fault with that individual rather than with the social system for placing roadblocks in his or her path.

3. *Hard work.* Americans expect people to work hard to achieve financial success and material comfort.

4. *Efficiency and practicality.* Americans award high marks for getting things done efficiently. Even in everyday life, Americans consider it important to do things fast, and they seek ways to increase efficiency.

5. *Science and technology*. Americans have a passion for applied science, for using science to control nature—to tame rivers and harness winds—and to develop new technology, from iPads to self-driving cars.

6. *Material comfort*. Americans expect a high level of material comfort. This includes not only plentiful food, fashionable clothing, and ample housing but also good medical care, late-model cars, and recreational playthings—from smartphones to motor homes.

7. *Freedom*. This core value pervades U.S. life. It underscored the American Revolution, and Americans pride themselves on their personal freedom.

8. *Democracy*. By this term, Americans refer to majority rule, to the right of everyone to express an opinion, and to representative government.

9. *Equality*. It is impossible to understand Americans without being aware of the central role that the value of equality plays in their lives. Equality of opportunity (part of the ideal culture discussed later) has significantly influenced U.S. history and continues to mark relations between the groups that make up U.S. society.

10. *Group superiority*. Although it contradicts the values of freedom, democracy, and equality, Americans regard some groups more highly than others and have done so throughout their history. The denial of the vote to women, the slaughter of Native Americans, and the enslavement of Africans are a few examples of how dominant groups considered themselves superior and denied equality, freedom, and even life to others.

In an earlier publication, I updated Williams' analysis by adding these three values.

1. *Education*. Americans are expected to go as far in school as their abilities and finances allow. Over the years, the definition of an "adequate" education has changed, and today a college education is considered an appropriate goal for most Americans. Those who have an opportunity for higher education and do not take it are sometimes viewed as doing something "wrong"—not merely as making a bad choice, but as somehow being involved in an immoral act.

2. *Religiosity*. There is a feeling that "every true American ought to be religious." This does not mean that everyone is expected to join a church, synagogue, or mosque, but that everyone ought to acknowledge a belief in a Supreme Being and follow some set of matching precepts. This value is so pervasive that Americans stamp "In God We Trust" on their money and declare in their national pledge of allegiance that they are "one nation under God."

3. *Romantic love*. Americans feel that the only proper basis for marriage is romantic love. Songs, literature, mass media, and folk beliefs all stress this value. Americans grow misty-eyed at the theme that "love conquers all."

Value Clusters

As you can see, values are not independent units; some cluster together to form a larger whole. In the **value cluster** that surrounds success, for example, we find education, hard work, material comfort, and individualism bound up together. Americans are expected to go far in school, to work hard afterward, and then to attain a high level of material comfort, which, in turn, demonstrates success. Success is attributed to the individual's efforts; lack of success is blamed on his or her faults.

value cluster
values that together form a larger whole

Value Contradictions

You probably were surprised to see group superiority on the list of dominant American values. This is an example of what I mentioned in Chapter 1, how sociology upsets people and creates resistance. Few people want to bring something like this into the open. It violates today's *ideal culture*, a concept we will discuss shortly. But this is what sociologists do—they look beyond the façade to penetrate what is really going on. And when you look at our history, there is no doubt that group superiority has been a dominant value. It still is, but values change, and this one is diminishing.

value contradiction

values that contradict one another; to follow the one means to come into conflict with the other

Value contradictions, then, are part of culture. Not all values come wrapped in neat, pretty packages, and you can see how group superiority contradicts freedom, democracy, and equality. There simply cannot be a full expression of freedom, democracy, and equality along with racism and sexism. Something has to give. One way in which Americans in the past sidestepped this contradiction was to say that freedom, democracy, and equality applied only to some groups. The contradiction was bound to surface over time, however, and so it did with the Civil War and the women's liberation movement. *It is precisely at the point of value contradictions, then, that you can see a major force for social change in a society.*

An Emerging Value Cluster

A value cluster of four interrelated core values—leisure, self-fulfillment, physical fitness, and youthfulness—is emerging in the United States. So is a fifth core value—concern for the environment.

1. *Leisure.* The emergence of leisure as a value is reflected in a huge recreation industry—from computer games, boats, vacation homes, and spa retreats to sports arenas, home theaters, adventure vacations, and luxury cruises.

2. *Self-fulfillment.* This value is reflected in the "human potential" movement, which emphasizes becoming "all you can be," and in magazine articles, books, and talk shows that focus on "self-help," "relating," and "personal development."

3. *Physical fitness.* Physical fitness is not a new U.S. value, but the greater emphasis on it is moving it into this emerging cluster. You can see this trend in the emphasis placed on nutrition, organic foods, weight, and diet; the many joggers, cyclists, and backpackers; the marathons; and the countless health clubs and physical fitness centers.

Physical fitness, as with this Zumba class, is part of an emerging value cluster.

4. *Youthfulness.* Valuing youth and disparaging old age are also not new, but some analysts note a sense of urgency in today's emphasis on youthfulness. They attribute this to the huge number of aging baby boomers, who, aghast at the physical changes that accompany their advancing years, are attempting to deny or at least postpone their biological fate. Some physicians even claim that aging is not a normal life event but a disease (Nieuwenhuis-Mark 2011).

5. *Concern for the environment.* During most of U.S. history, the environment was viewed as something to be exploited—a wilderness to be settled, forests to be cleared for farmland and lumber, rivers and lakes to be fished, and animals to be hunted. One result was the near extinction of the bison and the extinction in 1914 of the passenger pigeon, a species of bird previously so numerous that its annual migration would darken the skies for days. With their pollution laws and lists of endangered species, today's Americans have developed an apparently long-term concern for the environment.

IN SUM Values don't "just happen." They are related to conditions of society. This emerging value cluster is a response to fundamental changes in U.S. culture. Earlier generations of Americans were focused on forging a nation and fighting for economic survival. But today, millions of Americans are freed from long hours of work, and millions retire from work at an age when they anticipate decades of life ahead of them. This new value cluster centers on helping people maintain their health and vigor during their younger years and enabling them to enjoy their years of retirement.

Only when an economy produces adequate surpluses can a society afford these emerging values. To produce both longer lives and retirement, for example, requires a certain stage of economic development. Concern for the environment is another remarkable example. People act on environmental concerns only *after* they have met their basic needs. The world's poor nations have a difficult time "affording" this value at this point in their development (MacLennan 2012).

When Values Clash

Challenges in core values are met with strong resistance by the people who hold them dear. They see change as a threat to their way of life, an undermining of both their present and their future. Efforts to change gender roles, for example, arouse intense controversy, as do same-sex marriages. Alarmed at such onslaughts against their values, traditionalists fiercely defend the family relationships and gender roles they grew up with. Some use the term *culture wars* to refer to the clash in values between traditionalists and those advocating change, a term that is highly exaggerated. Compared with the violence directed against the Mormons, today's culture clashes are but mild disagreements.

Values as Distorting Lenses

Values and their supporting beliefs are lenses through which we see the world. The views that these lenses provide are often of what life *ought* to be like, not what it is. For example, Americans value individualism so highly that they tend to see almost everyone as free and equal in pursuing the goal of success. This value blinds them to the significance of the circumstances that keep people from achieving success. The dire consequences of family poverty, parents' low education, and dead-end jobs tend to drop from sight. Instead, Americans see the unsuccessful as not taking advantage of opportunities, or as having some inherent flaw, such as laziness or dull minds. And they "know" they are right, because the mass media dangle before their eyes enticing stories of individuals who have succeeded despite the greatest of handicaps.

"Ideal" Versus "Real" Culture

Many of the norms that surround cultural values are followed only partially. Differences always exist between a group's ideals and what its members actually do. Consequently, sociologists use the term **ideal culture** to refer to the values, norms, and goals that a

ideal culture

a people's ideal values and norms; the goals held out for them

Values, both those held by individuals and those that represent a nation or people, can undergo deep shifts. It is difficult for many of us to grasp the pride with which earlier Americans destroyed trees that took thousands of years to grow, are located only on one tiny speck of the globe, and that we today consider part of the nation's and world's heritage. But this is a value statement, representing current views. The pride expressed on these woodcutters' faces represents another set of values entirely.

group considers ideal, worth aiming for. Success, for example, is part of ideal culture. Americans glorify academic progress, hard work, and the display of material goods as signs of individual achievement. What people actually do, however, usually falls short of the cultural ideal. Compared with their abilities, for example, most people don't work as hard as they could or go as far as they could in school. Sociologists call the norms and values that people actually follow **real culture**.

real culture

the norms and values that people actually follow; as opposed to *ideal culture*

Cultural Universals

2.5   **Explain what cultural universals are and why they do not seem to exist.**

cultural universal

a value, norm, or other cultural trait that is found in every group

With the amazing variety of human cultures around the world, are there any **cultural universals**—values, norms, or other cultural traits that are found everywhere?

To answer this question, anthropologist George Murdock (1945) combed through the data that anthropologists had gathered on hundreds of groups around the world. He compared their customs concerning courtship, marriage, funerals, games, laws, music, myths, incest taboos, and even toilet training. He found that these activities are present in all cultures, but *the specific customs differ from one group to another.* There is no universal form of the family, no universal way of toilet training children, no universal music, and no universal way of disposing of the deceased.

Incest is another remarkable example. Groups don't even agree on what incest is. The Mundugumors of New Guinea extend the incest taboo so far that for each man, seven of every eight women are ineligible marriage partners (Mead 1935/1950). Other groups go in the opposite direction and allow some men to marry their own daughters (La Barre 1954). Some groups even *require* that brothers and sisters marry one another, although only in certain circumstances (Beals and Hoijer 1965). The Burundi of Africa even insist that a son have sex with his mother—but only to remove a certain curse (Albert 1963). Such sexual relations, so surprising to us, are limited to special people (royalty) or to extraordinary situations (such as the night before a dangerous lion hunt). No society permits generalized incest for its members.

IN SUM   Although there are universal human activities (singing, playing games, storytelling, preparing food, marrying, child rearing, disposing of the dead, and so on), there is no universal way of doing any of them.

Sociobiology and Human Behavior

2.6   **Explain why most sociologists consider genes to be an inadequate explanation of human behavior.**

sociobiology

a framework of thought in which human behavior is considered to be the result of natural selection and biological factors: a fundamental cause of human behavior

A controversial view of human behavior, called **sociobiology** (also known as neo-Darwinism and evolutionary psychology), provides a sharp contrast to the perspective of this chapter, that the key to human behavior is culture. Sociobiologists believe that because of natural selection, biology is a basic cause of human behavior (Wade 2014). In the following Thinking Critically section, let's consider this view.

Thinking Critically

Are We Prisoners of Our Genes?

Charles Darwin (1859), who, as we saw in Chapter 1, adopted Spencer's idea of *natural selection*, pointed out that the genes of a species—the units that contain an individual's traits—are not distributed evenly among a population. The characteristics that some members inherit make it easier for them to survive their environment, increasing the likelihood that they will pass their genetic traits to the next generation. Over thousands of generations, the genetic traits that aid survival become common in a species, while those that do not aid survival become less common or even disappear. Natural selection explains not only the physical characteristics of animals but also their behavior, since over countless generations, instincts emerged.

Edward Wilson (1975), an insect specialist, set off an uproar when he claimed that human behavior is like the behavior of cats, rats, bats, and gnats—bred into *Homo sapiens* through evolutionary principles. Wilson went on to claim that sociobiology can explain competition and cooperation, envy and altruism—even religion, slavery, genocide, and war and peace. He provocatively added that because genetic programming can explain human behavior, sociobiology will eventually absorb sociology, as well as anthropology and psychology.

Most sociologists think that this view is ridiculous. It is not that sociologists deny that biology is important in human behavior—at least in the sense that there would be no speech if humans had no tongue or larynx and that it takes a highly developed brain to develop human culture and abstract thought. We all know that to stay alive we must eat and keep from freezing and that this certainly motivates some of our behavior. Biology is so significant that it could

Unlike this beautiful ant, we humans are not controlled by instincts. Sociobiologists, though, are exploring the extent to which genes influence our behavior.

even underlie the origin of gender inequality, one of the theories we discuss in Chapter 10.

Some sociologists do emphasize the influence of genes on human behavior. Developing what they call *genetics-informed sociology*, they are coming up with interesting findings. For example, people with the gene DRD2 are more likely than people without this gene to abuse alcohol ("The Interaction of..." 2012). Similarly, males who have the gene 9R/9R average fewer sexual partners than people without this gene. The 9R/9R individuals are also less likely to binge drink and more likely to wear seat belts (Guo et al. 2008).

The response of most sociologists to this research is, where is the social? Simply put, *the genes don't determine people's behavior. Rather, the influence of genes is modified*

(continued)

by social experiences. On the obvious level, Arabs with the gene DRD2 who live in a society where alcohol is difficult to find are less likely to abuse alcohol than are Americans with this gene who hang around bars. Similarly, subcultures that encourage sexual behavior override the 9R/9R gene. To their surprise, researchers have even found that social experiences can change how genes influence behavior (Sapolsky 2014b).

IN SUM To say that genes have an influence on human behavior is a far cry from saying that genes determine human behavior,

that we act as we do because of our genes. On the contrary, pigs act like pigs and spiders act like spiders because instincts control their behavior. We humans, in contrast, possess a self and engage in abstract thought. We develop purposes and goals and discuss the reasons that we do things. Unlike pigs and spiders, we are immersed in a world of symbols that we use to consider, reflect, and make reasoned choices. Because we humans are not prisoners of our genes, we have developed fascinatingly diverse ways of life around the world—which we will be exploring in this text.

Technology in the Global Village

2.7 **Explain how technology changes culture and what cultural lag and cultural leveling are.**

The New Technology

The gestures, language, values, folkways, and mores that we have discussed—all are part of symbolic (nonmaterial) culture. Culture, as you recall, also has a material aspect: a group's *things*, from its houses to its toys. Central to a group's material culture is its technology. In its simplest sense, **technology** can be equated with tools. In a broader sense, technology also includes the skills or procedures necessary to make and use those tools.

We can use the term **new technology** to refer to an emerging technology that has a significant impact on social life. Although people develop minor technologies all the time, most are only slight modifications of existing technologies. Occasionally, however, they develop a technology that makes a major impact on human life. It is primarily to these innovations that the term *new technology* refers. Five hundred years ago, the new technology was the printing press. For us, the new technology consists of the microchip, computers, satellites, and the Internet.

The sociological significance of technology goes far beyond the tool itself. *Technology sets the framework for a group's nonmaterial culture.* It is obvious that if a group's technology changes, so do the ways people do things. But the effects of technology go far beyond this. Technology also influences how people think and how they relate to one another. An example is gender relations. Through the centuries and throughout the world, it has been the custom (nonmaterial culture) for men to dominate women. Today's global communications (material culture) make this custom more difficult to maintain. For example, when Arab women watch Western television, they observe an unfamiliar freedom in gender relations. As these women use e-mail and cell phones to talk about what they have seen, they both convey and create discontent, as well as feelings of sisterhood. These communications motivate some of them to agitate for social change.

In today's world, the long-accepted idea that it is proper to withhold rights on the basis of someone's sex can no longer be sustained. What usually lies beyond our awareness in this revolutionary change is the role of the new technology, which joins the world's nations into a global communications network.

The changes are so extensive that we can hardly keep up with them. For a glimpse of technology being developed that will affect your life, read the Sociology and the New Technology box on the next page.

Cultural Lag and Cultural Change

Three or four generations ago, sociologist William Ogburn (1922/1950) coined the term **cultural lag**. By this, Ogburn meant that not all parts of a culture change at the same pace. When one part of a culture changes, other parts lag behind.

technology

in its narrow sense, tools; its broader sense includes the skills or procedures necessary to make and use those tools

new technology

the emerging technologies of an era that have a significant impact on social life

cultural lag

Ogburn's term for human behavior lagging behind technological innovations

Sociology and the New Technology

How Smart Is Your Clothing?

"Google Glass" is world famous. Though a bit awkward, it does allow instantaneous communications via the Internet. A tremendous advancement: Eye movements become cursors.

But we have barely touched the surface. Despite its heralded advancements, today's Google Glass is destined to be a relic of the past, much as computers from the 1980s have become prized museum pieces.

Certainly not many of us want to walk around wearing this monstrosity. Although sleeker, more chic models are in the works, Google Glass remains an awkward device. In contrast, how about wearable computing items that are invisible? Ones that don't interfere with movement or appearance? They're on the way.

How about your T-shirt talking to you? Already developed. A company makes one that reports your heart beat, measures your breathing, and tells you how many calories you are burning (Bilton 2014).

How about a wonder bra? No that name was taken long ago. This coming "smart bra," which will give the wearer feedback about her physical fitness, is yet to be given a unique name.

"Smart textiles," clothing with sensors woven into them, are already in production. Some predict that within a decade all of our clothing will contain biofeedback sensors. First will

The implications of technology go far beyond "the thing," what you can see, such as this robot that serves food and drinks in a seafood restaurant in China. As technology changes, so do our ideas, values, and relationships.

come smart textiles for fitness buffs, then those for people with health problems. From there, smart clothing will go mainstream. The microsensors woven into smart clothing will be so fine that neither the wearer nor anyone else will be aware of them.

Unless the wearer wants someone to be aware, that is. In development is a marvelously strange item that stirs the imagination, a dress called Intimacy. The dress has an opaque fabric that turns transparent when its wearer becomes sexually aroused.

You can see that the term personal computing is likely to gain an entirely different meaning.

"Intimacy" is probably a specialty item that won't be in huge demand. Or it could indicate that society is on the cusp of another vast change.

We'll see—in more ways than one.

For Your Consideration

→ How do you think *your* life will be different in ten years because of developments in computing?

→ How do you think society will be different ten years from now because of developments in computing?

Ogburn pointed out that *a group's material culture usually changes first, with the nonmaterial culture lagging behind.* This leaves the nonmaterial (or symbolic) culture playing a game of catch-up. For example, when we get sick, we can type our symptoms into a computer and get an instant diagnosis and recommended course of treatment. In some tests, computer programs outperform physicians. Yet our customs have not caught up with our technology, and we continue to visit the doctor's office.

Sometimes nonmaterial culture never does catch up. We can rigorously hold onto some outmoded form—one that once was needed but that long ago was bypassed by technology. Have you ever wondered why our "school year" is nine months long, and why we take summers off? For most of us, this is "just the way it is," and we have never questioned it. But there is more to this custom than meets the eye. In the late 1800s, when universal schooling came about, the school year matched the technology of the time. Most parents were farmers, and for survival they needed their children's help at the crucial times of planting and harvesting. Today, generations later, when few people

Language is the basis of human culture. Our new technology makes it easy to talk with people across the globe, something new in human history. This development is changing cultures. Shown here is a Kayapo Indian talking on his cell phone at the National Indigenous Mobilization conference in Brazil.

"JUST THINK OF IT AS IF YOU'RE READING A LONG TEXT-MESSAGE."

Technological advances are now so rapid that there can be cultural gaps between generations.

cultural diffusion

the spread of cultural traits from one group to another; includes both material and nonmaterial cultural traits

farm and there is no need for the "school year" to be so short, we still live with this cultural lag.

Technology and Cultural Leveling

For most of human history, communication was limited and travel was slow. Consequently, in their smaller groups living in relative isolation, people developed highly distinctive ways of life as they responded to the particular situations they faced. The unique characteristics they developed that distinguished one culture from another tended to change little over time. The Tasmanians, who live on a remote island off the coast of Australia, provide an extreme example. For thousands of years, they had no contact with other people. They were so isolated that they did not even know how to make clothing or fire (Edgerton 1992).

Except in such rare instances, humans have always had *some* contact with other groups. During these contacts, people learned from one another, adopting things they found desirable. In this process, called **cultural diffusion**, groups are most open to changes in their technology or material culture. They usually are eager, for example, to adopt superior weapons and tools. In remote jungles in South America, one can find metal cooking pots, steel axes, and even bits of clothing spun in mills in South Carolina. Although the direction of cultural diffusion today is primarily from the West to other parts of the world, cultural diffusion is not a one-way street—as bagels, woks, hammocks, and sushi in the United States attest.

Cultural leveling is occurring rapidly, with some strange twists. These men from an Amazon tribe have just come back from a week hunting in the jungle. They are wearing traditional headdress and using traditional weapons, but you can easily spot things that are jarringly out of place.

With today's trade, travel, and communications, cultural diffusion is occurring rapidly. Jet planes have made it possible to journey around the globe in a matter of hours. Daily, we use products from around the world. In the not-so-distant past, a trip from the United States to Africa was so unusual that only a few adventurous people made it, so few that newspapers would herald their feat. Today, hundreds of thousands make the trip each year.

The changes in communication are no less vast. Communication used to be limited to face-to-face speech, written messages that were passed from hand to hand, and visual signals such as smoke or light reflected from mirrors. Despite newspapers and even the telegraph, people in some parts of the United States did not hear that the Civil War had ended until weeks and even months after it was over. Today's electronic communications transmit messages across the globe in seconds, and we learn almost instantaneously what is happening on the other side of the world. Reporters travel with U.S. soldiers, and the public is able to view videos of battles as they take place. When Navy Seals executed Osama bin Laden under President Obama's orders, Obama and Hillary Clinton watched the helicopter land in bin Laden's compound, listened to reports of the killing, and watched the Seals leave (Schmiddle 2011).

Travel and communication bridge time and space to such an extent that there is almost no "other side of the world" anymore. One result is **cultural leveling**, a process by which cultures become more and more similar to one another. The globalization of capitalism brings with it both technology and Western culture. Japan, for example, has adopted not only capitalism but also Western forms of dress and music, transforming it into a blend of Western and Eastern cultures.

Cultural leveling is apparent to any international traveler. The golden arches of McDonald's welcome visitors to Tokyo, Paris, London, Madrid, Moscow, Hong Kong, and Beijing. When I visited a jungle village in India—no electricity, no running water, and so remote that the only entrance was by a footpath—I saw a young man sporting a cap with the Nike emblem.

Although the bridging of geography, time, and culture by electronic signals and the adoption of Western icons do not in and of themselves mark the end of traditional cultures, the inevitable result is some degree of *cultural leveling*. We are producing a blander, less distinctive way of life—U.S. culture with French, Japanese, and Brazilian accents, so to speak. Although the "cultural accent" remains, something vital is lost forever.

cultural leveling

the process by which cultures become similar to one another; refers especially to the process by which Western culture is being exported and diffused into other nations

---

Summary and Review

What Is Culture?

2.1 **Explain what culture is, how culture provides orientations to life, and what practicing cultural relativism means.**

How do sociologists understand culture?

All human groups possess **culture**—language, beliefs, values, norms, and material objects that they pass from one generation to the next. **Material culture** consists of objects such as art, buildings, clothing, weapons, and tools. **Nonmaterial** (or **symbolic**) **culture** is a group's ways of thinking and its patterns of behavior. **Ideal culture** is a group's ideal values, norms, and goals. **Real culture** is people's actual behavior, which often falls short of their cultural ideals.

What are cultural relativism and ethnocentrism?

People are **ethnocentric**; that is, they use their own culture as a yardstick for judging the ways of others. In contrast,

those who embrace **cultural relativism** try to understand other cultures on those cultures' own terms.

Components of Symbolic Culture

2.2 **Know the components of symbolic culture: gestures, language, values, norms, sanctions, folkways, mores, and taboos; also explain the Sapir-Whorf hypothesis.**

What are the components of nonmaterial culture?

The central component of nonmaterial culture is **symbols**, anything to which people attach meaning and that they use to communicate with others. Universally, the symbols of nonmaterial culture are **gestures**, **language**, **values**, **norms**, **sanctions**, **folkways**, and **mores**.

Why is language so significant to culture?

Language allows human experience to be goal-directed, cooperative, and cumulative. It also lets humans move beyond the present and share a past, a future, and other common perspectives. According to the **Sapir-Whorf hypothesis**, language even shapes our thoughts and perceptions.

How do values, norms, sanctions, folkways, and mores reflect culture?

All groups have **values**, standards by which they define what is desirable or undesirable, and **norms**, expectations (or rules) about behavior. Groups use **positive sanctions** to show approval of those who follow their norms and **negative sanctions** to show disapproval of those who violate them. Norms that are not strictly enforced are called **folkways**, while **mores** are norms to which groups demand conformity because they reflect core values.

Many Cultural Worlds

2.3   Distinguish between subcultures and countercultures.

How do subcultures and countercultures differ?

A **subculture** is a group whose values and related behaviors distinguish its members from the general culture. A **counterculture** holds some values that stand in opposition to those of the dominant culture.

Values in U.S. Society

2.4   Discuss the major U.S. values and explain value clusters, value contradictions, value clashes, how values are lenses of perception, and ideal versus real culture.

What are some core U.S. values?

Although the United States is a **pluralistic society**, made up of many groups, each with its own set of values, certain values dominate. These are called **core values**. Core values do not change without opposition. Some values cluster together to form a larger whole called **value clusters**. **Value contradictions** (such as equality versus sexism and racism) indicate areas of tension, which are likely points

of social change. Leisure, self-fulfillment, physical fitness, youthfulness, and concern for the environment form an emerging value cluster.

Cultural Universals

2.5   Explain what cultural universals are and why they do not seem to exist.

Do cultural universals exist?

Cultural universal refers to a value, norm, or other cultural trait that is found in all cultures. Although all human groups have customs concerning cooking, childbirth, funerals, and so on, because these customs differ from one culture to another, there are no cultural universals.

Sociobiology and Human Behavior

2.6   Explain why most sociologists consider genes to be an inadequate explanation of human behavior.

Why don't sociologists say that genes control human behavior?

Genes certainly influence human behavior, but the rich diversity of human behavior indicates that culture overrides genetic influences.

Technology in the Global Village

2.7   Explain how technology changes culture and what cultural lag and cultural leveling are.

How is technology changing culture?

William Ogburn coined the term **cultural lag** to describe how a group's nonmaterial culture lags behind its changing technology. With today's technological advances in trade, travel, and communications, **cultural diffusion** is occurring rapidly. This leads to **cultural leveling**, groups becoming similar as they adopt items from other cultures. Much of the richness of the world's diverse cultures is being lost in the process.

Thinking Critically about Chapter 2

1. Do you favor ethnocentrism or cultural relativism? Explain your position.

2. Do you think that the language change in Miami, Florida, indicates the future of the United States? Why or why not?

3. What subculture are you a member of? Why do you think that your group is a subculture and not a counterculture? What is your group's relationship to the mainstream culture?

Chapter 3
Socialization

The old man was horrified when he found out. Life never had been good since his daughter lost her hearing when she was just 2 years old. She couldn't even talk—just fluttered her hands around trying to tell him things.

Over the years, he had gotten used to this. But now . . . he shuddered at the thought of her being pregnant. No one would be willing to marry her; he knew that. And the neighbors, their tongues would never stop wagging. Everywhere he went, he could hear people talking behind his back.

If only his wife were still alive, maybe she could come up with something. What should he do? He couldn't just kick his daughter out into the street.

After the baby was born, the old man tried to shake his feelings, but they wouldn't let loose. Isabelle was a pretty name, but every time he looked at the baby he felt sick to his stomach.

He hated doing it, but there was no way out. His daughter and her baby would have to live in the attic.

Unfortunately, this is a true story. Isabelle was discovered in Ohio in 1938 when she was about 6-and-a-half years old, living in a dark room with her deaf-mute mother. Isabelle couldn't talk, but she did use gestures to communicate with her mother. An inadequate diet and lack of sunshine had given Isabelle a disease called rickets.

Her behavior toward strangers, especially men, was almost that of a wild animal, manifesting much fear and hostility.

[Her legs] were so bowed that as she stood erect the soles of her shoes came nearly flat together, and she got about with a skittering gait. Her behavior toward strangers, especially men, was almost that of a wild animal, manifesting much fear and hostility. In lieu of speech she made only a strange croaking sound. (Davis 1940/2016)

When the newspapers reported this case, sociologist Kingsley Davis decided to find out what had happened to Isabelle after her discovery. We'll come back to that later, but first let's use the case of Isabelle to gain insight into human nature.

Society Makes Us Human

3.1   Explain how feral, isolated, and institutionalized children help us understand that "society makes us human."

"What do you mean, society makes us human?" is probably what you are asking. "That sounds ridiculous. I was born a human." The meaning of this statement will become more apparent as we get into the chapter. Let's start by considering what is human about human nature. How much of a person's characteristics comes from "nature" (heredity) and how much from "nurture" (the **social environment**, contact with others)? Experts are trying to answer the nature–nurture question by studying identical twins who were separated at birth and were reared in different environments, such as those discussed in the Down-to-Earth Sociology box on the next page.

Another way is to examine children who have had little human contact. Let's consider such children.

social environment

the entire human environment, including interaction with others

feral children

children assumed to have been raised by animals, in the wilderness, isolated from humans

Feral Children

The naked child was found in the forest, walking on all fours, eating grass and lapping water from the river. When he saw a small animal, he pounced on it. Growling, he ripped at it with his teeth. Tearing chunks from the body, he chewed them ravenously.

This is an accurate description of reports that have come in over the centuries. Supposedly, these **feral** (wild) **children** could not speak; they bit, scratched, growled, and walked on all fours. They drank by lapping water, ate grass, tore eagerly at raw meat, and showed insensitivity to pain and cold.

Why am I even mentioning stories that sound so exaggerated? Consider what happened in 1798. In that year, such a child was found in the forests of Aveyron, France. "The wild boy of Aveyron," as he became known, would have been written off as another folk myth, except that French scientists took the child to a laboratory and studied him. Like the feral children in the earlier informal reports, this child gave no indication of feeling the cold. Most startling, though, when he saw a small animal, the boy would growl, pounce on it, and devour it uncooked. Even today, the scientists' detailed reports make fascinating reading (Itard 1962).

Ever since I read Itard's account of this boy, I've been fascinated by the seemingly fantastic possibility that animals could rear human children. In 2002, I received a report from a contact in Cambodia that a feral child had been found in the jungle. When I had the opportunity the following year to visit the child and interview his caregivers, I grabbed it. The boy's photo is to the right.

If we were untouched by society, would we be like feral children? By nature, would our behavior be like that of wild animals? This is the sociological question. Unable to study feral children, sociologists have studied isolated children, like Isabelle in our opening vignette. Let's see what we can learn from them.

One of the reasons I went to Cambodia was to interview a feral child—the boy shown here—who supposedly had been raised by monkeys. When I arrived at the remote location where the boy was living, I was disappointed to find that the story was only partially true. When the boy was about two months old, the Khmer Rouge killed his parents and abandoned him. Months later, villagers shot the female monkey who was carrying the baby. Not quite a feral child—but Mathay is the closest I'll ever come to one.

Down-to-Earth Sociology

Heredity or Environment? The Case of Jack and Oskar, Identical Twins

Identical twins are almost identical in their genetic makeup. They are the result of one fertilized egg dividing to produce two embryos. (Some differences can occur as genetic codes are copied.) If heredity determines personality—or attitudes, temperament, skills, and intelligence—then identical twins should be identical, or almost so, not only in their looks but also in these characteristics.

The fascinating case of Jack and Oskar helps us unravel this mystery. From their experience, we can see the far-reaching effects of the environment—how social experiences override biology.

Jack Yufe and Oskar Stohr are identical twins. Born in 1932 to a Roman Catholic mother and a Jewish father, they were separated

The relative influence of heredity and the environment in human behavior has fascinated and plagued researchers. Twins intrigue researchers, especially twins who were separated at birth.

as babies after their parents divorced. Jack was reared in Trinidad by his father. There, he learned loyalty to Jews and hatred of Hitler and the Nazis. After the war, Jack and his father moved to Israel. When he was 17, Jack joined a kibbutz and later served in the Israeli army.

Oskar's upbringing was a mirror image of Jack's. Oskar was reared in Czechoslovakia by his mother's mother, who was a strict Catholic. When Oskar was a toddler, Hitler annexed this area of Czechoslovakia, and Oskar learned to love Hitler and to hate Jews. He joined the Hitler Youth. Like the Boy Scouts, this organization was designed to instill healthy living, love of the outdoors, friendships, and patriotism—but this one added loyalty to Hitler and hatred for Jews.

In 1954, the two brothers met. It was a short meeting, and Jack had been warned not to tell Oskar that they were Jews. Twenty-five years later, in 1979, when they were 47 years old, social scientists at the University of Minnesota brought them together again. These researchers figured

that because Jack and Oskar had the same genes, any differences they showed would have to be the result of their environment—their different social experiences.

Not only did Jack and Oskar hold different attitudes toward the war, Hitler, and Jews, but their basic orientations to life were also different. In their politics, Jack was liberal, while Oskar was more conservative. Jack was a workaholic, while Oskar enjoyed leisure. And, as you can predict, Jack was proud of being a Jew. Oskar, who by this time knew that he was a Jew, wouldn't even mention it.

That would seem to settle the matter. But there were other things. As children, Jack and Oskar had both excelled at sports but had difficulty with math. They also had the same rate of speech, and both liked sweet liqueur and spicy foods. Strangely, each flushed the toilet both before and after using it, and they each enjoyed startling people by sneezing in crowded elevators.

For Your Consideration

Heredity or environment? How much influence does each have? The question is far from settled, but at this point it seems fair to conclude that the *limits* of certain physical and mental abilities are established by heredity (such as ability at sports and aptitude for mathematics), while attitudes are the result of the environment. Basic temperament, though, seems to be inherited. Although the answer is still fuzzy, we can put it this way: For some parts of life, the blueprint is drawn by heredity; but even here the environment can redraw those lines. For other parts, the individual is a blank slate, and it is up to the environment to determine what is written on that slate.

SOURCES: Based on Begley 1979; Chen 1979; Wright 1995; Segal and Hershberger 2005; Ledger 2009; Johnson et al. 2009; Segal and Mulligan 2014.

Isolated Children

What can isolated children tell us about human nature? We can first conclude that humans have no natural language, for Isabelle in our opening vignette and others like her are unable to speak.

But maybe Isabelle was mentally impaired. Perhaps she simply was unable to progress through the usual stages of development. It certainly looked that way—she scored practically zero on her first intelligence test. But after a few months of language training, Isabelle was able to speak in short sentences. In just a year, she could write a few words, do simple addition, and retell stories after hearing them. Seven months later, she had a vocabulary of almost 2,000 words. In just two years, Isabelle reached the intellectual level that is normal for her age. She then went on to school, where she was "bright, cheerful, energetic . . . and participated in all school activities as normally as other children" (Davis 1940/2016).

As discussed in the previous chapter, language is the key to human development. Without language, people have no mechanism for developing thought and communicating their experiences. Unlike animals, humans have no instincts that take the place of language. If an individual lacks language, he or she lives in a world of internal silence, without shared ideas, lacking connections to others.

Without language, there can be no culture—no shared way of life—and culture is the key to what people become. Each of us possesses a biological heritage, but this heritage does not determine specific behaviors, attitudes, or values. It is our culture that superimposes the specifics of what we become onto our biological heritage.

Institutionalized Children

Other than language, what else is required for a child to develop into what we consider a healthy, balanced, intelligent human being? We find part of the answer in two intriguing experiments.

THE ORPHANAGE EXPERIMENT IN THE UNITED STATES   Back in the 1930s, orphanages were common because parents were more likely than now to die before their children were grown. Children reared in orphanages tended to have low IQs. "Common sense" (which we noted in Chapter 1 is unreliable) made it seem obvious that their low intelligence was because of poor brains ("They're just born that way"). But two psychologists, H. M. Skeels and H. B. Dye (1939), began to suspect a social cause.

Listen to Skeels (1966) describe a "good" orphanage in Iowa, one where he and Dye were consultants:

> *Until about six months, they were cared for in the infant nursery. The babies were kept in standard hospital cribs that often had protective sheeting on the sides, thus effectively limiting visual stimulation; no toys or other objects were hung in the infants' line of vision. Human interactions were limited to busy nurses who, with the speed born of practice and necessity, changed diapers or bedding, bathed and medicated the infants, and fed them efficiently with propped bottles.*

"Maybe it isn't the children's brains," thought Skeels and Dye. "It could be the absence of stimulating social interaction." To test their controversial idea, they left a control group of twelve infants at the orphanage and placed thirteen infants in an institution for low IQ women. They assigned each of these infants, then about 19 months old, to a separate ward of women who were between the ages of 18 and 50 but whose mental age was just 5 to 12. The women enjoyed taking care of the infants' physical needs—diapering, feeding, and so on—and they also loved the children. They played with them, cuddled them, and showered them with attention. They even competed to see which ward would have "its baby" walking or talking first. In each ward, one woman became particularly attached to the child and figuratively adopted him or her:

> *As a consequence, an intense one-to-one adult–child relationship developed, which was supplemented by the less intense but frequent interactions with the other adults in the environment. Each child had some one person with whom he [or she] was identified and who was particularly interested in him [or her] and his [or her] achievements. (Skeels 1966)*

Two-and-a-half years later, Skeels and Dye tested all the children's intelligence. Their findings are startling: Those who were cared for by the women in the institution gained an average of 28 IQ points while those who remained in the orphanage lost 30 points.

A child in an orphanage in Juba, Sudan. The treatment of this child is likely to affect his ability to reason and to function as an adult.

What happened after these children were grown? Did these initial differences matter? Twenty-one years later, Skeels and Dye did a follow-up study. The twelve in the control group, those who had remained in the orphanage, averaged less than a third-grade education. Four still lived in state institutions, and the others held low-level jobs. Only two had married. The thirteen in the experimental group, those cared for by the institutionalized women, had an average education of twelve grades (about normal for that period). Five had completed one or more years of college. One had even gone to graduate school. Eleven had married. All thirteen were self-supporting or were homemakers (Skeels 1966). Apparently, "high intelligence" depends on early, close relations with other humans.

THE ORPHANAGE EXPERIMENT IN ROMANIA   Under Romania's communist regime, tens of thousands of unwanted children were placed in government orphanages. After the people rose up against the hated dictator, Nicolae Ceausescu, and executed him and his wife in 1989, people were horrified when they learned how extensively these children had been neglected and abused.

In an experiment reminiscent of that by Skeels and Dye, doctors randomly divided the 2-year-old orphans in Bucharest into experimental and control groups. The sixty-nine children in the experimental group were placed in foster families, while the sixty-seven 2-year-olds in the control group remained in the orphanages. When they tested the children six years later, the children who had been placed in foster care were better adjusted socially. They even had more brain cells than the children who remained in the orphanage (Hamilton 2014; Bick et al. 2015).

Note the integrated looping—how social interaction influences physical development, which, in turn, influences social interaction. Attention from caring adults, their reassurances, and living with security apparently allow the brain to get "wired" in ways that produce more secure, caring people.

TIMING AND HUMAN DEVELOPMENT   The longer that children lack stimulating interaction, the more difficulty they have intellectually (Meese 2005; Li et al. 2013). Let's consider a classic, heart-wrenching case. From it, you can see how important timing is in the development of "human" characteristics.

Genie, a child in California, had been locked in a small room and tied to a potty chair since she was 20 months old. She was discovered when she was 13 years old:

> *Apparently, Genie's father (70 years old when Genie was discovered in 1970) hated children. He probably had caused the death of two of Genie's siblings. Her 50-year-old mother was partially blind and frightened of her husband. Genie could not speak, did not know how to chew, was unable to stand upright, and could not straighten her hands and legs. On intelligence tests, she scored at the level of a 1-year-old. After intensive training, Genie learned to walk and to put garbled, three-word sentences together. Genie's language remained primitive as she grew up. She would take anyone's property if it appealed to her, and she went to the bathroom wherever she wanted. At the age of 21, she was sent to a home for adults who cannot live alone. (Pines 1981)*

IN SUM   From the research on institutionalized and deprived children, we can conclude that the basic human traits of intelligence and the ability to establish close bonds with others depend on early interaction with other humans. From Genie's pathetic story, it also seems that children must learn language and experience human bonding before age 13 if they are to develop normal intelligence and the ability to be sociable and follow social norms.

Deprived Animals

Finally, let's consider animals that have been deprived of normal interaction. In a series of experiments with rhesus monkeys, psychologists Harry and Margaret Harlow demonstrated the importance of early learning. The Harlows (1962) raised baby monkeys in isolation. As shown in the photo on this page, they gave each monkey two artificial mothers. One "mother" was only a wire frame with a wooden head, but it did have a nipple from which the baby could nurse. The frame of the other "mother," which had no bottle, was covered with soft terrycloth. To obtain food, the baby monkeys nursed at the wire frame.

When the Harlows (1965) frightened the baby monkeys with a mechanical bear or dog, the babies did not run to the wire frame "mother." Instead, they would cling pathetically to their terrycloth "mother." The Harlows concluded that infant–mother bonding is not the result of feeding but, rather, of what they termed "intimate physical contact." To most of us, this phrase means cuddling.

The monkeys raised in isolation could not adjust to monkey life. Placed with other monkeys when they were grown, they didn't know how to participate in "monkey interaction"—to play and to engage in pretend fights—and the other monkeys rejected them. Despite their futile attempts, they didn't even know how to have sexual intercourse. The experimenters designed a special device that allowed some females to become pregnant. Their isolation, however, made them "ineffective, inadequate, and brutal mothers." They "struck their babies, kicked them, or crushed the babies against the cage floor."

In one of their many experiments, the Harlows isolated baby monkeys for different lengths of time and then put them in with other monkeys. Monkeys that had been isolated for shorter periods (about three months) were able to adjust to normal monkey life. They learned to play and engage in pretend fights. Those isolated for six months or more, however, couldn't make the adjustment, and the other monkeys rejected them. In other words, the longer the period of isolation, the more difficult its effects are to overcome. In addition, there seems to be a critical learning stage: If this stage is missed, it may be impossible to compensate for what has been lost. This seems to have been the case with Genie.

Because humans are not monkeys, we must be careful about extrapolating from animal studies to human behavior. The Harlow experiments, however, support what we know about children who are reared in isolation.

Like humans, monkeys need interaction to thrive. Those raised in isolation are unable to interact with other monkeys. In this photograph, we see one of the monkeys described in the text. Purposefully frightened by the experimenter, the monkey has taken refuge in the soft terrycloth draped over an artificial "mother."

In Sum Society Makes Us Human Babies do not develop "naturally" into social adults. If children are reared in isolation, their bodies grow, but they become little more than big animals. Without the concepts that language provides, they can't grasp relationships between people (the "connections" we call brother, sister, parent, friend, teacher, and so on). And without warm, friendly interactions, they can't bond with others. They don't become "friendly" or cooperate with others. In short, it is through human contact that people learn to be members of the human community. This process by which we learn the ways of society (or of particular groups), called **socialization**, is what sociologists have in mind when they say, "Society makes us human."

To add to our understanding of how society makes us human, let's look at how we develop our self-concept, our ability to "take the role of others," and our ability to reason.

socialization

the process by which people learn the characteristics of their group—the knowledge, skills, attitudes, values, norms, and actions thought appropriate for them

Socialization into the Self and Mind

3.2 Use the ideas and research of Cooley (looking-glass self), Mead (role taking), and Piaget (reasoning) to explain socialization into the self and mind.

When you were born, you had no ideas. You didn't know that you were a son or daughter. You didn't even know that you were a he or she. How did you develop a **self**, your image of who you are? And how did you develop your ability to reason? Let's find out.

Cooley and the Looking-Glass Self

self

the unique human capacity of being able to see ourselves "from the outside"; the views we internalize of how we think others see us

About a hundred years ago, Charles Horton Cooley (1864–1929), a symbolic interactionist who taught at the University of Michigan, concluded that producing a self is an essential part of how *society* makes us human. He said that *our sense of self develops from interaction with others*. To describe the process by which this unique aspect of "humanness" develops, Cooley (1902) coined the term **looking-glass self**.

He summarized this idea in the following couplet:

looking-glass self

a term coined by Charles Horton Cooley to refer to the process by which our self develops through internalizing others' reactions to us

Each to each a looking-glass
Reflects the other that doth pass.

The looking-glass self contains three elements:

1. *We imagine how we appear to those around us.* For example, we may think that others perceive us as witty or dull.
2. *We interpret others' reactions.* We come to conclusions about how others evaluate us. Do they like us for being witty? Do they dislike us for being dull?
3. *We develop a self-concept.* How we interpret others' reactions to us frames our feelings and ideas about ourselves. A favorable reflection in this *social mirror* leads to a positive self-concept; a negative reflection leads to a negative self-concept.

IN SUM *Although the self-concept begins in childhood*, it *is never a finished product*. All of our lives, we monitor how others react to us. Whether we are accurate in how we think others evaluate us does not change the process. Even if we grossly misinterpret how others think about us, those misjudgments become part of our self-concept. Because we are always monitoring others' reactions to us, we are continually modifying the self, even in our old age.

Mead and Role Taking

Another symbolic interactionist, George Herbert Mead (1863–1931), who taught at the University of Chicago, pointed out how important play is in developing a self. As we play with others, we learn to **take the role of the other**. That is, we learn to put ourselves in someone else's shoes—to understand how someone else feels and thinks and to anticipate how that person will act.

taking the role of the other

putting yourself in someone else's shoes; understanding how someone else feels and thinks, so you anticipate how that person will act

This doesn't happen overnight. We develop this ability over a period of years (Mead 1934; Denzin 2007). Psychologist John Flavel (1968) asked 8- and 14-year-olds to explain a board game to children who were blindfolded and also to others who were not. The 14-year-olds gave more detailed instructions to those who were blindfolded, but the 8-year-olds gave the same instructions to everyone. The younger children could not yet take the role of the other, while the older children could.

significant other

an individual who significantly influences someone else

As we develop this ability, at first we can take only the roles of **significant others**, individuals who significantly influence our lives, such as parents or siblings.

By assuming their roles during play, such as dressing up in our parents' clothing, we cultivate the ability to put ourselves in the place of significant others.

As our self gradually develops, we internalize the expectations of more and more people. Our ability to take the role of others eventually extends to being able to take the role of "the group as a whole." Mead used the term **generalized other** to refer to our perception of how people in general think of us.

Taking the role of others is essential if we are to become cooperative members of human groups—whether they are family, friends, or co-workers. This ability allows us to modify our behavior by anticipating how others will react—something Genie never learned.

As Figure 3.1 illustrates, we go through three stages as we learn to take the role of the other:

1. *Imitation.* Under the age of 3, we can only mimic others. We do not yet have a sense of self separate from others, and we can only imitate people's gestures and words. (This stage is actually not role taking, but it prepares us for it.)

2. *Play.* During the second stage, from the ages of about 3 to 6, we pretend to take the roles of specific people. We might pretend that we are a firefighter, a wrestler, a nurse, Supergirl, Spider-Man, a princess, and so on. We like costumes at this stage and enjoy dressing up in our parents' clothing or tying a towel around our neck to "become" Superman or Wonder Woman.

3. *Team Games.* This third stage, organized play, or team games, begins roughly when we enter school. The significance for the self is that to play these games, we must be able to take multiple roles. Baseball was one of Mead's favorite examples. To play baseball, each player must be able to take the role of any other player. It isn't enough that players know their own role; they also must be able to anticipate what everyone else on the field will do when the ball is hit or thrown.

Mead also said that the self has two parts, the "I" and the "me." The "I" is *the self as subject*, the active, spontaneous, creative part of the self. In contrast, the "me" is *the self as object*. It is made up of attitudes we internalize from our interactions with others. Mead chose these pronouns because in English, "I" is the active agent, as in "I shoved him," while "me" is the object of action, as in "He shoved me." Mead stressed that we are not passive in the socialization process. We are not like robots, with programmed software shoved into us. Rather, our "I" actively evaluates the reactions of others and organizes them into a unified whole. Mead added that the "I" even monitors the "me," fine-tuning our ideas and attitudes to help us better meet what others expect of us.

IN SUM In studying these details, be careful not to miss the main point, which some find startling: *Both our self and our mind are social products.* Mead stressed that we cannot think without symbols. But where do these symbols come from? Only from society, which gives us our symbols by giving us language. If society did not provide the symbols, we would not be able to think and so would not possess a self-concept or that entity we call the mind. The self and mind, then, like language, are products of society.

Mead analyzed taking the role of the other as an essential part of learning to be a full-fledged member of society. At first, we are able to take the role only of significant others, as this child is doing. Later we develop the capacity to take the role of the generalized other, which is essential not only for cooperation but also for the control of antisocial desires.

generalized other

the norms, values, attitudes, and expectations of people "in general"; the child's ability to take the role of the generalized other is a significant step in the development of a self

Figure 3.1 How We Learn to Take the Role of the Other: Mead's Three Stages

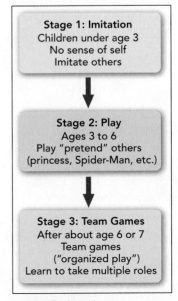

Stage 1: Imitation
Children under age 3
No sense of self
Imitate others

↓

Stage 2: Play
Ages 3 to 6
Play "pretend" others
(princess, Spider-Man, etc.)

↓

Stage 3: Team Games
After about age 6 or 7
Team games
("organized play")
Learn to take multiple roles

SOURCE: By the author.

To help his students understand the term *generalized other*, Mead used baseball as an illustration. Why are team sports and organized games excellent examples to use in explaining this concept?

Piaget and the Development of Reasoning

The development of the mind—specifically, how we learn to reason—was studied in detail by Jean Piaget (1896–1980). This Swiss psychologist noticed that when young children take intelligence tests, they often give similar wrong answers. This set Piaget to thinking that the children might be using some consistent, but incorrect, reasoning. It might even indicate that children go through some natural process as they learn how to reason.

Stimulated by this intriguing possibility, Piaget set up a laboratory where he could give children of different ages problems to solve (Piaget 1950, 1954; Flavel et al. 2002). After years of testing, Piaget concluded that children go through a natural process as they develop their ability to reason. This process has four stages. (If you mentally substitute "reasoning" or "reasoning skills" for the term *operational* as you review these stages, Piaget's findings will be easier to understand.)

1. *The sensorimotor stage* (from birth to about age 2).
   During this stage, our understanding is limited to direct contact—sucking, touching, listening, looking. We aren't able to "think." During the first part of this stage, we do not even know that our bodies are separate from the environment. Indeed, we have yet to discover that we have toes. Neither can we recognize cause and effect. That is, we do not know that our actions cause something to happen.

2. *The preoperational stage* (from about age 2 to age 7).
   During this stage, we *develop the ability to use symbols*. However, we do not yet understand common concepts such as size, speed, or causation. Although we are learning to count, we do not really understand what numbers mean.

3. *The concrete operational stage* (from about age 7 to age 12).
   Although our reasoning abilities are more developed, they remain *concrete*. We can now understand numbers, size, causation, and speed, and we are able to take the role of the other. We can even play team games. Unless we have concrete examples, however, we are unable to talk about concepts such as truth, honesty, or justice. We can explain why Jane's answer was a lie, but we cannot describe what truth itself is.

4. *The formal operational stage* (after the age of about 12).
   We now are capable of abstract thinking. We can talk about concepts, come to conclusions based on general principles, and use rules to solve abstract problems.

During this stage, we are likely to become young philosophers (Kagan 1984). If we were shown a photo of a slave during our concrete operational stage, we might have said, "That's wrong!" Now at the formal operational stage we are likely to add, "If our country was founded on equality, how could anyone own slaves?"

Global Aspects of the Self and Reasoning

Cooley's conclusions about the looking-glass self appear to be true for everyone around the world. So do Mead's conclusions about role taking and the mind and self as social products, although researchers are finding that the self may develop earlier than Mead indicated. Piaget's theory is also being refined (Burman 2013). Although children everywhere begin with the concrete and move to the abstract, researchers have found that the stages are not as distinct as Piaget concluded. The ages at which individuals enter the stages also differ from one person to another (Flavel et al. 2002). Even during the sensorimotor stage, for example, children show early signs of reasoning, which may indicate an innate ability that is wired into the brain.

Interestingly, some people seem to get stuck in the concreteness of the third stage and never reach the fourth stage of abstract thinking (Kohlberg and Gilligan 1971; Suizzo 2000). College, for example, nurtures the fourth stage, and people with this experience apparently have more ability for abstract thought. Social experiences, then, can modify these stages.

Jean Piaget in his office.

Learning Personality, Morality, and Emotions

3.3 **Explain how the development of personality and morality and socialization into emotions are part of how "society makes us human."**

As you know so well, our personality, morality, and emotions are also vital aspects of who we are. Let's look at how we learn these essential aspects of our being.

Freud and the Development of Personality

As the mind and the self develop, so does the personality. Sigmund Freud (1856–1939) developed a theory of the origin of personality that had a major impact on Western thought. Freud, a physician in Vienna in the early 1900s, founded *psychoanalysis*, a technique for treating emotional problems through long-term exploration of the subconscious mind. Let's look at his theory.

Freud believed that personality consists of three elements. Each child is born with the first element, an **id**. This was Freud's term for inborn drives that cause us to seek self-gratification. The pleasure-seeking id operates throughout life. It demands the immediate fulfillment of basic needs: food, safety, attention, sex, and so on. The id of the newborn is evident in its cries of hunger or pain.

The id's drive for immediate gratification, however, runs into a roadblock: primarily the needs of other people, especially those of the parents. To adapt to these constraints, a second component of the personality emerges, which Freud called the ego. The **ego** is the balancing force between the id and the demands of society that suppress it. The ego also

id

Freud's term for our inborn basic drives

ego

Freud's term for a balancing force between the id and the demands of society

Shown here is Sigmund Freud in 1931 as he poses for a sculptor in Vienna, Austria. Although Freud was one of the most influential theorists of the twentieth century, most of his ideas have been discarded.

superego

Freud's term for the conscience; the internalized norms and values of our social groups

serves to balance the id and the **superego**, the third component of the personality, more commonly called the *conscience*.

The superego represents *culture within us*, the norms and values we internalize from our social groups. As the *moral* component of the personality, the superego provokes feelings of guilt or shame when we break social rules or pride and self-satisfaction when we follow them.

According to Freud, when the id gets out of hand, we follow our desires for pleasure and break society's norms. When the superego gets out of hand, we become overly rigid in following those norms and end up wearing a straitjacket of rules that can make our lives miserable. The ego, the balancing force, tries to prevent either the superego or the id from dominating. In the emotionally healthy individual, the ego succeeds in balancing these conflicting demands of the id and the superego. In the maladjusted individual, the ego fails to control the conflict between the id and the superego. Either the id or the superego dominates this person, leading to internal confusion and problem behaviors.

SOCIOLOGICAL EVALUATION Sociologists appreciate Freud's emphasis on socialization—his assertion that the social group into which we are born transmits norms and values that restrain our biological drives. Sociologists, however, object to the view that inborn and subconscious motivations are the primary reasons for human behavior. *This denies the central principle of sociology*: that factors such as social class (income, education, and occupation) and people's roles in groups underlie their behavior (Epstein 1988; Bush and Simmons 1990).

Feminist sociologists have been especially critical of Freud. Although what I just summarized applies to both females and males, Freud assumed that "male" is "normal." He even referred to females as inferior, castrated males (Chodorow 1990; Gerhard 2000). It is obvious that sociologists need to continue to research how we develop personality.

Kohlberg and the Development of Morality

If you have observed young children, you know that they want immediate gratification and show little or no concern for others. ("Mine!" a 2-year-old will shout, as she grabs a toy from another child.) Yet, at a later age, this same child will be considerate of others and try to be fair in her play. How does this change happen?

KOHLBERG'S THEORY Psychologist Lawrence Kohlberg (1975, 1984, 1986; Reed 2008) concluded that we go through a sequence of stages as we develop morality. Building on Piaget's work, he found that children start in the *amoral stage* I just described. For them, there is no right or wrong, just personal needs to be satisfied. From about ages 7 to 10, children are in what Kohlberg called a *preconventional stage*. They have learned rules, and they follow them to stay out of trouble. They view right and wrong as what pleases or displeases their parents, friends, and teachers. Their concern is to get rewards and to avoid punishment. At about age 10, they enter the *conventional stage*. During this period, morality means following the norms and values they have learned. Then comes the *postconventional stage*: People are able to reflect on abstract principles of right and wrong and judge people's behavior according to these principles.

CRITICISMS OF KOHLBERG   To test Kohlberg's theory, researchers checked how it applies in different cultures. They found that the preconventional and conventional stages apply around the world. Most societies, though, do not have the postconventional stage of universal reasoning. This stage appears to be mostly a Western concept (Jensen 2009). Apparently, there is no universal, abstract way of figuring what is moral. Instead, different cultures have their own ways to determine morality, and each teaches its members to use its norms in deciding what is moral.

RESEARCH WITH BABIES   Researchers have developed ingenious experiments to see if babies have a morality (Bloom 2010; Hamlin and Wynn 2011). In one experiment, they showed babies a puppet that helps another puppet and one that interferes with that puppet. They found that babies—even under 1 year of age—prefer the "good" puppet and want the "bad" puppet punished. From these experiments, some draw the intriguing conclusion that we are born with a basic morality and a desire to punish those who break our moral codes. Others suggest that the experiments are flawed (Scarf et al. 2012). More research should eventually settle the question.

THE CULTURAL RELATIVITY OF MORALITY   If babies do have an inborn sense of fairness, it indicates that, like language, morality is a capacity hardwired in the brain. Just as society lays a particular language onto the child's linguistic capacity, so society lays its particular ideas of what is moral onto the child's moral capacity. As languages differ around the world, so do moralities. When people violate whatever morality they have learned, it arouses the emotions of guilt and shame. Sociologists are studying how people's sense of identity is connected to morality and these emotions (Stets and Carter 2012).

Let's turn to how we learn emotions, another essential element of who we are as humans.

Socialization into Emotions

Like our mind, personality, and morality, our emotions also reflect our socialization (Hochschild 2008; Stets 2012). Let's see why.

GLOBAL EMOTIONS   At first, it may look as though socialization is not relevant to our emotions, that we simply express feelings that everyone has. The research of Paul Ekman, a psychologist, seems to support this idea. After studying emotions in several countries, Ekman (1980) found that everyone experiences six basic emotions: anger, disgust, fear, happiness, sadness, and surprise. Ekman also found that people show the same facial expressions when they feel these emotions. A person from Peru, for example, can tell from just the look on an American's face that she is angry, disgusted, or fearful, and she can tell from the Peruvian's face that he is happy, sad, or surprised. Because we all show the same facial expressions when we experience these six emotions, Ekman concluded that they are hardwired into our biology.

A study of facial expressions at the Paralympics supports this observation (Matsumoto and Willingham 2009). Upon learning if they had won or lost, people who were blind from birth showed the same facial expressions as those of sighted people, something they could not have learned.

EXPRESSING EMOTIONS: "GENDER RULES."   What, then, does sociology have to do with emotions? If we have universal facial expressions to express our emotions, then this is biology. Facial expressions, however, are only one way by which we show our feelings. We also use our bodies, voices, and gestures.

Jane and Sushana have been best friends since high school. They were hardly ever apart until Sushana married and moved to another state a year ago. Jane has been waiting eagerly at the arrival gate for Sushana's flight, which has been delayed. When Sushana exits, she and Jane hug one another, giving out "squeals of glee" and even jumping a bit.

If you couldn't tell from their names that these were women, you could tell from their behavior. To express delight, U.S. women are allowed to give "out squeals of glee" in public places and to jump as they hug. In contrast, in the same circumstances, U.S. men are expected to shake hands or to give a brief hug. If they gave "squeals of glee," they would be violating fundamental "feeling rules" based on gender.

THE EXTENT OF "FEELING RULES."   Not only do the norms about how we express our feelings change with gender, but "feeling rules" are also based on culture, social class, relationships, and settings. Consider *culture*. Two close Japanese friends who meet after a long separation don't shake hands or hug—they bow. Two Arab men will kiss. *Social class* is so significant that it, too, cuts across other lines, even gender. Upon seeing a friend after a long absence, upper-class women and men are likely to be more reserved in expressing their delight than are lower-class women and men. *Relationships* also make a big difference. We express our feelings more openly if we are with close friends, more guardedly if we are at a staff meeting with the corporate CEO. The *setting*, then, is also important, with different settings having different "rules" about emotions. As you know, the emotions you can express at a rock concert differ considerably from those you express in a classroom. If you think about your childhood, you will realize that a good part of your early socialization centered on learning your culture's feeling rules.

What emotions are these people expressing? Are these emotions global? Is their way of expressing them universal?

WHAT WE FEEL

> *Joan, a U.S. woman who had been married for seven years, had no children. When she finally gave birth and the doctor handed her a healthy girl, she was almost overcome with joy. Tafadzwa, in Zimbabwe, had been married for seven years and had no children. When the doctor handed her a healthy girl, she was almost overcome with sadness.*

You can easily understand why the U.S. woman felt happy, but why did the woman in Zimbabwe feel sad? The effects of socialization on our emotions go much deeper than guiding how, where, and when we express our feelings. Socialization also affects *what* we feel (Clark 1997). In Zimbabwe culture, to not give birth to a male child lowers a woman's social status. It is even considered a good reason for her husband to divorce her (Horwitz and Wakefield 2007:43).

RESEARCH NEEDED   Ekman identified only six emotions as universal in facial expression, but I suspect there are more. It could be that the emotions of confusion, despair, disgust, helplessness, and shock also produce similar facial expressions around the world. This is a hypothesis, and we need cross-cultural research to find out whether the facial expressions of these emotions are universal. We also need more research into how culture guides people in how they express their feelings, even in what they feel—and how these might differ from one culture to another as well as by age, gender, social class, and race–ethnicity.

Society within Us: The Self and Emotions as Social Control

Much of our socialization is intended to turn us into conforming members of society. Socialization into the self and emotions is essential in this process, for *both the self and our emotions mold our behavior.* Although we like to think that we are "free," consider for a moment some of the factors that influence how you act: the expectations of your friends and parents; of neighbors and teachers; classroom norms and college rules; city, state, and federal laws. For example, if in a moment of intense frustration or out of a devilish desire to shock people, you wanted to tear off your clothes and run naked down the street, what would stop you?

The answer is your socialization—*society within you.* Your experiences in society have resulted in a self that thinks along certain lines and feels particular emotions. This helps to keep you in line. Thoughts such as "Would I get kicked out of school?" and "What would my friends (parents) think if they found out?" represent an awareness of the self in relationship to others. So does the desire to avoid feelings of shame and embarrassment. Your *social mirror,* then—the result of your being socialized into a self and emotions— sets up effective internal controls over your behavior. In fact, socialization into self and emotions is so effective that some people feel embarrassed just thinking about running naked in public!

IN SUM Socialization is essential for our development as human beings. From our interaction with others, we learn how to think, reason, and feel. The net result is the shaping of our behavior—including our thinking, morality, and emotions—according to cultural standards. This is what sociologists mean when they refer to *society within us.*

Do you remember how we began this chapter—that society makes us human? Socialization into emotions is part of this process.

Socialization into Gender

3.4 Discuss how gender messages from the family, peers, and the mass media teach us society's gender map.

As we just saw with emotions and gender, socialization into gender is part of the way that society turns us into certain types of people—and sets up deep controls over us. Let's get a glimpse of how this happens.

Learning the Gender Map

For a child, society is unexplored territory. A major signpost on society's map is **gender,** the attitudes and behaviors that are expected of us because we are a male or a female. In learning the *gender map* (called **gender socialization**), we are nudged into different lanes in life—into contrasting attitudes and behaviors. We take direction so well that, as adults, most of us act, think, and even feel according to our culture's guidelines regarding what is appropriate for our sex.

The significance of gender is emphasized throughout this book, and we focus on gender in Chapter 10. For now, though, let's briefly consider some of the *gender messages* that we get from our family and the mass media.

gender

the behaviors and attitudes that a society considers proper for its males and females; masculinity or femininity

gender socialization

learning society's "gender map," the paths in life set out for us because we are male or female

Gender Messages in the Family

PARENTS Our parents are the first to introduce us to the gender map. Sometimes they do this consciously, perhaps by bringing into play pink and blue, colors that have no meaning in themselves but that are now associated with gender. Our parents' own

It is in the family that we first learn how to do gender, how to match our ideas, attitudes, and behaviors to those expected of us because of our sex. This photo is from Papua New Guinea.

gender orientations are embedded so firmly that they do most of their gender teaching without being aware of what they are doing.

This is illustrated in a classic study by psychologists Susan Goldberg and Michael Lewis (1969), whose results have been confirmed by other researchers (Connors 1996; Clearfield and Nelson 2006; Best 2010).

Goldberg and Lewis asked mothers to bring their 6-month-old infants into their laboratory, supposedly to observe the infants' development. Covertly, however, they also observed the mothers. They found that the mothers kept their daughters closer to them. They also touched their daughters more and spoke to them more frequently than they did to their sons. By the time the children were 13 months old, the girls stayed closer to their mothers during play, and they returned to their mothers sooner and more often than the boys did.

Then Goldberg and Lewis did a little experiment. They set up a barrier to separate the children from their mothers, who were holding toys. The girls were more likely to cry and motion for help; the boys, to try to climb over the barrier.

Goldberg and Lewis concluded that the mothers had subconsciously rewarded their daughters for being passive and dependent, their sons for being active and independent.

TOYS AND PLAY   Our family's gender lessons are thorough. On the basis of our sex, our parents give us different kinds of toys. Boys are more likely to get guns and "action figures" that destroy enemies. Girls are more likely to be given dolls and jewelry. Some parents try to choose "gender neutral" toys, but kids know what is popular, and they feel left out if they don't have what the other kids have. The significance of toys in gender socialization can be summarized this way: Most parents would be upset if someone gave their son Barbie dolls.

We also learn gender through play. Parents subtly "signal" to their sons that it is okay for them to participate in more rough-and-tumble play. In general, parents expect their sons to get dirtier and to be more defiant, their daughters to be daintier and more compliant (Gilman 1911/1971; Nordberg 2010). And in large part, parents get what they expect.

Our experiences in socialization lie at the heart of the sociological explanation of male–female differences. For a fascinating account of how socialization can trump biology, read the following Cultural Diversity box.

Frank and Ernest

www.cartoonistgroup.com

The *gender roles* that we learn during childhood become part of our basic orientations to life. Although we refine these roles as we grow older, they remain built around the framework established during childhood.

Cultural Diversity around the World

When Women Become Men: The Sworn Virgins

"I will become a man," said Pashe. "I will do it."

The decision was final. Taking a pair of scissors, she soon had her long, black curls lying at her feet. She took off her dress—never to wear one again in her life—and put on her father's baggy trousers. She armed herself with her father's rifle. She would need it.

Going before the village elders, she swore to never marry, to never have children, and to never have sex.

Pashe had become a sworn virgin—and a man.

There was no turning back. The penalty for violating the oath was death.

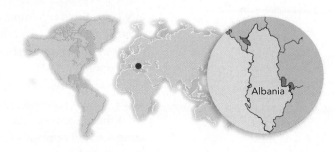

In northern Albania, where Pashe Keqi lives, and in parts of Bosnia and Serbia, some women become men. They are neither transsexuals nor lesbians. Nor do they have a sex-change operation, something which is unknown in those parts.

This custom, which goes back centuries, is a practical matter, a way to protect and support the family. In these traditional societies, women stay home and take care of the children and household. They can go hardly anywhere except to the market and mosque. Women depend on men for survival.

And when there is no man? This is the problem.

Pashe's father was killed in a blood feud. In these traditional groups, when the family patriarch (male head) dies and there are no male heirs, how are the women to survive? In the fifteenth century, people in this area hit upon a solution: One of the women gives an oath of lifelong virginity and takes over the man's role. She then becomes a social he—she wears male clothing, carries a gun, owns property, and moves freely throughout the society.

She drinks in the tavern with the men. She sits with the men at weddings. She prays with the men at the mosque. When a man wants to marry a girl of the family, she is the one who approves or disapproves of the suitor.

In short, the woman really becomes a man. Actually, a *social man*, sociologists would add. Her biology does not change, but her gender does. Pashe had become the man of the house, a status she occupied her entire life.

Taking this position at the age of 11—Pashe is in her 70s now—also made her responsible for avenging her father's murder. But when his killer was released from prison,

Sokol (Zhire) Zmajli, aged 80, changed her name from Zhire to the male name Sokol when she was young. She heads the family household consisting of her nephew, his wife, their sons, and their wives.

her 15-year-old nephew (she is his uncle) rushed in and did the deed instead.

Sworn virgins walk like men, they talk like men, and they hunt with the men. They also take up manly occupations. They become shepherds, security guards, truck drivers, and political leaders. Those around them know that they are biological women, but in all ways they treat them as men. When a sworn virgin talks to women, the women recoil in shyness.

The sworn virgins of Albania are a fascinating cultural contradiction: In the midst of a highly traditional group, one built around male superiority that severely limits women, we find both the belief and practice that a biological woman can do the work of a man and function in all of a man's social roles. The sole exception is marriage.

Under communist rule until 1985, with travel restricted by law and custom, mountainous northern Albania had been cut off from the rest of the world. Now there is a democratic government, and the region is connected to the world by better roads, telephones, and even television. As modern life trickles into these villages, few women want to become men. "Why should we?" they ask. "Now we have freedom. We can go to the city and work and support our families."

For Your Consideration

→ How do the sworn virgins of Albania help to explain what gender is?

→ Apply functionalism: How was the custom and practice of sworn virgins functional for this society?

→ Apply symbolic interactionism: How do symbols underlie and maintain a woman's shift to becoming a man in this society?

→ Apply conflict theory: How do power relations between men and women underlie the custom of sworn virgins?

SOURCES: Based on Zumbrun 2007; Bilefsky 2008; Paterniti 2014.

SAME-SEX PARENTS   Because parents give gender messages to their children, we might expect that the children of homosexual and heterosexual parents will learn different gender lessons and display different gender behaviors. Do they? The initial research findings are mixed. Some research indicates that the children of gay and lesbian couples show less gender stereotyping. That is, the boys show more behaviors that are traditionally considered feminine, and the girls display more behaviors that are traditionally considered masculine (Goldberg et al. 2012). In contrast, other research indicates that the children of gay and lesbian couples are more likely to reflect traditional ideas of gender (Fedewa et al. 2014).

This research is in its infancy. At this point we don't even know what gender messages same-sex parents give their children, much less how they give those messages and what the outcome is. We need rigorous research, including matching studies of how both same-sex and opposite-sex parents teach femininity and masculinity. Such research is not likely to be here soon.

Gender Messages from Peers

Sociologists stress how this sorting process into gender that begins in the family is reinforced as children are exposed to other aspects of society. Of those other influences, one of the most powerful is the **peer group**, individuals of roughly the same age who are linked by common interests. Examples of peer groups are friends, classmates, and "the kids in the neighborhood."

As you grew up, you saw girls and boys teach one another what it means to be female or male. You might not have recognized what was happening, however, so let's eavesdrop on a conversation between two eighth-grade girls studied by sociologist Donna Eder (2007).

peer group

a group of individuals, often of roughly the same age, who are linked by common interests and orientations

CINDY: The only thing that makes her look anything is all the makeup …
PENNY: She had a picture, and she's standing like this. (Poses with one hand on her hip and one by her head)
CINDY: Her face is probably this skinny, but it looks that big 'cause of all the makeup she has on it.
PENNY: She's ugly, ugly, ugly.

Do you see how these girls were giving gender lessons? They were reinforcing images of appearance and behavior that they thought were appropriate for females.

Boys, too, reinforce cultural expectations of gender (Carter 2014). When sociologist Melissa Milkie (1994) studied junior high school boys, she caught a glimpse of this in action. Much of their talk was about movies and TV programs. Of the many images they saw, the boys would single out those associated with sex and violence. They would amuse one another by repeating lines, acting out parts, and joking and laughing at what they had seen.

If you know boys in their early teens, you've probably seen a lot of behavior like this. You may have been amused or have even shaken your head in disapproval. But did you peer beneath the surface? Milkie did. What is really going on? The boys, she concluded, were using media images to develop their identity as males. They had gotten the message: "Real" males are obsessed with sex and violence. Not to joke and laugh about murder and promiscuous sex would have marked a boy as a "weenie" or a "nerd," labels to be avoided at all costs.

mass media

forms of communication, such as radio, newspapers, and television that are directed to mass audiences

Gender Messages in the Mass Media

As you can see with the boys Milkie studied, a major guide to the gender map is the **mass media**, forms of communication that are directed to large audiences. Let's look further at how media images help teach us **gender**, the behaviors and attitudes considered appropriate for our sex.

TELEVISION, MOVIES, AND CARTOONS   If you've watched youngsters while they are watching children's videos or television you've probably noticed how engrossed they are. They can hardly lift their eyes from "the action" when you try to get their attention. What are children learning through these powerful media that transmit ideas through words and moving images? One major lesson is that males are more important than females, as male characters outnumber female characters two to one (Ahmed and Wahab 2014).

In children's cartoons, females used to be portrayed as less brave and more dependent. Reflecting women's changing position in society, cartoons now feature more dominant, aggressive females. Kim Possible divides her time between cheerleading practice and saving the world from evil. With tongue in cheek, the Powerpuff Girls are touted as "the most elite kindergarten crime-fighting force ever assembled." This changed portrayal of gender is especially evident in the violent females who play lead characters in action movies, from Furiosa in *Mad Max: Fury Road* to Katnis Everdeen in *The Hunger Games*, whose athletic, archery, and fighting skills are nothing short of amazing.

A key part of gender is body image, and the mass media are effective in teaching us what we "should" look like. While girls are presented as more powerful than they used to be, they have to be skinny and gorgeous and wear the latest fashions. Such messages present a dilemma for girls: Continuously thrust before them is a model that is almost impossible to replicate in real life.

VIDEO GAMES

Chicago's Robert Morris University is the nation's first school to offer a sports scholarship in video games. When the basketball team protested, the sports director said "It used to be considered odd to throw a ball through a hoop, too." (Belkin 2014)

All over the nation, parents are concerned that their children are wasting their time playing video games. To the parent's dismay, with an athletic scholarship available, children can now mount a stronger defense.

Sociologists have found that the message of male dominance continues in this format, too—and overwhelmingly so. Females are even more underrepresented in video games than on television: 96 percent of the main characters are male—and most females, as usual, are portrayed as sexy (Kuchera 2013). Some video games, though, reflect cutting-edge changes in sex roles, the topic of the Mass Media in Social Life box on the next page.

ADVERTISING   From an early age, you have been bombarded with stereotypical images of gender. If you are average, you are exposed to a blistering 200,000 commercials a year (Kacen 2011). In commercials geared toward children, boys are more likely to be shown as competing in outdoor settings, while girls are more likely to be portrayed as cooperating in indoor settings. Action figures are pitched to boys, and dolls are directed to girls (Kahlenberg and Hein 2010).

Wasting time? Just fun? Improving hand–eye coordination? Parents' lament? Now so culturally integrated and gaining respect that a university (Robert Morris in Chicago) now calls playing video games a sport and awards a scholarship in video games. The newest position in coaching is e-sport coach.

Mass Media in Social Life

Lara Croft, Tomb Raider: Changing Images of Women in the Mass Media

With digital advances, video games have crossed the line from games to something that more closely resembles interactive movies. The games cost millions of dollars to produce and market. One game (*Grand Theft Auto 5*) cost $250 million (McLaughlin 2014). Sociologically, what is significant is not their cost but their *content*. Video games expose gamers not only to action but also to ideas and images. Just as in other forms of the mass media, the gender images in video games communicate powerful messages.

The message of changing gender is loud and clear with Lara Croft, an adventure-seeking archeologist and star of *Tomb Raider* and its many sequels. Lara is smart, strong, and able to utterly vanquish foes. With both guns blazing—or whatever weapons she happens to be using— Lara breaks stereotypical gender roles and dominates what usually is the domain of men. She was the first female protagonist in a field of muscle-rippling, gun-toting macho caricatures (the first was Samus Aran, an intergalactic bounty hunter).

Yet the old remains powerfully encapsulated in the new. As the photo here makes evident, Lara is a fantasy girl for young men of the digital generation. No matter her foe, no matter her predicament, Lara oozes sex. Her form-fitting outfits, which flatter her voluptuous figure, reflect the mental images of the men who created this digital character.

In 2013, these men gave Lara a makeover, presenting what they said was a "more vulnerable and realistic" Lara (Parker 2012). The new Lara, shown here, doesn't seem more vulnerable, as she still manages to kill a lot of men. She is more realistic in the sense that the new graphics make her look almost human, but she still manages to ooze sex whenever she moves. My best guess is that her creators have not had a mental makeover.

For Your Consideration

→ A sociologist who reviewed this text said, "It seems that for women to be defined as equal, we have to become symbolic males—warriors with breasts." Why is gender change mostly one-way—females adopting traditional male characteristics? These two questions should help: Who is moving into the traditional territory of the other? Do people prefer to imitate power or weakness?

As adults, we are still peppered with ads. Although their purpose is to sell products—from booze and bras to cigarettes and cell phones—these ads continue our gender lessons. The stereotypical images—from cowboys who roam the wide-open spaces to scantily clad women whose physical assets couldn't possibly be real—become part of our own images of the sexes. So do advertising's occasional attention-grabbing stereotype-breaking images.

IN SUM   "Male" and "female" are powerful symbols. When we learn that different behaviors and attitudes are expected of us because we are a girl or a boy, we learn to interpret the world in terms of gender. Whether overt and exaggerated or subtle and below our awareness, the mass media continue the gender lessons begun at home and reinforced by our peers. Gender serves as a primary basis for **social inequality**— giving privileges and obligations to one group of people while denying them to another, something we will analyze in following chapters.

social inequality

a social condition in which privileges and obligations are given to some but denied to others

Agents of Socialization

3.5 Explain why the family, the neighborhood, religion, day care, school, peer groups, and the workplace are agents of socialization.

Individuals and groups that influence our orientations to life—our self-concept, emotions, attitudes, and behavior—are called **agents of socialization**. We have already considered how three of these agents—the family, our peers, and the mass media—influence our ideas of gender. Now we'll look more closely at how agents of socialization prepare us in ways other than gender to take our place in society. We will consider the family, then the neighborhood, religion, day care, school and peers, and the workplace.

agents of socialization
people or groups that affect our self concept, attitudes, behaviors, or other orientations toward life

The Family

As you know, the first group to have a major impact on who you become is your family. Your experiences in the family are so intense that they last a lifetime. These experiences establish your initial motivations, values, and beliefs. In your family, you receive your basic sense of self, ideas about who you are and what you deserve out of life. It is here that you began to think of yourself as strong or weak, smart or dumb, good-looking or ugly—or more likely, somewhere in between.

Not all families are the same, of course. Let's look at the difference that social class makes in how families socialize their children.

SOCIAL CLASS AND TYPE OF WORK   Sociologist Melvin Kohn (1959, 1963, 1977, 2006) found that the main concern of working-class parents is that their children stay out of trouble. To keep them in line, they tend to use physical punishment. Middle-class parents, in contrast, focus more on developing their children's curiosity, self-expression, and self-control. They are more likely to reason with their children than to punish them physically.

Why should there be such differences? Kohn wondered. As a sociologist, he knew that the reason was life experiences of some sort, and he found the answer in the world of work. Blue-collar workers are usually told exactly what to do. Since they expect their children's lives to be like theirs, they stress obedience. In contrast, the work of middle-class parents requires more initiative, and these parents socialize their children into the qualities they find valuable.

Kohn was still puzzled. Some working-class parents act more like middle-class parents, and vice versa. As Kohn probed further, the pieces fell into place. The key turned out to be the parents' types of jobs. Middle-class office workers are supervised closely, and Kohn found that they follow the working-class pattern of child rearing, emphasizing conformity. And some blue-collar workers, such as those who do home repairs, have a good deal of freedom. These workers follow the middle-class model in rearing their children (Pearlin and Kohn 1966; Kohn and Schooler 1969).

SOCIAL CLASS AND PLAY   Working-class and middle-class parents also have different ideas of how children develop, ideas that have fascinating consequences for children's play (Lareau 2002, 2011; Stephens et al. 2014). Working-class parents see their children as being like wildflowers—they develop naturally. Since the child's development will take care of itself, good parenting primarily means providing food, shelter, and comfort. These parents set limits on their children's play ("Don't go near the railroad tracks") and let them play as they wish. To middle-class parents, in contrast, children are like tender houseplants—they need a lot of guidance if they are to flower.

This photo captures an extreme form of family socialization. The father seems to be more emotionally involved in the goal—and in more pain—than his daughter, as he pushes her toward the finish line in the Teen Tours of America Kid's Triathlon.

These parents want their children's play to accomplish something. They may want them to play baseball, for example, not for the enjoyment of the sport but to help them learn how to be team players.

The Neighborhood

As all parents know, some neighborhoods are better than others for children. Parents try to move to the better neighborhoods—if they can afford them. Their commonsense evaluations are borne out by sociological research. Children from poor neighborhoods are more likely to get in trouble with the law, to become pregnant, to drop out of school, and even to have worse mental health (Levanthal and Brooks-Gunn 2000; Wheaton and Clarke 2003; DeLuca and Dayton 2009; Rendon 2014).

Sociologists have found that parenting is easier in the more affluent neighborhoods. Among the major advantages these parents have are more employment, less crime, stronger ties among the neighbors, more support groups, and being able to rely more on one another in times of need (Byrnes and Miller 2012; Rendon 2014). There are also fewer families in transition, so the adults are more likely to know the local children and their parents. This better equips them to help keep the children safe and out of trouble.

Religion

How important is religion in your life? Most Americans report that religion is very important to them, but what if you are among the 22 percent who say that religion is not very important (Newport 2013)? We would miss the point if we were to assume that religion influences only people who are "religious." Religion plays a powerful role even for people who wouldn't be caught dead near a church, synagogue, or mosque. How? Religious ideas so pervade U.S. society that they provide the foundation of morality for both the religious and the nonreligious.

For many Americans, the influence of religion is more direct. This is especially true for the two of every five Americans who report that during a typical week they attend a religious service (Newport 2013). On the obvious level, through their participation in religious services, they learn doctrines, values, and morality, but the effects of religion on their lives go far beyond this. As they learn beliefs about the hereafter, for example, they also learn what kinds of clothing, speech, and manners are appropriate for formal occasions. Life in congregations also provides them a sense of identity, a feeling of belonging. Religious participation also helps to integrate immigrants into their new society, offers an avenue of social mobility for the poor, provides social contacts for jobs, and, for African Americans, has been a powerful influence in social change.

Day Care

It is rare for social science research to make national news, but occasionally it does. This is what happened when researchers published their findings on 1,200 kindergarten children they had studied since they were a month old. They observed the children multiple times both at home and at day care. They also videotaped the children's interactions with their mothers (National Institute of Child Health and Human Development 1999; Guensburg 2001). What caught the media's attention? Children who spend more time in day care have weaker bonds with their mothers and are less affectionate toward them. They are also less cooperative with others and more likely to fight and to be "mean." By the time they get to kindergarten, they are more likely to talk back to teachers and to disrupt the classroom. This holds true regardless of the quality of the day care, the family's social class, or whether the child is a girl or a boy (Belsky 2006). On the positive side, the children scored higher on language tests.

Are we producing a generation of "smart but mean" children? This is not an unreasonable question, since the study was well designed and an even larger study of children in England has come up with similar findings (Belsky 2006). Some point out that the differences between children who spend a lot of time in day care and those who spend less time are slight. Others stress that with 2 million children in day care (*Statistical Abstract* 2014:Table 604), slight differences can be significant for society.

The researchers continued to test these children as they went through school, and the surprise is that these initial effects of day care have continued. At age 15, the children who had spent more time in child care had slightly more behavioral problems and did slightly worse academically than those who had spent less time in day care (Vandell et al. 2010).

The School

Part of the **manifest function**, or *intended* purpose, of formal education is to teach knowledge and skills, such as reading, writing, and arithmetic. Schools also have **latent functions**, *unintended consequences* that help the social system. Let's look at this less obvious aspect of education. At home, children learn attitudes and values that match their family's situation in life. At school, they learn a broader perspective that helps prepare them to take a role in the world beyond the family. At home, a child may have been the almost exclusive focus of doting parents, but in school, the child learns *universality—* that the same rules apply to everyone, regardless of who their parents are or how special they may be at home. The Cultural Diversity box on the next page explores how these new values and ways of looking at the world sometimes even replace those the child learns at home.

Sociologists have also identified a *hidden curriculum* in our schools. This term refers to values that, although not taught explicitly, are part of a school's "cultural message." For example, the stories and examples that are used to teach math and English may bring with them lessons in patriotism, democracy, justice, and honesty. There is also a *corridor curriculum*, what students teach one another outside the classroom. The corridor curriculum is strikingly different: It includes racism, sexism, illicit ways to make money, coolness, and superiority (Hemmings 1999; Cross and Fletcher 2013). You can determine for yourself how each of these is functional and dysfunctional.

Conflict theorists point out that social class separates children into different educational worlds. Children of wealthy parents go to private schools, where they learn skills and values that match their higher position. Children of middle-class parents go to public schools, where they learn that good jobs, even the professions, beckon, while children from blue-collar families learn that not many of "their kind" will become professionals or leaders. This is one of the many reasons that children from blue-collar families are less likely to take college prep courses or to go to college. In short, our schools reflect and reinforce our social class divisions. We will return to this topic in Chapter 13.

Peer Groups

As a child's experiences with agents of socialization broaden, the influence of the family decreases. Entry into school marks one of many steps in this transfer of allegiance. One of the most significant aspects of education is that it exposes children to peer groups whose influences conflict with how parents and schools are trying to socialize them.

When sociologists Patricia and Peter Adler (1998) observed children at two elementary schools in Colorado, they saw how children separate themselves by sex and develop separate gender worlds. The norms that made boys popular were athletic ability, coolness, and toughness. For girls, popularity came from family background, physical appearance (clothing and use of makeup), and the ability to attract popular boys. In this children's subculture, academic achievement pulled in opposite directions: High grades lowered the popularity of boys, but for girls, good grades increased their standing among peers.

manifest functions

the intended beneficial consequences of people's actions

latent functions

unintended beneficial consequences of people's actions

Schools are a primary agent of socialization. One of their functions is to teach children the attitudes and skills they are thought to need as adults.

Cultural Diversity in the United States

Immigrants and Their Children: Caught between Two Worlds

It is a struggle to adapt to a new culture, to learn behaviors and ways of thinking that are at odds with those already learned. This exposure to two worlds can lead to inner turmoil. One way to handle the conflict is to cut ties with your first culture. Doing so, however, can create a sense of loss, one that is perhaps recognized only later in life.

Richard Rodriguez, a literature professor and essayist, was born to working-class Mexican immigrants. Wanting their son to be successful in their adopted land, his parents named him Richard instead of Ricardo. Although his English–Spanish hybrid name indicates his parents' aspirations for their son, it was also an omen of the conflict that Richard would experience.

Like other children of Mexican immigrants, Richard first spoke Spanish—a rich mother tongue that introduced him to the world. Until the age of 5, when he began school, Richard knew only fifty words in English. He describes what happened when he began school:

The change came gradually but early. When I was beginning grade school, I noted to myself the fact that the classroom environment was so different in its styles and assumptions from my own family environment that survival would essentially entail a choice between both worlds. When I became a student, I was literally "remade"; neither I nor my teachers considered anything I had known before as relevant. I had to forget most of what my culture had provided, because to remember it was a disadvantage. The past and its cultural values became detachable, like a piece of clothing grown heavy on a warm day and finally put away.

As happened to millions of immigrants before him, whose parents spoke German, Polish, Italian, and so on, learning English eroded family and class ties and ate away at his ethnic roots. For Rodriguez, language and education were not simply devices that eased the transition to the dominant culture. They also slashed at the roots that had given him life.

To face conflicting cultures is to confront a fork in the road. Some turn one way and withdraw from the new culture—a clue that helps to explain why so many Latinos drop out of U.S. schools. Others turn the other way. Cutting ties with their family and cultural roots, they embrace the new culture.

Rodriguez took the second road. He excelled in his new language—so much, in fact, that he graduated from Stanford University and then became a graduate student in English at the University of California at Berkeley. He was even awarded a Fulbright fellowship to study English Renaissance literature at the University of London.

But the past shadowed Rodriguez. Prospective employers were impressed with his knowledge of Renaissance literature. At job interviews, however, they would skip over the Renaissance training and ask him if he would teach the Mexican novel and be an advisor to Latino students. Rodriguez was also haunted by the image of his grandmother, the warmth of the culture he had left behind, and the language and ways of thinking to which he had become a stranger.

Richard Rodriguez represents tens of millions of immigrants—not just those of Latino origin but those from other cultures, too—who want to integrate into U.S. culture yet not betray their past. Fearing loss of their roots, they are caught between two cultures, each beckoning, each offering rich rewards. The choice is painful.

From his most recent writings, it is evident that even as he ages, the past and cultural contradictions still plague Rodriguez.

SOURCES: Based on Rodriguez 1975, 1982, 1990, 1991, 1995; Herrera and Rodriguez 2014.

For Your Consideration

→ I saw this conflict firsthand with my father, who did not learn English until after the seventh grade (his last in school). He left German behind, eventually coming to the point that he could no longer speak it, but broken English and awkward expressions remained for a lifetime. Then, too, there were the lingering emotional connections to old ways, as well as the haughtiness and slights of more assimilated Americans. He grasped security by holding on to the past, its ways of thinking and feeling, but at the same time he wanted to succeed in the everyday reality of the new culture. Have you seen similar conflicts?

You know from your own experience how compelling peer groups are. It is almost impossible to go against a peer group, whose cardinal rule seems to be "conformity or rejection." Anyone who doesn't do what the others want becomes an "outsider," a "non-member," an "outcast." For preteens and teens just learning their way around in the world, it is not surprising that the peer group rules. As you know, peer groups can be vicious in enforcing their norms, the focus of the following Down-to-Earth Sociology box.

Down-to-Earth Sociology

Gossip and Ridicule to Enforce Adolescent Norms

Adolescence is not known as the turbulent years for nothing. During this period of our lives, the security of a self identity rooted in parental relations and family life is being ripped from us as we attempt to piece together a strong sense of individual identity. This sense of who we are apart from our parents and siblings does not come easily. At this stage of life, we simply don't know who we yet are, and seldom do we have a good sense of whom we will become. The process of developing a sense of self by evaluating the reflections we receive from others is not new, but its severity at this point of life grows acute. Here is what sociologist Donna Eder said about her research on adolescent girls.

I became concerned while reading studies on adolescent girls. Many of these studies reported a drop in girls' self-esteem and self-image when they entered junior high school. I hired both female and male assistants to observe lunchtime interaction along with me as I wanted to study both girls and boys from different social class backgrounds. We also attended after-school sports events and cheerleading practices. All of us took field notes after we left the setting and tape-recorded lunchtime conversations.

Some of the things we observed were painful to watch. Through our recordings of gossip and ridicule, we learned a lot about what might make girls so insecure. For one thing, much of the gossip involved negative comments on other girls' appearances as well as their "stuck up" behavior. The only time that anyone disagreed with someone's negative evaluation was if they did so early on, right after the remark was made. Once even one other person agreed with it, no one seemed willing

to challenge the "group" view. So in order to participate in the gossip, you pretty much needed to join in with the negative comments or else be sure to speak up quickly.

When we studied teasing, we also saw the power of a response to shape the meaning of an exchange. One day during volleyball practice, a girl said that another girl was showing off her new bra through her white T-shirt. The girl responded by saying, "If I want to show off my bra, I'll do it like this," lifting her shirt up. By responding playfully, she disarmed the insulter, and her teammates all joined in on the laughter.

In this large middle school, status hierarchies were based on appearance, social class, and intelligence. Those at the bottom of the status rankings were isolates, eating lunch by themselves or with other low status students. As isolates, they were frequent targets of ridicule from students trying to build themselves up by putting others down. Both boys and girls picked on the isolates, most of whom lacked the skills to turn the exchanges into playful ones.

SOURCE: Redacted from Eder 2014.

Gossip and ridicule increase the status insecurity of this time of life.

For Your Consideration

→ What was school like for you at this age?

→ Did you observe anything like this?

→ Why do you think peer groups at this stage in life are so critical, even vicious?

→ Why do peer groups, at all stages of life, produce isolates?

As a result, the standards of our peer groups tend to dominate our lives. If your peers, for example, listen to rap, Nortec, death metal, rock and roll, country, or gospel, it is almost inevitable that you also prefer that kind of music. In high school, if your friends take math courses, you probably do, too (Crosnoe et al. 2008). It is the same for clothing styles and dating standards. Peer influences also extend to behaviors that violate social norms. If your peers are college-bound and upwardly striving, this is most likely what you will be; but if they use drugs, cheat, and steal, you are likely to do so, too.

The Workplace

Another agent of socialization that comes into play somewhat later in life is the workplace. Those initial jobs that we take in high school and college are much more than just a way to earn a few dollars. From the people we rub shoulders with at work, we learn not only a set of skills but also perspectives on the world.

Most of us eventually become committed to some particular type of work, often after trying out many jobs. This may involve **anticipatory socialization**, learning to play a role before entering it. Anticipatory socialization is a sort of mental rehearsal for some future activity. We may talk to people who work in a particular career, read novels about that type of work, or take a summer internship in that field. Such activities allow us to become aware of what would be expected of us. Sometimes this helps people avoid committing themselves to an empty career, as with some of my students who tried student teaching, found that they couldn't stand it, and then moved on to other fields more to their liking.

An intriguing aspect of work as a socializing agent is that the more you participate in a line of work, the more this work becomes part of your self-concept. Eventually, you come to think of yourself so much in terms of the job that if someone asks you to describe yourself, you are likely to include the job in your self-description. You might say, "I'm a teacher," "I'm a nurse," or "I'm a sociologist."

Resocialization

3.6   Explain what total institutions are and how they resocialize people.

What does a woman who has just become a nun have in common with a man who has just divorced? The answer is that they both are undergoing **resocialization**; that is, they are learning new norms, values, attitudes, and behaviors to match their new situation in life. In its most common form, resocialization occurs each time we learn something contrary to our previous experiences. A new boss who insists on a different way of doing things is resocializing you. Most resocialization is mild—only a slight modification of things we have already learned.

Resocialization can also be intense. People who join Alcoholics Anonymous (AA), for example, are surrounded by reformed drinkers who affirm the destructive consequences of excessive drinking. Some students experience an intense period of resocialization when they leave high school and start college—especially during those initially scary days before they find companions, start to fit in, and feel comfortable. The experiences of people who join a cult or begin psychotherapy are even more profound: They learn views that conflict with their earlier socialization. If these ideas "take," not only does the individual's behavior change but he or she also learns a fundamentally different way of looking at life.

Total Institutions

Relatively few of us experience the powerful agent of socialization that sociologist Erving Goffman (1961) called the **total institution**. He coined this term to refer to a place where people are cut off from the rest of society and where they come under almost total control of the officials who are in charge. Boot camps, prisons, concentration camps, convents, and some military schools, such as West Point, are total institutions.

A person entering a total institution is greeted with a **degradation ceremony** (Garfinkel 1956), an attempt to remake the self by stripping away the individual's current identity and stamping a new one in its place. This unwelcome greeting may involve fingerprinting, photographing, or shaving the head. Newcomers may be ordered to strip, undergo an examination (often in a humiliating, semipublic setting), and then put on a uniform that designates their new status. Officials also take away the individual's *personal identity kit*, items such as jewelry, hairstyles, clothing, and other body decorations used to express individuality.

anticipatory socialization
the process of learning in advance an anticipated future role or status

resocialization
the process of learning new norms, values, attitudes, and behaviors

total institution
a place that is almost totally controlled by those who run it, in which people are cut off from the rest of society and the society is mostly cut off from them

degradation ceremony
a term coined by Harold Garfinkel to refer to a ritual whose goal is to remake someone's self by stripping away that individual's self-identity and stamping a new identity in its place

Total institutions are isolated from the public. The bars, walls, gates, and guards not only keep the inmates in but also keep outsiders out. Staff members supervise the day-to-day lives of the residents. Eating, sleeping, showering, recreation—all are standardized. Inmates learn that their previous statuses—student, worker, spouse, parent—mean nothing. The only thing that counts is their current status.

No one leaves a total institution unscathed: The experience brands an indelible mark on the individual's self and colors the way he or she sees the world. Boot camp, as described in the Down-to-Earth Sociology box below, is brutal but swift. Prison, in contrast, is brutal and prolonged. Neither recruit nor prisoner, however, has difficulty in knowing that the institution has had profound effects on their attitudes and orientations to life.

Down-to-Earth Sociology

Boot Camp as a Total Institution

The bus arrives at Parris Island, South Carolina, at 3 A.M. The early hour is no accident. The recruits are groggy, confused. Up to a few hours ago, the young men were ordinary civilians. Now, as a sergeant sneeringly calls them "maggots," their heads are buzzed (25 seconds per recruit), and they are quickly thrust into the harsh world of Marine boot camp.

Buzzing the boys' hair is just the first step in stripping away their identity so that the Marines can stamp a new one in its place. The uniform serves the same purpose. There is a ban on using the first person "I." Even a simple request must be made in precise Marine style or it will not be acknowledged. ("Sir, Recruit Jones requests permission to make a head call, Sir.")

Every intense moment of the next eleven weeks reminds the recruits, men and women, that they are joining a subculture of self-discipline. Here, pleasure is suspect, and sacrifice is good. As they learn the Marine way of talking,

A recruit with a drill instructor.

walking, and thinking, they are denied the diversions they once took for granted: television, cigarettes, cars, candy, soft drinks, video games, music, alcohol, drugs, and sex.

Lessons are taught with fierce intensity. When Sergeant Carey checks brass belt buckles, Recruit Robert Shelton nervously blurts, "I don't have one." Sergeant Carey's face grows red as his neck cords bulge. "I?" he says, his face just inches from the recruit. With spittle flying from his mouth, he screams, "'I' is gone!"

"Nobody's an individual" is the lesson that is driven home again and again. "You are a team, a Marine. Not a civilian. Not black or white, not Hispanic or Indian or some hyphenated American—but a Marine. You will live like a Marine, fight like a Marine, and, if necessary, die like a Marine."

Each day begins before dawn with close-order formations. The rest of the day is filled with training in hand-to-hand combat, marching, running, calisthenics, Marine history, and—always—following orders.

"An M-16 can blow someone's head off at 500 meters," Sergeant Norman says. "That's beautiful, isn't it?"

"Yes, sir!" shout the platoon's fifty-nine voices.

"Pick your nose!" Simultaneously fifty-nine index fingers shoot into nostrils.

The pressure to conform is intense. Those who are sent packing for insubordination or suicidal tendencies are mocked in cadence during drills. ("Hope you like the sights you see/Parris Island casualty.") As lights go out at 9 P.M., the exhausted recruits perform the day's last task: The entire platoon, in unison, chants the virtues of the Marines.

Recruits are constantly scrutinized. Subpar performance is not accepted, whether a dirty rifle or a loose thread on a uniform. The underperformer is shouted at, derided, humiliated. The group suffers for the individual. If one recruit is slow, the entire platoon is punished.

The system works.

One of the new Marines (until graduation, they are recruits, not Marines) says, "I feel like I've joined a new society or religion."

He has.

SOURCES: Based on Garfinkel 1956; Goffman 1961; Ricks 1995; Dyer 2007.

For Your Consideration

Use concepts in this chapter to explain why the Marine system works.

→ Of what significance is the recruits' degradation ceremony?

→ Why are recruits not allowed video games, cigarettes, or calls home?

→ Why are the Marines so unfair as to punish an entire platoon for the failure of an individual?

Socialization through the Life Course

3.7 Identify major divisions of the life course and discuss the sociological significance of the life course.

life course

the stages of our life as we go from birth to death

You are at a particular stage in your life now, and college is a major part of it. You know that you have more stages ahead as you go through life. These stages, from birth to death, are called the **life course**. The sociological significance of the life course is twofold. First, as you pass through a stage, it affects your behavior and orientations. You simply don't think about life in the same way when you are 35, are married, and have a baby and a mortgage as you do when you are 18 or 20, single, and in college. (Actually, you don't even see life the same way as a freshman and as a senior.) Second, your life course differs by social location. Your social class, race–ethnicity, and gender, for example, map out distinctive worlds of experience.

This means that the typical life course differs for males and females, the rich and the poor, and so on. To emphasize this major sociological point, in the sketch that follows I will stress the *historical* setting of people's lives. Because of your particular social location, your own life course may differ from this sketch, which is a composite of stages that others have suggested (Levinson 1978; Carr et al. 1995; Quadagno 2010).

Childhood (from birth to about age 12)

Consider how remarkably different your childhood would have been if you had grown up in Europe a few hundred years ago. Historian Philippe Ariès (1965) noticed that in European paintings from about A.D. 1000 to 1800, children were always dressed in adult clothing. If they were not depicted stiffly posed, as in a family portrait, they were shown doing adult activities.

From this, Ariès drew a conclusion that sparked a debate among historians. He said that Europeans of this era did not regard childhood as a special time of life. They viewed children as miniature adults and put them to work at an early age. At the age of 7, for example, a boy might leave home for good to learn to be a jeweler or a stonecutter. A girl, in contrast, stayed home until she married, but by the age of 7, she assumed her share of the household tasks. Historians do not deny that these were the customs of that time, but some say that Ariès' conclusion is ridiculous, that other evidence indicates that these people viewed childhood as a special time of life (Orme 2002).

Until about 1900, having children work like adults was common around the world. Even today, children in the Least Industrialized Nations work in many occupations—from blacksmiths to waiters. As tourists are shocked to discover, children in these nations also work as street peddlers, hawking everything from shoelaces to chewing gum.

Child rearing, too, used to be remarkably different. Three hundred years ago, parents and teachers considered it their *moral* duty to *terrorize* children. To keep children from "going bad," they would frighten them with bedtime stories of death and hellfire, lock them in dark closets, and force them to witness events like this:

> *A common moral lesson involved taking children to visit the gibbet [an upraised post on which executed bodies were left hanging], where they were forced to inspect the rotting corpses as an example of what happens to bad children when they grow up. Whole classes were taken out of school to witness hangings, and parents would often whip their children afterwards to make them remember what they had seen. (DeMause 1975)*

Industrialization transformed the way we perceive children. When children had the leisure to go to school and postpone taking on adult roles, parents and officials came to think of them as tender and innocent, as needing more care, comfort, and protection.

Such attitudes of dependency grew, and today we view children as needing gentle guidance if they are to develop emotionally, intellectually, morally, even physically. We take our view for granted—after all, it is only "common sense." Yet, as you can see, our view is not "natural." It is rooted in society—in geography, history, and economic development.

IN SUM Childhood is more than biology. Everyone's childhood occurs at some point in history and is embedded in specific social locations, especially social class and gender. *These social factors are as vital as our biology, for they determine what our childhood will be like.* Although a child's *biological* characteristics (such as being small and dependent) are universal, the child's *social* experiences (the kind of life the child lives) are not. Because of this, sociologists say that childhood varies from culture to culture.

Adolescence (ages 13–17)

It might seem strange to you, but adolescence is a *social invention*, not a "natural" age division. In earlier centuries, people simply moved from childhood to young adulthood, with no stopover in between. The Industrial Revolution allowed adolescence to be invented. It brought such an abundance of material surpluses that for the first time in history people in their teens were not needed as workers. At the same time, education became more important for achieving success. As these two forces in industrialized societies converged, they created a gap between childhood and adulthood. The term *adolescence* was coined to indicate this new stage in life (Hall 1904), one that has become renowned for uncertainty, rebellion, and inner turmoil.

To mark the passage of children into adulthood, tribal societies hold *initiation rites.* This grounds the self-identity, showing these young people how they fit in the society. In the industrialized world, however, adolescents must "find" themselves. They grapple with the dilemma of "I am neither a child nor an adult. Who am I?" As they attempt to carve out an identity that is distinct from both the "younger" world being left behind and the "older" world that still lingers out of reach, adolescents develop their own subcultures, with distinctive clothing, hairstyles, language, gestures, and music. We usually fail to realize that contemporary society, not biology, created this period of inner turmoil that we call *adolescence.*

Transitional Adulthood (ages 18–29)

If society invented adolescence, can it also invent other periods of life? As Figure 3.2 illustrates, this is actually happening now. Postindustrial societies are adding a period of extended youth to the life course, which sociologists call **transitional adulthood** (also known as *adultolescence*). After high school, millions of young adults postpone adult responsibilities by going to college. They are mostly freed from the control of their parents, yet they don't have to support themselves. After college, many return home, so they

In many societies, manhood is not bestowed upon males simply because they reach a certain age. Manhood, rather, signifies a standing in the community that must be achieved. Shown here is an initiation ceremony in Indonesia, where boys, to lay claim to the status of manhood, must jump over this barrier.

Figure 3.2 Transitional Adulthood: A New Stage in the Life Course

Who has completed the transition?

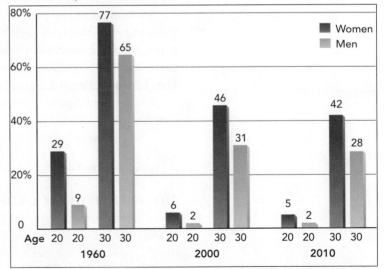

The bars show the percentage who have completed the transition to adulthood, as measured by leaving home, finishing school, getting married, having a child, and being financially independent.

SOURCE: Furstenberg et al. 2004. Year 2010 is the author's estimate based on Sironi and Furstenberg 2014.

A son at "Bring Your Parents to Work Day" showing his parents the hi-tech equipment he uses at work.

can live cheaply while they establish themselves in a career—and, of course, continue to "find themselves." During this time, people are "neither psychological adolescents nor sociological adults" (Keniston 1971). At some point during this period of extended youth, young adults ease into adult responsibilities. They take full-time jobs, become serious about a career, engage in courtship rituals, get married—and go into debt.

"BRING YOUR PARENTS TO WORK DAY." With this new stage of life come longer attachments to parents. Some companies find that worker morale and productivity increase if they incorporate the parents in the workplace. Some companies even send Mom and Dad notes when their child achieves work goals, and LinkedIn has begun a Bring Your Parents to Work Day (Hopschneider 2013).

The Middle Years (ages 30–65)

THE EARLY MIDDLE YEARS (AGES 30–49) During their early middle years, most people are more sure of themselves and of their goals in life. As with any point in the life course, however, the self can receive severe jolts. Common upheavals during this period are divorce and losing jobs. It may take years for the self to stabilize after such ruptures.

The early middle years pose a special challenge for many U.S. women, who have been given the message, especially by the media, that they can "have it all." They can be superworkers, superwives, and supermoms—all rolled into one superwoman. Reality, however, hits them in the face: too little time, too many demands, even too little sleep. Something has to give, and attempts to resolve this dilemma are anything but easy.

transitional adulthood

a term that refers to a period following high school when young adults have not yet taken on the responsibilities ordinarily associated with adulthood; also called *adultolescence*

THE LATER MIDDLE YEARS (AGES 50–65) During the later middle years, health issues and mortality begin to loom large as people feel their bodies change, especially if they watch their parents become frail, fall ill, and die. The consequence is a fundamental reorientation in thinking—*from time since birth to time left to live* (Neugarten 1976). With this changed orientation, people attempt to evaluate the past and come to terms with what lies ahead. They compare what they have accomplished with what they had hoped to achieve. Many people also find themselves caring not only for their own children but also for their aging parents. Because of this double burden, which is often crushing, people in the later middle years are sometimes called the "sandwich generation."

In contrast, many people experience few of these stresses and find the late middle years to be the most comfortable period of their lives. They enjoy job security or secure marriages and a standard of living higher than ever before. They live in a bigger house (one that may even be paid for), drive newer cars, and take longer and more exotic vacations. The children are grown, the self is firmly planted, and fewer upheavals are likely to occur.

As they anticipate the next stage of life, however, most people do not like what they see.

The Older Years (about age 65 on)

transitional older years

an emerging stage of the life course between retirement and when people are considered old; about age 65 to 74

THE TRANSITIONAL OLDER YEARS (AGES 65–74) In agricultural societies, when death came early, old age was thought to begin at around age 40. As industrialization brought improved nutrition, medicine, and public health, more people lived longer, and the beginning of "old age" gradually receded. Today, people who enjoy good health don't think of their 60s as old age but as an extension of their middle years. This change is so recent that another *new stage of life* seems to be evolving, the period between retirement and old age—which people are increasingly coming to see as beginning around age 75 ("Schwab Study" 2008). We can call this stage the *transitional older years*.

Researchers who are focusing on this transitional stage of life have found that social isolation harms both the body and brain, that people who are more integrated into social networks stay mentally sharper (Cacioppo and Cacioppo 2013). With improved health, most people between their late 60s and age 75 (two-thirds of the men and two-fifths of the women) continue to be sexually active (Lindau et al. 2007). Not only are people in this stage of life having more sex but they also are enjoying it more (Beckman et al. 2008).

Because we have a self and can reason abstractly, we can contemplate death. In our early years, we regard death as a vague notion, a remote possibility. As people see their parents and friends die and observe their own bodies no longer functioning as before, however, the thought of death becomes less abstract. During this stage in the life course, people feel that "time is closing in" on them.

THE LATER OLDER YEARS (AGE 75 OR SO ON)   As with the preceding periods of life, except the first one, there is no precise beginning point to this last stage. For some, the 75th birthday may mark entry into this period of life. For others, that marker may be the 80th or even the 85th birthday. For most, this stage is marked by growing frailty and illness. For all who reach this stage, it is ended by death. For some, the physical decline is slow, and a rare few manage to see their 100th birthday mentally alert and in good physical health.

Applying the Sociological Perspective to the Life Course

In Chapter 1, you learned about the sociological perspective, especially how your *social location* is vitally important for what you experience in life. Your social location, such as your social class, gender, and race–ethnicity, is also highly significant for your life course. If you are poor, for example, you likely will feel older sooner than most wealthy people for whom life is less harsh. Individual factors—such as your health or marrying early or entering college late—can also throw your life course "out of sequence."

As you learned, the sociological perspective stresses not just social location but also the broad streams of history. These, too drastically affect your life course. As sociologist C. Wright Mills (1959) would say, if employers are beating a path to your door, or failing to do so, you will be more inclined to marry, to buy a house, and to start a family—or to postpone these life course events.

This takes us to the sociological significance of the life course. Our life course does not merely reflect biology, things that occur naturally to all of us as we add years to our lives. Rather, *social* factors influence our life course. Since you live in a period of rapid social change, like a speeding car in a thunderstorm, you might find your life course skidding in unexpected directions.

This January 1937 photo from Sneedville, Tennessee, shows Eunice Johns, age 9, and her husband, Charlie Johns, age 22. The groom gave his wife a doll as a wedding gift. The new husband and wife planned to build a cabin, and, as Charlie Johns phrased it, "go to housekeepin'." This couple illustrates the cultural relativity of life stages, which we sometimes mistake as fixed. It also is interesting from a symbolic interactionist perspective— that of changing definitions.

Some students have asked what happened to this couple. The marriage lasted. Charlie and Eunice Johns had 7 children, 5 boys and 2 girls. Charlie died in 1997 at age 83, and Eunice in 2006 at age 78. The two were buried next to each other in the Johns Family Cemetery.

Are We Prisoners of Socialization?

3.8   Understand why we are not prisoners of socialization.

From our discussion of socialization, you might conclude that sociologists think of people as robots: The socialization goes in, and the behavior comes out. People cannot help what they do, think, or feel, as everything is a result of their exposure to socializing agents.

Sociologists do *not* think of people in this way. Although socialization is powerful, and affects all of us profoundly, we have a self. Established in childhood and continually modified by later experience, our self is dynamic. Our self is not a sponge that passively absorbs influences from the environment, but, rather, it is a vigorous, essential part of our being that allows us to act on our environment.

Precisely because people are not robots, individual behavior is hard to predict. The countless reactions of others merge in each of us. As the self develops, we each internalize or "put together" these innumerable reactions, which become the basis for how we reason, react to others, and make choices in life. The result is a unique whole called the *individual*.

Rather than being passive sponges in this process, *each of us is actively involved in the construction of the self.* Our experiences in the family and other groups during childhood lay down our basic orientations to life, but we are not doomed to keep these orientations if we do not like them. We can purposely expose ourselves to other groups and ideas. Those experiences, in turn, have their own effects on our self. In short, we influence our socialization as we make choices. We can change even the self within the limitations of the framework laid down by our social locations. And that self—along with the options available within society—is the key to our behavior.

Summary and Review

Society Makes Us Human

3.1 **Explain how feral, isolated, and institutionalized children help us understand that "society makes us human."**

How much of our human characteristics come from "nature" (heredity) and how much from "nurture" (the social environment)?

Observations of isolated, institutionalized, and **feral children** help to answer the nature–nurture question, as do experiments with monkeys that were raised in isolation. Language and intimate social interaction—aspects of "nurture"—are essential to the development of what we consider to be human characteristics.

Socialization into the Self and Mind

3.2 **Use the ideas and research of Cooley (looking-glass self), Mead (role taking), and Piaget (reasoning) to explain socialization into the self and mind.**

How do we acquire a self?

Humans are born with the *capacity* to develop a **self**, but the self must be socially constructed; that is, its contents depend on social interaction. According to Charles Horton Cooley's concept of the **looking-glass self**, our self develops as we internalize others' reactions to us. George Herbert Mead identified the ability to **take the role of the other** as essential to the development of the self. Mead concluded that even the mind is a social product.

How do children develop reasoning skills?

Jean Piaget identified four stages that children go through as they develop the ability to reason: (1) *sensorimotor*, in which understanding is limited to sensory stimuli such as touch and sight; (2) *preoperational*, the ability to use symbols; (3) *concrete operational*, in which reasoning ability is more complex but not yet capable of complex abstractions; and (4) *formal operational*, or abstract thinking.

Learning Personality, Morality, and Emotions

3.3 **Explain how the development of personality and morality and socialization into emotions are part of how "society makes us human."**

How do sociologists evaluate Freud's psychoanalytic theory of personality development?

Sigmund Freud viewed personality development as the result of our **id** (inborn, self-centered desires) clashing with the demands of society. The **ego** develops to balance the id and the **superego**, the conscience. Sociologists, in contrast, do not examine inborn or subconscious motivations but, instead, consider how *social* factors—social class, gender, religion, education, and so forth—underlie personality.

How do people develop morality?

That even babies exhibit a sense of morality seems to indicate that a basic morality could be inborn. Lawrence Kohlberg identified four stages children go through as they learn morality: amoral, preconventional, conventional, and postconventional. The answer to "What is moral?" differs from society to society.

How does socialization influence emotions?

Socialization influences not only *how we express our emotions* but also *what emotions we feel*. Socialization into emotions is one of the means by which society produces conformity.

Socialization into Gender

3.4 **Discuss how gender messages from the family, peers, and the mass media teach us society's gender map.**

How does gender socialization affect our sense of self?

Gender socialization—sorting males and females into different roles—is a primary way that groups control human behavior. Children receive messages about **gender** even in infancy. A society's ideals of sex-linked behaviors are reinforced by its social institutions.

Agents of Socialization

3.5 **Explain why the family, the neighborhood, religion, day care, school, peer groups, and the workplace are agents of socialization.**

What are the main agents of socialization?

The **agents of socialization** include the family, neighborhood, religion, day care, school, **peer groups**, the **mass media**, and the workplace. Each has its particular influences in socializing us into becoming full-fledged members of society.

Resocialization

3.6 **Explain what total institutions are and how they resocialize people.**

What is resocialization?

Resocialization is the process of learning new norms, values, attitudes, and behavior. Most resocialization is voluntary, but some, as with residents of **total institutions**, is involuntary.

Socialization through the Life Course

3.7 **Identify major divisions of the life course and discuss the sociological significance of the life course.**

Does socialization end when we enter adulthood?

Socialization occurs throughout the life course. In industrialized societies, the **life course** can be divided into childhood, adolescence, young adulthood, the middle years, and the older years. The West is adding two new stages, **transitional adulthood** and **transitional older years**. Using the sociological perspective, we can see how both the streams of history and social location—geography, gender, race–ethnicity, social class—influence the life course.

Are We Prisoners of Socialization?

3.8 **Understand why we are not prisoners of socialization.**

Although socialization is powerful, we are not merely the sum of our socialization experiences. Just as socialization influences our behavior, so we act on our environment and influence even our self-concept.

Thinking Critically about Chapter 3

1. What two agents of socialization have influenced you the most? Try to pinpoint their influence on specific attitudes, beliefs, values, or other of your orientations to life.

2. Summarize your views of the "proper" relationships of women and men. What in your socialization has led you to have these views?

3. How does the text's summary of the life course compare with your experiences? Use the sociological perspective to explain both the similarities and the differences.

Chapter 4
Social Structure and Social Interaction

Learning Objectives

4.1 Distinguish between macrosociology and microsociology. (p. 102)

4.2 Explain the significance of social structure. (p. 103)

4.3 Be able to identify the major components of social structure: culture, social class, social status, roles, groups, and social institutions. (p. 104)

4.4 Explain the significance of social institutions and compare the functionalist and conflict perspectives on social institutions. (p. 108)

4.5 Explain what holds society together. (p. 110)

4.6 Discuss what symbolic interactionists study and explain dramaturgy and ethnomethodology. (p. 113)

4.7 Be able to apply the social construction of reality to your own life. (p. 124)

4.8 Explain why we need both macrosociology and microsociology to understand social life. (p. 126)

My curiosity had gotten the better of me. When the sociology convention was over, I climbed aboard the first city bus that came along. I didn't know where the bus was going, and I didn't know where I would spend the night.

This was my first visit to Washington, D.C., so everything was unfamiliar to me. I had no destination, no plans, not even a map. I carried no billfold, just a driver's license shoved into my jeans for emergency identification, some pocket change, and a $10 bill tucked into my sock. My goal was simple: If I saw something interesting, I would get off the bus and check it out.

As we passed row after row of apartment buildings and stores, I could see myself riding buses the entire night. Then something caught my eye. Nothing spectacular—just groups of people clustered around a large circular area where several streets intersected.

I got off the bus and made my way to what turned out to be Dupont Circle. I took a seat on a sidewalk bench. As the scene came into focus, I noticed several streetcorner men drinking and joking with one another. One of the men broke from his companions and sat down next to me. As we talked, I mostly listened.

As night fell, the men said that they wanted to get another bottle of wine. I contributed. They counted their money and asked if I wanted to go with them. As we left the circle, the three men began to cut through an alley. "Oh, no," I thought. "This isn't what I had in mind."

I had but a split second to make a decision. I held back half a step so that none of the three was behind me. As we walked, they passed around the remnants of their bottle. When my turn came, I didn't know what to do. I shuddered to think about the diseases lurking

"Suddenly one of the men jumped up, smashed the empty bottle against the sidewalk, and. . . ."

within that bottle. In the semidarkness I faked it, letting only my thumb and forefinger touch my lips and nothing enter my mouth.

When we returned to Dupont Circle, we sat on the benches, and the men passed around their new bottle of Thunderbird. I couldn't fake it in the light, so I passed, pointing at my stomach to indicate that I was having digestive problems.

Suddenly one of the men jumped up, smashed the emptied bottle against the sidewalk, and thrust the jagged neck outward in a menacing gesture. He glared straight ahead at another bench, where he had spotted someone with whom he had some sort of unfinished business. As the other men told him to cool it, I moved slightly to one side of the group—ready to flee, just in case.

Levels of Sociological Analysis

4.1 Distinguish between macrosociology and microsociology.

On this sociological adventure, I almost got in over my head. Fortunately, it turned out all right. The man's "enemy" didn't look our way, the man put the broken bottle next to the bench "in case he needed it," and my intriguing introduction to a life that up until then I had only read about continued until dawn.

Sociologists Elliot Liebow (1967/1999), Mitchell Duneier (1999), and Elijah Anderson (1978, 1990, 1990/2006) have written fascinating accounts about men like my companions from that evening. Although streetcorner men may appear to be disorganized—simply coming and going as they please and doing whatever feels good at the moment—sociologists have analyzed how, like us, these men are influenced by the norms and beliefs of our society. This will become more apparent as we examine the two levels of analysis that sociologists use.

Macrosociology and Microsociology

The first level, **macrosociology**, focuses on broad features of society. Conflict theorists and functionalists use this approach to analyze such things as social class and how groups are related to one another. If they were to analyze streetcorner men, for example, they would stress that these men are located at the bottom of the U.S. social class system. Their low status means that many opportunities are closed to them: The men have few job skills, little education, hardly anything to offer an employer. As "able-bodied" men, however, they are not eligible for welfare—even for a two-year limit—so they hustle to survive. As a consequence, they spend their lives on the streets.

In the second level, **microsociology**, the focus is on **social interaction**, what people do when they come together. Sociologists who use this approach are likely to analyze the men's rules, or "codes," for getting along; their survival strategies ("hustles"); how they divide up money, wine, or whatever other resources they have; their relationships with girlfriends, family, and friends; where they spend their time and what they do there; their language; their pecking order; and so on. Microsociology is the primary focus of symbolic interactionists.

Because the different focuses of macrosociology and microsociology yield distinctive perspectives, we need both to gain an understanding of social life. We need macrosociology to place these men within the broad context of how groups in U.S. society are related to one another. This helps us to see how social class shapes their attitudes and behavior. We also need microsociology to understand these men: The everyday situations they face also shape their orientations to life—as they do for all of us.

Let's look in more detail at how these two approaches in sociology work together to help us understand social life. As we examine them more closely, you may find yourself feeling more comfortable

macrosociology

analysis of social life that focuses on broad features of society, such as social class and the relationships of groups to one another; usually used by functionalists and conflict theorists

microsociology

analysis of social life that focuses on social interaction; typically used by symbolic interactionists

social interaction

one person's actions influencing someone else; usually refers to what people do when they are in one another's presence, but also includes communications at a distance

Sociologists use both macro and micro levels of analysis to study social life. Those who use macrosociology to analyze the homeless (or any human behavior) focus on broad aspects of society, such as the economy and social classes. Sociologists who use the microsociological approach analyze how people interact with one another. This photo illustrates social structure (the disparities between power and powerlessness are amply evident). It also illustrates the micro level (the isolation of this man).

with one approach than the other. This is what happens with sociologists. For reasons that include personal background and professional training, sociologists find themselves more comfortable with one approach and tend to use it in their research. Both approaches, however, are necessary to understand life in society.

The Macrosociological Perspective: Social Structure

4.2   **Explain the significance of social structure.**

Why did the street people in our opening vignette act as they did, staying up all night drinking wine, prepared to use a lethal weapon? Why don't *we* act like this? Social structure helps us answer such questions.

The Sociological Significance of Social Structure

To better understand human behavior, we need to understand *social structure*, the framework of society that was already laid out before you were born. **Social structure** refers to the typical patterns of a group, such as the usual relationships between men and women or students and teachers. *The sociological significance of social structure is that it guides our behavior.*

Because this term may seem vague, let's consider how you experience social structure in your own life. As I write this, I do not know your race–ethnicity. I do not know your religion. I do not know whether you are young or old, tall or short, male or female. I do not know whether you were reared on a farm, in the suburbs, or in the inner city. I do not know whether you went to a public high school or to an exclusive prep school. But I do know that you are in college. And this, alone, tells me a great deal about you.

From this one piece of information, I can assume that the social structure of your college is now shaping what you do. For example, let's suppose that today you felt euphoric over some great news. I can be fairly certain (not absolutely, mind you, but relatively confident) that when you entered the classroom, social structure overrode your mood. That is, instead of shouting at the top of your lungs and joyously throwing this book into the air, you entered the classroom in a fairly subdued manner and took your seat.

The same social structure influences your instructor, even if he or she, on the one hand, is facing a divorce or has a child dying of cancer or, on the other, has just been awarded a promotion or a million-dollar grant. Your instructor may feel like either retreating into seclusion or celebrating wildly, but most likely he or she will conduct class in the usual manner. In short, social structure tends to override our personal feelings and desires.

And how about street people? Just as social structure influences you and your instructor, so it also establishes limits for them. They, too, find themselves in a specific location in the U.S. social structure—although it is quite different from yours or your instructor's. Consequently, they are affected in different ways. Nothing about their social location leads them to take notes or to lecture. *Their behaviors, however, are as logical an outcome of where they find themselves in the social structure as are your own.* In their position in the social structure, it is just as "natural" to drink wine all night as it is for you to stay up studying all night for a crucial examination. It is just as "natural" for them to break off the neck of a wine bottle and glare at an enemy as it is for you to nod and say, "Excuse me," when you enter a crowded classroom late and have to claim a desk on which someone has already placed books. To better understand social structure, read the Down-to-Earth Sociology box on the next page.

social structure

the framework of society that surrounds us; consists of the ways that people and groups are related to one another; this framework gives direction to and sets limits on our behavior

Down-to-Earth Sociology

College Football as Social Structure

To gain a better idea of *social structure*, let's use the example of college football (Dobriner 1969). You probably know the various positions on the team: center, guards, tackles, ends, quarterback, running backs, and the like. Each is a *status*; that is, each is a social position. For each of the statuses shown in Figure 4.1, there is a *role*; that is, each of these positions has certain expectations attached to it. The center is expected to snap the ball, the quarterback to pass it, the guards to block, the tackles to tackle or block, the ends to receive passes, and so on. These role expectations guide each player's actions; that is, the players try to do what their particular role requires.

Let's suppose that football is your favorite sport, and you never miss a home game at your college. Let's also suppose that you graduate, get a great job, and move across the country. Five years later, you return to your campus for a nostalgic visit. The climax of your visit is the biggest football game of the season. When you get to the game, you might be surprised to see a different coach, but you are not surprised that each playing position is occupied by people you don't know, since all the players you knew have graduated, and their places have been filled by others.

This scenario mirrors *social structure*, the framework around which a group exists. In football, this framework consists of the coaching staff and the eleven playing positions. The game does not depend on any particular individual but, rather, on *social statuses*, the positions that the individuals occupy. When someone leaves a position, the game can go on because someone else takes over that position or status and plays the role. The game will continue even though not a single individual remains from one period of time to the next. Notre Dame's football team endures today even though Knute Rockne, the Gipper, and his teammates are long dead.

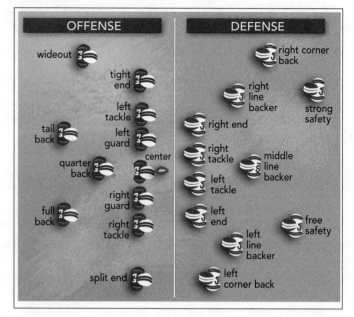

Figure 4.1 Team Positions (Statuses) in Football

SOURCE: By the author.

Even though you may not play football, you do live your life within a clearly established social structure. The statuses that you occupy and the roles you play were already in place before you were born. You take your particular positions in life, others do the same, and society goes about its business. Although the specifics change with time, the game—whether of life or of football—goes on.

For Your Consideration

→ How does social structure influence your life? To answer this question, you can begin by analyzing your social statuses.

IN SUM People learn behaviors and attitudes because of their location in the social structure (whether those are privileged, deprived, or in between), and they act accordingly. This is as true of street people as it is of us. *The differences in our behavior and attitudes are not because of biology (race–ethnicity, sex, or any other supposed genetic factors), but to our location in the social structure.* Switch places with street people and watch your behaviors and attitudes change!

4.3   **Be able to identify the major components of social structure: culture, social class, social status, roles, groups, and social institutions.**

Because social structure is so vital for us—affecting who we are and what we are like—let's look more closely at its major components: culture, social class, social status, roles, groups, and social institutions.

Culture

In Chapter 2, we considered culture's far-reaching effects on our lives. At this point, let's simply summarize its main impact. Sociologists use the term *culture* to refer to a group's language, beliefs, values, behaviors, and even gestures. Culture also includes the material objects that a group uses. Culture is the broadest framework that determines what kind of people we become. If we are reared in Chinese, Arab, or U.S. culture, we will grow up to be like most Chinese, Arabs, or Americans. On the outside, we will look and act like them, and on the inside, we will think and feel like them.

Social Class

To understand people, we must examine the social locations that they hold in life. Especially significant is *social class*, which is based on income, education, and occupational prestige. Large numbers of people who have similar amounts of income and education and who work at jobs that are roughly comparable in prestige make up a **social class**. It is hard to overemphasize this aspect of social structure, because our social class influences not only our behaviors but also our ideas and attitudes.

We have this in common, then, with the street people described in this chapter's opening vignette: We both are influenced by our location in the social class structure. Theirs may be a considerably less privileged position, but it has no less influence on their lives. Social class is so significant that we shall spend an entire chapter (Chapter 8) on this topic.

Social Status

When you hear the word *status*, you are likely to think of prestige. These two words are wedded together in people's minds. As you saw in the box on football, however, sociologists use **status** in a different way—to refer to the *position* that someone occupies. That position may carry a great deal of prestige, as in the case of a judge or an astronaut, or it may bring little prestige, as in the case of a convenience store clerk or a waitress at the local truck stop. The status may also be looked down on, as in the case of a streetcorner man, an ex-convict, or a thief.

Like other aspects of social structure, statuses are part of our basic framework of living in society. The example I gave of students and teachers who come to class and do what others expect of them despite their particular circumstances and moods illustrates how statuses affect our actions—and those of the people around us. Our statuses—whether daughter or son, teacher or student—*provide guidelines for how we are to act and feel*. Like other aspects of social structure, statuses set limits on what we can and cannot do. Because social statuses are an essential part of the social structure, all human groups have them.

STATUS SETS All of us occupy several positions at the same time. You may simultaneously be a son or daughter, a worker, a date, and a student. Sociologists use the term **status set** to refer to all the statuses or positions that you occupy. Obviously your status set changes as your particular statuses change. For example, if you graduate from college, take a full-time job, get married, buy a home, and have children, your status set changes to include the positions of worker, spouse, homeowner, and parent.

ASCRIBED AND ACHIEVED STATUSES An **ascribed status** is involuntary. You do not ask for it, nor can you choose it. At birth, you inherit ascribed statuses such as your race–ethnicity, sex, and the social class of your parents, as well as your statuses as female or male, daughter or son, niece or nephew. Others, such as teenager and senior citizen, are related to the life course we discussed in Chapter 3. They are given to you later in life.

social class

according to Weber, a large group of people who rank close to one another in property, power, and prestige; according to Marx, one of two groups: capitalists who own the means of production or workers who sell their labor

status

the position that someone occupies in a social group (also called *social status*)

status set

all the statuses or positions that an individual occupies

ascribed status

a position an individual either inherits at birth or receives involuntarily later in life

Social class and social status are significant factors in social life. Fundamental to what we become, they affect our orientations to life. Can you see how this photo illustrates this point?

achieved statuses

positions that are earned, accomplished, or involve at least some effort or activity on the individual's part

status symbols

indicators of a status; items that display prestige

master status

a status that cuts across the other statuses that an individual occupies

status inconsistency

ranking high on some dimensions of social status and low on others; also called *status discrepancy*

Achieved statuses, in contrast, are voluntary. These you earn or accomplish. As a result of your efforts, you become a student, a friend, a spouse, or a lawyer. Or, for lack of effort (or for efforts that others fail to appreciate), you become a school dropout, a former friend, an ex-spouse, or a debarred lawyer. As you can see, achieved statuses can be either positive or negative; both college president and bank robber are achieved statuses.

STATUS SYMBOLS People who are pleased with their social status often want others to recognize their position. To elicit this recognition, they use **status symbols**, signs that identify a status. For example, people wear wedding rings to announce their marital status; uniforms, guns, and badges to proclaim that they are police officers (and, not so subtly, to let you know that their status gives them authority over you); and "backward" collars to declare that they are Lutheran ministers or Roman Catholic or Episcopal priests.

Because some social statuses are negative, so are their status symbols. The scarlet letter in Nathaniel Hawthorne's book by the same title is one example. Another is the CONVICTED DUI (Driving Under the Influence) bumper sticker that some U.S. courts require convicted drunk drivers to display if they want to avoid a jail sentence.

All of us use status symbols. We use them to announce our statuses to others and to help smooth our interactions in everyday life. Can you identify your own status symbols and what they communicate? For example, how does your clothing announce your statuses of sex, age, and college student?

MASTER STATUSES A **master status** cuts across your other statuses. Some master statuses are ascribed. One example is your sex. Whatever you do, people perceive you as a male or a female. If you are working your way through college by flipping burgers, people see you not only as a burger flipper and a student but also as a *male* or *female* burger flipper and a *male* or *female* college student. Other ascribed master statuses are race–ethnicity and age.

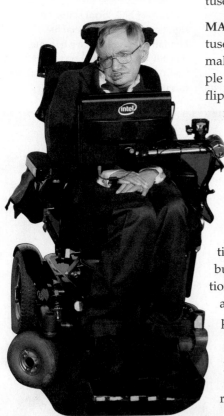

Some master statuses are achieved. If you become very, very wealthy (and it doesn't matter whether your wealth comes from a successful invention, a hit song, or from winning the lottery—it is still *achieved* as far as sociologists are concerned), your wealth is likely to become a master status. For example, people might say, "She is a very rich burger flipper"—or, more likely, "She's very rich, and she used to flip burgers!"

Similarly, people who become disfigured find, to their dismay, that their condition becomes a master status. For example, a person whose face is scarred from severe burns will be viewed through this unwelcome master status regardless of their occupation or accomplishments. In the same way, people who are confined to wheelchairs can attest to how their wheelchair overrides all their other statuses and influences others' perceptions of everything they do.

STATUS INCONSISTENCY Our statuses usually fit together fairly well, but some people have a mismatch among their statuses. This is known as **status inconsistency** (or discrepancy). A 14-year-old college student is an example. So is a 40-year-old married woman who is dating a 19-year-old college sophomore.

These examples reveal an essential aspect of social statuses: Like other components of social structure, our statuses come with built-in *norms* (that is, expectations) that guide our behavior. When statuses mesh well, as they usually do, we know what to expect of people. This helps social interaction to unfold smoothly. Status inconsistency, however, upsets our expectations. In the preceding examples, how are you supposed to act? Are you supposed to treat the 14-year-old as you would a young teenager, or as you would your college classmate? Do you react to the married woman as you would to the mother of your friend, or as you would to a classmate's date?

Master statuses are those that overshadow our other statuses. Shown here is Stephen Hawking, who is severely disabled by Lou Gehrig's disease. For some, his master status is that of a person with disabilities. Because Hawking is one of the greatest physicists who has ever lived, however, his outstanding achievements have given him another master status, that of a world-class physicist in the ranking of Einstein.

Roles

All the world's a stage
And all the men and women merely players.
They have their exits and their entrances;
And one man in his time plays many parts . . .

(William Shakespeare, As You Like It, Act II, Scene 7)

Like Shakespeare, sociologists see roles as essential to social life. When you were born, **roles**—the behaviors, obligations, and privileges attached to a status—were already set up for you. Society was waiting with outstretched arms to teach you how it expected you to act as a boy or a girl. And whether you were born poor, rich, or somewhere in between, that, too, attached certain behaviors, obligations, and privileges to your statuses.

The difference between role and status is that you *occupy* a status, but you *play* a role (Linton 1936). For example, being a son or daughter is your status, but your expectations of receiving food and shelter from your parents—as well as their expectations that you show respect to them—are part of your role. Or, again, your status is student, but your role is to attend class, take notes, do homework, and take tests.

Roles are like fences. They allow us a certain amount of freedom, but for most of us that freedom doesn't go very far. Suppose that a woman decides that she is not going to wear dresses—or a man that he will not wear suits and ties—regardless of what anyone says. In most situations, they'll stick to their decision. When a formal occasion comes along, however, such as a family wedding or a funeral, they are likely to cave in to norms that they find overwhelming. Almost all of us follow the guidelines for what is "appropriate" for our roles. Few of us are bothered by such constraints. Our socialization is so thorough that we usually *want* to do what our roles indicate is appropriate.

The sociological significance of roles is that they lay out what is expected of people. As individuals throughout society perform their roles, those many roles mesh together to form this thing called *society*. As Shakespeare put it, people's roles provide "their exits and their entrances" on the stage of life. In short, roles are remarkably effective at keeping people in line—telling them when they should "enter" and when they should "exit," as well as what to do in between.

role
the behaviors, obligations, and privileges attached to a status

Groups

A **group** consists of people who interact with one another and who feel that the values, interests, and norms they have in common are important. The groups to which we belong—just like social class, statuses, and roles—are powerful forces in our lives. By belonging to a group, we assume an obligation to affirm the group's values, interests, and norms. To remain a member in good standing, we need to show that we share those characteristics. This means that *when we belong to a group, we yield to others the right to judge our behavior*—even though we don't like it!

Although this principle holds true for all groups, some groups wield influence over only small segments of our behavior. For example, if you belong to a stamp collectors' club, the group's influence may center on your display of knowledge about stamps and perhaps your fairness in trading them. Other groups, in contrast, such as the family, control many aspects of our behavior. When parents say to their 15-year-old daughter, "As long as you are living under our roof, you had better be home by midnight," they show an expectation that their daughter, as a member of the family, will conform to their ideas about many aspects of life, including their views on curfew. They are saying that as long as the daughter wants to remain a member of the family in good standing, her behavior must conform to their expectations.

In Chapter 5, we will examine groups in detail. For now, let's look at the next component of social structure: social institutions.

group
people who interact with one another and who believe that what they have in common is significant; also called a *social group*

Social Institutions

4.4 **Explain the significance of social institutions and compare the functionalist and conflict perspectives on social institutions.**

social institution

the organized, usual, or standard ways by which society meets its basic needs

At first glance, the term *social institution* may seem cold and abstract—with little relevance to your life. In fact, however, **social institutions**—the standard or usual ways that a society meets its basic needs—vitally affect your life. They not only shape your behavior, but they even color your thoughts. How can this be?

The first step in understanding how this can be is to look at Figure 4.2. Look at what social institutions are: the family, religion, education, the economy, medicine, politics, law,

Figure 4.2 Social Institutions in Industrial and Postindustrial Societies

Social Institution	Basic Needs	Some Groups or Organizations	Some Statuses	Some Values	Some Norms
Family	Regulate reproduction, socialize and protect children	Relatives, kinship groups	Daughter, son, father, mother, brother, sister, aunt, uncle, grandparent	Sexual fidelity, providing for your family, keeping a clean house, respect for parents	Have only as many children as you can afford, be faithful to your spouse
Religion	Concerns about life after death, the meaning of suffering and loss; desire to connect with the Creator	Congregation, synagogue, mosque, denomination, charity, clergy associations	Priest, minister, rabbi, imam, worshipper, teacher, disciple, missionary, prophet, convert	Honoring God and the holy texts such as the Torah, the Bible, and the Qur'an	Attend worship services, contribute money, follow the teachings
Education	Transmit knowledge and skills across generations	School, college, student senate, sports team, PTA, teachers' union	Teacher, student, dean, principal, football player, cheerleader	Academic honesty, good grades, being "cool"	Do homework, prepare lectures, don't snitch on classmates
Economy	Produce and distribute goods and services	Credit unions, banks, credit card companies, buying clubs	Worker, boss, buyer, seller, creditor, debtor, advertiser	Making money, paying bills on time, producing efficiently	Maximize profits, "the customer is always right," work hard
Medicine	Heal the sick and injured, care for the dying	AMA, hospitals, pharmacies, HMOs, insurance companies	Doctor, nurse, patient, pharmacist, medical insurer	Hippocratic oath, staying in good health, following doctor's orders	Don't exploit patients, give best medical care available
Politics	Allocate power, determine authority, prevent chaos	Political party, congress, parliament, monarchy	President, senator, lobbyist, voter, candidate, spin doctor	Majority rule, the right to vote, loyalty to the constitution	Be informed about candidates, one vote per person
Law	Maintain social order, enforce norms	Police, courts, prisons	Judge, police officer, lawyer, defendant, prison guard	Trial by one's peers, innocence until proven guilty	Give true testimony, follow the rules of evidence
Science	Master the environment	Local, state, regional, national, and international associations	Scientist, researcher, technician, administrator, journal editor	Unbiased research, open dissemination of research findings, originality	Follow scientific method, be objective, disclose findings, don't plagiarize
Military	Provide protection from enemies, enforce national interests	Army, navy, air force, marines, coast guard, national guard	Soldier, recruit, enlisted person, officer, veteran, prisoner, spy	Willingness to die for one's country, obedience unto death	Follow orders, be ready to go to war, sacrifice for your buddies
Mass Media	Disseminate information, report events, mold public opinion	TV networks, radio stations, publishers, association of bloggers	Journalist, newscaster, author, editor, blogger	Timeliness, accuracy, freedom of the press	Be accurate, fair, timely, and profitable

SOURCE: By the author.

science, the military, and the mass media. *By weaving the fabric of society, social institutions set the context for your behavior and orientations to life. If your social institutions were different, your orientations to life would be different.*

Social institutions are so significant that an entire part of this book, Part IV, focuses on them.

Comparing Functionalist and Conflict Perspectives

The functionalist and conflict perspectives give us quite different views of social institutions. Let's compare their views.

THE FUNCTIONALIST PERSPECTIVE   Because the first priority of human groups is to survive, all societies establish customary ways to meet their basic needs. As a result, no society is without social institutions. In tribal societies, some social institutions are less visible because the group meets its basic needs in more informal ways. A society may be too small to have people specialize in education, for example, but it will have established ways of teaching skills and ideas to the young. It may be too small to have a military, but it will have some mechanism of self-defense.

What are society's basic needs? Functionalists identify five *functional requisites* (basic needs) that each society must meet if it is to survive (Aberle 1950; Mack and Bradford 1979).

1. *Replacing members.* Obviously, if a society does not replace its members, it cannot continue to exist. With reproduction fundamental to a society's existence and the need to protect infants and children universal, all groups have developed some version of the family. The family gives the newcomer to society a sense of belonging by providing a *lineage*, an account of how he or she is related to others. The family also functions to control people's sex drive and to maintain orderly reproduction.

2. *Socializing new members.* Each baby must be taught what it means to be a member of the group into which it is born. To accomplish this, each human group develops devices to ensure that its newcomers learn the group's basic expectations. As the primary "bearer of culture," the family is essential to this process, but other social institutions, such as religion and education, also help meet this basic need.

3. *Producing and distributing goods and services.* Every society must produce and distribute basic resources, from food and clothing to shelter and education. Consequently, every society establishes an *economic* institution, a means of producing goods and services along with routine ways of distributing them.

4. *Preserving order.* Societies face two threats of disorder: one internal, the potential for chaos, and the other external, the possibility of attack. To protect themselves from internal threat, they develop ways to police themselves, ranging from informal means, such as gossip, to formal means, such as armed groups. To defend themselves against external conquest, they develop a means of defense, some form of the military.

5. *Providing a sense of purpose.* Every society must get people to yield self-interest in favor of the needs of the group. To convince people to sacrifice personal gains, societies instill a sense of purpose. Human groups develop many ways to implant such beliefs, but a primary one is religion, which attempts to answer questions about ultimate meaning. Actually, all of a society's institutions are involved in meeting this functional requisite; the family provides one set of answers about the sense of purpose, the school another, and so on.

Functionalist theorists have identified *functional requisites* for the survival of society. One, providing a sense of purpose, is often met through religious groups. To most people, snake handling, as in this church service in the Appalachian mountains of West Virginia, is nonsensical. From a functionalist perspective, however, it makes a great deal of sense. Can you identify its sociological meanings?

THE CONFLICT PERSPECTIVE Although conflict theorists agree that social institutions were designed originally to meet basic survival needs, they do not view social institutions as working harmoniously for the common good. On the contrary, conflict theorists stress that powerful groups control our social institutions, manipulating them in order to maintain their own privileged position of wealth and power (Useem 1984; Domhoff 1999a, 1999b, 2006, 2007).

Conflict theorists point out that a fairly small group of people has garnered the lion's share of our nation's wealth. Members of this elite group sit on the boards of our major corporations and our most prestigious universities. They make strategic campaign contributions to influence (or control) our lawmakers, and it is they who are behind the nation's major decisions: to go to war or to refrain from war; to increase or to decrease taxes; to raise or to lower interest rates; and to pass laws that favor or impede moving capital, technology, and jobs out of the country.

Feminist sociologists (both women and men) have used conflict theory to gain a better understanding of how social institutions affect gender relations. Their basic insight is that gender is also an element of social structure, not simply a characteristic of individuals. In other words, throughout the world, social institutions divide males and females into separate groups, each with unequal access to society's resources.

IN SUM Functionalists view social institutions as working together to meet universal human needs, but conflict theorists regard social institutions as having a single primary purpose—to preserve the social order. For them, this means safeguarding the wealthy and powerful in their positions of privilege.

Changes in Social Structure

4.5 Explain what holds society together.

In the preceding chapter, you saw how technology led to deep transformations in societies. Our current society is also being transformed by new technology, changing values, and contact with cultures around the world. These changes have vital effects on our lives, sometimes dramatically so. Globalization is one of the best examples. As our economy adjusts to this fundamental change, we find our lives marked by uncertainty as jobs disappear and new requirements are placed on the careers we are striving for. Sometimes it seems that we have to move at a running pace just to keep up with the changes.

What Holds Society Together?

Not only are we in the midst of social change so extensive that it threatens to rip our society apart, but our society also has antagonistic groups that would love to get at one another's throats. In the midst of all this, how does society manage to hold together? Sociologists have proposed two answers. Let's examine them, starting with a bit of history.

MECHANICAL AND ORGANIC SOLIDARITY Sociologist Emile Durkheim (1893/1933) was interested in how societies manage to create **social integration**—their members united by shared values and other social bonds. He found the answer in what he called **mechanical solidarity**. By this term, Durkheim meant that people who perform similar tasks develop a shared way of viewing life. Think of a farming community in which everyone is involved in growing crops—planting, cultivating, and harvesting. Because they have so much in common, they share similar views about life. Societies with mechanical solidarity tolerate little diversity in behavior, thinking, or attitudes; their unity depends on sharing similar views.

social integration

the degree to which members of a group or a society are united by shared values and other social bonds; also known as *social cohesion*

mechanical solidarity

Durkheim's term for the unity (a shared consciousness) that people feel as a result of performing the same or similar tasks

Durkheim used the term *mechanical solidarity* to refer to the shared consciousness that develops among people who perform similar tasks. Can you see from this photo why this term applies so well to small farming groups, why they share such similar views about life? This photo was taken in Virginia.

As societies get larger, they develop different kinds of work, a specialized **division of labor**. Some people mine gold, others turn it into jewelry, and still others sell it. This disperses people into different interest groups where they develop different ideas about life. No longer do they depend on one another to have similar ideas and behaviors. Rather, they depend on one another to do specific work, with each person contributing to the group.

Durkheim called this new form of solidarity **organic solidarity**. To see why he used this term, think about your body. The organs of your body need one another. Your lungs depend on your heart to pump your blood, and your heart depends on your lungs to oxygenate your blood. To move from the physical to the social, think about how you need your teacher to guide you through this course and how your teacher needs students in order to have a job. You and your teacher are *like two organs in the same body*. (The "body" in this case is the college.) Like the heart and lungs, although you perform different tasks, you need one another.

The change to organic solidarity changed the basis for social integration. In centuries past, you would have had views similar to your neighbors because you lived in the same village, farmed together, and had relatives in common. But no longer does social integration require this. Like organs in a body, our separate activities contribute to the welfare of the group. The change from mechanical to organic solidarity allows our society to tolerate a wide diversity of orientations to life and still manage to work as a whole.

GEMEINSCHAFT **AND** *GESELLSCHAFT* Ferdinand Tönnies (1887/1988) also analyzed this fundamental shift in relationships. He used the term *Gemeinschaft* (Guh-MINE-shoft), or "intimate community," to describe village life, the type of society in which everyone knows everyone else. He noted that society was changing. The personal ties, kinship connections, and lifelong friendships that Tönnies had come to know in childhood were being replaced by short-term relationships, individual accomplishments, and self-interest. Tönnies called this new type of society *Gesellschaft* (Guh-ZELL-shoft), or "impersonal association." He did not mean that we no longer have intimate ties to family and friends but, rather, that our lives no longer center on them. Few of us take jobs in a family business, for example, and contracts replace handshakes. Much of our time is spent with strangers and short-term acquaintances.

HOW RELEVANT ARE THESE CONCEPTS TODAY? I know that *Gemeinschaft, Gesellschaft*, and *mechanical* and *organic solidarity* are strange terms and that Durkheim's and Tönnies' observations must seem like a dead issue. The concern these sociologists

division of labor
the splitting of a group's or a society's tasks into specialties

organic solidarity
Durkheim's term for the interdependence that results from the division of labor; as part of the same unit, we all depend on others to fulfill their jobs

Gemeinschaft
a type of society in which life is intimate; a community in which everyone knows everyone else and people share a sense of togetherness

Gesellschaft
a type of society that is dominated by impersonal relationships, individual accomplishments, and self-interest

The warm, more intimate relationships of *Gemeinschaft* society are apparent in the photo taken at this Amish market in Pennsylvania. The more impersonal relationships of *Gesellschaft* society are evident in this Internet cafe in Seattle, where customers are ignoring one another.

expressed, however—that their world was changing from a community in which people were united by close ties and shared ideas and feelings to an anonymous association built around impersonal, short-term contacts—is still very real. In large part, this same concern explains the rise of Islamic fundamentalism (Volti 1995). Islamic leaders fear that Western values will uproot their traditional culture, that cold rationality will replace the warm, informal, personal relationships among families and clans. They fear, rightly so, that this will also change their views on life and morality. Although the terms may sound strange, even obscure, you can see that the ideas remain a vital part of today's world.

IN SUM   Whether the terms are *Gemeinschaft* and *Gesellschaft* or *mechanical solidarity* and *organic solidarity*, they indicate that as societies change, so do people's orientations to life. *The sociological point is that social structure sets the context for what we do, feel, and think, and ultimately, then, for the kind of people we become.* The following Cultural Diversity box describes one of the few remaining *Gemeinschaft* societies in the United States. As you read it, think of how fundamentally different your life would be if you had been reared in an Amish family.

Cultural Diversity in the United States

The Amish: *Gemeinschaft* Community in a *Gesellschaft* Society

One of the best examples of a *Gemeinschaft* community in the United States is the Old Order Amish, followers of a group that broke away from the Swiss–German Mennonite church in the 1600s and settled in Pennsylvania around 1727. Most of today's 250,000 Old Order Amish live in just three states—Pennsylvania, Ohio, and Indiana.

Because Amish farmers use horses instead of tractors, most of their farms are 100 acres or less. To the ten million tourists who pass through Lancaster County each year, the rolling green pastures, white farmhouses, simple barns, horse-drawn buggies, and clotheslines hung with somber-colored garments convey a sense of innocence reminiscent of another era. Although just 65 miles from Philadelphia, "Amish country" is a world away.

The differences are striking: the horses and buggies from so long ago, the language (a dialect of German known as Pennsylvania Dutch), and the plain clothing—often black, no belt—whose style has remained unchanged for almost 300 years. Beyond these externals is a value system that binds the Amish together, with religion and discipline the glue that maintains their way of life.

Amish life is based on separation from the world—an idea taken from Christ's Sermon on

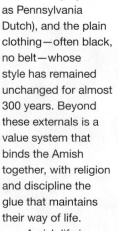

Photo taken in Nickel Mines, Pennsylvania

the Mount—and obedience to the church's teachings and leaders. This rejection of worldly concerns, writes sociologist Donald Kraybill (2002), "provides the foundation of such Amish values as humility, faithfulness, thrift, tradition, communal goals, joy of work, a slow-paced life, and trust in divine providence." The Amish believe that violence is bad, even self-defense, and they register as conscientious objectors during times of war. They pay no Social Security, and they receive no government benefits.

To maintain their separation from the world, Amish children attend schools that are run by the Amish, and they attend only until the age of 13. (In 1972, the Supreme Court ruled that Amish parents have the right to take their children out of school after the eighth grade.) To go to school beyond the eighth grade would expose the children to values that would drive a wedge between the children and their community.

The *Gemeinschaft* of village life that has been largely lost to industrialization remains a vibrant part of Amish life. The Amish make their decisions in weekly meetings, where, by consensus, they follow a set of rules, or *Ordnung*, to guide their behavior. The welfare of the community is a central value. In times of birth, sickness, and death, neighbors pitch in with the chores. The family is also vital for Amish life. Nearly all Amish marry, and divorce is forbidden. The major events of Amish life take place in the home, including weddings, births, funerals, and church services. In these ways, they maintain the bonds of an intimate community.

Because they cannot resist all change, the Amish try to adapt in ways that will least disrupt their core values. Urban sprawl poses a special threat, since it has driven up the price of farmland. Unable to afford farms, about half of Amish men now work at jobs other than farming. The men go to great lengths to avoid leaving the home. Most work in farm-related businesses or operate woodcraft shops, but some have taken jobs in factories. With intimate, or *Gemeinschaft*, society essential to the Amish way of life,

concerns have grown about how the men who work for non-Amish businesses are being exposed to the outside world. Some are using modern technology, such as cell phones and computers, at work. During the economic crisis, some who were laid off from their jobs even accepted unemployment checks—violating the fundamental principle of taking no help from the government.

Despite the threats posed by a materialistic and secular culture, the Amish are managing to retain their way of life. Perhaps the most poignant illustration of how greatly the Amish differ from the dominant culture is this: When in 2006 a non-Amish man shot several Amish girls and himself at a one-room school, the Amish community raised funds not only for the families of the dead children but also for the family of the killer.

SOURCES: Aeppel 1996; Kephart and Zellner 2001; Kraybill 2002; Johnson-Weiner 2007; Scolforo 2008; Buckley 2011; Donnermeyer et al. 2013.

For Your Consideration

→ If you had been reared in an Amish family, how would your ideas, attitudes, and behaviors be different?

→ What do you like and dislike about Amish life? Why?

The Microsociological Perspective: Social Interaction in Everyday Life

4.6   Discuss what symbolic interactionists study and explain dramaturgy and ethnomethodology.

As you have seen, macrosociologists focus on the broad features of society. Microsociologists, in contrast, examine narrower slices of social life. Their primary focus is *face-to-face interaction*—what people do when they are in one another's presence. Before you study the main features of social interaction, look at the photo essay on the next two pages. See if you can identify both social structure and social interaction in each of the photos.

Symbolic Interaction

Symbolic interactionists are especially interested in how people view things and how this, in turn, affects their behavior and orientations to life. Of the many areas of social interaction that symbolic interactionists study, let's look at just a few—stereotypes, personal space, eye contact, smiling, and body language.

STEREOTYPES IN EVERYDAY LIFE   You are familiar with how important first impressions are, how they set the tone for interaction. You also know that when you first meet someone, you notice certain features of the individual, especially the person's sex, race–ethnicity, age, height, body shape, and clothing. But did you know that this sets off a circular, self-feeding reaction? Your assumptions about these characteristics—many of which you don't even know you have—shape not only your first impressions but also how you act toward that person. This, in turn, influences how that person acts toward you, which then affects how you react, and so on. Most of this self-feeding cycle occurs without your being aware of it.

THROUGH THE AUTHOR'S LENS

Vienna: Social Structure and Social Interaction

We live our lives within social structure. Just as a road is to a car, providing limits to where it can go, so social structure limits our behavior. Social structure—our culture, social class, statuses, roles, group memberships, and social institutions—points us in particular directions in life. Most of this direction-giving is beyond our awareness. But it is highly effective, giving shape to our social interactions, as well as to what we expect from life.

These photos that I took in Vienna, Austria, make visible some of social structure's limiting, shaping, and direction-giving. Most of the social structure that affects our lives is not physical, as with streets and buildings, but social, as with norms, belief systems, obligations, and the goals held out for us because of our ascribed statuses. In these photos, you should be able to see how social interaction takes form within social structure.

Vienna provides a mixture of the old and the new. Stephan's Dom (Cathedral) dates back to 1230, the carousel to now.

And what would Vienna be without its wieners? The word *wiener* actually comes from the name Vienna, which is Wien in German. Wiener means "from Vienna."

The main square in Vienna, Stephan Platz, provides a place to have a cup of coffee, read the newspaper, enjoy the architecture, or just watch the hustle and bustle of the city.

Part of the pull of the city is its offering of rich culture. I took this photo at one of the many operas held in Vienna each night.

In the appealing street cafes of Vienna, social structure and social interaction are especially evident. Can you see both in this photo?

And what would Vienna be without its world-famous beers? The city's entrepreneurs make sure that the beer is within easy reach.

The city offers something for everyone, including unusual places for people to rest and to talk and to flirt with one another.

To be able to hang out with friends, not doing much, but doing it in the midst of stimulating sounds and sights—this is the vibrant city.

© James M. Henslin

stereotype
assumptions of what people are like, whether true or false

In the Down-to-Earth Sociology box on beauty, let's look at how people's attractiveness sets off this reciprocal reaction.

Down-to-Earth Sociology

Beauty May Be Only Skin Deep, But Its Effects Go On Forever: Stereotypes in Everyday Life

Mark Snyder, a psychologist, wondered whether **stereotypes**— our assumptions of what people are like—might be self-fulfilling. He came up with an ingenious way to test this idea. Snyder (1993) gave college men a Polaroid snapshot of a woman (supposedly taken just moments before) and told each man that he would be introduced to her after they talked on the telephone. Actually, the photographs—showing either a pretty or a homely woman—had been prepared before the experiment began. The photo was *not* of the woman the men would talk to.

Stereotypes came into play immediately. As Snyder gave each man the photograph, he asked him what he thought the woman would be like. The men who saw the photograph of the attractive woman said that they expected to meet a poised, humorous, outgoing woman. The men who had been given a photo of the unattractive woman described her as awkward, serious, and unsociable.

The men's stereotypes influenced the way they spoke to the women on the telephone, who did *not* know about the photographs. The men who had seen the photograph of a pretty woman were warm, friendly, and humorous. This, in turn, affected the women they spoke to: They responded in a warm, friendly, outgoing manner. And the men who had seen the photograph of a homely woman? On the phone, they were cold, reserved, and humorless, and the women they spoke to became cool, reserved, and humorless. Keep in mind that the women did not know that their looks had been evaluated. Keep in mind, too, that the photos that the men saw were not of these women. In short, stereotypes tend to produce behaviors that match the stereotype. Figure 4.3 illustrates this principle.

Beauty might be only skin deep, but it has real consequences. Attractive people are viewed as smarter, kinder, and more honest (Sapolsky 2014a). Judges and juries are more lenient with attractive people (Frevert and Walker 2014). Teacher evaluations follow the same pattern. Students give higher ratings to their better-looking teachers (Liu et al. 2013).

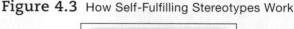

Figure 4.3 How Self-Fulfilling Stereotypes Work

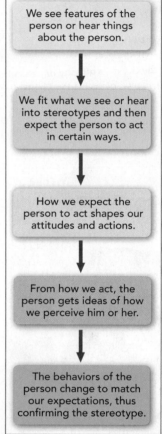

We see features of the person or hear things about the person.

We fit what we see or hear into stereotypes and then expect the person to act in certain ways.

How we expect the person to act shapes our attitudes and actions.

From how we act, the person gets ideas of how we perceive him or her.

The behaviors of the person change to match our expectations, thus confirming the stereotype.

SOURCE: By the author.

Then there is income. On average, more attractive people earn 10 to 15 percent more than plain folks. Over a lifetime, this comes to about $200,000 (Judge et al. 2009; Hamermesh 2011). Apparently, bosses are more willing to hire people whom they perceive as good-looking, others are more willing to interact with them, and the good-looking bring in more clients.

For Your Consideration

Stereotypes have a deep influence on how we react to one another. Instead of beauty, consider body shape, gender, and race–ethnicity.

→ How do you think these characteristics affect those who do the stereotyping?

→ How do you think these characteristics affect those who are stereotyped?

Based on the experiments summarized here, how do you think men would modify their interactions if they were to meet these two women? And if women were to meet these two women, would they modify their interactions in the same way?

PERSONAL SPACE   We all surround ourselves with a "personal bubble," and we go to great lengths to protect it. We open the bubble to intimates—to our friends, children, and parents—but we're careful to keep most people out of this space. In a crowded hallway between classes, we might walk with our books clasped in front of us (a strategy often chosen by females). When we stand in line, we make certain there is enough space so that we don't touch the person in front of us and aren't touched by the person behind us.

At times, we extend our personal space. In the library, for example, you might place your coat on the chair next to you—claiming that space for yourself even though you aren't using it. If you want to really extend your space, you might even spread books in front of the other chairs, keeping the whole table to yourself by giving the impression that others have just stepped away.

The amount of space that people prefer varies from one culture to another. South Americans, for example, like to be closer when they talk to others than do people reared in the United States. Anthropologist Edward Hall (1959; Hall and Hall 2014) recounts a conversation with a man from South America who had attended one of his lectures.

> *He came to the front of the class at the end of the lecture. . . . We started out facing each other, and as he talked I became dimly aware that he was standing a little too close and that I was beginning to back up. Fortunately I was able to suppress my first impulse and remain stationary because there was nothing to communicate aggression in his behavior except the conversational distance. . . .*
>
> *By experimenting I was able to observe that as I moved away slightly, there was an associated shift in the pattern of interaction. He had more trouble expressing himself. If I shifted to where I felt comfortable (about twenty-one inches), he looked somewhat puzzled and hurt, almost as though he were saying, "Why is he acting that way? Here I am doing everything I can to talk to him in a friendly manner and he suddenly withdraws. Have I done anything wrong? Said something I shouldn't?" Having ascertained that distance had a direct effect on his conversation, I stood my ground, letting him set the distance.*

As you can see, despite Hall's extensive knowledge of other cultures, he still felt uncomfortable in this conversation. He first interpreted the invasion of his personal space as possible aggression, since people get close (and jut out their chins and chests) when they are hostile. But when he realized that this was not the case, Hall resisted his impulse to move.

After Hall analyzed situations like this, he observed that North Americans use four different "distance zones."

1. *Intimate distance.* This is the zone that the South American had unwittingly invaded. It extends to about 18 inches from our bodies. We reserve this space for comforting, protecting, hugging, intimate touching, and lovemaking.

2. *Personal distance.* This zone extends from 18 inches to 4 feet. We reserve it for friends and acquaintances and ordinary conversations. This is the zone in which Hall would have preferred speaking with the South American.

3. *Social distance.* This zone, extending from about 4 to 12 feet, marks impersonal or formal relationships. We use this zone for such things as job interviews.

How people use space as they interact is studied by sociologists who have a microsociological focus. What do you see in common in these two photos?

4. *Public distance.* This zone, extending beyond 12 feet, marks even more formal relationships. It is used to separate dignitaries and public speakers from the general public.

EYE CONTACT   One way that we protect our personal bubble is by controlling eye contact. Letting someone gaze into our eyes—unless the person is an eye doctor—can be taken as a sign that we are attracted to that person, even as an invitation to intimacy. With the goal of becoming "the friendliest store in town," a chain of supermarkets in Illinois ordered its checkout clerks to make direct eye contact with each customer. Female clerks complained that male customers were taking their eye contact the wrong way, as an invitation to intimacy. Management said they were exaggerating. The clerks' reply was, "We know the kind of looks we're getting back from men," and they refused to continue making direct eye contact with them.

SMILING   In the United States, we take it for granted that clerks will smile as they wait on us. But it isn't this way in all cultures. Apparently, Germans aren't used to smiling clerks, and when Wal-Mart expanded into Germany, it brought its American ways with it. The company ordered its German clerks to smile at their customers. They did—and the customers complained. The German customers interpreted the smiles as flirting (Samor et al. 2006).

BODY LANGUAGE   While we are still little children, we learn to interpret **body language**, the ways people use their bodies to give messages to others. This skill in interpreting facial expressions, posture, and gestures is essential for getting through everyday life. Without it—as is the case for people with Asperger's syndrome—we wouldn't know how to react to others. It would even be difficult to know whether someone were serious or joking.

APPLIED BODY LANGUAGE   In an interesting twist for an area of sociology that had been entirely theoretical, interpreting body language has become a tool for both business and government. In some hotels, clerks are taught how to "read" the body language of arriving guests (head sunk into the shoulders, a springy step) to know how to greet them (Petersen 2012). The U.S. army is teaching soldiers in military zones how to interpret body language to alert them to danger when they are interacting with civilians (Yager et al. 2009). "Reading" body language has also become a tool in the fight against terrorism. Homeland Security spends $200 million a year on what it calls a behavior-detection program. Three thousand Behavior Detection Officers (their official title) are trained to look for ninety-four signs of deception by people who are going to board planes. A quick downturn of the mouth or rapid blinking might indicate nervousness or lying (McCartney 2014).

Let's turn to dramaturgy, a special area of symbolic interactionism.

body language

the ways in which people use their bodies to give messages to others

With the training of Homeland Security agents, body language has changed from being purely descriptive and theoretical to applied.

Dramaturgy: The Presentation of Self in Everyday Life

Have you noticed how some clothing simply doesn't "feel" right for certain occasions? Have you ever changed your mind about something you were wearing and decided to change your clothing? Or maybe you just switched shirts or added a necklace?

What you were doing was fine-tuning the impressions you wanted to make. Ordinarily, we are not this aware that we're working on impressions, but sometimes we are, especially those "first impressions"—the first day in college, a job interview, visiting the parents of our loved one for the first time, and so on. Usually we are so used to the roles we play in everyday life that we tend to think we are "just doing" things, not that we are actors on a stage who manage impressions. Yet every time we dress for school, or for any other activity, we are engaging in impression management.

dramaturgy

an approach, pioneered by Erving Goffman, in which social life is analyzed in terms of drama or the stage; also called *dramaturgical analysis*

Sociologist Erving Goffman (1922–1982) added a new twist to microsociology when he recast the theatrical term **dramaturgy** into a sociological term. Goffman (1959/1999) used the term to mean that social life is like a drama or a stage play: Birth ushers us onto the stage of everyday life, and our socialization consists of learning to perform on that stage. The self that we studied in the previous chapter lies at the center of our performances. We have ideas about how we want others to think of us, and we use our roles in everyday life to communicate these ideas. Goffman called our efforts to manage the impressions that others receive of us **impression management**.

STAGES   We do our impression management on **front stages**, places where we perform the roles assigned to us. Everyday life is filled with front stages. Where your teacher lectures is a front stage. And if you wait until your parents are in a good mood to tell them some bad news, you are using a front stage. We also have **back stages**, places where we retreat from performances and let our hair down. When you close the bathroom or bedroom door for privacy, for example, you are entering a back stage.

In *dramaturgy*, a specialty within sociology, social life is viewed as similar to the theater. In our everyday lives, we all are actors. Like those in the cast of *Orange Is the New Black*, we, too, perform roles, use props, and deliver lines to fellow actors—who, in turn, do the same.

The same setting can serve as both a back and a front stage. For example, when you get into your car and look over your hair in the mirror or check your makeup, you are using the car as a back stage. But when you wave at friends or if you give that familiar gesture to someone who has just cut in front of you in traffic, you are using your car as a front stage.

ROLE PERFORMANCE, CONFLICT, AND STRAIN   As discussed earlier, everyday life brings many statuses. We may be a student, a shopper, a worker, and a date, as well as a daughter or a son. Although the roles attached to these statuses lay down the basic outline for our performances, they also allow a great deal of flexibility. The particular interpretation that you give a role, your "style," is known as **role performance**. Consider how you play your role as a son or daughter. Perhaps you play the role of ideal daughter or son—being respectful, coming home at the hours your parents set, and happily running errands. Or this description may not even come close to your particular role performance.

Ordinarily, our statuses are separated sufficiently that we find little conflict between our role performances. Occasionally, however, what is expected of us in one status (our role) is incompatible with what is expected of us in another status. This problem, known as **role conflict**, is illustrated in Figure 4.4 on the next page, in which family, friendship, student, and work roles come crashing together. Usually, however, we manage to avoid role conflict by segregating our statuses, although doing so can require an intense juggling act.

Sometimes the *same* status contains incompatible roles, a conflict known as **role strain**. Suppose that you are exceptionally well prepared for a particular class assignment. Although the instructor asks an unusually difficult question, you find yourself knowing the answer when no one else does. If you want to raise your hand, yet don't want to make your fellow students look bad, you will experience role strain. As illustrated in Figure 4.4, the difference between role conflict and role strain is that role conflict is conflict *between* roles, while role strain is conflict *within* a role.

SIGN-VEHICLES   To communicate information about the self, we use three types of **sign-vehicles**: the social setting, our appearance, and our manner. The *social setting* is the place where the action unfolds. This is where the curtain goes up on your performance, where you find yourself on stage playing parts and delivering lines. A social setting might be an office, dorm, living room, classroom, church, or bar. It

impression management
people's efforts to control the impressions that others receive of them

front stages
places where people give performances

back stages
places where people rest from their performances, discuss their presentations, and plan future performances

role performance
the ways in which someone performs a role; showing a particular "style" or "personality"

role conflict
conflict that someone feels *between* roles because the expectations attached to one role are at odds with those attached to another role

role strain
conflicts that someone feels *within* a role

sign-vehicle
the term used by Goffman to refer to how people use social setting, appearance, and manner to communicate information about the self

Figure 4.4 Role Strain and Role Conflict

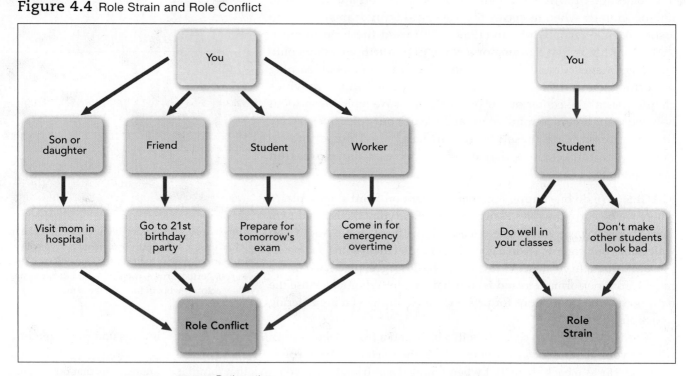

SOURCE: By the author.

is wherever you interact with others. The social setting includes *scenery*, the furnishings you use to communicate messages, such as desks, blackboards, scoreboards, couches, and so on.

The second sign-vehicle is *appearance*, or how you look when you play your roles. On the most obvious level is your choice of hairstyle to communicate messages about yourself. (You might be proclaiming "I'm wild and sexy" or "I'm serious and professional" and, quite certainly, "I'm masculine" or "I'm feminine"). Your appearance also includes props, which are like scenery except that they decorate your body rather than the setting. Your most obvious prop is your costume, ordinarily called clothing. You switch costumes as you play your roles, wearing different costumes for attending class, swimming, jogging, working out at the gym, and dating.

Your appearance lets others know what to expect from you and how they should react. Think of the messages that props communicate. Some people use clothing to say they are college students, others to say they are older adults. Some use clothing to let you know they are clergy, others to give the message that they are prostitutes. In the same way, people choose models of cars, brands of liquor, and the hottest cell phone to convey messages about the self.

The body itself is a sign-vehicle. Its shape proclaims messages about the self. The meanings that are attached to various shapes change over time, but, as explored in the Mass Media box on the next page, thinness currently screams desirability.

The third sign-vehicle is *manner*, the attitudes you show as you play your roles. You use manner to communicate information about your feelings and moods. When you show that you are angry or indifferent, serious or in good humor, you are indicating what others can expect of you as you play your roles.

TEAMWORK Being a good role player brings positive responses from others, something we all covet. To accomplish this, we use **teamwork**—two or more people working together to help a performance come off as planned. If you laugh at your boss's jokes, even though you don't find them funny, you are doing teamwork to help your boss give a good performance.

teamwork

the collaboration of two or more people to manage impressions jointly

Mass Media in Social Life

"Nothing Tastes as Good as Thin Feels": Body Images and the Mass Media

When you stand before a mirror, do you like what you see? Do you watch your weight or work out? Where did you get your ideas about what you should look like?

"Your body isn't good enough!" You are bombarded with this message. The way to improve your body is to buy the advertised products: hair extensions, "uplifting" bras, diet programs, exercise equipment, and according to your preference, butt reducers or enhancers. Muscular hulks on TV show off machines that magically produce "six-pack abs" and incredible biceps—in just a few minutes a day. Female celebrities go through tough workouts without even breaking into a sweat. Members of the opposite sex will flock to you if you purchase that wonder-working workout machine.

We try to shrug off such messages, knowing that they are designed to sell products, but the messages penetrate our thinking and feeling. They help to shape the ideal images we hold of how we "ought" to look. Those models so attractively clothed and coiffed as they walk down the runway, could they be any thinner? For women, the message is clear: You can't be thin enough. The men's message is also clear: You've got to be more muscular. Everybody loves a hulk.

These messages are powerful. Impossibly shaped models show off the latest lingerie for Victoria's Secret and the latest fashions in *Vogue* and *Seventeen*. Half of U.S. adolescent girls feel fat and count calories (Grabe et al. 2008). Sixty percent of girls think that the secret to popularity is being thin (Zaslow 2009). To look more feminine, each year about 8,000 teen girls have their breasts enlarged, while to look more masculine, about 14,000 teen boys have theirs reduced (Crerand and Magee 2013).

"Thinspiration" videos on YouTube feature emaciated girls proudly displaying their skeletal frames. "Pro-ana" (pro-anorexic) sites promote eating disorders as a lifestyle choice (Zaslow 2009). I took the title of this box, "Nothing Tastes as Good as Thin Feels," from one of these sites.

Attractiveness does pay off in cold cash. "Good-looking" men and women earn the most, "average-looking" men and women earn average amounts, and the "plain" and the "ugly" earn the least (Hamermesh 2011). Then there is that fascinating cash "bonus" available to "attractive" women: With the right facial features and shape, even the

bubble-heads can attract and marry higher-earning men (Kanazawa and Kovar 2004).

More popularity *and* more money? Maybe you can't be thin enough after all. Perhaps those exercise machines are a good investment. If only we could catch up with the Japanese, who have developed a soap that "sucks the fat right out of your pores" (Marshall 1995). Although we don't have such a soap, we do have liposuction. It's even easier. Just lie down, and a surgeon inserts a vacuum wand in your body and sucks the fat out of your hips, butt, stomach, or wherever you feel too plumpy. A bit more expensive than the soap, but you get immediate results.

For Your Consideration

→ How do cultural expectations of "ideal" bodies underlie the images you have of your body? What advertisements, television programs, movies, or celebrities have influenced your body images?

→ Most advertising that focuses on weight is directed at women. Women are more likely than men to be dissatisfied with their bodies and to have eating disorders (Honeycutt 1995; Austin et al. 2009). Do you think that targeting women in advertising creates these attitudes and behaviors? Or do you think that these attitudes and behaviors would exist even if there were no such ads? Why?

→ There is a backlash against featuring emaciated models who look as though they'll collapse on the runway. One reaction is to feature "plus-size" models in ads. What do you think about this?

All of us contrast the reality we see when we look in the mirror with our culture's ideal body types. The thinness craze, discussed in this box, encourages some people to extremes, as with model Gisele Bundchen. It also makes it difficult for larger people to have positive self-images. Overcoming this difficulty, Rebel Wilson is in the forefront of promoting an alternative image.

face-saving behavior

techniques used to salvage a performance (interaction) that is going sour

If a performance doesn't come off quite right, the team might try to save it by using **face-saving behavior**.

Suppose your teacher is about to make an important point. Suppose also that her lecturing has been outstanding and the class is hanging on every word. Just as she pauses for emphasis, her stomach lets out a loud growl. She might then use a face-saving technique by remarking, "I was so busy preparing for class that I didn't get breakfast this morning."

It is more likely, however, that both the teacher and class will simply ignore the sound, giving the impression that no one heard a thing—a face-saving technique called *studied nonobservance*. This allows the teacher to make the point or, as Goffman would say, it allows the performance to go on.

BECOMING THE ROLES WE PLAY   A fascinating characteristic of roles is that *we tend to become the roles we play.* That is, roles become incorporated into our self-concept, especially roles for which we prepare long and hard and that become part of our everyday lives. Helen Ebaugh (1988) experienced this firsthand when she quit being a nun to become a sociologist. With her own heightened awareness of *role exit*, she interviewed people who had left marriages, police work, the military, medicine, and religious vocations. Just as she had experienced, the role had become intertwined so extensively with the individual's self-concept that leaving it threatened the person's identity. The question these people struggled with was "Who am I, now that I am not a nun (or wife, police officer, colonel, physician, and so on)?"

A statement made by one of my respondents illustrates how roles become part of the person. Notice how a role can linger even after the individual is no longer playing that role:

After I left the ministry, I felt like a fish out of water. Wearing that backward collar had become a part of me. It was especially strange on Sunday mornings when I'd listen to someone else give the sermon. I knew that I should be up there preaching. I felt as though I had left God.

Phil blows his interview before even sitting down.

Both individuals and organizations do impression management, trying to communicate messages about the self (or organization) that best meets their goals. At times, these efforts fail.

APPLYING IMPRESSION MANAGEMENT.   I can just hear someone say, "Impression management is interesting, but is it really important?" It certainly is. Impression management can even make a vital difference for your career. To be promoted, you must be perceived as someone who *should* be promoted. You must appear dominant. For men, giving this impression is less of a problem because stereotypes join masculinity and dominance at the hip. For women, though, stereotypes separate femininity and dominance.

How can a woman appear dominant? She could swagger, curse, and tell dirty jokes. This would get her noticed—but it is not likely to put her on the path to promotion. To assist women, career coaches have appeared on the scene. These "image consultants," as they are known, have a grab bag of little sayings, such as "The more skin you show, the more power you give away." They tell women to tone down their femininity, but not give it up. Women should present a "subtle femininity, they say, by wearing "soft" fabrics. They should also use makeup that doesn't have to be reapplied during the day. During business meetings they should place their hands on the table, not in their laps. And they should stash their purse inside a briefcase. They also need to practice giving good handshakes. "Presenting the whole package," said one image consultant, "takes a lot of work." Indeed (Agins 2009; Agno and McEwen 2011; Chapman 2013).

A common saying is that much success in the work world depends not on what you know but on who you know. This is true, but let's add the sociological twist: Much success in the work world depends not on what you know, but on your ability to give the impression that you know what you should know.

Ethnomethodology: Uncovering Background Assumptions

Certainly one of the strangest words in sociology is *ethnomethodology*. To better understand this term, consider the word's three basic components. *Ethno* means "folk" or "people"; *method* means how people do something; *ology* means "the study of." Putting them together, then, *ethno–method–ology* means "the study of how people do things." What things? **Ethnomethodology** is the study of how people use commonsense understandings to make sense of life.

> *Let's suppose that during a routine office visit, your doctor remarks that your hair is rather long, then takes out a pair of scissors and starts to give you a haircut. You would feel strange about this, because your doctor would be violating* **background assumptions**— *your ideas about the way life is and the way things ought to work. These assumptions, which lie at the root of everyday life, are so deeply embedded in our consciousness that we are seldom aware of them, and most of us fulfill them unquestioningly. Thus, your doctor does not offer you a haircut, even if he or she is good at cutting hair and you need one!*

The founder of ethnomethodology, sociologist Harold Garfinkel, had his students do little exercises to uncover background assumptions. Garfinkel (1967, 2002) asked his students to act as though they did not understand the basic rules of social life. Some of his students tried to bargain with supermarket clerks; others would inch close to people and stare directly at them. They were met with surprise, bewilderment, even indignation and anger. In one exercise, Garfinkel asked students to act as though they were boarders in their own homes. They addressed their parents as "Mr." and "Mrs.," asked permission to use the bathroom, sat stiffly, were courteous, and spoke only when spoken to. As you can imagine, the other family members didn't know what to make of their behavior:

> *They vigorously sought to make the strange actions intelligible and to restore the situation to normal appearances. Reports (by the students) were filled with accounts of astonishment, bewilderment, shock, anxiety, embarrassment, and anger, and with charges by various family members that the student was mean, inconsiderate, selfish, nasty, or impolite. Family members demanded explanations: What's the matter? What's gotten into you? . . . Are you sick? . . . Are you out of your mind or are you just stupid?* (Garfinkel 1967)

In another exercise, Garfinkel asked students to take words and phrases literally. When one student asked his girlfriend what she meant when she said that she had a flat tire, she said:

> *What do you mean, "What do you mean?" A flat tire is a flat tire. That is what I meant. Nothing special. What a crazy question!*

Another conversation went like this:

ACQUAINTANCE: How are you?

STUDENT: How am I in regard to what? My health, my finances, my schoolwork, my peace of mind, my . . . ?

ACQUAINTANCE: (red in the face): Look! I was just trying to be polite. Frankly, I don't give a damn how you are.

Students can be highly creative when they are asked to break background assumptions. The young children of one of my students were surprised one morning when they came down for breakfast to find a sheet spread on the living room floor. On it were dishes, silverware, lit candles—and bowls of ice cream. They, too, wondered what was going on, but they dug eagerly into the ice cream before their mother could change her mind.

ethnomethodology
the study of how people use background assumptions to make sense out of life

background assumption
a deeply embedded, common understanding of how the world operates and of how people ought to act

All of us have *background assumptions*, deeply ingrained assumptions of how the world operates. What different background assumptions do you think are operating here? If the annual "No Pants! Subway Ride" gains popularity, will background assumptions for this day change?

This is a risky assignment to give students, because breaking some background assumptions can make people suspicious. When a colleague of mine gave this assignment, a couple of his students began to wash dollar bills in a Laundromat. By the time they put the bills in the dryer, the police had arrived.

IN SUM   Ethnomethodologists explore *background assumptions*, the taken-for-granted ideas about the world that underlie our behavior. Most of these assumptions, or basic rules of social life, are unstated. We learn them as we learn our culture, and we violate them only with risk. Deeply embedded in our minds, they give us basic directions for living everyday life.

The Social Construction of Reality

4.7   Be able to apply the social construction of reality to your own life.

On a visit to Morocco, in northern Africa, I decided to buy a watermelon. When I indicated to the street vendor that the knife he was going to use to cut the watermelon was dirty (encrusted with filth would be more apt), he was very obliging. He immediately bent down and began to swish the knife in a puddle on the street. I shuddered as I looked at the passing burros that were urinating and defecating as they went by. Quickly, I indicated by gesture that I preferred my melon uncut after all.

"If people define situations as real, they are real in their consequences," said sociologists W. I. and Dorothy S. Thomas in what has become known as *the definition of the situation*, or the **Thomas theorem**. For that vendor of watermelons, germs did not exist. For me, they did. And each of us acted according to our definition of the situation. My perception and behavior did not come from the fact that germs are real but, rather, from *my having grown up in a society that teaches that germs are real*. Microbes, of course, *objectively* exist, and whether or not germs are part of our thought world makes no difference as to whether we are infected by them. Our behavior, however, does not depend on the *objective* existence of something but, rather, on our *subjective interpretation*, on what sociologists call our *definition of reality*. In other words, it is not the reality of microbes that impresses itself on us, but society that impresses the reality of microbes on us.

Let's consider another example. Do you remember the identical twins, Oskar and Jack, who grew up so differently? As discussed in Chapter 3, Oskar was reared in Germany and learned to love Hitler, while Jack was reared in Trinidad and learned to hate Hitler. As you can see, what Hitler meant to Oskar and Jack (and what he means to us) depends not on Hitler's acts but, rather, on how we view his acts—that is, on our definition of the situation.

Sociologists call this the **social construction of reality**. From the social groups to which we belong (the *social* part of this process), we learn ways of looking at life. We learn ways to view Hitler and Osama bin Laden, the Palestinians and the Israelis (they're good, they're evil), germs (they exist, they don't exist), and *just about everything else in life*. In short, through our interaction with others, we *construct reality*; that is, we learn ways of interpreting our experiences in life.

The *social construction of reality* is sometimes difficult to grasp. We sometimes think that meanings are external to us, that they originate "out there" somewhere, rather than in our social group. To better understand the social construction of reality, let's consider pelvic examinations.

GYNECOLOGICAL EXAMINATIONS   When I interviewed a gynecological nurse who had been present at about 14,000 vaginal examinations, I analyzed *how doctors construct social reality in order to define the examination as nonsexual* (Henslin and Biggs 1971/2016). It became apparent that the pelvic examination unfolds much as a stage play does. I will use "he" to refer to the physician because only male physicians were part of this study. Perhaps the results would be different with female gynecologists.

Thomas theorem

William I. and Dorothy S. Thomas' classic formulation of the definition of the situation: "If people define situations as real, they are real in their consequences"

social construction of reality

the use of background assumptions and life experiences to define what is real

Scene 1 (the patient as person) In this scene, the doctor maintains eye contact with his patient, calls her by name, and discusses her problems in a professional manner. If he decides that a vaginal examination is necessary, he tells a nurse, "Pelvic in room 1." By this statement, he is announcing that a major change will occur in the next scene.

Scene 2 (from person to pelvic) This scene is the depersonalizing stage. In line with the doctor's announcement, the patient begins the transition from a "person" to a "pelvic." The doctor leaves the room, and a female nurse enters to help the patient make the transition. The nurse prepares the "props" for the coming examination and answers any questions the woman might have.

What occurs at this point is essential for the social construction of reality, for *the doctor's absence removes even the suggestion of sexuality*. To undress in front of the doctor could suggest either a striptease or intimacy, thus undermining the reality that the team is so carefully defining: that of nonsexuality.

The patient, too, wants to remove any hint of sexuality, and during this scene, she may express concern about what to do with her panties. Some mutter to the nurse, "I don't want him to see these." Most women solve the problem by either slipping their panties under their other clothes or placing them in their purse.

Scene 3 (the person as pelvic) This scene opens when the doctor enters the room. Before him is a woman lying on a table, her feet in stirrups, her knees tightly together, and her body covered by a drape sheet. The doctor seats himself on a low stool before the woman and says, "Let your knees fall apart" (rather than the sexually loaded "Spread your legs"), and begins the examination.

The drape sheet is crucial in this process of desexualization, because it *dissociates the pelvic area from the person*: Leaning forward and with the drape sheet above the doctor's head, the physician can see only the vagina, not the patient's face. Thus dissociated from the individual, the vagina is transformed dramaturgically into an object of analysis. To examine the patient's breasts, the doctor also dissociates them from her person by examining them one at a time, with a towel covering the unexamined breast. Like the vagina, each breast becomes an isolated item dissociated from the person.

In this third scene, the patient cooperates in being an object, becoming, for all practical purposes, a pelvis to be examined. She withdraws eye contact from the doctor and usually from the nurse, is likely to stare at a wall or at the ceiling, and avoids initiating conversation.

Scene 4 (from pelvic to person) In this scene, the patient is "repersonalized." The doctor has left the examining room; the patient dresses and fixes her hair and makeup. Her reemergence as a person is indicated by such statements to the nurse as "My dress isn't too wrinkled, is it?" showing a need for reassurance that the metamorphosis from "pelvic" back to "person" has been completed satisfactorily.

Scene 5 (the patient as person) In this final scene, sometimes with the doctor seated at a desk, the patient is once again treated as a person rather than as an object. The doctor makes eye contact with her and addresses her by name. She, too, makes eye contact with the doctor, and the usual middle-class interaction patterns are followed. She has been fully restored.

IN SUM   For an outsider to our culture, the custom of women going to strangers for a vaginal examination might seem bizarre. But not to us. We learn that pelvic examinations are nonsexual. To sustain this definition requires teamwork—doctors, nurses, and the patient working together to *socially construct reality*.

It is not just pelvic examinations or our views of germs that make up our definitions of reality. Rather, *our behavior depends on how we define reality*. Our definitions (our constructions of reality) provide the basis for what we do and how we view life. To understand human behavior, then, we must know how people define reality.

The Need for both Macrosociology and Microsociology

4.8   Explain why we need both macrosociology and microsociology to understand social life.

As noted earlier, we need both macrosociology and microsociology. Without one or the other, our understanding of social life would be vastly incomplete. The photo essay on the next two pages on people's activities following a tornado should help to make clear why we need *both* perspectives.

To illustrate this point, consider two groups of high school boys studied by sociologist William Chambliss (1973/2016). Both groups attended Hanibal High School. In one group were eight middle-class boys who came from "good" families and were perceived by the community as "going somewhere." Chambliss calls this group the "Saints." In the other group were six lower-class boys who were seen as headed down a dead-end road. Chambliss calls this group the "Roughnecks."

Boys in both groups skipped school, got drunk, got in fights, and vandalized property. The Saints were truant more often and involved in more vandalism, but the Saints had a good reputation. The Roughnecks, in contrast, were seen by teachers, the police, and the general community as no good and headed for trouble.

The boys' reputations set them on separate paths. Seven of the eight Saints went on to graduate from college. Three studied for advanced degrees: One finished law school and became active in state politics, one finished medical school, and one went on to earn a Ph.D. The four other college graduates entered managerial or executive training programs with large firms. After his parents divorced, one Saint failed to graduate from high school on time and had to repeat his senior year. Although this boy tried to go to college by attending night school, he never finished. He was unemployed the last time Chambliss saw him.

In contrast, two of the Roughnecks dropped out of high school. They were later convicted of separate murders and sent to prison. Of the four boys who graduated from high school, two had done exceptionally well in sports and were awarded athletic scholarships to college. They both graduated from college and became high school coaches. Of the two others who completed high school, one became a small-time gambler and the other disappeared "up north," where he was last reported to be driving a truck.

To understand what happened to the Saints and the Roughnecks, we need to grasp *both* social structure and social interaction. Using *macrosociology*, we can place these boys within the larger framework of the U.S. social class system. This reveals how opportunities open or close to people depending on their social class and how people learn different goals as they grow up in different groups. We can then use *microsociology* to follow their everyday lives. We can see how the Saints manipulated their "good" reputations to skip classes and how their access to automobiles allowed them to protect their reputations by spreading their troublemaking around different communities. In contrast, the Roughnecks, who did not have cars, were highly visible. Their lawbreaking, which was limited to a small area, readily came to the attention of the community. Microsociology also reveals how the boys' reputations opened doors of opportunity to the Saints while closing them to the Roughnecks.

It is clear that we need both kinds of sociology, and both are stressed in the following chapters.

THROUGH THE AUTHOR'S LENS

When a Tornado Strikes: Social Organization Following a Natural Disaster

As I was watching television on March 20, 2003, I heard a report that a tornado had hit Camilla, Georgia. "Like a big lawn mower," the report said, it had cut a path of destruction through this little town. In its fury, the tornado had left behind six dead and about 200 injured.

From sociological studies of natural disasters, I knew that immediately after the initial shock the survivors of natural disasters work together to try to restore order to their disrupted lives. I wanted to see this restructuring process first-hand. The next morning, I took off for Georgia.

These photos, taken the day after the tornado struck, tell the story of people in the midst of trying to put their lives back together. I was impressed at how little time people spent commiserating about their misfortune and how quickly they took practical steps to restore their lives.

As you look at these photos, try to determine why we need both microsociology and macrosociology to understand what occurs after a natural disaster.

For children, family photos are not as important as toys. This girl has managed to salvage a favorite toy, which will help anchor her to her previous life.

Personal relationships are essential in putting lives together. Consequently, reminders of these relationships are one of the main possessions that people attempt to salvage. This young man, having just recovered the family photo album, is eagerly reviewing the photos.

After making sure that their loved ones are safe, one of the next steps people take is to recover their possessions. The cooperation that emerges among people, as documented in the sociological literature on natural disasters, is illustrated here.

© James M. Henslin, all photos

In addition to the inquiring sociologist, television teams also were interviewing survivors and photographing the damage. This was the second time in just three years that a tornado had hit this neighborhood.

Formal organizations also help the survivors of natural disasters recover. In this neighborhood, I saw representatives of insurance companies, the police, the fire department, and an electrical co-op. The Salvation Army brought meals to the neighborhood.

No building or social institution escapes a tornado as it follows its path of destruction. Just the night before, members of this church had held evening worship service. After the tornado, someone mounted a U.S. flag on top of the cross, symbolic of the church members' patriotism and religiosity—and of their enduring hope.

The owners of this house invited me inside to see what the tornado had done to their home. In what had been her dining room, this woman is trying to salvage whatever she can from the rubble. She and her family survived by taking refuge in the bathroom. They had been there only five seconds, she said, when the tornado struck.

Like electricity and gas, communications need to be restored as soon as possible.

Summary and Review

Levels of Sociological Analysis

4.1 Distinguish between macrosociology and microsociology.

What two levels of analysis do sociologists use?

Sociologists use macrosociological and microsociological levels of analysis. In **macrosociology**, the focus is placed on large-scale features of social life, while in **microsociology**, the focus is on **social interaction**. Functionalists and conflict theorists tend to use a macrosociological approach, while symbolic interactionists are likely to use a microsociological approach.

The Macrosociological Perspective: Social Structure

4.2 Explain the significance of social structure.

How does social structure influence our behavior?

The term **social structure** refers to the social envelope that surrounds us and establishes limits on our behavior. Social structure consists of culture, social class, social statuses, roles, groups, and social institutions. Our location in the social structure underlies our perceptions, attitudes, and behaviors.

4.3 Be able to identify the major components of social structure: culture, social class, social status, roles, groups, and social institutions.

What are the major components of social structure?

Culture lays the broadest framework, while **social class** divides people according to income, education, and occupational prestige. Each of us receives **ascribed statuses** at birth; later we add **achieved statuses**. Our social statuses guide our **roles**, put boundaries around our behavior, and give us orientations to life. These are further influenced by the **groups** to which we belong and our experiences with social institutions. These components of society work together to help maintain social order.

4.4 Explain the significance of social institutions and compare the functionalist and conflict perspectives on social institutions.

What are social institutions?

Social institutions are the standard ways that a society develops to meet its basic needs. As summarized in Figure 4.2, industrial and postindustrial societies have ten social institutions—the family, religion, education, economy, medicine, politics, law, science, the military, and the mass media. From the functionalist perspective, social institutions meet universal group needs, or *functional requisites*. Conflict theorists stress how the elites of society use social institutions to maintain their privileged positions.

4.5 Explain what holds society together.

What holds society together?

According to Emile Durkheim, in agricultural societies, people are united by **mechanical solidarity** (having similar views and feelings). With industrialization comes **organic solidarity** (people depend on one another to do their more specialized jobs). Ferdinand Tönnies pointed out that the informal means of control in *Gemeinschaft* (small, intimate) societies are replaced by formal mechanisms in *Gesellschaft* (larger, more impersonal) societies.

The Microsociological Perspective: Social Interaction in Everyday Life

4.6 Discuss what symbolic interactionists study and explain dramaturgy and ethnomethodology.

What is the focus of symbolic interactionism?

In contrast to functionalists and conflict theorists, who as macrosociologists focus on the "big picture," symbolic interactionists tend to be microsociologists and focus on face-to-face social interaction. Symbolic interactionists analyze how people define their worlds, and how their definitions, in turn, influence their behavior.

How do stereotypes affect social interaction?

Stereotypes are assumptions of what people are like. When we first meet people, we classify them according to our perceptions of their visible characteristics. Our ideas about these characteristics guide our reactions to them. Our behavior, in turn, can influence them to behave in ways that reinforce our stereotypes.

Do all human groups share a similar sense of personal space?

In examining how people use physical space, symbolic interactionists stress that we have a "personal bubble" that we carefully protect. People from different cultures use "personal bubbles" of varying sizes, so the answer to the question is no. Americans typically use four different "distance zones": intimate, personal, social, and public.

What is body language?

Body language is using our bodies to give messages. We do this through facial expressions, posture, smiling, and eye contact. Interpreting body language is becoming a tool in business and in the fight against terrorism.

What is dramaturgy?

Erving Goffman developed **dramaturgy** (or dramaturgical analysis), in which everyday life is analyzed in terms of the stage. At the core of this analysis is **impression management**, our attempts to control the impressions we make on others. For this, we use the **sign-vehicles** of setting, appearance, and manner. Our **role performances** on the **front stages** of life often call for **teamwork** and **face-saving behavior**. They sometimes are hampered by **role conflict** or **role strain**.

What is ethnomethodology?

Ethnomethodology is the study of how people make sense of everyday life. Ethnomethodologists try to uncover **background assumptions**, the basic ideas about the way life is that guide our behavior.

4.7   Be able to apply the social construction of reality to your own life.

What is the social construction of reality?

The phrase **social construction of reality** refers to how we construct our views of the world, which, in turn, underlie our actions.

The Need for both Macrosociology and Microsociology

4.8   Explain why we need both macrosociology and microsociology to understand social life.

Why are both levels of analysis necessary?

Because macrosociology and microsociology focus on different aspects of the human experience, each is necessary for us to understand social life.

Thinking Critically about Chapter 4

1. The major components of social structure are culture, social class, social status, roles, groups, and social institutions. Use social structure to explain why Native Americans have such a low rate of college graduation. (See Table 9.3 on page 284.)

2. Dramaturgy is a form of microsociology. Use dramaturgy to analyze a situation with which you are intimately familiar (such as interaction with your family or friends or at work or in one of your college classes).

3. To illustrate why we need both macrosociology and microsociology to understand social life, analyze the situation of a student getting kicked out of college.

Chapter 5
Social Groups and Formal Organizations

Learning Objectives

After you have read this chapter, you should be able to:

5.1 Discuss the main characteristics of primary groups, secondary groups, in-groups and out-groups, reference groups, and social networks. (p. 133)

5.2 Summarize the characteristics of bureaucracies, their dysfunctions and goal displacement; also contrast ideal and real bureaucracy. (p. 141)

5.3 Discuss humanizing the work setting, fads in corporate culture, the "hidden" corporate culture, and worker diversity. (p. 146)

5.4 Summarize major issues in the technological control of workers. Explain how global competition is affecting corporations. (p. 148)

5.5 Be familiar with the effects of group size on stability, intimacy, attitudes, and behavior; types and styles of leaders; the Asch experiment on peer pressure; the Milgram experiment on authority; and the implications of groupthink. (p. 149)

When Kody Scott joined the L.A. Crips, his initiation had two parts. Here's the first:

> *"How old is you now anyway?"*
>
> *"Eleven, but I'll be twelve in November."*
>
> *I never saw the blow to my head come from Huck. Bam! And I was on all fours. . . . Kicked in the stomach, I was on my back counting stars in the blackness. A solid blow to my chest exploded pain on the blank screen that had now become my mind. Bam! Blows rained on me from every direction. . . .*
>
> *Then I just started swinging, with no style or finesse, just anger and the instinct to survive. . . . [This] reflected my ability to represent the set [gang] in hand-to-hand combat. The blows stopped abruptly. . . . My ear was bleeding, and my neck and face were deep red. . . .*

Scott's beating was followed immediately by the second part of his initiation. For this, he received the name *Monster*, which he carried proudly:

> *"Give Kody the pump" [12-gauge pump action shotgun] . . . "Tonight we gonna rock they world." . . . Hand slaps were passed around the room. . . . "Kody, you got eight shots, you don't come back to the car unless they all are gone."*
>
> *"Righteous," I said, eager to show my worth. . . .*
>
> *Hanging close to buildings, houses, and bushes, we made our way, one after the other, to within spitting distance of the Bloods. . . . Huck and Fly stepped from the shadows simultaneously. . . . Boom! Boom! Heavy bodies hitting the ground, confusion,*

"Bangin'. . . . It's gettin' caught and not tellin'. Killin' and not caring, and dyin' without fear."

yells of dismay, running. . . . By my sixth shot I had advanced past the first fallen bodies and into the street in pursuit of those who had sought refuge behind cars and trees. . . .

Back in the shack we smoked more pot and drank more beer. . . .

Tray Ball said, "You got potential, 'cause you eager to learn. Bangin' [being a gang member] ain't no part-time thang, it's full-time, it's a career. . . . It's gettin' caught and not tellin'. Killin' and not caring, and dyin' without fear. It's love for your set and hate for the enemy. You hear what I'm sayin'?"

Kody adds this insightful remark:

. . . The supreme sacrifice was to "take a bullet for a homie" [fellow gang member]. Nothing held a light to the power of the set. If you died on the trigger you surely were smiled upon by the Crip God.

Excerpts from Scott 1994:8–13, 103.

Could you be like Kody and shoot strangers in cold blood—just because others tell you to pull the trigger? Although none of us want to think that we could, don't bet on it. In this chapter, you are going to read some surprising things about groups.

Groups within Society

5.1   Discuss the main characteristics of primary groups, secondary groups, in-groups and out-groups, reference groups, and social networks.

Groups, people who think of themselves as belonging together and who interact with one another, are the essence of life in society. Groups are vital for our well-being. They provide intimate relationships and a sense of belonging, something that we all need. This chapter, then, is highly significant for your life.

Before we analyze groups, we should clarify the concept. Two terms sometimes confused with group are *aggregate* and *category*. An **aggregate** consists of people who temporarily share the same physical space but who do not see themselves as belonging together. Shoppers standing in a checkout line or drivers waiting at a red light are an aggregate. A **category** is simply a statistic. It consists of people who share similar characteristics, such as all college women who wear glasses or all men over 6 feet tall. Unlike group members, the individuals who make up a category don't think of themselves as belonging together, and they don't interact with one another. These concepts are illustrated in the photos on the next page.

Groups are so influential that they determine who you are. If you think that this is an exaggeration, recall what you read in Chapter 3, that even your mind is a product of society—or, more specifically phrased, of the groups to which you belong. To better understand the influence of groups on your life, let's begin by looking at the types of groups that make up our society.

Primary Groups

As you will recall from Chapter 3, a major point about socialization is that you didn't develop "naturally" into a human adult. Your social experiences shaped you into what you have become. In this shaping process, it is hard to overestimate how significant your family has been. It was your family that laid down your basic orientations to life. Then came friends, where your sense of belonging expanded. Family and friends are what sociologist Charles Cooley called **primary groups**. By providing intimate, face-to-face interaction, your primary groups have given you a self, an identity, a feeling of who you are. Here's how Cooley (1909) put it:

By primary groups I mean those characterized by intimate face-to-face association and cooperation. They are primary in several senses, but chiefly in that they are fundamental in forming the social nature and ideals of the individual.

From our opening vignette, you can see that youth gangs are also primary groups.

group
people who interact with one another and who believe that what they have in common is significant; also called a *social group*

aggregate
individuals who temporarily share the same physical space but who do not see themselves as belonging together

category
people, objects, and events that have similar characteristics and are classified together

primary group
a small group characterized by cooperative, intimate, long-term, face-to-face relationships

Groups have a deep impact on your actions, views, orientations, even what you feel and think about life. Yet, as illustrated by these photos, not everything that appears to be a group is actually a group in the sociological sense.

The outstanding trait that these three people have in common does not make them a group, but a **category**.

Why are these swimmers who are competing in the Ironman triathlon in Hawaii an example of a **secondary group**? Why are the onlookers an **aggregate**?

Primary groups such as the family play a key role in the development of the self. As a small group, the family also serves as a buffer from the often-threatening larger group known as society. The family has been of primary significance in forming the basic orientations of this couple, as it will be for their son.

Why are the members of this crowd taking photos of a black swan an **aggregate**?

PRODUCING A MIRROR WITHIN   We humans have intense emotional needs. Among them are a sense of belonging and feelings of self-esteem. Because primary groups provide intense face-to-face interaction as we are being introduced to the world, they are uniquely equipped to meet our basic needs. They can make us feel appreciated—even that we are loved. When primary groups are dysfunctional, however, and fail to meet these basic needs, they produce dysfunctional adults, wounded people who make life difficult for others.

Regardless of the levels at which your primary groups have functioned—and none is perfect—their values and attitudes have been fused into your identity. You have internalized their views, which are now lenses through which you view life. Even as an adult—no matter how far you move away from your childhood roots—your early primary groups remain "inside" you. There, they continue to form part of the perspective from which you look out onto the world. Your primary groups have become your *mirror within*.

Secondary Groups

Compared with primary groups, **secondary groups** are larger, more anonymous, and more formal and impersonal. Secondary groups are based on shared interests or activities, and their members are likely to interact on the basis of specific statuses, such as president, manager, worker, or student. Examples include college classes, the American Sociological Association, and political parties. Secondary groups are part of the way we get our education, make our living, spend our money, and use our leisure time.

Secondary groups are necessary for contemporary life, but they often fail to satisfy our deep needs for intimate association. Consequently, *secondary groups tend to break down into primary groups.* At school and work, we form friendships. Our interaction with our friends is so important that we sometimes feel that if it weren't for them, school or work "would drive us crazy." The primary groups that we form within secondary groups, then, serve as a buffer between ourselves and the demands that secondary groups place on us.

secondary group
compared with a primary group, a larger, relatively temporary, more anonymous, formal, and impersonal group based on some interest or activity

VOLUNTARY ASSOCIATIONS   A special type of secondary group is a **voluntary association**, a group made up of volunteers who organize on the basis of some mutual interest. Some groups are local, consisting of only a few volunteers; others are national, with a paid professional staff.

Americans love voluntary associations and use them to express a wide variety of interests. A visitor entering one of the thousands of small towns that dot the U.S. landscape is often greeted by a sign proclaiming some of the town's voluntary associations: Girl Scouts, Boy Scouts, Kiwanis, Lions, Elks, Eagles, Knights of Columbus, Chamber of Commerce, American Legion, Veterans of Foreign Wars, and perhaps a host of others. One type of voluntary association is so prevalent that a separate sign sometimes indicates which varieties the town offers: Roman Catholic, Baptist, Lutheran, Methodist, Episcopalian, and so on. Not listed on these signs are many other voluntary associations, such as political parties, unions, health clubs, National Right to Life, National Organization for Women, Alcoholics Anonymous, Gamblers Anonymous, Association of Pinto Racers, and Citizens United For or Against This and That.

voluntary associations
groups made up of people who voluntarily organize on the basis of some mutual interest; also known as *voluntary memberships* and *voluntary organizations*

THE INNER CIRCLE   The key members of a voluntary association, its inner circle, often grow distant from the regular members. They become convinced that only they can be trusted to make the group's important decisions. To see this principle at work, let's look at the Veterans of Foreign Wars (VFW).

Sociologists Elaine Fox and George Arquitt (1985) studied three local posts of the Veterans of Foreign Wars. They found that although the leaders of the VFW concealed their attitudes from the rank-and-file-members, the inner circle viewed them as a bunch of ignorant boozers. Because the leaders couldn't stand the thought that such people

"So long, Bill. This is my club. You can't come in."

How our participation in social groups shapes our self-concept is a focus of symbolic interactionists. In this process, knowing who we are *not* is as significant as knowing who we are.

iron law of oligarchy

Robert Michels' term for the tendency of formal organizations to be dominated by a small, self-perpetuating elite

in-group

a group toward which one feels loyalty

out-group

a group toward which one feels antagonism

In a process called the *iron law of oligarchy*, a small, self-perpetuating elite tends to take control of formal organizations. The text explains that the leaders of the local VFW posts separate themselves from the rank-and-file members, such as those shown here in Mokena, Illinois.

might represent them in the community and at national meetings, a curious situation arose. The rank-and-file members were eligible for top leadership positions, but they never became leaders. In fact, the inner circle was so effective in controlling these top positions that even before an election, they could tell you who was going to win. "You need to meet Jim," the sociologists were told. "He's the next post commander after Sam does his time."

At first, the researchers found this puzzling. The election hadn't been held yet. As they investigated further, they found that leadership was determined behind the scenes. The current leaders appointed their favored people to chair the key committees. This spotlighted their names and accomplishments, propelling the members to elect them. By appointing its own members to highly visible positions, then, the inner circle maintained control over the entire organization.

THE IRON LAW OF OLIGARCHY   Like the VFW, in most voluntary associations, an elite inner circle keeps itself in power by passing the leadership positions among its members. Sociologist Robert Michels (1876–1936) coined the term **the iron law of oligarchy** to refer to how organizations come to be dominated by a small, self-perpetuating elite. (*Oligarchy* means a system in which many are ruled by a few.)

What many find disturbing about the iron law of oligarchy is that people are excluded from leadership because they don't represent the inner circle's values, or, in some instances, their background or even the way they look. This is true even of organizations that are committed to democratic principles. For example, U.S. political parties—supposedly the backbone of the nation's representative government—are run by an inner circle that passes leadership positions from one elite member to another. This principle also shows up in the U.S. Congress. With their control of political machinery and access to free mailing, 90 to 95 percent of U.S. senators and representatives who choose to run are reelected (*Statistical Abstract* 2006:Table 394; Cillizza 2013).

The iron law of oligarchy is not without its limitations, of course. Regardless of their personal feelings, members of the inner circle must keep attuned to the opinions of the rank-and-file members. If the oligarchy gets too far out of line, it runs the risk of a grassroots rebellion that would throw the elite out of office. This threat softens the iron law of oligarchy by making the leadership responsive to the membership. The iron law of oligarchy, then, is actually more like a copper law of oligarchy. In addition, because not all organizations become captive to an elite, it is a strong tendency, not an inevitability.

In-Groups and Out-Groups

What groups do you identity with? Which groups in our society do you dislike?

We all have **in-groups**, groups toward which we feel loyalty. And we all have **out-groups**, groups toward which we feel antagonism. For Monster Kody in our opening vignette, the Crips were an in-group, while the Bloods were an out-group. That the Crips—and we—make such a fundamental division of the world has far-reaching consequences for our lives.

SHAPING PERCEPTION AND MORALITY   You know the sense of belonging that some groups give you. This can bring positive consequences, such as our tendency to excuse the faults of people we love and to encourage them to do better. Unfortunately, dividing the world into a "we" and "them" also leads to discrimination, hatred, and, as we saw in our opening vignette, even murder. From this, you can see *the* *sociological significance of in-groups: They shape your perception of the world, your views of right and wrong, and your behavior.*

A fascinating result of dividing the world into "we" and "they" is that it can nurture double standards, such as prejudice and discrimination on the basis of sex:

> *We tend to view the traits of our in-group as virtues, while we perceive those* **same** *traits as vices in out-groups. Men may perceive an aggressive man as assertive but an aggressive woman as pushy. They may think that a male employee who doesn't speak up "knows when to keep his mouth shut," while they consider a quiet woman as too timid to make it in the business world (Merton 1949/1968).*

The twisting of perceptions can be so severe that, as in our opening vignette, harming others can become viewed as right. The Nazis provide a startling example. For them, the Jews were an out-group who symbolized an evil that should be eliminated. Many ordinary, "good" Germans shared this view and defended the Holocaust as "dirty work" that someone had to do (Hughes 1962/2005).

An example from way back then, you might say—and the world has moved on. But our inclination to divide the world into in-groups and out-groups has not moved on—nor has the twisting of perception that accompanies it. When al-Qaeda became Americans' number one out-group after 9/11, top U.S. officials ordered "cruel and inhuman" treatment of al-Qaeda prisoners. Interrogators waterboarded one prisoner 83 times ("Ex-FBI Official . . ." 2015). (None of us would want to be waterboarded even once.)

Perhaps this prisoner's account of his treatment at U.S. hands at Guantanamo will provide more insight into the extreme consequences that can arise from out-group thinking:

> *Suddenly a commando team consisting of three soldiers and a German shepherd broke into our interrogation room. . . . _____ punched me violently, which made me fall face down on the floor. . . . His partner kept punching me everywhere, mainly on my face and my ribs. He, too, was masked from head to toe. . . The third man was not masked; he stayed at the door holding the dog's collar, ready to release it on me. . . . I saw the dog fighting to get loose.*
>
> *One of them hit me hard across the face, and quickly put the goggles on my eyes, ear muffs on my ears, and a small bag over my head. I couldn't tell who did what. They tightened the chains around my ankles and my wrists; afterwards, I started to bleed. All I could hear was _____ cursing, "F-this and F-that!" (Sandberg 2015)*

Shades of the Nazis!

In short, to divide the world into in-groups and out-groups, a natural part of social life, produces both functional and dysfunctional consequences.

Reference Groups

Suppose you have just been offered a good job. It pays double what you hope to make even after you graduate from college. You have only two days to make up your mind. If you accept the job, you will have to drop out of college. As you consider the offer, thoughts like this may go through your mind: "My friends will say I'm a fool if I don't take the job . . . but Dad and Mom will practically go crazy. They've made sacrifices for me, and they'll be crushed if I don't finish college. They've always said I've got to get my education first, that good jobs will always be there. . . . But, then, I'd like to see the look on the faces of those neighbors who said I'd never amount to much!"

EVALUATING OURSELVES This is an example of how people use **reference groups**, the groups we refer to when we evaluate ourselves. Your reference groups may include your family, neighbors, teachers, classmates, co-workers, or the members of your church, synagogue, or mosque. If you were like Monster Kody in our opening vignette, the "set" would be your main reference group. Even a group you don't belong to can be a reference group. For example, if you are thinking about going to graduate school,

reference group

a group whose standards we refer to as we evaluate ourselves

All of us have reference groups—the groups we use as standards to evaluate ourselves. How do you think the reference groups of these members of the KKK who are demonstrating in Jaspar, Texas, differ from those of the police officer who is protecting their right of free speech? Although the KKK and this police officer use different groups to evaluate their attitudes and behaviors, the process is the same.

social network

the social ties radiating outward from the self that link people together

clique

(cleek) a cluster of people within a larger group who choose to interact with one another

graduate students or members of the profession you want to join may form a reference group. You would consider their standards as you evaluate your grades or writing skills.

Reference groups exert tremendous influence on us. For example, if you want to become a corporate executive, you might start to dress more formally, try to improve your vocabulary, read the *Wall Street Journal*, and change your major to business or law. In contrast, if you want to become a rock musician, you might get elaborate tattoos and body piercings, dress in ways your parents and even many of your peers consider extreme, read *Rolling Stone*, drop out of college, and hang around clubs and rock groups.

EXPOSURE TO CONTRADICTORY STANDARDS IN A SOCIALLY DIVERSE SOCIETY From these examples, you can see how you use reference groups to evaluate your life. When you see yourself as measuring up to a reference group's standards, you feel pleased. But you can experience inner turmoil if your behavior—or aspirations—does not match the group's standards. Although wanting to become a corporate executive would create no inner turmoil for most of us, it would for someone who had grown up in an Amish home. The Amish strongly disapprove of such aspirations for their children. They ban high school and college education, suits and ties, and corporate employment. Similarly, if you want to join the military and your parents are dedicated pacifists, you likely would feel deep conflict, because your parents would have quite different aspirations for you.

Contradictions that lead to inner turmoil are common because of two chief characteristics of our society: social diversity and social mobility. These expose us to standards and orientations that are inconsistent with those we learned during childhood. The "internal recordings" that play contrasting messages from different reference groups, then, are one price we pay for our social mobility.

Social Networks

Although we live in a huge and diverse society, we don't experience social life as a sea of nameless, strange faces. This is because of the groups we have been discussing. Among these is our **social network**, people who are linked to one another. Your social network includes your family, friends, acquaintances, people at work and school, and even "friends of friends." Think of your social network as a spider's web. You are at the center, with lines extending outward, gradually encompassing more and more people.

If you are a member of a large group, you probably associate regularly with a few people within that group. In a sociology class I was teaching at a commuter campus, six women who didn't know one another ended up working together on a project. They got along well, and they began to sit together. Eventually, they planned a Christmas party at one of their homes. This type of social network, the clusters within a group, or its internal factions, is called a **clique** (cleek).

APPLIED NETWORK ANALYSIS The analysis of social networks has become part of applied sociology. An interesting application is its use to reduce gang violence. When a gang member is shot, the gang retaliates by shooting members of their rival gang. This leads to endless violence, as each tries to even the score. To try to break this cycle, when the Chicago police arrest a gang member, they add the person's name to a program that links people. When a gang member is shot, the police click the name of the individual. This person then appears at the center, with his associates and known enemies shown in

The smallest part of *social networks* is our friends and acquaintances, the people we hang out with. This part of our social networks overlaps with and forms a core part of our *reference groups*. From these two photos, can you see how the *reference groups* and *social networks* of these youths are not likely to lead them to the same social destination?

concentric circles. Click a name and a mug shot appears, with that person's gang affiliations. The police then know who might be seeking to avenge the shooting (Belkin 2012).

THE SMALL WORLD PHENOMENON If you list everyone you know, and each of these individuals lists everyone he or she knows, and all of you keep doing this, would almost everyone in the United States eventually be included on those lists? This takes us to a question social scientists have asked: Just how extensive are the connections among social networks?

It would be too cumbersome to test this question by drawing up such lists, but psychologist Stanley Milgram (1933–1984) came up with an interesting idea. In a classic study known as "the small world phenomenon," Milgram (1967) addressed a letter to "targets": the wife of a divinity student in Cambridge and a stockbroker in Boston. He didn't mail the letters to these people, but instead sent them to "starters"—people who did not know these individuals. He asked them to send the letter to someone they knew on a first-name basis who might know the "target." Those recipients, in turn, were asked to mail the letter to a friend or acquaintance who might know the "target," and so on. The question was, Would the letters ever reach the "target"? If so, how long would the chain be?

Think of yourself as part of this research. What would you do if you were a "starter," but the "target" lived in a state in which you knew no one? You would send the letter to someone that you think might know someone in that state. This, Milgram reported, is just what happened. Although none of the senders knew the targets, the letters reached the designated individual in an average of just six jumps.

Milgram's research caught the public's fancy, leading to the phrase "six degrees of separation." This expression means that, on average, everyone in the United States is separated by just six individuals. Milgram's conclusions have become so popular that a game, "Six Degrees of Kevin Bacon," was built around it.

IS THE SMALL WORLD PHENOMENON AN ACADEMIC MYTH? Psychologist Judith Kleinfeld (2002) decided to replicate Milgram's study. At Yale University Library, where she went to get more details, she went through Milgram's papers. To her surprise, she found that Milgram had stacked the deck in favor of finding a small world. As mentioned, one of the "targets" was a Boston stockbroker. Kleinfeld found that this person's "starters"

Photo taken at the funeral of a six-month old child in Chicago who was killed as she sat on her father's lap. A gang member fired a gun into the minivan. How is network analysis being used to reduce such senseless deaths?

were investors in blue-chip stocks. She also found that on average, only 30 percent of the letters reached their "target."

Since most letters did *not* reach their targets, even with the deck stacked in favor of success, we can draw the *opposite* conclusion: People who don't know one another are dramatically separated by social barriers. As Kleinfeld says, "Rather than living in a small world, we may live in a world that looks like a bowl of lumpy oatmeal, with many small worlds loosely connected and perhaps some small worlds not connected at all." Somehow, I don't think that the phrase "lumpy oatmeal phenomenon" will become standard, but it seems reasonable to conclude that we do *not* live in a small world where everyone is connected by six links.

But not so fast. The plot thickens. Although research with thousands of e-mail chains showed that only about 1 percent reached their targets (Dodds et al. 2003; Muhamad 2010), other research confirms Milgram's conclusions. Research on 250 million people who exchanged chat messages showed a link of less than seven, and a study of 700 million people on *Facebook* showed a connection of less than five (Markoff and Sengupta 2011).

Why such disparity? The problem seems to be the choice of samples and how researchers measure links. These definitions must be worked out before we can draw solid conclusions. But maybe Milgram did stumble onto the truth. We'll find out as the research continues.

BUILDING UNINTENTIONAL BARRIERS   Besides geography, the barriers that divide us into separate small worlds (lumpy or not) are primarily those of social class, gender, and race–ethnicity. Overcoming these social barriers is difficult because even our own social networks contribute to social inequality, a topic that we explore in the Cultural Diversity box that follows.

Cultural Diversity in the United States

Do Your Social Networks Perpetuate Social Inequality?

Suppose that an outstanding job—great pay, interesting work, opportunity for advancement—has just opened up where you work. Who are you going to tell?

Consider some of the principles we have reviewed. We are part of in-groups, people with whom we identify; we use reference groups to evaluate our attitudes and behavior; and we interact in social networks. Our in-groups, reference groups, and social networks are likely to consist of people whose backgrounds are similar to our own. For most of us, this means that just as social inequality is built into society, so it is built into our relationships. One consequence is that we tend to perpetuate social inequality.

Go back to the extract that opens this box. Who will you tell about the opening for this outstanding job? Will it be a stranger? Not likely. Most likely it will be a friend or someone to whom you owe a favor. And most likely your social network is made up of people who look much like yourself—similar to your age, education, social class, race–ethnicity, and, probably also, gender. You can see how *our social networks both reflect the inequality in our society and help to perpetuate it.*

Consider a network of white men in some corporation. As they learn of opportunities (jobs, investments, and so on), they share this information with their networks. This causes opportunities and good jobs to flow to people whose characteristics are similar to theirs. This perpetuates the "good old boy"' network, bypassing people who have different characteristics—in this example, women and minorities. No intentional discrimination need be involved. It is just a reflection of our contacts, of our everyday interactions.

To overcome this barrier and advance their careers, women and minorities do networking. They try to meet "someone who knows someone" (Kantor 2009). Like the "good old boys," they go to parties and join clubs, religious organizations, and political parties. They use *Facebook* and other online networking sites. One result is a "new girl" network in which women steer business to one another (Jacobs 1997). African American leaders have cultivated their own network, one so tight that one-fifth of the entire national African American leadership knows one another personally. Add some "friends of a friend," and *three-fourths* of the entire leadership belong to the same network (Taylor 1992).

For Your Consideration

The perpetuation of social inequality does not require intentional discrimination. Just as social inequality is built into society, so it is built into our personal relationships.

When people learn of opportunities, they share this information with their networks. Opportunities then flow to people whose characteristics are similar to theirs.

→ How do you think your social network helps to perpetuate social inequality?

→ How do you think we can break this cycle? How can we create diversity in our social networks?

→ Should we try to break this cycle? What are the assumptions on which your answer is based?

Bureaucracies

5.2   Summarize the characteristics of bureaucracies, their dysfunctions, and goal displacement; also contrast ideal and real bureaucracy.

About one hundred years ago, sociologist Max Weber analyzed *bureaucracy,* a type of organization that has since become dominant in social life. To achieve more efficient results, bureaucracies shift the emphasis from traditional relationships based on personal loyalties to the "bottom line." As we look at the characteristics of bureaucracies, we will also consider their implications for our lives.

The Characteristics of Bureaucracies

Do you know what the Russian army and the U.S. postal service have in common? Or the government of Mexico and your college?

The sociological answer to these questions is that all four of these organizations are *bureaucracies.* As Weber (1913/1947) pointed out, **bureaucracies** have:

1. *Separate levels, with assignments flowing downward and accountability flowing upward.* Each level assigns responsibilities to the level beneath it, and each lower level is accountable to the level above it for fulfilling those assignments. Figure 5.1 on the next page shows the bureaucratic structure of a typical university.

2. *A division of labor.* Each worker is assigned specific tasks, and the tasks of all the workers are coordinated to accomplish the purpose of the organization. In a college, for example, a teacher does not fix the heating system, the president does not approve class schedules, and a secretary does not evaluate textbooks. These tasks are distributed among people who have been trained to do them.

3. *Written rules.* In their attempt to become efficient, bureaucracies stress written procedures. In general, the longer a bureaucracy exists and the larger it grows, the more written

bureaucracy

a formal organization with a hierarchy of authority and a clear division of labor; emphasis on impersonality of positions and written rules, communications, and records

Today's armies, no matter what country they are from, are bureaucracies. They have a strict hierarchy of rank, division of labor, impersonality and replaceability (an emphasis on the office, not the person holding it), and they stress written records, rules, and communications—essential characteristics identified by Max Weber. This photo was taken in Pyongyang, North Korea.

Figure 5.1 The Typical Bureaucratic Structure of a Medium-Sized University

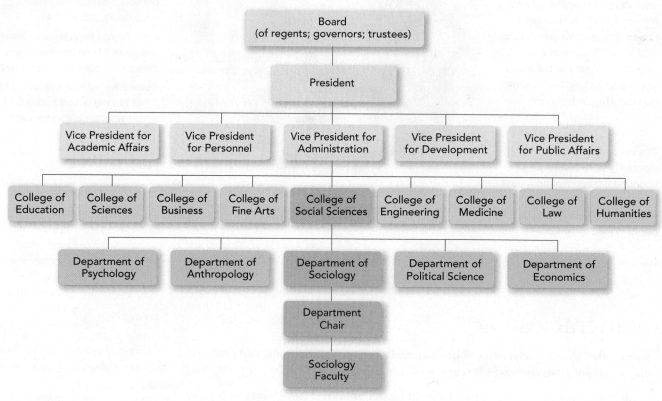

Source: By the author.

rules it has. The rules of some bureaucracies cover just about every imaginable situation. In my university, for example, the rules are published in handbooks: separate ones for faculty, students, administrators, civil service workers, and perhaps others that I don't even know about.

4. *Written communications and records.* Records are kept for much of what occurs in a bureaucracy ("Be sure to CC all immediate supervisors"). Some workers must detail their activities in written reports. My university, for example, requires that each semester, faculty members produce a summary of the number of hours they spent performing specified activities. They must also submit an annual report listing what they accomplished in teaching, research, and service—all accompanied by copies of publications, evidence of service, and written teaching evaluations from each course. Committees use these materials to evaluate the performance of each faculty member.

5. *Impersonality and replaceability.* The office is important, not the individual who holds the office. Each worker is a replaceable unit. You work for the organization, not for the replaceable person who holds some post in the organization. When a professor retires, for example, someone else is hired to take his or her place. This makes each person a small cog in a large machine.

These five characteristics help bureaucracies reach their goals. They also allow them to grow and endure. One bureaucracy in the United States, the postal service, has grown so large that 1 out of every 225 employed Americans works for it (*Statistical Abstract* 2014:Tables 642, 1150). If the head of a bureaucracy resigns, retires, or dies, the organization continues without skipping a beat. Unlike a "mom and pop" operation, a bureaucracy does not depend on the individual who heads it.

Bureaucracies have expanded to such an extent that they now envelop our entire lives, the topic of our Down-to-Earth Sociology box on the next page.

Down-to-Earth Sociology

The McDonaldization of Society

The significance of the McDonald's restaurants that dot the United States—and, increasingly, the world—goes far beyond quick hamburgers, milk shakes, and salads. As sociologist George Ritzer (1993, 1998, 2012) says, our everyday lives are being "McDonaldized." Let's see what he means.

The **McDonaldization of society** does not refer just to the robotlike assembly of food at McDonalds. This term refers to the standardization of everyday life, a process that is transforming our lives. Want to do some shopping? Shopping malls offer one-stop shopping in controlled environments. Planning a trip? Travel agencies offer "package" tours. They will transport middle-class Americans to ten European capitals in fourteen days. All visitors experience the same hotels, restaurants, and other scheduled sites—and no one need fear meeting a "real" native. Want to keep up with events? *USA Today* spews out McNews—short, bland, non-analytical pieces that can be digested between gulps of the McShake or the McBurger.

Efficiency brings dependability. You can expect your burger and fries to taste the same whether you buy them in Minneapolis or Moscow. Although efficiency also lowers prices, it does come at a cost. Predictability washes away spontaneity. It changes the quality of our lives by producing sameness—flat, bland versions of what used to be unique experiences. In my own travels, for example, had I taken packaged tours, I never would have had the eye-opening experiences that have added so much to my appreciation of human diversity. (Bus trips with chickens in Mexico, hitchhiking in Europe and Africa, sleeping on a

McDonald's delivery service in South Korea.

granite table in a nunnery in Italy and in a cornfield in Algeria are not part of tour agendas.)

For good or bad, our lives are being McDonaldized, and the predictability of packaged settings seems to be our social destiny. Education is being rationalized. When this process is complete, no longer will our children have to put up with real professors, who insist on discussing ideas endlessly, who never come to decisive answers, and who come saddled with idiosyncrasies. At some point, such an education is going to be like quill pens and ink wells, a bit of quaint history.

Our programmed education will eliminate the need for evaluating social issues. We will have packaged solutions to social problems, definitive answers that satisfy our need for closure, and the government's desire that we not explore its warts. Computerized courses will teach the same answers to everyone—"politically correct" ways to think about social issues. Mass testing will ensure that students regurgitate the programmed responses. Like carcasses of beef, our courses will be stamped "U.S. government approved."

Our looming prepackaged society will be efficient. But we will be trapped in the "iron cage" of bureaucracy—just as Weber warned would happen.

For Your Consideration

→ What do you like and dislike about the standardization of society?

→ What do you think about the author's comments on the future of education?

Goal Displacement and the Perpetuation of Bureaucracies

Bureaucracies are so good at harnessing people's energies to reach specific goals that they have become a standard feature of our lives. Once in existence, however, bureaucracies tend to take on a life of their own. In a process called **goal displacement**, even after an organization achieves its goal and no longer has a reason to continue, continue it does.

A classic example is the March of Dimes, organized in the 1930s with the goal of fighting polio (Sills 1957). At that time, the origin of polio was a mystery. The public was alarmed and fearful; overnight, a healthy child could be stricken with this crippling disease. To raise money to find a cure, the March of Dimes placed posters of children on crutches near cash registers in almost every store in the United States. The organization raised money beyond its wildest dreams. When Dr. Jonas Salk developed a vaccine for polio in the 1950s, the threat of polio was wiped out almost overnight.

goal displacement

an organization replacing old goals with new ones; also known as *goal replacement*

McDonaldization of society

the process by which ordinary aspects of life are rationalized and efficiency comes to rule them, including such things as food preparation

Did the staff that ran the March of Dimes hold a wild celebration and then quietly fold up their tents and slip away? Of course not. They had jobs to protect, so they targeted a new enemy—birth defects. But then, in 2001, another ominous threat of success reared its ugly head. Researchers finished mapping the human genome system, a breakthrough that held the possibility of eliminating birth defects—and their jobs. Officials of the March of Dimes had to come up with something new—and something that would last. Their new slogan, "Stronger, healthier babies," is so vague that it should ensure the organization's existence forever: We are not likely to ever run out of the need for "stronger, healthier babies." This goal displacement is illustrated in the photos that follow.

Then there is NATO (North Atlantic Treaty Organization), founded during the Cold War to prevent Russia from invading western Europe. The end of the Cold War removed the organization's purpose. But why waste a perfectly good bureaucracy? As with the March of Dimes, the western powers found a new goal: to combat terrorism and "rogue nations" (Tyler 2002). Russia poked a finger in NATO's eye over this very point, saying that because NATO is looking for a reason to exist it provokes tensions with Russia (RT 2014).

The March of Dimes was founded by President Franklin Roosevelt in the 1930s to fight polio. When a vaccine for polio was discovered in the 1950s, the organization did not declare victory and disband. Instead, its leaders kept the organization intact by creating new goals—first "fighting birth defects," and now "helping babies." Sociologists use the term *goal displacement* to refer to this process of adopting new goals.

Dysfunctions of Bureaucracies

Although in the long run no other form of social organization is more efficient, as Weber recognized, bureaucracies have a dark side. Let's look at some of their dysfunctions.

RED TAPE: A RULE IS A RULE   Bureaucracies can be so bound by rules that the results defy logic.

The Federal Aviation Administration (FAA) has authority over what flies in the U.S. air. One of its rules is that airplanes must carry a printed flight manual. When

Applewhite Aero applied for permission to test a drone it was developing, the FAA insisted that the drone carry a flight manual. "But there's no one to read it on a drone," the company objected. "But it's a rule," replied the FAA." You can't fly the drone without it."(Nicas 2014)

In Spain, I came across an example so ridiculous that it can make your head swim—if you don't burst from laughing first.

The Civil Registry of Barcelona recorded the death of a woman named Maria Antonieta Calvo in 1992. Apparently, Maria's evil brother had reported her dead so he could collect the family inheritance.

When Maria learned that she was supposedly dead, she told the Registry that she was very much alive. The bureaucrats at this agency looked at their records, shook their heads, and insisted that she was dead. Maria then asked lawyers to represent her in court. They all refused—because no dead person can bring a case before a judge.

When Maria's boyfriend asked her to marry him, the couple ran into a slight obstacle: No man in Spain (or most other places) can marry a dead woman—so these bureaucrats said, "So sorry, but no license."

After years of continuing to insist that she was alive, Maria finally got a hearing in court. When the judges looked at Maria, they believed that she really was a living person, and they ordered the Civil Registry to declare her alive.

The ending of this story gets even happier: Now that Maria was alive, she was able to marry her boyfriend. I don't know if the two lived happily ever after, but, after overcoming the bureaucrats, they at least had that chance ("Mujer 'resucite'" 2006).

Technology has changed our lives fundamentally. The connection to each telephone call used to have to be made by hand. As in this 1939 photo from London, England, these connections were made by women. Long-distance calls, with their numerous hand-made connections, not only were slow, but also expensive. In 1927, a call from New York to London cost $25 a minute. In today's money, this comes to $300 a minute!

BUREAUCRATIC ALIENATION Perceived in terms of roles, rules, and functions rather than as individuals, many workers in bureaucracies begin to feel more like objects than people. With boring, repetitive tasks—from factory workers inserting bolts to office workers filling out forms—workers can come to feel estranged from both their labor and their work environment. Marx termed these reactions **alienation**, a result, he said, of workers being cut off from the finished product of their labor. He pointed out that before industrialization workers used their own tools to produce an entire product, such as a chair or table. Now the capitalists own the tools (machinery, desks, computers) and assign each worker only a single step or two in the entire production process.

alienation

Marx's term for workers' lack of connection to the product of their labor; caused by workers being assigned repetitive tasks on a small part of a product—this leads to a sense of powerlessness and normlessness; others use the term in the general sense of not feeling a part of something

RESISTING ALIENATION Workers don't want to feel alienated. They want to feel valued and to have a sense of control over their work. So they resist alienation. A major form of their resistance is forming primary groups at work. They band together in informal settings—at lunch, around desks, or for a drink after work. There, they give one another approval for jobs well done and express sympathy for the shared need to put up with cantankerous bosses, meaningless routines, and endless rules. In these contexts, they relate to one another not just as workers but also as people who value one another. They flirt, laugh, tell jokes, and talk about their families and goals. Adding this multidimensionality to their work relationships helps them maintain their sense of being individuals rather than mere cogs in a machine.

How is this worker trying to avoid becoming a depersonalized unit in a bureaucratic-economic machine?

As in the photo you just viewed, workers often decorate their work areas with personal items. The sociological implication is that these workers are staking a claim to individuality. They are rejecting an identity as machines that exist to perform functions.

Working for the Corporation

5.3 **Discuss humanizing the work setting, fads in corporate culture, the "hidden" corporate culture, and worker diversity.**

Since you are likely to be working for a bureaucracy after college, let's examine some of its characteristics and how these might affect your career.

Self-Fulfilling Stereotypes in the "Hidden" Corporate Culture

As you might recall from Chapter 4, stereotypes can be self-fulfilling. That is, stereotypes can produce the very characteristics they are built around. The example used there was of stereotypes of appearance and personality. Sociologists have also uncovered **self-fulfilling stereotypes** in corporate life (Rivera 2012; Whiteley et al. 2012). Let's see how they might affect *your* career after college.

self-fulfilling stereotype preconceived ideas of what someone is like that lead to the person's behaving in ways that match the stereotype

SELF-FULFILLING STEREOTYPES AND PROMOTIONS   Corporate and department heads have ideas of "what it takes" to get ahead. Not surprisingly, since they themselves got ahead, they look for people who have characteristics similar to their own. They feed better information to workers who have these characteristics, bring them into stronger networks, and put them in "fast-track" positions. With such advantages, these workers perform better and become more committed to the company. This, of course, confirms the supervisor's expectations, the initial stereotype of a successful person.

But for workers who don't look or act like the corporate leaders, the opposite happens. Thinking of these people as less capable, the bosses give them fewer opportunities and challenges. When these workers realize that they are working beneath their abilities and they see others get ahead, they lose motivation, become less committed to the company, and don't perform as well. This, of course, confirms the stereotypes the bosses had of them in the first place.

In her research on U.S. corporations, Kanter (1977, 1983) found that such self-fulfilling stereotypes are part of a **"hidden" corporate culture**. That is, these stereotypes and their powerful effects on workers remain hidden to everyone, even the supervisors. What is visible is the surface—workers with superior performance and greater commitment to the company getting promoted. To bosses and workers alike, this seems to be just the way it should be. Hidden below this surface, however, are the higher and lower expectations and the opening and closing of opportunities that produce the attitudes and the accomplishments—or the lack of them.

"For the benefit of our new employees, we've simplified the corporate flow chart."

Conflict theorists would say that this cartoon is more realistic than the organization chart shown in Figure 5.1 (page 142). They would revise the cartoon, however, to show one big fish (owners) eating a lot of little fish (workers).

Diversity in the Workplace

At one point in U.S. history, most workers were white men. Over the years, this gradually changed, and now 47 percent of workers are women and 32 percent are minorities (*Statistical Abstract* 2014:Tables 620, 621). With such extensive diversity, the stereotypes in the hidden corporate culture will give way, although only grudgingly. In the following Thinking Critically section, let's consider diversity in the workplace.

hidden corporate culture stereotypes of the traits that make for high-performing and underperforming workers, which end up producing both types of workers

Thinking Critically

Managing Diversity in the Workplace

What is diversity? It certainly is much more than skin color. Diversity refers to differences in age, ethnicity, gender, religion, sexual orientation, and social class (Bezrukova et al. 2012). Here is an indication of how diverse the United States is: More than half of U.S. workers are minorities, immigrants, and women. The San Jose, California, electronic phone book lists *ten* times more *Nguyens* than *Joneses* (Albanese 2010).

It used to be assumed that immigrants and most minorities would join the "melting pot." They would give up their distinctive traits and become like the dominant group. Today, though, people are more likely to prize their distinctive traits. With assimilation (being absorbed into the dominant culture) not the wave of the future, most large companies have "diversity training" (Bendick 2013). They hold lectures and workshops so that employees can learn to work with colleagues of diverse cultures and racial–ethnic backgrounds.

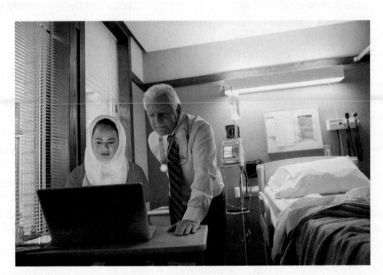

The cultural and racial–ethnic diversity of today's work force has led to the need for diversity training.

Coors Brewery is a prime example. In the 1980s, Coors was quite different than it is today. One of the Coors brothers even felt comfortable giving a racially charged speech. Today, Coors holds diversity workshops, sponsors gay dances, and pays for a corporate-wide mammography program. Coors even took a public stance against an amendment to the Colorado constitution that would have banned same-sex marriage. The company has rabbis certify its suds as kosher and sends employees to gay bars to promote its beer (Kim 2004). Quite a change.

Coors even adopted the slogan "Coors cares." Cute, but this slogan does not mean that Coors cares about diversity. What Coors cares about is the same as other corporations, the bottom line. Blatant racism and sexism once made no difference to profitability. Now they do. When the Coors brother gave that racially charged speech, boycotts went into effect, and Coors went into a financial tailspin. To promote diversity is to promote profitability, so companies must promote diversity—or at least give the appearance of doing so.

Pepsi provides a good example of a positive and effective approach to diversity training. Managers are given the assignment of sponsoring a group of employees who are unlike themselves. Men sponsor women, African Americans sponsor whites, and so on. The executives are expected to try to understand the work situation from the perspective of the people they sponsor, to identify key talent, and to mentor at least three people in their group. Accountability is built in: The sponsors are required to give updates of their mentoring to their own supervisory executives (Terhune 2005).

For Your Consideration

→ Do you think that corporations and government agencies need diversity training? Why or why not?

→ Can you suggest practical ways to overcome divisions of diversity among workers?

Technology and the Maximum-Security Society

5.4 **Summarize major issues in the technological control of workers. Explain how global competition is affecting corporations.**

The microchip is affecting all areas of society. One of the most ominous is its potential to create a police state. The Big Brother in Orwell's classic novel *1984* may turn out to be a master computer that makes servants of us all.

With computerized cameras monitoring the workplace and taking video images of us as we walk on the street and shop in stores and with smartphones constantly broadcasting our location, we seem to be moving toward a *maximum-security society* (Marx 1995; Hopkins et al. 2013), the topic of the New Technology box that follows.

Sociology and the New Technology

Welcome to the Memory Hole: Enjoy the Security State (SS)

Back in the early 1900s, Max Weber did his classic analysis of bureaucracy that you studied in this chapter. One of his observations was that the bureaucracy is so effective that it has the power to place us in little cages. Little did Weber realize how right he was.

In Weber's time, advanced technology was the typewriter and the fairly new things called electricity and cars. Today's pace of technological change is so fast that this week's "new thing" is outdated by next month. Or so it seems.

The primary technological change of our time is the computer. Not only has the computer made us more productive, but also it has transformed everyday life, changing even the ways we communicate at work and with our families. Its effects go deep, impacting even our way of thinking, our orientation to the world. These changes—deep and profound—are deserving of sociological study and intelligent analysis. After all, it is our lives that we are talking about.

But the computer presents a potent threat. Its power combined with bureaucracy along with the State's felt need for secrecy and security can destroy our freedom and make us slaves to the State.

We live in perilous times—ebola and its equivalents haunt the air we breathe, terrorists are ready to pounce, violent criminals lurk in the darkness. Or so it seems. We yearn for safety and security.

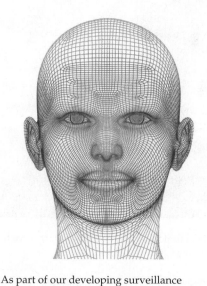

As part of our developing surveillance society, our government is accumulating images of faces. The goal is to have the faces of all citizens and residents in government computerized files so any person can be identified immediately by face recognition software, even if the individual is just one in a crowd of thousands.

And your friendly government is ready to provide it.

The uniformed personnel and the armored vehicles obligingly supplied by the military to local police departments are only part of our transition to the Security State. These are only physical manifestations of the deeper probe into our minds. In the background lies the computer, with its software of powerful algorithms that can sort billions of pieces of data in seconds. The face-recognition software, the files on citizens, the monitoring devices surreptitiously placed in strategic locations. But especially those files, those vast streams of information, inaccessible to those being monitored, even unknown to them. The individuals' names appeared in some intercepted message or computers indicated some sort of connection. No cumbersome court orders bothered with.

All citizens become suspects, because, after all, you never know. And it is the government's task to provide security. It must also secure its own agencies, that bureaucratic apparatus, until now so relatively weak.

Those pesky, intolerable, insolent whistleblowers. Instead of loyalty to the organization, they betray it. Snowden, Assange, Binney, Drake, and the others— letting people know they are being spied on, that their e-mail and telephone calls are algorithmically massaged. The surveillance machine works best in secret.

The power of these software programs is beyond comprehension. Just one example of what exists now, much less of what is to come. At the press of a button, Amazon can delete information from every Kindle anywhere in the world. No exaggeration. Amazon has already done this. When Amazon determined that the copies of some of its books were bootlegged, it vaporized them from everyone's Kindle (van Buren 2014). Great Britain is enshrouding its citizens within a protective shield that will prevent its people from viewing unapproved sites: pornography, violence, extremism, terrorism, anorexia, and suicide-related sites. Those that mention alcohol or smoking will be tolerated, but monitored.

Iran and North Korea, of course, also love filtering devices. The Chinese, Russians, Germans, and others are busy doing the same thing in their own way. And we can't forget the U.S. Army that protects its soldiers from what they see while abroad.

Back in 1948, George Orwell peered into the future through his novel *1984*. Orwell lived in a predigital world, and I'm amazed at his prescience. The future he envisioned is arriving rapidly. The bureaucracy paired with the computer will give us secure lives, very secure. Our acts will be monitored, all behind the scenes, not visible to us. With advances in brain research, the government should one day be able to monitor even our thoughts, for unapproved thinking can be dangerous to the Security State.

Eventually, the State will bring us what Orwell called the "memory hole." Orwell envisioned little slots where paper was inserted to be destroyed, with history rewritten to match the views approved by society's controllers. Computer programs make such slots antique relics. The new programs will be able to rewrite history, forcing unwanted information down the memory hole, thrust out of existence.

For Your Consideration

→ What do you think about the coming security state?

→ Do you find it comforting that the government wants to be your parent and decide what is proper and correct for you?

→ Does it give you a warm feeling that the government wants to protect you even from your own evil thoughts?

Actually, your feelings or opinions won't count for much. These decisions are being made for you.

Group Dynamics

5.5 Be familiar with the effects of group size on stability, intimacy, attitudes, and behavior; types and styles of leaders; the Asch experiment on peer pressure; the Milgram experiment on authority; and the implications of groupthink.

Group dynamics is a fascinating area of sociology. This term refers to how groups influence us and how we influence groups. Most of the ways that groups influence us lie below our sense of awareness, however, so let's see if we can bring some of this to the surface. Let's consider how even the size of a group makes a difference and then examine leadership, conformity, and decision making.

Before doing so, we should define **small group**, which is a group small enough so that each member can interact directly with all the others. Small groups can be either primary or secondary. A wife, husband, and children make up a *primary* small group, as do workers who take their breaks together. Students in a small introductory sociology class and bidders at an auction form *secondary* small groups. You might want to look again at the photos on page 134.

Effects of Group Size on Stability and Intimacy

Writing in the early 1900s, sociologist Georg Simmel (1858–1918) analyzed how group size affects people's behavior. He used the term **dyad** for the smallest possible group, which consists of two people. Dyads, which include marriages, love affairs, and close friendships,

group dynamics

the ways in which individuals affect groups and the ways in which groups influence individuals

small group

a group small enough for everyone to interact directly with all the other members

dyad

the smallest possible group, consisting of two persons

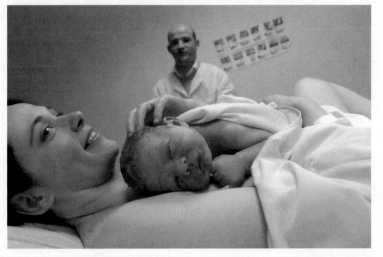

Group size has a significant influence on how people interact. When a group changes from a dyad (two people) to a triad (three people), the relationships among the participants undergo a shift. How do you think the birth of this child will change the relationship between the mother and father?

show two distinct qualities. First, they are the most intense or intimate of human groups. Because only two people are involved, the interaction is focused on both individuals. Second, dyads tend to be unstable. Because dyads require that both members participate, if one member loses interest, the dyad collapses. In larger groups, by contrast, if one person withdraws, the group can continue, since its existence does not depend on any single member (Simmel 1950).

triad

a group of three people

A **triad** is a group of three people. As Simmel noted, the addition of a third member changes the group in fundamental ways. One of the most significant changes is that interaction between the first two members of the group decreases. This can create strain. With the birth of a child, for example, hardly any aspect of a couple's relationship goes untouched. Attention focuses on the baby, and interaction between the husband and wife decreases. The marriage, though, usually becomes stronger. Although the intensity of interaction is less in triads, they are inherently stronger and give greater stability to a relationship.

coalition

the alignment of some members of a group against others

Yet, as Simmel noted, triads, too, are unstable. They tend to produce **coalitions**—two group members aligning themselves against one. This common tendency for two people to develop stronger bonds and prefer one another leaves the third person feeling hurt and excluded. Another characteristic of triads is that they often produce an arbitrator or mediator, someone who tries to settle disagreements between the other two. In one-child families, you can often observe both of these characteristics of triads—coalitions and arbitration.

The general principle is this: *As a small group grows larger, the group becomes more stable, but its intensity, or intimacy, decreases.* To see why, look at Figure 5.2. As each new person comes into a group, the connections among people multiply. In a dyad, there is only one relationship; in a triad, there are three; in a group of four, six; in a group of five, ten. If we expand the group to six, we have fifteen relationships, while a group of seven yields twenty-one relationships. If we continue adding members, we soon are unable to follow the connections: A group of eight has twenty-eight possible relationships; a group of nine, thirty-six; a group of ten, forty-five; and so on.

It is not only the number of relationships that makes larger groups more stable. As groups grow, they also tend to develop a more formal structure. For example, leaders emerge and more specialized roles come into play. This often results in such familiar offices as president, secretary, and treasurer. This structure provides a framework that helps the group survive over time.

Figure 5.2 The Effects of Group Size on Relationships

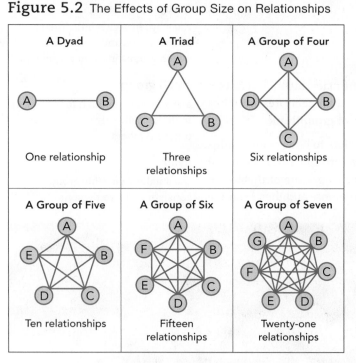

Effects of Group Size on Attitudes and Behavior

You probably have observed the first consequence of group size firsthand. When a group is small, its members act informally, but as the group grows, the members lose their sense of intimacy and become more formal with one another. No longer can the members assume that the others are "insiders" who agree with their views. Now they must take a "larger audience" into consideration, and instead of merely "talking," they begin to "address" the group. As their speech becomes more formal, their body language stiffens.

You probably have observed a second aspect of group dynamics, too. In the early stages of a party, when only a few people are present, almost everyone talks with everyone else. But as more people arrive, the guests break into smaller groups. Some hosts, who want their guests to mix together, make a nuisance of themselves trying to achieve *their* idea of what a group should be like. The division into small groups is inevitable, however: It follows the basic sociological principles that we have just reviewed. Because the addition of each person rapidly increases connections (in this case, "talk lines"), conversation becomes more difficult. The guests break into smaller groups in which they can look at each other directly and interact comfortably with one another.

Let's turn to a third consequence of group size:

> *Imagine that you are taking a team-taught course in social psychology, and your professors have asked you to join a few students to discuss how you are adjusting to college life. When you arrive, they tell you that to make the discussion anonymous, they want you to sit unseen in a booth. You will participate in the discussion over an intercom, talking when your microphone comes on. The professors say that they will not listen to the conversation, and they leave.*
>
> *You find the format somewhat strange, to say the least, but you go along with it. You have not seen the other students in their booths, but when they talk about their experiences, you find yourself becoming wrapped up in the problems they are sharing. One student even mentions how frightening it is to be away from home because of his history of epileptic seizures. Later, you hear this individual breathe heavily into the microphone. Then he stammers and cries for help. A crashing noise follows, and you imagine him lying helpless on the floor.*
>
> *Nothing but an eerie silence follows. What do you do?*

Your professors, John Darley and Bibb Latané (1968), staged the whole thing, but you don't know this. No one had a seizure. In fact, no one was even in the other booths. Everything, except your comments, was on tape.

Some participants were told that they would be discussing the topic with just one other student, others with two, and still others with three, four, or five. Darley and Latané found that all students who thought they were part of a dyad rushed out to help. If they thought they were in a triad, only 80 percent went to help—and they were slower in leaving the booth. In six-person groups, only 60 percent went to see what was wrong—and they were even slower.

This experiment demonstrates how deeply group size influences our attitudes and behavior: It even affects our willingness to help one another. Students in the dyad knew that no one else could help the student in trouble. The professor was gone, and it was up to them. In the larger groups, including the triad, students felt a *diffusion of responsibility*: Giving help was no more their responsibility than anyone else's.

LABORATORY FINDINGS AND THE REAL WORLD Experiments in social psychology can give insight into human behavior—but at the same time, they can woefully miss the mark. Darley and Latané's classic laboratory experiment has serious flaws when it comes to real life. Look at the photos on the next page that I snapped in Vienna, Austria, and you'll see something entirely different than what they reported. Many people—strangers to one another—were passing one another on the sidewalk. But as you can see, no diffusion of responsibility stopped them from immediately helping the man who had tripped and fallen. Other norms and values that people carry within them are also at work, ones that can trump the diffusion of responsibility.

Leadership

All of us are influenced by leaders, so it is important to understand leadership. Let's look at how people become leaders, the types of leaders, and different styles of leadership. Before we do this, though, it is important to clarify that leaders don't necessarily hold formal positions in a group. **Leaders** are people who influence the behaviors, opinions, or attitudes of others. Even a group of friends has leaders.

leader

someone who influences other people

WHO BECOMES A LEADER? Are leaders born with characteristics that propel them to the forefront of a group? No sociologist would agree with such an idea. In general,

THROUGH THE AUTHOR'S LENS

Helping a Stranger

Serendipity sometimes accompanies sociologists as they do their work, which was certainly the case here. The entire episode took no more than three minutes, and I was fortunate to capture it with my camera. Real life sometimes differs sharply from that portrayed in research laboratories.

As I was walking in Vienna, a city of almost 2 million people, I heard a crashing noise behind me. I turned, and seeing that a man had fallen to the sidewalk, quickly snapped this picture. You can see strangers beginning to help the man. This photo was taken about three seconds after the man fell.

The man is now on his feet, but still a bit shaky. The two who have helped him up are still expressing their concern, especially the young woman.

Two strangers are helping the man, with another two ready to pitch in. They have all stopped whatever they were doing to help a man they did not know.

By this point, the police officer has noticed that I have been taking photos. You can see him coming toward me, his hand on whatever he is carrying at his hip, his shoulders back, glowering and ready for a confrontation. He asked, "What are you doing?" I said, "I am taking pictures" (as though he couldn't see this). He asked, "Do you have to take pictures of this man?" I said, "Yes," and hoping to defuse the situation, added, "I'm a sociologist, and I'm documenting how people help each other in Vienna." He grunted and turned away.

This photo really completes the series, as this individual was acting as the guardian of the community, placing a barrier of protection around the participants in this little drama.

people who become leaders are perceived by group members as strongly representing their values or as able to lead a group out of a crisis (Trice and Beyer 1991). Leaders tend to be more talkative, outgoing, determined, and self-confident (Ward et al. 2010).

These findings may not be surprising, since such traits are related to what we expect of leaders. However, researchers have also discovered traits that seem to have no bearing on the ability to lead. For example, taller people and those judged better-looking are more likely to become leaders (Stodgill 1974; Judge and Cable 2004). Some of the factors that go into our choice of leaders are subtle. In a classic experiment, repeated many times, social psychologists Lloyd Howells and Selwyn Becker (1962) had five people who did not know one another sit at a small rectangular table. Three sat on one side and two on the other. After discussing a topic for a set period of time, the groups chose a leader. The findings are startling: Although only 40 percent of the people sat on the two-person side, 70 percent of the leaders emerged from there. The explanation is that we tend to interact more with people facing us than with people to our side.

TYPES OF LEADERS   Groups have two types of leaders (Bales 1950, 1953; Cartwright and Zander 1968; Emery et al. 2013). The first is easy to recognize. This person, called an **instrumental leader** (or *task-oriented leader*), tries to keep the group moving toward its goals. These leaders try to keep group members from getting sidetracked, reminding them of what they are trying to accomplish. The **expressive leader** (or *socioemotional leader*), in contrast, usually is not recognized as a leader, but he or she certainly is one. This person lifts the group's morale by such things as cracking jokes and offering sympathy. Both types of leadership are essential: The one keeps the group on track, and the other increases harmony and minimizes conflicts.

It is difficult for the same person to be both an instrumental and an expressive leader, since these roles tend to contradict one another. Because instrumental leaders are task-oriented, they sometimes create friction as they prod the group to get on with the job. Their actions often cost them popularity. Expressive leaders, in contrast, who stimulate personal bonds and reduce friction, are usually more popular (Olmsted and Hare 1978).

LEADERSHIP STYLES   Let's suppose that the president of your college has asked you to head a task force to determine how to improve race relations on campus. You can adopt a number of **leadership styles**, or ways of expressing yourself as a leader. Of the three basic styles, you could be an **authoritarian leader**, one who gives orders; a **democratic leader**, one who tries to gain consensus; or a **laissez-faire leader**, one who is highly permissive. Which style should you choose?

Social psychologists Ronald Lippitt and Ralph White (1958) carried out a classic study of these leadership styles. After matching a group of boys for IQ, popularity, physical energy, and leadership, they assigned them to "craft clubs" made up of five boys each. They trained men in the three leadership styles and then peered through peepholes, took notes, and made movies as the men rotated among the clubs. To control possible influences of the men's personalities, each man played all three styles.

The *authoritarian* leaders assigned tasks to the boys and told them what to do. They also praised or condemned the boys' work arbitrarily, giving no explanation for why they judged it good or bad. The *democratic* leaders discussed the project with the boys, outlining the steps that would help them reach their goals. When they evaluated the boys' work, they gave "facts" as the basis for their decisions. The *laissez-faire* leaders, who gave the boys almost total freedom to do as they wished, offered help when asked, but made few suggestions. They did not evaluate the boys' projects, either positively or negatively.

The results? The boys under authoritarian leaders grew dependent on their leader. They also became either apathetic or aggressive, with the aggressive boys growing hostile toward their leader. In contrast, the boys in the democratic clubs were friendlier and looked to one another for approval. When the leader left the room, they continued to work at a steady pace. The boys with laissez-faire management goofed off a lot and were notable for their lack of achievement. The researchers concluded that the democratic style of leadership works best. This conclusion, however, may be biased, as the

instrumental leader
an individual who tries to keep the group moving toward its goals; also known as a *task-oriented leader*

expressive leader
an individual who increases harmony and minimizes conflict in a group; also known as a *socioemotional leader*

leadership styles
ways in which people express their leadership

authoritarian leader
an individual who leads by giving orders

democratic leader
an individual who leads by trying to reach a consensus

laissez-faire leader
an individual who leads by being highly permissive

researchers favored a democratic style of leadership in the first place (Olmsted and Hare 1978). Apparently, this same bias in studies of leadership continues (Cassel 1999).

You may have noticed that only boys and men were involved in this experiment. What do you think would happen if we were to repeat the experiment with all-girl groups? With mixed groups of girls and boys? How about if we used both men and women as leaders? Perhaps you will become the sociologist who studies such variations of this classic experiment.

LEADERSHIP STYLES IN CHANGING SITUATIONS Different situations require different styles of leadership. Let's suppose that you are leading a dozen backpackers in the mountains, and it is time to make dinner. If the backpackers have brought their own food, a laissez-faire style would be appropriate. If everyone is expected to pitch in, perhaps a democratic style would be called for. Certainly authoritarian leadership—you telling the hikers how to prepare their meals—would create resentment. It would also interfere with the primary goal of the group, having a good time while enjoying nature.

Now assume you are leading this same group, but one of your party is lost, and a blizzard is on its way. This situation would call for you to exercise authority. If you simply shrugged your shoulders and said "You figure it out," you would invite disaster—and probably a lawsuit.

The Power of Peer Pressure: The Asch Experiment

How influential are groups in our lives? To answer this, let's look first at *conformity* in the sense of going along with our peers. Our peers have no authority over us, only the influence that we allow.

Adolf Hitler, shown here in Nuremberg in 1938, was one of the most influential—and evil—persons of the twentieth century. Why did so many people follow Hitler? This question stimulated the research by Stanley Milgram (discussed on pages 155–156).

Imagine again that you are taking a course in social psychology, this time with Dr. Solomon Asch. You have agreed to participate in an experiment. As you enter his laboratory, you see seven chairs, five of them already filled by other students. You are given the sixth. Soon the seventh person arrives. Dr. Asch stands at the front of the room next to a covered easel. He explains that he will show a large card with a vertical line on it, then another card with three vertical lines. Each of you is to tell him which of the three lines matches the line on the first card (see Figure 5.3).

Dr. Asch then uncovers the first card with the single line and the comparison card with the three lines. The correct answer is easy, for two of the lines are obviously wrong, and one is exactly right. Each person, in order, states his or her answer aloud. You all answer correctly. The second trial is just as easy, and you begin to wonder why you are there.

On the third trial, though, something strange happens. Just as before, it is easy to tell which lines match. The first student, however, gives a wrong answer. The second gives the same incorrect answer. So do the third and the fourth. By now, you are wondering what is wrong. How will the person next to you answer? You can hardly believe it when he, too, gives the same wrong answer. Then it is your turn, and you give what you know is the right answer. The seventh person also gives the same wrong answer.

On the next trial, the same thing happens. You know that the choice of the other six is wrong. They are giving what to you are obviously wrong answers. You don't know what to think. Why aren't they seeing things the same way you are? Sometimes they do, but in twelve trials they don't. Something is seriously wrong, and you are no longer sure what to do.

When the eighteenth trial is finished, you heave a sigh of relief. The experiment is finally over, and you are ready to bolt for the door. Dr. Asch walks over to you with a big smile on his face and thanks you for participating in the experiment. He explains that you were the only real subject in the experiment! "The other six were stooges. I paid them to give those answers," he says. Now you feel real relief. Your eyes weren't playing tricks on you after all.

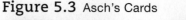

Figure 5.3 Asch's Cards

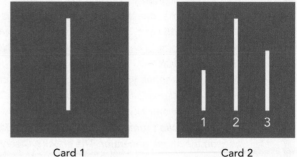

Card 1   Card 2

The cards used by Solomon Asch in his classic experiment on group conformity

What were the results? Asch (1952) tested fifty people. One-third (33 percent) gave in to the group half the time, providing what they knew to be wrong answers. Another two out of five (40 percent) gave wrong answers, but not as often. One-quarter (25 percent) stuck to their guns and always gave the right answer. I don't know how I would do on this test (if I knew nothing about it in advance), but I like to think that I would be part of the 25 percent. You probably feel the same way about yourself. But why should we feel that we wouldn't be like *most* people?

The results are disturbing, and researchers are still replicating Asch's experiment (Morl and Aral 2011). In our "land of individualism," the group is so powerful that most people are willing to say things that they know are not true. And this was a group of strangers! How much more conformity can we expect when our group consists of friends, people we value highly and depend on for getting along in life? Again, maybe you will become the sociologist who runs that variation of Asch's experiment, perhaps using both female and male subjects.

The Power of Authority: The Milgram Experiment

Let's look at the results of another experiment in the following Thinking Critically section.

Thinking Critically

If Hitler Asked You to Execute a Stranger, Would You? The Milgram Experiment

Stanley Milgram (1963, 1965) was a former student of Dr. Asch. Imagine that Dr. Milgram has asked you to participate in a study on punishment and learning. Assume that you do not know about the Asch

experiment and have no reason to be wary. When you arrive at the laboratory, you and a second student draw lots for the roles of "teacher" and "learner." You are to be the teacher. When you see that the learner's chair has protruding electrodes, you are glad that you are the teacher. Dr. Milgram shows you the machine you will run. You see that one side of the control panel is marked "Mild Shock, 15 volts," while the center says "Intense Shock, 350 Volts." The far right side reads "DANGER: SEVERE SHOCK."

"As the teacher, you will read aloud a pair of words," explains Dr. Milgram. "Then you will repeat the first word, and the learner will reply with the paired word. If the learner can't remember the word, you press this lever on the shock generator. The shock will serve as punishment, and we can then determine if punishment improves memory." You nod, relieved that you haven't been designated the learner.

"Every time the learner makes an error, increase the punishment by 15 volts," instructs Dr. Milgram. Then, seeing the look on your face, he adds, "The shocks can be painful, but they won't cause any permanent tissue damage." He pauses, and then says, "I want you to see." You follow him to the "electric chair," and Dr. Milgram gives you a shock of 45 volts. "There. That wasn't too bad, was it?" "No," you mumble.

The experiment begins. You hope for the learner's sake that he is bright, but, unfortunately, he turns out to be rather dull. He gets some answers right, but you have to keep turning up the dial. Each turn makes you more and more uncomfortable. You find yourself hoping that the learner won't miss another answer. But he does. When he received the first shocks, he let out some moans and groans, but now he is screaming in agony. He even protests that he suffers from a heart condition.

How far do you turn that dial?

By now, since you are only reading this, not doing it, you probably have guessed that there was no electricity attached to the electrodes and that the "learner" was a stooge who only pretended to feel pain. The purpose of the experiment was to find out at what point people refuse to participate. Does anyone actually turn the lever all the way to "DANGER: SEVERE SHOCK"?

Milgram wanted the answer because millions of ordinary people did nothing to stop the slaughter of people the Nazis designated as "inferior"—Jews, gypsies, Slavs, homosexuals, and people with disabilities. The cooperation of so many ordinary people in mass killing seemed bizarre, and Milgram wanted to see how Americans might react to orders from an authority (Russell 2010).

What Milgram found upset him. Some "teachers" broke into a sweat and protested that the experiment was inhuman and should be stopped. But when the experimenter calmly replied that the experiment must go on, this assurance from an "authority" ("scientist, white coat, university laboratory") was enough for most "teachers" to continue, even though the "learner" screamed in agony. Even "teachers" who were "reduced to twitching, stuttering wrecks" continued to follow orders.

In the 1960s, social psychologists did highly creative but controversial experiments. This photo, taken during Stanley Milgram's experiment, should give you an idea of how convincing the experiment was to the "teacher."

Milgram varied the experiments. He used both men and women. In some experiments, he put the "teachers" and "learners" in the same room, so the "teacher" could see the suffering. In others, he put the "learners" in an adjacent room and had them pound and kick the wall during the first shocks and then go silent. The results varied. When there was no verbal feedback from the "learner," 65 percent of the "teachers" pushed the lever all the way to 450 volts. Of those who could see the "learner," 40 percent turned the lever all the way. When Milgram added a second "teacher," a stooge who refused to go along with the experiment, only 5 percent of the "teachers" turned the lever all the way.

Milgram's research set off a stormy discussion about research ethics (Tolich 2014). Researchers agreed that to reduce subjects to "twitching, stuttering wrecks" was unethical, and almost all deception was banned. Universities began to require that subjects be informed of the nature and purpose of social research.

Although researchers were itching to replicate Milgram's experiment, it took almost fifty years before they found a way to satisfy the committees that approve research. The findings: People today obey the experimenter at about the same rate that people did in the 1960s (Burger 2009). The results were even higher on *The Game of Death*, a fake game show in France, where the contestants were prodded by the show's host and a shouting audience to administer shocks and win prizes. The contestants kept turning up the dial, with 80 percent of them giving victims what they thought were near lethal 450-volt shocks (Crumley 2010).

For Your Consideration

→ Taking into account the significance of Milgram's findings, do you think that the scientific community overreacted to these experiments? Should we allow such research?

→ Consider both the Asch and Milgram experiments, and use symbolic interactionism, functionalism, and conflict theory to explain why groups have such influence over us.

Global Consequences of Group Dynamics: Groupthink

Suppose you are a member of the U.S. president's inner circle. It is midnight, and the president has called an emergency meeting. There has just been a terrorist attack, and you must decide how to respond to it. You and the others suggest several options. Eventually, these are narrowed to only a couple of choices, and at some point, everyone seems to agree on what now appears to be "the only possible course of action." To criticize the proposed solution at this point will bring you into conflict with all the other important people in the room and mark you as "not a team player." So you keep your mouth shut. As a result, each step commits you—and them—more and more to the "only" course of action.

Under some circumstances, as in this example, the influence of authority and peers can lead to **groupthink**. Sociologist Irving Janis (1972, 1982) used this term to refer to the collective tunnel vision that group members sometimes develop. As they begin to think alike, they become convinced that there is only one "right" viewpoint, just a single course of action to follow. They take suggestions of alternatives as a sign of disloyalty. With their perspective narrowed, and fully convinced that they are right, they may disregard risk. They might also put aside moral judgments (Hart 1991; Kramer and Dougherty 2013).

Groupthink can bring catastrophe. Consider the *Columbia* space shuttle disaster of 2003.

> *Foam broke loose during launch, raising concerns that this might have damaged tiles on the nose cone, making reentry dangerous. Engineers sent e-mails to NASA officials, warning them about the risk. One suggested that the crew do a "space walk" to examine the tiles (Vartabedian and Gold 2003). The team in charge of the Columbia shuttle disregarded the warnings. Convinced that a piece of foam weighing less than 2 pounds could not seriously harm the shuttle, they refused to even consider the possibility (Wald and Schwartz 2003). The fiery results of their closed minds were transmitted around the globe.*

Groupthink can lead to consequences even greater than this. In 1941, President Franklin D. Roosevelt and his chiefs of staff had evidence that the Japanese were preparing to attack Pearl Harbor. Refusing to believe it, they decided to continue naval operations as usual. The destruction of the U.S. naval fleet ushered the United States into World War II. During the Vietnam War, U.S. officials had evidence of the strength and determination of the North Vietnamese military. These officials arrogantly threw the evidence aside, refusing to believe that "little, uneducated, barefoot people in pajamas" could defeat the mighty U.S. military.

In each of these cases, options closed as officials committed themselves to a single course of action. Questioning the decisions would have indicated disloyalty and disregard for "team play." No longer did those in power try to weigh events objectively. Interpreting ongoing events as supporting their one "correct" decision, they plunged ahead, blind to disconfirming evidence and alternative perspectives.

One of the fascinating aspects of groupthink is how it can lead "good" people to do "bad" things. After 9/11, U.S. government officials defended torture as "the lesser of two evils." Thought narrowed so greatly that the U.S. Justice Department ruled that the United States was not bound by the Geneva Convention that prohibits torture (Lewis 2005). Just as in Nazi Germany, medical professionals, trained to "help humanity," joined in. They advised the CIA interrogators, telling them when to stop waterboarding, slamming prisoners' heads into walls, or shackling a prisoner's arms to the ceiling—so there wouldn't be "permanent damage" (Shane 2009).

Do you see the power of groups and groupthink?

PREVENTING GROUPTHINK The leaders of a government tend to surround themselves with an inner circle that closely reflects their own views. In "briefings," written

groupthink
a narrowing of thought by a group of people, leading to the perception that there is only one correct answer and that to even suggest alternatives is a sign of disloyalty

summaries, and "talking points," this inner circle spoon-feeds the leaders information it has selected. As a result, the top leaders, such as the president, are largely cut off from information that does not support their own opinions. You can see how the mental captivity and intellectual paralysis known as groupthink is built into this arrangement.

Perhaps the key to preventing groupthink is the widest possible circulation—especially among a nation's top government officials—of research by social scientists independent of the government and information that media reporters have gathered freely. If this conclusion comes across as an unabashed plug for sociological research and the free exchange of ideas, it is. Giving free rein to diverse opinions can curb groupthink, which—if not prevented—can lead to the destruction of a society and, in today's world of nuclear, chemical, and biological weapons, the obliteration of Earth's inhabitants.

Summary and Review

Groups within Society

5.1 **Discuss the main characteristics of primary groups, secondary groups, in-groups and out-groups, reference groups, and social networks.**

How do sociologists classify groups?

Sociologists divide **groups** into primary groups, secondary groups, in-groups, out-groups, reference groups, and networks. The cooperative, intimate, long-term, face-to-face relationships provided by **primary groups** are fundamental to our sense of self. **Secondary groups** are larger, relatively temporary, and more anonymous, formal, and impersonal than primary groups. **In-groups** provide members with a strong sense of identity and belonging. **Out-groups** also foster identity by showing in-group members what they are *not*. **Reference groups** are groups whose standards we refer to as we evaluate ourselves. **Social networks** consist of social ties that link people together.

What is "the iron law of oligarchy"?

Sociologist Robert Michels noted that formal organizations have a tendency to become controlled by an inner circle that limits leadership to its own members. The dominance of a formal organization by an elite that keeps itself in power is called **the iron law of oligarchy**.

Bureaucracies

5.2 **Summarize the characteristics of bureaucracies, their dysfunctions, and goal displacement; also contrast ideal and real bureaucracy.**

What are bureaucracies?

Bureaucracies are social groups characterized by a hierarchy, division of labor, written rules and communications, and impersonality and replaceability of positions. These characteristics make bureaucracies efficient and enduring. In a process called **goal displacement**, bureaucracies are able to perpetuate themselves even after their purpose for existing ceases.

What dysfunctions are associated with bureaucracies?

The dysfunctions of bureaucracies include red tape, lack of communication between units, and alienation. In Weber's view, the impersonality of bureaucracies tends to produce **alienation** among workers—the feeling that no one cares about them and that they do not really fit in. Marx's view of alienation is somewhat different—workers do not identify with the product of their labor because they participate in only a small part of the production process.

Working for the Corporation

5.3 **Discuss humanizing the work setting, fads in corporate culture, the "hidden" corporate culture, and worker diversity.**

How does the corporate culture affect workers?

Within corporate culture are values and stereotypes that are not readily visible. Often, **self-fulfilling stereotypes** are at work: People who match a corporation's hidden values tend to be put on career tracks that enhance their chance of success, while those who do not match those values are set on a course that minimizes their performance.

Technology and the Control of Workers

5.4 **Summarize major issues in the technological control of workers. Explain how global competition is affecting corporations.**

What is the maximum security society?

Computers and surveillance devices are increasingly used to monitor people, especially in the workplace. This intrusive technology is being extended to monitoring our everyday lives.

Group Dynamics

5.5 **Be familiar with the effects of group size on stability, intimacy, attitudes, and behavior; types and styles of leaders; the Asch experiment on peer**

pressure; the Milgram experiment on authority; and the implications of groupthink.

How does a group's size affect its dynamics?

The term **group dynamics** refers to how individuals affect groups and how groups influence individuals. In a **small group**, everyone can interact directly with everyone else. As a group grows larger, its intensity decreases but its stability increases. A **dyad**, consisting of two people, is the most unstable of human groups, but it provides the most intense intimate relationships. The addition of a third person, forming a **triad**, fundamentally changes relationships. Triads are unstable, as **coalitions** (the alignment of some members of a group against others) tend to form.

What characterizes a leader?

A **leader** is someone who influences others. **Instrumental leaders** try to keep a group moving toward its goals, even though this causes friction and they lose popularity.

Expressive leaders focus on creating harmony and raising group morale. Both types are essential to the functioning of groups.

What are three leadership styles?

Authoritarian leaders give orders, **democratic leaders** try to lead by consensus, and **laissez-faire leaders** are highly permissive. An authoritarian style appears to be more effective in emergency situations, a democratic style works best for most situations, and a laissez-faire style is usually ineffective.

How do groups encourage conformity?

The Asch experiment was cited to illustrate the power of peer pressure, the Milgram experiment to illustrate the influence of authority. Both experiments demonstrate how easily we can succumb to **groupthink**, a kind of collective tunnel vision. Preventing groupthink requires the free circulation of diverse and opposing ideas.

Thinking Critically about Chapter 5

1. Identify your in-groups and your out-groups. How have your in-groups influenced the way you see the world? And how have your out-groups influenced you?

2. You are likely to work for a bureaucracy. How do you think this will affect your orientation to life?

3. How can you make the "hidden corporate culture" work to your advantage?

4. Asch's experiments illustrate the power of peer pressure. How has peer pressure operated in your life? Think about something that you did not want to do but did anyway because of peer pressure.

Chapter 6
Deviance and Social Control

In just a few moments I was to meet my first Yanomamö, my first primitive man. What would it be like? . . . I looked up [from my canoe] and gasped when I saw a dozen burly, naked, filthy, hideous men staring at us down the shafts of their drawn arrows. Immense wads of green tobacco were stuck between their lower teeth and lips, making them look even more hideous, and strands of dark-green slime dripped or hung from their noses. We arrived at the village while the men were blowing a hallucinogenic drug up their noses. One of the side effects of the drug is a runny nose. The mucus is always saturated with the green powder, and the Indians usually let it run freely from their nostrils. . . . I just sat there holding my notebook, helpless and pathetic. . . .

The whole situation was depressing, and I wondered why I ever decided to switch from civil engineering to anthropology in the first place. . . . [Soon] I was covered with red pigment, the result of a dozen or so complete examinations. . . . These examinations capped an otherwise grim day. The Indians would blow their noses into their hands, flick as much of the mucus off that would separate in a snap of the wrist, wipe the residue into their hair, and then carefully examine my face, arms, legs, hair, and the contents of my pockets. I said [in their language], "Your hands are dirty"; my comments were met by the Indians in the following way: they would "clean" their hands by spitting a quantity of slimy tobacco juice into them, rub them together, and then proceed with the examination.

"They would 'clean' their hands by spitting slimy tobacco juice into them."

161

This is how Napoleon Chagnon describes the culture shock he felt when he met the Yanomamö tribe of the rain forests of Brazil. His following months of fieldwork continued to bring surprise after surprise, and often Chagnon (1977) could hardly believe his eyes—or his nose.

If you were to list the deviant behaviors of the Yanomamö, what would you include? The way they appear naked in public? Use of hallucinogenic drugs? Let mucus hang from their noses? Or the way they rub hands filled with mucus, spittle, and tobacco juice over a frightened stranger who doesn't dare to protest? Perhaps. But it isn't this simple. As we shall see, deviance is relative.

deviance

the violation of norms (or rules or expectations)

crime

the violation of norms written into law

I took this photo on the outskirts of Hyderabad, India. Is this man deviant? If this were a U.S. street, he would be. But here? No houses have running water in his neighborhood, and the men, women, and children bathe at the neighborhood water pump. This man, then, would not be deviant in this culture. And yet, he is actually mugging for my camera, making the three bystanders laugh. Does this additional factor make this a scene of deviance?

What Is Deviance?

6.1   Summarize the relativity of deviance, the need for norms, and the types of sanctions; contrast sociobiological, psychological, and sociological explanations of deviance.

Sociologists use the term **deviance** to refer to any violation of norms, whether the infraction is as minor as driving over the speed limit, as serious as murder, or as humorous as Chagnon's encounter with the Yanomamö. This deceptively simple definition takes us to the heart of the sociological perspective on deviance, which sociologist Howard S. Becker (1966) described this way: *It is not the act itself, but the reactions to the act, that make something deviant.* What Chagnon saw disturbed him, but to the Yanomamö, those same behaviors represented normal, everyday life. What was deviant to Chagnon was *conformist* to the Yanomamö. From their viewpoint, you *should* check out strangers the way they did—and nakedness is good, as are hallucinogenic drugs. And it is natural to let mucus flow.

THE RELATIVITY OF DEVIANCE   Chagnon's abrupt introduction to the Yanomamö allows us to see the *relativity of deviance*, a major point made by symbolic interactionists. Because different groups have different norms, *what is deviant to some is not deviant to others.* This principle applies not just to cultures but also to groups within the same society. Look at the photo to the left and the one on page 164.

This principle also applies to norms of sexuality, the focus of the Cultural Diversity box on the next page.

The relativity of deviance also applies to **crime**, the violation of rules that have been written into law. In the extreme, an act that is applauded by one group may be so despised by another group that it is punishable by death. Making a huge profit on business deals is one example. Americans who do this are admired. Like Donald Trump and Warren Buffet, they may even write books about their exploits. In China, however, until recently, this same act was considered a crime called *profiteering*. Those found guilty were hanged in a public square as a lesson to all.

The Chinese example also lets us see how even within the same society, the meaning of an act can change over time. With China's switch to capitalism, making large profits has changed from a crime punishable by death to an act to be admired.

A NEUTRAL TERM   Unlike the general public, sociologists use the term *deviance* nonjudgmentally, to refer to any act to which people respond negatively. When sociologists use this term, it does *not* mean that they are saying that an act is bad, just that people judge it negatively. To sociologists, then, *all* of us are deviants of one sort or another, since we all violate norms from time to time.

Cultural Diversity around the World

Human Sexuality in Cross-Cultural Perspectives

Human sexuality illustrates how a group's *definition* of an act, not the act itself, determines whether it will be considered deviant. Let's look at some examples reported by anthropologist Robert Edgerton (1976).

Norms of sexual behavior vary so widely around the world that what is considered normal in one society may be considered deviant in another. In Kenya, a group called the Pokot place high emphasis on sexual pleasure, and they expect that both a husband and wife will reach orgasm. If a husband does not satisfy his wife, he is in trouble—especially if she thinks that his failure is because of adultery. If this is so, the wife and her female friends will sneak up on her husband when he is asleep. The women will tie him up, shout obscenities at him, beat him, and then urinate on him. As a final gesture of their contempt, before releasing him they will slaughter and eat his favorite ox. The husband's hours of painful humiliation are intended to make him more dutiful concerning his wife's conjugal rights.

People can also become deviants for following their group's ideal norms instead of its real norms. As with many groups, the Zapotec Indians of Mexico profess that sexual relations should take place exclusively between husband and wife. However, the Zapotec also have a covert norm, an unspoken understanding, that married people will have affairs but that they will be discreet about them. In one Zapotec community, the *only* person who did not have an extramarital affair was condemned by everyone in the village. The reason was not that she did not have an affair but that she told the other wives who their husbands were sleeping with. It is an

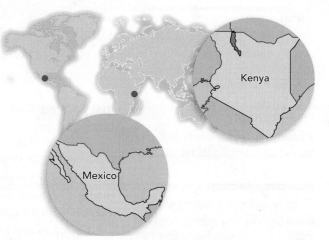

A Pokot woman in traditional dress.

interesting case; if this virtuous woman had had an affair—and kept her mouth shut—she would not have become a deviant. Clearly, real norms can conflict with ideal norms—another illustration of the gap between ideal and real culture.

For Your Consideration

→ How do the behaviors of the Pokot wives and husbands mentioned here look from the perspective of U.S. norms? What are those U.S. norms?

→ What norms did the Zapotec woman break?

→ How does cultural relativity apply to the Pokot and Zapotec? (We discussed this concept in Chapter 2.)

STIGMA To be considered deviant, a person does not even have to *do* anything. Sociologist Erving Goffman (1963) used the term **stigma** to refer to characteristics that discredit people. These include violations of norms of appearance (a facial birthmark, a huge nose, ears that stick out) and norms of ability (blindness, deafness, mental handicaps). Also included are involuntary memberships, such as being a victim of AIDS or the brother of a rapist. The stigma can become a person's master status, defining him or her as deviant. Recall from Chapter 4 that a master status cuts across all other statuses that a person occupies.

stigma

"blemishes" that discredit a person's claim to a "normal" identity

How Norms Make Social Life Possible

No human group can exist without norms: *Norms make social life possible by making behavior predictable.* What would life be like if you could not predict what others would do? Imagine for a moment that you have gone to a store to purchase milk:

Suppose the clerk says, "I won't sell you any milk. We're overstocked with soda, and I'm not going to sell anyone milk until our soda inventory is reduced."

You don't like it, but you decide to buy a case of soda. At the checkout, the clerk says, "I hope you don't mind, but there's a $5 service charge on every fifteenth customer." You, of course, are the fifteenth.

Just as you start to leave, another clerk stops you and says, "We're not working anymore. We decided to have a party." Suddenly a CD begins to blast, and everyone in the store starts to dance. "Oh, good, you've brought the soda," says a different clerk, who takes your package and passes sodas all around.

Life is not like this, of course. You can depend on grocery clerks to sell you milk. You can also depend on paying the same price as everyone else and not being forced to attend a party in a store. Why can you depend on this? Because we live in a world of norms that govern the behavior of both store clerks and ourselves. We are socialized to follow norms, to play the basic roles that society assigns to us.

Without norms, we would have social chaos. Norms lay out the basic guidelines for how we should play our roles and interact with others. In short, norms bring about **social order**, a group's customary social arrangements. Our lives are based on these arrangements, which is why deviance often is perceived as threatening: *Deviance undermines predictability, the foundation of social life.* Consequently, human groups developed a system of **social control**—formal and informal means of enforcing norms. At the center of social control are sanctions.

social order

a group's usual and customary social arrangements, on which its members depend and on which they base their lives

social control

a group's formal and informal means of enforcing its norms

negative sanction

an expression of disapproval for breaking a norm, ranging from a mild, informal reaction such as a frown to a formal reaction such as a fine or a prison sentence

positive sanction

an expression of approval for following a norm, ranging from a smile or a good grade in a class to a material reward such as a prize

Sanctions

As we discussed in Chapter 2, people do not enforce folkways strictly, but they become upset when people break mores (MO-rays). Expressions of disapproval for deviance, called **negative sanctions**, range from frowns and gossip for breaking folkways to imprisonment and death for violating mores. In general, the more seriously the group takes a norm, the harsher the penalty for violating it. In contrast, **positive sanctions**—from smiles to formal awards—are used to reward people for conforming to norms. Getting a raise is a positive sanction; being fired is a negative sanction. Getting an A in Intro to Sociology is a positive sanction; getting an F is a negative one.

Most negative sanctions are informal. You might stare if you observe someone dressed in what you consider to be inappropriate clothing, or you might gossip if a married person you know spends the night with someone other than his or her spouse. Whether you consider the breaking of a norm an amusing matter that warrants no sanction or a serious infraction that does, however, depends on your perspective. Let's suppose that a woman appears at your college graduation in a bikini. You might stare, laugh, and nudge the person next to you. If this is *your* mother, however, you are likely to feel that different sanctions are appropriate. Similarly, if it is *your* father who spends the night with an 18-year-old college freshman, you are likely to do more than gossip.

IN SUM In sociology, the term *deviance* refers to all violations of social rules, regardless of their seriousness. The term is neutral, not a judgment about the behavior. Deviance is so relative that what is deviant in one group may be conformist in another. Because of this, we must consider deviance from within a group's own framework: It is their meanings that underlie their behavior.

Competing Explanations of Deviance: Sociobiology, Psychology, and Sociology

If social life is to exist, norms are essential. So why do people violate them? To better understand the reasons, it is useful to know how sociological explanations differ from biological and psychological ones. Let's compare them.

Violating background assumptions is a common form of deviance. Although we have no explicit rule that says, "Do not put snakes through your nose," we all know that it exists (perhaps as a subcategory of "Don't do strange things in public"). Is this act also deviant for this man in Chennai, India?

BIOSOCIAL EXPLANATIONS *Sociobiologists* explain deviance by looking for answers *within* individuals. They assume that **genetic predispositions** lead people to such behaviors as juvenile delinquency and crime (Lombroso 1911; Wilson and Herrnstein 1985; Barnes and Jacobs 2013). An early explanation was that men with an extra Y chromosome (the "XYY" theory) were more likely to become criminals. Another was that people with "squarish, muscular" bodies were more likely to commit **street crime**—acts such as mugging, rape, and burglary. These theories were abandoned when research did not support them.

With advances in the study of genetics, biosocial explanations are being proposed to explain differences in crime by sex, race, social class, and age (juvenile delinquency) (Walsh and Beaver 2009; Stetler et al. 2014). The basic explanation is that over the millennia, people with certain characteristics were more likely to survive than were people with different characteristics. As a result, different groups today inherit different propensities (tendencies) for empathy, self-control, and risk-taking.

A universal finding is that in all known societies, men commit more violent crimes than women do. There are no exceptions. Here is how sociobiologists explain this. It took only a few pelvic thrusts for men to pass on their genes. After that, they could leave if they wanted to. The women, in contrast, had to carry, birth, and nurture the children. Women who were more empathetic (inclined to nurture their children) engaged in less dangerous behavior. These women passed genes for more empathy, greater self-control, and less risk-taking to their female children. As a result, all over the world, men engage in more violent behavior, which comes from their lesser empathy, lower self-control, and greater tendency for taking risks.

But behavior, whether deviant or conforming, does not depend only on genes, add the biosocial theorists (Barnes and Jacobs 2013). Our inherited propensities (the *bio* part) are modified and stimulated by our environment (the *social* part). Biosocial research holds the potential of opening a new understanding of deviance.

PSYCHOLOGICAL EXPLANATIONS Psychologists focus on abnormalities *within* the individual. Instead of genes, they examine what are called **personality disorders**. Their supposition is that deviating individuals have deviating personalities (Mayer 2007; Liu 2014) and that subconscious motives drive people to deviance.

Researchers have never found a specific childhood experience to be invariably linked with deviance. For example, some children who had "bad toilet training," "suffocating mothers," or "emotionally aloof fathers" become embezzling bookkeepers—but others become good accountants. Just as college students and police officers represent a variety of bad—and good—childhood experiences, so do deviants. Similarly, people with "suppressed anger" can become freeway snipers or military heroes—or anything else. In short, there is no inevitable outcome of any childhood experience. Deviance is not associated with any particular personality.

SOCIOLOGICAL EXPLANATIONS In contrast with both sociobiologists and psychologists, sociologists search for factors *outside* the individual. They look for social influences that "recruit" people to break norms. To account for why people commit crimes, for example, sociologists examine such external influences as socialization, membership in subcultures, and social class. *Social class*, a concept that we discuss in depth in Chapter 8, refers to people's relative standing in terms of education, occupation, and especially income and wealth.

To explain deviance, sociologists apply the three sociological perspectives—symbolic interactionism, functionalism, and conflict theory. Let's compare these three explanations.

The Symbolic Interactionist Perspective

6.2 **Apply the symbolic interactionist perspective to deviance by explaining differential association, control, and labeling.**

As we examine symbolic interactionism, it will become more evident why sociologists are not satisfied with explanations that are rooted in sociobiology or psychology. *A basic*

genetic predisposition

inborn tendencies (for example, a tendency to commit deviant acts)

street crime

crimes such as mugging, rape, and burglary

personality disorders

the view that a personality disturbance of some sort causes an individual to violate social norms *principle of symbolic interactionism is that we are thinking beings who act according to how we interpret situations.* Let's consider how our membership in groups influences how we view life and, from there, our behavior.

Differential Association Theory

THE THEORY   Going directly against the idea that biology or personality is the source of deviance, sociologists stress our experiences in groups (Deflem 2006; Chambliss 1973/2016). Consider an extreme: boys and girls who join street gangs and those who join the Scouts. Obviously, each will learn different attitudes and behaviors concerning deviance and conformity. Edwin Sutherland coined the term **differential association** to indicate this: From the *different* groups we *associate* with, we learn to deviate from or conform to society's norms (Sutherland 1924, 1947; Rendon 2014).

differential association

Edwin Sutherland's term to indicate that people who associate with some groups learn an "excess of definitions" of deviance, increasing the likelihood that they will become deviant

Sutherland's theory is more complicated than this, but he basically said that the different groups with which we associate (our "*different*(ial) association") give us messages about conformity and deviance. We may receive mixed messages, but we end up with more of one kind of message than the other (an "excess of definitions," as Sutherland put it). The end result is an imbalance—attitudes that tilt us in one direction or another. Consequently, we learn to either conform or to deviate.

FAMILIES   You know how important your family has been in forming your views toward life, so it probably is obvious to you that the family makes a big difference in whether people learn deviance or conformity. Researchers have confirmed this informal observation. Of the many studies, this one stands out: Of all prison inmates across the United States, about *half* have a father, mother, brother, sister, or spouse who has served time in prison (*Sourcebook of Criminal Justice Statistics* 2003:Table 6.0011; Glaze and Maruschak 2008:Table 11). In short, families that are involved in crime tend to set their children on a lawbreaking path.

FRIENDS, NEIGHBORHOODS, AND SUBCULTURES   Most people don't know the term *differential association*, but they do know how it works. Most parents want to move out of "bad" neighborhoods because they know that if their kids have delinquent friends, they are likely to become delinquent, too. Sociological research also supports this common observation (Miller 1958; Rendon 2014).

In some neighborhoods, violence is so woven into the subculture that even a wrong glance can mean your death ("Why ya lookin' at me?") (Gardiner and Fox 2010). If the neighbors feel that a victim deserved to be killed, they refuse to testify because "he got what was coming to him" (Kubrin and Weitzer 2003). Killing can even be viewed as honorable:

> *Sociologist Ruth Horowitz (1983, 2005), who did participant observation in a lower-class Chicano neighborhood in Chicago, discovered how the concept of "honor" propels young men to deviance. The formula is simple. "A real man has honor. An insult is a threat to one's honor. Therefore, not to stand up to someone is to be less than a real man."*
>
> *Now suppose you are a young man growing up in this neighborhood. You likely would do a fair amount of fighting, since you would interpret many things as attacks on your honor. You might even carry a knife or a gun, because words and fists wouldn't always be sufficient. Along with members of your group, you would define fighting, knifing, and shooting quite differently from the way most people do.*

Sociologist Victor Rios (2011), who did participant observation of young male African American and Latino gang members in Oakland, California, reports that these same ideas of masculinity continue. They also continue to produce high rates of violence, including homicide.

Members of the Mafia also intertwine ideas of manliness with killing. For them, *to kill is a measure of manhood*. If a Mafia member were to seduce the *capo*'s wife or girlfriend, for example, the seduction would slash at the *capo*'s manliness and honor. This would require swift, violent retaliation. The offender's body would be found in the trunk of a car somewhere with his penis stuffed in his mouth. Not all killings bring the same respect, for "the more awesome and potent the victim, the more worthy and meritorious the killer" (Arlacchi 1980).

From this example, you can again see the relativity of deviance. Killing is deviant in mainstream society, but for members of the Mafia, *not* to kill after certain of their norms are broken would be the deviant act.

DIFFERENTIAL ASSOCIATION IN THE CYBER AGE The computer has brought major changes to social interaction. I have seen people lying on the beach with friends, not interacting with those next to them, but each absorbed in communicating on a smartphone. I'm sure you have seen people walking on the sidewalk, engrossed in smartphones, barely aware of the presence of passersby. With whom are they associating?

Friends and family remain the focus of most of these communications. But the computer has also opened easy access to areas of life previously hidden and unavailable. Sociologists have begun to study how this can impact people's orientations to conformity. An example is how terrorist groups use the social media to motivate people to do violence (Castillo 2015). Differential association with the social media is new, and at this point everything about this intriguing topic is preliminary.

PRISON OR FREEDOM? As was mentioned in Chapter 3, an issue that comes up over and over again in sociology is whether we are prisoners of socialization. Symbolic interactionists stress that we are not mere pawns in the hands of others. We are not destined to think and act as our groups dictate. Rather, we *help to produce our own orientations to life*. By joining one group rather than another (differential association), for example, we help to shape the self. One college student may join a feminist group that is trying to change ideas about fraternities and rape, while another associates with women who shoplift on weekends. Their choices point them in different directions. The one who joins the feminist group may develop an even greater interest in producing social change, while the one who associates with shoplifters may become even more oriented toward criminal activities.

Control Theory

Do you ever feel the urge to do something that you know you shouldn't, something that would get you in trouble? Most of us fight temptations to break society's norms. We find that we have to stifle things inside us—urges, hostilities, raunchy desires of various sorts. And most of the time, we manage to keep ourselves out of trouble. The basic question that **control theory** tries to answer is, With the desire to deviate so common, why don't we all just "bust loose"?

THE THEORY Sociologist Walter Reckless (1973), who developed control theory, stressed that we have two control systems that work against our motivations to deviate. Our *inner controls* include our internalized morality—conscience, religious principles, ideas of right and wrong. Inner controls also include fears of punishment and the desire to be a "good" person (Hirschi

Do you understand how the definitions of deviance that Mafia members use underlie their behavior? Although their definitions are markedly different from ours, the process is the same. Shown here is the head of the Camorra, the Neapolitan version of the Mafia, as he is arrested near Naples, Italy. He was convicted of murder.

control theory

the idea that two control systems—inner controls and outer controls—work against our tendencies to deviate

The social control of deviance takes many forms. One of the most prominent is the actions of the police. This man tried to interfere with capitalism by participating in a demonstration to block Wall Street in Manhattan, New York.

1969; Gottfredson 2011). Our *outer controls* consist of people—such as family, friends, and the police—who influence us not to deviate.

As sociologist Travis Hirschi (1969) pointed out, the stronger our bonds are with society, the more effective our inner controls are. These bonds are based on *attachments* (our affection and respect for people who conform to mainstream norms), *commitments* (having a stake in society that you don't want to risk, such as your place in your family, being a college student, or having a job), *involvements* (participating in approved activities), and *beliefs* (convictions that certain actions are wrong).

This theory is really about *self*-control, said Hirschi. Where do we learn self-control? As you know, this happens during childhood, especially in the family when our parents supervise us and punish our deviant acts (Gottfredson 2011). Sometimes they use shame to keep us in line. You probably had that finger shaken at you. I certainly recall it aimed at me. Do you think that more use of shaming, discussed in the Down-to-Earth Sociology box on the next page, could help strengthen people's internal controls?

APPLYING CONTROL THEORY

Suppose that your friends invite you to go to a nightclub. When you get there, you notice that everyone seems unusually happy—almost giddy. They seem to be euphoric in their animated conversations and dancing. Your friends tell you that almost everyone here has taken the drug Ecstasy, and they invite you to take some with them.
    What do you do?

Let's not explore the question of whether taking Ecstasy in this setting is a deviant or a conforming act. This is a separate issue. Instead, concentrate on the pushes and pulls you would feel. The pushes toward taking the drug: your friends, the setting, and perhaps your curiosity. Then there are your inner controls—those inner voices of conscience and parents, perhaps of teachers, as well as your fears of arrest and the dangers of illegal drugs. There are also the outer controls—perhaps the uniformed security guard looking in your direction.

So, what *would* you decide? Which is stronger: your inner and outer controls or the pushes and pulls toward taking the drug? It is you who can best weigh these forces, since they differ with each of us. This little example puts you at the center of what control theory is all about.

Labeling Theory

Suppose for one undesirable moment that people think of you as a "whore," a "pervert," or a "cheat." (Pick one.) What power such a reputation would have—over both how others would see you and how you would see yourself. How about if you became known as "very intelligent," "truthful in everything," or "honest to the core"? (Choose one.) You can see how this type of reputation would give people different expectations of your character and behavior—and how the label would also shape the way you see yourself.

labeling theory

the view that the labels people are given affect their own and others' perceptions of them, thus channeling their behavior into either deviance or conformity

This is what **labeling theory** focuses on: the significance of reputations, how reputations or labels help set us on paths that propel us into deviance or divert us away from it.

REJECTING LABELS: HOW PEOPLE NEUTRALIZE DEVIANCE Not many of us want to be called "whore," "pervert," or "cheat." We resist negative labels, even lesser ones than these that others might try to pin on us. Did you know that some people are so successful at rejecting labels that even though they beat people up and vandalize property, they consider themselves to be conforming members of society? How do they do it?

Sociologists Gresham Sykes and David Matza (1957/1988) studied boys like this. They found that the boys used five **techniques of neutralization** to deflect society's norms.

techniques of neutralization

ways of thinking or rationalizing that help people deflect (or neutralize) society's norms

Denial of responsibility. Some boys said, "I'm not responsible for what happened because . . . ." And they were quite creative about the "becauses." Some said that what happened was an "accident." Other boys saw themselves as "victims" of society. What else could you expect? "I'm like a billiard ball shot around the pool table of life."

Down-to-Earth Sociology

Shaming: Making a Comeback?

Shaming can be effective, especially when members of a primary group use it. In some communities, where the individual's reputation was at stake, shaming was the centerpiece of the enforcement of norms. Violators were marked as deviant and held up for all the world to see. In Nathaniel Hawthorne's *The Scarlet Letter*, town officials forced Hester Prynne to wear a scarlet "A" sewn on her dress. The "A" stood for *Adulteress*. Wherever she went, Prynne had to wear this badge of shame—every day for the rest of her life.

As our society grew large and urban, the sense of community diminished, and shaming lost its effectiveness. Shaming is now starting to make a comeback.

- In Houston, Texas, a couple stole $265,000 from the crime victims' fund. The couple was sentenced to stand in front of a local mall for five hours every weekend for six years, each wearing a sign reading, "I am a thief." They also had to post a sign outside their house stating they were convicted thieves ("Woman Ordered to . . ." 2012).
- In Arizona, one sheriff parades the women prisoners in chain gangs, where they are forced to pick up street trash. He makes the men in his jail wear pink underwear. The men also wear pink striped prison uniforms while they work in chain gangs (Billeaud 2008).
- Online shaming sites have also appeared. Captured on cell phone cameras are bad drivers, older men who leer at teenaged girls, and people who don't pick up their dog's poop (Saranow 2007).
- In Spain, where one's reputation with neighbors still matters, debt collectors dress in tuxedos and top hats and walk slowly to the debtor's front door. The sight shames debtors into paying (Catan 2008).
- And as shown in the photo above, in Cleveland, Ohio, a judge ordered a woman who drove on a sidewalk in order to pass a school bus to hold a sign at the intersection reading, "Only an idiot would drive on the sidewalk to avoid a school bus" ("Woman Ordered to . . ." 2012).

Sociologist Harold Garfinkel (1956) gave the name **degradation ceremony** to an extreme form of shaming. The individual is called to account before the group, witnesses

For doing what the sign says, this woman must humiliate herself by holding the sign. The judge evidently neglected to tell the woman not to disguise herself by wearing sunglasses.

denounce him or her, the offender is pronounced guilty, and the individual is stripped of his or her identity as a group member. In some courts martial, officers who are found guilty stand at attention before their peers while others rip the insignia of rank from their uniforms. This ceremony screams that the individual is no longer a member of the group. Although Hester Prynne was not banished from the group physically, she was banished morally; her degradation ceremony proclaimed her a *moral* outcast from the community. The scarlet "A" marked her as not "one of them."

Although we don't use scarlet A's today, informal degradation ceremonies still occur. Consider what happened to this New York City police officer (Chivers 2001):

Joseph Gray had been a police officer in New York City for fifteen years. As with some of his fellow officers, alcohol and sex helped relieve the pressures of police work. After spending one afternoon drinking in a topless bar, bleary-eyed, Gray plowed his car into a vehicle carrying a pregnant woman, her son, and her sister. All three died. Gray was accused of manslaughter and drunk driving.

The New York newspapers and television stations kept hammering this story to the public. Three weeks later, as Gray left police headquarters after resigning, an angry crowd surrounded him. Gray hung his head in public disgrace as Victor Manuel Herrera, whose wife and son were killed in the crash, followed him, shouting, "You're a murderer!" (Gray was later convicted of drunk driving and manslaughter.)

For Your Consideration

→ How do you think law enforcement officials might use shaming to reduce law breaking?

→ How do you think school officials could use shaming?

→ Suppose that you were caught shoplifting at a store near where you live. Would you rather spend a week in jail with no one but your family knowing it or six hours a day for a week walking in front of the store you stole from wearing a placard that proclaims in bold red capital letters: "I AM A THIEF!" and in smaller letters says: "I am sorry for stealing from this store and making **you** pay higher prices"? Why?

degradation ceremony

a term coined by Harold Garfinkel to refer to a ritual whose goal is to remake someone's self by stripping away that individual's self-identity and stamping a new identity in its place

Denial of injury. A favorite explanation was "What I did wasn't wrong because no one got hurt." The boys would call vandalism "mischief," gang fights a "private quarrel," and stealing cars "borrowing." They might acknowledge that what they did was illegal but claim that they were "just having a little fun."

Denial of a victim. Some boys thought of themselves as avengers. Trashing a teacher's car was revenge for an unfair grade, while shoplifting was a way to get even with "crooked" store owners. In short, even if the boys did accept responsibility and admit that someone had gotten hurt, they protected their self-concept by claiming that the people "deserved what they got."

Condemnation of the condemners. Another technique the boys used was to deny that others had the right to judge them. They accused people who pointed fingers at them of being "hypocrites": The police were "on the take," teachers had "pets," and parents cheated on their taxes. In short, they said, "Who are *they* to accuse *me* of something?"

Appeal to higher loyalties. A final technique the boys used to justify their actions was to consider loyalty to the gang more important than the norms of society. They might say, "I had to help my friends. That's why I got in the fight." Not incidentally, the boy may have shot two members of a rival group, as well as a bystander!

APPLYING NEUTRALIZATION These techniques of neutralization have implications far beyond this group of boys, since it is not only delinquents who try to neutralize the norms of mainstream society. Look again at these techniques—don't they sound familiar? Consider how you might be using these same techniques. Let's take them one by one.

(1) "I was so mad that I couldn't help myself."

(2) "Who really got hurt?"

(3) "Don't you think she deserved that, after what she did?"

(4) "Who are you to talk?"

(5) "I had to help my friends—wouldn't you have done the same thing?"

All of us attempt to neutralize the moral demands of society; neutralization helps us to sleep at night.

EMBRACING LABELS: THE EXAMPLE OF OUTLAW BIKERS

Years ago, in a defensive statement, the American Motorcyclists' Association said that 99 percent of motorcyclists are law abiding citizens, that only 1 percent are thugs and criminals. The Outlaws, Hells Angels, and Warlocks then began to proudly display 1% on their uniforms (Stutzman 2014).

While most people resist labels of deviance, some embrace them. In what different ways do these photos illustrate the embracement of deviance?

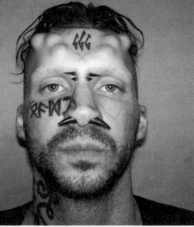

Sociologist Mark Watson (1980/2006) did participant observation with outlaw bikers. He rebuilt Harleys with them, hung around their bars and homes, and went on "runs" (trips) with them. He concluded that outlaw bikers see the world as "hostile, weak, and effeminate." Holding the conventional world in contempt, gang members pride themselves on breaking its norms and getting in trouble, laughing at death, and treating women as lesser beings whose primary value is to provide them with services—especially sex. They take pleasure in shocking people by their appearance and behavior. They pride themselves in looking "dirty, mean, and generally undesirable." Outlaw bikers also regard themselves as losers, a view that is woven into their unusual embrace of deviance.

Although most of us resist attempts to label us as deviant, it is not only outlaw bikers who revel in a deviant identity. Some teenagers make certain by their clothing, music, hairstyles, and body art that no one misses their rejection of adult norms. Their status among fellow members of a subculture—within which they are almost obsessive conformists—is vastly more important than any status outside it.

LABELS CAN BE POWERFUL   To label a teenager a delinquent can trigger a process that leads to greater involvement in deviance (Liberman 2014). Because of this, judges sometimes use *diversion*: To avoid the label of delinquent, they *divert* youthful offenders away from the criminal justice system. Instead of sending them to reform school or jail, they assign them to social workers and counselors. In the following Thinking Critically section, let's consider how powerful labeling can be.

Thinking Critically

The Saints and the Roughnecks: Labeling in Everyday Life

As you recall from Chapter 4, the Saints and the Roughnecks were high school boys. Both groups were "constantly occupied with truancy, drinking, wild parties, petty theft, and vandalism." Yet their teachers looked on the Saints as "headed for success" and the Roughnecks as "headed for failure." By the time they finished high school, not one Saint had been arrested, while the Roughnecks had been in constant trouble with the police.

Why did the members of the community perceive these boys so differently? Chambliss (1973/2016) concluded that *social class* created this split vision. As symbolic interactionists emphasize, social class is like a lens that focuses our perceptions. The Saints came from respectable, middle-class families, while the Roughnecks were from less respectable, working-class families. These backgrounds led teachers and the authorities to expect good things from the Saints but trouble from the Roughnecks. And, like the rest of us, teachers and police saw what they expected to see.

The boys' social class also affected their visibility. The Saints had automobiles, and they did their drinking and vandalism out of town. Without cars, the Roughnecks hung around their own street corners. There, their drinking and boisterous behavior drew the attention of police, confirming the negative impressions that the community already had of them.

The boys' social class also equipped them with distinct *styles of interaction*. When police or teachers questioned them, the Saints were apologetic. Their show of respect for authority elicited a positive reaction from teachers and police, allowing the Saints to escape school and legal problems. The Roughnecks, said Chambliss, were "almost the polar opposite." When questioned, they were hostile. Even when these boys tried to assume a respectful attitude, everyone could see through it. As a result, the teachers and police let the Saints off with warnings, but they came down hard on the Roughnecks.

Stereotypes, both positive and negative, help to form the perception and reaction of authorities. What stereotypes come to mind when you look at this photo?

Certainly, what happens in life is not determined by labels alone, but the Saints and the Roughnecks did live up to the labels that the community gave them. As you may recall, all but one of the Saints went on to college. One earned a Ph.D., one became a lawyer, one a doctor, and the others business managers. In contrast, only two of the Roughnecks went to college. They earned athletic scholarships and became coaches. The other Roughnecks did not fare so well. Two of them dropped out of high school, later became involved in separate killings, and were sent to prison. Of the final two, one became a local bookie, and no one knows the whereabouts of the other.

For Your Consideration

→ Did you see anything like the reactions to the Saints and the Roughnecks in your high school? If so, how did it work?

→ Besides labels, what else could have been involved in the life outcomes of these boys?

→ In what areas of life do you see the power of labels?

HOW DO LABELS WORK?   How labels work is complicated because they involve self-concepts and reactions that vary from one individual to another. To analyze this process would require a book. For our purposes, let's just note that unlike its meaning in sociology, in everyday life the term *deviant* is emotionally charged with a negative judgment. This label closes doors of opportunity. It can lock people out of conforming groups and push them into almost exclusive contact with people who have been similarly labeled.

IN SUM   Symbolic interactionists examine how people's definitions of the situation underlie their deviating from or conforming to social norms. They focus on group membership (differential association), how people balance pressures to conform and to deviate (control theory), and the significance of reputations (labeling theory).

The Functionalist Perspective

6.3   **Apply the functionalist perspective by explaining how deviance can be functional for society, how mainstream values can produce deviance (strain theory), and how social class is related to crime (illegitimate opportunities).**

When we think of deviance, its dysfunctions are likely to come to mind. Functionalists point out that deviance also has functions.

Can Deviance Really Be Functional for Society?

Most of us are upset by deviance, especially crime, and assume that society would be better off without it. In contrast to this common assumption, the classic functionalist theorist Emile Durkheim (1893/1933, 1895/1964) came to a surprising conclusion. Deviance, he said—including crime—is functional for society. Deviance contributes to the social order in three ways:

1. *Deviance clarifies moral boundaries and affirms norms.* By *moral boundaries*, Durkheim referred to a group's ideas about how people should think and act. Deviance challenges those boundaries. To call a member into account is to say, in effect, "You broke an important rule, and we cannot tolerate that." Punishing deviants affirms the group's norms and clarifies what it means to be a member of the group.

2. *Deviance encourages social unity.* To affirm the group's moral boundaries by punishing deviants creates a "we" feeling among the group's members. By saying, "You can't get away with that," the group affirms the rightness of its ways.

3. *Deviance promotes social change.* Not everyone agrees on what to do with people who push beyond the accepted ways of doing things. Some group members may even approve of the rule-breaking behavior. Boundary violations that gain enough support become new, acceptable behaviors. Deviance, then, may force a group to rethink and redefine its moral boundaries, helping groups—and whole societies—to adapt to changing circumstances.

In the Down-to-Earth Sociology box on the next page, you can see these three functions of deviance, as well as the central point of symbolic interactionism, that deviance involves a clash of competing definitions.

Down-to-Earth Sociology

Running Naked with Pumpkins on Their Heads: Deviance or Freedom of Self-Expression?

They can hardly sleep the night before Halloween, thinking about all the fun to come. When night falls, they put sneakers on their feet, their creatively carved pumpkins on their heads, and run into the street. There is nothing between the pumpkins and the sneakers—except whatever nature endowed them with (Simon 2009).

They join one another for their annual chilly, late-night run. Do the gawkers bother them? Maybe a little, but it's all in good fun. The crowd is waiting, hooting and hollering and waving them on. "Not so fast," replied the police in Boulder, Colorado, where the naked pumpkin run was held on the last day of each October. "You are breaking the law."

Although the Boulder police pride themselves on tolerance, they don't see the run in quite the same way as the participants do. "The law," they say, "clearly states that no one can show genitalia in public."

"Are women's breasts genitalia?" they've been asked. "No, those are okay," replied the police. "But watch the rest of it—uh, that is, don't watch . . . uh, that is, don't show anything else. You know what we mean. If you do, we will arrest you, and you'll end up on the sexual offenders list."

"Bad sports," replied the naked pumpkin runners, pouting just a bit. "You're trying to ruin our fun."

"We didn't make the laws," the police replied, not pleased about the many who became angry at their lack of understanding. "We just enforce them."

The police won. They made arrests. Some participants were found guilty. This scared the others, and no one was willing to organize another naked pumpkin run (Miller 2010). "I'm going to be a teacher," said one former participant. "I'd risk a hundred dollar fine for a good time, but having to register as a sex offender would trash my plans."

But the arrests did not turn out to be the end. The idea is catching on in some cities in California. Fremont and Greenlake have begun their own naked pumpkin runs.

Breaking the boundaries of conformance is part of social change. As with the naked pumpkin run, running naked, an expression of freedom and fun, can be a way of testing those boundaries. This photo was taken on an almost freezing October night in Boulder, Colorado.

For Your Consideration

→ Here is a basic principle of deviance: As people break rules, sometimes deliberately to test the boundaries of acceptable behavior, the group enforces its norms—or bends them to accommodate the deviants. How do the naked pumpkin runners illustrate this principle?

→ Can you apply control theory to the naked pumpkin runners? How about labeling theory? The conflict perspective?

Strain Theory: How Mainstream Values Produce Deviance

Functionalists argue that crime is a *natural* outcome of the conditions that people experience, not some alien element in our midst (Agnew 2012). Even mainstream values can generate crime. Consider what sociologists Richard Cloward and Lloyd Ohlin (1960) identified as the crucial problem of the industrialized world: the need to locate and train talented people—whether they were born into wealth or into poverty—so that they can take over the key technical jobs of society. When children are born, no one knows which ones will have the ability to become dentists, nuclear physicists, or engineers. To get the most talented people to compete with one another, society tries to motivate *everyone* to strive for success.

cultural goals

the objectives held out as legitimate or desirable for the members of a society to achieve

institutionalized means

approved ways of reaching cultural goals

strain theory

Robert Merton's term for the strain engendered when a society socializes large numbers of people to desire a cultural goal (such as success), but withholds from some the approved means of reaching that goal; one adaptation to the strain is crime, the choice of an innovative means (one outside the approved system) to attain the cultural goal

We are quite successful in getting almost everyone to want **cultural goals**, success of some sort, such as wealth or prestige. But we are far from successful when it comes to providing everyone access to the **institutionalized means**, the legitimate ways to reach success. People who find their way to success blocked can come to see the institutionalized goals (such as working hard or pursuing higher education) as not applying to themselves. Sociologist Robert Merton (1956, 1949/1968) referred to this situation as *anomie*, a sense of normlessness. These people experience frustration, or what Merton called *strain*.

Table 6.1 presents a summary of Merton's **strain theory**. The most common reaction to means and goals is *conformity*. Most people find at least adequate access to the institutionalized means and use them to try to reach cultural goals. They try to get a quality education, good jobs, and so on. If well-paid jobs are unavailable, they take less desirable jobs. If they can't get into Harvard or Stanford, they go to a state university. Others take night classes and go to vocational schools. In short, most people take the socially acceptable path.

Table 6.1 How People Match Their Goals to Their Means

Do They Feel the Strain That Leads to Anomie?	Mode of Adaptation	Cultural Goals	Institutionalized Means
No	Conformity	Accept	Accept
	Deviant Paths:		
Yes	1. Innovation	Accept	Reject
	2. Ritualism	Reject	Accept
	3. Retreatism	Reject	Reject
	4. Rebellion	Reject/Replace	Reject/Replace

SOURCE: Based on Merton 1968.

FOUR DEVIANT PATHS The next four responses in Table 6.1 represent deviant reactions to the gap that people find between the goals they want and their access to the institutionalized means to reach them. Let's look at each. *Innovators* are people who accept the goals of society but use illegitimate means to try to reach them. Embezzlers, for instance, accept the goal of achieving wealth, but they reject the legitimate avenues for doing so. Other examples are drug dealers, robbers, and con artists.

The second deviant path is taken by people who start out wanting the cultural goals but become discouraged and give up on achieving them. Yet they still cling to conventional rules of conduct. Merton called this response *ritualism*. Although ritualists have given up on getting ahead at work, they survive by rigorously following the rules of their job. Teachers whose idealism is shattered (who are said to suffer from "burnout"), for example, remain in the classroom, where they teach without enthusiasm. Their response is considered deviant because they cling to the job even though they have abandoned the goal, which may have been to stimulate young minds or to make the world a better place.

People who choose the third deviant path, *retreatism*, reject both the cultural goals and the institutionalized means of achieving them. Some people stop pursuing success and retreat into alcohol or drugs. Although their path to withdrawal is considerably different, women who enter a convent or men a monastery are also retreatists.

The final deviant response is *rebellion*. Convinced that their society is corrupt, rebels, like retreatists, reject both society's goals and its institutionalized means. Unlike retreatists, however, rebels seek to give society new goals, as well as new means for reaching them. Revolutionaries are the most committed type of rebels.

Merton either did not recognize *anarchy* as applying to his model or he did not think of it. In either case, the angry *anarchist* who wants to destroy society is not shown on Table 6.1. Like the retreatist and the rebel, anarchists have given up on both society's goals and means. Unlike the rebel, however, they do not want to replace the goals and means with anything. And unlike the retreatist, they do not want to withdraw and let others live in peace. Instead, they want to annihilate what exists and whoever stands in their way.

IN SUM Strain theory underscores the sociological principle that deviants are the product of society. Mainstream social values (cultural goals and institutionalized means to reach those goals) can produce strain (frustration, dissatisfaction). People who feel this strain are more likely than others to take deviant (nonconforming) paths.

Illegitimate Opportunity Structures: Social Class and Crime

Over and over in this text, you have seen the impact of social class on people's lives—and you will continue to do so in coming chapters. Let's look at how the social classes produce different types of crime.

STREET CRIME In applying strain theory, functionalists point out that industrialized societies have no trouble socializing the poor into wanting to own things. Like others, the poor are bombarded with messages urging them to buy everything from iPhones and iPads to designer jeans and new cars. Television and movies spew out images of middle-class people enjoying luxurious lives. The poor get the message—full-fledged Americans can afford society's many goods and services.

Yet, the most common route to success, education, presents a bewildering world to the poor. Run by the middle class, schools are at odds with their background. In the schools, what the poor take for granted is unacceptable, questioned, even mocked. Their speech, for example, is built around nonstandard grammar. It is also often laced with what the middle class considers obscenities. Their ideas of punctuality and their poor preparation in reading and paper-and-pencil skills also make it difficult to fit in. Facing such barriers, the poor are more likely than their more privileged counterparts to drop out of school. Educational failure, of course, slams the door on many legitimate avenues to success.

Not all doors slam shut, though. Woven into life in urban slums is what Cloward and Ohlin (1960) called an **illegitimate opportunity structure**. An alternative door to success opens: "hustles" such as robbery, burglary, drug dealing, prostitution, pimping, and gambling (Anderson 1978, 1990/2006; Duck and Rawls 2011). Pimps and drug dealers, for example, present an image of a glamorous life—people who are in control and have plenty of "easy money." For many of the poor, the "hustler" becomes a role model.

It should be easy to see, then, why street crime attracts disproportionate numbers of the poor. In the Down-to-Earth Sociology box on the next page, let's look at how gangs are part of the illegitimate opportunity structure that beckons disadvantaged youth.

illegitimate opportunity structure
opportunities for crimes that are woven into the texture of life

WHITE-COLLAR CRIME As with the poor, the *forms* of crime of the more privileged classes also match their life situation. And how different their illegitimate opportunities are! Physicians don't hold up cabbies, but they do cheat Medicare. Investment managers like Bernie Madoff don't rob gas stations, but they do run fraudulent schemes that cheat people around the world. Mugging, pimping, and burgling are not part of this more privileged world, but evading income tax, bribing public officials, and embezzling are. Sociologist Edwin Sutherland (1949) coined the term **white-collar crime** to refer to crimes that people of respectable and high social status commit in the course of their occupations.

A special form of white-collar crime is **corporate crime**, executives breaking the law in order to benefit their corporation. For example, to increase corporate profits, Sears executives defrauded $100 million from victims so poor that they had filed for bankruptcy. To avoid a criminal trial, Sears pleaded guilty. This frightened the parent companies of Macy's and Bloomingdales, which were doing similar things, and they

white-collar crime
Edwin Sutherland's term for crimes committed by people of respectable and high social status in the course of their occupations; for example, bribery of public officials, securities violations, embezzlement, false advertising, and price fixing

corporate crime
crimes committed by executives in order to benefit their corporation

Down-to-Earth Sociology

Islands in the Street: Urban Gangs in the United States

Gangs are part of urban life, but why do people join gangs?

For more than ten years, sociologist Martín Sánchez-Jankowski (1991) did participant observation of *thirty-seven* ethnic gangs: African American, Chicano, Dominican, Irish, Jamaican, and Puerto Rican. The members of these gangs in Boston, Los Angeles, and New York City earned money through gambling, arson, mugging, and armed robbery. They also sold moonshine, drugs, guns, stolen car parts, and protection. Sánchez-Jankowski ate, slept, and fought with the gangs, but by mutual agreement he did not participate in drug dealing or other illegal activities. He was seriously injured twice during the study.

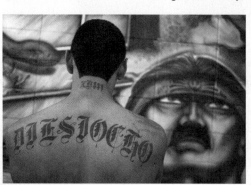

Contrary to stereotypes, Sánchez-Jankowski did not find that the motive for joining a gang was to escape a broken home (there were as many members from intact families as from broken homes) or to seek a substitute family (the same number of boys said they were close to their families as those who said they were not). Rather, the boys joined to gain access to money, sex, and drugs, to maintain anonymity in committing crimes, to get protection, and to help the community. This last reason may seem surprising, but in some neighborhoods, gangs protect residents from outsiders and spearhead political change (Kontos et al. 2003). The boys also saw the gang as an alternative to the boring, dead-end jobs held by their parents.

Neighborhood residents are ambivalent about gangs. Although they fear the violence, the gang members are the children of people who live in the neighborhood, and many of the adults once belonged to gangs. In addition, some gangs provide better protection than the police.

Particular gangs will come and go, but gangs are likely to remain part of the city. Why? As functionalists point out, gangs fulfill needs of poor youth who live on the margins of society.

For Your Consideration

→ What functions do gangs fulfill (what needs do they meet)?

→ Suppose that you have been hired as an urban planner for the city of Chicago. How could you arrange to meet the needs that gangs fulfill in ways that minimize violence and encourage youth to follow mainstream norms?

White collar crime can be deadly and yet the criminals go unpunished. Faulty ignition switches on GM cars, not fixed after the problem was known, killed over 100 people. This paralyzed child is looking at a photo of himself as a toddler before he became a victim of this crime.

settled out of court (McCormick 1999). *Not one of the corporate thieves at Sears, Macy's, or Bloomingdales spent even a day in jail.*

Citigroup, another household name, is notorious for breaking the law. In 2004, this company was caught stealing from the poor. For this crime, Citigroup paid $70 million (O'Brien 2004). In 2008, Citigroup was caught red-handed again, this time stealing money from its customers' credit cards. For these crimes, Citigroup was fined $18 million (Read 2008). Like a career criminal addicted to easy money, this company continued its lawbreaking ways. In 2014, Citigroup was fined *$7 billion* for deceiving investors in subprime mortgages (Grossman and Rexrode 2014). Another big-name criminal, Bank of America, paid *$17 billion* for its lawbreaking (Rexrode and Barrett 2014). *Not one of Citigroup's or BOA's corporate crime chiefs spent even a single day in jail.*

If these same executives had used guns to rob people on the street, you know what would have happened. White-collar crime, in contrast, is seldom taken seriously—even when those crimes result in death. In the 1930s, workers were hired to blast a tunnel through a mountain in West Virginia. The company knew the silica dust would kill the miners, and in just three months about six hundred died (Dunaway 2008). No owner went to jail. In the 1980s, Firestone executives recalled faulty tires in Saudi Arabia and Venezuela but allowed them to remain on U.S. vehicles. When their tires blew out, about two hundred Americans died (White et al. 2001). Not a single Firestone executive went to jail.

In 2001, General Motors found out that a jarring of the ignition key could shut down the car's engine and electrical system and disable the air bags. Did they fix the ignition? No. For a dozen years GM kept quiet. What did their decision makers care, as long as the profits and their bonuses kept rolling in? Their decision cost the lives of 124 people. No one went to jail. Not one person was even arrested. GM just paid a fine (Spector and Matthews 2015).

Consider this: Under federal law, causing the death of a worker by *willfully* violating safety rules is a misdemeanor punishable by up to six months in prison. Yet to harass a wild burro on federal lands is punishable by a year in prison (Barstow and Bergman 2003).

At $500 billion a year (Reiman and Leighton 2010), "crime in the suites" costs more than "crime in the streets." This refers only to dollar costs. The physical and emotional costs are another matter. For example, no one has figured out a way to compare the suffering of rape victims with the pain of elderly couples who lost their life savings to Madoff's white-collar fraud.

Fear, however, centers on street crime, especially the violent stranger who can change your life forever. As the Social Map shows, the chances of such an encounter depend on where you live. You can see that entire regions are safer—or more dangerous—than others. In general, the northern states are safer, the southern states more dangerous.

Figure 6.1 How Safe is Your State? Violent Crime in the United States

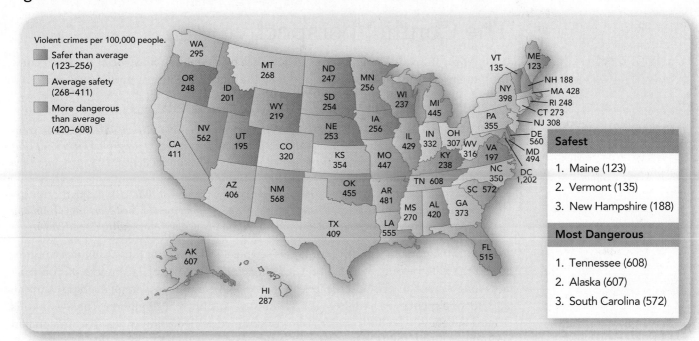

NOTE: Violent crimes are murder, rape, robbery, and aggravated assault. I estimated Minnesota's rate, based on earlier data and reduced rates since then. The chance of becoming a victim of a violent crime is five times higher in Tennessee, the most dangerous state, than in Maine, the safest state. Washington, D.C., not a state, is in a class by itself. Its rate of 1,202 is *ten* times higher than Maine's rate.

SOURCE: By the author. Based on *Statistical Abstract of the United States* 2014:Table 321.

GENDER AND CRIME.   Gender is not just something we do. Gender is a feature of society that surrounds us from birth. Gender pushes us, as male or female, into different corners in life, offering and nurturing some behaviors while it withdraws others. The opportunity to commit crime is one of the many consequences of how society sets up a *gender order*. The social changes that opened business and the professions to women also brought new opportunities for women to commit crime. From stolen property to illegal weapons, Table 6.2 on the next page shows how women have taken advantage of this new opportunity.

IN SUM   Functionalists stress that just as the social classes differ in opportunities for income and education, so they differ in opportunities for crime. As a result, street crime is greater among the lower social classes and white-collar crime greater among the higher social classes. The growing crime rates of women illustrate how changing gender roles have given women more access to what sociologists call "illegitimate opportunities."

Table 6.2 Women and Crime: What a Change

Of all those arrested, what percentage are women?			
Crime	1992	2012	Change
Burglary	9.2%	16.7%	+82%
Drunken driving	13.8%	24.5%	+78%
Car theft	10.8%	19.2%	+78%
Stolen property	12.5%	20.3%	+62%
Robbery	8.5%	13.3%	+56%
Aggravated assault	14.8%	22.7%	+53%
Larceny/theft	32.1%	43.4%	+35%
Arson	13.4%	18.1%	+35%
Illegal drugs	16.4%	20.5%	+25%
Illegal weapons	7.5%	8.2%	+9%
Forgery and counterfeiting	34.7%	37.3%	+7%
Fraud	42.1%	40.1%	−5%

SOURCE: By the author. Based on *Statistical Abstract of the United States* 2014:Table 342 and earlier years; FBI 2014:Table 33.

The Conflict Perspective

6.4 **Apply the conflict perspective to deviance by explaining how social class is related to the criminal justice system and how the criminal justice system is oppressive.**

Class, Crime, and the Criminal Justice System

> *TRW sold transistors to the federal government to use in its military satellites. The transistors failed, and the government had to shut down its satellite program. TRW said that the failure was a surprise, that it was due to some unknown defect. U.S. officials then paid TRW millions of dollars to investigate the failure.*
>
> *Then a whistle blower appeared, informing the government that TRW knew the transistors would fail in satellites even before it sold them. The government sued Northrop Grumman Corporation, which had bought TRW, and the corporation was found guilty (Drew 2009).*

What was the punishment for a crime this serious? The failure of these satellites compromised the defense of the United States. When the executives of TRW were put on trial, how long were their prison sentences? Actually, these criminals weren't even put on trial, and not one spent even a night in jail. Grumman was fined $325 million. Then—and this is hard to believe—on the same day, the government settled a lawsuit that Grumman had brought against it for $325 million. Certainly a rare coincidence.

Contrast this backdoor deal between influential people with what happens to the poor who break the law. A poor person who is caught stealing even a $1,000 car can end up serving years in prison. How can a legal system that proudly boasts "justice for all" be so inconsistent? According to conflict theory, this question is central to the analysis of crime and the **criminal justice system**—the police, courts, and prisons that deal with people who are accused of having committed crimes. Let's see what conflict theorists have to say about this.

The Criminal Justice System as an Instrument of Oppression

Conflict theorists regard power and social inequality as the main characteristics of society. The criminal justice system, they stress, is a tool designed by the powerful to maintain their power and privilege. For the poor, in contrast, the law is an instrument of oppression (Davis and Sorensen 2013; Chambliss 2000, 1973/2016). The idea that the law operates impartially to bring justice to all, they say, is a cultural myth promoted by the capitalist class to secure the cooperation of the poor in their own oppression.

criminal justice system

the system of police, courts, and prisons set up to deal with people who are accused of having committed a crime

The working poor and those below them pose a special threat to the power elite. Receiving the least of society's material rewards, they hold the potential to rebel and overthrow the current social order (see Figure 8.5 on page 236). To prevent this, the law comes down hard on the poor and the underclass. They are the least rooted in society. They have only low-paying, part-time, or seasonal work—if they have jobs at all. Because their street crimes threaten the social order that keeps the elite in power, they are punished severely. From this class come *most* of the prison inmates in the United States.

The criminal justice system, then, does not focus on the executives of corporations and the harm they do through manufacturing unsafe products, creating pollution, and manipulating prices. Yet the violations of the capitalist class cannot be ignored totally; if they become too extreme, they might outrage the working class, encouraging them to rise up and revolt. To prevent this, a flagrant violation by a member of the capitalist class is occasionally prosecuted. The publicity given to the case provides evidence of the "fairness" of the criminal justice system, which helps to stabilize the social system—and keeps the powerful in their positions of privilege.

The powerful are usually able to bypass the courts altogether, appearing instead before an agency that has no power to imprison (such as the Federal Trade Commission). These agencies are directed by people from wealthy backgrounds who sympathize with the intricacies of the corporate world. It is they who oversee most cases of price manipulation, insider stock trading, violations of fiduciary duty, and so on. Is it surprising, then, that the typical sanction for corporate crime is a token fine?

"If you want justice, it's two hundred dollars an hour. Obstruction of justice runs a bit more."

The cartoonist's hyperbole makes an excellent commentary on the social class disparity of our criminal justice system. Not only are the crimes of the wealthy not as likely to come to the attention of authorities as are the crimes of the poor, but when they do, the wealthy can afford legal expertise to wiggle around the law that the poor cannot.

In early capitalism, children worked alongside adults. At that time, just as today, most street criminals came from the *marginal working class*, as did these boys who worked 14 hours a day in the coal mines of Pennsylvania. This photo is from 1908.

IN SUM Conflict theorists stress that the power elite developed the legal system to stabilize the social order. They use it to control the poor, who pose a threat to the powerful. The poor hold the potential of rebelling as a group, which could dislodge the power elite from their place of privilege. To prevent this, the criminal justice system makes certain that heavy penalties come down on the poor.

Reactions to Deviance

6.5 Be able to discuss street crimes and imprisonment, the three-strikes laws, the decline in violent crime, recidivism, bias in the death penalty, the medicalization of deviance, and the need for a more humane approach.

Whether it involves cheating on a sociology quiz or holding up a liquor store, any violation of norms invites reaction. Before we turn to reactions to violent crimes, let's consider reactions to sexting in the Down-to-Earth Sociology box below.

Street Crime and Prisons

Here's a horrendous statistic for you to consider: The United States has only 5 percent of the world's population but about 25 percent of the world's prisoners (Brayne 2013). One

Down-to-Earth Sociology

Sexting: Getting on the Phone Isn't What It Used to Be

The eighth-grade girls were having a sleepover. As they talked about how they could impress the boys they were interested in, they came up with an idea. They took off their clothes, covered themselves with whipped cream, and sent pictures to boys of themselves licking it off.

It seemed like a good idea at the time, but the girls didn't think so the next day. As they walked to class, the boys stood around leering, laughing, and holding up the girls' images on their cell phones.

The boys who received the images had forwarded them to their friends—who forwarded them to their friends, and so on.

Even some parents received the photos on their cell phones, and, as they say, then all hell broke loose.

Sexting can be fun. It can also be dangerous. If a photo is of an underage person, an individual can be convicted of a sexual offense against a child. If only adults are involved, sexting can still be risky. This man, Anthony Weiner, might have been mayor of New York City, but the voters did not like his transmitting suggestive photos of himself to women.

If two people over the age of 18 sext, exchange sexually explicit electronic messages or images of themselves, this is a matter between them. If someone forwards those images, it is still a problem between those individuals. But since those under the age of 18 are legally minors, the law classifies their sexually explicit photos as child pornography. This means that both those who send the messages and those who pass them on to others are guilty of producing or disseminating child pornography. Anyone convicted of this form of sexting will have to register as sex offenders for decades!

"You're all getting excited about nothing," said one 17-year-old girl. "You're overlooking the positive side to sexting. You can't get pregnant from it, and you can't transmit STDs. It's a kind of safe sex."

Lawmakers and enforcers, who are grappling with sexting, don't agree. Some think that the current laws are just fine, but the general consensus seems to be that applying child pornography laws isn't the right road to follow. Most proposals for legal change center around educational programs and community service for minors who transmit images of "sexually explicit acts." Then, of course, there is the more severe penalty—taking their cell phones away.

For Your Consideration

→ Do you think there should be any sanctions for sexting by minors, or should this be a private matter, much as it is for adults?

→ If you think there should be sanctions, which ones? The same ones for sexters age 13 and age 17? The same sanctions for nudity or for the depiction of sexual intercourse?

of 35 adults, 7 million Americans, is on probation or parole or in jail or prison (*Statistical Abstract* 2014:Tables 363, 364, 369). No other country comes close to these totals.

To see how the number of prisoners has surged, look at Figure 6.2. Arrests and convictions have increased at such a torrid pace that the states and federal government haven't been able to build prisons fast enough to hold all of their incoming prisoners. To keep up, they have hired corporations to operate private prisons for them. About 133,000 prisoners are held in these "for-profit" prisons (Carson 2014).

As you can see from Figure 6.2, the number of prisoners peaked in 2009 and has dropped slightly since then. With the decline in violent crime, which we will review shortly, this decrease is likely to be permanent. The broken line on this figure gives a rough indication of what the future might look like.

Who are these prisoners? Let's compare them with the U.S. population. As you look at Table 6.3 on the next page, several things may strike you. Close to half (46 percent) of all prisoners are younger than 35, and almost all the prisoners are men. Then there is this remarkable statistic: Although African Americans make up just 12.5 percent of the U.S. population, there are more African American prisoners than white prisoners. On any given day, *one out of every eight* African American men in their twenties is in jail or prison. For Latinos, the rate is one of twenty-six; for whites, one of one hundred (Warren et al. 2008).

Figure 6.2 How Much Is Enough? The Explosion in the Number of U.S. Prisoners

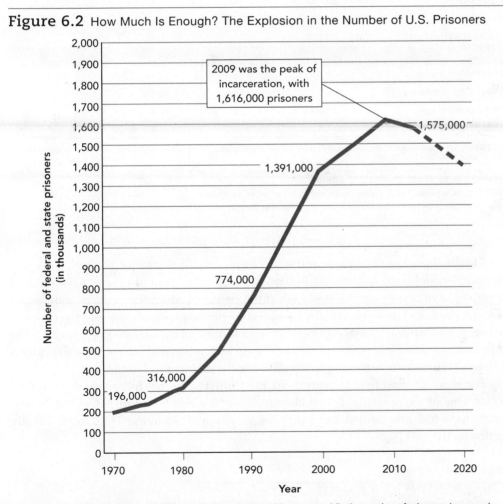

NOTE: Between 1970 and 2013, the U.S. population increased 55 percent, while the number of prisoners increased 800 percent, *fifteen times faster* than the population. If the number of prisoners had grown at the same rate as the U.S. population, we would have about 304,000 prisoners, about one-fifth of today's total. Or if the U.S. population had increased at the same rate as that of U.S. prisoners, the U.S. population would be 1,640,000,000—more than the population of China.

SOURCE: By the author. Based on *Statistical Abstract of the United States* 1995:Table 349; 2014:Tables 2, 6, 363; Carson 2014. The broken line is the author's estimate.

Table 6.3 Comparing Prison Inmates with the U.S. Population

Characteristics	Percentage of Prisoners with These Characteristics	Percentage of U.S. Population Age 18 and Over with These Characteristics[a]
Age		
18–24	13.4%	13.10%
25–34	32.6%	17.6%
35–44	26.4%	16.9%
45–54	19.2%	18.4%
55 and older	8.2%	34.0%
Race-Ethnicity		
African American	38.1%	12.5%
White	34.3%	66.1%
Latino	21.2%	14.8%
Other[b]	6.4%	6.5%
Sex		
Male	93.2%	49.2%
Female	6.8%	50.8%
Marital Status[c]		
Never married	54.7%	27.6%
Married	21.9%	56.0%
Divorced and Widowed	23.0%	16.4%
Education		
Less than high school	30.6%	12.4%
High school graduate	45.8%	30.4%
Some college	18.8%	26.3%
College graduate	4.8%	30.9%

SOURCE: By the author. Based on *Sourcebook of Criminal Justice Statistics* 2013:Tables 6.0001, 6.45, 6.81. *Statistical Abstract of the United States* 2014:Tables 11, 59, 243, 366.

[a]Because this column refers to Americans age 18 and over, the percentages will not agree with other totals in this book. For education, the percentages are based on Americans age 25 and over.

[b]By default, the remainder after *Sourcebook* lists African American, white, and Hispanic.

[c]The marital status of prisoners applies only to inmates on death row. Data not available for other inmates.

Finally, note how marriage and education—two of the major ways that society "anchors" people into mainstream behavior—keep people out of prison. About half of prisoners have never married. And look at the power of education, a major component of social class. As I mentioned earlier, social class funnels some people into the criminal justice system while it diverts others away from it. You can see how people who drop out of high school have a high chance of ending up in prison—and how unlikely it is for a college graduate to have this unwelcome destination in life.

For about the past twenty years or so, the United States has followed a "get tough" policy. One of the most significant changes was "three-strikes-and-you're-out" laws, which have had unintended consequences, as you will see in the Thinking Critically section on the next page.

The Decline in Violent Crime

As you have seen, judges have put more and more people in prison, and legislators have passed the three-strikes laws. As these changes took place, the crime rate dropped sharply. Sociologists conclude that getting tough on criminals reduced crime, but it is only

Thinking Critically

What Should We Do About Repeat Offenders? "Three Strikes" Laws

In the 1980s, violent crime soared. Americans grew fearful. When a rapist–molester on parole abducted, raped, and killed a 12-year-old, the public was outraged. In the midst of fear and outrage, politicians passed "three-strikes" laws: Anyone convicted of a third felony receives a mandatory sentence. California's version required twenty-five years to life.

- In Los Angeles, a 64-year-old man who stole a package of cigarettes was sentenced to twenty-five-years-to-life in prison (Phillips 2013).
- Another California man passed a bad check for $94. He was sentenced to twenty-five years to life (Jones 2008).
- A Florida man stored cocaine in his girlfriend's attic. He was sentenced to fifteen years in prison, but his 27-year-old girlfriend, a mother of three, was sent to prison for life. The judge said the sentence was unjust, but he had no choice (Tierney 2012).
- In New York City, a man who was about to be sentenced for selling crack said to the judge, "I'm only 19. This is terrible." He then hurled himself out of a courtroom window, plunging to his death sixteen stories below (Cloud 1998).

A sort of Oops! moment followed. This isn't quite what was intended. The public had in mind men convicted of a third brutal rape or a third murder being sent to prison

for life. In their haste to pass the three-strikes laws, however, the politicians neglected to limit them to *violent* crimes.

With the longer sentences taking many repeat offenders off the street, few felt rushed to change these laws. Judges, though, began to complain that these laws prevented them from taking into consideration basic circumstances that surround a crime. Eventually, the gap between justice and unfair sentencing became too great to bear, and in 2012 California softened its draconian law, limiting three-strikes to violent crimes. This made several thousand shoplifters, petty thieves, and the like eligible for release, but kept the murderers, child molesters, and rapists behind bars.

For Your Consideration

Apply the symbolic interactionist, functionalist, and conflict perspectives to the passage of the three-strikes laws and to their revision.

→ For *symbolic interactionism*, how does the meaning of these laws depend on where someone is in the criminal justice system?

→ For *functionalism*, what are some of the functions (benefits) of three-strikes laws? Their dysfunctions?

→ For the *conflict perspective*, which groups are in conflict? Who has the power to enforce their will on others?

---

one of the reasons that violent crime dropped (Baumer and Wolff 2013). Other reasons include higher employment, less illegal drug use, a lower birth rate, and even abortion. There are even those who say that the best explanation is the elimination of lead in gasoline (Drum 2013). We can rule out employment: When the unemployment rate shot up with the economic crisis, the lower crime rates continued (Oppel 2011). This matter is not yet settled. We'll see what answers future research brings.

Recidivism

If a goal of prisons is to teach their clients to stay away from crime, they are colossal failures. We can measure their failure by the **recidivism rate**—the percentage of released prisoners who are rearrested. Within just three years of their release, two out of three (68 percent) are rearrested, and half are back in prison (Durose et al. 2014). Looking at Figures 6.3 and 6.4, it is safe to conclude that prisons fail to teach people that crime doesn't pay.

recidivism rate
the percentage of released convicts who are rearrested

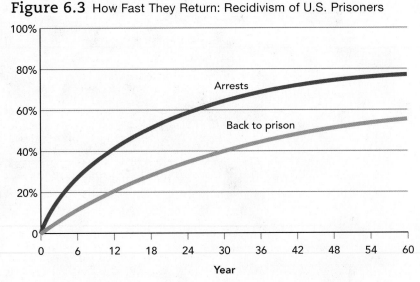

Figure 6.3 How Fast They Return: Recidivism of U.S. Prisoners

SOURCE: Modified by the author from Figure 1 of Durose et al. 2014.

Figure 6.4 Recidivism by Type of Crime

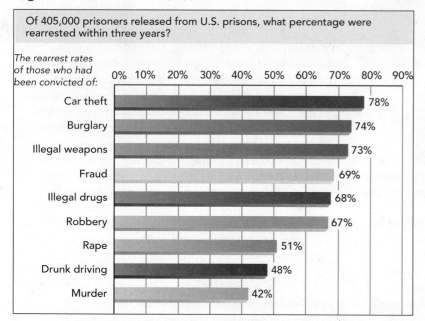

Of 405,000 prisoners released from U.S. prisons, what percentage were rearrested within three years?

The rearrest rates of those who had been convicted of:

- Car theft — 78%
- Burglary — 74%
- Illegal weapons — 73%
- Fraud — 69%
- Illegal drugs — 68%
- Robbery — 67%
- Rape — 51%
- Drunk driving — 48%
- Murder — 42%

SOURCE: By the author. Based on Durose et al. 2014:Table 8.

capital punishment

the death penalty

The Death Penalty and Bias

As you know, **capital punishment**, the death penalty, is the most extreme measure the state takes. As you also know, the death penalty arouses both impassioned opposition and support. Advances in DNA testing have given opponents of the death penalty a strong argument: Innocent people have been sent to death row, and some have been executed. Others are just as passionate about retaining the death penalty. They point to such crimes as those of the serial killers discussed in the Down-to-Earth Sociology box on the next page.

GEOGRAPHY It is clear that the death penalty is not administered evenly. Consider geography: You can see from the Social Map below that where people commit murder greatly affects their chances of being put to death.

SOCIAL CLASS The death penalty also shows social class bias. As you know from news reports, it is rare for a rich person to be sentenced to death. Although the government does not collect statistics on social class and the death penalty, this common observation is borne out by the education of the prisoners on death row. Half of the prisoners on death row (52 percent) have not finished high school (*Bureau of Justice Statistics* 2014).

GENDER There is also gender bias in the death penalty. Gender bias is so strong that it is almost unheard of for a woman to be sentenced to death, much less executed. Although women commit 9.6 percent of the murders, they make up only 1.8 percent of death row inmates (*Sourcebook of Criminal Justice Statistics* 2009:Table 6.81). Even on death row, the gender

Figure 6.5 Executions in the United States

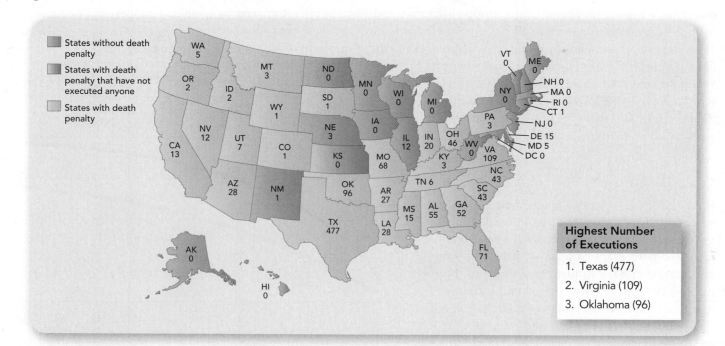

- States without death penalty
- States with death penalty that have not executed anyone
- States with death penalty

WA 5
OR 2
ID 2
MT 3
WY 1
ND 0
SD 1
MN 0
WI 0
MI 0
NV 12
UT 7
CO 1
NE 3
IA 0
IL 12
IN 20
OH 46
CA 13
AZ 28
NM 1
KS 0
MO 68
KY 3
WV 0
VA 109
TN 6
NC 43
OK 96
AR 27
SC 43
MS 15
AL 55
GA 52
TX 477
LA 28
FL 71
AK 0
HI 0
VT 0
NY 0
PA 3
ME 0
NH 0
MA 0
RI 0
CT 1
NJ 0
DE 15
MD 5
DC 0

Highest Number of Executions
1. Texas (477)
2. Virginia (109)
3. Oklahoma (96)

NOTE: Executions since 1977, when the death penalty was restored. The executions in states without the death penalty occurred before those states banned the death penalty.

SOURCE: By the author. Based on *Statistical Abstract of the United States* 2014:Table 368; Jones 2014.

Down-to-Earth Sociology

The Killer Next Door: Serial Murderers in Our Midst

Here is my experience with serial killers. As I was watching television one night, I was stunned by the images coming from Houston, Texas. Television cameras showed the police digging up dozens of bodies from under a boat storage shed. A few days later, I drove from Illinois, where I was teaching, to Houston, where 33-year-old Dean Corll had befriended Elmer Wayne Henley and David Brooks, two teenagers from broken homes. Together, they had killed twenty-seven boys. Elmer and David would pick up young hitchhikers and deliver them to Corll to rape and kill. They even brought him their neighbors and high school classmates.

On a city map, I plotted the locations of the homes of the local murder victims. Many clustered around the homes of the teenage killers. I then talked to one of Elmer's neighbors, as he was painting his front porch. His 15-year-old son had gone to get a haircut one Saturday morning. That was the last time he saw his son alive. The police refused to investigate. They insisted that his son had run away.

I decided to spend my coming sabbatical writing a novel on this case. To get into the minds of the killers, I knew that I would have to "become" them day after day. Corll kept a piece of plywood in his apartment. In each of its corners, he had cut a hole. He and the boys would spread-eagle their handcuffed victims on this board and torture them for hours. Sometimes, they would even pause to order pizza. I began to be concerned about immersing myself in torture and human degradation. Would I be the same person afterward? I decided not to write the book.

The three killers led double lives so successfully that their friends and family were unaware of their criminal activities. Henley's mother swore to me that her son couldn't possibly be guilty—he was a good boy. Some of Elmer's high school friends told me that his being involved in homosexual rape and murder was ridiculous—he was interested only in girls. I was interviewing them in Henley's bedroom, and for proof, they pointed to a pair of girls' panties that were draped across a lamp shade.

Ted Bundy is shown here on trial in Miami for killing two women, both college students. He often used charm and wit to win the confidence of his victims. Like most serial killers, he blended in with society. Bundy was executed for his murders.

Serial murder is killing three or more victims in separate events. The murders may occur over several days, weeks, or years. The elapsed time between murders distinguishes serial killers from *mass murderers*, those who do their killing all at once. Here are some infamous examples:

- During the 1960s and 1970s, Ted Bundy, shown below, raped and killed dozens of women in four states.
- Between 1974 and 1991, Dennis Rader killed ten people in Wichita, Kansas. Rader had written to the newspapers, proudly calling himself the BTK (Bind, Torture, and Kill) strangler.
- In the late 1980s and early 1990s, Aileen Wuornos hitchhiked along Florida's freeways. She killed seven men after having sex with them.
- In 2009, Anthony Sowell of Cleveland, Ohio, was discovered living with eleven decomposing bodies of women he had raped and strangled (UPI 2009).
- The serial killer with the most victims appears to be Virginia de Souza, a physician in Brazil, who, between 2006 and 2014, is thought to have killed 320 patients to "free up the wards." She injected her victims with muscle relaxants and then cut off their air supply (Roper 2013).

Is serial murder more common now than it used to be? Not likely. In the past, police departments had little communication with one another, and seldom did anyone connect killings in different jurisdictions. Today's more efficient communications and investigative techniques, coupled with DNA matching, make it easier for the police to know when a serial killer is operating in an area. Part of the perception that there are more serial killers today is also due to ignorance of our history: In our frontier past, for example, serial killers went from ranch to ranch.

For Your Consideration

→ Do you think that serial killers should be given the death penalty? Why or why not?

→ How does your social location influence your opinion on the death penalty?

serial murder

the killing of several victims in three or more separate events

Figure 6.6 Who Gets Executed? Gender Bias in Capital Punishment

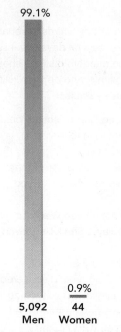

99.1%

0.9%

5,092   44
Men   Women

SOURCE: By the author. Based on *Statistical Abstract of the United States* 2014:Table 367.

bias continues: Of those condemned to death, the state is more likely to execute a man than a woman. As Figure 6.6 shows, only 0.9 percent of the 5,136 prisoners executed in the United States since 1930 have been women. Rather than gender bias, perhaps the chances of being sentenced to death or being executed reflect the women's previous offenses and the relative brutality of their murders. Not likely, but maybe. We need research to find out.

RACE–ETHNICITY At one point, racial-ethnic bias was so flagrant that the U.S. Supreme Court put a stop to the death penalty. Donald Partington (1965), a lawyer in Virginia, was shocked by the bias he saw in the courtroom, and he decided to document it. He found that 2,798 men had been convicted for rape and attempted rape in Virginia between 1908 and 1963—56 percent whites and 44 percent blacks. For rape, 41 men had been executed. For attempted rape, 13 had been executed. *All those executed were black.* Not one of the whites was executed.

After listening to evidence like this, in 1972 the Supreme Court ruled in *Furman v. Georgia* that the death penalty, as applied, was unconstitutional. The execution of prisoners stopped—but not for long. The states wrote new laws, and in 1977, they again began to execute prisoners. Since the death penalty was reinstituted, 62 percent of those put to death have been white and 38 percent African American (*Statistical Abstract* 2014:Table 367). (Latinos are evidently counted as whites in this statistic.) In North Carolina, African Americans who kill whites are three times as likely to be sentenced to death as are whites who kill African Americans (Radelet and Pierce 2011). We don't have this statistic for other states.

The official responses to deviance that we have discussed assume that the state (government) is functioning. What happens when the state breaks down? Let's consider this in the following Thinking Critically section.

Thinking Critically

Vigilantes: When the State Breaks Down

Many of us chafe under the coercive nature of the state: the IRS, Homeland Security, the NSA, the many police agencies from the CIA and FBI to who knows how many other groups that go by three capital letters. Little cameras litter society, seemingly recording our every move.

We certainly have given up a lot of freedoms—and we are likely to give up many more in the name of security. We can chafe and complain all we want, but as stressed at the end of the preceding chapter, this wave of surveillance is seemingly unstoppable.

There is another side to what is happening. The guns that the many uniformed and plainclothes men and women are carrying can also be aimed at us. But for now, they bring security. They indicate that the state is operating; perhaps overreacting, but operating nonetheless.

What happens when the state fails, when the men and women who are authorized to carry guns don't protect citizens from the bad guys who carry guns?

One reaction is vigilantism, people taking the law into their own hands. Remember what we call the Wild West? Citizens armed themselves, formed posses, chased the bad guys, and dispensed quick justice at the end of a rope. You've seen the movies.

And this is what is happening in Mexico right now.

From the local to the national, the Mexican government has failed. The drug lords have infiltrated the police and the politicians. The most wanted drug lord in Mexico, "El Chapo" Guzman, who headed the feared Sinaloa cartel, would drive openly into the state capital in an armored SUV. The police could never see him. Guzman would even meet with the state governor (Johnson 2014). The man who directed Mexico's national drug enforcement agency was on the drug lords' payroll. Army generals take money to protect drug deals. They even let dealers use army vehicles to transport drugs.

It is difficult to overstate the extent of corruption in Mexico, but let's add a couple more shocking findings. A secret *billion* dollar bank account was traced to the brother of Mexico's president. (But why rush to judgment? Perhaps some taxi driver gave the president's brother a billion-dollar tip because he was a good passenger.) In Gomez Palacio, prison administrators let prisoners out so they could kill members of a rival drug gang. They even loaned the prisoners their guns and cars to do the killing. Afterward, the men dutifully returned to the prison, turned in the cars and guns, and went back to their cells. Incredible, I know. But true.

The death toll is shocking. Shooting deaths by the police, the army, and the gangsters run over 100,000. In one town, Iguala in the state of Guerrero, the mayor is accused of ordering his police to arrest forty-three students and turn them over to the local drug cartel to be killed (de Cordoba and Montes 2014).

The Mexican people have begun to take the law into their own hands. In the state of Guerrero, country folk have put on masks, grabbed their old hunting rifles, raided the homes of drug dealers, and put them in makeshift jails. They have blockaded the roads leading to their little towns. They won't let drug dealers, or any strangers, in. They won't even let the federal police, the state police, or the army in. The official "enforcers of the law" are too corrupt, they say. They trust only the neighbors they grew up with.

The state can't tolerate competition in the use of violence. It claims this right for itself. A conflict, then, between the vigilantes and the state is inevitable. And it has begun. In the state of Michoacan, the people took up arms against the Knights Templar, the drug cartel that is terrorizing their area. As the citizen militias were gaining the upper hand, the military stepped in to stop them. This confused the people, who asked why the military was trying to disarm them and not the drug cartel. "First we must disarm you, so there won't be bloodshed," the military replied. "Then we can go after the drug dealers."

The vigilantes asked if they could accompany the police and military as they pursue the drug cartel. The reply, "No, that's our job. You go home."

This didn't make sense to the people, and they resisted. The military killed several of the citizens.

"Enough is enough!" This physician (center) in Michoacan, Mexico, organized vigilantes to replace the corrupt police. The police arrested him for carrying illegal guns.

The people still don't understand. The state isn't doing its job, their lives are in danger, and the local citizens think they know how to take care of the problem.

The reaction of the local police, the honest ones? "Maybe the citizens can do something about the problem. We can't. If we try, the drug dealers will go to our homes and kill our families. They don't know who these masked men are."

Based on Sheridan 1998; Malkin 2010; Archibold 2012; Casey 2013; Casey and Harrup 2014; Johnson 2014; Perez and Cordoba 2014.

For Your Consideration

→ We don't yet know the consequences of this incipient vigilante movement in Mexico. But what else can the citizens do?

→ How much freedom are you willing to give up to have security?

→ Where is a balance between personal freedom and state security?

The Trouble with Official Statistics

We must be cautious when it comes to official crime statistics. According to official statistics, working-class boys are more delinquent than middle-class boys. Yet, as we have seen, who actually gets arrested for what is influenced by social class, a point that has far-reaching implications. As symbolic interactionists point out, the police follow a symbolic system as they enforce the law. Ideas of "typical criminals" and "typical good citizens" permeate their work. The more a suspect matches their stereotypes of a lawbreaker (which they call "criminal profiles"), the more likely that person is to be arrested. **Police discretion**, the decision whether to arrest someone or even to ignore a matter, is a routine part of police work. Official crime statistics reflect these and many other biases.

Crime statistics do not have an objective, independent existence. They are not like oranges that you pick out in a grocery store. Rather, they are a human creation. If the police enforce laws strictly, crime statistics go up. Loosen up the enforcement, and crime

police discretion

the practice of the police, in the normal course of their duties, to either arrest or ticket someone for an offense or to overlook the matter statistics go down. New York City provides a remarkable example. To keep their crime statistics low, the police keep some crime victims waiting in the police station for hours. The victims give up and leave, and the crime doesn't enter their official records. In other cases, the police simply listen to crime victims but make no written record of the crime (Baker and Goldstein 2011). It is likely that such underreporting occurs in most places.

As a personal example, someone took my mailbox (rural, located on the street). When I called and reported the theft, a police officer arrived promptly. He was incredibly friendly. He looked around and spotted the mailbox in the ditch. He retrieved it and then personally restored it to its post. He even used his tools to screw it back on. He then said, "I'm chalking this one up to the wind." I didn't object. I knew what he was doing. No crime to report, no paperwork for him, and the area has one less incident to go into the crime statistics.

The Medicalization of Deviance: Mental Illness

When the woman drove her car into the river, drowning her two small children strapped to their little car seats, people said that she had "gone nuts," "went bonkers," and just plain "lost it."

medicalization of deviance

to make deviance a medical matter, a symptom of some underlying illness that needs to be treated by physicians

medicalization

the transformation of a human condition into a medical matter to be treated by physicians

People whose behaviors violate norms are sometimes called mentally ill. "Why else would they do such things?" is a common response to deviant behaviors that we don't understand. Mental illness is a label that contains the assumption that there is something wrong "within" people that "causes" their disapproved behavior. The surprise with this man, who changed his legal name to "Scary Guy," is that he speaks at schools across the country, where he promotes acceptance, awareness, love, and understanding.

NEITHER MENTAL NOR ILLNESS?   When people cannot find a satisfying explanation for why someone does something weird or is "like that," they often say that a "sickness in the head" is causing the unacceptable behavior. To *medicalize* something is to make it a medical matter, to classify it as a form of illness that properly belongs in the care of physicians. For the past hundred years or so, especially since the time of Sigmund Freud (1856–1939), the Viennese physician who founded psychoanalysis, there has been a growing tendency toward the **medicalization of deviance**. In this view, deviance, including crime, is a sign of mental sickness. Rape, murder, stealing, cheating, and so on are external symptoms of internal disorders, consequences of a confused or tortured mind, one that should be treated by mental health experts.

Thomas Szasz (1920–2012), a renegade in his profession of psychiatry, disagreed. He (1996, 1998, 2010) argued that what are called *mental illnesses are neither mental nor illnesses. They are simply problem behaviors.* Szasz broke these behaviors for which we don't have a ready explanation into two causes: physical illness and learned deviance.

Some behaviors that are called "mental illnesses" have physical causes. That is, something in an individual's body leads to unusual perceptions or behavior. For example, a chemical imbalance in the brain can cause depression. The individual's behaviors—crying, long-term sadness, or lack of interest in family, work, school, or grooming—are symptoms of this physical problem, one that can be treated by drugs.

Another example is attention-deficit hyperactivity disorder (ADHD), a "mental illness" that seems to have come out of nowhere (Saul 2014). As Szasz said, "No one explains where this disease came from or why it didn't exist 50 years ago. No one is able to diagnose it with objective tests." A teacher or parent complains that a child is misbehaving, and a psychiatrist or doctor says the child is suffering from ADD. Misbehaving children have been a problem throughout history, but now, with doctors looking to expand their territory, this problem behavior has become a sign of "mental illness" that they can treat.

All of us have troubles. Some of us face a constant barrage of problems as we go through life. Most of us continue the struggle, perhaps encouraged by relatives and friends and motivated by job, family responsibilities, religious faith, or life goals. Even when the odds seem hopeless, we carry on, not perfectly, but as best we can.

Some people, however, fail to cope well with life's challenges. Overwhelmed, they become depressed, uncooperative, or hostile. Some strike out at others, while some, in Merton's term, become retreatists and withdraw into their homes, refusing to come out. These may be inappropriate ways of coping, stressed Szasz, but they are *behaviors, not mental illnesses*. Szasz concluded that "mental illness" is a myth foisted on a naive public. Our medical profession uses pseudoscientific jargon that people don't understand so it can expand its area of control and force nonconforming people to accept society's definitions of "normal."

Szasz's controversial claims force us to look anew at the forms of deviance that we usually refer to as mental illness. To explain behavior that people find bizarre, he directs our attention not to disorders deep within the "subconscious" but, instead, to how people learn those behaviors. To ask, "What is the origin of someone's inappropriate or bizarre behavior?" then becomes similar to asking "Why do some women steal?" "Why do some men rape?" "Why do some teenagers cuss their parents and stalk out of the room?" The answers depend on those people's particular experiences in life, not on an illness in their mind. Some sociologists find Szasz's renegade analysis refreshing because it points us away from illnesses of the mind to *social experiences*. Others, however, are uncomfortable with it, and some disagree wholeheartedly. Regardless of these disagreements, Szasz's analysis applies not just to mental illness but also to deviance in general.

THE HOMELESS MENTALLY ILL

Jamie was sitting on a low wall surrounding the landscaped courtyard of an exclusive restaurant. She appeared unaware of the stares elicited by her layers of mismatched clothing, her matted hair and dirty face, and the shopping cart that overflowed with her meager possessions.

After sitting next to Jamie for a few minutes, I saw her point to the street and concentrate, slowly moving her finger horizontally. I asked her what she was doing.

"I'm directing traffic," she replied. "I control where the cars go. Look, that one turned right there," she said, now withdrawing her finger.

"Really?" I said.

After a while she confided that her cart talked to her.

"Really?" I said again.

"Yes," she replied. "You can hear it, too." At that, she pushed the shopping cart a bit.

"Did you hear that?" she asked.

When I shook my head, she demonstrated again. Then it hit me. She was referring to the squeaking wheels!

I nodded.

When I left Jamie, she was pointing a finger toward the sky, for, as she told me, she also controlled the flight of airplanes.

To most of us, Jamie's behavior and thinking are bizarre. They simply do not match any reality we know. Could you or I become like Jamie?

Suppose for a bitter moment that you are homeless and have to live on the streets. You have no money, no place to sleep, no bathroom. You do not know *if* you are going to eat, much less where. You have no friends or anyone you can trust. You live in constant fear of being beaten and raped. Do you think this might be enough to drive you over the edge?

Consider just the problems involved in not having a place to bathe. (Shelters are often so dangerous that many homeless people prefer to sleep in public settings.) At first, you try to wash in the restrooms of gas stations, bars, the bus station, or a shopping center. But you are dirty, and people stare when you enter and call the management when they see you wash your feet in the sink. You are thrown out and told in no uncertain terms never to come back. So you get dirtier and dirtier. Eventually, you come to think of being dirty as a fact of life. Soon, maybe, you don't even care. The stares no longer bother you—at least not as much.

Mental illness and drug/alcohol addiction are common among the homeless. This photo was taken in New York City, but it could have been taken in any large city in the United States.

No one will talk to you, and you withdraw more and more into yourself. You begin to build a fantasy life. You talk openly to yourself. People stare, but so what? They stare anyway. Besides, they are no longer important to you.

Jamie might be mentally ill. Some organic problem, such as a chemical imbalance in her brain, might underlie her behavior. But perhaps not. How long would it take you to exhibit bizarre behaviors if you were homeless—and hopeless? The point is that *living on the streets can cause mental illness*—or whatever we want to label socially inappropriate behaviors that we find difficult to classify. *Homelessness and mental illness are reciprocal:* Just as "mental illness" can cause homelessness, so the trials of being homeless, of living on cold, hostile streets, can lead to unusual thinking and behaviors.

The Need for a More Humane Approach

As Durkheim (1895/1964:68) pointed out, deviance is inevitable—even in a group of saints.

Imagine a society of saints, a perfect cloister of exemplary individuals. Crimes, properly so called, will there be unknown; but faults which appear invisible to the layman will create there the same scandal that the ordinary offense does in ordinary society.

With deviance inevitable, one measure of a society is how it treats its deviants. Our prisons certainly don't say much good about U.S. society. Filled with the poor, uneducated, and unskilled, they are warehouses of the unwanted. White-collar criminals continue to get by with a slap on the wrist while street criminals are punished severely. Some deviants, who fail to meet current standards of admission to either prison or mental hospitals, take refuge in shelters, as well as in cardboard boxes tucked away in urban recesses. Although no one has *the* answer, it does not take much reflection to see that there are more humane approaches than these.

Because deviance is inevitable, the larger issues are to find ways to protect people from deviant behaviors that are harmful to themselves or others, to tolerate behaviors that are not harmful, and to develop systems of fairer treatment for deviants. In the absence of fundamental changes that would bring about an equitable society, most efforts are, unfortunately, like putting a Band-Aid on a gunshot wound. What we need is a more humane social system, one that would prevent the social inequalities that are the focus of the next four chapters.

Summary and Review

What Is Deviance?

6.1   **Summarize the relativity of deviance, the need for norms, and the types of sanctions; contrast sociobiological, psychological, and sociological explanations of deviance.**

Deviance (the violation of norms) is relative. What people consider deviant varies from one culture to another and from group to group within the same society. As symbolic interactionists stress, it is not the act but the reactions to the act that make something deviant. All groups develop systems of **social control** to punish **deviants**—those who violate their norms.

How do sociological and individualistic explanations of deviance differ?

To explain why people deviate, sociobiologists and psychologists look for reasons *within* the individual, such as **genetic predispositions** or **personality disorders**. Sociologists, in contrast, look for explanations *outside* the individual, in social experiences.

The Symbolic Interactionist Perspective

6.2 **Apply the symbolic interactionist perspective to deviance by explaining differential association, control, and labeling.**

How do symbolic interactionists explain deviance?

Symbolic interactionists have developed several theories to explain deviance such as **crime** (the violation of norms that are written into law). According to **differential association** theory, people learn to deviate by associating with others. According to **control theory**, each of us is propelled toward deviance, but most of us conform because of an effective system of inner and outer controls. People who have less effective controls deviate.

Labeling theory focuses on how labels (names, reputations) help to funnel people into or divert them away from deviance. People often use **techniques of neutralization** to deflect social norms.

The Functionalist Perspective

6.3 **Apply the functionalist perspective by explaining how deviance can be functional for society, how mainstream values can produce deviance (strain theory), and how social class is related to crime (illegitimate opportunities).**

How do functionalists explain deviance?

Functionalists point out that deviance, including criminal acts, is functional for society. Functions include affirming norms and promoting social unity and social change. According to **strain theory**, societies socialize their members into desiring **cultural goals**. Many people are unable to achieve these goals in socially acceptable ways—that is, by **institutionalized means**. *Deviants*, then, are people who either give up on the goals or use disapproved means to attain them. Merton identified five types of responses to cultural goals and institutionalized means: conformity, innovation, ritualism, retreatism, and rebellion. Because of **illegitimate opportunity structures**, some people have easier access to illegal means of achieving goals.

The Conflict Perspective

6.4 **Apply the conflict perspective by explaining how social class is related to the criminal justice system and how the criminal justice system is oppressive.**

How do conflict theorists explain deviance?

Conflict theorists take the position that the group in power imposes its definitions of deviance on other groups. From this perspective, the law is an instrument of oppression used by the powerful to maintain their position of privilege. The ruling class, which developed the **criminal justice system**, uses it to punish the crimes of the poor while diverting its own criminal activities away from this punitive system.

Reactions to Deviance

6.5 **Be able to discuss street crime and imprisonment, the three-strikes laws, the decline in violent crime, recidivism, bias in the death penalty, the medicalization of deviance, and the need for a more humane approach.**

What are common reactions to deviance in the United States?

In following a "get-tough" policy, the United States has imprisoned millions of people. African Americans and Latinos make up a disproportionate percentage of U.S. prisoners. The death penalty shows biases by geography, social class, gender, and race–ethnicity.

Are official statistics on crime reliable?

The conclusions of both symbolic interactionists (that the police operate with a large measure of discretion) and conflict theorists (that a power elite controls the legal system) indicate that we must be cautious when using crime statistics.

What is the medicalization of deviance?

The medical profession has attempted to **medicalize** many forms of **deviance**, claiming that they represent mental illnesses. Thomas Szasz disagreed, asserting that these are problem behaviors, not mental illnesses. The situation of homeless people indicates that problems in living can lead to bizarre behavior and thinking.

What is a more humane approach?

Deviance is inevitable, so the larger issues are to find ways to protect people from deviance that harms themselves and others, to tolerate deviance that is not harmful, and to develop systems of fairer treatment for deviants.

Thinking Critically about Chapter 6

1. Select some deviance with which you are personally familiar. (It does not have to be your own—it can be something that someone you know did.) Choose one of the three theoretical perspectives to explain what happened.

2. As explained in the text, deviance can be mild. Recall some instance in which you broke a social rule in dress, etiquette, or speech. What was the reaction? Why do you think people reacted like that? What was your response to their reactions?

3. What do you think should be done about the U.S. crime problem? What sociological theories support your view?

Chapter 7
Global Stratification

Learning Objectives

7.1 Compare and contrast slavery (including bonded labor), caste, estate, and class systems of social stratification. (p. 194)

7.2 Contrast the views of Marx and Weber on what determines social class. (p. 202)

7.3 Contrast the functional and conflict views of why social stratification is universal. (p. 204)

7.4 Discuss the ways that elites keep themselves in power. (p. 207)

7.5 Contrast social stratification in Great Britain and the former Soviet Union. (p. 209)

7.6 Compare the three worlds of global stratification: the Most Industrialized Nations, the Industrializing Nations, and the Least Industrialized Nations. (p. 210)

7.7 Discuss how colonialism and world system theory explain how the world's nations became stratified. (p. 218)

7.8 Explain how neocolonialism, multinational corporations, and technology help to maintain global stratification. (p. 221)

7.9 Identify strains in today's system of global stratification. (p. 223)

Let's contrast two "average" families from around the world:

For Getu Mulleta, 33, and his wife, Zenebu, 28, of rural Ethiopia, life is a constant struggle to avoid starvation. They and their seven children live in a 320-square-foot manure-plastered hut with no electricity, gas, or running water. They have a radio, but the battery is dead. The family farms teff, a grain, and survives on $130 a year.

The Mulletas' poverty is not due to a lack of hard work. Getu works about eighty hours a week, while Zenebu puts in even more hours. Housework for Zenebu includes fetching water, cleaning animal stables, and making fuel pellets out of cow dung for the open fire over which she cooks the family's food. Like other Ethiopian women, she eats after the men.

In Ethiopia, the average male can expect to live to age 48, the average female to 50.

The Mulletas' most valuable possession is their oxen. Their wishes for the future: more animals, better seed, and a second set of clothing.

Springfield, Illinois, is home to the Kellys—Rick, 36, Patti, 34, Julie, 10, and Michael, 7. The Kellys live in a three-bedroom, 2½-bath, 2,505-square-foot ranch-style house with a fireplace, central heating and air conditioning, a basement, and a two-car garage. Their home is equipped with a refrigerator, freezer, washing machine, clothes dryer, dishwasher, garbage disposal, vacuum cleaner, food processor, microwave, and a convection stovetop and oven. They also own computers, cell phones, color televisions, a Kindle, several digital cameras,

They live in a 320-square-foot manure-plastered hut

an iPod, an iPad, a printer-scanner-fax machine, blow dryers, a juicer, an espresso coffee maker, a pickup truck, and an SUV.

Rick works forty hours a week as a cable splicer for a telephone company. Patti teaches school part-time. Together they make $60,974, plus benefits. The Kellys can choose from among dozens of superstocked supermarkets. They spend $5,411 for food they eat at home, and another $3,571 eating out, a total of 15 percent of their annual income.

In the United States, the average life expectancy is 77 for males, 82 for females.

On the Kellys' wish list are a solar car with Internet connection, another laptop computer (with a terabyte of memory and solid-state drive), a phablet, an Ultra HighDefinition bendable TV, a virtual reality simulator, a boat, a motor home, an ATV, and an in-ground heated swimming pool.

Menzel 1994; *Statistical Abstract* 2014:Tables 112, 717, 726, 996.

Systems of Social Stratification

7.1 **Compare and contrast slavery (including bonded labor), caste, estate, and class systems of social stratification.**

Some of the world's nations are wealthy, others poor, and some in between. This division of nations, as well as the layering of groups of people within a nation, is called *social stratification*. Social stratification is one of the most significant topics we will discuss in this book. As you saw in the opening vignette, social stratification profoundly affects our life chances—from our access to material possessions to the age at which we die.

Social stratification also affects the way we think about life. Look at the photo below. If you were born into this family, you would expect hunger to be a part of life and would not expect all of your children to survive. You would also be illiterate and would assume that your children would be as well. In contrast, if you are an average U.S. parent, you expect your children not only to survive but to be well fed, not only to be able to read but to go to college. You can see that social stratification brings with it not just material things but also ideas of what we can expect out of life.

The Mulleta family of Ethiopia, described in the opening vignette, displaying all of their possessions.

Social stratification is a system in which groups of people are divided into layers according to their relative property, power, and prestige. It is important to emphasize that social stratification does not refer to individuals. It is a way of ranking large groups of people into a hierarchy according to their relative privileges.

It is also important to note that *every society stratifies its members.* Some societies have more inequality than others, but social stratification is universal. In addition, in every society of the world, *gender* is a basis for stratifying people. On the basis of their gender, people are either allowed or denied access to the good things offered by their society.

Let's consider four major systems of social stratification: slavery, caste, estate, and class.

Slavery

Slavery, whose essential characteristic is that *some individuals own other people*, has been common throughout history. The Old Testament even lays out rules for how owners should treat their slaves. So does the Quran. The Romans had slaves, as did the Africans and Greeks. In classical Greece and Rome, slaves did the work, freeing citizens to engage in politics and the arts. Slavery was most widespread in agricultural societies and least common among nomads, especially hunters and gatherers (Landtman 1938/1968; Rowthorn et al. 2011).

Slaves are commodities, items for sale at the highest price. With the price of slaves higher in New Orleans than in Kentucky, Talbott became an arbitrageur, making a profit by buying slaves at a lower price in one area and selling them at a higher price in another area.

SOURCE: Corbis

Let's examine the causes and conditions of slavery. You probably will be surprised to learn how remarkably slavery has varied around the world.

CAUSES OF SLAVERY   Contrary to popular assumption, slavery was usually based not on racism but on one of three other factors. The first was *debt*. In some societies, creditors would enslave people who could not pay their debts. The second was *crime*. Instead of being killed, a murderer or thief might be enslaved by the victim's family as compensation for their loss. The third was *war*. When one group of people conquered another, they often enslaved some of the vanquished. Historian Gerda Lerner (1986) notes that women were the first people enslaved through warfare. When tribal men raided another group, they killed the men, raped the women, and then brought the women back as slaves. The women were valued for sexual purposes, for reproduction, and for their labor.

Roughly 2,500 years ago, when Greece was but a collection of city-states, slavery was common. A city that became powerful and conquered another city would enslave some of the vanquished. Both slaves and slaveholders were Greek. Similarly, when Rome became the supreme power of the Mediterranean area about two thousand years ago, following the custom of the time, the Romans enslaved some of the Greeks they had conquered. More educated than their conquerors, some of these slaves served as tutors in Roman homes. Slavery, then, was a sign of debt, of crime, or of defeat in battle. It was not a sign that the slave was viewed as inherently inferior.

CONDITIONS OF SLAVERY   The conditions of slavery have varied widely around the world. *In some places, slavery was temporary.* Slaves of the Israelites were set free in the year of jubilee, which occurred every fifty years. Roman slaves ordinarily had the right to buy themselves out of slavery. They knew what their purchase price was, and some were able to meet this price by striking a bargain with their owners and selling their services to others. In most instances, however, slavery was a lifelong condition. Some criminals, for example, became slaves when they were given life sentences as oarsmen on Roman warships. There they served until death, which often came quickly to those in this exhausting service.

social stratification

the division of large numbers of people into layers according to their relative property, power, and prestige; applies to both nations and to people within a nation, society, or other group

slavery

a form of social stratification in which some people own other people

Slavery was not necessarily inheritable. In most places, the children of slaves were slaves themselves. But in some instances, the child of a slave who served a rich family might even be adopted by that family, becoming an heir who bore the family name along with the other sons or daughters of the household. In ancient Mexico, the children of slaves were always free (Landtman 1938/1968:271).

Slaves were not necessarily powerless and poor. In almost all instances, slaves owned no property and had no power. Among some groups, however, slaves could accumulate property and even rise to high positions in the community. Occasionally, a slave might even become wealthy, loan money to the master, and, while still a slave, own slaves himself or herself (Landtman 1938/1968). This, however, was rare.

BONDED LABOR IN THE NEW WORLD   A gray area between slavery and contract labor is **bonded labor**, also called **indentured service**. People who wanted to start a new life in the American colonies but could not pay for their passage across the ocean would arrange for a ship captain to transport them on credit. When they arrived, wealthy colonists would pay the captain for the voyage, and these penniless people would become the colonists' servants for a set number of years. During this period, the servants were required by law to serve their masters. If they ran away, they became outlaws who were hunted down and forcibly returned. At the end of their period of indenture, they were free to work and to live where they chose (Main 1965; Post 2009).

SLAVERY IN THE NEW WORLD   When there were not enough indentured servants to meet the growing need for labor in the American colonies, some colonists tried to enslave Native Americans. This attempt failed, in part because Indians who escaped knew how to survive in the wilderness and were able to make their way back to their tribes. The colonists then turned to Africans, who were being brought to North and South America by the Dutch, English, Portuguese, and Spanish.

Because slavery has a broad range of causes, some analysts conclude that racism didn't lead to slavery but, rather, that slavery led to racism. To defend slavery, U.S. slave owners developed an **ideology**, beliefs that justify social arrangements, making those arrangements seem necessary and fair. They developed the view that their slaves were inferior. Some even said that they were not fully human. In short, the colonists wove elaborate justifications for slavery, built on the presumed superiority of their own group.

To make slavery even more profitable, slave states passed laws that made slavery *inheritable*; that is, the babies born to slaves became the property of the slave owners (Stampp 1956). These children could be sold, bartered, or traded. To strengthen their control, slave states passed laws making it illegal for slaves to hold meetings or to be away from the master's premises without carrying a pass (Lerner 1972). Sociologist W. E. B. Du Bois (1935/1992:12) noted that "gradually the entire white South became an armed camp to keep Negroes in slavery and to kill the black rebel."

The Civil War did not end legal discrimination. For example, until 1954, many states operated separate school systems for blacks and whites. Until the 1950s, in order to keep the races from "mixing," it was illegal in Mississippi for a white and an African American to sit together on the same seat of a car! There was no outright ban on blacks and whites being in the same car, however, so whites could employ African American chauffeurs.

SLAVERY TODAY   Slavery continues to rear its ugly head in several parts of the world (Crane 2012). The Ivory Coast, Mauritania, Niger, and Sudan have a long history of slavery, and not until the 1980s was slavery made illegal in Mauritania and Sudan

bonded labor (indentured service)
a contractual system in which someone sells his or her body (services) for a specified period of time in an arrangement very close to slavery, except that it is entered into voluntarily

During my research in India, I interviewed this 8-year-old girl. Mahashury is a bonded laborer who was exchanged by her parents for a 2,000 rupee loan (about $14). To repay the loan, Mahashury must do construction work for one year. She will receive one meal a day and one set of clothing for the year. Because this centuries-old practice is now illegal, the master bribes Indian officials, who inform him when they are going to inspect the construction site. He then hides his bonded laborers. I was able to interview and photograph Mahashury because her master was absent the day I visited the construction site.

(Ayittey 1998). It took until 2003 for slavery to be banned in Niger, where it still continues (Mwiti 2013). In 2015, in the Iraqi area, ISIS sold captured women as sex slaves.

The enslavement of children for work and sex is a problem in Africa, Asia, and South America (*Trafficking in Persons Report* 2015). A unique form of child slavery in some Mid-east countries involves buying little boys around the ages of 4 or 6 to race camels. Their screams of terror are thought to make the camels run faster. In Qatar and the United Arab Emirates, which recently banned this practice, robots have begun to replace the children (Rasni 2013).

Caste

The second system of social stratification is caste. In a **caste system**, birth determines status, which is lifelong. Someone who is born into a low-status group will always have low status, no matter how much that person may accomplish in life. In sociological terms, a caste system is built on ascribed status (discussed in Chapter 4). Achieved status cannot change an individual's place in this system.

Societies with this form of stratification try to make certain that the boundaries between castes remain firm. They practice **endogamy**, marriage within their own group, prohibiting the marriage of members of different castes. Rules about *ritual pollution* also keep contact between castes to a minimum. Touching someone from an inferior caste, for example, makes a member of the superior caste unclean.

INDIA'S RELIGIOUS CASTES   India provides the best example of a caste system. Based not on race but on religion, India's caste system has existed for almost three thousand years (Chandra 1993; Hnatkovska et al. 2012). Look at Table 7.1, which lists India's four main castes. These castes are subdivided into about three thousand subcastes, or *jati*. Each *jati* specializes in a particular occupation. For example, one subcaste washes clothes, another sharpens knives, and yet another repairs shoes.

The lowest group listed in Table 7.1, the Dalit, make up India's "untouchables." If a Dalit touches someone of a higher caste, that person becomes unclean. Even the shadow of an untouchable can contaminate. Early morning and late afternoons are especially risky, for the long shadows of these periods pose a danger to everyone higher up the caste system. Consequently, Dalits are not allowed in some villages during these times. Anyone who becomes contaminated must follow *ablution*, or washing rituals, to restore purity.

An untouchable summed up his situation this way:

> At the tea stalls, we have separate cups to drink from, chipped and caked with dirt. We have to walk for 15 minutes to carry water to our homes, because we're not allowed to use the taps in the village that the upper castes use. We're not allowed into temples. When I attended school, my friends and I were forced to sit outside the classroom. The upper caste children would not allow us even to touch the football they played with. We played with stones instead. (Guru and Sidhva 2001)

From personal observations in India, I can add that in some villages, Dalit children are not allowed in the government schools. If they try to enroll, they are beaten.

The Indian government formally abolished the caste system in 1949. However, these centuries-old practices continue, and the caste system remains part of everyday life in India. The ceremonies people follow at births, marriages, and deaths are dictated by caste (Chandra 1993). Caste is so ingrained in the Indian mind that when couples visit a sperm bank, they insist on knowing the caste of the donor (Tewary 2012).

India's caste system is changing, but only gradually. The federal government began an affirmative action plan that has increased education and jobs for the lower castes. Slowly, the caste system is giving way, being replaced by a social class system based on material wealth (Sankaran 2013).

ideology

beliefs about the way things ought to be that justify social arrangements

caste system

a form of social stratification in which people's statuses are lifelong conditions determined by birth

endogamy

the practice of marrying within one's own group

Table 7.1 India's Caste System

Caste	Occupation
Brahman	Priests and teachers
Kshatriya	Rulers and soldiers
Vaishya	Merchants and traders
Shudra	Peasants and laborers
Dalit (untouchables)	The outcastes; degrading or polluting labor

SOURCE: By the author.

apartheid

the government-approved-and-enforced separation of racial–ethnic groups as was practiced in South Africa

SOUTH AFRICA In South Africa, Europeans of Dutch descent, a numerical minority called Afrikaners, used to control the government, the police, and the military. They used these sources of power to enforce a system called **apartheid** (ah-PAR-tate), the separation of the races. Everyone was classified by law into one of four groups: Europeans (whites), Africans (blacks), Coloureds (mixed races), and Asians. These classifications determined where people could live, work, and go to school. It also established where they could swim or see movies; by law, whites and the others were not allowed to mix socially.

Listen to what an Anglican priest observed when he arrived in South Africa:

I went to the post office to send my mother a letter telling her that I had arrived safely. There were two entrances, one marked "Whites only" and the other, "Non-whites." . . . Durban is a seaside city and so I went off to explore the beach. There I discovered that even the sea was divided by race. The most beautiful beaches were where white people could swim; there was another for people of Indian descent, still another for people of mixed race, and far, far away, one for Africans. (Lapsley 2012)

After years of trade sanctions and sports boycotts, in 1990 Afrikaners began to dismantle their caste system, and in 1994, Nelson Mandela, a black, was elected president. Black Africans no longer have to carry special passes, public facilities are integrated, and all racial–ethnic groups have the right to vote and to hold office. Although apartheid has been dismantled, its legacy haunts South Africa. Whites still dominate the country's social institutions, and most blacks remain uneducated and poor. Many new rights—such as the rights to higher education, to eat in restaurants, even to see a doctor—are of little use to people who can't afford them. Political violence has been replaced by old-fashioned crime. Even though the U.S. murder rate is so high it intimidates foreigners, South Africa's murder rate is six times higher (South African Police Service 2013; *Statistical Abstract* 2014:Table 319). Apartheid's legacy of prejudice, bitterness, and hatred appears destined to fuel racial tensions for generations to come.

In a *caste system*, status is determined by birth and is lifelong. At birth, these women received not only membership in a lower caste but also, because of their gender, a predetermined position in that caste. When I photographed these women, they were carrying sand to the second floor of a house being constructed in Andhra Pradesh, India.

A U.S. RACIAL CASTE SYSTEM   Before leaving the subject of caste, we should note that when slavery ended in the United States, it was replaced by a *racial caste system*. From the moment of birth, race marked everyone for life (Berger 1963/2016). *All* whites, even if they were poor and uneducated, considered themselves to have a higher status than *all* African Americans. As in India and South Africa, the upper caste, fearing pollution from the lower caste, made intermarriage illegal. There were also separate schools, hotels, restaurants, and even toilets and drinking fountains for blacks and whites. In the South, when any white met any African American on a sidewalk, the African American had to move aside. The untouchables of India still must do this when they meet someone of a higher caste (Deliege 2001).

To see more parallels between the caste systems of the United States and India, see the Global Glimpse box below.

A Global Glimpse

Rape: Blaming the Victim and Protecting the Caste System

Shana, just 16 years old, was raped by four men in Mississippi. She was walking alongside the road leading to her house when a car stopped. The men got out, shoved her into the car, and drove about a mile down the road. For several hours, they took turns raping the terrified young woman. When the rape (and the other abuse that I won't describe) was over, they told Shana to keep her mouth shut. They would kill her if she told anyone.

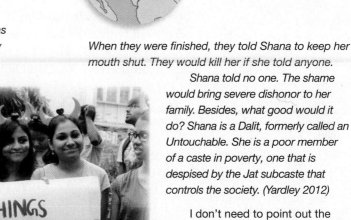

When they were finished, they told Shana to keep her mouth shut. They would kill her if she told anyone.

Fearful of what her parents would say and how the neighbors would gossip, Shana told no one. She also knew that it would do no good to report the rape to the police, since they would do nothing. Shana carried the shame—and the anger—of her rape with her the rest of her life.

This is a composite story. Shana is a combined version of the many young black women who were raped by white men in the U.S. South years ago, at a time when rape brought shame to any woman, black or white, and the rape and the rapists were enshrouded in silence. For black women in the South at this time, it was useless to report a rape. The prosecutors, judges, and juries—all were white. And none was about to take a black woman's word over that of white men.

This event just took place in India:

Shana, just 16 years old, was walking home when she was grabbed by several men and forced into a small stone shelter at the edge of a field. There, for three hours, eight men of the Jat subcaste raped her.

Students at Kolkata, India, protesting rape. Some people still blame the victim.

Shana told no one. The shame would bring severe dishonor to her family. Besides, what good would it do? Shana is a Dalit, formerly called an Untouchable. She is a poor member of a caste in poverty, one that is despised by the Jat subcaste that controls the society. (Yardley 2012)

I don't need to point out the parallels to you.

Then something unusual happened. One of the rapists from the Jat caste had used his cell phone to take trophy videos of the rape. As the video circulated, one man who saw it showed it to Shana's father. Dishonored by the rape of his daughter, he committed suicide.

His suicide and Shana's rape enraged the Dalits in the community. They marched to the police and demanded justice.

What did they get? One official said that the sexual drive of girls is causing rapes. He said that all girls should be married by the age of 16. Then there wouldn't be any rapes. Another said that they never used to have any rapes, that it must be the new fast food the young people are eating. The fast food causes hormonal imbalance, creating sexual urges in young women.

I know that these reactions to Shana's rape sound incredible, but they happened.

When another Dalit woman reported her rape by an upper caste man, the police officer asked how many children she had. When she said "Four," he asked how old the eldest was. When she said 14 or 15 (birthdays are not kept the same as in the West), the officer said, "Who would rape such an old woman?" and walked away (Pokharel and Lahiri 2013).

I want to add a personal note. Since I wrote this box, the daughter of a man I know in India was raped. After the rape, the rapists poured kerosene on the girl and set her afire. Her screams brought help, and the rapists fled. The young woman was taken to a hospital, where she died. As I write this personal note, the monsters have not been caught.

For Your Consideration

→ Can you compare the racial caste system that used to exist in the United States with the religious caste system that currently exists in India?

→ How does a caste system prevent people from receiving justice?

→ In what ways other than rape does a caste system tolerate and perhaps encourage exploitation?

→ Do you see how the ruling Jat subcaste "blamed the victim" instead of the rapists? How does this protect the caste system?

Estate

estate stratification system

the stratification system of medieval Europe, consisting of three groups or estates: the nobility, clergy, and commoners

During the middle ages, Europe developed an **estate stratification system**. There were three groups, or estates. The *first estate* was made up of the nobility, the wealthy families who ruled the country. This group owned the land, which was the source of wealth at that time. The nobility did no farming themselves, or any "work," for that matter. Work was considered beneath their dignity, something to be done by servants. The nobility's responsibility was to administer their lands, to defend the king (and, in doing so, their own position), and to live "genteel" lives worthy of their high position.

The *second estate* consisted of the clergy. The Roman Catholic Church was a political power at this time. It also owned vast amounts of land and collected taxes from everyone who lived within the boundaries of a parish. The church's power was so great that in order to be crowned, kings had to obtain the pope's permission.

To prevent their vast land holdings from being carved into smaller chunks, members of the nobility practiced *primogeniture*, allowing only firstborn sons to inherit land. The other sons had to find some way to support themselves, and joining the clergy was a favorite way. (Other ways included becoming an officer in the military or practicing law.) The church was appealing because priests held lifetime positions and were guaranteed a comfortable living. At that time, the church sold offices, and, for example, a wealthy man could buy the position of bishop for his son, which guaranteed a high income.

The *third estate* consisted of the commoners. Known as *serfs*, they belonged to the land. If someone bought or inherited land, the serfs came with it. Serfs were born into the third estate, and they died within it, too. The rare person who made it out of the third estate was either a man who was knighted for extraordinary bravery in battle or someone "called" into a religious vocation.

WOMEN IN THE ESTATE SYSTEM Women belonged to the estate of their husbands. Women in the first estate had no occupation, since, as in the case of their husbands, physical work was considered beneath their dignity. Their responsibility was to administer the household, overseeing the children and servants. The women in the second estate, nuns, were the exception to the rule that women belonged to the estate of their husbands, as the Roman Catholic clergy did not marry. Women of the third estate shared the hard life of their husbands, including physical labor and food shortages. In addition, they faced the peril of rape by men of the first estate. A few commoners who caught the eye of men of the first estate did marry and join them in the first estate. This was rare.

Class

As we have seen, stratification systems based on slavery, caste, and estate are rigid. The lines drawn between people are firm, and there is little or no movement from one group to another. A **class system**, in contrast, is much more open, because it is based primarily on money or material possessions, which can be acquired. This system, too, is in place at birth, when children are ascribed the status of their parents. Unlike the other systems, however, individuals can change their social class by what they achieve (or fail to achieve) in life. In addition, no laws specify people's occupations on the basis of birth or prohibit marriage between the classes.

A major characteristic of the class system, then, is its relatively fluid boundaries. A class system allows **social mobility**, movement up or down the class ladder. The potential for improving one's life—or for falling down the class ladder—is a major force that drives people to go far in school and to work hard. In the extreme, the family background that a child inherits at birth may present such obstacles that he or she has little chance of climbing very far—or it may provide such privileges that it is almost impossible to fall down the class ladder. Because social class is so significant for our own lives, we will focus on class in the next chapter.

In early industrialization, children worked alongside adults. They worked twelve hours a day Monday to Friday and fifteen hours on Saturday, often in dangerous, filthy conditions. This photo was taken at a U.S. cotton mill in 1911.

class system

a form of social stratification based primarily on income, education, and prestige of occupation

social mobility

movement up or down the social class ladder

Global Stratification and the Status of Females

In *every* society of the world, gender is a basis for social stratification. In no society is gender the sole basis for stratifying people, but gender cuts across *all* systems of social stratification—whether slavery, caste, estate, or class (Huber 1990). In all these systems, on the basis of their gender, people are sorted into categories and given different access to the good things available in their society.

Apparently, these distinctions always favor males. It is remarkable, for example, that in *every* society of the world, men's earnings are higher than women's. Men's dominance is even more evident when we consider female circumcision (see the box on page 308). That most of the world's illiterate are females also drives home women's relative position. Of the several hundred million adults who cannot read, about two-thirds are women (UNESCO 2012). Because gender is such a significant factor in what happens to us in life, we shall focus on it more closely in Chapter 10.

The Global Superclass

The growing interconnections among the world's wealthiest people have produced a *global superclass*, one in which wealth and power are more concentrated than ever before. There are only about 6,000 members of the global superclass. *The richest 1,000 of this superclass have more wealth than the 2½ billion poorest people on this planet* (Rothkopf 2008:37). Almost all are white, and, except as wives and daughters, few women are an active part of the global superclass. We will have more to say about the superclass in Chapter 11, but for now, let's just stress their incredible wealth. There is nothing in history to compare with what you see in Figure 7.1.

Figure 7.1 The Distribution of the Earth's Wealth

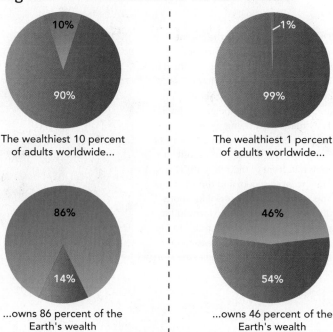

The wealthiest 10 percent of adults worldwide...

10%

90%

...owns 86 percent of the Earth's wealth

86%

14%

The wealthiest 1 percent of adults worldwide...

1%

99%

...owns 46 percent of the Earth's wealth

46%

54%

SOURCE: By the author. Based on Keating et al. 2013.

What Determines Social Class?

7.2 **Contrast the views of Marx and Weber on what determines social class.**

In the early days of sociology, a disagreement arose about the meaning of social class. Let's compare how Marx and Weber analyzed the issue.

Karl Marx: The Means of Production

As we discussed in Chapter 1, as agricultural society gave way to an industrial one, masses of peasants were displaced from their traditional lands and occupations. Fleeing to cities, they competed for the few available jobs. Paid only a pittance for their labor, they wore rags, went hungry, and slept under bridges and in shacks. In contrast, the factory owners built mansions, hired servants, and lived in the lap of luxury. Seeing this great disparity between owners and workers, Karl Marx (1818–1883) concluded that social class depends on a single factor: people's relationship to the **means of production**—the tools, factories, land, and investment capital used to produce wealth (Marx 1844/1964; Marx and Engels 1848/1967).

Marx argued that the distinctions people often make among themselves—such as their clothing, speech, education, and paycheck, or the neighborhood they live in and the car they drive—are superficial matters. These things camouflage the only dividing line that counts. There are just two classes of people, said Marx: the **bourgeoisie** (*capitalists*), those who own the means of production, and the **proletariat** (*workers*), those who work for the owners. In short, people's relationship to the means of production determines their social class.

Marx did recognize other groups: farmers and peasants; a *lumpenproletariat* (people living on the margin of society, such as beggars, vagrants, and criminals); and a middle group of self-employed professionals. Marx did not consider these groups social classes, however, because they lacked **class consciousness**—a shared identity based on their relationship to the means of production. In other words, they did not perceive themselves as exploited workers whose plight could be resolved by collective action. Marx thought of these groups as insignificant in the future he foresaw—a workers' revolution that would overthrow capitalism.

means of production

the tools, factories, land, and investment capital used to produce wealth

bourgeoisie

Marx's term for capitalists, those who own the means of production

proletariat

Marx's term for the exploited class, the mass of workers who do not own the means of production

class consciousness

Marx's term for awareness of a common identity based on one's position in the means of production

false class consciousness

Marx's term to refer to workers identifying with the interests of capitalists

These photos illustrate the contrasting worlds of social classes produced by early capitalism. The photo on the left was taken in 1890. These homeless boys who spent their nights sleeping on the sidewalk did not go to school. They made their living by selling newspapers. The children on the right, Cornelius and Gladys Vanderbilt, are shown in front of their parents' estate. They went to school and did not work. You can see how the social locations illustrated in these photos would have produced different orientations to life and, therefore, politics, ideas about marriage, values, and so on—the stuff of which life is made.

The capitalists will grow even wealthier, Marx said, and hostilities will increase. When workers come to realize that capitalists are the source of their oppression, they will unite and throw off the chains of their oppressors. In a bloody revolution, they will seize the means of production and usher in a classless society—and no longer will the few grow rich at the expense of the many. What holds back the workers' unity and their revolution is **false class consciousness**, workers mistakenly thinking of themselves as capitalists. For example, workers with a few dollars in the bank may forget that they are workers and instead see themselves as investors, or as capitalists who are about to launch a successful business.

The only distinction worth mentioning, then, is whether a person is an owner or a worker. This decides everything else, Marx stressed, because property determines people's lifestyles, establishes their relationships with one another, and even shapes their ideas.

Max Weber: Property, Power, and Prestige

Max Weber (1864–1920) was an outspoken critic of Marx. Weber argued that property is only part of the picture. *Social class*, he said, has three components: property, power, and prestige (Gerth and Mills 1958; Weber 1922/1978). Some call these the three P's of social class. (Although Weber used the terms *class*, *power*, and *status*, some sociologists find *property*, *power*, and *prestige* to be clearer terms. To make them even clearer, you may wish to substitute *wealth* for *property*.)

Property (or wealth), said Weber, is certainly significant in determining a person's standing in society. On this point he agreed with Marx. But, added Weber, ownership is not the only significant aspect of property. For example, some powerful people, such as managers of corporations, *control* the means of production even though they do not *own* them. If managers can control property for their own benefit—awarding themselves huge bonuses and magnificent perks—it makes no practical difference that they do not own the property that they use so generously for their own benefit.

Power, the second element of social class, is the ability to control others, even over their objections. Weber agreed with Marx that property is a major source of power, but he added that it is not the only source. For example, prestige can be turned into power. Two well-known examples are actors Arnold Schwarzenegger, who became governor of California, and Ronald Reagan, who was elected governor of California and president of the United States. Figure 7.2 shows how property, power, and prestige are interrelated.

Prestige, the third element in Weber's analysis, is often derived from property and power, since people tend to admire the wealthy and powerful. Prestige, however, can be based on other factors. Olympic gold medalists, for example, might not own property or be powerful, yet they have high prestige. Some are even able to exchange their prestige for property—such as those who are paid a small fortune for endorsing a certain brand of sportswear or for claiming that they start their day with "the breakfast of champions." In other words, property and prestige are not one-way streets: Although property can bring prestige, prestige can also bring property.

IN SUM   For Marx, the only distinction that counted was property, more specifically people's relationship to the means of production. People are either owners or workers, which sets them on contrasting paths in life. Their path determines their lifestyle and shapes their orientations to life. Weber, in contrast, argued that social class has three components—a combination of property, power, and prestige.

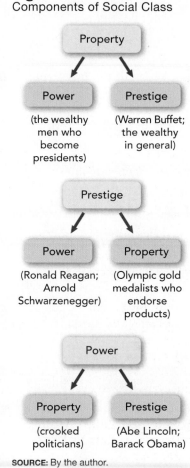

Figure 7.2 Weber's Three Components of Social Class

Property

Power
(the wealthy men who become presidents)

Prestige
(Warren Buffet; the wealthy in general)

Prestige

Power
(Ronald Reagan; Arnold Schwarzenegger)

Property
(Olympic gold medalists who endorse products)

Power

Property
(crooked politicians)

Prestige
(Abe Lincoln; Barack Obama)

SOURCE: By the author.

Prestige can sometimes be converted into property. Shown here is supermodel Rosie Huntington-Whiteley doing this as she launches her new perfume.

Why Is Social Stratification Universal?

7.3 Contrast the functional and conflict views of why social stratification is universal.

What is it about social life that makes all societies stratified? We will first consider the explanation proposed by functionalists, which has aroused much controversy in sociology, and then explanations proposed by conflict theorists.

The Functionalist View: Motivating Qualified People

Functionalists take the position that the patterns of behavior that characterize a society exist because they are functional for that society. Because social inequality is universal, inequality must help societies survive. But how?

DAVIS AND MOORE'S EXPLANATION   Two functionalists, Kingsley Davis and Wilbert Moore (1945, 1953), wrestled with this question. They concluded that stratification of society is inevitable because:

1. For society to function, its positions must be filled.
2. Some positions are more important than others.
3. The more important positions must be filled by the more qualified people.
4. To motivate the more qualified people to fill these positions, they must offer greater rewards.

To flesh out this functionalist argument, consider college presidents and military generals. The position of college president is more important than that of student because the president's decisions affect a large number of people, including many students. College presidents are also accountable for their performance to boards of trustees. It is the same with generals. Their decisions affect many people and sometimes even determine life and death. Generals are accountable to superior generals and to the country's leader.

Why do people accept demanding, high-pressure positions? Why don't they just take easier jobs? The answer, said Davis and Moore, is that these positions offer greater rewards—more prestige, pay, and benefits. To get highly qualified people to compete with one another, some positions offer a salary of $5 million a year, country club membership, a private jet and pilot, and a chauffeured limousine. For less demanding positions, a $40,000 salary without fringe benefits is enough to get hundreds of people to compete. If a job requires rigorous training, it, too, must offer more salary and benefits. If you can get the same pay with a high school diploma, why suffer through the many tests and term papers that college requires?

TUMIN'S CRITIQUE OF DAVIS AND MOORE   Davis and Moore did not attempt to justify social inequality. There were simply trying to explain *why* social stratification is universal. Nevertheless, their view makes many sociologists uncomfortable, because they see it as coming close to justifying the inequalities in society. Its bottom line seems to be: The people who contribute more to society are paid more, while those who contribute less are paid less.

Melvin Tumin (1953) was the first sociologist to point out what he saw as major flaws in the functionalist position. Here are three of his arguments.

First, how do we know that the positions that offer the higher rewards are more important? A heart surgeon, for example, saves lives and earns much more than a garbage collector, but this doesn't mean that garbage collectors are less important to society. By helping to prevent contagious diseases, garbage collectors save more lives than heart surgeons do. We need independent methods of measuring importance, and we don't have them.

Second, if stratification worked as Davis and Moore described it, society would be a **meritocracy**; that is, positions would be awarded on the basis of merit. But is this what we have? The best predictor of who goes to college, for example, is not ability but income: The more a family earns, the more likely their children are to go to college (Bailey and Dynarski 2011). Not merit, then, but money—another form of the inequality that is built into society. In short, people's positions in society are based on many factors other than merit.

Third, if social stratification is so functional, it ought to benefit almost everyone. Yet social stratification is *dysfunctional* for many. Think of the people who could have made valuable contributions to society had they not been born in slums, dropped out of school, and taken menial jobs to help support their families. Then there are the many who, born female, are assigned "women's work," thus ensuring that they do not maximize their mental abilities.

IN SUM   Functionalists argue that some positions are more important to society than others. Offering higher rewards for these positions motivates more talented people to take them. For example, to get highly talented people to become surgeons—to undergo years of rigorous training and then cope with life-and-death situations, as well as malpractice suits—that position must provide a high payoff.

Next, let's see how conflict theorists explain why social stratification is universal. Before we do, look at Table 7.2 which compares the functionalist and conflict views.

To determine the social class of athletes as highly successful as the Williams sisters presents a sociological puzzle. With their high prestige and growing wealth, what do you think their social class is? Why?

Table 7.2 Functionalist and Conflict Views of Stratification: The Distribution of Society's Resources

	Who Receives the Most Resources?	Who Receives the Least Resources?
The Functionalist View	Those who perform the more important functions (the more capable and more industrious)	Those who perform the less important functions (the less capable and less industrious)
The Conflict View	Those who occupy the more powerful positions	Those who occupy the less powerful positions

SOURCE: By the author.

The Conflict Perspective: Class Conflict and Scarce Resources

Conflict theorists don't just criticize details of the functionalist argument. Rather, they go for the throat and attack its basic premise. Conflict, not function, they stress, is the reason that we have social stratification. Let's look at the major arguments.

MOSCA'S ARGUMENT   Italian sociologist Gaetano Mosca argued that every society will be stratified by power. This is inevitable, he said in an 1896 book titled *The Ruling Class*, because:

1. No society can exist unless it is organized. This requires leadership to coordinate people's actions.

2. Leadership requires inequalities of power. By definition, some people lead, while others follow.

3. Because human nature is self-centered, people in power will use their positions to seize greater rewards for themselves.

meritocracy

a form of social stratification in which all positions are awarded on the basis of merit

There is no way around these facts of life, added Mosca. Social stratification is inevitable, and every society will stratify itself along lines of power.

MARX'S ARGUMENT   If he were alive to hear the functionalist argument, Karl Marx would be enraged. From his point of view, the people in power are not there because of superior traits, as the functionalists would have us believe. This view is an ideology that members of the elite use to justify their being at the top—and to seduce the oppressed into believing that their welfare depends on keeping quiet and following authorities. What is human history, Marx asked, except the chronicle of class struggle? All of human history is an account of small groups of people in power using society's resources to benefit themselves and to oppress those beneath them—and of oppressed groups trying to overcome that domination.

Marx predicted that the workers will revolt. Capitalist ideology now blinds them, but one day, class consciousness will rip that blindfold off and expose the truth. When workers realize their common oppression, they will rebel. The struggle to control the means of production may be covert at first, taking such forms as work slowdowns and industrial sabotage. Ultimately, however, resistance will break out into the open. But the revolution will not be easy, since the bourgeoisie control the police, the military, and even the educational system, where they implant false class consciousness in the minds of the workers' children.

CURRENT APPLICATIONS OF CONFLICT THEORY   Just as Marx focused on overarching historical events—the accumulation of capital and power and the struggle between workers and capitalists—so do some of today's conflict sociologists. In analyzing global stratification and global capitalism, they look at power relations among nations, how national elites control workers, and how power shifts as capital is shuffled among nations (Jessop 2010; Sprague 2012).

Other conflict sociologists, in contrast, examine conflict wherever it is found, not just as it relates to capitalists and workers. They examine how groups *within the same class* compete with one another for a larger slice of the pie (Collins 1999; King et al. 2010). Even within the same industry, for example, union will fight against union for higher salaries, shorter hours, and more power. Another focus of conflict theorists is conflict between racial–ethnic groups as they compete for education, housing, and even prestige—whatever rewards society has to offer. They also study the relations between women and men, which conflict theorists say are best understood as a conflict over power—over who controls society's resources. Unlike functionalists, conflict theorists say that just beneath the surface of what may appear to be a tranquil society lies conflict that is barely held in check.

Lenski's Synthesis

As you can see, functionalist and conflict theorists disagree sharply. Is it possible to reconcile their views? Sociologist Gerhard Lenski (1966) thought so. He suggested that surplus is the key. He said that the functionalists are right when it comes to *groups that don't accumulate a surplus*, such as hunting and gathering societies. These societies give a greater share of their resources to those who take on important tasks, such as warriors who risk their lives in battle. It is a different story, said Lenski, with *societies that accumulate surpluses*. In them, groups fight over the surplus, and the group that wins becomes an elite. This dominant group rules from the top, controlling the groups below it. In the resulting system of social stratification, where you are born in that society, not personal merit, is what counts.

IN SUM   Conflict theorists stress that in every society, groups struggle with one another to gain a larger share of their society's resources. Whenever a group gains power, it uses that power to extract what it can from the groups beneath it. This elite group also uses the social institutions to keep itself in power.

How Do Elites Maintain Stratification?

7.4   **Discuss the ways that elites keep themselves in power.**

Suppose that you are part of the ruling elite of your society. You want to make sure that you and your family and friends are going to be able to keep your privileged position for the next generation. How will you accomplish this?

You might think about passing laws and using the police and the military. After all, you are a member of the *ruling elite*, so you have this power. You could use force, but this can lead to resentment and rebellion. It is more effective to control people's ideas, information, and technology—which is just what the elite try to do. Let's look at some of their techniques.

Soft Control Versus Force

Let's start with medieval Europe, where we find an excellent example of "soft" control. At that time, land was the primary source of wealth—and only the nobility and the church could own land. Almost everyone was a peasant (a serf) who worked for these powerful landowners. The peasants farmed the land, took care of the livestock, and built the roads and bridges. Each year, they had to turn over a designated portion of their crops to their feudal lord. Year after year, for centuries, they did so. Why?

CONTROLLING PEOPLE'S IDEAS   Why didn't the peasants rebel and take over the land themselves? There were many reasons, not the least of which was that the nobility and church controlled the army. Coercion, however, goes only so far, because it breeds hostility and nourishes rebellion. How much more effective it is to get the masses to *want* to do what the ruling elite desires. This is where *ideology* (beliefs that justify the way things are) comes into play, and the nobility and clergy used it to great effect. They developed an ideology known as the **divine right of kings**—the idea that the king's authority comes directly from God. The king delegates authority to nobles, who, as God's representatives, must be obeyed. To disobey is to sin against God; to rebel is to merit physical punishment on earth and eternal suffering in hell.

Controlling people's ideas can be remarkably more effective than using brute force. Although this particular ideology governs few minds today, the elite in every society uses ideology to justify its position at the top. For example, around the world, schools teach that their country's form of government—*no matter what form of government it has*— is good. Religious leaders teach that we owe obedience to authority, that laws are to be obeyed. To the degree that their ideologies are accepted by the masses, the elite remains securely in power.

Ideology is so powerful that it even sets limits on the elite. Although leaders use ideas to control people, the people can also insist that their leaders conform to those same ideas. Pakistan is an outstanding example. If Pakistani leaders depart from fundamentalist Islamic ideology, their position is in jeopardy. For example, regardless of their personal views, Pakistani leaders cannot support Western ideas of morality. If they were to allow women to wear short skirts in public, for example, not only would they lose their positions of leadership but perhaps also

divine right of kings
the idea that the king's authority comes from God; in an interesting gender bender, also applies to queens

Louis IV as he is crowned the Holy Roman Emperor in 1328 in Rome.

their lives. To protect their position within a system of stratification, leaders, regardless of their personal opinions, must also conform at least outwardly to the controlling ideas.

CONTROLLING INFORMATION   To maintain their power, elites try to control information. Chinese leaders have put tight controls on Internet cafes and search engines, and they block access to Facebook, Twitter, and YouTube (Makinen 2014). For watching a Jackie Chan movie, North Koreans can be sentenced to six months of backbreaking work in a labor camp (LaFraniere 2010). Lacking such power in democracies, the ruling elites rely on covert means. A favorite tactic of U.S. presidents is to withhold information "in the interest of national security," a phrase that usually translates as "in the interest of protecting me."

STIFLING CRITICISM   Like the rest of us, the power elite doesn't like to be criticized. But unlike the rest of us, they have the power to do something about it. Fear is a favorite tactic. In Thailand, you can be put in prison for criticizing the king or his family (Hookway 2013). Poetry is dangerous, too. Judges in Qatar sentenced a poet to *life in prison* because one of his poems criticized "the ruling family" (Delmar-Morgan 2012). It can be worse. In Saddam Hussein's Iraq, the penalty for telling a joke about Hussein was having your tongue cut out (Nordland 2003).

In a democracy, the control of critics takes a milder form. When the U.S. Defense Department found out that an author had criticized its handling of 9/11, it bought and destroyed 9,500 copies of his book (Thompson 2010).

BIG BROTHER TECHNOLOGY   The new technology allows the elite to monitor citizens without anyone knowing they are being watched. Drones silently patrol the skies. The Picosecond laser scanner, able to read molecules, can sense from 150 feet away if you have gunpowder residue on your body, as well as report your adrenaline level (Compton 2012). Software programs can read the entire contents of a computer in a second—and not leave a trace. Security cameras—"Tiny Brothers"—have sprouted almost everywhere. The FBI is digitizing faces so its face-recognition system can scan crowds and instantly match those faces with its files (Brandom 2014). Eventually the facial image of every citizen will be in their files. Dictators have few checks on how they use this technology, but democracies do have some, such as requiring court orders for search and seizure. Such restraints on power frustrate officials, so they are delighted with our new Homeland Security laws that allow them to spy on citizens without their knowledge.

Just as with ideology, the new technology is a two-edged sword. It gives the elite powerful tools for monitoring citizens, but it also makes it difficult for the elite to control information. With international borders meaning nothing to the Internet, it takes but seconds for e-mail, tweets, and photos to fly around the globe. Encryption also frustrates governments and excites privacy advocates. *Silent Circle* shreds files into thousands of pieces as they are sent to the cloud. Only the recipient has the key, which is deleted automatically after a file is downloaded (Gallagher 2013). Governments have not been able to break *Silent Circle, PGP* (*Pretty Good Privacy,* a free code), or *Signal,* which scrambles messages until they reach the intended reader (Yadron 2015). The FBI became upset when Google and Apple added encryption to their mobile platforms (Nichols 2014). We will see how long these companies resist governmental pressure.

IN SUM   To maintain stratification, the elite tries to dominate its society's institutions. In a dictatorship, the elite makes the laws. In a democracy, the elite influences the laws. In both, the elite controls the police and military and can give orders to crush a rebellion—or to run the post office or air traffic control if workers strike. With force having its limits, especially the potential of provoking resistance, most power elites prefer to keep themselves in power by peaceful means, especially by influencing the thinking of their people.

Comparative Social Stratification

7.5   **Contrast social stratification in Great Britain and the former Soviet Union.**

Now that we have examined systems of social stratification, considered why stratification is universal, and looked at how elites keep themselves in power, let's compare social stratification in Great Britain and in the former Soviet Union. In the next chapter, we'll look at social stratification in the United States.

Social Stratification in Great Britain

Great Britain is often called England by Americans, but England is only one of the countries that make up the island of Great Britain. The others are Scotland and Wales. In addition, Northern Ireland is part of the United Kingdom of Great Britain and Northern Ireland.

Like other industrialized countries, Great Britain has a class system that can be divided into lower, middle, and upper classes. Great Britain's population is about evenly divided between the middle class and the lower (or working) class. A tiny upper class— wealthy, powerful, and highly educated—makes up perhaps 1 percent of the population.

Compared with Americans, the British are very class conscious (Lyall 2013). Like Americans, they recognize class distinctions on the basis of the type of car a person drives or the stores someone patronizes. But the most striking characteristics of the British class system are language and education. Because these often show up in distinctive speech, accent has a powerful impact on British life. Accent almost always betrays class. As soon as someone speaks, the listener is aware of that person's social class—and treats him or her accordingly (Sullivan 1998).

Education is the primary way by which the British perpetuate their class system from one generation to the next (Lindley and Machin 2013). Almost all children go to neighborhood schools. Great Britain's richest 5 percent, however—who own *half* the nation's wealth—send their children to exclusive private boarding schools. There the children of the elite are trained in subjects that are considered "proper" for members of the ruling class. An astounding 50 percent of the students at Oxford and Cambridge, the country's most elite universities, come from this 5 percent of the population. So do half of the prime minister's cabinet (Neil 2011). To illustrate how powerfully stratified education affects the national life of Great Britain, sociologist Ian Robertson (1987) said,

> *Eighteen former pupils of the most exclusive of [England's high schools], Eton, have become prime minister. Imagine the chances of a single American high school producing eighteen presidents!*

Social Stratification in the Former Soviet Union

Heeding Karl Marx's call for a classless society, Vladimir Ilyich Lenin (1870–1924) and Leon Trotsky (1879–1940) led a revolution in Russia in 1917. They, and the nations that followed their banner, never claimed to have achieved the ideal of communism, in which all contribute their labor to the common good and receive according to their needs. Instead, they used the term *socialism* to describe the intermediate step between capitalism and communism, in which social classes are abolished but some inequality remains.

To tweak the nose of Uncle Sam, the socialist countries would trumpet their equality and point a finger at glaring inequalities in the United States. These countries, however, also were marked by huge disparities in privilege. Their major basis of stratification was membership in the Communist party. Party members decided who would gain admission to the better schools or obtain the more desirable jobs and housing. The equally qualified son or daughter of parents who were not members of the Communist Party would be turned down, since such privileges came with demonstrated loyalty to the party.

The Communist party, too, was highly stratified. Most members occupied a low level, where they fulfilled such tasks as spying on fellow workers. For this, they might get easier jobs in the factory or occasional access to special stores to purchase hard-to-find goods. The middle level consisted of bureaucrats who were given better than average access to resources and privileges. At the top level was a small elite: party members who enjoyed not only power but also limousines, imported delicacies, vacation homes, and even servants and hunting lodges. As with other stratification systems around the world, women held lower positions in the party. This was evident at each year's May Day, when the top members of the party reviewed the latest weapons paraded in Moscow's Red Square. Photos of these events show only men.

The leaders of the USSR (Union of Soviet Socialist Republics) became frustrated as they saw the West thrive. They struggled with a bloated bureaucracy, the inefficiencies of central planning, workers who did the minimum because they could not be fired, and a military so costly that it spent one of every eight of the nation's rubles (*Statistical Abstract* 1993:1432, table dropped in later editions). Socialist ideology did not call for their citizens to be deprived, and, in an attempt to turn things around, the Soviet leadership allowed elections to be held in which more than one candidate ran for an office. (Before this, voters had a choice of only one candidate per office.) They also sold huge chunks of state-owned businesses to the public. Overnight, making investments to try to turn a profit changed from a crime into a respectable goal.

Russia's transition to capitalism took a bizarre twist. As authority broke down, powerful mafias emerged (Ahmari 2014). These criminal groups are headed by gangsters, crooked businessmen, and corrupt government officials (including members of the Russian secret police, the FSB). They assassinate business leaders, reporters, and politicians who refuse to cooperate. They launder money through banks they control and buy luxury properties in popular tourist areas in Europe and Asia. A favorite is Marbella, a watering and wintering spot on Spain's Costa del Sol.

As Moscow reestablished its authority, its criminal ties brought wealth to some members of the government (Dawisha 2014). This group of organized criminals is taking its place as part of Russia's new capitalist class.

Global Stratification: Three Worlds

7.6 Compare the three worlds of global stratification: the Most Industrialized Nations, the Industrializing Nations, and the Least Industrialized Nations.

Let's start this section a little differently. The Down-to-Earth Sociology box that follows should get you thinking.

Down-to-Earth Sociology

Inequality? What Inequality?

There is a lot of talk about social inequality. Like so many things, maybe it's overblown.

There are differences among us, of course. Some people do have newer cars than others. Some do have bigger houses, better clothing, and more expensive foods and drinks. We all know this.

So there are a few differences among us. But why the concern? Is this perhaps just a little rabble-rousing by a few radical sociologists and some other troublemakers?

Well, let's see. To be logical, perhaps even a bit scientific, we probably should start out by determining if there really is inequality. How can we do this? With all the statistical techniques available to us, things quickly could become mind-boggling. There must be a simpler way of doing this.

And there is. It turns out that *the 85 richest people in the world own as much of the world's wealth as the bottom half of the entire world's population* (Hardoon 2015).

Let's see. If eighty-five people have as much as three and a half billion people, then . . .

Hmm. Maybe there is inequality.

Ah, maybe not. Perhaps this is just the normal state of affairs of the world, just another fact like there are more cats than dogs in the world, or more mice than elephants.

Or perhaps this indicates that something is out of kilter in the world, an imbalance that doesn't seem quite right. Hmm. Could be.

For Your Consideration

→ I don't mean to skew this box too much in one direction. Or maybe I just sort of can't help it. This is perhaps one of the most mind-boggling statistics you will ever come across in your life, and I feel compelled to tell you about it. Anyway, what do you think?

THE PROBLEM WITH TERMS   As was noted at the beginning of this chapter, just as the people within a nation are stratified by property, power, and prestige, so are the world's nations. Until recently, a simple model consisting of First, Second, and Third Worlds was used to depict global stratification. *First World* referred to the industrialized capitalist nations, *Second World* to the communist (or socialist) countries, and *Third World* to any nation that did not fit into the first two categories. The breakup of the Soviet Union in 1989 made these terms outdated. In addition, although *first, second,* and *third* did not mean "best," "better," and "worst," they implied it. An alternative classification that some now use—developed, developing, and undeveloped nations—has the same drawback. By calling ourselves "developed," it sounds as though we are mature and the "undeveloped" nations are backward.

To resolve this problem, I use more neutral, descriptive terms: *Most Industrialized, Industrializing,* and *Least Industrialized* nations. We can measure industrialization with no judgment implied as to whether a nation's industrialization represents "development," ranks it "first," or is even desirable at all. The intention is to depict on a global level the three primary dimensions of social stratification: property, power, and prestige. The Most Industrialized Nations have much greater property (wealth), power (they usually get their way in international relations), and prestige (they are looked up to as world leaders).

As you read this analysis, don't forget the sociological significance of the stratification of nations, its far-reaching effects on people's lives, as illustrated by the two families sketched in our opening vignette.

The Most Industrialized Nations

The Most Industrialized Nations are the United States and Canada in North America; Great Britain, France, Germany, Switzerland, and the other industrialized countries of western Europe; Japan in Asia; and Australia and New Zealand in the area of the world known as Oceania. Although there are variations in their economic systems, these countries are capitalistic. As Table 7.3 shows, although these nations have only 16 percent of the world's people, they possess 31 percent of the Earth's land. Their wealth is so enormous that even their poor live better and longer lives than do the average citizens of the Least Industrialized Nations. The Social Map on the next two pages shows the tremendous disparities in income among the world's nations.

Table 7.3 Distribution of the World's Land and Population

	Land	Population
Most Industrialized Nations	31%	16%
Industrializing Nations	20%	16%
Least Industrialized Nations	49%	68%

SOURCES: By the author. Computed from Kurian 1990, 1991, 1992.

Figure 7.3 Global Stratification: Income of the World's Nations

The Most Industrialized Nations

	Nation	Income per Person
1	Luxembourg	$77,900
2	Singapore	$62,400
3	Norway	$55,400
4	Switzerland	$54,800
5	United States	$52,800
6	Hong Kong	$52,700
7	Netherlands	$43,300
8	Canada	$43,100
9	Australia	$43,000
10	Austria	$42,600
11	Sweden	$40,900
12	Iceland	$40,700
13	Taiwan	$39,600
14	Germany	$39,500
15	Greenland	$38,400
16	Belgium	$37,800
17	Denmark	$37,800
18	United Kingdom	$37,300
19	Japan	$37,100
20	Israel	$36,200
21	Finland	$35,900
22	France	$35,700
23	Korea, South	$33,200
24	New Zealand	$30,400
25	Italy	$29,600
26	Slovenia	$27,400
27	Czech Republic	$26,300

The Industrializing Nations

	Nation	Income per Person
28	Ireland	$41,300
29	Spain	$30,100
30	Slovakia	$24,700
31	Greece	$23,600
32	Portugal	$22,900
33	Lithuania	$22,600
34	Estonia	$22,400
35	Poland	$21,100
36	Trinidad	$20,300
37	Hungary	$19,800
38	Gabon	$19,200
39	Chile	$19,100
40	Latvia	$19,100
41	Argentina	$18,600
42	Russia	$18,100
43	Croatia	$17,800
44	Malaysia	$17,500
45	Mauritius	$16,100
46	Mexico	$15,600
47	Turkey	$15,300
48	Bulgaria	$14,400
49	Romania	$14,400
50	Venezuela	$13,600
51	Costa Rica	$12,900
52	Brazil	$12,100
53	South Africa	$11,500
54	Cuba	$10,200
55	China	$9,800

The Least Industrialized Nations

	Nation	Income per Person		Nation	Income per Person
56	Uruguay	$16,600	72	Turkmenistan	$9,700
57	Panama	$16,500	73	Jamaica	$9,000
58	Botswana	$16,400	74	Belize	$8,800
59	Belarus	$16,100	75	Guyana	$8,500
60	Lebanon	$15,800	76	Bosnia	$8,300
61	Kazakhstan	$14,100	77	Namibia	$8,200
62	Suriname	$12,900	78	Algeria	$7,500
63	Colombia	$11,100	79	El Salvador	$7,500
64	Peru	$11,100	80	Ukraine	$7,400
65	Azerbaijan	$10,800	81	Bhutan	$7,000
66	Macedonia	$10,800	82	Paraguay	$6,800
67	Albania	$10,700	83	Egypt	$6,500
68	Ecuador	$10,600	84	Sri Lanka	$6,500
69	Thailand	$9,900	85	Angola	$6,300
70	Tunisia	$9,900	86	Armenia	$6,300
71	Dominican Republic	$9,700	87	Georgia	$6,100
			88	Jordan	$6,100

SOURCE: By the author. Based on CIA World Factbook 2014.

Figure 7.3 (Continued)

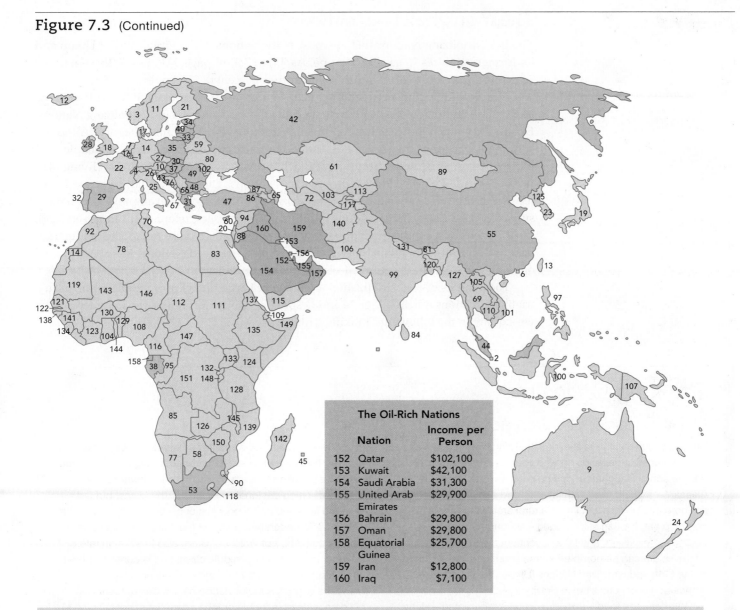

The Oil-Rich Nations

Nation	Income per Person
152 Qatar	$102,100
153 Kuwait	$42,100
154 Saudi Arabia	$31,300
155 United Arab Emirates	$29,900
156 Bahrain	$29,800
157 Oman	$29,800
158 Equatorial Guinea	$25,700
159 Iran	$12,800
160 Iraq	$7,100

The Least Industrialized Nations

Nation	Income per Person	Nation	Income per Person	Nation	Income per Person	Nation	Income per Person
89 Mongolia	$5,900	106 Pakistan	$3,100	122 Gambia	$2,000	138 Guinea-Bissau	$1,200
90 Swaziland	$5,700	107 Papua-New Guinea	$2,900	123 Cote d'Ivoire	$1,800	139 Mozambique	$1,200
91 Bolivia	$5,500			124 Kenya	$1,800	140 Afghanistan	$1,100
92 Morocco	$5,500	108 Nigeria	$2,800	125 Korea, North	$1,800	141 Guinea	$1,100
93 Guatemala	$5,300	109 Djibouti	$2,700	126 Zambia	$1,800	142 Madagascar	$1,100
94 Syria	$5,100	110 Cambodia	$2,600	127 Burma (Myanmar)	$1,700	143 Mali	$1,100
95 Congo	$4,800	111 Sudan	$2,600			144 Togo	$1,000
96 Honduras	$4,800	112 Chad	$2,500	128 Tanzania	$1,700	145 Malawi	$900
97 Philippines	$4,700	113 Kyrgyzstan	$2,500	129 Benin	$1,600	146 Niger	$800
98 Nicaragua	$4,500	114 Western Sahara	$2,500	130 Burkina Faso	$1,500	147 Central African Republic	$700
99 India	$4,000	115 Yemen	$2,500	131 Nepal	$1,500		
100 Indonesia	$4,000	116 Cameroon	$2,400	132 Rwanda	$1,500	148 Burundi	$600
101 Vietnam	$4,000	117 Tajikistan	$2,300	133 Uganda	$1,500	149 Somalia	$600
102 Moldova	$3,800	118 Lesotho	$2,200	134 Sierra Leone	$1,400	150 Zimbabwe	$600
103 Uzbekistan	$3,800	119 Mauritania	$2,200	135 Ethiopia	$1,300	151 Congo, Dem. Rep.	$400
104 Ghana	$3,500	120 Bangladesh	$2,100	136 Haiti	$1,300		
105 Laos	$3,100	121 Senegal	$2,100	137 Eritrea	$1,200		

The Industrializing Nations

The Industrializing Nations include most of the nations of the former Soviet Union and its former satellites in eastern Europe. As Table 7.3 on page 211 shows, these nations account for 20 percent of the Earth's land and 16 percent of its people.

The dividing points between the three "worlds" are soft, making it difficult to know how to classify some nations. This is especially the case with the Industrializing Nations. Exactly how much industrialization must a nation have to be in this category? Although soft, these categories do pinpoint essential differences among nations. Most people who live in the Industrializing Nations have much lower incomes and standards of living than do those who live in the Most Industrialized Nations. The majority, however, are better off than those who live in the Least Industrialized Nations. For example, on such measures as access to electricity, indoor plumbing, automobiles, telephones, and even food, most citizens of the Industrializing Nations rank lower than those in the Most Industrialized Nations but higher than those in the Least Industrialized Nations. As you saw in the opening vignette, stratification affects even life expectancy.

The benefits of industrialization are uneven. Large numbers of people in the Industrializing Nations remain illiterate and desperately poor. Conditions can be gruesome, as we explore in the following Thinking Critically section.

Thinking Critically

Open Season: Children as Prey

What is childhood like in the Industrializing Nations?

The answer depends on who your parents are. If you are the son or daughter of rich parents, childhood can be pleasant—a world filled with luxuries and servants. If you are born into poverty but live in a rural area where there is plenty to eat, life can still be good—although there may be no books, television, and little education. If you live in a slum, however, life can be horrible—worse even than in the slums of the Most Industrialized Nations (Lyons 2013). Let's take a glance at a notorious slum in Brazil.

Not enough food—this you can take for granted—along with wife abuse, broken homes, alcoholism, drug abuse, and a lot of crime: From your knowledge of slums in the Most Industrialized Nations, you would expect these things. What you may not expect, however, are the brutal conditions in which Brazilian slum (*favela*) children live.

Sociologist Martha Huggins (Huggins et al. 2002) reports that poverty is so deep that children and adults swarm through garbage dumps to try to find enough decaying food to keep them alive. You might also be surprised to discover that the owners

Early morning in a *favela* in Sao Paolo, Brazil.

of some of these dumps hire armed guards to keep the poor out—so that they can sell the garbage for pig food. And you might be shocked to learn that some shop owners hire hit men, auctioning designated victims to the *lowest* bidder!

Life is cheap in the poor nations—but death squads for children? To understand this, we must first note that Brazil has a long history of violence. Brazil also has a high rate of poverty, has only a tiny middle class, and is controlled by a small group of families who, under a veneer of democracy, make the country's major decisions. Hordes of homeless children, with no schools or jobs, roam the streets. To survive, they wash windshields, shine shoes, beg, and steal (Rosenblatt 2012).

The "respectable" classes see these children as nothing but trouble. They hurt business: Customers feel intimidated when they see begging children—especially teenaged boys—clustered in front of stores. Some shoplift. Others break into stores. With no effective social institutions to care for these children, one solution is to kill them. As Huggins notes, murder sends a clear message—especially if it is accompanied by ritual torture: gouging out the eyes, ripping open the chest, cutting off the genitals, raping the girls, and burning the victim's body.

Not all life is bad in the Industrializing Nations, but this is about as bad as it gets.

For Your Consideration

→ Do you think there is anything the Most Industrialized Nations can do about this situation? Or is it, though

unfortunate, just an "internal" affair that is up to Brazil to handle as it wishes?

→ Directed by the police, death squads in Brazil also assassinate criminals, while in the Philippine slums they kill rapists and drug dealers ("You Can Die Anytime" 2009; Lyons 2014). What do you think about this?

The Least Industrialized Nations

In the Least Industrialized Nations, most people live on small farms or in villages, have large families, and barely survive. These nations account for 68 percent of the world's people but only 49 percent of the Earth's land.

Poverty plagues these nations to such an extent that some families actually *live* in city dumps. This is hard to believe, but look at the photos on the next two pages, which I took in Phnom Penh, the capital of Cambodia. Although wealthy nations have their pockets of poverty, *most* people in the Least Industrialized nations are poor. *Most* of them have no running water, indoor plumbing, or access to trained teachers or doctors. As we will review in Chapter 14, most of the world's population growth occurs in these nations, placing even greater burdens on their limited resources and causing them to fall farther behind each year.

Modifying the Model

To classify countries into Most Industrialized, Industrializing, and Least Industrialized is helpful in that it pinpoints significant similarities and differences among groups of nations. But then there are the oil-rich nations of the Middle East, those that provide much of the gasoline that fuels the machinery of the Most Industrialized Nations. Although these nations are not industrialized, some are immensely wealthy. To classify them simply as Least Industrialized would gloss over significant distinctions, such as their modern hospitals, extensive prenatal care, desalinization plants, abundant food and shelter, high literacy, and computerized banking. On the Social Map on page 213, I classify them separately. Table 7.4 also reflects this distinction.

Table 7.4 An Alternative Model of Global Stratification

Four Worlds of Stratification
Most Industrialized Nations
Industrializing Nations
Least Industrialized Nations
Oil-rich, nonindustrialized nations

SOURCE: By the author.

Kuwait is an outstanding example. Kuwait is so wealthy that almost none of its citizens work for a living. The government simply pays them an annual salary just for being citizens. Everyday life in Kuwait still has its share of onerous chores, of course, but migrant workers from the poor nations do most of this work. To run the specialized systems that keep Kuwait's economy going, Kuwait imports trained workers from the Most Industrialized Nations.

The Dump People: Working and Living and Playing in the City Dump of Phnom Penh, Cambodia

I went to Cambodia to inspect orphanages, to see how well the children are being cared for. While in Phnom Penh, Cambodia's capital, I was told about people who live in the city dump. Live there? I could hardly believe my ears. I knew that people made their living by picking scraps from the city dump, but I didn't know they actually lived among the garbage. This I had to see for myself.

I did. And there I found a highly developed social organization—an intricate support system. Because words are inadequate to depict the abject poverty of the Least Industrialized Nations, these photos can provide more insight into these people's lives than anything I could say.

After the garbage arrives by truck, people stream around it, struggling to be the first to discover something of value. To sift through the trash, the workers use metal picks, like the one this child is holding. Note that children work alongside the adults.

The children who live in the dump also play there. These children are riding bicycles on a "road," a packed, leveled area of garbage that leads to their huts. The huge stacks in the background are piled trash. Note the ubiquitous Nike.

This is a typical sight—family and friends working together. The trash, which is constantly burning, contains harmful chemicals. Why do people work under such conditions? Because they have few options. It is either this or starve.

© James M. Henslin, all photos

One of my many surprises was to find food stands in the dump. Although this one primarily offers drinks and snacks, others serve more substantial food. One even has broken chairs salvaged from the dump for its customers.

The people live at the edge of the dump, in homemade huts (visible in the background). This woman, who was on her way home after a day's work, put down her sack of salvaged items to let me take her picture. She still has her pick in her hand.

CAMBODIA
★ Phnom Penh

I was surprised to learn that ice is delivered to the dump. This woman is using a hand grinder to crush ice for drinks for her customers. The customers, of course, are other people who also live in the dump.

At the day's end, the workers wash at the community pump. This hand pump serves all their water needs—drinking, washing, and cooking. There is no indoor plumbing. The weeds in the background serve that purpose. Can you imagine drinking water that comes from below this garbage dump?

Not too many visitors to Phnom Penh tell a cab driver to take them to the city dump. The cabbie looked a bit perplexed, but he did as I asked. Two cabs are shown here because my friends insisted on accompanying me.

I know my friends were curious themselves, but they had also discovered that the destinations I want to visit are usually not in the tourist guides, and they wanted to protect me.

Note the smoke from the smoldering garbage.

How Did the World's Nations Become Stratified?

7.7 Discuss how colonialism and world system theory explain how the world's nations became stratified.

How did the globe become stratified into such distinct worlds? The commonsense answer is that the poorer nations have fewer resources than the richer nations. As with many commonsense answers, this one falls short. Many of the Industrializing and Least Industrialized Nations are rich in natural resources, while one Most Industrialized Nation, Japan, has few. Three theories explain how global stratification came about.

Colonialism

The first theory, **colonialism**, stresses that the countries that industrialized first got a jump on the rest of the world. Beginning in Great Britain about 1750, industrialization spread throughout western Europe. Plowing some of their profits into powerful armaments and fast ships, these countries invaded weaker nations, making colonies out of them (Harrison 1993; Saikal 2014). After subduing these weaker nations, the more powerful countries left behind a controlling force in order to exploit the nations' labor and natural resources. At one point, there was even a free-for-all among the industrialized European countries as they rushed to divide up an entire continent. As they sliced Africa into pieces, even tiny Belgium got into the act and acquired the Congo, which was *seventy-five* times larger than itself.

The purpose of colonialism was to establish *economic colonies*—to exploit the nation's people and resources for the benefit of the "mother" country. The more powerful European countries would plant their national flags in a colony and send their representatives to run the government, but the United States usually chose to plant corporate flags in a colony and let these corporations dominate the territory's government. Central and South America are prime examples. There were exceptions, such as the U.S. army's conquest of the Philippines, which President McKinley said was motivated by the desire "to educate the Filipinos, and uplift and civilize and Christianize them" (Krugman 2002).

Colonialism, then, shaped many of the Least Industrialized Nations. In some instances, the Most Industrialized Nations were so powerful that when dividing their spoils, they drew lines across a map, creating new states without regard for tribal or cultural considerations (Kifner 1999). Britain and France did just this as they divided up North Africa and parts of the Middle East—which is why the national boundaries of Libya, Saudi Arabia, Kuwait, and other countries are so straight. This legacy of European conquests is a background factor in much of today's racial–ethnic and tribal violence: By the stroke of a pen, groups with no history of national identity were incorporated within the same political boundaries.

Homeless people sleeping on the streets is a common sight in India's cities. I took this photo in Chennai (formerly Madras).

colonialism

the process by which one nation takes over another nation, usually for the purpose of exploiting its labor and natural resources

world system theory

a theory of how economic and political connections developed and now tie the world's countries together

World System Theory

The second explanation of how global stratification came about was proposed by Immanuel Wallerstein (1979, 1990, 2011). According to **world system theory,** industrialization led to four groups of nations. The first group consists of the *core nations*, the countries that industrialized first (Britain, France, Holland, and, later, Germany), which grew rich and powerful. The second group is the *semiperiphery*. The economies of these nations, located around the Mediterranean, stagnated because they grew dependent on trade with the core nations. The economies of the third group, the *periphery*, or fringe nations, developed even less. These are the eastern European countries, which sold cash crops to the core nations. The fourth group of nations includes most of Africa and Asia. Called the *external area*, these nations were left out of the development of capitalism altogether. The current expansion of capitalism has changed the relationships among these groups. Most notably, eastern Europe and Asia are no longer left out of capitalism.

The **globalization of capitalism**—the adoption of capitalism around the world—has created extensive ties among the world's nations. Production and trade are now so interconnected that events around the globe affect us all. Sometimes this is immediate, as happens when a civil war disrupts the flow of oil, or—perish the thought—as would be the case if terrorists managed to get their hands on nuclear or biological weapons. At other times, the effects are like a slow ripple, as when a government adopts some policy that gradually impedes its ability to compete in world markets. All of today's societies, then, no matter where they are located, are part of a world system.

The interconnections are most evident among nations that do extensive trading with one another. The following Thinking Critically section explores implications of Mexico's *maquiladoras*.

globalization of capitalism
capitalism (investing to make profits within a rational system) becoming the globe's dominant economic system

Thinking Critically

When Globalization Comes Home: *Maquiladoras* South of the Border

Two hundred thousand Mexicans rush to Juarez each year, fleeing the hopelessness of the rural areas in pursuit of a better life. They have no running water or plumbing, but they didn't have any in the country either, and here they have the possibility of a job, a weekly check to buy food for the kids.

The pay is $100 for a 48-hour work week, about $2 an hour (Harris 2008).

This may not sound like much, but it is more than twice the minimum daily wage in Mexico.

Assembly-for-export plants, known as *maquiladoras*, dot the Mexican border (Archibald 2011). The North American Free Trade Agreement (NAFTA) allows U.S. companies to import materials to Mexico without paying tax and then to export the finished products into the United States, again without tax. It's a sweet deal: few taxes and $8 to $16 a day for workers starved for jobs.

That these workers live in shacks, with no running water or sewage disposal, is not the employers' concern.

Nor is the pollution. The stinking air doesn't stay on the Mexican side of the border. Neither does the garbage. Heavy rains wash torrents of untreated sewage and industrial wastes into the Rio Grande (Casey and Watkins 2014).

There is also the loss of jobs for U.S. workers. Six of the fifteen poorest cities in the United States are located along the sewage-infested Rio Grande. NAFTA didn't bring poverty to these cities. They were poor before this treaty, but residents resent the transfer of jobs across the border (Thompson 2001).

What if the *maquilas* (*maquiladora* workers) organize and demand better pay? Farther south, even cheaper labor beckons. Workers in Guatemala and Honduras, even more desperate than those in Mexico, will gladly take these jobs (Brown 2008). China, too, is competing for them (Utar and Ruiz 2010). And Vietnam and Cambodia are competing for China's jobs.

Many Mexican politicians would say that this presentation is one-sided. "Sure there are problems," they would say, "but this is how it always is when a country industrializes. Don't you realize that the *maquiladoras* bring jobs to people who have no work? They also bring roads, telephone lines, and electricity to undeveloped areas." "In fact," said Vicente Fox, when he was the president of Mexico, "workers at the *maquiladoras* make more than the average salary in Mexico—and that's what we call fair wages" (Fraser 2001).

For Your Consideration

Let's apply our three theoretical perspectives.

→ Some conflict theorists analyze how capitalists try to weaken the bargaining power of workers by exploiting divisions among them. In what is known as the *split labor market*, capitalists pit one group of workers against another to lower the cost of labor. How do you think *maquiladoras* fit this conflict perspective?

→ When functionalists analyze a situation, they identify its functions and dysfunctions. What functions and dysfunctions of *maquiladoras* do you see?

→ Symbolic interactionists analyze how people's experiences shape their views of the world. How would people's experiences in contrasting social locations lead to different answers to "Do *maquiladoras* represent exploitation or opportunity?" What multiple realities do you see here?

A *maquiladora* worker in Ciudad Juarez, Chihuahua. One of 3,000 employees at this cross-border plant.

Inside the home of a *maquiladora* worker in Nuevo Laredo, Mexico.

Culture of Poverty

The third explanation of global stratification is quite unlike colonialism and world system theory. Economist John Kenneth Galbraith (1979) claimed that the cultures of the Least Industrialized Nations hold them back. Building on the ideas of anthropologist Oscar Lewis (1966a, 1966b), Galbraith argued that some nations are crippled by a **culture of poverty**, a way of life that perpetuates poverty from one generation to the next. He explained it this way: Most of the world's poor people are farmers who live on little plots of land. They barely produce enough food to survive. Living on the edge of starvation, they have little room for risk—so they stick to tried-and-true, traditional ways. To experiment with new farming techniques is to court disaster, since failure would lead to hunger and death.

Their religion also encourages them to accept their situation. It teaches fatalism, the belief that an individual's position in life is God's will. For example, in India, the Dalits are taught that they must have done very bad things in a previous life to suffer so. They are supposed to submit to their situation, which they deserve—and in the next life, maybe they'll come back in a more desirable state.

culture of poverty

the assumption that the values and behaviors of the poor make them fundamentally different from other people, that these factors are largely responsible for their poverty, and that parents perpetuate poverty across generations by passing these characteristics to their children

Evaluating the Theories

Most sociologists prefer colonialism and world system theory. To them, an explanation based on a culture of poverty places blame on the victim—the poor nations themselves. It points to characteristics of the poor nations, rather than to international political arrangements that benefit the Most Industrialized Nations at the expense of the poor nations. But even taken together, these theories yield only part of the picture. None of these theories, for example, would have led anyone to expect that after World War II, Japan would become an economic powerhouse: Japan had a religion that stressed fatalism, two of its major cities had been destroyed by atomic bombs, and it had been stripped of its colonies.

Each theory, then, yields but a partial explanation, and the grand theorist who will put the many pieces of this puzzle together has yet to appear.

Maintaining Global Stratification

7.8   **Explain how neocolonialism, multinational corporations, and technology help to maintain global stratification.**

Regardless of how the world's nations became stratified, why do countries remain rich— or poor—year after year? Let's look at three explanations of how global stratification is maintained.

Neocolonialism

Sociologist Michael Harrington (1977) argued that when colonialism fell out of style, it was replaced by **neocolonialism**. When World War II changed public sentiment about sending soldiers to conquer weaker countries and colonists to exploit them, the Most Industrialized Nations turned to the international markets as a way of controlling the Least Industrialized Nations. By selling them goods on credit—especially weapons that the local elites desire so they can keep themselves in power—the Most Industrialized Nations entrap the poor nations within a circle of debt.

neocolonialism
the economic and political dominance of the Least Industrialized Nations by the Most Industrialized Nations

As many of us learn the hard way, owing a large debt puts us at the mercy of our creditors. So it is with neocolonialism. The *policy* of selling weapons and other manufactured goods to the Least Industrialized Nations on credit turns those countries into eternal debtors. The capital they need to develop their own industries goes instead as payments toward the debt, which becomes bloated with mounting interest. Keeping these nations in debt forces them to submit to trading terms dictated by the neocolonialists (Carrington 1993; Smith 2001).

RELEVANCE TODAY   Neocolonialism might seem remote from your life, but its heritage affects you directly. Consider the oil-rich Middle Eastern countries, our wars in the Persian Gulf, and the terrorism that emanates from this region (*Strategic Energy Policy* 2001; Mouawad 2007). Although this is an area of ancient civilizations, the countries themselves are recent. Great Britain created Saudi Arabia, drawing its boundaries and even naming the country after the man (Ibn Saud) whom British officials picked to lead it. This created a debt for the Saudi family. For decades, this family repaid its debt by providing low-cost oil, which the Most Industrialized Nations need to maintain their way of life. When other nations pumped less oil—no matter the cause, whether revolution or an attempt to raise prices—the Saudis helped keep prices low by making up the shortfall. In return, the United States (and other nations) overlooked the human rights violations of the Saudi royal family, keeping them in power by selling them the latest weapons. This mutually sycophantic arrangement continues.

Multinational Corporations

Multinational corporations, companies that operate across many national boundaries, also help to maintain the global dominance of the Most Industrialized Nations. In some cases, multinational corporations exploit the Least Industrialized Nations directly. A prime example is the United Fruit Company, a U.S. corporation that used to run Central American nations as its own fiefdoms. The CIA would plot and overthrow elected, but uncooperative, governments (CIA 2003), and an occasional invasion by Marines would remind area politicians of the military power that backed U.S. corporations.

multinational corporations
companies that operate across national boundaries; also called *transnational corporations*

Most commonly, however, it is simply by doing business that multinational corporations help to maintain international stratification. A single multinational corporation may manage mining operations in several countries, manufacture goods in others, and market its products around the globe. No matter where the profits are made, or where they are reinvested, the primary beneficiaries are the Most Industrialized Nations, especially the one in which the multinational corporation has its world headquarters.

BUYING POLITICAL STABILITY   In their pursuit of profits, the multinational corporations need cooperative power elites in the Least Industrialized Nations (Pariza 2011; Sprague 2012). In return for funneling money to the elites and selling them modern weapons, the corporations get a "favorable business climate"—that is, low taxes and cheap labor. The corporations politely call the money they pay to the elites "subsidies" and "offsets"—which ring prettier on the ear than "bribes." Able to siphon money from their country's tax collections and government budgets, these elites live a sophisticated upper-class life in the major cities of their home country. Although most of the citizens of these countries live a hard-scrabble life, the elites are able to send their children to prestigious Western universities, such as Oxford, the Sorbonne, and Harvard.

You can see how this cozy arrangement helps to maintain global stratification. The significance of these payoffs is not so much the genteel lifestyles that they allow the elites to maintain but the translation of the payoffs into power. They allow the elites to purchase high-tech weapons with which they preserve their positions of privilege, even though they must oppress their people to do so. The result is a political stability that keeps alive this diabolical partnership between the multinational corporations and the national elites.

UNANTICIPATED CONSEQUENCES   This, however, is not the full story. An unintentional by-product of the multinationals' global search for cheap resources and labor is to modify global stratification. When corporations move manufacturing from the Most Industrialized Nations to the Least Industrialized Nations, they not only exploit cheap labor, but they also bring jobs and money to these nations. Although workers in the Least Industrialized Nations are paid a pittance, it is more than they can earn elsewhere. With new factories come opportunities to develop skills, acquire technology, and accumulate a capital base from which local elites can launch their own factories.

The Pacific Rim nations provide a remarkable example. In return for providing the "favorable business climate" just mentioned, multinational corporations invested billions of dollars in the "Asian tigers" (Hong Kong, Singapore, South Korea, and Taiwan). These nations have developed such a strong capital base that, along with China, they have begun to rival the older capitalist countries. This has also made them subject to capitalism's "boom and bust" cycles. When capitalism suffers a downturn, workers and investors in these nations, including those in the *maquiladoras* that you just read about, have their dreams smashed.

Technology and Global Domination

The race between the Most and Least Industrialized Nations to develop and apply the new technologies might seem like a race between a marathon runner and someone with a broken leg. Can the outcome be in doubt? As the multinational corporations amass profits, they are able to invest huge sums in the latest technology while the Least Industrialized Nations are struggling to put scraps on the table.

So it would appear, but the race is not this simple. Although the Most Industrialized Nations have a seemingly insurmountable head start, some of the other nations are shortening the distance between themselves and the front-runners. With cheap labor making their manufactured goods inexpensive, China and India are exporting goods on a massive scale. They are using the capital from these exports to buy high technology so they can modernize their infrastructure (transportation, communication, electrical, and banking systems). Although global domination remains in the hands of the West, it could be on the verge of a major shift from West to East.

Strains in the Global System

7.9 **Identify strains in today's system of global stratification.**

It is never easy to maintain global stratification. At the very least, a continuous stream of unanticipated events forces the elite to stay on their toes, and at times, huge currents of history threaten to sweep them aside. No matter how secure a stratification system may seem, it always contains unresolved matters. These contradictions can be covered up for a while, but inevitably the discontent multiplies and the demand for change grows louder. Some are just little dogs nipping at the heels of the world's elites, bringing issues that can be resolved with a drone or a few tanks or bombs—or, better, with a scowl and the threat to bomb an opponent. Other issues are of a broader nature, part of huge historical shifts. Baring their teeth, both emerging and old unresolved contradictions snarlingly demand change, even the rearrangement of global power.

Historical shifts bring cataclysmic disruptions. We are now living through such a time. The far-reaching economic–political changes in Russia and China have been accompanied by huge cracks in a creaking global banking system. In desperation, the global powers have pumped trillions of dollars into their economic–political systems. As curious as we are about the outcome and as much as our welfare is at stake, we don't know the end point of this current strain in the global system and the power elites' attempts to patch up the most glaring inconsistencies in their global domination. As this process of realignment continues, however, it is likely to sweep all of us into its unwelcome net.

Summary and Review

Systems of Social Stratification

7.1 **Compare and contrast slavery (including bonded labor), caste, estate, and class systems of social stratification.**

What is Social Stratification?

Social stratification refers to a hierarchy of privilege based on property, power, and prestige. Every society stratifies its members, and in every society, men-as-a-group dominate women-as-a-group.

What are four major systems of social stratification?

Four major stratification systems are slavery, caste, estate, and class. The essential characteristic of **slavery** is that some people own other people. Initially, slavery was based not on race but on debt, punishment for crime, or defeat in battle. Slavery could be temporary or permanent and was not necessarily passed on to the children. North American slavery was gradually buttressed by a racist **ideology**. In a **caste system**, people's status, which is lifelong, is determined by their caste's relation to other castes. The **estate system** of feudal Europe consisted of three estates: the

nobility, clergy, and peasants (serfs). A **class system** is much more open than these other systems, since it is based primarily on money or material possessions. Industrialization encourages the formation of class systems. Gender cuts across all forms of social stratification.

What Determines Social Class?

7.2 **Contrast the views of Marx and Weber on what determines social class.**

Karl Marx argued that a single factor determines social class: If you own the means of production, you belong to the **bourgeoisie**; if you do not, you are one of the **proletariat**. Max Weber argued that three elements determine social class: property, power, and prestige.

Why Is Social Stratification Universal?

7.3 **Contrast the functional and conflict views of why social stratification is universal.**

To explain why stratification is universal, functionalists Kingsley Davis and Wilbert Moore argued that to attract the most capable people to fill its important positions, society must offer them greater rewards. Melvin Tumin said that if this view were correct, society would be a **meritocracy**, with positions awarded on the basis of merit. Gaetano Mosca argued that stratification is inevitable because every society must have leadership, which, by definition, means inequality. Conflict theorists argue that stratification is the outcome of an elite emerging as groups struggle for limited resources. Gerhard Lenski suggested a synthesis between the functionalist and conflict perspectives.

How Do Elites Maintain Stratification?

7.4   Discuss the ways that elites keep themselves in power.

To maintain social stratification within a nation, the ruling class adopts an ideology that justifies its current arrangements. It also controls information and uses technology. When all else fails, it turns to brute force.

Comparative Social Stratification

7.5   Contrast social stratification in Great Britain and the former Soviet Union.

What are key characteristics of stratification systems in other nations?

The most striking features of the British class system are speech and education. In Britain, accent reveals social class, and almost all of the elite attend private schools. In the former Soviet Union, communism was supposed to abolish class distinctions. Instead, it ushered in a different set of classes.

Global Stratification: Three Worlds

7.6   Compare the three worlds of global stratification: the Most Industrialized Nations, the Industrializing Nations, and the Least Industrialized Nations.

How are the world's nations stratified?

The model presented here divides the world's nations into three groups: the Most Industrialized, the Industrializing,

and the Least Industrialized. This layering represents relative property, power, and prestige. The oil-rich nations are an exception.

How Did the World's Nations Become Stratified?

7.7   Discuss how colonialism and world system theory explain how the world's nations became stratified.

The main theories that seek to account for global stratification are **colonialism**, **world system theory**, and the **culture of poverty**.

Maintaining Global Stratification

7.8   Explain how neocolonialism, multinational corporations, and technology help to maintain global stratification.

How do elites maintain global stratification?

There are two basic explanations for why the world's countries remain stratified. **Neocolonialism** is the ongoing dominance of the Least Industrialized Nations by the Most Industrialized Nations. The second explanation points to the influence of **multinational corporations**. The new technology gives further advantage to the Most Industrialized Nations.

Strains in the Global System

7.9   Identify strains in today's system of global stratification.

What strains are showing up in global stratification?

All stratification systems have contradictions that threaten to erupt, forcing the system to change. Currently, capitalism is in crisis, and we seem to be experiencing a global shift in economic (and, ultimately, political) power from the West to the East.

Thinking Critically about Chapter 7

1. How do slavery, caste, estate, and class systems of social stratification differ?

2. Why is social stratification universal?

3. How do elites maintain stratification (keep themselves in power)?

4. What shifts in global stratification seem to be taking place? Why?

Chapter 8
Social Class in the United States

Learning Objectives

8.1 Explain the three components of social class—property, power, and prestige; distinguish between wealth and income; explain how property and income are distributed; and describe the democratic façade, the power elite, and status inconsistency. (p. 227)

8.2 Contrast Marx's and Weber's models of social class. (p. 234)

8.3 Summarize the consequences of social class for physical and mental health, family life, education, religion, politics, and the criminal justice system. (p. 239)

8.4 Contrast the three types of social mobility, review gender issues in research on social mobility, and explain why social mobility brings pain. (p. 243)

8.5 Explain the problems in drawing the poverty line and how poverty is related to geography, race–ethnicity, education, feminization, and age. (p. 247)

8.6 Contrast the dynamics of poverty with the culture of poverty, explain why people are poor and how deferred gratification is related to poverty, and comment on the Horatio Alger myth. (p. 251)

8.7 Discuss the possibility that we are developing a three-tier society. (p. 255)

Ah, New Orleans, that fabled city on the Mississippi Delta. Images from its rich past floated through my head—pirates, treasure, intrigue. Memories from a pleasant vacation stirred my thoughts—the exotic French Quarter with its enticing aroma of Creole food and sounds of earthy jazz drifting through the air.

The shelter for the homeless forced me back to an unwelcome reality. The shelter was like those I had visited in the North, West, and East—only dirtier. The dirt, in fact, was the worst that I had encountered during my research. On top of that, this was the only shelter to insist on payment in exchange for sleeping in one of its filthy beds.

The men here looked the same as the homeless anywhere in the country—disheveled and haggard, wearing that unmistakable expression of sorrow and despair. Except for the accent, you wouldn't know what region you were in. Poverty wears the same tired face wherever you are, I realized. The accent may differ, but the look remains the same.

I had grown used to the sights and smells of abject poverty. Those no longer surprised me. But after my fitful sleep with the homeless that night, I saw something that did. Just a block or so from the shelter, I was startled by a sight so out of step with the misery and despair I had just experienced that I stopped and stared.

> "My mind refused to stop juxtaposing these images of extravagance with the suffering I had just seen."

I felt indignation swelling within me. Confronting me were life-sized, full-color photos mounted on the transparent Plexiglas shelter of a bus stop. Staring back at me were images of finely dressed men and women, proudly strutting about as they modeled elegant suits, dresses, diamonds, and furs.

A wave of disgust swept over me. "Something is cockeyed in this society," I thought, as my mind refused to stop juxtaposing these images of extravagance with the suffering I had just seen.

The disjunction—the mental distress—that I felt in New Orleans was triggered by the ads, but it was not the first time I had experienced this sensation. Whenever my research abruptly transported me from the world of the homeless to one of another social class, I experienced a sense of disjointed unreality. Each social class has its own way of thinking and behaving, and because these fundamental orientations to the world contrast so sharply, the classes do not mix well.

What Is Social Class?

8.1 **Explain the three components of social class—property, power, and prestige; distinguish between wealth and income; explain how property and income are distributed; and describe the democratic façade, the power elite, and status inconsistency.**

If you ask most Americans about their country's social class system, you are likely to get a blank look. If you press the matter, you are likely to get an answer like this: "There are the poor and the rich—and then there's us, neither poor nor rich." This is just about as far as most Americans' consciousness of social class goes. Let's try to flesh out this idea.

Our task is made somewhat difficult because sociologists have no clear-cut, agreed-on definition of social class (Sosnaud et al. 2013). As was noted in the last chapter, conflict sociologists (of the Marxist orientation) see only two social classes: those who own the means of production and those who do not. The problem with this view, say most sociologists, is that it lumps too many people together. Teenage "order takers" at McDonald's who work for $15,000 a year are lumped together with that company's executives who make $500,000 a year—because they both are workers at McDonald's, not owners.

Most sociologists agree with Weber that there is more to social class than just a person's relationship to the means of production. Consequently, most sociologists use the components Weber identified and define **social class** as a large group of people who rank closely to one another in property, power, and prestige. These three elements give people different chances in life, separate them into different lifestyles, and provide them with distinctive ways of looking at the self and the world.

Let's look at how sociologists measure these three components of social class.

Property

Property comes in many forms, such as buildings, land, animals, machinery, cars, stocks, bonds, businesses, furniture, jewelry, and bank accounts. When you add up the value of someone's property and subtract that person's debts, you have what sociologists call **wealth**. This term can be misleading, as some of us have little wealth—especially most college students. Nevertheless, if your net total comes to $10, then that is your wealth. (Obviously, *wealth* as a sociological term does not mean wealthy.)

DISTINGUISHING BETWEEN WEALTH AND INCOME Wealth and income are sometimes confused, but they are not the same. Where *wealth* is a person's net worth, **income** is a flow of money. Income has many sources: The most common is wages or a business, but other sources are rent, interest, and royalties. Even alimony, an allowance, and gambling winnings are part of income.

social class

according to Weber, a large group of people who rank close to one another in property, power, and prestige; according to Marx, one of two groups: capitalists who own the means of production or workers who sell their labor

property

material possessions: includes animals, bank accounts, bonds, buildings, businesses, cars, cash, commodities, copyrights, furniture, jewelry, land, and stocks

wealth

the total value of everything someone owns, minus the debts

income

money received, usually from a job, business, or assets

A mere one-half percent of Americans owns over a quarter of the entire nation's wealth. Very few minorities are numbered among this 0.5 percent. An exception is Oprah Winfrey, who has had an ultra-successful career in entertainment and investing. Worth $3.0 billion, she is the 215th richest person in the United States. Winfrey has given millions of dollars to help minority children.

Wealth and income usually go together, but not always. Some people have much wealth and little income. For example, a farmer may own a lot of land (a form of wealth), but bad weather can cause the income to dry up.

Then there are those who have a large income and no wealth. Here is a real-life example of someone who makes $375,000 a year and is dead broke:

> *Gregory Owens is a New York City lawyer who makes $375,000 a year. Yet he is broke. In his bankruptcy petition, Owens revealed that taxes, alimony, required retirement contributions, rent, food, and transportation eat up all his income. He spends $52 more a month than he earns. (Stewart 2014)*

DISTRIBUTION OF PROPERTY   If we add up the value of the property in the United States—all the houses, apartments, cars and trucks, farms, businesses, and bank accounts—the total comes to about $51 trillion (*Statistical Abstract* 2014:Table 751). This certainly is a hefty sum. And who owns this vast property? One answer, of course, is "everyone," as this $51 trillion is the total of what all Americans own. What this statement overlooks, though, is how the nation's property is divided among "everyone."

You might be surprised at how concentrated U.S. wealth is. Look at Figure 8.1. *Just 1 percent of Americans owns more than one-third of all real estate, stocks, bonds, and business assets in the entire country.* As you can also see from this figure, *10 percent* of Americans own *77 percent* of the nation's wealth.

Figure 8.1 Distribution of the Wealth of Americans

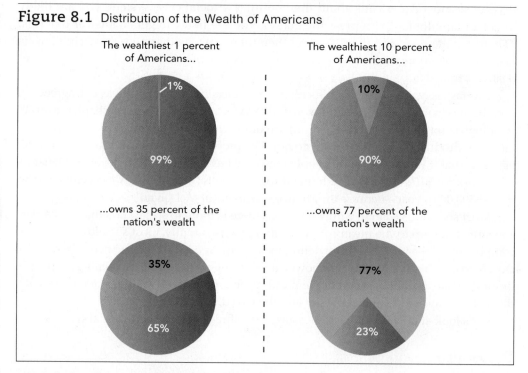

The wealthiest 1 percent of Americans...

1%

99%

...owns 35 percent of the nation's wealth

35%

65%

The wealthiest 10 percent of Americans...

10%

90%

...owns 77 percent of the nation's wealth

77%

23%

SOURCE: By the author. Based on Wolff 2013.

DISTRIBUTION OF INCOME   How is income distributed in the United States? Economist Paul Samuelson (Samuelson and Nordhaus 2005) put it this way: "If we made an income pyramid out of a child's blocks, with each layer portraying $500 of income, the peak would be far higher than Mount Everest, but most people would be within a few feet of the ground."

To better grasp this layering, look at Figure 8.2 on the next page. You can see that if each block were 1½ inches tall, the typical American would be just *11 feet off the ground*. This portrays the average income in the United States of about $43,000 per year. (This is per capita income, which includes every American, even children.) The typical family climbs a little higher, since most families have more than one worker; together, they average about $61,000 a year (*Statistical Abstract* 2014:Tables 709, 726). Compared with the few families who are on the mountain's peak, the average U.S. family would still find itself only 15 feet off the ground.

The fact that some Americans enjoy the peaks of Mount Everest while most—despite their efforts—make it only 11 to 15 feet up the slope presents a striking image of income inequality in the United States. Another picture emerges if we divide the U.S. population into five equal groups and rank them from highest to lowest income. As Figure 8.3 on the next page shows, the top 20 percent of the population receive *half* (51.0 percent) of all income in the United States. In contrast, the bottom 20 percent of Americans receive only 3.2 percent of the nation's income.

Two features of Figure 8.3, on the next page, stand out. First, look at how income inequality decreased from 1935 to 1970. Then notice how inequality has increased since 1970. *Since 1970, the richest 20 percent of U.S. families have grown richer, while the poorest 20 percent have grown poorer.* Despite numerous government antipoverty programs, the poorest 20 percent of Americans receive *less* of the nation's income today than they did decades ago. The richest 20 percent, in contrast, are receiving more, as much as they did in 1935.

The chief executive officers (CEOs) of the nation's largest corporations are especially affluent. The *Wall Street Journal* surveyed the 300 largest U.S. companies to find out what they paid their CEOs. Their median compensation (including salaries, bonuses, and stock options) came to $11,000,000 a year. (*Median* means that half received more than this amount, and half less.) On Table 8.1, you can see the pay of the five highest paid CEOs.

Table 8.1 The Five Highest-Paid CEOs

CEO	Company	Compensation
Michael Fries	Liberty Global	$112 Million
Satya Nadella	Microsoft	$84 Million
Lawrence Ellison	Oracle	$67 Million
Steven Mollenkopf	Qualcomm	$61 Million
Leslie Moonves	CBS	$57 Million

NOTE: Compensation is for 2014. It includes salary, bonuses, and stock options.
SOURCE: Canipe and Slobin 2015.

The average income of these highest-paid CEOs is *1,800 times* higher than the average pay of U.S. workers (*Statistical Abstract* 2014:Table 709). This does *not* include these CEOs' income from interest, dividends, or rents. Nor does it include the value of their company-paid limousines and chauffeurs, airplanes and pilots, and their private boxes at the symphony and sporting events. To really see the disparity, consider this:

Let's suppose that you started working the year Jesus was born and that you worked full time starting then. Let's also assume that each year you earned today's average per capita income of $42,693. As of this year, you would still have to work 600 more years to earn what the highest-paid executive listed in Table 8.1 earned in just one year.

Imagine how you could live with an income like Michael Fries'. And this is precisely the point. Beyond these cold numbers lies a dynamic reality that profoundly affects people's lives. The difference in wealth between those at the top and those at the bottom of the U.S. class structure means that people experience vastly different lives. For example,

a colleague of mine who was teaching at an exclusive Eastern university piqued his students' curiosity when he lectured on poverty in Latin America. That weekend, one of the students borrowed his parents' corporate jet and pilot, and in class on Monday, he and his friends related their personal observations on poverty in Latin America.

Figure 8.2 How the Income of Americans Is Distributed

Some U.S. families have incomes that exceed the height of Mt. Everest, 29,028 feet

Average U.S. family income $61,000 or 15 feet

Average U.S. individual income $43,000 or 11 feet

If a 1½-inch child's block equals $500 of income, the average individual's annual income of $43,000 would represent a height of 11 feet, and the average family's annual income of $61,000 would represent a height of 15 feet. The income of some families, in contrast, would represent a height greater than that of Mt. Everest.

SOURCE: By the author. Based on *Statistical Abstract of the United States* 2014:Tables 709, 726.

Figure 8.3 The More Things Change, the More They Stay the Same: Dividing the Nation's Income

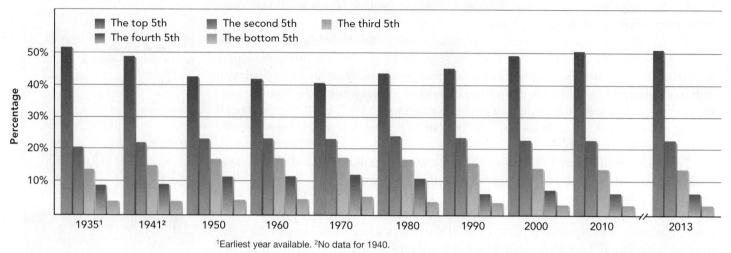

[1]Earliest year available. [2]No data for 1940.

SOURCE: By the author. Based on Statistical Abstract of the United States 1960:Table 417; 1970:Table 489; U.S. Census Bureau. Income, Poverty and Health Insurance Coverage in the United States: 2013. Historical Tables, Income, Households, Table H-2. 2014.

Few of us could ever say, "Mom and Dad, I've got to do a report for my soc class, so I need to borrow the jet—and the pilot—to run down to South America for the weekend." What a lifestyle! Contrast this with Americans at the low end of the income ladder who lack the funds to travel even to a neighboring town for the weekend. For parents in poverty, choices may revolve around whether to spend the little they have at the laundromat or on milk for the baby. The elderly poor might have to choose between purchasing the medicines they need or buying food. In short, divisions of wealth represent not "empty" numbers but choices that make vital differences in people's lives. Let's explore this topic in the Down-to-Earth Sociology box on the next page.

Power

Let's look at the second component of social class: power.

THE DEMOCRATIC FACADE Like many people, you may have said to yourself, "The big decisions are always made despite what I think. Certainly *I* don't make the decision to send soldiers to Afghanistan or Iraq. *I* don't order drones to launch missiles. *I* don't decide to raise taxes, lower interest rates, or spend billions of dollars to bail out Wall Street fools and felons."

And then another part of you may say, "But I do participate in these decisions through my representatives in Congress and by voting for president." True enough—as far as it goes. The trouble is, it doesn't go far enough. Such views of being a participant in the nation's "big" decisions are a playback of the ideology we learn at an early age—an ideology that is promoted by the elites to legitimate and perpetuate their power. Some sociologists call this the "democratic facade" that conceals the real source of power in the United States.

Following this conflict perspective, let's try to get a picture of where that power is located.

THE POWER ELITE In Chapter 1, I mentioned that in the 1950s, sociologist C. Wright Mills pointed out that **power**—the ability to get your way despite resistance—was concentrated in the hands of a few. Mills met heavy criticism, because his analysis contradicted the dominant view that "the people" make the country's decisions. This ideology is still dominant, and Mills' analysis continues to ruffle feathers. Some still choke on the term **power elite**, which Mills coined to refer to those who make the big decisions in U.S. society.

power

the ability to carry out your will, even over the resistance of others

power elite

C. Wright Mills' term for the top people in U.S. corporations, military, and politics who make the nation's major decisions

Down-to-Earth Sociology

How the Super-Rich Live

Larry Ellison, the top man on Table 8.1, loves basketball. And he's quite good at it, too. He loves this sport so much that he has his own basketball court on his yacht. When he misses the basket, a ball sometimes ends up in the ocean. Not to worry. Ellison has hired a man whose sole job is to drive a 44-foot powerboat behind the yacht to retrieve the errant balls.

And when Ellison gets bored with playing on his yacht's basketball court? He climbs in his personal helicopter flown by his personal pilot. Flying above the yacht, he shoots hoops to his heart's content. His personal basketball retriever faithfully trails the yacht, scooping up those errant balls. (Gay 2014)

As F. Scott Fitzgerald said in The Great Gatsby, *"The rich are different than you and me." And how!*

Let's take a glimpse at the lifestyle of another very rich man, John Castle (his real name). John has made more than $100 million in banking and securities (Lublin 1999). But the super-rich yearn for more than just money. Displayed in the right way, vast wealth can bring distinction and envy.

Wanting to be connected to someone famous, John bought President John F. Kennedy's "Winter White House," an oceanfront estate in Palm Beach, Florida. John spent $11 million to remodel the 13,000-square-foot house so that it would be more to his liking. Among those changes: adding bathrooms numbers 14 and 15. He likes to show off John F. Kennedy's bed and also the dresser that has the drawer labeled "black underwear," carefully hand-lettered by Rose Kennedy (Bloomfield 2012).

John has a yacht, too, a source of pleasure and pride. How much did his custom-built Hinckley yacht cost? John can't tell you. As he says, "I don't want to know what anything costs. When you've got enough money, price doesn't make a difference. That's part of the freedom of being rich."

Right. And for John, being rich also means paying $1,000,000 to charter a private jet to fly Spot, his Appaloosa horse, back and forth to the vet. John didn't want Spot to have

Billionaire software designer Charles Simonyi after his second $25 million ride in space.

to endure a long trailer ride. Oh, and of course, there was the cost of Spot's medical treatment, another $500,000.

Other wealthy people besides Ellison and Castle spend extravagantly, too. Lee Tachman threw a four-day party for three friends. They had massages; ate well; took rides in a helicopter, a fighter jet, Ferraris, and Lamborghinis; and did a little paintballing—all for the bargain price of $50,000. At the 1Oak Lounge in New York City, some customers pay $35,000 for a bottle of champagne (Haughney and Konigsberg 2008). Of course, it is a large bottle.

Parties are fun, but what if you want privacy? You can buy that, too. Wayne Huizenga, the founder of Blockbuster, who sold a half ownership in the Miami Dolphins for $550 million ("Builder Stephen . . ." 2008), bought a 2,000-acre country club, complete with an 18-hole golf course, a 55,000-square-foot-clubhouse, and 68 slips for visiting vessels. The club is so exclusive that its only members are Wayne and his wife (Fabrikant 2005).

Withdrawing behind gated estates is one way to gain privacy, but Microsoft co-founder Paul Allen has found another way. On his 414-foot yacht, the *Octopus,* are two helicopters, a swimming pool, and a submarine (Freeland 2011).

While the length of Allen's yacht creates envy among the plutocracy that would make Freud break into a sweat, some might say that Charles Simonyi has even outdone this. He bought a $25 million ticket for a rocket ride to the International Space Station. Simonyi liked the experience so much that he bought a second ticket (Leo 2008). No frequent flyer miles included. But at the pace that prices are increasing, $50 million isn't worth what it used to be anyway.

For Your Consideration

→ What effects has social class had on your life? (Go beyond possessions to values and how you view life.)

→ How do you think you would see the world differently if you were Larry Ellison, John Castle, Lee Tachman, Paul Allen, Charles Simonyi, or Mrs. Wayne Huizenga?

Mills and others have stressed how wealth and power coalesce in a group of people who look at the world in the same way—and view themselves as a special elite. They belong to the same private clubs, vacation at the same exclusive resorts, and even hire the same bands for their daughters' debutante balls (Domhoff 2006, 2014). This elite wields extraordinary power in U.S. society, so much so that many U.S. presidents have been millionaire white men from families with "old money."

Table 8.2 Occupational Prestige: How the United States Compares with Sixty Countries

Occupation	United States	Average of Sixty Countries
Physician	86	78
Supreme Court judge	85	82
College president	81	86
Astronaut	80	80
Lawyer	75	73
College professor	74	78
Airline pilot	73	66
Architect	73	72
Biologist	73	69
Dentist	72	70
Civil engineer	69	70
Clergy	69	60
Psychologist	69	66
Pharmacist	68	64
High school teacher	66	64
Registered nurse	66	54
Professional athlete	65	48
Electrical engineer	64	65
Author	63	62
Banker	63	67
Veterinarian	62	61
Police officer	61	40
Sociologist	61	67
Journalist	60	55
Classical musician	59	56
Actor or actress	58	52
Chiropractor	57	62
Athletic coach	53	50
Social worker	52	56
Electrician	51	44
Undertaker	49	34
Jazz musician	48	38
Real estate agent	48	49
Mail carrier	47	33
Secretary	46	53
Plumber	45	34
Carpenter	43	37
Farmer	40	47
Barber	36	30
Store sales clerk	36	34
Truck driver	30	33
Cab driver	28	28
Garbage collector	28	13
Waiter or waitress	28	23
Bartender	25	23
Lives on public aid	25	16
Bill collector	24	27
Factory worker	24	29
Janitor	22	21
Shoe shiner	17	12
Street sweeper	11	13
Janitor	22	21
Shoe shiner	17	12
Street sweeper	11	13

NOTE: The rankings are based on 1 to 100, from lowest to highest. For five occupations not located in the 1994 source, the 1991 ratings were used: Supreme Court judge, astronaut, athletic coach, lives on public aid, and street sweeper.

SOURCES: Treiman 1977: Appendices A and D; Nakao and Treas 1990, 1994: Appendix D.

Continuing in the tradition of Mills, sociologist William Domhoff (2006, 2014) argues that the power elite is so powerful that the U.S. government makes no major decision without its approval. He analyzed how this group works behind the scenes with elected officials to determine both foreign and domestic policy—from setting Social Security taxes to imposing tariffs on imported goods. Although Domhoff's conclusions are controversial—and alarming—they certainly follow logically from the principle that wealth brings power and extreme wealth brings extreme power.

Prestige

Let's look at the third component of social class, occupational prestige.

OCCUPATIONS AND PRESTIGE   What are you thinking about doing after college? Chances are, you don't have the option of lying in a hammock under palm trees in some South Pacific paradise. Almost all of us have to choose an occupation and go to work. Look at Table 8.2 to see how the career you are considering stacks up in terms of **prestige** (the respect or regard people give it). Because we are moving toward a global society, this table also shows how the rankings given by Americans compare with those of the residents of sixty other countries.

Why do people give more prestige to some jobs than to others? Look again at Table 8.2. The jobs at the top share four features:

1. They pay more.
2. They require more education.
3. They involve more abstract thought.
4. They offer greater autonomy (independence, or self-direction).

Now look at the bottom of the list. You can see that people give less prestige to jobs with the opposite characteristics: These jobs pay little, require less education, involve more physical labor, and are closely supervised. In short, the professions and the white-collar jobs are at the top of the list, the blue-collar jobs at the bottom.

One of the more interesting aspects of these rankings is how consistent they are across countries and over time. For example, people in every country rank college professors higher than nurses, nurses higher than social workers, and social workers higher than janitors. Similarly, the occupations that were ranked high twenty-five years ago still rank high today—and likely will rank high in the years to come.

DISPLAYING PRESTIGE   People want others to acknowledge their prestige. In times past, in some countries, only the emperor and his family could wear purple—it was the royal color. In France, only the nobility could wear lace. In England, no one could sit while the king was on his throne. Some kings and queens required that subjects walk backward as they left the room—so that they would not "turn their back" on the "royal presence."

Concern with displaying prestige has not let up. Military manuals specify who must salute whom. The U.S. president enters a room only after everyone else attending the function is present (to show that the president isn't waiting for others). Everyone must also be standing when the president enters. In the courtroom, bailiffs, some with a gun at the hip, make certain that everyone stands when the judge enters.

Status symbols vary with social class. People who are striving to be upwardly mobile flaunt labels on their clothing or carry shopping bags from prestigious stores to show that they have "arrived." The wealthy regard the status symbols of the "common" classes as cheap and tawdry. They, too, flaunt status symbols, but theirs are things like $100,000 Rolex watches and $50,000 diamond earrings. Like the other classes, the wealthy also try to outdo one another. They casually mention the length of their yacht or that a helicopter flew them to their golf game (Fabrikant 2005). Or they offhandedly bring up the $40,000-a-night penthouse suite at the Four Seasons in New York City, asking, "Have you tried it yet? It's 'rather nice'" (Clemence 2013). Some show off by buying their child an alligator backpack sold by Ashley and Mary-Kate Olsen: just $39,000 (R. Smith 2014).

How about yourself? How do you try to display prestige? Think about your clothing. How much more are you willing to pay for clothing that bears some hot "designer" label? Purses, shoes, jeans, and shirts—many of us pay more if they have some little symbol than if they don't. As we wear them proudly, aren't we actually proclaiming, "See, I had the money (and the in-vogue taste, of course) to buy this particular item!"? For many, prestige is a primary factor in deciding which college to attend. Everyone knows how the prestige of a generic sheepskin from Regional State College compares with a degree from Harvard, Princeton, Yale, or Stanford.

prestige
respect or regard

Status Inconsistency

Ordinarily, we have a similar rank on all three dimensions of social class—property, power, and prestige. The homeless men in the opening vignette are an example of these three dimensions lined up. Such people are **status consistent**. Some people, however, have a mixture of high and low ranks. This condition, called **status inconsistency**, leads to some interesting situations.

Sociologist Gerhard Lenski (1954, 1966) analyzed how people try to maximize their **status**, their position in a social group. Individuals who rank high on one dimension of social class but lower on others want people to judge them on the basis of their highest status. Others, however, are also trying to maximize their own positions, so they may respond according to these people's lowest rankings.

A classic study of status inconsistency was done by sociologist Ray Gold (1952). After apartment-house janitors unionized in Chicago, they made more money than some of the tenants whose garbage they carried out. Residents became upset when they saw janitors driving more expensive cars than they did. Some attempted to "put the janitor in his place" by making "snotty" remarks to him. For their part, the janitors took delight in finding "dirty" secrets about the tenants in their garbage.

People who are status inconsistent, then, are likely to confront one frustrating situation after another (Dogan 2011). They claim the higher status but are handed the lower one. This is so frustrating that the resulting tension can affect people's health. Researchers who studied the health of thousands of Europeans over a decade found that men who were status inconsistent were twice as likely to have heart attacks as men who were status consistent. For reasons that no one knows, status inconsistent women do not have a higher risk of heath attacks (Braig et al. 2011).

status consistency
ranking high or low on all three dimensions of social class

status inconsistency
ranking high on some dimensions of social class and low on others; also called *status discrepancy*

status
the position that someone occupies in a social group (also called *social status*)

There are other consequences as well. Lenski (1954) found that people who are status inconsistent tend to be more politically radical. An example is college professors. Their prestige is very high, as you saw in Table 8.2 on page 232, but their incomes are relatively low. Hardly anyone in U.S. society is more educated, and yet college professors don't even come close to the top of the income pyramid. In line with Lenski's prediction, the politics of most college professors are left of center. This hypothesis may also hold true among academic departments; that is, the higher a department's average pay, the more conservative are the members' politics. Teachers in departments of business and medicine, for example, are among the most highly paid in the university—and they also are the most politically conservative.

Instant wealth, the topic of the Down-to-Earth Sociology box on the next page, provides an interesting case of status inconsistency.

How do you set yourself apart in a country so rich that of its 4.6 million people 79,000 are millionaires? Saeed Khouri (on the right), at an auction in Abu Dhabi, paid $14 million for the license plate "1." His cousin was not as fortunate. His $9 million was enough to buy only "5."

anomie

Durkheim's term for a condition of society in which people become detached from the usual norms that guide their behavior

contradictory class locations

Erik Wright's term for a position in the class structure that generates contradictory interests

---

Figure 8.4 Marx's Model of the Social Classes

> **Capitalists**
> (*Bourgeoisie*, those who own the means of production)

> **Workers**
> (*Proletariat*, those who work for the capitalists)

> **Inconsequential Others**
> (beggars, etc.)

SOURCE: By the author.

Sociological Models of Social Class

8.2   Contrast Marx's and Weber's models of social class.

The question of how many social classes there are is a matter of debate. Sociologists have proposed several models, but no single one has gained universal support. There are two main models: One builds on Marx, the other on Weber.

Updating Marx

As Figure 8.4 illustrates, Marx argued that there are just two classes—capitalists and workers—with membership based solely on a person's relationship to the means of production. Sociologists have criticized this view, saying that these categories are too broad. For example, because executives, managers, and supervisors don't own the means of production, they would be classified as workers. But what do these people have in common with assembly-line workers? The category of "capitalist" is also too broad. Some people, for example, employ a thousand workers, and their decisions directly affect a thousand families. Others, in contrast, have very small businesses.

> *Consider a man I know in Godfrey, Illinois, who used to fix cars in his backyard. As Frank gained a following, he quit his regular job, and, in a few years, he put up a building with five bays and an office. Frank is now a capitalist: He employs five or six mechanics and owns the tools and the building (the "means of production").*

But what does this man have in common with a factory owner who controls the lives of one thousand workers? Not only is Frank's work different, so are his lifestyle and the way he looks at the world.

To resolve this problem, sociologist Erik Wright (1985) suggests that some people are members of more than one class at the same time. They occupy what he calls **contradictory class locations**. By this, Wright means that a person's position in the class structure can generate contradictory interests.

Down-to-Earth Sociology

The Big Win: Life after the Lottery

"If I just win the lottery, life will be good. These problems I've got, they'll be gone. I can just see myself now."

So goes the dream. And many people shell out megabucks every week, with the glimmering hope that "Maybe this week, I'll hit it big."

Most are lucky to get $20 or maybe just another scratch-off ticket.

But some do hit it big. What happens to these winners? Are their lives all wine, roses, and chocolate afterward?

We don't have any systematic studies of the big winners, so I can't tell you what life is like for the average winner. But several themes are apparent from reporters' interviews.

The most common consequence of hitting it big is that life becomes topsy-turvy (Susman 2012; Evans 2013). All of us are rooted somewhere. We have connections with others that provide the basis for our orientations to life and how we feel about the world. Sudden wealth can rip these moorings apart, and the resulting *status inconsistency* can lead to a condition sociologists call **anomie** (an`-uh-me).

First comes the shock. As Mary Sanderson, a telephone operator in Dover, New Hampshire, who won $66 million, said, "I was afraid to believe it was real and afraid to believe it wasn't." Mary says that she never slept worse than her first night as a multimillionaire. "I spent the whole time crying—and throwing up" (Tresniowski 1999).

Reporters and TV crews appear on your doorstep. "What are you going to do with all that money?" they demand. You haven't the slightest idea, but in a daze you mumble something.

Then come the calls. Some are welcome. Your Mom and Dad call to congratulate you. But long-forgotten friends and distant relatives suddenly remember how close they are to you—and strangely enough, they all have emergencies that your money can solve. You even get calls from strangers who have ailing mothers, terminally ill kids, sick dogs . . .

You have to turn off your phone and change your number.

You might be flooded with marriage proposals. You certainly didn't become more attractive or sexy overnight—or did you? Maybe money makes people sexy.

You can no longer trust people. You don't know what their real motives are. Before, no one could be after your money because you didn't have any. You may even fear kidnappers. Before, this wasn't a problem—unless some kidnapper wanted the ransom of a seven-year-old car.

Dung Trans, a U.S. immigrant from Vietnam, as he accepts his Powerball Jackpot check for $22 million. Dung worked at a meat plant in Lincoln, Nebraska. How do you think his life has changed?

The normal becomes abnormal. Even picking out a wedding gift becomes a problem. If you give the usual juicer, everyone will think you're stingy. But should you write a check for $25,000? If you do, you'll be invited to every wedding in town—and everyone will expect the same.

Here is what happened to some lottery winners:

Mack Metcalf, a forklift operator in Corbin, Kentucky, hit the jackpot for $34 million. To fulfill a dream, he built and moved into a replica of George Washington's Mount Vernon home. Then his life fell apart—his former wife sued him, his current wife divorced him, and his new girlfriend got $500,000 while he was drunk. Within three years of his "good" fortune, Metcalf had drunk himself to death. (Dao 2005).

When Abraham Shakespeare, a dead-broke truck driver's assistant, won $31 million in the Florida lottery, he bought a million dollar home in a gated community. He lent money to friends to start businesses, even paid for funerals (McShane 2010). This evidently wasn't enough. His body was found buried in the yard of a "friend," who was convicted of his murder. (Allen 2012).

Callie Rogers was just 16 years old when she won $3 million in the lottery. She proudly declared that she wouldn't change, that she'd drive a regular car, and so on. Then came the drugs ($380,000 on cocaine), the booze, the two boob jobs, and the four suicide attempts. Now broke, a mother, and married to a firefighter, she says, "I'm the happiest I've ever been in my life." (Evans 2013).

Winners who avoid *anomie* seem to be people who don't make sudden changes in their lifestyle or their behavior. They hold onto their old friends and routines—the anchors in life that give them identity and a sense of belonging. Some even keep their old jobs—not for the money, of course, but because the job anchors them to an identity with which they are familiar and comfortable.

Sudden wealth, in other words, poses a threat that has to be guarded against.

And I can just hear you say, "I'll take the risk!"

For Your Consideration

→ How do you think your life would change if you won a lottery jackpot of $10 million?

Figure 8.5 Wright's Modification of Marx's Model of the Social Class

1. Capitalists
2. Petty bourgeoisie
3. Managers
4. Workers

SOURCE: By the author.

For example, the automobile-mechanic-turned-business-owner may want his mechanics to have higher wages because he, too, has experienced their working conditions. At the same time, his current interests—making profits and remaining competitive with other repair shops—lead him to resist pressures to raise their wages.

Because of such contradictory class locations, Wright modified Marx's model. As summarized in Figure 8.5, Wright identifies four classes: (1) *capitalists*, business owners who employ many workers; (2) *petty bourgeoisie*, small business owners; (3) *managers*, who sell their own labor but also exercise authority over other employees; and (4) *workers*, who simply sell their labor to others. As you can see, this model allows finer divisions than the one Marx proposed, yet it maintains the primary distinction between employer and employee.

Problems persist, however. For example, in which category would we place college professors? And as you know, there are huge differences in the power of managers. An executive at Toyota, for example, may manage a thousand workers, while a shift manager at McDonald's may be responsible for only a handful. They, too, have little in common.

Updating Weber

Sociologists Joseph Kahl and Dennis Gilbert (Gilbert and Kahl 1998; Gilbert 2014) developed a six-tier model to portray the class structure of the United States and other capitalist countries. Think of this model, illustrated in Figure 8.6, as a ladder. Our discussion starts

Figure 8.6 The U.S. Social Class Ladder

Social Class	Education	Occupation	Income	Percentage of Population
Capitalist	Prestigious university	Investors and heirs, a few top executives	$1,000,000+	1%
Upper Middle	College or university, often with postgraduate study	Professionals and upper managers	$125,000+	15%
Lower Middle	High school or college; often apprenticeship	Semiprofessionals and lower managers, craftspeople, foremen	About $60,000	34%
Working	High school	Factory workers, clerical workers, low-paid retail sales, and craftspeople	About $36,000	30%
Working Poor	High school or just some high school	Laborers, service workers, low-paid salespeople	About $19,000	15%
Underclass	Some high school	Unemployed and part-time, on welfare	Under $12,000	5%

SOURCE: By the author. Based on Gilbert and Kahl 1998 and Gilbert 2014; income estimates are inflation-adjusted and modified from Duff 1995.

with the highest rung and moves downward. In line with Weber, on each lower rung, you find less property (wealth), less power, and less prestige. Note that in this model, education is also a primary measure of class.

THE CAPITALIST CLASS   Sitting on the top rung of the class ladder is a powerful elite that consists of just 1 percent of the U.S. population. As you saw in Figure 8.1 on page 228, this capitalist class is so wealthy that it owns one-third of the entire nation's wealth. *This tiny 1 percent is worth more than the entire bottom 90 percent of the country* (Beeghley 2008). One family, the Waltons of Wal-Mart fame, is worth more than the bottom 40 percent of all Americans (Magdoff and Bellamy 2014).

Power and influence cling to this small elite. Its members have access to top politicians, and their decisions open or close job opportunities for millions of people. They even help to shape the consciousness of the nation: They own our major media and entertainment outlets—newspapers, magazines, radio and television stations, and sports franchises. They also control the boards of directors of our most influential colleges and universities. The super-rich perpetuate themselves in privilege by passing on their assets and social networks to their children.

The capitalist class can be divided into "old" and "new" money. The longer that wealth has been in a family, the more it adds to the family's prestige. The children of "old" money seldom mingle with "common" folk. Instead, they attend exclusive private schools where they learn views of life that support their privileged position. They don't work for wages; instead, many study business or become lawyers so that they can manage the family fortune. These old-money capitalists (also called "blue bloods") wield vast power as they use their extensive political connections to protect their economic empires (Khan 2012; Domhoff 1990, 2006, 2014).

At the lower end of the capitalist class are the *nouveau riche*, those who have "new money." Although they have made fortunes in business, the stock market, inventions, entertainment, or sports, they are outsiders to the upper class (Peretz 2013). They have not attended the "right" schools, and they don't share the social networks that come with old money. Not blue bloods, they aren't trusted to have the right orientations to life. Even their "taste" in clothing and status symbols is suspect (Fabrikant 2005). Donald Trump, whose money is "new," is not listed in the *Social Register*, the "White Pages" of the blue bloods that lists the most prestigious and wealthy one-tenth of 1 percent of the U.S. population. Trump says he "doesn't care," but he reveals his true feelings by adding that his heirs will be in it (Kaufman 1996). He is probably right, since the children of new money can ascend into the top part of the capitalist class—*if* they go to the right schools *and* marry old money.

Many in the capitalist class are philanthropic. They establish foundations and give huge sums to "causes." Their motives vary. Some feel guilty because they have so much while others have so little. Others seek prestige, acclaim, or fame. Still others feel a responsibility—even a sense of fate or destiny—to use their money for doing good. Bill Gates, who has given more money to the poor and to medical research than anyone else in history, seems to fall into this latter category.

THE UPPER-MIDDLE CLASS   Of all the classes, the upper-middle class is the one most shaped by education. Almost all members of this class have at least a bachelor's degree, and many have postgraduate degrees in business, management, law, or medicine. These people manage the corporations owned by the capitalist class, operate their own businesses, or pursue professional careers. As Gilbert and Kahl (1998) say,

> *[These positions] may not grant prestige equivalent to a title of nobility in the Germany of Max Weber, but they certainly represent the sign of having "made it" in contemporary America . . . . Their income is sufficient to purchase houses and cars and travel that become public symbols for all to see and for advertisers to portray with words and pictures that connote success, glamour, and high style.*

The wealthiest person on the planet: Bill Gates, the cofounder of Microsoft, is worth $80 billion. He has also given away $30 billion, more than anyone in history.

Sociologists use income, education, and occupational prestige to measure social class. For most people, this works well, but not for everyone, especially entertainers. To what social class do DiCaprio, Smith, Swift, and Vergara belong? Leonardo DiCaprio makes about $37 million a year, Will Smith $32 million, Taylor Swift $80 million, and Sofia Vergara $37 million.

Consequently, parents and teachers push children to prepare for upper-middle-class jobs. Around 15 percent of the population belong to this class.

THE LOWER-MIDDLE CLASS   About 34 percent of the U.S. population are in the lower-middle class. Their jobs require that they follow orders given by members of the upper-middle class. With their technical and lower-level management positions, they can afford a mainstream lifestyle, although they struggle to maintain it. Many anticipate being able to move up the social class ladder. Feelings of insecurity are common, however, with the threat of inflation, recession, and job insecurity bringing a nagging sense that they might fall down the class ladder.

The distinctions between the lower-middle class and the working class on the next rung below are more blurred than those between other classes. In general, however, members of the lower-middle class work at jobs that have slightly more prestige, and their incomes are generally higher.

THE WORKING CLASS   About 30 percent of the U.S. population belong to this class of relatively unskilled blue-collar and white-collar workers. Compared with the lower-middle class, they have less education and lower incomes. Their jobs are also less secure, more routine, and more closely supervised. One of their greatest fears is that of being laid off during a recession. With only a high school diploma or a fleeting attempt at college, the average member of the working class has little hope of climbing up the class ladder. Job changes usually bring "more of the same," so most concentrate on getting ahead by achieving seniority on the job rather than by changing their type of work. They tend to think of themselves as having "real jobs" and regard the "suits" above them as paper pushers who have no practical experience and don't do "real work" (Morris and Grimes 2005).

THE WORKING POOR   Members of this class, about 15 percent of the population, work at unskilled, low-paying, temporary and seasonal jobs, such as sharecropping, migrant farm work, housecleaning, and day labor. Most are high school dropouts. Many are functionally illiterate, finding it difficult to read even the want ads. Believing that their situation won't change no matter what party is elected to office, they are less likely than other groups to vote (U.S. Census Bureau 2013c).

Although they work full time, millions of the working poor depend on food stamps (cards from the Supplemental Nutritional Assistance Program) and local food banks to survive on their meager incomes (O'Hare 1996b; Bello 2011). It is easy to see how you can work full time and still be poor. Suppose that you are married and have a baby 3 months old and another child 3 years old. Your spouse stays home to care for them, so earning the income is up to you. But as a high-school dropout, all you can get is a minimum wage job.

At $7.25 an hour, you earn $290 for 40 hours. In a year, this comes to $15,080—before deductions. Your nagging fear—and recurring nightmare—is of ending up "on the streets."

THE UNDERCLASS   On the lowest rung, and with next to no chance of climbing anywhere, is the **underclass**. Concentrated in the inner city, this group has little or no connection with the job market. Those who are employed—and some are—do menial, low-paying, temporary work. Welfare, if it is available, along with food stamps and food pantries, is their main support. Most members of other classes consider these people the "ne'er-do-wells" of society. Life is the toughest in this class, and it is filled with despair. About 5 percent of the population fall into this class.

The homeless men described in the opening vignette of this chapter, and the women and children like them, are part of the underclass. These are the people whom most Americans wish would just go away. Their presence on our city streets bothers passersby from the more privileged social classes—which includes just about everyone. "What are those obnoxious, dirty, foul-smelling people doing here, cluttering up my city?" appears to be a common response. Some people react with sympathy and a desire to do something. But what? Almost all of us just shrug our shoulders and look the other way, despairing of a solution and somewhat intimidated, perhaps irritated, by their presence. If only they would disappear.

The homeless are the "fallout" of our postindustrial economy. In another era, they would have had plenty of work. They would have tended horses, worked on farms, dug ditches, shoveled coal, and run the factory looms. Some would have explored and settled the West. The prospect of gold would have lured others to California, Alaska, and Australia. Today, however, with no frontiers to settle, factory jobs scarce, and farms that are becoming technological marvels, we have little need for unskilled labor.

"There are plenty of jobs around. People just don't want to work."

A primary sociological principle is that people's views are shaped by their social location. Many people from the middle and upper classes cannot understand how anyone can work and still be poor.

underclass

a group of people for whom poverty persists year after year and across generations

Consequences of Social Class

8.3   **Summarize the consequences of social class for physical and mental health, family life, education, religion, politics, and the criminal justice system.**

The man was a C student in school. As a businessman, he ran an oil company (Arbusto) into the ground. A self-confessed alcoholic until age forty, he was arrested for drunk driving. With this background, how did he become president of the United States?

Accompanying these personal factors was the power of social class. George W. Bush was born the grandson of a wealthy senator and the son of a businessman who, after serving as a member of the House of Representatives and director of the CIA, was elected president of the United States. For high school, he went to an elite private prep school, Andover; for his bachelor's degree to Yale; and for his MBA to Harvard. He was given $1 million to start his own business. When that business (Arbusto) failed, Bush fell softly, landing on the boards of several corporations. Taken care of even further, he was made the managing director of the Texas Rangers baseball team and allowed to buy a share of the team for $600,000, which he sold for $15 million.

When it was time for him to get into politics, Bush's connections financed his run for governor of Texas and then for the presidency.

Does social class matter? And how! Think of each social class as a broad subculture with distinct approaches to life, so significant that it affects our health, family life, education, religion, politics, and even our experiences with crime and the criminal justice system. Let's look at some of the ways that social class affects our lives.

With tough economic times, a lot of people have lost their jobs—and their homes. If this happens, how can you survive? Maybe a smile and a sense of humor to tap the kindness of strangers. I took this photo outside Boston's Fenway Park.

Physical Health

If you want to get a sense of how social class affects health, take a ride on Washington's Metro system. Start in the blighted Southeast section of downtown D.C. For every mile you travel to where the wealthy live in Montgomery County in Maryland, life expectancy rises about a year and a half. By the time you get off, you will find a twenty-year gap between the poor blacks where you started your trip and the rich whites where you ended it. (Cohen 2004)

The principle is simple: As you go up the social-class ladder, health improves. As you go down the ladder, health worsens (Masters et al. 2012). Age makes no difference. Infants born to the poor are more likely to die before their first birthday, and a larger percentage of poor people in their old age—whether 75 or 95—die each year than do the elderly who are wealthy.

How can social class have such dramatic effects? While there are many reasons, here are three. First, social class opens and closes doors to medical care. People with good incomes or with good medical insurance are able to choose their doctors and pay for whatever treatment and medications are prescribed. The poor, in contrast, don't have the money or insurance to afford this type of medical care. How much difference the new health reform will make is yet to be seen.

A second reason is lifestyle, which is shaped by social class. People in the lower classes are more likely to smoke, eat a lot of fats, be overweight, abuse drugs and alcohol, get little exercise, and practice unsafe sex (Chin et al. 2000; Dolnick 2010). This, to understate the matter, does not improve people's health.

There is a third reason, too. Life is hard on the poor. The persistent stresses they face weaken their immune systems, causing their bodies to wear out faster (Geronimus et al. 2010; John-Henderson et al. 2012; Magdoff and Foster 2014). For the rich, life is so much better. They have fewer problems and vastly more resources to deal with the ones they have. This gives them a sense of control over their lives, a source of both physical and mental health.

Mental Health

Sociological research from as far back as the 1930s has found that the mental health of the lower classes is worse than that of the higher classes (Faris and Dunham 1939; Srole and Fisher 1978; Funk et al. 2012). Greater mental problems are part of the higher stress that accompanies poverty. Compared with middle- and upper-class Americans, the poor have less job security and lower wages. They are more likely to divorce, to be the victims of crime, and to have more physical illnesses. Couple these conditions with bill collectors and the threat of eviction and you can see how they deal severe blows to people's emotional well-being.

People higher up the social class ladder experience stress in daily life, of course, but their stress is generally less, and their coping resources are greater. Not only can they afford vacations, psychiatrists, and counselors, but *their class position also gives them greater control over their lives, a key to good mental health.*

Family Life

Social class also makes a significant difference in our choice of spouse, our chances of getting divorced, and how we rear our children.

CHOICE OF HUSBAND OR WIFE Members of the capitalist class place strong emphasis on family tradition. They stress the family's history, even a sense of purpose or destiny in life (Baltzell 1979; Aldrich 1989). Children of this class learn that their choice of husband or wife affects not just them but the entire family, that it will have an impact on the "family line." These background expectations shrink the field of "eligible" marriage partners, making it narrower than it is for the children of any other social class. As a result, parents in this class play a strong role in their children's mate selection.

DIVORCE The more difficult life of the lower social classes, especially the many tensions that come from insecure jobs and inadequate incomes, leads to higher marital friction and a greater likelihood of divorce. Consequently, children of the poor are more likely to grow up in broken homes.

CHILD REARING Lower-class parents focus more on getting their children to follow rules and obey authority, while middle-class parents focus more on developing their children's creative and leadership skills (Lareau 2011). Sociologists have traced this difference to the parents' occupations (Kohn 1977; Stephens et al. 2014). Lower-class parents are closely supervised at work, and they anticipate that their children will have similar jobs. Consequently, they try to teach their children to defer to authority. Middle-class parents, in contrast, enjoy greater independence at work. Anticipating similar jobs for their children, they encourage them to be more creative. Out of these contrasting orientations arise different ways of disciplining children: Lower-class parents are more likely to use physical punishment, while the middle classes rely more on verbal persuasion.

Proudly posing in her exclusive Oleg Cassini Ballgown, this debutante's photo is being taken at her Manhattan home prior to her appearance at The International Debutante Ball in New York City. Her appearance there announces her eligibility to be courted for marriage. Like you, from her parents, peers, and education she has learned a view of where she belongs in life. How do you think her view differs from yours?

Education

In Figure 8.6, you saw how education increases as one goes up the social class ladder. It is not just the amount of education that changes but also the type of education. Children of the capitalist class bypass public schools. They attend exclusive private schools where they are trained to take a commanding role in society. These schools teach upper-class values and prepare their students for prestigious universities (Stevens 2009; Khan 2011).

Keenly aware that private schools can be a key to upward social mobility, some upper-middle-class parents do their best to get their children into the prestigious preschools that feed into these exclusive prep schools. Although some preschools cost $37,000 a year, they have a waiting list (Anderson 2011). Figuring that waiting until birth to enroll a child is too late, some parents-to-be enroll their child as soon as the wife knows she is pregnant (Ensign 2012). Other parents hire tutors to train their 4-year-olds in test-taking skills so they can get into public kindergartens for gifted students. Experts teach these preschoolers to look adults in the eye while they are being interviewed for these limited positions (Banjo 2010). You can see how such parental involvement and resources make it more likely that children from the more privileged classes go to college—and graduate.

Religion

One area of social life that we might think would not be affected by social class is religion. ("People are just religious, or they are not. What does social class have to do with it?") As we shall see in Chapter 13, however, the classes tend to cluster in different denominations. Episcopalians, for example, are more likely to attract the middle and upper classes, while Baptists draw heavily from the lower classes. Patterns of worship also follow class lines: The lower classes are attracted to more expressive worship services and louder music, while the middle and upper classes prefer more "subdued" worship.

Politics

As I have stressed throughout this text, people perceive events from their own corner in life. Political views are no exception to this symbolic interactionist principle, and the rich and the poor walk different political paths. The higher that people are on the social class ladder, the more likely they are to vote for Republicans (Gelman 2014). In contrast, most members of the working class believe that the government should intervene in the economy to provide jobs and to make citizens financially secure. They are more likely to vote for Democrats. Although the working class is more liberal on *economic* issues (policies that increase government spending), it is more conservative on *social* issues (such as opposing abortion and the Equal Rights Amendment) (Houtman 1995; Hout 2008). People toward the bottom of the class structure are also less likely to be politically active—to campaign for candidates or even to vote (Gilbert 2014).

Crime and Criminal Justice

If justice is supposed to be blind, it certainly is not when it comes to one's chances of being arrested (Henslin 2015). In Chapter 6, we discussed how the social classes commit different types of crime. The white-collar crimes of the more privileged classes are more likely to be dealt with outside the criminal justice system, while the police and courts deal with the street crimes of the lower classes. One consequence of this class standard is that members of the lower classes are more likely to be in prison, on probation, or on parole. In addition, since those who commit street crimes tend to do so in or near their own neighborhoods, the lower classes are more likely to be robbed, burglarized, or murdered.

On the left is a window seat in the Beverly Hills home of the comedian Joan Rivers (1933–2014). To the right is a couple who live in an old motor home parked in Santa Barbara, one of the wealthiest communities in California.

Social Mobility

8.4   Contrast the three types of social mobility, review gender issues in research on social mobility, and explain why social mobility brings pain.

No aspect of life, then—from work and family life to politics—goes untouched by social class. Because life is so much more satisfying in the more privileged classes, people strive to climb the social class ladder. What affects their chances?

Three Types of Social Mobility

Janice's mom, a single mother, sold used cars at a Toyota dealership. Janice worked summers and part-time during the school year, earned her BA, and then her MBA. After college, she worked at IBM, but she missed her home town. When her mom's boss retired, Janice grabbed the chance to put a down payment on the Toyota dealership. She has since paid the business off and has opened another at a second location.

When grown-up children like Janice end up on a different rung of the social class ladder from the one occupied by their parents, it is called **intergenerational mobility**. You can go up or down, of course. Janice experienced **upward social mobility**. If her mother had owned the dealership and Janice had dropped out of college and ended up selling cars, she would have experienced **downward social mobility**.

We like to think that individual efforts are the reason people move up the class ladder—and their faults the reason they move down. In this example, we can identify intelligence, hard work, and ambition. Although individual factors, such as these, do underlie social mobility, we must place Janice in the context of **structural mobility**. This second basic type of mobility refers to changes in society that allow large numbers of people to move up or down the class ladder.

Janice grew up during a boom time of easy credit and business expansion. Opportunities were abundant, and colleges were looking for women from working-class backgrounds. It is far different for people who grow up during an economic bust when opportunities are shrinking. As sociologists point out, in analyzing social mobility,

intergenerational mobility

the change that family members make in social class from one generation to the next

upward social mobility

movement up the social class ladder

downward social mobility

movement down the social class ladder

structural mobility

movement up or down the social class ladder that is due more to changes in the *structure* of society than to the actions of individuals

The term *structural mobility* refers to changes in society that push large numbers of people either up or down the social class ladder. A remarkable example was the stock market crash of 1929 when thousands of people suddenly lost their wealth. People who once "had it made" found themselves standing on street corners selling apples or, as depicted here, selling their possessions at fire-sale prices. The crash of 2008 brought similar problems to untold numbers of people.

we must always look at *structural mobility*, how changes in society (its *structure*) make opportunities plentiful or scarce.

The third type of social mobility is **exchange mobility**. This occurs when large numbers of people move up and down the social class ladder, but, on balance, the proportions of the social classes remain about the same. Suppose that a million or so working-class people are trained in some new technology, and they move up the class ladder. Suppose also that because of a surge in imports, about a million skilled workers have to take lower-status jobs. Although millions of people change their social class, there is, in effect, an exchange among them. The net result more or less balances out, and the class system remains basically untouched.

How much social mobility is there? The Down-to-Earth Sociology box on the next page should be quite encouraging to students who are striving for success.

exchange mobility

a large number of people moving up the social class ladder, while a large number move down; it is as though they have *exchanged* places, and despite much social mobility the social class system shows little change

Women in Studies of Social Mobility

> *About half of sons pass their fathers on the social class ladder, about one-third stay at the same level, and about one-sixth fall down the ladder. (Blau and Duncan 1967; Featherman 1979)*

"Only sons!" protested feminists in response to these classic studies on social mobility. "Do you think it is good science to ignore daughters? And why do you assign women the class of their husbands? Do you think that wives have no social class position of their own?" (Davis and Robinson 1988; Western et al. 2012). The male sociologists brushed off these objections, replying that there were too few women in the labor force to make a difference.

Obviously, the times have changed. Almost half of U.S. workers are now women, and sociologists include women in their research. However, sociologists sometimes still single out sons in their research (Lopoo and DeLeire 2012).

In recent decades, millions of white-collar jobs and the professions have opened up to women. Even with this vast *structural* change, there is *a gender gap in social mobility*: As adults, women are less likely than men to live in families with higher income than the one in which they grew up (Reeves and Venator 2013). Researchers have also found that behind upwardly mobile women are parents who encouraged their daughters to postpone marriage and get an education (Higginbotham and Weber 1992). For upwardly mobile African American women, strong mothers are especially significant (Robinson and Nelson 2010).

With research on the social class of women in its infancy, the social mobility of women is going to be a fruitful area of research in coming years.

Both downward and upward social mobility bring challenges that require life adjustments. An extreme instance is the case of Mikhail Khodorkovsky, the richest man in Russia, who made the mistake of challenging Vladimir Putin. He is shown here at his trial for tax evasion. After serving several years in prison, he was pardoned. He then fled Russia.

The Pain of Social Mobility

If you were to be knocked down the social class ladder, you know it would be painful. But are you aware that it also hurts to climb this ladder?

Sociologist Steph Lawler (1999) found that British women who had moved from the working class to the middle class were caught between two worlds—their working-class origin and their current middle-class life. Their mothers, still in the working class, were uncomfortable with their daughters' "uppity" new life. They felt that their daughters thought they were better than they were. The tension was high, and they criticized their daughters' preferences in furniture and food, their speech, even the way they reared their children. As you can expect, this strained the mother–daughter relationship.

Sociologists Richard Sennett and Jonathan Cobb (1972/1988) found something similar among working-class parents in Boston. So their children could go to college, the fathers had worked two jobs and even postponed

Down-to-Earth Sociology

"The American Dream": Social Mobility Today

What is "The American Dream"? For most people, this term means achieving a better life. The sociological definition of the American Dream is similar, but it is more specific: It refers to children being able to pass their parents as they climb the social class ladder. So how much upward mobility is there?

Vast Changes   Contrary to the many dismal reports of social life today, the American Dream remains vibrant. Let's look at national research that compares today's adult children with their parents. From Figure 8.7, you can see that whether children start life at the top of the nation's income or at the bottom, about the same percentage move from their starting point. Of those who start life at the bottom, 43 percent are still there when they grow up, but most, 57 percent, have moved up. Four percent even make it to the top fifth of the nation's income. Now look at those who start life at the top. When they grow up, 40 percent are still there, but most, 60 percent, have dropped down. Eight percent have dropped all the way to the bottom. Overall, thirty-five percent of adult children move up at least one rung past their parents on the social class ladder (Lopoo and DeLeire 2012).

Incomes   If we look at incomes, even though the income was not enough to move the adult child into a different quintile, we find something impressive: *84 percent of today's adults have family incomes higher than their parents had at the same age.* (The incomes of the parents and their adult child were adjusted for inflation, so the dollars have the same base.) One of the surprises is that the children most likely to surpass their parents were reared at the bottom of the nation's income ladder. Of the adult children who started life there,

Figure 8.7 Income of Adult Children Compared with that of their Parents

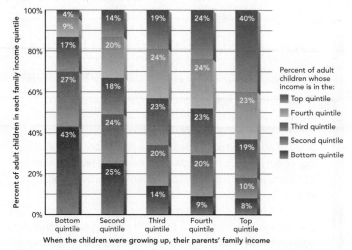

Chances of moving up or down the family income ladder, by parents' income

Percent of adult children whose income is in the:
- Top quintile
- Fourth quintile
- Third quintile
- Second quintile
- Bottom quintile

When the children were growing up, their parents' family income

SOURCE: Pursuing the American Dream: Economic Mobility Across Generations, p. 6. © July, 2013 the Pew Charitable Trusts.

93 percent have incomes higher than their parents did at the same age.

With incomes stagnating today, many fear that the "American Dream" has been shattered. Although poverty has increased, the Great Recession did not crush the dream, just deflated it (Chetty et al. 2014).

What Do These Findings Mean?   People have a lot of things they want to prove, and they like to use statistics to make their point. These data allow you to go either way. You can stress that 43 percent of the very poorest kids never get out of the bottom—or you can point to the 57 percent who do. It is the same with the richest kids: You can stress the 40 percent who stay at the top of the nation's income or the 60 percent who drop down. No matter what your opinion, any way you look at it this is a lot of social mobility.

You could get lost in the details, but don't lose sight of the broader principle: Children of high-income parents enjoy benefits that tend to keep them afloat, while children of low-income parents confront obstacles that tend to weigh them down. Yet, as you can see, the benefits don't keep most of the children up nor do the obstacles keep most of the children down.

For Your Consideration

→ How can you apply these findings to yourself?

→ In ten years, do you think your social class will be higher, lower, or the same as that of your parents? Why?

The main avenue to upward social mobility is education.

medical care. They expected their children to appreciate their sacrifice. But again, the result was two distinct worlds of experience. The children's educated world was so unlike that of their parents that it became awkward for them to even talk to one another. Not surprisingly, the parents felt betrayed and bitter. Their sacrifices had ripped their children from them.

Torn from their roots, some of those who make the jump from the working to the middle class never become comfortable with their new social class (Morris and Grimes 2005; Heller 2011). The Cultural Diversity box below discusses other costs that come with the climb up the social class ladder.

Cultural Diversity in the United States

Social Class and the Upward Social Mobility of African Americans

The overview of social class presented in this chapter doesn't apply equally to all the groups that make up U.S. society. Consider geography: What constitutes the upper class of a town of 5,000 people will differ from that of a city of a million. In small towns, which have fewer extremes of wealth and occupation, family background and local reputation are more significant.

So it is with racial–ethnic groups. All racial–ethnic groups are marked by social class, but what constitutes a particular social class can differ from one group to another—as well as from one historical period to another. Consider social class among African Americans (Landry and Marsh 2011).

The earliest class divisions can be traced to slavery—to slaves who worked in the fields and those who worked in the "big house." Those who worked in the plantation home were exposed more to the customs, manners, and forms of speech of wealthy whites. Their more privileged position—which brought with it better food and clothing, as well as lighter work—was often based on skin color. Mulattos, lighter-skinned slaves, were often chosen for this more desirable work. One result was the development of a "mulatto elite," a segment of the slave population that, proud of its distinctiveness, distanced itself from other slaves. At this time, there also were free blacks. Not only were they able to own property but some even owned black slaves.

After the War between the States (as the Civil War is known in the South), these two groups, the mulatto elite and the free blacks, formed an upper class that distanced itself from other blacks. By the 1870s, just ten or fifteen years after this war, some African Americans had become millionaires (Graham 1999). After World War II, the black middle class expanded as African Americans entered a wider range of occupations. Today, more than half of all African American adults work at white-collar jobs, about 22 percent at the professional or managerial level (Beeghley 2008).

An unwelcome cost greets many African Americans who move up the social class ladder: an uncomfortable distancing from their roots, a separation from significant others—parents, siblings, and childhood friends (Lacy 2007; Khare et al. 2014). The upwardly mobile enter a world unknown to those left behind, one that demands not only different appearance and speech, but also different values, aspirations, and ways of viewing the world. These are severe challenges to the self and often rupture relationships with those left behind.

An additional cost is a subtle racism that lurks beneath the surface of some work settings, poisoning what could be easy, mutually respectful interaction. To be aware that white co-workers perceive you as different—as a stranger, an intruder, or "the other"—engenders frustration, dissatisfaction, and cynicism (Carbado and Gulati 2014). To cope, many nourish their racial identity and stress the "high value of black culture and being black" (Lacy and Harris 2008). Some move to neighborhoods of upper-middle-class African Americans, where they can live among like-minded people who have similar experiences (Wiggins et al. 2011).

For Your Consideration

→ In the box on upward social mobility on page 90, we discussed how Latinos face a similar situation. Why do you think this is?

→ What connections do you see among upward mobility, frustration, and racial–ethnic identity?

→ How do you think that the costs of upward mobility of whites differ from those of Latinos and African Americans? Why?

Poverty

8.5   **Explain the problems in drawing the poverty line, how poverty is related to geography, race–ethnicity, education, feminization, and age.**

Many Americans find that the "limitless possibilities" of the American dream are quite elusive. As illustrated in Figure 8.6 on page 236, the working poor and underclass together form about one-fifth of the U.S. population. This translates into a huge number, over 60 million people. Who are these people?

Drawing the Poverty Line

To determine who is poor, the U.S. government draws a **poverty line**. This measure was set in the 1960s, when poor people were thought to spend about one-third of their incomes on food. On the basis of this assumption, each year, the government computes a low-cost food budget and multiplies it by 3. Families whose incomes are less than this amount are classified as poor; those whose incomes are higher—even by a dollar—are considered "not poor."

poverty line

the official measure of poverty; calculated to include incomes that are less than three times a low-cost food budget

High rates of rural poverty have been a part of the United States from its origin to the present. This 1937 photo shows a 32-year-old woman who had seven children and no food. She was part of a huge migration of people from the Dust Bowl of Oklahoma in search of a new life in California.

This official measure of poverty is grossly inadequate. Poor people actually spend only about one-fifth of their income on food, so to determine a poverty line, we ought to multiply their food budget by 5 instead of 3 (Chandy and Smith 2014). Another problem is that mothers who work outside the home and have to pay for child care are treated the same as mothers who don't have this expense. The poverty line is also the same for everyone across the nation, even though the cost of living is much higher in New York than in Alabama. On the other hand, much of the income of the poor is not counted: food stamps, rent assistance, subsidized child care, and the earned income tax credit (Short 2012). In the face of these criticisms, the Census Bureau has developed alternative ways to measure poverty. These show higher poverty, but the official measure has not changed.

That a change in the poverty line can instantly make millions of people poor—or take away their poverty—would be laughable, if it weren't so serious. Although this line is arbitrary, because it is the official measure of poverty, we'll use it to see who in the United States is poor. Before we do this, though, how do you think that your ideas of the poor match up with sociological findings? To find out, go to the Down-to-Earth Sociology box on the next page.

Who Are the Poor?

THE GEOGRAPHY OF POVERTY   The Social Map on page 250 illustrates how poverty varies by *region*. The striking clustering of poverty in the South has prevailed for more than 150 years.

A second aspect of geography is *rural poverty*. At 16 percent, rural poverty is higher than the national average of 15 percent. Helping to maintain this higher rate are the lower education of the rural poor and the scarcity of rural jobs (Latimer and Woldoff 2010).

A third aspect of geography is the *suburbanization of poverty*. With the extensive migration from cities to suburbs, *more* of the nation's poor now live in the suburbs than in the cities (Kneebone and Berube 2013). This major change is not likely to be temporary.

Geography, however, is not the main factor in poverty. The greatest predictors of poverty are race–ethnicity, education, and the sex of the person who heads the family. Let's look at these factors.

Down-to-Earth Sociology

What Do You Know about Poverty? A Reality Check

Can you tell which of these statements are true?

1. **Poverty is unusual.** *False.* Over a three-year period, *one-third* of all Americans experience poverty for at least two months (DeNavas-Walt, et al. 2013). About *half* of the entire U.S. population will experience poverty before they reach age 65 (Cellini et al. 2008).

2. **People with less education are more likely to be poor.** *True.* Most definitely. See Figure 8.10 on page 251.

3. **Most poor people are poor because they do not want to work.** *False.* About 40 percent of the poor are under age 18 and another 10 percent are age 65 or older. Most of the rest work at jobs that are seasonal, undependable, or pay poverty wages (O'Hare 1996a, 1996b; U.S. Bureau of Labor Statistics 2014).

4. **Most of the poor are trapped in a cycle of poverty.** *We have to go true and false on this one.* Most poverty lasts less than a year (DeNavas-Walt et al. 2013), but just over half of those who escape poverty will return to poverty within five years (Ratcliffe and McKernan 2010).

5. **The percentage of children who are poor is higher than that of adults in poverty.** *True.* Look at Figure 8.10.

6. **Most children who are born in poverty are poor as adults.** *False.* See Figure 8.7 on page 245.

7. **There is more poverty in urban than in rural areas.** *False.* We'll review this in the following section.

8. **Most African Americans are poor.** *False.* This one was easy. We just reviewed some statistics in the box on upward mobility—plus you have Figure 8.8 below.

9. **Most of the poor are African Americans.** *False.* There are many more poor whites than any other group. Look at Part 2 of Figure 8.8.

10. **Most of the poor live in the inner city.** *False.* Most of the poor live in the suburbs (Kneebone and Berube 2013).

11. **Most of the poor are single mothers and their children.** *False.* About 38 percent of the poor match this stereotype, but 34 percent of the poor live in married-couple families, 22 percent live alone or with nonrelatives, and 6 percent live in other settings (O'Hare 1996a, 1996b; U.S. Bureau of Labor Statistics 2014).

12. **Most of the poor live on welfare.** *False.* Most of the incomes of people in poverty come from wages, pensions, and Social Security. Somewhere between 11 percent and 25 percent come from welfare (O'Hare 1996a, 1996b; Lang 2012).

For Your Consideration

→ What stereotypes of the poor do you (or people you know) hold?

→ How would you test these stereotypes?

Figure 8.8 Race–Ethnicity and U.S. Poverty

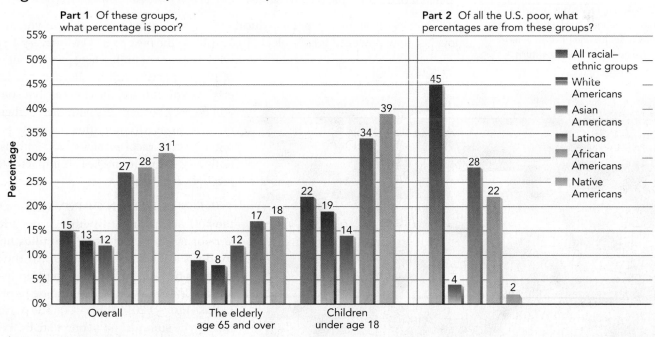

Part 1 Of these groups, what percentage is poor?

Part 2 Of all the U.S. poor, what percentages are from these groups?

- All racial–ethnic groups
- White Americans
- Asian Americans
- Latinos
- African Americans
- Native Americans

[1]The source does not break this total down by age.
NOTE: Only these groups are listed in the source. The poverty line is $22,314 for a family of four.
SOURCE: By the author. Based on *Statistical Abstract of the United States* 2014:Tables 6, 37, 38, 738, 739, and 741.

Figure 8.9 Patterns of Poverty

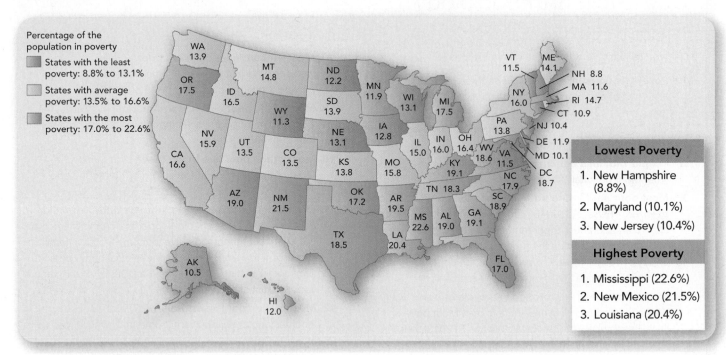

Percentage of the
population in poverty

- States with the least
poverty: 8.8% to 13.1%
- States with average
poverty: 13.5% to 16.6%
- States with the most
poverty: 17.0% to 22.6%

WA 13.9
OR 17.5
ID 16.5
MT 14.8
ND 12.2
MN 11.9
WI 13.1
MI 17.5
VT 11.5
ME 14.1
NH 8.8
MA 11.6
RI 14.7
CT 10.9
NJ 10.4
NY 16.0
PA 13.8
DE 11.9
MD 10.1
NV 15.9
UT 13.5
WY 11.3
SD 13.9
NE 13.1
IA 12.8
IL 15.0
IN 16.0
OH 16.4
WV 18.6
VA 11.5
CA 16.6
CO 13.5
KS 13.8
MO 15.8
KY 19.1
NC 17.9
DC 18.7
AZ 19.0
NM 21.5
OK 17.2
AR 19.5
TN 18.3
SC 18.9
MS 22.6
AL 19.0
GA 19.1
TX 18.5
LA 20.4
FL 17.0
AK 10.5
HI 12.0

Lowest Poverty

1. New Hampshire (8.8%)
2. Maryland (10.1%)
3. New Jersey (10.4%)

Highest Poverty

1. Mississippi (22.6%)
2. New Mexico (21.5%)
3. Louisiana (20.4%)

SOURCE: By the author. Based on *Statistical Abstract of the United States* 2014:Table 737.

RACE–ETHNICITY   One of the strongest factors in poverty is race–ethnicity. As you can see from Figure 8.8 on page 249, 12 percent of Asian Americans are poor, followed closely by whites at 13 percent. From there, the poverty rate jumps. Twenty-seven to 28 percent of Latino and African Americans and 31 percent of Native Americans live in poverty. Because whites are, by far, the largest group in the United States, their lower rate of poverty translates into larger numbers. As a result, there are many more poor whites than poor people of any other racial–ethnic group. As Part 2 of Figure 8.8 shows, 45 percent of all poor people are whites.

EDUCATION   You are aware that education is a vital factor in poverty, but you may not know just how powerful it is. Look at Figure 8.10 on the next page. One of every 4 people who drop out of high school is poor, but only 5 of 100 people who finish college end up in poverty. As you can see, the chances that someone will be poor become less with each higher level of education. Although this principle applies regardless of race–ethnicity, you can also see how race–ethnicity makes an impact at every level of education.

THE FEMINIZATION OF POVERTY   One of the best indicators of whether or not a family is poor is family structure. Families headed by both a mother and father are the least likely to be poor, while those headed by only a mother are the most likely to be poor (*Statistical Abstract* 2014:Table 744). The reason for this can be summed up in one statistic: Women average only 72 percent of what men earn. (If you want to jump ahead, go to Figure 10.8 on page 318.) With our high rate of divorce

Poverty comes in many forms. Families who go into debt to buy possessions squeak by month after month until a crisis turns their lives upside down. I took this photo of a family in Georgia, parked alongside a highway selling their possessions to survive our economic downturn.

Figure 8.10 Who Ends Up Poor? Poverty by Education and Race–Ethnicity

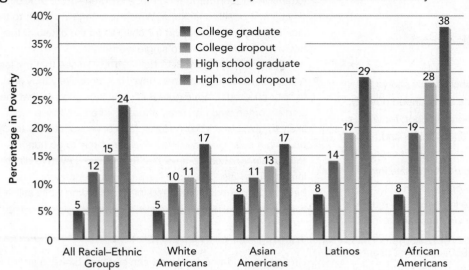

SOURCE: By the author. Based on U.S. Census Bureau 2014:Table POV29.

combined with the large number of births to single women, mother-headed families have become more common. Sociologists call this association of poverty with women the **feminization of poverty**.

OLD AGE   As Figure 8.8 on page 249 shows, the elderly are *less* likely than the general population to be poor. This is quite a change. It used to be that growing old increased people's chances of being poor, but government policies to redistribute income—Social Security and subsidized housing, food stamps, and medical care—slashed the rate of poverty among the elderly. Figure 8.8 also shows how the prevailing racial–ethnic patterns carry over into old age. You can see how much more likely elderly minorities are to be poor than elderly whites.

Children of Poverty

Children are more likely to live in poverty than are adults or the elderly. This holds true regardless of race–ethnicity, but from Figure 8.8, you can see how much greater poverty is among Latino and African American children. That millions of U.S. children are reared in poverty is shocking when one considers the wealth of this country and our supposed concern for the well-being of children. This tragic aspect of poverty is the topic of the following Thinking Critically section on the next page.

8.6   **Contrast the dynamics of poverty with the culture of poverty, explain why people are poor and how deferred gratification is related to poverty, and comment on the Horatio Alger myth.**

The Dynamics of Poverty versus the Culture of Poverty

Some have suggested that the poor get trapped in a **culture of poverty** (Lewis 1966a; Cohen 2010). They assume that the values and behaviors of the poor "make them fundamentally different from other Americans and that these factors are largely responsible for their continued long-term poverty" (Ruggles 1989:7). Lurking behind this concept is the idea that the poor are lazy people who bring poverty on themselves. Certainly, some individuals and families do match this stereotype—many of us have known them. But is a self-perpetuating culture—one that poor people transmit across generations and that locks them in poverty—the basic reason for U.S. poverty?

feminization of poverty

a condition of U.S. poverty in which most poor families are headed by women

culture of poverty

the assumption that the values and behaviors of the poor make them fundamentally different from other people, that these factors are largely responsible for their poverty, and that parents perpetuate poverty across generations by passing these characteristics to their children

Thinking Critically

The Nation's Shame: Children in Poverty

One of the most startling statistics in sociology is shown in Figure 8.8 on page 249. Look at the rate of childhood poverty: For Asian Americans, one of seven children is poor; for whites, one of five; for Latinos, an astounding one of three; and for African Americans, an even higher total, with two of every five children living in poverty. These percentages translate into incredible numbers—approximately *16 million* children.

Why do so many U.S. children live in poverty? A major reason is the large number of births to women who are not married, about 1.7 million a year. This number has increased sharply, going from *one of twenty* in 1960 to *eight of twenty* today. With the total jumping eight times, single women now account for 41 percent of all U.S. births (*Statistical Abstract* 2014:Table 92).

But do births to single women actually cause poverty? Consider the obvious: Children born to wealthy single women don't live in poverty. Then consider this: In some countries, such as Sweden, single women are more likely to give birth than are single women in the United States, *yet their rate of child poverty is lower than ours* (Garfinkel et al. 2010). The reason for this is because their governments provide extensive support for rearing these children—from providing day care to health checkups. Why, then, can't we point to the lack of government support for children as the cause of the poverty of children born to single women?

Now look at Figure 8.11 below. You can see that the less education that single women have, the more likely they are to bear children. From Figure 8.12, you can also see that the single women who can least afford children are those most likely to give birth. Their children face severe obstacles to building a satisfying life. They are more likely to go hungry, to be malnourished, to have health problems, even to die in infancy. They also are more likely to drop out of school, to become involved in crime, and to have children while still in their teens—perpetuating a cycle of poverty.

For Your Consideration

On Figures 8.11 and 8.12, you can see how births to single women drop as education and income increase. In answering these two questions be specific and practical.

→ What programs would you suggest to help women attain more education?

→ What other ways would you suggest to reduce child poverty?

Figure 8.11 How Does Education Influence Births to Single Women

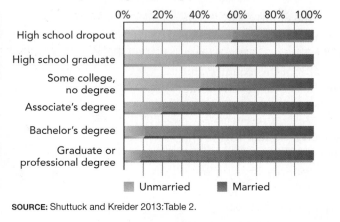

SOURCE: Shuttuck and Kreider 2013:Table 2.

Figure 8.12 How Does Income Influence Births to Single Women

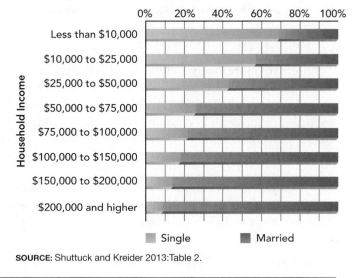

SOURCE: Shuttuck and Kreider 2013:Table 2.

Contrary to the stereotype of lazy people who contentedly sit back sucking welfare, poverty is dynamic. First, we should note that many people live on the edge of poverty. They manage to keep their heads above poverty, although barely, but then comes some dramatic life change, such as a divorce, an accident, an illness, or the loss of a job. The *poverty trigger* propels them over the edge they were holding onto, and they find themselves in the poverty they fiercely had been trying to avoid (Western et al. 2012).

Second, most poverty is short-lived, lasting less than a year. As Figure 8.13 shows, only 12 percent of poverty lasts five years or longer. Yet from one year to the next, the number of poor people remains about the same. This means that the people who move out of poverty are replaced by people who move into poverty. Most of these newly poor will also move out of poverty within a year. Some people even bounce back and forth, never quite making it securely out of poverty.

Few poor people enjoy poverty—and they do what they can to avoid being poor. In the end, though, poverty touches a lot more people than the official totals indicate. Although 15 percent of Americans may be poor at any one time, for those under age 30, 40 percent will be poor in the next ten years (Western et al. 2012). Before they turn 65, about half of the U.S. population will experience poverty (Cellini et al. 2008).

Why Are People Poor?

Two explanations for poverty compete for our attention. The first, which sociologists prefer, focuses on *social structure*. Sociologists stress that *features of society* deny some people access to education or training in job skills. They emphasize racial–ethnic, age, and gender discrimination, as well as changes in the job market—fewer unskilled jobs, businesses closing, and manufacturing jobs moving overseas. In short, some people find their escape route from poverty blocked.

A competing explanation focuses on the *characteristics of individuals*. Sociologists reject explanations, such as laziness and lack of intelligence, viewing these as worthless stereotypes. Individualistic explanations that sociologists reluctantly acknowledge include dropping out of school and bearing children in the teen years. Most sociologists are reluctant to speak of such factors in this context, since they appear to blame the victim, something that sociologists bend over backward not to do.

A third explanation is the *poverty triggers* that were just mentioned, the unexpected events in life that push people into poverty.

Deferred Gratification

One consequence of a life of deprivation punctuated by emergencies—*and of viewing the future as promising more of the same*—is a lack of **deferred gratification**, giving up things in the present for the sake of greater gains in the future. It is difficult to practice this middle-class virtue of deferring gratification if you do not have a middle-class surplus—or middle-class hope.

In a classic 1967 study of black street-corner men, sociologist Elliot Liebow noted that the men did not defer gratification. Their jobs were low-paying and insecure, their lives pitted with emergencies. With the future looking exactly like the present and any savings they did manage gobbled up by emergencies, it seemed pointless to save for the future. The only thing that made sense from their perspective was to enjoy what they could at the moment. Immediate gratification, then, was not the cause of their poverty but, rather, its consequence. Cause and consequence loop together, however: Their immediate gratification helped perpetuate their poverty. For another look at this "looping," see the Down-to-Earth Sociology box on the next page, in which I share my personal experience with poverty.

If both structural and personal causes are at work, why do sociologists emphasize the structural explanation? Reverse the situation for a moment. Suppose that members of the middle class drove old cars that broke down, faced threats from the utility company to shut off the electricity and heat, and had to make a choice between paying the rent or buying medicine and food and diapers. How long would they practice deferred gratification? Their orientations to life would likely make a sharp U-turn.

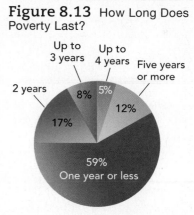

Figure 8.13 How Long Does Poverty Last?

Up to 3 years · Up to 4 years · Five years or more

2 years · 8% · 5% · 12%

17%

59% One year or less

SOURCE: Gottschalk et al. 1994:89.

deferred gratification

going without something in the present in the hope of achieving greater gains in the future

Sociologists, then, do not view the behaviors of the poor as the cause of their poverty but, rather, as the result of their poverty. Poor people would welcome the middle-class opportunities that would allow them the chance to practice the middle-class virtue of deferred gratification. Without those opportunities, though, they just can't afford it.

Where Is Horatio Alger? The Social Functions of a Myth

In the late 1800s, Horatio Alger was one of the country's most popular authors. The rags-to-riches exploits of his fictional boy heroes and their amazing successes in overcoming severe odds motivated thousands of boys of that period. Although Alger's characters have disappeared from U.S. literature, they remain alive and well in the psyche of Americans. From real-life examples of people of humble origin who climbed the social class ladder, Americans know that anyone who really tries can get ahead. In fact, they believe that most Americans, including minorities and the working poor, have an average or better-than-average chance of getting ahead—obviously a statistical impossibility (Kluegel and Smith 1986).

Down-to-Earth Sociology

Poverty: A Personal Journey

I was born in poverty. My parents, who could not afford to rent either a house or an apartment, rented the tiny office in their minister's house. That is where I was born.

My father, who had only a seventh grade education, began to slowly climb the social class ladder. His fitful odyssey took him from laborer to truck driver to the owner of a series of small businesses (tire repair shop, bar, hotel), and from there to vacuum cleaner salesman, and back to bar owner. He converted a garage into a house. Although it had no indoor plumbing, it was a start. Later, he bought a house, and then he built a new home. After that we moved into a trailer, and then back to a house. Although he never became wealthy, poverty eventually became a distant memory for him.

My social class took a leap—from working class to upper-middle class—when, after attending college and graduate school, I became a university professor. I entered a world that was unknown to my parents, one much more pampered and privileged. I had opportunities to do research, to publish, and to travel to exotic places. My reading centered on sociological research, and I read books in Spanish as well as in English. My father, in contrast, never read a book in his life, and my mother read only detective stories and romance paperbacks. One set of experiences isn't "better" than the other, just significantly different in determining what windows of perception it opens onto the world.

My interest in poverty, rooted in my own childhood experiences, stayed with me. I traveled to a dozen or so skid rows across the United States and Canada, talking to homeless people and staying in their shelters. In my own town, I spent considerable time with people on welfare, observing how they lived. I constantly marveled at the connections between *structural* causes of poverty (low education, low skills, low pay, the irregularity of unskilled jobs, undependable transportation) and *personal* causes (the *culture of poverty*—alcohol and drug abuse, multiple out-of-wedlock births, frivolous spending, all-night partying, domestic violence, criminal involvement, and a seeming incapacity to keep appointments—except to pick up the welfare check).

Sociologists haven't unraveled this connection, and as much as we might *like* for only structural causes to apply, *both* are at work (Duneier 1999:122; Gorski 2013). The situation can be illustrated by looking at the perennial health problems I observed among the poor—the constant colds, runny noses, backaches, and injuries. The health problems stem from the *social structure* (less access to medical care, less capable physicians, drafty houses, little knowledge about nutrition, and more dangerous jobs). At the same time, *personal* characteristics—hygiene, eating habits, drug and alcohol abuse—cause health problems. Which is the cause and which the effect? Both, of course: One loops into the other. The medical problems (which are based on both personal and structural causes) feed into the poverty these people experience, making them less able to perform their jobs successfully—or even to show up at work regularly. What an intricate puzzle for sociologists!

A society's dominant ideologies are reinforced throughout the society, including its literature. Horatio Alger provided inspirational heroes for thousands of boys. The central theme of these many novels, immensely popular in their time, was rags to riches. Through rugged determination and self-sacrifice, a boy could overcome seemingly insurmountable obstacles to reach the pinnacle of success. (Girls did not strive for financial success, but were dependent on fathers and husbands.)

The accuracy of the **Horatio Alger myth** is less important than the belief that surrounds it—that limitless possibilities exist for everyone. Functionalists would stress that this belief is functional for society. On the one hand, it encourages people to compete for higher positions, or, as the song says, "to reach for the highest star." On the other hand, it places blame for failure squarely on the individual. If you don't make it—in the face of ample opportunities to get ahead—the fault must be your own. The Horatio Alger myth helps to stabilize society: Since the fault is viewed as the individual's, not society's, current social arrangements can be regarded as satisfactory. This reduces pressures to change the system.

As Marx and Weber pointed out, social class penetrates our consciousness, shaping our ideas of life and our "proper" place in society. When the rich look at the world around them, they sense superiority and anticipate control over their own destiny. When the poor look around them, they are more likely to sense defeat and to anticipate that unpredictable forces will batter their lives. Both rich and poor know the dominant ideology: The reasons for success—or failure—lie solely with the self. Like fish that don't notice the water, people tend not to perceive the effects of social class on their own lives.

Horatio Alger myth

the belief that due to limitless possibilities anyone can get ahead if he or she tries hard enough

Peering into the Future: Will We Live in a Three-Tier Society?

8.7   Discuss the possibility that we are developing a three-tier society.

Now that we have looked at social class in the United States, you should be much more aware not only of how social class influences your life but also of American social structure, how the social classes fit together to form the whole that we call American society.

Let's go beyond this and in the following Thinking Critically section try to peer into the future. We will consider the disturbing possibility that society is being restratified—and that the picture coming into focus is not pleasant. Unfortunately, this will give us a much darker ending to this chapter than I prefer. But let's go on.

Thinking Critically

The Coming Three-Tier Society and the Militarization of the Police

A three-tier society seems to be looming over us. On the top tier will be the wealthy, who will live in luxury behind gated fortresses, protected from the prying eyes of the unwashed masses. On the middle tier will be the technically trained, an army of servants who will run the essential affairs of society. They will maintain the computers that control the financial system, the infrastructure of utilities, and the government surveillance. There will also be the teachers, the elite ones for the children of the elite and the regular ones whose task is to indoctrinate and control the children of the poor. These technical servants of society's controllers will be backed up by a police force that has come to look more like the military than the police.

And the third tier? This one will consist of the jobless poor. The need for unskilled work is drying up. We still need some fruit pickers and some house cleaners, and an occasional someone to hold up flags when a road is being constructed. But there is little of this kind of work. And most of what there is pays little. Enter one of today's new factories, and you will be struck by the absence of people. You will see untiring robots that never complain, don't take coffee breaks, and need neither vacations nor retirement pay. With each passing year, we need fewer human workers.

Widespread joblessness will trigger hopelessness and deep despair in some, resentment and hostility in others. To keep the lid on violence as long as possible, two solutions will be followed. The first will be to pacify the jobless through food stamps, subsidized housing, entertainment, and drugs. Videos and television will divert most of the "dangerous poor" from seeking political solutions. Drugs will be tolerated because the poor who flee into them to escape their misery do not threaten the top tier by agitating for political change. Not all will be hopeless: Powerball will remain.

The second solution, coexisting with the first, is the militarization of the police. That the police are beginning to look like the military is not incidental. This is preparation for the armed force that will be necessary to control the impoverished masses. The media have been willing handmaidens of the elite, preparing the public for the militarization of the police by stoking constant fears of "terrorists." This comes not without a plan from the controllers. The hostile elements of society—the masses left behind with little future, the resentful ones who do not choose to escape into drugs or television—pose a threat to the first tier. For most of the jobless poor, welfare food, televised sports, and the stream of "latest revelations" about vaunted celebrities provide escape adequate to keep them in line. But if what the Romans called food and circus fail to keep minds numb and wills weak, the militarized police with their powerful new weapons, armored vehicles, and trained snipers stand ready to take care of the rest.

For Your Consideration

This is not a pleasant picture of the future, but your author sees it as a looming possibility.

→ Do you think the three-tier society is our likely destiny? Why or why not?

→ What do you think we can do to produce a better future than the three-tier society?

Summary and Review

What Determines Social Class?

8.1   Explain the three components of social class—property, power, and prestige; distinguish between wealth and income; explain how property and income are distributed; and describe the democratic façade, the power elite, and status inconsistency.

What is meant by the term social class?

Most sociologists have adopted Weber's definition of **social class**: a large group of people who rank closely to one another in terms of property (wealth), power, and prestige. **Wealth**—consisting of the value of property and income—is concentrated in the upper classes. From the 1930s to the 1970s, the trend in the distribution of wealth in the United States was toward greater equality. Since that time, it has been toward greater inequality. **Power** is the ability to get your way even though others resist. C. Wright Mills coined the term **power elite** to refer to the small group that holds the reins of power in business, government, and the military. **Prestige** is linked to occupational status.

How does occupational prestige differ around the world?

From country to country, people rank occupational prestige similarly. Globally, the occupations that bring greater prestige are those that pay more, require more education and abstract thought, and offer greater independence.

What is meant by the term status inconsistency?

Status is social position. Most people are **status consistent**; that is, they rank high or low on all three dimensions of social class. People who rank higher on some dimensions than on others are status inconsistent. The frustrations of **status inconsistency** tend to produce political radicalism.

Sociological Models of Social Class

8.2 **Contrast Marx's and Weber's models of social class.**

What models are used to portray the social classes?

Erik Wright developed a four-class model based on Marx: (1) capitalists (owners of large businesses), (2) petty bourgeoisie (small business owners), (3) managers, and (4) workers. Kahl and Gilbert developed a six-class model based on Weber. At the top is the capitalist class. In descending order are the upper-middle class, the lower-middle class, the working class, the working poor, and the **underclass**.

Consequences of Social Class

8.3 **Summarize the consequences of social class for physical and mental health, family life, education, religion, politics, and the criminal justice system.**

How does social class affect people's lives?

Social class leaves no aspect of life untouched. It affects our chances of dying early, becoming ill, receiving good health care, and getting divorced. Social class membership also affects child rearing, educational attainment, religious affiliation, political participation, the crimes people commit, and their contact with the criminal justice system.

Social Mobility

8.4 **Contrast the three types of social mobility, review gender issues in research on social mobility, and explain why social mobility brings pain.**

What are three types of social mobility?

The term **intergenerational mobility** refers to changes in social class from one generation to the next. **Structural mobility** refers to changes in society that lead large numbers of people to change their social class. **Exchange mobility** is the movement of large numbers of people from one social class to another, with the net result that the relative proportions of the population in the classes remain about the same.

Poverty

8.5 **Explain the problems in drawing the poverty line, how poverty is related to geography, race–ethnicity, education, feminization, and age.**

Who are the poor?

The poverty line, although it has serious consequences, is arbitrary. Poverty is unequally distributed in the United States. Racial–ethnic minorities (except Asian Americans), children, households headed by women, and rural Americans are more likely than others to be poor. The poverty rate of the elderly is much less than that of the general population.

8.6 **Contrast the dynamics of poverty with the culture of poverty, explain why people are poor and how deferred gratification is related to poverty, and comment on the Horatio Alger myth.**

Why are people poor?

They dynamics of poverty (huge numbers moving into and out of poverty) indicate that the culture of poverty is not generally true. Rather than looking at the characteristics of *individuals* as the cause of poverty, sociologists stress the *structural* features of society, such as employment opportunities. There also are *poverty triggers*. Sociologists generally conclude that life orientations are a consequence, not the cause, of people's position in the social class structure.

How is the Horatio Alger myth functional for society?

The **Horatio Alger myth**—the belief that anyone can get ahead if only he or she tries hard enough—encourages people to strive to get ahead. It also stabilizes society by deflecting blame for failure from society to the individual.

8.7 **Discuss the possibility that we are developing a three-tier society.**

What is meant by a three-tier society?

Trends indicate an alarming future. In the top tier of a three-tier society will live a wealthy ruling elite. In the middle tier will be well-compensated people who serve this elite. At the bottom tier will be a large underclass considered dangerous to society. It will be kept under control by welfare, entertainment, drugs, and a militarized police force.

Thinking Critically about Chapter 8

1. The belief that the United States is the land of opportunity draws millions of legal and illegal immigrants to the United States. How do the materials in this chapter support or undermine this belief?

2. In what three ways is social class having an ongoing impact on your life?

3. What social mobility has your own family experienced? In what ways has this affected your life?

4. What indications do you see that we are or are not developing a three-tier society?

Chapter 9
Race and Ethnicity

Learning Objectives

9.1 Contrast the myth and reality of race; compare race and ethnicity and minority and dominant groups; discuss ethnic work. (p. 260)

9.2 Contrast prejudice and discrimination and individual and institutional discrimination; discuss learning prejudice, internalizing dominant norms, and institutional discrimination. (p. 265)

9.3 Contrast psychological and sociological theories of prejudice: include functionalism, conflict, and symbolic interactionism. (p. 271)

9.4 Explain genocide, population transfer, internal colonialism, segregation, assimilation, and multiculturalism. (p. 275)

9.5 Summarize the major patterns that characterize European Americans, Latinos, African Americans, Asian Americans, and Native Americans. (p. 278)

9.6 Discuss immigration, affirmative action, and a multicultural society. (p. 291)

Imagine that you are an African American man living in Macon County, Alabama, during the Great Depression of the 1930s. Your home is a little country shack with a dirt floor. You have no electricity or running water. You never finished grade school, and you make a living, such as it is, by doing odd jobs. You haven't been feeling too good lately, but you can't afford a doctor.

Then you hear incredible news. You rub your eyes in disbelief. It is just like winning the lottery! If you join *Miss Rivers' Lodge* (and it is free to join), you will get free physical examinations at Tuskegee University *for life.* You will even get free rides to and from the clinic, hot meals on examination days, and a lifetime of free treatment for minor ailments.

You eagerly join *Miss Rivers' Lodge.*

After your first physical examination, the doctor gives you the bad news. "You've got bad blood," he says. "That's why you've been feeling bad. Miss Rivers will give you some medicine and schedule you for your next exam. I've got to warn you, though. If you go to another doctor, there's no more free exams or medicine."

You can't afford another doctor anyway. You are thankful for your treatment, take your medicine, and look forward to the next trip to the university.

What has really happened? You have just become part of what is surely slated to go down in history as one of the most callous experiments of all time, outside of the infamous World War II Nazi and Japanese experiments. With heartless disregard for human life, the U.S. Public Health Service told 399 African American men that they had joined a social club and burial society called *Miss Rivers' Lodge.* What the men were *not* told was that they had syphilis, that there was no real Miss Rivers' Lodge, that the doctors were just using this term so they could study what happened when syphilis went untreated. For forty years, the "U.S. Public Health Service" allowed these men to go without treatment for their syphilis—and kept testing them

> "You have just become part of one of the most callous experiments of all time."

259

each year—to study the progress of the disease. The "U.S. public health" officials even had a control group of 201 men who were free of the disease (Jones 1993; Reverby 2014).

By the way, the men did receive a benefit from "Miss Rivers' Lodge," a free autopsy to determine the ravages of syphilis on their bodies.

Laying the Sociological Foundation

9.1   **Contrast the myth and reality of race; compare race and ethnicity and minority and dominant groups; discuss ethnic work.**

As unlikely as it seems, this is a true story. Rarely do racial-ethnic relations degenerate to this point, but reports of troubled race relations surprise none of us. Today's newspapers, TV, and Internet regularly report on racial problems. Sociology can contribute greatly to our understanding of this aspect of social life—and this chapter may be an eye-opener for you. To begin, let's consider to what extent race itself is a myth.

Race: Myth and Reality

race

a group whose inherited physical characteristics distinguish it from other groups

Humans show remarkable diversity. Shown here is just one example—He Pingping, from China, who at 2 feet 4 inches, was the world's shortest man, and Svetlana Pankratova, from Russia, who, according to the *Guinness Book of World Records*, is the woman with the longest legs. Race–ethnicity shows similar diversity.

THE REALITY OF HUMAN VARIETY   With its 7 billion people, the world offers a fascinating variety of human shapes and colors. Skin colors come in all shades between black and white, heightened by reddish and yellowish hues. Eyes come in shades of blue, brown, and green. Lips are thick and thin. Hair is straight, curly, kinky, black, blonde, red—and, of course, all shades of brown.

As humans spread throughout the world, their adaptations to diverse climates and other living conditions resulted in this profusion of colors, hair textures, and other physical variations. Genetic mutations added distinct characteristics to the peoples of the globe. In this sense, the concept of **race**—a group of people with inherited physical characteristics that distinguish it from another group—is a reality. Humans do, indeed, come in a variety of colors and shapes.

THE MYTH OF PURE RACES   Humans show such a mixture of physical characteristics that there are no "pure" races. Instead of falling into distinct types that are clearly separate from one another, human characteristics—skin color, hair texture, nose shape, head shape, eye color, and so on—flow endlessly together. The mapping of the human genome system shows that any two individuals in the world have 99.6 percent of their genetic material in common (Beauchamp et al. 2011). What are called racial groups differ from one another only once in a thousand subunits of the genome (Angler 2000; Frank 2007). As you can see from the example of Tiger Woods, discussed in the Cultural Diversity box on the next page, these minute gradations make any attempt to draw lines of pure race purely arbitrary.

THE MYTH OF A FIXED NUMBER OF RACES   Although large groupings of people can be classified by blood type and gene frequencies, even these classifications do not uncover "race." Rather, the term is so arbitrary that biologists and anthropologists cannot even agree on how many "races" there are (Glasgow 2013). Ashley Montagu (1964, 1999), a physical anthropologist, pointed out that some scientists have classified humans into only two "races," while others have found as many as two thousand. Montagu (1960) himself classified humans into forty "racial" groups.

"Race" is so fluid that even a plane ride can change someone's race. If you want to see how, read the Down-to-Earth Sociology box on page 262.

THE MYTH OF RACIAL SUPERIORITY   Regardless of what anthropologists, biologists, and sociologists say, however, people do divide one another into races, and we are stuck with this term. People also tend to see some races (mostly their own) as superior and others as inferior. As with language, however, no race is better than another. All races have their geniuses—and their idiots.

Cultural Diversity in the United States

Tiger Woods: Mapping the Changing Ethnic Terrain

Tiger Woods, perhaps the top golfer of all time, calls himself *Cablinasian*. Woods invented this term as a boy to try to explain to himself just who he was—a combination of Caucasian, Black, Indian, and Asian (Leland and Beals 1997; McKibbin 2014). Woods wanted to embrace all sides of his family.

Like many of us, Tiger Woods' heritage is difficult to specify. Analysts who like to quantify ethnic heritage put Woods at one-quarter Thai, one-quarter Chinese, one-quarter white, an eighth Native American, and an eighth African American. From this chapter, you know how ridiculous such computations are, but the sociological question is why many people consider Tiger Woods to be African American. The U.S. racial scene is indeed complex, but a good part of the reason is that Woods has dark skin, and this is the label the media placed on him. The attitude seems to be "Everyone has to fit somewhere." And for Tiger Woods, the media chose African American.

The United States once had a firm "color line"—barriers between racial–ethnic groups that you didn't dare cross, especially in dating or marriage. This invisible barrier has broken down, and today such marriages are common (*Statistical Abstract* 2014:Table 63). Children born in these marriages have a difficult time figuring out how to classify themselves (Saulny 2011). To help them make an adjustment in college, some colleges have interracial student organizations.

As we enter unfamiliar ethnic terrain, our classifications are bursting at the seams. Here is how Kwame Anthony Appiah, of Harvard's Philosophy and Afro-American Studies Departments, described his situation:

> My mother is English; my father is Ghanaian. My sisters are married to a Nigerian and a Norwegian. I have nephews who range from blond-haired kids to very black kids. They are all first cousins. Now according to the American scheme of things, they're all black—even the guy with blond hair who skis in Oslo. (Wright 1994)

I marvel at what racial experts the U.S. census takers once were. When they took the national census, which is done every ten years, they looked at people and assigned them a race. At various points, the census contained these categories: mulatto, quadroon, octoroon, Negro, black, Mexican, white, Indian, Filipino, Japanese, Chinese, and Hindu. Quadroon (one-fourth black and three-fourths white) and octoroon (one-eighth black and seven-eighths white) proved too difficult to "measure," and these categories were

Tiger Woods as he answers questions at a news conference.

used only in 1890. Mulatto appeared in the 1850 census and lasted until 1920. The Mexican government complained about Mexicans being treated as a race, and this category was used only in 1930. I don't know whose idea it was to make Hindu a race, but it lasted for three censuses, from 1920 to 1940 (Bean et al. 2004; Tafoya et al. 2005).

In the 2010 census, we were first asked to declare whether we were or were not "Spanish/Hispanic/Latino." After this, we were asked to check "one or more races" that we "consider ourselves to be." We could choose from White; Black, African American, or Negro; American Indian or Alaska Native; and Asian Indian, Chinese, Filipino, Japanese, Korean, Vietnamese, Native Hawaiian, Guamanian or Chamorro, or Samoan. There were boxes for Other Asian and Other Pacific Islander, with examples that listed Hmong, Pakistani, and Fijian as races. If these didn't do it, we could check a box called "Some Other Race" and then write whatever we wanted.

Perhaps the census should list Cablinasian, after all. We could also have ANGEL for African-Norwegian-German-English-Latino Americans, DEVIL for those of Danish-English-Vietnamese-Italian-Lebanese descent, and STUDENT for Swedish-Turkish-Uruguayan-Danish-English-Norwegian-Tibetan Americans. As you read farther in this chapter, you will see why these terms make as much sense as the categories we currently use.

For Your Consideration

Perhaps you can use the materials in this chapter to answer these questions:

→ Why do we count people by "race"? Why not eliminate race from the U.S. census? (Race became a factor in 1790 during the first census. To determine the number of representatives from each state, a slave was counted as three-fifths of a person!)

→ Why is race so important to some people?

Down-to-Earth Sociology

Can a Plane Ride Change Your Race?

At the beginning of this text, I mentioned that common sense and sociology often differ. This is especially so when it comes to race. According to common sense, our racial classifications represent biological differences between people. Sociologists, in contrast, stress that what we call races are *social* classifications, not biological categories.

Sociologists point out that *our "race" depends more on the society in which we live than on our biology*. For example, the racial categories common in the United States are only one of *numerous* ways by which people around the world classify physical appearances (Mukhopadhyay et al. 2014). Although various groups use different categories, each group assumes that its categories are natural, merely a response to visible biology.

To better understand this essential sociological point—that race is more social than it is biological—consider this: In the United States, children born to the same parents are all of the same race. "What could be more natural?" Americans assume. But in Brazil, children born to the same parents may be of different races—if their appearances differ. "What could be more natural?" assume Brazilians.

Consider how Americans usually classify a child born to a "black" mother and a "white" father. Why do they usually say that the child is "black"? Wouldn't it be equally as logical to classify the child as "white"? Similarly, if a child has one grandmother who is "black," but all her other ancestors are "white," the child is often considered "black." Yet she has much more "white blood" than "black blood." Why, then, is she considered "black"? Certainly not because of biology.

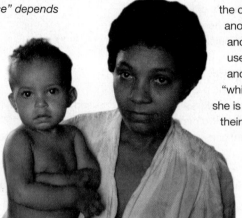

What "race" are these two Brazilians? Is the child's "race" different from her mother's "race"? The text explains why "race" is such an unreliable concept that it changes even with geography.

Such thinking is a legacy of slavery. In an attempt to preserve the "purity" of their "race" in the face of the many children whose fathers were white slave masters and whose mothers were black slaves, whites classified anyone with even a "drop of black blood" as black. They actually called this the "one-drop" rule.

Even a plane trip can change a person's race. In the city of Salvador in Brazil, people classify one another by color of skin and eyes, breadth of nose and lips, and color and curliness of hair. They use at least seven terms for what we call white and black. Consider again a U.S. child who has "white" and "black" parents. If she flies to Brazil, she is no longer "black"; she now belongs to one of their several "whiter" categories (Fish 1995).

If the girl makes such a flight, would her "race" actually change? Our common sense revolts at this, I know, but it actually would. We want to argue that because her biological characteristics remain unchanged, her race remains unchanged. This is because we think of race as biological, when *race is actually a label we use to describe perceived biological characteristics*. Simply put, the race we "are" depends on our social location—on who is doing the classifying.

"Racial" classifications are also fluid, not fixed. Even now, you can see change occurring in U.S. classifications. The category "multiracial," for example, indicates changing thought and perception.

For Your Consideration

→ How would you explain to someone that race is more a social classification than a biological one? Can you come up with any arguments to refute this statement?

→ How do you think our racial–ethnic categories will change in the future?

Yet the myth of racial superiority abounds, a myth that is particularly dangerous. Adolf Hitler, for example, believed that the Aryans were a superior race, destined to establish an advanced culture and a new world order. This destiny required them to avoid the "racial contamination" that would come from breeding with inferior races. The Aryans, then, had a "cultural duty" to isolate or destroy races that threatened their racial purity and culture.

Hitler's views, put into practice, were appalling. The Nazis slaughtered those they deemed inferior: Jews, Slavs, gypsies, homosexuals, and people with mental and physical disabilities. Horrific images of gas ovens and emaciated bodies stacked like cordwood have haunted the world's nations. At Nuremberg, the Allies, flush with victory, put the top Nazis on trial, exposing their heinous deeds to a shocked world. Their public executions, everyone assumed, marked the end of such grisly acts.

Obviously, they didn't.

The reason I selected these photos is to illustrate how seriously we must take all preaching of hatred and of racial supremacy, even though it seems to come from harmless or even humorous sources. The strange looking person with his hands on his hips, who is wearing *lederhosen*, traditional clothing of Bavaria, Germany, is Adolf Hitler. He caused this horrific carnage at the Landsberg concentration camp.

"Which one of your seven children are you going to throw into this grave?" the men asked the woman. "If you refuse to tell us, they'll all be buried alive." (Isaacs 2014)

This was fifty years later in Rwanda, when, over 100 days in 1994, Hutus slaughtered a million Tutsis—mostly with machetes (Kagame 2014). That same decade, Serbian leaders in Bosnia massacred Muslims, giving the world the term *ethnic cleansing*. In North Korea today, prisoners deemed genetically inferior—defiling the "sacred Korean race"—are tortured, raped, and starved to death (Eberstadt 2014a). As these events sadly attest, **genocide**, the attempt to destroy a group of people because of their presumed race or ethnicity, remains alive and well. Although more recent killings are not accompanied by swastikas and gas ovens, the perpetrators' goal is the same.

THE MYTH CONTINUES   The *idea* of race, of course, is far from a myth. Firmly embedded in our culture, it is a powerful force in our everyday lives. That no race is superior and that even biologists cannot decide how people should be classified into races is not what counts. "I know what I see, and you can't tell me any different" seems to be the common attitude. As was noted in Chapter 4, sociologists W. I. and D. S. Thomas (1928) observed, "If people define situations as real, they are real in their consequences." In other words, people act on perceptions and beliefs, not facts. As a result, we will always have people like Hitler and, as illustrated in our opening vignette, calloused bureaucrats like those in the U.S. Public Health Service who thought that it was fine to experiment with people whom they deemed inferior. Although few people hold such extreme views, most people appear to be ethnocentric enough to believe that their own race is—at least just a little—superior to others.

genocide

the annihilation or attempted annihilation of a people because of their presumed race or ethnicity

Ethnic Groups

In contrast to *race*, which people use to refer to supposed biological characteristics that distinguish one group of people from another, **ethnicity** and **ethnic** refer to cultural characteristics. Derived from the word *ethnos* (a Greek word meaning "people" or "nation"), *ethnicity* and *ethnic* refer to people who identify with one another on the basis of common ancestry and cultural heritage. Their sense of belonging may center on their nation or region of origin, distinctive foods, clothing, language, music, religion, or family names and relationships.

People often confuse the terms *race* and *ethnic group*. For example, many people, including many Jews, consider Jews a race. Jews, however, are more properly considered an ethnic group, since it is their cultural characteristics, especially their religion, that bind

ethnicity (and **ethnic**)

having distinctive cultural characteristics

Assumptions of race-ethnicity influence both perception and behavior. This photo is of Jews in Gondar, Ethiopia, awaiting their immigration to Israel. It took Israeli authorities several years to acknowledge that the Ethiopian Jews were "real Jews" and then allow them to immigrate.

minority group

people who are singled out for unequal treatment and who regard themselves as objects of collective discrimination

dominant group

the group with the most power, greatest privileges, and highest social status

them together. Wherever Jews have lived in the world, they have intermarried. Consequently, Jews in China may have Chinese features, while some Swedish Jews are blue-eyed blonds. The confusion of race and ethnicity is illustrated in the photo on the left.

Minority Groups and Dominant Groups

Sociologist Louis Wirth (1945) defined a **minority group** as people who are singled out for unequal treatment and who regard themselves as objects of collective discrimination. Worldwide, minorities share several conditions: Their physical or cultural traits are held in low esteem by the dominant group, which treats them unfairly, and they tend to marry within their own group (Wagley and Harris 1958). These conditions tend to create a sense of identity among minorities (a feeling of "we-ness"). In some instances, even a sense of common destiny emerges (Chandra 1993).

NOT SIZE, BUT DOMINANCE AND DISCRIMINATION   Surprisingly, a minority group is not necessarily a *numerical* minority. For example, before India's independence in 1947, a handful of British colonial rulers dominated tens of millions of Indians. Similarly, when South Africa practiced apartheid, a smaller group of Afrikaners, primarily Dutch, discriminated against a much larger number of blacks. And all over the world, as we discussed in the previous chapter, females are a minority group. Because of this, sociologists refer to those who do the discriminating not as the *majority* but, rather, as the **dominant group**. Regardless of its numbers, the dominant group has the greater power and privilege.

Possessing political power and unified by shared physical and cultural traits, the dominant group uses its position to discriminate against those with different—and supposedly inferior—traits. The dominant group considers its privileged position to be obvious proof of its own innate superiority.

EMERGENCE OF MINORITY GROUPS   A group becomes a minority in one of two ways. The *first* is through the expansion of political boundaries. With the exception of females, tribal societies contain no minority groups. There everyone shares the same culture, including the same language, and belongs to the same group. When a group expands its political boundaries, however, it produces minority groups if it incorporates people with different customs, languages, religions, values, or physical characteristics into the same political entity and discriminates against them. For example, in 1848, after defeating Mexico in war, the United States took over the Southwest. The Mexicans living there, who had been the dominant group prior to the war, were transformed into a minority group, a master status that has influenced their lives ever since. Referring to his ancestors, one Latino said, "We didn't move across the border—the border moved across us."

A *second* way in which a group becomes a minority is by migration. This can be voluntary, as with the Mexicans and South Americans who have chosen to move to the United States, or involuntary, as with the Africans who were brought in chains to the United States. (The way females became a minority group represents a third way, but, as discussed in the previous chapter, no one knows just how this occurred.)

Ethnic Work: Constructing Our Racial–Ethnic Identity

Some of us have a greater sense of ethnicity than others, and we feel firm boundaries between "us" and "them." Others of us have assimilated so extensively into the mainstream culture that we are only vaguely aware of our ethnic origins. With interethnic marriage common, some do not even know the countries from which their families originated—nor do they care. If asked to identify themselves ethnically, they respond with something like "I'm Heinz 57—German and Irish, with a little Italian and French thrown in—and I think someone said something about being one-sixteenth Indian, too."

Why do some people feel an intense sense of ethnic identity, while others feel hardly any? Figure 9.1 portrays four factors, identified by sociologist Ashley Doane, that heighten or reduce our sense of ethnic identity. From this figure, you can see that the keys are relative size, power, appearance, and discrimination. If your group is relatively small, has little power, looks different from most people in society, and is an object of discrimination, you will have a heightened sense of ethnic identity. In contrast, if you belong to the dominant group that holds most of the power, look like most people in the society, and feel no discrimination, you are likely to experience a sense of "belonging"—and to wonder why ethnic identity is such a big deal.

Figure 9.1 A Sense of Ethnicity

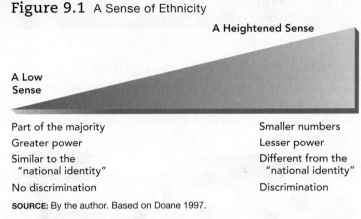

Part of the majority	Smaller numbers
Greater power	Lesser power
Similar to the "national identity"	Different from the "national identity"
No discrimination	Discrimination

SOURCE: By the author. Based on Doane 1997.

We can use the term **ethnic work** to refer to the way we construct our ethnicity. For people who have a strong ethnic identity, this term refers to how they enhance and maintain their group's distinctions—from clothing, food, and language to religious practices and holidays. For people whose ethnic identity is not as firm, it refers to attempts to recover their ethnic heritage, such as trying to trace family lines or visiting the country of their family's origin. As illustrated by the photo essay on the next page, many Americans do ethnic work. This has confounded the experts, who thought that the United States would be a *melting pot*, with most of its groups blending into a sort of ethnic stew. Because so many Americans have become fascinated with their "roots," some analysts suggest that "tossed salad" is a more appropriate term than "melting pot."

ethnic work

activities designed to discover, enhance, maintain, or transmit an ethnic or racial identity

Prejudice and Discrimination

9.2 Contrast prejudice and discrimination and individual and institutional discrimination; discuss learning prejudice, internalizing dominant norms, and institutional discrimination.

With prejudice and discrimination so significant in social life, let's consider the origin of prejudice and the extent of discrimination.

Learning Prejudice

DISTINGUISHING BETWEEN PREJUDICE AND DISCRIMINATION Prejudice and discrimination are common throughout the world. In Mexico, Mexicans of Hispanic descent discriminate against Mexicans of Native American descent; in Israel, Ashkenazi Jews, primarily of European descent, discriminate against Sephardic Jews, from the Middle East; in China, the Han discriminate against the Uighurs. In some places, the elderly discriminate against the young; in others, the young discriminate against the elderly. And all around the world, men discriminate against women.

Discrimination is an *action*—unfair treatment directed against someone. Discrimination can be based on many characteristics: age, sex, height, weight, skin color, clothing, speech, income, education, marital status, sexual orientation, disease, disability, religion, and politics. When the basis of discrimination is someone's perception of race, it is known as **racism**. Discrimination is often the result of an *attitude* called **prejudice**— a prejudging of some sort, usually in a negative way. There is also *positive prejudice*, which exaggerates the virtues of a group, as when people think that some group is superior to others. Most prejudice, however, is negative and involves prejudging a group as inferior.

discrimination

an act of unfair treatment directed against an individual or a group

racism

prejudice and discrimination on the basis of race

prejudice

an attitude or prejudging, usually in a negative way

Explorations in Cultural Identity

Ethnic work refers to the ways that people establish, maintain, and transmit their ethnic identity. As shown here, among the techniques people use to forge ties with their roots are dress, dance, and music.

Many African Americans are trying to get in closer contact with their roots. To do this, some use musical performances. This photo was taken in Philadelphia, Pennsylvania.

As some groups do ethnic work, they produce a mythical long-lost heritage, as in this photo of "1500s Spanish" that I took in St. Augustine, Florida.

Many European Americans are involved in ethnic work, attempting to maintain an identity more precise than "from Europe." These women of Czech ancestry are performing for a Czech community in a small town in Nebraska.

Many Native Americans have maintained continuous identity with their tribal roots. This woman in Brooklyn is playing a *towa*, a gourd wrapped in a beaded net.

The *Cinco de Mayo* celebration is used to recall roots and renew ethnic identities. This one was held in Los Angeles, California.

LEARNING PREJUDICE FROM ASSOCIATING WITH OTHERS As with our other attitudes, we are not born with prejudice. Rather, we learn prejudice from the people around us. You probably know this, but here is a twist that sociologists have found. Michael Kimmel (2007), who interviewed neo-Nazi skinheads in Sweden, found that the young men were attracted mostly by the group's tough masculinity, not its hatred of immigrants. Kathleen Blee (2005, 2011), who interviewed female members of the Ku Klux Klan (KKK) and Aryan Nations in the United States, found something similar. They were attracted to the hate group because someone they liked belonged to it. They learned to be racists *after* they joined the group. Both Blee and Kimmel found that the members' racism was not the *cause* of their joining but, rather, joining was the cause of their racism.

Just as our associations can increase prejudice, so they can reduce prejudice, the topic of our following Down-to-Earth Sociology box.

contact theory
the idea that prejudice and negative stereotypes decrease and racial–ethnic relations improve when people from different racial–ethnic backgrounds, who are of equal status, interact frequently

Down-to-Earth Sociology

Living in the Dorm: Contact Theory

From your own experience, you know that friends influence one another. Much of this influence comes from talking. As friends talk about their experiences and share their ideas, they help give shape to one another's views of life.

It is no different for friends who are from different racial–ethnic groups. As they interact with one another, their understandings change and their perspectives broaden. Over time, if they cannot see the world through each other's eyes, they at least get a glimpse of what that world looks like.

If one of the goals of college is to increase students' understanding of the world and change their attitudes while helping to integrate racial–ethnic groups—and this is a big if—then why do some colleges have separate dorms for African American students, Jewish students, and so on? And when there aren't separate dorms, why do some colleges assign roommates so blacks will room with blacks and whites with whites?

The goal of such room assignments, of course, is to make minority students feel comfortable and help prevent them from feeling lost in a sea of white faces and suffering from *anomie*, feelings of not belonging.

These good intentions have an unanticipated result. As African American students interact in these "little corners" of the campus, their interracial friendships decrease. At the end of their freshman year in college, African American students have about 10 percent fewer interracial friends than when they began college. What happens if colleges assign students of different racial–ethnic groups to the same dorm rooms? It is

Contact theory indicates that prejudice decreases and relations improve when individuals of different racial–ethnic backgrounds who are of equal status interact frequently. These two freshmen are roommates at DePaul University in Chicago.

not surprising, but these students end up with more interracial friendships than those who have roommates of their own race–ethnicity.

Mixed racial–ethnic roommate arrangements, though, are more likely to fail. About 17 percent end during the school year, compared to 10 percent of white–white pairings and 9 percent of black–black pairings. The dissatisfactions cut both ways, with blacks and whites requesting transfers at about the same rate.

But note that the vast majority of these interracial pairings last. They don't always blossom into friendships, of course, and like other roommate assignments, some roommates can barely tolerate one another. But contacts and cross-racial friendships do increase in most cases, changing understandings and perspectives. We need in-depth research to uncover who is changed in what ways.

To summarize the sociological research: Mutual understandings increase, prejudice decreases, and relations improve when people of equal status who are from different racial–ethnic backgrounds interact frequently and work toward mutual goals. The shorthand for these findings is **contact theory**.

SOURCE: Based on Riley 2009; King et al. 2013.

For Your Consideration

→ Do you think colleges should eliminate racially and ethnically themed dormitories?

→ What is your opinion about colleges assigning students of different racial–ethnic groups to the same dorm rooms?

THE FAR-REACHING NATURE OF PREJUDICE   It is amazing how much prejudice people can learn. In a classic article, psychologist Eugene Hartley (1946) asked people how they felt about several racial–ethnic groups. Besides Negroes, Jews, and so on, he included the Wallonians, Pireneans, and Danireans—names he had made up. Most people who expressed dislike for Jews and Negroes showed similar contempt for these three fictitious groups.

Hartley's study shows that prejudice does not depend on negative experiences with others. It also reveals that people who are prejudiced against one racial or ethnic group also tend to be prejudiced against other groups. People can be, and are, prejudiced against people they have never met—and even against groups that do not exist!

The neo-Nazis and the Ku Klux Klan base their existence on prejudice. These groups believe that race is real, that white is best, and that beneath society's surface is a murky river of mingling conspiracies (Ezekiel 1995). What would happen if a Jew attended their meetings? Would he or she survive? In the Down-to-Earth Sociology box on the next page, sociologist Raphael Ezekiel reveals some of the insights he gained during his remarkable study of these groups.

INTERNALIZING DOMINANT NORMS   People can even learn to be prejudiced against their own group. A national survey found that African Americans think that lighter-skinned African American women are more attractive than those with darker skin (Hill 2002). Participant observation in the inner city also reveals a preference for lighter skin (Jones 2010). Sociologists call this *internalizing the norms of the dominant group*.

To study the internalization of dominant norms, psychologists Mahzarin Banaji and Anthony Greenwald created the *Implicit Association Test*. In one version of this test,

This photo, taken in Birmingham, Alabama, provides a glimpse into the determination and bravery of the civil rights demonstrators of the 1960s and the severe opposition they confronted.

Down-to-Earth Sociology

The Racist Mind

Sociologist Raphael Ezekiel wanted to get a close look at the racist mind. The best way to study racism from the inside is to do participant observation (see page 28). But Ezekiel is a Jew. How could he study these groups by participant observation? To see if he could, Ezekiel simply told Ku Klux Klan and neo-Nazi leaders that he was a Jew and wanted to interview them and attend their meetings. Surprisingly, they agreed. Ezekiel published his path-breaking research in a book, *The Racist Mind* (1995). Here are some of the insights he gained during his fascinating sociological adventure:

Raphael Ezekiel

[The leader] builds on mass anxiety about economic insecurity and on popular tendencies to see an Establishment as the cause of economic threat; he hopes to teach people to identify that Establishment as the puppets of a conspiracy of Jews . . . . [He has a] belief in exclusive categories. For the white racist leader, it is profoundly true . . . that the socially defined collections we call races represent fundamental categories. A man is black or a man is white; there are no in-betweens. Every human belongs to a racial category, and all the members of one category are radically different from all the members of other categories. Moreover, race represents the essence of the person. A truck is a truck, a car is a car, a cat is a cat, a dog is a dog, a black is a black, a white is a white . . . . These axioms have a rock-hard quality in the leaders' minds; the world is made up of racial groups. That is what exists for them.

Two further beliefs play a major role in the minds of leaders. First, life is war. The world is made of distinct racial groups; life is about the war between these groups. Second, events have secret causes, are never what they seem superficially . . . . Any myth is plausible, as long as it involves intricate plotting . . . . It does not matter to him what others say . . . . He lives in his ideas and in the little world he has created where they are taken seriously . . . . Gold can be made from the tongues of frogs; Yahweh's call can be heard in the flapping swastika banner. (pp. 66–67)

Who is attracted to the neo-Nazis and Ku Klux Klan? Here is what Ezekiel discovered:

[There is a] ready pool of whites who will respond to the racist signal . . . . This population [is] always hungry for activity—or for the talk of activity— that promises dignity and meaning to lives that are working poorly in a highly competitive world . . . . Much as I don't want to believe it, [this] movement brings a sense of meaning—at least for a while—to some of the discontented. To struggle in a cause that transcends the individual lends meaning to life, no matter how ill-founded or narrowing the cause. For the young men in the neo-Nazi group . . . membership was an alternative to atomization and drift; within the group they worked for a cause and took direct risks in the company of comrades . . . .

When interviewing the young neo-Nazis in Detroit, I often found myself driving with them past the closed factories, the idled plants of our shrinking manufacturing base. The fewer and fewer plants that remain can demand better educated and more highly skilled workers. These fatherless Nazi youths, these high-school dropouts, will find little place in the emerging economy . . . a permanently underemployed white underclass is taking its place alongside the permanent black underclass. The struggle over race merely diverts youth from confronting the real issues of their lives. Not many seats are left on the train, and the train is leaving the station. (pp. 32–33)

For Your Consideration

→ Use functionalism, conflict theory, and symbolic interaction to explain how the leaders and followers of these hate groups view the world.

→ Use these same perspectives to explain why some people are attracted to the message of hate.

good and bad words are flashed on a screen along with photos of African Americans and whites (Blair et al. 2013). Most subjects are quicker to associate positive words (such as "love," "peace," and "baby") with whites and negative words (such as "cancer," "bomb," and "devil") with blacks. Here's the clincher: This is true for *both* whites and blacks (Dasgupta et al. 2000; Greenwald and Krieger 2006). Apparently, we all learn the *ethnic maps* of our culture and, along with them, their route to biased perception.

individual discrimination

person-to-person or face-to-face discrimination; the negative treatment of people by other individuals

institutional discrimination

negative treatment of a minority group that is built into a society's institutions; also called *systemic discrimination*

Individual and Institutional Discrimination

Sociologists stress that we should move beyond thinking in terms of **individual discrimination**, the negative treatment of one person by another. Although such behavior creates problems, it is primarily an issue between individuals. With their focus on the broader picture, sociologists encourage us to examine **institutional discrimination**, that is, to see how discrimination is woven into the fabric of society. Let's look at two examples.

HOME MORTGAGES   Bank lending provides an excellent illustration of institutional discrimination (Ropiequet et al. 2012). Reviewing national samples of loan applications, researchers found that bankers often refuse to make loans to minorities. When confronted, the bankers said they didn't have a discriminatory bone in their bodies—the whites simply had better credit history. The researchers retested their data. They found that even when applicants had identical credit, bankers were *60 percent* more likely to reject African Americans and Latinos (Thomas 1991, 1992). The problem continues. Look at Figure 9.2. You can see that *minorities are more likely to be turned down for a loan—and this is true whether their incomes are below or above the median income of their community.*

In the Great Recession that we have suffered through, African Americans and Latinos were hit harder than whites. The last set of bars on Figure 9.2 shows one of the reasons for this: *Banks purposely charged minorities higher interest rates, a practice called predatory lending.* When the economic crisis hit, the results were devastating. Many African Americans and Latinos who could have continued to make their house payments if they had the lower interest rates lost their homes (Ropiequet et al. 2012).

Would nice bankers really do predatory lending? After checking data like these, the Justice Department accused Countrywide Financial, a major mortgage lender, of discriminating against 200,000 Latino and African American borrowers. Countrywide agreed to pay a fine of $335 million, the largest fair-lending settlement in history (Savage 2011).

HEALTH CARE   Losing your home is devastating. Losing your mother or baby is even worse. Look at Table 9.1 on the next page. You can see that institutional discrimination can be a life-and-death matter. In childbirth, African American mothers are almost *three* times as likely to die as white mothers, while their babies are more than *twice* as

---

Figure 9.2 Buying a House: Institutional Discrimination and Predatory Lending

This figure, based on a national sample, illustrates *institutional discrimination*. Rejecting the loan applications of minorities and gouging minorities with higher interest rates are a nationwide practice, not the acts of a rogue banker here or there. Because the discrimination is part of the banking system, it is also called *systemic discrimination*.

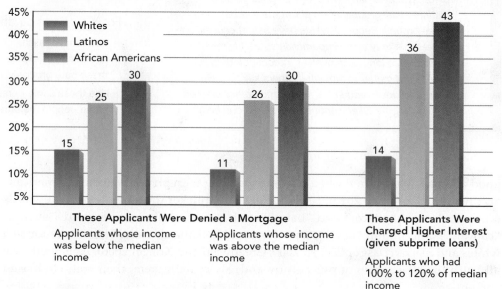

These Applicants Were Denied a Mortgage

Applicants whose income was below the median income

Applicants whose income was above the median income

These Applicants Were Charged Higher Interest (given subprime loans)

Applicants who had 100% to 120% of median income

SOURCE: By the author. Based on Kochbar and Gonzalez-Barrera 2009.

Table 9.1 Health and Race–Ethnicity

	Infant	Maternal	Life Expectancy	
	Deaths[1]	Deaths[2]	Male	Female
Whites	5.2	10.0	76.5	81.3
African Americans	11.6	26.5	71.8	78.0

[1]The death rates given here are the number per 1,000. Infant deaths refer to the number of infants under 1 year who die in a year per 1,000 live births. The source does not provide data for other racial–ethnic groups.

[2]The source has not updated maternal deaths since 2007. I expect they have dropped since then.

SOURCE: By the author. Based on *Statistical Abstract of the United States* 2014:Tables 111, 121.

likely to die during their first year of life. This is not a matter of biology, as though African American mothers and children are more fragile. It is a matter of *social* conditions, primarily nutrition and medical care.

Discrimination is not always deliberate. In some *unintentional discrimination*, no one is aware of it—neither those being discriminated against nor those doing the discriminating (Hausmann et al. 2014). Researchers studied the race–ethnicity of people who receive knee replacements and coronary bypass surgery. They found that white patients are more likely than Latino or African American patients to receive these procedures (Skinner et al. 2003; Popescu et al. 2007). They found a similar pattern in treatment after a heart attack: Whites are more likely than blacks to be given cardiac catheterization, a test to detect blockage of blood vessels. This study of 40,000 patients held a surprise: Both black and white doctors are more likely to give this preventive care to whites (Stolberg 2001).

Researchers are trying to figure out how race–ethnicity becomes a factor in medical decisions (Penner et al. 2014). With both white and black doctors involved, we can be certain that physicians do not *intend* to discriminate. Apparently, the implicit bias that comes with the internalization of dominant norms becomes a subconscious motivation for giving or denying access to advanced medical procedures. Race seems to work like gender: Just as women's higher death rates in coronary bypass surgery can be traced to implicit attitudes about gender (see pages 311–312), so also race–ethnicity becomes a subconscious motivation for giving or denying access to advanced medical procedures (Blair et al. 2013).

Theories of Prejudice

9.3 Contrast psychological and sociological theories of prejudice: include functionalism, conflict, and symbolic interactionism.

Social scientists have developed several theories to explain prejudice. Let's first look at psychological explanations, then at sociological ones.

Psychological Perspectives

FRUSTRATION AND SCAPEGOATS.

> *"Why are we having a depression? The answer is simple. The Jews have taken over the banking system, and they want to suck every dollar out of us."*

This was a common sentiment in Germany in the 1930s during the deep depression that helped propel Hitler to power. People often unfairly blame their troubles on a **scapegoat**—often a racial–ethnic or religious minority. Why do they do this? Psychologist John Dollard (1939) suggested that prejudice is the result of frustration. People who are unable to strike out at the real source of their frustration (such as unemployment) look for someone to blame. This person or group becomes a target on which they vent their frustrations. Gender and age are also the basis for scapegoating. Immigrants, too, often find that they are scapegoats.

scapegoat
an individual or group unfairly blamed for someone else's troubles

How easily frustration can lead to prejudice was illustrated in a simple, yet fascinating experiment. A team of psychologists measured the prejudice of a group of students (Cowen 1959). They then gave the students two puzzles to solve, making sure the students did not have enough time to finish. After the students had worked furiously on the puzzles, the experimenters shook their heads in disgust and expressed disbelief that the students couldn't complete such a simple task. They then retested the students. The results? Their scores on prejudice increased. The students had directed their frustrations outward, transferring them to people who had nothing to do with the contempt they had experienced.

THE AUTHORITARIAN PERSONALITY

"I don't like Swedes. They're too rigid. And I don't like the Italians. They're always talking with their hands. I don't like the Walloneans, either. They're always smiling at something. And I don't like librarians. And my job sucks. Hitler might have had his faults, but he put people to work during the Great Depression."

Have you ever wondered whether some people's personalities make them more inclined to be prejudiced and others more fair-minded? For psychologist Theodor Adorno, who had fled from the Nazis, this was no idle speculation. With the horrors he had observed still fresh in his mind, Adorno wondered whether there might be a certain type of person who is more likely to fall for the racist spewings of people like Hitler, Mussolini, and those in the Ku Klux Klan.

To find out, Adorno gave three tests to about two thousand people, ranging from college professors to prison inmates (Adorno et al. 1950). He measured their ethnocentrism, anti-Semitism (bias against Jews), and support for strong, authoritarian leaders. People who scored high on one test also scored high on the other two. For example, people who agreed with anti-Semitic statements also said that governments should be authoritarian and that foreign customs pose a threat to the "American way."

authoritarian personality
Theodor Adorno's term for people who are prejudiced and rank high on scales of conformity, intolerance, insecurity, respect for authority, and submissiveness to superiors

Adorno concluded that highly prejudiced people have deep respect for authority and are submissive to authority figures. He termed this the **authoritarian personality**. These people believe that things are either right or wrong. Ambiguity disturbs them, especially in matters of religion or sex. They become anxious when they confront norms and values that are different from their own. To view people who differ from themselves as inferior assures them that their own positions are right.

Adorno's research stimulated more than a thousand research studies. In general, the researchers found that people who are older, less educated, less intelligent, and from a lower social class are more likely to be authoritarian. Critics say that this doesn't indicate a particular personality, just that the less educated are more prejudiced—which we already knew (Yinger 1965; Ray 1991). Nevertheless, researchers continue to study this concept (Duncan and Peterson 2014).

Sociological Perspectives

Sociologists find psychological explanations inadequate. They stress that the key to understanding prejudice cannot be found by looking *inside* people but, rather, by examining conditions *outside* of them. For this reason, sociologists focus on how social environments influence prejudice. With this background, let's compare functionalist, conflict, and symbolic interactionist perspectives on prejudice.

FUNCTIONALISM

In a television documentary, journalist Bill Moyers interviewed Fritz Hippler, a Nazi who was just 29 when he was put in charge of the entire German film industry. When Hitler came to power, Hippler said, the Germans were no more anti-Semitic than the French. Hippler was told to increase anti-Semitism in Germany. Obediently, he produced movies that contained vivid scenes comparing Jews to rats—with their breeding threatening to infest the population.

Why was Hippler told to create hatred? Prejudice and discrimination were functional for the Nazis. Defeated in World War I and devastated by fines levied by the victors, Germany was on its knees. Runaway inflation was destroying its middle class. To help unite this fractured Germany, the Nazis created a scapegoat to blame for their troubles. In addition, the Jews owned businesses, bank accounts, fine art, and other property that the Nazis could confiscate. Jews also held key positions (as university professors, reporters, judges, and so on), which the Nazis could give as prizes to their followers. In the end, hatred also showed its dysfunctional face, as the Nazi officials hanged at Nuremberg discovered.

Prejudice becomes practically irresistible when state machinery is used to advance the cause of hatred. To produce prejudice, the Nazis harnessed government agencies, the schools, police, courts, and mass media. The results were devastating. Recall the identical twins featured in the Down-to-Earth Sociology box on page 70 of Chapter 3. Jack and Oskar had been separated as babies. Jack was brought up as a Jew in Trinidad, while Oskar was reared as a Catholic in Czechoslovakia. Under the Nazi regime, Oskar learned to hate Jews, unaware that he himself was a Jew.

That prejudice is functional and shaped by the social environment was demonstrated in another classical experiment by psychologists Muzafer and Carolyn Sherif (1953). In a boys' summer camp, the Sherifs assigned friends to different cabins and then had the cabin groups compete in sports. In just a few days, strong in-groups had formed. Even lifelong friends began to taunt one another, calling each other "crybaby" and "sissy."

The Sherif study teaches us important lessons about social life. Note how it is possible to arrange the social environment to generate either positive or negative feelings about people, and how prejudice arises if we pit groups against one another in an "I win, you lose" situation. You can also see that prejudice is functional, how it creates in-group solidarity. And, of course, it is obvious how dysfunctional prejudice is, when you observe the way it destroys human relationships.

CONFLICT THEORY

"The Japanese have gone on strike? They're demanding a raise? And they even want a rest period? We'll show them who's boss. Hire those Koreans who keep asking for work."

This did happen. When Japanese workers in Hawaii struck, owners of plantations hired Koreans (Jeong and You 2008). The division of workers along racial–ethnic and gender lines is known as a **split labor market** (Du Bois 1935/1992; Alimahomed-Wilson 2012). Although today's exploitation of these divisions is more subtle, whites are aware that other racial–ethnic groups are ready to take their jobs, African Americans often perceive Latinos as competitors (Glanton 2013), and men know that women are eager to get promoted. All of this helps to keep workers in line.

Conflict theorists, as you will recall, focus on how groups compete for scarce resources. Owners want to increase profits by holding costs down, while workers want better food, health care, housing, education, and leisure. Divided, workers are weak, but united, they gain strength. The *split labor market* is one way that owners divide workers so they can't take united action to demand higher wages and better working conditions.

Another tactic that owners use is the **reserve labor force**. This is simply another term for the unemployed. To expand production during economic booms, companies hire people who don't have jobs. When the economy contracts, they lay off unneeded workers. That there are desperate people looking for work is a lesson not lost on those who have jobs. They fear eviction and worry about having their cars and furniture repossessed. Many know they are just one or two paychecks away from ending up "on the streets."

Just like the boys in the Sherif experiment, African Americans, Latinos, whites, and others see themselves as able to make gains only at the expense of other groups.

split labor market

workers split along racial–ethnic, gender, age, or any other lines; this split is exploited by owners to weaken the bargaining power of workers

reserve labor force

the unemployed; unemployed workers are thought of as being "in reserve"—capitalists take them "out of reserve" (put them back to work) during times of high production and then put them "back in reserve" (lay them off) when they are no longer needed

Sometimes this rivalry shows up along very fine racial–ethnic lines, such as that in Miami between Haitians and African Americans, who distrust each other as competitors. Divisions among workers deflect anger and hostility away from the power elite and direct these powerful emotions toward other racial–ethnic groups. Instead of recognizing their common class interests and working for their mutual welfare, workers learn to fear and distrust one another.

SYMBOLIC INTERACTIONISM

"I know her qualifications are good, but yikes! She's ugly. I don't want to have to look at her every day. Let's hire the pretty one with the nice curves."

While conflict theorists focus on the role of the owner (or capitalist) class in exploiting racial–ethnic divisions, symbolic interactionists examine how labels affect perception and create prejudice.

selective perception

seeing certain features of an object or situation, but remaining blind to others

HOW LABELS CREATE PREJUDICE   Symbolic interactionists stress that *the labels we learn affect the ways we perceive people*. Labels create **selective perception**; that is, they lead us to see certain things while they blind us to others. If we apply a label to a group, we tend to perceive its members as all alike. We shake off evidence that doesn't fit (Simpson and Yinger 1972; Drakulich 2012). Shorthand for emotionally charged stereotypes, some racial–ethnic labels are especially powerful. As you know, the term *nigger* is not neutral. Nor are *cracker, dago, guinea, honky, kike, kraut, limey, mick, spic,* or any of the other scornful words people use to belittle other groups. As in the statement above, *ugly* can work in a similar way. Such words overpower us with emotions, blocking out rational thought about the people to whom they refer (Allport 1954).

LABELS AND SELF-FULFILLING STEREOTYPES   Some stereotypes not only justify prejudice and discrimination but also produce the behavior depicted in the stereotype. We examined this principle in Chapter 4 in the box on beauty. Let's consider Group X. According to stereotypes, the members of this group are lazy, so they don't deserve good jobs. ("They are lazy and wouldn't do the job well.") Denied the better jobs, most members of Group X do "dirty work," the jobs few people want. ("That's the right kind of work for that kind of people.") Since much "dirty work" is sporadic, members of Group X are often seen "on the streets." The sight of their idleness reinforces the original stereotype of laziness. The discrimination that created the "laziness" in the first place passes unnoticed.

To apply these three theoretical perspectives and catch a glimpse of how amazingly different things were in the past, read the following Down-to-Earth Sociology box.

Down-to-Earth Sociology

The Man in the Zoo

The Bronx Zoo in New York City used to keep a 22-year-old pygmy in the Monkey House. The man—and the orangutan he lived with—became the most popular exhibit at the zoo. Thousands of visitors would arrive daily and head straight for the Monkey House. Eyewitnesses to what they were told was a lower form of human in the long chain of evolution, the visitors were fascinated by the pygmy, especially by his sharpened teeth.

To make the exhibit even more alluring, the zoo director scattered animal bones in front of the man.

I know it sounds as though I must have made this up, but this is a true story. The World's Fair was going to be held in St. Louis in 1904, and the U.S. Department of Anthropology wanted to show villages from different cultures. They asked Samuel Verner, an explorer, if he could bring some pygmies to St. Louis to serve as live exhibits. Verner agreed, and on his next trip to Africa, in the Belgian Congo, he came across Ota Benga, a pygmy who had been enslaved by another tribe. Benga, then about age 20, said he was willing to go to St. Louis. After Verner bought Benga's freedom for some cloth and salt, Benga recruited several other pygmies to go with them.

After the World's Fair, Verner took the pygmies back to Africa. When Benga found out that a Belgian military had wiped out his village and killed his family, he asked Verner if he could return with him to the United States. Verner agreed.

When they returned to New York, Verner ran into financial trouble and wrote some bad checks. No longer able to care for Benga, Verner left him with the director of the American Museum of Natural History. Later, Benga was turned over to the Bronx Zoo, which put him on display in the Monkey House, with this sign:

The African Pygmy, "Ota Benga." Age 23 years. Height 4 feet 11 inches. Weight 103 pounds. Brought from the Kasai River, Congo Free State, South Central Africa by Dr. Samuel P. Verner. Exhibited each afternoon during September.

Exhibited with an orangutan, Benga became a sensation. An article in *The New York Times* said it was fortunate that Benga couldn't think very deeply or else living with monkeys might bother him.

When the Colored Baptist Ministers' Conference protested that exhibiting Benga was degrading, zoo officials replied that they were "taking excellent care of the little fellow." They added that "he has one of the best rooms at the primate house." (I wonder what animal had *the* best room.)

Not surprisingly, this reply didn't satisfy the ministers. When they continued to protest, zoo officials decided to let Benga out of his cage. They put a white shirt on him and let him walk around the zoo. At night, Benga slept in the monkey house.

Ota Benga, 1906, on exhibit in the Bronx Zoo.

Benga's life became even more miserable. Zoo visitors would follow him, howling, jeering, laughing, and poking at him. One day, Benga found a knife in the feeding room of the Monkey House and flourished it at the visitors. Unhappy zoo officials took the knife away.

Benga then made a little bow and some arrows and began shooting at the obnoxious visitors. This ended the fun for the zoo officials. They decided that Benga had to leave.

After living in an orphanage for African American children, Benga went to work as a laborer in a tobacco factory in Lynchburg, Virginia.

Always treated as a freak, Benga was desperately lonely. In 1916, at about the age of 32, in despair that he had no home or family to return to in Africa, Benga ended his misery by shooting himself in the heart.

SOURCE: Based on Bradford and Blume 1992; Crossen 2006; Bergman 2014.

For Your Consideration

→ See what different views emerge as you apply the three theoretical perspectives (functionalism, symbolic interactionism, and conflict theory) to exhibiting Benga at the Bronx Zoo.

→ How does the concept of ethnocentrism apply to this event?

→ Explain how the concepts of prejudice and discrimination apply to what happened to Benga.

Global Patterns of Intergroup Relations

9.4 Explain genocide, population transfer, internal colonialism, segregation, assimilation, and multiculturalism.

In their studies of racial–ethnic relations around the world, sociologists have found six basic ways that dominant groups treat minority groups. These patterns are shown in Figure 9.3 on the next page. Let's look at each.

Genocide

When gold was discovered in northern California in 1849, the fabled "Forty-Niners" rushed in. In this region lived 150,000 Native Americans. To get rid of them, the white government put a bounty on their heads. It even reimbursed the whites for their bullets. The result was the slaughter of 120,000 Native American men, women, and children. (Schaefer 2004)

Could you ever participate in genocide? Don't be too quick in answering. Gaining an understanding of how ordinary people take part in genocide will be our primary goal in this section. In the events depicted in the little vignette above, those who did the killing were regular people—people like you and I. The killing was promoted by calling the Native Americans "savages," making them seem inferior, somehow less

Figure 9.3 Global Patterns of Intergroup Relations: A Continuum

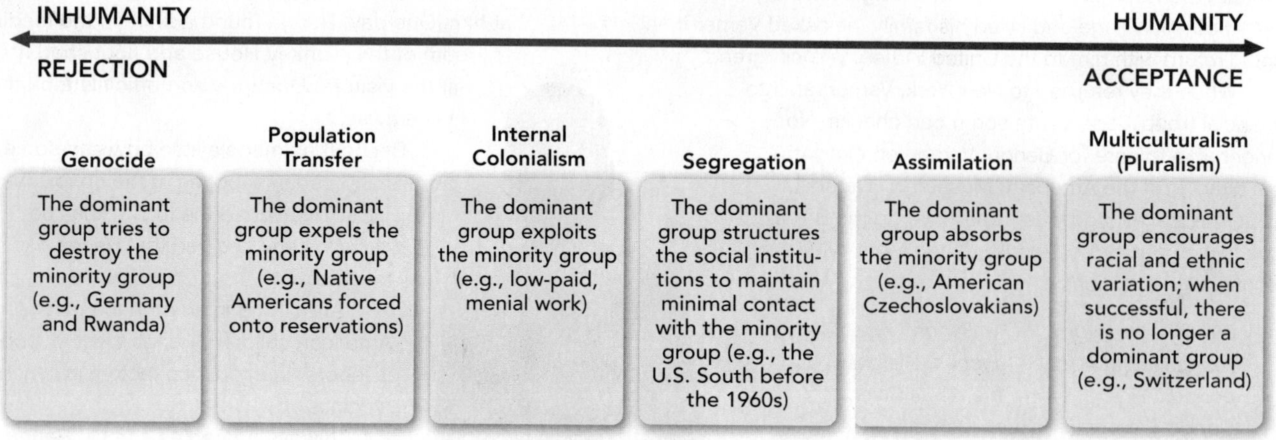

INHUMANITY → HUMANITY

REJECTION → ACCEPTANCE

Genocide	Population Transfer	Internal Colonialism	Segregation	Assimilation	Multiculturalism (Pluralism)
The dominant group tries to destroy the minority group (e.g., Germany and Rwanda)	The dominant group expels the minority group (e.g., Native Americans forced onto reservations)	The dominant group exploits the minority group (e.g., low-paid, menial work)	The dominant group structures the social institutions to maintain minimal contact with the minority group (e.g., the U.S. South before the 1960s)	The dominant group absorbs the minority group (e.g., American Czechoslovakians)	The dominant group encourages racial and ethnic variation; when successful, there is no longer a dominant group (e.g., Switzerland)

SOURCE: By the author.

than human. Killing them, then, didn't seem the same as killing whites in order to take their property.

Most Native Americans, though, died not from bullets but from the diseases the whites brought with them. Measles, smallpox, and the flu came from another continent, and the Native Americans had no immunity against them (Dobyns 1983). But disease wasn't enough. To accomplish the takeover of the Native Americans' resources, the settlers and soldiers destroyed their food supply (crops and buffalo). From all causes, about *95 percent* of Native Americans died (Thornton 1987; Schaefer 2012). Ordinary, "good" people were intent on destroying the "savages."

Now consider last century's two most notorious examples of genocide. In Germany during the 1930s and 1940s, Hitler and the Nazis attempted to destroy all Jews. In the 1990s, in Rwanda, the Hutus tried to destroy all Tutsis. One of the horrifying aspects of these two slaughters is that the killers did not crawl out from under a rock someplace. In some cases, it was even the victims' neighbors and friends who did the killing. *Their killing was facilitated by labels that marked the victims as enemies who deserved to die* (Huttenbach 1991; Browning 1993; Gross 2001).

compartmentalize

to separate acts from feelings or attitudes

IN SUM Labels are powerful; dehumanizing ones are even more so. They help people to **compartmentalize**—to separate their acts of cruelty from their sense of being good and decent people. To regard members of some group as inferior opens the door to treating them inhumanely. In some cases, these labels help people to kill—and to still retain a good self-concept (Bernard et al. 1971). In short, *labeling the targeted group as inferior or even less than fully human facilitates genocide.*

Population Transfer

population transfer

the forced transfer of a minority group

There are two types of **population transfer**: indirect and direct. *Indirect transfer* is achieved by making life so miserable for members of a minority that they leave "voluntarily." Under the bitter conditions of czarist Russia, for example, millions of Jews made this "choice." *Direct transfer* occurs when a dominant group expels a minority. Examples include the U.S. government relocating Native Americans to reservations and putting Americans of Japanese descent in internment camps during World War II.

In the 1990s, a combination of genocide and population transfer occurred in Bosnia and Kosovo, parts of the former Yugoslavia. A hatred nurtured for centuries had been kept under wraps by Tito's iron-fisted rule from 1944 to 1980. After Tito's death, these suppressed, smoldering hostilities soared to the surface, and Yugoslavia split into warring factions. When the Serbs gained power, Muslims rebelled and began guerilla warfare. The Serbs vented their hatred by what they termed **ethnic cleansing**: They terrorized villages with killing and rape, forcing survivors to flee in fear. In Iraq in 2014, ISIS began doing the same thing with ethnic/religious minorities.

Internal Colonialism

In Chapter 7 (page 218), the term *colonialism* was used to refer to one way that the Most Industrialized Nations exploit the Least Industrialized Nations. Conflict theorists use the term **internal colonialism** to describe how a country's dominant group exploits minority groups for its economic advantage. The dominant group manipulates the social institutions to suppress minorities and deny them full access to their society's benefits. Slavery, reviewed in Chapter 7, is an extreme example of internal colonialism, as was the South African system of *apartheid*. Although the dominant Afrikaners despised the minority, they found its presence necessary. As Simpson and Yinger (1972) put it, who else would do the hard work?

Segregation

Internal colonialism is often accompanied by **segregation**—the separation of racial or ethnic groups. Segregation allows the dominant group to maintain social distance from the minority and yet to exploit their labor as cooks, cleaners, chauffeurs, nannies, farmworkers, and so on. Even today, in some villages of India, an ethnic group, the Dalits (untouchables), is forbidden to use the village pump. Dalit women must walk long distances to streams or pumps outside of the village to fetch their water (author's notes).

Do you recall from Chapter 7 the account of *apartheid* in South Africa, where the beaches were divided by racial groups? It was once like this in parts of the United States, too. In St. Augustine, Florida, Butler Beach was reserved for blacks, while the area's many other beaches were for whites (author's notes). Until the 1960s, in the U.S. South, by law, African Americans and whites had to stay in separate hotels, go to separate schools, and use separate bathrooms and even drinking fountains. In thirty-eight states, laws prohibited marriage between blacks and whites. The punishment for violating these marriage laws? Prison. The last law of this type was repealed in 1967 (Baars 2009).

Assimilation

There are two types of **assimilation**, the process by which a minority group is absorbed into the mainstream culture. In *forced assimilation*, the dominant group refuses to allow the minority to practice its religion, to speak its language, or to follow its customs. Before the fall of the Soviet Union, for example, the dominant group, the Russians, required that Armenian children attend schools where they were taught in

ethnic cleansing
a policy of eliminating a population; includes forcible expulsion and genocide

internal colonialism
the policy of exploiting minority groups for economic gain

segregation
the policy of keeping racial–ethnic groups apart

assimilation
the process of being absorbed into the mainstream culture

Amid fears that Japanese Americans were "enemies within" who would sabotage industrial and military installations on the West Coast, in the early days of World War II Japanese Americans were transferred to "relocation camps." To make sure they didn't get lost, the children were tagged like luggage.

This is one of two major examples of population transfer in the United States. The other is transferring Native Americans to reservations.

Russian. Armenians could celebrate only Russian holidays, not Armenian ones. *Permissible assimilation*, in contrast, allows the minority to adopt the dominant group's patterns in its own way and at its own speed.

Multiculturalism (Pluralism)

multiculturalism (or pluralism)
a policy that permits or encourages ethnic differences

A policy of **multiculturalism**, also called **pluralism**, permits or even encourages racial–ethnic variation. The minority groups are able to maintain their separate identities, yet participate freely in the country's social institutions, from education to politics. Switzerland provides an outstanding example of multiculturalism. The Swiss population includes four ethnic groups: French, Italians, Germans, and Romansh. These groups have kept their own languages, and they live peacefully in political and economic unity. Multiculturalism has been so successful that none of these groups can properly be called a minority.

Racial–Ethnic Relations in the United States

9.5 Summarize the major patterns that characterize European Americans, Latinos, African Americans, Asian Americans, and Native Americans.

Writing about race–ethnicity is like stepping onto a minefield: One never knows where to expect the next explosion. Serbian students have written to me, saying that I have been unfair to their group. So have American whites. Even basic terms are controversial. Some people classified as *African Americans* reject this term because they identify themselves as blacks. Similarly, some Latinos prefer the term *Hispanic American*, but others reject it, saying that it ignores the Native American side of their heritage. Some would limit the term *Chicanos*—commonly used to refer to Americans from Mexico—to those who have a sense of ethnic oppression and unity; they say that it does not apply to those who have assimilated.

WASP
White Anglo-Saxon Protestant

white ethnics
white immigrants to the United States whose cultures differ from WASP culture

No term that I use here, then, will satisfy everyone. Racial–ethnic identity is fluid, constantly changing, and all terms carry a risk as they take on politically charged meanings. Nevertheless, as part of everyday life, we classify ourselves and one another as belonging to distinct racial–ethnic groups. As Figure 9.4 below and 9.5 on the next page show, on the basis of self-identity, whites make up 62 percent of the U.S. population, minorities (African Americans, Asian Americans, Latinos, and Native Americans) 36 percent. About 2 percent claim membership in two or more racial–ethnic groups.

As you can see from the Social Map on page 280, the distribution of dominant and minority groups among the states does not come close to the national average. This is because minority groups tend to be clustered in regions. The extreme distributions are found in Maine, where whites outnumber minorities 17 to 1, and Hawaii, where minorities outnumber whites 3 to 1. With this as background, let's review the major groups in the United States, going from the largest to the smallest.

Figure 9.4 Race–Ethnicity of the U.S. Population

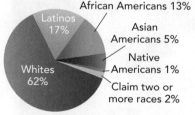

African Americans 13%
Latinos 17%
Asian Americans 5%
Native Americans 1%
Whites 62%
Claim two or more races 2%

SOURCE: By the author. See Figure 9.5.

European Americans

Benjamin Franklin said, "Why should the Palatine boors (Germans) be suffered (allowed) to swarm into our settlements and by herding together establish their language and manners to the exclusion of ours? Why should Pennsylvania, founded by the English, become a colony of aliens, who will shortly be so numerous as to germanize us instead of our anglifying them?" (in Alba and Nee 2003:17)

At the founding of the United States, White Anglo-Saxon Protestants (**WASPs**) held deep prejudices against other whites. There was practically no end to their disdainful stereotypes of **white ethnics**—immigrants from Europe whose language and other customs differed from theirs. The English despised the Irish, viewing them as dirty, lazy drunkards, but they also painted Poles, Jews, Italians, and others with similar disparaging brushstrokes. From what Benjamin Franklin said, you can see that they didn't like Germans either.

The political and cultural dominance of the WASPs placed intense pressure on immigrants to assimilate into the mainstream culture. The children of most immigrants embraced the new way of life and quickly came to think of themselves as Americans rather than as Germans, French, Hungarians, and so on. They dropped their distinctive customs, especially their languages, often viewing them as symbols of shame. This second generation of immigrants was sandwiched between two worlds: "the old country" of their parents and their new home. Their children, the third generation, had an easier adjustment, since they had fewer customs to discard. As white ethnics assimilated into this Anglo-American culture, the meaning of WASP expanded to include them.

And for those who weren't white? Perhaps the event that best illustrates the racial view of the nation's founders occurred when Congress passed the Naturalization Act of 1790, declaring that only white immigrants could apply for citizenship. Relationships between the various racial–ethnic groups since the founding of the nation have been, at best, tense and rocky.

Figure 9.5 U.S. Racial–Ethnic Groups[a]

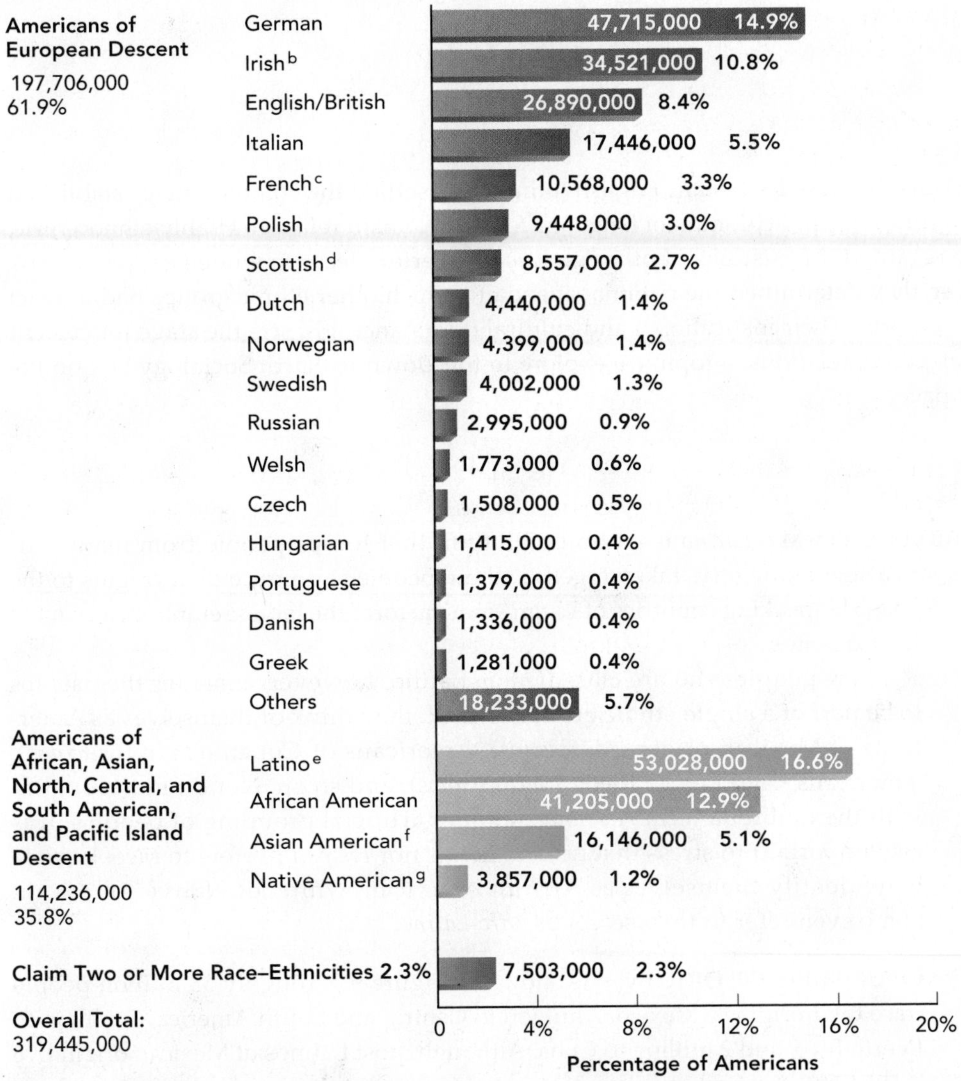

Americans of European Descent 197,706,000 61.9%

Group	Number	Percent
German	47,715,000	14.9%
Irish[b]	34,521,000	10.8%
English/British	26,890,000	8.4%
Italian	17,446,000	5.5%
French[c]	10,568,000	3.3%
Polish	9,448,000	3.0%
Scottish[d]	8,557,000	2.7%
Dutch	4,440,000	1.4%
Norwegian	4,399,000	1.4%
Swedish	4,002,000	1.3%
Russian	2,995,000	0.9%
Welsh	1,773,000	0.6%
Czech	1,508,000	0.5%
Hungarian	1,415,000	0.4%
Portuguese	1,379,000	0.4%
Danish	1,336,000	0.4%
Greek	1,281,000	0.4%
Others	18,233,000	5.7%

Americans of African, Asian, North, Central, and South American, and Pacific Island Descent 114,236,000 35.8%

Group	Number	Percent
Latino[e]	53,028,000	16.6%
African American	41,205,000	12.9%
Asian American[f]	16,146,000	5.1%
Native American[g]	3,857,000	1.2%

Claim Two or More Race-Ethnicities 2.3% 7,503,000 2.3%

Overall Total: 319,445,000

Percentage of Americans

[a]Only groups with 1,000,000 or more are shown. The total U.S. population listed here is the total of all groups, which does not necessarily match the total U.S. population given in the sources.
[b]Interestingly, this total is six times higher than all the Irish who live in Ireland.
[c]Includes French Canadian.
[d]Includes "Scottish–Irish."
[e]Most Latinos trace at least part of their ancestry to Europe.
[f]In descending order, the largest groups of Asian Americans are from China, India, Philippines, Vietnam, Korea, and Japan. See Figure 9.9 on page 287. Also includes those who identify themselves as Native Hawaiian or Pacific Islander.
[g]Includes Native Alaskan.

SOURCE: By the author. Based on *Statistical Abstract of the United States* 2014:Tables 10, 55.

USA—the land of diversity.

Figure 9.6 The Distribution of Dominant and Minority Groups

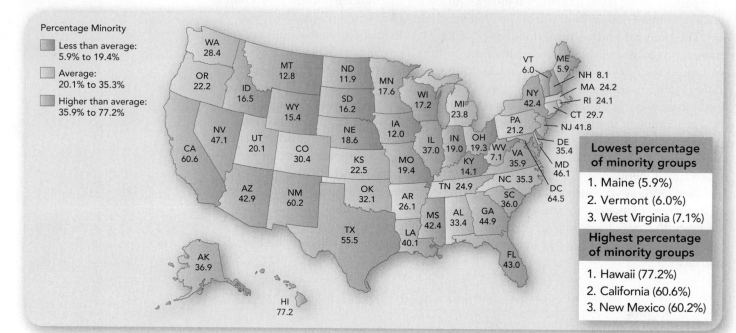

SOURCE: By the author. Based on *Statistical Abstract of the United States* 2014:Table 19.

IN SUM Because Protestant English immigrants settled the colonies, they established the culture—from the dominant language to the dominant religion. Highly ethnocentric, they regarded the customs of other groups as inferior. Because white Europeans took power, they determined the national agenda to which other ethnic groups had to react and conform. Their institutional and cultural dominance still sets the stage for current racial–ethnic relations, a topic we explore in the Down-to-Earth Sociology box on the next page.

Latinos (Hispanics)

UMBRELLA TERM *Latino* is an umbrella term that lumps people from many cultures into a single category. Taken together, these people, who trace their origins to the Spanish-speaking countries of Latin America, form the largest ethnic group in the United States.

Few people who are classified as Latino, however, consider themselves to be part of a single ethnic group. Instead, they think of themselves as Americans of Mexican origin (*Mexicanos*), Americans of Cuban origin (*Cubanos*), Americans from Puerto Rico (*Puertoricanos*), and so on. Nor do most identify with the umbrella term *Hispanic*, another artificial grouping of peoples. It is also important to stress that neither *Latino* nor *Hispanic* refers to race. Latinos may identify themselves as African American, white, or Native American. Some even refer to themselves as *Afro Latino*.

Figure 9.7 Geographical Origins of U.S. Latinos

Other countries
1,700,000 3%

Cuba
2,300,000 5%

Mexico
32,500,000
68%

Puerto Rico 4,600,000
10%

Central and South
America 7,000,000
10%

NOTE: Strangely, Cuban Americans were dropped from the Hispanic table of the 2013 edition. I added this group from Table 615 in the 2014 edition, after adjusting for civilian workers and children.

SOURCE: By the author. Based on *Statistical Abstract of the United States* 2014:Tables 38, 615.

COUNTRIES OF ORIGIN As shown in Figure 9.7, roughly 33 million people trace their origin to Mexico, 7 million to Central and South America, 5 million to Puerto Rico, and 2 million to Cuba. Although most Latinos of Mexican origin live in the Southwest, most Latinos from Puerto Rico live in New York City, and those from Cuba live primarily in Florida.

Down-to-Earth Sociology

Unpacking the Invisible Knapsack: Exploring Cultural Privilege

Overt racism in the United States has dropped sharply, but doors still open and close on the basis of the color of our skin. Whites have a difficult time grasping the idea that good things come their way because they are white. They usually fail to perceive how "whiteness" operates in their own lives.

Peggy McIntosh, of Irish descent, began to wonder why she was so seldom aware of her race–ethnicity, while her African American friends were so conscious of theirs. She realized that people are not highly aware of things that they take for granted—and that "whiteness" is a "taken-for-granted" background assumption of U.S. society. (You might want to review Figure 9.1 on page 265.) To explore this, she drew up a list of taken-for-granted privileges that come with her "whiteness," what she calls her "invisible knapsack." Because she is white, McIntosh (1988) says:

1. When I go shopping, store detectives don't follow me.
2. If I don't do well as a leader, I can be sure people won't say that it is because of my race.
3. When I watch television or look at the front page of the paper, I see people of my race presented positively.

One of the cultural privileges of being white in the United States is less suspicion of wrongdoing.

4. When I study our national heritage, I see people of my color and am taught that they made our country great.
5. To protect my children, I do not have to teach them to be aware of racism.
6. I can talk with my mouth full and not have people put this down to my color.
7. I can speak at a public meeting without putting my race on trial.
8. I can achieve something and not be "a credit to my race."
9. If a traffic cop pulls me over, I can be sure that it isn't because I'm white.
10. I can be late to a meeting without people thinking I was late because "That's how *they* are."

For Your Consideration

→ Can you think of other "background privileges" that come to whites because of their skin color? (McIntosh's list contains forty-six items.)

→ Why are whites seldom aware that they carry an "invisible knapsack"?

UNAUTHORIZED IMMIGRANTS Officially tallied at 53 million, the number of Latinos in the United States is likely higher than this. Although most Latinos are U.S. citizens, about 9 million have entered the country illegally (7 million from Mexico and 2 million from Central and South America) (*Statistical Abstract* 2014:Table 48). Although the economic crisis shrank the number of unauthorized immigrants, each year about 265,000 people are arrested at the border and returned to Mexico (U.S. Border Patrol 2014). Some come to the United States for temporary work and then return home. Most do not.

One reaction to this massive unauthorized entry into the United States has been welcoming. Ten states, for example, offer drivers licenses (Coffman 2014). In 2012, President Obama signed an executive order allowing work permits to certain unauthorized immigrants who were not over the age of 30 and who arrived here before the age of 16 (Preston and Cushman 2012). In 2014, Obama issued another executive order allowing over 4 million unauthorized immigrants to apply legally for jobs (Holland and Rampton 2014).

Another reaction is to prevent illegal entry. Immigration officers check documents at entry points and patrol the borders. With this being ineffective, the United States began building a wall along its 2,000-mile border with Mexico. After 53 miles at the horrendous cost of $1 billion, the wall was cancelled (Preston 2011). Citizen groups jumped in to offer their mostly unwelcome help. A group called the Minutemen patrolled the border for

As immigrants assimilate into a new culture, they learn and adapt new customs. This photo was taken in New York City at the annual American Muslim Parade.

several years, but gave up. A group called The Border Control is using drones and small planes to monitor the border, but it has only seven members (Murphy 2014).

Still another response has come from Arizona, where many of the illegal crossings take place. This state passed a law that gives its police the power to detain anyone suspected of being in the country illegally. When the U.S. Supreme Court reviewed the law, it upheld the state's right to check the immigration status of anyone the police stop or arrest (Liptak 2012).

To gain insight into why this vast subterranean migration exists and will continue, see the Cultural Diversity box below.

Cultural Diversity in the United States

The Illegal Travel Guide

Manuel was a drinking buddy of José, a man I had met in Colima, Mexico. At 45, Manuel was friendly, outgoing, and enterprising.

Manuel, who had lived in the United States for seven years, spoke fluent English. Preferring to live in his hometown in Colima, where he palled around with his childhood friends, Manuel always seemed to have money and free time.

When Manuel invited me to go on a business trip with him, I accepted. I never could figure out what he did for a living or how he could afford a car, a luxury that none of his friends had. As we traveled from one remote village to another, Manuel would sell used clothing that he had heaped in the back of his older-model Ford station wagon.

At one stop, Manuel took me into a dirt-floored, thatched-roof hut. While chickens ran in and out, Manuel whispered to a slender man who was about 23 years old. The poverty was overwhelming. Juan, as his name turned out to be, had a partial grade school education. He also had a wife, four hungry children under the age of 5, and two pigs—his main food supply. Although eager to work, Juan had no job; there was simply no work available in this remote village.

Crossing the border at Calexico, California.

As we were drinking a Coke, which seems to be the national beverage of Mexico's poor, Manuel explained to me that he was not only selling clothing—he was also lining up migrants to the United States. For a fee, he would take a man to the border and introduce him to a "wolf," who would help him cross into the promised land.

When I saw the hope in Juan's face, I knew nothing would stop him. He was borrowing every cent he could from every friend and relative to scrape the money together. Although Juan would be facing dangers and risked losing everything if apprehended, he would make the trip: Beckoning to him was a future with opportunity, perhaps even with wealth. He knew people who had been to the United States

and spoke glowingly of its opportunities. Manuel, of course, salesman as he was, stoked the fires of hope.

Looking up from the little children playing on the dirt floor with chickens pecking about them, I saw a man who loved his family. In order to make the desperate bid for a better life, he would suffer an enforced absence, as well as the uncertainties of a foreign culture whose language he did not know.

Juan opened his billfold, took something out, and slowly handed it to me. I looked at it curiously. I felt tears as I saw the tenderness with which he handled this piece of paper. It was his passport to the land of opportunity: a Social Security card made out in his name, sent by a friend who had already made the trip and who was waiting for Juan on the other side of the border.

It was then that I realized that the thousands of Manuels scurrying about Mexico and the millions of Juans they are transporting can never be stopped, since only the United States can fulfill their dreams of a better life.

For Your Consideration

The vast stream of immigrants illegally crossing the Mexican–U.S. border has become a national issue.

→ What do you think is the best way to deal with this issue? Why?

→ How does your social location affect your view?

RESIDENCE As Figure 9.8 shows, seven of every ten Latinos live in just six states—California, Texas, Florida, New York, Illinois, and Arizona. With its prominent Latino presence, Miami has been called "the capital of South America."

SPANISH The factor that clearly distinguishes Latinos from other U.S. minorities is the Spanish language. Although not all Latinos speak Spanish, most do. About 38 million Latinos speak Spanish at home (*Statistical Abstract* 2014:Table 56). Many cannot speak English or can do so only with difficulty. Being fluent only in Spanish in a society where English is spoken almost exclusively remains an obstacle.

Despite the 1848 Treaty of Hidalgo, which guarantees Mexicans the right to maintain their culture, from 1855 until 1968 California banned teaching in Spanish in school. In a 1974 decision (*Lau v. Nichols*), the U.S. Supreme Court ruled that using only English to teach Spanish-speaking students violated their civil rights. This decision paved the way for bilingual instruction for Spanish-speaking children (Vidal 1977; Lopez 1980).

The use of Spanish has provoked an "English-only" movement. Although the constitutional amendment that was proposed never got off the ground, thirty states have passed laws that declare English their official language (Newman et al. 2012).

ECONOMIC WELL-BEING To see how Latinos are doing on major indicators of well-being, look at Table 9.2. Their family income averages only three-fifths that of whites, and they are twice as likely as whites to be poor. On the positive side, one of every eight Latino families has an income higher than $100,000 a year (see Table 9.4 on page 286).

From Table 9.3 on the next page, you can see that Latinos are the most likely to drop out of high school. They also tie with Native Americans as the least likely to graduate from college. In a postindustrial society that increasingly requires advanced skills, these totals indicate that huge numbers of Latinos are being left behind.

POLITICS Because of their huge numbers, we might expect sixteen or seventeen of the one hundred U.S. senators to be Latino. How many are there? *Two.* In addition, Latinos hold only 7 percent of the seats in the U.S. House of Representatives (*Statistical Abstract* 2014:Table 432). Yet, compared with the past, even these small totals represent substantial gains. On the positive side, several Latinos have been elected as state governors. The first Latina to become a governor is Susana Martinez of New Mexico, who was elected in 2010.

It is likely that Latinos soon will play a larger role in U.S. politics, perhaps one day even beyond their overall numbers. This is because the six states in which they are concentrated hold one-third of the country's 538 electoral votes: California (55), Texas (38), Florida (29), New York (29), Illinois (20), and Arizona (11). Latinos have received presidential appointments to major federal positions, such as Secretary of the Interior, Secretary of Transportation, and Secretary of Housing and Urban Development.

Figure 9.8 Where U.S. Latinos Live

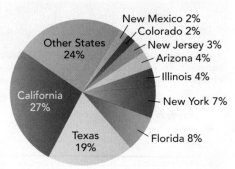

New Mexico 2%
Colorado 2%
New Jersey 3%
Arizona 4%
Illinois 4%
New York 7%
Florida 8%
Texas 19%
California 27%
Other States 24%

SOURCE: By the author. Based on *Statistical Abstract of the United States* 2014:Table 19.

Table 9.2 Indicators of Relative Economic Well-Being

	Family Income		Families In Poverty	
	Median Family Income	Compared to Whites	Percentage Below Poverty	Compared to Whites
Whites	$69,700		12.8%	
Asian Americans	$77,700	11% higher	12.3%	4% lower
Latinos	$41,000	41% lower	25.3%	106% higher
African Americans	$40,100	42% lower	27.6%	124% higher
Native Americans	$41,000	41% lower	29.1%	137% higher

NOTE: These totals are for families, which have less poverty than "persons," the unit of the tables in Chapter 7.
SOURCE: By the author. Based on *Statistical Abstract of the United States* 2014:Tables 37, 739; Krogstad 2014.

Table 9.3 Race–Ethnicity and Education

Racial–Ethnic Group	Education Completed					Doctorates	
	Less Than High School	High School	Some College	Associate's Degree	College (BA or Higher)	Percentage of all U.S. Doctorates[1]	Percentage of U.S. Population
Whites	8.8%	29.1%	21.8%	8.3%	31.9%	73.8%	61.9%
Latinos	36.8%	27.1%	17.4%	5.5%	13.2%	6.0%	16.6%
Country or Area of Origin							
Cuba	NA[2]	NA	NA	NA	26.2%	NA	0.6%
Puerto Rico	NA	NA	NA	NA	17.5%	NA	1.4%
Central and South America	NA	NA	NA	NA	18.9%	NA	2.2%
Mexico	NA	NA	NA	NA	10.6%	NA	10.4%
African Americans	17.5%	31.5%	25.0%	7.5%	18.4%	7.6%	12.9%
Asian Americans	14.9%	15.7%	12.9%	6.6%	50.0%	11.9%	5.1%
Native Americans	21.1%	31.4%	26.2%	8.3%	13.2%	0.7%	1.2%

[1]Percentage after the doctorates awarded to nonresidents are deducted from the total.
[2]Not Available.

SOURCE: By the author. Based on *Statistical Abstract of the United States* 2014:Tables 37, 38, 340, and Figure 9.5 of this chapter.

What holds back the political power of Latinos? It is primarily the divisions based on country of origin. As I mentioned, Latinos do not think of themselves as a single people, and national origin remains highly significant. People from Puerto Rico, for example, feel little sense of unity with people from Mexico. It is similar with those from Venezuela, Colombia, or El Salvador. It used to be the same with European immigrants. Those who came from Germany and Sweden or from England and France did not identify with one another. With time, the importance of the country of origin was lost, and the Europeans came to think of themselves as Americans. Perhaps this will happen to Latinos as well, but for now, these distinctions nourish disunity and create political disagreements.

African Americans

It was 1955, in Montgomery, Alabama. As specified by law, whites took the front seats of the bus and blacks went to the back. As the bus filled up, blacks had to give up their seats to whites.

When Rosa Parks, a 42-year-old African American woman and secretary of the Montgomery NAACP, was told that she would have to stand so white folks could sit, she refused (Bray 1995). She stubbornly sat there while the bus driver raged and whites felt insulted. Her arrest touched off mass demonstrations, led 50,000 blacks to boycott the city's buses for a year, and thrust an otherwise unknown preacher into a historic role.

Rev. Martin Luther King, Jr., who had majored in sociology at Morehouse College in Atlanta, Georgia, took control. He organized car pools and preached nonviolence. Incensed at this radical organizer and at the stirrings in the normally compliant black community, segregationists also put their beliefs into practice—by bombing the homes of blacks and dynamiting their churches.

For millions of people, the United States represents a land of opportunity and freedom from oppression. Shown here are Cubans who reached the United States by transforming their 1950s truck into a boat.

After slavery was abolished, the Southern states passed legislation (*Jim Crow* laws) to segregate blacks and whites. In 1896, the U.S. Supreme Court ruled in *Plessy v. Ferguson* that it was a reasonable use of state power to require "separate but equal" accommodations for blacks. Whites used this ruling to strip blacks of the political power they had gained after the Civil War. Declaring political primaries to be "white," they prevented blacks from voting in them. Not until 1944 did the Supreme Court rule that political primaries were not "white" and were open to all voters. White politicians then passed laws that restricted voting only to people who could read—and they determined that most African Americans were illiterate. Not until 1954 did African Americans gain the legal right to attend the same public schools as whites, and, as recounted in the vignette you just read, even later to sit where they wanted on a bus.

rising expectations

the sense that better conditions are soon to follow, which, if unfulfilled, increases frustration

RISING EXPECTATIONS AND CIVIL STRIFE   The barriers came down, but they came down slowly. In 1964, Congress passed the Civil Rights Act, making it illegal to discriminate on the basis of race. African Americans were finally allowed in "white" restaurants, hotels, theaters, and other public places. Then in 1965, Congress passed the Voting Rights Act, banning the fraudulent literacy tests that the Southern states had used to keep African Americans from voting.

African Americans then experienced what sociologists call **rising expectations**. They expected that these sweeping legal changes would usher in better conditions in life. However, the lives of the poor among them changed little, if at all. Frustrations built up,

Until the 1960s, the South's public facilities were segregated. Some were reserved for whites, others for blacks. This *apartheid* was broken by blacks and whites who worked together and risked their lives to bring about a fairer society. Shown here is a 1963 sit-in at a Woolworth's lunch counter in Jackson, Mississippi. Sugar, ketchup, and mustard are being poured over the heads of the demonstrators.

Table 9.4 Race–Ethnicity and Income Extremes

	Less than $15,000	Over $100,000
Asian Americans	6.3%	35.5%
Whites	7.0%	28.3%
African Americans	18.4%	14.1%
Latinos	14.3%	12.7%

NOTE: These are family incomes. Only these groups are listed in the source.

SOURCE: By the author: *Based on Statistical Abstract of the United States* 2014:Table 726.

exploding in Watts in 1965, when people living in that ghetto of central Los Angeles took to the streets in the first of what were termed the *urban revolts*. When a white supremacist assassinated King on April 4, 1968, inner cities across the nation erupted in fiery violence. Under threat of the destruction of U.S. cities, Congress passed the sweeping Civil Rights Act of 1968.

CONTINUED GAINS   Since then, African Americans have made remarkable gains in politics, education, and jobs. At 10 percent, the number of African Americans in the U.S. House of Representatives is *two to three times* what it was a generation ago (*Statistical Abstract* 1989:Table 423; 2014:Table 432). As college enrollments increased, the middle class expanded, and today half (50 percent) of all African American families make more than $40,000 a year. As you can see from Table 9.4, one in seven has an income over $100,000 a year.

African Americans have become prominent in politics. Jesse Jackson (another sociology major) competed for the Democratic presidential nomination in 1984 and 1988. In 1989, L. Douglas Wilder was elected governor of Virginia, and in 2006, Deval Patrick became governor of Massachusetts. These accomplishments, of course, pale in comparison to the election of Barack Obama as president of the United States in 2008 and his reelection in 2012.

CURRENT LOSSES   Despite these remarkable gains, African Americans continue to lag behind in politics, economics, and education. According to their share of the population, we would expect about thirteen African American senators. How many are there? *Zero*. There have been only six in U.S. history. As Tables 9.2 and 9.3 on pages 283 and 284 show, African Americans average only 59 percent of white income, experience much more poverty, and are less likely to have a college education. That one of seven African American families has an income over $100,000 is only part of the story. Table 9.4 also shows the other part—that one of every five or six African American families makes less than $15,000 a year.

RACE OR SOCIAL CLASS? A SOCIOLOGICAL DEBATE   Let's turn to an ongoing disagreement in sociology. Sociologist William Julius Wilson (1978, 2000, 2007) argues that social class is more important than race in determining the life chances of African Americans. Some sociologists disagree.

For background on why Wilson makes his argument, let's start with civil rights. Prior to the civil rights laws, African Americans were excluded from avenues of economic advancement: good schools and good jobs. When civil rights laws opened new opportunities, African Americans seized them, and millions entered the middle class. As the better-educated African Americans obtained white-collar jobs, they moved to better areas of the city and to the suburbs.

Left behind in the inner city were the less educated and less skilled, who depended on blue-collar jobs. At this time, a second transition was taking place: Manufacturing was moving from the city to the suburbs. This took away those blue-collar jobs. Without work, those in the inner city have the least hope, the most despair, and the violence that so often dominates the evening news.

This is the basis of Wilson's argument. The upward mobility of millions of African Americans into the middle class created two worlds of African American experience—one educated and affluent, the other uneducated and poor. Those who have moved up the social class ladder live in comfortable homes in secure neighborhoods. Their jobs provide decent incomes, and they send their children to good schools. The group that is stuck in the inner city has

In 2008, Barack Obama was elected president of the United States, the first minority to achieve this office. In 2012, he was reelected.

little opportunity for work, lives in depressing poverty, and attends poor schools. This group is filled with hopelessness and despair, combined with apathy or hostility.

Our experiences shape our views on life, our attitudes, our values, and our behavior. Look at how vastly different these two worlds of experiences are. Those who learn middle-class views, with its norms, aspirations, and values, have little in common with the orientations to life that arise from living in neighborhoods of deep poverty. Wilson, then, stresses that social class—not race—has become the more significant factor in the lives of African Americans.

Some sociologists reply that this analysis overlooks the discrimination that continues to underlie the African American experience. They note that African Americans who do the same work as whites average less pay (Willie 1991; Herring 2002) and even receive fewer tips (Lynn et al. 2008). Others document how young black males experience daily indignities and are objects of suspicion and police brutality (Rios 2011). These, they argue, point to racial discrimination, not to social class.

What is the answer to this debate? Wilson would reply that it is not an either-or question. My book is titled *The **Declining Significance** of Race*, he would say, not *The **Absence** of Race*. Certainly racism is still alive, he would add, but today, social class is more central to the African American experience than is racial discrimination.

Sociologists disagree about the relative significance of race and social class in determining social and economic conditions of African Americans. William Julius Wilson, shown here, is an avid proponent of the social class side of this debate.

RACISM AS AN EVERYDAY BURDEN

Researchers sent out 5,000 résumés in response to help wanted ads in the Boston and Chicago Sunday papers. The résumés were identical, except some applicants had white-sounding names, such as Emily and Brandon, while others had black-sounding names, such as Lakisha and Jamal. Although the qualifications of these supposed job applicants were identical, the white-sounding names elicited 50 percent *more callbacks than the black-sounding names (Bertrand and Mullainathan 2002).*

Certainly racism continues as a regular feature of society, often something that whites, not subjected to it, are only vaguely aware of. But for those on the receiving end, racism can be an everyday burden. Here is how an African American professor describes his experiences:

[One problem with] being black in America is that you have to spend so much time thinking about stuff that most white people just don't even have to think about. I worry when I get pulled over by a cop . . . . I worry what some white cop is going to think when he walks over to our car, because he's holding on to a gun. And I'm very aware of how many black folks accidentally get shot by cops. I worry when I walk into a store, that someone's going to think I'm in there shoplifting . . . . And I get resentful that I have to think about things that a lot of people, even my very close white friends whose politics are similar to mine, simply don't have to worry about. (Feagin 1999:398)

Asian Americans

I have stressed in this chapter that our racial–ethnic categories are based more on social factors than on biological ones. Perhaps this point will become less foreign to your thinking when we examine the category Asian American. As Figure 9.9 shows, those who are called Asian Americans came to the United States from many nations. *With no unifying culture or "race," why should people from so many backgrounds be clustered together and assigned a single label?* Think about it. What culture or race–ethnicity do Samoans and Vietnamese have in common? Or Laotians and Pakistanis? Or people from Guam and those from China? Those from Japan and those from India? Yet all these groups—and more—are lumped together

Figure 9.9 Countries of Origin of Asian Americans

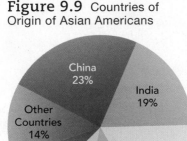

China 23%
India 19%
Other Countries 14%
Philippines 18%
Japan 5%
Korea 10%
Vietnam 11%

SOURCE: By the author. Based on U.S. Census Bureau 2010.

and called Asian Americans. Apparently, the U.S. government is not satisfied until it is able to pigeonhole everyone into some racial–ethnic category.

Since *Asian American* is a standard term, however, let's look at the characteristics of the 16 million people who are lumped together and assigned this label.

A BACKGROUND OF DISCRIMINATION

Lured by gold strikes in the West and an urgent need for unskilled workers to build the railroads, 200,000 Chinese immigrated between 1850 and 1880. When the famous golden spike was driven at Promontory, Utah, in 1869 to mark the completion of the railroad to the West Coast, white workers prevented Chinese workers from being in the photo—even though Chinese made up 90 percent of Central Pacific Railroad's labor force (Hsu 1971).

After the transcontinental railroad was complete, the Chinese competed with whites for other jobs. Anglos then formed vigilante groups to intimidate them. They also used the law. California's 1850 Foreign Miners Act required Chinese (and Latinos) to pay $20 a month in order to work—when wages were a dollar a day. The California Supreme Court ruled that Chinese could not testify against whites (Carlson and Colburn 1972). In 1882, Congress passed the Chinese Exclusion Act, suspending all Chinese immigration for ten years. Four years later, the Statue of Liberty was dedicated. The tired, the poor, and the huddled masses it was intended to welcome were obviously not Chinese.

When immigrants from Japan arrived, they encountered *spillover bigotry*, a stereotype that lumped Asians together, depicting them as sneaky, lazy, and untrustworthy. After Japan attacked Pearl Harbor in 1941, conditions grew worse for the 110,000 Japanese Americans who called the United States their home. U.S. authorities feared that Japan would invade the United States and that the Japanese Americans would fight on Japan's side. They also feared that Japanese Americans would sabotage military installations on the West Coast. Although no Japanese American had been involved in even a single act of sabotage, on February 19, 1942, President Franklin D. Roosevelt ordered that everyone who was *one-eighth Japanese or more* be confined in detention centers (called "internment camps"). These people were charged with no crime, and they were allowed no trials. Japanese ancestry was sufficient cause for being imprisoned.

DIVERSITY   As you can see from Tables 9.2 and 9.4 on pages 283 and 286, the income of Asian Americans has outstripped that of all groups, including whites. This has led to the stereotype that all Asian Americans are successful. Are they? From Table 9.2, you can see that one of eight Asian American families lives in poverty. As with Latinos, country of origin is significant: Poverty is lower for Chinese and Japanese Americans, but it clusters among Americans from Southeast Asia. Altogether, almost 2 million Asian Americans live in poverty.

REASONS FOR FINANCIAL SUCCESS   The remarkably high average incomes of Asian Americans can be traced to three major factors: family life, education, and assimilation into mainstream culture. Of all ethnic groups, including whites, Asian American children are the most likely to grow up with two parents and the least likely to be born to a single mother (*Statistical Abstract* 2014:Table 72). Common in these families is a stress on self-discipline, thrift, and hard work (Suzuki 1985; Bell 1991). This early socialization provides strong impetus for the other two factors.

The second factor is their unprecedented rate of college graduation. As Table 9.3 on page 284 shows, 50 percent of Asian Americans complete college. To realize how stunning this is, compare their rate with those of the other groups shown on this table. Educational achievement, in turn, opens doors to economic success.

The most striking indication of the third factor, assimilation, is a high rate of intermarriage. Of all racial–ethnic groups, Asian Americans are the most likely to marry someone of a different racial–ethnic group (Wang 2012). Of Asian Americans who graduate from college, about 40 percent of the men and 60 percent of the women marry a non–Asian American (Qian and Lichter 2007). The intermarriage of Japanese Americans is so extensive that two of every three of their children have one parent who is not of Japanese descent (Schaefer 2012). The Chinese are close behind (Alba and Nee 2003).

POLITICS   Asian Americans are becoming more prominent in politics. With about half of its citizens being Asian American, Hawaii has elected Asian American governors and sent several Asian American senators to Washington, including the one now serving there (Lee 1998; *Statistical Abstract* 2014:Table 432). The first Asian American governor outside of Hawaii was Gary Locke, who served from 1997 to 2005 as governor of Washington, a state in which Asian Americans make up less than 6 percent of the population. In 2008, Bobby Jindal became the first Indian American governor when he was elected governor of Louisiana, a state in which Asian Americans make up less than 2 percent of the population.

Mazie Hirono, the first Japanese American woman to be elected a U.S. senator.

Native Americans

"I don't go so far as to think that the only good Indians are dead Indians, but I believe nine out of ten are—and I shouldn't inquire too closely into the case of the tenth."

—Teddy Roosevelt, 1886 (President of the United States 1901–1909)
(As cited in "Past Imperfect" 2012)

DIVERSITY OF GROUPS   This quote from Teddy Roosevelt provides insight into the rampant racism of earlier generations. Yet, even today, thanks to countless grade B Westerns, some Americans view the original inhabitants of what became the United States as uncivilized savages, a single group of people subdivided into separate tribes. The European immigrants to the colonies, however, encountered diverse groups of people who spoke over seven hundred languages. Their variety of cultures ranged from nomadic hunters and gatherers to farmers who lived in wooden houses (Schaefer 2004). Each group had its own norms and values—and the usual ethnocentric pride in its own culture. Consider what happened in 1744 when the colonists of Virginia offered college scholarships for "savage lads." The Iroquois replied:

> *"Several of our young people were formerly brought up at the colleges of Northern Provinces. They were instructed in all your sciences. But when they came back to us, they were bad runners, ignorant of every means of living in the woods, unable to bear either cold or hunger, knew neither how to build a cabin, take a deer, or kill an enemy . . . . They were totally good for nothing."*
>
> They added, *"If the English gentlemen would send a dozen or two of their children to Onondaga, the great Council would take care of their education, bring them up in really what was the best manner and make men of them."* (Nash 1974; in McLemore 1994)

Native Americans, who numbered about 10 million, had no immunity to the diseases the Europeans brought with them. With deaths due to disease—and warfare, a much lesser cause—their population plummeted (Schaefer 2012). The low point came in 1890, when the census reported only 250,000 Native Americans. If the census and the estimate of the original population are accurate, Native Americans had been reduced to about *one-fortieth* their original size. The population has never recovered, but Native Americans now number close to 4 million (see Figure 9.5 on page 279). Native Americans, who today speak 169 different languages, do not think of themselves as a single people who fit neatly within a single label (Siebens and Julian 2011).

This depiction breaks stereotypes, but is historically accurate. Shown here is an Iroquois fort. Can you guess who the attackers are?

FROM TREATIES TO GENOCIDE AND POPULATION TRANSFER At first, the Native Americans tried to accommodate the strangers, since there was plenty of land for both the few newcomers and themselves. Soon, however, the settlers began to raid Indian villages and pillage their food supplies (Horn 2006). As wave after wave of settlers arrived, Pontiac, an Ottawa chief, saw the future—and didn't like it. He convinced several tribes to unite in an effort to push the Europeans into the sea. He almost succeeded, but failed when the English were reinforced by fresh troops (McLemore 1994).

A pattern of deception evolved. The U.S. government would make treaties to buy some of a tribe's land, with the promise to honor forever the tribe's right to what it had not sold. European immigrants, who continued to pour into the United States, would then disregard these boundaries. The tribes would resist, with death tolls on both sides. The U.S. government would then intervene—not to enforce the treaty it had made but to force the tribe off its lands.

In its relentless drive westward, the U.S. government embarked on a policy of genocide. It assigned the U.S. cavalry the task of "pacification," which translated into slaughtering Native Americans who "stood in the way" of this territorial expansion.

The acts of cruelty perpetrated by the Europeans against Native Americans appear endless, but two are especially notable. The first is the Trail of Tears. The U.S. government adopted a policy of population transfer (see Figure 9.3 on page 276), which it called *Indian Removal*. The goal was to confine Native Americans to specified areas called *reservations*. In the winter of 1838–1839, the U.S. Army rounded up 15,000 Cherokees and forced them to walk a thousand miles from the Carolinas and Georgia to Oklahoma. Conditions were so brutal that about 4,000 of those who were forced to make this midwinter march died along the way. The second notable act of cruelty also marked the symbolic end of Native American resistance to the European expansion. In 1890 at Wounded Knee, South Dakota, the U.S. cavalry gunned down three hundred men, women, and children of the Dakota Sioux tribe. After the massacre, the soldiers threw the bodies into a mass grave (Thornton 1987; DiSilvestro 2006; Demos 2014).

THE INVISIBLE MINORITY AND SELF-DETERMINATION Native Americans can truly be called the invisible minority. Because about half live in rural areas and one-third in just three states—Oklahoma, California, and Arizona—most other Americans are hardly aware of a Native American presence in the United States. The isolation of about one-third of Native Americans on reservations further reduces their visibility (Schaefer 2012).

The systematic attempts of European Americans to destroy the Native Americans' way of life and their forced resettlement onto reservations continue to have deleterious effects. The rate of suicide among Native Americans is higher than that of any other group, and their life expectancy is lower than that of the nation as a whole (Crosby et al. 2011; CDC 2014c). Table 9.3 on page 284 shows that their educational attainment also lags behind most groups: Only 13 percent graduate from college.

Native Americans are experiencing major changes. In the 1800s, U.S. courts ruled that Native Americans did not own the land on which they had been settled and had no right to develop its resources. They made Native Americans wards of the state, and the Bureau of Indian Affairs treated them like children (Mohawk 1991; Schaefer 2012).

Then, in the 1960s, Native Americans won a series of legal victories that gave them control of reservation lands. With this legal change, many Native American tribes have opened businesses—ranging from fish canneries to industrial parks that serve metropolitan areas. The Skywalk, opened by the Hualapai, which offers breathtaking views of the Grand Canyon, gives an idea of the varieties of businesses to come (Audi 2012).

THE CASINOS   It is the casinos operated by over two hundred tribes, though, that have attracted the most attention. These casinos *bring in $27 billion a year, more than all the casinos in Las Vegas combined* (Lovett 2014; *Statistical Abstract* 2014:Table 1285). Some tribes located near large cities have made a killing. California's United Auburn tribe has only two hundred adult members; its casino nets $30,000 *a month* for each member (Onishi 2012). To get part of the action, some tribes have bought land to build casinos. The land is not part of their reservation, but they have obtained "off reservation" permits to build casinos. The rich gambling revenues have led to intense envy among tribes. Those that operate casinos, the "haves," fight in court to keep the "have-nots" casinoless (Lovett 2014).

Another controversy is the *separatism* embraced by some Native Americans. Because Native Americans were independent peoples when the Europeans arrived and they never willingly joined the United States, many tribes maintain the right to remain separate from the U.S. government. The chief of the Onondaga tribe in New York, a member of the Iroquois Federation, summarized the issue this way:

> *For the whole history of the Iroquois, we have maintained that we are a separate nation. We have never lost a war. Our government still operates. We have refused the U.S. government's reorganization plans for us. We have kept our language and our traditions, and when we fly to Geneva to UN meetings, we carry Hau de no sau nee passports. We made some treaties that lost some land, but that also confirmed our separate-nation status. That the U.S. denies all this doesn't make it any less the case. (Mander 1992)*

The success of Native American casinos has created intense envy. Some non-Native Americans resent the new wealth that the casinos have brought tribes that were in poverty, and some Native American tribes are suing other tribes to prevent them from opening rival casinos.

DETERMINING IDENTITY AND GOALS   Native Americans have formed national and regional organizations, but their most common cooperative organization is intertribal councils (National Congress . . . 2014). Although these organizations represent a diversity of cultures and contrasting ideas, through them runs this common sentiment: "It is we who must determine whether to establish a common identity and work together or to stress separatism and identify solely with individual tribes. It is up to us to assimilate into the dominant culture or to stand apart from it; to move to cities or to remain on reservations; or to operate casinos or to engage only in traditional activities. We are sovereign nations, separate governments guaranteed by treaties, and we will not take orders from the victors of past wars."

Looking toward the Future

9.6   Discuss immigration, affirmative action, and a multicultural society.

Back in 1903, sociologist W. E. B. Du Bois said, "The problem of the twentieth century is the problem of the color line—the relation of the darker to the lighter races." Incredibly, over a hundred years later, the color line remains one of the most volatile topics facing the United States. From time to time, the color line takes on a different complexion, as with the war on terrorism and the corresponding discrimination directed against people of Middle Eastern descent.

In another hundred years, will yet another sociologist lament that the color of people's skins still affects human relationships? Given our past, it seems that although racial–ethnic walls will diminish, some even crumbling, the color line is not likely to disappear. Let's close this chapter by looking at two issues we are currently grappling with, immigration and affirmative action.

The Immigration Controversy

Throughout its history, the United States has both welcomed immigration and feared its consequences. The gates opened wide (numerically, if not in attitude) for waves of immigrants in the 1800s and early 1900s. During the past twenty years, a new wave of immigration has brought close to a million new residents to the United States each year. Today, more immigrants (38 million) live in the United States than at any other time in the country's history (*Statistical Abstract* 2007:Table 5; 2014:Table 41).

In contrast to earlier waves, in which immigrants came almost exclusively from western Europe, the current wave of immigrants is changing the U.S. racial–ethnic mix. If current trends in immigration (and birth) persist, in about fifty years, the "average" American will trace his or her ancestry to Africa, Asia, South America, the Pacific Islands, the Middle East—almost anywhere but white Europe. This change is discussed in the Cultural Diversity box on the next page.

In some states, the future is arriving much sooner than this. In California, racial–ethnic minorities have become the majority. California has 23 million minorities and 15 million whites (*Statistical Abstract* 2014:Table 19). Californians who request new telephone service from Pacific Bell can speak to customer service representatives in Spanish, Korean, Vietnamese, Mandarin, Cantonese—or English.

As in the past, there is concern that "too many" immigrants will change the character of the United States. "Throughout the history of U.S. immigration," write sociologists Alejandro Portés and Rubén Rumbaut (1990), "a consistent thread has been the fear that the 'alien element' would somehow undermine the institutions of the country and would lead it down the path of disintegration and decay." A hundred years ago, the widespread fear was that the immigrants from southern Europe would bring communism with them. Today, some fear that Spanish-speaking immigrants threaten the primacy of the English language. In addition, the age-old fear that immigrants will take jobs away from native-born Americans remains strong. Finally, minority groups that struggled for political representation fear that newer groups will gain political power at their expense.

The Affirmative Action Controversy

For decades, affirmative action has been at the center of a national debate about racial–ethnic relations. In this policy, initiated by President Kennedy in 1961, goals based on race and sex were used in hiring, promotion, and college admissions. As liberals, both white and minority, put it at the time: Affirmative action is the most direct way to level the playing field of economic opportunity. If whites are passed over, this is an unfortunate but necessary cost to make up for past discrimination. As conservatives, both white and minority, put it: Opportunity should be open to all, but to place race or sex ahead of an individual's ability is reverse discrimination. It discriminates against qualified people who had nothing to do with past inequality.

This national debate led to a series of U.S. Supreme Court rulings. One of the most significant was upholding the 1996 amendment to the California state constitution, called *Proposition 209*, which made it illegal to give preference to minorities and women in hiring,

Cultural Diversity in the United States

Glimpsing the Future: The Shifting U.S. Racial–Ethnic Mix

During the next twenty-five years, the population of the United States is expected to grow by about 22 percent. To see what the U.S. population will look like at that time, can we simply add 22 percent to our current racial–ethnic mix? The answer is a resounding no. As you can see from Figure 9.10, some groups will grow much more than others, giving us a different-looking United States. Some of the changes in the U.S. racial–ethnic mix will be dramatic. By 2050, one of every thirteen or fourteen Americans is expected to have an Asian background, and, in the most dramatic change, about one of three or four is expected to be of Latino ancestry.

The basic causes of this fundamental shift are the racial–ethnic groups' different rates of immigration and birth. Both will change the groups' proportions of the U.S. population, but immigration is by far the more important. From Figure 9.10, you can see that the proportion of non-Hispanic whites is expected to shrink, that of African Americans and Native Americans to remain about the same, and that of Latinos to increase sharply.

For Your Consideration

This shifting racial–ethnic mix is one of the most significant events occurring in the United States. To better understand its implications, apply the three theoretical perspectives.

→ Use the *conflict perspective* to identify the groups that are likely to be threatened by this change. Over what resources are struggles likely to develop? What impact do you think this changing mix might have on European Americans? On Latinos? On African Americans? On Asian Americans? On Native Americans? What changes in immigration laws (or their enforcement) can you anticipate?

→ To apply the *symbolic interactionist perspective*, consider how groups might perceive one another differently as their proportions of the population change. How do you think that these changed perceptions will affect people's behavior?

→ To apply the *functionalist perspective*, try to determine how each racial–ethnic group will benefit from this changing mix. How will other parts of society (such as businesses) benefit? What functions and dysfunctions can you anticipate for politics, economics, education, or religion?

Figure 9.10 Projections of the Racial–Ethnic Makeup of the U.S. Population

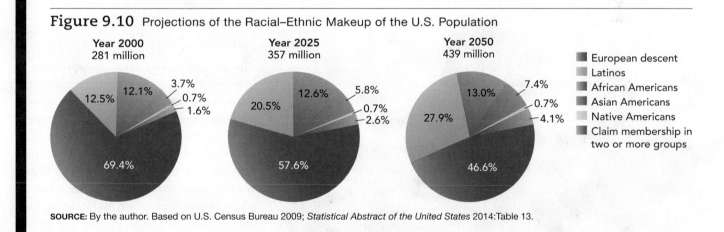

SOURCE: By the author. Based on U.S. Census Bureau 2009; *Statistical Abstract of the United States* 2014:Table 13.

promotion, and college admissions. In 2003, the Court ruled that universities can consider race a "plus factor" in admissions, but they cannot use a point system to give minorities an edge. After this ruling, Michigan and several other states amended their constitutions to make it illegal for public institutions to consider race or sex in college admissions and in hiring and issuing contracts. After years of legal battles, the U.S. Supreme Court ruled in 2014 that voters have the right to ban affirmative action (Bravin 2014).

The answer to this meaty problem can be social class. One of the most significant cases decided by the Court was *Fisher v. University of Texas* in 2013. The Court ruled that diversity is an excellent goal of colleges, but they should find paths to reach this goal that don't explicitly weigh race. Giving a hand to qualified applicants who come from low-income homes, regardless of their race–ethnicity, will provide college access and upward social mobility to those most in need. Apparently, it will also increase the number of minorities who are admitted to college (Kahlenberg 2014).

As leaders search for ways to overcome the effects of past discrimination and at the same time to offer fair means to do so, further Supreme Court rulings are inevitable, making it certain that affirmative action in our multicultural society will remain center stage for quite some time.

Less Racism

One of the more positive aspects of today's race–ethnic relations is the reduction of prejudice and discrimination. These problems continue to exist, as we have reviewed in this chapter, but their reduction is extraordinary. The quote by Teddy Roosevelt indicates how socially acceptable racism used to be. To get a broader picture, consider this:

> *In 1876, a white mob burned down a Chinese immigrant community in Antioch, California. An editorial in The San Francisco Chronicle, Northern California's main newspaper, said that this attack should "meet with the hearty approval of every man, woman, and child on the Pacific coast." (Stein 2014)*

Compare this with today when Donald Sterling, the multimillionaire owner of the Los Angeles Clippers, a professional basketball team, made a racist comment to his girlfriend. The National Basketball Association banned Sterling from professional basketball for life and fined him $2.5 million.

From approval of burning down homes and businesses to severe sanctions for making a comment—what an extraordinary, fundamental change. We can expect even less racism in the future.

The United States is the most racially–ethnically diverse society in the world. This can be our central strength, with our many groups working together to build a harmonious society, a stellar example for the world. Or it can be our Achilles heel, with us breaking into feuding groups, a Balkanized society that marks an ill-fitting end to a grand social experiment. Our reality will probably fall somewhere between these extremes.

Toward a True Multicultural Society

The United States has the potential to become a society in which racial–ethnic groups not only coexist but also respect one another—and thrive—as they work together for mutually beneficial goals. In a true multicultural society, the minority groups that make up the United States would participate fully in the nation's social institutions while maintaining their cultural integrity. Reaching this goal will require that we understand that "the biological differences that divide one race from another add up to a drop in the genetic ocean." For a long time, we have given racial categories an importance they never merited. Now we need to figure out how to reduce them to the irrelevance they deserve. In short, we need to make real the abstraction called equality that we profess to believe (Cose 2000).

Summary and Review

Laying the Sociological Foundation

9.1 **Contrast the myth and reality of race; compare race and ethnicity and minority and dominant groups; discuss ethnic work.**

How is race both a reality and a myth?

In the sense that different groups inherit distinctive physical traits, race is a reality. There is no agreement regarding what makes up a particular race, however, or even how many races there are. In the sense of one race being superior to another and of there being pure races, race is a myth. The *idea* of race is powerful, shaping basic relationships among people.

How do race and ethnicity differ?

Race refers to inherited biological characteristics, **ethnicity** to cultural ones. Members of ethnic groups identify with one another on the basis of common ancestry and cultural heritage.

What are minority and dominant groups?

Minority groups are people who are singled out for unequal treatment by members of the **dominant group**, the group with more power and privilege. Minorities originate with migration or the expansion of political boundaries.

What heightens ethnic identity, and what is "ethnic work"?

A group's ethnic identity is heightened or reduced by its relative size, power, and physical characteristics, as well as the amount of discrimination it faces. **Ethnic work** is the process of constructing and maintaining an ethnic identity. For people without a firm ethnic identity, ethnic work is an attempt to recover their ethnic heritage. For those with strong ties to their culture of origin, ethnic work involves enhancing group distinctions.

Prejudice and Discrimination

9.2 **Contrast prejudice and discrimination and individual and institutional discrimination; discuss learning prejudice, internalizing dominant norms, and institutional discrimination.**

Why are people prejudiced?

Prejudice is an attitude, and **discrimination** is an action. Like other attitudes, prejudice is learned in association with others. Prejudice is so extensive that people can show prejudice against groups that don't even exist. Minorities also internalize the dominant norms, and some show prejudice against their own group.

How do individual and institutional discrimination differ?

Individual discrimination is the negative treatment of one person by another, while **institutional discrimination** is negative treatment that is built into social institutions. Institutional discrimination can occur without the awareness of either those who do the discriminating or those who are discriminated against. Discrimination in health care is one example.

Theories of Prejudice

9.3 **Contrast psychological and sociological theories of prejudice: include functionalism, conflict, and symbolic interactionism.**

How do psychologists explain prejudice?

Psychological theories of prejudice stress the **authoritarian personality** and frustration displaced toward **scapegoats**.

How do sociologists explain prejudice?

Sociological theories focus on how different social environments increase or decrease prejudice. *Functionalists* stress the benefits and costs that come from discrimination. *Conflict theorists* look at how the groups in power exploit racial–ethnic divisions in order to control workers and maintain power. *Symbolic interactionists* stress how labels create **selective perception** and self-fulfilling prophecies.

Global Patterns of Intergroup Relations

9.4 **Explain genocide, population transfer, internal colonialism, segregation, assimilation, and multiculturalism.**

What are the major patterns of minority and dominant group relations?

Beginning with the least humane, they are **genocide**, **population transfer**, **internal colonialism**, **segregation**, **assimilation**, and **multiculturalism (pluralism)**.

Racial–Ethnic Relations in the United States

9.5 **Summarize the major patterns that characterize European Americans, Latinos, African Americans, Asian Americans, and Native Americans.**

What are the major racial–ethnic groups in the United States?

From largest to smallest, the major groups are European Americans, Latinos, African Americans, Asian Americans, and Native Americans.

What are some issues in racial–ethnic relations and characteristics of minority groups?

Latinos are divided by social class and country of origin. African Americans are increasingly divided into middle and lower classes, with two sharply contrasting worlds of experience. On many measures, Asian Americans are better off than white Americans, but their well-being varies with country of origin. For Native Americans, the primary issues are poverty, nationhood, and settling treaty obligations. The overarching issue for minorities is overcoming discrimination.

Looking toward the Future

9.6 Discuss immigration, affirmative action, and a multicultural society.

What main issues dominate U.S. racial–ethnic relations?

The main issues are immigration, affirmative action, and how to develop a true multicultural society. We can expect racism to decline.

Thinking Critically about Chapter 9

1. How many races do your friends or family think there are? Do they think that one race is superior to the others? What do you think their reaction would be to the sociological position that racial categories are primarily social?

2. A hundred years ago, sociologist W. E. B. Du Bois said, "The problem of the twentieth century is the problem of the color line—the relation of the darker to the lighter races." Why do you think that the color line remains one of the most volatile topics facing the nation?

3. If you were appointed head of the U.S. Civil Service Commission, what policies would you propose to reduce racial–ethnic strife in the United States? Be ready to explain the sociological principles that might give your proposals a higher chance of success.

Chapter 10
Gender and Age

In Tunis, the capital of Tunisia on Africa's northern coast, I met some U.S. college students and spent a couple of days with them. They wanted to see the city's red light district, but I wondered whether it would be worth the trip. I already had seen other red light districts, including the unusual one in Amsterdam where a bronze statue of a female prostitute lets you know you've entered the area; the state licenses of the women and men, requiring that they have medical checkups (certificates must be posted); and the prostitutes add sales tax to the receipts they give customers. The prostitutes sit behind lighted picture windows while customers stroll along the narrow canalside streets and "window shop" from the outside. Tucked among the brothels are day care centers, bakeries, and clothing stores. Amsterdam itself is an unusual place—in cafes, you can smoke marijuana but not tobacco.

The prostitutes sit behind lighted picture windows while customers stroll along the narrow canal side streets and "window shop" from the outside.

I decided to go with the students. We ended up on a wharf that extended into the Mediterranean. Each side was lined with a row of one-room wooden shacks, one crowding against the next. In front of each open door stood a young woman. Peering from outside into the dark interiors, I could see that each door led to a tiny room with an old, well-worn bed.

The wharf was crowded with men who were eyeing the women and negotiating prices. Many of the men wore sailor uniforms from countries that I couldn't identify.

As I looked more closely, I could see that some of the women had running sores on their legs. Incredibly, with such visible evidence of their disease, men still sought them out.

Somewhere nearby, out of sight, I knew that there were men whose wealth derived from exploiting these women who were condemned to short lives punctuated by fear and misery.

In the previous chapter, we considered how race–ethnicity affects people's well-being and their position in society. In this chapter, we examine **gender stratification**—males' and females' unequal access to property, power, and prestige. We also explore the prejudice and discrimination directed to people because of their age.

Gender and age are especially significant because, like race–ethnicity, they are *master statuses*; that is, they cut across *all* aspects of social life. We all are labeled male or female and are assigned an age category. These labels are powerful. Not only do they convey images and expectations about how we should act, but they also serve as a basis for distributing property, power, and prestige.

gender stratification
males' and females' unequal access to property, power, and prestige

■ Inequalities of Gender

Let's begin by considering the distinctions between sex and gender.

Issues of Sex and Gender

10.1 Distinguish between sex and gender; use research on Vietnam veterans and testosterone to explain why the door to biology is opening in sociology.

When we consider how females and males differ, the first thing that usually comes to mind is **sex**, the *biological characteristics* that distinguish males and females. *Primary sex characteristics* consist of a vagina or a penis and other organs related to reproduction. *Secondary sex characteristics* are the physical distinctions between males and females that are not directly connected with reproduction. These characteristics become clearly evident at puberty when males develop larger muscles, lower voices, more body hair, and greater height, while females develop breasts and form more fatty tissue and broader hips.

sex
biological characteristics that distinguish females and males, consisting of primary and secondary sex characteristics

Gender, in contrast, is a *social*, not a biological characteristic. **Gender** consists of whatever behaviors and attitudes a group considers proper for its males and females. *Sex* refers to male or female, and *gender* refers to masculinity or femininity. In short, you inherit your sex, but you learn your gender as you learn the behaviors and attitudes your culture asserts are appropriate for your sex.

gender
the behaviors and attitudes that a society considers proper for its males and females; masculinity or femininity

As the photo montage on the next page illustrates, the expectations associated with gender differ around the world. They vary so greatly that some sociologists replace the terms *masculinity* and *femininity* with *masculinities* and *femininities*.

THE SOCIOLOGICAL SIGNIFICANCE OF GENDER   *The sociological significance of gender is this: Gender is a device by which society controls its members.* Gender sorts us, on the basis of sex, into different life experiences. It opens and closes doors to property, power, and prestige. Like social class, gender is a structural feature of society.

Before examining inequalities of gender, let's consider why the behaviors of men and women differ.

Standards of Gender

Each human group determines its ideas of "maleness" and "femaleness." As you can see from these photos of four women and four men, standards of gender are arbitrary and vary from one culture to another. Yet, in its ethnocentrism, each group thinks that its preferences reflect what gender "really" is. As indicated here, around the world men and women try to make themselves appealing by aspiring to their group's standards of gender.

Mexico

Jordan

Kenya

Ethiopia

Brazil

Papua New Guinea

India

China

Gender Differences in Behavior: Biology or Culture?

Why are most males more aggressive than most females? Why do women enter "nurturing" occupations, such as teaching young children and nursing, in far greater numbers than men? To answer such questions, many people respond with some variation of "They're born that way."

Is this the correct answer? Certainly biology plays a significant role in our lives. Each of us begins as a fertilized egg. The egg, or ovum, is contributed by our mother, the sperm that fertilizes the egg by our father. At the very instant the egg is fertilized, our sex is determined. Each of us receives twenty-three chromosomes from the ovum and twenty-three from the sperm. The egg has an X chromosome. If the sperm that fertilizes the egg also has an X chromosome, the result is a girl (XX). If the sperm has a Y chromosome, the result is a boy (XY).

Differences in how we display gender often lie below our awareness. How males and females use social space is an example. In this unposed photo from Grand Central Station in New York City, you can see how males tend to sprawl out, females to enclose themselves. Why do you think this difference exists? Biology? Socialization? Both?

THE DOMINANT POSITION IN SOCIOLOGY   That's the biology. Now, the sociological question is: Does this biological difference control our behavior? Does it, for example, make females more nurturing and submissive and males more aggressive and domineering? Here is the quick sociological answer: The dominant sociological position is that *social* factors, not biology, are the reasons people do what they do.

Let's apply this position to gender. If biology were the principal factor in human behavior, all around the world we would find women behaving in one way and men in another. Men and women would be just like male spiders and female spiders, whose genes tell them what to do. In fact, however, ideas of gender vary greatly from one culture to another—and, as a result, so do male–female behaviors.

Despite this, to see why the door to biology is opening just slightly in sociology, let's consider a medical accident and a study of Vietnam veterans.

Opening the Door to Biology

A MEDICAL ACCIDENT

In 1963, 7-month-old identical twin boys were taken to a doctor for a routine circumcision. The physician, not the most capable person in the world, was using a heated needle. He turned the electric current too high and accidentally burned off the penis of one of the boys.

You can imagine the parents' disbelief—and then their horror—as the truth sank in. What could they do? After months of soul-searching and tearful consultations with experts, the parents decided that their son should have a sex-change operation (Money and Ehrhardt 1972). When he was 22 months old, surgeons castrated the boy, using the skin to construct a vagina. The parents then gave the child a new name, Brenda, dressed him in frilly clothing, let his hair grow long, and began to treat him as a girl. Later, physicians gave Brenda female steroids to promote female puberty (Colapinto 2001).

At first, the results were promising. When the twins were 4 years old, the mother said (remember that the children are biologically identical):

One thing that really amazes me is that she is so feminine. I've never seen a little girl so neat and tidy. . . . She likes for me to wipe her face. She doesn't like to be dirty, and yet my son is quite different. I can't wash his face for anything. . . . She is very proud of herself, when she puts on a new dress, or I set her hair. . . . She seems to be daintier. (Money and Ehrhardt 1972)

David Reimer, whose story is recounted here.

If the matter were this clear-cut, we could use this case to conclude that gender is determined entirely by nurture. Seldom are things in life so simple, however, and a twist occurs in this story.

Despite this promising start and her parents' coaching, Brenda did not adapt well to femininity. She preferred to mimic her father shaving, rather than her mother putting on makeup. She rejected dolls, favoring guns and her brother's toys. She liked rough-and-tumble games and insisted on urinating standing up. Classmates teased her and called her a "cavewoman" because she walked like a boy. At age 14, she was expelled from school for beating up a girl who teased her. Despite estrogen treatment, she was not attracted to boys. At age 14, when despair over her inner turmoil brought her to the brink of suicide, her father, in tears, told Brenda about the accident and her sex change.

"All of a sudden everything clicked. For the first time, things made sense, and I understood who and what I was," the twin said of this revelation. David (his new name) was given testosterone shots and, later, had surgery to partially reconstruct a penis. At age 25, David married a woman and adopted her children (Diamond and Sigmundson 1997; Colapinto 2001). There is an unfortunate end to this story, however. In 2004, David committed suicide.

THE VIETNAM VETERANS STUDY   Time after time, researchers have found that boys and men who have higher levels of testosterone tend to be more dominant and aggressive (Turan et al. 2014). In one study, researchers compared the testosterone levels of college men in a "rowdy" fraternity with those of men in a fraternity that had a reputation for academic achievement. Men in the "rowdy" fraternity had higher levels of testosterone (Dabbs et al. 1996). In another study, researchers found that prisoners who had committed sex crimes and other crimes of violence had higher levels of testosterone than those who had committed property crimes (Dabbs et al. 1995). The samples were small, however, leaving the nagging uncertainty that these findings might be due to chance.

Then in 1985, the U.S. government began a health study of Vietnam veterans. To be certain that the study was representative, the researchers chose a random sample of 4,462 men. Among the data they collected was a measurement of testosterone. This sample supported the earlier studies. When the veterans with higher testosterone levels were boys, they were more likely to get in trouble with parents and teachers and to become delinquents. As adults, they were more likely to use hard drugs, to get into fights, to end up in lower-status jobs, and to have more sexual partners. Those who married were more likely to have affairs, to hit their wives, and, it follows, to get divorced (Dabbs and Morris 1990; Mazur and Booth 2014).

This 1966 photo shows a U.S. soldier taking care of a wounded buddy.

This makes it sound like biology is the basis for behavior. Fortunately for us sociologists, there is another side to this research, and here is where *social class*, the topic of Chapter 8, comes into play. The researchers compared high-testosterone men from higher and lower social classes. The men from lower social classes were more likely to get in trouble with the law, do poorly in school, and mistreat their wives (Dabbs and Morris 1990). You can see, then, that *social* factors, such as socialization, subcultures, life goals, and self-definitions were significant in these men's behavior.

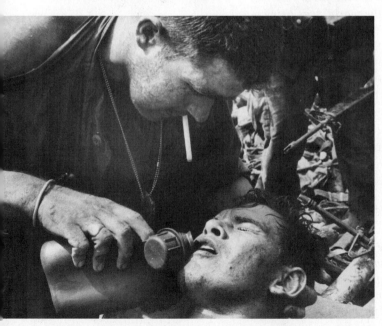

MORE RESEARCH ON HUMANS   Research on the effects of testosterone in humans continues. The results are intriguing. Not only do higher levels of testosterone lead to higher dominance but the reverse is also true: Dominance behavior, such as winning a game, also produces higher levels of testosterone. So does holding a real gun (Klinesmith et al. 2006). This has made it difficult to determine which causes which. Controlled studies in which cause can be determined help. When researchers administer single doses of testosterone, dominance behavior increases. This is true of *both* males and females, who then seek higher status and show less concern for the feelings of others (Eisenegger et al. 2011). Researchers are investigating how the testosterone changes people's behaviors, which they think might be by triggering other hormones.

IN SUM   Sociologists acknowledge that biological factors are involved in some human behavior other than reproduction and childbearing (Freese 2008; Horowitz et al. 2014). Years back, one of the first sociologists to open this issue was Alice Rossi, a feminist sociologist and former president of the American Sociological Association.

Perhaps Rossi (1977, 1984) expressed it best when she said that the issue is not either biology or society. Instead, whatever biological predispositions nature provides are overlaid with culture. A task of sociologists, then, is to discover how social factors modify biology, especially, as sociologist Janet Chafetz (1990:30) said, to determine how "different" becomes translated into "unequal."

The sociological perspective—that of social factors in human behavior—dominates this book, and in the Thinking Critically section that follows, we will explore how gender is changing.

Thinking Critically

New Masculinities and Femininities Are on Their Way

Facebook *has changed its classifications from male/female to, well, here is part of the list: agender, androgyne, gender fluid, gender queer, gender variant, intersex, neutrois, non-binary, and trans man. Facebook *offers another forty categories of gender.*

Social change is so fast-paced and extensive that it is hard to count on anything from one year to the next. From the new *Facebook* classifications, you can see that even *gender*, what we consider masculine or feminine, is changing. This helps let us know that sexual identity is complicated: There are *many* ways of identifying with being male or female—and in some instances of not quite identifying with either.

Powerfully entrenched in our culture, the traditional models of the aggressive-dominant male and the compassionate-submissive female will not disappear. For most males, life will remain cast as a form of struggle, of adversaries pitted against one another. These males will try to live up to the expectations of endurance and stamina, victory in competition, and achievement despite obstacles. They will continue to mask compassion and avoid even the appearance of weakness, fear, and vulnerability. For most women, the dominant model will also hold, and they will show—and probably feel—more emotions than men. They will express greater compassion and more fears and weaknesses.

As new models of gender take their place alongside the traditional ones, it is likely that a softer masculinity will become a viable model for men. Men will feel freer to ask for help, to form emotional bonds with other men, even to tenderly touch both women and men—and still be masculine. Women will have more options to fight hard in the rough-and-tumble competitive world of business and the professions—and still be feminine.

Maria, a member of the male-dominated Chicanos por Vida in Yakima, Washington. A "tough femininity" that incorporates masculine violence is emerging among female juvenile delinquents.

As the developing masculinities incorporate behaviors previously considered undesirable, off limits, or even taboo, we can expect a decrease of homophobia (dislike and fear of homosexuals). Homophobia seems to be based on a need to mark a sharp distance between the self and anyone who threatens the dominant model of masculinity or femininity. As cultural attitudes shift, fewer will feel an urgent need to maintain gender boundaries, to demonstrate to the self and others that "I'm not gay."

For Your Consideration

→ What have you experienced to indicate that the dominant forms of masculinity and femininity are changing?

→ Do you think we are developing femininities and masculinities?

→ Do you agree with the author, that homophobia will decrease?

Gender Inequality in Global Perspective

10.2 Discuss the origin of gender discrimination and review global aspects of violence against women.

Around the world, gender is *the* primary division between people. To catch a glimpse of how remarkably gender expectations differ with culture, look at the photo essay on the next two pages. Every society sorts men and women into separate groups and gives them different access to property, power, and prestige. These divisions *always* favor men-as-a-group. After reviewing the historical record, historian and feminist Gerda Lerner (1986) concluded that "there is not a single society known where women-as-a-group have decision-making power over men (as a group)." Consequently, sociologists classify females as a *minority group*. Because females outnumber males, you may find this strange. This term applies, however, because *minority group* refers to people who are discriminated against on the basis of physical or cultural characteristics, regardless of their numbers (Hacker 1951).

How Did Females Become a Minority Group?

Have females always been a minority group? Some analysts speculate that in hunting and gathering societies, women and men were social equals and that horticultural societies also had less gender discrimination than is common today (Wilson 2013). In these societies, women may have contributed about 60 percent of the group's total food. Yet, around the world, gender is the basis for discrimination.

Men's work? Women's work? Customs in other societies can blow away stereotypes. As is common throughout India, these women are working on road construction.

Work and Gender: Women at Work in India

Traveling through India was both a pleasant and an eye-opening experience. The country is incredibly diverse, the people friendly, and the land culturally rich. For this photo essay, wherever I went—whether city, village, or countryside—I took photos of women at work.

From these photos, you can see that Indian women work in a wide variety of occupations. Some of the jobs that women in India do match traditional Western expectations, and some diverge sharply from our gender stereotypes.

Although women in India remain subservient to men—with the women's movement hardly able to break the cultural surface—women's occupations are hardly limited to the home. I was surprised at some of the hard, heavy labor that Indian women do.

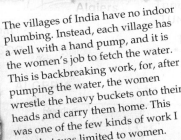

The villages of India have no indoor plumbing. Instead, each village has a well with a hand pump, and it is the women's job to fetch the water. This is backbreaking work, for, after pumping the water, the women wrestle the heavy buckets onto their heads and carry them home. This was one of the few kinds of work I saw that was limited to women.

I visited quarries in different parts of India, where I found men, women, and children hard at work in the tropical sun. This woman works 8 ½ hours a day, six days a week. She earns 40 rupees a day (about ninety cents). Men make 60 rupees a day (about $1.35). Like many quarry workers, this woman is a bonded laborer. She must give half of her wages to her master.

Indian women are highly visible in public places. A storekeeper is as likely to be a woman as a man. This woman is selling glasses of water at a beach on the Bay of Bengal. The structure on which her glasses rest is built of sand.

Women also take care of livestock. It looks as though this woman dressed up and posed for her photo, but this is what she was wearing and doing when I saw her in the field and stopped to talk to her. While the sheep are feeding, her job is primarily to "be" there, to make certain the sheep don't wander off or that no one steals them.

© James M. Henslin, all photos

Sweeping the house is traditional work for Western women. So it is in India, but the sweeping has been extended to areas outside the home. These women are sweeping a major intersection in Chennai. When the traffic light changes here, the women will continue sweeping, with the drivers swerving around them. This was one of the few occupations that seems to be limited to women.

As in the West, food preparation in India is traditional women's work. Here, however, food preparation takes an unexpected twist. Having poured rice from the 60-pound sack onto the floor, these women in Chittoor search for pebbles or other foreign objects that might be in the rice.

When I saw this unusual sight, I had to stop and talk to the workers. From historical pictures, I knew that belt-driven machines were common on U.S. farms 100 years ago. This one in Tamil Nadu processes sugar cane. The woman feeds sugar cane into the machine, which disgorges the stalks on one side and sugar cane juice on the other.

This woman belongs to the Dhobi subcaste, whose occupation is washing clothes. She stands waist deep at this same spot doing the same thing day after day. The banks of this canal in Hyderabad are lined with men and women of her caste, who are washing linens for hotels and clothing for more well-to-do families.

A common sight in India is women working on construction crews. As they work on buildings and on highways, they mix cement, unload trucks, carry rubble, and, following Indian culture, carry loads of bricks atop their heads. This photo was taken in Raipur, Chhattisgarh.

How, then, did it happen that women became a minority group? The main theory that has been proposed to explain the origin of **patriarchy**—men dominating society—centers on human reproduction (Baumeister 2013). In early human history, life was short. Because people died young, if the group were to survive, women had to give birth to many children. This brought severe consequences for women. To survive, an infant needed a nursing mother. If there were no woman to nurse the child, it died. With a child at her breast or in her uterus, or one carried on her hip or on her back, women were not able to stay away from camp for as long as the men could. They also had to move slower. Around the world, then, women assumed the tasks that were associated with the home and child care, while men hunted the large animals and did other tasks that required greater speed and longer absences from the base camp.

This led to men becoming dominant. When the men left the camp to hunt animals, they made contact with other groups. They traded with them, gaining new possessions—and they also quarreled and waged war with them. It was also the men who made and controlled the instruments of power and death, the weapons that were used for hunting and warfare. The men heaped prestige upon themselves as they returned triumphantly to the camp, leading captured prisoners and displaying their new possessions or the large animals they had killed to feed themselves and the women and children.

Contrast this with the women. Their activities were routine, dull, and taken for granted. The women kept the fire going, took care of the children, and did the cooking. There was nothing triumphant about what they did—and they were not perceived as risking their lives for the group. The women were "simply there," awaiting the return of their men, ready to acclaim their accomplishments.

Men, then, took control of society. Their sources of power were their weapons, items of trade, and the knowledge they gained from their contact with other groups. Women did not have access to these sources of power, which the men enshrouded in secrecy. The women became second-class citizens, subject to whatever the men decided.

GLOBAL VIOLENCE AGAINST WOMEN   A global human rights issue is violence against women. Historical examples include foot binding in China, witch burning in Europe, and, in India, *suttee,* burning the living widow with the body of her dead husband. Today, we have rape, wife beating, female infanticide, and the kidnapping of women to be brides. There is also forced prostitution, which was probably the case in our opening vignette. There is also *swara,* a practice in tribal areas of Pakistan: Unmarried girls, even children, are given as brides to compensate a family for a man's crime (Symington 2014). Another notorious example is female circumcision, the topic of the Cultural Diversity box on the next page.

"Honor killings" are another form of violence against women. In some societies, such as Afghanistan, India, Jordan, Kurdistan, and Pakistan, a woman who is thought to have brought disgrace on her family is killed by a male relative—usually a brother or her husband, but sometimes her father or uncles. What threat to a family's honor can be so severe that a man would kill his own daughter, wife, or sister? The usual reason is sex outside of marriage. Virginity at marriage is so prized in these societies that even a woman who has been raped is in danger of becoming the victim of an honor killing (Falkenberg 2008; McCoy 2014). Another offense worthy of death is refusing to marry the man the father picked out (Nordland 2014). Killing the girl or woman—even one's own sister or mother—removes the "stain" she has brought to the family and restores its honor in the community. Sharing this view, the police generally ignore honor killings, considering them to be private family matters.

IN SUM   Gender inequality is not some accidental, hit-or-miss affair. Rather, each society's institutions work together to maintain the group's particular forms of inequality. Customs, often venerated throughout history, both justify and maintain these arrangements. In some cases, the prejudice and discrimination directed at females are so extreme that they lead to enslavement and death.

It is the job of these women in Kenya to get the water for their families. They carry not only the water, but also their young children.

patriarchy

men-as-a-group dominating women-as-a-group; authority is vested in males

Swara, an ancient custom, includes both adult males marrying female children and marrying children to one another. In compensation for a murder committed by her father, this Pakistani woman, now 19, was married to a man four times her age when she was nine years old.

Cultural Diversity around the World

Female Circumcision (Genital Cutting)

"Lie down there," the excisor suddenly said to me [when I was 12], pointing to a mat on the ground. No sooner had I laid down than I felt my frail, thin legs grasped by heavy hands and pulled wide apart. . . . Two women on each side of me pinned me to the ground. . . . I underwent the ablation of the labia minor and then of the clitoris. The operation seemed to go on forever. I was in the throes of agony, torn apart both physically and psychologically. It was the rule that girls of my age did not weep in this situation. I broke the rule. I cried and screamed with pain . . . !

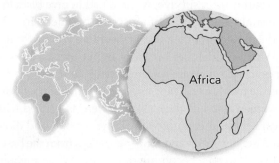

Afterwards they forced me, not only to walk back to join the other girls who had already been excised, but to dance with them. I was doing my best, but then I fainted. . . . It was a month before I was completely healed. When I was better, everyone mocked me, as I hadn't been brave, they said. (Walker and Parmar 1993:107–108)

Worldwide, about 125 million females have been circumcised, mostly in Muslim Africa and in some parts of Malaysia and Indonesia (Dugger 2013). In Egypt and Indonesia, about 91 percent of the women have been circumcised. At 98 percent, the highest rate is in Somalia (Turkewitz 2014). In most cultures, the surgery takes place between the ages of 4 and 8, but in some, it is not performed until the girls reach adolescence. Because the surgery is usually done without anesthesia, the pain is excruciating and adults hold the girls down. In urban areas, physicians sometimes perform the operation; in rural areas, a neighborhood woman usually does it, often with a razor blade.

In some cultures, only the girl's clitoris is cut off; in others, more is removed. In Sudan, the Nubians cut away most of the girl's genitalia, then sew together the outer edges. They bind the girl's legs from her ankles to her waist for several weeks while scar tissue closes up the vagina. They leave a small opening the diameter of a pencil for the passage of urine and menstrual fluids. When a woman marries, the opening is cut wider to permit sexual intercourse. Before she gives birth, the opening is enlarged further. After birth, the vagina is again sutured shut. This cycle of surgically closing and opening begins anew with each birth.

Why are girls circumcised? Some groups believe that it reduces sexual desire, making it more likely that a woman will be a virgin at marriage and, afterward, remain faithful to her husband. Others think that women can't bear children if they aren't circumcised (Kindzeka 2014).

In some societies, uncircumcised women are considered impure, and men do not want them as wives. Concerned that

An excisor displaying the razor blades she will use to circumcise teenage girls of the Sebei tribe in Uganda.

their daughters marry well, the mothers insist that this custom continue.

Feminists have campaigned against female circumcision, calling it a form of ritual torture to control female sexuality. They point out that men dominate the societies that practice it.

Change is on the way. A social movement to ban female circumcision has emerged, and the World Health Organization has even declared that female circumcision is a human rights issue. Fifteen African countries have made the circumcision of females illegal. Without sanctions, though, these laws accomplish little.

Health workers have hit upon a strategy that is meeting with some success. They begin by teaching village women about germs and hygiene. Then they trace the women's current health problems, such as incontinence to female circumcision. When enough support has been gained, an entire village will publicly abandon the practice. As other villages do the same, the lack of circumcision no longer remains an obstacle to marriage.

The most powerful indicator of the future is this: Compared to their mothers, fewer young women support circumcision and fewer have been circumcised (Dugger 2013). Yet we must balance this statement with this one: In Bandung, Indonesia, hospitals offer package deals: a special price if you combine infant vaccinations, ear piercing, and genital cutting (Haworth 2012).

SOURCES: As cited, and Lightfoot-Klein 1989; Merwine 1993; Tuhus-Dubrow 2007; Lazaro 2011; Sacirbey 2012.

For Your Consideration

→ Do you think that the members of one culture have the right to judge the customs of another culture as inferior or wrong and to then try to get rid of them? If so, under what circumstances? What makes us right and them wrong?

→ Let's go further. Some are trying to ban the circumcision of boys. One court in Germany even ruled that the circumcision of boys "amounts to bodily harm even if the parents consent to the circumcision" ("German Court…" 2012). Why shouldn't the same principle apply to both female and male circumcision?

Gender Inequality in the United States

10.3 Review the rise of feminism and summarize gender inequality in health care and education.

As we review gender inequality in the United States, let's begin by taking a brief look at how change in this vital area of social life came about.

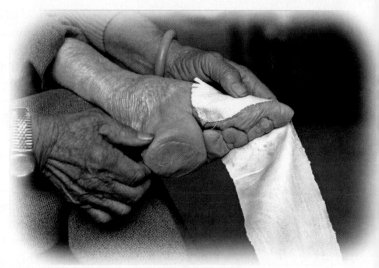

Fighting Back: The Rise of Feminism

In the early history of the United States, the second-class status of women was taken for granted. A husband and wife were legally one person—him (Chafetz and Dworkin 1986). Women could not vote, buy property in their own names, make legal contracts, or serve on juries. How could relationships have changed so much in the last hundred years or so that these examples sound like fiction?

A central lesson of conflict theory is that power brings privilege. Like a magnet, power draws society's best resources to the elite. Because men tenaciously held onto their privileges and used social institutions to maintain their dominance, basic rights for women came only through prolonged and bitter struggle.

Feminism—the view that biology is not destiny, that stratification by gender is wrong and should be resisted, and that men and women should be equal—met with strong opposition, both by men who had privilege to lose and by women who accepted their status as morally correct. In 1894, for example, Jeannette Gilder said that women should not have the right to vote: "Politics is too public, too wearing, and too unfitted to the nature of women" (Crossen 2003).

Feminists, known at that time as suffragists, struggled against such views. In 1916, they founded the National Woman's Party, and in 1917, they began to picket the White House. After picketing for six months, the women were arrested. Hundreds were sent to prison, including Lucy Burns, a leader of the National Woman's Party. The extent to which these women had threatened male privilege is demonstrated by how they were treated in prison.

> *Two men brought in Dorothy Day [the editor of a periodical that promoted women's rights], twisting her arms above her head. Suddenly they lifted her and brought her body down twice over the back of an iron bench. . . . They had been there a few minutes when Mrs. Lewis, all doubled over like a sack of flour, was thrown in. Her head struck the iron bed and she fell to the floor senseless. As for Lucy Burns, they handcuffed her wrists and fastened the handcuffs over [her] head to the cell door. (Cowley 1969)*

This *first wave* of the women's movement had a radical branch that wanted to reform all the institutions of society and a conservative branch whose goal was to win the vote for women (Freedman 2001). The conservative branch dominated, and after winning the right to vote in 1920, the movement basically dissolved.

Inequality continued, of course, and even social science was part of the problem. In what is historically humorous, male social scientists paraded themselves as experts on the essence of womanhood. Here is what a renowned psychologist wrote in the 1960s, the paternalism oozing out of his well-intentioned statement: "We must start with the realization that, as much as we want women to be good scientists or engineers, they want first and foremost to be womanly companions of men and to be mothers" (Bettelheim 1965:15 in Eagly et al. 2012).

Photo of Xiao Xiuxiang, taken in 2002. Foot binding was banned by the Chinese government in 1911, but continued to be practiced in some places for several decades. Tiny feet were a status symbol. Making it difficult for a woman to walk; small feet indicated that a woman's husband did not need his wife's labor. To make the feet even smaller, sometimes the baby's feet were broken and wrapped tightly. In some cases, the baby's toes were cut off.

feminism

the philosophy that men and women should be politically, economically, and socially equal; organized activities on behalf of this principle

This man knew what women wanted—and in the 1960s, almost everyone else made the same assumption. From infancy, women were immersed in the idea that their purpose in life was to be "womanly companions of men and mothers." Even children's books reinforced such thinking, as you can see from Figure 10.1 on the facing page.

Reared with this idea, most women thought of work as a temporary activity intended to fill the time between completing school—usually high school—and getting married (Chafetz 1990). Then, as more women took jobs, they began to regard them as careers. This fundamental shift in perspective ushered in huge discontent. Women compared their working conditions with those of men, and they didn't like what they saw. The result was a *second wave* of protest against gender inequalities, roughly from the 1960s to the 1980s (Eagly et al. 2012). The goals of this second wave (which continue today) were broad, ranging from raising women's pay to changing policies on violence against women and legalizing abortion.

About 1990, the second wave gradually merged into a *third wave* (Byers and Crocker 2012). This current wave has many divisions, but three main aspects are apparent. The first is a greater focus on the problems of women in the Least Industrialized Nations (Lövheim 2013). Women there are struggling against conditions overcome long ago by women in the Most Industrialized Nations. The second is a criticism of the values that dominate work and society. Some feminists argue that competition, toughness, and calloused emotions represent "male" qualities that need to be replaced with cooperation, connection, and openness (England 2000). A third aspect is an emphasis on women's freedom to explore sexual pleasure (Nguyen 2013).

Sharp disagreements have arisen among feminists (Kantor 2013). Some in the third wave promote what is called "girlie feminism" (Nguyen 2013). They say that women should declare the battle for equality won and move on to confidently enjoy the "pink things" of childhood. Women should focus on self-fulfillment and sexual pleasure. They

The "first wave" of the U.S. women's movement met enormous opposition. The women in this 1920 photo had just been released after serving two months in jail for picketing the White House. Lucy Burns, mentioned on the previous page, is the second woman on the left. Alice Paul, who was placed in solitary confinement and is a subject of this 1920 protest, is featured in the photo wheel of early female sociologists in Chapter 1, page 9.

ALICE PAUL
GOT SEVEN MONTHS
BECAUSE
SHE OPPOSED A POLITICAL PARTY
WE DEMAND
THAT SHE BE TREATED AS A
POLITICAL OFFENDER

THE SUFFRAGE PRISONERS
WERE ARRESTED FOR A
POLITICAL OFFENSE.
WE DEMAND
THAT THEY BE TREATED AS
POLITICAL OFFENDERS.

TO ASK FREEDOM
FOR WOMEN IS NOT
A CRIME
SUFFRAGE PRISONER
SHOULD NOT BE TREATED
AS CRIMINALS

Figure 10.1 Teaching Gender

Mother and Sally

The "Dick and Jane" readers were the top selling readers in the United States in the 1940s and 1950s. In addition to reading, they taught "gender messages." What gender message do you see here?

Mother can sew.
Jane can sew.

What gender lesson is being taught here?

"I will help," said Dick.
"I will help you with the pigs."

Besides learning words like "pigs" (relevant at that historical period), boys and girls also learned that rough outside work was for men.

Father

What does this page teach children other than how to read the word "Father"? (Look to the far left to see what Jane and Mother are doing.)

SOURCE: From *Dick and Jane: Fun with Our Family,* Illustrations © copyright 1951, 1979, and *Dick and Jane: We Play Outside,* copyright © 1965, Pearson Education, Inc., published by Scott, Foresman and Company. Used with permission.

should also embrace their "erotic capital," using their sexual attractiveness and seductiveness to get ahead at work. Those who struggled in the second wave are shocked by these younger feminists. Such attitudes, they say, are a denial of women's ability to compete with men on equal terms, a betrayal of the equality women have fought for (Hakim 2010).

Although U.S. women enjoy fundamental rights today, we are far from having reached the goal of gender inequality. Let's first consider gender inequality in health care.

Gender Inequality in Health Care

Medical researchers were perplexed. Reports were coming in from all over the country: Women were twice as likely as men to die after coronary bypass surgery. Researchers at Cedars-Sinai Medical Center in Los Angeles checked their own records. They found that of 2,300 coronary bypass patients, 4.6 percent of the women died as a result of the surgery, compared with 2.6 percent of the men.

The researchers faced a sociological puzzle. To solve it, they first turned to biology (Bishop 1990). In coronary bypass surgery, a blood vessel is taken from one part of the body and stitched to an artery on the surface of the heart. Perhaps the surgery was more difficult to do on women because of their smaller arteries. To find out, researchers measured the amount of time that surgeons kept patients on the heart-lung machine. They were surprised to learn that women spent *less* time on the machine than men. This indicated that the surgery was not more difficult to perform on women.

As the researchers probed further, a surprising answer unfolded: unintended sexual discrimination. When women complained of chest pains, their doctors took them only *one-tenth as seriously* as when men had the same complaints. How do we know this? Doctors were *ten* times more likely to give men exercise stress tests and radioactive heart scans. They also sent men to surgery on the basis of abnormal stress tests, but they waited until women showed clear-cut symptoms of heart disease before sending them to surgery. Patients with more advanced heart disease are more likely to die during and after heart surgery.

Although these findings have been publicized, the problem continues (Varughese et al. 2014). Perhaps as more women become physicians, the situation will change, since female doctors are more sensitive to women's health problems (Tabenkin et al. 2010). For example, they are more likely to order Pap smears and mammograms (Lurie et al. 1993). In addition, as more women join the faculties of medical schools, we can expect women's health problems to receive more attention in the training of physicians. Even this might not do it, however, as women, too, hold our cultural stereotypes.

In contrast to unintentional sexism in heart surgery, let's look at a type of surgery that is a blatant form of discrimination against women. This is the focus of the Down-to-Earth Sociology box below.

Down-to-Earth Sociology

Cold-Hearted Surgeons and Their Women Victims

While doing participant observation in a hospital, sociologist Sue Fisher (1986) was surprised to hear surgeons recommend a total hysterectomy (removal of both the uterus and the ovaries) *when no cancer was present*. When she asked why, the male doctors explained that the uterus and ovaries are "potentially disease producing." They also said that these organs are unnecessary after the childbearing years, so why not remove them? Doctors who reviewed hysterectomies confirmed this gender-biased practice. *Ninety percent* of hysterectomies are avoidable. Only 10 percent involve cancer (Costa 2011).

Greed is a powerful motivator in many areas of social life, and it rears its ugly head in surgical sexism (Domingo and Pellicer 2009). Surgeons make money when they do hysterectomies. The more hysterectomies they do, the more money they make. Since women, to understate the matter, are reluctant to part with these organs, surgeons have to "sell" this operation. Here is how one resident explained the "hard sell" to sociologist Diana Scully (1994):

> You have to look for your surgical procedures; you have to go after patients. Because no one is crazy enough to come and say, "Hey, here I am. I want you to operate on me." You have to sometimes convince the patient that she is really sick—if she is, of course [laughs], and that she is better off with a surgical procedure.

Used-car salespeople would love to have the powerful sales weapon that surgeons have at their disposal: To "convince" a woman to have this surgery, the doctor puts on a serious face and tells her that the examination has turned up *fibroids* in her uterus—and these lumps might turn into *cancer*. This statement is often sufficient to get the woman to buy the surgery. She starts to picture herself lying at death's door, her sorrowful family gathered at her death bed. Then the used-car salesperson—I mean, the surgeon—moves in to clinch the sale. Keeping a serious face and displaying an "I-know-how-you-feel" look, the surgeon starts to make arrangements for the surgery. What the surgeon withholds is the rest of the truth—that uterine fibroids are common, that they usually do *not* turn into cancer, and that the patient has several alternatives to surgery.

In case it is difficult to see how this is sexist, let's change the context just a little. Let's suppose that the income of some female surgeon depends on selling a specialized operation. To sell it, she systematically suggests to older men the benefits of castration—since "those organs are no longer necessary and might cause disease."

For Your Consideration

→ Hysterectomies have become so common that by age 60, *one of three* U.S. women has had her uterus surgically removed (Rabin 2013). Why do you think that surgeons are so quick to operate?

→ How can women find alternatives to surgery?

Gender Inequality in Education

THE PAST

Until 1832, women were not allowed to attend college with men. When women were admitted to colleges attended by men—first at Oberlin College in Ohio—they had to wash the male students' clothing, clean their rooms, and serve them their meals (Flexner 1971/1999).

How times have changed—so much so that this quote sounds like it is a joke. But there is more. The men who controlled education were bothered by female organs. They said that women's minds were dominated by their organs, making women less qualified than men for higher education. The men considered menstruation to be a special obstacle to women's success in education: It made women so feeble that they could hardly continue with their schooling, much less anything else in life. Here is how Dr. Edward Clarke, of Harvard University, put it:

A girl upon whom Nature, for a limited period and for a definite purpose, imposes so great a physiological task, will not have as much power left for the tasks of school, as the boy of whom Nature requires less at the corresponding epoch. (Andersen 1988)

Because women are so much weaker than men, Clarke urged them to study only one-third as much as young men. And, of course, in their weakened state, they were advised to not study at all during menstruation.

THE CHANGE Like out-of-fashion clothing, such ideas were discarded. As Figure 10.2 shows, by 1900 one-third of college students were women. Today, far more women than men attend college, but the overall average differs with racial–ethnic groups. As you can see from Figure 10.3 on the next page, African Americans have the most women relative to men, and Asian Americans the least. Another indication of how extensive the change is: Women now earn an astounding 57 percent of all bachelor's

Figure 10.2 Changes in College Enrollment, by Sex

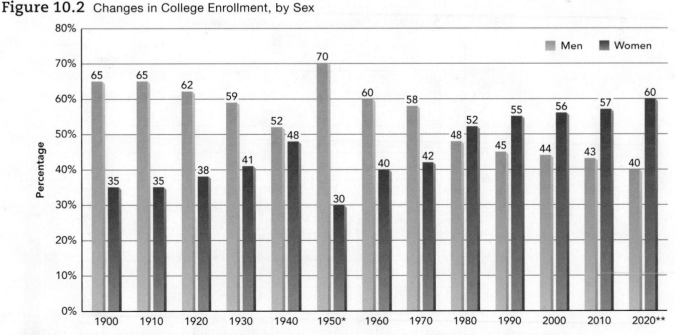

*This sharp drop in women's enrollment occurred when large numbers of male soldiers returned from World War II and attended college under the new GI Bill of Rights.
**Author's estimate.

SOURCES: By the author. Based on *Statistical Abstract of the United States* 1938:Table 114; 1959:Table 158; 1991:Table 261; 2011:Table 273; 2014:Table 282.

Figure 10.3 College Students, by Sex and Race–Ethnicity

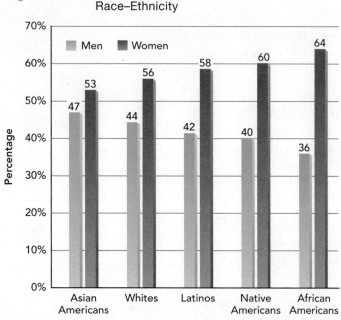

SOURCE: By the author. Based on *Statistical Abstract of the United States* 2014:Table 283.

degrees and 60 percent of all master's degrees (*Statistical Abstract* 2014:Table 303). As discussed in the Down-to-Earth Sociology box on the next page, could it be time to apply affirmative action to men?

Figure 10.4 below illustrates another major change—how women have increased their share of professional degrees. The greatest change is in dentistry: In 1970, across the entire United States, only thirty-four women earned degrees in dentistry. Today, that total has jumped to 2,300 a year. As you can also see, almost as many women as men now become dentists, lawyers, and physicians. It is likely that women will soon outnumber men in earning these professional degrees.

GENDER TRACKING With such extensive change, it would seem that gender equality has been achieved, or at least almost so. In some instances—as with the changed sex ratio in college—we even have a new form of gender inequality. If we look closer, however, we can see *gender tracking*. That is, college degrees tend to follow gender, which reinforces male–female distinctions. Here are two extremes: Men earn 95 percent of the associate's degrees in the "masculine" field of construction trades, while women are awarded 96 percent of the associate's degrees in the "feminine" field of "family and consumer sciences" (*Statistical Abstract* 2014:Table 306). Because gender socialization gives men and women different orientations to life, they enter college with gender-linked aspirations. Socialization—not some presumed innate characteristic—channels men and women into different educational paths.

Figure 10.4 Gender Changes in Professional Degrees*

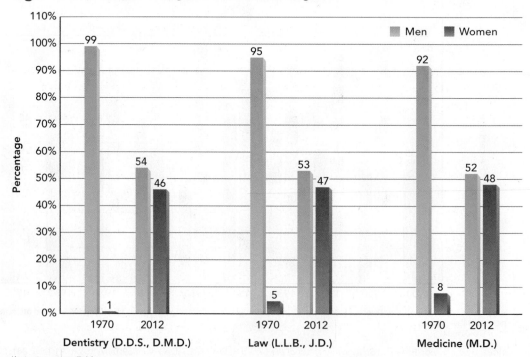

*Latest year available.

SOURCES: By the author. Based on *Digest of Education Statistics* 2007:Table 269; 2014:Table 318:30.

Down-to-Earth Sociology

Affirmative Action for Men?

When psychologist Judith Kleinfeld (2002) suggested the need of affirmative action *for men* in college, she was met by laughter. After all, men dominate societies around the world, as they have for millennia. To think that men would need affirmative action seemed humorous at best.

But let's pause, step back, and try to see whether the idea has merit. Look again at Figures 10.2 and 10.3 on pages 313 and 314. Look at how women have passed men in enrollment and how this is true of all racial–ethnic groups. This is not something temporary, like lead cars changing place at the Indy 500. The trend is strong. For decades, women have been adding to their share of college enrollment and the degrees they earn.

With colleges open to both women and men, why don't enrollment and degrees match the proportions of women and men in the population (51 percent and 49 percent)? Although no one yet knows the reasons—and many suggestions are being thrown

With fewer men than women in college, is it time to consider affirmative action for men?

around—some colleges consider this imbalance a problem searching for a solution. They are putting affirmative action for men into practice, trying to get a male–female balance. To do so, some reject more highly qualified women (Kingsbury 2007; Lam 2013). Because men on average are underperforming women in the classroom, some colleges have begun to offer study groups and mentoring programs for men (Hass 2012; Vendituoli 2013). Others, concerned about men's emotional state, their feelings of being a minority on campus, even that they are discriminated against, have started men's centers, support programs for men, even student associations for men (Gibbs 2008; Rosin 2010; Vendituoli 2013).

For Your Consideration

→ Why do you think that men are falling behind in education?

→ What implications could men falling behind have for the future of society?

→ Do you think that special programs for men are desirable? Why or why not?

Gender Inequality in the Workplace

10.4   Explain reasons for the pay gap; discuss the glass ceiling and sexual harassment.

To examine the work setting is to make visible basic relations between men and women. Let's begin with one of the most remarkable areas of gender inequality at work, the pay gap.

The Pay Gap

After college, you might like to take a few years off, travel around Europe, sail the oceans, or maybe sit on a beach in some South American paradise and drink piña coladas. But chances are, you are going to go to work instead. Since you have to work, how would you like to make an extra $712,000 on your job? If this sounds appealing, read on. I'm going to reveal how you can average an extra $1,484 a month between the ages of 25 and 65.

HISTORICAL BACKGROUND   First, let's get a broad background to help us understand today's situation. One of the chief characteristics of the U.S. workforce is the steady increase in the numbers of women who work for wages outside the home. Figure 10.5 on the next page shows that in 1890, about one of every five paid workers was a woman. By 1940, this ratio had grown to one of four; by 1960 to one of three; and today, it is almost one of two. As you can see from this Figure, 53 percent of U.S. workers are men, and 47 percent are women. During the next few years, we can expect little change in this ratio.

Figure 10.5 Proportion of Men and Women in the U.S. Labor Force

SOURCES: By the author. Based on *Women's Bureau of the United States* 1969: 10; *Manpower Report to the President*, 1971: 203, 205; *Mills and Palumbo* 1980: 6, 45; *Statistical Abstract of the United States* 2014:Table 614.

GEOGRAPHICAL FACTORS   Women who work for wages are not distributed evenly throughout the United States. From the Social Map below, you can see that where a woman lives makes a difference in how likely she is to work outside the home. Why is there such a clustering among the states? The geographical patterns that you see on this map reflect regional subcultural differences about which we currently have little understanding.

THE "TESTOSTERONE BONUS"   Now, back to how you can make an extra $712,000 at work—maybe even more. You might be wondering if this is hard to do. Actually, it is simple for some and impossible for others. Look at Figure 10.7 on the next page.

Figure 10.6 Women in the Workforce

SOURCE: By the author. Based on *Statistical Abstract of the United States* 2014:Table 621.

Figure 10.7 The Gender Pay Gap, by Education[1]

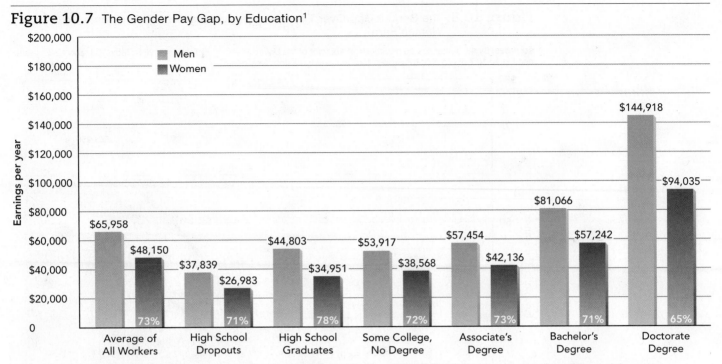

[1]Mean earnings of full-time year-around workers. The percentage at the bottom of each purple bar indicates the women's percentage of the men's income.

SOURCE: By the author. Based on U.S. Census Bureau, *Current Population Survey*, Annual Social and Economic (ASEC) Supplement, 2014:Table PINC-04.

All you have to do is be born a male. If we compare full-time workers, based on current differences in earnings, this is how much more the *average male* can expect to earn over the course of his career. Now, if you want to boost that difference to $23,800 a year for a whopping career total of $953,000 extra, be both a male and a college graduate. Hardly any single factor pinpoints gender discrimination better than these totals. As you can see from Figure 10.7, the pay gap shows up at *all* levels of education.

For college students, the gender gap in pay begins with the first job after graduation. You might know of a particular woman who was offered a higher salary than most men in her class, but she would be an exception. On average, employers start men out at higher salaries than women, and women never catch up with the men's starting "testosterone bonus" (Weinberger 2011; R. Smith 2012). Depending on your sex, then, you will either benefit from the pay gap or be victimized by it.

The pay gap is so great that U.S. women who work full time average *only 73 percent* of what men are paid. As you can see from Figure 10.8 on the next page, this low percentage is actually the smallest gender pay gap the United States has ever had. And it isn't only the United States. A gender gap in pay occurs in *all* industrialized nations.

REASONS FOR THE GENDER PAY GAP   What logic can underlie the gender pay gap? As we just saw, college degrees are gender linked, so perhaps this gap is due to career choices. Maybe women are more likely to choose lower-paying jobs, such as teaching grade school, while men are more likely to go into better-paying fields, such as business and engineering. Actually, this is true, and researchers have found that about *half* of the gender pay gap is due to such factors. And the balance? It consists of a combination of gender discrimination (Jacobs 2003; Roth 2003) and what is called the "child penalty"— women missing out on work experience and opportunities while they care for children (Gough and Noonan 2013).

Another reason has also become apparent. Let's look at this in the Down-to-Earth Sociology box on the next page.

Figure 10.8 The Gender Gap Over Time: What Percentage of Men's Income Do Women Earn?

SOURCES: By the author. Based on *Statistical Abstract of the United States* 1995:Table 739; 2014:Table 733, and earlier years; and Figure 10.7 of this chapter. Broken lines indicate the author's estimate.

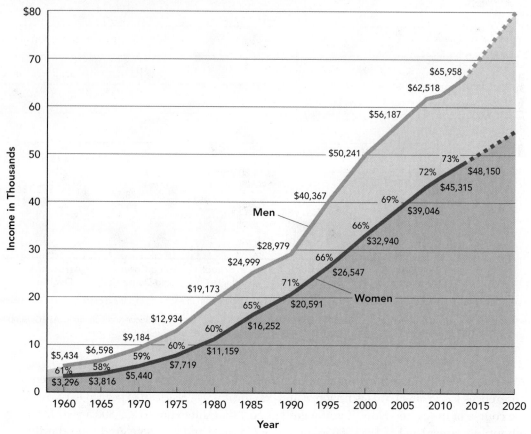

Down-to-Earth Sociology

Applying Sociology: How to Get a Higher Salary

It will take years of united effort to overcome the powerful structural factors that hold down women's pay at work. But to increase your own pay, you don't have to wait for this to happen.

Let's apply sociology to see what steps you can take. As you just read, when college students take their first jobs, most women start at lower salaries than men do. Apart from the structural reasons such as men being perceived as more valuable workers, another factor is that women aren't as good as men at negotiating salaries. Women are more likely to accept the first offer or to negotiate a little and be happy with the small increase that comes with a second offer (Bennett 2012; Lipman 2014).

Why be satisfied with less? If you are a woman, remember that the first offer is usually negotiable. The hiring agent will

be happy if you accept the offer, but usually is willing to add considerably to it if you negotiate strongly. Negotiating is like riding a bike. It is simply a skill that you can learn. So learn it. Read books on how to negotiate. Also, practice with a partner. Role-play until you are good at it.

Then, during your career, continue to promote yourself. You might think that the system will automatically reward hard work. It should, but things don't work this way in real life. Don't be afraid to bring your accomplishments to the attention of your supervisors. You need to show them that you deserve higher raises. If you don't, you run the risk of what you have done getting lost in the shuffle of the accomplishments of the workers around you.

On top of this, be bold and ask for large raises. When

women ask for raises, they ask for 30 percent less than what men ask for (Lipman 2014). If asking large makes you uncomfortable, then overcome that discomfort. *Remember this simple rule: Ask more, and you get more. Ask less, and you get less.* Again, read books on how to negotiate, and practice your negotiating skills with others. (And copy this box and put it into practice.)

Does this application of sociology apply only to women? Of course not. Even though men on average are less reluctant to bring their accomplishments to the attention of supervisors and to ask for and negotiate salaries, many men also hesitate to do so. They can use these same techniques to overcome their reluctance. All workers, male and female, can hone up on their negotiating skills. It's worth the time you put into improving this skill. It can pay off in your weekly paycheck.

Sociology isn't something to lock up in an ivory tower. Sociology is about life. As you can see, you can even apply its insights into achieving success at work and increasing your standard of living.

For Your Consideration

→ How do you think you can improve your negotiating skills?

→ For practice, what partner do you think you should choose?

→ If you practice, how can you evaluate what you are learning?

→ What other insights of sociology do you think you can apply to your career?

THE CEO POWER GAP As is obvious to all, men have more power than women in the corporate world. To see the gender gap in power, consider this. Women head only fourteen of the nation's largest three hundred corporations. The surprising positive news: With today's corporate boards more sensitive to gender, the median pay of these women equals that of their male peers (Murray 2014).

I examined the names of the CEOs of the 350 largest U.S. corporations, and I found that your best chance to reach the top is to be named (in this order) John, Robert, James, William, or Charles. Edward, Lawrence, and Richard are also advantageous names. Amber, Katherine, Leticia, and Maria apparently draw a severe penalty. Naming your baby girl John or Robert might seem a little severe, but it could help her reach the top. (I say this only slightly tongue in cheek. One of the few women to head a Fortune 500 company—before she was fired and given $21 million severance pay—had a man's first name: Carleton Fiorina of Hewlett-Packard. Carleton's first name is actually Cara, but knowing what she was facing in the highly competitive business world, she dropped this feminine name to go by her masculine middle name.)

Is the Glass Ceiling Cracking?

"First comes love, then comes marriage,
then comes flex time and a baby carriage."

—*Said by a supervisor at Novartis who refused to hire women (Carter 2010)*

This supervisor's statement reflects blatant discrimination. Most gender discrimination in the workplace, however, seems to be unintentional, with much of it based on gender stereotypes.

Apart from cases of discrimination, then, what keeps women from breaking through the **glass ceiling**, the mostly invisible barrier that prevents women from reaching the executive suite? Stereotypes are part of the reason (Isaac 2012). It is common for men, who dominate leadership, to have the stereotype that women are good at "support" but less capable than men of leadership. They steer women into human resources or public relations. This keeps many away from the "pipelines" that lead to the top of a company— marketing, sales, and production—positions that produce profits for the company and bonuses for the managers (Hymowitz 2004; DeCrow 2005).

Another reason that the glass ceiling is so strong is that women lack mentors— successful executives who take an interest in them and teach them the ropes. Lack of a mentor is no trivial matter, since mentors can provide opportunities to develop leadership skills that open the door to the executive suite (Hymowitz 2007; Yakaboski and Reinert 2011).

glass ceiling

the mostly invisible barrier that keeps women from advancing to the top levels at work

As the glass ceiling slowly cracks, women are gaining entry into the top positions of society. Shown here is Indra Nooyi, Chairperson and Chief Executive Officer of PepsiCo.

sexual harassment

the abuse of one's position of authority to force unwanted sexual demands on someone

Sexual Harassment—and Worse

Sexual harassment—unwelcome sexual attention at work or at school that may affect job or school performance or create a hostile environment—was not recognized as a problem until the 1970s. Before this, a woman considered unwanted sexual comments, touches, looks, and pressure to have sex as a personal matter, something between her and some "turned on" man—or an obnoxious one.

With the prodding of feminists, women began to perceive unwanted sexual advances at work and school as part of a *structural* problem. That is, they began to realize that the issue was more than a man here or there doing obnoxious things because he was attracted to a woman; rather, men were using their positions of authority to pressure women for sex.

LABELS AND PERCEPTION As symbolic interactionists stress, labels affect the way we see things. Because we have the term *sexual harassment*, we perceive actions in a different light than people used to. We are now more apt to perceive the sexual advances of a supervisor toward a worker not as sexual attraction but as a misuse of authority.

NOT JUST A "MAN THING" It is important to add that sexual harassment is not just a "man thing." Unlike the past, many women today are in positions of authority, and in those positions, they, too, sexually harass subordinates (McLaughlin et al. 2012). With most authority still vested in men, however, most sexual harassers are men.

SEXUAL ORIENTATION Originally, sexual desire was an element of sexual harassment, but no longer. This changed when the U.S. Supreme Court considered the lawsuit of a homosexual who had been tormented by his supervisors and fellow workers. The Court ruled that sexual desire is not necessary—that sexual harassment laws also apply to homosexuals who are harassed by heterosexuals while on the job (Felsenthal 1998; Ramakrishnan 2011). By extension, the law applies to heterosexuals who are sexually harassed by homosexuals.

Gender and Violence

10.5 **Summarize violence against women: rape, murder, and violence in the home.**

One of the consistent characteristics of violence in the United States—and the world—is its gender inequality. That is, females are more likely to be the victims of males, not the other way around. Let's briefly review this almost one-way street in gender violence as it applies to the United States.

Violence against Women

We have already examined violence against women in other cultures. On page 312, we reviewed a form of surgical violence in the United States, and in Chapter 12, we will review violence in the home. Here we briefly review some primary features of gender violence.

FORCIBLE RAPE The fear of rape is common among U.S. women, a fear that is far from groundless. The U.S. rate is 1 per 2,000 females age 12 and older (*Statistical Abstract* 2014:Table 327). This means that 1 of every 2,000 U.S. girls and women ages 12 and older is raped *each year*. Despite this high number, women are much safer now than they were twenty-five or so years ago, when many think society was so much safer. Today's rape rate is only *one-third* of what it was in 1990.

"Of course it isn't a case of sexual discrimination. We just don't think you're the right man for the job."

Although crassly put by the cartoonist, behind the glass ceiling lies this background assumption.

Although any woman can be a victim of sexual assault—and victims include babies and elderly women—the typical victim is 16 to 19 years old. As you can see from Table 10.1, sexual assault peaks at those ages and then declines.

Women's most common fear seems to be an attack by a stranger—a sudden, violent abduction and rape. However, contrary to the stereotypes that underlie these fears, most victims know their attackers. As you can see from Table 10.2, about one of three rapes is committed by strangers.

Males are also victims of rape, which is every bit as devastating for them as it is for female victims (Dao 2013). The rape of males in the military and in jails and prisons is a special problem. An astounding finding is that about as many prisoners are raped by prison staff as by other prisoners (Holland 2012).

Table 10.1 Rape Victims

Age	Rate per 1,000 Females
12–15	1.6
16–19	2.7
20–24	2.0
25–34	1.3
35–49	0.8
50–64	0.4
65 and Older	0.1

SOURCES: By the author. A ten-year average based on *Statistical Abstract of the United States* 2005:Table 306; 2006:Table 308; 2007:Table 311; 2008:Table 313; 2009:Table 305; 2010:Table 305; 2011:Table 312; 2012:Table 316; 2013:Table 278; 2014:Table 328.

Table 10.2 Relationship of Victims and Rapists

Relationship	Percentage
Relative	6%
Known Well	33%
Casual Acquaintance	23%
Stranger	34%
Not Reported	3%

SOURCES: By the author. A ten-year average based on *Statistical Abstract of the United States* 2005:Table 307; 2006:Table 311; 2007: Table 315; 2008:Table 316; 2009:Table 306; 2010:Table 306; 2011:Table 313; 2012:Table 317; 2013:Table 323; 2014:Table 329.

DATE (ACQUAINTANCE) RAPE

At the peer workshop on sexual assault at the University of California at Berkeley, the student leader was talking to fraternity members. When she explained that sex with someone who has blacked out from drinking is rape, "jaws dropped." "They didn't even know this was illegal or wrong," she said. (Phillips 2014).

Date rape (also known as *acquaintance rape*) is common. Based on a nationally representative sample of women college students, 1.7 percent have been raped during the preceding six months. Another 1.1 percent were victims of attempted rape (Fisher et al. 2000).

These are *huge* numbers. With 12 million women enrolled in college, 2.8 percent (1.7 plus 1.1) means that over a quarter of a million college women were victims of sexual assault *in just the past six months.* (The research was based on colleges with more than 1,000 students, so this assumes that the same rates apply to smaller colleges.)

You can assume, then, that tens of thousands of men were arrested. Not really, though. Most of the women told a friend what happened, but only *5 percent* reported the crime to the police (Fisher et al. 2003). (In another study, 11.5 percent reported their rape [Wolitzky-Taylor et al 2011]). Most did not consider the event "serious enough" to report. Many were uncertain that a crime had been committed. Others were embarrassed and wanted to keep it from their families. Some felt helpless, that "It would be my word against his." Some victims even feel responsible for their own rape: They were drinking with the man, went to his place, or invited him

The most common drug used to facilitate date rape is alcohol, not GHB.

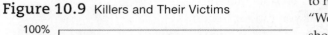

Figure 10.9 Killers and Their Victims

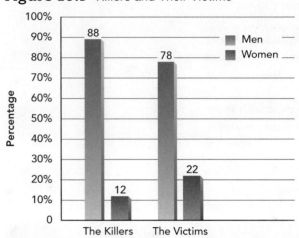

SOURCE: By the author. Based on *Statistical Abstract of the United States* 2014:Tables 324, 342.

to her place. As a physician who treats victims of sexual assault said, "Would you feel responsible if someone hit you over the head with a shovel—just because you knew the person?" (Carpenito 1999).

MURDER   All over the world, men are more likely than women to be killers. Figure 10.9 illustrates this gender pattern in U.S. murders. Note that although females make up about 51 percent of the U.S. population, they don't even come close to making up 51 percent of the nation's killers. As you can see from this Figure, when women are murdered, about nine times out of ten the killer is a man.

VIOLENCE IN THE HOME   In the family, too, women are the typical victims. Spouse battering, marital rape, and incest are discussed in Chapter 12. Two forms of violence against women—honor killings and female circumcision—are discussed on pages 307 and 308.

FEMINISM AND GENDERED VIOLENCE   Feminist sociologists have been especially effective in bringing violence against women to the public's attention. Some use symbolic interactionism, pointing out that to associate strength and virility with violence—as is done in many cultures—is to promote violence. Others employ conflict theory. They argue that men are losing power and that some men turn violently against women as a way to reassert their declining power and status (Reiser 1999; Meltzer 2002; Xie et al. 2011).

SOLUTIONS   There is no magic bullet for the problem of gendered violence, but to be effective, any solution must break the connection between violence and masculinity. This would require an educational program that encompasses schools, churches, homes, and the media. Given the gunslinging heroes of the Wild West and other American icons, as well as the violent messages that are so prevalent in the mass media, including video games, it is difficult to be optimistic that a change will come any time soon.

Our next topic, women in politics, however, gives us much more reason for optimism.

Angela Merkel, the world's most powerful woman, broke through the German glass ceiling in politics. Serving her third 4-year term as Chancellor of Germany, she is shown here on a visit to New Zealand, greeting a Maori leader in their traditional manner of rubbing noses.

The Changing Face of Politics

10.6   Discuss changes in gender and politics.

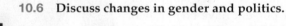

Women could take over the United States! Think about it. There are eight million more women than men of voting age. But look at Table 10.3 on the next page. Although women voters greatly outnumber men voters, men greatly outnumber women in political office. The remarkable gains women have made in recent elections can take our eye off the broader picture. Since 1789, about two thousand men have served in the U.S. Senate. And how many women? Only forty-four, including the twenty current senators. Not until 1992 was the first African American woman (Carol Brown) elected to the U.S. Senate. It took until 2013 for the first Asian American woman (Mazie Hirono) to be sworn in to the Senate. No Latina has yet been elected to the Senate (National Women's Political Caucus 1998, 2013; *Statistical Abstract* 2014:Table 432).

We are in the midst of fundamental change. In 2002, Nancy Pelosi was the first woman to be elected by her colleagues as minority leader of the House of Representatives. Five years later, in 2007, they chose her as the first female Speaker of the House. These posts made her the most powerful woman ever in Congress. Another significant event occurred in 2008 when Hillary Clinton came within a hair's breadth of becoming the presidential nominee of the Democratic Party. That same year, Sarah Palin was chosen as the Republican vice-presidential candidate. We can also note that more women are becoming corporate executives, and, as indicated in Figure 10.4

Table 10.3 U.S. Women in Political Office

	Offices Held by Women (Percentage)	Offices Held by Women (Number)
National Office		
U.S. Senate	20%	20
U.S. House of Representatives	18%	79
State Office		
Governors	10%	5
Lt. Governors	22%	11
Attorneys General	16%	8
Secretaries of State	22%	11
Treasurers	14%	7
State Auditors	16%	8
State Legislators	24%	1,789

SOURCE: By the author. Based on Center for American Women and Politics 2014.

on page 314, more women are also becoming lawyers. In these positions, women are traveling more and making statewide and national contacts. Along with other social changes that give women more freedom, such as more people seeing child care as the responsibility of both mother and father, it is only a matter of time until a woman occupies the Oval Office.

Glimpsing the Future—with Hope

Women's fuller participation in the decision-making processes of our social institutions has shattered stereotypes that tended to limit females to "feminine" activities and push males into "masculine" ones. As structural barriers continue to fall and more activities are degendered, both males and females will have greater freedom to pursue activities that are more compatible with their abilities and desires as individuals.

As females and males develop a new consciousness both of their capacities and of their potential, relationships will change. Distinctions between the sexes will not disappear, but there is no reason for biological differences to be translated into social inequalities. The potential, as sociologist Alison Jaggar (1990) observed, is for gender equality to become less a goal than a background condition for living in society.

■ Inequalities of Aging

In 1928, Charles Hart, who was working on his Ph.D. in anthropology, did fieldwork with the Tiwi people, who live on an island off the northern coast of Australia. Because every Tiwi belongs to a clan, they assigned Hart to the bird (Jabijabui) clan and told him that a particular woman was his mother. Hart described the woman as "toothless, almost blind, withered." He added that she was "physically quite revolting and mentally rather senile." He then recounted this remarkable event:

> *Toward the end of my time on the islands an incident occurred that surprised me because it suggested that some of them had been taking my presence in the kinship system much more seriously than I had thought. I was approached by a group of about eight or nine senior men. . . . They were the senior members of the Jabijabui clan and they had decided among themselves that the time had come to get rid of the decrepit old woman who had first called me son and whom I now called mother. . . . As I knew, they said, it was Tiwi custom, when an old woman became too feeble to look after herself, to "cover her up." This could only be done by her sons and brothers and all of them had to agree beforehand, since once it was done, they did not want any dissension among the brothers or*

clansmen, as that might lead to a feud. My "mother" was now completely blind, she was constantly falling over logs or into fires, and they, her senior clansmen, were in agreement that she would be better out of the way. Did I agree?

I already knew about "covering up." The Tiwi, like many other hunting and gathering peoples, sometimes got rid of their ancient and decrepit females. The method was to dig a hole in the ground in some lonely place, put the old woman in the hole and fill it in with earth until only her head was showing. Everybody went away for a day or two and then went back to the hole to discover to their great surprise, that the old woman was dead, having been too feeble to raise her arms from the earth. Nobody had "killed" her; her death in Tiwi eyes was a natural one. She had been alive when her relatives last saw her. I had never seen it done, though I knew it was the custom, so I asked my brothers if it was necessary for me to attend the "covering up."

They said no and that they would do it, but only after they had my agreement. Of course I agreed, and a week or two later we heard in our camp that my "mother" was dead, and we all wailed and put on the trimmings of mourning. **(C. W. M. Hart in Hart and Pilling 1979:125–126.)**

Aging in Global Perspective

10.7 **Understand how attitudes toward the elderly vary around the world; explain how industrialization led to a graying globe.**

We won't deal with the question of whether it was moral or ethical for Hart to agree that the old woman should be "covered up." What is of interest for our purposes is how the Tiwi treated their frail elderly—or, more specifically, their frail *female* elderly. You probably noticed that the Tiwi "covered up" only old women. As was noted earlier, females are discriminated against throughout the world. As this incident makes evident, in some places that discrimination extends even to death.

Every society must deal with the problem of people growing old and of some becoming frail. Although few societies choose to bury old people alive, all societies must decide how to allocate limited resources among their citizens. With more people around the world making it to old age, these decisions are producing tensions between the generations on a global level.

Extremes of Attitudes and Practices

The way the Tiwi treated frail elderly women reflects one extreme of how societies cope with aging. Another extreme, one that reflects a sharply different attitude, is illustrated by the Abkhasians, an agricultural people who live in Georgia, a republic of the former Soviet Union. The Abkhasians pay their elderly high respect and look to them for guidance (Gurian 2013). They would no more dispense with their elderly by "covering them up" than we would "cover up" a sick child in our culture.

The Abkhasians may be the longest-lived people on Earth. Many claim to live past 100—some beyond 120 and even 130 (Benet 1971; Robbins 2006). Although researchers have concluded that the extreme claims are bogus (Young et al. 2010), government records do indicate that many Abkhasians do live to a very old age.

Three main factors appear to account for their long lives. The first is their diet, which consists of little meat and much fresh fruit, vegetables, garlic, goat cheese, cornmeal, buttermilk, and wine. The second is their lifelong physical activity. They do slow down after age 80, but even after the age of 100, they still work about four hours a day. The third factor—a highly developed sense of community—lies at the very heart of the Abkhasian culture. From childhood, each individual is integrated into a primary group and remains so throughout life. There is no such

Among some groups, the elderly don't retire. They continue their traditional tasks, but they do slow down. This ethnic Miao woman in China continues to harvest grain, as she has done since her childhood.

thing as a nursing home nor do the elderly live alone. Because they continue to work and contribute to the group's welfare, the elderly aren't a burden to anyone. They don't vegetate, nor do they feel the need to "fill time" with bingo and shuffleboard. In short, the elderly feel no sudden rupture between what they "were" and what they "are."

IN SUM Contrasting the Tiwi and the Abkhasians reveals an important sociological principle: Like gender, aging is *socially constructed*. That is, nothing in the nature of aging summons forth any particular viewpoint. Rather, attitudes toward the aged are rooted in society. They differ with groups around the world.

Industrialization and the Graying of the Globe

In 1900, the average person in the world was dead by the age of 30! Today the average person lives to 70! **(Eberstadt 2014b)**

What happened to bring about such a remarkable change? The one-word answer is industrialization. Industrialization brings not only more material goods but also a higher standard of living: more food, a purer water supply, better housing, and more effective ways of fighting the diseases that kill children. As a result, when a country industrializes, its people live longer. The Social Map provides a good illustration. As you can see, the industrialized countries have the highest percentage of elderly.

Because industrialization is uneven around the world, the percentage of elderly differs sharply among the world's nations. In nonindustrialized Uganda, just one of forty-five citizens is age 65 or older, but in postindustrial Japan one of every four persons is elderly (*Statistical Abstract* 2014:Table 1367). The graying of the globe is so new that *two-thirds of all people who have ever passed age 50 in the history of the world are alive today* (Zaslow 2003).

Figure 10.10 The Graying of the Globe

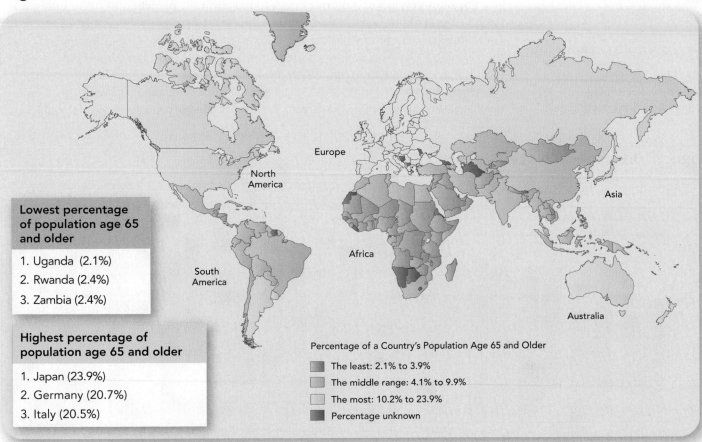

Lowest percentage of population age 65 and older

1. Uganda (2.1%)
2. Rwanda (2.4%)
3. Zambia (2.4%)

Highest percentage of population age 65 and older

1. Japan (23.9%)
2. Germany (20.7%)
3. Italy (20.5%)

Percentage of a Country's Population Age 65 and Older

- The least: 2.1% to 3.9%
- The middle range: 4.1% to 9.9%
- The most: 10.2% to 23.9%
- Percentage unknown

SOURCE: By the author. Based on *Statistical Abstract of the United States* 2014:Table 1367.

Except for interaction within families, age groups in Western culture are usually kept fairly separate. The idea of having a day care center in the same building as a nursing home breaks this tradition. This photo was taken in Seattle, Washington.

life span

the maximum length of life of a species; for humans, the longest that a human has lived

life expectancy

the number of years that an average person at any age, including newborns, can expect to live

graying of America

the growing percentage of older people in the U.S. population

As the number of elderly continues to grow, analysts have become alarmed about future liabilities for their care. This issue is especially troubling in western Europe and Japan, which have the largest percentage of citizens over age 65. The basic issue is: How can these large numbers of elderly be provided high-quality care without burdening future generations with impossible taxes? The many nations confronting this issue have not yet found a solution.

THE LIFE SPAN   Although more people are living to old age, the maximum length of life possible, the **life span**, has not increased. No one knows, however, just what that maximum is. We do know that it is at least 122: This was the well-documented age of Jeanne Louise Calment of France at her death in 1997. The birth certificate of Tuti Yusupova in Uzbekistan, who has a one-hundred-year-old daughter, shows her birth year as 1880. If this turns out to be genuine, then the human life span exceeds 122 by a comfortable margin. It is also likely that advances in genetics will extend the human life span—maybe even to hundreds of years.

The Graying of America

From Figure 10.11, you can see how the United States is part of this global trend. This Figure shows how U.S. **life expectancy**, the number of years people can expect to live, has increased since 1900. To me, and perhaps to you, it is startling to realize that a hundred years or so ago, the average U.S. woman and man didn't live long enough to celebrate their 50th birthday. Since then, we've added about *thirty years* to our life expectancy, and Americans born today can expect to live into their 70s or 80s.

The term **graying of America** refers to this growing percentage of older people in the U.S. population. Look at Figure 10.12 on the next page. In 1900, only 4 percent of Americans were age 65 and older. Today, 14 percent are. U.S. society has become so "gray" that, as Figure 10.13 on the next page shows, the median age has almost *doubled* since 1850. Today, there are fourteen million *more* elderly Americans than there are teenagers (*Statistical Abstract* 2014:Tables 11, 111). Despite this vast change, as Figure 10.14 on the next page shows, the United States ranks just twelfth in life expectancy on a global level.

Figure 10.11 U.S. Life Expectancy by Year of Birth

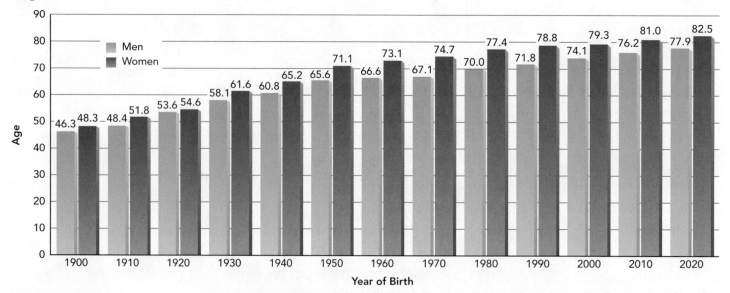

SOURCES: By the author. Based on *Historical Statistics of the United States, Colonial Times to 1970*, Bicentennial Edition, Part I, Series B, 107–115; *Statistical Abstract of the United States* 2014:Table 112.

Figure 10.12 The Graying of America: Americans Age 65 and Older

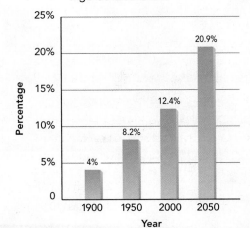

SOURCE: By the author. Based on *Statistical Abstract of the United States* 2014:Table 9, and earlier years.

Figure 10.13 The Median Age of the U.S. Population

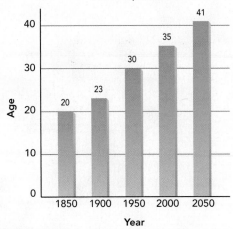

SOURCE: By the author. Based on *Statistical Abstract of the United States* 2000:Table 14; 2014:Table 9, and earlier years.

Figure 10.14 Life Expectancy in Global Perspective

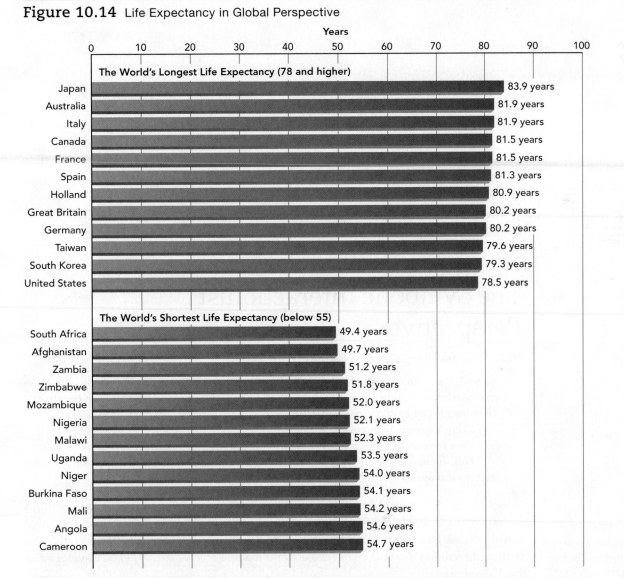

NOTE: The countries listed in the source are those with a life expectancy longer than the United States and those with a life expectancy less than 55 years. All the countries in the top group are industrialized, and none of those in the bottom group are.

SOURCE: By the author. Based on *Statistical Abstract of the United States* 2014:Table 1368.

Figure 10.15 As Florida Goes, So Goes the Nation

SOURCE: By the author. Based on *Statistical Abstract of the United States* 2014:Table 17.

As anyone who has ever visited Florida knows, the elderly population is not distributed evenly around the country. (As Jerry Seinfeld sardonically noted, "There's a law that when you get old, you've got to move to Florida.") The Social Map above shows how uneven this distribution is.

Let's see the different pictures of aging that emerge when we apply the three theoretical perspectives.

The Symbolic Interactionist Perspective

10.8 Discuss changes in perceptions of the elderly.

> *At first, the audience sat quietly as the developers explained their plans to build a high-rise apartment building. After a while, people began to shift uncomfortably in their seats. Then they began to show open hostility.*
>
> *"That's too much money to spend on those people," said one.*
>
> *"You even want them to have a swimming pool?" asked another incredulously.*
>
> *Finally, one young woman put their attitudes in a nutshell when she asked, "Who wants all those old people around?"*

ageism

prejudice and discrimination directed against people because of their age; can be directed against any age group, including youth

When physician Robert Butler (1975, 1980) heard these complaints about plans to build apartments for senior citizens, he began to realize how deeply antagonistic feelings toward the elderly can run. He coined the term **ageism** to refer to prejudice and discrimination directed against people because of their age. Let's see how ageism developed in the United States.

Shifting Meanings of Growing Old

As we have seen, there is nothing inherent in old age to produce any particular attitude, negative or not. Some historians point out that in early U.S. society, old age was regarded positively (Greenstein and Holland 2015). In colonial times, growing old was seen as an accomplishment because so few people made it to old age. With no pensions, the elderly continued to work. Their jobs changed little over time, and they were viewed as storehouses of knowledge about work skills and sources of wisdom about how to live a long life.

The coming of industrialization eroded these bases of respect. With better sanitation and medical care, more people reached old age, and being elderly lost its uniqueness and the honor it had brought. Industrialization's new forms of mass production also made young workers as productive as the elderly. Coupled with mass education, this stripped away the elderly's superior knowledge (Cowgill 1974; Cruikshank 2013).

A basic principle of symbolic interactionism is that we perceive both ourselves and others according to the symbols of our culture. When the meaning of old age changed from an asset to a liability, not only did younger people come to view the elderly differently but so did the elderly. They, too, began to perceive themselves in a new light. This shift in meaning is demonstrated in the way people lie about their age: They used to say that they were older than they were but now claim to be younger than their true ages (Clair et al. 1993).

Today, the meaning of old age is shifting once again—this time in a positive direction. More positive images of the elderly are developing, largely because most of today's U.S. elderly enjoy good health and can take care of themselves financially. If this symbolic shift continues, the next step—now in process—will be to view old age not as a period that precedes death but, rather, as a new stage of growth. We will return to this topic.

Even theories of old age have taken a more positive tone. A theory that goes by the mouthful *gerotranscendence* was developed by Swedish sociologist Lars Tornstam (2011). The thrust of this theory is that as people grow old, they transcend their limited views of life. They become less self-centered and begin to feel more at one with the universe. Coming to see things as less black and white, they develop subtler ways of viewing right and wrong and tolerate more ambiguity. However, this theory seems to miss the mark. Some elderly people do grow softer and more spiritual, but I have seen others turn bitter, close up, and become even more judgmental of others. The theory's limitations should become apparent shortly.

When does old age begin? And what activities are appropriate for the elderly? From this photo that I took of Munimah, a 65-year-old bonded laborer in Chennai, India, you can see how culturally relative these questions are. No one in Chennai thinks it is extraordinary that this woman makes her living by carrying heavy rocks all day in the burning, tropical sun. Working next to her in the quarry is her 18-year-old son, who breaks the rocks into the size that his mother carries.

The Influence of the Mass Media

In Chapter 3 (pages 84–86), we noted that the mass media help to shape our ideas about both gender and relationships between men and women. As a powerful source of symbols, the media also influence our ideas of the elderly, the topic of the Mass Media box on the next page.

IN SUM Symbolic interactionists stress that old age has no inherent meaning. There is nothing about old age to automatically summon forth responses of honor and respect, as with the Abkhasians, or any other response. Our culture shapes how we perceive the elderly, including the ways we view our own aging. In short, the social modifies the biological.

Mass Media in Social Life

The Cultural Lens: Shaping Our Perceptions of the Elderly

The mass media profoundly influence our perception of people (Levy et al. 2013). What we hear and see on television and in the movies, the songs we listen to, the books and magazines we read—all become part of the cultural lens through which we view the world. The media shape our images of minorities and dominant groups; men, women, and children; people with disabilities; those from other cultures—and the elderly.

The shaping of our images and perception of the elderly is subtle, so much so that it usually occurs without our awareness. The elderly, for example, are underrepresented on television and in most popular magazines (Barrett et al. 2014). This omission transmits a covert message—that the elderly are of little consequence and can be safely ignored.

The media also reflect and reinforce stereotypes of *gender age*. Older male news anchors are likely to be retained, while female anchors who turn the same age are more likely to be transferred to less visible positions. Similarly, in movies, older men are more likely to play romantic leads—and to play them opposite much younger rising stars.

The message might be subtle, but it is not lost. The more television that people watch, the more they perceive the elderly in negative terms. The elderly, too, internalize these negative images, which, in turn, influences the ways they view themselves. These images are so powerful that

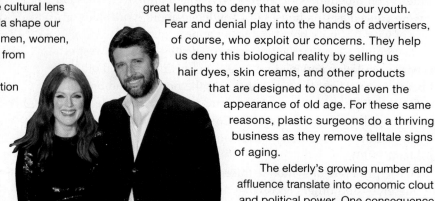

When does "old" begin? Until recently, Julianne Moore, age 54, would have been considered elderly. No longer. In some cultures yet today, her partner, Bart Freundlich, age 45, would be considered elderly.

they affect the elderly's health, even the way they walk (Donlon et al. 2005).

We become fearful of growing old, and we go to great lengths to deny that we are losing our youth. Fear and denial play into the hands of advertisers, of course, who exploit our concerns. They help us deny this biological reality by selling us hair dyes, skin creams, and other products that are designed to conceal even the appearance of old age. For these same reasons, plastic surgeons do a thriving business as they remove telltale signs of aging.

The elderly's growing number and affluence translate into economic clout and political power. One consequence is more positive images of the elderly in the mass media (Balazs 2014). An indication of this change is shown in the photo at the left.

For Your Consideration

→ What other examples of fear and denial of growing old are you familiar with?

→ What examples of older men playing romantic leads with younger women can you give? Of older women and younger men?

→ Why do you think we have gender age stereotypes?

→ How do you think age stereotypes are changing?

The Functionalist Perspective

10.9   Summarize theories of disengagement, activity, and continuity.

Functionalists analyze how the parts of society work together. Among the components of society are **age cohorts**—people who were born at roughly the same time and who pass through the life course together. This term might strike you as something divorced from your life, but age cohorts actually affect your life deeply. For example, when you finish college, if the age cohort that is retiring is large (a "baby boom" generation), jobs will be plentiful. In contrast, if the age cohort is small (a "baby bust" generation), your opportunities for good jobs will shrink.

Let's consider theories that focus on retirement.

Disengagement Theory

Think about how disruptive it would be if the elderly left their jobs only when they died or became incompetent. How does society get the elderly to leave their positions so younger people can take them? According to **disengagement theory**, developed by Elaine Cumming and William Henry (1961), this is the function of pensions. Pensions

age cohort

people born at roughly the same time who pass through the life course together

disengagement theory

the view that society is stabilized by having the elderly retire (disengage from) their positions of responsibility so the younger generation can step into their shoes get the elderly to *disengage* from their positions and hand them over to younger people. Retirement, then, is a mutually beneficial arrangement between two parts of society.

EVALUATION OF THE THEORY   Certainly pensions do entice the elderly to leave their jobs so a younger generation can step in. I think we all know this, so it isn't much of a theory. Critics have also pointed out that the elderly don't really "disengage." People who quit their jobs don't sit in rocking chairs and watch the world go by. Instead of disengaging, the retired *exchange* one set of roles for another (Tadic et al. 2012). They find these new ways of conducting their lives, which often center on friendship, no less satisfying than their earlier roles. In addition, the meaning of retirement has changed since this "theory" was developed. Less and less does retirement mean an end to work. Many people stay at their jobs, but they slow down, putting in fewer hours. Others remain as part-time consultants. Some use the Internet to explore new areas of work. Others switch careers, even in their 60s, some even in their 70s. If disengagement theory is ever resurrected, it must come to grips with our new patterns of retirement.

This Japanese woman competed in the 1,500 meter race. Her time was 1 hour, 54.39 seconds. She is 100 years old.

Activity Theory

Are retired people more satisfied with life? (All that extra free time and not having to kowtow to a boss must be nice.) Are intimate activities more satisfying than formal ones? Such questions are the focus of **activity theory**. Although we could consider this theory from other perspectives, we are examining it from the functionalist perspective because its focus is how disengagement is functional or dysfunctional.

EVALUATION OF THE THEORY   When it comes to retired people, it is the same as with young people: No one size fits all. Some people are happier when they are more active, but others prefer less involvement (Keith 1982; Levy et al. 2013). Similarly, many people find informal, intimate activities, such as spending time with friends, to be more satisfying than formal activities. But not everyone does. In one study, two thousand retired U.S. men reported formal activities to be just as satisfying as informal ones. Even solitary tasks, such as doing home repairs, had about the same impact as intimate activities on these men's life satisfaction (Beck and Page 1988). It is the same for spending time with adult children. "Often enough" for some parents is "not enough" or even "too much" for others. In short, researchers have discovered the obvious: What makes life satisfying for one person doesn't work for another. (This, of course, can be a source of intense frustration for couples, retired or not.)

activity theory

the view that satisfaction during old age is related to a person's amount and quality of activity

Stereotypes, which play such a profound role in social life, are a basic area of sociological investigation. In contemporary society, the mass media are a major source of stereotypes.

During their elderly years, men and women continue to exhibit aspects of the gender roles that they learned and played in their younger years.

Continuity Theory

As its name implies, a theory of aging called **continuity theory** focuses on how the elderly continue ties with their past (Goth and Smaland 2014). When they retire, people like to preserve positive mental images of themselves. One way they do this is to take on new roles that are similar to the ones they have given up. For example, a former CEO might serve as a consultant, a retired electrician might do small electrical repairs, or a pensioned banker might take over the finances of her church. Researchers have found that people who are active in multiple roles (wife, author, mother, intimate friend, church member, etc.) are better equipped to handle the changes that come with growing old. Social class is also significant: With their greater resources, people from higher social classes adjust better to the challenges of aging.

continuity theory

a theory focusing on how people adjust to retirement by continuing aspects of their earlier lives

EVALUATION OF THE THEORY   The basic criticism of continuity theory is that it is too broad (Hatch 2000). We all have anchor points based on our particular experiences in life, and we all rely on them to make adjustments to what we confront in life. This applies to people of all ages beyond infancy. This theory is really a collection of loosely connected ideas, with no specific application to the elderly.

IN SUM   The *broader* perspective of the functionalists is how society's parts work together to keep society running smoothly. If younger workers had to fight to take over the jobs of the elderly, it would be disruptive to society. To smooth the transition, the elderly are offered pensions that entice them to leave their positions. Functionalists also use a *narrower* perspective, focusing on how individuals adjust to retirement. The basic finding that seems to run through the research is this: Regardless of the form it takes, activity that provides meaning helps the aged reconstruct their identities, promotes satisfaction and happiness, and leads to a more successful retirement (Newman et al. 2013).

The Conflict Perspective

10.10   Explain the conflict perspective on Social Security and discuss intergenerational competition and conflict.

As you know, the conflict perspective's guiding principle is how social groups compete with one another to control power and resources. How does this apply to society's age groups? As conflict theorists stress, regardless of whether the young and old recognize it, they are opponents in a struggle that threatens to throw society into turmoil. Let's look at how the passage of Social Security legislation fits the conflict view.

Fighting for Resources: Social Security Legislation

In the 1920s, before Social Security provided an income for the aged, two-thirds of all citizens over 65 had no savings and could not support themselves (Holtzman 1963; Crossen 2004). Then came the Great Depression. The situation grew even worse, and in 1930 Francis Townsend, a physician, started a movement to rally older citizens. He soon had one-third of all Americans over age 65 enrolled in his Townsend Clubs.

They demanded that the federal government impose a national sales tax of 2 percent to provide $200 a month for every person over 65 ($2,100 a month in today's money). In 1934, the Townsend Plan went before Congress. Because it called for such high payments and many were afraid that it would destroy people's incentive to save for the future, members of Congress looked for a way to reject the plan without appearing to oppose the elderly. When President Roosevelt announced his own, more modest Social Security plan in 1934, Congress embraced it (Schottland 1963; Amenta 2006).

To provide jobs for younger people, the new Social Security law required that workers retire at age 65. It did not matter how well people did their work or how much they needed the pay. For decades, the elderly protested. Finally, in 1986, Congress eliminated mandatory retirement. Today, almost 90 percent of Americans retire by age 65, but most do so voluntarily. No longer can they be forced out of their jobs simply because of age.

Intergenerational Competition and Conflict

"Old people are tax burdens who should hurry up and die."

Taro Aso, the Finance Minister of Japan

Could conflict between the elderly and the young be in your future? As conflict theorists stress, equilibrium between competing groups is only a temporary balancing of oppositional forces. Since the balance can be upset at any time, let's consider this possibility.

Actually, the first shots have already been fired. They started with mild complaints that the elderly were getting more than their fair share of society's resources. This has escalated. Some now accuse the elderly of *generational theft*. They say that they are running up a national debt that coming generations will have to pay (Freeman 2013). One article is even titled, *Old People Are Sucking Us Dry* (Altman 2014).

Smoldering behind these charges are the gigantic costs of Social Security and Medicare. As incredible as it may seem, *97 percent of the nation's total income tax is spent on these two programs.* Of the nation's *total revenue* from all sources, these two programs take one of every two dollars (49 percent) (*Statistical Abstract* 2014:Tables 488, 492, 499). Look at Figure 10.16. You can see that Social Security payments are now more than *one thousand times* higher than they were in 1950. To see the nation's huge medical bill to care for the elderly, look at Figure 10.17 on the next page. Like gasoline poured on a fire, these soaring costs may fuel intergenerational conflict.

Some are also resentful that the condition of the elderly has improved while that of the nation's children has deteriorated. To see this, look at Figure 10.18 on page 335. As the government transferred resources to the elderly, their poverty rate dropped by *two-thirds*. Now compare the path of childhood poverty. It is now *higher* than it was in 1967—and in all the years in between.

Some think that the drop in the elderly's poverty came at the expense of the nation's children. Did it? Ask yourself: Could Congress have funded

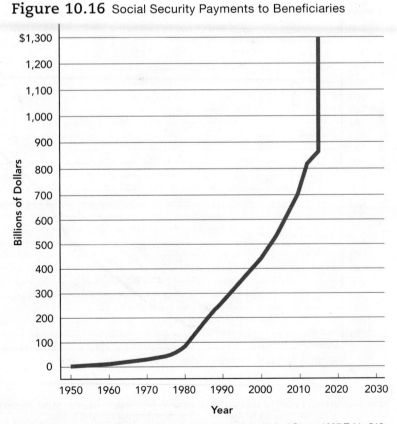

Figure 10.16 Social Security Payments to Beneficiaries

SOURCE: By the author. Based on *Statistical Abstract of the United States* 1997:Table 518; 2014:Table 492. Broken line indicates the author's projections.

In old age, as in all other stages of the life course, people find life more pleasant if they have friends and enough money to meet their needs. How do you think the elderly man to the left finds life? How about the elderly men in the photo to the right? While neither welcomes old age, you can see what a difference social factors make in how people experience this time of life.

Figure 10.17 Health Care Costs for the Elderly and Disabled

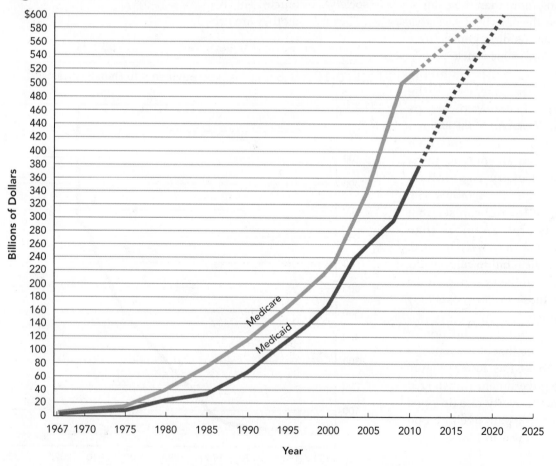

NOTE: Medicare is intended for the elderly and disabled, Medicaid for the poor. About 19 percent of Medicaid payments ($64 billion) go for medical care for the elderly (*Statistical Abstract* 2014:Table 156).

SOURCE: By the author. Based on *Statistical Abstract of the United States* various years, and 2014:Table 145. Broken lines indicate the author's projections.

Figure 10.18 Age and Trends in Poverty

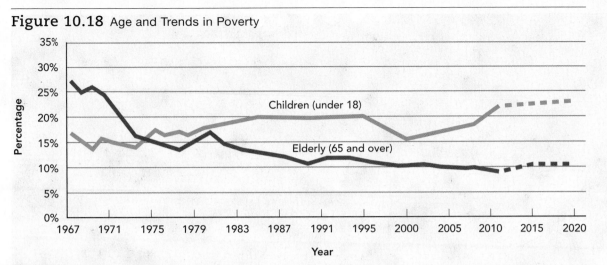

SOURCE: By the author. Based on *Statistical Abstract of the United States*, various years, and 2014:Table 741. Broken lines indicate the author's projections.

the welfare of children just as it did that of the elderly? Of course. But it chose not to. Why? *The elderly, not the children, launched a broad assault on Congress.* The elderly threatened to vote politicians out of office, and their lobbyists put a lot of grease in the political reelection machine. The children, in contrast, can't vote, and they didn't offer a payoff to the politicians.

Let's suppose that the country gets serious about reducing childhood poverty. Watch out for politicians saying that to improve the children's welfare we must take money from the elderly. What a choice: either pathetic children or suffering old folks. If you ever hear this, you will know it is a false choice. It will simply be politicians trying to manipulate your emotions.

From the quote that opened this section, you can see that intergenerational conflict has begun to heat up in Japan, where 23 percent of the population are elderly (Bennett-Smith 2013). Could it happen here? What do you think?

IN SUM   People of different ages (cohorts) are among society's many groups that are competing for scarce resources. As more demands are placed on these resources, the opposing interests of these groups will become more apparent.

Looking Toward the Future

10.11   Discuss developing views of aging and the impact of technology on how long people live.

Let's not lose sight of one of the major changes stressed in this chapter—that for the first time in human history, huge numbers of people are becoming elderly. It is inevitable that such a fundamental change will have a powerful impact on societies around the world, so much so that it might even transform them. We don't have space to explore such potential transformations, so let's try to catch a glimpse of what is happening with the elderly themselves.

Changing Views of Aging

The huge numbers of Americans moving into old age are changing our views of the elderly. The new views reject the idea that old age is "a-time-close-to-death," placing the emphasis on the elderly years as a time to be enjoyed, even celebrated. One view, called *creative aging*, stresses the unique opportunities that the elderly years provide to pursue

With longer lives, better health, and more resources, the elderly years are becoming a stage of life in which people explore and develop new dimensions of their selves. Shown here is the world's oldest hip hop group as they perform in Las Vegas.

interests, to develop creativity, and to enhance the appreciation of life's beauty and one's place in it.

This changing perspective is new, so we don't yet know the directions it will take. But if this emphasis continues, it will change how younger people view the elderly—as well as how the elderly view themselves. Stereotypes of despondent, disengaged old folks are already giving way to stereotypes of affluent, thriving, engaged older adults who are enjoying a life of leisure and the time to pursue personal interests. No stereotype will encompass the reality of the elderly years, of course, as the aged differ among themselves as much as younger people do.

There is also the matter of social class. Creative aging and the other more positive views apply mainly to the middle and upper classes. Those trapped in poverty often find old age to be a time of ill health and despair. This leaves us with a serious issue as a society: How can we increase health and the opportunity to enjoy life for all the elderly, no matter their social class?

Summary and Review

Gender and Age

10.1 Distinguish between sex and gender; use research on Vietnam veterans and testosterone to explain why the door to biology is opening in sociology.

What is gender stratification?

The term **gender stratification** refers to unequal access to property, power, and prestige on the basis of sex. Each

society establishes a structure that, on the basis of sex and gender, opens and closes doors to its privileges.

How do sex and gender differ?

Sex refers to biological distinctions between males and females. It consists of both primary and secondary sex characteristics. **Gender**, in contrast, is what a society considers proper behaviors and attitudes for its male and female members. *Sex* physically distinguishes males from females; *gender* refers to what people call "masculine" and "feminine."

Why do the behaviors of males and females differ?

The "nature versus nurture" debate refers to whether differences in the behaviors of males and females are caused by inherited (biological) or learned (cultural) characteristics. Almost all sociologists take the side of nurture. In recent years, however, sociologists have begun to cautiously open the door to biology.

Gender Inequality in Global Perspective

10.2 Discuss the origin of gender discrimination and review global aspects of violence against women.

How did females become a minority group?

Patriarchy, or male dominance, appears to be universal. The origin of discrimination against females is lost in history, but the primary theory of how females became a minority group in their own societies focuses on the physical limitations imposed by childbirth.

What are some forms of global violence against females?

The major forms discussed are honor killing and female circumcision.

Gender Inequality in the United States

10.3 Review the rise of feminism and summarize gender inequality in health care and education.

Is the feminist movement new?

In what is called the "first wave," feminists made political demands for change in the early 1900s—and were met with hostility and even violence. The "second wave" began in the 1960s and continues today. A "third wave" has emerged.

What forms do gender inequality in health care and education take?

Physicians don't take women's health complaints as seriously as those of men, and they exploit women's fears, performing unnecessary hysterectomies. More women than men attend college, and there is a tendency to select fields that are categorized as "feminine" or "masculine."

10.4 Explain reasons for the pay gap; discuss the glass ceiling and sexual harassment.

How does gender inequality show up in the workplace?

All occupations show a gender gap in pay. For college graduates, the lifetime pay gap runs over a million dollars in favor of men. Women often confront a **glass ceiling**. **Sexual harassment** also continues to be a reality of the workplace.

10.5 Summarize violence against women: rape, murder, and violence in the home.

What is the relationship between gender and violence?

Overwhelmingly, the victims of rape, murder, and spouse abuse are females. Conflict theorists point out that men use violence to maintain their power and privilege.

10.6 Discuss changes in gender and politics.

What is the trend in gender inequality in politics?

Women continue to be underrepresented in politics, but the trend toward greater political equality is firmly in place.

Aging in Global Perspective

10.7 Understand how attitudes toward the elderly vary around the world; explain how industrialization led to a graying globe.

How are the elderly treated around the world, and why are there more elderly?

There is no single set of attitudes, beliefs, or policies regarding the aged. Rather, they vary around the world, ranging from exclusion and killing to integration and honor. Industrialization, bringing more resources, has created a global trend for more people to live longer.

The Symbolic Interactionist Perspective

10.8 Discuss changes in perceptions of the elderly.

What does the social construction of aging mean?

Nothing in the nature of aging produces any particular set of attitudes. Rather, attitudes toward the elderly are rooted in society and differ from one social group to another.

The Functionalist Perspective

10.9 Summarize theories of disengagement, activity, and continuity.

How is retirement functional for society?

Functionalists focus on how the withdrawal of the elderly from positions of responsibility benefits society. **Disengagement theory** examines retirement as a device for ensuring that a society's positions of responsibility will be passed smoothly from one generation to the next. **Activity theory** examines how people adjust when they retire. **Continuity theory** focuses on how people adjust to growing old by maintaining their roles and coping techniques.

The Conflict Perspective

10.10 Explain the conflict perspective on Social Security and discuss intergenerational competition and conflict.

Is there conflict among different age groups?

Social Security legislation is an example of one generation making demands on another generation for limited resources. As the number of retired people grows, there are relatively fewer workers to support them.

Looking Toward the Future

10.11 Discuss developing views of aging and the impact of technology on how long people live.

What trends indicate the future for gender and aging?

The trends are positive: Increasing equality and political participation for women and, for the elderly, longer lives, less poverty, and the development of creative aging.

Thinking Critically about Chapter 10

1. What is your position on the "nature versus nurture" (biology or culture) debate? What materials in this chapter support your position?

2. Why do you think that the gender gap in pay exists all over the world?

3. How does culture influence our ideas about the elderly?

4. How can we solve the problem of caring for the elderly and not burdening future generations?

Chapter 11
Politics and the Economy

In 1949, George Orwell wrote *1984*, a book about a time in the future when a government known as "Big Brother" spies on everyone and dictates almost every aspect of each individual's life. Even loving someone is considered sinister—a betrayal of the supreme love and total allegiance that all citizens owe Big Brother.

Despite the danger, Winston and Julia fall in love. They delight in each other, but they must meet furtively, always with the threat of discovery hanging over their heads. When informers turn them in, interrogators separate Julia and Winston and try to destroy their affection and restore their loyalty to Big Brother.

Winston's tormentor is O'Brien, who straps Winston into a chair so tightly that he can't even move his head. O'Brien explains that inflicting pain is not always enough to break a person's will, but everyone has a breaking point. There is some worst fear that will push anyone over the edge.

O'Brien tells Winston that he has discovered his worst fear. Then he sets a cage with two starving giant sewer rats on the table next to Winston. O'Brien picks up a hood connected

Even loving someone is considered sinister—a betrayal of the supreme love and total allegiance that all citizens owe Big Brother.

to the door of the cage and places it over Winston's head. He then explains that when he presses the lever, the door of the cage will slide up, and the rats will shoot out like bullets and bore straight into Winston's face. Winston's eyes, the only part of his body that he can move, dart back and forth, revealing his terror. Speaking so quietly that Winston has to strain to hear him, O'Brien adds that the rats sometimes attack the eyes first, but sometimes they burrow through the cheeks and devour the tongue. When O'Brien places his hand on the lever, Winston realizes that the only way out is for someone else to take his place. But who? Then he hears his own voice screaming, "Do it to Julia! . . . Tear her face off. Strip her to the bones. Not me! Julia! Not me!"

Orwell does not describe Julia's interrogation, but when Julia and Winston see each other later, they realize that each has betrayed the other. Their love is gone. Big Brother has won.

Winston and Julia's misplaced loyalty had made them political heretics, a danger to the state. Every citizen had the duty to place the state above all else in life, pledging love and loyalty to an individual was a threat to the state's dominance. Their allegiance to one another had to be stripped from them. As you see, it was.

■ Politics: Establishing and Exercising Leadership

Although seldom as dramatic as the interrogations of Winston and Julia, **politics** is always about power and authority. Let's explore this topic that is so significant for our lives.

politics

the exercise of power, leadership, influence, and authority

Power, Authority, and Violence

11.1 Contrast power, authority, and violence; compare traditional, rational–legal, and charismatic authority.

To exist, every society must have a system of leadership. Some people must have **power** over others. As Weber (1913/1947) pointed out, we perceive power as either legitimate or illegitimate. *Legitimate* power is called **authority**. This is power that people accept as right. In contrast, *illegitimate* power—called **coercion**—is power that people do not accept as just.

power

the ability to carry out your will, even over the resistance of others

authority

power that people consider legitimate, as rightly exercised over them; also called *legitimate power*

> *Imagine that you are on your way to buy the hot new cell phone that is on sale for $250. As you approach the store, a man jumps out of an alley and shoves a gun in your face. He demands your money. Frightened for your life, you hand over your $250. After filing a police report, you head back to college to take a sociology exam. You are running late, so you step on the gas. As you hit 85, you see flashing blue and red lights in your rearview mirror. Your explanation about being robbed doesn't faze the officer—or the judge who hears your case a few weeks later. She first lectures you on safety and then orders you to pay $50 in court costs plus $10 for every mile over 65. You pay the $250.*

coercion

power that people do not accept as rightly exercised over them; also called *illegitimate power*

The mugger, the police officer, and the judge—all have power, and in each case you part with $250. What, then, is the difference? The difference is that the mugger has no authority. His power is *illegitimate*—he has no *right* to do what he did. In contrast, you acknowledge that the officer has the right to stop you and that the judge has the right to fine you. They have authority, or *legitimate* power.

state

a political entity that claims monopoly on the use of violence in some particular territory; commonly known as a country

Authority and Legitimate Violence

As sociologist Peter Berger observed, it makes little difference whether you willingly pay the fine that the judge levies against you or refuse to pay it. The court will get its money one way or another.

traditional authority

authority based on custom

rational–legal authority

authority based on law or written rules and regulations; also called *bureaucratic authority*

> *There may be innumerable steps before its application [of violence], in the way of warnings and reprimands. But if all the warnings are disregarded, even in so slight a matter*

The ultimate foundation of any political order is violence, no more starkly demonstrated than when a government takes a human life. This iconic photo from the war in Vietnam shows the chief of the national police shooting a suspected Viet Cong officer.

as paying a traffic ticket, the last thing that will happen is that a couple of cops show up at the door with handcuffs and a Black Maria [paddy wagon]. Even the moderately courteous cop who hands out the initial traffic ticket is likely to wear a gun—just in case. (Berger 1963)

The *government*, then, also called the **state**, claims a monopoly on legitimate force or violence. This point, made by Max Weber (1946, 1922/1978)—that the state claims both the exclusive right to use violence and the right to punish everyone else who uses violence—is crucial to our understanding of politics. If someone owes you $100, you cannot take the money by force, much less imprison that person. The state, in contrast, can. The ultimate proof of the state's authority is that you cannot kill someone because he or she has done something that you consider absolutely horrible—but the state can. As Berger (1963) summarized this matter, "*Violence is the ultimate foundation of any political order.*"

But just why do people accept power as legitimate? Max Weber (1922/1978) identified three sources of authority: traditional, rational–legal, and charismatic. Let's examine each.

Traditional Authority

Throughout history, the most common basis for authority has been tradition. **Traditional authority**, which is based on custom, is the hallmark of tribal groups. In these societies, custom dictates basic relationships. For example, birth into a particular family makes an individual the chief, king, or queen. As far as members of that society are concerned, this is the right way to determine who rules because "We've always done it this way."

Although traditional authority declines with industrialization, it never dies out. Even though we live in a postindustrial society, parents continue to exercise authority over their children *because* parents always have had such authority. From generations past, we inherit the idea that parents should discipline their children, choose their doctors and schools, and teach them religion and morality.

Rational–Legal Authority

The second type of authority, **rational–legal authority**, is based not on custom but on written rules. *Rational* means reasonable, and *legal* means part of law. Thus, *rational–legal* refers to matters that have been agreed to by reasonable people and written into law (or regulations of some sort). The matters that are agreed to may be as broad as a

For centuries, widows in the Mediterranean countries, such as this widow in Italy, were expected to dress in black and to mourn for their husbands the rest of their lives. Widows conformed to this expression of lifetime sorrow not because of law, but because of custom. As industrialization erodes traditional authority, fewer widows follow this practice.

constitution that specifies the rights of all members of a society or as narrow as a contract between two individuals. Because bureaucracies are based on written rules, rational–legal authority is also called *bureaucratic authority*.

Rational–legal authority comes from the *position* that someone holds, not from the person who holds that position. In the United States, for example, the president's authority comes from the legal power assigned to that office, as specified in a written constitution, not from custom or the individual's personal characteristics. In rational–legal authority, everyone—no matter how high the office—is subject to the organization's written rules. In governments based on traditional authority, the ruler's word may be law; but in those based on rational–legal authority, the ruler's word is subject to the law.

Charismatic Authority

A few centuries back, in 1429, the English controlled large parts of France. When they prevented the coronation of a new French king, a farmer's daughter heard a voice telling her that God had a special assignment for her—that she should put on men's clothing, recruit an army, and go to war against the English. Inspired, Joan of Arc raised an army, conquered cities, and defeated the English. Later that year, her visions were fulfilled as she stood next to Charles VII while he was crowned king of France. (Bridgwater 1953)

Joan of Arc is an example of **charismatic authority**, the third type of authority Weber identified. (*Charisma* is a Greek word that means a gift freely and graciously given [Arndt and Gingrich 1957].) People are drawn to a charismatic individual because they believe that individual has been touched by God or has been endowed by nature with exceptional qualities (Lipset 1993). The armies did not follow Joan of Arc because it was the custom to do so, as in traditional authority. Nor did they risk their lives fighting alongside her because she held a position defined by written rules, as in rational–legal authority. Instead, people followed her because they were attracted by her outstanding traits. They saw her as a messenger of God, fighting on the side of justice, and they accepted her leadership because of these appealing qualities.

charismatic authority
authority based on an individual's outstanding traits, which attract followers

One of the best examples of charismatic authority is Joan of Arc, a teenager who changed the history of France. In this painting from 1900s, she is shown leading the French army in a battle against the British.

THE THREAT POSED BY CHARISMATIC LEADERS Kings and queens owe allegiance to tradition, and presidents to written laws. To what, however, do charismatic leaders owe allegiance? Their authority resides in their ability to attract followers, which is often based on their sense of a special mission or calling. Not tied to tradition or the regulation of law, charismatic leaders pose a threat to the established political order. Following their personal goals, charismatic leaders can inspire followers to disregard—or even to overthrow—traditional and rational–legal authorities.

This threat does not go unnoticed, and traditional and rational–legal authorities often oppose charismatic leaders. If they are not careful, however, their opposition can arouse even more positive sentiment in favor of the charismatic leader, who might be viewed as an underdog persecuted by the powerful. Occasionally, the Roman Catholic Church faces such a threat, as when a priest claims miraculous powers that appear to be accompanied by amazing healings. As people flock to this individual, they bypass parish priests and the formal ecclesiastical structure. This transfer of allegiance from the organization to an individual threatens the church hierarchy. Consequently, church officials may encourage the priest to withdraw from the public eye, perhaps to a monastery, to rethink matters. This defuses the threat, reasserts rational–legal authority, and maintains the stability of the organization.

The Transfer of Authority

The orderly transfer of authority from one leader to another is crucial for social stability. Under traditional authority, people know who is next in

Charismatic authorities can be of any morality, from the saintly to the most bitterly evil. Like Joan of Arc, Adolf Hitler attracted throngs of people, providing the stuff of dreams and arousing them from disillusionment to hope. This poster from the 1930s, titled *Es Lebe Deutschland* ("Long Live Germany"), illustrates the qualities of leadership that Germans of that period saw in Hitler.

routinization of charisma

the transfer of authority from a charismatic figure to either a traditional or a rational–legal form of authority

city-state

an independent city whose power radiates outward, bringing the adjacent area under its rule

monarchy

a form of government headed by a king or queen

line. Under rational–legal authority, people might not know who the next leader will be, but they do know how that person will be selected. South Africa provides a remarkable example of the orderly transfer of authority under a rational–legal organization. This country had been ripped apart by decades of racial–ethnic strife, including horrible killings committed by each side. Yet, by maintaining its rational–legal authority, the country was able to transfer power peacefully from the dominant group led by President de Klerk to the minority group led by Nelson Mandela.

Charismatic authority has no rules of succession, making it less stable than either traditional or rational–legal authority. Because charismatic authority is built around a single individual, the death or incapacitation of a charismatic leader can mean a bitter struggle for succession. To avoid this, some charismatic leaders make arrangements for an orderly transition of power by appointing a successor. This step does not guarantee orderly succession, since the followers may not share the leader's confidence in the designated heir. A second strategy is for the charismatic leader to build an organization. As the organization develops rules or regulations, it transforms itself into a rational–legal organization. Weber used the term **routinization of charisma** to refer to the transition of authority from a charismatic leader to either traditional or rational–legal authority.

The transfer of authority in Cuba after Fidel Castro became ill is a remarkable example. Castro was a charismatic leader, attracting enough followers to overthrow Cuba's government. He ruled through a combination of personal charisma and bureaucratic machinery. Castro set up an organized system to transfer authority to his noncharismatic brother, Raul, who, in turn, made certain that authority was transferred in an orderly manner to the state bureaucracies (Hoffman 2011).

Types of Government

11.2 Compare monarchies, democracies, dictatorships, and oligarchies.

How do the various types of government—monarchies, democracies, dictatorships, and oligarchies—differ? As we compare them, let's also look at how the state arose and why the concept of citizenship was revolutionary.

Monarchies: The Rise of the State

Early societies were small and needed no extensive political system. They operated more like an extended family. As surpluses developed and societies grew larger, cities evolved—perhaps around 3500 b.c. (Ur 2010). **City-states** then came into being, with power radiating outward from the city like a spider's web. Although the ruler of each city controlled the immediate surrounding area, the land between cities remained in dispute. Each city-state had its own **monarchy**, a king or queen whose right to rule was passed on to the monarch's children. If you drive through Spain, France, or Germany, you can still see evidence of former city-states. In the countryside, you will see only scattered villages. Farther on, your eye will be drawn to the outline of a castle on a faraway hill. As you get closer, you will see that the castle is surrounded by a city. Several miles farther, you will see another city, also dominated by a castle. Each city, with its castle, was once a center of power.

City-states often quarreled, and wars were common. The victors extended their rule, and eventually a single city-state was able to wield power over an entire region. As the size of these regions grew, the people slowly began to identify with the larger region. That is, they began to see distant inhabitants as "we" instead of "they." What we call the *state*—the political entity that claims a monopoly on the use of violence within a territory—came into being.

Democracies: Citizenship as a Revolutionary Idea

The United States had no city-states. Each colony, however, was small and independent like a city-state. After the American Revolution, the colonies united. With the greater strength and resources that came from political unity, they conquered almost all of North America, bringing it under the power of a central government.

The government formed in this new country was called a **democracy** (derived from two Greek words—*demos* [common people] and *kratos* [power]—democracy literally means "power to the people"). Because of the bitter antagonisms associated with the revolution against the British king, the founders of the new country were distrustful of monarchies. They wanted to put political decisions into the hands of the people.

This was not the first democracy the world had seen, but such a system had been tried before only with smaller groups. Athens, a city-state of Greece, practiced democracy 2,500 years ago, with each free male above a certain age having the right to be heard and to vote. Members of some Native American tribes, such as the Iroquois, also elected their chiefs, and, in some, women were able to vote and to hold the office of chief. (The Incas and Aztecs of Mexico and Central America had monarchies.)

Because of their small size, tribes and cities were able to practice **direct democracy**. That is, they were small enough for the eligible voters to meet together, express their opinions, and then vote publicly—much like a town hall meeting today. As populous

democracy

a government whose authority comes from the people; the term, based on two Greek words, translates literally as "power to the people"

direct democracy

a form of democracy in which the eligible voters meet together to discuss issues and make their decisions

This classic painting, "Siege at Yorktown" by Louis Coulder, depicts George Washington and Jean de Rochambeau giving the final orders for the attack on Yorktown in 1781. This turned out to be the decisive battle of the American Revolution, allowing the fledgling U.S. democracy to proceed.

Democracy (or "democratization") is a global social movement. People all over the world yearn for the freedoms that are taken for granted in the Western democracies. Shown here is a tribal leader voting in the Philippines.

representative democracy

a form of democracy in which voters elect representatives to meet together to discuss issues and make decisions on their behalf

citizenship

the concept that birth (and residence or naturalization) in a country imparts basic rights

universal citizenship

the idea that everyone has the same basic rights by virtue of being born in a country (or by immigrating and becoming a naturalized citizen)

dictatorship

a form of government in which an individual has seized power

oligarchy

a form of government in which a small group of individuals holds power; the rule of the many by the few

totalitarianism

a form of government that exerts almost total control over people

and spread out as the United States was, however, direct democracy was impossible, and the founders invented **representative democracy**. Certain citizens (at first only white men who owned property) voted for other white men who owned property to represent them. Later, the vote was extended to men who didn't own property, then to African American men, and, finally, to women.

Today we take the concept of citizenship for granted. What is not evident to us is that this idea had to be envisioned in the first place. There is nothing natural about citizenship; it is simply one way in which people choose to define themselves. Throughout most of human history, people were thought to *belong* to a clan, to a tribe, or even to a ruler. The idea of **citizenship**—that by virtue of birth and residence, people have basic rights—is quite new to the human scene.

The concept of representative democracy based on citizenship— perhaps the greatest gift the United States has given to the world—was revolutionary. Power was to be vested in the people themselves, and government was to flow from the people. That this concept was revolutionary is generally forgotten, but its implementation meant *the reversal of traditional ideas. It made the government responsive to the people's will, rather than the people being responsive to the government's will*. To keep the government responsive to the needs of its citizens, people were expected to express dissent. In a widely quoted statement, Thomas Jefferson observed:

> *A little rebellion now and then is a good thing. . . . It is a medicine necessary for the sound health of government. . . . God forbid that we should ever be twenty years without such a rebellion. . . . The tree of liberty must be refreshed from time to time with the blood of patriots and tyrants. (In Hellinger and Judd 1991)*

The idea of **universal citizenship**—of *everyone* having the same basic rights by virtue of being born in a country (or by immigrating and becoming a naturalized citizen)— flowered slowly and came into practice only through fierce struggle. When the United States was founded, for example, this idea was still in its infancy. Today, it seems inconceivable to Americans that sex or race–ethnicity should be the basis for denying anyone the right to vote, hold office, make a contract, testify in court, or own property. For earlier generations of property-owning white American men, however, it seemed just as inconceivable that women, racial–ethnic minorities, and the poor should be *allowed* such rights.

Dictatorships and Oligarchies: The Seizure of Power

If an individual seizes power and then dictates his or her will to the people, the government is known as a **dictatorship**. If a small group seizes power, the government is called an **oligarchy**. The occasional coups in Central and South America and Africa, in which military leaders seize control of a country, are often oligarchies. Although one individual may be named president, often it is military officers, working behind the scenes, who make the decisions. If their designated president becomes uncooperative, they remove that person from office and appoint another.

Monarchies, dictatorships, and oligarchies vary in the amount of control they wield. **Totalitarianism** is almost *total* control of a people by the government. In Nazi Germany, Hitler organized a ruthless secret police force, the Gestapo, which searched for any sign of dissent. Spies even watched how moviegoers reacted to newsreels, reporting those who did not respond "appropriately" (Hippler 1987). Saddam Hussein acted just as ruthlessly toward Iraqis. The lucky ones who opposed Hussein were shot; the unlucky ones had their eyes gouged out, were bled to death, or were buried alive (Amnesty International 2005). We have not come to the end of totalitarianism. As I write this, an organization calling itself Islamic State (ISIS) is beheading men and turning girls and women into sex slaves.

People around the world find great appeal in the freedom that is inherent in citizenship and representative democracy. Those who have no say in their government's decisions, or who face prison, torture, or death for expressing dissent, find in these ideas the hope for a brighter future. With today's electronic communications, people no longer remain ignorant of whether they are more or less politically privileged than others. This knowledge produces pressure for greater citizen participation in government—and for governments to respond to their citizens' concerns. The communist rulers of China are sensitive to online communications and will sometimes change course if they sense strong sentiment in some direction (Areddy 2012). As electronic communications develop further, this pressure will increase.

The U.S. Political System

11.3 **Discuss voting patterns, lobbyists, and PACs.**

With this global background, let's turn to the U.S. political system. We shall consider the two major political parties, examine voting patterns, and evaluate the role of lobbyists and PACs.

Political Parties and Elections

After the founding of the United States, numerous political parties emerged. By the time of the Civil War, however, two parties dominated U.S. politics: the Democrats and the Republicans (Burnham 1983). Each party draws from all social classes, but the working class leans toward the Democrats and wealthier people toward the Republicans. In pre-elections, called *primaries*, the voters decide who will represent their party. The candidates chosen by each party then campaign, trying to appeal to the most voters. The Social Map below shows how Americans align themselves with political parties.

Figure 11.1 Which Political Party Dominates?

SOURCE: By the author. Based on *Book of the States* 2014:Table 3.3.

NOTE: Domination by a political party does not refer to votes for president or Congress. This social map is based on the composition of the states' upper and lower houses. When different parties dominate a state's houses, the total number of legislators was used. In Nebraska, where no parties are designated, the percentage vote for president was the determining factor.

Although the Democrats and the Republicans represent slightly different slices of the center, those differences arouse extreme emotions, pandered to by both parties.

SLICES FROM THE CENTER Although the Democrats and Republicans have somewhat contrasting philosophical principles, each party represents *slightly different slices of the center*. Each party may ridicule the other and promote different legislation—and they do fight hard battles—but they both firmly support such fundamentals of U.S. political philosophy as free public education; a strong military; freedom of religion, speech, and assembly; and, of course, capitalism—especially the private ownership of property. This makes it difficult to distinguish a conservative Democrat from a liberal Republican.

The extremes are easy to see, however. Deeply committed Democrats support legislation that transfers income from those who are richer to those who are poorer or that controls wages, working conditions, and competition. Deeply committed Republicans, in contrast, oppose such legislation.

Those who are elected to Congress may cross party lines. That is, some Democrats vote for legislation proposed by Republicans, and vice versa. This happens because office-holders support their party's philosophy but not necessarily its specific proposals. When it comes to a particular bill, such as raising the minimum wage, some conservative Democrats may view the measure as unfair to small employers and vote with the Republicans against the bill. At the same time, liberal Republicans—feeling that the proposal is just or sensing a dominant sentiment in voters back home—may side with its Democratic backers.

THIRD PARTIES Third parties sometimes play a role in U.S. politics, but, to gain power, they must also support these centrist themes. Any party that advocates radical change is doomed to a short life. Because most Americans consider votes for third parties as wasted, they do not do well at the polls. Two exceptions are the Bull Moose party, whose candidate, Theodore Roosevelt, won more votes in 1912 than William Howard Taft, the Republican presidential candidate, and the United We Stand (Reform) party, founded by billionaire Ross Perot, which won 19 percent of the vote in 1992. Amid internal bickering, the Reform Party declined rapidly and fell off the political map (Bridgwater 1953; *Statistical Abstract* 1995:Table 437; 2014:Table 422).

Voting Patterns

Year after year, Americans show consistent voting patterns. From Table 11.1 on the next page, you can see how the percentage of people who vote increases with age. This table also shows how significant race–ethnicity is. Although non-Hispanic whites are more likely to vote than are African Americans, when Barack Obama ran for president, African Americans voted at higher rates than whites. You can also see that both whites and African Americans are much more likely to vote than are Latinos and Asian Americans.

Look at education on Table 11.1 on the next page. Notice how voting increases with each level of education. Education is so significant that college graduates are more than twice as likely to vote as are high school dropouts. You can also see

Table 11.1 Who Votes for President?

	1988	1992	1996	2000	2004	2008	2012
Overall							
Americans Who Voted	57%	61%	54%	55%	58%	58%	57%
Age							
18–20	33%	39%	31%	28%	41%	41%	35%
21–24	46%	46%	33%	35%	43%	47%	40%
25–34	48%	53%	43%	44%	47%	49%	46%
35–44	61%	64%	55%	55%	57%	55%	53%
45–64	68%	70%	64%	64%	67%	65%	63%
65 and older	69%	70%	67%	68%	69%	68%	70%
Sex							
Male	56%	60%	53%	53%	56%	56%	54%
Female	58%	62%	56%	56%	60%	60%	59%
Race–Ethnicity							
Whites	64%	70%	56%	56%	60%	60%	58%
African Americans	55%	59%	51%	54%	56%	61%	62%
Asian Americans	NA	54%	NA	25%	30%	32%	31%
Latinos	48%	52%	27%	28%	28%	32%	32%
Education							
Some high school	41%	41%	34%	34%	35%	34%	32%
High school graduates	55%	58%	49%	49%	52%	51%	49%
Some college	65%	69%	61%	60%	66%	65%	62%
College graduates	78%	81%	73%	72%	74%	73%	72%
Marital Status							
Married	NA	NA	66%	67%	71%	70%	63%
Divorced	NA	NA	50%	53%	58%	59%	56%
Labor Force							
Employed	58%	64%	55%	56%	60%	60%	59%
Unemployed	39%	46%	37%	35%	46%	49%	46%
Income[1]							
Under $20,000	NA	NA	NA	NA	48%	52%	48%
$20,000 to $30,000	NA	NA	NA	NA	58%	56%	56%
$30,000 to $40,000	NA	NA	NA	NA	62%	62%	58%
$40,000 to $50,000	NA	NA	NA	NA	69%	65%	63%
$50,000 to $75,000	NA	NA	NA	NA	72%	71%	68%
$75,000 to $100,000	NA	NA	NA	NA	78%	76%	74%
Over $100,000	NA	NA	NA	NA	81%	92%	79%

[1]The primary source changed the income categories in 2004, making the data from earlier presidential election years incompatible.

SOURCES: By the author. Based on Casper and Bass 1998; Jamieson et al. 2002; Holder 2006; *Current Population Survey*: Voting and Registration Supplement, 2012; *Statistical Abstract of the United States* 1991:Table 450; 1997:Table 462; 2014:Table 418.

how much more likely the employed are to vote. And look at how powerful income and age are in determining voting. At each higher level, people are more likely to vote. Finally, note that women are more likely than men to vote.

SOCIAL INTEGRATION   How can we explain these voting patterns? It is useful to look at the extremes. You can see from this table that those who are most likely to vote are the older, more educated, affluent, and employed. Those who are least likely to vote are the younger, less educated, poor, and unemployed. From these extremes, we can draw this principle: The more that people feel they have a stake in the political system, the more likely they are to vote. They have more to protect, and they feel that voting can make a difference. In effect, people who have been rewarded more by the political and economic system feel more socially integrated. They vote because they perceive that elections make a difference in their lives, including the type of society in which they and their children live.

ALIENATION In contrast, those who gain less from the system—in terms of education, income, and jobs—are more likely to feel alienated from politics. Perceiving themselves as outsiders, many feel hostile toward the government. Some feel betrayed, believing that politicians have sold out to special-interest groups. They ask, "How can you tell when politicians are lying?" and reply, "When you see their lips moving."

voter apathy

indifference and inaction on the part of individuals or groups with respect to the political process

APATHY But we must go beyond this. From Table 11.1, you can see that many highly educated people with good incomes also stay away from the polls. They are not alienated, but many do not vote because of **voter apathy**, or indifference. Their view is that "next year will just bring more of the same, regardless of who is in office." A common attitude of those who are apathetic is "What difference will my one vote make when there are millions of voters?" Many also see little difference between the two major political parties. Only about *half* of the nation's eligible voters cast ballots in presidential elections (*Statistical Abstract* 2014:Table 417).

THE GENDER AND RACIAL–ETHNIC GAPS IN VOTING Historically, men and women voted the same way, but now we have a *political gender gap*. That is, men and women are somewhat more likely to vote for different presidential candidates. As you can see from Table 11.2 below, men are more likely to favor the Republican candidate, while women are more likely to vote Democratic. This table also illustrates the much larger racial–ethnic gap in politics. Note how few African Americans vote for a Republican presidential candidate.

You can use Table 11.1 to help explain Table 11.2. You just saw that voting patterns reflect life experiences, especially people's economic conditions. On average, women earn less than men, and African Americans earn less than whites. As a result, at this point

Table 11.2 How the Two-Party Presidential Vote Is Split

	1988	1992	1996	2000	2004	2008	2012
Women							
Democrat	50%	61%	65%	56%	53%	57%	55%
Republican	50%	39%	35%	44%	47%	43%	44%
Men							
Democrat	44%	55%	51%	47%	46%	52%	45%
Republican	56%	45%	49%	53%	54%	48%	52%
African Americans							
Democrat	92%	94%	99%	92%	90%	99%	93%
Republican	8%	6%	1%	8%	10%	1%	6%
Whites							
Democrat	41%	53%	54%	46%	42%	44%	39%
Republican	59%	47%	46%	54%	58%	56%	59%
Latinos							
Democrat	NA	NA	NA	61%	58%	66%	71%
Republican	NA	NA	NA	39%	42%	34%	27%
Asian Americans							
Democrat	NA	NA	NA	62%	77%	62%	73%
Republican	NA	NA	NA	38%	23%	38%	26%

SOURCES: By the author. Based on Gallup Poll 2008; *Statistical Abstract of the United States* 1999:Table 464; 2002:Table 372; 2014:Table 423; Roper Center 2013.

in history, women and African Americans tend to look more favorably on government programs that redistribute income, and they are more likely to vote for Democrats. As you can see in this table, Asian American voters, with their higher average incomes, are an exception to this pattern. Attempted explanations are far from satisfactory (Logan et al. 2012), but the reason could be a lesser emphasis on individualism in the Asian American subculture.

Lobbyists and Special-Interest Groups

Suppose that you are president of the United States, and you want to make milk more affordable for the poor. As you check into the matter, you find that part of the reason prices are high is because the government is paying farmers billions of dollars a year in price supports. You propose to eliminate these subsidies.

Immediately, large numbers of people leap into action. They contact their senators and representatives and hold news conferences. Your office is flooded with calls, faxes, and e-messages.

Reuters and the Associated Press distribute pictures of farm families—their Holsteins grazing contentedly in the background—and inform readers that your harsh proposal will destroy these hard-working, healthy, happy, good Americans who are struggling to make a living. President or not, you have little chance of getting your legislation passed.

LOBBYING BY SPECIAL-INTEREST GROUPS   What happened? The dairy industry went to work to protect its special interests. A **special-interest group** consists of people who think alike on a particular issue and can be mobilized for political action. The dairy industry is just one of thousands of such groups that employ **lobbyists**, people who are paid to influence legislation on behalf of their clients. Members of Congress must pay attention to lobbyists, since they represent voters who share an interest in some proposed legislation. Able to hand over huge chunks of money, lobbyists can deliver votes to you—or to your opponent.

Lobbying has opened a *revolving door*. Former assistants to the president or to powerful senators are sought after as lobbyists (Lipton and Protess 2014). With their contacts swinging open the doors to the money vault, some even go to work for the same companies they regulated when they worked for the president (Delaney 2010).

To try to reign in some of this influence peddling, Congress made it illegal for former senators to lobby for two years after they leave office. Yet senators do lobby immediately after leaving office. How do you suppose they dance around the law and spin through this revolving door? It's all in the name. They hire themselves out to lobbying firms as *strategic advisors*. They then lobby—excuse me, "strategically advise"—their former colleagues ("It's So Much Nicer . . ." 2008). And they laugh all the way to the bank.

THE MONEY   Buying votes is what especially bothers people. In response to publicity, Congress passed laws that limit the amount that corporations and individuals can give to candidates. To get around this law, special-interest groups form **political action committees (PACs)** to solicit contributions from many and then hand over huge sums to politicians. The amounts are mind-boggling. Each year, about 4,500 PACs shell out more than a half billion dollars to politicians (*Statistical Abstract* 2014:Tables 441, 442). A few PACs represent broad social interests such as environmental protection. Most, however, represent the financial interests of specific groups, such as the banking, dairy, defense, and oil industries.

special-interest group

a group of people who support a particular issue and who can be mobilized for political action

lobbyists

people who influence legislation on behalf of their clients

political action committee (PAC)

an organization formed by one or more special-interest groups to solicit and spend funds for the purpose of influencing legislation

In 2010, the Supreme Court opened the floodgates to bankrolling politicians. In *Citizens United v. Federal Election Commission*, the Court ruled that laws that limit the amount corporations can contribute to politicians violate the First Amendment, which guarantees the right to political speech (Liptak 2010). This has led to the creation of *Super PACS* that raise huge amounts for a single candidate (Kaplan 2014). At this point in the strange history of politics, corporations have more legal rights to fund candidates than individuals do.

Who Rules the United States?

11.4 Compare the functionalist (pluralist) and conflict (power elite) perspectives on U.S. power.

With lobbyists and PACs wielding such influence, just whom do U.S. senators and representatives really represent? This question has led to a lively debate among sociologists. Let's compare the functionalist and conflict perspectives.

The Functionalist Perspective: Pluralism

anarchy

a condition of lawlessness or political disorder caused by the absence or collapse of governmental authority

pluralism

the diffusion of power among many interest groups that prevents any single group from gaining control of the government

checks and balances

the separation of powers among the three branches of U.S. government—legislative, executive, and judicial—so that each is able to nullify the actions of the other two, thus preventing any single branch from dominating the government

Functionalists view the state as having arisen out of the basic needs of the social group. To protect themselves from oppressors, people formed a government and gave it the monopoly on violence. The risk is that the state can turn that force against its own citizens. To return to the example used earlier, states have a tendency to become muggers. Thus, people must find a balance between having no government—which would lead to **anarchy**, a condition of disorder and violence—and having a government that protects them from violence, but that also may turn against them. When functioning well, then, the state is a balanced system that protects its citizens both from one another *and* from government.

What keeps the U.S. government from turning against its citizens? Functionalists say that **pluralism**, a diffusion of power among many special-interest groups, prevents any one group from gaining control of the government and using it to oppress the people (Bentley 1908; Dahl 1961, 1982; Muniz-Fraticelli 2014). To keep the government from coming under the control of any one group, the founders of the United States set up three branches of government: the executive branch (the president), the judiciary branch (the courts), and the legislative branch (the Senate and House of Representatives). Each is sworn to uphold the Constitution, which guarantees rights to citizens, and each can nullify the actions of the other two. This system, known as **checks and balances**, was designed to ensure that no one branch of government dominates the others.

IN SUM Our pluralist society has many parts—women, men, racial–ethnic groups, farmers, factory and office workers, religious organizations, bankers, bosses, the unemployed, the retired—as well as such broad categories as the rich, middle class, and poor. As each group pursues its own interests, it is balanced by other groups that are pursuing theirs. To attain their goals, groups must make compromises and work together. Because these many groups have political muscle to flex at the polls, politicians try to design policies that please as many groups as they can. This, say functionalists, makes the political system responsive to the people, and no group dominates.

The Conflict Perspective: The Power Elite

If you focus on the lobbyists scurrying around Washington, conflict theorists stress, you get a blurred image of superficial activities. What really counts is the big picture, not its fragments. The important question is, Who holds the power that determines the country's overarching policies? For example, who determines interest rates and their impact on the price of our homes? Who sets policies that encourage the transfer of jobs from the United States to countries where labor costs less? And the ultimate question of power: Who is behind the decision to go to war?

Sociologist C. Wright Mills (1956) took the position that the country's most important matters are not decided by lobbyists or even by Congress. Rather, the decisions that have the greatest impact on the lives of Americans—and people across the globe—are made by a **power elite**. As depicted in Figure 11.2, the power elite consists of the top leaders of the largest corporations, the most powerful generals and admirals of the armed forces, and certain elite politicians—the president, the president's cabinet, and senior members of Congress who chair the major committees. It is they who wield power, who make the decisions that direct the country and shake the world.

Are the three groups that make up the power elite— the top business, political, and military leaders—equal in power? Mills said that they were not, but he didn't point to the president and his staff or even to the generals and admirals as the most powerful. Instead, he said that the corporate leaders are the most dominant. Because all three segments of the power elite view capitalism as essential to the welfare of the country, Mills said that business interests take center stage in setting national policy.

Sociologist William Domhoff (2010) uses the term **ruling class** to refer to the power elite. He focuses on the 1 percent of Americans who belong to the superrich, the powerful capitalist class analyzed in Chapter 8 (page 237). Members of this class control our top corporations and foundations, even the boards that oversee our major universities. It is no accident, says Domhoff, that from this group come most members of the president's cabinet and the ambassadors to the most powerful countries of the world.

power elite

C. Wright Mills' term for the top people in U.S. corporations, military, and politics who make the nation's major decisions

Figure 11.2 Power in the United States: The Model Proposed by C. Wright Mills

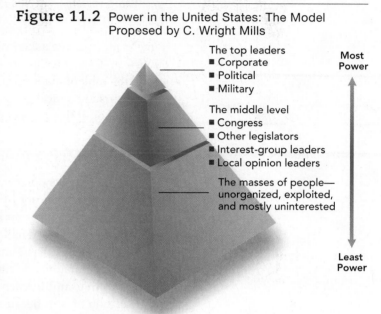

SOURCE: By the author. Based on Mills 1956.

ruling class

another term for the power elite

IN SUM Conflict theorists take the position that a *power elite* dominates the United States. With connections that extend to the highest centers of power, this ruling class determines the economic and political conditions under which the rest of the country operates. They say that we should not think of the power elite (or ruling class) as some secret group that meets to agree on specific matters. Rather, the group's unity springs from its members having similar backgrounds and orientations to life. They have attended prestigious private schools, belong to exclusive clubs, and are millionaires many times over. Their behavior stems not from some grand conspiracy to control the country but from a mutual interest in solving the problems that face big business.

Which View Is Right?

The functionalist and conflict views of power in U.S. society cannot be reconciled. Either competing interests block any single group from being dominant, as functionalists assert, or a power elite oversees the major decisions of the United States, as conflict theorists maintain. After years of rancorous arguments by proponents of each view, researchers seem to have come up with the answer. Political scientists Martin Gilens and Benjamin Page (2014) reviewed 1,800 policy decisions made by the U.S. government. The evidence overwhelmingly indicates that the wealthy and business groups are the major influence in U.S. policy.

Because this is such significant research, it is certain that other researchers will retest the Gilens-Page data to see if there are flaws in their data or conclusions.

War and Terrorism: Implementing Political Objectives

11.5   Explain why countries go to war and why some groups choose terrorism; discuss targeted killings.

"War is merely a continuation of politics by other means."

Carl von Clausewitz, 1918

Some students have asked why I include war and terrorism as topics of politics. The quote from Carl von Clausewitz, who entered the Prussian military at the age of 12 and rose to the rank of major-general, gives the succinct answer. War and terrorism are tools used to pursue political goals.

Let's look at this aspect of politics.

Why Countries Go to War

Why do countries choose war as a means to handle disputes? As usual, sociologists answer this question not by focusing on factors *within* humans, such as aggressive impulses, but by looking for *social* causes—conditions in society that encourage or discourage combat between nations.

Sociologist Nicholas Timasheff (1965) identified three essential conditions for war. The *first* is an antagonistic situation in which two or more states confront incompatible objectives. For example, each may want the same land or resources. The *second* is a cultural tradition of war. Because their nation has fought wars in the past, the leaders of a group see war as an option for dealing with serious disputes with other nations. The *third* is a "fuel" that heats the antagonistic situation to a boiling point, so that politicians cross the line from thinking about war to actually waging it.

Timasheff identified seven such "fuels." He found that war is likely if a country's leaders see the antagonistic situation as an opportunity to achieve one or more of these objectives:

1. *Power*: dominating a weaker nation
2. *Unity*: uniting rival groups within their country
3. *Revenge*: settling "old scores" from earlier conflicts
4. *Prestige*: defending the nation's "honor"
5. *Leaders*: protecting or exalting the leaders' positions
6. *Ethnicity*: bringing under their rule "our people" who are living in another country
7. *Beliefs*: converting others to religious or political beliefs

You can use these three essential conditions and seven fuels to analyze any war. They will help you understand why politicians at that time chose this political action.

THE FLESH AND BLOOD OF WAR   Sociological analysis can be cold and dispassionate. These "fuels" of war are like this: accurate and insightful, but cold. Throughout this book, I've tried to bring you the flesh and blood of topics, to help you see the ways that people experience life. So let's do this again.

Behind these "fuels" are politicians who make the bloody choice to go to war. They do not fight the war themselves, of course. They sit back and watch it from the comfort of their homes and offices. Some even profit from the war by making investments in companies that produce weapons. For most politicians, the deaths are bloodless affairs. It is young men, and increasingly young women, who do the killing—and dying—for them. Some soldiers are killed on the battlefield; others survive but are mutilated for the rest of

Few want to say that we honor war and killing, but we do. Its centrality in the teaching of history and the honoring of the patriots who founded a country are two indications. A third is the display of past weapons in parks and museums. A fourth is the monuments that commemorate wars and battles. In this photo from Papua New Guinea, you can see the next generation being primed for warfare.

their lives. Many who survive with their body intact suffer emotionally. Some of my students have shared their suffering with me, but let me close this section with one of the most powerful statements I have come across. A soldier from California wrote this just before he put a bullet through his brain (Smith 1980):

> I can't sleep anymore. When I was in Vietnam, we came across a North Vietnamese soldier with a man, a woman, and a three- or four-year-old girl. We had to shoot them all. I can't get the little girl's face out of my mind. I hope that God will forgive me . . . I can't.

A boy soldier in Liberia.

Terrorism

> *Mustafa Jabbar, in Najaf, Iraq, is proud of his firstborn, a baby boy. Yet he said, "I will put mines in the baby and blow him up." (Sengupta 2004)*

Can feelings really run so deep that a father would sacrifice his only son? Some groups nourish hatred, endlessly chronicling the injustices and atrocities of their archenemy. Stirred in a cauldron of bitter hatred, antagonism can span generations, its embers sometimes burning for centuries. The combination of perceived injustice and righteous hatred fuels the desire to strike out—but what can a group do if it is weaker than its enemy? Unable to meet its more powerful opponent on the battlefield, one option is **terrorism**, violence intended to create fear in order to bring about political objectives. And, yes, if the hatred is strong enough, this can mean blowing up your only child.

Suicide terrorism, a weapon sometimes chosen by the weaker group, captures headlines around the world. Among the groups that have used suicide terrorism are the Palestinians against the Israelis and the Iraqis against U.S. troops. The suicide terrorism that has had the most profound effects on our lives is the attack on the World Trade Center and the Pentagon under the direction of Osama bin Laden. What kind of sick people become suicide terrorists? This is the topic of the Down-to-Earth Sociology box below.

terrorism
the use of violence or the threat of violence to produce fear in order to attain political objectives

Down-to-Earth Sociology

Who Are the Suicide Terrorists? Testing Your Stereotypes

We carry a lot of untested ideas around in our heads, and we use those ideas to make sense out of our experiences. When something happens, we place the event into a mental file of "similar events" that gives us a way of interpreting it. This is a normal process. We all do it all the time. Without stereotypes—ideas of what people, things, and events are like—we could not get through everyday life.

As we traverse society, our files of "similar people" and "similar events" are usually adequate. That is, the explanations we get from our interpretations usually satisfy our "need to understand." Sometimes, however, our files for classifying people and events leave us perplexed, not knowing what to make of things. For most of us, suicide terrorism is like this. We don't know any terrorists or suicide bombers, so it is hard to imagine someone becoming one.

Let's see if we can flesh out our mental files a bit. Sociologist Marc Sageman (2008, 2011) wondered about terrorists, too. Finding that his mental files were inadequate to understand them, he decided that research might provide the answer. Sageman had an unusual

advantage for gaining access to data—he had been in the CIA. Through his contacts, he studied 400 al-Qaeda terrorists who had targeted the United States. He was able to examine thousands of pages of their trial records.

So let's use Sageman's research to test some common ideas. I think you'll find that the data blow away stereotypes of terrorists.

- Here's a common stereotype. Terrorists come from backgrounds of poverty. Cunning leaders take advantage of their frustration and direct it toward striking out at an enemy.

  Not true. Three-quarters of the terrorists came from middle and upper classes.

- How about the deranged loner, then? We carry around images like this concerning serial and mass murderers. It is a sort of catch-all stereotype that we have. These people can't get along with anyone; they stew in their loneliness and misery, and all this bubbles up in misapplied violence. You know, the workplace killer sort of image, loners "going postal."

Not true, either. Sageman found that 90 percent of the terrorists came from caring, intact families. On top of this, 73 percent were married, and most of them had children.

- Let's try another one. Terrorists are uneducated, ignorant people, so those cunning leaders can manipulate them easily.

We have to drop this one, too. Sageman found that 63 percent of the terrorists had gone to college. Three-quarters worked in professional and semiprofessional occupations. Some were scientists, engineers, and architects.

What? Most terrorists are intelligent, educated, family-oriented, professional people? How can this be?

Sageman found that these people had gone through a process of radicalization. Here was their trajectory:

1. *Moral outrage.* They became angry, even enraged, about something they felt was terribly wrong.
2. *Ideology.* They interpreted their moral outrage within a radical, militant understanding of Islamic teachings.
3. *Shared outrage and ideology.* They found like-minded people, often on the Internet, especially in chat rooms.
4. *Group support for radical action.* They decided that thinking and talking were not enough. The moral wrong

After kissing her daughter, this mother blew herself up at a crossing point in the Gaza Strip. For some, she is a heroic martyr because she killed four Israelis. No one knows how to stop the hatred and killing.

needed dramatic action. The choice was an act of terrorism.

To understand terrorists, then, it is not the individual that we need to look at. We need to focus on *group dynamics*, how the group influences the individual and how the individual influences the group (as we studied in Chapter 5).

In one sense, however, the image of the loner does come close. Seventy percent of these terrorists committed themselves to extreme acts while they were living away from the country where they grew up. They became homesick, sought out people like themselves, and ended up at radical mosques where they learned a militant script.

Constantly, then, sociologists seek to understand the relationship between the individual and the group. This fascinating endeavor sometimes blows away stereotypes.

For Your Consideration

→ How do you think we can help eliminate the process of radicalization that turns people into terrorists?

→ Sageman concludes that this process of radicalization has sprouted networks of homegrown, leaderless terrorists who don't need al-Qaeda to direct them. He also concludes that this process will eventually wear itself out. Do you agree? Why or why not?

Targeted Killings

To U.S. officials, al-Qaeda has become a multiheaded snake. Over and over, the U.S. military has targeted and killed the head of some al-Qaeda group. In each instance, like Wack-a-Mole, a replacement head pops up to take over. Although this process of targeting, killing, and replacement seems endless, it continues. A new element has been added, however, which we explore in the following Thinking Critically section.

Thinking Critically

Targeted Killings

"I wonder if I should kill her?" the president of the United States asks himself as he sits in the Oval Office. "Let's see the record," he says to his advisor whose job it is to add names to the president's "kill list."

"She's only 17," says the president.

"She's young, but a killer—and a threat to the security of our troops," replies the advisor.

"Yes, she's a valid target. Keep her on the list. But remember—no collateral damage. If she's with her family, no strike. That goes for all."

For the record, not to be revealed to the public, the president initials the list and the date.

The advisor leaves the office, the "kill list" tucked in his briefing book.

"Did he approve the list?"

The advisor nods.

"Did he keep her on it?"

"Who?"

"You know who I mean. Don't play games."

"Yes, sir. She's still on it."

"I wonder why he wants to approve each kill himself?"

"He said something about 'The buck stops here,'" said the advisor.

"Right. Truman's statement will live forever."

The order was given. The drones flew to their target. And to the next one. And to the next. Each killing personally approved by the president of the United States.

The advisor watched the monitor, much like a video game. The explosions were silent.

He nodded, grim-faced, then went to his office to prepare the next kill list. This one had an American on it. The president approved this list, too.

Never in the history of the United States have we had something like this. The president is both judge and jury—and he sends the executioner. This bothers even top military officers who are concerned that we are waging "a secret war governed by secret law" (Mulrine 2014).

Based on Savage 2011; Becker and Shane 2012; Savage 2012.

For Your Consideration

This is not a transcript of a recording, so the conversation in the Oval Office will differ from this vignette. But it is based on actual events. The president of the United States personally authorizes the names of the people he wants killed in other countries. An American citizen can

At this end, drone strikes are like a video game: looking at images, pressing a button, and seeing a puff of dust. The other end is remarkably different—real death and destruction.

be targeted. No trial. No lawyers. Just some men, and an occasional woman, I presume, poring over reports and deciding what names to suggest to the president. The president reviews the report and approves or disapproves each name.

The rationale? It's necessary to cripple al-Qaeda and ISIS and protect the United States.

→ What do you think?

The Economy: Work in the Global Village

If you are like most students, you are wondering how changes in the economy are going to affect your chances of getting a good job. Let's see if we can shed some light on this question. We'll begin with this story:

"Not Monday already," Kim groaned as the alarm went off. "There must be a better way of starting the week." With her eyes still closed, she pressed the snooze button on the clock (from Germany) to sneak another ten minutes' sleep. In what seemed like just thirty seconds, the alarm once again shrilly insisted that she get up and face the week.

Still bleary-eyed after her shower, Kim peered into her closet and picked out a silk blouse (from China), a plaid wool skirt (from Scotland), and leather shoes (from Italy). She nodded, satisfied, as she added a pair of simulated pearls (from Taiwan). Running late, she hurriedly ran a brush (from Mexico) through her hair. As Kim wolfed down a bowl of cereal (from the United States) topped with milk (from the United States), bananas (from Costa Rica), and sugar (from the Dominican Republic), she turned on her kitchen television (from Korea) to listen to the weather forecast.

Gulping the last of her coffee (from Brazil), Kim grabbed her briefcase (from India), purse (from Spain), and jacket (from Malaysia), left her house, and quickly climbed into her car (from Japan). As she glanced at her watch (from Switzerland), she hoped that the traffic would be in her favor. She muttered to herself as she pulled up at a stoplight (from Great Britain) and eyed her gas gauge. She muttered again when she pulled into a station and paid for gas (from Saudi Arabia), because the price had risen over the weekend. "My paycheck never keeps up with prices," she moaned.

When Kim arrived at work, she found the office abuzz. Six months ago, New York headquarters had put the company up for sale, but there had been no takers. The big news was that both a Chinese company and a Canadian company had put in bids over the weekend. No one got much work done that day, as the whole office speculated about how things might change.

The Transformation of Economic Systems

11.6 Summarize the broad historical shifts in economic systems; emphasize inequality.

economy

a system of producing and distributing goods and services

Although this vignette may be slightly exaggerated, many of us are like Kim: We use a multitude of products from around the world, and yet we're concerned about our country's ability to compete in global markets. Today's **economy**—our system of producing and distributing goods and services—differs radically from past economies. The products that Kim uses make it apparent that today's economy knows no national boundaries. To better understand how global forces affect the U.S. economy—and your life—let's begin by summarizing the sweeping historical changes that have led to the society we live in today.

Preindustrial Societies: The Birth of Inequality

subsistence economy

a type of economy in which human groups live off the land and have little or no surplus

The earliest human groups, *hunting and gathering societies*, had a **subsistence economy**. In small groups of about twenty-five to forty, people lived off the land. They gathered plants and hunted animals in one location and then moved to another place as these sources of food ran low. Having few possessions, they did little trading with one another. With no excess to accumulate, everybody owned as much (or, really, as little) as everyone else.

Then people discovered how to breed animals and cultivate plants. The more dependable food supply in what became *pastoral and horticultural societies* allowed humans to settle down in a single place. Human groups grew larger, and for the first time in history, it was no longer necessary for everyone to work at producing food. Some people became leather workers, others made weapons, and so on. This new division of labor produced a surplus, and groups traded items with one another. The primary sociological significance of surplus and trade is this: They fostered *social inequality*, since some people accumulated more possessions than others. The effects of that change remain with us today.

The plow brought the next major change, ushering in *agricultural societies*. Plowing made land more productive, allowing even more people to specialize in activities other than producing food. More specialized divisions of labor followed, and trade expanded. Trading centers then developed, which turned into cities. As power passed from the heads of families and clans to a ruling elite, social, political, and economic inequalities grew.

The commonsense meaning of market is a place where people exchange or buy and sell goods. Such old-fashioned markets remain common in the Least Industrialized Nations, such as this one in Vietnam. I took this photo in a village market outside Ho Chi Minh City. The customer (squatting, as is customary in Vietnam) does not have to wonder if her chicken is fresh.

Industrial Societies: The Birth of the Machine

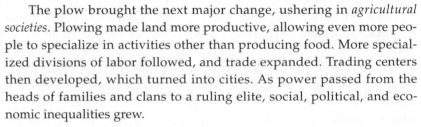

The steam engine, invented in 1765, ushered in *industrial societies*. Based on machines powered by fuels, these societies created a surplus unlike anything the world had seen. This, too, stimulated trade among nations and brought even more social inequality. A handful of individuals opened factories and exploited the labor of many.

Then came more efficient machines. As the surpluses grew even larger, the emphasis gradually changed—from producing goods to consuming them. In 1912, sociologist Thorstein Veblen coined the term **conspicuous consumption** to describe this fundamental change in people's orientations. By this term, Veblen meant that the Protestant ethic identified by Weber—an emphasis on hard work, savings, and a concern for salvation (discussed on page 8)—was being replaced with an eagerness to show off wealth by the "elaborate consumption of goods."

conspicuous consumption

Thorstein Veblen's term for a change from the thrift, savings, and investments of the Protestant ethic to showing off wealth through spending and the display of possessions

Postindustrial Societies: The Birth of the Information Age

In 1973, sociologist Daniel Bell noted that *a new type of society was emerging*. This new society, which he called the *postindustrial society*, has six characteristics: (1) a service sector so large that *most* people work in it, (2) a vast surplus of goods, (3) even more extensive trade among nations, (4) a wider variety and quantity of goods available to the average person, (5) an information explosion, and (6) an interconnected *global village*—that is, the world's nations are linked by fast communications, transportation, and trade.

To see why analysts use the term *postindustrial society* to describe the United States, look at Figure 11.3. The change shown in this figure is without parallel in human history. In the 1800s, most U.S. workers were farmers. Today, farmers make up about 1 percent of the workforce. With the technology of the 1800s, a typical farmer produced enough food to feed five people. With today's powerful machinery and hybrid seeds, a farmer now feeds about eighty. In 1940, about half of U.S. workers wore a blue collar. As changing technology shrank the market for blue-collar jobs, white-collar work continued its ascent, reaching the dominant position it holds today.

Biotech Societies: The Merger of Biology and Economics

We may be on the verge of yet another new type of society. If so, this one is being ushered in by advances in biology, especially the deciphering of the human genome system. Although the specifics of this new society have yet to unfold, the marriage of biology and economics is likely to yield even greater surpluses and more extensive trade. The technological advances that will emerge in this new society may allow us to lead longer, healthier lives. Its effects on inequality between the nations are likely to be spotty. Some poorer nations may be able to import the new technology and develop their economies, while others will remain in poverty.

Implications for Your Life

The broad changes in societies that I have just sketched may seem to be merely abstract matters, but they are far from irrelevant to your life. Changes in society directly affect you. Consider the information explosion. When you graduate from college, you will most likely do some form of "knowledge work." Instead of working in a factory, you will manage information or you will design, sell, or service products. The type of work you do has profound implications for your life. It produces social networks, creates attitudes, and even affects how you view yourself and the world. To better understand this, consider how vastly different your outlook on life would be if you were one of the children discussed in the Cultural Diversity box on the next page.

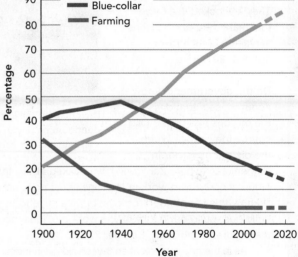

Figure 11.3 The Revolutionary Change in the U.S. Workforce

SOURCE: By the author. Based on *Statistical Abstract of the United States*, various years, and 2014:Tables 642, 648.

Cultural Diversity around the World

The Child Workers

In Beirut, Lebanon, 10-year-old Mohammed Huzaifa goes from bar to bar with a little vase of red roses. He stands on street corners, too, selling the roses one by one. It sometimes takes the boy until 3 A.M. to sell them all. If he fails to sell all the roses, his mother beats him. Without the money from her son's sales, she won't be able to pay the rent on their one-room apartment where ten people live (Morris 2014).

* * * * *

In Afghanistan, Zar Muhammad said he felt guilty that his 7- and 8-year-old sons work 12 hours a day making bricks in the mud. Zar borrowed 10,000 rupees ($165) to get married. He now owes 150,000 rupees ($2,500). The children have to work alongside him to try to pay the debt. But the debt continues to grow: rent to the kiln owner for their mud house, electricity, and food, and sometimes emergency medicine for the children. They are locked in a cycle that makes Zar and his sons servants/slaves forever (Kamber 2011).

* * * * *

Do the governments know about these situations and the millions like them? Of course they know. When the district governor in Afghanistan (where Zar works), was asked about the 5,000 children who work in the kilns in his area, he said, "I know this is not good for kids, but we have to build our buildings, build our country. The work provides income for the children's families" (Kamber 2011).

As in the photo I took of an 8-year-old girl in India (page 196), some children work in construction. Others work in factories, as miners, and pesticide sprayers. They weave carpets in India, race camels in the Middle East, and, all over the world, work as street vendors, household servants, and prostitutes. In the poverty-stricken areas of some of these

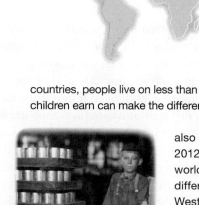

The photo on the left of a child worker in a Bangladesh aluminum pot factory is current. On the right is a boy working in a U.S. canning factory about 1908.

countries, people live on less than $1 a day. The few dollars the children earn can make the difference between life and death.

Besides poverty, there is also a cultural factor (Hilson 2012). In many parts of the world, people view children differently than we do in the West. Fairly new in history is the idea that children have the right to be educated and to be spared from adult burdens. A major factor shaping our views of life is economics, and when prosperity comes to these other countries, so will this new perspective. In fact, with the world's increasing material prosperity, the number of the world's child workers is dropping (Barta and Okeeffe 2013).

For Your Consideration

→ How do you think the wealthier nations can help alleviate the suffering of child workers?

→ Before industrialization, and for a period afterward, having children work was common in the West, including the United States. Advanced industrialization brought different ideas of childhood and of the rights of children. What gives us the right to impose our changed ideas on other nations?

Think of the globe as being divided into three neighborhoods—the three worlds of industrialization that we reviewed in Chapter 7. Some nations are located in the poor part of the village. Their citizens do menial work and barely eke out a living. Life is so precarious that some even starve to death, while their fellow villagers in the rich neighborhood feast on steak and lobster, washed down with vintage Chateau Lafite Rothschild. It's the same village, but what a difference the neighborhood makes.

Now visualize any one of the three neighborhoods. Again you will see gross inequalities. Not everyone who lives in the poor neighborhood is poor, and some areas of the rich neighborhood are packed with poor people. The United States is the global economic leader, occupying the most luxurious mansion in the best neighborhood and spearheading the new biotech society.

World Economic Systems

11.7 Contrast capitalism and socialism: their components, ideologies, criticisms, and convergence.

Now that we have sketched the major historical changes in world economic systems and their means of exchange, let's compare capitalism and socialism, the two main economic systems in force today. This will help us to understand where the United States stands in the world economic order.

Capitalism

WHAT CAPITALISM IS People who live in a capitalist society may not understand its basic tenets, even though they see them reflected in their local shopping malls and fast-food chains. Table 11.3 distills the many businesses of the United States down to their basic components. As you can see, **capitalism** has three essential features: (1) *private ownership of the means of production* (individuals own the land, machines, and factories), (2) *market competition* (competing with one another, the owners decide what to produce and set the prices for their products), and (3) *the pursuit of profit* (the owners try to sell their products for more than they cost).

capitalism
an economic system built around the private ownership of the means of production, the pursuit of profit, and market competition

Table 11.3 Comparing Capitalism and Socialism

Capitalism	Socialism
1. Individuals own the means of production.	1. The public owns the means of production.
2. Based on competition, the owners determine production and set prices.	2. Central committees plan production and set prices; no competition.
3. The pursuit of profit is the reason for distributing goods and services.	3. No profit motive in the distribution of goods and services.

SOURCE: By the author.

WHAT STATE CAPITALISM IS No country has pure capitalism. Pure capitalism, known as **laissez-faire capitalism** (literally "hands off" capitalism), means that the government doesn't interfere in the market. The current form of U.S. capitalism is *state (or welfare) capitalism*. Private citizens own the means of production and pursue profits, but they do so within a vast system of laws designed to protect the welfare of the population, and—not incidentally—ensure that the government can collect taxes.

Consider this example:

laissez-faire capitalism
literally "hands off" capitalism, meaning that the government doesn't interfere in the market

Suppose that you discover what you think is a miracle tonic: It will grow hair, erase wrinkles, and dissolve excess fat. If your product works, you will become an overnight sensation—not only a multimillionaire but also the toast of television talk shows and the darling of Hollywood.

But don't count on your money or fame yet. You still have to reckon with market restraints, the laws and regulations of welfare capitalism that limit your capacity to produce and sell. First, you must comply with local and state laws. You must obtain a business license and a state tax number that allows you to buy your ingredients without paying sales taxes. Then come the federal regulations. You cannot simply take your product to local stores and ask them to sell it; you first must seek approval from federal agencies that monitor compliance with the Pure Food and Drug Act. This means that you must prove that your product will not cause harm to the public. Your manufacturing process is also subject to federal, state, and local laws concerning fraud, hygiene, and the disposal of hazardous wastes.

Suppose that you overcome these obstacles, and your business prospers. Other federal agencies will monitor your compliance with laws concerning minimum wages, Social Security taxes, and discrimination on the basis of race, gender, religion, or disability. State agencies will examine your records to see whether you have paid unemployment and sales taxes. Finally, as your shadowy but ever-present business partner, the Internal Revenue Service will look over your shoulder and demand about 35 percent of your profits.

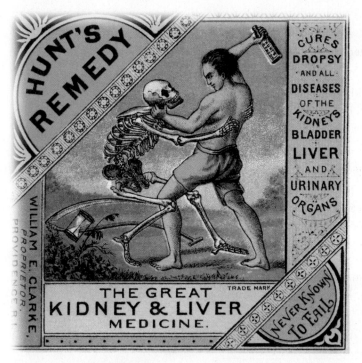

This advertisement from about 1885 represents an early stage of capitalism when individuals were free to manufacture and market products with little or no interference from the government. Today, the production and marketing of goods take place under detailed, complicated government laws and regulations.

socialism

an economic system built around the public ownership of the means of production, central planning, and the distribution of goods without a profit motive

market forces

the law of supply and demand

democratic socialism

a hybrid economic system in which the individual ownership of businesses is mixed with the state ownership of industries thought essential to the public welfare, such as the postal service, natural resources, the medical delivery system, and mass transportation

In short, the U.S. economic system is highly regulated and is far from an example of laissez-faire capitalism.

Socialism

WHAT SOCIALISM IS As Table 11.3 on page 361 shows, **socialism** also has three essential components: (1) public ownership of the means of production, (2) central planning, and (3) the distribution of goods without a profit motive.

In socialist economies, the government owns the means of production—not only the factories but also the land, railroads, oil wells, and gold mines. Unlike capitalism in which **market forces**—supply and demand—determine both what will be produced and the prices that will be charged, in socialism a central committee decides that the country needs X number of toothbrushes, Y toilets, and Z shoes. The committee decides how many of each will be produced, which factories will produce them, what price will be charged for the items, and where they will be distributed.

Socialism is designed to eliminate competition: Goods are sold at predetermined prices regardless of the demand for an item or the cost of producing it. The goal is not to make a profit, nor is it to encourage the consumption of goods that are in low demand (by lowering the price) or to limit the consumption of hard-to-get goods (by raising the price). Rather, the goal is to produce goods for the general welfare and to distribute them according to people's needs, not their ability to pay.

In a socialist economy, *everyone* in the economic chain works for the government. The members of the central committee who set production goals are government employees, as are the supervisors who implement their plans, the factory workers who produce the merchandise, the truck drivers who move it, and the clerks who sell it. Those who buy the items may work at different jobs—in offices, on farms, or in day care centers—but they, too, are government employees.

SOCIALISM IN PRACTICE Just as capitalism does not exist in a pure form, neither does socialism. Although the ideology of socialism calls for resources to be distributed according to need and not the ability to pay, socialist countries found it necessary to pay higher salaries for some jobs in order to entice people to take on greater responsibilities. Factory managers, for example, always earned more than factory workers. These differences in pay follow the functionalist argument of social stratification presented in Chapter 7 (pages 204–205). By narrowing the huge pay gaps that characterize capitalist nations, however, socialist nations established considerably greater equality of income.

DEMOCRATIC SOCIALISM Dissatisfied with the greed and exploitation of capitalism and the lack of freedom and individuality of socialism, Sweden and Denmark developed **democratic socialism** (also called *welfare socialism*). In this form of socialism, both the state and individuals produce and distribute goods and services. The government owns and runs the steel, mining, forestry, and energy concerns, as well as the country's telephones, television stations, and airlines. Remaining in private hands are the retail stores, farms, factories, and most service industries.

Ideologies of Capitalism and Socialism

Not only do capitalism and socialism have different approaches to producing and distributing goods, but they also represent opposing belief systems. *Capitalists* believe that market forces should determine both products and prices. They also believe that profits are good for humanity. The potential to make money stimulates people to produce and distribute goods, as well as to develop new products. Society benefits, as the result is a more abundant supply of goods at cheaper prices.

Socialists take an opposite view of profits. They consider profits to be immoral. An item's value is based on the work that goes into it, said Karl Marx. The only way there can be profit, he stressed, is by paying workers less than the value of their labor. Profit, he said, is the *excess value* that has been withheld from workers. Socialists believe that the government should protect workers from this exploitation. To do so, the government should own the means of production, using them not to generate profit but to produce items that match people's needs, not their ability to pay.

Capitalists and socialists paint each other in such stark colors that *each perceives the other system as one of exploitation.* Capitalists believe that socialists violate people's basic right to make their own decisions and to pursue opportunity. Socialists believe that capitalists violate people's basic right to be free from poverty. With each side claiming moral superiority while viewing the other as a threat to its very existence, the last century witnessed the world split into two main blocs. In what was known as the *Cold War*, the West armed itself to defend and promote capitalism, the East to defend and promote socialism.

Criticisms of Capitalism and Socialism

In India, an up-and-coming capitalist giant, the construction of a 27-story building is almost complete (Yardley 2010b). It comes with a grand ballroom, nine elevators, a fifty-seat theater, a six-story garage, and three helipads on the roof.

The occupants are ready to move in—all five of them—a husband and wife and their three children. From their elegant perch, they will be able to view the teeming mass of destitute people below.

The primary criticism leveled against capitalism is that it leads to social inequality. Capitalism, say its critics, produces a tiny top layer of wealthy people who exploit an immense bottom layer of poorly paid workers. Another criticism is that the tiny top layer wields vast political power. Those few who own the means of production reap huge profits, accrue power, and get legislation passed that goes against the public good.

The first criticism leveled against socialism is that it does not respect individual rights. Others (in the form of some government agency) control people's lives. They decide where people will live, work, and go to school. In China, government officials even determine how many children women may bear (Mosher 1983, 2006). Critics make a second point—that central planning is grossly inefficient and that socialism is not capable of producing much wealth. They say that its greater equality really amounts to giving almost everyone an equal chance to be poor.

Propaganda to influence public opinion surrounds us, but most propaganda is covert, difficult to recognize. During economic–political conflicts, much propaganda moves into the open. The anti-German poster on the left is from Russia. It reads: "Father, kill the Germans" (who have just killed my mother). The anti-Russian poster on the right is from Germany. It reads: "Bolshevism means the world will drown in blood." To arouse their people, each accuses the other of horrible motives and acts.

The Convergence of Capitalism and Socialism

Regardless of the validity of these mutual criticisms, as nations industrialize they come to resemble one another. They urbanize, encourage education, and produce similar divisions of labor (such as professionals and technicians; factory workers and factory managers). Despite their incompatible ideologies, both capitalist and socialist systems have adopted features from the other. That capitalism and socialism are growing similar is known as **convergence theory** (Form 1979).

convergence theory

the view that as capitalist and socialist economic systems each adopt features of the other, a hybrid (or mixed) economic system will emerge

CHANGES IN SOCIALIST COUNTRIES   In the 1980s and 1990s, the rulers of Russia abandoned communism. Making a profit had been a crime, but practically overnight profits were encouraged. Chinese leaders saw the potential and joined the change. However, they kept a communist government. Their encouragement of profits unleashed an entrepreneurial energy that, with its new businesses, rapid industrialization, and vast exports, has transformed the country. As a sign of the fundamental change, China's new capitalists have joined the Communist party.

The switch to capitalism has produced these amazing numbers: 2.4 million millionaires ("Global Wealth…" 2014) and 152 billionaires (Flannery 2014). Some Chinese textbooks even praise Bill Gates as a model for youth (Guthrie 2008). As in the West, Chinese capital moves to the cheapest labor. You know that American capitalists have moved millions of jobs to China, but did you know that Chinese capitalists are now moving factories from China to Africa? And for the same reason: They can pay African workers less than Chinese workers (Wonacott 2014).

For a glimpse of the new capitalism in China, read the Cultural Diversity box on the next page.

CHANGES IN CAPITALISM   The United States has adopted many socialist practices. One of the most obvious is that the government collects money from some individuals to pay for benefits it gives to others. When the country was founded, it had none of these: unemployment compensation (taxes paid by workers are distributed to those who no longer produce a profit); subsidized housing, food, and medical care (paid for by the many and given to the poor and elderly with no motive of profit); welfare (taxes from the many are distributed to the needy); a minimum wage (the government, not the employer, determines the minimum that workers are paid); and Social Security (the retired do not receive what they paid into the system but, rather, money that the government collects from current workers).

Convergence is continuing. In 2008, when Wall Street and auto firms started to buckle, the U.S. government stepped in to shore up these businesses. The government even bought some companies, fired CEOs, and set salary limits. This extended embrace of socialist principles indicates that the United States has produced its own version of a mixed economy.

IN SUM   Capitalist and socialist countries are converging. On the one hand, capitalists have assumed, reluctantly, that their system should provide workers with at least minimal support during unemployment, illness, and old age—and, in some instances, that the government should bail out private companies that are going bankrupt. On the other hand, wanting to increase the nation's wealth and standard of living, socialist leaders have reluctantly embraced profit-making and private property.

The Globalization of Capitalism

11.8   Discuss the globalization of capitalism, including its effects on workers, the divisions of wealth, and the global superclass.

Capitalism has made the world's countries part of the same broad economic unit. When the economic crisis hit the United States, it spread quickly around the world. To decide what they should do, the leaders of the top 20 producers of consumer goods met in

Cultural Diversity around the World

The New Competitor: The Chinese Capitalists

Socialism has the virtue of making people more equal. Socialism's equality, however, translates into making almost everyone equally poor.

Capitalism has the virtue of producing wealth. A lot of people remain poor, however, leaving deep gaps between wealth and poverty.

Realizing that their country was mired in poverty and that capitalism has such capacity to produce wealth, Chinese leaders turned to capitalism. One consequence has been an astonishing growth of wealth. The irony is thick. China's capitalism directed by communists has lifted *a half billion people* out of poverty ("China Overview" 2014).

This new capitalism has also produced extravagant ostentatiousness. In Beijing, the capital of China, Zhang Yuchen built a mansion. This is no ordinary mansion, like those built by China's other newly rich. It is a reproduction of the Chateau de Maisons-Laffitte, an architectural landmark on the Seine River outside Paris. At a cost of $50 million, the Beijing replica matches the original edifice detail for detail. The architects followed the original blueprints of the French chateau, even using the same Chantilly stone (Kahn 2004, 2007).

In the midst of this transition to capitalism, poor farmers have remained poor farmers. This has fueled anger and resentment, which have kept the Party busy sending out the army to squelch riots. It turns out that to make themselves wealthy the powerful have taken the farmers' land. To replicate the Maisons-Laffitte chateau and its nearby luxury homes turned eight hundred farmers into landless peasants. The spiked fence, the moat, and the armed guards—looking sharp in their French-style uniforms complete with capes and kepis—are not just decorative. They also keep the peasants out.

In most places, you need connections to become wealthy. It is the same in China. There, connections refer

As China has embraced its version of capitalism, wealth has grown, as has consumption. Luxury goods from the West are considered prestigious and are highly desired.

to the Communist Party, since this group holds the power. Yuchen has those connections. His job as a member of the Party was to direct Beijing's construction projects.

Yuchen's connections allowed him to get the peasants' wheat fields rezoned from farmland to a "conservation area." He was even able to divert a river so he could build a moat around the chateau, one of the finishing touches on his architectural wonder.

Beneath such capitalistic excesses lies this irony: China is doing capitalism better than the capitalist countries are. Harnessing the state machinery, the Chinese leaders have proven themselves nimble at seizing opportunities for profit, in reacting to competition, and in accumulating vast amounts of capital. The capitalist nations have become envious, especially as the Chinese model of capitalism—at least at this historical point—is proving competitively superior (Bremmer 2011; Karon 2011).

For Your Consideration

→ When China has completed its transition to capitalism, what do you think the final version will look like (that is, what characteristics do you think it will have)?

→ Where will the top Party leaders fit in the class system that is emerging? Why? (To answer this, consider the connections and resources of the Chinese elite.)

Washington. The Chinese leaders said that no one should worry about them not being a team player; they knew that their actions would affect other nations. (Yardley and Bradsher 2008)

The globalization of capitalism is so significant that its ultimate impact on our lives may rival that of the Industrial Revolution. As Louis Galambos, a historian of business, says, "This new global business system will change the way everyone lives and works" (Zachary 1995).

Let's look, then, at how capitalism is changing the face of the globe.

A New Global Structure and its Effects on Workers

The globalization of capitalism is producing a new world structure, one that integrates the world's nations into a global production and distribution system. Three primary trading blocs have emerged: North and South America, dominated by the United States; Europe, dominated by Germany; and Asia, dominated by China and Japan. Functionalists stress that this new global division benefits not only the multinational giants but also the citizens of the world.

Consider free trade. Free trade increases competition, which, in turn, drives the search for greater productivity. This lowers prices and brings a higher standard of living. Free trade also has dysfunctions. As production moves to countries where labor costs are lower, millions of U.S., U.K., French, and Spanish workers lose their jobs. Functionalists point out that this is a temporary dislocation. As the Most Industrialized Nations lose factory jobs, their workers shift into service and high-tech jobs. Perhaps. But the millions of workers searching in vain for jobs that no longer exist would disagree.

The adjustment certainly is not easy. As the U.S. steel industry lost out to global competition, for example, the closing of plants created "rust belts" in the northern states. The globalization of capitalism has also brought special challenges to small towns, which were already suffering long-term losses because of urbanization. Their struggle to survive is the topic of the photo essay on the next two pages.

Figure 11.4 Average Hourly Earnings of U.S. Workers in Current and Constant Dollars

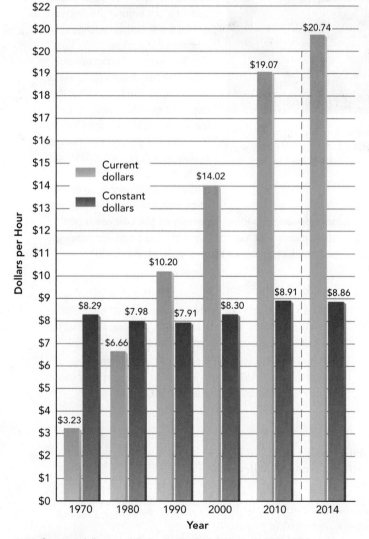

NOTE: Constant dollars are dollars adjusted for inflation with 1982–1984 as the base.

SOURCE: By the author. Based on *Statistical Abstract of the United States* 1992:Table 650; 1999:Table 698; U.S. Bureau of Labor Statistics 2014b.

Stagnant Paychecks

With extensive automation, the productivity of U.S. workers has increased year after year, making them some of the most productive in the world (*Statistical Abstract* 2014:Tables 668, 1383). One might think, therefore, that their pay would be increasing. This brings us to a disturbing trend, one that bothers Americans and is an underlying reason that so many workers lost their homes to foreclosure.

Look at Figure 11.4. The gold bars show current dollars. These are the dollars the average worker finds in his or her paycheck. You can see that since 1970 the average pay of U.S. workers has soared from just over $3 an hour to almost $21 an hour. Workers today are bringing home more than *six* times as many dollars as workers used to.

But let's strip away the illusion. Look at the purple bars that show these dollars adjusted for inflation, the *buying power* of those paychecks. You can see how inflation has suppressed the value of the dollars that workers earn. Today's workers, with their $21 an hour, can buy little more than workers in 1970 could with their "measly" $3 an hour. The question is not "How could workers live on just $3 an hour back then?" but, rather, *"How can workers get by on a 57-cent-an-hour raise that took 44 years to get?"* That's only slightly more than a penny an hour per year! Incredibly, despite workers having more years of college and more technical training, despite the use of computers, and much higher productivity, the workers' purchasing power increased just 57 cents an hour between 1970 and 2014. What can you buy with those 57 cents?

Actually, after taxes and Social Security deductions, we should ask, What can you buy with those four or five dimes?

Small Town USA: Struggling to Survive

All across the nation, small towns are struggling to survive. Parents and town officials are concerned because so few young adults remain in their home town. There is little to keep them there, and when they graduate from high school, most move to the city. With young people leaving and old ones dying, the small towns are shriveling.

How can small towns contend with cut-throat global competition when workers in some countries are paid just a few dollars a day? Even if you open a store, down the road Wal-Mart sells the same products for about what you pay for them—and offers much greater variety.

There are exceptions: Some small towns are located close to a city, and they receive the city's spillover. A few possess a rare treasure—some unique historical event or a natural attraction—that draws visitors with money to spend. Most of the others, though, are drying up, left in a time warp as history shifts around them. This photo essay tells the story.

I was struck by the grandiosity of people's dreams, at least as reflected in the names that some small-towners give their businesses. Donut Palace has a nice ring to it—inspiring thoughts of wealth and royalty (note the crowns). Unfortunately, like so many others, this business didn't make it.

People do whatever they can to survive. This enterprising proprietor uses the building for an unusual combination of purposes: a "plant world," along with the sale of milk, eggs, bread, and, in a quaint southern touch, cracking pecans.

The small towns are filled with places like this—small businesses, locally owned, that have enough clientele for the owner and family to eke out a living. They have to offer low prices because there is a fast-food chain down the road. Fixing the sign? That's one of those "I'll get-to-its."

In striking contrast to the grandiosity of some small town business names is the utter simplicity of others. Cafe tells everyone that some type of food and drinks are served here. Everyone in this small town knows the details.

© James M. Henslin, all photos

One of the few buildings consistently in good repair in the small towns is the U.S. Post Office. Although its importance has declined in the face of telecommunications, for "small towners" the post office still provides a vital link with the outside world.

With little work available, it is difficult to afford adequate housing. This house, although cobbled together and in disrepair, is a family's residence.

This general store used to be the main business in the area: It even has a walk-in safe. This store has been owned by the same family since the 1920s, but is no longer successful. To get into the building, I had to find out where the owner (shown here) lived, knock on her door, and then wait while she called around to find out who had the keys.

There is no global competition for this home-grown business. Shirley has located her sign on a main highway just outside Niceville, Florida. By the looks of the building, business could be better.

This is a successful business. The store goes back to the early 1900s, and the proprietors have capitalized on the "old timey" atmosphere.

The New Economic System and the Old Divisions of Wealth

Suppose that you own a business that manufactures widgets. You are paying your workers an average $166 a day ($20.70 an hour, including vacation pay, sick pay, unemployment benefits, Social Security, and so on). Widgets similar to yours are being manufactured in Thailand, where workers are paid $8 a day. Those imported widgets are being sold in the same stores that feature your widgets.

How long do you think you could stay in business? Even if your workers were willing to cut their pay in half—which they aren't willing to do—you still couldn't compete.

What do you do? Your choices are simple. You can continue as you are and go broke, try to find some other product to manufacture (which, if successful, will soon be made in Thailand or India or China)—or you can close up your plant here and manufacture your widgets in Thailand.

These are not easy times for workers. One disruption after another. High insecurity with layoffs, plant closings, and the prospect of more of the same. The insecurity is especially hard-hitting on the most desperate of workers, the less skilled and those who live from paycheck to paycheck. How can they compete with people overseas who work for peanuts? They suffer the wrenching adjustments that come from having their jobs pulled out from under them, looking for work and finding only jobs that pay lower wages—if that—watching their savings go down the drain, postponing their retirement, and seeing their children disillusioned about the future. The photo below indicates some of the effects on the workers in the Least Industrialized Nations.

What about the wealthy? In these tough economic times, aren't they being hurt, too? Some rich individuals do get on the wrong side of investments and lose their collective shirts. In general, though, the wealthy do just fine in these challenging times.

What happens when oil tankers wear out? They go to Bangladesh, where they are turned into scrap. These workers, an expendable part of the global economic system that we are all a part of, are exposed to PCBs, asbestos, and other toxins. For this, they earn $1 a day.

How can I be so sure?, you probably wonder. Take a look at Figure 11.5. Each rectangle on the left of this figure represents a fifth of the U.S. population, about 63 million people. The rectangles of the inverted pyramid on the right show the percentage of the nation's income that goes to each fifth of the population. You can see that half (51 percent) of the entire country's income goes to the richest fifth of Americans. Only 3 percent goes to the poorest fifth.

This gap has been growing over the years, and it is now *greater* than it has been in generations. The transition to a postindustrial economy and the globalization of capitalism have increased our income inequalities. The common folk saying that the rich are getting richer and the poor are getting poorer is certainly an apt observation, well supported by social research. What implications of this division of the nation's wealth do you see for our future?

Figure 11.5 The Inverted Income Pyramid: The Proportion of Income Received by Each Fifth of the U.S. Population

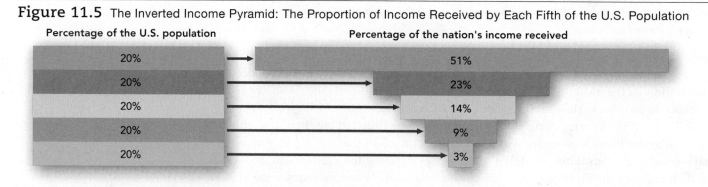

SOURCE: By the author. Based on *Statistical Abstract of the United States* 2014:Table 724.

The Global Superclass

global superclass

the top members of the capitalist class, who, through their worldwide interconnections, make the major decisions that affect the world

The overlapping memberships of the globe's top multinational companies enfold their leaders into a small circle. This group, called the **global superclass**, is extremely wealthy. To see how wealthy, look at Figure 7.1 on page 201). Because its members have access to the top circles of political power around the world, the global superclass is also extremely powerful.

This group shies away from researchers, but here is your chance to listen to a member of the global superclass describe their tight connections:

> *Every country has its large financial institutions that are central to the development of that country, and everyone else in finance knows somebody who will know the head of one of those companies. That person knows a senior person in their government that could be useful in a situation. . . . the key is the network. . . . it is twenty, thirty, fifty people worldwide who ultimately drive the decisions. (Rothkopf 2008:129–130)*

Twenty to fifty individuals who make the world's major decisions! Could this possibly be true? The person who said this, Stephen Schwarzman, is one of those insiders (Freeland 2011). Worth about $11 billion, he is the 114th richest person in the world (Dolan and Kroll 2014). Here is a real-life example of how this interconnected global power works:

> *When Schwarzman, a co-founder of Blackstone, an investment company, had a problem with some policy of the German government, he called a German friend. The friend arranged for Schwarzman to meet with the chancellor of Germany. After listening to Schwarzman, the chancellor agreed to support a change in Germany's policy.*

Do you see the power that is concentrated in this small group? The U.S. members can call the U.S. president, the English members can ring up the British prime minister, and so on. They know how to get and give favors, to move vast amounts of capital from country to country, and to open and close doors to investments around the world. This concentration of power is new to the world scene. Working behind the scenes, the global superclass affects our present and our future.

To close this chapter, let's look at this aspect of our changing political and economic order.

A New World Order?

11.9 **Explain how the globalization of capitalism might be bringing a New World Order—and why It might not be.**

So far, the use of war and terrorism to try to dominate the globe has failed. A New World Order, however, might be on its way, ushered in not by violence, but by nations cooperating for economic reasons. Let's examine this possibility, as well as consider its opposite.

Trends Toward Unity

The world's nations have made huge strides toward cooperation. Especially prominent is the economic and political unit called the European Union (EU). Twenty-eight countries with a combined population of 450 million, which in years past have gone to bitter war with each other, have adopted a single currency, the Euro, displacing their marks, francs, liras, lats, and pesetas. Major regional trading partnerships also indicate unity, from the formation of NAFTA (North American Free Trade Agreement) that binds the United States, Canada, and Mexico in a trading partnership to ASEAN (Association of Southeast Asian Nations) which unites ten Asian countries with a combined population of a half billion people.

Could rivalries and tensions be overcome and economic-political alignments continue to form until just one state or empire envelops the earth? It is possible. The

We are in the midst of the globalization of capitalism. The explosion that is sending products around the world brings new ways of thinking to people in the Least Industrialized Nations. Many ideas are subtle, such as what refreshing drinks are.

United Nations (UN) is striving to become the legislative body of the world, wanting its decisions to supersede those of any individual nation. The UN operates a World Court (The International Court of Justice). There is even a World Bank.

Perhaps, then, the globalization of capitalism and its encompassing trade organizations will eventually lead to a single world government.

Strains in the Global System

Trends toward divisions, however, are also strong. The developing global system is experiencing strains that threaten to rip the system apart. Unresolved conflicts constantly rear up, demanding realignments of the current arrangements of power. These pressures are always resolved on a short-term, emergency basis that satisfies few, sowing the seeds of discontent that lead to future disruptions.

Economic crises have exposed a debt-ridden financial system teetering on the edge of global disaster. The European Union is barely held together, its growing debt and conflicting views of how to get its economic engine roaring again, threatening to rip its fragile unity apart. Greece, on the verge of walking out, pinches Germany's nose by demanding that the Germans pay reparations for what the Nazis did to Greece 70 years ago. Although the United States is a debtor nation, it has poured billions of dollars into the European Central Bank and the International Monetary Fund. This has helped European banks keep credit flowing, holding the fragile economic-political union together for the moment. Larger and larger Band-Aids are needed to patch this tattered union together.

Russia, convinced that the West has plans for war against it, seized the Crimea and demanded that the West stop encircling it. Meanwhile, China is threatening its smaller Asian neighbors. In other regions, al-Qaeda, Boko Haram, ISIS, and other groups appear on the global scene, each venting their historical grievances by their preferred ways of killing. The issues, enemies, and demands seem endless.

Which Way?

It is certain that our current economic and political arrangements will change. Just as all economic-political dominators in human history have been swept into the dustbin of history, so will the present dominance of the United States. We don't know the particular shape of future global stratification, but whatever it turns out to be, it is likely to be led by a super-dominant group of more-or-less integrated economic-political elites. This super-group will not belong to any single nation, and the alliances that forge its dominance in the new global scheme of things will pay little attention to international borders. If this process does lead to a one-world government, the dissenting nations will be controlled by a dominant military. If the final form is a dictatorship that controls the world's resources and people, we could end up living under a government like that of Winston and Julia.

Summary and Review

Power, Authority, and Violence

11.1 Contrast power, authority, and violence; compare traditional, rational–legal, and charismatic authority.

How are authority and coercion related to power?

Authority is **power** that people view as legitimately exercised over them, while **coercion** is power they consider unjust. The **state** is a political entity that claims a monopoly on violence over some territory.

What kinds of authority are there?

Max Weber identified three types of authority. In **traditional authority**, power is derived from custom—patterns set down in the past serve as rules for the present. In **rational–legal authority** (also called *bureaucratic authority*), power is based on law and written rules. In **charismatic authority**, power is derived from loyalty to an individual to whom people are attracted. Charismatic authority, which undermines traditional and rational–legal authority, has built-in problems in transferring authority to a new leader.

Types of Government

11.2　**Compare monarchies, democracies, dictatorships, and oligarchies.**

How are the types of government related to power?

In a **monarchy,** power is based on hereditary rule; in a **democracy,** power is given to the ruler by citizens; in a **dictatorship,** power is seized by an individual; and in an **oligarchy,** power is seized by a small group.

The U.S. Political System

11.3　**Discuss voting patterns, lobbyists, and PACs.**

What are the main characteristics of the U.S. political system?

The U.S. political system is dominated by the Democratic and Republican parties that represent slightly different centrist positions. The differences are most obvious in those who take extreme positions.

　　Voter turnout is higher among people who are more socially integrated—those who sense a greater stake in the outcome of elections, such as the more educated and well-to-do. **Lobbyists** and **special-interest groups,** such as **political action committees** (PACs), play a significant role in U.S. politics.

Who Rules the United States?

11.4　**Compare the functionalist (pluralist) and conflict (power elite) perspectives on U.S. power.**

Is the United States controlled by a ruling class?

In a view known as **pluralism,** functionalists say that no one group holds power, that the country's many competing interest groups balance one another. Conflict theorists, who focus on the top level of power, say that the United States is governed by a **power elite,** a **ruling class** made up of the top corporate, political, and military leaders. At this point, the matter is not settled.

War and Terrorism: Implementing Political Objectives

11.5　**Explain why countries go to war and why some groups choose terrorism; discuss targeted killings.**

How are war and terrorism related to politics?

War and **terrorism** are both means of attempting to accomplish political objectives. Timasheff identified three essential conditions of war and seven fuels that bring about war. His analysis can be applied to terrorism. A controversial response to terrorism is targeted killing.

The Transformation of Economic Systems

11.6　**Summarize the broad historical shifts in economic systems; emphasize inequality.**

How are economic systems linked to types of societies?

In the earliest societies (hunting and gathering), small groups lived off the land and produced little or no surplus. Economic systems grew more complex as people discovered how to domesticate animals and grow plants (pastoral and horticultural societies), farm (agricultural societies), and manufacture (industrial societies). As people produced, a *surplus,* trade developed. Trade, in turn, brought social inequality as some people accumulated more than others. Service industries dominate the postindustrial societies. If a biotech society is emerging, its consequences, too, will be far reaching.

World Economic Systems

11.7　**Contrast capitalism and socialism: their components, ideologies, criticisms, and convergence.**

How do the major economic systems differ?

The world's two major economic systems are capitalism and socialism. In **capitalism,** private citizens own the means of production and pursue profits. In **socialism,** the state owns the means of production and has no goal of profit. Adherents of each have developed ideologies that defend their own systems and paint the other as harmful or even evil. As expected from **convergence theory,** each system has adopted features of the other.

The Globalization of Capitalism

11.8　**Discuss the globalization of capitalism, including its effects on workers, the divisions of wealth, and the global superclass.**

What is the new global structure?

The world's nations are forming major trading blocs. As multinational corporations seek the lowest costs of production, millions of jobs are transferred to nations where workers are paid little. This is causing great suffering to workers who are losing their jobs and to those whose pay is stagnant. At the same time, an ultra-wealthy and powerful **global superclass** has risen.

A New World Order?

11.9 Explain how the globalization of capitalism might be bringing a New World Order—and why it might not be.

Is humanity headed toward a world political system?

The globalization of capitalism, the global superclass, and the trend toward regional economic and political unions may indicate that a world economic-political system is developing. Competing interests and internal contradictions might prevent a New World Order from developing, but if one does emerge, the consequences for human welfare could be calamitous.

Thinking Critically about Chapter 11

1. What are the three sources of authority, and how do they differ from one another?

2. Apply the three essential conditions of war and its seven fuels to a recent (or current) war that the United States has been (or is) a part of.

3. What global forces are affecting the U.S. economy? What consequences are they having? How might they affect your own life?

Chapter 12
Marriage and Family

I was living in a remote village in the state of Colima, Mexico. I had chosen this nondescript town a few kilometers from the ocean because it had no other Americans, and I wanted to immerse myself in the local culture.

The venture was successful. I became friends with my neighbors, who were curious about why a gringo was living in their midst. After all, there was nothing about their drab and dusty town to attract tourists. So why was this gringo there, this guy who looked so different from them and who had the unusual custom of jogging shirtless around the outskirts of town and among the coconut and banana trees? This was their burning question, while mine was "What is your life like?"

We satisfied one another. I explained to them what a sociologist is. Although they never grasped why I would want to know about *their* way of life, they accepted my explanation. And I was able to get my questions answered. I was invited into their homes—by the men. The women didn't talk to men outside the presence of their husbands, brothers, or other women. The women didn't even go out in public unless they were accompanied by someone. Another woman would do, just so they weren't alone. The women did the cooking, cleaning, and child care. The men worked in the fields.

I was culturally startled one day at my neighbor's house. The man had retired from the fields, and he and his wife, as the custom was, were being supported by their sons who worked in the fields. When I saw the bathroom, with a homemade commode made

---

It was his wife's job to pick up the used toilet paper.

---

of clay—these were poor people—I asked him about the used toilet paper heaped in a pile on the floor. He explained that the sewer system couldn't handle toilet paper. He said that I should just throw mine onto the pile, adding that it was his wife's job to pick up the used toilet paper and throw it out.

I became used to the macho behavior of the men. This wasn't too unlike high-school behavior—a lot of boisterous man-to-man stuff—drinking, joking, and bragging about sexual conquests. The sex was vital for proving manhood. When the men took me to a whorehouse (to help explain their culture, they said), they couldn't understand why I wouldn't have sex with a prostitute. Didn't I find the women attractive? Yes, they were good looking. Weren't they sexy? Yes, very much so. Was I a real man? Yes. Then why not? My explanation about being married didn't faze them one bit. They were married, too—and a real man had to have sex with more women than just his wife.

Explanations of friendship with a wife and respect for her fell on deaf cultural ears.

Marriage and Family in Global Perspective

12.1   Define marriage and family and summarize their common cultural themes.

These men and I were living in the same physical space, but our cultural space—which we carry in our heads and show in our behavior—was worlds apart. My experiences with working-class men in this remote part of Mexico helped me understand how marriage and family can differ vastly from one culture to another. To broaden our perspective for understanding this vital social institution, let's look at how marriage and family customs differ around the world.

What Is a Family?

"What is a family, anyway?" *Family* should be easy to define, since it is so significant to humanity that it is universal. Although every human group organizes its members in families, the world's cultures display an incredible variety of family forms. The Western world regards a family as a husband, wife, and children, but in some groups, men have more than one wife (**polygyny**) or women more than one husband (**polyandry**). How about the obvious? Can we define the family as the approved group into which children are born? If so, we would overlook the Banaro of New Guinea. In this group, a young woman must give birth *before* she can marry—and she *cannot* marry the father of her child (Murdock 1949).

What if we were to define the family as the unit in which parents are responsible for disciplining children and providing for their material needs? This, too, seems obvious, but it is not universal. Among the Trobriand Islanders, it is not the parents but the wife's eldest brother who is responsible for providing the children's discipline and their food (Malinowski 1927).

Such remarkable variety means that we have to settle for a broad definition. A **family** consists of people who consider themselves related by blood, marriage, or adoption. A **household**, in contrast, consists of people who occupy the same housing unit—a house, apartment, or other living quarters.

We can classify families as **nuclear** (husband, wife, and children) and **extended** (including people such as grandparents, aunts, uncles, and cousins in addition to the nuclear unit). Sociologists also refer to the **family of orientation** (the family in which an individual grows up) and the **family of procreation** (the family that is formed when a couple has its first child).

polygyny
a form of marriage in which men have more than one wife

polyandry
a form of marriage in which women have more than one husband

family
two or more people who consider themselves related by blood, marriage, or adoption

household
people who occupy the same housing unit

nuclear family
a family consisting of a husband, wife, and child(ren)

extended family
a family in which relatives, such as the "older generation" or unmarried aunts and uncles, live with the parents and their children

family of orientation
the family in which a person grows up

family of procreation
the family formed when a couple's first child is born

Often one of the strongest family bonds is that of mother–daughter. The young artist, an eleventh grader, wrote: "This painting expresses the way I feel about my future with my child. I want my child to be happy and I want her to love me the same way I love her. In that way we will have a good relationship so that nobody will be able to take us apart. I wanted this picture to be alive; that is why I used a lot of bright colors."

marriage

a group's approved mating arrangements, usually marked by a ritual of some sort

endogamy

the practice of marrying within one's own group

exogamy

the practice of marrying outside of one's group

incest taboo

the rule that prohibits sex and marriage among designated relatives

system of descent

how kinship is traced over the generations

What Is Marriage?

We have the same problem in defining marriage. For just about every element you might regard as essential to marriage, some group has a different custom.

Consider the sex of the bride and groom. Until recently, opposite sex was taken for granted. Then in the 1980s and 1990s, several European countries legalized same-sex marriages. Canada and several U.S. states followed.

Same-sex marriages sound so new, but when Columbus landed in the Americas, some Native American tribes already had same-sex marriages. Through a ceremony called the *berdache*, a man or woman who wanted to be a member of the opposite sex was officially *declared* to have his or her sex changed. The "new" man or woman put on the clothing and performed the tasks associated with his or her new sex and was allowed to marry.

Even sexual relationships don't universally characterize marriage. The Nayar of Malabar don't allow a bride and groom to have sex. After a three-day celebration of the marriage, they send the groom packing—and he can never see his bride again (La Barre 1954). This can be a little puzzling to figure out, but it works like this: The groom is "borrowed" from another tribe for the ceremony. Although the Nayar bride can't have sex with her husband, after the wedding she can have approved lovers from her tribe. This system keeps family property intact—along matrilineal lines.

At least one thing has to be universal in marriage: We can at least be sure that the bride and groom are alive. So you would think. But even for this there is an exception. On the Loess Plateau in China, if a son dies without a wife, his parents look for a dead woman to be his bride. After buying one—from the parents of a dead unmarried daughter—the dead man and woman are married and then buried together. Happy that their son will have intimacy in the afterlife, the parents throw a party to celebrate the marriage (Fremson 2006).

With such tremendous cultural variety, we can define **marriage** this way: a group's approved mating arrangements, usually marked by a ritual of some sort (the wedding) to indicate the couple's new public status.

Common Cultural Themes

Despite this diversity, several common themes run through marriage and family. As Table 12.1 on the next page illustrates, all societies use marriage and family to establish patterns of mate selection, descent, inheritance, and authority. Let's look at these patterns.

MATE SELECTION   Each human group establishes norms to govern who marries whom. If a group has norms of **endogamy**, it specifies that its members must marry *within* their group. For example, some groups prohibit interracial marriage. In some societies, these norms are written into law, but in most cases, they are informal. In the United States, most whites marry whites, and most African Americans marry African Americans—not because of any laws but because of informal norms. In contrast, norms of **exogamy** specify that people must marry *outside* their group. The best example of exogamy is the **incest taboo**, which prohibits sex and marriage among designated relatives.

As you can see from Table 12.1, how people find mates varies around the world, from fathers selecting them to the highly personal choices common in Western cultures. Changes in mate selection are the focus of the Sociology and the New Technology box on page 380.

DESCENT   How are you related to your father's father or to your mother's mother? You would think that the answer to this question would be the same all over the world—but it isn't. Each society has a **system of descent**, the way people trace kinship over generations.

Table 12.1 Common Cultural Themes: Marriage in Traditional and Industrialized Societies

Characteristic	Traditional Societies	Industrial (and Postindustrial) Societies
What is the structure of marriage?	*Extended* (marriage embeds spouses in a large kinship network of explicit obligations)	*Nuclear* (marriage brings fewer obligations toward the spouse's relatives)
What are the functions of marriage?	Encompassing (see the six functions listed on page 381)	More limited (many functions are fulfilled by other social institutions)
Who holds authority?	*Patriarchal* (authority is held by males)	Although some patriarchal features remain, authority is divided more equally
How many spouses at one time?	Most have one spouse (*monogamy*), while some have several (*polygamy*)	One spouse
Who selects the spouse?	Parents, usually the father, select the spouse	Individuals choose their own spouses
Where does the couple live?	Couples usually reside with the groom's family (*patrilocal residence*), less commonly with the bride's family (*matrilocal residence*)	Couples establish a new home (*neolocal residence*)
How is descent figured?	Usually figured from male ancestors (*patrilineal kinship*), less commonly from female ancestors (*matrilineal kinship*)	Figured from male and female ancestors equally (*bilineal kinship*)
How is inheritance figured?	Rigid system of rules; usually patrilineal, but can be matrilineal	Highly individualistic; usually bilineal

SOURCE: By the author.

We use a **bilineal system**; that is, we think of ourselves as related to both our mother's and our father's sides of the family. This is so obvious. Doesn't everyone do it this way? Actually, no. Ours is only one way that people reckon descent. Some groups use a **patrilineal system**, tracing descent only on the father's side—they don't think of children as being related to their mother's relatives. Others don't consider children to be related to their father's relatives and follow a **matrilineal system**, tracing descent only on the mother's side. The Naxi of China don't even have a word for father (Hong 1999).

INHERITANCE   Marriage and family are also used to determine rights of inheritance. In a bilineal system, property is passed to both males and females; in a patrilineal system, only to males; and in a matrilineal system (the rarest form), only to females. No system is natural. Rather, each matches a group's ideas of justice and logic.

AUTHORITY   Some form of **patriarchy**, men-as-a-group dominating women-as-a-group, runs through all societies. Contrary to what some think, there are no historical records of a society that was a true **matriarchy**, where women-as-a-group dominated men-as-a-group. Although U.S. family patterns are becoming more **egalitarian**, or equal, some of today's customs still reflect their patriarchal origin. One of the most obvious is the U.S. naming pattern: Despite some changes, the typical bride still takes the groom's last name, and children usually receive the father's last name.

Marriage and Family in Theoretical Perspective

12.2   **Contrast the functionalist, conflict, and symbolic interactionist perspectives on marriage and family.**

As we have seen, human groups around the world have many forms of mate selection, ways to view the parent's responsibility and ways to trace descent. Although these

bilineal system

(of descent) a system of reckoning descent that counts both the mother's and the father's side

patrilineal system

(of descent) a system of reckoning descent that counts only the father's side

matrilineal system

(of descent) a system of reckoning descent that counts only the mother's side

patriarchy

men-as-a-group dominating women-as-a-group; authority is vested in males

matriarchy

a society in which women-as-a-group dominate men-as-a-group; authority is vested in females

egalitarian

authority more or less equally divided between people or groups (in heterosexual marriage, for example, between husband and wife)

Sociology and the New Technology

Online Dating: Risks and Rewards

There are over 1,000 online dating sites. Some are general—they try to appeal to everyone. Others are niche, targeting people by age, race, or religion. Still others are super-niche. There are sites for Goths, military widows, and pet lovers (Broughton 2013). One targets "green singles," people for whom environmental, vegetarian, and animal rights are central. Another targets women who like men with mustaches (Cole 2012; Webb 2013).

Electronic matchmaking is changing the way many find mates. Online dating has become so popular that one-third of singles meet their first dates through the Internet (Fisher 2014). But first they have to traverse that pesky matter of gender, which we reviewed in Chapter 10. No longer will that dichotomy, either-male-or-female, work. To keep up with changing times, OkCupid has added androgynous, asexual, genderqueer, transman, transsexual, transmasculine, heteroflexible, pansexual, bigender, and sapiosexual (Ulaby 2014). The last one refers to people who are attracted to smart people.

It isn't difficult to see the appeal of dating sites. They offer thousands of potential companions, lovers, or spouses. For a low monthly fee, you can meet the person of your dreams—or so the promise goes.

The photos on these sites are fascinating. Some seem to be lovely people—warm, attractive, and vivacious. Others seem okay, although perhaps a bit needy. Then there are the desperate, begging for someone—anyone—to contact them: women who try for sexy poses, their exposed flesh suggesting the promise of a good time, and men who do their best to look like hulks, their muscular presence promising the same.

If you want to meet a mate online, you can expect to be fed a few lies. To "put their best foot forward," women say they weigh less than they do. And men? They say they are taller than they are (D'Costa 2014). Since the correspondence is via computer, they can get away with it. But isn't this similar to what you can expect wherever people seek mates? To make a good impression, most people stretch the truth. They try to match their presentation of self to what they think the other expects.

Snapshots

© Jason Love/www.CartoonStock.com

Tall, Dark, and Handsome chats with Buxom Blonde.

Are there dangers? The rapists of Craig's List and all that? Certainly there are, and you have to watch out for shady characters lurking on the Net. How do you know that the engaging person you are corresponding with is not already married, does not have a dozen kids, or is not a child molester or a rapist? But what makes such concerns unique to Internet dating? Aren't these the same kind of issues you need to be concerned about when meeting someone at school, a party, or even in the supermarket?

Even though the form is changing, the substance appears to be about the same. Maybe Internet dating is just tradition dressed up in technological clothing.

For Your Consideration

→ Have you used an online dating site? Why or why not?
→ Would you consider using one (if you were single and unattached)? Why or why not?

---

patterns are arbitrary, each group perceives its own forms of marriage and family as natural. Now let's see what pictures emerge when we view marriage and family theoretically.

The Functionalist Perspective: Functions and Dysfunctions

Functionalists stress that to survive, a society must fulfill basic functions (that is, meet its basic needs). When functionalists look at marriage and family, they examine how they are related to other parts of society, especially the ways that marriage and family contribute to the well-being of society.

WHY THE FAMILY IS UNIVERSAL Although the form of marriage and family varies from one group to another, the family is universal. The reason for this, say functionalists, is that the family fulfills six needs that are basic to the survival of every society. These needs, or functions, are (1) economic production, (2) socialization of children, (3) care of the sick and aged, (4) recreation, (5) sexual control, and (6) reproduction. To make certain that these functions are performed, every human group has adopted some form of the family.

FUNCTIONS OF THE INCEST TABOO Functionalists note that the incest taboo helps families to avoid *role confusion*. This, in turn, helps parents socialize children. For example, if father–daughter incest were allowed, how should a wife treat her daughter—as a daughter or as a second wife? Should the daughter consider her mother as a mother or as the first wife? Would her father be a father or a lover? And would the wife be the husband's main wife or the "mother of the other wife"? And if the daughter had a child by her father, what relationships would everyone have? Maternal incest would also lead to complications every bit as confusing as these.

The incest taboo also forces people to look outside the family for marriage partners. Anthropologists theorize that *exogamy* was especially functional in tribal societies, because it forged alliances between tribes that otherwise might have killed each other off. Today, exogamy still extends both the bride's and the groom's social networks by building relationships with their spouse's family and friends.

ISOLATION AND EMOTIONAL OVERLOAD As you know, functionalists also analyze dysfunctions. The relative isolation of today's nuclear family creates one of those dysfunctions. Because the members of extended families are embedded in a larger kinship network, they can count on many people for material and emotional support. In nuclear families, in contrast, the stresses that come with crises—the loss of a job, a death, or even family quarrels—are spread among fewer people. This places greater strain on each family member, creating *emotional overload*. In addition, the relative isolation of the nuclear family makes it vulnerable to a "dark side"—incest and other forms of abuse, matters that we examine later in this chapter.

The Conflict Perspective: Struggles between Husbands and Wives

Anyone who has been married or who has seen a marriage from the inside knows that—despite a couple's best intentions—conflict is a part of marriage. Conflict inevitably arises between two people who live intimately and who share most everything in life—from their goals and checkbooks to their bedroom and children. At some point, their desires and approaches to life clash, sometimes mildly, at other times quite harshly. Conflict among married people is so common that it is the grist of soap operas, movies, songs, and novels.

Power is the source of much conflict in marriage. Who has it? And who resents not having it? Throughout history, husbands have had more power, and wives have resented it. In the United States, as I'm sure you know, wives have gained more and more power in marriage. Do you think that one day wives will have more power than their husbands?

You probably are saying that such a day will never come. But could wives *already* have reached this point? From time to time, you've seen some surprising things in this book. Now look at Figure 12.1. Based on a national sample, this figure shows who makes decisions concerning the family's finances and purchases, what to do on the weekends, and even what to watch on television. As you can see, wives now have *more* control over the family purse and make *more* of these decisions than do their husbands. These findings are such a surprise that we await confirmation by future studies.

Figure 12.1 Who Makes the Decisions at Home?

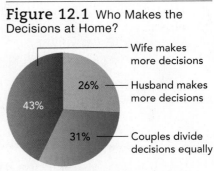

- Wife makes more decisions
- 26% — Husband makes more decisions
- 43%
- 31% — Couples divide decisions equally

NOTE: Based on a nationally representative sample, with questions on who chooses weekend activities, buys things for the home, decides what to watch on television, and manages household finances.

SOURCE: Morin and Cohn 2008.

The Symbolic Interactionist Perspective: Gender, Housework, and Child Care

CHANGES IN TRADITIONAL GENDER ORIENTATIONS   This chapter's opening vignette gave you a glimpse into extreme gender roles. Apart from the specifics mentioned there, throughout the generations, housework and child care have been regarded as "women's work." As times changed and women put in more hours at paid work, men gradually did more housework and took more responsibility for the care of their children. Ever so slowly, cultural ideas shifted, with housework, care of children, and paid labor coming to be regarded as the responsibilities of both men and women. Let's examine this shift.

PAID WORK AND HOUSEWORK   Figure 12.2 below illustrates major changes that have taken place in U.S. families. The first is startling—how wives have traded housework for paid work. They have cut down the amount of time they spend doing housework by 14.5 hours a week, while they have increased the time they spend at paid work by 14.9 hours a week. From this figure, you can see that husbands have done just the opposite. They have increased the time they spend on housework and child care, while they have dropped their paid work hours slightly.

From Figure 12.2, you can see that the total hours husbands and wives spend on housework have dropped by 9.4 hours a week. This is a lot less housework—*about 500 hours a year* of less washing, vacuuming, dusting, and so on. Does this mean that today's homes are dirtier and messier than those of the past? This is one possibility. But it is likely that the explanation lies in changed technology (Bianchi et al. 2006). Our microwaves, dishwashers, washing machines, clothes dryers, and wrinkle-free clothing save hours of drudgery. The "McDonaldization" we discussed in Chapter 5, which has led to so many "fast-food" meals, also reduces the time it takes to prepare food and clean up. Home hygiene could well be about the same as in years past.

In Hindu marriages, the roles of husband and wife are firmly established. Neither this woman, whom I photographed in Chittoor, India, nor her husband question whether she should carry the family wash to the village pump. Women here have done this task for millennia. As India industrializes, as happened in the West, who does the wash will be questioned—and may eventually become a source of strain in marriage.

Figure 12.2 In Two-Paycheck Marriages, How Do Wives and Husbands Divide Their Responsibilities?

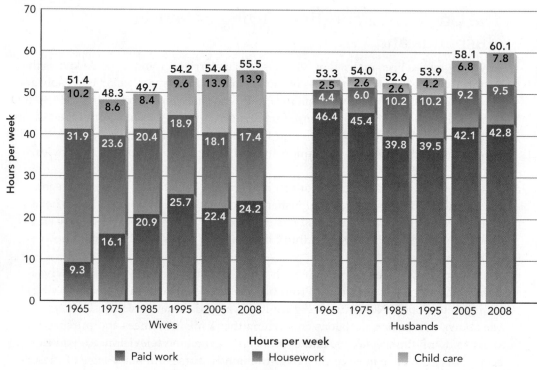

Wives

	1965	1975	1985	1995	2005	2008
Total	51.4	48.3	49.7	54.2	54.4	55.5
Child care	10.2	8.6	8.4	9.6	13.9	13.9
Housework	31.9	23.6	20.4	18.9	18.1	17.4
		16.1	20.9	25.7	22.4	24.2
Paid work	9.3					

Husbands

	1965	1975	1985	1995	2005	2008
Total	53.3	54.0	52.6	53.9	58.1	60.1
Child care	2.5	2.6	2.6	4.2	6.8	7.8
Housework	4.4	6.0	10.2	10.2	9.2	9.5
Paid work	46.4	45.4	39.8	39.5	42.1	42.8

Hours per week

■ Paid work   ■ Housework   ■ Child care

SOURCE: By the author. Based on Bianchi 2010:Tables 1, 2.

MORE CHILD CARE   From this figure, you can see another significant change: *Both* husbands and wives are spending more time on child care. How can children be getting *more* attention from their parents than they used to? This flies in the face of our mythical past, the *Leave It to Beaver* images that color our perception of the present. We know that today's families are not strolling leisurely through life as huge paychecks flow in. So if parents are spending more time with their children, just where is that time coming from?

The answer isn't very exciting, but researchers know what it is. Today's parents have squeezed out some of the extra time for their children by cutting down on their reading and the time they spend on preparing meals. However, the main way that parents are getting the extra time is by spending about 5 hours a week less visiting with friends and relatives (Bianchi 2010). We don't yet know the implications of the individual family withdrawing more into itself, but it could be increasing the family's "emotional overload."

TOTAL HOURS   Figure 12.2 holds another surprise. You can see that *both* husbands and wives are now putting in more hours taking care of family responsibilities. However, each week husbands average 4.6 hours more than their wives. This comes to 240 hours a year, the equivalent of today's husbands spending thirty 8-hour days a year more than their wives.

A GENDER DIVISION OF LABOR   Something else is evident from Figure 12.2. Look at how differently husbands and wives spend their time. Sociologists call this a *gendered division of labor*. You can see that husbands still take the primary responsibility for earning the income and wives the primary responsibility for taking care of the house and children. You have seen, however, the major shift that is taking place in this traditional gender orientation: Wives are spending more time earning the family income, while husbands are spending more time on housework and child care. In light of these trends and with changing ideas of gender—of what is considered appropriate for husbands and wives—we can anticipate greater marital equality in the future.

The Family Life Cycle

12.3   **Summarize research on love and courtship, marriage, childbirth, child rearing, and family transitions.**

We have seen how the forms of marriage and family vary widely, looked at marriage and family theoretically, including major shifts in gender. Now let's discuss love, courtship, and the family life cycle.

Love and Courtship in Global Perspective

Have you ever been "love sick"? Some people can't eat, and they are obsessed with thoughts of the one they love. Some neuroscientists decided to study "love sickness," and they found that it is both real and extreme: Love feelings release dopamine and light up the same area of the brain that lights up when heroin addicts are craving heroin (Bernstein 2015).

Evidently, then, love can be an addiction. From your own experience, you probably know the power of **romantic love**—mutual sexual attraction and idealized feelings about one another. Although people in most cultures talk about similar experiences, ideas of love can differ dramatically from one society to another (Jankowiak and Fischer 1992; Munck et al. 2011). In the Cultural Diversity box on the next page, we look at a society where people don't expect love to occur until *after* marriage.

romantic love

feelings of erotic attraction accompanied by an idealization of the other

Cultural Diversity around the World

East Is East and West Is West: Love and Arranged Marriage in India

After Arun Bharat Ram returned to India with a degree from the University of Michigan, his mother announced that she wanted to find him a wife. Arun would be a good catch anywhere: 27 years old, educated, intelligent, handsome— and, not incidentally, heir to a huge fortune.

Arun's mother already had someone in mind. Manju came from a middle-class family and was a college graduate. Arun and Manju met in a coffee shop at a luxury hotel—along with both sets of parents. He found her pretty and quiet. He liked that. She was impressed that he didn't boast about his background.

After four more meetings, including one at which the two young people met by themselves, the parents asked their children whether they were willing to marry. Neither had any major objections.

The prime minister of India and 1,500 other guests came to the wedding.

"I didn't love him," Manju says. "But when we talked, we had a lot in common." She then adds, "But now I couldn't live without him. I've never thought of another man since I met him."

Despite India's many changes, parents still arrange about 70 percent of marriages. Unlike the past, however, today's couples have veto power over their parents' selection. Another innovation is that the prospective bride and groom can talk to each other before the wedding—unheard of a generation or two ago.

Why do Indians have arranged marriages? And why does this practice persist, even among the educated and upper classes? We can also ask why the United States has such an individualistic approach to marriage.

Two Sociological Principles.   The answers to these questions take us to two sociological principles. First, *a group's marriage practices match its values*. Individual mate selection matches U.S. values of individuality and independence, while arranged marriages match the Indian value of children deferring to parental authority. To Indians, allowing unrestricted dating would mean entrusting important matters to inexperienced young people.

Second, *a group's marriage practices match its patterns of social stratification*. Arranged marriages in India affirm caste lines by channeling marriage within the same caste.

This billboard in India caught my attention. As the text indicates, even though India is industrializing, most of its people still follow traditional customs. This billboard is a sign of changing times.

Unchaperoned dating would encourage premarital sex, which, in turn, would break down family lines. Virginity at marriage, in contrast, assures the upper castes that they know who fathered the children. Consequently, Indians socialize their children to think that parents have superior wisdom in these matters. In the United States, where family lines are less important and caste is an alien concept, the practice of young people choosing their own dating partners mirrors the relative openness of our social class system.

Two Ideas of Love.   These different backgrounds have produced contrasting ideas of love. Americans idealize love as something mysterious, a passion that seizes an individual. Indians view love as a peaceful feeling that develops when a man and a woman are united in intimacy and share life's interests and goals. For Americans, love just "happens," while for Indians, the right conditions create love. Marriage is one of those right conditions.

The end result is this startling difference: *For Americans, love produces marriage—while for Indians, marriage produces love.*

SOURCES: Based on Gupta 1979; Bumiller 1992; Sprecher and Chandak 1992; Dugger 1998; Gautham 2002; Swati 2008; Harris 2013; "Most Indians . . ." 2014.

For Your Consideration

→ What advantages do you see to the Indian approach to love and marriage?

→ Could the Indian system work in the United States? Why or why not?

→ Do you think that love can be created? Or does love "seize" people?

→ What do you think love is, anyway?

Because romantic love plays such a significant role in Western life—and often is regarded as the *only* proper basis for marriage—social scientists have probed this concept with the tools of the trade: experiments, questionnaires, interviews, and observations (Hatfield et al. 2012; Bolmont et al. 2014). In a fascinating experiment, psychologists Donald Dutton and Arthur Aron discovered that fear can produce romantic love (Rubin 1985). Here's what they did.

> *A rickety footbridge sways in the wind about 230 feet above the Capilano River in North Vancouver, British Columbia. Walking on it makes you feel like you might fall into the rocky gorge below. A more solid footbridge crosses only 10 feet above the shallow stream.*
>
> *The researchers had an attractive woman approach men who were crossing these bridges. She told them she was studying "the effects of exposure to scenic attractions on creative expression." She showed them a picture, and they wrote down their associations. The sexual imagery in their stories showed that the men on the unsteady, frightening bridge were more sexually aroused than were the men on the solid bridge. More of these men also called the young woman afterward—supposedly to get information about the study.*

You may have noticed that this research was really about sexual attraction, not love. The point, however, is that romantic love usually begins with sexual attraction. Finding ourselves sexually attracted to someone, we spend time with that person. If we discover mutual interests, we may label our feelings "love." Apparently, then, *romantic love has two components*. The first is emotional, a feeling of sexual attraction. The second is cognitive, a label that we attach to our feelings. If we attach this label, we describe ourselves as being "in love."

Marriage

Ask Americans why they married, and they will say that they were "in love." Contrary to folklore, whatever love is, it certainly is not blind. That is, love does not hit us willy-nilly, as if Cupid had shot darts blindly into a crowd. If it did, marital patterns would be unpredictable. When we look at who marries whom, however, we can see that love follows social channels.

THE SOCIAL CHANNELS OF LOVE AND MARRIAGE The most highly predictable social channels are age, education, social class, and race–ethnicity. For example, a Latina with a college degree whose parents are both physicians is likely to fall in love with and marry a Latino slightly older than herself who has graduated from college. Similarly, a girl who drops out of high school and whose parents are on welfare is likely to fall in love with and marry a man who comes from a background similar to hers.

Sociologists use the term **homogamy** to refer to the tendency of people who have similar characteristics to marry one another. Homogamy occurs largely as a result of *propinquity*, or spatial nearness. This is a sociological way of saying that we tend to "fall in love" with and marry someone who lives near us or someone we meet at school, church, work, or a neighborhood bar. The people with whom we associate are far from a random sample of the population, since social filters produce neighborhoods, schools, and places of worship that follow racial–ethnic and social class lines.

As with all social patterns, there are exceptions. Although most Americans marry someone of their same racial–ethnic background, 8 percent do not. Eight percent is a lot of people. With 60 million married couples in the United States, this comes close to 5 million couples (*Statistical Abstract* 2014:Table 63).

One of the more dramatic changes in U.S. marriage is the increase in marriages between African Americans and whites. Today it is difficult to realize how norm-shattering such marriages used to be, but they were once illegal in forty states (Staples 2008). In Mississippi, the penalty for interracial marriage was *life in prison* (Crossen 2004b).

homogamy
the tendency of people with similar characteristics to marry one another

Michael Jordan and Yvette Prieto are an example of the most common pattern of marriages between African Americans and whites.

Despite the risks, a few couples crossed the "color line," but it took the social upheaval of the 1960s to shatter this barrier. In 1967, the U.S. Supreme Court struck down the state laws that prohibited such marriages.

Figure 12.3 shows this change. Look at the race–ethnicity of the husbands and wives in these marriages, and you will see that here, too, Cupid's arrows don't hit random targets. Why do you think this particular pattern exists? Why do you think it is changing?

For a surprising effect of marriage—that it helps people live longer—look at the Down-to-Earth Sociology box on the next page.

Childbirth

IDEAL FAMILY SIZE The number of children that Americans consider ideal has changed over the years. You can track these changes in Figure 12.5 on the next page. Note the sharp change in the 1970s. I can't specify with certainty the reasons for this abrupt change of wanting fewer children, but I expect it had to do with three major events of that time: the birth control pill, the sexual revolution, and women's changed perceptions of work—from a temporary activity before marriage to long-term careers.

The research shows an interesting religious divide in the number of children that people want, not between Protestants and Roman Catholics, who give the same answers, but by church attendance. Those who attend services more often prefer larger families than those who attend less often. The last couple of polls reveal an unexpected change: Younger Americans (ages 18 to 34) prefer larger families than do those who are older than 34 (Gallup Poll 2011a).

Figure 12.3 Marriages between Whites and African Americans: The Race–Ethnicity of the Husbands and Wives

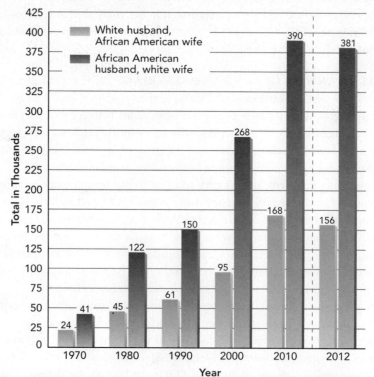

SOURCE: By the author. Based on *Statistical Abstract of the United States* 1990:Table 53; 2014:Table 63.

Down-to-Earth Sociology

Health Benefits of Marriage: Living Longer

An old joke goes like this.

Joe: Do married people really live longer?

Mary: Not really. Marriage is so boring that it just feels that way.

Jokes about marriage aside, marriage brings health benefits, and the married really do live longer than the unmarried. This has been observed since the 1800s and confirmed in study after study. Look at Figure 12.4 to see the results of recent research. The follow-up years shown on this figure began at age 18.

From this figure, you can see that marriage actually does bring health benefits. You can see that the greatest benefits, in terms of length of life, go to those who marry and stay married. They live the longest. You can see that those who remarry also live considerably longer. People who divorce and stay single don't live as long, but even the marriage they once had adds years to their lives. The worst for health is never getting married. At each age, people who remain single are the most likely to die.

Among the health benefits of marriage is a longer life.

Why does marriage help people live longer? Beyond practical matters, such as husbands and wives encouraging one another to exercise and eat regularly, the primary reason seems to be the support they give one another. Married couples have someone who means a lot to them (sometimes called "a significant other") to help them get through the problems of everyday life. The touches, kisses, sex, and encouragement are good for health.

For Your Consideration

→ With more people staying single longer, how do you think this might affect the data shown in Figure 12.4? How about cohabitation?

→ Singles also develop social support systems. Why do you think they fall short when compared with the social support of marriage?

Figure 12.4 Health Benefits of Marriage

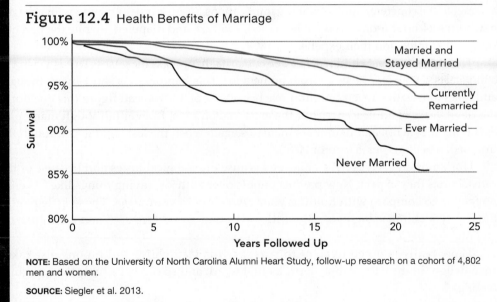

NOTE: Based on the University of North Carolina Alumni Heart Study, follow-up research on a cohort of 4,802 men and women.

SOURCE: Siegler et al. 2013.

If they had their way, some couples would specify not just the number of children but also their characteristics, the topic of the Sociology and the New Technology box on page 389.

MARITAL SATISFACTION   Sociologists have found that after the birth of a child, marital satisfaction usually decreases (Twenge et al. 2003; Dew and Wilcox 2011). To understand why, recall from Chapter 5 that a dyad (two persons) provides greater intimacy than a triad (after adding a third person, interaction must be shared). In addition, the

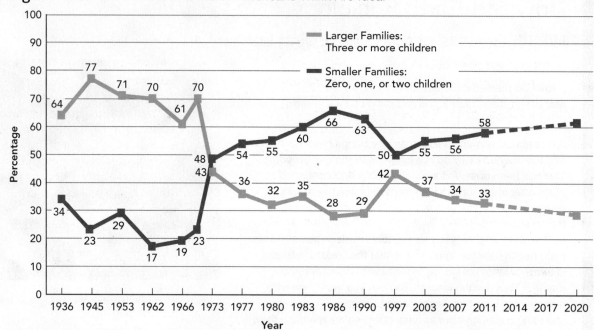

Figure 12.5 The Number of Children Americans Think Are Ideal

SOURCE: Gallup Poll 2011b. 2011 is the last year for which we have data. The broken lines are the author's projections.

birth of a child unbalances the life that the couple has worked out. To move from the abstract to the concrete, think about the implications for marriage of coping with a fragile newborn's 24-hour-a-day needs of being fed, soothed, and diapered—while the parents' sleep is disrupted and their expenses grow.

Then when the last child reaches age 6, marital happiness increases. This is when the child starts school and is away from home a lot. This happiness is short-lived, though, and takes a nosedive when the child reaches age 12 or 13. You can figure this one out—the devil years of adolescence. But those years don't last forever (although many parents think they will), and happiness increases again when the last child gets through the troubled, rebellious years (Senior 2010).

Husbands and wives have children because of biological urges and because of the satisfactions they expect. New parents bubble over with joy, saying things like "There's no feeling to compare with holding your own child in your arms. Those little hands, those tiny feet, those big eyes, that little nose, that sweet face . . ." and they gush on and on.

There really is no equivalent to parents. It is *their* child, and no one else takes such delight in the baby's first steps, its first word, and so on. Let's turn, then, to child rearing.

Child Rearing

As you saw in Figure 12.2 on page 382, today's parents are spending more time with their children than parents did in earlier decades. But they are also spending huge amounts of time at work. This includes a large percentage of mothers of single children. Let's ask, then: Who's minding the kids while the parents are at work?

MARRIED COUPLES AND SINGLE MOTHERS Figure 12.7 on page 390 compares the child care of babies of single and married mothers. As you can see, their overall arrangements are similar. A main difference, though, is that when married women are at work, the father is more likely to be taking care of the baby. To help single mothers, grandparents and other relatives tend to fill in for the absent father.

Sociology and the New Technology

What Color Eyes? How Tall? Designer Babies on the Way

Ready to shop for your child? You might begin by browsing the online catalogue of sperm donors at the London Sperm Bank. With a few clicks, you can check the donor's race–ethnicity, eye color, hair color, and height—even the man's religion, education, and TV preferences (de Lange 2014).

Satisfied? Click "Add to Cart" and go to Check Out.

Actually, they haven't added those check-out clicks yet. But the list of donor characteristics is there. In the coming world of Designer Baby Clinics, you will be able to put in your order. Not like fast food, of course, since it will still take the usual nine months.

The allure of choosing a daughter who will be a scientist, a son who will be musical—or a basketball star—is apparent. To pick superior qualities for your child, isn't this like being able to pick a superior college?

But with this allure comes moral dilemmas. Let's suppose that a couple wants a green-eyed blond girl. As Figure 12.6 shows, the technicians will fertilize several eggs, test the embryos, and plant the one(s) with the desired characteristics in a uterus. And the embryos that are not used?

They will be flushed down the toilet. Some people find this objectionable.

Others are concerned that selecting certain characteristics represents a bias against people who have different characteristics. To order a tall designer baby, for example, is this a bias against short people?

If it isn't quite clear why this is a bias, perhaps this will help. If there is a preference for boys, a lot of female embryos will be flushed down the toilet.

Or consider this: Two deaf parents want a deaf child. They fear that if their child is part of the hearing world it will drive a wedge between them (Fordham 2011). Would it be moral or immoral to produce a deaf child?

Oh, the moral dilemmas our new technologies bring!

For Your Consideration

→ What are your answers to the questions raised in this box? On what do you base your answers?

→ One more moral issue to consider: a super race. If we can produce people who are superior physically, intellectually, and emotionally, would it be wrong to do so? Or would it be immoral *not* to do this if this is within our capacity?

Figure 12.6 On the Way to Designer Babies

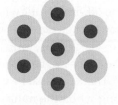 

A woman's eggs are fertilized with sperm in a lab, creating several embryos.

A single cell is removed from each embryo, and then tested for biomarkers associated with females, green eyes, and blond hair.

Only embryos with the biomarkers for the required traits are placed in the woman's womb.

The procedure virtually guarantees that the child will be female and increases the probability she will have green eyes and blond hair.

SOURCE: Adapted from Naik 2009. Reproduced with permission.

SINGLE FATHERS   But what about single fathers? These are the men who have sole custody of their children, usually because the mothers have abandoned the children or the court has declared them unfit as parents. While we don't have space to explore this in detail, read what a student who read this text, a 40-year-old father who has custody of his 8-year-old son wrote to me. This will help you gain insight into their conflicts and difficulties.

My son is being raised by his father, me. I do not have the social network that I used to have because my life consists of cooking, cleaning, playtime, and schoolwork. I am not accepted by other mothers, and while I am respected by most men, they aren't interested in hearing about domestic life. This has started to impact my son because I can't really model relationships for him being in this awkward state of mother–dad.

Figure 12.7 Who Takes Care of the Babies While Their Mothers Are at Work?

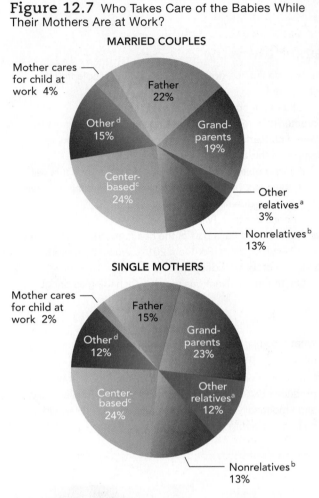

MARRIED COUPLES

Mother cares for child at work 4%

Father 22%

Other[d] 15%

Grand-parents 19%

Center-based[c] 24%

Other relatives[a] 3%

Nonrelatives[b] 13%

SINGLE MOTHERS

Mother cares for child at work 2%

Father 15%

Other[d] 12%

Grand-parents 23%

Center-based[c] 24%

Other relatives[a] 12%

Nonrelatives[b] 13%

[a]Includes siblings.
[b]Includes in-home babysitters and other nonrelatives providing care in either the child's or the provider's home.
[c]Includes day care centers, nursery schools, preschools, and Head Start programs.
[d]Includes no regular arrangement.

SOURCE: *America's Children* 2014:Table FAM3A.

The single father with custody of his child(ren) has unique role conflicts. Just what is a mother–dad?

DAY CARE   You know that quality child care is important, but did you know that children who receive quality care do better at language, math, and reading? They even have better memories (Li et al. 2013). About one of five U.S. children is in day care, but only a minority of these children receives high-quality care—stimulating learning activities, emotional warmth, and attentiveness to their needs (Bergmann 1995; Blau 2000; Belsky 2009; *Statistical Abstract* 2014:Table 604). A primary reason for this dismal situation is the low salaries paid to day care workers. They average only about $10 an hour ("Child Care Workers" 2013).

With many parents doing shift work (evening and midnight work), some "day care" centers are open 24 hours a day. The workers brush the children's teeth, read them bedtime stories, and tuck them in. The parents pick their children up whenever they get off work, whether this is midnight or 6 A.M. (Tavernise 2012).

It is difficult for parents to judge the quality of day care, since they don't know what takes place when they are not there. If you ever need day care, what should you look for? Here are the two factors that best predict quality care: a staff that has taken courses in early childhood development and a low ratio of children per staff member (Belsky et al. 2007; Sosinsky and Kim 2013). If you have nagging fears that your children might be neglected or even abused, choose a center that streams live Web cam images on the Internet. While at work, you can "visit" the day care center via cyberspace and monitor your child's activities and care.

NANNIES   For upper-middle-class parents, nannies have become a popular alternative to day care centers. Parents love the one-on-one care and the convenience of not having to drive the child to a day care center or having to take time off from work when the child becomes ill. A recurring problem, however, is tensions between the parents and the nanny: disagreements over discipline styles and jealousy that the nanny might see the first step, hear the first word, or—worse yet—be called "mommy." There can also be what parents find heart-breaking—the child crying when the nanny leaves but not when the mother goes to work.

UBER AS A PARENT SUBSTITUTE   A major complaint of parents is the vast amount of time it takes to run their kids to their many after-school activities. If parents have two or three children near the same age, the scheduling can become herculean—how to get one to soccer while the other is due at play practice, and so on. To the relief of many parents, technology to the rescue.

Parents are increasingly turning to Uber (Kapp 2014). When they open an account with Uber, they download an app that lets them see the driver's name, cell phone number, and license plate. When their child enters the car, they can follow its route and know when the child exits the car. If they want to, they can also text with their children during their ride. To get their children to that soccer game or play practice, they don't have to leave work or get into convoluted planning. In some ways, Uber is becoming a parent substitute.

SOCIAL CLASS   Do you think that social class makes a difference in how people rear their children? If you answered "yes," you are right. But what difference? And why? Besides such things as middle-class parents being able to afford generous use of Uber, sociologists have found fundamental differences in how parents view children.

Working-class parents tend to think of children as wildflowers that develop naturally, while in the middle-class mind, children are like tender garden flowers that need careful nurturing if they are to bloom (Lareau 2011). These contrasting views make a world of difference in how people rear their children (Treas et al. 2014). Working-class parents are more likely to set limits for their children and then let them choose their own activities, while middle-class parents are more likely to try to push their children into activities that they think will develop their thinking and social skills.

Sociologist Melvin Kohn (1963, 1977; Kohn and Schooler 1969) also found that the type of work that parents do has an impact on how they rear their children. Because members of the working class are closely supervised on their jobs, where they are expected to follow explicit rules, their concern is less with their children's motivation and more with their outward conformity. These parents are more apt to use physical punishment, which brings about outward conformity, and may or may not change attitudes. Middle-class workers, in contrast, are expected to take more initiative on the job. This leads them to have more concern that their children develop curiosity and self-expression. Middle-class parents are less likely to use physical punishment and more likely to withdraw privileges or affection.

Family Transitions

The later stages of family life bring their own pleasures to be savored and problems to be solved. Let's look at two transitions—children staying home longer and adults adjusting to widowhood.

TRANSITIONAL ADULTHOOD AND THE NOT-SO-EMPTY NEST Adolescents, especially young men, used to leave home after finishing high school. When the last child left home at about age 17 to 19, the husband and wife were left with what was called an *empty nest*. Today's nest is not as empty as it used to be. With prolonged education and the higher cost of establishing a household, U.S. children are leaving home later. Many stay home during college, while others who strike out on their own find the cost or responsibility too great and return home. Much to their own disappointment, some even leave and return to the parents' home several times. As a result, 18 percent of all U.S. 25- to 29-year-olds are living with their parents. About 11 percent of this still-at-home group have their own children (U.S. Census Bureau 2012:Table A2).

This major historical change in how people become adult, which we call *transitional adulthood*, is playing out before our eyes. With the path to adulthood changing abruptly, its contours—its roadmap—are still being worked out. Although "adultolescents" enjoy the protection of home, they have to work out issues about privacy, authority, and responsibilities—items that both the children and parents thought were resolved long ago. You might want to look again at Figure 3.2 on page 95.

WIDOWHOOD As you know, women are more likely than men to become widowed. There are two reasons for this: On average, women live longer than men, and they usually marry men older than they are. For either women or men, the death of a spouse tears at the self, clawing at identities that merged through the years. With the one who had become an essential part of the self gone, the survivor, as in adolescence, once again confronts the perplexing question "Who am I?"

The death of a spouse produces what is called the *widowhood effect*: The impact of the death is so strong that surviving spouses tend to die earlier than expected. The widowhood effect is not even across the board, however. There are almost twice as many "excess deaths," as sociologists call them, among widowed men than among widowed women (Shor et al 2012). This indicates that marriage brings greater health benefits to elderly men.

Diversity in U.S. Families

12.4 Summarize research on families: African American, Latino, Asian American, Native American, one-parent, couples without children, blended, and gay and lesbian.

As we review some of the vast diversity of U.S. families, it is important to note that we are not comparing any of them to *the* American family. There is no such thing. Rather, family life varies widely throughout the United States. In several contexts, we have seen how significant social class is in our lives. Its significance will continue to be evident as we examine diversity in U.S. families.

African American Families

Note that the heading reads African American *families*, not *the* African American family. There is no such thing as *the* African American family any more than there is *the* white family or *the* Latino family. The primary distinction is not between African Americans and other groups but between social classes (Hattery and Smith 2012). Because African Americans who are members of the upper class follow the class interests reviewed in Chapter 8—preservation of privilege and family fortune—they are especially concerned about the family background of those whom their children marry (Gatewood 1990). To them, marriage is viewed as a merger of family lines. Children of this class marry later than children of other classes.

Middle-class African American families focus on achievement and respectability. Both husband and wife are likely to work outside the home. A central concern is that their children go to college, get good jobs, and marry well—that is, marry people like themselves, respectable and hardworking, who want to get ahead in school and pursue a successful career.

African American families in poverty face all the problems that cluster around poverty (Smith-Bynum 2013). Because the men have few marketable skills and few job prospects, it is difficult for them to fulfill the cultural roles of husband and father. Consequently, these families are likely to be headed by a woman and to have a high rate of births to single women. Divorce and desertion are also more common than among other classes. Sharing scarce resources and "stretching kinship" are primary survival mechanisms. People who have helped out in hard times are considered brothers, sisters, or cousins to whom one owes obligations as though they are blood relatives. Men who are not the biological fathers of their children are given fatherhood status (Stack 1974; Nelson 2013). Sociologists use the term *fictive kin* to refer to this stretching of kinship.

From Figure 12.8 on the next page, you can see that, compared with other groups, African American families are the least likely to be headed by married couples and the most likely to be headed by women. Because African American women tend to go farther in school than African American men, they face a *marriage squeeze*. That is, their pool of eligible partners with characteristics that match theirs has shrunk, and they are more likely than women in other racial–ethnic groups to marry men who are less educated than themselves (Smith-Bynum 2013).

There is no such thing as *the* African American family, any more than there is *the* Native American, Asian American, Latino, or Irish American family. Rather, each racial–ethnic group has different types of families, with the primary determinant being social class.

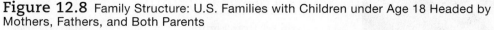

Figure 12.8 Family Structure: U.S. Families with Children under Age 18 Headed by Mothers, Fathers, and Both Parents

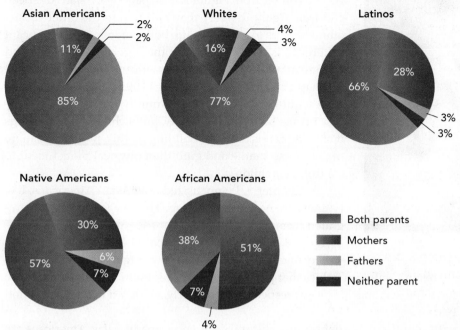

Asian Americans
- 2%
- 2%
- 11%
- 85%

Whites
- 4%
- 3%
- 16%
- 77%

Latinos
- 28%
- 66%
- 3%
- 3%

Native Americans
- 30%
- 6%
- 7%
- 57%

African Americans
- 38%
- 51%
- 7%
- 4%

Legend:
- Both parents
- Mothers
- Fathers
- Neither parent

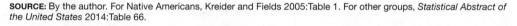

SOURCE: By the author. For Native Americans, Kreider and Fields 2005:Table 1. For other groups, *Statistical Abstract of the United States* 2014:Table 66.

Latino Families

As Figure 12.8 shows, the proportion of Latino families headed by married couples and women falls in between that of whites and Native Americans. The effects of social class on families, which I just sketched, also apply to Latinos. In addition, families differ by country of origin. Families from Mexico, for example, are more likely to be headed by a married couple than are families from Puerto Rico (*Statistical Abstract* 2014:Table 38). The longer that Latinos live in the United States, the more their families resemble those of middle-class Americans (Falicov 2010).

Researchers disagree on what is distinctive about Latino families (Cabrera and Bradley 2012). Some indicate that Latino families are set apart by the Spanish language, the Roman Catholic religion, and a strong family orientation coupled with a disapproval of divorce. True in a general sort of way, but this overlooks the Latino families that are Protestants, don't speak Spanish, and so on. Some point to loyalty to the extended family, with an obligation to support relatives in times of need (Cauce and Domenech-Rodriguez 2002). This, too, is hardly unique to Latino families. Descriptions of Latino families used to include **machismo**—an emphasis on male strength, sexual vigor, and dominance, like that recounted in the chapter's opening vignette—but *machismo* decreases with each generation in the United States and is certainly not limited to Latinos (Hurtado et al. 1992; Wood 2001; Torres et al. 2002).

With such diversity among Latino families, you can see why researchers are unable to generalize about all or even most Latino families. However, there is a central sociological point that runs through the studies of Latino families: Social class is more important in determining family life than is either being Latino or a family's country of origin.

machismo

an emphasis on male strength and dominance

As with other groups, there is no such thing as *the* Latino family. Some Latino families speak little or no English, while others have assimilated into U.S. culture to such an extent that they no longer speak Spanish.

It is easy to see why there is no *the* Asian American family when you realize that Asian American is a general census category that lumps together groups from many nations. Shown here is an Asian American family, this one from Iran.

Asian American Families

As you can see from Figure 12.8 on page 393, Asian American children are more likely than children in the other racial–ethnic groups to grow up with both parents. This significant difference is a foundation for the higher educational and income attainments of Asian Americans that we discussed in Chapter 9. In addition, parents stress that their children represent the family in the community, that the child's success brings honor to the family, but a child's failure brings it shame (Zamiska 2004). Building on this, parents are more likely to use shame and guilt than physical punishment to control their children.

In Chapter 9, I emphasized how Asian Americans, like Latinos, are not a single group. That Asian Americans emigrated from many different countries means that their family life reflects not only differences of social class but also a variety of cultures. Families whose origin is Japan, for example, tend to retain Confucian values that provide a framework for family life: humanism, collectivity, self-discipline, hierarchy, respect for the elderly, moderation, and obligation (Suzuki 1985).

But with country of origin bringing cultural differences, many Asian Americans are not even familiar with Confucianism. Asian American family life also differs by length of residence in the United States. As with immigrants everywhere, recent immigrants continue their old patterns, while the family life of Asian Americans who have been here for generations reflects few of the patterns of their country of origin.

Native American Families

To search for *the* Native American family would be fruitless. There are rural, urban, single-parent, extended, nuclear, rich, poor, traditional, and assimilated Native American families, to name just a few. This photo was taken on the Big Cypress Reservation near Hollywood, Florida.

Perhaps the most significant issue that Native American families face is whether to follow traditional values or to assimilate into the dominant culture (Johnson 2014). This primary distinction creates vast differences among families. The traditionals speak native languages and emphasize distinctive Native American values and beliefs. Those who have assimilated into the broader culture do not.

Figure 12.8 on page 394 depicts the structure of Native American families. You can see that it is closest to those of Latinos and African Americans. In general, Native American parents are permissive with their children and avoid physical punishment. Elders play a much more active role in their children's families than they do in most U.S. families. Elders, especially grandparents, not only provide child care but also teach and discipline children. Like others, Native American families differ by social class.

IN SUM From this brief review, you can see that race–ethnicity signifies little for understanding family life. Rather, social class and culture hold the keys. The more resources a family has, the more it assumes the characteristics of a middle-class nuclear family. Regardless of race–ethnicity, compared with the poor, middle-class families have fewer children and fewer unmarried mothers. They also place greater emphasis on educational achievement and deferred gratification.

One-Parent Families

An indication of how extensively U.S. families are changing is the increase in one-parent families. Look at Figure 12.9. You can see the decline in the percentage of U.S. children who live with two parents. Divorce is not the only reason for this change. Another is that single women who give birth are taking longer to get married (Gibon-Davis 2011). Because women head most one-parent families, these families tend to be poor. Even though most divorced women earn less than their former husbands, four of five children of divorce live with their mothers (U.S. Census Bureau 2013:Table C3). The concerns—even alarm—that many express about one-parent families may have more to do with their poverty than with children being reared by one parent.

Couples without Children

While most married women give birth, a large number of women—about one of six (15.7 percent)—do not (Martinez et al. 2012). This number is *double* what it was thirty years ago. From Figure 12.10, you can see that childlessness varies by racial–ethnic group, with Latinas the least likely to be childless. You can also see that the more education women have, the less likely they are to have children.

Some couples are infertile, but most childless couples have made a *choice* to not have children—and they prefer the term *childfree* rather than *childless*. Some decide before marriage that they will never have children, often to attain a sense of freedom—to pursue a career, to travel, and to have less stress. Other couples keep postponing the time when they will have their first child until either it is too late to have children, or it seems too uncomfortable to add a child to their lifestyle.

And the future? We have several indicators that the percentage of women who never bear children will increase: women going to school longer, more women career-oriented, contraception and legal abortion, the high cost of rearing children, and an emphasis on possessing material things. Here is how one woman expressed her view:

> *I'd rather continue traveling the world, running my business, getting massages, getting pedicures and manicures, working out with my trainer, enjoying great dining experiences and enjoying life to the fullest.*

A couple summed up their reasons for choosing not to have children this way:

> *We are DINKS (Dual Incomes, No Kids). We are happily married. I am 43; my wife is 42. We have been married for almost twenty years . . . . Our investment strategy has a lot to do with our personal philosophy: "You can have kids—or you can have everything else!" (in a newsletter).*

Blended Families

The **blended family**, one whose members were once part of other families, is an increasingly important type of family in the United States. Two divorced people who marry and each bring their children into a new family unit form a blended family. With divorce common, millions of children spend some of their childhood in blended families. I've never seen a better explanation of how blended

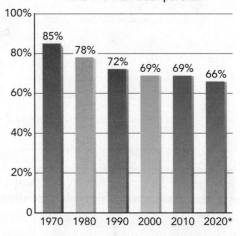

Figure 12.9 The Decline of Two-Parent Families

The percentage of children under 18 who live with both parents

- 1970: 85%
- 1980: 78%
- 1990: 72%
- 2000: 69%
- 2010: 69%
- 2020*: 66%

*Author's estimate.

SOURCE: By the author. *Based on Statistical Abstract of the United States* 1995:Table 79; 2014:Table 72.

blended family

a family whose members were once part of other families

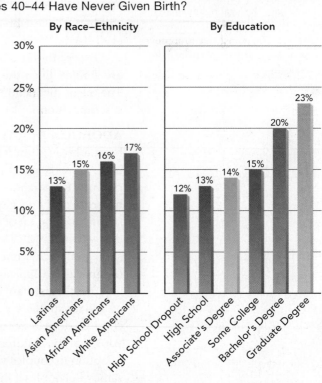

Figure 12.10 What Percentage of U.S. Married Women Ages 40–44 Have Never Given Birth?

By Race–Ethnicity

- Latinas: 13%
- Asian Americans: 15%
- African Americans: 16%
- White Americans: 17%

By Education

- High School Dropout: 12%
- High School: 13%
- Associate's Degree: 14%
- Some College: 15%
- Bachelor's Degree: 20%
- Graduate Degree: 23%

SOURCE: Monte and Ellis 2014:Table 2.

families can complicate family relationships than this description written by one of my freshman students:

> *I live with my dad. I should say that I live with my dad, my brother (whose mother and father are also my mother and father), my half sister (whose father is my dad, but whose mother is my father's last wife), and two stepbrothers and stepsisters (children of my father's current wife). My father's wife (my current stepmother, not to be confused with his second wife who, I guess, is no longer my stepmother) is pregnant, and soon we all will have a new brother or sister. Or will it be a half brother or half sister?*
>
> *If you can't figure this out, I don't blame you. I have trouble myself. It gets very complicated around Christmas. Should we all stay together? Split up and go to several other homes? Who do we buy gifts for, anyway?*

Gay and Lesbian Families

Until 2015, same-sex marriages were legal only in some states, but with the historic ruling of *Obergefell v. Hodges*, same-sex marriages became legal throughout the United States. Just as with heterosexual couples, for same-sex couples marriage is a big step as it immerses them in legal ties and obligations. Like heterosexual couples, gay and lesbian couples hope that marriage will make their relationship even more solid. Let's see what researchers have found about same-sex relationships.

If you expect exotic differences of some sort, you are in for a disappointment. Researchers have found that the main struggles of same-sex couples are housework, money, careers, problems with relatives, and sexual adjustment (Blumstein and Schwartz 1985). If these sound familiar, they should, as these are the same problems that heterosexual couples face. A major difference is that many same-sex couples face a stigma, sometimes accompanied by discrimination. As you can imagine, this complicates a couple's relationship.

The similarity continues when it comes to relationships that sour. Breakups occur among same-sex couples for the same reasons they do among heterosexual couples: disagreements about sex, how to spend money, how to rear children, romantic triangles, and so on. About 30 percent of lesbian couples and 17 percent of gay couples are rearing children, so these breakups bring the usual problems of custody and visitation (Gartrell et al. 2011).

Except for the sex of the individuals, then, same-sex and heterosexual relationships are similar. Even the rate at which they break up is about the same (Rosenfeld 2014). The major distinction centers not on the sex of the couples but on social acceptance and discrimination.

ADOPTION BY GAY AND LESBIAN COUPLES   Adoption by same-sex couples has been a hot-button issue. A concern is that children reared by same-sex parents will have worse social-psychological adjustments than children reared by two biological parents. Researchers have tried to answer this question by comparing the children of heterosexual and gay and lesbian couples. The first comparisons indicated that the sexual orientation of the parents made no difference in the children's adjustment (Gelderen et al. 2012). Then a storm erupted among sociologists when a large-scale study showed that children reared by gay and lesbian parents do have slightly more problems (Regnerus 2012).

Sociologist Paul Amato (2012) points out that because of statistical reasons none of this research can determine causation. The research can determine that one group of children does better or worse, but it leaves the reasons for those differences unclear. He adds that the children of divorced parents do slightly less well, but we would not deny adoption to couples who had divorced. Why, then, he asks, would we deny adoption to same-sex couples if their children do slightly less well. With the arguments on either side of this issue rooted not in science but in people's values, future research, no matter its particular findings, is destined to stir more controversy.

Views on whether same-sex couples should have the legal right to marry are marked by an age gap. Younger Americans are more likely to approve of same-sex marriages than are older Americans.

Trends in U.S. Families

12.5 **Discuss changes in the timetable of family life, cohabitation, and elder care.**

As is apparent from our discussion, marriage and family life in the United States is undergoing fundamental change. Let's look at other major trends.

The Changing Timetable of Family Life: Marriage and Childbirth

Figure 12.11 below illustrates another profound change in U.S. marriage. As you can see, the average age of first-time brides and grooms declined from 1890 to about 1950. In 1890, the typical first-time bride was 22, but by 1950, she had just left her teens. For about twenty years, there was little change. Then in 1970, the average age took a sharp turn upward, and *today's average first-time bride and groom are older than at any other time in U.S. history.*

Since postponing marriage is today's norm, it may surprise you to learn that *most* U.S. women used to marry before they turned 24. To see this remarkable change, look at Figure 12.12 on the next page. The percentage of men between 20 and 24 who are married is now *less than a fourth* of what it was in 1970. For women, it is *less than a third.* Just as couples are postponing marriage, so they are putting off having children. Today's average U.S. woman now has her first child at age 26, the highest age in U.S. history (Martin et al. 2013).

Why have these changes occurred? The primary reason is cohabitation. Although Americans have postponed the age at which they first marry, they have *not* postponed the age at which they first set up housekeeping with someone of the opposite sex. Let's look at this change.

Cohabitation

To see one of the most remarkable trends in the United States, look at Figure 12.13 on the next page. This figure shows the increase in **cohabitation**, adults living together in a sexual relationship without being married. I know of no other social trend that has risen this steeply and consistently. Cohabitation, once a furtive activity, has moved into

cohabitation
unmarried couples living together in a sexual relationship

Figure 12.11 When Do Americans Marry? The Changing Age at First Marriage

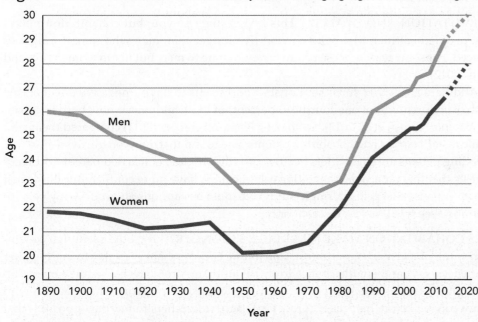

NOTE: This is the median age at first marriage. The broken lines indicate the author's estimate.

SOURCES: By the author. Based on U.S. Census Bureau 2010; Fry 2014.

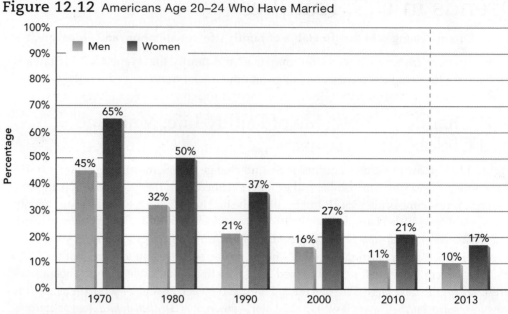

Figure 12.12 Americans Age 20–24 Who Have Married

NOTE: Includes widowed and divorced.

SOURCE: By the author. Based on *Statistical Abstract of the United States* 1993:Table 60; 2002:Table 48; 2012:Table 57; 2014:Table 60; U.S. Census Bureau 2014.

Figure 12.13 Cohabitation in the United States

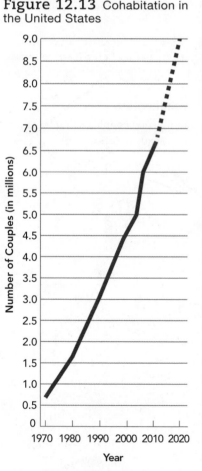

NOTE: Broken line indicates author's estimate

SOURCE: By the author. Based on U.S. Census Bureau 2007 and *Statistical Abstract of the United States* 1995:Table 60; 2014:Table 66.

the mainstream. Today, somewhere between one-half and two-thirds of couples cohabit before marriage (Huang et al. 2011; Copen et al. 2013).

COHABITATION AND MARRIAGE: THE ESSENTIAL DIFFERENCE   The essential difference between cohabitation and marriage is *commitment*. In marriage, the assumption is permanence; in cohabitation, couples agree to remain together for "as long as it works out." For marriage, individuals make public vows that legally bind them as a couple; for cohabitation, they simply move in together. Marriage requires a judge to authorize its termination, but if a cohabiting relationship sours, the couple separates, telling friends and family that "it didn't work out."

Within three years of cohabiting, 40 percent of couples decide to make this commitment, and they marry. Another 27 percent break up, and the rest continue to cohabit (Copen et al. 2013).

COHABITATION AND HEALTH   This might surprise you, but cohabitation makes some people healthier. Men who cohabit live longer than men who remain single or divorced. For some reason, these health benefits come to men, but not to women (Liu and Reczek 2012).

And here is another surprise: Cohabitation seems to have a negative effect on the health of children. About one-fourth (23 percent) of U.S. children are now born to cohabiting parents (Copen et al. 2013). Sociologist Kammi Schmeer (2011) compared the health of children of married and cohabiting parents. She found that, on average, the children of cohabiting parents are slightly less healthy than the children of married parents. Schmeer suggests that this is because cohabiting relationships have more conflict. But this is just a guess. Because this is just a single study, we must be cautious about drawing conclusions. We'll see what further research brings.

DOES COHABITATION MAKE MARRIAGE STRONGER?   It would seem that cohabitation would make marriage stronger. Cohabiting couples share everyday living-together experiences, giving them the chance to work out many problems before they marry. So are couples who live together before marriage less likely to divorce than couples who did not cohabit before marriage? A few years ago, researchers found the opposite—that couples who cohabited before marriage were *more* likely to divorce (Osborne et al. 2007; Lichter and Qian 2008). The latest research, however, shows that their divorce rate is about the same (Manning and Cohen 2011). If this finding holds, we can conclude that cohabitation neither weakens nor strengthens marriage.

The "Sandwich Generation" and Elder Care

The "sandwich generation" refers to people who find themselves sandwiched between and responsible for two other generations, their children and their own aging parents. Typically between the ages of 40 and 55, these people find themselves pulled in two directions. Many feel overwhelmed as these competing responsibilities collide. Some are plagued with guilt and anger because they can be in only one place at a time and are left with little time to pursue personal interests—or to just "get away from it all." As during the child-rearing years, women provide more emotional support than men to both grown children and aging parents (Parker and Patten 2013).

With people living longer, this issue is likely to become increasingly urgent.

Divorce and Remarriage

12.6 **Summarize problems in measuring divorce, research findings on children and grandchildren of divorce, fathers' contact after divorce, ex-spouses, and remarriage.**

The topic of family life would not be complete without considering divorce. Let's first try to determine how much divorce there is.

Ways of Measuring Divorce

You probably have heard that the U.S. divorce rate is 50 percent, a figure that is popular with reporters. The statistic is true in the sense that each year about half as many divorces are granted as there are marriages performed. The totals are about 2 million marriages and 1 million divorces (*Statistical Abstract* 2014:Table 138).

What is wrong, then, with saying that the divorce rate is about 50 percent? Think about it for a moment. Why should we compare the number of divorces and marriages that take place during the same year? The couples who divorced do not—with rare exceptions—come from the group that married that year. The one number has *nothing* to do with the other, so in no way do these two statistics reveal the divorce rate.

What figures should we compare, then? Couples who divorce come from the entire group of married people in the country. Since the United States has 61,000,000 married couples and about 1 million of them get divorced in a year, the divorce rate for any given year is less than 2 percent. A couple's chances of still being married at the end of a year are over 98 percent—not bad odds—and certainly much better odds than the mass media would have us believe. As the Social Map on the next page shows, the "odds"—if we want to call them that—depend on where you live.

Over time, of course, each year's small percentage adds up. A third way of measuring divorce, then, is to ask, "Of all U.S. adults, what percentage is divorced?" Figure 12.15 on the next page answers this question. You can see how divorce has increased over the years and how race–ethnicity makes a difference for the likelihood that couples will divorce. But this figure only shows us the percentage of Americans who are currently divorced. Those who have remarried don't show up here.

This fanciful depiction of marital trends may not be too far off the mark.

© Sidney Harris, ScienceCartoonPlus.com

" I NOW PRONOUNCE YOU SECOND HUSBAND AND FOURTH WIFE."

Figure 12.14 The "Where" of U.S. Divorce

NOTE: Data for several states are incomplete. For these, best estimates are used.

SOURCE: By the author. Based on *Statistical Abstract of the United States* 1995:Table 149; 2002:Table 111; 2014:Table 137.

Figure 12.15 The Increase in Divorce

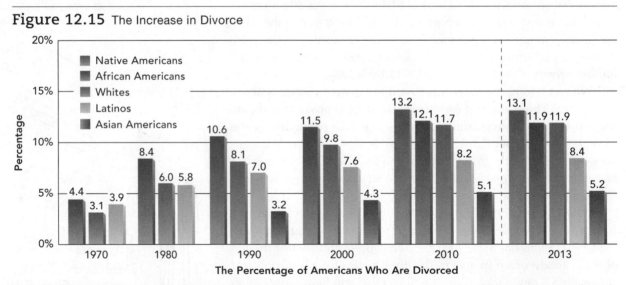

NOTE: This figure shows the percentage of those who are divorced and have not remarried, not the percentage of those who have ever divorced. Only these racial–ethnic groups are listed in the source. The source only recently added data on Asian Americans and Native Americans.

SOURCE: By the author. Based on *Statistical Abstract of the United States* 1995:Table 58; 2014:Table 59; U.S. Census Bureau 2014d.

We get yet another answer if we ask the question, "What percentage of Americans has ever been divorced?" This percentage increases with each age group, peaking when people reach their 50s ("Marital History . . ." 2004). Overall, about 43 to 46 percent of marriages end in divorce (Amato 2010), so a divorce rate of 50 percent is actually fairly accurate.

National statistics are fine, but you probably want to know if sociologists have found anything that will tell you about *your* chances of divorce. This is the topic of the Down-to-Earth Sociology box on the next page.

Down-to-Earth Sociology

"What Are *Your* Chances of Getting Divorced?"

As you have seen, over a lifetime, about half of all marriages fail. If you have that 50 percent figure dancing in your head while you are getting married, you might as well make sure that you have an escape hatch open even while you're saying "I do."

Not every group carries the same risk of divorce. For some, the risk is much higher; for others, much lower.

Let's look at some factors that reduce people's risk. As Table 12.2 shows, sociologists have worked out percentages that you might find useful. As you can see, people who go to college, participate in a religion, wait until marriage before having children, and earn higher incomes have a much better chance that their marriages will last. You can also see that having parents who did not divorce is significant. If you reverse these factors, you will see how the likelihood of divorce increases for people who have a baby before they

Divorce often summarizes nasty, bitter feelings. What feelings do you think Kevin Cotter was expressing when he posed his ex-wife's wedding dress as Darth Vader? He has also dragged the dress behind his car.

marry, who marry in their teens, and so on. It is important to note, however, that *these factors reduce the risk of divorce for groups of people, not for any particular individual.*

Other factors also increase the risk for divorce, but sociologists have not computed percentages for them. Here is one that might strike you as strange: Divorce is higher among couples whose firstborn child is a girl (Ananat and Michaels 2007; Dahl and Moretti 2008). The reason is probably that men prefer sons, and if the firstborn is a boy, the father is more likely to stick around (Gallup Poll 2011b). A second factor is more obvious: The more co-workers you have who are of the opposite sex, the more likely you are to get divorced (McKinnish 2007). (I'm sure you can figure out why.) Another factor is marrying someone of a different race–ethnicity, which leads to more incompatible backgrounds. (But on the next page, you will see an exception to this.) Another factor that no one knows the reason for is working with people who are recently divorced (Aberg 2003). It could be that divorced people are more likely to "hit on" their fellow workers—and human nature being what it is . . . .

Table 12.2 What Reduces the Risk of Divorce?

Factors That Reduce People's Chances of Divorce	How Much Does This Decrease the Risk of Divorce?
Some college (vs. high-school dropout)	–13%
Affiliated with a religion (vs. none)	–14%
Parents not divorced	–14%
Age 25 or over at marriage (vs. under 18)	–24%
Having a baby 7 months or longer after marriage (vs. before marriage)	–24%
Annual income over $25,000 (vs. under $25,000)	–30%

NOTE: These percentages apply to the first ten years of marriage.
SOURCE: Whitehead and Popenoe 2004; Copen et al. 2013.

For Your Consideration

→ Why do you think that people who go to college have a lower risk of divorce?

→ How would you explain the other factors shown in Table 12.2 or discussed in this box?

→ Why can't you figure your own chances of divorce by starting with some percentage (say 14 percent less likelihood of divorce if your parents are not divorced, another 13 percent for going to college, and so on)? To better understand this, you might want to read the section on the misuse of statistics on page 406.

Divorce and Mixed Racial–Ethnic Marriages

It is "common knowledge" that people who marry outside their racial–ethnic group have a higher divorce rate. This is true in general, but it is not quite this simple (Wang 2012). Researchers have found that it depends on "who marries whom." The marriages most likely to break up are those between African American men and white women.

Their rate is much higher than the national average. For marriages between Latinos and whites, the divorce rate is less than this, but it is still higher than the U.S. average.

The researchers also came up with a major surprise: Some mixed marriages, as they are called, have a *lower* divorce rate than the U.S. average. The marriages that are more durable than the national average are those between Asian Americans and whites and those in which the husband is white and the wife is African American. Why these marriages are stronger is not known at present.

Children of Divorce

NEGATIVE EFFECTS Divorce takes a toll on children's well-being. Children whose parents divorce are more likely than children reared by both parents to have behavioral problems, to get poor grades and drop out of high school, and to get in trouble with the law (Amato 2000, 2010). They are also more likely to divorce, perpetuating a marriage–divorce cycle (Cui and Fincham 2010). The negative effects are worse for children in poverty (Mandemakers and Kalmijn 2014).

Is the greater maladjustment of the children of divorce a serious problem? This question initiated a lively debate between two psychologists. Judith Wallerstein claims that divorce scars children, making them depressed and leaving them with insecurities that follow them into adulthood (Wallerstein et al. 2001). Mavis Hetherington replies that 75 to 80 percent of children of divorce function as well as children who are reared by both of their parents (Hetherington and Kelly 2003).

Without meaning to weigh in on either side of this debate, it doesn't seem to be a simple case of the glass being half empty or half full. If 75 to 80 percent of children of divorce don't suffer long-term harm, this leaves one-fourth to one-fifth who do. Any way you look at it, one-fourth or one-fifth of a million children *each year* is a lot of kids who are having a lot of problems.

WHAT HELPS CHILDREN ADJUST TO DIVORCE? The children who feel close to both parents make the best adjustment, and those who don't feel close to either parent make the worst adjustment (Richardson and McCabe 2001). Children have an especially

It is difficult to capture the anguish of the children of divorce, but when I read these lines by the fourth-grader who drew these two pictures, my heart was touched:

Me alone in the park . . .
All alone in the park.
My Dad and Mom are divorced
that's why I'm all alone.

This is me in the picture with my son.
We are taking a walk in the park.
I will never be like my father.
I will never divorce my wife and kid.

difficult time when one parent tries to undermine the other. These children are more likely to be depressed and insecure—even after they are grown up (Ben-Ami and Baker 2012). Children adjust well if they experience little conflict, feel loved, live with a parent who is making a good adjustment, and have consistent routines. It also helps if their family has adequate money to meet its needs. Children also adjust better if a second adult can be counted on for support (Hayashi and Strickland 1998). Urie Bronfenbrenner (1992) says this person is like the third leg of a stool, giving stability to the smaller family unit. Any adult can be the third leg, he says—a relative, friend, or even a former mother-in-law—but the most powerful stabilizing third leg is the father, the ex-husband. (For children living with their father, it is the mother, of course.)

PERPETUATING DIVORCE   As you saw in Table 12.2 on page 401, when the children of divorce grow up and marry, they are more likely to divorce than are adults who grew up in intact families. Have researchers found any factors that increase the chances that the children of divorce will have successful marriages? Actually, they have. Children of divorce are more likely to have a lasting marriage if they marry someone whose parents did not divorce. These marriages have more trust and less conflict. If both husband and wife come from broken families, however, it is not good news. Those marriages tend to have less trust and more conflict, leading to a higher chance of divorce (Wolfinger 2003).

Grandchildren of Divorce: Ripples to the Future

Paul Amato and Jacob Cheadle (2005), the first sociologists to study the grandchildren of couples who had divorced, found that the effects of divorce continue across generations. Using a national sample, they compared grandchildren—those whose grandparents had divorced with those whose grandparents had not divorced. Their findings are astounding. The grandchildren of divorce have weaker ties to their parents, don't go as far in school, and don't get along as well with their spouses. As these researchers put it, when parents divorce, the consequences ripple through the lives of children who are not yet born.

Fathers' Contact with Children after Divorce

With most children living with their mothers after divorce, how often do fathers see their children? As you can see from Table 12.3, researchers have found four main patterns. The most common pattern is for fathers to see their children frequently after the divorce and to keep doing so. But as you can see, a similar number of fathers have little contact with their children both right after the divorce and in the following years.

Which fathers are more likely to see and talk often to their children? It is men who were married to the mothers of the children, especially those who are older, more educated, and have higher incomes. In contrast, men who were cohabiting with the mothers, as well as younger, less educated men with lower incomes, tend to have less contact with their children. If his former wife marries, the father tends to see his children less (Berger et al. 2012).

Table 12.3 Fathers' Contact with their Children after Divorce

Frequent[1]	Minimal[2]	Decrease[3]	Increase[4]
38%	32%	23%	8%

[1]Maintains contact once a week or more through the years.
[2]Little contact after the divorce, maybe 2 to 6 times a year.
[3]Has frequent contact after the divorce but decreases it through the years.
[4]Has little contact after the divorce but increases it through the years. Sometimes called the "divorce activated" father.

SOURCE: By the author: Based on Cheadle et al. 2010.

The Ex-Spouses

Anger, depression, and anxiety are common feelings at divorce. But so is relief. Women are more likely than men to feel that divorce is giving them a "new chance" in life. A few couples manage to remain friends through it all—but they are the exception. The spouse who initiates the divorce usually gets over it sooner (Kelly 1992; Wang and Amato 2000) and remarries sooner (Sweeney 2002).

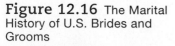

Figure 12.16 The Marital History of U.S. Brides and Grooms

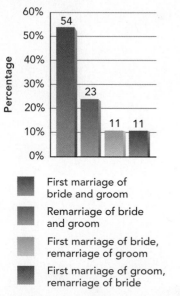

- First marriage of bride and groom
- Remarriage of bride and groom
- First marriage of bride, remarriage of groom
- First marriage of groom, remarriage of bride

SOURCE: By the author. Based on *Statistical Abstract of the United States* 2000:Table 145. Table dropped in later editions.

Divorce does not necessarily mean the end of a couple's relationship. Many divorced couples maintain contact because of their children. For others, the *continuities*, as sociologists call them, represent lingering attachments (Vaughan 1985; Masheter 1991; author's file 2005). The former husband may help his former wife paint a room or move furniture; she may invite him over for a meal or to watch television. They might even go to dinner or to see a movie together. Some couples even continue to make love after they divorce.

Remarriage

How common is remarriage? Look at Figure 12.16. As you can see, only a little more than half (54 percent) of today's newly married couples said "I do" for the first time. In about one-fifth of new marriages, either the bride or the groom was married previously, and in about one-fourth, both the bride and the groom were married before.

How do remarriages work out? The divorce rate of remarried people *without children* is about the same as that of first marriages. But bringing children into a marriage complicates family life, and with the added stress, these couples are more likely to divorce (MacDonald and DeMaris 1995). One complication is that these families lack clear norms—how they are related to one another and what those relationships require. As sociologist Andrew Cherlin (1989) noted, the names step-mothers, step-fathers, step-brothers, step-sisters, step-aunts, step-uncles, step-cousins, and step-grandparents are not only awkward, but they also represent ill-defined relationships.

Two Sides of Family Life

12.7 Summarize the dark and bright sides of family life.

Let's first look at situations in which marriage and family have gone seriously wrong and then try to answer the question of what makes marriage work.

The Dark Side of Family Life: Battering, Child Abuse, Marital Rape, and Incest

The dark side of family life involves events that people would rather keep in the dark. We will look at spouse battering, child abuse, rape, and incest.

SPOUSE BATTERING   This might surprise you, but based on a national sample, in one of four cases of domestic violence it is the man who is the victim (Truman and Morgan 2014). From his own research, sociologist Murray Straus (2011) concludes that wives attack their husbands as often as husbands attack their wives. With most men bigger and stronger than most women, however, women are more likely to be injured.

That women initiate domestic violence as often as men do blows away stereotypes. It also has serious implications: If we want to curb violence, we should *not* concentrate on men but, instead, on both men and women. The basic sociological question, then, is how to socialize *both* males and females to handle frustration and disagreements without resorting to violence. We do not yet have this answer.

CHILD ABUSE

I answered an ad about a lakeside house in a middle-class neighborhood that was for sale by owner. As the woman showed me through her immaculate home, I was surprised to see a plywood box in the youngest child's bedroom. About 3 feet high, 3 feet wide, and 6 feet long, the box was perforated with holes and had a little door with a padlock. Curious, I asked what it was. The woman replied matter-of-factly that her son had a behavior problem, and this was where they locked him for "time out." She

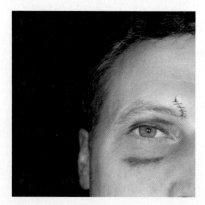

Wives and husbands are equally as likely to initiate violence, but unlike this photo, wives are more likely to be injured.

added that sometimes they would tie him to a float, attach a line to the dock, and put him in the lake.

I left as soon as I could. With thoughts of a terrorized child filling my head, I called the state child abuse hotline.

As you can tell, what I saw upset me. Most of us are bothered by child abuse—helpless children being victimized by their parents and other adults who are supposed to love, protect, and nurture them. The most gruesome of these cases make the evening news: The 4-year-old girl who was beaten and raped by her mother's boyfriend, passed into a coma, and three days later passed out of this life; the 6- to 10-year-old children whose stepfather videotaped them engaging in sex acts. Unlike these cases, which made headlines in my area, most child abuse is never brought to our attention: the children who live in filth, who are neglected—left alone for hours or even days at a time—or who are beaten with extension cords—cases like the little boy I learned about when I went house hunting.

Child abuse is extensive. Each year, U.S. authorities receive about 2 million reports of children being abused or neglected. Over 3 million children are involved in these reports. After investigating, authorities find that about 700,000 of the children have been abused or neglected (National Center 2014). The excuses that parents make are incredible. Of those I have read, the most fantastic is what a mother said to a Manhattan judge: "I slipped in a moment of anger, and my hands accidentally wrapped around my daughter's windpipe" (LeDuff 2003).

MARITAL AND INTIMACY RAPE Marital rape seems to be more common than is usually supposed, but we have no national totals. Sociologist Diana Russell (1990) used a sampling technique that allows generalization, but only to San Francisco. Fourteen percent of married women told her that their husbands had raped them. In interviews with a representative sample of Boston women, 10 percent reported that their husbands had used physical force to compel them to have sex (Finkelhor and Yllo 1985, 1989). Compared with victims of rape by strangers or acquaintances, victims of marital rape are less likely to report the rape (Mahoney 1999).

With the huge numbers of couples who are cohabiting, we need a term that includes sexual assault in intimate but nonmarital relationships. Let's use the term *intimacy rape* (Walters et al. 2013). This term will apply to both heterosexual and homosexual relationships. Sociologist Lori Girshick (2002) interviewed women who had been sexually assaulted by their female partners. Girshick points out that if the pronoun "he" were substituted for "she" in her interviews, a reader would believe that the events were told by women who had been raped by male partners. Just as in heterosexual rape, these victims suffered from shock, depression, and self-blame.

INCEST Sexual relations between certain relatives (for example, between brothers and sisters or between parents and children) constitute **incest**. Incest is most likely to occur in families that are socially isolated (Smith 1992). Sociologist Diana Russell (n.d.) found that incest victims who experience the greatest trauma are those who were victimized the most often, whose assaults occurred over longer periods of time, and whose incest was "more intrusive"—for example, sexual intercourse as opposed to sexual touching.

Incest can occur between any family members, but apparently the most common form is sex between children. An analysis of 13,000 cases of sibling incest showed that three-fourths of the incest was initiated by a brother who was five years older than his sister (Krienert and Walsh 2011). In one-fourth of the cases, the victim was a younger brother, and in 13 percent of the cases, the offender was an older sister. Most offenders are between the ages of 13 and 15, and most victims are age 12 or younger. Most parents treat incest as a family matter to be dealt with privately.

incest
sexual relations between specified relatives, such as brothers and sisters or parents and children

What is unusual about this German couple is not that they have four children but that they are brother and sister. The European Court ruled against their challenge to Germany's incest laws. They insist they have done nothing wrong and they are in love. What do you think?

The Bright Side of Family Life: Successful Marriages

On the bright side, marriage improves people's health, which we reviewed in the box on page 386. Compared with single people, married people on average also have more sex, are happier, have less depression, and are less likely to abuse drugs (Emery et al. 2012). And the more successful the marriage, the better all of these good things are.

But what makes marriage successful? Let's try to find out.

SUCCESSFUL MARRIAGES Sociologists Jeanette and Robert Lauer (1992) interviewed 351 couples who had been married fifteen years or longer. Fifty-one of these marriages were unhappy. The couples had stayed together for religious reasons, because of family tradition, or "for the sake of the children."

What about the 300 happy couples? They all

1. Consider their spouse to be their best friend
2. Like their spouse as a person
3. Think of marriage as a long-term commitment
4. Believe that marriage is sacred
5. Agree on aims and goals
6. Believe that their spouse has grown more interesting over the years
7. Strongly want the relationship to succeed
8. Laugh together

Sociologist Nicholas Stinnett (1992) studied 660 families from the United States and South America. He found that the happy families

1. Spend a lot of time together
2. Are quick to express appreciation
3. Promote one another's welfare
4. Do a lot of talking and listen to one another
5. Are religious
6. Deal with crises in a positive manner

Here are three more important factors, which won't surprise you: Marriages are happier when couples enjoy leisure activities together (Crawford et al. 2002), agree on how to spend money (Bernard 2008), and get along with their in-laws (Bryant et al. 2001).

Symbolic Interactionism and the Misuse of Statistics

Many students are concerned that divorce statistics mean they won't have a successful marriage. Because sociology is not just about abstract ideas but is really about our lives, it is important to stress that you are an individual, not a statistic. That is, if the divorce rate were 33 percent or 50 percent, this would *not* mean that if you marry, your chances of getting divorced are 33 percent or 50 percent. This is a misuse of statistics—and a common one at that. Divorce statistics represent all marriages and have absolutely *nothing* to do with any individual marriage. Our own chances depend on our own situations—especially the way we approach marriage.

To make this point clearer, let's apply symbolic interactionism. From a symbolic interactionist perspective, we create our own worlds. That is, because our experiences don't come with built-in meanings, we interpret our experiences and act accordingly. As we do so, we can create a self-fulfilling prophecy. For example, if we think that our marriage might fail, we are more likely to run when things become difficult. If we think that our marriage is going to work out, we are more likely to stick around and do things to make the marriage successful. The folk saying "There are no guarantees in life" is certainly true, but it does help to have a vision that a good marriage is possible and that it is worth the effort to work things out.

The Future of Marriage and Family

12.8 Explain the likely future of marriage and family.

What can we expect of marriage and family in the future? We can first note that marriage is so functional that it exists in every society. Despite its many problems, then, marriage is in no danger of becoming a relic of the past, and the vast majority of Americans will continue to find marriage vital to their welfare.

We can catch a glimpse of the future by considering trends that are firmly in place. Cohabitation, births to single women, and the age at first marriage will increase. As more married women join the workforce, wives will continue to gain marital power. As the number of elderly increase, more couples will find themselves sandwiched between caring for their parents and rearing their own children.

Our culture will continue to be haunted by distorted images of marriage and family: the bleak ones portrayed in the mass media and the rosy ones perpetuated by cultural myths. Sociological research can help correct these distortions and allow us to see how our own family experiences fit into the patterns of our culture. Sociological research can also help to answer the big question: How do we formulate social policies that support and enhance the quality of family life?

Summary and Review

Marriage and Family in Global Perspective

12.1 Define marriage and family and summarize their common cultural themes.

What is a family, and what themes are universal?

Family is difficult to define because there are exceptions to every element that you might consider essential. Consequently, **family** is defined broadly—as people who consider themselves related by blood, marriage, or adoption. Universally, **marriage** and family are mechanisms for governing mate selection, reckoning descent, and establishing inheritance and authority.

Marriage and Family in Theoretical Perspective

12.2 Contrast the functionalist, conflict, and symbolic interactionist perspectives on marriage and family.

What is a functionalist perspective on marriage and family?

Functionalists examine the functions and dysfunctions of family life. Examples include the **incest taboo** and how weakened family functions increase divorce.

What is a conflict perspective on marriage and family?

Conflict theorists focus on inequality in marriage, especially unequal and changing power between husbands and wives.

What is a symbolic interactionist perspective on marriage and family?

Symbolic interactionists examine the contrasting experiences and perspectives of men and women in marriage. They stress that only by grasping the perspectives of wives and husbands can we understand their behavior.

The Family Life Cycle

12.3 Summarize research on love and courtship, marriage, childbirth, child rearing, and family transitions.

What are the major elements of the family life cycle?

The major elements are love and courtship, marriage, childbirth, child rearing, and the family in later life. Most mate selection follows patterns of age, social class, and race–ethnicity. Child-rearing patterns vary by social class.

Diversity in U.S. Families

12.4 Summarize research on families: African American, Latino, Asian American, Native American, one-parent, couples without children, blended, and gay and lesbian.

How significant is race–ethnicity in family life?

The primary distinction is social class, not race–ethnicity. Families of the same social class are likely to be similar, regardless of their race–ethnicity.

What other diversity do we see in U.S. families?

Also discussed are one-parent, childless, **blended**, and gay and lesbian families. Each has its unique characteristics, but social class is important in determining their primary characteristics. Poverty is especially significant for one-parent families, most of which are headed by women.

Trends in U.S. Families

12.5 Discuss changes in the timetable of family life, cohabitation, and elder care.

What major changes characterize U.S. families?

Three major changes are postponement of first marriage, an increase in **cohabitation**, and having the first child at a later age. With more people living longer, many middle-aged couples find themselves sandwiched between rearing their children and taking care of their aging parents.

Divorce and Remarriage

12.6 Summarize problems in measuring divorce, research findings on children and grandchildren of divorce, fathers' contact after divorce, ex-spouses, and remarriage.

What is the current divorce rate?

Depending on what numbers you choose to compare, you can produce rates between 2 percent and 50 percent.

How do children and their parents adjust to divorce?

Divorce is difficult for children whose adjustment problems often continue into adulthood. Consequences of divorce are passed on to grandchildren. Fathers who have frequent contact with their children after a divorce are likely to maintain it.

Two Sides of Family Life

12.7 Summarize the dark and bright sides of family life.

What are the two sides of family life?

The dark side is abuse—spouse battering, child abuse, marital rape, and **incest**, all a misuse of family power. The bright side is that most people find marriage and family to be rewarding.

The Future of Marriage and Family

12.8 Explain the likely future of marriage and family.

What is the likely future of marriage and family?

We can expect cohabitation, births to unmarried women, and age at first marriage to increase. The growing numbers of women in the workforce are likely to continue to shift the balance of marital power.

Thinking Critically about Chapter 12

1. Functionalists stress that the family is universal because it provides basic functions for individuals and society. What functions does *your* family provide? *Hint:* In addition to the section "The Functionalist Perspective," also consider the section "Common Cultural Themes."

2. Explain why social class is more important than race–ethnicity in determining a family's characteristics.

3. Apply this chapter's contents to your own experience with marriage and family. What social factors affect your family life? In what ways is your family life different from that of your grandparents when they were your age?

Chapter 13
Education and Religion

"Kathy's 11-year-old twins were disturbing other children and the teacher— and what was Kathy going to do about this?"

Kathy Spiegel was upset. Horace Mann, the school principal in her hometown in Oregon, had asked her to come to his office. He explained that Kathy's 11-year-old twins had been acting up in class. They were disturbing other children and the teacher—and what was Kathy going to do about this?

Kathy didn't want to tell Mr. Mann what he could do with the situation. *That* would have gotten her kicked out of the office. Instead, she bit her tongue and said she would talk to her daughters.

* * * * *

On the other side of the country, Jim and Julia Attaway were pondering their own problem. When they visited their son's school in the Bronx, they didn't like what they saw. The boys looked like they were little gangsta wannabes, and the girls dressed and acted as though they were sexually active. Their own 13-year-old son had started using street language at home, and it was becoming increasingly difficult to talk to him.

* * * * *

In Minneapolis, Denzil and Tamika Jefferson were facing a much quieter crisis. They found life frantic as they hurried from one school activity to another. Their 13-year-old son attended a private school, and the demands were so intense that it felt like the junior year in high school. They no longer seemed to have any relaxed family time together.

* * * * *

In Atlanta, Jaime and Maria Morelos were upset at the ideas that their 8-year-old daughter had begun to express at home. As devout first-generation Protestants, Jaime and Maria felt moral issues were a top priority, and they didn't like what they were hearing.

* * * * *

Kathy talked the matter over with her husband, Bob. Jim and Julia discussed their problem, as did Denzil and Tamika and Jaime and Maria. They all came to the same conclusion: The problem was not their children. The problem was the school their children attended. All four sets of parents also came to the same solution: home schooling for their children.

Home schooling might seem to be a radical solution to today's education problems, but it is one that the parents of 1½ million U.S. children have chosen. We'll come back to this topic, but, first, let's take a broad look at education.

Education: Transferring Knowledge and Skills

Education in Global Perspective

13.1 **Understand how education is related to a nation's culture and economy; compare education in Japan, Russia, and Egypt.**

Have you ever wondered why people need a high school diploma to sell cars or to join the U.S. Marines? You will learn what you know on the job. Why do employers insist on diplomas and degrees? Why don't they simply use on-the-job training?

In some cases, job skills must be mastered before you are allowed to do the work. On-the-job training was once adequate to become an engineer or an airline pilot, but with changes in information and technology, it is no longer sufficient. This is precisely why doctors display their credentials so prominently. Their framed degrees declare that an institution of higher learning has certified them to work on your body.

But testing in algebra or paragraph construction to sell sheets at K-Mart or serve burritos at Chipotle? Sociologist Randall Collins (1979) observed that industrialized nations have become **credential societies**. By this, he meant that employers use diplomas and degrees as *sorting devices* to determine who is eligible for a job. Because employers don't know potential workers, they depend on schools to weed out the incapable. For example,

credential society

the use of diplomas and degrees to determine who is eligible for jobs, even though the diploma or degree may be irrelevant to the actual work

As you can see from this 1899 cooking class in Washington, D.C., early public education had a focus on practical matters. The skills children needed as adults differed markedly from those they need today.

when you graduate from college, potential employers will presume that you are a responsible person—that you have shown up for numerous classes, have turned in scores of assignments, and have demonstrated basic writing and thinking skills. They will then graft their particular job skills onto this foundation that has been certified by your college.

Education and Industrialization

INDUSTRIALIZATION AND MANDATORY EDUCATION In the early years of the United States, most people worked on farms, and there was no free public education. But by 1918, all U.S. states had **mandatory education laws** requiring children to attend school, usually until they completed the eighth grade or turned 16, whichever came first. Graduation from the eighth grade marked the end of education for most people. "Dropouts" at that time were students who did not complete grade school.

It is no coincidence that universal education and industrialization occurred at the same time. The economy was changing from farm to factory, and as political and civic leaders observed this transformation, they recognized the need for an educated workforce. They also feared the influx of "foreign" values and looked at public education as a way to "Americanize" immigrants (Jones and Meyer 2010).

mandatory education laws

laws that require all children to attend school until a specified age or until they complete a minimum grade in school

THE EXPANSION OF EDUCATION As industrialization progressed and fewer people made their living from farming, even more years of formal education came to be regarded as essential to the well-being of society. Graduation from high school became more common, and more students wanted a college education. Free education stopped with high school, however, and with the distance to the nearest college too far and the cost of tuition and lodging too great, few high school graduates were able to attend college. As discussed in the Down-to-Earth Sociology box that follows, this predicament gave birth to community colleges.

Down-to-Earth Sociology

Community Colleges: Facing Old and New Challenges

I attended a junior college in Oakland, California. From there, with fresh diploma in hand, I transferred to a senior college—a college in Fort Wayne, Indiana, that had no freshmen or sophomores.

I didn't realize that my experimental college matched the vision of some of the founders of the community college movement. In the early 1900s, they foresaw a system of local colleges that would be accessible to the average high school graduate—a system so extensive that it would be unnecessary for universities

Community colleges have opened higher education to millions of students who would not otherwise have access to college because of cost or distance.

to offer courses at the freshman and sophomore levels (Handel 2013).

A group with an equally strong opinion questioned whether preparing high school graduates for entry to four-year colleges and universities should be the goal of junior colleges. They insisted that the purpose of junior colleges should be vocational preparation, to equip people for the job market as electricians and other technicians. In some regions, where the proponents of transfer dominated, the admissions requirements for junior colleges were higher than those of Yale (Pedersen 2001). This debate was never won by either side, and you can still hear its echoes today (Handel 2013).

The name *junior* college also became a problem. Some felt that the word *junior* made their institution sound as though it weren't quite a real college. A struggle to change the name ensued, and several decades ago, *community* college won out. The name change didn't settle the debate about whether the purpose was preparing students to transfer to universities or training them for jobs, however. Community colleges continue to serve this dual purpose.

Community colleges have become such an essential part of the U.S. educational system that 36 percent of all undergraduates in the United States are enrolled in them (*Statistical Abstract* 2014:Table 283). They have become the major source of the nation's emergency medical technicians, firefighters, nurses, and police officers. Most students are *nontraditional* students: Many are age 25 or older, come from the working class, have jobs and children, and attend college part-time (Bellafante 2014).

To help students who are not seeking occupational certificates transfer to four-year colleges and universities, many community colleges work closely with four-year public and private universities. Some provide admissions guidance on how to enter flagship state schools. Others coordinate courses, making sure they match the university's title and numbering system, as well as its rigor of instruction and grading. Many offer honors programs that prepare talented students to transfer with ease into these schools.

An emerging trend is for community colleges to become four-year colleges without changing their names. Some are now granting work-related baccalaureate degrees in such areas as teaching, nursing, and public safety (Hanson 2010). This raises the question: Will these community colleges eventually develop into full four-year colleges, perhaps even creating the need to establish two-year community colleges to replace them? Community colleges face continuing challenges. They must secure adequate funding in the face of declining resources, adjust to changing job markets, and maintain quality instruction and campus security. Other challenges include offering financial aid, remedial and online courses, and flex schedules. Still other challenges are teaching students for whom English is a second language and providing on-campus day care for parents. A pressing need is to increase graduation rates. For this, community colleges are improving their orientation programs and developing better ways to monitor their students' progress (Dunn 2013; Wang 2013).

For Your Consideration

→ Do you think the primary goal of community colleges should be to train students for jobs or to prepare them to transfer to four-year colleges and universities? Why?

Figure 13.1 shows the incredible change in educational achievement. As you can see, receiving a bachelor's degree is now more than *twice* as common as completing high school used to be. Two of every three (68 percent) high school graduates enter college (*Statistical Abstract* 2014:Table 280).

Figure 13.1 Educational Achievement in the United States

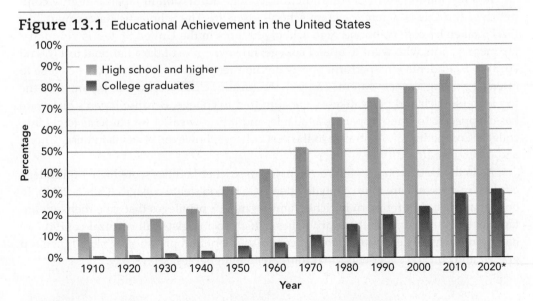

NOTE: *Americans 25 years and over. Asterisk indicates author's estimate. College graduates are included in both categories (High school and higher, and College graduates).

SOURCE: By the author. Based on National Center for Education Statistics 1991:Table 8; *Statistical Abstract of the United States* 2014:Table 243.

To place our own educational system in global perspective, let's look at education in three countries at different levels of industrialization. This will help us see how education is related to a nation's culture and its economy.

Education in the Most Industrialized Nations: Japan

School is over—but not for this student. After the regular school day, hundreds of thousands in Japan attend 50,000 cram (*juku*) schools.

The yells of children pierce the night, belting out the elements—"Lithium! Magnesium!"—as an instructor displays abbreviations from the periodic table.

Japanese students outscore U.S. students. Why? One reason is that hardly any nation takes education as seriously as Japan does. Japan has 50,000 (juku) cram schools. These schools operate *after* the regular school day. Let's peer inside one:

An instructor flashes an abbreviation from the periodic table. The grade school children shout "Magnesium!" Then come shouts of "Lithium!" "Gadolinium!" "Tantalum!" As a stream of flags passes by, the students shout out the names of the countries. When the instructor displays photos of the stars, the students shout the names of constellations they have memorized.

Older students use timers. Each night, they try to get faster in their answers and to memorize more materials for more tests ("Testing Times" 2011).

Japan's *juku* aren't free. The parents pay over $3,000 a year to enroll a child in one. And one in five first graders is enrolled in a cram school. Another unique aspect of Japanese education is that during the regular school day, all grade school children study the same page from the same textbook ("Less Rote . . ." 2000). This vast uniformity is accompanied by a personal touch: Teachers are required to visit each student's home once a year (Yamamoto and Brinton 2010).

A central sociological principle of education is that a nation's education reflects its culture. Studying the same materials at the same time reflects the core Japanese value of solidarity with the group. In the workforce, people who are hired together are not expected to compete with one another for promotions. Instead, they are promoted as a group (Inatsugu 2011). Japanese education reflects this group-centered approach to life.

In a fascinating cultural contradiction, college admission in Japan is highly competitive, and this is where the cram schools come in. The Scholastic Assessment Test (SAT), taken by college-bound high school students in the United States, is voluntary. Japanese seniors who want to attend college, however, must take a national test (Osaki 2013). U.S. students who perform poorly on their tests can usually find some college to attend—as long as their parents can pay the tuition. Until recently, in Japan, only the top scorers—rich and poor alike—were admitted to college. Because Japan's birth rate has dropped so low, more space is available, and it is now easier for students to get into college. Competition for entrance to the best colleges, however, remains intense (Zhang and McCornac 2014).

As in the United States, children from Japan's richer families score higher on college admission tests and are more likely to attend the nation's elite colleges (Okada 2012). In both countries, children born in richer families inherit privileges that give them advantages over others. Among these privileges, which sociologists call **cultural capital**, are having more highly educated parents, encouragement and pressure to bring home top grades, and cultural experiences that translate into higher test scores.

cultural capital

privileges accompanying a social location that help someone in life; included are more highly educated parents, from grade school through high school being pushed to bring home high grades, and enjoying cultural experiences that translate into higher test scores, better jobs, and higher earnings

Education in the Industrializing Nations: Russia

Before the Russian Revolution of 1917, the czar had been expanding Russia's educational system beyond the children of the elite (Andreev 2012). The Soviet Communist party continued this expansion until education encompassed all children. True to the sociological principle that education reflects culture, the new government saw education as a way to undergird the new political system and made certain that socialist values dominated its schools. Schoolchildren were taught that capitalism was evil and communism was the salvation of the world. Every classroom was required to prominently display photographs of Lenin and Stalin.

Under the Soviets, education, including college, was free. Just as the economy was directed from central headquarters in Moscow, so was education. Each school followed the same state-prescribed curriculum, and all students in the same grade used the same textbooks. Schools stressed mathematics and the natural sciences. To prevent critical thinking, which might lead to criticisms of communism, there were few courses in the social sciences. Students memorized course materials, repeating lectures on oral exams (Deaver 2001).

Russia's switch from communism to capitalism brought a change in culture—especially new ideas about profit, private property, and personal freedom. This, in turn, meant that the educational system had to adjust to the country's changing values and views of the world. Not only did the photos of Lenin and Stalin come down, but also, for the first time, private, religious, and even foreign-run schools were allowed. For the first time as well, teachers were able to encourage students to think for themselves.

The problems that Russia confronted in "reinventing" its educational system were mind-boggling. Tens of thousands of teachers who had been teaching students to memorize Party-dictated political answers had to learn new methods of teaching. As the economy faltered during Russia's early transition to capitalism, school budgets dwindled. Some teachers went unpaid for months; instead of money, at one school, teachers were paid in toilet paper and vodka (Deaver 2001). Teachers are now paid regularly (and in money), but the salaries are low. University professors average only $1,000 a month (Agranovich 2012).

With teachers and texts able to shape minds, politicians are interested in their country's educational system. Russia is no exception. After Vladimir Putin, the president of Russia, declared that the new history books did not do justice to Russia's glorious past (Rapoport 2009), he eliminated most of the publishing competition and arranged for his old friend and judo partner to become the publisher of "patriotic" texts that "match Russian values" (Becker and Myers 2014). With or without Putin, we can be certain that Russia's educational system will glorify Russia's history and reinforce its values and world views—no matter what direction those values and views may take.

Vladimir Putin, Russia's president, detests the weakness that led to the breakup of the Soviet empire. To make up for this humiliation, he ordered Russia's textbooks revised to glorify the country. He also projects an image of strength to Russian citizens and to the world through confrontations with the West and, as you can see, by publicity photos of his own macho persona.

The poverty of the Least Industrialized Nations carries over to their educational systems. This photo was taken in Cambodia.

Education in the Least Industrialized Nations: Egypt

Education in the Least Industrialized Nations stands in sharp contrast to education in the industrialized world. Because most of the citizens of these nations work the land or take care of families, there is little emphasis on formal schooling. As we saw in Figure 7.3 (pages 212–213), many people in the Least Industrialized Nations live on less than $1,000 a year. Amid such poverty, many children don't even finish grade school. As was once common around the globe, it is primarily the wealthy in the Least Industrialized Nations who have the means and the leisure for formal education—especially anything beyond the basics. As an example, let's look at education in Egypt.

Several centuries before the birth of Christ, Egypt's centers of learning were world renowned.

They produced such acclaimed scientists as Archimedes and Euclid. During this classic period, Egypt excelled in astronomy, geography, geometry, mathematics, medicine, philosophy, and physics. The world's largest library was at Alexandria. This library burned to the ground, but fragments from its papyri manuscripts have helped scholars decipher ancient manuscripts. After Rome defeated Egypt, education declined, never to regain its former prominence.

Education in Egypt is free, but qualified teachers are few, and classrooms are crowded (Hussein 2014). As a result, one-third to one-half of Egyptians are illiterate, with more women than men unable to read and write (UNESCO 2012; UNICEF 2015). After the six years of grade school, students are tracked. Most study technical subjects for three years, and at about the age of 14 are done with school. Others go on to high school for three years. Those who score the highest on national exams are admitted to college.

The emphasis has not been on thinking, but on memorizing facts to pass national tests. With concerns growing that this approach leaves minds less capable of evaluating life and opens the door to religious extremism, Egyptian educators are rethinking their educational system. They want to remold it, patterning it after the educational system in Great Britain (Reisz 2014). These are the goals, but to implement them will take a great deal of money, making it unlikely that serious reform will follow. The general low quality of education in Egypt, including at the university level, leaves Egypt uncompetitive in the global economy. Without fundamental reforms, Egypt will continue to lag behind in the global race for economic security.

manifest functions

the intended beneficial consequences of people's actions

latent functions

unintended beneficial consequences of people's actions

cultural transmission of values

the process of transmitting values from one group to another; often refers to how cultural traits are transmitted across generations; in education, the ways in which schools transmit a society's culture, especially its core values

The cartoonist captures a primary reason that we have become a credential society.

"Hey, how come no diplomas?" "Oh, I'm self-taught."

©Robert Mankoff/The New Yorker Collection/www.cartoonbank.com

The Functionalist Perspective: Providing Social Benefits

13.2 Explain the functions of education: knowledge and skills, values, social integration, gatekeeping, and replacing family functions.

A central position of functionalism is that when the parts of society are working properly, each contributes to the well-being or stability of that society. The positive things that people intend their actions to accomplish are known as **manifest functions**. The positive consequences they did not intend are called **latent functions**. Let's begin by looking at the functions of education.

Teaching Knowledge and Skills

Education's most obvious manifest function is to teach knowledge and skills—whether the traditional three R's or their more contemporary counterparts, such as computer literacy. Each generation must train the next to fill the group's significant positions. Because our postindustrial society needs highly educated people, the schools supply them.

Cultural Transmission of Values

Another manifest function of education is the **cultural transmission of values**, a process by which schools pass on a society's core values from one generation to the next. Schools in a socialist society stress values that support socialism, while schools in a capitalist society teach values that support capitalism. U.S. schools, for example, stress the significance of private property, individualism, and competition.

Regardless of a country's economic system, loyalty to the state is a cultural value, Schools around the world teach patriotism. U.S. schools—as well as those of Russia, France, China, and other countries around the world—extol the society's founders, their struggle for freedom from oppression, and the goodness of the country's social institutions. Seldom is this function as explicit as it is in Japan, where the law requires that schools "cultivate a respect for tradition and culture, and love for the nation and homeland" (Nakamura 2006).

To better understand what the functionalists mean by transmitting values in education, consider how different a course in U.S. history would be if it were taught in Cuba, Iran, and Muncie, Indiana.

Social Integration

Schools also bring about *social integration.* Among the ways they promote a sense of national identity is by having students salute the flag and sing the national anthem.

INTEGRATING IMMIGRANTS   One of the best examples of how U.S. schools promote political integration is their teaching of mainstream ideas and values to tens of millions of immigrants. The schools help the immigrants regard themselves as Americans and give up their earlier national and cultural identities (Westheimer 2012).

STABILIZING SOCIETY: MAINTAINING THE STATUS QUO   This integrative function of education goes far beyond making people similar in their appearance, speech, or even ways of thinking. *To forge a national identity is to stabilize the political system.* If people identify with a society's institutions and *perceive them as the basis of their own welfare,* they have no reason to rebel. This function is especially significant when it comes to the lower social classes, from which most social revolutionaries emerge. The wealthy already have a vested interest in maintaining the status quo, but getting the lower classes to identify with a social system *as it is* goes a long way toward preserving the system as it is.

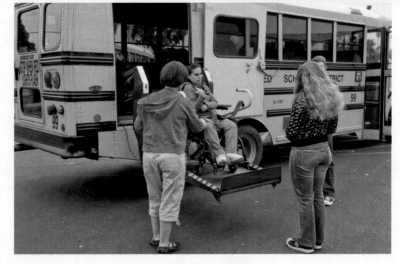

Children with disabilities used to be sent to special schools. In a process called *mainstreaming* or inclusion, they now attend regular schools.

INTEGRATING PEOPLE WITH DISABILITIES   People with disabilities often have found themselves left out of the mainstream of society. As a matter of policy, students with special needs used to be placed in special classes or schools. There, however, they learned to adjust to a specialized situation, leaving them ill prepared to cope with the dominant world. To overcome this, U.S. schools have added a manifest function, **inclusion**, or mainstreaming. As in the photo to the right, this means that educators try to incorporate students with disabilities into regular school activities. Wheelchair ramps are provided for people who cannot walk; interpreters who use sign language may attend classes with students who cannot hear. About 90 percent of students with disabilities spend at least some of their days in regular classrooms, with over half there most of the time (IES 2010). Exceptions include most blind students, who attend special schools, as well as people with severe learning disabilities. Most inclusion goes fairly smoothly, but mainstreaming students with serious emotional and behavioral problems disrupts classrooms, frustrates teachers, and increases teacher turnover (Tomsho and Golden 2007; Logan and Winner 2013).

inclusion

helping people to become part of the mainstream of society; also called *mainstreaming*

social placement

a function of education—funneling people into a society's various positions

Gatekeeping (Social Placement)

Sociologists Talcott Parsons (1940), Kingsley Davis, and Wilbert Moore (Davis and Moore 1945) analyzed **social placement** as a function of schools. They pointed out that some

gatekeeping

the process by which education opens and closes doors of opportunity; another term for the social placement function of education

tracking

the sorting of students into different educational programs on the basis of real or perceived abilities

jobs require few skills and can be performed by people of lesser intelligence. Other jobs, such as that of physician, require high intelligence and advanced education. The schools sort the capable from the incapable. They do this, say the functionalists, on the basis of merit, the students' abilities and ambitions.

As you can see, social placement, more commonly known as **gatekeeping**, means to open the doors of opportunity for some and to close them to others. What opens and closes those doors? Is it merit, as the functionalists argue? To accomplish gatekeeping, schools use some form of **tracking**, sorting students into different educational "tracks" or programs on the basis of their perceived abilities. Some U.S. high schools funnel students into one of three tracks: general, college prep, or honors. Students on the lowest track are likely to go to work after high school or to take vocational courses. Those on the highest track usually attend prestigious colleges. Those in between usually attend a local college or regional state university.

You can also see that the impact of gatekeeping is lifelong. Tracking affects people's opportunities for jobs, income, and lifestyle. When tracking was challenged—that it is based more on social class than merit, which perpetuates social inequality—schools retreated from formal tracking. Placing students in "ability groups" and "advanced" classes, however, serves the same purpose (Yee 2013b).

Replacing Family Functions

Over the years, the functions of U.S. schools have expanded, even replacing some family functions. Child care, for example, has always been a latent function of formal education, since it was an unintended consequence. Now, however, with two wage earners in most families, child care has become a manifest function, and some schools offer child care both before and after the school day. Some high schools provide nurseries for the children of their teenaged students (Bosman 2007). Some provide three meals a day for students in poverty (Hollingsworth 2012).

Another function is providing sex education, and, in some school-based health centers, making condoms and birth control pills available (Hartocollis 2012). This has stirred controversy, since some families resent schools taking this function away from them. Disagreement over values has fueled the social movement for home schooling, featured in our opening vignette.

IN SUM Functionalists analyze the functions, the benefits, that schools provide to society. Not only do the schools teach the knowledge and skills needed by the next generation, but they also stabilize society by forging a national identity, providing work for millions, and keeping other millions out of the workforce. A controversial function is gatekeeping, sorting students for various levels of jobs. Schools have expanded their domain, taking over some functions formerly performed by families.

The Conflict Perspective: Perpetuating Social Inequality

13.3   Explain how the educational system reproduces the social class structure.

Unlike functionalists, who look at the benefits of education, conflict theorists examine how *the educational system reproduces the social class structure.* By this phrase, they mean that schools perpetuate the social divisions of society and help members of the elite maintain their dominance.

Let's look, then, at how education is related to social classes, how it helps people inherit *cultural capital,* the life opportunities that were laid down before they were born.

The Hidden Curriculum: Reproducing the Social Class Structure

The term **hidden curriculum** refers to the attitudes and the unwritten rules of behavior that schools teach in addition to the formal curriculum. Examples are obedience to authority and conformity to mainstream norms. Conflict theorists stress that the hidden curriculum helps to perpetuate social inequalities.

hidden curriculum
the unwritten goals of schools, such as teaching obedience to authority and conformity to cultural norms

To understand this central point, consider the way English is taught. Schools for the middle class—whose teachers know where their students are headed—stress "proper" English and "good" manners. In contrast, the teachers in inner-city schools—who also know where *their* students are headed—allow ethnic and street language in the classroom. *Each type of school is helping to reproduce the social class structure.* That is, each is preparing students to work in positions similar to those of their parents. The social class of some children destines them for higher positions. For these jobs, they need "refined" speech and manners. The social destiny of others is low-status jobs. For this type of work, they need only to obey rules (Bowles and Gintis 1976, 2002; Stephens et al. 2014). Teaching these students "refined" speech and manners would be wasted effort. In other words, even the teaching of English and manners helps keep the social classes intact across generations.

Tilting the Tests: Discrimination by IQ

Even intelligence tests help to keep the social class system intact. Let's look at an example. How would you answer this question?

> *A symphony is to a composer as a book is to a(n) ___*
> ___ *paper*   ___ *sculptor*   ___ *musician*   ___ *author*   ___ *man*

You probably had no difficulty coming up with "author" as your choice. Wouldn't any intelligent person have done so?

In point of fact, this question raises a central issue in intelligence testing. Not all intelligent people would know the answer. This question contains *cultural biases.* Children from some backgrounds are more familiar with the concepts of symphonies, composers, and sculptors than are other children. This tilts the test in their favor.

To make the bias clearer, try to answer this question:

> *If you throw two dice and "7" is showing on the top, what is facing down?*
> ___ *seven*   ___ *snake eyes*   ___ *box cars*   ___ *little Joes*   ___ *eleven*

Adrian Dove (n.d.), a social worker in Watts, a poor area of Los Angeles, suggested this question. Its cultural bias should be obvious—that it allows children from some social backgrounds to perform better than others. Unlike the first question, this one is not tilted to the middle-class experience. In other words, IQ (intelligence quotient) tests measure not only intelligence but also acquired knowledge.

You should now be able to perceive the bias of IQ tests that use such words as *composer* and *symphony.* A lower-class child may have heard about rap, rock, gangsta, or jazz, but not about symphonies. One consequence of this bias to the middle-class experience is that the children of the poor score lower on IQ tests. Then, to match their supposedly inferior intelligence, these children are assigned to less demanding courses. Their inferior education helps them reach their social destiny, their lower-paying jobs in adult life. As conflict theorists view them, then, IQ tests are another weapon in an arsenal designed to maintain the social class structure across the generations.

Stacking the Deck: Unequal Funding

Conflict theorists stress that the way schools are funded stacks the deck against the poor. Because public schools are supported largely by local property taxes, the richer

Figure 13.2 Parents' Income and the Quality of Their Children's College

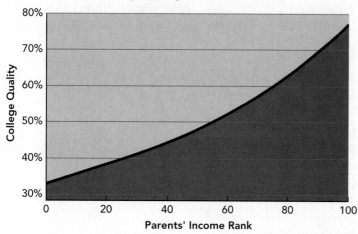

College Quality and Parents' Income

SOURCE: Modified from Chetty et al. 2014.

communities (where property values and incomes are higher) have more to spend on their children's schools, and the poorer communities have less to spend on theirs. The richer communities, then, can offer higher salaries and take their pick of the most highly qualified and motivated teachers. They can also afford to buy the latest textbooks, computers, and software, as well as offer courses in foreign languages, music, and the arts. This, stress conflict theorists, means that in *all* states the deck is stacked against the poor.

The Bottom Line: Family Background

REPRODUCING THE SOCIAL CLASS STRUCTURE   As sociologists found a long time ago, when it comes to attending college, money is more important than ability. Whether children have high or low ability, they are more likely to go to college if their parents have high income (Bowles 1977; Chetty et al. 2014).

When we look at the quality of the colleges that students attend, we find the same relationship. As you can see from Figure 13.2, the higher the parents' income, the better the quality of their children's college. This piles advantage upon advantage. The children of richer parents are more likely to go to college, they go to higher quality and more prestigious colleges, and they get higher-paying and more prestigious jobs when they graduate.

In short, colleges, too, help to reproduce the social class structure. The elite colleges are the icing on the cake for students who have won the lottery of more privileged birth.

REPRODUCING THE RACIAL–ETHNIC STRUCTURE   Conflict theorists point out that the educational system reproduces not only the U.S. social class structure but also its racial–ethnic divisions. From Figure 13.3, you can see that, compared with whites, African Americans and Latinos are less likely to complete high school and, of those who do, less likely to go to college. Because adults with only a high school diploma usually end up with low-paying, dead-end jobs, you can see how this supports the conflict view—that education is helping to reproduce the racial–ethnic structure for the next generation.

Figure 13.3 The Funneling Effects of Education: Race-Ethnicity

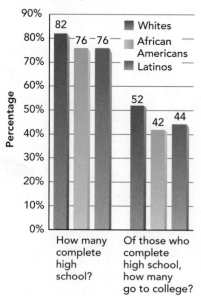

NOTE: The source gives totals only for these groups.

SOURCE: By the author. Based on *Statistical Abstract of the United States* 2014:Table 277.

IN SUM   U.S. schools closely reflect the U.S. social class system. They equip the children of the elite with the tools they need to maintain their dominance, while they prepare the children of the poor for lower-status positions. Because education's doors of opportunity swing wide open for some but have to be pried open by others, conflict theorists stress that the educational system perpetuates social inequality across generations (or, as they often phrase it, helps to reproduce the social class structure). In fact, they add, this is one of its primary purposes.

The Symbolic Interactionist Perspective: Teacher Expectations

13.4   **Explain the significance of teacher expectations and give examples.**

As you have seen, functionalists look at how education benefits society, and conflict theorists examine how education perpetuates social inequality. Symbolic interactionists, in contrast, study face-to-face interaction in the classroom. They have found that what teachers expect of their students has profound consequences for how students do in school.

The Rist Research

Why do some people get tracked into college prep courses and others into vocational ones? There is no single answer, but in what has become a classic study, sociologist Ray Rist came up with some intriguing findings. Rist (1970, 2007) did participant observation in an African American grade school with an African American faculty. He found that after only eight days in the classroom, the kindergarten teacher felt that she knew the children's abilities well enough to assign them to three separate worktables. To Table 1, Mrs. Caplow assigned those she considered to be "fast learners." They sat at the front of the room, closest to her. Those whom she saw as "slow learners," she assigned to Table 3, located at the back of the classroom. She placed "average" students at Table 2, in between the other tables.

This seemed strange to Rist. He knew that the children had not been tested for ability, yet their teacher was certain that she could identify the bright and slow children. Investigating further, Rist found that social class was the underlying basis for assigning the children to the different tables. Middle-class students were separated out for Table 1, and children from poorer homes were assigned to Tables 2 and 3. The teacher paid the most attention to the children at Table 1, who were closest to her, less to Table 2, and the least to Table 3. It didn't take long for the children at Table 1 to perceive that they were treated better and come to see themselves as smarter. They became the leaders in class activities and even called children at the other tables "dumb." Eventually, the children at Table 3 disengaged themselves from many classroom activities. At the end of the year, only the children at Table 1 had completed the lessons that prepared them for reading.

This early tracking stuck. Their first-grade teacher looked at the work these students had done, and she placed students from Table 1 at her Table 1. She treated her tables much as the kindergarten teacher had, and the children at Table 1 again led the class.

The children's reputations continued to follow them. The second-grade teacher reviewed the children's scores and also divided her class into three groups. The first she named the "Tigers" and, befitting their name, gave them challenging readers. Not surprisingly, the Tigers came from the original Table 1 in kindergarten. The second group she called the "Cardinals." They came from the original Tables 2 and 3. Her third group consisted of children she had failed the previous year, whom she called the "Clowns." The Cardinals and Clowns were given less advanced readers.

Rist concluded that *each child's journey through school was determined by the eighth day of kindergarten!* As we saw with the Saints and Roughnecks in Chapter 4, labels can be so powerful that they can set people on courses of action that affect the rest of their lives.

What occurred was a **self-fulfilling prophecy**. This term, coined by sociologist Robert Merton (1949/1968), refers to a false assumption of something that is going to happen, which comes true simply because it was predicted. For example, if people believe an unfounded rumor that a credit union is going to fail because its officers have embezzled their money, they all rush to the credit union to demand their money. The prediction—although originally false—is now likely to come true.

self-fulfilling prophecy
Robert Merton's term for an originally false assertion that becomes true simply because it was predicted

How do Teacher Expectations Work?

Sociologist George Farkas (Farkas et al. 1990a; Farkas et al. 1990b; Farkas 1996) became interested in how teacher expectations affect grades. Using a stratified sample of students in a large school district in Texas, he found that teacher expectations produce gender and racial–ethnic biases. *On the gender level:* When boys and girls have the *same* test scores, girls, on average, are given higher course grades. *On the racial–ethnic level:* Asian Americans who have the *same* test scores as the other groups average higher grades.

At first, this may sound like more of the same old news—another case of discrimination. But this explanation doesn't fit, which is what makes the finding fascinating. Look at

Why do some students with the same test scores receive higher grades? "Signaling" that one is a "good student" may influence teacher perceptions.

who the victims are. It is most unlikely that the teachers would be prejudiced against boys and whites. To interpret these unexpected results, Farkas used symbolic interactionism. He observed that some students "signal" to their teachers that they are "good students." They show an eagerness to cooperate, and they quickly agree with what the teacher says. They also show that they are "trying hard." The teachers pick up these signals and reward these "good students" with better grades. Girls and Asian Americans, Farkas concluded, are better at giving these signals so coveted by teachers.

So much for Texas. How about the other states? Their interest piqued, other researchers examined data from a national sample of students from kindergarten to the fifth grade. The results? The same. Regardless of race—ethnicity, if girls and boys have the same test scores, the girls, on average, receive higher grades (Cornwell et al. 2013). The researchers asked the teachers to rank their students on their "interpersonal skills," how often they "lose control," and how "engaged" they are in the classroom. The teachers reported that the girls had a "better attitude toward learning." Like the Texas researchers, these researchers conclude that the teachers are responding to the children's behavior.

We do not have enough information on how teachers communicate their expectations to students. Nor do we know much about how students "signal" messages to their teachers. Perhaps you will become the educational sociologist who sheds more light on this interesting area of human behavior.

Self-Expectations

In the section on conflict theory, you read about how social class affects students' chances of going to college. In this section on symbolic interactionism, you just read about how teachers' expectations influence students' performance. Now let's switch the topic just slightly to self-expectations, which are even more powerful than teachers' expectations. In the following Down-to-Earth Sociology box, let's see how self-expectations can help you get through college.

Down-to-Earth Sociology

You Want to Get Through College? Let's Apply Sociology

As you just read, students from low-income homes are less likely to go to college than students from more privileged backgrounds. And if they do go to college, they are more likely to drop out. Why? On average, their scores on the SAT tests are lower, so perhaps this indicates that they aren't as intelligent. This, in fact, is close to the main problem—but not in the way you might think. These students are not less intelligent. Rather, the problem is that they *think* they are less intelligent.

Students from low-income homes arrive at college with more self-doubts than do students from higher-income homes. When problems occur, as they will, such as doing badly on a test, students from higher-income homes tend to say to themselves, "It's just a situation. I didn't study enough." Or maybe: "The teacher threw in some unexpected material." Thinking like this *deflects* blame away from the self. It moves the fault away from their abilities and places it on a temporary situation.

However, when the same thing happens to students from low-income backgrounds, self-doubts creep in. These students are more likely to see *the self* as the problem. They are more likely to think something like this: "I'm not sure I'm smart enough to get through college. Maybe this is the wrong place for me." This, in turn, sets these students on a self-defeating course: They come to see problems as a sign of self-deficiency.

Look at how vitally different these self-expectations are. Students from the more privileged backgrounds tend to shrug off the problem as a temporary situation. Students from the less privileged backgrounds tend to see the cause as flaws within the self. These contrasting self-expectations direct students onto different paths, ones that have resounding consequences for the students' lives.

What I have just told you is not simply an idea. It has been demonstrated in a remarkable set of experiments run by David Laude at the University of Texas (Tough 2014).

Laude followed good scientific methods. He randomly divided incoming freshmen according to their SAT scores and parents' income. During their orientation, the control group of students read neutral essays, while the experimental group read an essay about how intelligence increases as people study and learn. The low-scoring students from low-income homes who read the essay about intelligence got better grades as they went through college and were more likely to graduate than students from this same background who did not read that essay.

Hardly anybody could believe the results of Laude's experiment. Could reading a little essay really have such a deep impact on students? It did. But how? Without the student realizing it, the essay changed self-expectations. It provided a new way to interpret problem situations in college. "Ah, my brain can grow. My intelligence can change. I can get smarter." If there is a low grade on a test, the self, then, is not the problem. The problem is the low test score, a temporary situation to overcome.

For Your Consideration

I wrote this box with two purposes in mind. The first is to illustrate the power of self-expectations. I find this to be a fascinating application of symbolic interactionism. You can apply it to many situations in life, not just to college.

The second reason is to encourage students. It is good to realize that how you think about the problems you face makes all the difference in the world. Scientific research shows that your brain continues to develop and your intelligence can continue to increase. When you confront obstacles in college—such as a low test score or doing poorly on a term paper—do not think of the problem as your lack of ability. Rather, think of the problem as a particular situation that you can overcome. *You can make it in college.* So do it.

If this box turns out to make a difference in someone's life, helping to set positively predictive self-expectations and self-interpretations, my ultimate purpose, I will be most pleased.

Let's apply sociology, then, the most interesting of all academic subjects—or at least this is how I think of sociology.

Problems in U.S. Education—and Their Solutions

13.5 **Discuss mediocrity in education, grade inflation, social promotion, raising standards, cheating by administrators, and violence in schools.**

Now that we've looked at some of the dynamics within the classroom, let's turn to three problems facing U.S. education—mediocrity, cheating, and violence—and consider potential solutions.

Mediocrity

THE RISING TIDE OF MEDIOCRITY Since I know you love taking tests, let's see how you do on these three questions:

1. *How many goals are on a basketball court? a. 1   b. 2   c. 3   d. 4*
2. *How many halves are in a college basketball game? a. 1   b. 2   c. 3   d. 4*
3. *How many points does a three-point field goal account for in a basketball game?*
   a. 1   b. 2   c. 3   d. 4

I know this sounds like a joke, but it isn't. Sociologist Robert Benford (2007) got his hands on a copy of a twenty-question final examination given to basketball players who took a credit course on coaching principles at the University of Georgia. It is often difficult to refer to athletes, sports, and academics in the same breath, but this is about as mediocre as mediocrity can get.

Let's move to a broader view of the mediocrity that plagues our educational system like pollution plagues gasoline engines:

- Arizona officials gave their high school sophomores a math test covering the math that sophomores should know. One of ten passed.
- Arkansas officials get their students out of high school by dropping the passing score in math to 24 out of 100 (Urbina 2010).

- In Washington, D.C., most of the students who graduate from high school operate at about the *fifth grade* level. How do they graduate? When they fail a course, they take something called "Credit Recovery," which does not require a test (Rossiter 2012).
- In Florida, only 27 percent of the state's fourth graders passed the reading test. That didn't sound good, so the state dropped the passing grade, and suddenly 80 percent passed (Kristoff 2012). Much better.

Figure 13.4 National Results of the Scholastic Assessment Test (SAT)

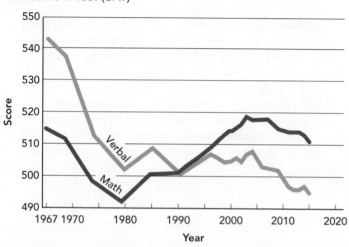

NOTE: Possible scores range from 200 to 800.

SOURCE: By the author. Based on College Board 2014; *Statistical Abstract of the United States* 2014:Table 271; 2015 test results.

THE SATs How are we doing on the SATs? Look at Figure 13.4. You can see how the scores dropped from the 1960s to 1980. At that point, educators sounded an alarm—and even Congress expressed concern. School officials decided they had better do something if they didn't want to lose their jobs.

Here's the good news. When school officials raised their standards, the SAT scores in math started to climb, and they continued going up for 25 years. Although scores have dropped recently, today's high school seniors score about the same in math as seniors did in the 1960s. Administrators are requiring more of math teachers, who, in turn, are demanding more of their students. Each is performing according to these higher expectations.

But there is also the *bad* news. Look at the verbal scores on Figure 13.4. Not only have they stayed down, but now they have dropped even more. No one knows why, but the usual suspects have been rounded up: "dummied down" textbooks, less rigorous teaching, and less reading because of television, videos, and computer games.

The news is actually worse than what you see on this figure. To accommodate today's less prepared students, those who develop the SAT have made it easier. They shortened the test, dropped the section on analogies and antonyms, and gave students more time to take the test. The test makers then "rescored" the totals of previous years to match the easier test. This "dummying down" of the SAT is a form of grade inflation, the topic to which we shall now turn.

GRADE INFLATION, SOCIAL PROMOTION, AND FUNCTIONAL ILLITERACY

Some graduates of prestigious law schools were having difficulty getting jobs. This reflected badly on these proud law schools—Georgetown, Golden Gate University, Loyola Law School, Tulane University, and New York University. They found a quick solution. To make their graduates look better, they raised everyone's grades (Rampell 2010). Much better-looking transcripts—all in a flash.

grade inflation

higher grades given for the same work; a general rise in student grades without a corresponding increase in learning

The letter grade C used to indicate average. Since more students are average than superior, high school teachers used to give about twice as many C's as A's. Now they give more A's than C's. Students aren't smarter—grading is just easier. **Grade inflation** is so pervasive that *50 percent* of all college freshmen have an overall high school grade point average of A. This is about twice what it was in 1980 (*Statistical Abstract* 2014:Table 290). Unfortunately, some of today's A's are the C's of years past.

social promotion

passing students on to the next level even though they have not mastered basic materials

Easy grades and declining standards have been accompanied by **social promotion**, passing students from one grade to the next despite their failure to learn the basic materials. One result is **functional illiteracy**, high school graduates who have never mastered things they should have learned in grade school. Some even have difficulty with reading and writing. Some high school graduates can't fill out job applications; others can't even figure out whether they get the right change at the grocery store.

functional illiteracy

refers to high school graduates who have difficulty with basic reading and math

RAISING STANDARDS FOR TEACHERS It is one thing to identify problems, quite another to find solutions for them. How can we solve mediocrity? To offer a quality education, we need quality teachers. Don't we already have them? Most teachers are qualified and, if motivated, can do an excellent job. But a large number of teachers are not qualified. Consider what happened in California, where teachers must pass an educational skills test. The teachers did so poorly that to fill the classrooms, officials had to drop the passing grade to the tenth-grade level. These are college graduates who are teachers—and they are expected to perform at the tenth-grade level (Schemo 2002). I don't know about you, but I think this situation is a national disgrace. If we want to improve teaching, we need to insist that teachers meet high standards.

RAISING STANDARDS FOR STUDENTS What else can we do to improve the quality of education? An older study by sociologists James Coleman and Thomas Hoffer (1987) provides helpful guidelines. They wanted to see why the test scores of students in Roman Catholic schools average 15 to 20 percent higher than those of students in public schools. Is it because Catholic schools attract better students, while public schools have to put up with everyone? To find out, they tested 15,000 students in public and Catholic high schools.

Their findings? From the sophomore through the senior years, students at Catholic schools pull ahead of public school students by a full grade in verbal and math skills. The superior test performance of students in Catholic schools, they concluded, is not due to better students, but to higher standards. Catholic schools have not watered down their curricula as have public schools. The researchers also underscored the importance of parental involvement. Parents and teachers in Catholic schools reinforce each other's commitment to learning.

These findings support the basic principle reviewed earlier about teacher expectations: Students perform better when they are expected to meet higher standards. To this, you might want to reply, "Of course. I knew that. Who wouldn't?" Somehow, however, this basic principle is lost on many teachers who expect little of their students and have supervisors who accept low performance from students. The reason, actually, is probably not their lack of awareness of such basics, but, rather, the organization that entraps them, a bureaucracy in which ritual replaces performance. To understand this point better, you may want to review Chapter 5.

A WARNING ABOUT HIGHER STANDARDS If we raise standards, we can expect to upset students and their parents. It is soothing to use low standards and to pat students on the head and tell them they are doing well. But it upsets people if you do rigorous teaching and use high standards to measure performance. When Florida decided that its high school seniors needed to pass an assessment test in order to receive a diploma, 13,000 students across the state failed the test. Parents of failed students protested. Did they demand better teaching? No. What they wanted was for the state to drop the test. In their anger, they asked people to boycott Disney World and to not buy Florida orange juice (Canedy 2003). What positive steps to improve their children's learning!

Let's look at a second problem in education.

Cheating

The cheating I'm referring to is not what you might have seen in your social studies or math class in high school. I'm referring to cheating by *teachers and school administrators* (Banchero 2014). Listen to this:

> *The state school board of Georgia ordered an investigation after computer scanners showed that teachers in **191 schools** had erased students' answers on reading and math tests and penciled in correct ones (Gabriel 2010). Thirty-four teachers were charged with conspiracy. Twenty-one pleaded guilty (McWhirter and Porter 2014). The cheating was apparently led by **the superintendent** of Atlanta's school system. She was charged with several crimes, including theft for taking $500,000 in bonuses for producing good test scores (Winerip 2013).*

The school district was facing pressure to show that their teaching had improved, and this was a quick way to do it. Now look at this:

> *Mississippi keeps two sets of books: The one sent to Washington reports the state's graduation rate at 87 percent. The other, which the state keeps, reports that 63 percent of its students graduate. Other states do the same. California reports its totals at 83 percent and 67 percent. (Dillon 2008)*

Why do high school administrators across the nation fake their graduation rates? The reason is that federal agencies publish these reports, and states don't want to look bad. Also, Washington might reduce the money it gives them. It's like a girl telling her parents that she received a B in English when she really received a D. She doesn't want to look bad, and her allowance might be cut.

School administrators can be quite creative in faking their numbers. Some count the number of students who begin their senior year and report the percentage of these seniors who graduate. This conveniently overlooks those who drop out in their freshman, sophomore, and junior years. Some even encourage high school students who are doing poorly to drop out before they reach their senior year. This way, they won't be counted as dropouts (Dillon 2008).

THE SOLUTION TO CHEATING   The solution to this cheating is fairly simple. Zero tolerance. Require all states to follow the same measurement of student performance and high school graduation, and fire teachers and administrators who cheat. A simple measure is to compare the number of those who graduate from high school with the number who entered high school in the ninth grade, minus those who died and those who transferred out, plus those who transferred in. Federal officials can spot-check records across the nation. With loss of job the punishment, we could expect honesty in reporting to jump immediately. Knowing students' real performance and real graduation rates can help pinpoint where the problems are, letting us know where to focus solutions. If you don't know where it's broken, you don't know where to fix it.

Let's turn to the third problem.

Violence

> *The man stalked the high school's hallways. He pressed his ear against a door, trying to determine if students were in the classroom. Hearing nothing, he moved silently to another classroom and did the same thing. Going from one locked door to another, he proceeded down the length of the entire hallway. Students were behind each door, but they remained absolutely quiet.*
>
> *Still hearing nothing, the man smiled.*

The man smiled? Yes, because he was not a sociopath seeking random victims. This was a teacher checking how well the school was performing in a "Code Blue" drill. In some schools, the safety of students and teachers is so precarious that armed guards, metal detectors, and drug-sniffing dogs are permanent fixtures. In an era of bomb threats and armed sociopaths, some states require lockdown, or "Code Blue," drills: The classrooms—each equipped with a phone—are locked. Shades or blinds on the windows are closed. The students are told to remain absolutely silent, while a school official wanders the halls, like an armed intruder, listening for the slightest sound that would indicate that someone is in a classroom (Kelley 2008). Students are even warned that the glow of their cell phones could make them targets (Healy 2014).

Although hope springs eternal in the human breast, it is unlikely that we will return to a time when school shootings are unknown. But certainly a good teaching-learning environment starts with safety.

How much worse are school shootings getting? The answer—in the Mass Media box on the next page—might surprise you.

Mass Media in Social Life

School Shootings: Exploding a Myth

The media sprinkle their reports of school shootings with such dramatic phrases as "alarming proportions," "outbreak of violence," and "out of control." They give us the impression that wackos walk our hallways, ready to spray students with gunfire. Parents used to consider schools safe havens, but no longer. Those naïve thoughts have been shattered by the media accounts of bullets ripping through our schools, children hovering in fear, and little bloody bodies strewn across classroom floors.

Have our schools really become war zones, as the mass media would have us believe? Certainly events, such as those at Sandy Hook Elementary School, Columbine High School, and Virginia Tech, are disturbing, but we need to probe deeper than screaming headlines and startling images.

When we do, we find that the media's sensationalism has created a myth. Contrary to "what everyone knows," *there is no trend toward greater school violence*. In fact, we find just the opposite—*the trend is toward greater safety at school*. Despite the occasional dramatic school shooting

This frame from a home video shows Eric Harris (on the left) and Dylan Klebold (on the right) smiling as they pretend that they are searching for victims. They put their desires into practice in the infamous Columbine High School shootings.

Table 13.1 Exploding a Myth: Murders at U.S. Schools[1]

School Year	Murders
1992–93	47
1993–94	38
1994–95	39
1995–96	46
1996–97	45
1997–98	47
1998–99	38
1999–2000	26
Mean of 1992–2000:	**40.8**
2000–01	26
2001–02	27
2002–03	25
2003–04	37
2004–05	40
2005–06	37
2006–07	48
2007–08	39
2008–09	29
2009–10	27
Mean of 2000–2010:	**33.5**
2010–11	25

[1]Homicides at U.S. elementary or secondary schools, "while the victim was on the way to or from regular sessions at school, or while the victim was attending or traveling to or from an official school-sponsored event." The totals include students, staff, and other nonstudents. These are the latest totals available in the source. The twenty deaths at Sandy Hook in Connecticut are not yet included.

SOURCE: National Center for Education Statistics. "Digest of Education Statistics." Table 228.10, 2014.

that makes the screaming headlines, as you can see from Table 13.1, deaths at schools are *decreasing*. Because school homicides are high one year and low another, to see trends we need to average them out. Here is where we get the surprising results. The average number of annual murders in U.S. schools for 1992 to 2000 is forty-one. For 2000 to 2010, it is thirty-four, a drop of 17 percent.

I don't think you've seen any screaming headlines proclaiming this decrease in school killings, right?

Violent deaths at school are a serious problem. Even one student being wounded or killed is too many. But contrary to the impression fostered by the media, school deaths have dropped. Headlines like "No Shootings This Month!" or "Schools Safer Than Ever!" simply don't get much attention—nor bring in much advertising money.

Can you see why we need sociology? Sociologists can search behind the headlines to quietly, dispassionately do research that helps us better understand the events that shape our lives. The first requirement for solving any problem is accurate data. How can we create solutions based on hysteria? The information presented in this box may not make for sensational headlines, but it does serve to explode one of the myths that the media have created.

For Your Consideration

→ How do you think we can reduce school shootings? How about school violence of any sort?

→ Why are people's ideas often based more on headlines than on facts?

The Need for Educational Reform

Most of the changes in education are merely minor adjustments to a flawed system: giving this test instead of that test, requiring more memorizing or less memorizing, measuring progress this way instead of that way, tinkering with the curriculum or motivating teachers and students by this carrot or that carrot. Each might be important in its own way, but each is but a minute adjustment to the details of a system that needs to be overhauled from top to bottom.

We are unlikely to do this.

■ Religion: Establishing Meaning

13.6 **Explain what Durkheim meant by sacred and profane; discuss the three elements of religion.**

Let's look at the main characteristics of a second significant social institution.

WHAT IS RELIGION? Religion was one of Emile Durkheim's major interests. For whatever reason—likely because he was reared in a mixed-religion family, by a Protestant mother and a Jewish father—Durkheim decided to find out what all religions have in common.

After surveying religions around the world, Durkheim published his findings in a 1912 book, *The Elementary Forms of the Religious Life*. This book is complicated, but here are three of Durkheim's main conclusions. The first is that there is no particular belief or practice common to all religions. The second is that despite their diversity, all religions develop a community that centers on their beliefs and practices. And third, all religions separate the sacred from the profane. By **sacred**, Durkheim meant things that have to do with the supernatural, things that inspire awe, reverence, deep respect, or even fear. By **profane**, he meant things that are not concerned with religion but, instead, are part of ordinary, everyday life.

After he did his research, here is how Durkheim (1912/1965) defined religion:

A religion is a unified system of beliefs and practices relative to sacred things, that is to say, things set apart and forbidden—beliefs and practices which unite into one single moral community called a Church, all those who adhere to them.

Religion, then, has three elements:

1. *Beliefs* that some things are sacred (forbidden, set apart from the profane)
2. *Practices* (rituals) centering on the things considered sacred
3. *A moral community* (a church) that results from a group's shared beliefs and practices

Durkheim used the word **church** in an unusual sense, to refer to any "moral community" centered on a group's beliefs and practices regarding the sacred. In Durkheim's sense, *church* refers to Buddhists bowing before a shrine, Hindus dipping in the Ganges River, and Confucians offering food to their ancestors. Similarly, the term *moral community* does not mean morality in the sense familiar to most of us—of ethical conduct. Rather, a moral community is simply a group of people who are united by their religious practices—and that would include sixteenth-century Aztec priests who each day gathered around an altar to pluck out the beating heart of a virgin.

To better understand the sociological approach to religion, let's see what pictures emerge when we apply the three theoretical perspectives.

sacred

Durkheim's term for things set apart or forbidden that inspire fear, awe, reverence, or deep respect

profane

Durkheim's term for common elements of everyday life

religion

according to Durkheim, beliefs and practices that separate the profane from the sacred and unite its adherents into a moral community

church

according to Durkheim, one of the three essential elements of religion—a moral community of believers; also refers to a large, highly organized religious group that has formal, sedate worship services with little emphasis on evangelism, intense religious experience, or personal conversion

Parents around the world teach their children their religious beliefs and practices. This mother in Thailand is teaching her daughter how to celebrate the Taoist vegetarian festival.

The Functionalist Perspective

13.7   Apply the functionalist perspective to religion: functions and dysfunctions.

Functionalists stress that religion is universal because it meets universal human needs. Let's look at some of the functions—and dysfunctions—of religion.

Functions of Religion

MEANING AND PURPOSE   Around the world, religions provide answers to perplexing questions about ultimate meaning. What is the purpose of life? Why do people suffer? Is there an afterlife? The answers to questions like these give followers a sense of purpose, a framework for living. Instead of seeing themselves buffeted by random events in an aimless existence, believers see their lives as fitting into a divine plan.

EMOTIONAL COMFORT   The answers that religion provides about ultimate meaning bring comfort by assuring people that there is a purpose to life, even to suffering. The religious rituals that enshroud crucial events, such as illness and death, assure the individual that others care.

SOCIAL SOLIDARITY   Religious teachings and practices unite believers into a community that shares values and perspectives ("we Jews," "we Christians," "we Muslims"). The religious rituals that surround marriage, for example, link the bride and groom with a broader community that wishes them well. So do other religious rituals, such as those that celebrate birth and mourn death.

GUIDELINES FOR EVERYDAY LIFE   The teachings of religion are not all abstractions. They also provide practical guidelines for everyday life. For example, four of the ten commandments delivered by Moses to the Israelites concern God, but the other six contain instructions for getting along with others, from how to avoid problems with parents and neighbors, to warnings about lying, stealing, and having affairs.

Many consequences for people who follow these guidelines can be measured. For example, people who attend church are less likely to abuse alcohol, nicotine, and illegal drugs than are people who don't go to church. They are also more likely to exercise (Gillum 2005; Wallace et al. 2007; Newport et al. 2012). In general, churchgoers follow a healthier lifestyle than people who don't go to church—and they live longer.

SOCIAL CONTROL   Although a religion's guidelines for everyday life usually apply only to its members, nonmembers feel a spillover. Religious teachings, for example, are incorporated into criminal law. In the American colonial period, people could be arrested

One of the functions of religion is providing emotional support. Shown here is a girl in Nicaragua being hugged by Sister Nirmala, who replaced Mother Teresa as head of the Missionaries of Charity order of nuns.

Religion can promote social change, as was evident in the U.S. civil rights movement. Dr. Martin Luther King, Jr., a Baptist minister, shown here in his famous "I have a dream" speech, was the foremost leader of this movement.

for blasphemy and adultery. As a carryover today, some states have laws that prohibit the sale of alcohol before noon on Sunday. The original purpose of these laws was to get people out of the saloons and into the churches.

SOCIAL CHANGE   Although religion is often so bound up with the prevailing social order that it resists social change, religious activists sometimes spearhead change. In the 1960s, for example, the civil rights movement, whose goals were to desegregate public facilities and abolish racial discrimination in voting, was led by religious leaders. African American churches served as centers where demonstrators were trained and rallies were organized. Other churches were centers for resisting this change.

Dysfunctions of Religion

Functionalists also examine ways in which religion is *dysfunctional*, that is, how religion can bring harmful results. Two dysfunctions are persecution and war and terrorism.

RELIGION AS JUSTIFICATION FOR PERSECUTION   Religion is sometimes a motivation for harming people. Beginning in the 1100s and continuing into the 1800s, in what has become known as the Inquisition, special commissions of the Roman Catholic Church tortured accused heretics and burned them at the stake. In 1692, Protestant leaders in Salem, Massachusetts, executed twenty-one women and men who were accused of being witches. The Aztec religion also had its dysfunctions—at least for the young virgins who were offered to appease angry gods.

I would like to say that this dysfunction of persecution and killing was all in the past, but it continues yet today. In Papua New Guinea, accused witches are tortured, doused with gasoline, and set on fire (Chumley 2013). As I write this, ISIS, an Islamic group, is beheading enemies in the name of their God. In short, religion is used to justify oppression and any number of brutal acts.

WAR AND TERRORISM   History is filled with wars based on religion—commingled with politics. Between the eleventh and fourteenth centuries, for example, Christian monarchs conducted nine bloody Crusades in an attempt to wrest control of the region they called the Holy Land from the Muslims. The suicide terrorists we focused on in Chapter 11 are a current example.

The Symbolic Interactionist Perspective

13.8   Apply the symbolic interactionist perspective to religion: symbols, rituals, beliefs, and religious experience.

Symbolic interactionists focus on the meanings that people give their experiences, especially how they use symbols. Let's apply this perspective to religious symbols, rituals, and beliefs to see how they help to forge a community of like-minded people.

Religious Symbols

Suppose that it is about two thousand years ago and you have just joined a new religion. You have come to believe that a recently crucified Jew named Jesus is the Messiah, the Lamb of God offered for your sins. The Roman leaders are persecuting the followers of Jesus. They hate your religion because you and your fellow believers will not acknowledge Caesar as God.

Christians are few in number, and you are eager to have fellowship with other believers. But how can you tell who is a believer? Spies are everywhere. The government has sworn to destroy this new religion, and you do not relish the thought of being fed to lions in the Colosseum.

You use a simple technique. While talking with a stranger, as though doodling absentmindedly in the sand or dust, you casually trace the outline of a fish. Only fellow believers know the meaning—that, taken together, the first letter of each word in the Greek sentence "Jesus (is) Christ the Son of God" spell the Greek word for fish. If the other person gives no response, you rub out the outline and continue the interaction as usual. If there is a response, you eagerly talk about your new faith.

All religions use symbols to provide identity and create social solidarity for their members. For Muslims, the primary symbol is the crescent moon and star; for Jews, the Star of David; for Christians, the cross. For members, these are not ordinary symbols, but sacred emblems that evoke feelings of awe and reverence. In Durkheim's terms, religions use symbols to represent what the group considers sacred and to separate the sacred from the profane.

A symbol is a condensed way of communicating. Worn by a fundamentalist Christian, for example, the cross says, "I am a follower of Jesus Christ. I believe that he is the Messiah, the promised Son of God, that he loves me, that he died to take away my sins, that he rose from the dead and is going to return to Earth, and that through him I will receive eternal life."

That is a lot to pack into one symbol—and it is only part of what this symbol means to a fundamentalist believer. To people in other traditions of Christianity, the cross conveys somewhat different meanings—but to all Christians, the cross is a shorthand way of expressing many meanings. So it is with the Star of David, the crescent moon and star, the cow (expressing to Hindus the unity of all living things), and the various symbols of the world's many other religions.

Symbolic interactionists stress that a basic characteristic of humans is that they attach meaning to objects and events and then use representations of those objects or events to communicate with one another. Michelangelo's *Pietà*, depicting Mary tenderly holding her son, Jesus, after his crucifixion, is one of the most acclaimed symbols in the Western world. It is admired for its beauty by believers and nonbelievers alike.

Rituals

Rituals, ceremonies or repetitive practices, are also symbols that help to unite people into a moral community. Some rituals, such as the bar mitzvah of Jewish boys and the holy communion of Christians, are designed to create in devout believers a feeling of closeness with God and unity with one another. Rituals include kneeling and praying at set times; bowing; crossing oneself; singing; lighting candles and incense; reading scripture; and following prescribed traditions at processions, baptisms, weddings, and funerals. The photo essay on the next two pages features photos I took of annual rituals held in Spain during Holy Week (the week that precedes the Christian holiday of Easter).

rituals

ceremonies or repetitive practices; in religion, observances or rites often intended to evoke a sense of awe of the sacred

Beliefs

Symbols, including rituals, develop from beliefs. The belief may be vague ("God is") or highly specific ("God wants us to prostrate ourselves and face Mecca five times each day"). Religious beliefs include not only *values* (what is considered good and desirable in life—how we ought to live) but also a **cosmology**, a unified picture of the world. For example, the Jewish, Christian, and Muslim belief that there is only one God, the creator of the universe, who is concerned about the actions of humans and who will hold us accountable for what we do, is a cosmology. It presents a unifying picture of the universe.

cosmology

teachings or ideas that provide a unified picture of the world

Religious Experience

The term **religious experience** refers to becoming aware of the supernatural or a feeling of coming into contact with God. Some people undergo a mild version, such as feeling closer to God when they look at a mountain, watch a sunset, or listen to a certain piece of music. Others report a life-transforming experience. St. Francis of Assisi, for example, said that he became aware of God's presence in every living thing.

religious experience

a sudden awareness of the supernatural or a feeling of coming in contact with God

THROUGH THE AUTHOR'S LENS

Holy Week in Spain

Religious groups develop rituals designed to evoke memories, create awe, inspire reverence, and stimulate social solidarity. One of the primary means by which groups, religious and secular, accomplish these goals is through the display of symbols.

I took these photos during Holy Week in Spain—in Malaga and Almuñecar. Throughout Spain, elaborate processions feature tronos that depict the biblical account of Jesus' suffering, death, and resurrection During the processions in Malaga, the participants walk slowly for about two minutes; then because of the weight of the tronos, they rest for about two minutes. They repeat this process for about six hours a day.

© Jim Henslin, all photos

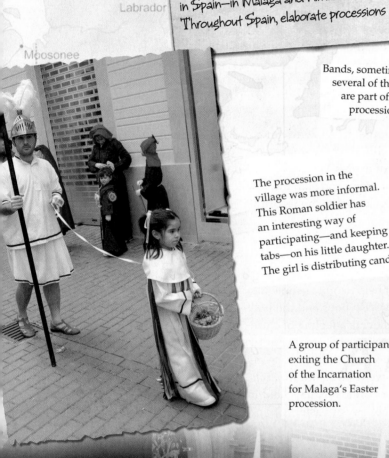

Bands, sometimes several of them, are part of the processions.

The procession in the village was more informal. This Roman soldier has an interesting way of participating—and keeping tabs—on his little daughter. The girl is distributing candy.

A group of participants exiting the Church of the Incarnation for Malaga's Easter procession.

Parents gave a lot of attention to their children both during the preparations and during the processions. This photo was taken during one of the repetitive two-minute breaks.

Beneath the costumes are townspeople and church members who know one another well. They enjoy themselves prior to the procession. This man is preparing to put on his hood.

During the short breaks at the night processions, children from the audience would rush to collect dripping wax to make wax balls. This was one way that the audience made themselves participants in the drama.

Some *tronos* are so heavy that they require many men to carry them. (Some were carried by over 100 men.) This photo was taken in Malaga, on Monday of Holy Week.

For the Good Friday procession, I was fortunate to be able to photograph the behind-the-scenes preparations, which are seldom seen by visitors. Shown here are finishing touches being given to the Mary figure.

The town square was packed with people awaiting the procession. From one corner of the square, the *trono* of Jesus was brought in. Then from another, that of Mary ("reuniting" them, as I was told). During this climactic scene, the priest on the balcony on the left read a message.

born again

a term describing Christians who have undergone a religious experience so life transforming that they feel they have become new persons

Some Protestants use the term **born again** to describe people who have undergone a life-transforming religious experience. These people say that they came to the realization that they had sinned, that Jesus had died for their sins, and that God wants them to live a new life. Their worlds become transformed. They look forward to the Resurrection and to a new life in heaven. They see relationships with spouses, parents, children, and even bosses in a new light. They also report a need to change how they interact with people so that their lives reflect their new, personal commitment to Jesus as their "Savior and Lord." They describe a feeling of beginning life anew—which is why they use the term *born again*.

The Conflict Perspective

13.9   Apply the conflict perspective to religion: opium of the people and legitimating social inequalities.

In general, conflict theorists are highly critical of religion. They stress that religion supports the status quo and helps to maintain social inequalities. Let's look at some of their analyses.

Opium of the People

Karl Marx, an avowed atheist who believed that the existence of God was impossible, set the tone for conflict theorists with this statement: "Religion is the sigh of the oppressed creature, the sentiment of a heartless world. . . . It is the opium of the people" (Marx 1844/1964). Marx meant that for oppressed workers, religion is like a drug that helps addicts forget their misery. By diverting thoughts toward future happiness in an afterlife, religion takes the workers' eyes off their suffering in this world, reducing the possibility that they will overthrow their chains by rebelling against their oppressors.

Legitimating Social Inequalities

Conflict theorists stress that religion legitimates social inequalities. By this, they mean that religion teaches that the existing social arrangements represent what God desires. For example, during the Middle Ages, Christian theologians decreed the *divine right of kings*. This doctrine meant that God determined who would become king and set him on the throne. The king ruled in God's place, and it was the duty of a king's subjects to be loyal to him (and to pay their taxes). To disobey the king was to disobey God.

In what was perhaps the supreme technique of legitimating the social order (one that went even farther than the divine right of kings), the religion of ancient Egypt held that the pharaoh was a *god*. The emperor of Japan was similarly declared divine. If this were so, who could ever question his decisions? Today's politicians would give their right arms for such a religious teaching.

Conflict theorists point to many other examples of how religion legitimates the social order. In India, Hinduism supports the caste system by teaching that anyone who tries to change caste will come back in the next life as a member of a lower caste—or even as an animal. In the decades before the American Civil War, southern ministers used scripture to defend slavery, saying that it was God's will—while northern ministers legitimated *their* region's social structure by using scripture to denounce slavery as evil (Ernst 1988; White 1995; Riley 2012).

Religion and the Spirit of Capitalism

13.10 **Explain Weber's analysis of how religion broke tradition and brought capitalism.**

Max Weber disagreed with the conflict perspective. Religion, he said, does not merely reflect and legitimate the social order and impede social change. Rather, religion's focus on the afterlife is a source of profound social change.

Like Marx, Weber observed the early industrialization of Europe. As he did so, he began to wonder why some societies embraced capitalism while others held onto their traditional ways. Tradition was strong in all these countries, yet capitalism transformed some while others remained untouched. As Weber explored this puzzle, he concluded that religion held the key to **modernization**—the transformation of traditional societies to industrial societies.

To explain his conclusions, Weber wrote *The Protestant Ethic and the Spirit of Capitalism* (1904–1905, 2011). He said that:

1. Capitalism represents a fundamentally different way of thinking about work and money. *Traditionally, people worked just enough to meet their basic needs, not so that they could have a surplus to invest.* To accumulate money (capital) as an end in itself, not just to spend it, was a radical departure from traditional thinking. People even came to consider it a duty to invest money so they could make profits. They reinvested these profits to make even more profits. Weber called this new approach to work and money the **spirit of capitalism**.

2. Why did the spirit of capitalism develop in Europe and not, for example, in China or India, where people had similar material resources and education? According to Weber, *religion was the key.* The religions of China and India, and indeed Roman Catholicism in Europe, encouraged a traditional approach to life, not thrift and investment. Capitalism appeared when Protestantism came on the scene.

3. What was different about Protestantism, especially Calvinism? John Calvin taught that God had predestined some people to go to heaven and others to hell. Neither church membership nor feelings about your relationship with God could assure you that you were saved. You wouldn't know your fate until after you died.

4. "Am I predestined to hell or to heaven?" Calvin's followers wondered. As they wrestled with this question, they concluded that church members have a duty to live as though they are predestined to heaven—for good works are a demonstration of salvation.

5. This conclusion motivated Calvinists to lead moral lives *and* to work hard, to use their time productively, and to be frugal—since idleness and needless spending were signs of worldliness. Weber called this self-denying approach to life the **Protestant ethic**.

6. As people worked hard and spent money only on necessities (a pair of earrings or a second pair of dress shoes would have been defined as sinful luxuries), they had money left over. Because the money couldn't be spent on personal items, this capital was invested, which led to a surge in production.

7. Weber's analysis can be summed up this way: The change in religion (from Catholicism to Protestantism, especially Calvinism) led to a fundamental change in thought and behavior (the *Protestant ethic*). The result was the *spirit of capitalism.*

"We're thinking maybe it's time you started getting some religious instruction. There's Catholic, Protestant, and Jewish—any of those sound good to you?"

For some Americans, religion is an "easy-going, makes-little-difference" matter, as expressed in this cartoon. For others, religious matters are firmly held, and followers find even slight differences of faith to be significant.

modernization

the transformation of traditional societies into industrial societies

spirit of capitalism

Weber's term for the desire to accumulate capital—not to spend it, but as an end in itself—and to constantly reinvest it

Protestant ethic

Weber's term to describe the ideal of a self–denying, highly moral life accompanied by thrift and hard work

For this reason, capitalism originated in Europe and not in places where religion did not encourage capitalism's essential elements: the accumulation of capital and its investment and reinvestment.

Although Weber's analysis has been influential, it has not lacked critics. Hundreds of scholars have attacked it, some for overlooking the lack of capitalism in Scotland (a Calvinist country), others for failing to explain why the Industrial Revolution was born in England (not a Calvinist country). Hundreds of other scholars have defended Weber's argument, and sociologists continue to test Weber's theory (Basten and Betz 2011). Currently, sociologists are not in agreement on this matter.

At this point in history, the Protestant ethic and the spirit of capitalism are not confined to any specific religion or even to any one part of the world. Rather, they have become cultural traits that have spread to societies around the globe (Greeley 1964; Yinger 1970). U.S. Catholics have about the same approach to life as do U.S. Protestants. In addition, Hong Kong, Japan, Malaysia, Singapore, South Korea, and Taiwan—not exactly Protestant countries—have embraced capitalism. China, Russia, and Vietnam are in the midst of doing so.

Types of Religious Groups

13.11 Compare cult, sect, church, and ecclesia.

Sociologists have identified four types of religious groups: cult, sect, church, and ecclesia. Why do some of these groups meet with hostility, while others tend to be accepted? For an explanation, look at Figure 13.5.

Let's explore what sociologists have found about these four types of religious groups. The summary that follows is a modification of analyses by sociologists Ernst Troeltsch (1931), Liston Pope (1942), and Benton Johnson (1963).

Cult

The word *cult* conjures up bizarre images. Shaven heads, weird music, brainwashing—even ritual suicide—may come to mind. Cults, however, are not necessarily weird, and

cult

a new religion with few followers, whose teachings and practices put it at odds with the dominant culture and religion

---

Figure 13.5 Religious Groups: From Hostility to Acceptance

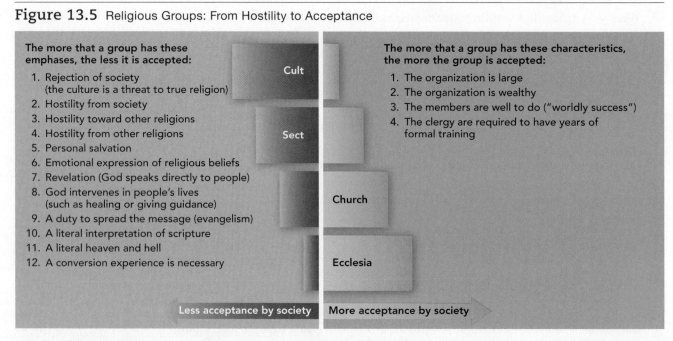

The more that a group has these emphases, the less it is accepted:
1. Rejection of society (the culture is a threat to true religion)
2. Hostility from society
3. Hostility toward other religions
4. Hostility from other religions
5. Personal salvation
6. Emotional expression of religious beliefs
7. Revelation (God speaks directly to people)
8. God intervenes in people's lives (such as healing or giving guidance)
9. A duty to spread the message (evangelism)
10. A literal interpretation of scripture
11. A literal heaven and hell
12. A conversion experience is necessary

The more that a group has these characteristics, the more the group is accepted:
1. The organization is large
2. The organization is wealthy
3. The members are well to do ("worldly success")
4. The clergy are required to have years of formal training

Cult

Sect

Church

Ecclesia

Less acceptance by society | More acceptance by society

NOTE: Any religious organization can be placed somewhere on this continuum, based on its having "more" or "less" of these characteristics and emphases. The varying proportions of the rectangles are intended to represent the group's relative characteristics and emphases.

SOURCE: By the author. Based on Troeltsch 1931; Pope 1942; Johnson 1963.

few practice "brainwashing" or bizarre rituals. In fact, *all religions began as cults* (Stark 1989). A **cult** is simply a new or different religion whose teachings and practices put it at odds with the dominant culture and religion. Because the term *cult* arouses negative associations in the public mind, however, some scholars prefer to use the term *new religion* instead. As is evident from the Cultural Diversity box below, "new" can mean that an old religion is making its appearance in a culture that is not familiar and is uncomfortable with it.

Cults often originate with a **charismatic leader**, an individual who inspires people because he or she seems to have extraordinary gifts, qualities, or abilities. **Charisma** refers to an outstanding gift or to some exceptional quality. People feel drawn to both the person and the message because they find something highly appealing about the individual—in some instances, almost a magnetic charm.

charismatic leader

literally, someone to whom God has given a gift; in its extended sense, someone who exerts extraordinary appeal to a group of followers

charisma

literally, an extraordinary gift from God; more commonly, an outstanding, "magnetic" personality

Cultural Diversity in the United States

Human Heads and Animal Blood: Testing the Limits of Tolerance

As the U.S. customs officials looked over the line of people who had just gotten off the plane from Haiti, there was nothing to make this particular woman stand out. She would have passed through without a problem, except for one thing: A routine search turned up something that struck the custom agents as somewhat unusual—a human head.

The head had teeth, hair, pieces of skin, and some dirt. It had evidently been dug up from some grave, probably in Haiti.

The thirty-year-old woman, who lives in Florida, practiced voodoo. The head was for her religious rituals.

The woman was arrested. Her crime? Not filing a report that she was carrying "organic material" ("Mujer con Cabeza . . ." 2006).

* * * * *

The Santeros from Cuba who live in Florida sacrifice animals. They meet in apartments, where, following a Yoruba religion, they kill goats and chickens. Calling on their gods, they first ask permission to sacrifice the animals. After sacrificing them, they pour out the animals' blood, which opens and closes the doors of their destiny. They also cut off the animals' heads and place them at locations in the city that represent the four directions of the compass. This is done to terrorize their enemies and give them safety. The heads also protect the city from hurricanes and other destructive forces.

When city officials in Hialeah, Florida, learned that the Santeros were planning to build a church in their city, they passed a law against the sacrifice of animals within the city limits. The Santeros appealed to the U.S. Supreme Court,

A Santeria priest in Havana, Cuba, stirring the blood of sacrificed animals. The blood is used to bathe a statue of their god, Eshu-Elegbara, the protector of the universe.

claiming discrimination, because the law was directed against them. The Court ruled in their favor.

City officials of Euless, Texas, were shocked when they learned that Jose Merced was sacrificing goats in his home. They sent in the police (Rassbach 2009). Merced appealed to the federal circuit court, saying that the officials were violating his rights as a Santeria priest. He can now sacrifice goats at home.

For Your Consideration

→ What do you think the limitations on religious freedom should be? Should people be allowed to sacrifice animals as part of their religious practices?

→ If the Santeros can sacrifice animals, why shouldn't people who practice voodoo be able to use human heads in their rituals if they want to? (Assume that the relatives of the dead person have given their permission.)

The most popular religion in the world began as a cult. Its handful of followers believed that an unschooled carpenter who preached in remote villages in a backwater country was the Son of God and that he was killed and came back to life. Those beliefs made the early Christians a cult, setting them apart from the rest of their society. Persecuted by both religious and political authorities, these early believers clung to one another for support. Many cut off associations with friends who didn't accept the new message. To others, the early Christians must have seemed deluded and brainwashed.

So it was with Islam. When Muhammad revealed his visions and said that God's name was really Allah, only a few people believed him. To others, he must have seemed crazy, deranged.

Each cult (or new religion) is met with rejection on the part of society. Its message is considered bizarre, its approach to life strange. Its members antagonize the majority, who are convinced that they have a monopoly on the truth. The new religion may claim messages from God, visions, visits from angels—some form of enlightenment or seeing the true way to God. The cult demands intense commitment, and its followers, who are confronting a hostile world, pull together in a tight circle, separating themselves from nonbelievers. Most cults fail. Not many people believe the new message, and the cult fades into obscurity. Some, however, succeed and make history. Over time, large numbers of people may come to accept the message and become followers of the religion. If this happens, the new religion changes from a cult to a sect.

Sect

sect

a religious group larger than a cult that still feels substantial hostility from and toward society

A **sect** is larger than a cult, but its members still feel tension between their views and the prevailing beliefs and values of the broader society. A sect may even be hostile to the society in which it is located. At the very least, its members remain uncomfortable with many of the emphases of the dominant culture; in turn, nonmembers tend to be uncomfortable with members of the sect.

If a sect grows, its members tend to gradually make peace with the rest of society. To appeal to a broader base, the sect shifts some of its doctrines, redefining matters to remove some of the rough edges that create tension between it and the rest of society. As the members become more respectable in the eyes of the society, they feel less hostility and little, if any, isolation. If a sect follows this course, as it grows and becomes more integrated into society, it changes into a church.

Like other aspects of culture, religion is filled with background assumptions that usually go unquestioned. In this photo, which I took in Amsterdam, what background assumption of religion is this woman violating? (See pages 440–441.)

Church

At this point, the religious group is highly bureaucratized—probably with national and international headquarters that give direction to the local congregations, enforce rules about who can be ordained, and control finances. The relationship with God has grown less intense. The group is likely to have less emphasis on personal salvation and emotional expression. Worship services are likely to be more sedate, with formal sermons and written prayers read before the congregation. Rather than being recruited from the outside by personal evangelism, most new members now come from within, from children born to existing members. Rather than joining through conversion—seeing the new truth—children may be baptized, circumcised, or dedicated in some other way. At some designated age, children may be asked to affirm the group's beliefs in a ceremony, such as a confirmation or bar mitzvah.

Ecclesia

Finally, some religions become so well integrated into a culture, and allied so strongly with their government, that it is difficult to tell where one leaves off and the other takes over. In these *state religions*, also called **ecclesia**, the government and religion work together to try to shape society. Since citizenship makes everyone a member, there is no recruitment of members. For most people in the society, the religion is part of a cultural identity, not an eye-opening experience. Sweden provides a good example of how extensively religion and government intertwine in an ecclesia. In the 1860s, all citizens had to memorize Luther's *Small Catechism* and be tested on it annually (Anderson 1995). Today, Lutheranism is still associated with the state, but most Swedes come to church only for baptisms, marriages, and funerals.

Unlike cults and sects, which perceive God as personally involved with and concerned about people, ecclesia envision God as more impersonal and remote. Reflecting this view of the supernatural, church services tend to be highly formal, directed by ministers or priests who, after undergoing training in approved schools or seminaries, follow prescribed rituals.

ecclesia

a religious group so integrated into the dominant culture that it is difficult to tell where the one begins and the other leaves off; also called a *state religion*

Religion in the United States

13.12 **Summarize the main features of religion in the United States.**

To better understand religion in the United States, let's first find out who belongs to religious groups and then look at the groups themselves.

Characteristics of Members

About 65 percent of Americans belong to a church, synagogue, or mosque. What are the characteristics of people who hold formal membership in a religion?

SOCIAL CLASS Religion in the United States is stratified by social class. As you can see from Figure 13.6 on the next page, some religious groups are "top-heavy," and others are "bottom-heavy." The most top-heavy are Jews and Episcopalians; the most bottom-heavy are the Assembly of God, Southern Baptists, and Jehovah's Witnesses. This figure provides further confirmation that churchlike groups tend to appeal to people who have more "worldly" success, while the more sectlike groups attract people who have less "worldly" success.

From this figure, you can see how *status consistency* (a concept we reviewed in Chapter 8, page 233) applies to religious groups. If a group ranks high (or low) on education, it is also likely to rank high (or low) on income and occupational prestige. Jews, for example, rank the highest on education, income, and occupational prestige, while Jehovah's Witnesses rank the lowest on these three measures of social class. As you can see, the Mormons are status inconsistent. They rank second in income, fourth in education, and tie for sixth in occupational prestige. Even more status inconsistent is the Assembly of God. Their members tie for third in occupational prestige but rank only eighth in income and ninth in education. This inconsistency is so jarring that there could be a problem with the sample.

RACE–ETHNICITY Many religions are associated with race–ethnicity: Islam with Arabs, Judaism with Jews, Hinduism with Indians, and Confucianism with Chinese. In the United States, all major religious groups draw from the nation's many

Figure 13.6 Social Class and Religious Affiliation

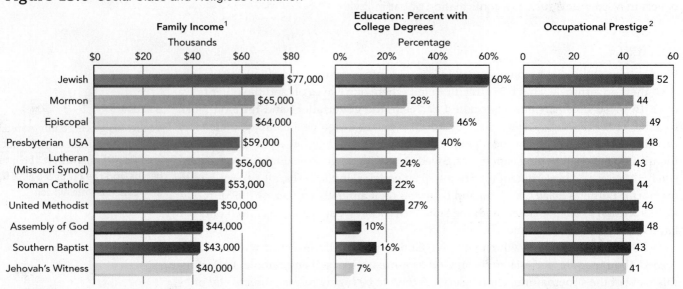

[1] The family incomes reported here must be taken as approximate. The original totals were from 1996. I increased them by 48 percent, the inflation rate reported by the Bureau of Labor Statistics for 1996 to 2013.

[2] Higher numbers mean that more of the group's members work at occupations that have higher prestige, generally those that require more education and offer higher pay. For more information on occupational prestige, see Table 8.2 on page 232.

SOURCE: By the author. Based on Smith and Faris 2005.

racial–ethnic groups. Like social class, however, race–ethnicity tends to cluster. People of Irish descent are likely to be Roman Catholics; those with Greek ancestors are likely to belong to the Greek Orthodox Church. African Americans are likely to be Protestants—more specifically, Baptists—or to belong to fundamentalist sects.

Although many churches are integrated, it is with good reason that Sunday morning between 10 and 11 A.M. has been called "the most segregated hour in the United States." African Americans tend to belong to African American churches, while most whites see only whites in theirs. The segregation of churches is based on custom, not on law.

Characteristics of Religious Groups

Let's examine features of the religious groups in the United States.

DIVERSITY Two of three Americans (63 percent) are members of a church, synagogue, or mosque, but with hundreds of denominations, no religious group comes even close to being a dominant religion in the United States (*Statistical Abstract* 2014:Tables 81, 82). Table 13.2 on the next page illustrates some of this remarkable diversity.

PLURALISM AND FREEDOM It is the U.S. government's policy not to interfere with religions. The government's position is that its obligation is to ensure an environment in which people can worship as they see fit. Religious freedom is so extensive that anyone can start a church and proclaim himself or herself a minister, revelator, or any other desired term. The exceptions to this hands-off policy are startling. The most notorious exception in recent times occurred in Waco, Texas. Armed agents of the Bureau of Alcohol, Tobacco, and Firearms attacked the Branch Davidians, an obscure religious group. Eighty-two men, women, and children were victims, some killed by bullets but most burned to death. A second example is the government's infiltration of mosques to monitor the activities of Arab immigrants (Audi and Jordan 2014). Other limitations to this policy are discussed in the Cultural Diversity box on page 437.

TOLERATION The general religious toleration of Americans can be illustrated by three prevailing attitudes: (1) "All religions have a right to exist—as long as they don't try to brainwash or hurt anyone." (2) "With all the religions to choose from, how can

Table 13.2 How Americans Age 18 and Over Identify with Religion

Religious Group	Number of Members	Percentage of U.S. Adults
Christian	**174,300,000**	**70.6%**
Protestant	115,000,000	46.5%
Evangelical churches	60,500,000	25.4%
Mainline churches	36,300,000	14.7%
Historical black churches	16,000,000	6.5%
Roman Catholic	51,300,000	20.8%
Mormon	4,000,000	1.6%
Jehovah's Witness	2,000,000	0.8%
Orthodox: Greek, Russian	1,250,000	0.5%
Other Christian	1,000,000	0.4%
Other Religions	**14,600,000**	**5.9%**
Jewish	4,700,000	1.9%
Muslim	2,200,000	0.9%
Buddhist	1,700,000	0.7%
Hindu	1,700,000	0.7%
Other faiths (Unitarians, New Age, Native American religions, Liberal)	3,700,000	1.5%
Other world religions (Sikhs, Baha'is, Jains, others)	700,000	.03%
No Identity with a Religion	**56,500,000**	**22.8%**
Nothing in particular	39,000,000	15.8%
Agnostic	10,000,000	4.0%
Atheist	7,700,0000	3.1%
Don't Know or Refused	**1,500,000**	**0.6%**

NOTE: These data are based on a telephone survey of a nationally representative sample of 35,000 adult Americans. The population base on which I computed the numbers of members is 246,745,000. Because of rounding the totals do not equal 100.

SOURCES: Totals computed by the author based on *Statistical Abstract of the United States* 2014: Table 12; *America's Changing Religious Landscape* 2015.

anyone tell which one—if any—is true?" (3) "Each of us may be convinced about the truth of our religion—and that is good—but don't be obnoxious by trying to convince others that you have the exclusive truth."

THE ELECTRONIC CHURCH   What began as a ministry to shut-ins and those who do not belong to a church blossomed into its own type of church. Its preachers, called "televangelists," reach millions of viewers and raise millions of dollars. Some of its most famous ministers are Joel Osteen, Kenneth Copeland, Creflo Dollar, Benny Hinn, Joyce Meyers, and Pat Robertson.

Many local ministers view the electronic church as a competitor. They complain that it competes for the attention and dollars of their members. Leaders of the electronic church reply that the money goes to good causes and that through its conversions, the electronic church feeds members into the local churches, strengthening, not weakening them.

Participating in a religion helps mold identities and bond people to one another. The participation consists of much more than attending worship services, as you can see from this photo of an evangelical children's parade in East Harlem, New York.

The Future of Religion

13.13   Discuss the likely future of religion.

Religion thrives in the most advanced scientific nations—and, as officials of Soviet Russia and communist China were disheartened to learn—even in ideologically

A basic principle of symbolic interactionism is that meaning is not inherent in an object or event, but is determined by people as they interpret the object or event. Does this dinosaur fossil "prove" evolution? Does it "disprove" creation? Such "proof" and "disproof" lie in the eye of the beholder, based on the background assumptions by which it is interpreted.

hostile climates. Although the Soviet and Chinese authorities threw believers into prison, people continued to practice their religion. Humans are inquiring creatures. As they reflect on life, they ask, What is the purpose of it all? Why are we born? Is there an afterlife? If so, where are we going? Out of these concerns arises this question: If there is a God, what does God want of us in this life? Does God have a preference about how we should live?

Science, including sociology, cannot answer such questions. By its very nature, science cannot tell us about four main concerns that many people have:

1. *The existence of God.* About this, science has nothing to say. No test tube has either isolated God or refuted God's existence.

2. *The purpose of life.* Although science can provide a definition of life and describe the characteristics of living organisms, it has nothing to say about ultimate purpose.

3. *An afterlife.* Science can offer no information on this at all, since it has no tests to prove or disprove a "hereafter."

4. *Morality.* Science can demonstrate the consequences of behavior, but not the moral superiority of one action compared with another. This means—to use an extreme example—that science cannot even prove whether loving your family and neighbor is morally superior to hurting and killing them.

There is no doubt that religion will last as long as humanity lasts—what could replace it? And if something did and answered such questions, would it not be religion under a different name?

To close this chapter, let's try to glimpse the cutting edge of religious change.

The Mass Media in Social Life

God on the Net: The Online Marketing of Religion

In Thailand: *Teenaged Buddhist monks post videos of themselves on YouTube playing air guitar and reciting religious chants to hip-hop beats. This upsets older Buddhists who feel that the young monks are being disrespectful (Hookway 2012).*

In Israel: *You want to pray here at the Holy Land, but you can't leave home? No problem. Buy our special telephone card—available at your local 7-11. Just record your prayer, and we'll broadcast it via the Internet at the site you choose. Press 1 for the holy site of Jerusalem, press 2 for the holy site of the Sea of Galilee, press 3 for the birthplace of Jesus, press 4 for. . . . (Rhoads 2007).*

In India: *You moved to Kansas, but you want to pray in Chennai? No problem. Order your pujas (prayers), and a priest will say them in the temple of your choice. Just click how many you want. Food offerings for Vishnu included in the price. All major credit cards accepted (Sullivan 2007).*

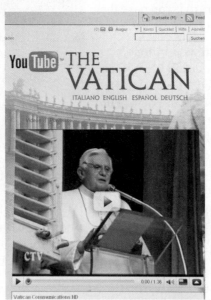

In our pluralist society, religions compete for members. The Internet is another venue for this competition.

In Rome: *The Pope tries to reach out to younger Roman Catholics by tweeting, little religious messages in 145 characters or less. The Pope doesn't actually write the tweets, but he "is involved" in what they say (Moloney 2012).*

In the United States: *Erin Polzin, a 20-year-old college student, listens to a Lutheran worship service on the radio, confesses online, and uses PayPal to tithe. "I don't like getting up early," she says. "This is like going to church without really having to" (Bernstein 2003).*

In Europe: *Muslims download sermons and join an invisible community of worshippers at virtual mosques. Jews type messages that fellow believers in Jerusalem download and insert in the Western Wall.*

Everywhere: No matter where you are, virtual church services are available. Just choose an avatar, and you can sing, kneel, pray, and listen to virtual sermons. And if you get bored, you don't have to continue to sit. You can walk around the virtual church and talk to other avatars (Feder 2004). And, of course, you can use your credit card—a real one, not the virtual kind.

The changes are far-reaching. An app for Jews shows a replica of the frond of a palm tree—with instructions how to swing it during Sukkot ("Study Finds. . ." 2014). One rabbi has congregants text anonymous messages regarding their reactions to what is being discussed. The cell phone messages are projected onto a screen in front of the congregation (Alvarez 2012).

Some say that the microchip has put us on the verge of a religious reformation that will turn out to be as big as the one set off by Gutenberg's invention of the printing press. This is likely an exaggeration, but perhaps not.

For Your Consideration

We are gazing into the future of religious practices as they change with technology.

→ How do you think that the Internet might change religion?

→ Do you think electronically-practiced religion can replace the warm embrace of fellow believers? Will tweets bring comfort to someone who is grieving for a loved one?

Summary and Review

Education in Global Perspective

13.1 Understand how education is related to a nation's culture and economy; compare education in Japan, Russia, and Egypt.

What is a credential society, and how did it develop?

A **credential society** is one in which employers use diplomas and degrees to determine who is eligible for a job. One reason that credentialism developed is that large, anonymous societies lack the personal knowledge common to smaller groups. Educational certification is taken as evidence of a person's ability.

How does education compare among the Most Industrialized, Industrializing, and Least Industrialized Nations?

In general, formal education reflects a nation's economy. Consequently, education is extensive in the Most Industrialized Nations, undergoing vast changes in the Industrializing Nations, and spotty in the Least Industrialized Nations. Japan, Russia, and Egypt provide examples of education in countries at three levels of industrialization.

The Functionalist Perspective: Providing Social Benefits

13.2 Explain the functions of education: knowledge and skills, values, social integration, gatekeeping, and replacing family functions.

What is the functionalist perspective on education?

Among the functions of education are the teaching of knowledge and skills, providing credentials, **cultural transmission of values,** social integration, **social placement (gatekeeping),** and **mainstreaming.** Functionalists also note that education has replaced some traditional family functions.

The Conflict Perspective: Perpetuating Social Inequality

13.3 Explain how the educational system reproduces the social class structure.

What is the conflict perspective on education?

The basic view of conflict theorists is that *education reproduces the social class structure;* that is, through such mechanisms as unequal funding and operating different schools for the elite and for the masses, education perpetuates a society's basic social inequalities from one generation to the next.

The Symbolic Interactionist Perspective: Teacher Expectations

13.4 Explain the significance of teacher expectations and give examples.

What is the symbolic interactionist perspective on education?

Symbolic interactionists focus on face-to-face interaction. In examining what occurs in the classroom, they have found that student performance tends to conform to teacher expectations, whether they are high or low.

Problems in U.S. Education—and Their Solutions

13.5 Discuss mediocrity in education, grade inflation, social promotion, raising standards, cheating by administrators, and violence in schools.

What are the chief problems that face U.S. education?

The major problems are mediocrity (low achievement as shown by standardized tests and SAT scores), **grade inflation, social promotion, functional illiteracy,** faked data reported by school administrators, and violence.

What are the potential solutions to these problems?

To restore high educational standards will require that we expect more of *both* students and teachers; school administrators can be required to use a single reporting measure based on objective, verifiable data; and, although we cannot prevent all school violence, for an effective learning environment, we can and must provide basic security for students.

Religion: Establishing Meaning

13.6 Explain what Durkheim meant by sacred and profane; discuss the three elements of religion.

What Is Religion?

Durkheim identified three essential characteristics of **religion:** beliefs that set the **sacred** apart from the **profane, rituals,** and a moral community (a **church**).

The Functionalist Perspective

13.7 Apply the functionalist perspective to religion: functions and dysfunctions.

What are the functions and dysfunctions of religion?

Among the functions of religion are answering questions about ultimate meaning; providing emotional comfort, social solidarity, guidelines for everyday life, social control, and social change. Among the dysfunctions of religion are religious persecution and war and terrorism.

The Symbolic Interactionist Perspective

13.8 Apply the symbolic interactionist perspective to religion: symbols, rituals, beliefs, and religious experience.

What aspects of religion do symbolic interactionists study?

Symbolic interactionists focus on the meanings of religion for its followers. They examine religious symbols, **rituals,** beliefs, and **religious experiences.**

The Conflict Perspective

13.9 Apply the conflict perspective to religion: opium of the people and legitimating social inequalities.

What aspects of religion do conflict theorists study?

Conflict theorists examine the relationship of religion to social inequalities, especially how religion reinforces a society's stratification system.

Religion and the Spirit of Capitalism

13.10 Explain Weber's analysis of how religion broke tradition and brought capitalism.

What does the spirit of capitalism have to do with religion?

Max Weber saw religion as a primary source of social change. He analyzed how Calvinism gave rise to the **Protestant ethic,** stimulating what he called the **spirit of capitalism.** The result was capitalism, which transformed society.

Types of Religious Groups

13.11 Compare cult, sect, church, and ecclesia.

What types of religious groups are there?

Sociologists divide religious groups into cults, sects, churches, and ecclesias. All religions began as **cults.** Those that survive tend to develop into **sects** and eventually into **churches.** Sects, often led by **charismatic leaders,** are unstable. Some are perceived as threats and are persecuted by the state. **Ecclesias,** or state religions, are rare.

Religion in the United States

13.12 Summarize main features of religion in the United States.

What are the main characteristics of religion in the United States?

Membership varies by social class and race–ethnicity. Major characteristics are diversity, pluralism and freedom, tolerance, and the electronic church.

The Future of Religion

13.13 Discuss the likely future of religion.

Because science cannot answer questions about ultimate meaning, the existence of God, or an afterlife, or provide guidelines for morality, the need for religion will remain. In any foreseeable future, religion will prosper. The Internet is likely to have far-reaching consequences on religion.

Thinking Critically about Chapter 13

1. How does education in the United States compare with education in Japan, Russia, and Egypt?

2. How have your experiences in education (including teachers and assignments) influenced your goals, attitudes, and values? How have your classmates influenced you? Be specific.

3. Why do the functionalist, symbolic interactionist, and conflict perspectives produce such different pictures of religion?

4. Why is religion likely to remain a strong feature of U.S. life—and remain strong in people's lives around the globe?

Chapter 14
Population and Urbanization

The image still haunts me. There stood Celia, age 30, her distended stomach visible proof that her thirteenth child was on its way. Her oldest was only 14 years old! A mere boy by our standards, he had already gone as far in school as he ever would. Each morning, he joined the men to work in the fields. Each evening around twilight, I saw him return home, exhausted from hard labor in the subtropical sun.

I was living in Colima, Mexico, and Celia and her husband Angel had invited me for dinner. Their home clearly reflected the family's poverty. A thatched hut consisting of only a single room served as home for all fourteen members of the family. At night, the parents and younger children crowded into a double bed, while the eldest boy slept in a hammock. As in many homes in the village, the other children slept on mats spread on the dirt floor—despite the crawling scorpions.

The home was meagerly furnished. It had only a gas stove, a table, and a cabinet where Celia stored her few cooking utensils and clay dishes. There were no closets; clothes hung on pegs in the walls. There also were no chairs, not even one. I was used to the poverty in the village, but this really startled me. The family was too poor to afford even a single chair.

Celia beamed as she told me how much she looked forward to the birth of her next child. Could she really mean it? It was hard to imagine that any woman would want to be in her situation.

"There stood Celia, age 30, her distended stomach visible proof that her thirteenth child was on its way."

Yet Celia meant every word. She was as full of delighted anticipation as she had been with her first child—and with all the others in between.

How could Celia have wanted so many children—especially when she lived in such poverty? This question bothered me. I couldn't let it go until I understood why.

This chapter helps to provide an answer.

Population in Global Perspective

Celia's story takes us to the heart of **demography**, the study of the size, composition, growth (or shrinkage), and distribution of human populations. It brings us face to face with the question of whether we are doomed to live in a world so filled with people that there will be little space for anybody. Will our planet be able to support its growing population? Or are chronic famine and mass starvation the sorry fate of most earthlings?

Let's look at how concern about population growth began.

demography

the study of the size, composition, growth (or shrinkage), and distribution of human populations

A Planet with No Space for Enjoying Life?

14.1 Contrast the views of the New Malthusians and Anti-Malthusians on population growth and the food supply; explain why people are starving.

The story begins with the lowly potato. When the Spanish *conquistadores* found that people in the Andes Mountains ate this vegetable that was unknown in Europe, they brought some home with them. At first, Europeans viewed the potato with suspicion, but gradually it became the main food of the lower classes. With a greater abundance of food, fertility increased, and the death rate dropped. Europe's population soared, almost doubling during the 1700s (McKeown 1977; McNeill 1999).

This surging growth alarmed Thomas Malthus (1766–1834), an English economist, who saw it as a sign of doom. In 1798, he wrote *An Essay on the Principle of Population* (1798/1926). In this book, which became world famous, Malthus proposed what became known as the **Malthus theorem**. He argued that although population grows geometrically (from 2 to 4 to 8 to 16 and so forth), the food supply increases only arithmetically (from 1 to 2 to 3 to 4 and so on). This meant, he claimed, that if births go unchecked, the population will outstrip its food supply.

Malthus theorem

an observation by Thomas Malthus that although the food supply increases arithmetically (from 1 to 2 to 3 to 4 and so on), population grows geometrically (from 2 to 4 to 8 to 16 and so forth)

The New Malthusians

Was Malthus right? This question has provoked heated debate among demographers. One group, which can be called the *New Malthusians*, is convinced that today's situation is at least as grim as—if not grimmer than—Malthus ever imagined (Emmott 2013). For example, *the world's population is growing so fast that in just the time it takes you to read this chapter, another 20,000 to 40,000 babies will be born!* By this time tomorrow, Earth will have about 237,000 more people to feed. This increase goes on hour after hour, day after day, without letup. For an illustration of this growth, see Figure 14.1 on the next page.

The New Malthusians point out that the world's population is following an **exponential growth curve**. This means that if growth doubles during approximately equal intervals of time, it suddenly accelerates. To illustrate the far-reaching implications of exponential growth, sociologist William Faunce (1981) retold an old parable about a poor man who saved a rich man's life. The rich man was grateful and said that he wanted to reward the man for his heroic deed.

exponential growth curve

a pattern of growth in which numbers double during approximately equal intervals, showing a steep acceleration in the later stages

The man replied that he would like his reward to be spread out over a four-week period, with each day's amount being twice what he received on the preceding day. He also said he would be happy to receive only one penny on the first day. The rich man immediately handed over the penny and congratulated himself on how cheaply he had gotten by.

Figure 14.1 How Fast Is the World's Population Growing?

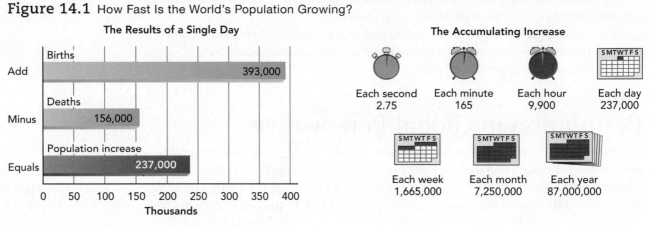

SOURCE: By the author. Based on Haub and Kaneda 2014.

At the end of the first week, the rich man checked to see how much he owed and was pleased to find that the total was only $1.27. By the end of the second week he owed only $163.83. On the twenty-first day, however, the rich man was surprised to find that the total had grown to $20,971.51. When the twenty-eighth day arrived the rich man was shocked to discover that he owed $1,342,177.28 for that day alone and that the total reward had jumped to $2,684,354.56!

This is precisely what alarms the New Malthusians. They claim that humanity has just entered the "fourth week" of an exponential growth curve. To see why they think the day of reckoning is just around the corner, look at Figure 14.2. *It took from the beginning of time until 1800 for the world's population to reach its first billion.* It then took only 130 years (1930) to add the second billion. Just 30 years later (1960), the world population hit 3 billion. The time it took to reach the fourth billion was cut in half, to only 15 years (1975). Then just 12 years later (in 1987) the total reached 5 billion, in another 12 years it hit 6 billion (in 1999), and in yet another 12 years it hit 7 billion (in 2011).

Another way to put this is that in the past 43 years, the world's population has doubled—going from 3.5 billion to over 7 billion. On average, every minute of every day,

Figure 14.2 World Population Growth

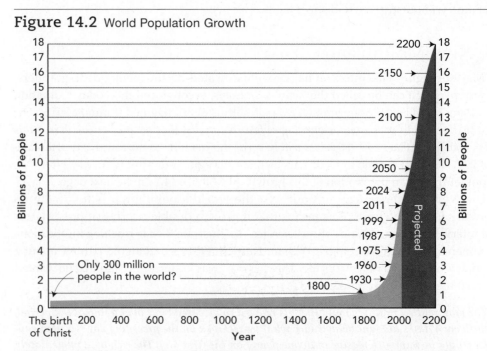

SOURCES: Modified from Piotrow 1973; McFalls 2007; based on projections from Haub and Kaneda 2015.

165 babies are born. As Figure 14.1 shows, at each sunset, the world has 237,000 more people than it did the day before. In a year, this comes to 87 million people. During the next four years, this increase will total more than the entire U.S. population. Think of it this way: *In the next dozen years, the world will add as many people as it did during the entire time from when the first humans began to walk the earth until the year 1800.*

These totals terrify the New Malthusians. They are convinced that we are headed toward a showdown between population and food. In the year 2050, the population of just India and China is expected to be as large as the entire world population was in 1960 (Haub and Kaneda 2015). It is obvious that we will run out of food if we don't curtail population growth. Soon we are going to see more televised images of pitiful, starving children.

The Anti-Malthusians

All of this seems obvious, and no one wants to live shoulder-to-shoulder and fight for scraps. How, then, can anyone argue with the New Malthusians?

To find out, let's turn to a much more optimistic group of demographers, whom we can call the *Anti-Malthusians*. For them, the future is painted in much brighter colors. They believe that Europe's **demographic transition** provides a more accurate glimpse into the future. This transition is diagrammed in Figure 14.3 on the next page. During most of its history, Europe was in Stage 1. Europe's population remained about the same from year to year, because its high death rates offset its high birth rates. Then came Stage 2, the "population explosion" that so upset Malthus. Europe's population surged because birth rates remained high while death rates went down. Finally, Europe made the transition to Stage 3: The population stabilized as people brought their birth rates into line with their lower death rates.

This, say the Anti-Malthusians, will also happen in the Least Industrialized Nations. Their current surge in population growth simply indicates that they have reached Stage 2 of the demographic transition. Hybrid seeds, medicine from the Most Industrialized Nations, and purer public drinking water have cut their death rates, while their birth

demographic transition

a three-stage historical process of change in the size of populations: first, high birth rates and high death rates; second, high birth rates and low death rates; and third, low birth rates and low death rates; a fourth stage of *population shrinkage* in which deaths outnumber births has made its appearance in the Most Industrialized Nations

Large families on U.S. farms used to be common. Children helped plant and harvest crops, take care of animals, and prepare food. As the country industrialized and urbanized, children became nonproducers, making them expensive to have around. Consequently, the size of families shrank as we entered Stage 3 of the demographic transition. The two adult sons in this 1890s Minnesota farm family are likely from their father's first wife who died.

Figure 14.3 The Demographic Transition

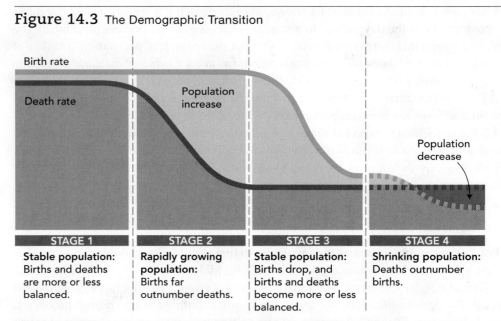

NOTE: The standard demographic transition is depicted by Stages 1–3. Stage 4 has been suggested by some Anti-Malthusians.

SOURCE: Standard presentation modified by the author to add Stage 4.

rates have remained high. When they move into Stage 3, as surely they will, we will wonder what all the fuss was about. In fact, their growth is already slowing.

Who Is Correct?

As you can see, both the New Malthusians and the Anti-Malthusians have looked at historical trends and projected them onto the future. The New Malthusians project continued world growth and are alarmed. The Anti-Malthusians project Stage 3 of the demographic transition onto the Least Industrialized Nations and are reassured.

There is no question that the Least Industrialized Nations are in Stage 2 of the demographic transition. The question is, Will these nations enter Stage 3? After World War II, the West exported its hybrid seeds, herbicides, and techniques of public hygiene around the globe. Death rates plummeted in the Least Industrialized Nations as their food supply increased and health improved. Because their birth rates stayed high, their populations mushroomed. This alarmed demographers, just as it had Malthus 200 years earlier. Some predicted worldwide catastrophe if something were not done immediately to halt the population explosion (Ehrlich and Ehrlich 1972, 1978).

We can use the conflict perspective to understand what happened when this message reached the leaders of the industrialized world. They saw the mushrooming populations of the Least Industrialized Nations as a threat to the global balance of power they had so carefully worked out. With swollen populations, the poorer countries might demand a larger share of Earth's resources. The leaders found the United Nations to be a willing tool, and they used it to spearhead efforts to reduce world population growth. The results have been remarkable. The annual growth of the Least Industrialized Nations has dropped one-third (33 percent), from an average of 2.1 percent a year in the 1960s to 1.4 percent today (Haub and Yinger 1994; Haub and Kaneda 2015).

The New Malthusians and Anti-Malthusians have greeted this news with incompatible interpretations. For the Anti-Malthusians, this slowing of growth is the signal they were waiting for: Stage 3 of the demographic transition has begun. First, the death rates in the Least Industrialized Nations fell; now, just as they predicted, birth rates are also falling. Did you notice, they would say if they looked at Figure 14.2, that it took twelve years to add the fifth billion to the world's population—and also twelve years to add the sixth billion—and also twelve years to add the seventh billion? Despite millions upon millions of more women of childbearing age, population growth has leveled off. The New Malthusians reply that a slower growth rate still spells catastrophe—it will just take longer for it to hit.

Then the Anti-Malthusians drop a bombshell, making the New Malthusians moan in disbelief. They say that our future will be the *opposite* of what the New Malthusians worry about: There are going to be too few children in the world, not too many. The world's problem will not be a population explosion, but **population shrinkage**—populations getting smaller. Births in 83 countries have already dropped so low that these countries no longer produce enough children to maintain their populations. Another seven countries are on the verge of dropping this low. If it weren't for immigration from Africa, all the countries of Europe would fill more coffins than cradles (Haub and Kaneda 2015).

Some Anti-Malthusians even predict a *demographic free fall* (Mosher 1997). As more nations enter Stage 4 of the demographic transition, the world's population will peak and then begin to grow smaller. Two hundred years from now, they say, we will have a lot fewer people on Earth.

Who is right? It simply is too early to tell. Like the proverbial pessimists who see the glass of water half empty, the New Malthusians interpret changes in world population growth negatively. And like the eternal optimists who see the same glass half full, the Anti-Malthusians view the figures positively. Sometime during our lifetimes, we should know the answer.

population shrinkage

the process by which a country's population becomes smaller because its birth rate and immigration are too low to replace those who die and emigrate

Why Are People Starving?

Pictures of starving children gnaw at our conscience. We live in such abundance, while these children and their parents starve before our very eyes. Why don't they have enough food? Is it because there isn't enough food in the world to feed them or because the abundant food the world produces does not reach them?

The Anti-Malthusians make a point that seems irrefutable. As Figure 14.4 shows, *there is much more food for each person in the world now than there was in 1950. Despite the billions of additional people who now live on this planet*, improved seeds and fertilizers have

Figure 14.4 How Much Food Does the World Produce per Person?

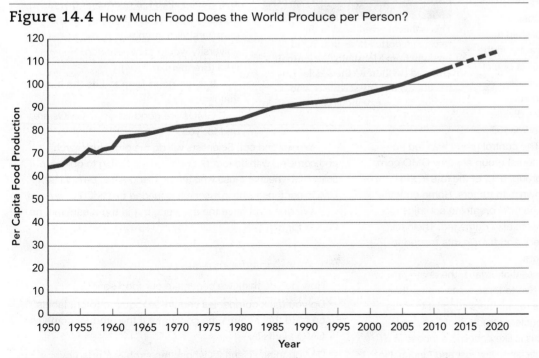

NOTE: 2004–2006 equals 100. Projections by the author.

SOURCES: By the author. Based on Simon 1981; *Statistical Abstract of the United States* 2010:Table 1335; Food and Agriculture Organization of the United Nations 2013.

made more food available for *each* person on Earth. Since the 1990s, world hunger has dropped 40 percent (Stone 2014). And, with bioengineers making breakthroughs in agriculture, even more food is on the way.

But will bioengineered foods live up to their promise? A slight problem seems to be emerging, the focus of our Down-to-Earth Sociology box below.

Down-to-Earth Sociology

BioFoods: What's in *Your* Future? Threats to Scientific Research

Luddites are people who fear change. They oppose anything new.

You can expect Luddites to complain about bioengineered foods. Biofoods, also called genetically modified organisms (GMOs), are a radical departure from the past. Until a few years ago, biofoods were just a gleam in the eyes of scientists. They experimented and came up with seeds that vastly increased harvests. Good enough. Then they came up with seeds that could withstand drought. Then seeds whose added genetic materials could even produce insecticides.

Crops kept increasing. And the Luddites kept shouting warnings about contaminating nature, about humans playing God. Scientists and the public shrugged them off. And Monsanto and the other agricultural conglomerates kept doing their research, developing new seeds that would allow the world's population to keep growing—and company profits, too.

Then scientific controversy hit full force, a storm that has not subsided. Some Italian researchers published a study that was anything but pretty. In the last edition, I reprinted a photo of one of their sick, tumor-filled rats, but now I've been denied permission to do so.

Basically, the researchers divided the rats into control and experimental groups (Seralini et al 2012). The control group was fed non-GMO corn, while the experimental group ate only GMO corn. Compared with the control group, a lot of the rats in the experimental group came down with tumors. Some growths were large enough to block the rats' breathing and digestion. The rats' kidneys and livers were also damaged. Their sex hormones were also disturbed. And female rats tended to come down with breast tumors.

With such damage to essential organs, the death rate of the experimental group was two to three times higher than that of the control group. The researchers suggest that the GMO corn disturbs the subnuclear structure of body cells.

To publish a study like this is like dangling a mouse in front of a starving cat. The criticisms flew fast and furious. Not enough rats were used in the research. The wrong rats were

This is the rat breed used in the research reported here. Bowing to pressure from Monsanto, the journal retracted (withdrew) the article. This has outraged many scientists who deplore this as egregious contamination of scientific research.

used. The statistics were flawed. These scientists are opposed to GMOs. And even, the rats were treated inhumanely.

In the midst of all the pressure, the editors of the scientific journal, a good one, said they made a mistake in publishing the article and retracted it.

The researchers stood by their research, defending it. Some scientists took their side.

Some demanded that Monsanto publish the full results of their own research. Monsanto did not do so. Apparently, Monsanto had released only selective findings. Not exactly good science, but apparently allowed when it comes to getting government approval to sell GMOs (Casassus 2013; Philpott 2014; Brenneman et al. 2014).

There's a lot at stake here—billions of dollars. With the Italian research posing a threat to those billions, the reaction was not unexpected.

This was not the first time researchers challenged Monsanto and lost. Back in 2004, a microbiologist at Berkeley pointed out that the millions of dollars Monsanto was giving the university would taint research. He was fired (Brenneman 2004).

It is not good form to bite the hand that feeds you.

GMOs are good for you? GMOs are bad for you?

We will find out. Scientists will do the proper research and come up with correct answers. I am referring to objective scientists—neither those who are predisposed to be against GMOs nor those whose research is funded by GMO companies.

We don't yet have the answers, but in the meantime, no GMOs for me.

For Your Consideration

→ How do you think we can make our food safe?

→ Do you think companies should be required to put labels on food that informs the consumer if the product contains GMO plants?

→ Do you think scientists whose research is funded by Monsanto can be objective?

Photos of starving children, such as this child in Somalia, haunt Americans and other members of the Most Industrialized Nations. Many of us wonder why, when some are starving, we should live in the midst of such abundance, often overeating and even casually scraping excess food into the garbage. As in this photo from Toronto, Ontario, Canada, we even have eating contests to see which *competitive eater* can eat the most food in the least amount of time.

If the earth is so productive, why do people die of hunger? From Figure 14.4, which you viewed on page 451, we can conclude that people don't starve because the Earth produces too little food, but because particular places lack food. Droughts and wars are the main reasons. Just as droughts slow or stop food production, so does war. In nations ravaged by civil war, opposing sides confiscate and burn crops, and farmers flee to the cities (Gettleman 2009; Stone 2014).

The New Malthusians counter with the argument that the world's population is still growing and that we don't know how long Earth will continue to produce enough food. They add that the recent policy of turning food (such as corn and sugar cane) into bio-fuels (such as gasoline and diesel) poses a threat to the world's food supply. *A bushel of corn that goes into someone's gas tank is a bushel of corn that does not go on people's dinner plates.*

Both the New Malthusians and the Anti-Malthusians have contributed significant ideas, but theories will not eliminate famines. Starving children are going to continue to peer out at us from our televisions and magazines, their tiny, shriveled bodies and bloated stomachs nagging at our consciences, imploring us to do something. Regardless of the underlying causes of this human misery, the solution is twofold: first, to transfer food from nations that have a surplus to those that have a shortage, and second, where needed, to teach more efficient farming techniques.

The pictures of starving Africans leave the impression that Africa is overpopulated. Why else would all those people be starving? The truth, however, is far different. There are 37 people per square kilometer in Africa, only slightly more than the 33 people per square kilometer in the United States. At 136 people per square kilometer, Asia's population is three-and-a-half times as concentrated as Africa's, and people there are not starving (Haub and Kaneda 2015). Africa even has vast areas of fertile land that have not yet been farmed. The reason for famines in Africa, then, *cannot* be too many people living on too little land.

Population Growth

14.2 Explain why the Least Industrialized Nations have so many children, consequences of rapid population growth, population pyramids, the three demographic variables, and problems in forecasting population growth.

Even if starvation is the result of a maldistribution of food rather than overpopulation, the Least Industrialized Nations are still growing much faster than the Most Industrialized Nations. Without immigration, it would take several hundred years for the average

Figure 14.5 World Population Growth, 1750–2150

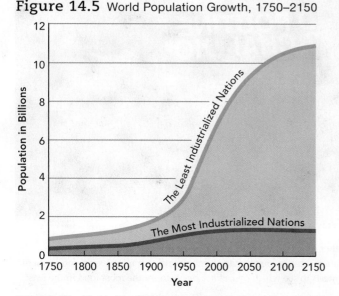

SOURCES: "The World of the Child 6 Billion" 2000; Haub and Kaneda 2015.

Most Industrialized Nation to double its population, but just fifty years for the average Least Industrialized Nation to do so (Haub and Kaneda 2015). Figure 14.5 puts the matter in stark perspective.

Why the Least Industrialized Nations Have So Many Children

Why do people in the countries that can least afford it have so many children? Let's go back to the chapter's opening vignette and try to figure out why Celia was so happy about having her thirteenth child. It will help if we apply the symbolic interactionist perspective. We must take the role of the other so that we can understand the world of Celia and Angel as *they* see it.

As our culture does for us, their culture provides a perspective on life that guides their choices. Celia and Angel's culture tells them that twelve children are *not* enough, that they ought to have a thirteenth—as well as a fourteenth and fifteenth. How can this be? Let's consider three reasons why bearing many children is important to Celia and Angel—and to millions upon millions of poor people around the world.

First is the status of parenthood. In the Least Industrialized Nations, motherhood is the most prized status a woman can achieve. The more children a woman bears, the more she is thought to have achieved the purpose for which she was born. Similarly, a man proves his manhood by fathering children. The more children he fathers, especially sons, the better: Through them, his name lives on.

Second, the community supports this view. Celia and those like her live in *Gemeinschaft* communities, where people share similar views of life. To them, children are a sign of God's blessing. By producing children, people reflect the values of their community, achieve status, and are assured that they are blessed by God. It is the barren woman, not the woman with a dozen children, who is to be pitied.

You can see how these factors provide strong motivations for bearing many children. There is also another powerful incentive: For poor people in the Least Industrialized Nations, children are *economic assets*. Look at Figure 14.6 on the next page. Like Celia's and Angel's eldest son, children begin contributing to the family income at a young age. But even more important: *Children are their equivalent of our Social Security.* In the Least Industrialized Nations, the government does not provide social security or medical and unemployment insurance. This motivates people to bear *more* children, because when parents become too old to work or when no work is to be found, their children take care of them. The more children they have, the broader their base of support and the more secure their future.

To those of us who live in the Most Industrialized Nations, it seems irrational to have many children. And *for us, it would be*. Understanding life from the framework of people who are living it, however—the essence of the symbolic interactionist perspective—reveals how it makes perfect sense to have many children. Consider this report by a government worker in India:

> *Thaman Singh (a very poor man, a water carrier) … welcomed me inside his home, gave me a cup of tea (with milk and "market" sugar, as he proudly pointed out later), and said: "You were trying to convince me that I shouldn't have any more sons. Now, you see, I have six sons and two daughters and I sit at home in leisure. They are grown up and they bring me money. One even works outside the village as a laborer. You told me I was a poor man and couldn't support a large family. Now, you see, because of my large family I am a rich man." (Mamdani 1973)*

Conflict theorists offer a different view of why women in the Least Industrialized Nations bear so many children. Feminists argue that women like Celia have internalized

Figure 14.6 Why the Poor Need Children

Children are an economic asset in the Least Industrialized Nations. Based on a survey in Indonesia, this figure shows that boys and girls can be net income earners for their families by the age of 9 or 10.

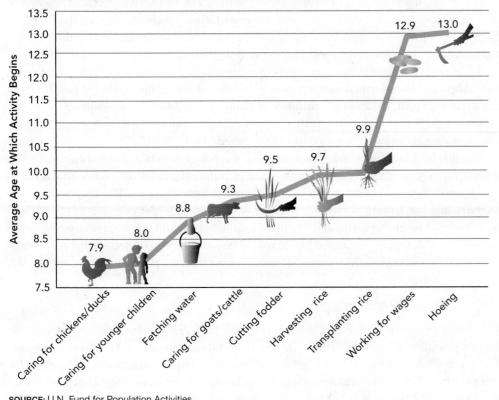

SOURCE: U.N. Fund for Population Activities.

values that support male dominance. In Latin America, *machismo*—an emphasis on male virility and dominance—is common. To father many children, especially sons, shows that a man is *macho*, strong and sexually potent, giving him higher status in the community. From a conflict perspective, then, the reason poor people have so many children is that men control women's reproductive choices.

Consequences of Rapid Population Growth

The result of Celia's and Angel's desire for many children—and of the millions of Celias and Angels like them—is that the population of the average Least Industrialized Nation will double in fifty years. In contrast, women in the United States are having so few children that if it weren't for immigration, the U.S. population would start to shrink.

The implications of a doubling population are mind-boggling. *Just to stay even*, within fifty years, a country must double the number of available jobs and housing facilities; its food production; its transportation and communication facilities; its water, gas, sewer, and electrical systems; and its schools, hospitals, churches, civic buildings, theaters, stores, and parks. If a country fails to maintain this growth, its already meager standard of living will drop even farther.

Conflict theorists point out that a declining standard of living poses the threat of political instability—protests, riots, even revolution—and, in response, repression by the government. Political instability in one country can spill into others, threatening an entire region's balance of power. Fearing such disruptions, leaders of the Most Industrialized Nations are using the United Nations to direct a campaign of worldwide birth control. With one hand, they give agricultural aid, IUDs, and condoms to the masses in the Least Industrialized Nations—while, with the other, they sell weapons to the elites in these countries. Both actions, say conflict theorists, serve the same purpose: promoting political stability in order to maintain the dominance of the Most Industrialized Nations in global stratification.

Population Pyramids as a Tool for Understanding

Although changes in population bring serious consequences, both on a personal and a political level, the reasons underlying these changes can be elusive. To illustrate one of these significant reasons, demographers use **population pyramids**, figures that depict a country's population by age and sex. Look at Figure 14.7, which compares the population pyramids of the United States, Mexico, and the world.

Let's see why population pyramids are important. Imagine a miracle—that overnight, Mexico is transformed into a nation as industrialized as the United States. Imagine also that overnight, the average number of children per Mexican woman drops to 1.9, the same as in the United States. If this happened, it is obvious that Mexico's population would change at the same rate as that of the United States, right?

But this isn't what would happen. Instead, the population of Mexico would continue to grow rapidly. To see why, look again at the population pyramids. Notice that a much higher percentage of Mexican women are in their childbearing years. This means that even if Mexico and the United States had the same birth rate, a larger percentage of Mexican women would be giving birth, and Mexico's population would grow rapidly while, without immigration, that of the United States would be standing still or decreasing. As demographers like to phrase this, Mexico's *age structure gives it greater population momentum.*

The Three Demographic Variables

How many people will live in the United States fifty years from now? What will the world's population be then? These are important questions. Educators want to know how many schools to build. Manufacturers want to anticipate changes in the market for their products. The government needs to know how many doctors, engineers, and executives to train. Politicians want to know how many people will be paying taxes—and how many young people will be available to fight their wars.

To project the future of populations, demographers use three **demographic variables**: fertility, mortality, and migration. Let's look at each.

FERTILITY   The number of children that the average woman bears is called the **fertility rate**. The world's overall fertility rate is 2.5, which means that during her lifetime, the average woman in the world bears 2.5 children (Haub and Kaneda 2015). A term that is sometimes confused with fertility is **fecundity**, the number of children that women

population pyramid

a graph that represents the age and sex of a population (see Figure 14.7)

demographic variables

the three factors that change the size of a population: fertility, mortality, and net migration

fertility rate

the number of children that the average woman bears

fecundity

the number of children that women are capable of bearing

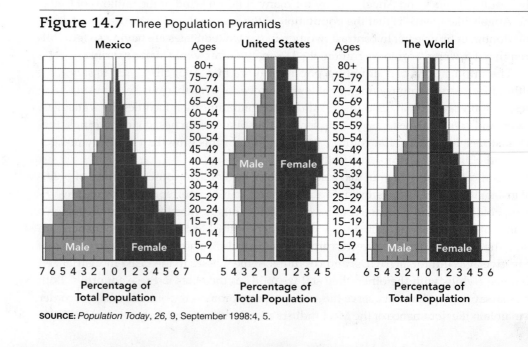

Figure 14.7 Three Population Pyramids

SOURCE: *Population Today, 26,* 9, September 1998:4, 5.

are *capable* of bearing. This number is rather high, as some women have given birth to 30 children (McFalls 2007).

To see which countries have the highest and lowest low birth rates, look at Table 14.1. You can see that three countries tie for the world's lowest fertility rate. In Andorra, Hong Kong, and Taiwan, the average woman gives birth to only 1.1 children. Five of the lowest-birth countries are in Europe (with three tied for tenth place). The other five are located in Asia. Now look at the countries with the highest birth rates. *All* of them are in Africa. Niger in West Africa holds the record for the world's highest birth rate. There, the average woman gives birth to 7.6 children, seven times as many children as the average woman in Andorra, Hong Kong, and Taiwan.

To compute the fertility rate of a country, demographers analyze the government's records of births. From these, they figure the country's **crude birth rate**, the annual number of live births per 1,000 people.

crude birth rate

the annual number of live births per 1,000 population

crude death rate

the annual number of deaths per 1,000 population

Table 14.1 Extremes in Childbirth

Where Do Women Give Birth to the Fewest Children?		Where Do Women Give Birth to the Most Children?	
Country	Number of Children	Country	Number of Children
Andorra	1.1	Niger	7.6
Hong Kong	1.1	South Sudan	7.0
Taiwan	1.1	Chad	6.6
Macao	1.2	Congo, Dem. Republic	6.6
Moldova	1.2	Somalia	6.6
Poland	1.2	Angola	6.2
Portugal	1.2	Central African Rep.	6.2
Singapore	1.2	Burundi	6.1
South Korea	1.2	Mali	6.1
Greece	1.3	Zambia	6.0

NOTE: Six European countries tie for tenth place of 1.3: Bosnia-Herzegovina, Greece, Hungary, Romania, Slovakia, and Spain.
SOURCE: Haub and Kaneda 2015.

MORTALITY   The second demographic variable is measured by the **crude death rate**, the annual number of deaths per 1,000 people. The highest death rate is 21, a record held by Lesotho, in Africa. The lowest death rate is 1, a record held by two Asian countries, Qatar and United Arab Emirates (Haub and Kaneda 2015).

MIGRATION   The third demographic variable is *migration*, the movement of people from one area to another. There are two types of migration. The first type occurs when people move from one region to another within the same country. During and after World War II, in what U.S. demographers call "The Great Migration," millions of African Americans moved from the South to the North. In a historical shift, many are now returning to the South to participate in its growing economy, to enjoy its warmer climate, and to renew ties with family roots (Graves 2014).

The second type of migration occurs when people move from one country to another. Demographers use the term **net migration rate** to refer to the difference between the number of *immigrants* (people moving into a country) and *emigrants* (people moving out of a country) per 1,000 people. Unlike fertility and mortality, migration does not affect the global population: People are simply shifting their residence from one country or region to another.

net migration rate

the difference between the number of immigrants and emigrants per 1,000 population

What motivates people to give up the security of their family and friends to move to a country with a strange language and unfamiliar customs? To understand migration, we need to look at both "pushes" and "pulls." The *pushes* are the things people want to escape: poverty, violence, war, or persecution for their religious and political ideas. The *pulls* are the magnets that draw people to a new land, such as opportunities for education, better jobs, the freedom to worship or to discuss political ideas, and a more promising future for their children. After "migrant paths" are established, immigration often accelerates—networks of kin and friends attract more people from the same nation, even from the same villages.

Around the world, the flow of migration is from the Least Industrialized Nations to the industrialized countries. By far, the United States is the world's number one choice. The United States admits more immigrants each year than all the other nations of the world combined. *Thirty-eight million residents*—one of every eight Americans—were born in other countries (*Statistical Abstract* 2014:Table 42). Table 14.2 below shows where recent U.S. immigrants were born. One major change is that more immigrants are from Asia than any other continent.

To escape grinding poverty, such as that which surrounds Celia and Angel, millions of people also enter the United States illegally. Although it may seem surprising, as Figure 14.8 shows, U.S. officials have sufficient information on these approximately 12 million people to estimate their countries of origin.

Experts cannot agree on whether immigrants are net contributors to the U.S. economy or a drain on it. Adding what immigrants produce in jobs and taxes and subtracting what they cost in welfare and the medical and school systems, some economists conclude that immigrants produce more than they cost (Council of Economic Advisers 2007; Parker 2013). Other economists conclude that immigrants cost taxpayers trillions of dollars (Davis and Weinstein 2002; Rector and Richwine 2013). Determining the costs or benefits of immigrants has become a highly charged political matter. I shake my head in wonder as I see political liberals and conservatives look at the same data and arrive at opposite conclusions. In the midst of this controversy, the fairest conclusion seems to be that the more educated immigrants produce more than they cost, while the less educated cost more than they produce.

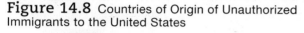

Figure 14.8 Countries of Origin of Unauthorized Immigrants to the United States

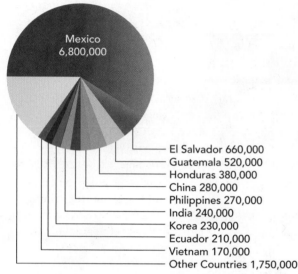

Mexico 6,800,000

El Salvador 660,000
Guatemala 520,000
Honduras 380,000
China 280,000
Philippines 270,000
India 240,000
Korea 230,000
Ecuador 210,000
Vietnam 170,000
Other Countries 1,750,000

SOURCE: *Statistical Abstract of the United States* 2014:Table 48.

Problems in Forecasting Population Growth

Russia's population is falling. We've got to do something. Let's give $5,000 to every woman who has a first child—and $15,000 to women who have a second child. And let men have two wives.

—*Vladimir Zhirinovsky, Russian politician, January 2010*

Table 14.2 Country of Birth of Authorized U.S. Immigrants

Asia	**3,785,000**	El Salvador	252,000	**South America**	**906,000**
China	663,000	Haiti	214,000	Colombia	251,000
India	663,000	Jamaica	181,000	Peru	146,000
Philippines	587,000	Canada	168,000	Brazil	124,000
Vietnam	306,000	Guatemala	161,000	Ecuador	113,000
Korea	222,000			Venezuela	85,000
Pakistan	157,000	**Europe**	**1,264,000**	Guyana	76,000
Iran	126,000	Ukraine	149,000	Argentina	51,000
Bangladesh	107,000	United Kingdom	154,000		
Taiwan	88,000	Russia	140,000	**Africa**	**860,000**
Japan	76,000	Poland	117,000	Nigeria	111,000
		Bosnia and Herzegovina	89,000	Ethiopia	110,000
North America	**3,605,000**	Germany	78,000	Egypt	73,000
Mexico	1,693,000	Romania	54,000	Somalia	64,000
Cuba	318,000	Albania	51,000	Ghana	65,000
Dominican Republic	329,000				

NOTE: Totals are for the top countries of origin for 2001–2010.

SOURCE: By the author. Based on *Statistical Abstract of the United States* 2014:Table 53. The totals for China and India are not in error; they are the same.

Here's another idea. Let's have a National Day of Conception. Workers can go home early and make love. Any woman who has a child 9 months later will get a free refrigerator.

—*Another politician in Russia*

If population growth depended only on biology, making projections of the future population would be easy. Just use the **basic demographic equation**. Add and subtract the three demographic variables—fertility, mortality, and net migration—and you get a country's **growth rate**, the net change after people have been added to and subtracted from a population. Here is how the demographers put it:

Growth rate equals births minus deaths plus net migration.

Then you project the results into the future—because current rates indicate future rates.

Or they *usually* do, and here is the rub. Some politician can come along and push those rates in an unexpected direction. As you read in the quotes that open this section, Russian politicians are worried about their shrinking population. In one city, women who give birth on Russia Day, June 12, win prizes—video cameras, TVs, refrigerators ("Russians Given Day Off" 2007; Salyer 2013). The photo below shows the grand prize.

When Hitler decided that Germany needed more "Aryans," the government outlawed abortion and offered not refrigerators but cash to women who gave birth. Germany's population increased. Today, trying to increase their country's population, Turkey's politicians proudly pin a gold medal on women who give birth to their first child. More gold medals and cash follow if they have more children (Buchanan 2015).

Some politicians go in the other direction and try to slow births. The Indian government is offering $106 to each newlywed woman who waits two years to get pregnant (Yardley 2010). As you probably know, China has a "one couple, one child" policy, but you might not know how ruthlessly officials have enforced this policy. Steven Mosher (2006), an anthropologist who did fieldwork in China, reports that if a woman gets pregnant without government permission (yes, you read that right!), doctors abort the fetus—even if the woman is nine months pregnant. The woman has no say in the matter. After the birth of her first child, each woman—whether she wants it or not—is fitted with an IUD (intrauterine device). Every three months, she must have a sonogram to verify that she is not pregnant (Chang 2013). If a woman has a second child, she is sterilized.

Chinese officials are easing up a bit. Concerned that there will not be enough young workers to support their rapidly aging population, officials allow rural couples to have a second child—if their first one was a girl (Greenhalgh 2009). Another exception is allowing a second child if both the husband and wife are only children ("China to Broaden . . ." 2014). Some couples with higher-paying jobs are having a second child and paying the fine (Chang 2013).

As you might suppose, wars, economic booms and busts, plagues, and famines also affect population growth. So does sexism, which we discuss in the following Cultural Diversity box.

We are in the midst of a large wave of immigration. Shown here is one of our newest citizens.

basic demographic equation
the growth rate equals births minus deaths plus net migration

growth rate
the net change in a population after adding births, subtracting deaths, and either adding or subtracting net migration; can result in a negative number

This couple is sitting in the grand prize they won for participating in the Day of Conception and giving birth on Russia Day.

Cultural Diversity around the World

Killing Little Girls: An Ancient and Thriving Practice

"The Mysterious Case of the Missing Girls" could have been the title of this box. Around the globe, for every 100 births of girls, about 105 boys are born. In China, however, for every 100 baby girls, the total jumps to 121 baby boys (Last 2011). Given China's huge population, this means that China has about *30 million* fewer females than males under the age of 20. What happened to the 30 million girls?

The answer is *female infanticide*, the killing of baby girls. When a Chinese woman goes into labor, the village midwife sometimes grabs a bucket of water. If the newborn is a girl, she is plunged into the water before she can draw her first breath.

At the root of China's sexist infanticide is economics. The people are poor, and they have no pensions. When parents can no longer work, sons support them. In contrast, a daughter must be married off, at great expense, and at that point, her obligations transfer to her husband and his family.

"Raising a girl is like watering someone else's plant," as they say in India, where female infanticide is also common.

In China, the past few years have brought even larger percentages of boy babies. The reason, again, is economics, but this time with a new twist. When China adopted capitalism, travel and trade opened up— but primarily to men, since it is not thought appropriate for women to travel alone. With men finding themselves in a better position to bring money home, parents have one more reason to want boys.

The gender ratio is so lopsided that for Chinese in their 20s, there are six bachelors for every five potential brides. Politicians fear that the men who cannot marry—"bare branches," as they call them—will become disgruntled. Lacking the stabilizing influences of marriage and children, these bare branches might become a breeding ground for political dissent. To head this off,

Because of female infanticide and sex-selection abortion, millions of men in China have no one to marry. Shown here is a "collective blind date," in which men try to impress eligible women that they would make good husbands. These four men are trying to get this woman to accept their flowers.

officials have begun a campaign to stop the drowning of girl babies and the aborting of female fetuses.

We find a similar situation in India. For the same reasons, India has an extra 37 million men. Officials there, too, are concerned. These additional men who cannot find wives, they say, are a major reason for sexual harassment and rape.

SOURCES: Jordan 2000; Dugger 2001; Riley 2004; Yardley 2007, 2011; Sharma 2013; Nelson 2014.

For Your Consideration

→ What do you think can be done to reduce female infanticide?

→ Why do you think sex-selection abortion receives so little publicity and is not a priority with world leaders?

As you can see, government policies can change a country's growth rate. The main factor, though, is not the government, but industrialization. *In every country that industrializes, the birth rate declines.* Why? One reason is that industrialization makes rearing children more expensive. They require more education and remain dependent longer. Another reason is that the basis for conferring status changes—from having many children to attaining education and displaying material wealth. As people like Celia and Angel in our opening vignette begin to see life differently, their motivation to have many children drops sharply. Not knowing how rapidly industrialization will progress or how quickly changes in values and reproductive behavior will follow adds to the difficulty of making accurate projections.

Chinese officials have become concerned about the lopsided gender ratio that their "one couple, one child" policy has produced. Their recent billboards continue to promote this policy, but by featuring a female child they are trying to reduce female infanticide.

Consider how difficult it is to estimate U.S. population growth. During the next fifty years, will we have **zero population growth**? (Every 1,000 women would give birth to 2,100 children, the extra 100 children making up for those who do not survive or reproduce.) Will more women go to college? (Educated women bear fewer children.) How many immigrants will we have? Will some devastating disease appear? Because of these many unknowns, demographers play it safe by making several projections of population growth, each depending on an "if" scenario. Figure 14.9 shows three projections of U.S. population.

Let's turn to a different aspect of population: where people live. Because more and more people around the world are living in cities, let's look at urban trends and urban life.

zero population growth

women bearing only enough children to reproduce the population

---

Figure 14.9 Population Projections of the United States

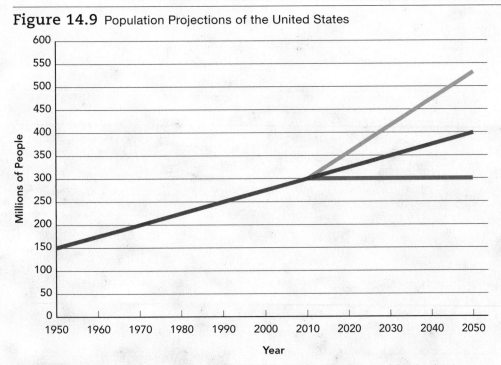

NOTE: The projections are based on different assumptions of fertility, mortality, and especially migration.

SOURCE: By the author. Based on Day 2010.

Urbanization

14.3 Summarize the development of cities, the process of urbanization, U.S. urban patterns, and the rural rebound.

As I was climbing a steep hill in Medellin, Colombia, in a district called El Tiro, my informant, Jaro, said, "This used to be a garbage heap." I stopped to peer through the vegetation alongside the path we were on, and sure enough, I could see bits of refuse still sticking out of the dirt. The "town" had been built on top of garbage.

This was just the first of my many revelations that day. The second was that the Medellin police refused to enter El Tiro because it was so dangerous. I shuddered for a moment, but I had good reason to trust Jaro. He had been a pastor in El Tiro for several years, and he knew the people well. I was confident that if I stayed close to him, I would be safe.

Actually, El Tiro was safer now than it had been. A group of young men had banded together to make it so, Jaro told me. A sort of frontier justice prevailed. The vigilantes told the prostitutes and drug dealers that there would be no prostitution or drug dealing in El Tiro and to "take it elsewhere." They killed anyone who robbed or murdered someone. And they even made families safer—they would beat up any man who got drunk and battered "his" woman. With the threat of instant justice, the area had become much safer.

Jaro then added that each household had to pay the group a monthly fee, which turned out to be less than a dollar in U.S. money. Each business had to pay a little more. For this, they received security.

As we wandered the streets of El Tiro, it did look safe—but I still stayed close to Jaro. And I wondered about this group of men who had made the area safe. What kept them from turning on the residents? Jaro had no answer. When Jaro pointed to two young men, who he said were part of the ruling group, I asked if I could take their picture. They refused. I did not try to snap one on the sly.

My final revelation was El Tiro itself. On pages 464-465, you can see some of the things I saw that day.

Early cities were small economic centers surrounded by walls to keep out enemies. These cities had to be fortresses, for they were constantly under threat. This photo is of Ávila, Spain, whose walls date from 1090.

In this second part of the chapter, I will try to lay the context for understanding urban life—and El Tiro. Let's begin by first finding out how the city itself came about.

The Development of Cities

Cities are not new to the world scene. Perhaps as early as 7,000 years ago, people built small cities with massive defensive walls, such as biblically famous Jericho (Homblin 1973). Cities on a larger scale appeared about 3500 B.C., around the time that writing was invented (Chandler and Fox 1974; Hawley 1981). The earliest cities emerged in several parts of the world—in Asia (China, India, Iran, and Iraq), West Africa (Egypt), Europe, and Central and South America (Fischer 1976; Palen 2012).

About 6,500 years ago, Bulgaria was home to the oldest town in Europe (Toshkov 2012). Its massive walls were 10 feet high and 6 feet thick. Its 350 residents made their living producing salt for trade. Another city that goes back 5,500 years was discovered in 2010 in Norway (Goll 2010). The city had been buried under sand. In the Americas, the first city was Caral, in what is now Peru (Fountain 2001). It was also discovered recently, covered by jungle growth.

The key to the origin of cities is the development of more efficient agriculture. Only when farming produces a surplus can some people stop producing food and gather in cities to spend time in other economic pursuits. A **city**, in fact, can be defined as a place in which a large number of people are permanently based and do not produce their own food. The invention of the plow about 5,000 years ago created widespread agricultural surpluses, stimulating the development of towns and cities.

Most early cities were small, merely a collection of a few thousand people in agricultural centers or on major trade routes. The most notable exceptions are two cities that reached 1 million residents for a brief period of time before they declined—Changan (Xi'an) in China about A.D. 800 and Baghdad in Persia (Iraq) about A.D. 900 (Chandler and Fox 1974). Even Athens at the height of its power in the fifth century B.C. had only about 250,000 inhabitants. Rome, at its peak, may have had a million people or more, but as the Roman Empire declined, the city of Rome became only a collection of villages (Palen 2012).

Two hundred years ago, the only city in the world that had a population of more than a million was Beijing (Peking), China (Chandler and Fox 1974). But today, as you can see from Figure 14.10, the world has about 500 cities with more than a million residents. Behind this urban surge lies the Industrial Revolution, which not only drew people to cities by providing work but also stimulated rapid transportation and communication. These, in turn, allowed the efficient movement of people, resources, products, and, especially today, information—essential factors (called *infrastructure*) that allow large cities to exist.

Urbanization

Although cities are not new to the world scene, quite recent in world history is **urbanization**—the movement of masses of people to cities, which then have a growing influence on society. In 1800, only 3 percent of the world's population lived in cities (Hauser and Schnore 1965). The watershed year was 2008, when for the first time in history, more people lived in cities than in rural areas. Urbanization continues strongly, and today 53% of the world's people live in cities (Haub and Kaneda 2015). From Figure 14.11, you can see how urbanization has accelerated—and how uneven it is. Note especially the rapid increase of urbanization in the Least Industrialized Nations.

THE APPEAL OF CITIES   To understand the city's attraction, we need to consider the "pulls" of urban life. Because of its exquisite division of labor, the city offers incredible variety—music ranging from rap and salsa to death metal and classical, shops that feature imported delicacies from around the world and those that sell special foods for vegetarians and diabetics. Cities also offer anonymity, which so many find refreshing in light of the tighter controls of village and small-town life. And, of course, the city offers work.

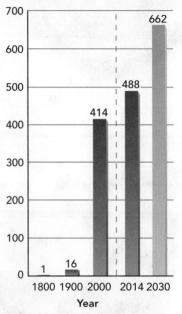

Figure 14.10 A Global Boom: Cities with over One Million Residents

SOURCES: By the author. Based on Chandler and Fox 1974; Brockerhoff 2000; United Nations 2014:Figure 8.

city

a place in which a large number of people are permanently based and do not produce their own food

urbanization

the process by which an increasing proportion of a population lives in cities and has a growing influence on the culture

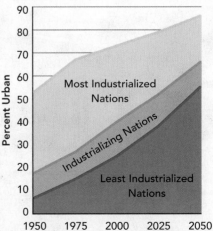

Figure 14.11 How the World Is Urbanizing

SOURCE: By the author. Based on United Nations 2010.

Medellin, Colombia: A Walk Through El Tiro

One of the most significant changes in our time is the global rush of poor, rural people to the cities of the Least Industrialized Nations. Some of these settlements are dangerous. I was fortunate to be escorted by an insider through this section of Medellin, Colombia.

Almost at the top of the garbage heap, I saw this boy in front of his house. His mother hung out the family's wash to dry.

Kids are kids the world over. These children don't know they are poor. They are having a great time playing on a pile of dirt in the street.

This is the "richer" area below El Tiro. As you can see, some of the residents own cars.

This is one of my favorite photos. The woman is happy that she has a home—and proud of what she has done with it. What I find remarkable is the flower garden she so carefully tends, and has taken great effort to protect from children and dogs. I can see the care she would take of a little suburban home.

◄ The road to El Tiro. On the left, going up the hill, is a board walk. To the right is a meat market (carnicería). Note the structure above the meat market, where the family that runs the store lives.

El Tiro has home delivery.

It doesn't take much skill to build your own house in El Tiro. A hammer and saw, some nails, and used lumber will provide most of what you need. This man is building his house on top of another house.

An infrastructure has developed to serve El Tiro. This woman is waiting in line to use the only public telephone.

"What does an El Tiro home look like inside?" I kept wondering. Then Jaro, my guide (on the left), took me inside the home of one of his parishioners. Amelia keeps a neat house, with everything highly organized.

© James M. Henslin, all photos

What do people do to make a living in El Tiro? Anything they can. This man is sharpening a saw in front of his home.

FORCED URBANIZATION An interesting twist has just occurred. Knowing that urbanization fuels economic growth, China's leaders are forcing villagers to move to the city. In some cases, they send demolition crews and tear down the villagers' houses. Since the government owns the land, the villagers cannot rebuild, and they have no choice but to move to the city (Johnson 2014). With both voluntary and forced urbanization, China's villages are shrinking by *300 a day*.

METROPOLISES Some cities have grown so large and have so much influence over a region that the term *city* is no longer adequate to describe them. The term **metropolis** is used instead, referring to a central city surrounded by smaller cities and their suburbs. Metropolises are linked by transportation, communication, and economics. Sometimes politics also binds them through county boards and regional governing bodies. St. Louis is an example.

metropolis

a central city surrounded by smaller cities and their suburbs

> *Although the name St. Louis officially refers to a city of 350,000 people in Missouri, in common usage St. Louis also refers to another 3 million people who live in more than a hundred separate towns in both Missouri and Illinois. Altogether, the region is known as the "St. Louis or Bi-State Area." Although these towns are independent politically, they form an economic unit. They are linked by work (many people in the smaller towns work in St. Louis or are served by industries from St. Louis), by communications (they share the same area newspaper and radio and television stations), and by transportation (they use the same interstate highways, the Bi-State Bus system, and the international airport). As symbolic interactionists would note, shared symbols (the Arch, the Mississippi River, Busch Brewery, the Cardinals, the Rams, and the Blues—both the hockey team and the music) provide the residents a common identity.*

MEGALOPOLISES Some metropolises have grown so large and influential that the term **megalopolis** is used to describe them. A megalopolis is an overlapping area of at least two metropolises and their many suburbs. The three largest megalopolises in the United States are the Eastern seaboard running from Maine to Virginia, the area in Florida between Miami, Orlando, and Tampa, and California's coastal area between San Francisco and San Diego. The California megalopolis extends into Mexico and includes Tijuana and its suburbs.

megalopolis

an urban area consisting of at least two metropolises and their many suburbs

MEGACITIES This process of urban areas turning into a metropolis, and a metropolis developing into a megalopolis, is occurring worldwide. When a city's population reaches 10 million, it is called a **megacity**. In 1950, New York City and Tokyo were the only megacities in the world. Today, the world has twenty-eight, with most located in the Least Industrialized Nations. Megacities are growing so fast that by 2030 there will be forty-one (United Nations 2014). The ten largest are shown on Figure 14.12 on the next page.

megacity

a city of 10 million or more residents

MEGAREGIONS With today's vast population growth and massive movement of people to cities, some megacities have begun to merge into one another. The resulting mass of people is called a **megaregion** (also called an *endless city*). Apparently, the world now has six megaregions, the largest being Hong Kong-Shenzhen-Guangzhou in China. This megaregion is home to 120 million people (Vidal 2010).

megaregion

a merging of megacities and nearby populated areas into an even larger mass of people

U.S. Urban Patterns

FROM COUNTRY TO CITY In its early years, the United States was almost exclusively rural. In 1790, only about 5 percent of Americans lived in cities. By 1920, this figure had jumped to 50 percent. Urbanization has continued without letup, and today, about 80 percent of Americans live in cities.

The U.S. Census Bureau divides the country into 274 **metropolitan statistical areas (MSAs)**. Each MSA consists of a central city of at least 50,000 people and the urbanized areas linked to it. About three of five Americans live in just fifty or so MSAs. As you

metropolitan statistical area (MSA)

a central city and the urbanized counties adjacent to it

Figure 14.12 The World's 10 Largest Megacities

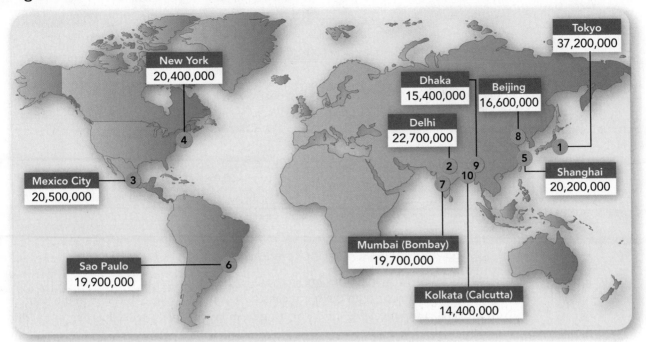

can see from the Social Map below, like our other social patterns, urbanization is uneven across the United States.

FROM CITY TO CITY   As Americans migrate in search of work and better lifestyles, some cities grow while others shrink. Table 14.3 on the next page compares the fastest-growing U.S. cities with those that are losing people. This table reflects a major shift of people, resources, and power between regions of the United States. As you can see, six

Figure 14.13 How Urban Is Your State? The Rural–Urban Makeup of the United States

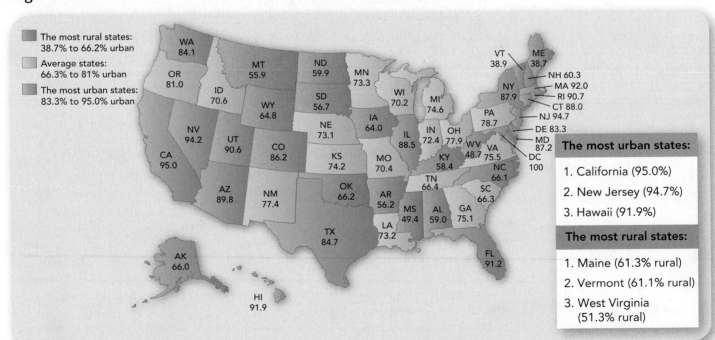

Table 14.3 The Shrinking and the Fastest-Growing Cities

	The Shrinking Cities		The Fastest-Growing Cities
1. −8.0%	New Orleans, LA	1. +51.3%	Las Vegas, NV
2. −7.5%	Youngstown, OH	2. +46.9%	Raleigh, NC
3. −4.1%	Flint, MI	3. +44.6%	Cape Coral–Ft. Myers, FL
4. −4.0%	Cleveland, OH	4. +44.4%	Provo, UT
5. −3.6%	Detroit, MI	5. +44.3%	Myrtle Beach, SC
6. −3.1%	Buffalo–Niagara Falls, NY	6. +44.2%	Austin, TX
7. −2.9%	Pittsburgh, PA	7. +44.0%	Greeley, CO
8. −1.3%	Toledo, OH	8. +40.2%	McAllen, TX
9. −0.8%	Canton, OH	9. +38.0%	Kennewick, WA
10. −0.6%	Utica-Rome, NY	10. +37.6%	Fayetteville, AR

NOTE: Population change from 2000 to 2012, the latest years available.

SOURCE: By the author. Based on *Statistical Abstract of the United States* 2014:Table 21.

of the ten fastest-growing cities are in the West and four are in the South. Of the ten shrinking cities, seven are in the Northeast, two in the Midwest, and one in the South. New Orleans, a unique case, still recovering from Hurricane Katrina, has begun to add population.

edge city

a large clustering of service facilities and residential areas near highway intersections that provides a sense of place to people who live, shop, and work there

BETWEEN CITIES   As Americans migrate, **edge cities** have appeared—clusters of buildings and services near the intersections of major highways. These areas of shopping malls, hotels, office parks, and apartment complexes are not cities in the traditional sense. Rather than being political units with their own mayors or city managers, edge cities, such as Tysons Corner outside of Washington, D.C., overlap political boundaries and include parts of several cities or towns.

Edge cities are changing. Clusters of buildings don't meet deeper human needs, and edge cities have proven disappointing. One drawback has been their lack of a "downtown," an area that provides identity, where people can go to bars and restaurants and socialize. Another is a lack of attractive parks. These are being added to Tysons Corner. So are sidewalks and rectangular blocks (Brown 2014). The goal is to create the familiar look and feel of traditional cities.

gentrification

middle-class people moving into a rundown area of a city, displacing the poor as they buy and restore homes

WITHIN THE CITY   Another U.S. urban pattern is **gentrification**, the movement of middle-class people into rundown areas of a city. What draws the middle class are the low prices for large houses that, although deteriorated, can be restored. With gentrification comes an improvement in the appearance of the neighborhood—freshly painted buildings, well-groomed lawns, and the absence of boarded-up windows.

As a neighborhood improves, property prices go up, driving many of the poor out of their neighborhood. This creates tensions between the poorer residents and the newcomers (Anderson 2006; S. Brown 2014). These social class tensions are often tinged with racial–ethnic antagonisms, as the residents usually are minorities while the middle-class newcomers usually are whites. Beneath this surface, though, is a more positive factor. Sociologists have found that gentrification also draws middle-class minorities to the neighborhood and improves their incomes (McKinnish et al. 2008).

Among the exceptions to the usual pattern of the gentrifiers being whites and the earlier residents being minorities is Harlem in New York City. We examine this change in the Down-to-Earth Sociology box on the next page.

Down-to-Earth Sociology

Reclaiming Harlem: A Twist in the Invasion–Succession Cycle

The story is well known. The inner city is filled with crack, crime, and corruption. It stinks from foul, festering filth strewn on its dangerous streets and piled up around burned-out buildings. Only people who have no choice live in these despairing areas where predators stalk their prey. Danger lurks around every corner.

What is not so well known is that affluent African Americans are reclaiming some of these areas.

Howard Sanders was living the American Dream. After earning a degree from Harvard Business School, he took a position with a Manhattan investment firm. He lived in an exclusive apartment on Central Park West, but he missed Harlem, where he had grown up. He moved back, along with his wife and daughter.

African American lawyers, doctors, professors, and bankers are doing the same.

What's the attraction? The first is nostalgia, a cultural yearning for Harlem past, the time of legend and folklore. It was here that black writers and artists lived in the 1920s, here that the blues and jazz attracted young and accomplished musicians.

The second reason is that Harlem offered housing values. Some homes, built in the 1800s, boasted five bedrooms and 6,000 square feet. They sold for a song, even with Honduran mahogany. Some brownstones were in good condition, although others were only shells and had to be rebuilt from the inside out.

Rebuilding Communities

What happened was the rebuilding of a community. Some people who had succeeded in business and the professions wanted to be role models. They wanted children in the community to see them going to and returning from work.

When the middle class moved out of Harlem and the area was taken over by drug dealers and prostitutes, the amenities moved out, too. When the young professionals moved back in, the amenities returned. There were no coffee shops, restaurants, jazz clubs, florists, copy centers, dentist and optometrist offices, or art galleries—the types of things urbanites take for granted. Now there are.

There is also a Whole Foods market, an American Eagle, and a Burlington Coat Factory. There is even a 95 square block of free Wi-Fi. Quite a change.

The police have also helped to change Harlem. No longer do they rush in, sirens wailing and guns drawn, to confront emergencies and shootouts. Instead, the police have become a normal part of this urban scene. Not only did they shut down the open-air drug markets, but they

For over 80 years, the Apollo Theater has been a landmark in Harlem. Still functioning today, the Apollo has nurtured many music legends.

also began enforcing laws against urinating on the streets, something they used to ignore as too trivial to matter for "that area." The greater safety of the area has attracted even more of the middle class. The change is so extensive that former President Clinton chose to locate his office there, and Magic Johnson opened a Starbucks and a multiplex.

Social Class Tensions

Another side of the story has emerged—tension between the people who were already living in Harlem and the newcomers. Social class is often the source of the irritation. Each class has its own ways, and the classes often grate on each other's nerves. The old-timers like loud music, for example, while the newcomers prefer a more sedate lifestyle. Then there is the old power establishment. They feel slighted if the newcomers don't ask for approval before they open a business. For their part, the new business owners feel they don't need to get those old people's permission to open anything.

There is another issue as well. The large houses built in the 1800s used to sell for a song. No longer. Vacant lots now bring a million dollars. Rents have shot upward, of course. Tenants' associations protest, their moans mostly muffled and unheard.

And the poor? The same as happened in other gentrified areas. Most are pushed out, block by block, forced into adjoining rundown streets.

The in-fighting of this emerging drama mostly involves African Americans. The issue is not race but social class. The "invasion–succession cycle," as sociologists call it, is continuing, but this time with a twist—a flight back in.

A New Pattern

It isn't just Harlem. In the Boyle Heights area of Los Angeles, for example, more well-to-do Chicanos are moving back. As this run-down barrio is being transformed, property prices are rising, and tensions there, too, are flaring (Medina 2013b). We can expect this twist in the invasion–succession cycle to be a new pattern that will occur throughout the country.

SOURCES: Based on Leland 2003; Hyra 2006; Williams 2008; Gayles 2014; Kravitz 2014.

For Your Consideration

→ Would you be willing to move into an area of high crime in order to get a housing bargain?

→ How do you think the current residents of an area being gentrified can be protected from rising rents so they can continue to live in the area? Should they be?

suburbanization

the migration of people from the city to the suburbs

suburb

a community adjacent to a city

FROM CITY TO SUBURB AND BACK   The term **suburbanization** refers to people moving from cities to **suburbs**, the communities located just outside a city. Suburbanization is not new. The Mayan city of Caracol (in what is now Belize) had suburbs, perhaps even with specialized subcenters, the equivalent of today's strip malls (Wilford 2000). The extent to which people have left U.S. cities in search of their dreams is remarkable. In 1920, only about 15 percent of Americans lived in the suburbs, while today, over half of all Americans live in them (Palen 2012).

After the racial integration of U.S. schools in the 1950s and 1960s, suburbanization sped up as whites fled the city. A few years later, around 1970, minorities also began to move to the suburbs. This, too, has been extensive, and in some suburbs, minorities have become the majority. Whites are now returning to the city. In a remarkable switch, some black churches and businesses in Washington, D.C., and San Francisco, California, are making the switch to a white clientele. In another reversal of patterns, some black churches are fleeing the city, following their parishioners to the suburbs.

SMALLER CENTERS   Another trend is the development of *micropolitan areas*. A *micropolis* is a city of 10,000 to 50,000 residents that is not a suburb, such as Gallup, New Mexico, or Carbondale, Illinois. Most micropolises are located "next to nowhere." They are fairly self-contained in terms of providing work, housing, and entertainment, and few of their residents commute to urban centers for work. Today's micropolises are stagnant, neither growing nor shrinking (Badger 2014).

Models of Urban Growth

14.4   Compare the models of urban growth.

In the 1920s, Chicago was a vivid mosaic of immigrants, gangsters, prostitutes, the homeless, the rich, and the poor—much as it is today. Sociologists at the University of Chicago studied these contrasting ways of life. One of these sociologists, Robert Park, coined the term **human ecology** to describe how people adapt to their environments (Park and Burgess 1921; Park 1936). (This concept is also known as *urban ecology*.) The process of urban growth is of special interest to sociologists. Let's look at four main models they developed.

human ecology

Robert Park's term for the relationship between people and their environment (such as land and structures); also known as *urban ecology*

The Concentric Zone Model

To explain how cities expand, sociologist Ernest Burgess (1925) proposed a *concentric-zone model*. As shown in part A of Figure 14.13, Burgess noted that a city expands outward from its center. Zone 1 is the central business district. Zone 2, which encircles the downtown area, is in transition. It contains rooming houses and deteriorating housing, which Burgess said breed poverty, disease, and vice. Zone 3 is the area to which thrifty workers have moved in order to escape the zone in transition and yet maintain easy access to their work. Zone 4 contains more expensive apartments, 2 residential hotels, single-family homes, and exclusive areas where the wealthy live. Commuters live in Zone 5, which consists of suburbs or satellite cities that have grown up around transportation routes.

Burgess said that no "city perfectly fits this ideal scheme." Some cities have physical obstructions, such as a lake, river, or railroad, that cause their expansion to depart from the model. Burgess also noticed another deviation from the model, that businesses were beginning to locate in outlying zones (see Zone 10). This was in 1925. Burgess didn't know it, but he was seeing the beginning of a major shift that led businesses away from downtown areas to suburban shopping malls. Today, these malls account for most of the country's retail sales.

The Sector Model

Sociologist Homer Hoyt (1939, 1971) modified Burgess's model of urban growth. As shown in part B of Figure 14.14 on the next page, he noted that a concentric zone can

Figure 14.14 How Cities Develop: Models of Urban Growth

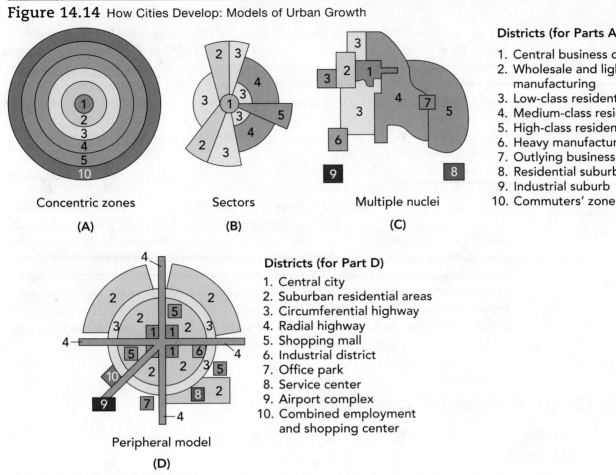

Concentric zones
(A)

Sectors
(B)

Multiple nuclei
(C)

Districts (for Parts A, B, C)

1. Central business district
2. Wholesale and light manufacturing
3. Low-class residential
4. Medium-class residential
5. High-class residential
6. Heavy manufacturing
7. Outlying business district
8. Residential suburb
9. Industrial suburb
10. Commuters' zone

Peripheral model
(D)

Districts (for Part D)

1. Central city
2. Suburban residential areas
3. Circumferential highway
4. Radial highway
5. Shopping mall
6. Industrial district
7. Office park
8. Service center
9. Airport complex
10. Combined employment and shopping center

SOURCE: Cousins and Nagpaul 1970; Harris 1997.

contain several sectors—one of working-class housing, another of expensive homes, a third of businesses, and so on—all competing for the same land.

In this dynamic competition comes the **invasion–succession cycle**. Poor immigrants and rural migrants settle in low-rent areas. As their numbers grow, they spill over into adjacent areas. Upset by their presence, the middle class moves out, which expands the sector of low-cost housing. The invasion–succession cycle is never complete, since later, another group will replace this earlier one. As you read in the Down-to Earth Sociology box on page 469, in Harlem, there has been a switch in the sequence: The "invaders" are the middle class.

invasion–succession cycle

the process of one group of people displacing another group whose racial–ethnic or social class characteristics differ from their own

The Multiple-Nuclei Model

Geographers Chauncy Harris and Edward Ullman noted that some cities have several centers or nuclei (Harris and Ullman 1945; Ullman and Harris 1970). As shown in part C of Figure 14.14, each nucleus contains some specialized activity. A familiar example is the clustering of fast-food restaurants in one area and automobile dealers in another. Sometimes similar activities are grouped together because they profit from cohesion; retail districts, for example, draw more customers if there are more stores. Other clustering occurs because some types of land use, such as factories and expensive homes, are incompatible with one another. One result is that services are not spread evenly throughout the city.

The Peripheral Model

Chauncy Harris (1997) also developed the peripheral model shown in part D of Figure 14.14. This model portrays the impact of radial highways on the movement of people and services away from the central city to the city's periphery, or outskirts. It also shows the development of industrial and office parks.

Critique of the Models

These models tell only part of the story. They are time bound: Medieval cities didn't follow these patterns (see the photo on page 462). In addition, they do not account for urban planning. Most European cities have laws that preserve green belts (forested areas and farmlands) around the city. This prevents urban sprawl: Wal-Mart cannot buy land outside the city and put up a store; instead, it must locate in the downtown area with the other stores. Norwich has 250,000 people—yet the city ends abruptly in a green belt where pheasants skitter across plowed fields while sheep graze in verdant meadows (Milbank 1995).

Another challenge to these models is the huge, sprawling areas that have sprung up around older cities. These sprawls seem to have no distinct form (Florida 2013). If sociologists ever discern clear patterns in these sprawls, they will develop new urban models to account for them. If you were to depend on these classic models, you would be surprised when you visit the cities of the Least Industrialized Nations. There, the wealthy often claim the inner city, where fine restaurants and other services are readily accessible. Tucked behind walls and protected from public scrutiny, they enjoy luxurious homes and gardens. The poor, in contrast, especially rural migrants, settle in areas outside the city—or, as in the case of El Tiro, featured in the photo essay on pages 464–465, on top of piles of garbage in what used to be the outskirts of a city. The vast movement of rural migrants to the city is the topic of the Cultural Diversity box that follows.

Cultural Diversity around the World

Why City Slums Are Better Than the Country: Urbanization in the Least Industrialized Nations

At the bottom of a ravine near Mexico City is a bunch of shacks. Some of the parents have 14 children. "We used to live up there," Señora Gonzalez gestured toward the mountain, "in those caves. Our only hope was one day to have a place to live. And now we do." She smiled with pride at the jerry-built shacks . . . each one had a collection of flowers planted in tin cans. "One day, we hope to extend the water pipes and drainage—perhaps even pave. . . ."

And what was the name of her community? Señora Gonzalez beamed. "Esperanza!" (McDowell 1984:172) Esperanza means hope in Spanish.

What started as a trickle has become a torrent. In 1930, only one Latin American city had over a million people—now fifty do. The world's cities are growing by more than one million people each week (Moreno et al. 2012). The rural poor are flocking to the cities at such a rate that, as you saw in Figure 14.12 on page 467, most of the world's largest cities are located in the Industrializing or the Least Industrialized Nations.

When migrants move to U.S. cities, they usually settle in rundown housing near the city's center. The wealthy live in suburbs and luxurious city enclaves. Migrants to cities of the Least Industrialized Nations, in contrast, establish illegal squatter settlements outside the city. There, they build shacks from scrap boards, cardboard, and bits of corrugated metal. Even flattened tin cans are scavenged for building material.

It is difficult for Americans to grasp the depth of the poverty that is the everyday life of hundreds of millions of people across the globe. These children are playing in an open drainage ditch while it is being repaired in Manila, the capital of the Philippines.

The squatters enjoy no city facilities—roads, public transportation, water, sewers, or garbage pickup. After thousands of squatters have settled an area, the city reluctantly acknowledges their right to live there and adds bus service and minimal water lines. Hundreds of people use a single spigot. About 5 million of Mexico City's residents live in such squalid conditions, with hundreds of thousands more pouring in each year.

Why this rush to live in the city under such miserable conditions? On the one hand are the "push" factors that come from the breakdown of traditional rural life. More children are surviving because of a safer water supply and modern medicine. As rural populations multiply, the parents no longer have enough land to divide among their children. With neither land nor jobs, there is hunger and despair. On the other hand are the "pull" factors that draw people to the cities—jobs, schools, housing, and even a more stimulating life.

How will the Least Industrialized Nations adjust to this vast migration? Removing the migrants by force doesn't work. Authorities in Brazil, Guatemala, Venezuela, and other countries have sent in the police and even the army to evict the settlers. After a violent dispersal, the settlers return—and others stream in. The roads, water and sewer lines, electricity, schools, and public facilities must be built. But these poor countries don't have the resources to build them. As wrenching as the adjustment will be, these countries must—and somehow will—make the transition. They have no choice.

For Your Consideration

→ What are the reasons that the world is urbanizing so rapidly?

→ What solutions do you see for this vast flow of migration to the cities of the Least Industrialized Nations?

City Life

14.5   Discuss alienation and community, types of people who live in the city, the norm of noninvolvement, and the diffusion of responsibility.

Life in cities is filled with contrasts. Let's look at two of those contrasts: alienation and community.

Alienation in the City

In a classic essay, sociologist Louis Wirth (1938) noted that urban dwellers live anonymous lives marked by segmented and superficial encounters. This type of relationship, he said, undermines kinship and neighborhood, the traditional bases of social control and feelings of solidarity. Urbanites then grow aloof and indifferent to other people's problems. In short, the price of the personal freedom that the city offers is **alienation**.

Alienation takes many forms, such as the "road rage" that makes the evening news. You can be following your usual routine, such as driving home from work, when the unexpected erupts, changing your life forever.

> *In crowded traffic on a bridge going into Detroit, Deletha Word bumped the car ahead of her. The damage was minor, but the driver, Martell Welch, jumped out. Cursing, he pulled Deletha from her car, pushed her onto the hood, and began beating her. Martell's friends got out to watch. One of them held Deletha down while Martell took a car jack and smashed Deletha's car. Scared for her life, Deletha broke away, fleeing to the bridge's railing. Martell and his friends taunted her, shouting, "Jump, bitch, jump!" Deletha plunged to her death. (Stokes and Zeman 1995). Welch was convicted of second-degree murder and sentenced to 16 to 40 years in prison.*

This certainly is not an ordinary situation, but anyone who lives in a large city knows that even a minor traffic accident can explode into murderous road rage. And you never know who that stranger in the mall—or even next door—really is. The most common reason for impersonality and self-interest is not fear of danger, however, but the impossibility of dealing with crowds as individuals and the need to tune out many of the stimuli that come buzzing in from the bustle of the city (Berman et al. 2008).

alienation

Marx's term for workers' lack of connection to the product of their labor; caused by workers being assigned repetitive tasks on a small part of a product, which leads to a sense of powerlessness and normlessness; others use the term in the general sense of not feeling a part of something

Community in the City

I don't want to give the impression that the city is inevitably alienating. Far from it. Many people find community in the city. There are good reasons that millions around the globe are rushing to the world's cities. And there is another aspect of the attack on Deletha Word. After Deletha went over the railing, two men jumped in after her, risking injury and their own lives in a futile attempt to save her.

Sociologist Herbert Gans, a symbolic interactionist who did participant observation in the West End of Boston, was so impressed with the area's sense of community that he titled his book *The Urban Villagers* (1962). In this book, which has become a classic in sociology, Gans said:

> *After a few weeks of living in the West End, my observations—and my perceptions of the area—changed drastically. The search for an apartment quickly indicated that the individual units were usually in much better condition than the outside or the hallways of the buildings. Subsequently, in wandering through the West End, and in using it as a resident, I developed a kind of selective perception, in which my eye focused only on those parts of the area that were actually being used by people. Vacant buildings and boarded-up stores were no longer so visible, and the totally deserted alleys or streets were outside the set of paths normally traversed, either by myself or by the West Enders. The dirt and spilled-over garbage remained, but, since they were concentrated in street gutters and empty lots, they were not really harmful to anyone and thus were not as noticeable as during my initial observations.*
>
> *Since much of the area's life took place on the street, faces became familiar very quickly. I met my neighbors on the stairs and in front of my building. And, once a shopping pattern developed, I saw the same storekeepers frequently, as well as the area's "characters" who wandered through the streets everyday on a fairly regular route and schedule. In short, the exotic quality of the stores and the residents also wore off as I became used to seeing them.*

SLUM OR LOW-RENT AREA?   In short, Gans found a *community*, people who identified with the area and with one another. Its residents enjoyed networks of friends and acquaintances. Despite the area's substandard buildings, most West Enders had chosen to live here. *To them, this was a low-rent district, not a slum.*

Most West Enders had low-paying, insecure jobs. Other residents were elderly, living on small pensions. Unlike the middle class, these people didn't care about their "address." The area's inconveniences were something they put up with in exchange for cheap housing. In general, they were content with their neighborhood.

Who Lives in the City?

Whether people find alienation or community in the city depends on whom you are talking about. As with almost everything in life, social class is especially significant. The greater security enjoyed by the city's wealthier residents removes alienation and increases satisfaction with city life (Santos 2009). There also are different types of urban dwellers, each with distinctive experiences. As we review the five types that Gans (1962, 1968, 1991) identified, try to see where you fit.

THE COSMOPOLITES   These are the intellectuals, professionals, artists, and entertainers who have been attracted to the city. They value its conveniences and cultural benefits.

THE SINGLES   Usually in their early 20s to early 30s, the singles have settled in the city temporarily. For them, urban life is a stage in their life course. Businesses and services, such as singles' bars and apartment complexes, cater to their needs and desires. After they marry, many move to the suburbs.

THE ETHNIC VILLAGERS   Feeling a sense of identity, working-class members of the same ethnic group band together. They form tightly knit neighborhoods that resemble villages and small towns. Family- and peer-oriented, they try to isolate themselves from the dangers and problems of urban life.

THE DEPRIVED   Destitute, emotionally disturbed, and having little income, education, or work skills, the deprived live in neighborhoods that are more like urban jungles than urban villages. Some of them stalk those jungles in search of prey. Neither predator nor prey has much hope for anything better in life—for themselves or for their children.

THE TRAPPED   These people don't live in the area by choice, either. Some were trapped when an ethnic group "invaded" their neighborhood, and they could not afford to move. Others found themselves trapped in a downward spiral. They started life in a higher social class, but because of personal problems—mental or physical illness or addiction to alcohol or other drugs—they drifted downward. There also are the elderly who are trapped by poverty and not wanted elsewhere. Like the deprived, the trapped suffer from high rates of assault, mugging, and rape.

This man is a member of the Lubavitch, an ultra-orthodox Jewish sect in Crown Heights, New York. Where do you think he fits in Gans' classification of urban dwellers?

CRITIQUE   You probably noticed this inadequacy in Gans' categories, that you can be both a cosmopolite and a single. You might have noticed also that you can be these two things and an ethnic villager as well. Gans also seems to have missed an important type of city dweller—the people living in the city who don't stand out in any way. They work and marry there and quietly raise their families. They aren't cosmopolites, singles, or ethnic villagers. Neither are they deprived nor trapped. Perhaps we can call these the "Just Plain Folks."

IN SUM   Within the city's rich mosaic of social diversity, not all urban dwellers experience the city in the same way. Each group has its own lifestyle, and each has distinct experiences. Some people welcome the city's cultural diversity, and they mix with several groups. Others find community by retreating into the security of ethnic enclaves. Still others feel trapped and deprived. To them, the city is an urban jungle. It poses threats to their health and safety, and their lives are filled with despair.

The Norm of Noninvolvement and the Diffusion of Responsibility

TUNING OUT: THE NORM OF NONINVOLVEMENT   To avoid intrusions from strangers, urban dwellers follow a *norm of noninvolvement*.

> *To do this, we sometimes use props such as newspapers to shield ourselves from others and to indicate our inaccessibility for interaction. In effect, we learn to "tune others out." In this regard, we might see the [iPod] as the quintessential urban prop in that it allows us to be tuned in and tuned out at the same time. It is a device that allows us to enter our own private world and thereby effectively to close off encounters with others. The use of such devices protects our "personal space," along with our body demeanor and facial expression (the passive "mask" or even scowl that persons adopt on subways). (Karp et al. 1991)*

Social psychologists John Darley and Bibb Latané (1968) ran the series of experiments featured in Chapter 5 (page 151). They uncovered the *diffusion of responsibility*—the more bystanders there are, the less likely people are to help. As a group grows, people's sense of responsibility becomes diffused, with each person assuming that *another* will do the responsible thing. "With these other people here, it is not *my* responsibility," they reason.

The diffusion of responsibility helps to explain why people can ignore the plight of others. Those who did nothing to intervene in the attack on Deletha Word were *not* uncaring people. Each felt that others might do something. Then, too, there was the norm of noninvolvement—helpful for getting people through everyday city life but, unfortunately, dysfunctional in some crucial situations.

As mentioned in Chapter 5, laboratory experiments can give insight into human behavior—but they can also woefully miss the mark. Recall the photo sequence I took in Vienna of the man who fell in Vienna, Austria (see page 152). That these people were strangers who were simply passing one another on the sidewalk didn't stop them from immediately helping the man who tripped and fell. We carry many norms within us, some of which can trump the diffusion of responsibility and the norm of noninvolvement.

Urban Problems and Social Policy

14.6 Explain the effects of suburbanization, disinvestment and deindustrialization, and the potential of urban revitalization.

To close this chapter, let's look at the primary reasons that U.S. cities have declined and then consider how they can be revitalized.

Suburbanization

We have discussed the transition to the suburbs. The U.S. city has been the loser in this transition. As people moved out of the city, businesses and jobs followed. Insurance companies and others that employ white-collar workers were the first to move their offices to the suburbs. They were soon followed by manufacturers and their blue-collar workers. This process has continued so relentlessly that today, twice as many manufacturing jobs are located in the suburbs as in the city (Palen 2012). This transition hit the city's tax base hard, leaving a budget squeeze that affected not only parks, zoos, libraries, and museums but also the city's basic services—its schools, streets, sewer and water systems, and police and fire departments.

Left behind were people who had no choice but to stay in the city. As we reviewed in Chapter 9, sociologist William Julius Wilson says that this exodus transformed the inner city into a ghetto. Individuals who lacked training and skills were trapped by poverty, unemployment, and welfare dependency. Also left behind were those who prey on others through street crime. The term *ghetto*, says Wilson, "suggests that a fundamental social transformation has taken place . . . that groups represented by this term are collectively different from and much more socially isolated from those that lived in these communities in earlier years" (quoted in Karp et al. 1991).

CITY VERSUS SUBURB Suburbanites want the city to keep its problems to itself. They reject proposals to share suburbia's revenues with the city and oppose measures that would allow urban and suburban governments joint control over what has become a contiguous mass of people and businesses (Innes et al. 2011). They do not mind going to the city to work or venturing there on weekends for the diversions it offers, but they do not want to help pay the city's expenses.

It is likely that the mounting bill ultimately will come due, however, and that suburbanites will have to pay for their uncaring attitude toward the urban disadvantaged. Sociologist David Karp and colleagues (1991) put it this way:

It may be that suburbs can insulate themselves from the problems of central cities, at least for the time being. In the long run, though, there will be a steep price to pay for the failure of those better off to care compassionately for those at the bottom of society.

Our occasional urban riots may be part of that bill—perhaps just the down payment.

As cities evolve, so does architecture. This building is in Baku, Azerbaijan.

SUBURBAN FLIGHT In some places, the bill is coming due quickly. As they age, some suburbs are becoming mirror images of the city that their residents so despise. Suburban crime, the flight of the middle class, a shrinking tax base, and eroding services create a spiraling sense of insecurity, stimulating more middle-class flight (Katz and Bradley 2009; Palen 2012). Figure 14.15 illustrates this process, which is new to the urban–suburban scene.

LIVING AT THE MALL To attract the middle class, some cities are turning their aging shopping malls into town centers that feature homes, offices, and parks (Whelan 2014). We will have to await the outcome of this new suburban experiment, but the first residents of the mall-turned-town-center at Edina, Minnesota, seem pleased at having restaurants and happy hour at their doorstep.

Figure 14.15 Urban Growth and Urban Flight

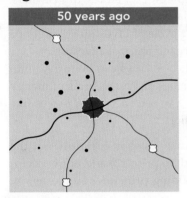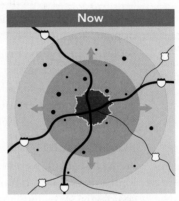

50 years ago	25 years ago	Now

At first, the city and surrounding villages grew independently.

As city dwellers fled urban decay, they created a ring of suburbs.

As middle-class flight continues outward, urban problems are arriving in the outer rings.

Disinvestment and Deindustrialization

As the cities' tax bases shrank and neighborhoods deteriorated, banks began **redlining**: Afraid of loans going bad, bankers would draw a line around a problem area on a map and refuse to make loans for housing or businesses there (Andriotis and Ensign 2015). This **disinvestment** (withdrawal of investment) pushed these areas into further decline. Youth gangs, muggings, and murders are common in these areas, but good jobs are not. All are woven into this process of disinvestment.

Redlining is illegal, and banks do not practice it openly. Without calling it redlining, though, they still target areas to disinvest. In Rhode Island, for example, Banco Santander was sued after its mortgages in white neighborhoods increased 25 percent while at the same time its mortgages in black neighborhoods declined by 63 percent (Dewan 2014).

The globalization of capitalism has also left a heavy mark on U.S. cities. As we reviewed in Chapter 11, to compete in the global market, many U.S. companies moved their factories to countries where labor costs are lower. This process, called **deindustrialization**, made U.S. industries more competitive, but it eliminated millions of U.S. manufacturing jobs. Lacking training in the new information technologies, many poor people are locked out of the benefits of the postindustrial economy that is engulfing the United States. Left behind in the inner cities, many live lives of quiet and not-so-quiet despair.

The Potential of Urban Revitalization

Social policy usually takes one of two forms. The first is to tear down and rebuild— something that is fancifully termed **urban renewal**. The result is the renewal of an

redlining
a decision by the officers of a financial institution not to make loans in a particular area

disinvestment
the withdrawal of investments by financial institutions, which seals the fate of an urban area

deindustrialization
the process of industries moving out of a country or region

urban renewal
the rehabilitation of a rundown area, which usually results in the displacement of the poor who are living in that area

U.S. suburbs were once unplanned, rambling affairs that took irregular shapes as people moved away from the city. Today's suburbs are planned to precise details even before the first foundation is laid. This photo is of a suburb in the Arizona desert.

enterprise zone
the use of economic incentives in a designated area to encourage investment

area—but *not* for the benefit of its inhabitants. Stadiums, high-rise condos, luxury hotels, and boutiques replace run-down, cheap housing. Outpriced, the area's inhabitants are displaced into adjacent areas.

The second is to attract businesses to an area by offering them reduced taxes. This program, called **enterprise zones**, usually fails because most businesses refuse to locate in high-crime areas. They know that the high costs of security and the losses from crime can eat up the tax savings.

A highly promising form of the enterprise zone, called the *Federal Empowerment Zone*, is the opposite of disinvestment. It targets the redevelopment of an area by adding low-interest loans to the tax breaks. The renaissance of Harlem, featured in the Down-to-Earth Sociology box on page 469, was stimulated by designating Harlem a Federal Empowerment Zone. The low-interest loans brought grocery stores, dry cleaners, and video stores, attracting the middle class. As they moved back in, the demand for more specialty shops followed. A self-feeding cycle of investment and hope replaced the self-feeding cycle of despair and crime that accompanies disinvestment.

If they become top agenda items of the government, U.S. cities can be turned into safe and decent places to live and enjoy. This will require not just huge sums of money but also creative urban planning. That we are beginning to see success in places like Harlem indicates that we can accomplish this transformation.

PUBLIC SOCIOLOGY Replacing old buildings with new ones is certainly not the answer. Instead, we need to do *public sociology* (discussed on page 12) and apply sociological principles to build community. Here are three guiding principles suggested by sociologist William Flanagan (1990):

Scale Regional and national planning is necessary. Local jurisdictions, with their many rivalries, competing goals, and limited resources, end up with a hodgepodge of mostly unworkable solutions.

Livability Cities must be appealing and meet human needs, especially the need for community. This will attract the middle classes into the city, which will increase its tax base. In turn, this will help finance the services that make the city more livable.

Social justice In the final analysis, social policy must be evaluated by how it affects people. "Urban renewal" programs that displace the poor for the benefit of the middle class and wealthy do not pass this standard. The same would apply to solutions that create "livability" for select groups but neglect the poor and the homeless.

Most actions taken to solve urban problems are window dressing by politicians who want to *appear* as though they are doing something constructive. The solution is to avoid Band-Aids that cover up the problems that hurt our quality of life and to address their *root* causes—poverty, poor schools, crime, lack of jobs, and an inadequate tax base to provide the amenities that enhance our quality of life and attract people to the city.

Summary and Review

A Planet with No Space for Enjoying Life?

14.1 **Contrast the views of the New Malthusians and Anti-Malthusians on population growth and the food supply; explain why people are starving.**

What debate did Thomas Malthus initiate?

In 1798, Thomas Malthus analyzed the surge in Europe's population. He concluded that the world's population will outstrip its food supply. The debate between today's New Malthusians and those who disagree, the Anti-Malthusians, continues.

Why are people starving?

Starvation is not due to a lack of food in the world: There is now *more* food for each person in the entire world than there was fifty years ago. Rather, starvation is the result of a maldistribution of food, which is primarily due to drought and civil war.

Population Growth

14.2 **Explain why the Least Industrialized Nations have so many children, consequences of rapid population growth, population pyramids, the three demographic variables, and problems in forecasting population growth.**

Why do people in the poor nations have so many children?

In the Least Industrialized Nations, children are often viewed as gifts from God. In addition, they cost little to rear, contribute to the family income at an early age, and provide the parents' social security. These are powerful motivations to have large families.

What are the three demographic variables?

To compute population growth, demographers use *fertility*, *mortality*, and *migration*. They follow the **basic demographic equation**, births minus deaths plus net migration equals the growth rate.

Why is forecasting population difficult?

A nation's growth rate is affected by changing conditions—from economic cycles, wars, and famines to industrialization and government policies.

Urbanization

14.3 **Summarize the development of cities, the process of urbanization, U.S. urban patterns, and the rural rebound.**

How are cities related to farming and the Industrial Revolution?

Cities can develop only if there is an agricultural surplus large enough to free people from food production. The primary impetus to the development of cities was the invention of the plow. After the Industrial Revolution stimulated rapid transportation and communication, cities grew quickly. Today, **urbanization** is so extensive that some cities have become **metropolises**, dominating the areas adjacent to them. Some metropolises spill over into each other, forming a **megalopolis**.

What is the rural rebound?

As people flee cities and suburbs, the population of many U.S. rural counties is growing. This is a fundamental departure from a trend that had been in place for a couple of hundred years.

Models of Urban Growth

14.4 **Compare the models of urban growth.**

What models of urban growth have been proposed?

The primary models are concentric zone, sector, multiple-nuclei, and peripheral. These models fail to account for ancient and medieval cities, many European cities, cities in the Least Industrialized Nations, and urban planning.

City Life

14.5 **Discuss alienation and community, types of people who live in the city, the norm of noninvolvement, and the diffusion of responsibility.**

Who lives in the city?

Some people experience **alienation** in the city; others find **community** in it. What people find depends largely on their backgrounds and urban networks. Five types of people who live in cities are cosmopolites, singles, ethnic villagers, the deprived, and the trapped.

Urban Problems and Social Policy

14.6 **Explain the effects of suburbanization, disinvestment and deindustrialization, and the potential of urban revitalization.**

Why have U.S. cities declined?

Three primary reasons for the decline of U.S. cities are **suburbanization** (as people moved to the suburbs, the tax base of cities eroded and services deteriorated), **disinvestment** (banks withdrew their financing), and **deindustrialization** (which caused a loss of jobs).

What social policy can salvage U.S. cities?

Three guiding principles for developing urban social policy are scale, livability, and social justice.

Thinking Critically about Chapter 14

1. Do you think the world is threatened by a population explosion? Use data from this chapter to support your position.

2. Explain the causes of food shortages that lead to starvation.

3. Why do people find alienation or community in the city?

4. What are the causes of urban problems, and what can we do to solve those problems?

Chapter 15
Social Change and the Environment

 Learning Objectives

15.1 Summarize how social change transforms society; include the four social revolutions, *Gemeinschaft* and *Gesellschaft*, capitalism, social movements, and global politics. (p. 482)

15.2 Summarize theories of social change: social evolution, natural cycles, conflict over power and resources, and Ogburn's theory. (p. 486)

15.3 Use the examples of the automobile and the microchip to illustrate the sociological significance of technology; include changes in ideology, norms, human relationships, education, work, business, war, and social inequality. (p. 490)

15.4 Explain how industrialization is related to environmental problems; contrast the environmental movement and environmental sociology; discuss the goal of harmony. (p. 497)

The job seemed to go on forever. Two archeologists and their team spent *25 years* mapping Caracol, perhaps the oldest and largest city in the Americas. This city in Belize, where people had lived from 600 BC to AD 900, when it was mysteriously abandoned, lay under thick jungle cover. The vegetation was so thick that the city had not been discovered until 1938, when some loggers stumbled onto it.

Year after year, the archeologists slaved away. Each year, they were able to map just a small part of the city. They knew that there were roads leading to the city, also hidden by thick jungle. And what else?

At the pace they were going, maybe archeologists would know the answer in 100 years or so.

But only if more teams of archeologists joined the project.

And only if they could survive the jungle's heat, insects, animals, and disease.

This is the traditional archeological way. Dig and document. What else can there be? Even attempts at using radar to map the site had failed. The jungle was too thick to penetrate.

Diane and Arlen Chase, the wife-and-husband team who had been slogging away in the jungle for 25 years, searched for alternatives. "Let's try LiDAR (light detection and ranging)," they concluded. "We can try it in the dry spring, when the vegetation is somewhat lighter."

When spring came, a little plane flew back and forth a half mile above the area. For four days, it sent laser beams onto the ground. The Chases grew anxious. Would the laser beams bounced back from the ground show anything besides vegetation? If so, what?

> At the pace they were going, maybe archeologists would know the answer in 100 years or so . . . if they could survive the jungle's heat, insects, animals, and disease.

The results were astounding: high-quality 3-D images of what lay beneath the jungle. And not just in the area near the excavated site. LiDAR also revealed intriguing things hidden in an *80-square-mile area*. You could see crisp images of house mounds, roadways, and agricultural terraces.

In just four days, the new technology revealed much more than the archeologists had discovered by slaving away for 25 years.

Based on Chase et al. 2010; Handwerk 2010; Wilford 2010.

If you want a better understanding of society—and your own life—you need to understand social change, probably the main characteristic of social life today. As you will see in this chapter, technology, such as the laser imagery that reveals ancient cities hidden beneath thick jungle, is the driving force behind this change.

Let's begin by reviewing how social change transforms social life.

How Social Change Transforms Social Life

15.1 **Summarize how social change transforms society; include the four social revolutions, *Gemeinschaft* and *Gesellschaft*, capitalism, social movements, and global politics.**

social change

the alteration of culture and societies over time

Social change, a shift in the characteristics of culture and society, is such a vital part of social life that it has been a recurring theme throughout this book. To make this theme more explicit, let's review the main points about social change that we have looked at in the preceding chapters.

The Four Social Revolutions

Rapid social change is part of your everyday life. Why? To understand why our society is changing so fast, we need to go back in history a bit. Let's start with forces that were set in motion thousands of years ago when humans domesticated plants and animals. This first social revolution allowed hunting and gathering societies to develop into horticultural and pastoral societies. The plow brought about the second social revolution, from which agricultural societies emerged. The third social revolution, prompted by the invention of the steam engine, ushered in the Industrial Revolution. Now we are in the midst of the fourth social revolution, stimulated by the invention of the microchip. The process of change has accelerated so greatly that the mapping of the human genome system could be pushing us into yet another new type of society, one based on biotechnology.

From *Gemeinschaft* to *Gesellschaft*

Although our society has changed extensively—think of how life was for your grandparents when they were children—we have seen only the tip of the iceberg. Based on what happened in earlier social revolutions, we know that by the time this fourth—and perhaps fifth—social revolution is full-blown, little of our current way of life will remain.

Consider the change from agricultural to industrial society. This transition didn't just touch the surface. It was not simply that people changed where they lived, moving from the farm to the city. The change was so extensive and deep that it transformed peoples' relationships. Lives had been built around the reciprocal obligations (such as exchanging favors) that are essential to kinship, social status, and friendship. Moving to the city broke many intimate relationships, replacing them with impersonal associations built around paid work, contracts, and money. As reviewed on pages 111–113, sociologists use the terms *Gemeinschaft* and *Gesellschaft* to indicate this fundamental shift in society.

Traditional, or *Gemeinschaft*, societies are small, rural, and slow-changing. Men dominate social life, and the divisions of labor between men and women are rigid. People live in extended families, have little formal education, treat illness at home, tend to see morals in absolute terms, and consider the past the key for dealing with the present. In contrast, modern, or *Gesellschaft*, societies are large, urbanized, and fast-changing, with more fluid divisions of labor between the sexes. When a group reaches the third stage of the demographic transition, people have smaller families and low rates of infant mortality. They prize formal education, are future-oriented, have higher incomes, and enjoy vastly more material possessions.

The evolution of societies has been so thorough that this scene—once common for all humanity—has become strange, exotic. Our type of society, too, will be replaced by some new type yet to appear.

The Industrial Revolution and Capitalism

As you can see, these are not mere surface changes. The switch from *Gemeinschaft* to *Gesellschaft* society transformed people's social relationships and their orientations to life. In his analysis of this transition, Karl Marx stressed that when feudal society broke up, it threw people off the land, creating a surplus of labor. When these desperate masses moved to cities, they were exploited by capitalists, the owners of the means of production (factories, machinery, and tools). This set in motion antagonistic relationships between capitalists and workers that remain today.

Max Weber traced capitalism to the Protestant Reformation. He noted that the Reformation stripped Protestants of the assurance that church membership saved them. As they agonized over heaven and hell, they concluded that God did not want the elect to live in uncertainty. Surely God would give them a sign that they were predestined to heaven. That sign, they decided, was prosperity. An unexpected consequence of the Reformation, then, was to make Protestants hard-working and thrifty. This created an economic surplus that stimulated capitalism. In this way, Protestantism laid the groundwork for the Industrial Revolution that transformed the world.

The sweeping changes ushered in by the Industrial Revolution, called **modernization**, are summarized in Table 15.1 on the next page. The traits listed in this table are *ideal types* in Weber's sense of the term, since no society exemplifies all of them to the maximum degree. Actually, our new technology has created a remarkable unevenness in the characteristics of nations, making them a mixture of the traits shown in this table. For example, Uganda is a traditional society, but the elite have smaller families, emphasize formal education, and use computers. The characteristics shown in Table 15.1 should be interpreted as "more" or "less," not "either–or."

When technology changes, societies change. Consider how technology from the industrialized world transforms traditional societies. When the West exports medicine to the Least Industrialized Nations, for example, death rates drop while birth rates remain high. As a result, the population

modernization

the transformation of traditional societies into industrial societies

The Protestant Reformation ushered in not only religious change but also, as Max Weber analyzed, fundamental change in economics. This painting by Johann Zoffany from about 1775 is of Sir Lawrence Dundas, a Scottish merchant. Note the wealth that he enjoyed.

Table 15.1 Comparing Traditional and Industrialized (and Information) Societies

Characteristics	Traditional Societies	Industrialized (and Information) Societies
General Characteristics		
Social change	Slow	Rapid
Size of group	Small	Large
Religious orientation	More	Less
Education	Informal	Formal
Place of residence	Rural	Urban
Family size	Larger	Smaller
Infant mortality	High	Low
Life expectancy	Short	Long
Health care	Home	Hospital
Temporal orientation	Past	Future
Demographic transition	First stage	Third stage (or Fourth)
Material Relations		
Industrialized	No	Yes
Technology	Simple	Complex
Division of labor	Little	Extensive
Income	Low	High
Material possessions	Few	Many
Social Relationships		
Basic organization	*Gemeinschaft*	*Gesellschaft*
Families	Extended	Nuclear
Respect for elders	More	Less
Social stratification	Rigid	More open
Social mobility	Little	Much
Statuses	More ascribed	More achieved
Gender equality	Less	More
Norms		
View of morals	Absolute	Relativistic
Social control	Informal	Formal
Tolerance of differences	Less	More

SOURCE: By the author.

explodes, bringing hunger and uprooting masses of people who migrate to cities that have little industrialization to support them. The photo essay on pages 464–465 and the Cultural Diversity box on pages 472–473 focus on some of these problems.

Social Movements

Social movements reveal the cutting edge of social change. Upset by some aspect of society, people band together to demand some change they want or to resist some change they don't want. With today's globalization, social movements often sweep across national borders. They can be subdued affairs or so dynamic that they upend the way of life of people in different cultures. The underlying issue can be something that has simmered for generations, but then, bursting onto the scene, a social movement can generate such enthusiasm that it topples governments. Such was the case with the Arab uprisings across North Africa in 2011.

Conflict, Power, and Global Politics

In our fast-paced world, we pay most attention to changes that directly affect our own lives or that make headlines. But largely out of sight lies one of the most significant changes of all, the shifting arrangements of power among nations. Let's look at some of these changes.

A BRIEF HISTORY OF GEOPOLITICS By the sixteenth century, global divisions of power had begun to emerge. Nations with the most advanced technology (at that time, the swiftest ships and the most powerful cannons) became wealthy through *colonialism*, conquering other nations and taking control of their resources. As the Industrial Revolution began in the eighteenth century, the nations that industrialized first exploited the resources of countries that had not yet industrialized. According to *world system theory*, this made the nonindustrialized nations dependent and unable to develop their own resources (see pages 218–219). The consequences of this early domination remain with us today, including the recurring conflicts over oil in the Middle East and the Arab uprisings in North Africa, but we'll get to this shortly.

G7 PLUS Since World War II, a realignment of the world's powers has created a triadic division of the globe: a Japan-centered East (with China in the process of replacing Japan), a Germany-centered Europe, and a U.S.-centered western hemisphere. In an effort to align power and divide global areas of dominance, these three powers, along with four lesser ones—Canada, France, Great Britain, and Italy—formed G7, meaning the "Group of 7." Fear of Russia's nuclear arsenal prompted G7 to let Russia join this elite club, creating G8. Currently, Russia is no longer welcome, and it looks as though the membership has dropped back to G7.

DIVIDING UP THE WORLD The heads of G7 (presidents, prime ministers) hold annual meetings at which they set policies to guide global economic/political affairs. (Representatives of major capitalist interests also hold more informal annual meetings at Davos, Switzerland.) Their goal is to perpetuate their global dominance. Essential to this goal is maintaining access to abundant, cheap oil—which requires that they dominate the Middle East. If the Arab nations became an independent power, it would sabotage this goal. The policies and international relations they develop to perpetuate their power and interests are known by the term the New World Order.

FOUR THREATS TO THIS COALITION OF POWERS   The global divisions that G8 has been trying to work out face four major threats. The first is dissension within. Currently, Russia and the West are in the midst of a bitter intrafamilial feud. Still stinging from the loss of its empire, in 2014 Russia seized the Crimea, a part of the Ukraine. To avoid war, the West's response was trade and banking sanctions. Coupled with a huge drop in the price of oil, Russia's main export, Russia's economy was damaged severely. As I write this, the snarling has grown so bitter that the United States and Russia are fighting a proxy war in Syria, with these two countries on opposite sides of the Assad regime.

Each year, the leaders of the most powerful nations meet in a secluded, secure place to make world-controlling decisions. This photo was taken at their 2015 meeting in the Bavarian Alps. With the striking absence of Russia, G8 has now shrunk to G7. (The additional two persons at the main table are the presidents of the European Union Commission and the European Council.)

The second threat is the growing military power of China. From a huge but sleepy, backwater nation, China is emerging as a giant on the world stage (Jacobs 2015). China's transition also threatens G7's (formerly G8's) plans, especially those concerning Asia and Africa. So far, the struggle between these rival powers has been limited to bidding wars for natural resources, threats about the sea lanes in the South China Sea, and mutual accusations about cyberespionage. If this competition were to erupt into real war, however, all bets would be off concerning G7's success.

In a sign of changes to come, G7 is gradually—but with severe reluctance—bowing to the inevitable. Attempting to reduce the likelihood of conflict as China steps onto turf claimed by others, G7 has allowed China to become an observer at its annual summits. If China cooperates adequately, the next step will be to add China to this exclusive club, transforming the group back into a G8. Unless China decides to go it alone—or pairs with Russia and the two split off—China will be incorporated into the coming New World Order.

The third threat is the resurgence of ethnic rivalries and conflicts. In Europe, Muslim immigrants feel unwelcome. In Africa, the Igbo in Nigeria won't let the government count them because, as they say, "We are not Nigerian." In North America, ethnic conflicts flare up in the United States and Mexico, and in Asia, they occur in China and Vietnam. We do not know how long the lid can be kept on the seemingly bottomless ethnic antagonisms or whether they will ever play themselves out. The end of these hostilities will certainly not come during our lifetimes.

For global control, G7 requires political and economic stability, both in its members' own backyards and in those countries that provide the raw materials that fuel its giant industrial machine. This explains why G7 cares little when African nations self-destruct in ethnic slaughter but refuses to tolerate interethnic warfare in its own neighborhoods. To allow warfare between different groups in Bosnia, Kosovo, or Georgia to go unchecked would be to tolerate conflict that could spread and engulf Europe. In contrast, the deaths of hundreds of thousands of Tutsis in Rwanda carried little or no political significance for these powerful countries.

The fourth threat comes from the smoldering embers of the Cold War that threaten to burst into flames. The United States thinks that Russia wants to invade Europe, and Russia suspects that the United States is planning to attack it with nuclear weapons (Kozin 2013). When the United States announced that to prevent attacks from "rogue nations" it was going to place "missile interceptors" in Poland and Romania, Russia suspected that the missiles were intended for it and threatened to bomb the bases (Boudreaux 2012). The West's suspicions were confirmed when Russia invaded the Ukraine, and Russia's suspicions were confirmed when NATO officials said the "nuclear defense system" system should be directed against Russia ("Baltic Fears" 2014). It is chilling to recall that Russia

To maintain global power requires the continuous development of weapons. Shown here is the F-35 Lightning II, an all-weather stealth fighter. The United States spent more to develop and deploy this plane than it did to land a man on the moon.

and the United States both claim the *right of first strike*, the right to strike the other with nuclear weapons even though the other has not launched any (Kozin 2013).

THE GROWING RELEVANCE OF AFRICA No longer can G7 safely ignore Africa, once a remote continent but now transformed by globalization into a neighbor. In the scramble to secure resources, G7 increasingly views Africa as significant to its own well-being. These global powers are realizing that African poverty and political corruption breed political unrest that can come back to haunt them. In addition to Africa's vast natural resources, including oil reserves that could counterbalance those of the unstable Middle East, Africa is also the world's last largely untapped market. Political stability in Africa could go a long way toward transforming this continent into a giant outlet for the products of G7's economic machinery. This combination of resources and markets helps explain why the United States has raised funds for African AIDS victims and, as in Liberia, Somalia, and Darfur, has begun to intervene in African politics.

To gain and maintain dominance over Africa and to send a not-so-subtle signal to China, its chief competitor for Africa's resources, the U.S. government has formed AFRICOM (African Command). This special command unit of the U.S. Marines was "sold" to the U.S. Congress as a "soft force." It would specialize in humanitarian missions, such as bringing medical assistance to Africa (Vandiver 2013a, 2013b). Finding a humanitarian mission less than macho and a civilian staff cumbersome, the Marines succeeded in shedding its softer side. AFRICOM now proudly boasts of having changed its focus to one more to its liking: combat-ready Marines ready to strike specific targets at a moment's notice. AFRICOM has forged relationships with most African leaders and is training Africans to fight rebels in their own countries. With its rapid-reaction, crisis-response units and its new drones and Ospreys (planes that can take off and land vertically), AFRICOM is now "military ready," and is zeroing in on groups that threaten U.S. access to Africa's resources. Currently, those groups are Islamic radicals, especially those in Nigeria and Mali, not surprisingly, oil-rich countries.

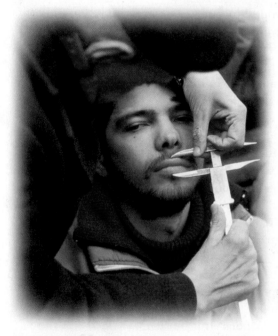

Despite the globe's vast social change, people all over the world continue to make race a fundamental distinction. Shown here is a Ukrainian being measured to see if he is really "full lipped" enough to be called a Tartar.

Theories and Processes of Social Change

15.2 Summarize theories of social change: social evolution, natural cycles, conflict over power and resources, and Ogburn's theory.

Social change has always fascinated theorists. Earlier in the text, we reviewed the theories of Karl Marx and Max Weber, which I just summarized. Of the many other attempts to explain why societies change, we will consider just four: the evolution of societies, natural cycles, conflict and power, and the pioneering views of sociologist William Ogburn.

Evolution from Lower to Higher

Evolutionary theories of how societies change are of two types, unilinear and multilinear. *Unilinear* theories assume that all societies follow the same path: Each evolves from simpler to more complex forms. This journey takes each society through uniform sequences (Barnes 1935). Of the many versions of this theory, the one proposed by Lewis Morgan

(1877) once dominated Western thought. Morgan said that all societies go through three stages: savagery, barbarism, and civilization. In Morgan's eyes, England, his own society, was the epitome of civilization. All other societies were destined to follow England's path.

Multilinear views of evolution replaced unilinear theories. Instead of assuming that all societies follow the same sequence, multilinear theorists proposed that different routes lead to the same stage of development. Although the paths all lead to industrialization, societies need not pass through the same sequence of stages on their journey (Sahlins and Service 1960; Lenski and Lenski 1987).

Central to all evolutionary theories, whether unilinear or multilinear, is the assumption of *cultural progress*. Tribal societies are assumed to have a primitive form of human culture. As these societies evolve, they reach a higher state—the supposedly advanced and superior form that characterizes the Western world. Growing appreciation of the rich diversity—and complexity—of tribal cultures discredited this idea. In addition, Western culture is now in crisis: poverty, racism, sexual assaults, unsafe streets, a fragile banking system, war, and terrorism. Consequently, the idea of cultural progress and Western culture as the apex of human civilization has been cast aside, and evolutionary theories have been rejected (Eder 1990; Smart 1990).

Natural Cycles

Cyclical theories attempt to account for the rise of entire civilizations. Why, for example, did Egypt, Greece, and Rome wield such power and influence, only to crest and then decline? Cyclical theories assume that civilizations are like organisms: They are born, enjoy an exuberant youth, come to maturity, and then decline as they reach old age. Finally, they die (Hughes 1962).

The cycle does exist, but why? Historian Arnold Toynbee (1946) said that each civilization faces challenges to its existence. Groups work out solutions to these challenges, as they must if they are to continue. But these solutions are not satisfactory to all. The ruling elite manages to keep the remaining oppositional forces under control, even though they "make trouble" now and then. At a civilization's peak, however, when it has become an empire, the ruling elite loses its capacity to keep the masses in line "by charm rather than by force." Gradually, the fabric of society rips apart. Force may hold the empire together for hundreds of years, but the civilization is doomed.

In a book that provoked widespread controversy, *The Decline of the West* (1926–1928), Oswald Spengler, a high school teacher in Germany, proposed that Western civilization had passed its peak and was in decline. Although the West succeeded in overcoming the crises provoked by Hitler and Mussolini, as Toynbee noted, civilizations don't end in sudden collapse. Because the decline can last hundreds of years, perhaps the crisis in Western civilization mentioned earlier (poverty, rape, murder, and so on) indicates that Spengler was right, and we are now in decline. If so, it appears that China is waiting on the horizon to seize global power and to forge a new civilization.

Conflict over Power and Resources

Long before Toynbee, Karl Marx identified a recurring process of social change. He said that each *thesis* (a current arrangement of power) contains its own *antithesis* (contradiction or opposition). A struggle develops between the thesis and its antithesis, leading to a *synthesis* (a new arrangement of power). This new social order, in turn, becomes a thesis that will be challenged by its own antithesis, and so on. Figure 15.1 gives a visual summary of this process.

According to Marx's view (called a **dialectical process of history**), each ruling group sows the seeds of its own destruction. Consider capitalism. Marx said that capitalism (the thesis) is built on the exploitation of workers (an antithesis, or built-in opposition).

dialectical process (of history) each arrangement of power (a thesis) contains contradictions (antitheses) which make the arrangement unstable and which must be resolved; the new arrangement of power (a synthesis) contains its own contradictions; this process of balancing and unbalancing continues throughout history as groups struggle for power and other resources

Figure 15.1 Marx's Model of Historical Change

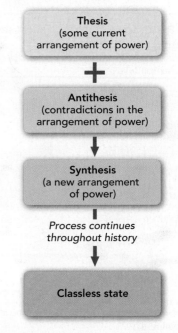

SOURCE: By the author.

With workers and owners on a collision course, the dialectical process will not stop until workers establish a classless state (the synthesis).

The analysis of G7/G8 in the previous section follows conflict theory. G7's current division of the globe's resources and markets is a thesis. Resentment on the part of have-not nations is an antithesis. The demand to redistribute power and resources will come from any Least Industrialized or Industrializing Nation that gains military power. With their nuclear weapons, China, India, and Pakistan fit this scenario. Russia, Iran, and North Korea present especially threatening antitheses, as do ISIS and the al-Qaedas and their desire to change the balance of power between the Middle East and the industrialized West.

Eventually, a new arrangement of power will form. Like the old, this new synthesis will contain its own antitheses, such as ethnic hostilities or leaders who feel their countries have been denied a fair share of resources. These contradictions will haunt the rearrangement of power, which at some point will be resolved into another synthesis. The process repeats, a continual cycle of thesis, antithesis, and synthesis.

Ogburn's Theory

Sociologist William Ogburn (1922/1950, 1961, 1964) proposed a theory of social change that is based largely on technology. As you can see from Table 15.2 below, he said that technology changes society by three processes: invention, discovery, and diffusion. Let's consider each.

INVENTION   Ogburn defined **invention** as a combining of existing elements and materials to form new ones. We usually think of inventions only as material items, such as computers, but there also are *social inventions*. We have considered many social inventions in this text, including democracy and citizenship (pages 345–346), capitalism (pages 361–362), socialism (page 362), bureaucracy (pages 141–146), the corporation (pages 146–147), and, in Chapter 10, gender equality. We saw how these social inventions had far-reaching consequences for people's lives. Material inventions can also affect social life deeply, and, in this chapter, we will examine how the automobile and the microchip have transformed society.

invention

the combining of existing elements and materials to form new ones; identified by William Ogburn as one of three processes of social change

Table 15.2 Ogburn's Processes of Social Change

Process of Change	What It Is	Examples	Social Changes
Invention	Combination of existing elements to form new ones	1. Cars 2. Microchip 3. Graphite composites	1. Urban sprawl and long commutes to work 2. Telecommuting and cyber warfare 3. New types of building construction
Discovery	New way of seeing some aspect of the world	1. Columbus—North America 2. Gold in California 3. DNA	1. Realignment of global power 2. Westward expansion of the U.S. 3. Positive identification of criminals
Diffusion	Spread of an invention or discovery	1. Airplanes 2. Money 3. Condom	1. Global tourism 2. Global trade 3. Smaller families

NOTE: For each example, there are many changes. For some of the changes ushered in by the automobile and microchip, see pages 492–497. You can also see that any particular change, such as global trade, depends not just on one item but also on several preceding changes.

SOURCE: By the author.

DISCOVERY Ogburn identified **discovery**, a new way of seeing reality, as a second process of change. The reality is already present, but people see it for the first time. An example is Columbus's "discovery" of North America, which had consequences so huge that they altered the course of human history. This example also illustrates another principle: A discovery brings extensive change only when it comes at the right time. Other groups, such as the Vikings, had already "discovered" North America in the sense of learning that a new land existed—obviously no discovery to the Native Americans already living there. Viking settlements disappeared into history, however, and Norse culture was untouched by the discovery.

DIFFUSION Ogburn stressed how **diffusion**, the spread of an invention or discovery from one area to another, can deeply affect people's lives. Consider an object as simple as the axe. When missionaries introduced steel axes to the Aborigines of Australia, it upset their whole society. Before this, the men controlled axe-making. They used a special stone that was available only in a remote region, and fathers passed axe-making skills on to their sons. Women had to request permission to use the axe. When steel axes became common, women also possessed them, and the men lost both status and power (Sharp 1995).

Diffusion also includes the spread of social inventions and ideas. As we saw in Chapter 11, the idea of citizenship changed political structures around the world. It swept away monarchs as an unquestioned source of authority. The idea of gender equality is now circling the globe. To those who live where this concept is taken for granted, it is surprising to think that opposition to withholding rights on the basis of someone's sex can be revolutionary. Like citizenship, gender equality is destined to transform human relationships and entire societies.

CULTURAL LAG Ogburn coined the term **cultural lag** to refer to how some elements of culture lag behind the changes that come from invention, discovery, and diffusion. Technology, he suggested, usually changes first, with culture lagging behind. In other words, we play catch-up with changing technology, adapting our customs and ways of life to meet its needs.

EVALUATION OF OGBURN'S THEORY Some find Ogburn's analysis too one-directional, saying that it makes technology the cause of almost all social change. They point out that people also take control over technology, developing or adapting the technology they need, and then selectively using it. You read about the Amish on pages 112–113, an example of people rejecting technology that they perceive as threatening to their culture.

Technology and social change are certainly not one-directional. Rather, they are like a two-way street: Just as technology stimulates social change, so social change stimulates technology. The Nazi armies that marched across Europe last century and the Japanese atrocities across the Pacific stimulated the United States to build the atomic bomb and led to nuclear power. Today, the growing number of elderly is spurring the development of new medical technologies, such as treatments for Alzheimer's disease. Similarly, ideas about people with disabilities are changing—that instead of being shunted aside, they should participate in society's mainstream. This, in turn, has triggered the development of new types of wheelchairs and prosthetic devices that allow people who cannot move their legs to play basketball, participate in the Paralympics, and even compete in downhill wheelchair races. The street is so two-way that this greater visibility and participation, in turn, is changing attitudes toward people with disabilities.

In fairness to Ogburn, we must note that he never said that technology is the only force for social change. Nor did he assert that people are passive pawns in the face of overwhelming technological forces. He did stress, though, that the material culture (technology) usually changes first, and the symbolic culture (people's ideas and ways of life) follows.

discovery

a new way of seeing reality; identified by William Ogburn as one of three processes of social change

diffusion

the spread of an invention or a discovery from one area to another; identified by William Ogburn as one of three processes of social change

cultural lag

Ogburn's term for human behavior lagging behind technological innovations

Diffusion refers not only to technology spreading from one group to another but also to the cultural diffusion of ideas. Women's rights, for example, taken for granted in the West, is a new idea in some parts of the world. This martial arts class for high school girls in Hyderabad, India, indicates that this new idea is reshaping views of the world. That women have the right to organize to defend themselves is a powerful transformation.

This direction still holds. Technology underlies the rapid changes that are engulfing us today. And we are still playing catch-up with technology, with the microchip especially, which is transforming society and, with it, our way of life.

How Technology Is Changing Our Lives

15.3 **Use the examples of the automobile and the microchip to illustrate the sociological significance of technology; include changes in ideology, norms, human relationships, education, work, business, war, and social inequality.**

Extending Human Abilities

postmodern society

another term for postindustrial society; a chief characteristic is the use of tools that extend human abilities to gather and analyze information, to communicate, and to travel

To understand what *technology* is, let's look at its three meanings. Its first meaning refers to *tools*, the items used to accomplish tasks. The tools can be as simple as a comb or as complicated as a computer. Technology's second meaning refers to the *procedures* necessary to produce tools: in this case, the ways we manufacture combs and computers. Technology's third meaning refers to the *skills* needed to use tools: in this case, the skills we need to "produce" an acceptable hairdo or to do research online.

No matter what tools, procedures, or skills we are talking about, technology always refers to *artificial means of extending human abilities*. Consider our opening vignette about the archeologists uncovering a hidden city in the jungle. The essence of the story is how greatly our new technology has extended human abilities.

All human groups make and use technology. They all have tools, procedures, and skills. The chief characteristic of technology in postindustrial societies (also called **postmodern societies**) is that it greatly extends our abilities to communicate, to travel, and to retrieve and analyze information. These *new technologies*, as they are called, extend our abilities beyond anything known in human history. We can now do what has never

Do you know what that large object in the center of the photo is? In the 1920s, 30s, and 40s, middle-class families would gather in the living room after dinner and listen to the radio. (It was a sit-down dinner served by the wife and assisted by the daughters.) Can you see how technology is influencing this 1940s family? How about yourself?

been done before: transplant organs from one human to another, communicate almost instantaneously anywhere on the globe, probe space, and travel vast distances quickly. And, as in our opening vignette, we can produce, store, retrieve, and analyze vast amounts of information, even if we must penetrate thick jungles to do so.

The Sociological Significance of Technology: How Technology Changes Social Life

Our journey to the future is going to have so many twists and turns that no one knows what our lives will be like. It is intriguing, however, to try to peer over the edge of the present to catch a glimpse of that future. But because this text is about sociology, we cannot lose sight of the sociological significance of technology—*how it changes our way of life*. When a technology is introduced into a society, it forces other parts of society to give way. In fact, *new technologies can reshape society*. Let's look at four ways that technology changes social life.

CHANGES IN PRODUCTION Technology changes how people organize themselves. In Chapter 11, we discussed how, before machine technology was developed, most people worked at home; the new power-driven machinery required them to leave their families and go to a place called a factory. In the first factories, each worker still made an entire item. Then it was discovered that production increased if each worker performed only a specific task. One worker would hammer on a single part or turn a certain number of bolts; then someone else would go to the item and do some other repetitive task on it; a third person would then take over; and so on. Henry Ford built on this innovation by developing the assembly line: Instead of workers moving to the parts, machines moved the parts to the workers. In addition, the parts were made interchangeable and easy to attach (Cwiek 2014).

CHANGES IN WORKER–OWNER RELATIONS Karl Marx noted that before factories came on the scene, workers owned their tools. This made them independent. If workers didn't like something, they would pack up their hammers and saws and leave. They would build a wagon or make a table for someone else. The factory brought fundamental change: The capitalists now owned the tools and machinery. This ownership transferred power to the capitalists. The workers had to submit, since desperate, unemployed workers were lined up, eager to take the place of anyone who left.

Marx also noted that workers who perform repetitive tasks on just a small part of a product do not feel connected to the finished product. No longer do they think of the product as "theirs." As Marx put it, workers become *alienated* from the product of their labor, an **alienation** that breeds dissatisfaction and unrest. With alienation, exploitation, and vast differences in power, basic antagonisms developed between workers and owners.

CHANGES IN IDEOLOGY The new technology that led to factories also led to a change in ideology. On one side came an ideology that praised capitalism. Making huge profits came to be viewed as a moral, even spiritual, endeavor. Profits benefited society—and pleased God as well.

On the other side were followers of Marx, who built ideologies in opposition to capitalism. In their view, profit comes from exploiting workers. Workers are the true owners of society's resources, and it is their labor that produces profits. This exploitation, Marx believed, would bring on a workers' revolution: One day, deciding that they had enough, workers would unite, violently take over the means of production, and establish a workers' state.

CHANGES IN CONSPICUOUS CONSUMPTION Just as ideology follows technology, so does conspicuous consumption. If technology is limited to clubbing animals, then animal skins are valued. No doubt primitive men and women who wore the skins of some especially unusual or dangerous animal walked with their heads held high—while their neighbors, wearing the same old sheepskins, looked on in envy. With technological change, Americans make certain that their clothing and accessories (sunglasses, handbags, and watches) have trendy labels prominently displayed. They also proudly

alienation

Marx's term for workers' lack of connection to the product of their labor; caused by workers being assigned repetitive tasks on a small part of a product—this leads to a sense of powerlessness and normlessness; others use the term in the general sense of not feeling a part of something display their cars, boats, and second homes. In short, while envy and pride may be basic to human nature, the particular material display depends on the state of technology.

CHANGES IN FAMILY RELATIONSHIPS Technology also changes how people relate to one another. When men left home to work in factories, they became isolated from much of the everyday lives of their families. One consequence of becoming relative strangers to their wives and children was more divorce. As more women were drawn from the home to offices and factories, there were similar consequences—greater isolation from husbands and children and even more fragile marriages. A counter-trend is now under way, as the newer technology allows millions of people to work at home. One consequence may be a strengthening of families and a reduction of divorce.

To get a better idea of how technology shapes our way of life, let's consider the changes ushered in by the automobile and the computer.

When Old Technology Was New: The Impact of the Automobile

About 100 years ago, the automobile was a new technology. You might be surprised at some of the ways in which this invention shaped U.S. society. Let's look at them.

DISPLACEMENT OF EXISTING TECHNOLOGY In a process that began in earnest when Henry Ford began to mass-produce the Model T in 1908, the automobile gradually pushed aside the old technology. People found automobiles to be cleaner, more reliable, and less expensive than horses. People even thought that cars would lower their taxes, since no longer would the public have to pay to clean up the tons of horse manure that accumulated on city streets (Flink 1990). Humorous as it sounds now, they also thought that automobiles would eliminate the cities' parking problems, since an automobile took up only half as much space as a horse and buggy.

EFFECTS ON CITIES The automobile stimulated suburbanization (Kopecky and Suen 2010). By the 1920s, Americans had begun to leave the city. They found that they could live in outlying areas where housing was more affordable and commute to jobs in the city. Eventually, this exodus to the suburbs produced urban sprawl and reduced the cities' tax base. As discussed in Chapter 14, suburbanization contributed to many of the problems that U.S. cities experience today.

In the photo on the left, Henry Ford proudly displays his 1905 car, the latest in automobile technology. As is apparent, especially from the spokes on the car's wheels, new technology builds on existing technology. At the time this photo was taken, who could have imagined that this vehicle would transform society? The photo on the right is of BMW's H2R, which runs on liquid hydrogen.

CHANGES IN ARCHITECTURE   The automobile's effects on commercial architecture are easy to see—from the huge parking lots that loop around shopping malls to the drive-up windows at banks and fast-food restaurants. Not so apparent is how the automobile altered the architecture of U.S. homes (Flink 1990). Before cars came on the scene, each home had a stable in the back where the family kept its horse and buggy. At first, people parked their cars there, as it required no change in architecture.

Then, in three steps, home architecture changed. First, new homes were built with a detached garage. It was located, like the stable, at the back of the home. As the automobile became more essential to the U.S. family, the garage was incorporated into the home. It was moved from the backyard to the side of the house, where it was connected by a breezeway. In the final step, the breezeway was removed, and the garage was integrated into the home, letting people enter their automobiles without going outside.

CHANGED COURTSHIP CUSTOMS AND SEXUAL NORMS   By the 1920s, the automobile was used extensively for dating. This removed young people from the watchful eye of parents and undermined parental authority. The police began to receive complaints about "night riders" who parked their cars along country lanes, "doused their lights, and indulged in orgies" (Brilliant 1964). Automobiles became so popular for courtship that by the 1960s, about 40 percent of marriage proposals took place in them (Flink 1990).

In 1925, Jewett introduced cars with a foldout bed, as did Nash in 1937. The Nash version became known as "the young man's model" (Flink 1990). Mobile lovemaking has declined since the 1970s, not because there is less premarital sex but because the change in sexual norms has made bedrooms easily accessible to the unmarried.

EFFECTS ON WOMEN'S ROLES   The automobile also lies at the heart of the change in women's roles. To see how, we first need to get a picture of what a woman's life was like before the automobile. Historian James Flink (1990) described it this way:

> *Until the automobile revolution, in upper-middle-class households groceries were either ordered by phone and delivered to the door or picked up by domestic servants or the husband on his way home from work. Iceboxes provided only very limited space for the storage of perishable foods, so shopping at markets within walking distance of the home was a daily chore. The garden provided vegetables and fruits in season, which were home-canned for winter consumption. Bread, cakes, cookies, and pies were home-baked. Wardrobes contained many home-sewn garments.*
>
> *Mother supervised the household help and worked alongside them preparing meals, washing and ironing, and housecleaning. In her spare time she mended clothes, did decorative needlework, puttered in her flower garden, and pampered a brood of children. Generally, she made few family decisions and few forays alone outside the yard. She had little knowledge of family finances and the family budget. The role of the lower-middle-class housewife differed primarily in that far less of the household work was done by hired help, so that she was less a manager of other people's work, more herself a maid-of-all-work around the house.*

Because automobiles required skill to operate rather than strength, women were able to drive as well as men. This new mobility freed women physically from the narrow confines of the home. As Flink (1990) observed, the automobile changed women "from producers of food and clothing into consumers of national-brand canned goods, prepared foods, and ready-made clothes. The automobile permitted shopping at self-serve supermarkets outside the neighborhood and in combination with the electric refrigerator made buying food a weekly rather than a daily activity." When women began to do the shopping, they gained greater control over the family budget, and, as their horizons extended beyond the confines of the home, they also learned different views of life.

IN SUM   The automobile helped transform society, including views of courtship and sexuality. It had a special impact on a woman's role at home, including the relationship with her husband. It altered women's attitudes as it transformed their opportunities and stimulated them to participate in areas of social life not connected with the home.

From this 1946 photo, you can see how computers have changed. This is the ENIAC, the world's first computer, which weighed 30 tons, was 8 feet high, 3 feet deep, and 100 feet long. Most cell phones have more computing power than this monstrosity.

This robot allows a child to participate in class even though the child is ill and in the hospital. The child can listen to the teacher, follow the teacher's movements by controlling the robot's eyes, and can even raise "his" or "her" hand and ask questions.

No one attributes such fundamental changes in relationships and values solely to the automobile, of course. Many historical events and other technological changes occurred during this same period, each making its own contribution to social change. Even this brief overview of the social effects of the automobile, however, illustrates that technology is much more than just a tool: It exerts profound influence on social life.

The New Technology: The Microchip and Social Life

Ten years ago, landlines were so limited in Mongolia that it was difficult to make a telephone call. Then came the technological leap. Investing heavily in information technology, the country now has an extensive 3G network. Most homes in the capitol city now have Internet connections, and most Mongols have cell phones. Even the nomads tending their sheep on the remote steppe are using cell phones. (Pappano 2013)

With technology changing so rapidly, the future greets us with unexpected twists and turns. Although we don't know where those twists and turns will lead us, it is intriguing to peer over the edge of the present to catch a glimpse of how our future is being shaped.

Let's do this by focusing on the microchip. We will begin with the effects of this marvelous device on education, business, and the waging of war. We'll then consider the chip's impact on social inequality.

COMPUTERS IN EDUCATION   Because of computers, students can take courses in Russian, German, and Spanish—even when their schools have no teachers who speak these languages. If their school also lacks sociology instructors, they can still study the sociology of gender, race, social class, or even sex, and sports. (The comma is important. It isn't sex and sports. That course isn't offered—yet.)

We've barely begun to harness the power of computers, but I imagine that the day will come when you will be able to key in the terms *social interaction* and *gender*, select your preference of historical period, geographical site, age, and ethnic group—and the computer will spew out text, maps, moving images, and sounds. You will be able to compare sexual discrimination in the military in 1985 and today or the price of marijuana in Los Angeles and New Orleans. If you wish, the computer will give you a test—geared to the level of difficulty you choose—so that you can check your mastery of the material.

Distance learning, courses taught to students who are not physically present with their instructor, will integrate students around the world. Using apps and their laptop cameras, everyone in the class will be able to see everyone else, even though the students live in different countries. Imagine this—and likely it soon will be a reality: Your fellow students in a course on human culture will be living in Thailand, South Africa, Latvia, Egypt, China, and Australia. With zero-cost conference calls and e-mail and file sharing, you will compare your countries' customs on eating, dating, marriage, family, or burial— whatever is of interest to you. You will then write a term paper in which you apply the theories in the text to what you have learned from your fellow students. With a flourish and a smile, you then e-mail the paper to your instructor. (Okay, forget the flourish and smile, but from this, you can catch a glimpse of the future.)

COMPUTERS IN BUSINESS AND FINANCE   The advanced technology of businesses used to consist of cash registers and adding machines. Connections to the outside world were managed by telephone. Today, businesses are electronically "wired" to suppliers, salespeople, and clients around the country—and around the world. Computers track sales of items, tabulate inventory, and set in motion the process of reordering and restocking. Sales reports alert managers to changes in their customers' tastes or preferences. For retail giants like Wal-Mart, the computer reports regional changes in preferences of products.

National borders are rendered meaningless as computers instantaneously transfer billions of dollars from one country to another. No "cash" changes hands in these transactions. The money consists of digits in computer memory banks. In the same day, digitized money can be transferred from the United States to Switzerland, from there to the Grand Cayman Islands, and then to the Isle of Man. Its zigzag, encrypted path around the globe leaves few traces for sleuths to follow. "Where's my share?" governments around the world are grumbling, as they consider how to control—and tax—this new technology.

COMPUTERS IN INTERNATIONAL CONFLICT   Computers are also having a major impact on war. Many of the changes, fortunately for us, are still theoretical. When the application arrives, the loss of lives will be horrendous. In the following Thinking Critically section we'll look at cyber war. After that, we'll consider drones and warfare in space.

Flying bicycles? This bike actually flies—thanks to six horizontal propellers and a battery-powered motor. Changing technology changes not only the way we do things, such as travel, but also the way we think about life and the self and the way we relate to others.

Thinking Critically

Cyberwar and Cyber Defense

Iran's nuclear enrichment program had progressed quite well. But as five thousand centrifuges were whirring away, Iranian scientists stared in disbelief. Although their computers reported that everything was fine, the centrifuges suddenly sped up and slowed down, ripping their delicate parts into shreds.

Iran had been hit by the Stuxnet worm, a malware that the United States and Israel had surreptitiously entered into Iran's computer codes. Iran's goal of producing material for a nuclear bomb had been set back by months, perhaps by years. (Sanger 2012)

Every country in conflict with another looks for an edge. The computer's marvelous strength—its capacity to store and retrieve information and to execute commands—can be turned into a weakness, an Achilles heel that can bring down the powerful.

To turn strength into weakness brings both delight and fear to generals around the world. Their delight comes from the mouthwatering anticipation that they might use this capacity against their enemies. Their fear? That their enemies might turn this capacity against them.

Cyber weapons offer intriguing potential for warfare. Missiles that have been ordered airborne to strike enemy targets

This military command post is in South Korea, with both U.S. and South Korean personnel. South Korea and North Korea accuse one another of attacking the other's communication systems. Each accusation is likely true.

can be made to sit in their silos like wounded birds taking refuge in their nests. If an enemy were to disrupt vital communications, they could transform computer screens into windows of darkness. Or they could fill military files with false information. Easy attack could follow. This fear pervades the military—on both sides, wherever those fluid sides line up today.

This is not some far-off future. As the Iranians discovered, cyber war has begun. The United States, too, is a victim with thousands of attacks launched against its military computers. The attacker? Just round up the usual suspects, China and Russia. The purpose of the attacks seems to be to find chinks in the armor, the spots where malicious code can be installed unawares—like Stuxnet to be unleashed at some designated moment. The targets extend beyond the military: a nation's electrical grid, its banking system, stock exchange, oil and gas pipelines, air traffic control systems, and Internet and cell phone communications.

The United States is spending billions of dollars preparing for cyber war. The U.S. Air Force runs an Office for Cyberspace Operations, while the Navy operates an aptly named Center for Information Dominance. An overarching group, the U.S. Cyber Command, has the assignment to integrate the cyber warfare capacities of the military with those of the National Security Agency (Barnes 2012; Sanger and Shanker 2013).

China has attempted to turn the tables, accusing the United States of tens of thousands of cyber attacks against its military Web sites (Mozur 2013). It is likely that this accusation is correct. Like China, the United States is breaking into the computers of other nations with the goal of "destroying, disrupting, degrading, deceiving, and corrupting" the ability of potential enemies (Gjelten 2013).

The games have begun. The outcome, unfortunately, might not resemble a game.

For Your Consideration

→ Do you think the United States should insert dormant malicious codes in Russia's and China's military and central civilian computers, so it can unleash them during some future conflict?

→ If such a code were discovered, what do you think the consequences might be?

At this point, the skirmishes are digital and bloodless, but this can change in a moment. In the Sociology and the New Technology box on the next page, we will look at how the microchip is bringing space weapons, destined as an essential part of future war.

Cyberspace and Social Inequality

We've already stepped into the future. The Net gives us access to digitized libraries. We utilize software that sifts, sorts, and transmits text, photos, sound, and video. We zap messages, images, and digitized money to people on the other side of the globe—or even in our own homes, dorm, or office. Our world has become linked by almost instantaneous communications, with information readily accessible around the globe. Few places can still be called "remote."

The offspring of the microchip—from computers to cell phones—offer access to vast information and efficiency of communication, manufacturing, and transportation. Will this fundamental change bring greater equality to the world's nations? This photo was taken in the Philippines.

This new technology carries severe implications for national and global stratification. On the national level, computer technology could perpetuate our current inequalities: We could end up with information have-nots, people cut off from the flow of information on which prosperity depends. Or this technology could provide an opportunity for the inner city and the rural areas to break out of poverty. On the global level, the question is similar, but on a grander scale, taking us to one of the more profound issues of this century: Will unequal access to advanced technology destine the Least Industrialized Nations to a perpetual pauper status? Or will access to this new technology be their passport to affluence?

IN SUM As technology wraps itself around us, transforming society, culture, and our everyday lives, we confront four primary issues: What type of future will technology lead us to? Will technology liberate us or make us slaves of Big Brother? Will the new technology perpetuate or alleviate social inequalities on both national and global levels? Finally, and perhaps most ominously, will the technology that is transforming war and which the United States is using to wage constant war "over there" come back to haunt us in our own land?

Sociology and the New Technology

The Coming Star Wars

Star Wars is on its way.

The Predator is an unmanned plane that flies thousands of feet above the ground. Operators at a base search its streaming video. When they identify what they call "the kill shot," they press a button. At this signal, the Predator beams a laser onto the target and launches guided bombs. The enemy sees neither the Predator nor the laser. Perhaps, however, an instant before they are blown to bits, they do hear the sound of the incoming bomb (Barry 2001).

The Pentagon plans to "weaponize" space far beyond the Predator. The Pentagon's X-47B is a "space plane:" It has an airplane's agility and a spacecraft's capacity to travel 5 miles per second in space (Cooper 2010). The Pentagon is also building its own Internet, the Global Information Grid (GIG). The goal of GIG is to encircle the globe and give the Pentagon a "God's eye view" of every enemy everywhere (Weiner 2004). An arsenal of space weapons is ready: microsatellites the size of a suitcase that can pull alongside enemy satellites and, using microwave guns, fry their electronics; a laser whose beam will bounce off a mirror in space, making the night battlefield visible to ground soldiers who are wearing special goggles; pyrotechnic electromagnetic pulsers; holographic decoys; oxygen suckers—and whatever else the feverish imaginations of military planners can devise.

The Air Force has nicknamed one of its space programs "Rods from God," tungsten cylinders to be hurled from space at targets on the ground. Striking at speeds of 7,000 miles an hour, the rods would have the force of a small nuclear weapon. In another program, radio waves would be directed to targets on Earth. As the Air Force explains it, the power of the radio waves could be "just a tap on the shoulder—or they could turn you into toast" (Weiner 2005).

But what happens when enemy, or even rival, nations develop similar capacities—or even greater ones? We are beginning to see an ominous transition in international technological expertise. Already there is the Pterodactyl, China's answer to the Predator. China has advanced its technology to the point that its unmanned aerial vehicles (UAVs) have begun to rival those of the United States

This pilotless drone, the Navy's X-47B, is being refueled in midair from a tanker plane.

(Page 2010; Wall 2010). China has even begun to flaunt its space weapons in the face of the Pentagon, a not-too-subtle warning not to mess with China as its leaders expand their territorial ambitions.

Weapons are made to be used—despite the constant polite rhetoric about their defensive purposes. On both sides are itchy trigger fingers, and now that China is becoming an ominous threat to U.S. space superiority, the Pentagon faces a new challenge. How will it be able to contain China's political ambitions if Star Wars looms?

For Your Consideration

→ Do you think we should militarize space?

→ What do you think of this comment, made to Congress by the head of the U.S. Air Force Space Command? "We must establish and maintain space superiority. It's the American way of fighting" (Weiner 2005).

→ Is it rational for the United States to think that it can always maintain technological superiority? What happens if it cannot?

The Growth Machine versus the Earth

15.4   Explain how industrialization is related to environmental problems; contrast the environmental movement and environmental sociology; discuss the goal of harmony.

After a frustrating struggle of twenty years, Russian environmentalists finally won a court order to stop Baikalsk Paper Mill from dumping its wastes into Lake Baikal. When the mill filed for bankruptcy, Vladimir Putin, the prime minister of Russia, boarded

a minisub and said, "I'll see if the lake has been damaged." At the bottom of Lake Baikal, Putin said, "It's clean. I can see the bottom." He then told Oleg Deripaska, the major owner of the paper mill, "You can dump your wastes in the lake." (Boudreaux 2010)

Politicians are usually more subtle than this, but, befitting his power and position, Putin doesn't have to be. He can crown himself an environmental expert and give personal permission to pollute. Although the specifics differ, in country after country, similar battles are being waged. While environmentalists struggle for a clean Earth, politicians fight for jobs and votes—and while doing so, some line the pockets of their friends and their own as well.

THE GLOBALIZATION OF CAPITALISM AND THE RACE FOR ECONOMIC GROWTH   Like drivers and cars spinning around a NASCAR racetrack, we are in the midst of a global economic race that threatens to destroy the Earth. The racetrack is the Earth, and the cars and drivers are the Earth's nations. At the head of the pack are the Most Industrialized Nations. To maintain their lead—and cheered on by their sponsors, the multinational corporations—they continue to push for economic growth. Without an annual increase in production, the economic engines of the Most Industrialized Nations falter, sputtering into recession or depression. Behind them, furiously trying to catch up, are the Industrializing Nations. To develop their economies, China and the others strive for even larger percentage growth. Meanwhile, the Least Industrialized Nations, lagging farther behind and envious of the others, do their best to rev up their economic engines.

A SUSTAINABLE ENVIRONMENT   Many people are convinced that the Earth cannot withstand such an onslaught. Global economic production creates global pollution; faster-paced production that feeds the globalization of capitalism, means faster-paced destruction of our environment. In this relentless pursuit of economic development, many animal species have been destroyed. Others, hanging by a claw or a wounded wing, are on the verge of extinction. If the goal is a **sustainable environment**, a world system in which we use our physical environment to meet our needs without destroying humanity's future, we cannot continue to trash the Earth. In short, the ecological message is incompatible with an economic message that implies it is okay to rape the Earth if it makes someone rich.

Before looking at the social movement that has emerged around this issue, let's examine some major environmental problems.

Environmental Problems and Industrialization

Although even tribal groups produced pollution, the frontal assault on the natural environment did not begin in earnest until nations industrialized. Industrialization was equated with progress and prosperity. For the Most Industrialized Nations, the slogan has been "Growth at any cost."

TOXIC WASTES   Industrial growth did come, but at a high cost. Despite their harm to the environment and the dangers they pose to people's health, much toxic waste has been dumped onto the land, into the oceans, and, with the occasional permission of Putin and other politicians, into our lakes. Formerly pristine streams have been turned into

sustainable environment a world system that takes into account the limits of the environment, produces enough material goods for everyone's needs, and leaves a heritage of a sound environment for the next generation

Sumatran Tiger
Fewer than 400, Indonesia

Texas Ocelot
Fewer than 250, southern United States, northern Mexico

Mountain Bongo
About 50, Kenya

Gaur
About 36,000, Southeast Asia

Figure 15.2 The Worst Hazardous Waste Sites

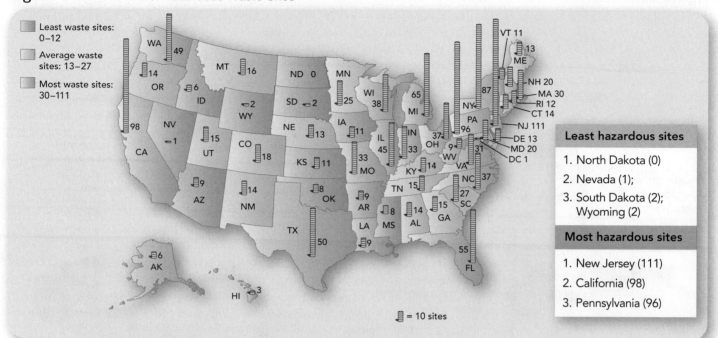

Least waste sites: 0–12
Average waste sites: 13–27
Most waste sites: 30–111

WA 49
OR 14
ID 6
MT 16
ND 0
MN 25
WI 38
MI 65
VT 11
ME 13
NH 20
MA 30
RI 12
CT 14
NY 87
PA 96
NJ 111
DE 13
MD 20
DC 1
NV 1
CA 98
UT 15
WY 2
CO 18
NE 13
IA 11
IL 45
IN 33
OH 37
WV 9
VA 31
AZ 9
NM 14
KS 11
MO 33
KY 14
TN 15
NC 37
SC 27
TX 50
OK 8
AR 9
LA 9
MS 8
AL 14
GA 15
FL 55
AK 6
HI 3
SD 2

= 10 sites

Least hazardous sites

1. North Dakota (0)
2. Nevada (1);
3. South Dakota (2); Wyoming (2)

Most hazardous sites

1. New Jersey (111)
2. California (98)
3. Pennsylvania (96)

SOURCE: By the author. Based on Environmental Protection Agency 2013.

polluted sewers. The disease-ridden water supply of some cities is unfit to drink. The Social Map above shows the locations of the worst hazardous waste sites in the United States. Keep in mind that these are just the worst. There are thousands of others.

Nuclear power plants are a special problem. They produce wastes that remain lethal for thousands of years. We simply don't know what to do with these piles of deadly garbage. In addition, these nuclear factories, supposedly built with redundant safety features, are vulnerable. Certainly the nuclear catastrophe at Fukushima, Japan, which continues to spew radiation, is mute testimony to nuclear folly.

We certainly can't lay the cause of our polluted Earth solely at the feet of the Most Industrialized Nations. The Industrializing Nations also do their share, with China the most striking offender. Here is a shocking figure: Of the world's ten most polluted cities, *seven* are in China (Staedter 2013). Here is another: With *nine thousand* chemical plants lining its banks, China's major waterway, the Yangtze River, has been turned into an industrial sewer (Zakaria 2008). Now that China has secured its place in the industrialized world, its leaders are placing more emphasis on reducing pollution (Chen 2015). However, the harm done to our planet is incalculable.

With limited space to address this issue, let's focus on fossil fuels, the energy shortage, and the rain forests.

FOSSIL FUELS AND CLIMATE CHANGE Burning fossil fuels to run motorized vehicles, factories, and power plants has been especially harmful to our Earth. Figure 15.3 on the next page illustrates how burning fossil fuels produces **acid rain** that kills animal and plant life. The harm is so extensive that fish can no longer survive in some lakes in Canada and the northeastern United States.

Global warming is producing many problems for Earth's inhabitants, but with the limited space we have, in the Thinking Critically section on the next page, we will consider just one of them.

acid rain

rain containing sulfuric and nitric acids (burning fossil fuels releases sulfur dioxide and nitrogen oxide that become sulfuric and nitric acids when they react with moisture in the air)

Pollution in the Industrializing Nations has become a major problem. The air in Beijing is hazardous to health.

Figure 15.3 Acid Rain

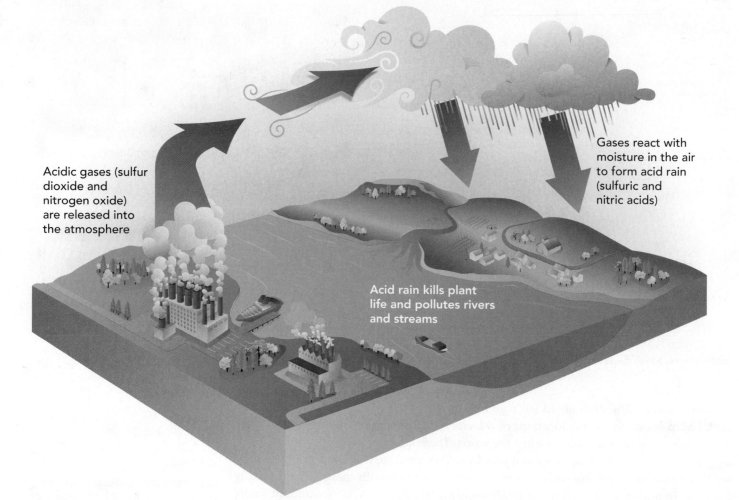

Acidic gases (sulfur dioxide and nitrogen oxide) are released into the atmosphere

Gases react with moisture in the air to form acid rain (sulfuric and nitric acids)

Acid rain kills plant life and pollutes rivers and streams

SOURCE: By the author.

Thinking Critically

Climate Controversy, the Island Nations, and You

The Problem The case seems clear-cut. As the United Nations Panel on Climate Change (2014) reported, food shortages, mass flooding, and mass extinction of plants and animals are on their way. Global warming is melting the world's glaciers. The ice caps at the North and South Poles store such incredible amounts of water that if they melt, the level of the world's oceans will rise by several feet. Low-lying areas in the United States, such as the bayous around New Orleans and Mississippi, will go under water. Barrier islands off the coast of the United States will disappear. The oceans will reclaim Florida's Everglades.

Then there are the world's island nations. The highest point on some of these nations is just six feet higher than the level of the ocean. *All* of their land mass will end up below water.

What are these nations going to do? Their residents cannot live in wet suits, so to survive, they have to come up with something. But so far, nothing, even though their survival is at stake. The Maldives, an island nation in the Indian Ocean, did come up with a cute tongue-in-cheek slogan to promote tourism: "Come see us while we're still here" (Dickey and Rogers 2002).

No one has taken the Maldives' ministry of tourism suggestion seriously, so the Maldives aren't using this slogan. But it does point to the severity of the problem. Since no one other than a few divers and surfers wants to wear those wet suits, just what will these island nations do?

The Controversy Not all climate scientists agree on global warming. As a top climate scientist pointed out, scientific consensus is limited to two matters: The world's climate is changing, and human activity is part of this change (Koonin 2014). Beyond these two points, there is little consensus. Climate scientists use computer models to predict the future.

Maldives

Nature, however, has produced inconsistencies that are confounding these models. During the last part of the 1900s, for example, carbon dioxide increased and so did global warming. This is what the models predict. But during the past sixteen years when carbon dioxide increased even more, the rate of warming slowed. Then another event has climate scientists shaking their collective heads: The polar ice caps at the Arctic are shrinking, but the polar ice caps at the Antarctic are growing. These ice caps have even reached record thickness.

For Your Consideration

If only life were as simple as we would like it to be—not just in our finances and relationships, but also in what science knows and how this knowledge can guide us in making life choices. But to our dismay, life is seldom as simple or as clear as we would like it to be. When it comes to global climate change, it is so much simpler to skip over inconsistencies and agree that unless we take action now, doomsday is just around the corner. Climate scientists want closure, too, and facing inconsistencies, they have taken sides and begun to hurl insults at one another. Eventually, however, all the facts will be in and the inconsistencies explained.

→ So what do you think about this?

THE ENERGY SHORTAGE AND INTERNAL COMBUSTION ENGINES   If you ever read about an energy shortage, you can be sure that what you read is false. There is no energy shortage, nor can there ever be. We have access to unlimited low-cost power that can help to raise the living standards of humans across the globe. The Sun, for example, produces more energy than humanity could ever use. Boundless energy is also available from the tides and the winds. In some cases, we need better technology to harness these sources of energy; in others, we need only apply the technology we already have.

Burning fossil fuels in internal combustion engines is the main source of pollution in the Most Industrialized Nations. Changes are on the way: car and truck engines that burn natural gas, a cleaner and lower-priced fossil fuel; battery powered cars; and cars powered by hydrogen fuel cells that use a chemical reaction to produce electricity. With hydrogen fuel cells converting hydrogen into electricity, water, not carbon monoxide, comes out of a car's exhaust pipe (Ramsey 2014).

THE RAIN FORESTS   Of special concern are the world's rain forests. Although these forests cover just 6 percent of the Earth's land area, they are home to *one-half* of all the Earth's plant and animal species (Frommer 2007). Despite knowing the rain forests' essential role for humanity's welfare, we seem bent on destroying them for the sake of timber and farms. In the process, we extinguish plant and animal species, perhaps thousands a year. As biologists remind us, once a species is lost, it is gone forever.

As the rain forests disappear, so do the Indian tribes who live in them. With their extinction goes their knowledge of the environment, the topic of the Cultural Diversity box on the next page. Like Esau who traded his birthright for a bowl of porridge, we are exchanging our future for lumber, farms, and pastures.

The Environmental Movement

Concern about environmental problems has touched such a nerve that it has produced a worldwide social movement. In Europe, *green parties*, political groups whose central concern is the environment, have become a force for change. Germany's Green Party, for example, holds seats in the national legislature and negotiates on major issues (Thomas 2013). In the United States, in contrast, green parties have had little success.

Cultural Diversity around the World

The Rain Forests: Lost Tribes, Lost Knowledge

In the past hundred years, 90 of Brazil's 270 Indian tribes have disappeared. Other tribes have moved to villages as ranchers and gold miners have taken over their lands. Tribal knowledge is lost as a tribe's members adapt to village life.

Contrary to some stereotypes, tribal groups are not ignorant people who barely survive. On the contrary, these groups have developed intricate forms of social organization and possess knowledge that has accumulated over thousands of years (Briand 2013). The Kayapo Indians, for example, who belong to one of the Amazon's endangered tribes, use 250 types of wild fruit and hundreds of nut and tuber species. They cultivate thirteen types of bananas, eleven kinds of manioc (cassava), sixteen strains of sweet potato, and seventeen kinds of yams. Many of these varieties are unknown to non-Indians. The Kayapo also use thousands of plants as medicine, one of which contains a drug that is effective against intestinal parasites.

Western scientists used to dismiss tribal knowledge as superstitious and worthless. Some still do, but others have come to realize that to lose tribes is to lose valuable knowledge.

> *In the Central African Republic, a man whose chest was being eaten away by an amoeboid infection lay dying because the microbes did not respond to drugs. Out of desperation, the Roman Catholic nuns who were treating him sought the advice of a native doctor. He applied crushed termites to the open wounds. To the amazement of the nuns, the man made a remarkable recovery.*

A member of the Quintana Roo in Yucatan, Mexico. The way of life of the world's few remaining rain forest tribes is threatened.

The disappearance of the rain forests means the destruction of plant species that may have healing properties. I don't mean to imply that these tribes have medicine superior to ours, just that we can learn from their experience with nature.

Some of the discoveries from the rain forests have been astounding. The needles from a Himalayan tree in India contain taxol, a drug that is effective against ovarian and breast cancer. A flower from Madagascar is used in the treatment of leukemia. A frog in Peru produces a painkiller that is more powerful, but less addictive, than morphine (Wolfensohn and Fuller 1998). A researcher noticed that the Mapuche people in the rain forests of Chile were using an avocado plant to heal wounds. Tests showed that this plant overcomes the bacteria's resistance, allowing antibiotics to work ("Rain Forest Plant" 2012).

On average, one tribe of Amazonian Indians has been lost each year for the past century—because of violence, greed for their lands, and exposure to infectious diseases against which these people have little resistance. Ethnocentrism underlies some of this assault. Perhaps the extreme is represented by the cattle ranchers in Colombia who killed eighteen Cueva Indians. The cattle ranchers were perplexed when they were put on trial for murder. They asked why they should be charged with a crime, since everyone knew that the Cuevas were animals, not people. They pointed out that there was even a verb in Colombian Spanish, *cuevar*, which means "to hunt Cueva Indians." So what was their crime, they asked? The jury found them not guilty because of "cultural ignorance."

SOURCES: Durning 1990; Gorman 1991; Linden 1991; Stipp 1992; Nabhan 1998; Simons 2006; Okpiliya 2014.

For Your Consideration

→ What do you think we can do to stop the destruction of the rain forests?

(Go back to page 501)

One concern of the environmental movement in the United States is **environmental injustice**, minorities and the poor being the ones who suffer the most from the effects of pollution (Lerner 2010). Industries locate where land is cheaper, which, as you know, is *not* where the wealthy live. Nor will the rich allow factories to spew pollution near their homes. As a result, pollution is more common in low-income communities. Sociologists have studied, formed, and joined *environmental justice* groups that fight to close polluting plants and block construction of polluting industries. As with the defeat at Lake Baikal, with Putin a friend of the mill owner, this often pits environmentalists against politicians and those connected to them.

Like the members of last century's civil rights movement, environmentalists are certain that they stand for what is right and just. Most activists seek quiet solutions in politics, education, and legislation. Despairing that pollution continues, that the rain forests are still being cleared, and that species continue to become extinct, others are convinced that the planet is doomed unless we take immediate action. This conviction motivates some to choose a more radical course, to use extreme tactics to try to arouse indignation among the public and to force the government to act. Such activists are featured in the following Thinking Critically section.

environmental injustice

refers to how minorities and the poor are harmed the most by environmental pollution

eco-sabotage

actions taken to sabotage the efforts of people who are thought to be legally harming the environment

Thinking Critically

Eco-sabotage

Chaining oneself to a giant Douglas fir that is slated for cutting, tearing down power lines and ripping up survey stakes, driving spikes into redwood trees, sinking whaling vessels, and torching SUVs and Hummers—are these the acts of dangerous punks who have little understanding of the needs of modern society? Or are they the efforts of brave men and women who are willing to put their freedom, and even their lives, on the line on behalf of Earth itself?

To understand why **eco-sabotage**—actions taken to sabotage the efforts of people who are thought to be legally harming the environment— is taking place, consider the Medicine Tree, a 3,000-year-old redwood in the Sally Bell Grove near the northern California coast. Georgia Pacific, a lumber company, was going to cut down the Medicine Tree, the oldest and largest of the region's redwoods, which grows in a sacred site of the Sinkyone Indians. Members of Earth First! chained themselves to the tree. After they were arrested, the sawing began. Other protesters jumped over the police-lined barricade and stood defiantly in the path of men wielding axes and chain saws. A logger swung an axe and barely missed a demonstrator. At that moment, the sheriff radioed a restraining order, and the cutting stopped.

How many 3,000-year-old trees remain on our planet? Does our desire for fences and picnic tables for backyard barbecues justify cutting them down? Issues like these—as well as the slaughter of seals and whales, the destruction of

Environmental activism is going global. These eco-warriors, as they are called, have chained themselves to a cottonwood tree in Stuttgart, Germany. They oppose the construction of a railway terminal that will destroy this tree.

the rain forests, and the drowning of dolphins in mile-long drift nets—spawned Earth First! and other organizations devoted to preserving the environment, such as Greenpeace, the Rainforest Action Network, the Ruckus Society, and the Sea Shepherds.

"We feel like there are insane people who are consciously destroying our environment, and we are compelled to fight back," explains a member of one of the militant groups. "No compromise in defense of Mother Earth!" says another. "With famine and death approaching, we're in the early stages of World War III," adds another.

We can't paint all radical environmentalists with the same brush. They are united neither on tactics nor on goals. Most envision a simpler lifestyle that will consume less energy and reduce pressure on the Earth's resources. Some try to stop specific activities, such as the killing of whales. For others, the goal is to destroy all nuclear weapons and dismantle nuclear power plants. Some would like to see everyone become a vegetarian. Still others want the Earth's population to drop to 1 billion, roughly what it was in 1800. Some even want humans to return to hunting and gathering societies. These groups are so splintered that Dave Foreman—the founder of Earth First!—quit his own organization when it became too confrontational for his taste.

Radical groups have had some successes. They have brought a halt to the killing of dolphins off Japan's Iki Island, achieved a ban on whaling, established trash/recycling programs, and saved hundreds of thousands of acres of trees, including the Medicine Tree.

SOURCES: Eder 1990; Foote 1990; Parfit 1990; Reed and Benet 1990; Knickerbocker 2003; Gunther 2004; Fattig 2007; Grigoriadis 2011; Oxalis 2014.

For Your Consideration

→ What is your view of eco-saboteurs?

→ As symbolic interactionists stress, it all depends on how you view their actions. And as conflict theorists emphasize, your view depends on your social location. That is, if you own a lumber company, you will see eco-saboteurs differently than a camping enthusiast will. How does your view of eco-saboteurs depend on your life situation?

→ What effective alternatives to eco-sabotage are there for people who are convinced that we are destroying the life support system of our planet?

Environmental Sociology

environmental sociology

a specialty within sociology whose focus is how humans affect the environment and how the environment affects humans

A specialization within sociology, **environmental sociology** focuses on the relationship between human societies and the environment (Dunlap and Catton 1979, 1983; Bell 2009). Environmental sociology is built around these key ideas:

1. The physical environment should be a significant variable in sociological research.

2. Human beings are but one species among many that depend on the natural environment.

3. Human actions have unintended consequences, many of which have an impact on nature.

4. The world is finite, so there are physical limits to economic growth.

5. Economic expansion requires the increased extraction of resources from the environment.

6. Increased extraction of resources leads to ecological problems.

7. These ecological problems place limits on economic expansion.

8. Governments create environmental problems by encouraging the accumulation of capital.

9. For the welfare of humanity, environmental problems must be solved.

The goal of environmental sociology is not to stop pollution or nuclear power but, rather, to study how humans (their cultures, values, and behavior) affect the physical environment and how the physical environment affects human activities. Not surprisingly, environmental sociology attracts activists, and the Section on Environment and Technology of the American Sociological Association tries to influence governmental policies (American Sociological Association n.d.).

Pollution in the Least Industrialized Nations has become a major problem. This boy is "swimming" in the Philippines' Manila Bay, a formerly pristine body of water that has been turned into a festering garbage dump.

Technology and the Environment: The Goal of Harmony

It is inevitable that humans will develop new technologies. But the abuse of our environment by those technologies is not inevitable. To understate the matter, the destruction of our planet is an unwise choice.

If we are to live in a world worth passing on to coming generations, we must seek harmony between technology and the natural environment. This will not be easy. At one extreme are people who claim that to protect the environment, we must eliminate industrialization and go back to a tribal way of life. At the other extreme are people who are blind to the harm being done to the natural environment, who want the entire world to industrialize at full speed. Somewhere, there must be a middle ground, one that recognizes not only that industrialization is here to stay but also that we *can* control it. After all, it is our creation. Controlled, industrialization can enhance our quality of life; uncontrolled, it will destroy us.

It is essential, then, that we develop ways to reduce or eliminate the harm that technology does to the environment. This includes mechanisms to monitor the production and use of technology and the disposal of its wastes. The question, of course, is whether we have the resolve to take the steps necessary to preserve the environment for future generations. What is at stake is nothing less than the welfare of planet Earth. Surely this should be enough to motivate us to make wise choices.

The social movement that centers on the environment has become global. In all nations, people are concerned about the destruction of the earth's resources. This photo is a sign of changing times. Instead of jumping on this beached whale and carving it into pieces, these Brazilians are doing their best to save its life.

Summary and Review

How Social Change Transforms Social Life

15.1 **Summarize how social change transforms society; include the four social revolutions, *Gemeinschaft* and *Gesellschaft*, capitalism, social movements, and global politics.**

What major trends have transformed the course of human history?

The primary changes in human history are the four social revolutions (domestication, agriculture, industrialization, and information); the change from *Gemeinschaft* to *Gesellschaft* societies; capitalism and industrialization; and global stratification. Social movements indicate cutting edges of social change. Ethnic conflicts and power rivalries threaten the global divisions that the Most Industrialized Nations have worked out. We may also be on the cutting edge of a new biotech society.

Theories and Processes of Social Change

15.2 **Summarize theories of social change: social evolution, natural cycles, conflict over power and resources, and Ogburn's theory.**

What are the main theories of social change?

Evolutionary theories hold that societies move from the same starting point to some similar ending point. *Unilinear* theories assume that every society follows the same evolutionary path, while *multilinear* theories conclude that different paths lead to the same stage of development. *Cyclical* theories view civilizations as going through a process of birth, youth, maturity, decline, and death. Conflict theorists see social change as inevitable, because each *thesis* (basically an arrangement of power) contains *antitheses* (contradictions). A new *synthesis* develops to resolve these contradictions, but it, too, contains contradictions that must be resolved, and so on. This is called a **dialectical process**.

What is Ogburn's theory of social change?

William Ogburn identified technology as the basic cause of social change, which comes through three processes: **invention, discovery**, and **diffusion**. The term **cultural lag** refers to symbolic culture lagging behind changes in technology.

How Technology Is Changing Society

15.3 **Use the examples of the automobile and the microchip to illustrate the sociological significance of technology; include changes in ideology, norms, human relationships, education, work, business, war, and social inequality.**

How does new technology affect society?

Because technology is an organizing force of social life, changes in technology can bring profound effects. The automobile and the microchip were used as extended examples. The computer is changing the ways we interact with one another, learn, work, do business, and fight wars. We don't yet know whether information technologies will help to perpetuate or to reduce social inequalities on national and global levels.

The Growth Machine versus the Earth

15.4 **Explain how industrialization is related to environmental problems; contrast the environmental movement and environmental sociology; discuss the goal of harmony.**

What are the environmental problems of the Most Industrialized Nations?

Among the most serious of the environmental problems of the most industrialized nations is **global warming**, which is likely to have severe consequences for the world. Burning fossil fuels in internal combustion engines lies at the root of many environmental problems. The location of factories and hazardous waste sites creates **environmental injustice**, with environmental problems having a greater impact on minorities and the poor.

Do the Industrializing and Least Industrialized Nations have environmental problems?

The rush of the Least Industrialized Nations to industrialize and the push of the Industrializing Nations to industrialize even faster are adding to the planet's environmental decay. The world is facing a basic conflict between the lust for profits through the exploitation of the Earth's resources and the need to establish a **sustainable environment**.

What is the environmental movement?

The environmental movement is an attempt to restore a healthy environment for the world's people. This global social movement takes many forms, from peaceful attempts to influence the political process to **eco-sabotage**.

What is environmental sociology?

Environmental sociology is not an attempt to change the environment but, rather, a study of the relationship between humans and the environment. Environmental sociologists are generally also environmental activists.

What is the goal of harmony between technology and the environment?

The goal of harmony is to control industrialization so it doesn't harm the environment, resulting in a world worth passing on to the next generation.

Thinking Critically about Chapter 15

1. How has social change affected your life? Be specific—what changes, how? Does Ogburn's theory help to explain your experiences? Why or why not?

2. In what ways does technology change society?

3. Do you think that a sustainable environment should be a goal of the world's societies? Why or why not? If so, what practical steps do you think we can take to produce a sustainable environment?

Epilogue: Why Major in Sociology?

As you explored social life in this textbook, I hope that you found yourself thinking along with me. If so, you should have gained a greater understanding of why people think, feel, and act as they do—as well as insights into why *you* view life the way you do. Developing your sociological imagination was my intention in writing this book. I have sincerely wanted to make sociology come alive for you.

Majoring in Sociology

If you feel a passion for peering beneath the surface—for seeking out the social influences in people's lives and for seeing these influences in your own life—this is the best reason to major in sociology. As you take more courses in sociology, you will continue this enlightening process of social discovery. Your sociological perspective will grow, and you will become increasingly aware of how social factors underlie human behavior.

In addition to people who have a strong desire to continue this fascinating process of social discovery, there is a second type of person whom I also urge to major in sociology. Let's suppose that you have a strong, almost unbridled sense of wanting to explore many aspects of life. Let's also assume that because you have so many interests, you can't make up your mind about what you want to do with your life. You can think of so many things you'd like to try, but for each one there are other possibilities that you find equally as compelling. Let me share what one student wrote me:

I'd love to say what my current major is—if only I truly knew. I know that the major you choose to study in college isn't necessarily the field of work you'll be going into. I've heard enough stories of grads who get jobs in fields that are not even related to their majors to believe it to a certain extent. My only problem is that I'm not even sure what it is I want to study or what I truly want to be in the future for that matter.

The variety of choices I have left open for myself are very wide, which creates a big problem, because I know I have to narrow it down to just one, which isn't something easy at all for me. It's like I want to be the best and do the best (medical doctor), yet I also wanna do other things (such as being a paramedic, or a cop, or a firefighter, or a pilot), but I also realize I've only got one life to live. So the big question is: What's it gonna be?

This note reminded me of myself. In my reply, I said:

You sound so much like myself when I was in college. In my senior year, I was plagued with uncertainty about what would be the right course for my life. I went to a counselor and took a vocational aptitude test. I still remember the day when I went in for the test results. I expected my future to be laid out for me, and I hung on every word. But then I heard the counselor say, "Your tests show that mortician should be one of your vocational choices."

Mortician! I almost fell off my chair. That choice was so far removed from anything that I wanted that I immediately gave up on such tests.

I like your list of possibilities: physician, cop, firefighter, and paramedic. In addition to these, mine included cowboy, hobo, and beach bum. One day, I was at the dry cleaners (end of my sophomore year in college), and the guy standing next to me was a cop. We talked about his job, and when I left the dry cleaners, I immediately went to the police station to get an application. I found out that I had to be 21, and I was just 20. I went back to college.

I'm very happy with my choice. As a sociologist, I am able to follow my interests. I was able to become a hobo (or at least a traveler and able to experience different cultural settings). As far as being a cop, I developed and taught a course in the sociology of law.

One of the many things I always wanted to be was an author. I almost skipped graduate school to move to Greenwich Village and become a novelist. The problem was that I was too timid, too scared of the unknown—and I had no support at all—to give it a try. My ultimate choice of sociologist has allowed me to fulfill this early dream.

It is sociology's breadth that is so satisfying to those of us who can't seem to find the limit to our interests, who can't pin ourselves down to just one thing in life. Sociology covers *all* of social life. Anything and everything that people do is part of sociology. For those of us who feel such broad, and perhaps changing, interests, sociology is a perfect major.

But what if you already have a major picked out, yet you really like thinking sociologically? You can *minor* in sociology. Take sociology courses that continue to pique your sociological imagination. Then after college, continue to stimulate your sociological interests through your reading, including novels. This ongoing development of your sociological imagination will serve you well as you go through life.

But What Can You Do with a Sociology Major?

I can just hear someone say: "That's fine for you, since you became a sociologist. I don't want to go to graduate school, though. I just want to get my bachelor's degree and get out of college and get on with life. So, how can a bachelor's in sociology help me?"

This is a fair question. Just what can you do with a bachelor's degree in sociology?

A few years ago, in my sociology department we began to develop a concentration in applied sociology. At that time, since this would be a bachelor's degree, I explored this very question. I was surprised at the answer: The short answer is: *Almost anything!*

Most employers don't care what you major in. (Exceptions are some highly specialized fields, such as nursing, computers, and engineering.) *Most* employers just want to make certain that you have completed college, and, for most of them, one degree is the same as another. *College provides the base on which the employer builds.*

Because you have your bachelor's degree—no matter what it is in—employers assume that you are a responsible person. This credential implies that you have proven yourself: You were able to stick with a four-year course, you showed up for classes, listened to lectures, took notes, passed tests, and carried out whatever assignments you were given. On top of this base of presumed responsibility, employers add the specifics necessary for you to perform their particular work, whether that be in sales or service, in insurance, banking, retailing, marketing, product development, or whatever.

If you major in sociology, you don't have to look for a job as a sociologist. If you ever decide to go on for an advanced degree, that's fine. But such plans are not necessary. The bachelor's in sociology can be your passport to most types of work in society.

Final Note

I want to conclude by stressing the reason to major in sociology that goes far beyond how you are going to make a living. It is the sociological perspective itself, the way of thinking and understanding that sociology provides. Wherever your path in life may lead, the sociological perspective will accompany you.

You are going to live in a fast-paced, rapidly changing society that, with all its conflicting crosscurrents, is going to be in turmoil. The sociological perspective will cast a different light on life's events, allowing you to perceive them in more insightful ways. As you watch television, attend a concert, converse with a friend, listen to a boss or coworker—you will be more aware of the social contexts that underlie such behavior. The sociological perspective that you develop as you major in sociology will equip you to view what happens in life differently from someone who does not have your sociological background. Even events in the news will look different to you.

There is one more benefit of majoring in sociology. Much of the insight and understanding that I have just described can be applied in your work setting to advance your career.

The final question that I want to leave you with, then, is, "If you enjoy sociology, why not major in it?"

With my best wishes for your success in life,

Jim Henslin

Glossary

achieved statuses positions that are earned, accomplished, or involve at least some effort or activity on the individual's part

acid rain rain containing sulfuric and nitric acids (burning fossil fuels release sulfur dioxide and nitrogen oxide that become sulfuric and nitric acids when they react with moisture in the air)

activity theory the view that satisfaction during old age is related to a person's amount and quality of activity

age cohort people born at roughly the same time who pass through the life course together

ageism prejudice and discrimination directed against people because of their age; can be directed against any age group, including youth

agents of socialization people or groups that affect our self concept, attitudes, behaviors, or other orientations toward life

aggregate individuals who temporarily share the same physical space but who do not see themselves as belonging together

agricultural revolution the second social revolution, based on the invention of the plow, which led to agricultural societies

agricultural society a society based on large-scale agriculture

alienation Marx's term for workers' lack of connection to the product of their labor; caused by workers being assigned repetitive tasks on a small part of a product, which leads to a sense of powerlessness and normlessness; others use the term in the general sense of not feeling a part of something

anarchy a condition of lawlessness or political disorder caused by the absence or collapse of governmental authority

animism the belief that all objects in the world have spirits, some of which are dangerous and must be outwitted

anomie (AN-uh-mee) Durkheim's term for a condition of society in which people become detached from the usual norms that guide their behavior

anticipatory socialization the process of learning in advance an anticipated future role or status

apartheid the government-approved-and-enforced separation of racial–ethnic groups as was practiced in South Africa

applied sociology the use of sociology to solve problems—from the micro level of classroom interaction and family relationships to the macro level of crime and pollution

ascribed status a position an individual either inherits at birth or receives involuntarily later in life

assimilation the process of being absorbed into the mainstream culture

authoritarian leader an individual who leads by giving orders

authoritarian personality Theodor Adorno's term for people who are prejudiced and rank high on scales of conformity, intolerance, insecurity, respect for authority, and submissiveness to superiors

authority power that people consider legitimate, as rightly exercised over them; also called *legitimate power*

back stages places where people rest from their performances, discuss their presentations, and plan future performances

background assumption a deeply embedded, common understanding of how the world operates and of how people ought to act

barter the direct exchange of one item for another

basic (or pure) sociology sociological research for the purpose of making discoveries about life in human groups, not for making changes in those groups

basic demographic equation the growth rate equals births minus deaths plus net migration

bilineal system (of descent) a system of reckoning descent that counts both the mother's and the father's side

biotech society a society whose economy increasingly centers on modifying genetics to produce food, medicine, and materials

blended family a family whose members were once part of other families

body language the ways in which people use their bodies to give messages to others

bonded labor (indentured service) a contractual system in which someone sells his or her body (services) for a specified period of time in an arrangement very close to slavery, except that it is entered into voluntarily

born again a term describing Christians who have undergone a religious experience so life transforming that they feel they have become new persons

bourgeoisie (boo r-zhwah-ZEE) Marx's term for capitalists, those who own the means of production

bureaucracy a formal organization with a hierarchy of authority and a clear division of labor; emphasis on impersonality of positions and written rules, communications, and records

capital punishment the death penalty

capitalism an economic system built around the private ownership of the means of production, the pursuit of profit, and market competition

case study an intensive analysis of a single event, situation, or individual

caste system a form of social stratification in which people's statuses are lifelong conditions determined by birth

category people, objects, and events that have similar characteristics and are classified together

charisma literally, an extraordinary gift from God; more commonly, an outstanding, "magnetic" personality

charismatic authority authority based on an individual's outstanding traits, which attract followers

charismatic leader literally, someone to whom God has given a gift; in its extended sense, someone who exudes extraordinary appeal to a group of followers

checks and balances the separation of powers among the three branches of U.S. government—legislative, executive, and judicial—so that each is able to nullify the actions of the other two, thus preventing any single branch from dominating the government

church according to Durkheim, one of the three essential elements of religion—a moral community of believers; also refers to a large, highly organized religious group that has formal, sedate worship services with little emphasis on evangelism, intense religious experience, or personal conversion

citizenship the concept that birth (and residence or naturalization) in a country imparts basic rights

city a place in which a large number of people are permanently based and do not produce their own food

city-state an independent city whose power radiates outward, bringing the adjacent area under its rule

class conflict   Marx's term for the struggle between capitalists and workers

class consciousness   Marx's term for awareness of a common identity based on one's position in the means of production

class system   a form of social stratification based primarily on income, education, and prestige of occupation

clique (cleek)   a cluster of people within a larger group who choose to interact with one another

coalition   the alignment of some members of a group against others

coercion   power that people do not accept as rightly exercised over them; also called *illegitimate power*

cohabitation   unmarried couples living together in a sexual relationship

colonialism   the process by which one nation takes over another nation, usually for the purpose of exploiting its labor and natural resources

common sense   those things that "everyone knows" are true

compartmentalize   to separate acts from feelings or attitudes

conflict theory   a theoretical framework in which society is viewed as composed of groups that are competing for scarce resources

conspicuous consumption   Thorstein Veblen's term for a change from the thrift, saving, and investing of the Protestant ethic to showing off wealth through spending and the display of possessions

contact theory   the idea that prejudice and negative stereotypes decrease and racial–ethnic relations improve when people from different racial–ethnic backgrounds, who are of equal status, interact frequently

continuity theory   a theory focusing on how people adjust to retirement by continuing aspects of their earlier lives

contradictory class locations   Erik Wright's term for a position in the class structure that generates contradictory interests

control group   the subjects in an experiment who are not exposed to the independent variable

control theory   the idea that two control systems—inner controls and outer controls—work against our tendencies to deviate

convergence theory   the view that as capitalist and socialist economic systems each adopt features of the other, a hybrid (or mixed) economic system will emerge

core values   the values that are central to a group, those around which people build a common identity

corporate capitalism   the domination of an economic system by giant corporations

corporate crime   crimes committed by executives in order to benefit their corporation

corporation   a business enterprise whose assets, liabilities, and obligations are separate from those of its owners; as a legal entity, it can enter into contracts, assume debt, and sue and be sued

correspondence principle   the sociological principle that schools correspond to (or reflect) the social structure of their society

cosmology   teachings or ideas that provide a unified picture of the world

counterculture   a group whose values, beliefs, norms, and related behaviors place its members in opposition to the broader culture

creative aging   the view that old age is a time for personal development, for greater creativity and learning new skills and outlooks on life

credential society   the use of diplomas and degrees to determine who is eligible for jobs, even though the diploma or degree may be irrelevant to the actual work

credit card   a device that allows its owner to purchase goods and to be billed later

crime   the violation of norms written into law

criminal justice system   the system of police, courts, and prisons set up to deal with people who are accused of having committed a crime

crude birth rate   the annual number of live births per 1,000 population

crude death rate   the annual number of deaths per 1,000 population

cult   a new religion with few followers, whose teachings and practices put it at odds with the dominant culture and religion

cultural capital   privileges accompanying a social location that help someone in life; included are more highly educated parents, from grade school through high school being pushed to bring home high grades, and enjoying cultural experiences that translate into higher test scores, better jobs, and higher earnings

cultural diffusion   the spread of cultural traits from one group to another; includes both material and nonmaterial cultural traits

cultural goals   the objectives held out as legitimate or desirable for the members of a society to achieve

cultural lag   Ogburn's term for human behavior lagging behind technological innovations

cultural leveling   the process by which cultures become similar to one another; refers especially to the process by which Western culture is being exported and diffused into other nations

cultural relativism   not judging a culture but trying to understand it on its own terms

cultural transmission of values   the process of transmitting values from one group to another; often refers to how cultural traits are transmitted across generations; in education, the ways in which schools transmit a society's culture, especially its core values

cultural universal   a value, norm, or other cultural trait that is found in every group

culture   the language, beliefs, values, norms, behaviors, and even material objects that characterize a group and are passed from one generation to the next

culture of poverty   the assumption that the values and behaviors of the poor make them fundamentally different from other people, that these factors are largely responsible for their poverty, and that parents perpetuate poverty across generations by passing these characteristics to their children

culture shock   the disorientation that people experience when they come in contact with a fundamentally different culture and can no longer depend on their taken-for-granted assumptions about life

currency   paper money

debit card   a device that electronically withdraws the cost of an item from the cardholder's bank account

deferred gratification   going without something in the present in the hope of achieving greater gains in the future

degradation ceremony   a term coined by Harold Garfinkel to refer to a ritual whose goal is to remake someone's self by stripping away that individual's self-identity and stamping a new identity in its place

deindustrialization   the process of industries moving out of a country or region

democracy   a government whose authority comes from the people; the term, based on two Greek words, translates literally as "power to the people"

democratic leader   an individual who leads by trying to reach a consensus

democratic socialism   a hybrid economic system in which the individual ownership of businesses is mixed with the state ownership of industries thought essential to the public welfare, such as the postal service, natural resources, the medical delivery system, and mass transportation

demographic transition a three-stage historical process of change in the size of populations: first, high birth rates and high death rates; second, high birth rates and low death rates; and third, low birth rates and low death rates; a fourth stage of population shrinkage in which deaths outnumber births has made its appearance in the Most Industrialized Nations

demographic variables the three factors that change the size of a population: fertility, mortality, and net migration

demography the study of the size, composition, growth (or shrinkage), and distribution of human populations

dependency ratio the number of workers who are required to support each dependent person—those 65 and older and those 15 and under

dependent variable a factor in an experiment that is changed by an independent variable

deposit receipt a receipt stating that a certain amount of goods are on deposit in a warehouse or bank; the receipt is used as a form of money

deviance the violation of norms (or rules or expectations)

dialectical process (of history) each arrangement of power (a thesis) contains contradictions (antitheses) which make the arrangement unstable and which must be resolved; the new arrangement of power (a synthesis) contains its own contradictions; this process of balancing and unbalancing continues throughout history as groups struggle for power and other resources

dictatorship a form of government in which an individual has seized power

differential association Edwin Sutherland's term to indicate that people who associate with some groups learn an "excess of definitions" of deviance, increasing the likelihood that they will become deviant

diffusion the spread of an invention or a discovery from one area to another; identified by William Ogburn as one of three processes of social change

direct democracy a form of democracy in which the eligible voters meet together to discuss issues and make their decisions

discovery a new way of seeing reality; identified by William Ogburn as one of three processes of social change

discrimination an act of unfair treatment directed against an individual or a group

disengagement theory the view that society is stabilized by having the elderly retire (disengage from) their positions of responsibility so the younger generation can step into their shoes

disinvestment the withdrawal of investments by financial institutions, which seals the fate of an urban area

divine right of kings the idea that the king's authority comes from God; in an interesting gender bender, also applies to queens

division of labor the splitting of a group's or a society's tasks into specialties

documents in its narrow sense, written sources that provide data; in its extended sense, archival material of any sort, including photographs, movies, CDs, DVDs, and so on

domestication revolution the first social revolution, based on the domestication of plants and animals, which led to pastoral and horticultural societies

dominant group the group with the most power, greatest privileges, and highest social status

downward social mobility movement down the social class ladder

dramaturgy an approach, pioneered by Erving Goffman, in which social life is analyzed in terms of drama or the stage; also called *dramaturgical analysis*

dyad the smallest possible group, consisting of two persons

e-cash digital money that is stored on computers

ecclesia a religious group so integrated into the dominant culture that it is difficult to tell where the one begins and the other leaves off; also called a *state religion*

economy a system of producing and distributing goods and services

eco-sabotage actions taken to sabotage the efforts of people who are thought to be legally harming the environment

edge city a large clustering of service facilities and residential areas near highway intersections that provides a sense of place to people who live, shop, and work there

education a formal system of teaching knowledge, values, and skills

egalitarian authority more or less equally divided between people or groups (in heterosexual marriage, for example, between husband and wife)

ego Freud's term for a balancing force between the id and the demands of society

endogamy the practice of marrying within one's own group

enterprise zone the use of economic incentives in a designated area to encourage investment

environmental injustice refers to how minorities and the poor are harmed the most by environmental pollution

environmental sociology a specialty within sociology whose focus is how humans affect the environment and how the environment affects humans

estate stratification system the stratification system of medieval Europe, consisting of three groups or estates: the nobility, clergy, and commoners

ethnic cleansing a policy of eliminating a population; includes forcible expulsion and genocide

ethnic work activities designed to discover, enhance, maintain, or transmit an ethnic or racial identity

ethnicity (and ethnic) having distinctive cultural characteristics

ethnocentrism the use of one's own culture as a yardstick for judging the ways of other individuals or societies, generally leading to a negative evaluation of their values, norms, and behaviors

ethnomethodology the study of how people use background assumptions to make sense out of life

exchange mobility a large number of people moving up the social class ladder, while a large number move down; it is as though they have *exchanged* places, and the social class system shows little change

exogamy the practice of marrying outside of one's group

experimental group the group of subjects in an experiment who are exposed to the independent variable

exponential growth curve a pattern of growth in which numbers double during approximately equal intervals, showing a steep acceleration in the later stages

expressive leader an individual who increases harmony and minimizes conflict in a group; also known as a *socioemotional leader*

extended family a family in which relatives, such as the "older generation" or unmarried aunts and uncles, live with the parents and their children

face-saving behavior techniques used to salvage a performance (interaction) that is going sour

false class consciousness Marx's term to refer to workers identifying with the interests of capitalists

family two or more people who consider themselves related by blood, marriage, or adoption

family of orientation the family in which a person grows up

family of procreation the family formed when a couple's first child is born

fecundity the number of children that women are capable of bearing

feminism the philosophy that men and women should be politically, economically, and socially equal; organized activities on behalf of this principle

feminization of poverty a condition of U.S. poverty in which most poor families are headed by women

feral children children assumed to have been raised by animals, in the wilderness, isolated from humans

fertility rate the number of children that the average woman bears

fiat money currency issued by a government that is not backed by stored value

folkways norms that are not strictly enforced

front stages places where people give performances

functional analysis a theoretical framework in which society is viewed as composed of various parts, each with a function that, when fulfilled, contributes to society's equilibrium; also *known as functionalism* and *structural functionalism*

functional illiteracy refers to high school graduates who have difficulty with basic reading and math

gatekeeping the process by which education opens and closes doors of opportunity; another term for the *social placement* function of education

Gemeinschaft (guh-MAHYN-shahft) a type of society in which life is intimate; a community in which everyone knows everyone else and people share a sense of togetherness

gender the behaviors and attitudes that a society considers proper for its males and females; masculinity or femininity

gender age the relative value placed on men's and women's ages

gender socialization learning society's "gender map," the paths in life set out for us because we are male or female

gender stratification males' and females' unequal access to property, power, and prestige

generalization a statement that goes beyond the individual case and is applied to a broader group or situation

generalized other the norms, values, attitudes, and expectations of people "in general"; the child's ability to take the role of the generalized other is a significant step in the development of a self

genetic predisposition inborn tendencies (for example, a tendency to commit deviant acts)

genocide the annihilation or attempted annihilation of a people because of their presumed race or ethnicity

gentrification middle-class people moving into a rundown area of a city, displacing the poor as they buy and restore homes

Gesellschaft (guh-ZEL-shahft) a type of society that is dominated by impersonal relationships, individual accomplishments, and self-interest

gestures the ways in which people use their bodies to communicate with one another

glass ceiling the mostly invisible barrier that keeps women from advancing to the top levels at work

global superclass the top members of the capitalist class, who, through their worldwide interconnections, make the major decisions that affect the world

globalization the growing interconnections among nations due to the expansion of capitalism

globalization of capitalism capitalism (investing to make profits within a rational system) becoming the globe's dominant economic system

goal displacement an organization replacing old goals with new ones; also known as *goal replacement*

gold standard paper money backed by gold

grade inflation higher grades given for the same work; a general rise in student grades without a corresponding increase in learning

graying of America the growing percentage of older people in the U.S. population

gross domestic product (GDP) the amount of goods and services produced by a nation

group people who interact with one another and who believe that what they have in common is significant; also called a *social group*

group dynamics the ways in which individuals affect groups and the ways in which groups influence individuals

groupthink a narrowing of thought by a group of people, leading to the perception that there is only one correct answer and that to even suggest alternatives is a sign of disloyalty

growth rate the net change in a population after adding births, subtracting deaths, and either adding or subtracting net migration; can result in a negative number

hidden corporate culture stereotypes of the traits that make for high-performing and underperforming workers, which end up producing both types of workers

hidden curriculum the unwritten goals of schools, such as teaching obedience to authority and conformity to cultural norms

homogamy the tendency of people with similar characteristics to marry one another

Horatio Alger myth the belief that due to limitless possibilities anyone can get ahead if he or she tries hard enough

horticultural society a society based on cultivating plants by the use of hand tools

hospice care professional care given to dying people at home. Originally referred to a place, a *hospice*, but now refers to home care

household people who occupy the same housing unit

human ecology Robert Park's term for the relationship between people and their environment (such as land and structures); also known as *urban ecology*

hunting and gathering society a human group that depends on hunting and gathering for its survival

hypothesis a statement of how variables are expected to be related to one another, often according to predictions from a theory

id Freud's term for our inborn basic drives

ideal culture a people's ideal values and norms; the goals held out for them

ideology beliefs about the way things ought to be that justify social arrangements

illegitimate opportunity structure opportunities for crimes that are woven into the texture of life

impression management people's efforts to control the impressions that others receive of them

incest sexual relations between specified relatives, such as brothers and sisters or parents and children

incest taboo the rule that prohibits sex and marriage among designated relatives

inclusion helping people to become part of the mainstream of society; also called *mainstreaming*

income money received, usually from a job, business, or assets

independent variable a factor that causes a change in another variable, called the *dependent variable*

individual discrimination person-to-person or face-to-face discrimination; the negative treatment of people by other individuals

Industrial Revolution the third social revolution, occurring when machines powered by fuels replaced most animal and human power

industrial society a society based on the harnessing of machines powered by fuels

inflation an increase in prices; technically, an increase in the amount of money in circulation, which leads to an increase in prices

in-group a group toward which one feels loyalty

institutional discrimination negative treatment of a minority group that is built into a society's institutions; also called *systemic discrimination*

institutionalized means approved ways of reaching cultural goals

instrumental leader an individual who tries to keep the group moving toward its goals; also known as a *task-oriented leader*

intergenerational mobility the change that family members make in social class from one generation to the next

interlocking directorates the same people serving on the boards of directors of several companies

internal colonialism the policy of exploiting minority groups for economic gain

invasion–succession cycle the process of one group of people displacing a group whose racial–ethnic or social class characteristics differ from their own

invention the combination of existing elements and materials to form new ones; identified by William Ogburn as one of three processes of social change

iron law of oligarchy Robert Michels' term for the tendency of formal organizations to be dominated by a small, self-perpetuating elite

labeling theory the view that the labels people are given affect their own and others' perceptions of them, thus channeling their behavior into either deviance or conformity

laissez-faire capitalism literally "hands off" capitalism, meaning that the government doesn't interfere in the market

laissez-faire leader an individual who leads by being highly permissive

language a system of symbols that can be combined in an infinite number of ways and can represent not only objects but also abstract thought

latent functions unintended beneficial consequences of people's actions

leader someone who influences other people

leadership styles ways in which people express their leadership

life course the stages of our life as we go from birth to death

life expectancy the number of years that an average person at any age, including newborns, can expect to live

life span the maximum length of life of a species; for humans, the longest that a human has lived

lobbyists people who influence legislation on behalf of their clients

looking-glass self a term coined by Charles Horton Cooley to refer to the process by which our self develops through internalizing others' reactions to us

machismo an emphasis on male strength and dominance

macro-level analysis an examination of large-scale patterns of society; such as how Wall Street and the political establishment are interrelated

macrosociology analysis of social life that focuses on broad features of society, such as social class and the relationships of groups to one another; usually used by functionalists and conflict theorists

Malthus theorem an observation by Thomas Malthus that although the food supply increases arithmetically (from 1 to 2 to 3 to 4 and so on), population grows geometrically (from 2 to 4 to 8 to 16 and so forth)

mandatory education laws laws that require all children to attend school until a specified age or until they complete a minimum grade in school

manifest functions the intended beneficial consequences of people's actions

market forces the law of supply and demand

marriage a group's approved mating arrangements, usually marked by a ritual of some sort

mass media forms of communication, such as radio, newspapers, and television that are directed to mass audiences

master status a status that cuts across the other statuses that an individual occupies

material culture the material objects that distinguish a group of people, such as their art, buildings, weapons, utensils, machines, hairstyles, clothing, and jewelry

matriarchy a society in which women-as-a-group dominate men-as-a-group; authority is vested in females

matrilineal system (of descent) a system of reckoning descent that counts only the mother's side

McDonaldization of society the process by which ordinary aspects of life are rationalized and efficiency comes to rule them, including such things as food preparation

means of production the tools, factories, land, and investment capital used to produce wealth

mechanical solidarity Durkheim's term for the unity (a shared consciousness) that people feel as a result of performing the same or similar tasks

medicalization of deviance to make deviance a medical matter, a symptom of some underlying illness that needs to be treated by physicians

medium of exchange the means by which people place a value on goods and services in order to make an exchange—for example, currency, gold, and silver

megacity a city of 10 million or more residents

megalopolis an urban area consisting of at least two metropolises and their many suburbs

megaregion a merging of megacities and nearby populated areas into an even larger mass of people

meritocracy a form of social stratification in which all positions are awarded on the basis of merit

metropolis a central city surrounded by smaller cities and their suburbs

metropolitan statistical area (MSA) a central city and the urbanized counties adjacent to it

micro-level analysis an examination of small-scale patterns of society; such as how the members of a group interact

microsociology analysis of social life that focuses on social interaction; typically used by symbolic interactionists

minority group people who are singled out for unequal treatment and who regard themselves as objects of collective discrimination

modernization the transformation of traditional societies into industrial societies

monarchy a form of government headed by a king or queen

money any item (from sea shells to gold) that serves as a medium of exchange

monopoly the control of an entire industry by a single company

mores norms that are strictly enforced because they are thought essential to core values or the well-being of the group

multiculturalism (or pluralism)   a policy that permits or encourages ethnic differences

multinational corporations   companies that operate across national boundaries; also called *transnational corporations*

natural sciences   the intellectual and academic disciplines designed to comprehend, explain, and predict events in our natural environments

negative sanction   an expression of disapproval for breaking a norm, ranging from a mild, informal reaction such as a frown to a formal reaction such as a fine or a prison sentence

neocolonialism   the economic and political dominance of the Least Industrialized Nations by the Most Industrialized Nations

net migration rate   the difference between the number of immigrants and emigrants per 1,000 population

new technology   the emerging technologies of an era that have a significant impact on social life

nonmaterial culture   a group's ways of thinking (including its beliefs, values, and other assumptions about the world) and doing (its common patterns of behavior, including language and other forms of interaction); also called *symbolic culture*

nonverbal interaction   communication without words through gestures, use of space, silence, and so on

norms   expectations of "right" behavior

nuclear family   a family consisting of a husband, wife, and child(ren)

objectivity   value neutrality in research

oligarchy   a form of government in which a small group of individuals holds power; the rule of the many by the few

operational definition   the way in which a researcher measures a variable

organic solidarity   Durkheim's term for the interdependence that results from the division of labor; as part of the same unit, we all depend on others to fulfill their jobs

out-group   a group toward which one feels antagonism

participant observation (or fieldwork)   research in which the researcher participates in a research setting while observing what is happening in that setting

pastoral society   a society based on the pasturing of animals

patriarchy   men-as-a-group dominating women-as-a-group; authority is vested in males

patrilineal system (of descent)   a system of reckoning descent that counts only the father's side

patterns of behavior   recurring behaviors or events

peer group   a group of individuals, often of roughly the same age, who are linked by common interests and orientations

personality disorders   the view that a personality disturbance of some sort causes an individual to violate social norms

pluralism   the diffusion of power among many interest groups that prevents any single group from gaining control of the government

pluralistic society   a society made up of many different groups

police discretion   the practice of the police, in the normal course of their duties, to either arrest or ticket someone for an offense or to overlook the matter

political action committee (PAC)   an organization formed by one or more special-interest groups to solicit and spend funds for the purpose of influencing legislation

politics   the exercise of power, leadership, influence, and authority

polyandry   a form of marriage in which women have more than one husband

polygyny   a form of marriage in which men have more than one wife

population   a target group to be studied

population pyramid   a graph that represents the age and sex of a population (see Figure 20.7)

population shrinkage   the process by which a country's population becomes smaller because its birth rate and immigration are too low to replace those who die and emigrate

population transfer   the forced transfer of a minority group

positive sanction   a reward or positive reaction for following norms, ranging from a smile to a material reward

positivism   the application of the scientific approach to the social world

postindustrial (information) society   a society based on information, services, and high technology, rather than on raw materials and manufacturing

postmodern society   another term for postindustrial society; a chief characteristic is the use of tools that extend human abilities to gather and analyze information, to communicate, and to travel

poverty line   the official measure of poverty; calculated to include incomes that are less than three times a low-cost food budget

power   the ability to carry out your will, even over the resistance of others

power elite   C. Wright Mills' term for the top people in U.S. corporations, military, and politics who make the nation's major decisions

prejudice   an attitude or prejudging, usually in a negative way

prestige   respect or regard

primary group   a small group characterized by cooperative, intimate, long-term, face-to-face relationships

profane   Durkheim's term for common elements of everyday life

proletariat   Marx's term for the exploited class, the mass of workers who do not own the means of production

property   material possessions: includes animals, bank accounts, bonds, buildings, businesses, cars, cash, commodities, copyrights, furniture, jewelry, land, and stocks

Protestant ethic   Weber's term to describe the ideal of a self-denying, highly moral life accompanied by thrift and hard work

public sociology   applying sociology for the public good; especially the use of the sociological perspective (how things are related to one another) to guide politicians and policy makers

quiet revolution   the fundamental changes in society that follow when vast numbers of women enter the workforce

race   a group whose inherited physical characteristics distinguish it from other groups

racism   prejudice and discrimination on the basis of race

random sample   a sample in which everyone in the target population has the same chance of being included in the study

rapport (ruh-POUR)   a feeling of trust between researchers and the people they are studying

rationalization of society   a widespread acceptance of rationality and social organizations that are built largely around this idea

rational–legal authority   authority based on law or written rules and regulations; also called *bureaucratic authority*

real culture   the norms and values that people actually follow; as opposed to *ideal culture*

recidivism rate   the percentage of released convicts who are rearrested

redlining   a decision by the officers of a financial institution not to make loans in a particular area

reference group a group whose standards we refer to as we evaluate ourselves

reliability the extent to which research produces consistent or dependable results

religion according to Durkheim, beliefs and practices that separate the profane from the sacred and unite its adherents into a moral community

religious experience a sudden awareness of the supernatural or a feeling of coming in contact with God

replication the repetition of a study in order to test its findings

representative democracy a form of democracy in which voters elect representatives to meet together to discuss issues and make decisions on their behalf

research method (or research design) one of seven procedures that sociologists use to collect data: surveys, participant observation, case studies, secondary analysis, analysis of documents, experiments, and unobtrusive measures

reserve labor force the unemployed; unemployed workers are thought of as being "in reserve"—capitalists take them "out of reserve" (put them back to work) during times of high production and then put them "back in reserve" (lay them off) when they are no longer needed

resocialization the process of learning new norms, values, attitudes, and behaviors

respondents people who respond to a survey, either in interviews or by self-administered questionnaires

rising expectations the sense that better conditions are soon to follow, which, if unfulfilled, increases frustration

rituals ceremonies or repetitive practices; in religion, observances or rites often intended to evoke a sense of awe of the sacred

role the behaviors, obligations, and privileges attached to a status

role conflict conflicts that someone feels *between* roles because the expectations are at odds with those attached to another role

role performance the ways in which someone performs a role; showing a particular "style" or "personality"

role strain conflicts that someone feels *within* a role

romantic love feelings of erotic attraction accompanied by an idealization of the other

routinization of charisma the transfer of authority from a charismatic figure to either a traditional or a rational–legal form of authority

ruling class another term for the power elite

sacred Durkheim's term for things set apart or forbidden that inspire fear, awe, reverence, or deep respect

sample the individuals intended to represent the population to be studied

sanctions either expressions of approval given to people for upholding norms or expressions of disapproval for violating them

Sapir–Whorf hypothesis Edward Sapir and Benjamin Whorf's hypothesis that language creates ways of thinking and perceiving

scapegoat an individual or group unfairly blamed for someone else's troubles

science the application of systematic methods to obtain knowledge and the knowledge obtained by those methods

scientific method the use of objective, systematic observations to test theories

secondary group compared with a primary group, a larger, relatively temporary, more anonymous, formal, and impersonal group based on some interest or activity

sect a religious group larger than a cult that still feels substantial hostility from and toward society

segregation the policy of keeping racial–ethnic groups apart

selective perception seeing certain features of an object or situation, but remaining blind to others

self the unique human capacity of being able to see ourselves "from the outside"; the views we internalize of how we think others see us

self-fulfilling prophecy Robert Merton's term for an originally false assertion that becomes true simply because it was predicted

self-fulfilling stereotype preconceived ideas of what someone is like that lead to the person's behaving in ways that match the stereotype

serial murder the killing of several victims in three or more separate events

sex biological characteristics that distinguish females and males, consisting of primary and secondary sex characteristics

sexual harassment the abuse of one's position of authority to force unwanted sexual demands on someone

significant other an individual who significantly influences someone else

sign-vehicle the term used by Goffman to refer to how people use social setting, appearance, and manner to communicate information about the self

slavery a form of social stratification in which some people own other people

small group a group small enough for everyone to interact directly with all the other people

social change the alteration of culture and societies over time

social class according to Weber, a large group of people who rank close to one another in property, power, and prestige; according to Marx, one of two groups: capitalists who own the means of production or workers who sell their labor

social construction of reality the use of background assumptions and life experiences to define what is real

social control a group's formal and informal means of enforcing its norms

social environment the entire human environment, including interaction with others

social facts Durkheim's term for a group's patterns of behavior

social inequality a social condition in which privileges and obligations are given to some but denied to others

social institution the organized, usual, or standard ways by which society meets its basic needs

social integration the degree to which members of a group or a society are united by shared values and other social bonds; also known as social cohesion

social interaction one person's actions influencing someone else; usually refers to what people do when they are in one another's presence, but also includes communications at a distance

social location the group memberships that people have because of their location in history and society

social mobility movement up or down the social class ladder

social network the social ties radiating outward from the self that link people together

social order a group's usual and customary social arrangements, on which its members depend and on which they base their lives

social placement a function of education—funneling people into a society's various positions

social promotion passing students on to the next level even though they have not mastered basic materials

social sciences the intellectual and academic disciplines designed to understand the social world objectively by means of controlled and repeated observations

social stratification the division of large numbers of people into layers according to their relative property, power, and prestige; applies to both nations and to people within a nation, society, or other group

social structure the framework of society that surrounds us; consists of the ways that people and groups are related to one another; this framework gives direction to and sets limits on our behavior

socialism an economic system built around the public ownership of the means of production, central planning, and the distribution of goods without a profit motive

socialization the process by which people learn the characteristics of their group—the knowledge, skills, attitudes, values, norms, and actions thought appropriate for them

society people who share a culture and a territory

sociobiology a framework of thought in which human behavior is considered to be the result of natural selection and biological factors: a fundamental cause of human behavior

sociological perspective understanding human behavior by placing it within its broader social context

sociology the scientific study of society and human behavior

special-interest group a group of people who support a particular issue and who can be mobilized for political action

spirit of capitalism Weber's term for the desire to accumulate capital—not to spend it, but as an end in itself—and to constantly reinvest it

split labor market workers split along racial–ethnic, gender, age, or any other lines; this split is exploited by owners to weaken the bargaining power of workers

state a political entity that claims monopoly on the use of violence in some particular territory; commonly known as a country

status the position that someone occupies in a social group (also called *social status*)

status consistency ranking high or low on all three dimensions of social class

status inconsistency ranking high on some dimensions of social class and low on others; also called *status discrepancy*

status set all the statuses or positions that an individual occupies

status symbols indicators of a status; items that display prestige

stereotype assumptions of what people are like, whether true or false

stigma "blemishes" that discredit a person's claim to a "normal" identity

stockholders' revolt refusal by stockholders at their annual meetings to approve management's recommendations

stored value the goods that are stored and held in reserve that back up (or provide the value for) a deposit receipt or a currency

strain theory Robert Merton's term for the strain engendered when a society socializes large numbers of people to desire a cultural goal (such as success), but withholds from some the approved means of reaching that goal; one adaptation to the strain is crime, the choice of an innovative means (one outside the approved system) to attain the cultural goal

stratified random sample a sample from selected subgroups of the target population in which everyone in those subgroups has an equal chance of being included in the research

street crime crimes such as mugging, rape, and burglary

structural mobility movement up or down the social class ladder that is due more to changes in the *structure* of society than to the actions of individuals

subculture the values and related behaviors of a group that distinguish its members from the larger culture; a world within a world

subjective meanings the meanings that people give their own behavior

subsistence economy a type of economy in which human groups live off the land and have little or no surplus

suburb a community adjacent to a city

suburbanization the migration of people from the city to the suburbs

superego Freud's term for the conscience; the internalized norms and values of our social groups

survey the collection of data by having people answer a series of questions

sustainable environment a world system that takes into account the limits of the environment, produces enough material goods for everyone's needs, and leaves a heritage of a sound environment for the next generation

symbol something to which people attach meaning and then use to communicate with one another

symbolic culture another term for *nonmaterial culture*

symbolic interactionism a theoretical perspective in which society is viewed as composed of symbols that people use to establish meaning, develop their views of the world, and communicate with one another

system of descent how kinship is traced over the generations

taboo a norm so strong that it brings extreme sanctions, even revulsion, if violated

taking the role of the other putting yourself in someone else's shoes; understanding how someone else feels and thinks, so you anticipate how that person will act

teamwork the collaboration of two or more people to manage impressions jointly

techniques of neutralization ways of thinking or rationalizing that help people deflect (or neutralize) society's norms

technology in its narrow sense, tools; its broader sense includes the skills or procedures necessary to make and use those tools

terrorism the use of violence or the threat of violence to produce fear in order to attain political objectives

theory a general statement about how some parts of the world fit together and how they work; an explanation of how two or more facts are related to one another

Thomas theorem William I. and Dorothy S. Thomas' classic formulation of the definition of the situation: "If people define situations as real, they are real in their consequences"

total institution a place that is almost totally controlled by those who run it, in which people are cut off from the rest of society and the society is mostly cut off from them

totalitarianism a form of government that exerts almost total control over people

tracking the sorting of students into different educational programs on the basis of real or perceived abilities

traditional authority authority based on custom

transitional adulthood a term that refers to a period following high school during which young adults have not yet taken on the responsibilities ordinarily associated with adulthood; also called *adultolescence*

transitional older years an emerging stage of the life course between retirement and when people are considered old; about age 63 to 74

triad a group of three people

underclass a group of people for whom poverty persists year after year and across generations

underground economy exchanges of goods and services that escape taxes because they are not reported to the government

universal citizenship the idea that everyone has the same basic rights by virtue of being born in a country (or by immigrating and becoming a naturalized citizen)

unobtrusive measures ways of observing people so they do not know they are being studied

upward social mobility movement up the social class ladder

urban renewal the rehabilitation of a rundown area, which usually results in the displacement of the poor who are living in that area

urbanization the process by which an increasing proportion of a population lives in cities and has a growing influence on the culture

validity the extent to which an operational definition measures what it is intended to measure

value cluster values that together form a larger whole

value contradiction values that contradict one another; to follow the one means to come into conflict with the other

value free the view that a sociologist's personal values or beliefs should not influence social research

values the standards by which people define what is desirable or undesirable, superior or inferior, good or bad, beautiful or ugly

variable a factor thought to be significant for human behavior, which can vary (or change) from one case to another

Verstehen a German word used by Weber that is perhaps best understood as "to have insight into someone's situation"

voluntary associations groups made up of people who voluntarily organize on the basis of some mutual interest; also known as *voluntary memberships* and *voluntary organizations*

voter apathy indifference and inaction on the part of individuals or groups with respect to the political process

WASP White Anglo-Saxon Protestant

wealth the total value of everything someone owns, minus the debts

white ethnics white immigrants to the United States whose cultures differ from WASP culture

white-collar crime Edwin Sutherland's term for crimes committed by people of respectable and high social status in the course of their occupations; for example, bribery of public officials, securities violations, embezzlement, false advertising, and price fixing

world system the economic, political, and cultural connections that tie the world's countries together

world system theory a theory of how the economic and political connections developed that now tie the world's countries together

zero population growth women bearing only enough children to reproduce the population

References

All new references are printed in cyan.

Aaron, Henry J., William B. Schwartz, and Melissa Cox. *Can We Say No? The Challenge of Rationing Health Care.* Washington, D.C.: Brookings Institution Press, 2005.

AAUP (American Association of *University* Professors). "Annual Report on the Economic Status of the Profession, 2013–2014." Washington, D.C.: American Association of University Professors, 2014.

Abelson, Reed, and Patricia Leigh Brown. "Alternative Medicine Is Finding Its Niche in Nation's Hospitals." *New York Times*, April 14, 2002.

Aberg, Yvonne. *Social Interactions: Studies of Contextual Effects and Endogenous Processes.* Doctoral dissertation, Department of Sociology, Stockholm University, 2003.

Aberle, David F. *The Peyote Religion among the Navaho.* Chicago: Aldine, 1966.

Aberle, David F., A. K. Cohen, A. K. David, M. J. Leng, Jr., and F. N. Sutton. "The Functional Prerequisites of a Society." *Ethics, 60,* January 1950:100–111.

Abi-Habib, Maria. "The Child Soldiers Who Escaped Islamic State." *Wall Street Journal,* December 26, 2014.

Ackernecht, Erwin H. "The Role of Medical History in Medical Education." *Bulletin of the History of Medicine, 21,* 1947:135–145.

Adams, Noah. "All Things Considered." *New England Journal of Medicine* report, January 12, 2000.

Addams, Jane. *Twenty Years at Hull-House.* New York: Signet, 1981. Originally published 1910.

Adler, Patricia A., and Peter Adler. *Peer Power: Preadolescent Culture and Identity.* New Brunswick, N.J.: Rutgers University Press, 1998.

Adorno, Theodor W., Else Frenkel-Brunswick, D. J. Levinson, and R. N. Sanford. *The Authoritarian Personality.* New York: Harper & Row, 1950.

Aeppel, Timothy. "More Amish Women Are Tending to Business." *Wall Street Journal,* February 8, 1996:B1, B2.

"Affordable Care Act." Washington, D.C.: Treasury Inspector General for Tax Administration, June 14, 2012.

Agins, Teri. "When to Carry a Purse to a Meeting." *Wall Street Journal,* October 1, 2009.

Agnew, Robert. "Reflections on 'A Revised Strain Theory of Delinquency.'" *Social Forces, 91,* 1, September 2012:33–38.

Agno, John, and Barb McEwen. *Decoding the Executive Woman's Dress Code.* Seattle, Wash.: Signature e-Books, 2011.

Agranovich, Maria. "Should Russian Universities Pay Much Attention to Rankings?" *Rossiyskaya Gazeta,* July 9, 2012.

Aguirre, Benigno E. "The Conventionalization of Collective Behavior in Cuba." In *Collective Behavior and Social Movements,* Russell L. Curtis, Jr., and Benigno E. Aquirre, eds. Boston: Allyn and Bacon, 1993:413–428.

Ahmari, Sohrab. "Russia's Polonium Widow." *Wall Street Journal,* July 26–27, 2014.

Ahmed, Nafeez. "Pentagon Preparing for Mass Civil Breakdown." *The Guardian,* June 12, 2014.

Ahmed, Shumaila, and Juliana Abdul Wahab. "Animation and Socialization Process: Gender Portrayal on Cartoon Network." *Asian Social Science, 10,* 3, 2014:44–53.

Alba, Richard, and Victor Nee. *Remaking the American Mainstream: Assimilation and Contemporary Immigration.* Cambridge, Mass.: Harvard University Press, 2003.

Albanese, Jennifer. Personal research for the author. 2010.

Albert, Ethel M. "Women of Burundi: A Study of Social Values." In *Women of Tropical Africa,* Denise Paulme, ed. Berkeley: University of California Press, 1963:179–215.

"Alcohol: Balancing Risks and Benefits." Harvard School of Public Health. Unpublished paper. January 9, 2009.

Aldrich, Nelson W., Jr. *Old Money: The Mythology of America's Upper Class.* New York: Vintage Books, 1989.

Alesina, Alberto Francisco. "Women, Fertility, and the Rise of Modern Capitalism." *Science, 342,* 2014.

Alger, Selim, and Erin Calabrese. "Nursing Home Residents Voted to Bring in Strippers." *New York Post,* April 8, 2014.

Alimahomed-Wilson, Jake. "Black Longshoremen and the Fight for Equality in an 'Anti-Racist' Union." *Race and Class, 53,* 4, 2012:39–53.

Allen, Nick. "Lottery Winner Murderer Jailed for Life." *Telegraph,* December 11, 2012.

Allport, Floyd. *Social Psychology.* Boston: Houghton Mifflin, 1954.

Alter, Alexandra. "Is This Man Cheating on His Wife?" *Wall Street Journal,* August 10, 2007.

"Alternative Investment Market Letter," November 1991.

Altman, Daniel. "Old People Are Sucking Us Dry." *Foreign Policy,* March 5, 2014.

Alvarez, Lizette. "For Young Jews, a Service Says, 'Please, Do Text.'" *New York Times,* September 17, 2012.

Amato, Paul. "Research on Divorce: Continuing Trends and New Developments." *Journal of Marriage and Family, 72,* 3, June 2010:650–666.

Amato, Paul R. "The Consequences of Divorce for Adults and Children." *Journal of Marriage and Family, 62,* 2000:1269–1287.

Amato, Paul R. "The Well-Being of Children with Gay and Lesbian Parents." *Social Science Research, 41,* 2012:771–774.

Amato, Paul R., and Jacob Cheadle. "The Long Reach of Divorce: Divorce and Child Well-Being across Three Generations." *Journal of Marriage and Family, 67,* February 2005:191–206.

Amenta, Edwin. "The Social Security Debate, Now, and Then." *Contexts, 5,* 3, Summer 2006.

America's Changing Religious Landscape. Washington, D.C.: Pew Research Center, May 12, 2015.

America's Children: Key National Indicators of Well-Being. Washington, D.C.: Federal Interagency Forum on Child and Family Statistics, 2014.

American Sociological Association. "An Invitation to Public Sociology." Washington, D.C.: American Sociological Association, 2004.

American Sociological Association. *Code of Ethics and Policies and Procedures of the ASA Committee on Professional Ethics.* Washington, D.C.: American Sociological Association, 1999.

American Sociological Association. "Section on Environment and Technology." Pamphlet. Washington, D.C.: American Sociological Association, no date.

Ananat, Elizabeth O., and Guy Michaels. "The Effect of Marital Breakup on the Income Distribution of Women with Children."

Centre for Economic Performance, CEP Discussion Paper dp0787, April 2007.

Andersen, Margaret L. *Thinking about Women: Sociological Perspectives on Sex and Gender*. New York: Macmillan, 1988.

Andersen, Stacy L., Paola Sebastiani, and Thomas T. Perls. "Health Span Approximates Life Span among Many Supercentenarians: Compression of Morbidity at the Approximate Limit of Life Span." *Journal of Gerontology and Biological Sciences*, 67A, April 2013:305–405.

Anderson, Cameron, and Jessica A. Kennedy. "Micropolitics: A New Model of Status Hierarchies in Teams." *Research on Managing Groups and Teams*, 15, 2012:49–80.

Anderson, Chris. "NORC Study Describes Homeless." *Chronicle*, 1986:5, 9.

Anderson, Elijah. *A Place on the Corner*. Chicago: University of Chicago Press, 1978.

Anderson, Elijah. "Streetwise." In *Exploring Social Life: Readings to Accompany Essentials of Sociology, Sixth Edition*, 2nd ed., James M. Henslin, ed. Boston: Allyn and Bacon, 2006:147–156. Originally published 1990.

Anderson, Elijah. *Streetwise: Race, Class, and Change in an Urban Community*. Chicago: University of Chicago Press, 1990.

Anderson, Jenny. "She's Warm, Easy to Talk to, and a Source of Terror for Private-School Parents." *New York Times*, December 18, 2011.

Anderson, Nels. *Desert Saints: The Mormon Frontier in Utah*. Chicago: University of Chicago Press, 1966. Originally published 1942.

Anderson, Philip. "God and the Swedish Immigrants." *Sweden and America*, Autumn 1995:17–20.

Andreev, A. L. "On the Modernization of Education in Russia: A Historical Sociological Analysis." *Russian Education and Society*, 54, 10, October 2012:53–70.

Andriotis, AnnaMaria, and Rachel Louise Ensign. "Loan-Bias Allegations Settled for $33 Million." *Wall Street Journal*, September 25, 2015.

Angler, Natalie. "Do Races Differ? Not Really, DNA Shows." *New York Times*, August 22, 2000.

Apple, Michael W., and Lois Weiss. "Seeing Education Rationally: The Stratification of Culture and People in the Sociology of School Knowledge." In *History of Multicultural Education. Vol. 2, Foundations and Stratifications*, Carl A. Grant and Thandeka K. Chapman, eds. New York: Routledge, 2008:133–148.

Aptheker, Herbert. "W. E. B. Du Bois: Struggle Not Despair." *Clinical Sociology Review*, 8, 1990:58–68.

Archibold, Randal C. "Despite Violence, U.S. Firms Expand in Mexico." *New York Times*, July 10, 2011.

Archibold, Randal C. "Mexico Holds 4 High-Ranking Army Officers." *New York Times*, May 18, 2012.

Areddy, James T. "Chinese Concern on Inequality Rises." *Wall Street Journal*, October 17, 2012.

Arías, Jesús. "La Junta rehabilita en Grenada casas que deberá tirar por ruina." *El Pais*, January 2, 1993:1.

Ariès, Philippe. *Centuries of Childhood*, R. Baldick, trans. New York: Vintage Books, 1965.

Arlacchi, P. *Peasants and Great Estates: Society in Traditional Calabria*. Cambridge, England: Cambridge University Press, 1980.

Armstrong, David. "Hard Case: When Academics Double as Expert Witnesses." *Wall Street Journal*, June 22, 2007.

Arndt, William F., and F. Wilbur Gingrich. *A Greek-English Lexicon of the New Testament and Other Early Christian Literature*. Chicago: University of Chicago Press, 1957.

Arrison, Sonia. "Living to 100 and Beyond." *Wall Street Journal*, August 29, 2011.

Asch, Solomon. "Effects of Group Pressure upon the Modification and Distortion of Judgments." In *Readings in Social Psychology*, Guy Swanson, Theodore M. Newcomb, and Eugene L. Hartley, eds. New York: Holt, Rinehart and Winston, 1952.

Ashley, Richard. *Cocaine: Its History, Uses, and Effects*. New York: St. Martin's, 1975.

Associated Press. "Sarasota Doctor Loses License for Terminating Wrong Fetus." *Palm Beach Post*, April 13, 2010.

Audi, Tamara. "A Canyon Separates Foes in Grand Battle." *Wall Street Journal*, March 22, 2012.

Audi, Tamara, and Miriam Jordan. "U.S. Engages with Muslims." *Wall Street Journal*, November 13, 2014.

Augoustinos, Martha, Ameilia Russin, and Amanda LeCouteur. "Representations of the Stem-Cell Cloning Fraud: From Scientific Breakthrough to Managing the Stake and Interest of Science." *Public Understanding of Science*, 18, 6, 2009:687–703.

Austin, S. Byrn, Jess Haines, and Paul J. Veuglers. "Body Satisfaction and Body Weight: Gender Differences and Sociodemographic Determinants." *BMC Public Health*, 9, August 2009.

Ayittey, George B. N. "Black Africans Are Enraged at Arabs." *Wall Street Journal*, interactive edition, September 4, 1998.

Baars, Madeline. "Marriage in Black and White: Women's Support for Law Against Interracial Marriage, 1972–2000." *Intersections*, 10, 1, 2009:219–238.

Badger, Emily. "Metropolitan Areas Are Now Fueling Virtually All of America's Population Growth." *Washington Post*, March 27, 2014.

Bailey, Martha J., and Susan M. Dynarski. "Gains and Gaps: Changing Inequality in U.S. College Entry and Completion." In *Whither Opportunity?: Rising Inequality, Schools, and Children's Life Chances*, Greg J. Duncan and Richard J. Murnane, eds. Russell Sage, September 2011.

Bainbridge, William Sims. "Collective Behavior and Social Movements." In *Sociology*, Rodney Stark, ed. Belmont, Calif.: Wadsworth, 1989:608–640.

Baker, Al, and Joseph Goldstein. "Police Tactic: Keeping Crime Reports off the Books." *New York Times*, December 30, 2011.

Baker, Julie. "EMU: Dismissal Email Sent to Students by Mistake Caused 'Undue Alarm.'" www.annarbor.com, May 5, 2012.

Balazs, A. E., "Forever Young: The New Aging Consumer in the Marketplace." In *Aging, Media, and Culture*, C. L. Harrington, D. D. Bielby, and A. R. Bardo, eds. London: Lexington Books, 2014:25–36.

Bales, Robert F. *Interaction Process Analysis*. Reading, Mass.: Addison-Wesley, 1950.

Bales, Robert F. "The Equilibrium Problem in Small Groups." In *Working Papers in the Theory of Action*, Talcott Parsons et al., eds. New York: Free Press, 1953:111–115.

Ball, Aimee Lee. "Who Are You on Facebook Now?" *New York Times*, April 4, 2014.

"Baltic Fears: NATO Debates Directing Missile Shield against Russia." August 25, 2014.

Baltzell, E. Digby. *Puritan Boston and Quaker Philadelphia*. New York: Free Press, 1979.

Banchero, Stephanie. "Cheating Probe Roils Philadelphia School System." *Wall Street Journal*, January 23, 2014.

Banjo, Shelly. "Prepping for the Playdate Test." *Wall Street Journal*, August 19, 2010.

Barnes, Fred. "How to Rig a Poll." *Wall Street Journal*, June 14, 1995:A14.

Barnes, Harry Elmer. *The History of Western Civilization*, Vol. 1. New York: Harcourt, Brace, 1935.

Barnes, Helen. "A Comment on Stroud and Pritchard: Child Homicide, Psychiatric Disorder and Dangerousness." *British Journal of Social Work*, 31, 3, June 2001.

Barnes, J. C., and Bruce A. Jacobs. "Genetic Risk for Violent Behavior and Environmental Exposure to Disadvantage and Violent Crime: The

Case for Gene-Environment Interaction." *Journal of Interpersonal Violence,* 18, 1, 2013:92–120.

Barnes, Julian A. "Pentagon Digs in on Cyberwar Front." *Wall Street Journal,* July 6, 2012.

Barreto, Matt. *Ethnic Cues: The Role of Shared Ethnicity in Latino Political Participation.* Ann Arbor: University of Michigan Press, 2010.

Barrett, A. E., A. Raphael, and J. Gunderson. "Reflections of Old Age, Constructions of Aging Selves: Drawing Links between Media Images and Views of Aging." In *Aging, Media, and Culture,* C. L. Harrington, D. D. Bielby, and A. R. Bardo, eds. London: Lexington Books, 2014:39–50.

Barrett, Devlin, and Michael Howard Saul. "Weiner Now Says He Sent Photos." *Wall Street Journal,* June 7, 2011.

Barry, John. "A New Breed of Soldier." *Newsweek,* December 10, 2001:24–31.

Barstow, David, and Lowell Bergman. "Death on the Job, Slaps on the Wrist." *Wall Street Journal,* January 10, 2003.

Barta, Patrick, and Kate O'Keeffe. "Use of Child Workers Is Declining." *Wall Street Journal,* September 23, 2013.

Basten, Christoph, and Frank Betz. *Marx vs. Weber: Does Religion Affect Politics and the Economy?* Florence, Italy: European University Institute, 2011.

Bates, Marston. *Gluttons and Libertines: Human Problems of Being Natural.* New York: Vintage Books, 1967. Quoted in Crapo, Richley H. *Cultural Anthropology: Understanding Ourselves and Others,* 5th ed. Boston: McGraw Hill, 2002.

Baumeister, Roy F. "Gender Differences in Motivation Shape Social Interaction Patterns, Sexual Relationships, Social Inequality, and Cultural History." In *Handbook of Gender and Psychology,* M. K. Ryan, and N. R. Branscombe, eds. Los Angeles: Sage, 2013:270–286.

Baumer, Eric P., and Kevin T. Wolff. "Evaluating the Contemporary Crime Drop(s) in America, New York City, and Many Other Places." *Justice Quarterly,* 2013. (in press)

Baylis, Francois. "The Ethics of Creating Children with Three Genetic Parents." *Reproductive BioMedicine Online,* 26, 6, June 2013:531–534.

Beachy, Lester. *Our Amish Values: Who We Are and What We Believe.* Eugene, Ore.: Harvest House, 2015.

Beah, Ishmael. *A Long Way Gone: Memoirs of a Boy Soldier.* New York: Farrar, Straus and Giroux, 2007.

Beals, Ralph L., and Harry Hoijer. *An Introduction to Anthropology,* 3rd ed. New York: Macmillan, 1965.

Bean, Frank D., Jennifer Lee, Jeanne Batalova, and Mark Leach. *Immigration and Fading Color Lines in America.* Washington, D.C.: Population Reference Bureau, 2004.

Bearak, Barry. "For Some Bushmen, a Homeland Worth a Fight." *New York Times,* November 5, 2010.

Bearak, Barry. "In Crisis, Zimbabwe Asks: Could Mugabe Lose?" *New York Times,* March 7, 2008.

Beauchamp, Jonathan P., David Cesarini, and Nicholas A. Christakis. "Molecular Genetics and Economics." *Journal of Economic Perspectives,* 25, 4, Fall 2011:57–82.

Beck, Melinda. "Virtual Doctor Visits: What's Treated and What's the Cost?" *Wall Street Journal,* May 8, 2014.

Beck, Scott H., and Joe W. Page. "Involvement in Activities and the Psychological Well-Being of Retired Men." *Activities, Adaptation, & Aging,* 11, 1, 1988:31–47.

Becker, Gary S., and Julio J. Elias. "Cash for Kidneys." *Wall Street Journal,* January 18–19, 2014.

Becker, George. "The Continuing Path of Distortion: The Protestant Ethic and Max Weber's School Enrollment Statistics." *Acta Sociologica,* 52, 3, September 2009:195–212.

Becker, Howard S. *Outsiders: Studies in the Sociology of Deviance.* New York: Free Press, 1966.

Becker, Jo, and Scott Shane. "Secret 'Kill List' Proves a Test of Obama's Principles and Will." *New York Times,* May 29, 2012.

Becker, Jo, and Steven Lee Myers. "Putin's Friend Profits in Purge of Schoolbooks." *New York Times,* November 1, 2014.

Beckman, Nils, Magda Waerm, Deborah Gustafson, and Ingmar Skoog. "Secular Trends in Self Reported Sexual Activity and Satisfaction in Swedish 70 Year Olds: Cross Sectional Survey of Four Populations, 1971–2001." *British Medical Journal,* 2008:1–7.

Beeghley, Leonard. *The Structure of Social Stratification in the United States,* 5th ed. Boston: Allyn & Bacon, 2008.

Begley, Sharon. "Twins: Nazi and Jew." *Newsweek,* 94, December 3, 1979:139.

Belkin, Douglas. "Chicago Hunts for Answers to Gang Killings." *Wall Street Journal,* July 13, 2012.

Belkin, Douglas. "Liberal Education: At This College, Videogames Are a Varsity Sport." *Wall Street Journal,* September 2, 2014.

Bell, Daniel. *The Coming of Post-Industrial Society: A Venture in Social Forecasting.* New York: Basic Books, 1973.

Bell, David A. "An American Success Story: The Triumph of Asian-Americans." In *Sociological Footprints: Introductory Readings in Sociology,* 5th ed., Leonard Cargan and Jeanne H. Ballantine, eds. Belmont, Calif.: Wadsworth, 1991:308–316.

Bell, Michael Mayerfeld. *An Invitation to Environmental Sociology.* Los Angeles: Pine Forge Press, 2009.

Bellafante, Ginia. "Community College Students Face a Very Long Road to Graduation." *New York Times,* October 3, 2014.

Bellah, Robert N. *Beyond Belief.* New York: Harper & Row, 1970.

Bello, Marisol. "Poverty Affects 46 Million Americans." *USA Today,* September 30, 2011.

Belluck, Pam. "Prosecutors Say Greed Drove Pharmacist to Dilute Drugs." *New York Times,* August 18, 2001.

Belsky, Jay. "Early Child Care and Early Child Development: Major Findings of the NICHD Study of Early Child Care." *European Journal of Developmental Psychology,* 3, 1, 2006:95–110.

Belsky, Jay. "Effects of Child Care on Child Development: Give Parents Real Choice." Unpublished paper, March 2009.

Belsky, Jay, Deborah Lowe Vandell, Margaret Burchinall, K. Alison Clarke-Stewart, Kathleen McCartney, and Margaret Tresch Owen. "Are There Long-Term Effects of Early Child Care?" *Child Development,* 78, 2, March/April 2007:681–701.

Ben-Ami, Naomi, and Amy J. L. Baker. "The Long-Term Correlates of Childhood Exposure to Parental Alienation on Adult Self-Sufficiency and Well-Being." *American Journal of Family Therapy,* 40, 2012:169–183.

Bendavid, Naftali. "EU Gears Up for Central Africa Force." *Wall Street Journal,* January 18–19, 2014.

Benet, Sula. "Why They Live to Be 100, or Even Older, in Abkhasia." *New York Times Magazine,* December 26, 1971.

Benford, Robert D. "The College Sports Reform Movement: Reframing the 'Educational' Industry." *The Sociological Quarterly,* 48, 2007:1–28.

Bennett, Brian, and Michael Weisskopf. "The Sum of Two Evils." *Time,* May 25, 2003.

Bennett, Jessica. "How to Attack the Gender Wage Gap? Speak Up." *New York Times,* December 15, 2012.

Bennett-Smith, Meredith. "Taro Aso, Japanese Finance Minster, Says Country Should Let Old People 'Hurry Up and Die.'" *Huffington Post,* January 23, 2013.

Bentley, Arthur Fisher. *The Process of Government: A Study of Social Pressures.* Chicago: University of Chicago Press, 1908.

Berger, Jeffrey T., Fred Rasner, and Eric J. Cassell. "Ethics of Practicing Medical Procedures on Newly Dead and Nearly Dead Patients." *Journal of General Internal Medicine,* 17, 2002:774–778.

Berger, Lawrence M., Maria Cancian, and Daniel R. Meyer. "Maternal Re-Partnering and New-Partner Fertility: Associations with Nonresident Father Investments in Children." *Children and Youth Services Review, 34*, 2012:426–436.

Berger, Peter. "Invitation to Sociology." In *Down to Earth Sociology: Introductory Readings*, 15th ed., James M. Henslin, ed. New York: Free Press, 2016. Originally published 1963.

Berger, Peter L. *Invitation to Sociology: A Humanistic Perspective*. New York: Doubleday, 1963.

Bergman, Jerry. "Ota Benga: The Pygmy Displayed in a Zoo." In *The Darwin Effect*. Green Forest, Ark.: New Leaf Publishing, 2014:175–198.

Bergmann, Barbara R. "The Future of Child Care." Paper presented at the annual meetings of the American Sociological Association, 1995.

Berk, Richard A. *Collective Behavior*. Dubuque, Iowa: Brown, 1974.

Berle, Adolf, Jr., and Gardiner C. Means. *The Modern Corporation and Private Property*. New York: Harcourt, Brace and World, 1932. (As cited in Useem 1980:44.)

Berman, Marc G., John Jonides, and Stephen Kaplan. "The Cognitive Benefits of Interacting with Nature." *Psychological Science, 19*, 12, 2008:1207–1212.

Bernard, Tara Siegel. "The Key to Wedded Bliss? Money Matters." *New York Times*, September 10, 2008.

Bernard, Viola W., Perry Ottenberg, and Fritz Redl. "Dehumanization: A Composite Psychological Defense in Relation to Modern War." In *The Triple Revolution Emerging: Social Problems in Depth*, Robert Perucci and Marc Pilisuk, eds. Boston: Little, Brown, 1971:17–34.

Bernstein, Elizabeth. "More Prayer, Less Hassle." *Wall Street Journal*, June 27, 2003:W3, W4.

Bernstein, Marc F. "Where All the Teachers Are Above Average." *Wall Street Journal*, September 30, 2014.

Bertrand, Marianne, and Sendhil Mullainathan. "Are Emily and Brendan More Employable than Lakish and Jamal? A Field Experiment on Labor Market Discrimination." Unpublished paper, November 18, 2002.

Bertrand, Natasha. "Here's the Average SAT Score for Every College Major." *Business Insider*, October 24, 2014.

Best, Deborah L. "The Contribution of the Whitings to the Study of the Socialization of Gender." *Journal of Cross-Cultural Psychology, 41*, 2010:534–545.

Bettelheim, Bruno. "The Commitment Required of a Woman Entering a Scientific Profession in Present-Day American Society." In *Women and the Scientific Professions*, Jacquelyn A. Mattfield and Carol G. Van Aken, eds. Cambridge, Mass.: MIT Press, 1965.

Bezrukova, Katerinma, Karen A. Jehn, and Chester S. Spell. "Reviewing Diversity Training: Where We Have Been and Where We Should Go." *Academy of Management Learning and Education, 11*, 2, 2012:207–227.

Bialik, Carl. "Hurdles for New Line on Poverty." *Wall Street Journal*, September 21–22, 2013.

Bianchi, Suzanne M. "Family Change and Time Allocation in American Families." Washington, D.C.: Alfred P. Sloan Foundation, November 29–30, 2010.

Bianchi, Suzanne M., John P. Robinson, and Melissa A. Milkie. *Changing Rhythms of American Family Life*. New York: Russell Sage Foundation, 2006.

Bick, Johanna, Tong Zhu, Catherine Stamoulis, et al. "Effect of Early Institutionalization and Foster Care on Long-Term White Matter Development: A Randomized Clinical Trial." *J.A.M.A. Pediatrics*, January 26, 2015.

Bilefsky, Dan. "Albanian Custom Fades: Woman as Family Man." *New York Times*, June 25, 2008.

Bilefsky, Dan. "An Abused Wife? Or an Executioner?" *New York Times*, September 25, 2011a.

Bilefsky, Dan. "5-Year Term for Woman Who Killed Her Husband." *New York Times*, November 10, 2011b.

Bilefsky, Dan. "In Mother's Trial, Man Tells of His Father's Rage." *New York Times*, September 21, 2011c.

Bilefsky, Dan. "Wife Who Fired 11 Shots Is Acquitted of Murder." *New York Times*, October 6, 2011d.

Billeaud, Jacques. "Arizona Sheriff Defends Illegal-Immigrant Sweeps." *Seattle Times*, April 26, 2008.

Bilton, Nick. "My T-Shirt Told Me to Take a Chill Pill." *New York Times*, May 25, 2014.

Bishop, Jerry E. "Study Finds Doctors Tend to Postpone Heart Surgery for Women, Raising Risk." *Wall Street Journal*, April 16, 1990:B4.

Blair, Irene V., John F. Steiner, D. L. Fairclough, et al. "Clinicians' Implicit Ethnic/Racial Bias and Perceptions of Care among Black and Latino Patients." *Annals of Family Medicine, 11*, 2013:43–52.

Blankstein, Andrew, and Richard Winton. "Paraplegic Allegedly 'Dumped' on Skid Row." *Los Angeles Times*, February 9, 2007.

Blau, David M. "The Production of Quality in Child-Care Centers: Another Look." *Applied Developmental Science, 4*, 3, 2000:136–148.

Blau, Peter M., and Otis Dudley Duncan. *The American Occupational Structure*. New York: John Wiley, 1967.

Blee, Kathleen M. "Inside Organized Racism." In *Life in Society: Readings to Accompany Sociology: A Down-to-Earth Approach, Seventh Edition*, James M. Henslin, ed. Boston: Allyn and Bacon, 2005:46–57.

Blee, Kathleen M. "Trajectories of Ideologies and Action in US Organized Racism." In *Identity and Participation in Culturally Diverse Societies: A Multidisciplinary Perspective*. Assaad E. Azzi, Xenia Chryssochoou, Bert Klandermans, and Bernd Simon, eds. Oxford, U.K.: Blackwell Publishing, 2011.

Bloom, Paul. "The Moral Life of Babies." *New York Times Magazine*, May 3, 2010.

Bloomfield, Ruth. "Where Did the Time Go?" *Wall Street Journal*, November 23, 2012.

Blumenthal, Ralph. "Court Says Texas Illegally Seized Sect's Children." *New York Times*, May 23, 2008a.

Blumenthal, Ralph. "52 Girls Are Taken from Polygamist Sect's Ranch in Texas." *New York Times*, April 5, 2008b.

Blumer, Herbert George. "Collective Behavior." In *Principles of Sociology*, Robert E. Park, ed. New York: Barnes and Noble, 1939:219–288.

Blumer, Herbert George. *Industrialization as an Agent of Social Change: A Critical Analysis*, David R. Maines and Thomas J. Morrione, eds. Hawthorne, N.Y.: Aldine de Gruyter, 1990.

Blumstein, Philip, and Pepper Schwartz. *American Couples: Money, Work, Sex*. New York: Pocket Books, 1985.

Bolmont, Mylene, John T. Cacioppo, and Stephanie Cacioppo. "Love Is in the Gaze: An Eye-Tracking Study of Love and Sexual Desire." *Psychological Science, 25*, 9, September 2014:1748–1756.

Book of the States. Washington, D.C.: The Council of State Governments, 2014.

Boorstein, Michelle. "Many U.S. Latinos Shift from Catholicism to Pentecostalism, Other Choices, Survey Finds." *The Washington Post*, May 7, 2014.

Borger, Julian. "The Truth about Israel's Secret Nuclear Arsenal." *The Guardian*, January 15, 2014.

Boroditsky, Lera. "Lost in Translation." *Wall Street Journal*, July 24, 2010.

Bosman, Julie. "New York Schools for Pregnant Girls Will Close." *New York Times*, May 24, 2007.

"Boston Scientific and Subsidiaries Pay $30 Million for Guidant's Sale of Defective Heart Devices for Use in Medicare Patients." Department of Justice Press Release, October 17, 2013.

Boudreaux, Richard. "Moscow Raises Alarm over Missile-Defense Plan for Europe." *Wall Street Journal*, May 3, 2012.

Boudreaux, Richard. "Putin Move Stirs Russian Environmentalist Row." *New York Times*, January 20, 2010.

Boulding, Elise. *The Underside of History*. Boulder, Colo.: Westview Press, 1976.

Bowles, Hannah Riley. "Claiming Authority: How Women Explain Their Ascent to Top Business Leadership Positions." *Harvard Kennedy School Faculty Research Working Paper Series RWP12-047*, Cambridge, Mass.: Harvard University, October 2012.

Bowles, Hannah Riley, and Linda Babcck. "How Can Women Escape the Compensation Negotiation Dilemma? Relational Accounts Are One Answer." *Psychology of Women Quarterly*, 37, 1, 2012:80–96.

Bowles, Samuel. "Unequal Education and the Reproduction of the Social Division of Labor." In *Power and Ideology in Education*, J. Karabel and A. H. Halsely, eds. New York: Oxford University Press, 1977.

Bowles, Samuel, and Herbert Gintis. *Schooling in Capitalist America*. New York: Basic Books, 1976.

Bowles, Samuel, and Herbert Gintis. "*Schooling in Capitalist America* Revisited." *Sociology of Education*, 75, 2002:1–18.

Bradford, Phillips Verner, and Harvey Blume. *Ota Benga: The Pygmy in the Zoo*. New York: Delta, 1992.

Braig, Stefanie, Richard Peter, Gabriele Nagel, et al. "The Impact of Social Status Inconsistency on Cardiovascular Risk Factors, Myocardial Infarction and Stroke in the EPIC-Heidelberg Cohort." *BMC Public Health*, 11, 2011:104.

Brajuha, Mario, and Lyle Hallowell. "Legal Intrusion and the Politics of Fieldwork: The Impact of the Brajuha Case." *Urban Life*, 14, 4, January 1986:454–478.

Bramlett, Matthew D., and Laura F. Radel. "Adverse Family Experiences among Children in Nonparental Care, 2011–2012." *National Health Statistics Report*, 74, May 7, 2014.

Brandom, Russell. "The FBI Just Finished Building Its Facial Recognition System." *The Verge*, September 15, 2014.

Bravin, Jess. "Supreme Court Upholds Michigan's Affirmative Action Ban." *Wall Street Journal*, April 23, 2014.

Bray, Rosemary L. "Rosa Parks: A Legendary Moment, a Lifetime of Activism." *Ms.*, 6, 3, November–December 1995:45–47.

Brayne, Sarah. "Explaining the United States' Penal Exceptionalism: Political, Economic, and Social Factors." *Sociology Compass*, 7, 2, 2013:75–86.

Brecher, Edward M., and the Editors of Consumer Reports. *Licit and Illicit Drugs*. Boston: Little, Brown, 1972.

Bremmer, Ian. "The Secret to China's Boom: State Capitalism." Thomson-Reuters, 2011.

Brenneman, Richard. "Ignacio Chapela: Ousted Professor Holds Final Class." *Berkeley Daily Planet*, December 10, 2004.

Briand, Frederic. "Silent Plains . . . The Fading Sounds of Native Languages." *National Geographic News Watch*, February 28, 2013.

Bridgwater, William, ed. *The Columbia Viking Desk Encyclopedia*. New York: Viking Press, 1953.

Brilliant, Ashleigh E. *Social Effects of the Automobile in Southern California during the 1920s*. Unpublished doctoral dissertation, University of California at Berkeley, 1964.

Brinton, Crane. *The Anatomy of Revolution*. New York: Vintage Books, 1965.

Broad, William J., and David E. Sanger. "With Eye on Iran, Rivals Also Want Nuclear Power." *New York Times*, April 15, 2007.

Brockerhoff, Martin P. "An Urbanizing World." *Population Bulletin*, 55, 3, September 2000:1–44.

Bromley, David G. "The Satanic Cult Scare." *Culture and Society*, May–June 1991:55–56.

Bronfenbrenner, Urie. "Principles for the Healthy Growth and Development of Children." In *Marriage and Family in a Changing Society*, 4th ed., James M. Henslin, ed. New York: Free Press, 1992:243–249.

Broughton, Philip Delves. "When Two People Click." *Wall Street Journal*, January 29, 2013.

Brown, Alan S. "Mexico Redux." *Mechanical Engineering*, January 2008.

Brown, Eliot. "Suburbia Looks to Grow Up." *Wall Street Journal*, January 18–19, 2014.

Brown, Fred. "Maverick Doctor's Revolution: Services-for-Fee Clinic." *Knoxville News Sentinel*, August 20, 2007.

Brown, Stephanie. "Strategies for Guiding the Conversation and Redirecting the Outcomes of Community Transition." Paper submitted to Harvard's Joint Center for Housing Studies and Neighbor Works America, July 2014.

Browning, Christopher R. *Ordinary Men: Reserve Police Battalion 101 and the Final Solution in Poland*. New York: HarperPerennial, 1993.

Brunvand, Jan Harold. *Be Afraid, Be Very Afraid: The Book of Scary Urban Legends*. New York: W. W. Norton, 2004.

Brunvand, Jan Harold. *The Choking Doberman and Other "New" Urban Legends*. New York: Norton, 1984.

Brunvand, Jan Harold. *The Vanishing Hitchhiker: American Urban Legends and Their Meanings*. New York: Norton, 1981.

Bryant, Chalandra M., Rand D. Conger, and Jennifer M. Meehan. "The Influence of In-Laws on Changes in Marital Success." *Journal of Marriage and the Family*, 63, 3, August 2001:614–626.

Buchanan, Elsa. "Turkey: PM Pledges Dowry of Gold to Young Women Who Have Children." *IBTimes*, February 10, 2015.

Buckley, Cara. "Among Victims, an Amish Farmer Quick to Adapt." *New York Times*, July 21, 2011.

"Builder Stephen Ross Buys Half of Dolphins from Huizenga." *International Herald Tribune*, February 22, 2008.

Bumiller, Elisabeth. "First Comes Marriage—Then, Maybe, Love." In *Marriage and Family in a Changing Society*, 4th ed., James M. Henslin, ed. New York: Free Press, 1992:120–125.

Bumiller, Elisabeth. "Records Show Doubts on '64 Vietnam Crisis." *New York Times*, July 14, 2010.

Burawoy, Michael. "The Field of Sociology: Its Power and Its Promise." In *Public Sociology: Fifteen Eminent Sociologists Debate Politics and the Profession in the Twenty-First Century*. Berkeley: University of California Press, 2007:241–258.

Burger, Jerry M. "Replicating Milgram: Would People Still Obey Today?" *American Psychologist*, 64, 1, January 2009:1–11.

Burgess, Ernest W. "The Growth of the City: An Introduction to a Research Project." In *The City*, Robert E. Park et al., eds. Chicago: University of Chicago Press, 1925:47–62.

Burgess, Ernest W., and Harvey J. Locke. *The Family: From Institution to Companionship*. New York: American Book, 1945.

Burkitt, Laurie. "China Abandons One-Child Policy." *Wall Street Journal*, October 30, 2015.

Burman, Jeremy Trevelyan. "Updating the Baldwin Effect: The Biological Levels behind Piaget's New Theory." *New Ideas in Psychology*, 2013. (in press)

Burnham, Walter Dean. *Democracy in the Making: American Government and Politics*. Englewood Cliffs, N.J.: Prentice Hall, 1983.

Burns, Frances. "Texas Seizes Yearning for Zion Ranch, HQ of Imprisoned Polygamist Warren Jeffs." United Press International, April 18, 2014.

Bush, Diane Mitsch, and Robert G. Simmons. "Socialization Processes over the Life Course." In *Social Psychology: Sociological Perspectives*, Morris Rosenberger and Ralph H. Turner, eds. New Brunswick, N.J.: Transaction, 1990:133–164.

Butler, Robert N. "Ageism: Another Form of Bigotry." *Gerontologist*, 9, Winter 1980:243–246.

Butler, Robert N. *Why Survive? Being Old in America*. New York: Harper & Row, 1975.

Byers, Michele, and Diane Crocker. "Feminist Cohorts and Waves: Attitudes of Junior Female Academics." *Women's Studies International Forum*, 35, 2012:1–11.

Bynum, Bill. "Discarded Diagnoses." *Lancet*, 358, 9294, November 17, 2001:1736.

Byrnes, Hilary F., and Breda A. Miller. "The Relationship between Neighborhood Characteristics and Effective Parenting Behaviors: The Role of Social Support." *Journal of Family Issues*, 33, 12, 2012:1658–1687.

Cabrera, Natasha J., and Robert H. Bradley. "Latino Fathers and Their Children." *Child Development Perspectives*, 6, 3, 2012:232–238.

Cacioppo, John T., and Stephanie Cacioppo. "Older Adults Reporting Social Isolation or Loneliness Show Poorer Cognitive Function 4 Years Later." *Evidence-Based Nursing*, June 8, 2013.

Campbell, James D., Dong Phil Yoon, and Brick Johnstone. "Determining Relationships between Physical Health and Spiritual Experience, Religious Practices, and Congregational Support in a Heterogeneous Medical Sample." *Journal of Religion and Health*, 49, 2010:3–17.

Campbell, Karen E., and Holly J. McCammon. "Elizabeth Blackwell's Heirs: Women as Physicians in the U.S., 1880–1920." Unpublished paper, 2005.

Canedy, Dana. "Critics of Graduation Exam Threaten Boycott in Florida." *New York Times*, May 13, 2003.

Canipe, Chris, and Sarah Slobin. "CEO Pay vs. Performance." *Wall Street Journal*, June 24, 2015.

Cannon, Lou. *Official Negligence: How Rodney King and the Riots Changed Los Angeles and the LAPD*. New York: Times Books, 1998.

Cantril, Hadley. *The Psychology of Social Movements*. New York: Wiley, 1941.

Caproni, Paula J. "Work/Life Balance: You Can't Get There from Here." *Journal of Applied Behavioral Science*, 40, 2, June 2004:208–218.

Carbado, Devon W., and Mitu Gulati. "Acting White?" Unpublished paper, 2014.

Carey, Benedict. "In the Hospital, a Degrading Shift from Person to Patient." *New York Times*, August 16, 2005.

Carlson, Lewis H., and George A. Colburn. *In Their Place: White America Defines Her Minorities, 1850–1950*. New York: Wiley, 1972.

Carpenito, Lynda Juall. "The Myths of Acquaintance Rape." *Nursing Forum*, 34, 4, October–December 1999:3.

Carr, Deborah. "Death and Dying in the Contemporary United States: What Are the Psychological Implications of Anticipated Death?" *Social and Personality Psychology Compass*, 6, 2, 2012:184–195.

Carr, Deborah, Carol D. Ryff, Burton Singer, and William J. Magee. "Bringing the 'Life' Back into Life Course Research: A 'Person-Centered' Approach to Studying the Life Course." Paper presented at the annual meetings of the American Sociological Association, 1995.

Carreyrou, John. "U.S. Sues Surgeon over Spinal Operations." *Wall Street Journal*, September 10, 2014.

Carreyrou, John, and Tom McGinty. "Top Spine Surgeons Reap Royalties, Medicare Bounty." *Wall Street Journal*, December 20, 2010.

Carrington, Tim. "Developed Nations Want Poor Countries to Succeed on Trade, but Not Too Much." *Wall Street Journal*, September 20, 1993:A10.

Carson, E. Ann. "Prisoners in 2013." *Bureau of Justice Statistics Bulletin*, September 2014.

Carter, Michael J. "Gender Socialization and Identity Theory." *Social Sciences*, 3, 2014:242–263.

Carter, Nancy M. "Pipeline's Broken Promise." New York: Catalyst, 2010.

Cartwright, Dorwin, and Alvin Zander, eds. *Group Dynamics*, 3rd ed. Evanston, Ill.: Peterson, 1968.

Casey, Edward S., and Mary Watkins. *Up against the Wall: Re-Imagining the U.S.-Mexico Border*. Austin: University of Texas Press, 2014.

Casey, Nicholas. "Mexico's Masked Vigilantes Defy Drug Gangs—and the Law." *Wall Street Journal*, February 2–3, 2013.

Casey, Nicholas, and Anthony Harrup. "Mexico Confront Cartel-Fighting Militias." *Wall Street Journal*, January 14, 2014.

Casper, Lynne M., and Loretta E. Bass. "Voting and Registration in the Election of November 1996." Washington, D.C.: U.S. Census Bureau, 1998.

Casper, Monica J. *The Making of the Unborn Patient: A Social Anatomy of Fetal Surgery*. New Brunswick, N.J.: Rutgers University Press, 1998.

Cassasus, Barbara. "Study Linking Genetically Modified Corn to Rat Tumors Is Retracted." *Scientific American*, November 29, 2013.

Cassel, Russell N. "Examining the Basic Principles for Effective Leadership." *College Student Journal*, 33, 2, June 1999:288–301.

Castells, Manuel. Occupy *Networks of Outrage and Hope: Social Movements in the Internet Age*. Cambridge, U.K.: Polity Press.

Castillo, Isabella. "ASU Chosen to Study How Terrorists Use Social Media to Recruit New Members." *The State Press*, July 9, 2015.

Catan, Thomas. "Spain's Showy Debt Collectors Wear a Tux, Collect the Bucks." *Wall Street Journal*, October 11, 2008.

Cauce, Ana Mari, and Melanie Domenech-Rodriguez. "Latino Families: Myths and Realities." In *Latino Children and Families in the United States: Current Research and Future Directions*, Josefina M. Contreras, Kathryn A. Kerns, and Angela M. Neal-Barnett, eds. Westport, Conn.: Praeger, 2002:3–25.

CDC. See Centers for Disease Control and Prevention.

Cellini, Stephanie R., Signe-Mary McKernan, and Caroline Ratcliffe. "The Dynamics of Poverty in the United States: A Review of Data, Methods, and Findings." *Journal of Policy Analysis and Management*, 27, 2008:577–605.

Center for American Women in Politics. "Women in Elective Office 2013." New Brunswick, N.J.: Rutgers University, 2013.

Center for Injury Prevention and Control. NCHS Vital Statistics System for Numbers of Deaths, 2013.

Centers for Disease Control and Prevention. "*2001 Surveillance Report*." Divisions of HIV/AIDS Prevention, 2003.

Centers for Disease Control and Prevention. "*HIV/AIDS Surveillance Report*." Divisions of HIV/AIDS Prevention, 1997.

Centers for Disease Control and Prevention. "HIV among African Americans." Hyattsville, MD: Department of Health and Human Services, 2010.

Centers for Disease Control and Prevention. "*Economic Facts about U.S. Tobacco Production and Use*." February 6, 2014a.

Centers for Disease Control and Prevention. *HIV Surveillance Report*. "Diagnoses of HIV Infection in the United States and Dependent Areas, 2012. October 2014b.

Centers for Disease Control and Prevention. "National Suicide Statistics at a Glance." January 2, 2014c.

Centers for Disease Control and Prevention. "National Vital Statistics System: Historical Data 1900–1998: Leading Causes of Death." Atlanta, Ga.: Centers for Disease Control and Prevention, 2009.

Centers for Disease Control and Prevention. "*Secondhand Smoke (SHS) Facts*." April 11, 2014d.

Centers for Disease Control and Prevention. "Summary Health Statistics for U.S. Adults: National Health Interview Survey, 2011." *Vital Health Statistics*, 10, 256, December 2012.

Centers for Disease Control and Prevention. "Summary Health Statistics for U.S. Adults: National Health Interview Survey, 2012." *Vital Health Statistics, 10*, 260, January 2014e.

Cerulo, Karen A., and Janet M. Ruane. "Death Comes Alive: Technology and the Re-Conception of Death." *Science as Culture, 6*, 28, 1996:444–466.

Chafetz, Janet Saltzman. *Gender Equity: An Integrated Theory of Stability and Change.* Newbury Park, Calif.: Sage, 1990.

Chafetz, Janet Saltzman, and Anthony Gary Dworkin. *Female Revolt: Women's Movements in World and Historical Perspective.* Totowa, N.J.: Rowman & Allanheld, 1986.

Chagnon, Napoleon A. *Yanomamo: The Fierce People*, 2nd ed. New York: Holt, Rinehart and Winston, 1977.

Chalfant, H. Paul. "Stepping to Redemption: Twelve-Step Groups as Implicit Religion." *Free Inquiry in Creative Sociology, 20*, 2, November 1992:115–120.

Chambliss, William J. *Power, Politics, and Crime.* Boulder: Westview Press, 2000.

Chambliss, William J. "The Saints and the Roughnecks." In *Down to Earth Sociology: Introductory Readings*, 15th ed., James M. Henslin, ed. New York: The Free Press, 2016.

Chandler, Tertius, and Gerald Fox. *3000 Years of Urban Growth.* New York: Academic Press, 1974.

Chandy, Laurence, and Cory Smith. "How Poor Are America's Poorest? U.S. $2 a Day Poverty in a Global Context." Washington, D.C.: The Bookings Institution, August 2014.

Chang, Iris. *The Rape of Nanking.* New York: Basic Books, 1997.

Chang, Leslie T. "Why the One-Child Policy Has Become Irrelevant." *Atlantic*, March 20, 2013.

Chapman, Catherine. "Women Learn to Dress for Success." *New York Times*, November 13, 2013.

Chase, Arlen F., Diane Z. Chase, and John F. Weishampel. "Lasers in the Jungle." *Archeology, 63*, 4, July/August 2010.

Cheadle, Jacob, Paul R. Amato, and Valarie King. "Patterns of Nonresident Father Involvement." *Demography, 47*, 2010:205–226.

Chen, Edwin. "Twins Reared Apart: A Living Lab." *New York Times Magazine*, December 9, 1979:112.

Chen, Kathy. "China's Growth Places Strains on a Family's Ties." *Wall Street Journal*, April 13, 2005.

Chen, Te-Ping. "China Sees More Cases against Polluters." *Wall Street Journal*, March 13, 2015.

Chen, Te-Ping. "In Hong Kong, Inflation Fears Spook the Spirit World." *Wall Street Journal*, August 20, 2013.

Cherlin, J. Andrew. "Remarriage as an Incomplete Institution." In *Marriage and Family in a Changing Society*, 3rd ed., James M. Henslin, ed. New York: Free Press, 1989:492–501.

Chetty, Raj, Nathaniel Hendren, Patrick Kline, Emmanuel Saez, and Nicholas Turner, "Is the United States Still a Land of Opportunity? Recent Trends in Intergenerational Mobility." Working Paper 19844, National Bureau of Economic Research, January 2014.

"Child Care Workers." In *2012–13 Occupational Outlook Handbook.* Washington, D.C.: Bureau of Labor Statistics, 2013.

Chin, Nancy P., Alicia Monroe, and Kevin Fiscella. "Social Determinants of (Un)Healthy Behaviors." *Education for Health: Change in Learning and Practice, 13*, 3, November 2000:317–328.

"China Overview." World Bank, February 28, 2014.

"China to Broaden Two-Child Policy in 2 Years, Adviser Says." *Bloomberg News*, October 17, 2014.

Chivers, C. J. "Officer Resigns before Hearing in D.W.I. Case." *New York Times*, August 29, 2001.

Chodorow, Nancy J. "What Is the Relation between Psychoanalytic Feminism and the Psychoanalytic Psychology of Women?" In *Theoretical Perspectives on Sexual Difference*, Deborah L. Rhode, ed. New Haven, Conn.: Yale University Press, 1990:114–130.

Chumley, Cheryl K. "Suspected Witch Bound, Tortured, Burned Alive in Papua New Guinea." *Washington Times*, February 8, 2013.

CIA (Central Intelligence Agency). "Report of Questionable Activity in Connection with Project PBSuccess." Washington, D.C.: Central Intelligence Agency, 2003.

CIA (Central Intelligence Agency). *The World Factbook.* Washington, D.C.: U.S. Government Printing Office, 2014. Published annually.

Cillizza, Chris. "People Hate Congress. But Most Incumbents Get Re-Elected. What Gives?" *Washington Post*, May 9, 2013.

Clair, Jeffrey Michael, David A. Karp, and William C. Yoels. *Experiencing the Life Cycle: A Social Psychology of Aging*, 2nd ed. Springfield, Ill.: Thomas, 1993.

Clark, Candace. *Misery and Company: Sympathy in Everyday Life.* Chicago: University of Chicago Press, 1997.

Clarke, Lee. "Panic: Myth or Reality?" *Contexts*, Fall 2002:21–26.

Clearfield, Melissa W., and Naree M. Nelson. "Sex Differences in Mothers' Speech and Play Behavior with 6-, 9-, and 14-Month-Old Infants." *Sex Roles, 54*, 1–2, January 2006:127–137.

Cleeland, Nancy. "Slowdown's Silent Victims." *Los Angeles Times*, October 21, 2001.

Clemence, Sara. "Suites Get Even Sweeter." *Wall Street Journal*, August 24–25, 2013.

Cloud, John. "For Better or Worse." *Time*, October 26, 1998:43–44.

Cloward, Richard A., and Lloyd E. Ohlin. *Delinquency and Opportunity: A Theory of Delinquent Gangs.* New York: Free Press, 1960.

Coffman, Keith. "Colorado Rolls Out Driver's Licenses for Illegal Immigrants." Reuters, August 2, 2014.

Cohen, Patricia. "'Culture of Poverty' Makes a Comeback." *New York Times*, October 17, 2010.

Cohen, Patricia. "Forget Lonely. Life Is Healthy at the Top." *New York Times*, May 15, 2004.

Colapinto, John. *As Nature Made Him: The Boy Who Was Raised as a Girl.* New York: HarperCollins, 2001.

Cole, Diane. "When Romance Is a Click Away." *Wall Street Journal*, July 11, 2012.

Coleman, James William. "Politics and the Abuse of Power." In *Down to Earth Sociology: Introductory Readings*, 8th ed., James M. Henslin, ed. New York: Free Press, 1995:442–450.

College Board. "2014 College-Bound Seniors: Total Group Profile Report." New York: College Board, October 7, 2014.

Collins, Randall. "Socially Unrecognized Cumulation." *American Sociologist, 30*, 2, Summer 1999:41–61.

Collins, Randall. *The Credential Society: An Historical Sociology of Education.* New York: Academic Press, 1979.

Compton, Allie. "Is the U.S. Government Planning to Implement Secret Scanners That Can Detect Anything?" *Huffington Post*, July 10, 2012.

Conahan, Frank C. "Human Experimentation: An Overview on Cold War Era Programs." Washington, D.C.: U.S. General Accounting Office, September 28, 1994:1–11.

Connors, L. "Gender of Infant Differences in Attachment: Associations with Temperament and Caregiving Experiences." Paper presented at the Annual Conference of the British Psychological Society, Oxford, England, 1996.

Cook, Robin, and Eric Topol. "How Digital Medicine Will Soon Save Your Life." *Wall Street Journal*, February 22–23, 2014.

Cooley, Charles Horton. *Human Nature and the Social Order.* New York: Scribner's, 1902.

Cooley, Charles Horton. *Social Organization.* New York: Schocken Books, 1962. Originally published by Scribner's, 1909.

Cooper, Charles. "Unmanned Space Plane Opening Door to Space Weaponization?" *CBS News,* April 22, 2010.

Copen, Casey E., Kimberly Daniels, and William D. Mosher. "First Premarital Cohabitation in the United States: Data from the 2006–2010 National Survey of Family Growth." *National Health Statistics Reports, 64,* Washington, D.C.: National Center for Health Statistics, April 4, 2013.

Cornwell, Christopher, David B. Mustard, and Jessica Van Parys. "Noncognitive Skills and the Gender Disparities in Test Scores and Teacher Assessments: Evidence from Primary School." *Journal of Human Resources, 48,* 1, 2013:236–264.

Cose, Ellis. "What's White Anyway?" *Newsweek,* September 18, 2000:64–65.

Coser, Lewis A. *Masters of Sociological Thought: Ideas in Historical and Social Context,* 2nd ed. New York: Harcourt Brace Jovanovich, 1977.

Costa, Stephanie. "Where's the Outrage?" *Ms. Magazine Blog.* September 12, 2011.

Costantini, Cristina. "Spanish in Miami: Diciendo 'Hola' or Saying 'Hello.'" *Huffpost Miami,* November 29, 2011.

Cottin, Lou. *Elders in Rebellion: A Guide to Senior Activism.* Garden City, N.Y.: Anchor Doubleday, 1979.

Council of Economic Advisers. "Immigration's Economic Impact." Washington, D.C., June 20, 2007.

Cousins, Albert N., and Hans Nagpaul. *Urban Man and Society: A Reader in Urban Sociology.* New York: McGraw-Hill, 1970.

Cowan, Tadlock. "Biotechnology in Animal Agriculture: Status and Current Issues." *Congressional Research Service Reports, 32,* Washington, D.C.: Congressional Research Service, September 10, 2010.

Cowen, Emory L., Judah Landes, and Donald E. Schaet. "The Effects of Mild Frustration on the Expression of Prejudiced Attitudes." *Journal of Abnormal and Social Psychology,* January 1959:33–38.

Cowgill, Donald. "The Aging of Populations and Societies." *Annals of the American Academy of Political and Social Science, 415,* 1974:1–18.

Cowley, Joyce. *Pioneers of Women's Liberation.* New York: Merit, 1969.

Cox, Daniel, Robert P. Jones, and Juhem Navarro-Rivera. "I Know What You Did Last Sunday: Measuring Social Desirability Bias in Self-Reported Religious Behavior, Belief, and Identity." Public Religion Research Institute, May 17, 2014.

Crane, Andrew. "Modern Slavery as a Management Practice: Exploring the Conditions and Capabilities for Human Exploitation." *Academy of Management Review, 38,* 1, 2012:49–69.

Crawford, Duane W., Renate M. Houts, Ted L. Huston, and Laura J. George. "Compatibility, Leisure, and Satisfaction in Marital Relationships." *Journal of Marriage and Family, 64,* May 2002:433–449.

Crerand, Canice E., and Leanne Magee. "Cosmetic and Reconstructive Breast Surgery in Adolescents: Psychological, Ethical, and Legal Considerations." *Seminars in Plastic Surgery, 27,* 1, 2013:72–78.

Critcher, Chas, Jason Hughes, Julian Petley, and Amanda Rohloff, eds. *Moral Panics in the Contemporary World.* New York: Bloomsbury, 2013.

Crosby, Alex E., LaVonne Ortega, and Mark R. Stevens. "Suicide: United States, 1999–2007." *Morbidity and Mortality Weekly Report, 60,* 1, Supplements, January 4, 2011:56–59.

Crosnoe, Robert, Catherine Riegle-Crumb, Sam Field, Kenneth Frank, and Chandra Muller. "Peer Group Contexts of Girls' and Boys' Academic Experiences." *Child Development, 79,* 1, February 2008:139–155.

Cross, Jennifer Riedl, and Kathryn L. Fletcher. "Associations of Parental and Peer Characteristics with Adolescents' Social Dominance Orientation." *Journal of Youth and Adolescence, 40,* 2011:694–706.

Crossen, Cynthia. "Before Social Security, Most Americans Faced Very Bleak Retirement." *Wall Street Journal,* September 15, 2004a.

Crossen, Cynthia. "Déjà Vu." *New York Times,* February 25, 2004b.

Crossen, Cynthia. "Deja Vu." *Wall Street Journal,* March 5, 2003.

Crossen, Cynthia. "How Pygmy Ota Benga Ended up in Bronx Zoo as Darwinism Dawned." *Wall Street Journal,* February 6, 2006.

Crossen, Cynthia. "Margin of Error: Studies Galore Support Products and Positions, but Are They Reliable?" *Wall Street Journal,* November 14, 1991:A1.

Cruikshank, Margaret. *Learning to Be Old: Gender, Culture, and Aging, 3rd ed..* Lanham, Md.: Rowman & Littlefield, 2013.

Crumley, Bruce. "The Game of Death: France's Shocking TV Experiment." *Time,* March 17, 2010.

Cui, Ming, and Frank D. Fincham. "The Differential Effects of Parental Divorce and Marital Conflict on Young Adult Romantic Relationships." *Personal Relationships, 17,* 3, September 2010:331–343.

Cumming, Elaine. "Further Thoughts on the Theory of Disengagement." In *Aging in America: Readings in Social Gerontology,* Cary S. Kart and Barbara B. Manard, eds. Sherman Oaks, Calif.: Alfred Publishing, 1976:19–41.

Cumming, Elaine, and William E. Henry. *Growing Old: The Process of Disengagement.* New York: Basic Books, 1961.

Current Population Survey: Voting and Registration Supplement. Washington, D.C.: Bureau of the Census, November 2012.

Cussins, Jessica. "'World's First GM Babies Born': 12-Year-Old Article Continues to Cause Confusion." *Biopolitical Times,* April 25, 2013.

Cwiek, Sarah. "The Middle Class Took off 100 Years Ago . . . Thanks to Henry Ford." *NPR,* January 27, 2014.

D'Costa, Krystal. "Catfishing: The Truth about Deception Online." *Scientific American,* April 25, 2014.

Dabbs, James M., Jr., and Robin Morris. "Testosterone, Social Class, and Antisocial Behavior in a Sample of 4,462 Men." *Psychological Science, 1,* 3, May 1990:209–211.

Dabbs, James M., Jr., Marian F. Hargrove, and Colleen Heusel. "Testosterone Differences among College Fraternities: Well-Behaved vs. Rambunctious." *Personality and Individual Differences, 20,* 1996:157–161.

Dabbs, James M., Jr., Timothy S. Carr, Robert L. Frady, and Jasmin K. Riad. "Testosterone, Crime, and Misbehavior among 692 Male Prison Inmates." *Personality and Individual Differences, 18,* 1995:627–633.

Daggett, Stephen. "Costs of Major U.S. Wars." Washington, D.C.: Congressional Research Service, June 29, 2010.

Dahl, Gordon B., and Enrico Moretti. "The Demand for Sons." *Review of Economic Studies, 75,* 2008:1085–1120.

Dahl, Robert A. *Dilemmas of Pluralist Democracy: Autonomy vs. Control.* New Haven, Conn.: Yale University Press, 1982.

Dahl, Robert A. *Who Governs?* New Haven, Conn.: Yale University Press, 1961.

Dao, James. "In Debate over Military Sexual Assault, Men Are Overlooked Victims." *New York Times,* June 23, 2013.

Dao, James. "Instant Millions Can't Halt Winners' Grim Side." *New York Times,* December 5, 2005.

Darley, John M., and Bibb Latané. "Bystander Intervention in Emergencies: Diffusion of Responsibility." *Journal of Personality and Social Psychology, 8,* 4, 1968:377–383.

Darwin, Charles. *The Origin of Species.* Chicago: Conley, 1859.

Dasgupta, Nilanjana, Debbie E. McGhee, Anthony G. Greenwald, and Mahzarin R. Banaji. "Automatic Preference for White Americans: Eliminating the Familiarity Explanation." *Journal of Experimental Social Psychology, 36,* 3, May 2000:316–328.

Davis, Donald R., and David E. Weinstein. "Technological Superiority and the Losses from Migration." National Bureau of Economic Research, Working Paper, June 2002.

Davis, Jaya, and Jon R. Sorensen. "Disproportionate Juvenile Minority Confinement: A State-Level Assessment of Racial Threat." *Youth Violence and Juvenile Justice*, 11, 2013:296–312.

Davis, Kingsley. "Extreme Isolation." In *Down to Earth Sociology: Introductory Readings*, 15th ed., James M. Henslin, ed. New York: Free Press, 2016. Originally published as "Extreme Social Isolation of a Child." *American Journal of Sociology*, 45, January 4, 1940:554–565.

Davis, Kingsley, and Wilbert E. Moore. "Reply to Tumin." *American Sociological Review*, 18, 1953:394–396.

Davis, Kingsley, and Wilbert E. Moore. "Some Principles of Stratification." *American Sociological Review*, 10, 1945:242–249.

Davis, Nancy J., and Robert V. Robinson. "Class Identification of Men and Women in the 1970s and 1980s." *American Sociological Review*, 53, February 1988:103–112.

Davis, R. E., M. P. Couper, N. K. Janz, C. H. Caldwell, and K. Resnicow. "Interviewer Effects in Public Health Surveys." *Health Education Research*, 25, 1, 2010:14–28.

Davis, Stan. *Lessons from the Future: Making Sense of a Blurred World.* New York: Capstone Publishers, 2001.

Dawisha, Karen. *Gangster's Paradise: Putin's Kleptocracy.* New York: Simon and Schuster, 2014.

Day, Jennifer Chesseman. "Population Profile of the United States: National Population Projections." Washington, D.C.: U.S. Census Bureau, 2010.

de Cordoba, José, and Juan Montes. "Mexican Mayor Is Detained in Case of Missing Students." *Wall Street Journal*, November 5, 2014.

De Lange, Catherine. "Startup Offering DNA Screening of 'Hypothetical Babies' Raises Fears over Designer Children." *Guardian*, April 7, 2014.

de Tocqueville, Alexis. *Democracy in America*, J. P. Mayer and Max Lerner, eds. New York: Harper & Row, 1966. Originally published 1835.

de Tocqueville, Alexis. *The Old Regime and the French Revolution.* Stuart Gilbert, trans. Garden City, N.Y.: Doubleday Anchor, 1955. First published in 1856.

Deaver, Michael V. "Democratizing Russian Higher Education." *Demokratizatsiya*, 9, 3, Summer 2001:350–366.

DeCrow, Karen. Foreword to *Why Men Earn More* by Warren Farrell. New York: AMACOM, 2005:xi–xii.

Deegan, Mary Jo. "W. E. B. Du Bois and the Women of Hull-House, 1895–1899." *American Sociologist*, Winter 1988:301–311.

Deflem, Mathieu, ed. *Sociological Theory and Criminological Research: Views from Europe and the United States.* San Diego: JAI Press, 2006.

Delaney, Arthur. "Revolving Door: 1447 Former Government Workers Lobby for Wall Street." *Huffington Post*, June 3, 2010.

Deliege, Robert. *The Untouchables of India.* New York: Berg Publishers, 2001.

Delmar-Morgan, Alex. "Qatari Poet Sentenced to Life in Prison." *Wall Street Journal*, November 30, 2012.

DeLuca, Stephanie, and Elizabeth Dayton. "Switching Social Contexts: The Effects of Housing Mobility and School Choice Programs on Youth Outcomes." *Annual Review of Sociology*, 35, 2009:457–491.

DeMartini, Joseph R. "Basic and Applied Sociological Work: Divergence, Convergence, or Peaceful Co-Existence?" *The Journal of Applied Behavioral Science*, 18, 2, 1982:203–215.

DeMause, Lloyd. "Our Forebears Made Childhood a Nightmare." *Psychology Today 8*, 11, April 1975:85–88.

Demos, John. *The Heathen School.* New York: Knopf, 2014.

DeNavas-Walt, Carmen, Bernadette D. Proctor, and Jessica C. Smith. "Income, Poverty, and Health Insurance Coverage in the United States: 2012." *Current Population Reports*, September 2013.

Denzin, Norman K. *Symbolic Interactionism and Cultural Studies: The Politics of Interpretation.* Cambridge, Mass.: Blackwell 2007.

Dew, Jeffrey, and W. Bradford Wilcox. "If Momma Ain't Happy: Explaining Declines in Marital Satisfaction among New Mothers." *Journal of Marriage and Family*, 73, February 2011:1–12.

Dewan, Shaila. "Santander Bank to Face Suit Claiming Bias in Mortgages." *New York Times*, May 28, 2014.

DeWitt, Larry. "The Development of Social Security in America." *Social Security Bulletin, 70, 3*, 2010.

Diamond, Milton, and Keith Sigmundson. "Sex Reassignment at Birth: Long–Term Review and Clinical Implications." *Archives of Pediatric and Adolescent Medicine, 151,* March 1997:298–304.

Dickey, Christopher, and Adam Rogers. "Smoke and Mirrors." *Newsweek*, February 25, 2002.

Dickey, Christopher, and John Barry. "Iran: A Rummy Guide." *Newsweek*, May 8, 2006.

Digest of Education Statistics. Washington, D.C.: National Center for Education Statistics, 2007.

Dillon, Sam. "States' Data Obscure How Few Finish High School." *New York Times*, March 20, 2008.

Dingwall, Robert. *Essays on Professions.* Farnham, United Kingdom: Ashgate Publishing, 2008.

DiSilvestro, Roger L. *In the Shadow of Wounded Knee: The Untold Final Chapter of the Indian Wars.* New York: Walker & Co., 2006.

Doane, Ashley W., Jr. "Dominant Group Ethnic Identity in the United States: The Role of 'Hidden' Ethnicity in Intergroup Relations." *The Sociological Quarterly, 38*, 3, Summer 1997:375–397.

Dobriner, William M. *Social Structures and Systems.* Pacific Palisades, California: Goodyear, 1969.

Dobyns, Henry F. *Their Numbers Became Thinned: Native American Population Dynamics in Eastern North America.* Knoxville: University of Tennessee Press, 1983.

"Doctor Leading Fight against Ebola in Sierra Leone Dies after Contracting Virus." *Wall Street Journal*, July 30, 2014.

Dodds, Peter Sheridan, Roby Muhamad, and Duncan J. Watts. "An Experimental Study of Search in Global Social Networks." *Science, 301*, August 8, 2003:827–830.

Dogan, Mattei. "Status Incongruence in Advanced Societies." *Societamutamentopolitica, 2*, 3, 2011:285–294.

Dolan, Kerry A., and Luisa Kroll, eds. "The Richest People on the Planet 2014." *Forbes* 2014.

Dollard, John, Leonard William Doob, Neal Elgar Miller, Orval Hobart Mowrer, and Robert Richardson Sears. *Frustration and Aggression.* New Haven, Conn.: Yale University Press, 1939.

Dolnick, Sam. "The Obesity-Hunger Paradox." *New York Times*, March 12, 2010.

Domhoff, G. William. "C. Wright Mills, Power Structure Research, and the Failures of Mainstream Political Science." *New Political Science, 29*, 2007:97–114.

Domhoff, G. William. "State and Ruling Class in Corporate America (1974): Reflections, Corrections, and New Directions." *Critical Sociology*, 25, 2–3, July 1999a:260–265.

Domhoff, G. William. "The Bohemian Grove and Other Retreats." In *Down to Earth Sociology: Introductory Readings*, 10th ed., James M. Henslin, ed. New York: Free Press, 1999b:391–403.

Domhoff, G. William. *Who Rules America? Power, Politics, and Social Change*, 5th ed. New York: McGraw-Hill, 2006.

Domhoff, G. William. *Who Rules America? The Triumph of the Corporate Rich,* 7th ed. New York: McGraw-Hill, 2014.

Domingo, Santiago, and Antonio Pellicer. "Overview of Current Trends in Hysterectomy." *Expert Review of Obstetrics and Gynecology*, 4, 6, 2009:673–685.

Donlon, Margie M., Ori Ash, and Becca R. Levy. "Re-Vision of Older Television Characters: A Stereotype-Awareness Intervention." *Journal of Social Issues*, 61, 2, June 2005.

Donnermeyer, Joseph F., Cory Anderson, and Elizabeth C. Cooksey. "The Amish Population: County Estimates and Settlement Patterns." *Journal of Amish and Plain Anabaptist Studies*, 1, 1, April 2013:72–109.

Doorenspleet, Renske, and Huib Pellikaan. "Which Type of Democracy Performs Best?" *Acta Politica*, 2013. (in press)

Douthat, Ross. "Abortion Politics Didn't Doom the G.O.P." *New York Times*, December 7, 2008.

Dove, Adrian. "Soul Folk 'Chitling' Test or the Dove Counterbalance Intelligence Test." Mimeo, no date.

Drakulich, Kevin M. "Strangers, Neighbors, and Race: A Contact Model of Stereotypes and Racal Anxieties about Crime." *Race and Justice*, 2, 4, 2012:322–355.

Drape, Joe. "Growing Cheers for the Home-Schooled Team." *New York Times*, March 16, 2008.

Drew, Christopher. "Military Contractor Agrees to Pay $325 Million to Settle Whistle-Blower Lawsuit." *New York Times*, April 2, 2009.

Drucker, Peter F. "There's More than One Kind of Team." *Wall Street Journal*, February 11, 1992:A16.

Drum, Kevin. "America's Real Criminal Element: Lead." *Mother Jones*, January/February 2013.

Du Bois, W. E. B. *Black Reconstruction in America: An Essay toward a History of the Part Which Black Folk Played in the Attempt to Reconstruct Democracy in America, 1860–1880.* New York: Atheneum, 1992. Originally published 1935.

Du Bois, W. E. B. *The Philadelphia Negro: A Social Study.* Philadelphia, Pennsylvania: University of Pennsylvania Press, 2011. Originally published in 1899.

Du Bois, W. E. B. *The Souls of Black Folk: Essays and Sketches.* Chicago: McClurg, 1903.

Duck, W. O., and Anne W. Rawls, "Interaction Orders of Drug Dealing Spaces: Local Orders of Sensemaking in a Poor Black American Place." *Crime, Law and Social Change*, 2011.

Dugger, Celia W. "Abortion in India Is Tipping Scales Sharply against Girls." *New York Times*, April 22, 2001.

Dugger, Celia W. "Report Finds Gradual Fall in Female Genital Cutting." July 22, 2013.

Dugger, Celia W. "Wedding Vows Bind Old World and New." *New York Times*, July 20, 1998.

Dunaway, Wilma A. *Women, Work, and Family in the Antebellum Mountain South.* New York: Cambridge University Press, 2008.

Duncan, Lauren E., and Bill E. Peterson. "Authoritarianism, Cognitive Rigidity, and the Processing of Ambiguous Visual Information." *Journal of Social Psychology*, 154, 2014:480–490.

Duneier, Mitchell. *Sidewalk.* New York: Farrar, Straus and Giroux, 1999.

Dunlap, Riley E., and William R. Catton, Jr. "Environmental Sociology." *Annual Review of Sociology*, 5, 1979:243–273.

Dunlap, Riley E., and William R. Catton, Jr. "What Environmental Sociologists Have in Common Whether Concerned with 'Built' or 'Natural' Environments." *Sociological Inquiry*, 53, 2–3, 1983:113–135.

Dunn, Hank. "Time to Hold Students Accountable for Their Own Success." *Community College Week*, March 18, 2013.

Durkheim, Emile. *Suicide: A Study in Sociology*, John A. Spaulding and George Simpson, trans. New York: Free Press, 1966. Originally published 1897.

Durkheim, Emile. *The Division of Labor in Society*, George Simpson, trans. New York: Free Press, 1933. Originally published 1893.

Durkheim, Emile. *The Elementary Forms of the Religious Life.* New York: Free Press, 1965. Originally published 1912.

Durkheim, Emile. *The Rules of Sociological Method*, Sarah A. Solovay and John H. Mueller, trans. New York: Free Press, 1938, 1958, 1964. Originally published 1895.

Durning, Alan. "Cradles of Life." In *Social Problems 90/91*, LeRoy W. Barnes, ed. Guilford, Conn.: Dushkin, 1990:231–241.

Durose, Matthew R., Alexia D. Cooper, and Howard N. Snyder. "Recidivism of Prisoners Released in 30 States in 2005: Patterns from 2005 to 2010." Bureau of Justice Statistics, April 2014.

Dwyer, Jim. "A Court Battle over a Husband's Rage and a Wife Who'd Had Enough." *New York Times*, April 26, 2011.

Dychtwald, Ken. "Remembering Maggie Kuhn: Gray Panther Founder on the 5 Myths of Aging." *Huffington Post*, May 31, 2012.

Dyer, Gwynne. "Anybody's Son Will Do." In *Down to Earth Sociology: Introductory Readings*, 14th ed., James M. Henslin, ed. New York: Free Press, 2007.

Eagly, Alice H., Asia Eaton, Suzanna M. Rose, et al. "Feminism and Psychology: Analysis of a Half-Century of Research on Women and Gender." *American Psychologist*, 67, 3, 2012:211–230.

Ebaugh, Helen Rose Fuchs. *Becoming an Ex: The Process of Role Exit.* Chicago: University of Chicago Press, 1988.

Eberstadt, Nicholas. "How the World Is Becoming More Equal." *Wall Street Journal*, August 27, 2014a.

Eberstadt, Nicholas. "Time for the 'Never Agains' on North Korea." *Wall Street Journal*, February 10, 2014b.

Eder, Donna. "On Becoming Female: Lessons Learned in School." In *Down to Earth Sociology: Introductory Readings*, 14th ed., James M. Henslin, ed. New York: Free Press, 2007.

Eder, Donna. *School Talk: Gender and Adolescent Culture.* New Brunswick, N.J.: Rutgers University Press, 1995.

Eder, Donna. "Sitting in on Adolescent Conversations." In *Social Problems: A Down-to-Earth Approach*, 11th ed., James M. Henslin, ed. Boston: Pearson, 2014.

Eder, Klaus. "The Rise of Counter-Culture Movements against Modernity: Nature as a New Field of Class Struggle." *Theory, Culture & Society*, 7, 1990:21–47.

Edgerton, Robert B. *Deviance: A Cross-Cultural Perspective.* Menlo Park, Calif.: Benjamin/Cummings, 1976.

Edgerton, Robert B. *Sick Societies: Challenging the Myth of Primitive Harmony.* New York: Free Press, 1992.

Editorial Board. "Tortured Doctors and Psychologists." *New York Times*, December 16, 2014.

Ehrenreich, Barbara, and Deidre English. *Witches, Midwives, and Nurses: A History of Women Healers.* Old Westbury, N.Y.: Feminist Press, 1973.

Ehrlich, Paul R., and Anne H. Ehrlich. "Humanity at the Crossroads." *Stanford Magazine*, Spring–Summer 1978:20–23.

Ehrlich, Paul R., and Anne H. Ehrlich. *Population, Resources, and Environment: Issues in Human Ecology*, 2nd ed. San Francisco: Freeman, 1972.

Eibl-Eibesfeldt, Irrenäus. *Ethology: The Biology of Behavior.* New York: Holt, Rinehart, and Winston, 1970.

Eisenegger, Christoph, Johannes Haushofer, and Ernst Fehr. "The Role of Testosterone in Social Interaction." *Trends in Cognitive Sciences*, 15, 6, 2011:263–271.

Eisenhart, R. Wayne. "You Can't Hack It, Little Girl: A Discussion of the Covert Psychological Agenda of Modern Combat Training." *Journal of Social Issues, 31*, Fall 1975:13–23.

Ekman, Paul. *Faces of Man: Universal Expression in a New Guinea Village.* New York: Garland Press, 1980.

Ekman, Paul, Wallace V. Friesen, and John Bear. "The International Language of Gestures." *Psychology Today*, May 1984:64.

Emanuel, Ezekiel J. "Sex and the Single Senior." *New York Times*, January 18, 2014.

Emery, Cécile, Thomas S. Calvard, and Meghan E. Pierce. "Leadership as an Emergent Group Process: A Social Network Study of Personality and Leadership." *Group Processes and Intergroup Relations, 16*, 1, 2013:28–45.

Emery, Robert E., Erin E. Horn, and Christopher R. Beam." Marriage and Improved Well-Being." In *Marriage at the Crossroads: Law, Policy, and the Brave New World of Twenty-First Century Families*, Marsha Garrison and Elizabeth S. Scott, eds. New York: Cambridge University Press, 2012:126–141.

Emmott, Stephen. *Ten Billion*. New York: Vintage, 2013.

Emsden, Christopher, and Matthew Dalton. "Europe Loosens Reins on National Budgets." *Wall Street Journal*, May 30, 2013.

England, Paula. "The Impact of Feminist Thought on Sociology." *Contemporary Sociology: A Journal of Reviews*, 2000:263–267.

Ensign, Rachel Louise. "It's Now a Grind for 2-Year-Olds." *New York Times*, March 12, 2012.

Environmental Protection Agency. "Final National Priorities List." Washington, D.C.: Environmental Protection Agency, March 29, 2013.

Epstein, Cynthia Fuchs. *Deceptive Distinctions: Sex, Gender, and the Social Order*. New Haven, Conn.: Yale University Press, 1988.

Erdbrink, Thomas. "Woman in Iran Sent to Prison after Going to Sports Event." *New York Times*, November 2, 2014.

Erikson, Kai T. *Everything in Its Path: Destruction of Community in the Buffalo Creek Flood*. New York: Simon and Schuster, 1978.

Ernst, Eldon G. "The Baptists." In *Encyclopedia of the American Religious Experience: Studies of Traditions and Movements*, Vol. 1, Charles H. Lippy and Peter W. Williams, eds. New York: Scribners, 1988:555–577.

Estes, Larissa J., Linda E. Lloyd, Michelle Teti, et al. "Perceptions of Audio Computer-Assisted Self-Interviewing (ACASI) among Women in an HIV-Positive Prevention Program." *PLoS ONE, 5*, 2, February 10, 2010:e9149.

Estruch, Ramón, Emilio Ros, Jordi Salas-Salvadó, et al. "Primary Prevention of Cardiovascular Disease with a Mediterranean Diet." *New England Journal of Medicine, 368*, 2013:1279–1290.

Evans, Natalie. "Britain's Youngest Lottery Winner Callie Rogers: 'I Have £2K Left in the Bank but I've Never Been Happier.'" *Mirror*, July 16, 2013.

"Ex-FBI Official: "We Left Our Most Important Prisoners to Amateurs.'" *Der Spiegel*, January 23, 2015.

Ezekiel, Raphael S. *The Racist Mind: Portraits of American Neo-Nazis and Klansmen*. New York: Viking, 1995.

Fabrikant, Geraldine. "Old Nantucket Warily Meets the New." *New York Times*, June 5, 2005.

Fahrenthold, David A. "A Medicare Scam That Just Kept Rolling." *Washington Post*, August 16, 2014.

Falicov, Celia Jaes. "Changing Constructions of Machismo for Latino Men in Therapy: 'The Devil Never Sleeps.'" *Family Process, 49*, 3, 2010:309–329.

Falkenberg, Katie. "Pakistani Women Victims of 'Honor.'" *Washington Times*, July 23, 2008.

Fan, Maureen. "After Quake, China's Elderly Long for Family." *Washington Post*, June 3, 2008.

Fang, Lee. "The Scholars Who Shill for Wall Street." *The Nation*, October 23, 2013.

Faris, Robert E. L., and Warren Dunham. *Mental Disorders in Urban Areas*. Chicago: University of Chicago Press, 1939.

Farkas, George. *Human Capital or Cultural Capital?: Ethnicity and Poverty Groups in an Urban School District*. New York: Walter DeGruyter, 1996.

Farkas, George, Daniel Sheehan, and Robert P. Grobe. "Coursework Mastery and School Success: Gender, Ethnicity, and Poverty Groups within an Urban School District." *American Educational Research Journal, 27*, 4, Winter 1990a:807–827.

Farkas, George, Robert P. Grobe, Daniel Sheehan, and Yuan Shuan. "Cultural Resources and School Success: Gender, Ethnicity, and Poverty Groups within an Urban School District." *American Sociological Review, 55*, February 1990b:127–142.

Fathi, Nazila. "Starting at Home, Iran's Women Fight for Rights." *New York Times*, February 12, 2009.

Fattig, Paul. "Good Intentions Gone Bad." *Mail Tribune*, June 6, 2007.

Faunce, William A. *Problems of an Industrial Society*, 2nd ed. New York: McGraw-Hill, 1981.

FBI. *Crime in the United States 2013*, 2014:Table 33.

Feagin, Joe. *Racist America*. New York: Routledge, 2014.

Feagin, Joe R. "The Continuing Significance of Race: Antiblack Discrimination in Public Places." In *Majority and Minority: The Dynamics of Race and Ethnicity in American Life*, 6th ed., Norman R. Yetman, ed. Boston: Allyn and Bacon, 1999:384–399.

Featherman, David L. "Opportunities Are Expanding." *Society, 13*, 1979:4–11.

Feder, Barnaby J. "Services at the First Church of Cyberspace." *New York Times*, May 15, 2004.

Fedewa, Alicia L., Whitney W. Black, and Soyeon Ahn."Children and Adolescents with Same-Gender Parents: A Meta-Analytic Approach in Assessing Outcomes." *Journal of GLBT Family Studies*, 2014:1–34.

Feeney, Nolan. "NSA Collects Millions of Facial Photos Daily, Snowden Documents Say." *Time*, June 1, 2014.

Feiler, Bruce. "Family Inc." *Wall Street Journal*, February 9–10, 2013.

Felsenthal, Edward. "Justices' Ruling Further Defines Sex Harassment." *Wall Street Journal*, March 5, 1998:B1, B2.

Finke, Roger, and Rodney Stark. *The Churching of America, 1776–1990: Winners and Losers in Our Religious Economy*. New Brunswick, N.J.: Rutgers University Press, 1992.

Finkelhor, David, and Kersti Yllo. *License to Rape: Sexual Abuse of Wives*. New York: Henry Holt, 1985.

Finkelhor, David, and Kersti Yllo. "Marital Rape: The Myth versus the Reality." In *Marriage and Family in a Changing Society*, 3rd ed., James M. Henslin, ed. New York: Free Press, 1989:382–391.

Fischer, Claude S. *The Urban Experience*. New York: Harcourt, 1976.

Fish, Jefferson M. "Mixed Blood." *Psychology Today, 28*, 6, November–December 1995:55–58, 60, 61, 76, 80.

Fisher, Bonnie S., Francis T. Cullen, and Michael G. Turner. *The Sexual Victimization of College Women*. Washington, D.C.: U.S. Department of Justice, 2000.

Fisher, Bonnie S., Leah E. Daigle, Francis T. Cullen, and Michael G. Turner. "Reporting Sexual Victimization to the Police and Others: Results from a National-Level Study of College Women." *Criminal Justice and Behavior, 30*, 1, February 2003:6–38.

Fisher, Helen. "Love, Prehistoric Style." *Wall Street Journal*, July 8, 2014.

Fisher, Helen E., Lucy L. Brown, Arthur Aron, Greg Strong, and Deborah Masek. "Reward, Addiction, and Emotion Regulation Systems Associated with Rejection in Love." *Journal of Neurophysiology*, 104, 2010:51–60.

Fisher, Sue. *In the Patient's Best Interest: Women and the Politics of Medical Decisions*. New Brunswick, N.J.: Rutgers University Press, 1986.

Flanagan, William G. *Urban Sociology: Images and Structure*. Boston: Allyn and Bacon, 1990.

Flannery, Russell. "2014 Forbes Billionaires List: Growing China's 10 Richest." *Forbes*, March 3, 2014.

Flavel, John H., et al. *The Development of Role-Taking and Communication Skills in Children*. New York: Wiley, 1968.

Flavel, John, Patricia H. Miller, and Scott A. Miller. *Cognitive Development*, 4th ed. Upper Saddle River, N.J.: Prentice Hall, 2002.

Flegal, Katherine M., and Karen Hunter. "Higher Levels of Obesity Associated with Increased Risk of Death; Being Overweight Associated with Lower Risk of Death." *Journal of American Medical Association*, 309, 1, 2013:87–88.

Flexner, Abraham. *Medical Education in the United States and Canada: A Report to the Carnegie Foundation for the Advancement of Teaching*. Bulletin No. 4. Boston: Merrymount Press, 1910.

Flexner, E. *Century of Struggle*. Cambridge, Mass.: Belknap, 1971. In Claire M. Renzetti and Daniel J. Curran, *Women, Men, and Society*, 4th ed. Boston: Allyn and Bacon, 1999.

Fligstein, Neil, and Jacob Habinek. "Sucker Punched by the Invisible Hand: The World Financial Markets and the Globalization of the U.S. Mortgage Crisis." *Socio-Economic Review*, 2014:1–29.

Flink, James J., *The Automobile Age*. Cambridge, Mass.: MIT Press, 1990.

Florida, Richard. "The Most Famous Models for How Cities Grow Are Wrong." *The Atlantic*, August 9, 2013.

Foley, Douglas E. "The Great American Football Ritual." In *Society: Readings to Accompany Sociology: A Down-to-Earth Approach, Core Concepts*, James M. Henslin, ed. Boston: Allyn and Bacon, 2006:64–76. Originally published 1990.

Foote, Jennifer. "Trying to Take Back the Planet." *Newsweek*, 115, 6, February 5, 1990:24–25.

Fordham, Brigham A. "Disability and Designer Babies." *Valparaiso University Law Review*, 45, 4, 2011:1473–1528.

Form, William. "Comparative Industrial Sociology and the Convergence Hypothesis." *Annual Review of Sociology*, 5, 1, 1979.

Forsyth, Jim. "Proabortion Group Asks Judge to Block Texas Sonogram Law." *Reuters*, July 6, 2011.

Fountain, Henry. "Archaeological Site in Peru Is Called Oldest City in Americas." *New York Times*, April 27, 2001.

Fowler, Geoffrey A., and Amy Chozick. "Cartoon Characters Get Big Makeover for Overseas Fans." *Wall Street Journal*, October 16, 2007.

Fox, Elaine, and George E. Arquitt. "The VFW and the 'Iron Law of Oligarchy.'" In *Down to Earth Sociology*, 4th ed., James M. Henslin, ed. New York: Free Press, 1985:147–155.

Francis, Theo, and Joann S. Lublin. "CEO Pay Rises Moderately: A Few Reap Huge Rewards." *Wall Street Journal*, May 27, 2014.

Frank, Reanne. "What to Make of It? The (Re)emergence of a Biological Conceptualization of Race in Health Disparities Research." *Social Science & Medicine*, 64, 2007:1977–1983.

Franklin, John Hope, and John Whittington Franklin. *My Life and an Era: The Autobiography of Buck Colbert Franklin*. Baton Rouge: Louisiana State University, 1997.

Franzosi, Roberto, Gianluca De Fazio, and Stefania Vicari. "Ways of Measuring Agency: An Application of Quantitative Analysis to Lynchings in Georgia (1875–1930). *Sociological Methodology*, 42, 1, 2012:1–42.

Fraser, Graham. "Fox Denies Free Trade Exploiting the Poor in Mexico." *Toronto Star*, April 20, 2001.

Frayer, Lauren. "Police: Baby Starved as Couple Nurtured Virtual Kid." *AOL News*, March 5, 2010.

Freedman, Jane. *Feminism*. Philadelphia: Open University Press, 2001.

Freeland, Chrystia. "The Rise of the New Global Elite." *Atlantic*, January/February 2011.

Freeman, James. "How Washington Really Redistributes Income." *Wall Street Journal*, October 19–20, 2013.

Freese, Jeremy." Genetics and the Social Science Explanation of Individual Outcomes." *American Journal of Sociology*, 114, S1, 2008:S1–S35.

Freidson, Eliot. *Professionalism: The Third Logic*. Chicago: University of Chicago Press, 2001.

Fremson, Ruth. "Dead Bachelors in Remote China Still Find Wives." *New York Times*, October 5, 2006.

Frevert, Tonya K., and Lisa Slattery Walker. "Physical Attractiveness and Social Status." *Sociology Compass*, 8, 3, 2014:313–323.

Friedl, Ernestine. "Society and Sex Roles." In *Conformity and Conflict: Readings in Cultural Anthropology*, James P. Spradley and David W. McCurdy, eds. Glenview, Ill.: Scott, Foresman, 1990:229–238.

Frommer, Arthur. *Peru*. New York: Wiley, 2007.

Frumkin, Robert M. "Early English and American Sex Customs." In *Encyclopedia of Sexual Behavior*, Vol. 1. New York: Hawthorne Books, 1967.

Fry, Richard. "New Census Data Show More Americans Are Tying the Knot, but Mostly It's the College-Educated." Pew Research Center, February 6, 2014.

Funk, Michelle, Natalie Drew, and Martin Knapp. "Mental Health, Poverty and Development." *Journal of Public Mental Health*, 11, 4, 2012:166-185.

Furstenberg, Frank F. "Fifty Years of Family Change: From Consensus to Complexity." *Annals of the American Academy of Political and Social Science*, 654, July 2014:12–30.

Furstenberg, Frank F., Jr., Sheela Kennedy, Vonnie C. McLoyd, Ruben G. Rumbaut, and Richard A. Settersten, Jr. "Growing up Is Harder to Do." *Contexts*, 3, 3, Summer 2004:33–41.

Gabriel, Trip. "Under Pressure, Teachers Tamper with Test Scores." *New York Times*, June 10, 2010.

Gahima, Lilian. "Prepex Device: Rwanda Targets to Circumcise over a Million Men." KT Press (Rwandan News Service), December 12, 2014.

Gaither, Milton. "Homeschooling in the USA: Past, Present, and Future." *Theory and Research in Education*, 7, 2009:331–346.

Galbraith, John Kenneth. *The Nature of Mass Poverty*. Cambridge, Mass.: Harvard University Press, 1979.

Gallagher, Ryan. "The Threat of Silence." *Future Tense*, February 4, 2013.

Galliher, John F. *Deviant Behavior and Human Rights*. Englewood Cliffs, N.J.: Prentice Hall, 1991.

Gallmeier, Charles P. "Methodological Issues in Qualitative Sport Research: Participant Observation among Hockey Players." *Sociological Spectrum*, 8, 1988:213–235.

Gallup, George, Jr. *The Gallup Poll: Public Opinion 1989*. Wilmington, Del.: Scholarly Resources, 1990.

Gallup Poll. "America's Preference for Smaller Families Edge Higher." Princeton, N.J. Gallup Organization, June 30, 2011a.

Gallup Poll. "Americans More Likely to Believe in God than the Devil, Heaven More than Hell." June 13, 2007.

Gallup Poll. "Americans See Religion Losing Influence." Princeton, N.J.: Gallup Organization, January 26, 2011b.

Gallup Poll. "Election Polls—Vote by Groups, 2008." Princeton, N.J.: Gallup Organization, 2008.

Gallup Poll. "Prefer Boys to Girls Just as They Did in 1941." Princeton, N.J.: Gallup Organization, June 23, 2011c.

Gallup Poll. "Very Religious Americans Lead Healthier Lives." Princeton, N.J.: Gallup Organization, December 23, 2010.

Gampbell, Jennifer. "In Northeast Thailand, a Cuisine Based on Bugs." *New York Times,* June 22, 2006.

Gans, Herbert J. *People, Plans, and Policies: Essays on Poverty, Racism, and Other National Urban Problems.* New York: Columbia University Press, 1991.

Gans, Herbert J. *People and Plans: Essays on Urban Problems and Solutions.* New York: Basic Books, 1968.

Gans, Herbert J. "Sociology as a Vocation: Looking to the Future." *Global Dialogue: Newsletter for the International Sociological Association, 4,* 2, June 2014.

Gans, Herbert J. *The Urban Villagers.* New York: Free Press, 1962.

Gardiner, Sean, and Alison Fox. "Glance May Have Led to Murder." *New York Times,* December 6, 2010.

Garfinkel, Harold. "Conditions of Successful Degradation Ceremonies." *American Journal of Sociology, 61,* 2, March 1956:420–424.

Garfinkel, Harold. *Ethnomethodology's Program: Working out Durkheim's Aphorism.* Lanham, Md.: Rowman & Littlefield, 2002.

Garfinkel, Harold. *Studies in Ethnomethodology.* Englewood Cliffs, N.J.: Prentice Hall, 1967.

Garfinkel, Irwin, Lee Rainwater, and Timothy Smeeding. *Wealth and Welfare States: Is America a Laggard or a Leader?* New York: Oxford University Press, 2010.

Gartrell, Nanette, Henny Bos, Heidi Peyser, Amalia Deck, and Carla Rodas. "Family Characteristics, Custody Arrangements, and Adolescent Psychological Well-Being after Lesbian Mothers Break Up." *Family Relations, 60,* December 2011:572–585.

Gates, Eddie Faye. "The Oklahoma Commission to Study the Tulsa Race Riot of 1921." *Harvard Black Letter Law Journal, 20,* 2004:83–89.

Gatewood, Willard B. *Aristocrats of Color: The Black Elite, 1880–1920.* Bloomington, Ind.: Indiana University Press, 1990.

Gautham, S. "Coming Next: The Monsoon Divorce." *New Statesman, 131,* 4574, February 18, 2002:32–33.

Gawande, Atul. "Letting Go." *New Yorker,* August 2, 2010.

Gay, Jason. "Larry Ellison's Basketball Retriever Tells All." *Wall Street Journal,* May 2, 2014.

Gayles, Contessa. "Harlem: New York's New Tech Hub?" CNN Money, July 21, 2014.

Geis, Gilbert, Robert F. Meier, and Lawrence M. Salinger. *White-Collar Crime: Classic and Contemporary Views,* 3rd ed. New York: Free Press, 1995.

Gelderen, Loes, Henny M. W. Bos, Nanette Gartrell, Jo Hermanns, and Ellen C. Perrin. "Quality of Life of Adolescents Raised from Birth by Lesbian Mothers: The U.S. National Longitudinal Family Study." *Journal of Developmental and Behavioral Pediatrics, 33,* 1, January 2012.

Gelman, Andrew. "How Bayesian Analysis Cracked the Red-State, Blue-State Problem." *Statistical Sciences, 29,* 1, 2014:28–35.

Gerhard, Jane. "Revisiting 'The Myth of the Vaginal Orgasm': The Female Orgasm in American Sexual Thought and Second Wave Feminism." *Feminist Studies, 26,* 2, Fall 2000:449–477.

Geronimus, Arline T., Margaret T. Hicken, Jay A. Pearson, Sarah J. Seashols, Kelly L. Brown, and Tracy Dawson Cruz. "Do US Black Women Experience Stress-Related Accelerated Biological Aging?" *Human Nature, 21,* 2010:19–38.

Gerth, H. H., and C. Wright Mills. *From Max Weber: Essays in Sociology.* New York: Galaxy, 1958.

Gettleman, Jeffrey. "Starvation and Strife Menace Torn Kenya." *New York Times,* February 28, 2009.

Gibbs, Nancy. "Affirmative Action for Boys." *Time,* April 3, 2008.

Gibson-Davis, Christina. "Mothers but Not Wives: The Increasing Lag between Nonmarital Births and Marriage." *Journal of Marriage and Family, 73,* 1, February 2011:264–278.

Gilbert, Dennis. *The American Class Structure in an Age of Growing Inequality,* 9th ed. New York: Sage, 2014.

Gilbert, Dennis, and Joseph A. Kahl. *American Class Structure.* 4th ed. Belmont: Wadsworth, 1998.

Gilens, Martin, and Benjamin Page. "Testing Theories of American Politics: Elites, Interest Groups, and Average Citizens." *Perspectives on Politics,* Fall 2014.

Gillis, Justin. "U.N. Panel Issues Its Starkest Warning Yet on Global Warming." *New York Times,* November 2, 2014.

Gillum, R. F. "Frequency of Attendance at Religious Services and Smoking: The Third National Health and Nutrition Examination Survey." *Preventive Medicine, 41,* 2005:607–613.

Gilman, Charlotte Perkins. *The Man-Made World or, Our Androcentric Culture.* New York: 1971. Originally published 1911.

Girshick, Lori B. *Woman-to-Woman Sexual Violence: Does She Call It Rape?* Boston: Northeastern University Press, 2002.

Gitlin, Todd. *The Twilight of Common Dreams: Why America Is Wracked by Culture Wars.* New York: Metropolitan Books, 1997.

Gjelten, Tom. "First Strike: US Cyber Warriors Seize the Offensive." *World Affairs Journal,* January/February 2013.

Glanton, Dahleen. "Hispanic Influx Causes Tensions with Blacks." *Daily Press* (Virginia), May 23, 2013.

Glasgow, Joshua M. "On the New Biology of Race." In *Arguing about Science,* Alexander Bird and James Ladyman, eds. New York: Routledge, 2013:170–184.

Glaze, Lauren E., and Laura M. Maruschak. "Parents in Prison and Their Minor Children." Bureau of Justice Statistics Special Report, August 2008:1–25.

"Global 2000." *Forbes,* March 29, 2007.

"Global 2000." *Forbes,* May 7, 2014.

"Global Wealth 2014: Riding a Wave of Growth." Boston Consulting Group, 2014.

Gloeckner, Gene W., and Paul Jones. "Reflections on a Decade of Changes in Homeschooling and the Homeschooled into Higher Education." *Peabody Journal of Education, 88,* 3, 2–13, July 2013:309–323.

Goffman, Erving. *Asylums: Essays on the Social Situation of Mental Patients and Other Inmates.* Chicago: Aldine, 1961.

Goffman, Erving. *The Presentation of Self in Everyday Life.* New York: Peter Smith, 1999. Originally published 1959.

Gold, Ray. "Janitors versus Tenants: A Status-Income Dilemma." *American Journal of Sociology, 58,* 1952:486–493.

Goldberg, Abbie E., Deborah A. Kashy, and JuliAnna Z. Smith. "Gender-Typed Play Behavior in Early Childhood: Adopted Children with Lesbian, Gay, and Heterosexual Parents." *Sex Roles, 67,* 2012:503–515.

Goldberg, Susan, and Michael Lewis. "Play Behavior in the Year-Old Infant: Early Sex Differences." *Child Development, 40,* March 1969:21–31.

Goldstein, Jacob. "A Simple Surgical Checklist Saves Lives." *Wall Street Journal,* January 15, 2009.

Goleman, Daniel. "Pollsters Enlist Psychologists in Quest for Unbiased Results." *New York Times,* September 7, 1993:C1, C11.

Goll, Sven. "Archaeologists Find 'Mini-Pompeii.'" *View and News from Norway*, October 1, 2010.

Gorman, Peter. "A People at Risk: Vanishing Tribes of South America." *The World & I*, December 1991:678–689.

Gorski, Philip S. "What Is Critical Realism? And Why Should You Care?" *Contemporary Sociology*, 42, 5, September 2013:658–670.

Goth, Ursula S., and Erik Smaland. "The Role of Civic Engagement for Men's Health and Well Being in Norway—A Contribution to Public Health." *International Journal of Environmental Research and Public Health*, 11, 2014:6375–6387.

Gottfredson, Michael R. "Sanctions, Situations, and Agency in Control Theories of Crime." *European Journal of Criminology*, 8, 2, 2011:128–143.

Gottschalk, Peter, Sara McLanahan, and Gary Sandefur, "The Dynamics and Intergenerational Transmission of Poverty and Welfare Participation." In *Confronting Poverty: Prescriptions for Change*, Sheldon H. Danziger, Gary D. Sandefur, and Daniel H. Weinberg, eds. Cambridge, Mass.: Harvard University Press, 1994.

Gough, Margaret, and Mary Noonan. "A Review of the Motherhood Wage Penalty in the United States." *Sociology Compass*, 7, 4, 2013:328–342.

Grabe, Shelly, L. Monique Ward, and Janet Shibley Hyde. "The Role of the Media in Body Image Concerns among Women: A Meta-Analysis of Experimental and Correlational Studies." *Psychological Bulletin*, 134, 3:2008:460–476.

Graham, L. O. *Our Kind of People: Inside America's Black Upper Class*. New York: HarperPerennial, 1999.

Grammich, Clifford, Kirk Hadaway, Richard Houseal, et al. *U.S. Religion Census: Religious Congregations and Membership Study, 2010*. Lenexa, Kansas: Association of Statisticians of American Religious Bodies, 2012.

Graves, Earl G. "Migration in Reverse: Blacks Are Leaving Major Cities and Heading South." *African Globe*, September 25, 2014.

Gray Panthers. "Age and Youth in Action." No date.

Greeley, Andrew M. "The Protestant Ethic: Time for a Moratorium." *Sociological Analysis*, 25, Spring 1964:20–33.

Greenhalgh, Susan. "The Chinese Biopolitical: Facing the Twenty-First Century." *New Genetics and Society*, 28, 3, September 2009:205–222.

Greenstein, Mindy, and Jimmie Holland. *Lighter as We Go: Virtues, Character Strengths, and Aging*. New York: Oxford University Press, 2015.

Greenwald, Anthony G., and Linda Hamilton Krieger. "Implicit Bias: Scientific Foundations." *California Law Review*, July 2006.

Grigoriadis, Vanessa. "The Rise and Fall of the Eco-Radical Underground." *Rolling Stone*, June 21, 2011.

Gross, Jan T. *Neighbors*. New Haven: Yale University Press, 2001.

Grossman, Andrew, and Christina Rexrode. "Citi to Pay $7 Billion to Settle Loan Probe." *Wall Street Journal*, July 15, 2014.

Grossman, Zoltán. "From Wounded Knee to Syria: A Century of U.S. Military Interventions." http://academic.evergreen.edu/g/grossmaz/interventions.html. 2014.

Guensburg, Carol. "Bully Factories." *American Journalism Review*, 23, 6, 2001:51–59.

"Guilds." *Encyclopedia Britannica*, 2014.

Gunther, Marc. "The Mosquito in the Tent." *Fortune*, 149, 11, May 31, 2004:158.

Guo, Guang, Yuying Tong, and Tianji Cai. "Gene by Social Context Interactions for Number of Sexual Partners among White Male Youths: Genetics-Informed Sociology." *American Journal of Sociology*, 114, Supplement, 2008:S36–S66.

Gupta, Giri Raj. "Love, Arranged Marriage, and the Indian Social Structure." In *Cross-Cultural Perspectives of Mate Selection and Marriage*, George Kurian, ed. Westport, Conn.: Greenwood Press, 1979.

Gurian, Michael. *The Wonder of Aging: A New Approach to Embracing Life after Fifty*. New York: Simon & Schuster, 2013.

Guru, Gopal, and Shiraz Sidhva. "India's 'Hidden Apartheid.'" *UNESCO Courier*, September 2001:27.

Gurven, Michael, and Hillard Kaplan. "Longevity among Hunter-Gatherers: A Cross-Cultural Examination." *Population and Development Review*, 33, 2, June 2007:321–365.

Gutek, Gerald L. *An Historical Introduction to American Education*, 3rd ed. Long Grove, Ill.: Waveland Press, 2013.

Guthrie, Doug. "The Great Helmsman's Cultural Death." *Contexts*, 7, 3, Summer 2008:26–31.

Gutner, Toddi. "Team Building—but Fun." *Wall Street Journal*, April 28, 2014.

Haas, Jack, and William Shaffir. "The Cloak of Competence." In *Down-to-Earth Sociology: Introductory Readings*, 7th ed. New York: Free Press, 1993:432–441.

Hacker, Helen Mayer. "Women as a Minority Group." *Social Forces*, 30, October 1951:60–69.

Hafner, Katie. "In Ill Doctor, a Surprise Reflection of Who Picks Assisted Suicide." *New York Times*, August 11, 2012.

Hagerty, James R. "As America Ages, Shortage of Help Hits Nursing Homes." *Wall Street Journal*, April 15, 2013.

Hakim, Catherine. "Erotic Capital." *European Sociological Review*, 2010:499–518.

Hall, Edward T. *The Silent Language*. New York: Doubleday, 1959.

Hall, Edward T., and Mildred R. Hall. "The Sounds of Silence." In *Down to Earth Sociology: Introductory Readings*, 15th ed., James M. Henslin, ed. New York: Free Press, 2016.

Hall, G. Stanley. *Adolescence: Its Psychology and Its Relations to Physiology, Anthropology, Sociology, Sex, Crime, Religion, and Education*. New York: Appleton, 1904.

Hall, Richard H. "The Concept of Bureaucracy: An Empirical Assessment." *American Journal of Sociology*, 69, July 1963:32–40.

Hallin, Daniel C. *The Uncensored War: The Media and Vietnam*. New York: Oxford University Press, 1986.

Halpern, Jack. "Iceland's Big Thaw." *New York Times*, May 13, 2011.

Hamermesh, Daniel. *Beauty Pays: Why Attractive People Are More Successful*. Princeton, N.J.: Princeton University Press, 2011.

Hamilton, Jon. "Orphans' Lonely Beginnings Reveal How Parents Shape a Child's Brain." *NPR News*, February 24, 2014.

Hamlin, J. Kiley, and Karen Wynn. "Young Infants Prefer Prosocial to Antisocial Others." *Cognitive Development*, 26, 1, 2011:30–39.

Handel, Stephen J. "Recurring Trends and Persistent Themes: A Brief History of Transfer." New York: College Board Advocacy and Policy Center, March 2013.

Handwerk, Brian. "Maya City in 3-D." *National Geographic Daily News*, May 20, 2010.

Hansen, Casper Worm, Peter S. Jensen, and Christian Skovsgaard. "Modern Gender Roles and Agricultural History: The Neolithic Inheritance." *Social Science Research Network*, November 4, 2012.

Hanson, Chad. *The Community College and the Good Society*. New Brunswick, N.J.: Transaction Publishers, 2010.

Hardoon, Deborah. "Wealth: Having It All and Wanting More." Oxford: Oxfam House, January 2015.

Hardy, Dorcas. *Social Insecurity: The Crisis in America's Social Security and How to Plan Now for Your Own Financial Survival*. New York: Villard Books, 1991.

Harlow, Harry F., and Margaret K. Harlow. "Social Deprivation in Monkeys." *Scientific American*, 207, 1962:137–147.

Harlow, Harry F., and Margaret K. Harlow. "The Affectional Systems." In *Behavior of Nonhuman Primates: Modern Research Trends*, Vol. 2,

Allan M. Schrier, Harry F. Harlow, and Fred Stollnitz, eds. New York: Academic Press, 1965:287–334.

Harper, Charles L., and Kevin T. Leicht. *Exploring Social Change: America and the World*. Upper Saddle River, N.J.: Prentice Hall, 2002.

Harrington, Charlene, Helen Carrillo, Megan Dowdell, et al. *Nursing Facilities, Staffing, Residents and Facility Deficiencies, 2005 through 2010*. San Francisco, Calif.: University of California, October 2011.

Harrington, Michael. *The Vast Majority: A Journey to the World's Poor*. New York: Simon & Schuster, 1977.

Harris, Chauncey D. "The Nature of Cities and Urban Geography in the Last Half Century." *Urban Geography*, 18, 1997.

Harris, Chauncey D., and Edward Ullman. "The Nature of Cities." *Annals of the American Academy of Political and Social Science*, 242, 1945:7–17.

Harris, Craig. "Fallout from Ariz. Employer Sanctions Law." *Arizona Republic*, September 15, 2008.

Harris, Gardiner. "Drug Makers Told Studies Would Aid It, Papers Say." *New York Times*, March 19, 2009.

Harris, Gardiner. "In India, Kisses Are on Rise, Even in Public." *New York Times*, February 13, 2013.

Harris, Jerry. "Global Monopolies and the Transnational Capitalist Class." *International Critical Thought*, 2, 1, March 2012:1–6.

Harris, Marvin. "Why Men Dominate Women." *New York Times Magazine*, November 13, 1977:46, 115, 117–123.

Harris, Shane. "Snowdenfreude." *Foreign Policy: Situation Report*, July 16, 2014.

Harrison, Paul. *Inside the Third World: The Anatomy of Poverty*, 3rd ed. London: Penguin Books, 1993.

Hart, Charles W. M., and Arnold R. Pilling. *The Tiwi of North Australia*, Fieldwork Edition. New York: Holt, Rinehart and Winston, 1979.

Hart, D. G. "The Eating of Sausages." *Wall Street Journal*, August 20, 2013.

Hart, Hornell. "Acceleration in Social Change." In *Technology and Social Change*, Francis R. Allen, Hornell Hart, Delbert C. Miller, William F. Ogburn, and Meyer F. Nimkoff, eds. New York: Appleton, 1957:27–55.

Hart, Paul. "Groupthink, Risk-Taking and Recklessness: Quality of Process and Outcome in Policy Decision Making." *Politics and the Individual*, 1, 1, 1991:67–90.

Hartley, Eugene. *Problems in Prejudice*. New York: King's Crown Press, 1946.

Hartocollis, Anemona. "More Access to Contraceptives in City Schools." *New York Times*, September 23, 2012.

Hass, Marjorie. "A College 'Reset' with Young Men in Mind." *Dallas News*, February 2, 2012.

"Harvard Medical School: Osher Research Center." http://www.osher.hms.harvard.edu/history.asp. 2011.

Hatch, Laurie Russell. *Beyond Gender Differences: Adaptation to Aging in Life Course Perspective*. Amityville, N.Y.: Baywood Publishing Company, 2000.

Hatfield, Elaine, Lisamarie Bensman, and Richard L. Rapson "A Brief History of Social Scientists' Attempts to Measure Passionate Love." *Journal of Social and Personal Relationships*, 29, 2, 2012:143–164.

Hattery, Angela, and Earl Smith. *African American Families Today: Myths and Realities*. Lanham, Md.: Rowman and Littlefield, 2012.

Haub, Carl, and Nancy Yinger. "The U.N. Long-Range Population Projections: What They Tell Us." Washington, D.C.: Population Reference Bureau, 1994.

Haub, Carl, and Toshiko Kaneda. "World Population Data Sheet, 2014." Washington, D.C.: Population Reference Bureau, 2015.

Haughney, Christine, and Eric Konigsberg. "Despite Tough Times, Ultrarich Keep Spending." *New York Times*, April 14, 2008.

Hauser, Philip, and Leo Schnore, eds. *The Study of Urbanization*. New York: Wiley, 1965.

Hausman, Daniel M. "Health, Naturalism, and Functional Efficiency." *Philosophy of Science*, 79, 4, October 2012:519–541.

Hausmann, Leslie R. M., Larissa Myaskovsky, Christian Niyonkuru, et al. "Examining Bias of Physicians Who Care for Individuals with Spinal Cord Injury: A Pilot Study and Future Directions." *Journal of Spinal Cord Medicine*, 2014. (In press)

Havrilla, Karina. "A Sociological Influence in Dora the Explorer." *ASA Footnotes*, 38, 2, February 2010.

Hawdon, James. "Applying Differential Association Theory to Online Hate Groups: A Theoretical Statement." *Research on Finnish Society*, 5, 2012:39–47.

Hawkes, Nigel. "Asbestos-Related Diseases Will Rise for 20 Years." *The Times*, September 25, 2001.

Hawkins, Harry. "Care Home Inviting in Prostitutes for Residents Is under Investigation." *Sun* (U.K.), January 28, 2013.

Hawley, Amos H. *Urban Society: An Ecological Approach*. New York: Wiley, 1981.

Haworth, Abigail. "The Day I Saw 248 Girls Suffering Genital Mutilation." *The Guardian*, November 17, 2012.

Hayashi, Gina M., and Bonnie R. Strickland. "Long-Term Effects of Parental Divorce on Love Relationships: Divorce as Attachment Disruption." *Journal of Social and Personal Relationships*, 15, 1, February 1998:23–38.

Hays-Thomas, Rosemary, and Marc Bendick, Jr. "Professionalizing Diversity and Inclusion Practice: Should Voluntary Standards Be the Chicken or the Egg?" *Industrial and Organizational Psychology*, 6, 2013:193–205.

Healy, Jack. "In Age of School Shootings, Lockdown is the New Fire Drill." *New York Times*, January 16, 2014.

Heller, Jennifer Lynn. "The Enduring Problem of Social Class Stigma Experienced by Upwardly Mobile White Academics." *McGill Sociological Review*, 2, April 2011:19–38.

Helliker, Kevin. "Body and Spirit: Why Attending Religious Services May Benefit Health." *Wall Street Journal*, May 3, 2005.

Hellinger, Daniel, and Dennis R. Judd. *The Democratic Facade*. Pacific Grove, Calif.: Brooks/Cole, 1991.

Hemmings, Annette. "The 'Hidden' Corridor Curriculum." *High School Journal*, 83, December 1999:1–12.

Hendin, Herbert. "Euthanasia and Physician-Assisted Suicide in the Netherlands." *New England Journal of Medicine*, 336, 19, May 8, 1997:1385–1387.

Hendin, Herbert. "Suicide, Assisted Suicide, and Medical Illness." *Harvard Mental Health Letter*, 16, 7, January 2000:4–7.

Henley, Nancy, Mykol Hamilton, and Barrie Thorne. "Womanspeak and Manspeak." In *Beyond Sex Roles*, Alice G. Sargent, ed. St. Paul, Minn: West, 1985.

Henslin, James M. *Social Problems: A Down-to-Earth Approach*, 12th edition. Boston: Pearson, 2015.

Henslin, James M., and Mae A. Biggs. "Behavior in Pubic Places: The Sociology of the Vaginal Examination." In *Down to Earth Sociology: Introductory Readings*, 15th ed., James M. Henslin, ed. New York: Free Press, 2016. Originally published 1971.

Herba, Catherine M., Richard E. Tremblay, et al. "Maternal Depressive Symptoms and Children's Emotional Problems: Can Early Child Care Help Children of Depressed Mothers?" JAMA Psychiatry, 70, 8, 2013:830–838.

Herrera, Spencer, and Richard Rodriguez. "The Desertification of Society: A Conversation with Richard Rodriguez." *World Literature Today*, 88, 2, March–April 2014:14–19.

Herring, Cedric. "Is Job Discrimination Dead?" *Contexts*, Summer 2002: 13–18.

Herz, Rachel. "You Eat That?" *Wall Street Journal*, January 28, 2012.

Hetherington, Mavis, and John Kelly. *For Better or for Worse: Divorce Reconsidered*. New York: W. W. Norton, 2003.

Higginbotham, Elizabeth, and Lynn Weber. "Moving with Kin and Community: Upward Social Mobility for Black and White Women." *Gender and Society*, 6, 3, September 1992:416–440.

Hill, Kim R., Robert S. Walker, Miran Bozicevic, et al. "Co-Residence in Hunter-Gatherer Societies Show Unique Human Social Structure." *Science*, 331, March 2011.

Hill, Mark E. "Skin Color and the Perception of Attractiveness among African Americans: Does Gender Make a Difference?" *Social Psychology Quarterly*, 65, 1, 2002:77–91.

Hilson, Gavin. "Family Hardship and Cultural Values: Child Labor in Malian Small-Scale Gold Mining Communities." *World Development*, 40, 8, 2012:1663–1674.

Himes, Christine L. "Elderly Americans." *Population Bulletin*, 56, 1, December 2001:1–40.

Hinshaw, Drew. "For Want of Gloves, Ebola Doctors Die." *Wall Street Journal*, August 16–17, 2014.

Hinshaw, Drew, and Betsy McKay. "Deadly Disappointment Awaits at Ebola Clinics." *Wall Street Journal*, September 8, 2014.

Hirschi, Travis. *Causes of Delinquency*. Berkeley: University of California Press, 1969.

Hnatkovska, Viktoria, Amartya Lahiri, and Sourabh Paul. "Castes and Labor Mobility." *American Economic Journal: Applied Economics*, 4, 2 2012:274–307.

Hochschild, Arlie. "Feelings around the World." *Contexts*, 7, 2, Spring 2008:80.

Hoffman, Bert. "The International Dimensions of Authoritarian Legitimation: The Impact of Regime Evolution." Leibnitz: German Institute of Global and Area Studies. Working Paper No. 182, December 2011.

Holder, Kelly. "Voting and Registration in the Election of November 2004." *Current Population Reports*, March 2006.

Holland, Jesse J. "Prison Rape: Department of Justice Orders Increase in Anti-Rape Efforts." Associated Press, May 12, 2012.

Holland, Steve, and Roberta Rampton. "Obama Unveils U.S. Immigration Reform, Setting up Fight with Republicans." Reuters, November 21, 2014.

Hollingsworth, Heather. "Dinner at School: More Public Schools Dish up 3 Meals a Day." *Huffington Post*, February 18, 2012.

Holtzman, Abraham. *The Townsend Movement: A Political Study*. New York: Bookman, 1963.

Homblin, Dora Jane. *The First Cities*. Boston: Little, Brown, Time-Life Books, 1973.

Honeycutt, Karen. "Disgusting, Pathetic, Bizarrely Beautiful: Representations of Weight in Popular Culture." Paper presented at the 1995 meetings of the American Sociological Association.

Hong, Lawrence. "Marriage in China." In *Til Death Do Us Part: A Multicultural Anthology on Marriage*, Sandra Lee Browning and R. Robin Miller, eds. Stamford, Conn.: JAI Press, 1999.

Hookway, James. "Editor Gets 10 Years in Jail for Thai Royal Insult." *Wall Street Journal*, January 23, 2013.

Hookway, James. "In Thailand Today, Teen Monks Express the Spirit to a Rock Beat." *Wall Street Journal*, August 15, 2012.

Hopschneider, Anita. "Hiring Millennials? Meet the Parents." *Wall Street Journal*, September 11, 2013.

Horn, James P. *Land as God Made It: Jamestown and the Birth of America*. New York: Basic Books, 2006.

Horobin, William. "French in Uproar over Train Snafu." *Wall Street Journal*, May 22, 2014.

Horowitz, Mark, William Yaworsky, and Kenneth Kickham. "Whither the Blank Slate? A Report on the Reception of Evolutionary Biological Ideas among Sociological Theorists." *Sociological Spectrum*, 34, 2014:489–509.

Horowitz, Ruth. *Honor and the American Dream: Culture and Identity in a Chicano Community*. New Brunswick, N.J.: Rutgers University Press, 1983.

Horowitz, Ruth. "Studying Violence among the 'Lions.'" In *Social Problems*, James M. Henslin, ed. Upper Saddle River, N.J.: Prentice Hall, 2005:135.

Horwitz, Allan V., and Jerome C. Wakefield. *The Loss of Sadness: How Psychiatry Transformed Normal Sorrow into Depressive Disorder*. New York: Oxford University Press, 2007.

Hotz, Robert Lee. "Practice Personalities: What an Avatar Can Teach You." *Wall Street Journal*, January 20, 2015.

Hout, Michael. "How Class Works: Objective and Subjective Aspects of Class since the 1970s." In *Social Class: How Does It Work?* Annette Lareau and Dalton Conley, eds. New York: Russell Sage, 2008:52–64.

Houtman, Dick. "What Exactly Is a 'Social Class'?: On the Economic Liberalism and Cultural Conservatism of the 'Working Class.'" Paper presented at the annual meetings of the American Sociological Association, 1995.

Howells, Lloyd T., and Selwyn W. Becker. "Seating Arrangement and Leadership Emergence." *Journal of Abnormal and Social Psychology*, 64, February 1962:148–150.

Hoyt, Homer. "Recent Distortions of the Classical Models of Urban Structure." In *Internal Structure of the City: Readings on Space and Environment*, Larry S. Bourne, ed. New York: Oxford University Press, 1971:84–96.

Hoyt, Homer. *The Structure and Growth of Residential Neighborhoods in American Cities*. Washington, D.C.: Federal Housing Administration, 1939.

Hsu, Francis L. K. *The Challenge of the American Dream: The Chinese in the United States*. Belmont, Calif.: Wadsworth, 1971.

Huang, Penelope M., Pamela J. Smock, Wendy D. Manning, and Cara A. Bergstrom-Lynch. "He Says, She Says: Gender and Cohabitation." *Journal of Family Issues*, 32, February 2011.

Hubbard, Ben. "Hajj Tragedy Inflames Schisms during a Pilgrimage Designed for Unity." *New York Times*, September 25, 2015.

Huber, Joan. "Micro-Macro Links in Gender Stratification." *American Sociological Review*, 55, February 1990:1–10.

HUD (U.S. Department of Housing and Urban Development) "The 2013 Annual Homeless Assessment Report (AHAR) to Congress." November 2013.

Huggins, Martha K., Mika Haritos-Fatouros, and Philip G. Zimbardo. *Violence Workers: Police Torturers and Murderers Reconstruct Brazilian Atrocities*. Berkeley: University of California Press, 2002.

Hughes, Everett C. "Good People and Dirty Work." In *Life in Society: Readings to Accompany Sociology: A Down-to-Earth Approach*, 7th ed. James M. Henslin, ed. Boston: Allyn and Bacon, 2005:125–134. Article originally published 1962.

Hughes, H. Stuart. *Oswald Spengler: A Critical Estimate*, rev. ed. New York: Scribner's, 1962.

Hughes, John. "Bush Had Good Reason to Believe There Were WMDs in Iraq." *Christian Science Monitor*, April 12, 2006.

Hummer, Robert A., Christopher G. Ellison, Richard G. Rogers, Benjamin E. Moulton, and Ron R. Romero. "Religious Involvement and Adult Mortality in the United States: Review and Perspective." *Southern Medical Journal*, 97, 2004:1223–1230.

Hummer, Robert A., Richard G. Rogers, Charles B. Nam, and Christopher G. Ellison. "Religious Involvement and U.S. Adult Mortality." *Demography* 36, 1999:273–285.

Humphreys, Laud. *Tearoom Trade: Impersonal Sex in Public Places*, enlarged ed. Chicago: Aldine, 1975. Originally published 1970.

Hunt, Darnell. "American Toxicity: Twenty Years after the 1992 Los Angeles 'Riots.'" *Amerasia Journal*, 38, 1, 2012:ix–xviii.

Hurdley, Rachel. "In the Picture or off the Wall? Ethical Regulation, Research Habitus, and Unpeopled Ethnography." *Qualitative Inquiry*, 16, 2010:517–528.

Hurtado, Aída, David E. Hayes-Bautista, R. Burciaga Valdez, and Anthony C. R. Hernández. *Redefining California: Latino Social Engagement in a Multicultural Society*. Los Angeles: UCLA Chicano Studies Research Center, 1992.

Hussein, Hayat. "Can Egypt Afford Quality Education?" *Al-Ahram Weekly*, April 17, 2014.

Huttenbach, Henry R. "The Roman *Porajmos*: The Nazi Genocide of Europe's Gypsies." *Nationalities Papers*, 19, 3, Winter 1991:373–394.

Hylton, Hillary. "Turning up the Heat on Polygamists." *Time*, July 24, 2008.

Hymowitz, Carol. "Raising Women to Be Leaders." *Wall Street Journal*, February 12, 2007.

Hymowitz, Carol. "Through the Glass Ceiling." *Wall Street Journal*, November 8, 2004.

Hyra, Derek S. "Racial Uplift? Intra-Racial Class Conflict and the Economic Revitalization of Harlem and Bronzeville." *City and Community*, 5, 1, March 2006:71–92.

IES (Institute of Education Sciences). *Digest of Education Statistics*. Washington, D.C.: U.S. Department of Education, 2010.

Inatsugu, Hiraoiki. "The System of Bureaucrats in Japan." In *Japanese Politics Today: From Karaoke to Kabuki Democracy*, Takashi Inoguchi and Purnendra Jain, eds. New York: Palgrave Macmillan, 2011:29–50.

Innes, Judith E., David E. Booher, and Sarah Di Vittorio. "Strategies for Megaregion Governance—Collaborative Dialogue, Networks, and Self-Organization." *Journal of the American Planning Association*, 77, 1, 2011:55–67.

Interlandi, Jeneen. "Not Just Urban Legend." *Newsweek*, January 10, 2009.

Inter-Parliamentary Union. "Women in National Parliaments." Geneva, Switzerland: Inter-Parliamentary Union, February 1, 2013.

Isaac, Carol A., Anna Kaatz, and Molly Carnes. "Deconstructing the Glass Ceiling." *Sociology Mind*, 2, 1, 2012:80–86.

Isaacs, Ken. "The Rwandan Genocide: 20 Years Later, We're No Wiser." *Wall Street Journal*, April 5–6, 2014.

"It's So Much Nicer on K Street." *New York Times*, June 8, 2008.

Itard, Jean Marc Gospard. *The Wild Boy of Aveyron*, George and Muriel Humphrey, trans. New York: Appleton-Century-Crofts, 1962.

Jacobs, Andrew. "Chinese Workers Say Illness Is Real, Not Hysteria." *New York Times*, July 29, 2009.

Jacobs, Margaret A. "'New Girl' Network Is Boon for Women Lawyers." *Wall Street Journal*, March 4, 1997:B1, B7.

Jaggar, Alison M. "Sexual Difference and Sexual Equality." In *Theoretical Perspectives on Sexual Difference*, Deborah L. Rhode, ed. New Haven, Conn.: Yale University Press, 1990:239–254.

Jakab, Spencer. "An Offal Tale: For This Club, Everything Is on the Menu." *Wall Street Journal*, June 25, 2012.

James, John. "More than 1,000 Preventable Deaths a Day Is Too Many: The Need to Improve Patient Safety." Senate Subcommittee Hearing on Primary Health and Aging, July 17, 2014.

Jamieson, Amie, Hyon B. Shin, and Jennifer Day. "Voting and Registration in the Election of November 2000." *Current Population Reports*, February 2002.

Janis, Irving L. *Victims of Groupthink*. Boston, Mass.: Houghton Mifflin, 1972.

Janis, Irving. L. *Groupthink: Psychological Studies of Policy Decisions and Fiascoes*. Boston: Houghton Mifflin, 1982.

Jankowiak, William R., and Edward F. Fischer. "A Cross-Cultural Perspective on Romantic Love." *Journal of Ethnology*, 31, 2, April 1992:149–155.

Jasper, James M. "Emotions and Social Movements: Twenty Years of Theory and Research." Unpublished paper, 2012.

Jasper, James M. "Moral Dimensions of Social Movements." Paper presented at the annual meetings of the American Sociological Association, 1991.

Jasper, James M. "Social Movements." *Blackwell Encyclopedia of Sociology*, January 2007:4443–4451.

Jauhar, Sandeep. "Our Ailing Medical System." *Wall Street Journal*, August 30–31, 2014.

Jeavens, Christine. "Hajj: Jamaret Bridge, a Deadly Pinch Point." BBCNews, September 25, 2015.

Jenkins, Philip. "The Next Christianity." *Atlantic Monthly*, October 2002:53–68.

Jensen, Lene Arnett. "Through Two Lenses: A Cultural-Developmental Approach to Moral Psychology." *Developmental Review*, 28, 2009:289–315.

Jeong, Yu-Jin, and Hyun-Kyung You. "Different Historical Trajectories and Family Diversity among Chinese, Japanese, and Koreans in the United States." *Journal of Family History*, 33, 3, July 2008:346–356.

Jessop, Bob, "The Return of the National State in the Current Crisis of the World Market." *Capital and Class*, 34, 1, 2010:38–43.

Jewkes, Rachel. "Rape Perpetration: A Review." *Pretoria, South Africa: Sexual Violence Research Initiative*, July 2012:1–45.

Johannes, Laura. "On the Heels of AARP." *Wall Street Journal*, March 31, 2014.

John-Henderson, Neha, Emily G. Jacobs, Rodolfo Mendoza-Denton, and Darlene D. Francis. "Wealth, Health, and the Moderating Role of Implicit Social Class Bias." *Annals of Behavioral Medicine*, 45, 2013: 173–179.

Johnson, Benton. "On Church and Sect." *American Sociological Review*, 28, 1963:539–549.

Johnson, Norris R. "Panic at 'The Who Concert Stampede': An Empirical Assessment." In *Collective Behavior and Social Movements*, Russell L. Curtis, Jr., and Benigno E. Aguirre, eds. Boston: Allyn and Bacon, 1993:113–122.

Johnson, Tim. "On Drug Lord's Mexican Turf, Lines Blur among Cops, Pols, Cartel." *Wall Street Journal*, March 1, 2014.

Johnson, Troy R., ed. *Native American Family Life*. Broomall, Pa.: Mason Crest, 2014.

Johnson, Wendy, Eric Turkheimer, Irving I. Gottesman, and Thomas J. Bouchard, Jr. "Beyond Heritability: Twin Studies in Behavioral Research." *Current Directions in Psychological Science*, 18, 4, 2009:217–220.

Johnson-Weiner, Karen. *Train up a Child: Old Order Amish and Mennonite Schools*. Baltimore: Johns Hopkins University Press, 2007.

Johnston, Drue M., and Norris R. Johnson. "Role Extension in Disaster: Employee Behavior at the Beverly Hills Supper Club Fire." *Sociological Focus*, 22, 1, February 1989:39–51.

Johnston, Lloyd D., Patrick M. O'Malley, Jerald G. Bachman, and John E. Schulenberg. *Monitoring the Future, National Survey Results on Drug Use, 1975–2011. Volume II: College Students and Adults Ages 19–50*. Ann Arbor, Mich.: Institute for Social Research, 2012.

Johnston, Lloyd D., Patrick M. O'Malley, Jerald G. Bachman, and John E. Schulenberg, and R.A. *Monitoring the Future, National Survey Results on Drug Use, 1975–2013. Volume II: College Students and Adults Ages 19–55*. Ann Arbor: Institute for Social Research, University of Michigan, 2014.

Johnston, Lloyd D., Patrick M. O'Malley, R. A. Miech, Jerald G. Bachman, and John E. Schulenberg. *Monitoring the Future, National Results on Adolescent Drug Use: Overview of Key Findings, 2014.* Ann Arbor: Institute for Social Research, University of Michigan, 2015.

Jones, Adrienne L., Abigail J. Moss, and Lauren D. Harris-Kojetin. "Use of Advance Directives in Long-Term Care Populations." *NCHS Data Brief, 54,* January 2011.

Jones, Allen. "Let Nonviolent Prisoners Out." *Los Angeles Times,* June 12, 2008.

Jones, Ashby. "Executions, Death Penalties Hit Multiyear Lows in U.S." *Wall Street Journal,* December 18, 2014.

Jones, James H. *Bad Blood: The Tuskegee Syphilis Experiment,* 2nd ed. New York: Free Press, 1993.

Jones, Jeffrey Owen, and Peter Meyer. *The Pledge: A History of the Pledge of Allegiance.* New York: St. Martin's Press, 2010.

Jones, Nikki. *Between Good and Ghetto: African American Girls and Inner-City Violence.* New Brunswick, N.J.: Rutgers University Press, 2010.

Jordan, Miriam. "Among Poor Villagers, Female Infanticide Still Flourishes in India." *Wall Street Journal,* May 9, 2000:A1, A12.

Josephson, Matthew. "The Robber Barons." In *John D. Rockefeller: Robber Baron or Industrial Statesman?* Earl Latham, ed. Boston: Heath, 1949:34–48.

Joungtrakul, Jamnean, and Bobbie McGhie Allen. "Research Ethics: A Comparative Study of Qualitative Doctoral Dissertations Submitted to Universities in Thailand and the USA." *Science Journal of Business Management,* 2012, 2012:1–11.

Judge, Timothy A., and Daniel M. Cable. "The Effect of Physical Height on Workplace Success and Income: Preliminary Test of a Theoretical Model." *Journal of Applied Psychology,* 89, 3, 2004:428–441.

Judge, Timothy A., Charlice Hurst, and Lauren S. Simon. "Does It Pay to Be Smart, Attractive, or Confident (or All Three)? Relationships among General Mental Ability, Physical Attractiveness, Core Self-Evaluations, and Income." *Journal of Applied Psychology,* 94, 3, 2009:742–755.

Juergensmeyer, Mark. *Terror in the Mind of God: The Global Rise of Religious Violence.* Berkeley: University of California Press, 2000.

Kacen, Jacqueline J. "Advertising Effectiveness." New York: Wiley International Encyclopedia of Marketing, 2011.

Kaestle, C. E. "Selling and Buying Sex: A Longitudinal Study of Risk and Protective Factors in Adolescence." *Preventive Science,* 13, 2012:314–322.

Kagame, Paul. "Building a Future after Rwanda's Genocide." *Wall Street Journal,* April 7, 2014.

Kagan, Donald. "Democracy Requires a Patriotic Education." *Wall Street Journal,* September 27–28, 2014.

Kagan, Jerome. "The Idea of Emotions in Human Development." In *Emotions, Cognition, and Behavior,* Carroll E. Izard, Jerome Kagan, and Robert B. Zajonc, eds. New York: Cambridge University Press, 1984:38–72.

Kahlenberg, Richard D. *The Future of Affirmative Action: New Paths to Higher Education Diversity after Fisher v. University of Texas.* Washington, D.C.: Century Foundation and Lumina Foundation, 2014.

Kahlenberg, Susan G., and Michelle M. Hein, "Progression on Nickelodeon? Gender-Role Stereotypes in Toy Commercials." *Sex Roles,* 62, 2010:830–847.

Kahn, Joseph. "China's Elite Learn to Flaunt It While the New Landless Weep." *New York Times,* December 25, 2004.

Kahn, Joseph. "Thousands Reportedly Riot in China." *International Herald-Tribune,* March 13, 2007.

Kaku, Michio. "The Golden Age of Neuroscience Has Arrived." *Wall Street Journal,* August 21, 2014.

Kalb, Claudia. "Faith and Healing." *Newsweek,* November 10, 2003:44–56.

Kalinovsky, Artemy. "Soviet War in Afghanistan (1979–1992)." In *The Encyclopedia of War,* 1st ed., Gordon Martel, ed. London: Blackwell Publishing, 2012.

Kamber, Michael. "In Afghan Kilns, a Cycle of Debt and Servitude." *New York Times,* March 15, 2011.

Kaminer, Ariel. "Columbia's Gang Scholar Lives on the Edge." *New York Times,* November 30, 2012.

Kanazawa, Satoshi, and Jody L. Kovar. "Why Beautiful People Are More Intelligent." *Intelligence,* 32, 2004:227–243.

Kanter, Rosabeth Moss. *Men and Women of the Corporation.* New York: Basic Books, 1977.

Kanter, Rosabeth Moss. *Supercorp: How Vanguard Companies Create Innovation, Profits, Growth, and Social Good.* New York: Random House, 2009.

Kanter, Rosabeth Moss. *The Change Masters: Innovation and Entrepreneurship in the American Corporation.* New York: Simon & Schuster, 1983.

Kanter, Rosabeth Moss. "Why Global Companies Will Behave More and More Alike." *Wall Street Journal,* July 8, 2014.

Kantor, Jodi. "In First Family, a Nation's Many Faces." *New York Times,* January 16, 2009.

Kantor, Jodi. "On the Job, Nursing Mothers Find a 2-Class System." *New York Times,* September 1, 2006.

Kaplan, Robert M., Michael L. Spittel, and Tia L. Zeno. "Educational Attainment and Life Expectancy." *Policy Insights from the Behavioral and Brain Sciences,* 1, 1, October 2014:189–194.

Kaplan, Thomas. "Judge Rejects New York Limit on Donations to 'Super PACs.'" *New York Times,* April 24, 2014.

Kapp, Diana. "When Uber Is the Family Chauffeur." *Wall Street Journal,* December 18, 2014.

Karon, Tony. "Why China Does Capitalism Better than the U.S." *Time,* January 20, 2011.

Karp, David A., Gregory P. Stone, and William C. Yoels. *Being Urban: A Sociology of City Life,* 2nd ed. New York: Praeger, 1991.

Katz, Bruce, and Jennifer Bradley. "The Suburban Challenge." *Newsweek,* January 26, 2009.

Katz, Jonathan M., and Erik Eckholm. "DNA Evidence Clears Two Men in 1983 Murder." *New York Times,* September 2, 2014.

Katz, Richard S. "Electoral Reform in Italy: Expectations and Results." *Acta Politica,* 41, 2006:285–299.

Kaufman, Joanne. "Married Maidens and Dilatory Domiciles." *Wall Street Journal,* May 7, 1996:A16.

Keating, Giles, Michael O'Sullivan, Anthony Shorrocks, et al. *Global Wealth Report 2013.* Zurich: Credit Suisse Research Institute, October 2013.

Keith, Jennie. *Old People, New Lives: Community Creation in a Retirement Residence,* 2nd ed. Chicago: University of Chicago Press, 1982.

Kelley, Tina. "In an Era of School Shootings, a New Drill." *New York Times,* March 25, 2008.

Kelly, Benjamin, and Khostrow Farahbakhsh. "Public Sociology and the Democratization of Technology: Drawing on User-Led Research to Achieve Mutual Education." *American Sociologist,* 44, 1, 2013:42–53.

Kelly, Joan B. "How Adults React to Divorce." In *Marriage and Family in a Changing Society,* 4th ed., James M. Henslin, ed. New York: Free Press, 1992:410–423.

Kempner, Joanna. "The Chilling Effect: How Do Researchers React to Controversy?" *PLoS Medicine,* 5, 11, November, 2008:1571–1578.

Keniston, Kenneth. *Youth and Dissent: The Rise of a New Opposition.* New York: Harcourt, Brace, Jovanovich, 1971.

Kent, Mary, and Robert Lalasz. "In the News: Speaking English in the United States." Washington, D.C.: Population Reference Bureau, January 18, 2007.

Kephart, William M., and William W. Zellner. *Extraordinary Groups: An Examination of Unconventional Life-Styles*, 7th ed. New York: Worth Publishing, 2001.

Khan, Shamus Rahman. *Privilege: The Making of an Adolescent Elite at St. Paul's School*. Princeton, N.J.: Princeton University Press, 2011.

Khan, Shamus Rahman. "The Sociology of Elites." *Annual Review of Sociology*, 38, 2012:361–377.

Khare, Amy T., Mark L. Joseph, and Robert J. Chaskin. "The Enduring Significance of Race in Mixed-Income Developments." *Urban Affairs Review*, 2014:1–30.

Kim, Richard. "The L Word." *The Nation*, October 19, 2004.

Kimes, Mina. "America's Hottest Export: Weapons—Full Version." *Fortune*, February 24, 2011.

Kimmel, Michael. "Racism as Adolescent Male Rite of Passage." *Journal of Contemporary Ethnography*, 36, 2, April 2007:202–218.

Kindzeka, Moki Edwin. "Cameroon, WHO Push for End to Female Circumcision." Voice of America, June 17, 2014.

King, Eden B., Jennifer L. Knight, and Michelle R. Hebl. "The Influence of Economic Conditions on Aspects of Stigmatization." *Journal of Social Issues*, 66, 3, September 2010:446–460.

King, Patricia M., Rosemary J. Perez, and Woo-jeong Shim. "How College Students Experience Intercultural Learning: Key Features and Approaches." *Journal of Diversity in Higher Education*, 6, 2, 2013:69–83.

Kingsbury, Alex, "Many Colleges Reject Women at Higher Rates than for Men." *U.S. News & World Report*, June 17, 2007.

Kingston, Maxine Hong. *The Woman Warrior*. New York: Vintage Books, 1975:108. Quoted in Frank J. Zulke and Jacqueline P. Kirley. *Through the Eyes of Social Science*, 6th ed. Prospect Heights, Ill.: Waveland Press, 2002.

Kissinger, Henry. "Henry Kissinger on the Assembly of a New World Order." *Wall Street Journal*, August 29, 2014.

Klandermans, Bert. *The Social Psychology of Protest*. Cambridge, Mass.: Blackwell, 1997.

Kleinfeld, Judith S. "Gender and Myth: Data about Student Performance." In *Through the Eyes of Social Science*, 6th ed., Frank J. Zulke and Jacqueline P. Kirley, eds. Prospect Heights, Ill.: Waveland Press, 2002a:380–393.

Kleinfeld, Judith S. "The Small World Problem." *Society*, January–February, 2002b:61–66.

Klinesmith, Jennifer, Tim Kasser, and Francis T. McAndrew. "Guns, Testosterone, and Aggression." *Psychological Science*, 17, 7, 2006:568–571.

Kluegel, James R., and Eliot R. Smith. *Beliefs about Inequality: America's Views of What Is and What Ought to Be*. Hawthorne, N.Y.: Aldine de Gruyter, 1986.

Knapp, Daniel. "What Happened When I Took My Sociological Imagination to the Dump." *Footnotes*, May–June, 2005:4.

Kneebone, Elizabeth, and Alan Berube. *Confronting Suburban Poverty in America*. Washington, D.C.: Brookings Institute, 2013.

Knickerbocker, Brad. "Firebrands of 'Ecoterrorism' Set Sights on Urban Sprawl." *Christian Science Monitor*, August 6, 2003.

Kochbar, Rakesh, and Ana Gonzalez-Barrera. "Through Boom and Bust: Minorities, Immigrants and Homeownership." Washington, D.C.: Pew Hispanic Center, May 12, 2009.

Kohlberg, Lawrence. "A Current Statement on Some Theoretical Issues." In *Lawrence Kohlberg: Consensus and Controversy*, Sohan Modgil and Celia Modgil, eds. Philadelphia: Falmer Press, 1986:485–546.

Kohlberg, Lawrence. "Moral Education for a Society in Moral Transition." *Educational Leadership*, 33, 1975:46–54.

Kohlberg, Lawrence. *The Psychology of Moral Development: Moral Stages and the Life Cycle*. San Francisco: Harper and Row, 1984.

Kohlberg, Lawrence, and Carol Gilligan. "The Adolescent as a Philosopher: The Discovery of the Self in a Postconventional World." *Daedalus*, 100, 1971:1051–1086.

Kohn, Alfie. "Make Love, Not War." *Psychology Today*, June 1988:35–38.

Kohn, Melvin L. *Change and Stability: A Cross-National Analysis of Social Structure and Personality*. Boulder, Colo.: Paradigm, 2006.

Kohn, Melvin L. *Class and Conformity: A Study in Values*, 2nd ed. Homewood, Ill.: Dorsey Press, 1977.

Kohn, Melvin L. "Social Class and Parental Values." *American Journal of Sociology*, 64, 1959:337–351.

Kohn, Melvin L. "Social Class and Parent–Child Relationships: An Interpretation." *American Journal of Sociology*, 68, 1963:471–480.

Kohn, Melvin L., and Carmi Schooler. "Class, Occupation, and Orientation." *American Sociological Review*, 34, 1969:659–678.

Kolata, Gina. "The Genesis of an Epidemic: Humans, Chimps and a Virus." *New York Times*, September 4, 2001.

Kontos, Louis, David Brotherton, and Luis Barrios, eds. *Gangs and Society: Alternative Perspectives*. New York: Columbia University Press, 2003.

Koonin, Steven E. "Climate Science Is Not Settled." *Wall Street Journal*, September 19, 2014.

Kopecky, Karen A., and Richard M. H. Suen. "A Quantitative Analysis of Suburbanization and the Diffusion of the Automobile." *International Economic Review*, 51, 4, 2010:1003–1037.

Kotz, David M. *The Rise and Fall of Neoliberal Capitalism*. Boston: Harvard University Press, 2015.

Kozin, Vladimir. "U.S.-NATO Missile System: First-Strike Potential Aimed at Russia." *Global Research*, March 2, 2013.

Kramer, Michael W., and Debbie S. Dougherty. "Groupthink as Communication Process, Not Outcome." *Communication and Social Change*, 1, 1, October 2013:44–62.

Kramer, Ronald. "Moral Panics and Urban Growth Machines: Official Reactions to Graffiti in New York City, 1990–2005." *Qualitative Sociology*, 33, 2010:297–311.

Krause, Neal, and Christopher G. Ellison. "Forgiveness by God, Forgiveness of Others, and Psychological Well-Being in Late Life." *Journal for the Scientific Study of Religion*, 42, 1, 2003:77–93.

Kravitz, Derek. "Harlem's Mount Morris Park Sees More Change." *Wall Street Journal*, January 30, 2014.

Kraybill, Donald B. *The Riddle of Amish Culture*, rev. ed. Baltimore, Md.: Johns Hopkins University Press, 2002.

Kreider, Rose M., and Jason Fields. "America's Living Arrangements: 2001." *Current Population Reports*, July 2005.

Krienert, Jessie L., and Jeffrey A. Walsh. "Characteristics and Perceptions of Child Sexual Abuse." *Journal of Child Sexual Abuse*, 20, 2011:353–372.

Kristof, Gregory. "FCAT Scores Lower for Third Graders, State Drops Standards for More Students to Pass." *Huffington Post*, May 24, 2012.

Kristoff, Nicholas D. "Interview with a Humanoid." *New York Times*, July 23, 2002.

Kroeger, Brooke. "When a Dissertation Makes a Difference." *New York Times*, March 20, 2004.

Krogstad, Jens Manuel. "1-in-4 Native Americas and Alaska Natives Are Living in Poverty." PEW Research Center, June 13, 2014.

Krugman, Paul. "White Man's Burden." *New York Times*, September 24, 2002.

Kübler-Ross, Elisabeth. *On Death and Dying*. New York: Macmillan, 1969. 40th anniversary edition published by Routledge in 2008.

Kubrin, Charis E., and Ronald Weitzer. "Retaliatory Homicide: Concentrated Disadvantage and Neighborhood Culture." *Social Problems*, 50, 2, May 2003:157–180.

Kuchera, Ben. "Games with Exclusively Female Heroes Don't Sell (Because Publishers Don't Support Them)." *The Penny Arcade Report*, November 21, 2013.

Kuhn, Peter J., and Marie-Claire Villeval. "Are Women More Attracted to Cooperation than Men?" National Bureau of Economic Research, Working Paper 19277, August 2013.

Kulish, Nicholas. "German Ruling against Circumcising Boys Draws Criticism." *New York Times*, June 26, 2012.

Kuperberg, Arielle. "Age at Coresidence, Premarital Cohabitation, and Marriage Dissolution: 1995–2009." *Journal of Marriage and Family, 76*, April 2014.

Kurian, George Thomas. *Encyclopedia of the First World*, Vols. 1, 2. New York: Facts on File, 1990.

Kurian, George Thomas. *Encyclopedia of the Second World*. New York: Facts on File, 1991.

Kurian, George Thomas. *Encyclopedia of the Third World*, Vols. 1, 2, 3. New York: Facts on File, 1992.

Kushkush, Isma'il. "In South Sudan, a Ghost of Wars Past: Child Soldiers." *New York Times*, June 7, 2014.

La Barre, Weston. *The Human Animal*. Chicago: University of Chicago Press, 1954.

Lacy, Karyn R. *Blue-Chip Black: Class and Status in the New Black Middle Class*. Berkeley: University of California Press, 2007.

LaFraniere, Sharon. "Views of North Korea Show How a Policy Spread Misery." *New York Times*, June 9, 2010.

Lam, Dottie. "Are Men the Forgotten Minority?" *Denver Post*, July 14, 2013.

Lanbewiesche, William. "The Accuser." *The Atlantic*, March 2005.

Landau, Elizabeth. "When 'Life Support' Is Really 'Death Support.'" CNN, December 29, 2013.

Landry, Bart, and Kris Marsh. "The Evolution of the New Black Middle Class." *Annual Review of Sociology*, 37, 2011:373–394.

Landtman, Gunnar. *The Origin of the Inequality of the Social Classes*. New York: Greenwood Press, 1968. Originally published 1938.

Lang, Kevin. "Poverty and the Labor Market." In *The Oxford Handbook of the Economics of Poverty*, P. N. Jefferson, ed. London: Oxford University Press, 2012.

Lang, Kurt, and Gladys E. Lang. *Collective Dynamics*. New York: Crowell, 1961.

Lapsley, Michael. *Redeeming the Past: My Journey from Freedom Fighter to Healer*. Maryknoll, N.Y.: Orbis Books, 2012.

Lareau, Annette. "Invisible Inequality: Social Class and Childrearing in Black Families and White Families." *American Sociological Review*, 67, October 2002:747–776.

Lareau, Annette. *Unequal Childhoods: Race, Class, and Family Life*, 2nd ed. Berkeley: University of California Press, 2011.

Last, Jonathan V. "The War against Girls." *Wall Street Journal*, June 24, 2011.

Latimer, Melissa, and Rachael A. Woldoff. "Good Country Living? Exploring Four Housing Outcomes among Poor Appalachians." *Sociological Forum*, 25, 2, June 2010:315–333.

Lauer, Jeanette, and Robert Lauer. "Marriages Made to Last." In *Marriage and Family in a Changing Society*, 4th ed., James M. Henslin, ed. New York: Free Press, 1992:481–486.

Laumann, E. O., S. A. Leitsch, and L. J. Waite. "Elder Mistreatment in the United States: Prevalence Estimates from a Nationally Representative Study." *The Journals of Gerontology, 63*, 4, July 2008: S248–S254.

Lawler, Steph. "'Getting Out and Getting Away': Women's Narratives of Class Mobility." *Feminist Review*, 63, Autumn 1999:3–24.

Lazaro, Fred de Sam. "In Senegal, a Movement to Reject Circumcision." *PBS Hour*, August 12, 2011.

Lazarsfeld, Paul F., and Jeffrey G. Reitz. "History of Applied Sociology." *Sociological Practice*, 7, 1989:43–52.

Leacock, Eleanor. *Myths of Male Dominance*. New York: Monthly Review Press, 1981.

Leahey, Colleen, and Caroline Fairchild. "Women CEOs in the Fortune 500." *Fortune*, January 6, 2015.

Ledger, Kate. "Sociology and the Gene." *Contexts*, 8, 3, 2009:16–20.

LeDuff, Charlie. "Handling the Meltdowns of the Nuclear Family." *New York Times*, May 28, 2003.

Lee, Alfred McClung, and Elizabeth Briant Lee. *The Fine Art of Propaganda: A Study of Father Coughlin's Speeches*. New York: Harcourt Brace, 1939.

Lee, Raymond M. *Unobtrusive Methods in Social Research*. Philadelphia: Open University Press, 2000.

Lee, Sharon M. "Asian Americans: Diverse and Growing." *Population Bulletin*, 53, 2, June 1998:1–39.

Lehnert, Thomas, Diana Sonntag, Alesander Konnopka, et al. "Economic Costs of Overweight and Obesity." *Best Practice & Research Clinical Endocrinology & Metabolism*, 27, 2013:105–115.

Leland, John. "A New Harlem Gentry in Search of Its Latte." *New York Times*, August 7, 2003.

Leland, John, and Gregory Beals. "In Living Colors." *Newsweek*, May 5, 1997:58–60.

Lengermann, Madoo, and Gillian Niebrugge. *The Women Founders: Sociology and Social Theory, 1830–1930*. Prospect Heights, Ill.: Waveland Press, 2007.

Lenski, Gerhard. *Power and Privilege: A Theory of Social Stratification*. New York: McGraw-Hill, 1966.

Lenski, Gerhard. "Status Crystallization: A Nonvertical Dimension of Social Status." *American Sociological Review*, 19, 1954:405–413.

Lenski, Gerhard, and Jean Lenski. *Human Societies: An Introduction to Macrosociology*, 5th ed. New York: McGraw-Hill, 1987.

Leo, Jen. "Google's Space Explorer Sergey Brin." *Los Angeles Times*, June 12, 2008.

Lerner, Gerda. *Black Women in White America: A Documentary History*. New York: Pantheon Books, 1972.

Lerner, Gerda. *The Creation of Patriarchy*. New York: Oxford, 1986.

Lerner, Steve. *Sacrifice Zones: The Front Lines of Toxic Chemical Exposure in the United States*. Cambridge, Mass.: MIT Press, 2010.

"Less Rote, More Variety: Reforming Japan's Schools." *The Economist*, December 16, 2000:8.

Lesser, Alexander. "War and the State." In *War: The Anthropology of Armed Conflict and Aggression*, Morton Fried, Marvin Harris, and Robert Murphy, eds. Garden City, N.Y.: Natural History, 1968:92–96.

Levanthal, Tama, and Jeanne Brooks-Gunn. "The Neighborhood They Live In: Effects of Neighborhood Residence on Child and Adolescent Outcomes." *Psychological Bulletin*, 126, 2000:309–337.

Levi, Ken. "Becoming a Hit Man." In *Down to Earth Sociology: Introductory Readings*, 15th ed., James M. Henslin, ed. New York: Free Press, 2015. Originally published 1981.

Levine, Alan, and Sidney Wolfe. "Hospitals Drop the Ball on Physician Oversight." *PublicCitizen*, May 27, 2009.

Levinson, D. J. *The Seasons of a Man's Life*. New York: Knopf, 1978.

Levy, Becca R., Pil H. Chung, T. Bedford, et al. "Facebook as a Site for Negative Age Stereotypes." *Gerontologist*, 2013.

Levy, Clifford J. "Doctor Admits He Did Needless Surgery on the Mentally Ill." *New York Times*, May 20, 2003.

Lewin, Tamar. "After Home Schooling, Pomp and Traditional Circumstances." *New York Times*, June 18, 2011.

Lewis, Neil A. "Justice Dept. Toughens Rules on Torture." *New York Times*, January 1, 2005.

Lewis, Oscar. *La Vida*. New York: Random House, 1966a.

Lewis, Oscar. "The Culture of Poverty." *Scientific American*, 115, October 1966b:19–25.

Li, Weilin, George Farkas, Greg J. Duncan, et al. "Timing of High-Quality Care and Cognitive, Language, and Preacademic Development." *Developmental Psychology*, 49, 8, August 2013:1440–1451.

Liberman, Akiva M., David S. Kirk, and Kim Kideuk. "Labeling Effects of First Juvenile Arrests: Secondary Deviance and Secondary Sanctioning." *Criminology*, 2014:1–26.

Liebow, Elliott. *Tally's Corner: A Study of Negro Streetcorner Men*. Boston: Little, Brown, 1999. Originally published 1967.

Lightfoot-Klein, A. "Rites of Purification and Their Effects: Some Psychological Aspects of Female Genital Circumcision and Infibulation (Pharaonic Circumcision) in an Afro-Arab Society (Sudan)." *Journal of Psychological Human Sexuality*, 2, 1989:61–78.

Lindau, Stacy Tessler, L. Philip Schumm, Edward O. Laumann, Wendy Levinson, Colm A. O'Muircheartaigh, and Linda J. Waite. "A Study of Sexuality and Health among Older Adults in the United States." *New England Journal of Medicine*, 357, 8, August 23, 2007:762–774.

Linden, Eugene. "Lost Tribes, Lost Knowledge." *Time*, September 23, 1991:46, 48, 50, 52, 54, 56.

Lindley, Joanne, and Stephen Machin. "The Postgraduate Premium: Revisiting Trends in Social Mobility and Educational Inequalities in Britain and America." London: Sutton Trust, February 2013.

Linton, Ralph. *The Study of Man*. New York: Appleton-Century-Crofts, 1936.

Linz, Daniel, Bryant Paul, Kenneth C. Land, Jay R. Williams, and Michael E. Ezell. "An Examination of the Assumption That Adult Businesses Are Associated with Crime in Surrounding Areas: A Secondary Effects Study in Charlotte, North Carolina." *Law & Society*, 38, 1, March 2004:69–104.

Lipman, "Women at Work: A Guide for Men." *Wall Street Journal*, December 13–14, 2014.

Lippitt, Ronald, and Ralph K. White. "An Experimental Study of Leadership and Group Life." In *Readings in Social Psychology*, 3rd ed., Eleanor E. Maccoby, Theodore M. Newcomb, and Eugene L. Hartley, eds. New York: Holt, Rinehart and Winston, 1958:340–365. (As summarized in Olmsted and Hare 1978:28–31.)

Lipset, Seymour Martin. "The Social Requisites of Democracy Revisited." Presidential address to the American Sociological Association, Boston, Massachusetts, 1993.

Liptak, Adam. "Blocking Parts of Arizona Law, Justices Allow Its Centerpiece." *New York Times*, June 25, 2012.

Liptak, Adam. "Justices, 5–4, Reject Corporate Spending Limit." *New York Times*, January 21, 2010.

Lipton, Eric, and Ben Protess. "Law Doesn't End Revolving Door on Capitol Hill." *New York Times*, February 1, 2014.

Liu, Hui, and Corinne Reczek. "Cohabitation and U.S. Adult Mortality: An Examination by Gender and Race." *Journal of Marriage and Family*, 74, August 2012:794–811.

Liu, J., J. Hu, and O. Furutan. "The Influence of Student Perceived Professors' 'Hotness' on Expertise, Motivation, Learning Outcomes, and Course Satisfaction." *Journal of Education for Business*, 88, 2013:94–100.

Liu, Jianqing. "Analyses on Criminal Personality and Its Typical Category." *Frontiers of Legal Research*, 2, 1, 2014:75–82.

Lofland, John F. *Protest: Studies of Collective Behavior and Social Movements*. New Brunswick, N.J.: Transaction Books, 1985.

Logan, Brenda E., and Gregory Winner. "Tracing Inclusion: Determining Teacher Attitudes." *Research in Higher Education Journal*, 20, 2013:1–10.

Logan, John R., Jennifer Darrah, and Sookhee Oh. "The Impact of Race and Ethnicity, Immigration and Political Context on Participation in American Electoral Politics." *Social Forces*, 90, 3, 2012:993–1022.

Lombroso, Cesare. *Crime: Its Causes and Remedies*, H. P. Horton, trans. Boston: Little, Brown, 1911.

Longman, Jeré. "Home Schoolers Are Hoping to Don Varsity Jackets in Virginia." *New York Times*, February 8, 2012.

López, Adalberto, ed. *The Puerto Ricans: Their History, Culture, and Society*. Cambridge, Mass.: Schenkman, 1980.

Lopoo, Leonard, and Thomas DeLeire. "Pursuing the American Dream: Economic Mobility across Generations." Washington, D.C.: PEW Charitable Trust, 2012.

Lovett, Ian. "Tribes Clash as Casinos Move Away from Home." *New York Times*, March 3, 2014.

Lövheim, M. "Media and Religion through the Lens of Feminist and Gender Theory." In *Media, Religion and Gender: Key Issues and New Challenges*. New York: Routledge, 2013.

Lublin, Joann S. "CEO Pay in 2010 Jumped 11%." *Wall Street Journal*, May 9, 2011.

Lublin, Joann S. "Living Well." *Wall Street Journal*, April 8, 1999.

Lublin, Joann S. "Trying to Increase Worker Productivity, More Employers Alter Management Style." *Wall Street Journal*, February 13, 1991:B1, B7.

Luke, Timothy W. *Ideology and Soviet Industrialization*. Westport, Conn.: Greenwood Press, 1985.

Lurie, Nicole, Jonathan Slater, Paul McGovern, Jacqueline Ekstrum, Lois Quam, and Karen Margolis. "Preventive Care for Women: Does the Sex of the Physician Matter?" *New England Journal of Medicine*, 329, August 12, 1993:478–482.

Lyall, Sarah H. "Multiplying the Old Divisions of Class in Britain." *New York Times*, April 3, 2013.

Lynn, Michael, Michael Sturman, Christie Ganley, Elizabeth Adams, Mathew Douglas, and Jessica McNeil. "Consumer Racial Discrimination in Tipping: A Replication and Extension." *Journal of Applied Social Psychology*, 38, 4, 2008:1045–1060.

Lyons, John. "As Crime Rattles Brazil, Killings by Police Turn Routine." *Wall Street Journal*, July 13, 2013.

Lyons, John. "Brazil Police Called among World's Deadliest." *Wall Street Journal*, November 11, 2014.

Ma, Wayne, and Chuin-Wei Yap. "China's 'War on Pollution' Hits Big Firms." *Wall Street Journal*, March 7, 2014.

MacDonald, William L., and Alfred DeMaris. "Remarriage, Stepchildren, and Marital Conflict: Challenges to the Incomplete Institutionalization Hypothesis." *Journal of Marriage and the Family*, 57, May 1995:387–398.

MacFarquhar, Neil. "Many Muslims Turn to Home Schooling." *New York Times*, March 26, 2008.

Mack, Raymond W., and Calvin P. Bradford. *Transforming America: Patterns of Social Change*, 2nd ed. New York: Random House, 1979.

Mackay, Charles. *Memories of Extraordinary Popular Delusions and the Madness of Crowds*. London: Office of the National Illustrated Library, 1852.

MacLean, Alair, and Meredith Kleykamp. "Coming Home: Attitudes toward U.S. Veterans Returning from Iraq." *Social Problems*, 61, 1, 2014:131–154.

MacLennan, Michael. "Locating the Policy Space for Inclusive Green Growth within the SADC Extractive Sector." *International Policy Centre for Inclusive Growth*, 38, December 2012:1–7.

Magdoff, Fred, and John Bellamy Foster. "The Plight of the U.S. Working Class." *Monthly Review*, 65, 8, January 2014.

Mahoney, Patricia. "High Rape Chronicity and Low Rates of Help-Seeking among Wife Rape Survivors in a Nonclinical Sample: Implications for Research and Practice." *Violence against Women*, 5, 9, September 1999:993–1016.

Main, Jackson Turner. *The Social Structure of Revolutionary America.* Princeton, N.J.: Princeton University Press, 1965.

Makinen, Julie. "China Broadens Crackdown on Google Services." *Los Angeles Times*, June 13, 2014.

Makinen, Julie. "China's 'Visit Your Parents' Law Weighs on Many in One-Child Nation." *Los Angeles Times*, July 29, 2013.

Malinowski, Bronislaw. *Sex and Repression in Savage Society.* Cleveland, Ohio: World, 1927.

Malkin, Elisabeth. "Mexican Officials Say Prisoners Acted as Hit Men." *New York Times*, July 25, 2010.

Malthus, Thomas Robert. *First Essay on Population 1798.* London: Macmillan, 1926. Originally published 1798.

Mamdani, Mahmood. "The Myth of Population Control: Family, Caste, and Class in an Urban Village." New York: Monthly Review Press, 1973.

Mandemakers, Jornt J., and Matthijs Kalmijn. "Do Mother's and Father's Education Condition the Impact of Parental Divorce on Child Well-Being?" *Social Science Research*, 44, 2014:187–199.

Mander, Jerry. *In the Absence of the Sacred: The Failure of Technology and the Survival of the Indian Nations.* San Francisco, Calif.: Sierra Club Books, 1992.

Manheimer, Ronald J. "The Older Learner's Journey to an Ageless Society." *Journal of Transformative Education*, 3, 3, 2005.

Manning, Wendy D., and Jessica A. Cohen. "Premarital Cohabitation and Marital Dissolution: An Examination of Recent Marriages." *Journal of Marriage and Family*, 74, April 2012:377–387.

"Manpower Report to the President." Washington, D.C.: U.S. Department of Labor, Manpower Administration, April 1971.

Manza, Jeff, and Michael A. McCarthy. "The Neo-Marxist Legacy in American Sociology." *Annual Review of Sociology*, 37, 2011:155–183.

Manzano, Sylvia, and Gabriel R. Sanchez. "Take One for the Team? Limits of Shared Ethnicity and Candidate Preferences." *Political Research Quarterly*, 63, 3, 2010:568–580.

"Marital History for People 15 Years Old and over by Age, Sex, Race and Ethnicity: 2001." Annual Demographic Survey, Bureau of Labor Statistics and U.S. Census Bureau, 2004.

Markoff, John, and Somini Sengupta. "Separating You and Me? 4.74 Degrees." *New York Times*, November 21, 2011.

Marshall, Samantha. "It's So Simple: Just Lather Up, Watch the Fat Go down the Drain." *Wall Street Journal*, November 2, 1995:B1.

Martin, Andrew W., John D. McCarthy, and Clark McPhail. "Why Targets Matter: Toward a More Inclusive Model of Collective Violence." *American Sociological Review*, 74, 2009:821–841.

Martin, David S. "Vets Feel Abandoned after Secret Drug Experiments." *CNN*, March 1, 2012.

Martin, Joyce A., Brady E. Hamilton, Michelle J. K. Osterman, Sally C. Curtin, and T. J. Matthews. "Births: Final Data for 2012." *National Vital Statistics Reports*, 62, 9, August, 2013.

Martineau, Harriet. *Society in America.* Garden City, N.Y.: Doubleday 1962. Originally published 1837.

Martinez, Barbara. "Cash before Chemo: Hospitals Get Tough." *Wall Street Journal*, April 28, 2008.

Martinez, Gladys, Kimberly Daniels, and Anjani Chandra. "Fertility of Men and Women Aged 15–44 Years in the United States." *National Health Statistics Reports*, 51, April 12, 2012.

Marx, Karl. "Contribution to the Critique of Hegel's Philosophy of Right." In *Karl Marx: Early Writings*, T. B. Bottomore, ed. New York: McGraw-Hill, 1964:45. Originally published 1844.

Marx, Karl, and Friedrich Engels. *Communist Manifesto.* New York: Pantheon, 1967. Originally published 1848.

Masheter, Carol. "Postdivorce Relationships between Ex-Spouses: The Role of Attachment and Interpersonal Conflict." *Journal of Marriage and the Family*, 53, February 1991:103–110.

Massey, Douglas S. "Inheritance of Poverty or Inheritance of Place? The Emerging Consensus on Neighborhoods and Stratification." *Contemporary Sociology*, 42, 5, Summer 2013:690–695.

Massoglia, Michael, Glenn Firebaugh, and Cody Warner. "Racial Variation in the Effect of Incarceration on Neighborhood Attainment." *American Sociological Review*, 78, 1, February 2013:142–165.

Masters, Ryan K., Robert A. Hummer, and Daniel A. Powers. "Educational Differences in U.S. Adult Mortality: A Cohort Perspective." *American Sociological Review*, 77, 4, 2012:548–572.

Mathews, Anna Wilde. "Doctors Move to Webcams." *Wall Street Journal*, December 21, 2012.

Matsumoto, D., and B. Willingham. "Spontaneous Facial Expressions of Emotion of Congenitally and Noncongenitally Blind Individuals." *Journal of Personality and Social Psychology*, 96, 2009:1–10.

Matthews, Warren." Religions Arising in India." In *World Religions*, 7th ed., Belmont, Calif.: Wadsworth, 2013:69–174.

Mauss, Armand. *Social Problems as Social Movements.* Philadelphia, Pa.: Lippincott, 1975.

Mayer, Anita P., Julia A. Files, Marcia G. Ko, and Janis E. Blair. "Academic Advancement of Women in Medicine: Do Socialized Gender Differences Have a Role in Mentoring?" *Mayo Clinic Proceedings*, 83, 2, February 2008:204–207.

Mayer, John D. *Personality: A Systems Approach.* Boston: Allyn and Bacon, 2007.

Mazur, Allan, and Alan Booth. "Testosterone Is Related to Deviance in Male Army Veterans, but Relationships Are Not Moderated by Cortisol." *Biological Psychology*, 96, 2014:72–76.

McCabe, J. Terrence, and James E. Ellis. "Pastoralism: Beating the Odds in Arid Africa." In *Conformity and Conflict: Readings in Cultural Anthropology*, James P. Spradley and David W. McCurdy, eds. Glenview, Ill.: Scott, Foresman, 1990:150–156.

McCarthy, John D., and Mayer N. Zald. "Resource Mobilization and Social Movements: A Partial Theory." *American Journal of Sociology*, 82, 6, 1977:1212–1241.

McCarthy, Justin. "Seven in 10 Americans Back Euthanasia." Gallup, June 18, 2014.

McCartney, Scott. "Subtle Signs That May Mark You a Security Risk." *Wall Street Journal*, January 22, 2014.

McCormick, John. "The Sorry Side of Sears." *Newsweek*, February 22, 1999:36–39.

McCoy, Terrence. "In Pakistan, 1,000 Women Die in 'Honor Killings' Annually. Why Is This Happening?" *Washington Post*, May 28, 2014.

McCracken, Harry. "The Mystery of Minecraft." *Time*, June 3, 2013.

McDowell, Bart. "Mexico City: An Alarming Giant." *National Geographic*, 166, 1984:139–174.

McFalls, Joseph A., Jr. "Population: A Lively Introduction, 5th ed." *Population Bulletin*, 62, 1, March 2007:1–30.

McIntosh, Peggy. "White Privilege and Male Privilege: A Personal Account of Coming to See Correspondences through Work in Women's

Studies." Wellesley College Center for Research on Women, Working Paper 189, 1988.

McKay, Betsy. "New Tack on Vaccine for HIV: Molecule Shown to Block Virus." *Wall Street Journal*, February 19, 2015.

McKay, Betsy, and Jenifer S. Forsyth. "Ebola Pledges Lagged as Epidemic Widened." *Wall Street Journal*, September 16, 2014.

McKay, Betsy, and Peter Wonacott. "After Slow Ebola Response, World Seeks to Avoid Repeat." *Wall Street Journal*, December 30, 2014.

McKeown, Thomas. *The Modern Rise of Population*. New York: Academic Press, 1977.

McKibbin, Molly Littlewood. "The Current State of Multiracial Discourse." *Journal of Critical Mixed Race Studies, 1*, 1, 2014:183–202.

McKinnish, Terra G. "Sexually Integrated Workplaces and Divorce: Another Form of on-the-Job Search." *Journal of Human Resources, 42*, 2, 2007:331–352.

McKinnish, Terra, Randall Walsh, and Kirk White. "Who Gentrifies Low-Income Neighborhoods?" National Bureau of Economic Research, Working Paper 14036, May 2008.

McKown, Clark, and Rhona S. Weinstein. "Modeling the Role of Child Ethnicity and Gender in Children's Differential Response to Teacher Expectations." *Journal of Applied Social Psychology, 32*, 1, 2002:159–184.

McKown, Clark, and Rhona S. Weinstein. "Teacher Expectations, Classroom Context, and the Achievement Gap." *Journal of School Psychology, 46*, 2008:235–261.

McLaughlin, Heather, Christopher Uggen, and Amy Blackstone. "Sexual Harassment, Workplace Authority, and the Paradox of Power." *American Sociological Review, 77*, 4, 2012:625–647.

McLaughlin, Martyn. "New GTAV Release Tipped to Rake in £1 in Sales." *The Scotsman*, August 16, 2014.

McLemore, S. Dale. *Racial and Ethnic Relations in America*. Boston: Allyn and Bacon, 1994.

McNeil, Donald G., Jr. "Precursor to H.I.V. Was in Monkeys for Millennia." *New York Times*, September 16, 2010.

McNeill, William H. "How the Potato Changed the World's History." *Social Research, 66*, 1, Spring 1999:67–83.

McPhail, Clark. "Blumer's Theory of Collective Behavior: The Development of a Non-Symbolic Interaction Explanation." *Sociological Quarterly, 30*, 3, 1989:401–423.

McPhail, Clark. *The Myth of the Madding Crowd*. Hawthorne, N.Y.: Aldine de Gruyter, 1991.

McShane, Larry. "Abraham Shakespeare, $31M Florida Lottery Winner, Found Dead 9 Months after Disappearing." *Daily News*, January 30, 2010.

McVeigh, Rory. *The Rise of the Ku Klux Klan: Right-Wing Movements and National Politics*. Minneapolis: University of Minnesota Press, 2009.

McWhirter, Cameron. "Educators Get Prison Terms." *Wall Street Journal*, April 15, 2015.

McWhirter, Cameron, and Caroline Porter. "Schools' Test: Beat the Cheat." *Wall Street Journal*, September 27–28, 2014.

Mead, George Herbert. *Mind, Self and Society*. Chicago: University of Chicago Press, 1934.

Mead, Margaret. *Sex and Temperament in Three Primitive Societies*. New York: New American Library, 1950. Originally published 1935.

Medicare Newsgroup. "Medicare FAQs." Online. January 9, 2015.

Medina, Jennifer. "Los Angeles Neighborhood Tries to Change, but Avoid the Pitfalls." *New York Times*, September 20, 2013.

Meese, Ruth Lyn. "A Few New Children: Postinstitutionalized Children of Intercountry Adoption." *Journal of Special Education, 39*, 3, 2005:157–167.

Meier, Barry. "Health Studies Suggest Asbestos Substitutes Also Pose Cancer Risk." *Wall Street Journal*, May 12, 1987:1, 21.

"Melee Breaks out at Retirement Home." *The Daily News*, March 5, 2004.

Menzel, Peter. *Material World: A Global Family Portrait*. San Francisco: Sierra Club, 1994.

Mermin, Jonathan. "In Wake of Latest Trial Results, CDC Stresses That Consistent Use Is Imperative When Using Pre-Exposure Prophylaxis to Prevent HIV Infection." Atlanta, Ga.: CDC Division of HIV/AIDS Prevention, March 4, 2013.

Merton, Robert K. *Social Theory and Social Structure*. Glencoe, Ill.: Free Press, 1949. Enlarged ed., 1968.

Merton, Robert K. "The Social-Cultural Environment and *Anomie*." In *New Perspectives for Research on Juvenile Delinquency*, Helen L. Witmer and Ruth Kotinsky, eds. Washington, D.C.: U.S. Department of Health, Education, and Welfare, 1956:24–50.

Merwine, Maynard H. "How Africa Understands Female Circumcision." *New York Times*, November 24, 1993.

Meyer, Julie. "Centenarians: 2010." U.S. Census Bureau, December 2012.

Michaels, Robert J. *Transactions and Strategies: Economics for Management*. Mason, Ohio: South-Western Cengage, 2011.

Mickle, Tripp. "Teens' Use of E-Cigarettes Seen Topping Regular Smokes." *Wall Street Journal*, December 17, 2014.

Milbank, Dana. "Guarded by Greenbelts, Europe's Town Centers Thrive." *Wall Street Journal*, May 3, 1995:B1, B4.

Milgram, Stanley. "Behavioral Study of Obedience." *Journal of Abnormal and Social Psychology, 67*, 4, 1963:371–378.

Milgram, Stanley. "Some Conditions of Obedience and Disobedience to Authority." *Human Relations, 18*, February 1965:57–76.

Milgram, Stanley. "The Small World Problem." *Psychology Today, 1*, 1967:61–67.

Milkie, Melissa A. "Social World Approach to Cultural Studies." *Journal of Contemporary Ethnography, 23*, 3, October 1994:354–380.

Miller, Laura L. "Women in the Military." In *Down to Earth Sociology: Introductory Readings*, 14th ed., James M. Henslin, ed. New York: Free Press, 2007. Originally published 1997.

Miller, Stephen. "Ensure Compliance with Reform Law's Lactation Room Requirements." Alexandria, Va.: Society for Human Resource Management, March 8, 2012.

Miller, Vanessa. "Boulder Police Ready, with Less Severe Penalties, for Naked Pumpkin Run." *Colorado Daily*, October 1, 2010.

Miller, Walter B. "Lower Class Culture as a Generating Milieu of Gang Delinquency." *Journal of Social Issues, 14*, 3, 1958:5–19.

Miller-Loessi, Karen. "Toward Gender Integration in the Workplace: Issues at Multiple Levels." *Sociological Perspectives, 35*, 1, 1992:1–15.

Mills, C. Wright. *The Power Elite*. New York: Oxford University Press, 1956.

Mills, C. Wright. *The Sociological Imagination*. New York: Oxford University Press, 1959.

Mills, Karen M., and Thomas J. Palumbo. *A Statistical Portrait of Women in the United States: 1978*. Current Population Reports, Series P-23, Number 100, U.S. Census Bureau, 1980.

Miner, Horace. "Body Ritual among the Nacirema." In *Down to Earth Sociology: Introductory Readings*, 14th ed., James M. Henslin, ed. New York: Free Press, 2007. Originally published 1956.

Mirola, William A. "Asking for Bread, Receiving a Stone: The Rise and Fall of Religious Ideologies in Chicago's Eight-Hour Movement." *Social Problems*, 50, 2, May 2003:273–293.

Mishin, Stanislav. "American Capitalism Gone with a Whimper." *Pravda*, April 27, 2009.

Mitchum, Preston D. "Slapping the Hand of Cultural Relativism: Female Genital Mutilation, Male Dominance, and Health as a Human Rights Framework." *William & Mary Journal of Women and Law*, 19, 3–4, 2013.

Mohawk, John C. "Indian Economic Development: An Evolving Concept of Sovereignty." *Buffalo Law Review*, 39, 2, Spring 1991:495–503.

Moloney, Liam. "Pope to Spread the Faith through Twitter." *Wall Street Journal*, December 3, 2012.

Monahan, Brian A., Joseph A. Marolla, and David G. Bromley. "Constructing Coercion: The Organization of Sexual Assault." *Journal of Contemporary Ethnography*, 34, 3, June 2005:284–316.

Money, John, and Anke A. Ehrhardt. *Man and Woman, Boy and Girl.* Baltimore: Johns Hopkins University Press, 1972.

"'Monkey' Gives Delhi Claws for Alarm." *The Australian*, May 17, 2001.

Montagu, M. F. Ashley. *Introduction to Physical Anthropology*, 3rd ed. Springfield, Ill.: Thomas, 1960.

Montagu, M. F. Ashley, ed. *Race and IQ: Expanded Edition.* New York: Oxford University Press, 1999.

Montagu, M. F. Ashley. *The Concept of Race.* New York: Free Press, 1964.

Monte, Lindsay M., and Renee R. Ellis. "Fertility of Women in the United States, 2012." U.S. Census Bureau, July 2014.

Moreno, Eduardo Lopez, Oyebanji Oyeyinka, and Gora Mboup. *State of the World's Cities 2010/2011: Bridging the Urban Divide.* London: UN Habitat, 2012.

Morgan, Lewis Henry. *Ancient Society.* New York: Holt, 1877.

Mori, Kazuo, Akina Ito-Koyama, Miho Arai, and Aiko Hanayama. "Boys, Be Independent! Conformity Development of Japanese Children in the Asch Experiment without Using Confederates." *Psychology*, 2014:617–623.

Morin, Monte. "$1.7 Million Awarded in Retirement Home Death." *Los Angeles Times*, October 17, 2001.

Morin, Rich, and D'Vera Cohn. "Women Call the Shots at Home; Public Mixed on Gender Roles in Jobs." Pew Research Center Publications, September 25, 2008.

Morris, Aldon. "Black Southern Student Sit-In Movement: An Analysis of Internal Organization." In *Collective Behavior and Social Movements*, Russell L. Curtis, Jr., and Benigno E. Aguirre, eds. Boston: Allyn and Bacon, 1993:361–380.

Morris, Joan M., and Michael D. Grimes. "Moving up from the Working Class." In *Down to Earth Sociology: Introductory Readings*, 13th ed., James M. Henslin, ed. New York: Free Press, 2005:365–376.

Morris, Loveday. "In Lebanon, Syrian Refugee Children Find Safety from War but New Dangers on the Streets." *Washington Post*, April 3, 2014.

Morrow, Betty Hearn. "Urban Families as Support after Disaster: The Case of Hurricane Andrew." Paper presented at the annual meetings of the American Sociological Association, 1995.

Mosca, Gaetano. *The Ruling Class.* New York: McGraw-Hill, 1939. Originally published 1896.

Mosher, Steven W. "China's One-Child Policy: Twenty-Five Years Later." *Human Life Review*, Winter 2006:76–101.

Mosher, Steven W. "Too Many People? Not by a Long Shot." *Wall Street Journal*, February 10, 1997:A18.

Mosher, Steven W. "Why Are Baby Girls Being Killed in China?" *Wall Street Journal*, July 25, 1983:9.

"Most Indians Still Prefer Arranged Marriages." *Times of India*, September 2, 2014.

Mouawad, Jad. "Saudi Officials Seek to Temper the Price of Oil." *Bloomberg News*, January 27, 2007.

Mouawad, Jad. "Shell to Pay $15.5 Million to Settle Nigerian Case." *New York Times*, June 8, 2009.

Moulton, Benjamin E., and Darren E. Sherkat. "Specifying the Effects of Religious Participation and Educational Attainment on Mortality Risk for U.S. Adults." *Sociological Spectrum*, 32, 2012:1–19.

Mozur, Paul. "China Alleges Cyberattacks Originated in U.S." *Wall Street Journal*, March 1, 2013.

Muhamad, Roby. "Search in Social Networks." Ph.D. dissertation, Columbia University, 2010.

Mukhopadhyay, Carol C., Rosemary Henze, and Yolanda T. Moses. *How Real Is Race?: A Sourcebook on Race, Culture, and Biology.* Lanham, Md.: Rowman & Littlefield, 2014.

Mulrine, Anna. "US Drone Killings: 'A Secret War Governed by Secret Law'?" *Christian Science Monitor*, June 26, 2014.

Muniz-Fraticelli, Victor M. *The Structure of Pluralism.* New York: Oxford University Press, 2014.

"Mujer con cabeza humana alega religion en defensa." AOL Online News, February 14, 2006.

"Mujer 'resucite blye' en España." *BBC Mundo*, February 17, 2006.

Muntaner, Charles, Edwin Ng, Christophe Vanroelen, et al. "Social Stratification, Social Closure, and Social Class as Determinants of Mental Health Disparities." In *Handbook of the Sociology of Mental Health*, 2nd ed., C. S. Aneshensel et al., eds. New York: Springer, 2013:205–227.

Murdock, George Peter. "Comparative Data on the Division of Labor by Sex." *Social Forces*, 15, 4, May 1937:551–553.

Murdock, George Peter. *Social Structure.* New York: Macmillan, 1949.

Murdock, George Peter. "The Common Denominator of Cultures." In *The Science of Man and the World Crisis*, Ralph Linton, ed. New York: Columbia University Press, 1945.

Murphy, Tim. "The Meltdown of the Anti-Immigration Minuteman Militia." *Mother Jones*, August 4, 2014.

Murray, G. W. *Sons of Ishmael.* London: Routledge, 1935.

Murray, Rheana. "Girls Who Mysteriously Developed Tourette's-like Symptoms Are Suffering from Mass Hysteria: Doctor." *New York Daily News*, January 18, 2012.

Murray, Sara. "Gains for Women, but Pay Gap Persists." *Wall Street Journal*, May 28, 2014.

Mwiti, Neva. "Hadijatou Mani: A Slave to Freedom." *Afritorial*, January 8, 2013.

Nabhan, Gary Paul. *Cultures in Habitat: On Nature, Culture, and Story.* New York: Counterpoint, 1998.

NACE (National Association of College and Employers), "Salary Survey: Starting Salaries for New College Graduates." 2014.

Naik, Gautam. "A Baby, Please. Blond, Freckles—Hold the Colic." *Wall Street Journal*, February 12, 2009.

Nakamura, Akemi. "Abe to Play Hardball with Soft Education System." *The Japan Times*, October 27, 2006.

Nakao, Keiko, and Judith Treas. "Occupational Prestige in the United States Revisited: Twenty-Five Years of Stability and Change." Paper presented at the annual meetings of the American Sociological Association, 1990. (As cited in Kerbo, Harold R. *Social Stratification and Inequality: Class Conflict in Historical and Comparative Perspective*, 2nd ed. New York: McGraw-Hill, 1991:181.)

Narvaez, Darcia. "The 99 Percent—Development and Socialization within an Evolutionary Context." In *War, Peace, and Human Nature: The*

Convergence of Evolutionary and Cultural Views, Douglas P. Fry, ed. New York: Oxford University Press, 2013:341–357.

Nash, Gary B. *Red, White, and Black*. Englewood Cliffs, N.J.: Prentice Hall, 1974.

National Alliance to End Homelessness. "The State of Homelessess in America 2015." Washington, D.C., April 21, 2015.

National Center for Education Statistics. *Digest of Education Statistics*. Washington, D.C.: U.S. Government Printing Office, 1991.

National Center for Injury Prevention and Control. "Child Maltreatment: Facts at a Glance." Centers for Disease Control, 2014.

National Coalition for the Homeless. NCH Fact Sheet #2, June 2008.

National Congress of American Indians (NCAI). "Tribal Organizations." Online. 2014.

National Institute of Child Health and Human Development. "Child Care and Mother–Child Interaction in the First 3 Years of Life." *Developmental Psychology*, 35, 6, November 1999:1399–1413.

National Women's Political Caucus. "Factsheet on Women's Political Progress." Washington, D.C., June 1998.

Nauman, Qasim, Safdar Dawar, and Saeed Shah. "Taliban Militants Attack Pakistan School." *Wall Street Journal*, December 17, 2014.

Neil, Andrew. "Does a Narrow Social Elite Run the Country?" *BBC*, January 26, 2011.

Nelson, Dean. "Infanticide May Be behind Boys Outnumbering Girls in Indian Village." *Telegraph Media Group*, February 3, 2014.

Nelson, Margaret K. "Whither Fictive Kin? Or, What's in a Name?" *Journal of Family Issues*, 2013.

Neugarten, Bernice L. "Middle Age and Aging." In *Growing Old in America*, Beth B. Hess, ed. New Brunswick, N.J.: Transaction, 1976:180–197.

Newman, Benjamin J., Todd K. Hartman, and Charles S. Taber. "Foreign Language Exposure, Cultural Threat, and Opposition to Immigration." *Political Psychology*, 33, 5, 2012:635–657.

Newman, David B., Louis Tay, and Ed Diener. "Leisure and Subjective Well-Being: A Model of Psychological Mechanisms as Mediating Factors." *Journal of Happiness Studies*, April 16, 2013.

Newman, Rick. "The New Underground Economy." *U.S. News & World Report*, March 18, 2013.

Newport, Frank. "In U.S., Four in 10 Report Attending Church in Last Week." Gallup Poll, December 24, 2013a.

Newport, Frank. "U.S. Catholic Population Less Religious, Shrinking." Princeton, N.J.: Gallup Poll, February 25, 2013b.

Newport, Frank, Dan Witters, and Sangeeta Agrawal. "Religious Americans Enjoy Higher Wellbeing." Princeton, N.J.: Gallup Poll, February 16, 2012.

Newport, Frank, Sangeeta Agrawal, and Dan Witters. "Very Religious Americans Report Less Depression, Worry." Gallup Poll, December 1, 2010.

Nguyen, Tram. "From SlutWalks to SuicideGirls: Feminist Resistance in the Third Wave and Postfeminist Era." *Women's Studies Quarterly*, 41, 3&4, Fall/Winter 2013:157–172.

Nicas, Jack. "U.S. Rules Clip Drone Makers' Wings." *Wall Street Journal*, October 6, 2014.

Nichol, Jim. "Russian Political, Economic, and Security Issues and U.S. Interests." Washington, D.C.: Congressional Research Service, November 4, 2011.

Nichols, Shaun. "US Attorney Gen Latest to Roast Apple, Google Mobile Encryption." *The Register*, October 1, 2014.

Niebuhr, H. Richard. *The Social Sources of Denominationalism*. New York: Holt, 1929.

Nieuwenhuis-Mark, Ruth Elaine. "Healthy Aging as Disease?" *Frontiers in Aging Neuroscience*, 3, 3, February 22, 2011.

Noah, Timothy. "White House Forms Panel to Investigate Cold War Radiation Tests on Humans." *Wall Street Journal*, January 4, 1994:A12.

Nordberg, Jenny. "In Afghanistan, Boys Are Prized and Girls Live the Part." *New York Times*, September 20, 2010.

Nordland, Rod. "In Spite of the Law, Afghan 'Honor Killings' of Women Continue." *New York Times*, May 3, 2014.

Nordland, Rod. "That Joke Is a Killer." *Newsweek*, May 19, 2003:10.

Norton, Steven. "A Post-PC CEO: No Desk, No Desktop." *Wall Street Journal*, November 20, 2014.

Nuland, Sherwin B. "The Debate over Dying." *USA Weekend*, February 3–5, 1995:4–6.

Nuwer, Rachel. "Keeping Track of the Oldest People in the World." *Smithsonian*, July 8, 2014.

O'Brien, John E. "Violence in Divorce-Prone Families." In *Violence in the Family*, Suzanne K. Steinmetz and Murray A. Straus, eds. New York: Dodd, Mead, 1975:65–75.

O'Brien, Timothy L. "Fed Assesses Citigroup Unit $70 Million in Loan Abuse." *New York Times*, May 28, 2004.

O'Hanlon, Michael E., and Ian Livingston. "Iraq Index: Tracking Variables of Reconstruction & Security in Post-Saddam Iraq." Washington, D.C.: Brookings Institute, May 25, 2010.

O'Hare, William P. "A New Look at Poverty in America." *Population Bulletin*, 51, 2, September 1996a:1–47.

O'Hare, William P. "U.S. Poverty Myths Explored: Many Poor Work Year-Round, Few Still Poor after Five Years." *Population Today: News, Numbers, and Analysis*, 24, 10, October 1996b:1–2.

OECD (Organization for Economic Co-Operation and Development). "Hours Worked: Average Annual Hours Actually Worked," *OECD Employment and Labour Market Statistics* (database), 2014.

Ogburn, William F. *On Culture and Social Change: Selected Papers*, Otis Dudley Duncan, ed. Chicago: University of Chicago Press, 1964.

Ogburn, William F. *Recent Social Trends in the United States*. New York: McGraw-Hill, 1933.

Ogburn, William F. *Social Change with Respect to Culture and Human Nature*. New York: W. B. Huebsch, 1922. (Other editions by Viking in 1927, 1938, and 1950.)

Ogburn, William F. "The Hypothesis of Cultural Lag." In *Theories of Society: Foundations of Modern Sociological Theory*, Vol. 2, Talcott Parsons, Edward Shils, Kaspar D. Naegele, and Jesse R. Pitts, eds. New York: Free Press, 1961:1270–1273.

Okada, Akito. "Education Reform and Equal Opportunity in Japan." *Journal of International and Comparative Education*, 1, 2, 2012:116–129.

Okpiliya, F. I. "The Allure of Flora Species in the Tropical Rainforest Ecosystem: The Need for Concern in a Global Context." *Global Journal of Science Frontier Research: Environment and Earth Science*, 14, 4, 2014.

Olmsted, Michael S., and A. Paul Hare. *The Small Group*, 2nd ed. New York: Random House, 1978.

"111 Health-Care Professionals Charged in $225 Million Medicare Scam." Associated Press, February 17, 2011.

Onishi, Norimitsu. "Lucrative Gambling Pits Tribe against Tribe." *New York Times*, August 4, 2012.

Orme, Nicholas. *Medieval Children*. New Haven: Yale University Press, 2002.

Orwell, George. *1984*. New York: Harcourt Brace, 1949.

Osaki, Tomohiro. "Entrance Exams Get Failing Grade." *Japan Times*, December 2, 2013.

Osborne, Cynthia, Wendy D. Manning, and Pamela J. Smock. "Married and Cohabiting Parents' Relationship Stability: A Focus on Race and Ethnicity." *Marriage and Family*, 69, December 2007:1345–1366.

Osborne, Lawrence. "Got Silk." *New York Times Magazine*, June 15, 2002.

Oxalis. "Two Steps Back: The Return of Nonviolence in Ecological Resistance." *Black Seed*, May 5, 2014.

Page, Jeremy. "China's New Drones Raise Eyebrows." *Wall Street Journal*, November 18, 2010.

Page, Jeremy, and Chan Han Wong. "Beijing Flexes Muscle Amid Rifts with West." *Wall Street Journal*, September 4, 2015.

Pager, Devah. "The Mark of a Criminal Record." *American Journal of Sociology*, 108, 5, March 2003:937–975.

Pager, Devah, Bruce Western, and Bart Bonikowski. "Discrimination in a Low-Wage Labor Market: A Field Experiment." *American Sociological Review*, 74, 5, October 2009:777–799.

Palen, J. John. *The Urban World*, 9th ed. Boulder: Paradigm Publishers, 2012.

Pappano, Laura. "The Boy Genius of Ulan Bator." *New York Times*, September 13, 2013.

Parfit, Michael, "Earth First!ers Wield a Mean Monkey Wrench." *Smithsonian*, 21, 1, April 1990:184–204.

Pariza, Geoffrey. "Genocide, Inc.: Corporate Immunity to Violations of International Law after *Kiobel v. Royal Dutch Petroleum.*" *Loyola University Chicago International Law Review, 8*, 2, Summer 2011:229–254.

Park, Alice. "Why Circumcision Lowers Risk of HIV." *Time*, April 17, 2013.

Park, Robert Ezra, and Ernest W. Burgess. *Human Ecology*. Chicago: University of Chicago Press, 1921.

Parker, Chris. "Medicare Fraud Is Sweetest Crime in South Florida." Broward-Palm Beach New Times, May 2, 2013.

Parker, Kim, and Eileen Patten. "The Sandwich Generation: Rising Financial Burdens for Middle-Aged Americans." Washington, D.C.: PEW Research Center, January 30, 2013.

Parker, Laura. "It's Hard to Believe in the New Lara Croft." *Gamespot*, December 5, 2012.

Parsons, Talcott. "An Analytic Approach to the Theory of Social Stratification." *American Journal of Sociology, 45*, 1940:841–862.

Partington, Donald H. "The Incidence of the Death Penalty for Rape in Virginia." *Washington and Lee Law Review, 22*, 1965:43–75.

"Past Imperfect: Geronimo's Appeal to Theodore Roosevelt." *Smithsonian*, November 9, 2012.

Paterniti, Michael. "The Mountains Where Women Live as Men." *GQ*, March 2014.

Pearlin, L. I., and Melvin L. Kohn. "Social Class, Occupation, and Parental Values: A Cross-National Study." *American Sociological Review, 31*, 1966:466–479.

Pedersen, R. P. "How We Got Here: It's Not How You Think." *Community College Week, 13*, 15, March 15, 2001:4–5.

Pelletier, Dick. "Indefinite Lifespan in Our Future; Experts Ponder Responses." *Ethical Technology*, May 25, 2014.

Pennar, Karen, and Christopher Farrell. "Notes from the Underground Economy." *Business Week*, February 15, 1993:98–101.

Penner, Louis A., Irene V. Blair, Terrance L. Albrecht, and John F. Dovidio. "Reducing Racial Health Care Disparities: A Social Psychological Analysis." *Policy Insights from the Behavioral and Brain Sciences, 1*, 1, October 2014:204–212.

Pentland, Alex. "The New Science of Building Great Teams." *Harvard Business Review*, April 2012.

Peretz, Evgenia. "Bluebloods and Billionaires." *Vanity Fair*, October 2013.

Perez, Santiago, and Jose de Cordoba. "Executive Slaying Sparks New Fears." *Wall Street Journal*, January 10, 1014.

Perrow, Charles. "A Society of Organizations." *Theory and Society, 20*, 6, December 1991:725–762.

Pescosolido, Bernice. "Theories and the Rise and Fall of the Medical Profession." In *Medical Sociology on the Move*, William C. Cockerham, ed. New York: Springer, 2013:173–194.

Peter, Laurence J., and Raymond Hull. *The Peter Principle: Why Things Always Go Wrong*. New York: HarperBusiness, 2011.

Petersen, Andrea. "Checking In? Hidden Ways Hotels Court Guests Faster." *Wall Street Journal*, April 11, 2012.

Petty, Gregory C., Doo Hun Lim, Seung Won Yoon, and Johnny Fontan. "The Effect of Self-Directed Work Teams on Work Ethic." *Performance Improvement Quarterly, 21*, 2, 2008:49–63.

Pflanz, Mike. "Rwanda's Women Lead the Miraculous Recovery." *Telegraph*, October 17, 2008.

Phillips, Erica E. "Campus Sexual Assault Draws Greater Scrutiny." *Wall Street Journal*, September 30, 2014.

Phillips, Erica E. "'Three-Strikes' Prisoners Drawing a Walk." *Wall Street Journal*, April 1, 2013.

Phillips, Linda, Guifang Guo, and Haesook Kim. "Elder Mistreatment in U.S. Residential Care Facilities: The Scope of the Problem." *Journal of Elder Abuse and Neglect, 25*, 1, 2013:19–39.

Phillips, Mary. "Midwives versus Medics: A 17th-Century Professional Turf War." *Management and Organizational History, 2*, 1, 2007:27–44.

Philpott, Tom. "The Making of an Agribusiness Apologist." *Mother Jones*, February 24, 2012.

Piaget, Jean. *The Construction of Reality in the Child*. New York: Basic Books, 1954.

Piaget, Jean. *The Psychology of Intelligence*. London: Routledge & Kegan Paul, 1950.

"Piden en Holanda Aplicar la Eutanasia Infantil." *BBC Mundo*, December 15, 2004.

Pillemer, Karl, and J. Jill Suitor. "Violence and Violent Feelings: What Causes Them among Family Caregivers?" *Journal of Gerontology, 47*, 4, 1992:165–172.

Pines, Maya. "The Civilizing of Genie." *Psychology Today, 15*, September 1981:28–34.

Piotrow, Phylis Tilson. *World Population Crisis: The United States' Response*. New York: Praeger, 1973. *Population Today 4*, 5, September 1998.

Piven, Frances Fox. "Can Power from below Change the World?" *American Sociological Review, 73*, 1, February 2008:1–14.

Pokharel, Krishna, and Tripti Lahiri. "India Rape Cases Colored by Caste." *Wall Street Journal*, December 31, 2013.

Pollack, Andrew. "Looking for a Superbug Killer." *New York Times*, November 5, 2010.

Pollard, Zane F. "The Bureaucrat Sitting on Your Doctor's Shoulder." *Wall Street Journal*, May 22, 2014.

Poole, Steven. "Programmer Bob Who Outsourced His Job Was a Model Modern Employee." *Guardian*, January 17, 2013.

Pope, Liston. *Millhands and Preachers: A Study of Gastonia*. New Haven, Conn.: Yale University Press, 1942.

Porter, Caroline. "More Schools Open Their Doors to the Whole Community: States and Towns Deliver an Array of Government Services on Campus." *Wall Street Journal*, July 28, 2014.

Porter, Eduardo. "A Smart Way to Skip College in Pursuit of a Job." *New York Times*, June 17, 2014.

Portes, Alejandro, and Rubén G. Rumbaut. *Immigrant America*. Berkeley: University of California Press, 1990.

Post, Charles. "Agrarian Class Structure and Economic Development in Colonial British North America: The Place of the American Revolution in the Origins of US Capitalism." *Journal of Agrarian Change, 9*, 4, October 2009:453–483.

Powell, Lynda H., Leila Shahabi, and Carl E. Thoresen. "Religion and Spirituality: Linkages to Physical Health." *American Psychologist, 58*, 1, January 2003:36–52.

Preston, Julia. "Homeland Security Cancels 'Virtual Fence' after Billion Is Spent." *New York Times*, January 14, 2011.

Preston, Julia, and John H. Cushman, Jr. "Obama to Permit Young Migrants to Remain in U.S." *New York Times*, June 16, 2012.

Proctor, Robert N. *The Nazi War on Cancer*. Princeton, N.J.: Princeton University Press, 1999.

Qian, Zhenchao, and Daniel T. Lichter. "Social Boundaries and Marital Assimilation: Interpreting Trends in Racial and Ethnic Intermarriage." *American Sociological Review*, 72, February 2007:68–94.

Quammen, David. *Spillover: Animal Infections and the Next Human Pandemic*. New York: Norton, 2012.

Quinet, Kenna. "The Problem of Missing Persons." *Guide 66*, Washington, D.C.: Center for Problem-Oriented Policing, 2012.

Rabin, Roni Caryn. "Health Researchers Will Get $10.1 Million to Counter Gender Bias in Studies." *New York Times*, September 23, 2014.

Rabin, Roni Caryn. "Questions about Robotic Hysterectomy." *New York Times*, February 25, 2013.

Radelet, Michael L., and Glenn L. Pierce. "Race and Death Sentencing in North Carolina, 1980–2007." *North Carolina Law Review*, 89, 2011:2119–2159.

Ramakrishnan, Kavita B. "Inconsistent Legal Treatment of Unwanted Sexual Advances." *Berkeley Journal of Gender, Law, and Justice, 26*, 2, 2011:291–355.

Rampell, Catherine. "In Law Schools, Grades Go up, Just like That." *New York Times*, June 21, 2010.

Ramsey, Mike. Hydrogen Cars to Challenge Hybrids." *Wall Street Journal*, February 25, 2014.

Ramstad, Evan. "Big Brother, Now at the Mall." *Wall Street Journal*, October 9, 2012.

Rapoport, Anatoli. "Patriotic Education in Russia: Stylistic Move or a Sign of Substantive Counter-Reform." *Educational Forum*, 73, 2009:141–152.

Rasmussen, R., A. Mylonas, and H. Beck. *Investigating Business Communication and Technologies*. New York: Cambridge University Press, 2012.

Rasni, Ada. *The Daily Beast*, "Dubai's Camel Races Embrace Robot Jockeys." December 7, 2013.

Rassbach, Eric. "Why I Defend Goat Sacrifice." *Wall Street Journal*, August 7, 2009.

Ratcliffe, Caroline, and Signe-Mary McKernan. "Childhood Poverty Persistence: Facts and Consequences." The Urban Institute, Brief 14, June 2010:1–10.

Ray, Brian D. "Homeschooling Associated with Beneficial Learner and Societal Outcomes but Educators Do Not Promote It." *Peabody Journal of Education*, 88, 3, 2013.

Ray, Brian D. "Research Facts on Homeschooling." National Home Education Research Institute, January 2014.

Ray, J. J. "Authoritarianism Is a Dodo: Comment on Scheepers, Felling and Peters." *European Sociological Review*, 7, 1, May 1991:73–75.

Read, Madlen. "Citi Pays $18M for Questioned Credit Card Practice." Associated Press, August 26, 2008.

Reckless, Walter C. *The Crime Problem*, 5th ed. New York: Appleton, 1973.

Rector, Robert, and Jason Richwine. "The Fiscal Cost of Unlawful Immigrants and Amnesty to the U.S. Taxpayer." Report #133. The Heritage Foundation, May 6, 2013.

Reddy, Movindri. "The Transnationalization of Social Movements." In *Handbook of Political Citizenship and Social Movements*, Hein-Anton van der Heijden, ed. Cheltenham, U.K.: Edward Elgar Publishing, 2014:334–358.

Reed, Don Collins. "A Model of Moral Stages." *Journal of Moral Education, 37*, 3, September 2008:357–376.

Reed, Susan, and Lorenzo Benet. "Ecowarrior Dave Foreman Will Do Whatever It Takes in His Fight to Save Mother Earth." *People Weekly*, 33, 15, April 16, 1990:113–116.

Reeves, Richard V., and Joanna Venator. "Gender Gaps in Relative Mobility." *Social Mobility Memos*, November 12, 2013.

Regalado, Antonio. "Seoul Team Creates Custom Stem Cells from Cloned Embryos." *Wall Street Journal*, May 20, 2005.

Regnerus, Mark. "How Different Are the Adult Children of Parents Who Have Same-Sex Relationships? Findings from the New Family Structures Study." *Social Science Research, 41*, 4, July 2012:752–770.

Reiman, Jeffrey, and Paul Leighton. *The Rich Get Richer and the Poor Get Prison: Ideology, Class, and Criminal Justice*, 9th ed. Boston: Allyn and Bacon, 2010.

Reiser, Christa. *Reflections on Anger: Women and Men in a Changing Society*. Westport, Conn.: Praeger Publishers, 1999.

Reisz, Matthew. "Egypt Tailors Reforms on UK Model." *The Times Higher Education*, September 25, 2014.

Rendon, Maria G. "'Caught Up'" How Urban Violence and Peer Ties Contribute to High School Noncompletion." *Social Problems, 61*, 1, February 2014:61–82.

"'Renzie,' Italy's New Premier, Grabs the Reins: Can a Young Man Run a Country Dominated by the Old?" *Huffington Post*, March 19, 2014.

Resnik, David B. "Financial Interests and Research Bias." *Perspectives on Science, 8*, 3, Fall 2000:255–283.

Reverby, Susan M. "Enemy of the People/Enemy of the State: Two Great(ly Infamous) Doctors, Passions, and the Judgment of History." *Bulletin of the History of Medicine, 88*, 3, Fall 2014.

Rexrode, Christina, and Devlin Barrett. "BofA Sets Record $17 Billion Settlement." *Wall Street Journal*, August 21, 2014.

Rhoads, Christopher. "Web Site to Holy Site: Israeli Firm Broadcasts Prayers for a Fee." *Wall Street Journal*, January 25, 2007.

Rhone, Nedra. "Widespread Violations Found at Care Homes." *Los Angeles Times*, April 18, 2001.

Richardson, Stacey, and Marita P. McCabe. "Parental Divorce during Adolescence and Adjustment in Early Adulthood." *Adolescence, 36*, Fall 2001:467–489.

Ricks, Thomas E. "'New' Marines Illustrate Growing Gap between Military and Society." *Wall Street Journal*, July 27, 1995:A1, A4.

Riessman, Catherine Kohler. "Women and Medicalization: A New Perspective." In *Dominant Issues in Medical Sociology*, 3rd ed., Howard D. Schwartz, ed. New York: McGraw-Hill, 1994:190–211.

Riley, Nancy E. "China's Population: New Trends and Challenges." *Population Bulletin*, 59, 2, June 2004:3–36.

Riley, Naomi Schaefer. "Not Your Grandfather's Southern Baptist." *Wall Street Journal*, March 2, 2012.

Riley, Naomi Schaefer. "The Real Path to Racial Harmony." *Wall Street Journal*, August 14, 2009.

Rios, Victor M. *Punished: Policing the Lives of Black and Latino Boys*. New York: New York University Press, 2011.

Rist, Ray. "Student Social Class and Teacher Expectations: The Self-Fulfilling Prophecy in Ghetto Education." *Harvard Educational Review*, reprinted in *Opportunity Gap: Achievement and Inequality in Education*, Carol DeShano, James Philip Huguley, Zenub Kakli, Radhika Rao, and Ronald F. Ferguson, eds. Cambridge, Mass.: Harvard Education Publishing Group, 2007:187–225.

Ritzer, George. "The McDonaldization of Society." In *Down to Earth Sociology: Introductory Readings*, 11th ed., James M. Henslin, ed. New York: Free Press, 2001:459–471.

Ritzer, George. *The McDonaldization of Society*, 7th ed. Thousand Oaks, Calif.: Sage, 2012.

Ritzer, George. *The McDonaldization of Society: An Investigation into the Changing Character of Contemporary Life.* Thousand Oaks, Calif.: Pine Forge Press, 1993.

Rivera, Lauren A. "Hiring as Cultural Matching: The Case of Elite Professional Service Firms." *American Sociological Review,* 77, 6, 2012:999–1022.

Robbins, John. *Healthy at 100.* New York: Random House, 2006.

Roberts, Andrew. "Bionic Mannequins Spy on Shoppers to Boost Luxury Sales." *Bloomberg News,* November 21, 2012.

Robertson, Christopher, Susannah Rose, and Aaron S. Kesselheim. "Effect of Financial Relationships on the Behaviors of Health Care Professionals: A Review of the Evidence." *Journal of Law, Medicine, and Ethics,* 452, 2012:452–466.

Robertson, Ian. *Sociology,* 3rd ed. New York: Worth, 1987.

Robinson, Gail, and Barbara Mullins Nelson. "Pursuing Upward Mobility: African American Professional Women Reflect on Their Journey." *Journal of Black Studies,* 40, 6, 2010:1168–1188.

Robinson, William I. *Global Capitalism and the Crisis of Humanity.* New York: Cambridge University Press, 2014.

Rodriguez, Richard. *Hunger of Memory: The Education of Richard Rodriguez.* Boston: Godine, 1982.

Rodriguez, Richard. "Mixed Blood." *Harper's Magazine,* 283, November 1991:47–56.

Rodriguez, Richard. "Searching for Roots in a Changing Society." In *Down to Earth Sociology: Introductory Readings,* 8th ed., James M. Henslin, ed. New York: Free Press, 1995:486–491.

Rodriguez, Richard. "The Education of Richard Rodriguez." *Saturday Review,* February 8, 1975:147–149.

Rodriguez, Richard. "The Late Victorians: San Francisco, AIDS, and the Homosexual Stereotype." *Harper's Magazine,* October 1990:57–66.

Rodríguez, Victor M. "Los Angeles, U.S.A. 1992: 'A House Divided against Itself . . .' ?" *SSSP Newsletter,* Spring 1994:5–12.

Rohter, Larry. "For Chilean Coup, Kissinger Is Numbered among the Hunted." *New York Times,* March 28, 2002.

Roper Center. "U.S. Elections: How Groups Voted in 2012." Storrs, Conn.: Roper Center, 2013.

Roper, Matt. "Is This the Most Prolific Serial Killer of All Time?" *Daily Mail,* March 27, 2013.

Ropiequet, John L., Christopher S. Naveja, and L. Jean Noonan. "Fair Lending Developments: Testing the Limits of Statistical Evidence." *Business Lawyer,* 67, February 2012:575–584.

Rosaldo, Michelle Zimbalist. "Women, Culture and Society: A Theoretical Overview." In *Women, Culture, and Society,* Michelle Zimbalist Rosaldo and Louise Lamphere, eds. Stanford: Stanford University Press, 1974.

Rose, Frederick. "Los Angeles Tallies Losses; Curfew Is Lifted." *Wall Street Journal,* May 5, 1992:A3, A18.

Rosenberg, Charles E. *The Care of Strangers: The Rise of America's Hospital System.* New York: Basic Books, 1987.

Rosenblatt, Fernanda Fonseca. "A Youth Justice Approach to the Street Children Phenomenon in Brazil: A Critical Review." *Youth Justice,* 12, 3, 2012:229–244.

Rosenfeld, Michael J. "Couple Longevity in the Era of Same-Sex Marriage in the United States." *Journal of Marriage and Family,* 76, 5, October 2014:905–918.

Rosenthal, Elisabeth. "Can a Computer Replace Your Doctor?" *New York Times,* September 20, 2014.

Rosenthal, Robert. "Covert Communication in Classrooms, Clinics, and Courtrooms." *Eye on Psi Chi,* 3, 1, Fall 1998:18–22.

Rosenthal, Robert, and Lenore Jacobson. *Pygmalion in the Classroom: Teacher Expectation and Pupils' Intellectual Development.* New York: Holt, Rinehart, and Winston, 1968.

Rosin, Hanna. "The End of Men." *Atlantic,* July/August 2010.

Rossi, Alice S. "A Biosocial Perspective on Parenting." *Daedalus,* 106, 1977:1–31.

Rossi, Alice S. "Gender and Parenthood." *American Sociological Review,* 49, 1984:1–18.

Rossi, Peter H. *Down and out in America: The Origins of Homelessness.* Chicago: University of Chicago Press, 1989.

Rossi, Peter H. "Going Along or Getting It Right?" *Journal of Applied Sociology,* 8, 1991:77–81.

Rossi, Peter H. "Half Truths with Real Consequences: Journalism, Research, and Public Policy." *Contemporary Sociology,* 1999:1–5.

Rossiter, Caleb. "How Washington, D.C., Schools Cheat Their Students Twice." *Wall Street Journal,* December 1, 2012.

Rothkopf, David. *Superclass: The Global Power Elite and the World They Are Making.* New York: Farrar, Straus and Giroux, 2008.

Rothman, Barbara Katz. "Midwives in Transition: The Structure of a Clinical Revolution." In *Dominant Issues in Medical Sociology,* 3rd ed., Howard D. Schwartz, ed. New York: McGraw-Hill, 1994: 104–112.

Rothschild, Joyce, and J. Allen Whitt. *The Cooperative Workplace: Potentials and Dilemmas of Organizational Democracy and Participation.* Cambridge, England: Cambridge University Press, 1986.

Rowthorn, Robert, Ricardo Andres Guzman, and Carolos Rodriguez-Sickert. "The Economies of Social Stratification in Premodern Societies." *MPRA Paper 35567,* Munich, Germany: Munich Personal RePEc Archive, November 28, 2011.

RT. "Ukraine a Pretext: Russian FM Accuses NATO of Using Conflict to Justify Its Existence." August 4, 2014.

Rubin, Zick. "The Love Research." In *Marriage and Family in a Changing Society,* 2nd ed., James M. Henslin, ed. New York: Free Press, 1985.

Rudner, Lawrence M. "The Scholastic Achievement of Home School Students." *ERIC/AE Digest,* September 1, 1999.

Ruggles, Patricia. "Short and Long Term Poverty in the United States: Measuring the American 'Underclass.'" Washington, D.C.: Urban Institute, June 1989.

Russell, Diana E. H. "Preliminary Report on Some Findings Relating to the Trauma and Long-Term Effects of Intrafamily Childhood Sexual Abuse." Unpublished paper, no date.

Russell, Diana E. H. *Rape in Marriage.* Bloomington: Indiana University Press, 1990.

Russell, Nestar John Charles. "Milgram's Obedience to Authority Experiments: Origins and Early Evolution." *British Journal of Social Psychology,* 2010:1–23.

"Russians Given Day off Work to Make Babies." *Guardian,* September 12, 2007.

Sacirbey, Omar. "Religion Is Key in Combating Female Genital Mutilation According to Activists." *Religion News Service,* October 28, 2012.

Sack, Kevin. "Transplant Brokers in Israel Lure Desperate Kidney Patients to Costa Rica." *New York Times,* August 17, 2014.

Sacks, Jonathan. "A New Movement against Religious Persecution." *Wall Street Journal,* December 12, 2014.

Sageman, Marc. "Explaining Terror Networks in the 21st Century." *Footnotes,* May–June 2008a:7.

Sageman, Marc. *Leaderless Jihad: Terror Networks in the Twenty-First Century.* Philadelphia: University of Pennsylvania Press, 2008b.

Sageman, Marc. "Ripples in the Waves: Fantasies and Fashions." In *Terrorism, Identity, and Legitimacy: The Four Waves—Theory and Political Violence,* Jean E. Rosenfeld, ed. New York: Routledge, 2011:97–92.

Sahlins, Marshall D. *Stone Age Economics.* Chicago: Aldine, 1972.

Sahlins, Marshall D., and Elman R. Service. *Evolution and Culture.* Ann Arbor: University of Michigan Press, 1960.

Saidak, Tom. "GMO Tobacco Plants Produce Antibodies to Treat Rabies." *BioBased Digest,* February 5, 2013.

Saikal, Amin. *Zone of Crisis: Afghanistan, Pakistan, Iraq and Iran.* London: I. B. Tauris, 2014.

Salomon, Gisela, "In Miami, Spanish Is Becoming the Primary Language." Associated Press, May 29, 2008.

Salyer, Kirsten. "In Russia, Valentine Day Is for Making Babies." *Bloomberg News,* February 4, 2013.

Samor, Geraldo, Cecilie Rohwedder, and Ann Zimmerman. "Innocents Abroad?" *Wall Street Journal,* May 5, 2006.

Samuelson, Paul Anthony, and William D. Nordhaus. *Economics,* 18th ed. New York: McGraw Hill, 2005.

Sánchez-Jankowski, Martín. "Gangs and Social Change." *Theoretical Criminology,* 7, 2, 2003:191–216.

Sandberg, Britta. "Guantanamo Prisoner Diary: 'We're Gonna Teach You about Great American Sex.'" *Der Spiegel,* January 17, 2015.

Sanger, David E. "Obama Order Sped Up Waves of Cyberattacks against Iran." *New York Times,* June 1, 2012.

Sanger, David E., and Thom Shanker. "Broad Powers Seen for Obama in Cyberstrikes." *New York Times,* February 3, 2013.

Sankaran, Lavanya. "Caste Is Not Past." *New York Times,* June 15, 2013.

Sanneh, Kelefa. "The Intensity Gap." *New Yorker,* October 27, 2014.

Santos, Fernanda. "Are New Yorkers Satisfied? That Depends." *New York Times,* March 7, 2009.

Sapir, Edward. *Selected Writings of Edward Sapir in Language, Culture, and Personality,* David G. Mandelbaum, ed. Berkeley: University of California Press, 1949.

Sapolsky, Robert M. "Pretty Smart? Why We Equate Beauty with Truth." *Wall Street Journal,* January 18–19, 2014a.

Sapolsky, Robert M. "Sperm Can Carry Dad's Stress as Well as Genes." *Wall Street Journal,* September 5, 2014b.

Saranow, Jennifer. "The Snoop Next Door." *Wall Street Journal,* January 12, 2007.

Saul, Richard. *ADHD Does Not Exist.* New York: Harper, 2014.

Saulny, Susan. "Black? White? Asian? More Young Americans Choose All of the Above." *New York Times,* January 29, 2011.

Savage, Charlie. "Countrywide Will Settle a Bias Suit." *New York Times,* December 21, 2011.

Savage, Charlie. "U.S. Law May Allow Killings, Holder Says." *New York Times,* March 5, 2012.

Scarf, Damian, Kana Imuta, Michael Colombo, and Harlene Hayne. "Social Evaluation or Simple Association? Simple Associations May Explain Moral Reasoning in Infants." *Plos One,* 7, 8, e42698, 2012.

Schaefer, Richard T. *Racial and Ethnic Groups,* 9th ed. Upper Saddle River, N.J.: Prentice Hall, 2004.

Schaefer, Richard T. *Racial and Ethnic Groups,* 13th ed. Boston: Pearson, 2012.

Schaefer, Richard T. *Sociology,* 3rd ed. New York: McGraw-Hill, 1989.

Scheff, Thomas J. *Being Mentally Ill: A Sociological Theory,* 3rd ed. New York: Aldine de Gruyter, 1999.

Schemo, Diana Jean. "Education Dept. Says States Have Lax Standard for Teachers." *New York Times,* June 13, 2002.

Schmeer, Kammi K. "The Child Health Disadvantage of Parental Cohabitation." *Journal of Marriage and Family,* 73, February 2011: 181–193.

Schmiddle Nicholas. "Getting Bin Laden." *The New Yorker,* August 8, 2011.

Schoofs, Mark. "Scientists See Breakthrough in the Global AIDS Battle." *Wall Street Journal,* May 12, 2011.

Schottland, Charles I. *The Social Security Plan in the U.S.* New York: Appleton, 1963.

"Schwab Study Finds Four Generations of American Adults Fundamentally Rethinking Planning for Retirement." *Reuters,* July 15, 2008.

Scolforo, Mark. "Amish Population Nearly Doubles in 16 Years." *Chicago Tribune,* August 20, 2008.

Scott, Monster Cody. *Monster: The Autobiography of an L.A. Gang Member.* New York: Penguin Books, 1994.

Scott, Susie. "The Medicalization of Shyness: From Social Misfits to Social Fitness." *Sociology of Health and Illness,* 28, 2, 2006:133–153.

Scully, Diana. "Negotiating to Do Surgery." In *Dominant Issues in Medical Sociology,* 3rd ed., Howard D. Schwartz, ed. New York: McGraw-Hill, 1994:146–152.

Scully, Diana, and Joseph Marolla. "Convicted Rapists' Vocabulary of Motive: Excuses and Justifications." *Social Problems,* 31, 5, June 1984:530–544.

Scully, Diana, and Joseph Marolla. "'Riding the Bull at Gilley's': Convicted Rapists Describe the Rewards of Rape." In *Down to Earth Sociology: Introductory Readings,* 15th ed., James M. Henslin, ed. New York: Free Press, 2016.

Segal, Nancy L., and Christy A. Mulligan. "Twins Reunited: Scientific and Personal Perspectives." *Twin Research and Human Genetics,* 17, 2, 2014:134.

Segal, Nancy L., and Scott L. Hershberger. "Virtual Twins and Intelligence." *Personality and Individual Differences,* 39, 6, 2005:1061–1073.

Seiden, Samuel C., and Paul Barach. "Wrong-Side/Wrong-Site, Wrong Procedure, and Wrong-Patient Adverse Events." *Archives of Surgery,* 141, 2006:931–939.

Sellers, Patricia. "New Yahoo CEO Mayer Is Pregnant." *Fortune,* July 16, 2012.

Semple, Kirk. "Idea of Afghan Women's Rights Starts Taking Hold." *New York Times,* March 2, 2009.

Senders, John W., and Regine Kanzki. "The Egocentric Surgeon or the Roots of Wrong Side Surgery." *Quality and Safety in Health Care,* 17, 2008:396–400.

Sengupta, Somini. "In the Ancient Streets of Najaf, Pledges of Martyrdom for Cleric." *New York Times,* July 10, 2004.

Senior, Jennifer. "All Joy and No Fun." *New York,* July 4, 2010.

Sennett, Richard, and Jonathan Cobb. "Some Hidden Injuries of Class." In *Down to Earth Sociology: Introductory Readings,* 5th ed., James M. Henslin ed. New York: Free Press, 1988:278–288. Excerpts from Richard Sennett and Jonathan Cobb. *The Hidden Injuries of Class.* New York: Knopf, 1972.

Séralini, Gilles-Eric, Emile Clair, Robin Mesnage, et al. "Long Term Toxicity of a Roundup Herbicide and a Roundup-Tolerant Genetically Modified Maize." *Food and Chemical Toxicology,* 50, 11, November 2012:4221–4231.

Shane, Scott. "Report Outlines Medical Workers' Role in Torture." *New York Times,* April 6, 2009.

Shanker, Thom. "U.S. Troops Were Subjected to a Wider Toxic Testing." *New York Times,* October 8, 2002.

Shapiro, Joseph P. "Euthanasia's Home." *U.S. News and World Report,* 122, 1, January 13, 1997:24–27.

Sharma, Amol, Biman Mukherji, and Rupa Subramanya. "On India's Streets, Women Run Gauntlet of Harassment." *Wall Street Journal,* February 28, 2013.

Sharp, Lauriston. "Steel Axes for Stone-Age Australians." In *Down to Earth Sociology: Introductory Readings*, 8th ed., James M. Henslin, ed. New York: Free Press, 1995:453–462.

Shattuck, Rachel M., and Rose M. Kreider. "Social and Economic Characteristics of Currently Unmarried Women with a Recent Birth: 2011." American Community Survey Reports. Washington, D.C.: U.S. Census Bureau, May 2013.

Shefner, Jon. "The New Left in Latin America and the Opportunity for a New U.S. Foreign Policy." In *Agenda for Social Justice: Solutions 2008*, Robert Perrucci, Kathleen Ferraro, JoAnn Miller, and Glenn Muschert, eds. Knoxville, Tenn.: Society for the Study of Social Problems, 2008:16–22.

Shellenbarger, Sue. "What's a Reasonable Break?" *Wall Street Journal*, June 13, 2011.

Sheridan, Mary Beth. "Salinas Warns Mexico against Drug Probe." *Los Angeles Times*, September 22, 1998.

Sherif, Muzafer, and Carolyn Sherif. *Groups in Harmony and Tension*. New York: Harper & Row, 1953.

Shipler, David K. "Robert McNamara and the Ghosts of Vietnam." *New York Times Magazine*, August 10, 1997.

Shor, Eran, David J. Roelfs, Misty Currell, L. Clemow, M. M. Burg, and J. E. Schwartz. "Widowhood and Mortality: A Meta-Analysis and Meta-Regression." *Demography*, 49, 2012:575–606.

Short, Kathleen. "The Research Supplemental Poverty Measure: 2011." *Current Population Reports P60-244*, Washington, D.C.: U.S. Census Bureau, November 2012.

Shute, Nancy. "Doctors Say Don't Give Birth to Baby in a Tub, but Midwives Disagree." *National Public Radio*, March 23, 2014.

Siebens, Julie, and Tiffany Julian. "Native North American Languages Spoken at Home in the United States and Puerto Rico: 2006–2010." Washington, D.C.: U.S. Census Bureau, December 2011.

Siegler, Ilene C., Beverly H. Brummett, Peter Martin, and M. J. Helms. "Consistency and Timing of Marital Transitions and Survival during Midlife: The Role of Personality and Health Risk Behaviors." *Annals of Behavioral Medicine*, 45, 3, 2013:338–347.

Sills, David L. *The Volunteers*. Glencoe, Ill.: Free Press, 1957.

Sills, David L. "Voluntary Associations: Sociological Aspects." In *International Encyclopedia of the Social Sciences*, Vol. 16, David L. Sills, ed. New York: Macmillan, 1968:362–379.

Silverman, Ed. "How Illinois Allocates $84,000 Drug for Hepatitis C." *Wall Street Journal*, August 3, 2014.

Simmel, Georg. *The Sociology of Georg Simmel*, Kurt H. Wolff, ed. and trans. Glencoe, Ill.: Free Press, 1950. Originally published between 1902 and 1917.

Simon, Stephanie. "Naked Pumpkin Run." *Wall Street Journal*, October 31, 2009.

Simonds, Wendy. "Presidential Address: The Art of Activism." *Social Problems*, 60, 1, 2013:1–26.

Simons, Andre B., and Jeannine Willie. "Runaway or Abduction. Assessment Tools for the First Responder." *FBI Law Enforcement Bulletin*, November 2000:1–7.

Simons, Marlise. "Social Change and Amazon Indians." In *Exploring Social Life: Readings to Accompany Essentials of Sociology: A Down-to-Earth Approach*, Sixth Edition, 2nd ed., James M. Henslin, ed. Boston: Allyn and Bacon, 2006:157–165.

Simpson, George Eaton, and J. Milton Yinger. *Racial and Cultural Minorities: An Analysis of Prejudice and Discrimination*, 4th ed. New York: Harper & Row, 1972.

Singer, Natasha. "Lawmakers Seek to Curb Drug Commercials." *New York Times*, July 28, 2009.

Singer, Natasha. "Shoppers Who Can't Have Secrets." *New York Times*, April 30, 2010.

SIPRI (Stockholm International Peace Research Institute). SIPRI Arms Transfers Database, January 2015.

Sironi, Maria, and Frank F. Furstenberg. "Trends in the Economic Independence of Young Adults in the United States: 1973–2007." *Population and Development Review*, 38, 4, December 2012:609–630.

Skeels, H. M. "*Adult Status of Children with Contrasting Early Life Experiences: A Follow-up Study*." Monograph of the Society for Research in Child Development, 31, 3, 1966.

Skeels, H. M., and H. B. Dye. "A Study of the Effects of Differential Stimulation on Mentally Retarded Children." *Proceedings and Addresses of the American Association on Mental Deficiency*, 44, 1939:114–136.

Sledzik, Paul S., and Nicholas Bellantoni. "Bioarcheological and Biocultural Evidence for the New England Vampire Folk Belief." *American Journal of Physical Anthropology*, 94, 1994.

Sloan, Allan. "A Lot of Trust, but No Funds." *Newsweek*, July 30, 2001:34.

Smart, Barry. "On the Disorder of Things: Sociology, Postmodernity and the 'End of the Social.'" *Sociology*, 24, 3, August 1990:397–416.

Smith, Beverly A. "An Incest Case in an Early 20th-Century Rural Community." *Deviant Behavior*, 13, 1992:127–153.

Smith, Christian, and Robert Faris. "Socioeconomic Inequality in the American Religious System: An Update and Assessment." *Journal for the Scientific Study of Religion*, 44, 1, 2005:95–104.

Smith, Clark. "Oral History as 'Therapy': Combatants' Account of the Vietnam War." In *Strangers at Home: Vietnam Veterans since the War*, Charles R. Figley and Seymore Leventman, eds. New York: Praeger, 1980:9–34.

Smith, Dave. "Lost in Translation: Nokia Lumia, and the 5 Worst Name Oversights." *International Business Times*, October 26, 2011.

Smith, Harold. "A Colossal Cover-up." *Christianity Today*, December 12, 1986:16–17.

Smith, Kevin R., Sarah Chan, and John Harris. "Human Germline Genetic Modification: Scientific and Bioethical Perspectives." *Archives of Medical Research*, 43, 2012:491–513.

Smith, Ray A. "A Stealth Luxury Brand Expands." *Wall Street Journal*, May 15, 2014.

Smith, Ryan A. "A Test of the Glass Ceiling and Glass Escalator Hypotheses." *Annals of the American Academy of Social Sciences*, 639, January 2012:149–172.

Smith, Simon C. "The Making of a Neo-Colony? Anglo-Kuwaiti Relations in the Era of Decolonization." *Middle Eastern Studies*, 37, 1, January 2001:159–173.

Smith, Wesley J. "Dependency or Death? Oregonians Make a Chilling Choice." *Wall Street Journal*, February 25, 1999.

Smith-Bynum, Mia A., "African American Families: Research Progress and Potential in the Age of Obama." In *Handbook of Marriage and the Family*, G. W. Peterson and K. R. Bush, eds. New York: Springer, 2013:683–704.

Snow, David A., Louis A. Zurcher, Jr., and Sheldon Ekland-Olson. "Social Networks and Social Movements: A Microstructural Approach to Differential Recruitment." In *Collective Behavior and Social Movements*, Russell L. Curtis, Jr., and Benigno E. Aguirre, eds. Boston: Allyn and Bacon, 1993:323–334.

Snyder, Mark. "Self-Fulfilling Stereotypes." In *Down to Earth Sociology: Introductory Readings*, 7th ed., James M. Henslin, ed. New York: Free Press, 1993:153–160.

Sorokin, Pitirim A. *Social and Cultural Dynamics*, 4 vols. New York: American Book Company, 1937–1941.

Sosinsky, Laura Stout, and Se-Kang Kim. "A Profile Approach to Child Care Quality, Quantity, and Type of Setting: Parent Selection of Infant Child Care Arrangements." *Applied Development Science*, 17, 1, 2013:39–56.

Sosnaud, Benjamin, David Brady, and Steven M. Frenk. "Class in Name Only: Subjective Class Identity, Objective Class Position, and Vote Choice in American Presidential Elections." *Social Problems*, 60, 1, 2013:81–99.

"Sourcebook of Criminal Justice Statistics." Washington, D.C.: U.S. Government Printing Office, published annually.

South African Police Service. *Crime Statistics 2011/2012*. Pretoria, South Africa: South African Police Service, 2013.

Spector, Malcolm, and John Kitsuse. *Constructing Social Problems*. Menlo Park, Calif.: Cummings, 1977.

Spector, Mike, and Christopher M. Matthews. "GM Admits to Criminal Wrongdoing." *Wall Street Journal*, September 18, 2015.

Spence, David B., and Robert Prentice. "The Transformation of American Energy Markets and the Problem of Market Power." *Boston College Law Review*, 53, 1, 2012:131–202.

Spengler, Oswald. *The Decline of the West*, 2 vols., Charles F. Atkinson, trans. New York: Knopf, 1926–1928. Originally published 1919–1922.

Sprague, Jeb. "Transnational State." *Wiley-Blackwell Encyclopedia of Globalization*, George Ritzer, ed. Hoboken, N.J.: Blackwell Publishing, 2012.

Sprecher, Susan, and Rachita Chandak. "Attitudes about Arranged Marriages and Dating among Men and Women from India." *Free Inquiry in Creative Sociology*, 20, 1, May 1992:59–69.

Srole, Leo, and Anita K. Fisher. *Mental Health in the Metropolis: The Midtown Manhattan Study*. Albany, N.Y.: New York University Press, 1978.

Stack, Carol B. *All Our Kin: Strategies for Survival in a Black Community*. New York: Harper, 1974.

Staedter, Tracy. "7 of 10 Most Air-Polluted Cities Are in China." *Discovery News*, January 16, 2013.

Stampp, Kenneth M. *The Peculiar Institution: Slavery in the Ante-Bellum South*. New York: Vintage Books, 1956.

Stansberry, Porter. "Correspondence." *S&A Digest Premium*, December 19, 2012.

Staples, Brent. "Loving v. Virginia and the Secret History of Race." *New York Times*, May 14, 2008.

Stark, Rodney. *Sociology*, 3rd ed. Belmont, Calif.: Wadsworth, 1989.

Starr, Paul. *The Social Transformation of American Medicine*. New York: Basic Books, 1982.

Statham, Anne, Eleanor M. Miller, and Hans O. Mauksch. "The Integration of Work: Second-Order Analysis of Qualitative Research." In *The Worth of Women's Work: A Qualitative Synthesis*, Anne Statham, Eleanor M. Miller, and Hans O. Mauksch, eds. Albany, N.Y.: State University of New York Press, 1988:11–35.

"Statistical Abstract of the United States." Washington, D.C.: U.S. Census Bureau, published annually.

Stayner, Leslie, Laura S. Welch, and Richard Lemen. "The Worldwide Pandemic of Asbestos-Related Diseases." *Annual Review of Public Health*, 34, 2013:205–216.

Stein, Mark. "The Sum of All Fears." *Wall Street Journal*, May 23, 2014.

Steinhauer, Jennifer, and Ford Fessenden. "Medical Retreads: Doctor Punished by State but Prized at the Hospitals." *New York Times*, March 27, 2001.

Stempel, Jonathan. "Citigroup to Pay Freddie Mac $395 Million on Suspect Mortgages." *Reuters*, September 26, 2013.

Stephens, Nicole M., Hazel Rose Markus, and L. Taylor Phillips. "Social Class Culture Cycles: How Three Gateway Contexts Shape Selves and Fuel Inequality." *Annual Review of Psychology*, 65, 2014:611–634.

Stetler, Dean A., Chad Davis, Kathryn Leavitt, et al. "Association of Low-Activity MAOA Allelic Variants with Violent Crime in Incarcerated Offenders." *Journal of Psychiatric Research*, 58, November 2014:69–75.

Stets, Jan E. "Current Emotion Research in Sociology: Advances in the Discipline." *Emotion Review*, 4, 3, July 2012:326–334.

Stets, Jan E., and Michael J. Carter. "A Theory of the Self for the Sociology of Morality." *American Sociological Review*, 77, 1, 2012:120–140.

Stevens, Amy, and Sarah Lubman. "Deciding Moment of the Trial May Have Been Five Months Ago." *Wall Street Journal*, May 1, 1992:A6.

Stevens, Mitchell. *Creating a Class: College Admissions and the Education of Elites*. Cambridge, Mass.: Harvard University Press, 2009.

Stevens, Mitchell L. *Kingdom of Children: Culture and Controversy in the Homeschooling Movement*. Princeton: N.J.: Princeton University Press, 2001.

Stevenson, Richard W. "U.S. Debates Investing in Stock for Social Security." *New York Times*, July 27, 1998.

Stewart, James B. "A Lawyer and Partner, and Also Bankrupt." *New York Times*, January 25, 2014.

Stewart, Phil. "U.S. Can Intercept North Korean Missiles but May Opt Not to, Says Admiral Samuel Locklear." *Reuters*, April 9, 2013.

Stinnett, Nicholas. "Strong Families." In *Marriage and Family in a Changing Society*, 4th ed., James M. Henslin, ed. New York: Free Press, 1992:496–507.

Stipp, David. "Himalayan Tree Could Serve as Source of Anti-Cancer Drug Taxol, Team Says." *Wall Street Journal*, April 20, 1992:B4.

Stockard, Jean, and Miriam M. Johnson. *Sex Roles: Sex Inequality and Sex Role Development*. Englewood Cliffs, N.J.: Prentice Hall, 1980.

Stockwell, John. "The Dark Side of U.S. Foreign Policy." *Zeta Magazine*, February 1989:36–48.

Stodgill, Ralph M. *Handbook of Leadership: A Survey of Theory and Research*. New York: Free Press, 1974.

Stokes, Myron, and David Zeman. "The Shame of the City." *Newsweek*, September 4, 1995.

Stokes, Randall. "Over 60 Years of Sociology at UMass–Amherst." *ASA Footnotes*, May–June 2009:6.

Stone, Daniel. "Enough to Go Around." *National Geographic*, December 2014:18.

Stouffer, Samuel A., Arthur A. Lumsdaine, Marion Harper Lumsdaine, Robin M. Williams, Jr., M. Brewster Smith, Irving L. Janis, Shirley A. Star, and Leonard S. Cottrell, Jr. *The American Soldier: Combat and Its Aftermath*, Vol. 2. New York: Wiley, 1949.

Strategic Energy Policy: Challenges for the 21st Century. New York: Council on Foreign Relations, 2001.

"Strategic Maneuvers: The Revolving Door from the Pentagon to the Private Sector." Washington, D.C.: Citizens for Responsibility and Ethics in Washington, November 16, 2012.

Straus, Murray A. "Gender Symmetry and Mutuality in Perpetration of Clinical-Level Partner Violence: Empirical Evidence and Implications for Prevention and Treatment." *Aggression and Violent Behavior*, 16, 2011:279–288.

"Study Finds Religious Apps Helps User Practice Mobile Faith." *Religion News Services*, May 7, 2014.

Stutzman, Rene. "Biker Gangs Thrive in Central Florida." *Orlando Sentinel*, May 26, 2014.

Suizzo, Marie-Anne. "The Social-Emotional and Cultural Contexts of Cognitive Development: Neo-Piagetian Perspectives." *Child Development*, 71, 4, August 2000:846–849.

Sullivan, Andrew. "What We Look up to Now." *New York Times Magazine*, November 15, 1998.

Sullivan, Kevin. "India Embraces Online Worship." *Washington Post,* March 15, 2007.

Sulzberger, A. G. "As Survivors Dwindle, Tulsa Confronts Past." *New York Times,* June 19, 2011.

Sumner, William Graham. *Folkways: A Study in the Sociological Importance of Usages, Manners, Customs, Mores, and Morals.* New York: Ginn, 1906.

Sun, Lena H. "China Seeks Ways to Protect Elderly." *Washington Post,* October 23, 1990:A1.

Sunstein, Cass R. *Rumors.* Princeton, N.J.: Princeton University Press, 2014.

Surowiecki, James. *The Wisdom of Crowds.* New York: Anchor Books, 2005.

Susman, Tina. "Lottery Winner Who Drew Outrage for Getting Welfare Is Found Dead." *Los Angeles Times,* October 2, 2012.

Sutherland, Edwin H. *Criminology.* Philadelphia: Lippincott, 1924.

Sutherland, Edwin H. *Principles of Criminology,* 4th ed. Philadelphia: Lippincott, 1947.

Sutherland, Edwin H. *White Collar Crime.* New York: Dryden Press, 1949.

Suzuki, Bob H. "Asian-American Families." In *Marriage and Family in a Changing Society,* 2nd ed., James M. Henslin, ed. New York: Free Press, 1985:104–119.

Swaim, Barton. "Book Review: *Inventing Freedom* by Daniel Hannan." *Wall Street Journal,* November 29, 2013.

Swati, Pandey. "Do You Take This Stranger?" *Los Angeles Times,* June 26, 2008.

Sweeney, Megan M. "Remarriage and the Nature of Divorce: Does It Matter Which Spouse Chose to Leave?" *Journal of Family Issues,* 23, 3, April 2002:410–440.

Sykes, Gresham M., and David Matza. "Techniques of Neutralization." In *Down to Earth Sociology: Introductory Readings,* 5th ed., James M. Henslin, ed. New York: Free Press, 1988:225–231. Originally published 1957.

Symington, Annabel. "Forced to Wed to Settle a Feud." *Wall Street Journal,* May 6, 2014.

Szasz, Thomas. "Fifty Years after *The Myth of Mental Illness.*" In *The Myth of Mental Illness: Foundations of a Theory of Personal Conduct,* 50th Anniversary Edition. New York: Harper Perennial, 2010.

Szasz, Thomas S. *Cruel Compassion: Psychiatric Control of Society's Unwanted.* Syracuse, N.Y.: Syracuse University Press, 1998.

Szasz, Thomas S. "Mental Illness Is Still a Myth." In *Deviant Behavior 96/97,* Lawrence M. Salinger, ed. Guilford, Conn.: Dushkin, 1996:200–205.

Tabenkin, H., C. B. Eaton, M. B. Roberts, D. R. Parker, J. H. McMurray, and J. Borkan. "Differences in Cardiovascular Disease Risk Factor Management in Primary Care by Sex of Physician and Patient." *Annals of Family Medicine,* 8, 1, January–February 2010:25–32.

Tadic, Maja, Wido G. M. Oerlemans, Arnold B. Bakker, and Ruut Veenhoven. "Daily Activities and Happiness in Later Life: The Role of Work Status." *Journal of Happiness Studies,* September 28, 2012.

Tafoya, Sonya M., Hans Johnson, and Laura E. Hill. "Who Chooses to Choose Two?" Washington, D.C.: Population Reference Bureau, 2005.

"Tales of Saddam's Brutality." Washington, D.C.: White House, September 29, 2003.

Taormino, Tristan, Celine Parrenas Shimizu, Constance Penley, and Mireille Miller-Young, eds. *The Feminist Porn Book.* New York: The Feminist Press, 2013.

Tavernise, Sabrina. "Day Care Centers Adapt to Round-the-Clock Demand." *New York Times,* January 15, 2012.

Taylor, Howard F. "The Structure of a National Black Leadership Network: Preliminary Findings." Unpublished manuscript, 1992. (As cited in Margaret L. Andersen and Howard F. Taylor, *Sociology: Understanding a Diverse Society.* Belmont, Calif.: Wadsworth, 2000.)

Terhune, Chad. "Pepsi, Vowing Diversity Isn't Just Image Polish, Seeks Inclusive Culture." *Wall Street Journal,* April 19, 2005.

"Testing Times." *The Economist,* December 31, 2011.

"Testosterone and Aggression." *Psychological Science,* 17, 7, 2006:568–571.

Tewary, Amarnath. "At a Sperm Bank in Bihar, Caste Divisions Start before Birth." *New York Times,* July 12, 2012.

"The Interaction of Genes, Behavior, and Social Environment." *Today's Research on Aging,* 27, December 2012:1–6.

"The World of the Child 6 Billion." Washington, D.C.: Population Reference Bureau, 2000.

Thomas, Andrea. "Germans Explore Coalitions." *Wall Street Journal,* October 5–6, 2013.

Thomas, Paulette. "Boston Fed Finds Racial Discrimination in Mortgage Lending Is Still Widespread." *Wall Street Journal,* October 9, 1992:A3.

Thomas, Paulette. "U.S. Examiners Will Scrutinize Banks with Poor Minority-Lending Histories." *Wall Street Journal,* October 22, 1991:A2.

Thomas, W. I., and Dorothy Swaine Thomas. *The Child in America: Behavior Problems and Programs.* New York: Alfred A. Knopf, 1928.

Thompson, Ginger. "Chasing Mexico's Dream into Squalor." *New York Times,* February 11, 2001.

Thompson, Paul. "Pentagon Buys and Destroys 9,500 Copies of Soldier's Afghanistan Book 'to Protect Military Secrets.'" *Mail Online,* September 27, 2010.

Thornton, Russell. *American Indian Holocaust and Survival: A Population History since 1492.* Norman: University of Oklahoma Press, 1987.

Tierney, John. "For Lesser Crimes, Rethinking Life behind Bars." *New York Times,* December 11, 2012.

Tilly, Charles. *Social Movements, 1768–2004.* Boulder, Colo.: Paradigm Publishers, 2004.

Timasheff, Nicholas S. *War and Revolution.* Joseph F. Scheuer, ed. New York: Sheed & Ward, 1965.

Tokc-Wilde, Iwona. "Workforce Surveillance: Is Your Boss Keeping a Private Eye on You?" *The Guardian,* May 7, 2011.

Tolich, Martin. "What Can Milgram and Zimbardo Teach Ethics Committees and Qualitative Researchers about Minimizing Harm?" *Research Ethics,* 10, 2, 2014:86–96.

Tomsho, Robert, and Daniel Golden. "Educating Eric." *Wall Street Journal,* May 12, 2007.

Tönnies, Ferdinand. *Community and Society (Gemeinschaft und Gesellschaft),* with a new introduction by John Samples. New Brunswick, N.J.: Transaction, 1988. Originally published 1887.

Tornstam, Lars. "Maturing into Gerotranscendence." *Journal of Transpersonal Psychology,* 43, 2, 2011:166–180.

Torres, Blanca. "Employers Bring Childcare Onsite to Keep Workers' Lives Balanced." *San Francisco Business Times,* August 9, 2012.

Torres, Jose B., V. Scott H. Solberg, and Aaron H. Carlstrom. "The Myth of Sameness among Latino Men and Their Machismo." *American Journal of Orthopsychiatry,* 72, 2, 2002:163–181.

Toshkov, Veselin. "Europe's 'Oldest Town' Identified Near Provadia in Eastern Bulgaria." *Huffington Post,* November 1, 2012.

Tough, Paul. "Who Gets to Graduate?" *New York Times,* May 15, 2014.

Toynbee, Arnold. *A Study of History,* D. C. Somervell, abridger and ed. New York: Oxford University Press, 1946.

Trafficking in Persons Report. Washington, D.C: U.S. State Department, June 2015.

Treas, Judith, Jacqueline Scott, and Martin Richard, eds. *Wiley-Blackwell Companion to the Sociology of Families.* New York: Wiley, 2014.

Treiman, Donald J. *Occupational Prestige in Comparative Perspective.* New York: Academic Press, 1977.

Tresniowski, Alex. "Payday or Mayday?" *People Weekly,* May 17, 1999:128–131.

Trice, Harrison M., and Janice M. Beyer. "Cultural Leadership in Organization." *Organization Science,* 2, 2, May 1991:149–169.

Troeltsch, Ernst. *The Social Teachings of the Christian Churches.* New York: Macmillan, 1931.

Trofimov, Yaroslav. "The Fractured Legacy of the Mapmakers." *Wall Street Journal,* April 11–12, 2015.

Troianovski, Anton. "New Wi-Fi Pitch: Tracker." *Wall Street Journal,* June 19, 2012.

Truman, Jennifer L., and Rachel E. Morgan. "Nonfatal Domestic Violence, 2003–2012." Bureau of Justice Statistics, April 2014.

Tugend, Alina. "Its Unclearly Defined, but Telecommuting Is Fast on the Rise." *New York Times,* March 7, 2014.

Tuhus-Dubrow, Rebecca. "Rites and Wrongs." *Boston Globe,* February 11, 2007.

Turan, Bulent, Jinhong Guo, Mary M. Boggiano, and Deidra Bedgood. "Dominant, Cold, Avoidant, and Lonely: Basal Testosterone as a Biological Marker for an Interpersonal Style." *Journal of Research in Personality,* 50, 2014:84–89.

Turkewitz, Julie. "A Fight as U.S. Girls Face Genital Cutting Abroad." *New York Times,* June 10, 2014.

Turner, Jonathan H. *The Structure of Sociological Theory.* Homewood, Ill.: Dorsey, 1978.

Turner, Ralph H., and Lewis M. Killian. *Collective Behavior,* 2nd ed. Englewood Cliffs, N.J.: Prentice Hall, 1987.

Twenge, J. M., W. K. Campbell, and C. A. Foster. "Parenthood and Marital Satisfaction: A Meta-Analytic Review." *Journal of Marriage and Family,* 65, 2003:574–583.

Tyler, Patrick E. "A New Life for NATO? But It's Sidelined for Now." *New York Times,* November 20, 2002.

U.S. Border Patrol. Apprehensions—Sector Profile. 2013 Fiscal Year, 2014.

U.S. Bureau of Labor Statistics. "A Profile of the Working Poor 2012." Report 1047, March 2014a.

U.S. Bureau of Labor Statistics. "Economic News Release." Table A-2, November 20, 2014b.

U.S. Census Bureau. "50 Million Children Lived with Married Parents in 2007." Washington, D.C.: U.S. Government Printing Office, 2007.

U.S. Census Bureau. "America's Families and Living Arrangements: 2012." Washington, D.C.: U.S. Census Bureau, 2013a.

U.S. Census Bureau. "America's Families and Living Arrangements: 2013." August 2014a.

U.S. Census Bureau. "Annual Social and Economic Supplement to Current Population Survey." Washington, D.C.: U.S. Government Printing Office, 2010.

U.S. Census Bureau. "*Current Population Survey, 2012 Annual Social and Economic (ASEC) Supplement,*" Washington, D.C.: U.S. Census Bureau, November 2012.

U.S. Census Bureau. Current Population Survey. Annual Social and Economic Supplement, 2013 Poverty, 2014b.

U.S. Census Bureau. "Marital Status." American Community Survey 2013, December 2014c.

U.S. Census Bureau, Population Division. "Percent of the Projected Population by Race and Hispanic Origin for the United States: 2010 to 2050." Constant Net International Migration Series (NP2009-T6-C): Table 6-C, December 16, 2009.

U.S. Census Bureau. "Voting and Registration in the Election of November 2012": Table 7, 2013b.

U.S. Department of Defense. "Operation Iraqi Freedom: U.S. Casualty Status." Washington, D.C.: U.S. Department of Defense, 2015.

U.S. Department of Energy, Advisory Committee on Human Radiation Experiments. Final Report, 1995. Washington, D.C.: U.S. Government Printing Office, 1995.

U.S. Department of State. "2010 Human Rights Report: Iran." 2010 Country Reports on Human Rights Practices, April 8, 2011.

U.S. Surgeon General. *The Health Consequences of Smoking—50 Years of Progress.* Washington, D.C.: U.S. Department of Health and Human Services, 2014.

Udy, Stanley H., Jr. "Bureaucracy and Rationality in Weber's Organizational Theory: An Empirical Study." *American Sociological Review,* 24, December 1959:791–795.

Ulaby, Neda. "Sapiosexual Seeks Same: A New Lexicon Enters Online Dating Mainstream." American University Radio, December 4, 2014.

Ullman, Edward, and Chauncey Harris. "The Nature of Cities." In *Urban Man and Society: A Reader in Urban Ecology,* Albert N. Cousins and Hans Nagpaul, eds. New York: Knopf, 1970:91–100.

UNAIDS. *The Gap Report,* 2014.

UNESCO. "Adult and Youth Literacy." Paris: UNESCO, September 2012.

UNESCO. "Adult and Youth Literacy: National, Regional and Global Trends, 1985–2015." UNESCO Institute for Statistics, June 2013.

UNESCO. "Education for All: Global Monitoring Report: Regional Overview: Arab States." 2015.

United Nations. "A Changing Climate Creates Pervasive Risks but Opportunities Exist for Effective Responses." Intergovernmental Panel on Climate Change, March 31, 2014.

United Nations. *World Urbanization Prospects: The 2014 Revision.* U.N. Department of Economic and Social Affairs, 2014.

UnitedHealthCare. Survey of Centenarians. March 2014.

UPI. "Experts: Cleveland Killer a Sexual Sadist." November 9, 2009.

Ur, Jason A. "Cycles of Civilization in Northern Mesopotamia, 4400–2000 BC." *Journal of Archaeological Research,* 18, 4, 2010:387–431.

Urbach, David R., Anand Govindarajan, et al. "Introduction of Surgical Checklists in Ontario, Canada." *New England Journal of Medicine,* 370, March 13, 2014:1029–1038.

Urbina, Ian. "As School Exit Tests Prove Tough, States Ease Standards." *New York Times,* January 11, 2010.

Useem, Michael. *The Inner Circle: Large Corporations and the Rise of Business Political Activity in the U.S. and U.K.* New York: Oxford University Press, 1984.

Utar, Hale, and Luis Bernardo Torres Ruiz. "International Competition and Industrial Evolution: Evidence from the Impact of Chinese Competition on Mexican Maquiladoras." University of Colorado at Boulder and Banco de Mexico, July 2010.

Van Buren, Peter. "Welcome to the Memory Hole: Disappearing Snowden." TomDispatch.com, April 28, 2014.

"VA Testing Drugs on War Veterans." *Washington Post,* June 17, 2008.

Vandell, Deborah Lowe, Jay Belsky, Margaret Burchinal, Laurence Steinberg, and Nathan Vandergrift. "No Effects of Early Child Care Extend to Age 15 Years? Results from the NICHD Study of Early Child Care and Youth Development." *Child Development,* 81, 3, May/June 2010:737–756.

Vandiver, John. "550 Marines Head to Spain in Support of AFRICOM." *Stars and Stripes,* April 25, 2013a.

Vandiver, John. "New Combat Focus for U.S. Africa Command." *Stars and Stripes,* April 5, 2013b.

Vartabedian, Ralph, and Scott Gold. "New Questions on Shuttle Tile Safety Raised." *Los Angeles Times*, February 27, 2003.

Varughese C. J., R. Pinnelas, J. Yu, and R. Mehran. "PCI Considerations in Women: Gender-Specific Outcomes and Challenges." In *Textbook of Cardiovascular Intervention*. New York: Springer, 2014:227–241.

Vaughan, Diane. "Uncoupling: The Social Construction of Divorce." In *Marriage and Family in a Changing Society*, 2nd ed., James M. Henslin, ed. New York: Free Press, 1985:429–439.

Veblen, Thorstein. *The Theory of the Leisure Class*. New York: Macmillan, 1912.

Vendituoli, Monica. "Are Men's Centers Essential for College Campuses?" *USA Today*, October 2, 2013.

Venkatesh, Sudhir. *Gang Leader for a Day: A Rogue Sociologist Takes to the Streets*. New York: Penguin, 2008.

Vergakis, Brock. "Utah High Court: Polygamist Leader Can Go to Texas." Associated Press, November 23, 2010.

Vidal, David. "Bilingual Education Is Thriving but Criticized." *New York Times*, January 30, 1977.

Vidal, John. "U.N. Report: World's Biggest Cities Merging into 'Mega-Regions.'" *The Guardian*, March 22, 2010.

Vidal, Jordi Blanes, Mirko Draca, and Christian Fons-Rosen. "Revolving Door Lobbyists." Center for Economic Performance, Discussion Paper 993, August 2010.

Volti, Rudi. *Society and Technological Change*, 3rd ed. New York: St. Martin's Press, 1995.

Von Hoffman, Nicholas. "Sociological Snoopers." *Transaction 7*, May 1970:4, 6.

Wade, Nicholas. *A Troublesome Inheritance: Genes, Race and Human History*. New York: Penguin Press, 2014.

Wagley, Charles, and Marvin Harris. *Minorities in the New World*. New York: Columbia University Press, 1958.

Wald, Matthew L., and John Schwartz. "Alerts Were Lacking, NASA Shuttle Manager Says." *New York Times*, July 23, 2003.

Walker, Alice, and Pratibha Parmar. *Warrior Marks: Female Genital Mutilation and the Sexual Blinding of Women*. New York: Harcourt Brace, 1993.

Walker, Marcus, and Andrew Higgins. "Zimbabwe Can't Paper over Its Million Percent Inflation Anymore." *Wall Street Journal*, July 2, 2008.

Wall, Robert. "China's Armed Predator." *Aviation Week*, November 17, 2010.

Wallace, John M., Ryoko Yamaguchi, Jerald G. Bachman, Patrick M. O'Malley, John E. Schulenberg, and Lloyd D. Johnston. "Religiosity and Adolescent Substance Use: The Role of Individual and Contextual Influences." *Social Problems*, 54, 2, 2007:308–327.

Wallerstein, Immanuel. "Culture as the Ideological Battleground of the Modern World-System." In *Global Culture: Nationalism, Globalization, and Modernity*, Mike Featherstone, ed. London: Sage, 1990:31–55.

Wallerstein, Immanuel. *Modern World System I: Capitalist Agriculture and the Origins of the European World-Economy in the Sixteenth Century*. Berkeley, Calif.: University of California Press, 2011.

Wallerstein, Immanuel. *The Capitalist World-Economy*. New York: Cambridge University Press, 1979.

Wallerstein, Judith S., Sandra Blakeslee, and Julia M. Lewis. *The Unexpected Legacy of Divorce: A 25-Year Landmark Study*. Concord, N.H.: Hyperion Press, 2001.

Walsh, Anthony, and Kevin M. Beaver. "Biosocial Criminology." In *Handbook on Crime and Deviance*, M. D. Krohn et al., eds. Dordrecht, New York: Springer, 2009:79–101.

Walters, Mike L., Jieru Chen, and Matthew J. Breiding. "The National Intimate Partner and Sexual Violence Survey (NISVS)." Atlanta, Georgia: National Center for Injury Prevention and Control, January 2013.

Wang, Hongyu, and Paul R. Amato. "Predictors of Divorce Adjustment: Stressors, Resources, and Definitions." *Journal of Marriage and the Family*, 62, 3, August 2000:655–668.

Wang, Stephanie. "Colleges Divided over Value of Free Online Classes." *Community College Week*, April 1, 2013.

Wang, Wendy. "The Rise of Intermarriage: Rates, Characteristics Vary by Race and Gender." Washington, D.C.: PEW Research Center, February 16, 2012.

Ward, Rose Marie, Halle C. Popson, and Donald G. DiPaolo. "Defining the Alpha Female: A Female Leadership Measure." *Journal of Leadership and Organizational Studies 17*, 3, 2010:309–320.

Warren, Jennifer, Adam Gelb, Jake Horowitz, and Jessica Riordan. "One in 100: Behind Bars in America 2008." Washington, D.C.: Pew Charitable Trust, February 2008.

Watson, J. Mark. "Outlaw Motorcyclists." In *Society: Readings to Accompany Sociology: A Down-to-Earth Approach, Core Concepts*, James M. Henslin, ed. Boston: Allyn and Bacon, 2006:105–114. Originally published 1980 in *Deviant Behavior*, 2, 1.

Webb, Amy. *Data, A Love Story: How I Gamed Online Dating to Meet My Match*. New York: Dutton, 2013.

Weber, Max. *Economy and Society*, G. Roth and C. Wittich, eds. Berkeley: University of California Press, 1978. Originally published 1922.

Weber, Max. *From Max Weber: Essays in Sociology*, Hans Gerth and C. Wright Mills, trans. and ed. New York: Oxford University Press, 1946.

Weber, Max. *The Protestant Ethic and the Spirit of Capitalism*. New York: Scribner's, 1958. Originally published 1904–1905.

Weber, Max. *The Theory of Social and Economic Organization*, A. M. Henderson and Talcott Parsons, trans., Talcott Parsons, ed. Glencoe, Ill.: Free Press, 1947. Originally published 1913.

Weinberger, Catherine. "In Search of the Glass Ceiling: Gender and Earnings Growth among U.S. College Graduates in the What Is This?" *Industrial and Labor Relations Review*, 64, 5, October 2011.

Weiner, Jill Caryl. "The Home-Schooled Don't Just Stay at Home." *New York Times*, March 14, 2012.

Weiner, Tim. "Air Force Seeks Bush's Approval for Space Weapons Programs." *New York Times*, May 18, 2005.

Weiner, Tim. "Pentagon Envisioning a Costly Internet for War." *New York Times*, November 13, 2004.

Weiss, Karen G. "'Boys Will Be Boys' and Other Gendered Accounts: An Exploration of Victims' Excuses and Justifications for Unwanted Sexual Contact and Coercion." *Violence against Women*, 15, 2009:810–834.

Weiss, Rick. "Mature Human Embryos Cloned." *Washington Post*, February 12, 2004:A1.

Welker, Marina, Damani J. Partridge, and Rebecca Hardin. "Corporate Lives: New Perspectives on the Social Life of the Corporate Form." *Current Anthropology*, 52, 3, April 2011:S3–S16.

Wertz, Richard W., and Dorothy C. Wertz. "Notes on the Decline of Midwives and the Rise of Medical Obstetricians." In *The Sociology of Health and Illness: Critical Perspectives*, Peter Conrad and Rochelle Kern, eds. New York: St. Martin's Press, 1981:165–183.

Western, Bruce, Deirdre Bloome, Benjamin Sosnaud, and Laura Tach. "Economic Insecurity and Social Stratification." *Annual Review of Sociology*, 38, 2012:341–359.

Westheimer, J. "Patriotism, Diversity, and Education." *Encyclopedia of Diversity in Education*, James A. Banks, ed. Thousand Oaks, Calif.: Sage, 2012:1653–1657.

"What Scares Doctors? Being the Patient." *Time*, May 1, 2006.

Wheaton, Blair, and Philippa Clarke. "Space Meets Time: Integrating Temporal and Contextual Influences on Mental Health in Early Adulthood." *American Sociological Review*, 68, 2003:680–706.

Whelan, Robbie. "Home Is Where the Mall Is." *Wall Street Journal*, October 14, 2014.

Whipple, Tom. "Nursing Home Defends Prostitutes' Visits." *Times*, January 29, 2013.

White, Jack E. "Forgive Us Our Sins." *Time*, July 3, 1995:29.

White, Joseph B., Stephen Power, and Timothy Aeppel. "Death Count Linked to Failures of Firestone Tires Rises to 203." *Wall Street Journal*, June 19, 2001:A4.

Whitehead, Barbara Dafoe, and David Popenoe. "The Marrying Kind: Which Men Marry and Why." *The State of Our Unions: The Social Health of Marriage in America*, Rutgers University, 2004.

Whiteley, Paul, Thomas Sy, and Stefanie K. Johnson. "Leaders' Conceptions of Followers: Implications for Naturally Occurring Pygmalion Effects." *Leadership Quarterly*, 23, 2012:822–834.

Whorf, Benjamin. *Language, Thought, and Reality*, J. B. Carroll, ed. Cambridge, MA: MIT Press, 1956.

Whyte, William Foote. "Street Corner Society." In *Down to Earth Sociology: Introductory Readings*, 11th ed., James M. Henslin, ed. New York: Free Press, 2001:61–69.

Wiener, Ron. "Acting against Ageing: The Theatre Group Helping Older People Stay Creative." *The Guardian*, July 29, 2014.

Wiggins, Ovetta, Carol Morello, and Dan Keating. "Prince George's County: Growing, and Growing More Segregated, Census Shows." *Washington Post*, October 30, 2011.

Wilford, John Noble. "In Maya Ruins, Scholars See Evidence of Urban Sprawl." *New York Times*, December 19, 2000.

Wilford, John Noble. "Mapping Ancient Civilization, in a Matter of Days." *New York Times*, May 10, 2010.

Williams, Jasmin K. "Utah—The Beehive State." *New York Post*, June 12, 2007.

Williams, Rhys H. "Constructing the Public Good: Social Movements and Cultural Resources." *Social Problems*, 42, 1, February 1995:124–144.

Williams, Robin M., Jr. *American Society: A Sociological Interpretation*, 2nd ed. New York: Knopf, 1965.

Williams, Timothy. "Old Sound in Harlem Draws New Neighbors' Ire." *New York Times*, July 6, 2008.

Willie, Charles Vert. "Caste, Class, and Family Life Experiences." *Research in Race and Ethnic Relations*, 6, 1991:65–84.

Willser, Kim. "French Railway Operator SNCF Orders Hundreds of New Trains That Are Too Big." *The Guardian*, May 21, 2014.

Wilson, Colin. "Sexuality in Pre-Class Society: A Response to Sheila McGregor." *International Socialism*, 139, Summer 2013.

Wilson, Duff. "Cigarette Giants in a Global Fight on Tighter Rules." *New York Times*, November 13, 2010.

Wilson, Duff. "Harvard Medical School in Ethics Quandary." *New York Times*, March 2, 2009.

Wilson, Edward O. *Sociobiology: The New Synthesis*. Cambridge, Mass.: Harvard University Press, 1975.

Wilson, James Q., and Richard J. Herrnstein. *Crime and Human Nature*. New York: Simon & Schuster, 1985.

Wilson, William Julius. "Jobless Poverty: A New Form of Social Dislocation in the Inner-City Ghetto." In *The Inequality Reader: Contemporary and Foundational Readings in Race, Class and Gender*, David B. Grusky and Szonja Szelenyi, eds. Boulder: Westview Press, 2007:142–152.

Wilson, William Julius. *The Bridge over the Racial Divide: Rising Inequality and Coalition Politics*. Berkeley: University of California Press, 2000.

Wilson, William Julius. *The Declining Significance of Race: Blacks and Changing American Institutions*. Chicago: University of Chicago Press, 1978.

Wimmer, Andreas, and Kevin Lewis. "Beyond and below Racial Homophily: ERG Models of a Friendship Network Documented on Facebook." *American Journal of Sociology*, 116, 2, 2010: 583–642.

Wines, Michael. "How Bad Is Inflation in Zimbabwe?" *Wall Street Journal*, May 2, 2006.

"Winner, Dumbest Moment, Marketing." CNN, February 1, 2006.

Wirth, Louis. "The Problem of Minority Groups." In *The Science of Man in the World Crisis*, Ralph Linton, ed. New York: Columbia University Press, 1945.

Wirth, Louis. "Urbanism as a Way of Life." *American Journal of Sociology*, 44, July 1938:1–24.

Wolfe, Alexandra. "Nathan Wolfe." *Wall Street Journal*, December 13–14, 2014a.

Wolfe, Alexandra. "Ray Kurzweil." *Wall Street Journal*, May 31–June 1, 2014b.

Wolfensohn, James D., and Kathryn S. Fuller. "Making Common Cause: Seeing the Forest for the Trees." *International Herald Tribune*, May 27, 1998:11.

Wolff, Edward N. "The Asset Price Meltdown and the Wealth of the Middle Class." National Bureau of Economic Research Working Paper No. 18559, January 2013.

Wolfinger, Nicholas H. "Family Structure Homogamy: The Effects of Parental Divorce on Partner Selection and Marital Stability." *Social Science Research*, 32, 2003:80–97.

Wolinsky, Frederic D., Timothy E. Stump, and Christopher M. Callahan. "Does Being Placed in a Nursing Home Make You Sicker and More Likely to Die?" In *Societal Mechanisms for Maintaining Competence in Old Age*, Sherry L. Willis, K. Warner Schaie, and Mark Hayward, eds. New York: Springer Publishing Company, 1997:94–130.

Wolitzky-Taylor, Kate B., Heidi S. Resnick, Amanda B. Amstadter, et al. "Reporting Rape in a National Sample of College Women." *Journal of American College Health*, 59, 7, 2011:582–587.

"Woman Ordered to Hold 'Idiot' Sign and 6 Other Cases of Court-Ordered Shaming." Associated Press, November 13, 2012.

Women's Bureau of the United States, Department of Labor. *Handbook on Women Workers*. Washington, D.C.: U.S. Government Printing Office, 1969.

Wonacott, Peter. "China Inc. Moves the Factory Floor to Africa." *Wall Street Journal*, May 15, 2014.

Wong, Chun Han. "Death of Elderly Man Denied a Bus Seat Sets off Introspection in China." *Wall Street Journal*, September 15, 2014.

Wood, Daniel B., "Latinos Redefine What It Means to Be Manly." *Christian Science Monitor*, 93, 161, July 16, 2001.

World Health Organization. *Constitution of the World Health Organization*. New York: World Health Organization. Washington, D.C.: Interim Commission, 1946.

World Health Organization (WHO). "Ebola Virus Disease in West Africa—The First 9 Months of the Epidemic and Forward Projections." *New England Journal of Medicine*, September 23, 2014.

Worsley, Peter M. "50 Years Ago: Cargo Cults of Melanesia." *Scientific American*, April 24, 2009. A reprint of an article that appeared in *Scientific American*, May 1959.

Worsley, Peter. *The Trumpet Shall Sound*. London: MacGibbon and Kee, 1957.

Wright, Erik Olin. *Class*. London: Verso, 1985.

Wright, Lawrence. "Double Mystery." *New Yorker*, August 7, 1995:45–62.

Wright, Lawrence. "One Drop of Blood." *New Yorker*, July 25, 1994: 46–50, 52–55.

Xie, Min, Karen Heimer, and Janet L. Lauritsen. "Violence against Women in U.S. Metropolitan Areas: Change in Women's Status and Risk, 1980–2004." *Criminology*, 2011:1–38.

Yager, Mark, Beret Strong, Linda Roan, David Matsumoto, and Kimberly A. Metcalf. "Nonverbal Communication in the Contemporary Operating Environment." United States Army Research Institute for the Behavioral and Social Sciences, Technical Report 1238, January 2009.

Yakaboski, Tamara, and Leah Reinert. "Review of Women in Academic Leadership: Professional Strategies, Personal Choices." *Women in Higher Education*, 4, 1, 2011.

Yamamoto, Yoko, and Mary C. Brinton. "Cultural Capital in East Asian Educational Systems: The Case of Japan." *Sociology of Education*, 83, 1, 2010:67–83.

Yardley, Jim. "A Village Rape Shatters a Family, and India's Traditional Silence." *New York Times*, October 27, 2012.

Yardley, Jim. "As Wealth and Literacy Rise in India, Report Says, So Do Sex-Selective Abortions." *New York Times*, May 24, 2011.

Yardley, Jim. "Faces of Abortion in China: A Young, Single Woman." *New York Times*, May 13, 2007.

Yardley, Jim. "India Tries Using Cash Bonuses to Slow Birthrates." *New York Times*, August 21, 2010a.

Yardley, Jim. "Soaring above India's Poverty, a 27-Story Home." *New York Times*, October 28, 2010b.

Yardley, Jim, and Keith Bradsher. "China, an Engine of Growth, Faces a Global Slump." *New York Times*, October 22, 2008.

Yadron, Danny. "The Coder Who Encrypted Your Text." *Wall Street Journal*, July 10, 2015.

Yarris, Lynn. "New Synthetic Biology Technique Boosts Microbial Production of Diesel Fuel." Berkeley, Calif.: Berkeley Lab News Center, March 26, 2012.

Yearbook of American and Canadian Churches. Washington, D.C.: National Council of Churches, 2012.

Yee, Vivian. "Flash Mob in Times Square Honors Victims of Newtown." *New York Times*, February 24, 2013a.

Yee, Vivian. "Grouping Students by Ability Regains Favor in Classroom." *New York Times*, June 9, 2013b.

Yinger, J. Milton. *The Scientific Study of Religion*. New York: Macmillan, 1970.

Yinger, J. Milton. *Toward a Field Theory of Behavior: Personality and Social Structure*. New York: McGraw-Hill, 1965.

"'You Can Die Anytime.' Death Squad Killings in Mindanao." New York: Human Rights Watch, 2009.

Young, Robert D., Bertrand Desjardins, Kirsten McCaughlin, Michel Poulain, and Thomas T. Perls. "Typologies of Extreme Longevity Myths." *Current Gerontology and Geriatrics Research*, 2010:1–12.

Zachary, G. Pascal. "Behind Stocks' Surge Is an Economy in Which Big U.S. Firms Thrive." *Wall Street Journal*, November 22, 1995:A1, A5.

Zakaria, Fareed. *The Post-American World*. New York: W. W. Norton, 2008.

Zald, Mayer N. "Looking Backward to Look Forward: Reflections on the Past and the Future of the Resource Mobilization Research Program." In *Frontiers in Social Movement Theory*, Aldon D. Morris and Carol McClurg Mueller, eds. New Haven, Conn.: Yale University Press, 1992:326–348.

Zald, Mayer N., and John D. McCarthy, eds. *Social Movements in an Organizational Society*. New Brunswick, N.J.: Transaction, 1987.

Zamiska, Nicholas. "Pressed to Do Well on Admissions Tests, Students Take Drugs." *Wall Street Journal*, November 8, 2004.

Zaslow, Jeffrey. "Thinness, Women, and School Girls: Body Image." *Wall Street Journal*, September 2, 2009.

Zaslow, Jeffrey. "Will You Still Need Me When I'm . . . 84? More Couples Divorce after Decades." *Wall Street Journal*, June 17, 2003:D1.

Zellner, William W. *Countercultures: A Sociological Analysis*. New York: St. Martin's, 1995.

Zerubavel, Eviatar. *The Fine Line: Making Distinctions in Everyday Life*. New York: Free Press, 1991.

Zhang, Rong, and Dennis McCornac. "Private Universities in Japan: A Race to the Bottom?" *The Diplomat*, September 3, 2014.

Zhang, Yuanting, and Franklin W. Goza. "Who Will Care for the Elderly in China?" Bowling Green, Ohio: Center for Family and Demographic Research, May 2007.

Zuboff, Shoshanna. "New Worlds of Computer-Mediated Work." In *Down to Earth Sociology: Introductory Readings*, 6th ed., James M. Henslin, ed. New York: Free Press, 1991:476–485.

Zumbrun, Joshua. "The Sacrifices of Albania's 'Sworn Virgins.'" *Washington Post*, August 11, 2007.

Name Index

Subject Index

Credits

Photo Credits

Chapter 1 p.1: Luca Tettoni/Robert Harding World Imagery/Corbis; p.3: Robert Geiss/Newscom; p.4: Martin Harvey/Corbis; p.5: Prisma/Newscom; p.5: Roger Viollet/The Image Works; p.6: Hulton-Deutsch Collection/Corbis; p.6: World History Archive/Newscom; p.7: Bettmann/Corbis; p.8.akg-images/Newscom; p.9: ullstein bild/Getty Images; p.9: Pearson; p.9: Pictorial Press Ltd/Alamy; p.9: Bettmann/Corbis; p.9: Mary Evans Picture Library/The Image Works; p.9: Courtesy of Wellesley College Archives; p.9: Bettmann/Corbis; p.9: The University of Chicago Library Special Collections Research Center; p.9: The University of Chicago Library Special Collections Research Center; p.9: Bettmann/Corbis; p.9: Everett Collection/Newscom; p.10: Picture History/Newscom; p.11: Everett Collection/Newscom; p.12: Fritz Goro/The LIFE Picture Collection/Getty Images; p.14: University of Chicago; p.16: Pictorial Parade/Getty Images; p.17: TopFoto/The Image Works; p.23: See Li/Demotix/Corbis; p.26: DOONESBURY © 1989 G. B. Trudeau. Reprinted with permission of UNIVERSAL UCLICK. All rights reserved; p.26: Anu Boro/Demotix/Corbis; p.27: C.M. Holmgren; p.28: Dinodia/The Image Works; p.29: Stephen Lovekin/WireImage/Getty Images; p.30: Doctor Stock/SuperStock; p.32: Bebert Bruno/SIPA/AP Images; p.34: Zoriah/EyePress/Newscom.

Chapter 2 p.39: Grant Rooney/age fotostock/SuperStock; p.41: Karim Sahib/AFP Photo/Newscom; p.43: Imaginechina/Corbis; p.43: Javier Lizon/EPA/Landov; p.44: OSTILL/Getty Images; p.46: C.M. Holmgren; p.46: C.M. Holmgren; p.46: C.M. Holmgren; p.46: Steve Hamblin/Alamy; p.46: C.M. Holmgren; p.46: jackhollingsworth.com/Shutterstock; p.46: James M. Henslin; p.48: Ruaridh Stewart/ZUMA Press/Newscom; p.51: Nick Tomecek/AP Images; p.50: The Post-Standard/Landov; p.51: Dan Riedlhuber/Reuters/Landov; p.53: Jaime Saldarriaga/Reuters/Landov; p.53: Valua Vitaly/Shutterstock; p.53: Asia Images/Superstock; p.53: Panorama/The Image Works; p.53: Piers Cavendish/Impact/HIP/The Image Works; p.53: Tom Cockrem/Lonely Planet Images/Getty Images; p.53: Dallas and John Heaton/Travel Pictures/Alamy; p.53: Bill Bachmann/Design Pics/Newscom; p.54: Boris Roessler/Epa/Corbis; p.56: Sergio Azenha/Alamy; p.58: Courtesy of Clarke Historical Museum; p.59 Tomatito/Shutterstock; p.60: Eraldo Peres/AP Images; p.61: Barcroft Media/Landov; p.61: Dave Carpenter/www.CartoonStock.com; p.62: Paulo Santos/Reuters/Landov.

Chapter 3 p.67: Kymri Wilt/DanitaDelimont.com "Danita Delimont Photography"/Newscom; p.68: Thomas Wanstall/The Image Works; p.67: James M. Henslin; p.70: Cai Yang/Xinhua/Landov; p.71: Nina Leen/The LIFE Picture Collection/Getty Images; p.73: Jacky Lam/EyeEm/Getty Images; p.74: Blend Images/Alamy; p.74: Bill Anderson/Science Source; p.76: Mary Evans Picture Library/The Image Works; p.78: Jim Marshall/The Image Works; p.78: Elie Bernager/Photodisc/Getty Images; p.78: Mary A ltaffer/AP Images; p.78: Laurent Rebours/AP Images; p.78: Pool/Tim Graham Picture Library/Getty Images; p.80: Frank and Ernest used with the permission of the Thaves and the Cartoonist Group. All rights reserved; p.80: Gavriel Jecan/Danita Delimont Photography/Newscom; p.81: Ben Speck/Getty Images; p.83: Chris Ryan/OJO Images Ltd/Alamy; p.84: Moviestore Collection Ltd/Alamy; p.85: Lannis Waters/The Palm Beach Post/Zuma Press; p.87: Asia Images Group/Getty Images; p.88: Katrina Wittkamp/Digital Vision/Getty Images; p.89: Image Source/Getty Images; p.91: US Marines Photo/Alamy; p.91: Michael MacIntyre/Eye Ubiquitous; p.94: Jonathan Kirn/Newscom; p.95: AP Images.

Chapter 4 p.100: Fred Dufour/AFP/Getty Images; p.100: Bettmann/Corbis; p.103: Jochem Wijnands/Horizons WWP/Alamy; p.104: Peter/Barcroft Media/Landov; p.107: Jim Lo Scalzo/EPA/Landov; p.108: Visions of America/Universal Images Group/Getty Images; p.109: Dorothy Alexander/Alamy; p.109: Tim Graham/Robert Harding/Newscom; p.110: Matthew Cavanaugh/EPA/Newscom; p.112: James M. Henslin; p.112: James M. Henslin; p.112: James M. Henslin; p.113: James M. Henslin; p.113: James M. Henslin; p.113: James M. Henslin; p.113: James M. Henslin; p.113: James M. Henslin; p.114: Dmitri Mihhailov/ShutterStock; p.114: Fotosearch/SuperStock; p.115: Ng Han Guan/AP Images; p.115: Solent News/Splash News/Newscom; p.116: Joshua Roberts/Reuters/Corbis; p.117: JoJo Whilden/Netflix/Everett Collection; p.119: Marka/SuperStock; p.119: Lexie Appleby/Geisler-Fotopress/DPA /Landov; p.120: McPherson, John/www.CartoonStock.com; p.121: Nir Alon/Alamy; p.125: James M. Henslin; p.125: James M. Henslin; p.125: James M. Henslin; p.126: James M. Henslin; p.126: James M. Henslin; p.126: James M. Henslin; p.126: James M. Henslin; p.126: James M. Henslin.

Chapter 5 p.131: Matt Crossick/PA Photos/Landov; p.134: John Birdsall/The Image Works; p.134: Konstantin Sutyagin/Shutterstock; p.134: Michael N. Paras/Veer/Corbis; p.134: Stan Carroll/The Commercial Appeal/Landov; p.134: Patrick Mcfeeley/National Geographic/SuperStock; p.134: Victoria Jones/SN /Landov; p.136: Robert Weber/The New Yorker Collection/The Cartoon Bank; p.136: Scott Olson/Getty Images; p.138: David J. Phillip/AP Images; p.139:

Blend Images/SuperStock; p.139: Ericsphotography/Getty Images; p.139: Paul Beaty/AP Images; p.141: KCNA/AFP/Getty Images; p.143: Daniel Kalker/DPA/Landov; p.144: Bettmann/Corbis; p.144: Damon Higgins/ZUMApress/Newscom; p.145: Keystone/Corbis; p.145: Solent News/Splash News/Corbis; p.147: Hero Images Inc./Corbis; p.148: Science Photo Library/Superstock; p.149: Villareal/BSIP/The Image Works; p.152: James M. Henslin; p.152: James M. Henslin; p.152: James M. Henslin; p.152: James M. Henslin; p.154: Pictorial Press Ltd/Alamy; p.156: Courtesy of Alexandra Milgram. Copyright 1968 by Stanley Milgram. Copyright renewed 1993 by Alexandra Milgram. From the film OBEDIENCE, distributed by Penn State Media Sales.

Chapter 6 p.160: Jack Kurtz/UPI Photo Service/Newscom; p.162: James M. Henslin; p.163: Martin Harvey/Corbis; p.164: Babu/Reuters/Landov; p.167: Cesare Abbate/EPA/Landov; p.167: Dress LatifF/Reuters/Landov; p.169: Marvin Fong/The Plain Dealer/Landov; p.170: Booking Photo/PacificCoastNews/Newscom; p.170: Ronaldo Schemidt/AFP/GettyImages; p.171: Lucy Nicholson/Reuters/Corbis; p.172: Jonathan Brady/PA Photos/Landov; p.175: Jonathan Ernst/Reuters/Corbis; p.176: PhotoEdit, Inc; p.179: Niday Picture Library/Alamy; p.179: Leo Cullum The New Yorker Collection/The Cartoon Bank; p.180: John Angelillo/UPI/Landov; p.185: AP Images; p.187: Jorge Lopez/Reuters/Corbis; p.188: Wenn Ltd/Alamy; p.190: Andy Levin/Science Source.

Chapter 7 p.192: Jack Kurtz/The Image Works; p.194: Shawn G. Henry; p.195: GraphicaArtis/Corbis; p.196: James M. Henslin; p.198: James M. Henslin; p.199: Chandan Ghosh/Demotix/Corbis; p.201: Lewis W. Hine/Buyenlarge/Getty Images; p.202: Jacob August Riis/Bettmann/Corbis; p.202: Bettmann/Corbis; p.203: Fred Duval/FilmMagic/Getty Images; p.205: Xinhua/Alamy; p.207: Lebrecht Music and Arts Photo Library/Alamy; p.214: Mike Goldwater/Alamy; p.216: James M. Henslin; p.216: James M. Henslin; p.216: James M. Henslin; p.217: James M. Henslin; p.217: James M. Henslin; p.217: James M. Henslin; p.217: James M. Henslin; p.217: James M. Henslin; p.218: James M. Henslin; p.219: Jesus Alcazar/AFP/Getty Images; p.219: Paul S. Howell/Getty Images.

Chapter 8 p.225: Niebrugge Images/Alamy; p.227: Mario Anzuoni/Reuters/Corbis; p.231: Mikhail Metzel/Pool/epa/Corbis; p.234: KARIM SAHIB/AFP/Getty Images; p.235: Stringer/USA/Reuters/Corbis; p.237: Francois Lenoir/Reuters/Corbis; p.238: Junko Kimura/ZUMA Press/Corbis; p.238: Splash News/Corbis; p.238: Kristin Callahan/Everett Collection/Newscom; p.238: Splash News/Corbis; p.239: Boris Drucker/The New Yorker Collection/The Cartoon Bank; p.240: James M. Henslin; p.241: William Geddes/Beateworks/Corbis Outline; p.241: David Bacon/The Image Works; p.242: Matt Peyton/Invision/AP Images; p.242: Bettmann/Corbis; p.245: Hill Street Studios/Blend Images/Alamy; p.280: Misha Japaridze/AP Images; p.246: Corbis/SuperStock; p.247: Lange/Dorothea/Library of Congress; p.248: By permission of John L. Hart FLP and Creators Syndicate, Inc; p.250: James M. Henslin; p.255: James M. Henslin.

Chapter 9 p.258: Alex Milan Tracy/Sipa/AP Images; p.260: John Stillwell/PA Photos/Landov; p.261: Doug Murray/SMI/Newscom; p.262: Didi/Alamy; p.263: Time Life Pictures/Getty Images; p.263: Akg-images/Newscom; p.264: Eliana Aponte/Reuters/Landov; p.266: Ken Blackbird/AP Images; p.266: James M. Henslin; p.266: Robert Galbraith/Reuters/Corbis; p.266: Lisa Dejong/The Plain Dealer/Landov; p.266: Rick Wilking/Reuters/Landov; p.267: Charles Moore/Black Star/Alamy; p.268: Bill Hogan/KRT/Newscom; p.275: Library of Congress Prints and Photographs Division Washington [LC-DIG-ggbain-22741]; p.277: AP Images; p.278: Momentimages/Tetra Images/Corbis; p.280: Jim West imageBroker/Newscom; p.281: Arianne Starnes/UPI/Landov; p.282: David McNew/Getty Images; p.284: U.S. Coast Guard/Landov; p.285: Photo by Fred Blackwell; p.286: Brooks Kraft/Corbis; p.287: Ted Thai/Getty images; p.289: Kyodo/Newscom; p.290: SuperStock; p.291: Antonio Ribeiro/Getty Images; p.294: Momentimages/Tetra Images/Newscom.

Chapter 10 p.297: Picavet/Getty Images; p.300: Monica Rodriguez/Getty Images; p.300: Nevada Wier/Getty Images; p.300: Jake Warga/Corbis; p.300: Bill Bachmann/The Image Works; p.300: Wilson Melo/Reuters/Corbis; p.300: Art Wolfe/Science Source; p.300: Doug Pearson/JAI/Corbis; p.300: Melvyn Longhurst China/Alamy; p.301: Monika Graff//UPI/Landov; p.302: Thomas Dallal/Sipa Press; p.302: Martin Gershen/Science Source; p.303: Gordon King/AP Images; p.304: Jeremy Horner/Corbis; p.305: James M. Henslin; p.305: James M. Henslin; p.305: James M. Henslin; p.305: James M. Henslin; p.306: James M. Henslin; p.306: James M. Henslin; p.306: James M. Henslin; p.306: James M. Henslin; p.306: James M. Henslin; p.307: Ton Koene/age fotostock/Superstock; p.307: Ali Imam/Reuters/Corbis; p.308: Sala Lewis/PA Photos/Landov; p.309: Francoise Sylvie/SIPA/Newscom; p.310: Hulton-Deutsch/Hulton-Deutsch Collection/Corbis; p.311: From Dick and Jane: Fun with Our Family, Illustrations © copyright 1951, 1979, and Dick and Jane: We Play Outside, copyright © 196. Pearson Education, Inc., published by Scott Foresman and Company. Used with permission; p.312: Frank and Helena/cultura/Corbis; p.315: AberCPC/Alamy; p.318:

Text Credits

Chapter 1: p.3: Source: Mills, C. Wright. The Sociological Imagination. New York: Oxford University Press, 1959; p.7: Fig01-01: Source: By the author. Based on Centers for Disease Control and Prevention. "Summary Health Statistics for U.S. Adults: National Health Interview Survey, 2011." Vital Health Statistics, 10, 256, December 2012. and earlier years; Center for Injury Prevention and Control 2013; p.8: UNDoc01.03: Source: Max Weber; p.9: Fig01-02: Source: Photo wheel copyright 2016 © James M. Henslin; p.9: UNDoc01.04: Source: Harriet Martineau; p.11: UNBox01-02: Source: W. E. B. Du Bois, The Souls of Black Folk (1903); p.12: Fig01-03: Source: By the author. Based on DeMartini, Joseph R. "Basic and Applied Sociological Work: Divergence, Convergence, or Peaceful Co-existence?" The Journal of Applied Behavioral Science, 18, 2, 1982: 203–215., plus events since then; p.13: Fig01-04: Source: Courtesy of Pager, Devah. "The Mark of a Criminal Record." American Journal of Sociology, 108, 5, March

2003: 937–975. (c) 2003 by University of Chicago Press. Reproduced by permission; p.15: Fig01-05: Source: By the author. Based on Statistical Abstract of the United States 1998: Table 92 and 2014: Tables 84, 137; earlier editions for earlier years. The broken lines indicate the author's estimates; p.19: TBL01-01: Source: By the author.

Chapter 2: p.40: Source: Linton, Ralph. The Study of Man. New York: Appleton-Century-Crofts, 1936; p.31: Source: Sumner, William Graham. Folkways: A Study in the Sociological Importance of Usages, Manners, Customs, Mores, and Morals. New York: Ginn, 1906; p.44: Source: Bates, Marston. Gluttons and Libertines: Human Problems of Being Natural. New York: Vintage Books, 1967. Quoted in Crapo, Richley H. Cultural Anthropology: Understanding Ourselves and Others, 5th ed. Boston: McGraw Hill, 2002; p.44: Source: Dusty Friedman; p.44: Source: Kingston, Maxine Hong. The Woman Warrior. New York: Vintage Books, 1975: 108. Quoted in Frank J. Zulke and Jacqueline P. Kirley. Through the Eyes of Social Science, 6th ed. Prospect Heights, Ill.: Waveland Press, 2002; p.47: Fig02-01: Source: By the author; p.47: Source: Ekman, Paul, Wallace V. Friesen, and John Bear. "The International Language of Gestures." Psychology Today, May 1984: 64; p.49: UNBox02-01: Source: Based on Kent, Mary, and Robert Lalasz. "In the News: Speaking English in the United States." Washington, D.C.: Population Reference Bureau, January 18, 2007; Salomon, Gisela, "In Miami, Spanish Is Becoming the Primary Language." Associated Press, May 29, 2008; Costantini, Cristina. "Spanish in Miami: Diciendo 'Hola' Or Saying 'Hello.'" Huffpost Miami, November 29, 2011; Nelson, Margaret K. "Whither Fictive Kin? Or, What's in a Name?" Journal of Family Issues, 2013; p.52: Source: Robertson, Ian. Sociology, 3rd ed. New York: Worth, 1987: 62; p.53: Source: Donald Rumsfeld, quoted in Dickey, Christopher, and John Barry. "Iran: A Rummy Guide." Newsweek, May 8, 2006: 38; p.53: Source: Jessop, Bob, "The Return of the National State in the Current Crisis of the World Market." Capital and Class, 34, 1, 2010: 38–43; p.56: Source: Zellner, William W. Countercultures: A Sociological Analysis. New York: St. Martin's, 1995: 58, 65; p.62: Source: Ogburn, William F. Social Change with Respect to Culture and Human Nature. New York: W. B. Huebsch, 1922.

Chapter 3: p.69: Source: Kingsley Davis, Kingsley Davis: A Biography And Selections From His Writings, Transaction Publishers, 2004; p.70: UNBox03-01: Sources: Based on Begley, Sharon. "Twins: Nazi and Jew." Newsweek, 94, December 3, 1979: 139; Chen, Edwin. "Twins Reared Apart: A Living Lab." New York Times Magazine. December 9, 1979: 112; Wright, Lawrence. "Double Mystery." New Yorker, August 7, 1995: 45–62; Segal, Nancy L., and Scott L. Hershberger. "Virtual Twins and Intelligence." Personality and Individual Differences, 39, 6, 2005: 1061–1073; Ledger, Kate. "Sociology and the Gene." Contexts, 8, 3, 2009: 16–20; Johnson et al. 2009; Segal and Mulligan 2014; p.71: Source: Skeels, H. M. "Adult Status of Children with Contrasting Early Life Experiences: A Follow-up Study." Monograph of the Society for Research in Child Development, 31, 3, 1966; p.72: Source: Pines, Maya. "The Civilizing of Genie." Psychology Today, 15, September 1981: 28–34; p.74: Source: Cooley, Charles Horton. Human Nature and the Social Order. New York: Scribner's, 1902; p.75: Fig03-01: Source: By the author; p.83: UNBox03-02: Source: Based on Zumbrun, Joshua. "The Sacrifces of Albania's 'Sworn Virgins.'" Washington Post, August 11, 2007; Bilefsky, Dan. "Albanian Custom Fades: Woman as Family Man." New York Times, June 25, 2008; Paterniti 2014; p.84: Source: Eder, Donna. "On Becoming Female: Lessons Learned in School." In Down to Earth Sociology: Introductory Readings, 14th ed., James M. Henslin, ed. New York: Free Press, 2007; p.86: Source: Parker, Laura. "It's Hard to Believe in the New Lara Croft." Gamespot, December 5, 2012; p.90: UNBox03-03: Source: Based on Rodriguez, Richard. "The Education of Richard Rodriguez." Saturday Review, February 8, 1975: 147–149; Rodriguez, Richard. Hunger of Memory: The Education of Richard Rodriguez. Boston: Godine, 1982; Rodriguez, Richard. "The Late Victorians: San Francisco, AIDS, and the Homosexual Stereotype." Harper's Magazine, October 1990: 57–66; Rodriguez, Richard. "Mixed Blood." Harper's Magazine, 283, November 1991: 47–56; Rodriguez, Richard. "Searching for Roots in a Changing Society." In Down to Earth Sociology: Introductory Readings, 8th ed., James M. Henslin, ed. New York: Free Press, 1995: 486–491; Herrera and Rodriguez 2014; p.91: UNBox03-04: Source: Redacted from Eder, Donna. "Sitting in on Adolescent Conversations." In Social Problems: A Down-to-Earth Approach, 11th ed., James M. Henslin, ed. Boston: Pearson, 2014; p.93: UNBox03-05: Sources: Based on Garfnkel, Harold. "Conditions of Successful Degradation Ceremonies." American Journal of Sociology, 61, 2, March 1956: 420–424; Ricks, Thomas E. "'New' Marines Illustrate Growing Gap between Military and Society." Wall Street Journal, July 27, 1995: A1, A4; Goffman, Erving. Asylums: Essays on the Social Situation of Mental Patients and Other Inmates. Chicago: Aldine, 1961; Dyer, Gwynne. "Anybody's Son Will Do." In Down to Earth Sociology: Introductory Readings, 14th ed., James M. Henslin, ed. New York: Free Press, 2007; Source: DeMause, Lloyd. "Our Forebears Made Childhood a Nightmare." Psychology Today 8, 11, April 1975: 85–88; p.95: Fig03-02: Source: Furstenberg, Frank F., Jr., Sheela Kennedy, Vonnie C. McLoyd, Ruben G. Rumbaut, and Richard A. Settersten, Jr. "Growing Up Is Harder to Do." Contexts, 3, 3, Summer 2004: 33–41. Year 2010 is the author's estimate based on Sironi and Furstenberg 2014; p.96: Source: Keniston, Kenneth. Youth and Dissent: The Rise of a New Opposition. New York: Harcourt, Brace, Jovanovich, 1971.

Chapter 4: p.104: Fig04-01: Source: By the author; p.107: Source: William Shakespeare, As You Like It, Act II, Scene 7; p.108: Fig04-02: Source: By the author; p.109: Source: Based on Aberle et al. 1950; Mack and Bradford 1979; pp.112-113: UNBox04-01: Sources: Based on Aeppel 1996; Kephart and Zellner 2001; Kraybill 2002; Johnson-Weiner 2007; Scolforo 2008; Buckley 2011; Donnermeyer et al. 2013; pp.112-113: Source: Kraybill, Donald B. The Riddle of Amish

Culture, rev. ed. Baltimore, Md.: Johns Hopkins University Press, 2002; p.116: Fig04-03: Source: By the author; p.120: Fig04-04: Source: By the author; p.121: Source: Marshall, Samantha. "It's So Simple: Just Lather Up, Watch the Fat Go Down the Drain." Wall Street Journal, November 2, 1995: B1; p.123: Source: Garfnkel, Harold. Studies in Ethnomethodology. Englewood Cliffs, N.J.: Prentice Hall, 1967; p.124: Source: W.I. Thomas and D.S. Thomas, The child in America: Behavior problems and programs. New York: Knopf, 1928: 571-572.

Chapter 5: pp.132-133: Source: Excerpt from MONSTER: THE AUTOBIOGRAPHY OF AN L.A. GANG MEMBER by Sanyika Shakur, copyright © 1993 by Kody Scott. Used by permission of Grove/Atlantic, Inc. Any third party use of this material, outside of this publication, is prohibited; p.133: Source: Cooley, Charles Horton. Social Organization. New York: Schocken Books, 1962. Originally published by Scribner's, 1909; p.137: Source: Merton, Robert K. Social Theory and Social Structure. Glencoe, Ill.: Free Press, 1949. Enlarged ed. 1968; p.137: Source: Britta Sandberg," Guantanamo Prisoner Diary: 'We're Gonna Teach You About Great American Sex'". Spiegel online International, January 20, 2015; p.139: Source: Kleinfeld, Judith S. "The Small World Problem." Society, January–February, 2002b: 61–66; p.140: Source: Kantor, Jodi. "In First Family, a Nation's Many Faces." New York Times, January 16, 2009; p.141: Source: Based on Weber, Max. The Theory of Social and Economic Organization, A. M. Henderson and Talcott Parsons, trans., Talcott Parsons, ed. Glencoe, Ill.: Free Press, 1947. Originally published 1913; p.142: Fig05-01: Source: By the author; p.143: Source: Based on Sills, David L. "Voluntary Associations: Sociological Aspects." In International Encyclopedia of the Social Sciences, Vol 16, David L. Sills, ed. New York: Macmillan, 1968: 362–379; p.150: Fig05-02: (c) Pearson Education, Inc; p.155: Fig05-03: Source: Asch, Solomon. "Effects of Group Pressure upon the Modifcation and Distortion of Judgments." In Readings in Social Psychology, Guy Swanson, Theodore M. Newcomb, and Eugene L. Hartley, eds. New York: Holt, Rinehart and Winston, 1952; p.155: UNDoc06-04: Solomon E. Asch, "Opinions and Social Pressure," Scientific American 193 no. 5, (1955): 31-35; pp.155-156: Source: Based on Milgram, Stanley. "Behavioral Study of Obedience." Journal of Abnormal and Social Psychology, 67, 4, 1963: 371–378; Milgram, Stanley. "Some Conditions of Obedience and Disobedience to Authority." Human Relations, 18, February 1965: 57–76.

Chapter 6: p.162: Source: Chagnon, Napoleon A. Yanomamo: The Fierce People, 2nd ed. New York: Holt, Rinehart and Winston, 1977; p.162: Source: Becker, Howard S. Outsiders: Studies in the Sociology of Deviance. New York: Free Press, 1966; p.166: Source: Kubrin, Charis E., and Ronald Weitzer. "Retaliatory Homicide: Concentrated Disadvantage and Neighborhood Culture." Social Problems, 50, 2, May 2003: 157–180; p.166: Source: Based on Horowitz, Ruth. Honor and the American Dream: Culture and Identity in a Chicano Community. New Brunswick, N.J.: Rutgers University Press, 1983; Horowitz, Ruth. "Studying Violence among the 'Lions.'" In Social Problems, James M. Henslin, ed. Upper Saddle River, N.J.: Prentice Hall, 2005: 135; p.167: Source: Arlacchi, P. Peasants and Great Estates: Society in Traditional Calabria. Cambridge, England: Cambridge University Press, 1980; p.168: Source: Based on Sykes, Gresham M., and David Matza. "Techniques of Neutralization." In Down to Earth Sociology: Introductory Readings, 5th ed., James M. Henslin, ed. New York: Free Press, 1988: 225–231. Originally published 1957; p.169: Source: "Woman Ordered to Hold 'Idiot' Sign and 6 Other Cases of Court-Ordered Shaming." Associated Press, November 13, 2012; p.169: Source: Based on Chivers, C. J. "Officer Resigns before Hearing in D.W.I. Case." New York Times, August 29, 2001; p.170: Source: Rene Stutzman, "Biker gangs thrive in Central Florida", Orlando Sentinel, May 26, 2014; p.172: Source: Based on Durkheim, Emile. The Division of Labor in Society, George Simpson, trans. New York: Free Press, 1933. Originally published 1893; Durkheim, Emile. The Rules of Sociological Method, Sarah A. Solovay and John H. Mueller, trans. New York: Free Press, 1938, 1958, 1964. Originally published 1895; p.174: TBL06-01: Source: Based on Merton, Robert K. Social Theory and Social Structure. Glencoe, Ill.: Free Press, 1949. Enlarged ed., 1968; p.177: Fig06-01: Source: By the author. Based on Statistical Abstract of the United States 2014: Table 321; p.178: TBL06-02: Source: By the author. Based on Statistical Abstract of the United States 2014: Table 342 and earlier years; FBI 2014: Table 33; p.178: Source: Based on Drew, Christopher. "Military Contractor Agrees to Pay $325 Million to Settle Whistle-Blower Lawsuit." New York Times, April 2, 2009; p.181: Fig06-02: Source: By the author. Based on Statistical Abstract of the United States 1995: Table 349; 2014: Tables 2, 6, 363; Carson 2014. The broken line is the author's estimate; p.182: TBL06-03: Source: By the author. Based on Sourcebook of Criminal Justice Statistics 2013: Tables 6.0001, 6.45, 6.81.Statistical Abstract of the United States 2014: Tables 11, 59, 243, 366; p.183: Fig06-03: Source: Modified Figure 1 from Durose et al. 2014; p.184: Fig06-04: Source: By the author. Based on Durose et al. 2014: Table 8; p.184: Fig06-05: Source: By the author. Based on Statistical Abstract of the United States 2014: Table 368; Jones 2014; p.186: Fig06-06: Source: By the author. Based on Statistical Abstract of the United States 2014: Table 367; pp.186-187: UNBox06-01: Source: Based on Sheridan, Mary Beth. "Salinas Warns Mexico Against Drug Probe." Los Angeles Times, September 22, 1998; Malkin, Elisabeth. "Mexican Offcials Say Prisoners Acted as Hit Men." New York Times, July 25, 2010; Archibold, Randal C. "Mexico Holds 4 High-Ranking Army Offcers." New York Times, May 18, 2012; Casey, Nicholas. "Mexico's Masked Vigilantes Defy Drug Gangs—And the Law." Wall Street Journal, February 2–3, 2013; Casey and Harrup 2014; Johnson 2014; Perez and Cordoba 2014; p.188: Source: Thomas Szasz; p.190: Source: Durkheim, Emile. The Rules of Sociological Method, Sarah A. Solovay and John H. Mueller, trans. New York: Free Press, 1938, 1958, 1964: 68. Originally published 1895.

Chapter 7: p.194: Source: Based on Menzel, Peter. Material World: A Global Family Portrait. San Francisco: Sierra Club, 1994; Statistical Abstract 2014: Tables 112, 717, 726, 996; p.196: Source: Du Bois, W. E. B. Black Reconstruction in America: An Essay toward a History of the Part Which Black Folk Played in the Attempt to Reconstruct Democracy in America, 1860–1880. New York: Atheneum, 1992. Originally published 1935; p.197: TBL07-01: (c) Pearson Education, Inc; p.197: Source: Guru, Gopal, and Shiraz Sidhva. "India's 'Hidden Apartheid.'" UNESCO Courier, September 2001: 27; p.198: Source: Lapsley, Michael. Redeeming the Past: My Journey from Freedom Fighter to Healer. Maryknoll, N.Y.: Orbis Books, 2012; p.201: Source: Rothkopf, David. Superclass: The Global Power Elite and the World They Are Making. New York: Farrar, Straus and Giroux, 2008; p.201: Fig07-01: Source: By the author. Based on Keating et al. 2013; p.203: Fig07-02: Source: By the author; p.204: Source: Based on Davis, Kingsley, and Wilbert E. Moore. "Reply to Tumin." American Sociological Review, 18, 1953: 394–396; Davis, Kingsley, and Wilbert E. Moore. "Some Principles of Stratifcation." American Sociological Review, 10, 1945: 242–249; p.205: TBL07-02: Source: By the author; p.205: Source: Based on Gaetano Mosca, The Ruling Class, McGraw Hill, 1939; p.209: Source: Robertson, Ian. Sociology, 3rd ed. New York: Worth, 1987; p.211: TBL07-03: Source: By the author. Computed from Kurian, George Thomas. Encyclopedia of the First World, Vols. 1, 2. New York: Facts on File, 1990; Kurian, George Thomas. Encyclopedia of the Second World. New York: Facts on File, 1991; Kurian, George Thomas. Encyclopedia ofthe Third World, Vols. 1, 2, 3. New York: Facts on File, 1992; pp.212-213: Fig07-03: Source: By the author. Based on CIA World Factbook 2014; p.215: TBL07-04: Source: By the author; p.218: Source: Krugman, Paul. "White Man's Burden." New York Times, September 24, 2002; p.219: Source: Fraser, Graham. "Fox Denies Free Trade Exploiting the Poor in Mexico." Toronto Star, April 20, 2001.

Chapter 8: p.228: Source: Based on James B. Stewart, "A Lawyer and Partner, and Also Bankrupt", New York Times, January, 24, 2014; p.228: Fig08-01: Source: By the author. Based on Wolff 2013; p.228: Source: Samuelson, Paul Anthony, and William D. Nordhaus. Economics, 18th ed. New York: McGraw Hill, 2005; p.229: Fig08-02: Source: By the author. Based on Statistical Abstract of the United States 2013: Tables 709, 726; p.229: TBL08-01: Source: Based on Theo Francis and Joann Lublin, "Pay Check: A Few CEOs Dominate Ranking," Wall Street Journal, May 28, 2014; p.230: Fig08-03: Source: By the author. Based on Statistical Abstract of the United States 1960: Table 417; 1970: Table 489; U.S. Census Bureau. Income, Poverty and Health Insurance Coverage in the United States: 2013. Historical Tables, Income, Households, Table H-2. 2014; p.231: Source: F. Scott Fitzgerald, The Great Gatsby. Charles Scribner's Sons, 1925; p.232: TBL08-02: Sources: Based on Treiman, Donald J. Occupational Prestige in Comparative Perspective. New York: Academic Press, 1977: Appendices A and D; Nakao, Keiko, and Judith Treas. "Occupational Prestige in the United States Revisited: Twenty-Five Years of Stability and Change." Paper presented at the annual meetings of the American Sociological Association, 1990; Nakao, Keiko, and Judith Treas. "Updating Occupational Prestige and Socioeconomic Scores: How the New Measures Measure Up." Sociological Methodology, 24, 1994: 1–72: Appendix D; p.234: Fig08-04: Source: By the author; p.235: Source: Tresniowski, Alex. "Payday or Mayday?" People Weekly, May 17, 1999: 128–131; p.235: Source: Based on Dao, James. "Instant Millions Can't Halt Winners' Grim Side." New York Times, December 5, 2005; p.235: Source: Sara Evans, 2013; p.236: Fig08-05: Source: By the author; p.236: Fig08-06: Source: By the author. Based on Gilbert and Kahl 1998; Gilbert 2014; income estimates are inflation-adjusted and modified from Duff 1995; p.237: Source: Beeghley, Leonard. The Structure of Social Stratification in the United States, 5th ed. Boston: Allyn & Bacon, 2008; p.237: Gilbert, Dennis, and Joseph A. Kahl, American Class Structure, 4th Edition. Belmont: Wadsworth, 1998; p.240: Source: Cohen, Patricia. "Forget Lonely. Life Is Healthy at the Top." New York Times, May 15, 2004; p.244: Source: Blau, Peter M., and Otis Dudley Duncan. The American Occupational Structure. New York: John Wiley, 1967; p.244: Source: Davis, Nancy J., and Robert V. Robinson. "Class Identifcation of Men and Women in the 1970s and 1980s." American Sociological Review, 53, February 1988: 103–112; p.245: Fig08-07: Source: Based on Pursuing the American Dream: Economic Mobility Across Generations, p. 6. © July, 2013 the Pew Charitable Trusts; p.249: Fig08-08: Source: By the author. Based on Statistical Abstract of the United States 2014: Tables 6, 37, 38, 738, 739, and 741; p.250: Fig08-09: Source: By the author. Based on Statistical Abstract of the United States 2014: Table 737; p.251: Fig08-10: Source: By the author. Based on U.S. Census Bureau 2014: Table POV29; p.251: Source: Ruggles, Patricia. "Short and Long Term Poverty in the United States: Measuring the American 'Underclass.'" Washington, D.C.: Urban Institute, June 1989. 7; p.252: Fig08-11: Source: Based on Shuttuck and Kreider 2013: Table 2; p.252: Fig08-12: Source: Based on Shuttuck and Kreider 2013: Table 2; p.253: Fig08-13: Source: Based on Gottschalk, Peter, Sara McLanahan, and Gary Sandefur, "The Dynamics and Intergenerational Transmission of Poverty and Welfare Participation." In Confronting Poverty: Prescriptions for Change, Sheldon H. Danziger, Gary D. Sandefur, and Daniel H. Weinberg, eds. Cambridge, Mass.: Harvard University Press, 1994: 89.

Chapter 9: p.261: Source: Wright, Lawrence. "One Drop of Blood." New Yorker, July 25, 1994: 46–50, 52–55; p.262: Source: Thomas, W. I., and Dorothy Swaine Thomas. The Child in America: Behavior Problems and Programs. New York: Alfred A. Knopf, 1928; p.265: Fig09-01: Source: By the author. Based on Doane, Ashley W., Jr. "Dominant Group Ethnic Identity in the United States: The Role of 'Hidden' Ethnicity in Intergroup Relations." The Sociological Quarterly, 38, 3, Summer 1997: 375–397; p.267: Source: Based on Riley, Naomi Schaefer. "The Real Path to Racial Harmony." Wall Street Journal, August 14, 2009; King et al. 2013; p.268: Source: From RACIST MIND by Raphael S. Ezekiel, copyright (c) 1995 by Raphael S. Ezekiel. Used by permission of Viking Books, an imprint of Penguin Publishing Group, a division of Penguin Random House LLC; p.269: Source: Ezekiel, Raphael S. The Racist Mind: Portraits of American

Neo-Nazis and Klansmen. New York: Viking, 1995. pp. 66–67; p.269: Source: Ezekiel, Raphael S. The Racist Mind: Portraits of American Neo-Nazis and Klansmen. New York: Viking, 1995. pp. 32–33; p.270: Fig09-02: Source: By the author. Based on Kochbar, Rakesh, and Ana Gonzalez-Barrera. "Through Boom and Bust: Minorities, Immigrants and Homeownership." Washington, D.C.: Pew Hispanic Center, May 12, 2009; p.271: TBL09-01: Source: By the author. Based on Statistical Abstract of the United States 2014: Tables 111, 121; p.275: Source: Based on Bradford, Phillips Verner, and Harvey Blume. Ota Benga: The Pygmy in the Zoo. New York: Delta, 1992; Crossen, Cynthia. "How Pygmy Ota Benga Ended Up in Bronx Zoo as Darwinism Dawned." Wall Street Journal, February 6, 2006; Bergman 2014; p.276: Fig09-03: Source: By the author; p.276: Source: Schaefer, Richard T. Racial and Ethnic Groups, 9th ed. Upper Saddle River, N.J.: Prentice Hall, 2004; p.278: Fig09-04: Source: By the author. See Figure12.5; p.278: Source: Alba, Richard, and Victor Nee. Remaking the American Mainstream: Assimilation and Contemporary Immigration. Cambridge, Mass.: Harvard University Press, 2003: 17; p.279: Fig09-05: Source: By the author. Based on Statistical Abstract of the United States 2013: Tables 10, 52; p.280: Fig09-06: Source: By the author. Based on Statistical Abstract of the United States 2013: Table 18; p.280: Fig09-07: Source: By the author. Based on Statistical Abstract of the United States 2013: Table 37; p.281: Source: McIntosh, Peggy. "White Privilege and Male Privilege: A Personal Account of Coming to See Correspondences through Work in Women's Studies." Wellesley College Center for Research on Women, Working Paper 189, 1988; p.283: Fig09-08: Source: By the author. Based on Statistical Abstract of the United States 2013: Table 18; p.283: TBL09-02: Source: By the author. Based on Statistical Abstract of the United States 2014: Tables 37, 739; Krogstad 2014; p.284: TBL09-03: Source: By the author. Based on Statistical Abstract of the United States 2014: Tables 37, 38, 340, and Figure12.5 of this chapter; p.286: TBL09-04: Source: By the author: Based on Statistical Abstract of the United States 2014: Table 726; p.287: Source: Bertrand, Marianne, and Sendhil Mullainathan. "Are Emily and Brendan More Employable than Lakish and Jamal? A Field Experiment on Labor Market Discrimination." Unpublished paper, November 18, 2002; p.287: Source: Feagin, Joe R. "The Continuing Signifcance of Race: Antiblack Discrimination in Public Places." In Majority and Minority: The Dynamics of Race and Ethnicity in American Life, 6th ed., Norman R. Yetman, ed. Boston: Allyn and Bacon, 1999: 384–399. p.398; p.287: Fig09-09: Source: By the author. Based on U.S. Census Bureau 2010; p.288: Source: Hsu, Francis L. K. The Challenge of the American Dream: The Chinese in the United States. Belmont, Calif.: Wadsworth, 1971; p.289: Source: Teddy Roosevelt, 1886 (President of the United States 1901–1909) (As cited in "Past Imperfect: Geronimo's Appeal to Theodore Roosevelt." Smithsonian, November 9, 2012.); p.289: Source: Nash, Gary B. Red, White, and Black. Englewood Cliffs, N.J.: Prentice Hall, 1974; p.291: Source: Mander, Jerry. In the Absence of the Sacred: The Failure of Technology and the Survival of the Indian Nations. San Francisco, Calif.: Sierra Club Books, 1992; p.291: Source: W. E. B. Du Bois, The Souls of Black Folk (1903); p.292: Source: Portes, Alejandro, and Rubén G. Rumbaut. Immigrant America. Berkeley: University of California Press, 1990; p.293: Fig09-10: Source: By the author. Based on U.S. Census Bureau 2009; Statistical Abstract of the United States 2013: Tables 5, 12. I modified the projections based on the new census category of membership in two or more groups and trends in interethnic marriage; p.294: Source: Mark Stein, American Panic: A History of Who Scares Us and Why (Palgrave Macmillan, 2014).

Chapter 10: p.301: Source: Money, John, and Anke A. Ehrhardt. Man and Woman, Boy and Girl. Baltimore: Johns Hopkins University Press, 1972; p.304: Source: Lerner, Gerda. The Creation of Patriarchy. New York: Oxford, 1986; p.308: Source: As cited, and Lightfoot-Klein, A. "Rites of Purifcation and Their Effects: Some Psychological Aspects of Female Genital Circumcision and Infbulation (Pharaonic Circumcision) in an Afro-Arab Society (Sudan)." Journal of Psychological Human Sexuality, 2, 1989: 61–78; Merwine, Maynard H. "How Africa Understands Female Circumcision." New York Times, November 24, 1993; Tuhus-Dubrow, Rebecca. "Rites and Wrongs." Boston Globe, February 11, 2007; Lazaro, Fred de Sam. "In Senegal, a Movement to Reject Circumcision." PBS Hour, August 12, 2011; Sacirbey, Omar. "Religion is Key in Combating Female Genital Mutilation According to Activists." Religion News Service, October 28, 2012; p.308: Source: Walker, Alice, and Pratibha Parmar. Warrior Marks: Female Genital Mutilation and the Sexual Blinding of Women. New York: Harcourt Brace, 1993: 107–108; p.309: Source: Crossen, Cynthia. "Deja Vu." Wall Street Journal, March 5, 2003; p.309: Source: Cowley, Joyce. Pioneers of Women's Liberation. New York: Merit, 1969; p.309: Source: Bettelheim, Bruno. "The Commitment Required of a Woman Entering a Scientifc Profession in Present-Day American Society." In Women and the Scientific Professions, Jacquelyn A. Mattfeld and Carol G. Van Aken, eds. Cambridge, Mass.: MIT Press, 1965: 15; p.311: Fig10-01: Source: From Dick and Jane: Fun with Our Family, Illustrations © copyright 1951, 1979, and Dick and Jane: We Play Outside, copyright © 1965, Pearson Education, Inc., published by Scott, Foresman and Company. Used with permission; p.312: Source: Scully, Diana. "Negotiating to Do Surgery." In Dominant Issues in Medical Sociology, 3rd ed., Howard D. Schwartz, ed. New York: McGraw-Hill, 1994: 146–152; p.313: Source: Flexner, E. Century of Struggle. Cambridge, Mass.: Belknap, 1971. In Claire M. Renzetti and Daniel J. Curran, Women, Men, and Society, 4th ed. Boston: Allyn and Bacon, 1999; p.313: Source: Andersen, Margaret L. Thinking about Women: Sociological Perspectives on Sex and Gender. New York: Macmillan, 1988; p.313: Fig10-02: Source: By the author. Based on Statistical Abstract of the United States 1938: Table 114; 1959: Table 158; 1991: Table 261; 2011: Table 273; 2014: Table 282; p.314: Fig10-03: Source: By the author. Based on Statistical Abstract of the United States 2014: Table 283; p.316: Fig10-05: Source: By the author. Based on Women's Bureau of the United States 1969: 10; Manpower Report to the President, 1971: 203, 205; Mills and Palumbo 1980: 6, 45; Statistical Abstract of the United States 2014: Table 614; p.316: Fig10-06: Source: By the author. Based on Statistical Abstract of the United States 2014: Table 621; p.317: Fig10-07: Source: By the author. Based on U.S. Census Bureau, Current Population Survey, Annual Social and Economic (ASEC) Supplement, 2014: Table PINC-04; p.318: Fig10-08: Source: By the author. Based on Statistical Abstract of the United States 1995: Table 739; 2014: Table 733, and earlier years; and Figure11.7 of this chapter. Broken lines indicate the author's estimate; p.319: Source: Said by a supervisor at Novartis who refused to hire women (Carter, Nancy M. "Pipeline's Broken Promise." New York: Catalyst, 2010.); p.321: TBL10-01: Source: By the author. A ten-year average, based on Statistical Abstract of the United States 2005: Table 306; 2006: Table 308; 2007: Table 311; 2008: Table 313; 2009: Table 305; 2010: Table 305; 2011: Table 312; 2012: Table 316; 2013: Table 278; 2014: Table 328; p.321: TBL10-02: Source: By the author. A ten-year average, based on Statistical Abstract of the United States 2005: Table 307; 2006: Table 311; 2007: Table 315; 2008: Table 316; 2009: Table 306; 2010: Table 306; 2011: Table 313; 2012: Table 317; 2013: Table 323; 2014: Table 329; p.322: Source: Carpenito, Lynda Juall. "The Myths of Acquaintance Rape." Nursing Forum, 34, 4, October–December 1999: 3; p.322: Fig10-09: Source: By the author. Based on Statistical Abstract of the United States 2014: Tables 324, 342; p.323: TBL10-03: Source: Center for American Women and Politics 2014; p.325: Source: Zaslow, Jeffrey. "Will You Still Need Me When I'm … 84? More Couples Divorce after Decades." Wall Street Journal, June 17, 2003: D1; p.327: Fig10-12: Source: By the author. Based on Statistical Abstract of the United States 2013: Table 9, and earlier years; p.327: Fig10-13: Source: By the author. Based on Statistical Abstract of the United States 2000: Table 14; 2013: Table 9, and earlier years; p.328: Source: Jerry Seinfeld; p.335: Source: Bennett-Smith, Meredith. "Taro Aso, Japanese Finance Minster, Says Country Should Let Old People 'Hurry Up and Die.'" Huffington Post, January 23, 2013.

Chapter 11: p.360: Source: Kamber, Michael. "In Afghan Kilns, a Cycle of Debt and Servitude." New York Times, March 15, 2011; p.363: Source: Yardley, Jim, and Keith Bradsher. "China, an Engine of Growth, Faces a Global Slump." New York Times, October 22, 2008; p.365: Source: Zachary, G. Pascal. "Behind Stocks' Surge Is an Economy in Which Big U.S. Firms Thrive." Wall Street Journal, November 22, 1995: A1, A5; p.366: Fig11-04: Source: By the author. Based on Statistical Abstract of the United States 1992: Table 650; 1999: Table 698; 2013: Table 656; p.370: Source: Rothkopf, David. Superclass: The Global Power Elite and the World They Are Making. New York: Farrar, Straus and Giroux, 2008: 129–130; p.370: Source: Freeland, Chrystia. "The Rise of the New Global Elite." Atlantic, January/February 2011; p.341: Source: Weber, Max. The Theory of Social and Economic Organization, A. M. Henderson and Talcott Parsons, trans., Talcott Parsons, ed. Glencoe, Ill.: Free Press, 1947. Originally published 1913; p.341: Source: Berger, Peter L. Invitation to Sociology: A Humanistic Perspective. New York: Doubleday, 1963; p.343: Source: Bridgwater, William, ed. The Columbia Viking Desk Encyclopedia. New York: Viking Press, 1953; p.346: Source: Thomas Jefferson, in Hellinger, Daniel, and Dennis R. Judd. The Democratic Facade. Pacifc Grove, Calif.: Brooks/Cole, 1991; p.349: TBL11-01: Source: By the author. Based on Casper, Lynne M., and Loretta E. Bass. "Voting and Registration in the Election of November 1996." Washington, D.D.: U.S. Census Bureau, 1998; Jamieson, Amie, Hyon B. Shin, and Jennifer Day. "Voting and Registration in the Election of November 2000." Current Population Reports, February 2002; Holder, Kelly. "Voting and Registration in the Election of November 2004." Current Population Reports, March 2006; Current Population Survey: Voting and Registration Supplement 2012; Statistical Abstract of the United States 1991: Table 450; 1997: Table 462; 2014: Table 418; p.350: TBL11-02: Source: By the author. Based on Gallup Poll. "Election Polls—Vote by Groups, 2008." Princeton, N.J.: Gallup Organization, 2008; Statistical Abstract of the United States 1999: Table 464; 2002: Table 372; 2014: Table 423; Roper Center. "U.S. Elections: How Groups Voted in 2012." Storrs, Conn.: Roper Center, 2013; p.353: Fig11-02: Source: By the author. Based on Mills, C. Wright. The Power Elite. New York: Oxford University Press, 1956; p.354: Source: Carl von Clausewitz, Howard, Michael; Paret, Peter, eds. On War [Vom Krieg] (Indexed ed.). New Jersey: Princeton University Press. p. 87; p.355: Source: Smith, Clark. "Oral History as 'Therapy': Combatants' Account of the Vietnam War." In Strangers at Home: Vietnam Veterans Since the War, Charles R. Figley and Seymore Leventman, eds. New York: Praeger, 1980: 9–34; p.355: Source: Sengupta, Somini. "In the Ancient Streets of Najaf, Pledges of Martyrdom for Cleric." New York Times, July 10, 2004; pp.356-357: UNBox11-01: Source: Based on Savage, Charlie. "Countrywide Will Settle a Bias Suit." New York Times, December 21, 2011; Becker, Jo, and Scott Shane. "Secret 'Kill List' Proves a Test of Obama's Principles and Will." New York Times, May 29, 2012; Savage, Charlie. "U.S. Law May Allow Killings, Holder Says." New York Times, March 5, 2012.

Chapter 12: p.379: TBL12-01: Source: By the author; p.380: Source: Based on Cole, Diane. "When Romance Is a Click Away." Wall Street Journal, July 11, 2012; Webb, Amy. Data, A Love Story: How I Gamed Online Dating to Meet My Match. New York: Dutton, 2013; p.381: Fig12-01: Source: Morin, Rich, and D'Vera Cohn. "Women Call the Shots at Home; Public Mixed on Gender Roles in Jobs." Pew Research Center Publications: September 25, 2008; p.382: Fig12-02: Source: By the author. Based on Bianchi, Suzanne M. "Family Change and Time Allocation in American Families." Washington, D.C.: Alfred P. Sloan Foundation, November 29–30, 2010: Tables 1, 2; p.384: Source: Based on Gupta, Giri Raj. "Love, Arranged Marriage, and the Indian Social Structure." In Cross-Cultural Perspectives of Mate Selection and Marriage, George Kurian, ed. Westport, Conn.: Greenwood Press, 1979; Bumiller, Elisabeth. "First Comes Marriage—Then, Maybe, Love." In Marriage and Family in a Changing Society, 4th ed., James M. Henslin, ed. New York: Free Press, 1992: 120–125; Sprecher, Susan, and Rachita Chandak. "Attitudes about Arranged Marriages and Dating among Men and Women from India." Free Inquiry in Creative Sociology, 20, 1, May

1992: 59–69; Dugger, Celia W. "Wedding Vows Bind Old World and New." New York Times, July 20, 1998; Gautham, S. "Coming Next: The Monsoon Divorce." New Statesman, 131, 4574, February 18, 2002: 32–33; Swati, Pandey. "Do You Take This Stranger?" Los Angeles Times, June 26, 2008; Harris, Gardiner. "In India, Kisses Are on Rise, Even in Public." New York Times, February 13, 2013; "Most Indians…" 2014; p.386: Fig12-03: Source: By the author. Based on Statistical Abstract of the United States 1990: Table 53; 2013: Table 60; p.387: Fig12-04: Source: Siegler, Ilene C., Beverly H. Brummett, Peter Martin, and M. J. Helms. "Consistency and Timing of Marital Transitions and Survival During Midlife: The Role of Personality and Health Risk Behaviors." Annals of Behavioral Medicine, 45, 3, 2013: 338–347; p.388: Fig12-05: Source: Gallup Poll. "Prefer Boys to Girls Just as They Did in 1941." Princeton, N.J.: The Gallup Organization, June 23, 2011b; p.389: Fig12-06: Source: Adapted from Naik, Gautam. "A Baby, Please. Blond, Freckles—Hold the Colic." Wall Street Journal, February 12, 2009; p.390: Fig12-07: Source: "America's Children in Brief: Key National Indicators of Well-Being, 2010." www.childstats.gov, July 2010: Table FAM3A; p.393: Fig12-08: Source: By the author. For Native Americans, Kreider and Elliott 2009: Table 1. For other groups, Statistical Abstract of the United States 2013: Table 69; p.395: Fig12-09: Source: By the author. Based on Statistical Abstract of the United States 1995: Table 79; 2013: Table 69; p.395: Fig12-10: Source: By the Author. Based on Livingston, Gretchen, and D'Vera Cohn. "Childlessness Up among All Women; Down among Women with Advanced Degrees." Washington, D.C.: PEW Research Center, June 25, 2010; p.397: Fig12-11: Source: By the author. Based on U.S. Census Bureau. "Annual Social and Economic Supplement to Current Population Survey." Washington, D.C.: U.S. Government Printing Office, 2010; Elliott, Diana B., Kristy Krivickas, Matthew W. Brault, et al. "Historical Marriage Trends from 1890–2010. A Focus on Race Differences." Paper presented at the annual meeting of the Population Association of America, San Francisco, Calif., May 3–5, 2012; p.398: Fig12-12: Source: By the author. Based on Statistical Abstract of the United States 1993: Table 60; 2002: Table 48; 2012: Table 57; 2013: Table 57; p.398: Fig12-13: Source: By the author. Based on U.S. Census Bureau. "50 Million Children Lived with Married Parents in 2007." Washington, D.C.: U.S. Government Printing Office, 2007 and Statistical Abstract of the United States 1995: Table 60; 2013: Table 63; p.400: Fig12-14: Source: By the author. Based on Statistical Abstract of the United States 1995: Table 149; 2002: Table 111; 2013: Table 134; p.400: Fig12-15: Source: By the author. Based on Statistical Abstract of the United States 1995: Table 58; 2013: Table 56; p.401: TBL12-02: Source: Based on Whitehead, Barbara Dafoe, and David Popenoe. "The Marrying Kind: Which Men Marry and Why." Rutgers University: The State of Our Unions: The Social Health of Marriage in America, 2004; Copen et al. 2013; p.403: TBL12-03: Source: By the author: Based on Cheadle, Jacob, Paul R. Amato, and Valarie King. "Patterns of Nonresident Father Involvement." Demography, 47, 2010: 205–226; p.405: Source: LeDuff, Charlie. "Handling the Meltdowns of the Nuclear Family." New York Times, May 28, 2003.

Chapter 13: p.413: Fig13-01: Source: By the author. Based on National Center for Education Statistics 1991: Table 8; Statistical Abstract of the United States 2013: Table 236; p.417: Source: Nakamura, Akemi. "Abe to Play Hardball with Soft Education System." The Japan Times, October 27, 2006; p.413: Source: By the author. Based on Statistical Abstract of the United States 2014: Table 283; p.426: Source: Dillon, Sam. "States' Data Obscure How Few Finish High School." New York Times, March 20, 2008; p.427: TBL13-01: Source: National Center for Education Statistics. "Digest of Education Statistics." Table 228.10, 2014; p.428: Source: Durkheim, Emile. The Elementary Forms of the Religious Life. New York: Free Press, 1965. Originally published 1912; p.434: Source: Marx, Karl. "Contribution to the Critique of Hegel's Philosophy of Right." In Karl Marx: Early Writings, T. B. Bottomore, ed. New York: McGraw-Hill, 1964: 45. Originally published 1844; p.435: Weber, Max. The Protestant Ethic and the Spirit of Capitalism, translated by Talcott Parsons (Charles Scribner's Sons, 1930); p.436: Fig13-05: Source: By the author. Based on Troeltsch, Ernst. The Social Teachings of the Christian Churches. New York: Macmillan, 1931; Pope, Liston. Millhands and Preachers: A Study of Gastonia. New Haven, Conn.: Yale University Press, 1942; Johnson, Benton. "On Church and Sect." American Sociological Review, 28, 1963: 539–549; p.440: Fig13-06: Source: By the author. Based on Smith, Christian, and Robert Faris. "Socioeconomic Inequality in the American Religious System: An Update and Assessment." Journal for the Scientific Study of Religion, 44, 1, 2005: 95–104; p.442: Source: Hookway, James. "In Thailand Today, Teen Monks Express the Spirit to a Rock Beat." Wall Street Journal, August 15, 2012; p.442: Source: Rhoads, Christopher. "Web Site to Holy Site: Israeli Firm Broadcasts Prayers for a Fee." Wall Street Journal, January 25, 2007; p.442: Source: Sullivan, Kevin. "India Embraces Online Worship." Washington Post, March 15, 2007; p.442: Source: Moloney, Liam. "Pope to Spread the Faith through Twitter." Wall Street Journal, December 3, 2012; p.442: Source: Bernstein, Elizabeth. "More Prayer, Less Hassle." Wall Street Journal, June 27, 2003: W3, W4.

Chapter 14: p.448: Fig14-01: Source: By the author. Based on Haub, Carl, and Toshiko Kaneda. "World Population Data Sheet 2012." Washington, D.C.: Population Reference Bureau, 2012; p.448: Fig14-02: Source: Modified from Piotrow, Phylis Tilson. World Population Crisis: The United States' Response. New York: Praeger, 1973. Population Today 4, 5, September 1998; McFalls, Joseph A., Jr. "Population: A Lively Introduction, 5th ed." Population Bulletin, 62, 1, March 2007: 1–30; based on projections from Haub, Carl, and Toshiko Kaneda. "World Population Data Sheet 2012." Washington, D.C.: Population Reference Bureau, 2012; p.451: Fig14-04: Source: By the author. Based on Simon 1981; Statistical Abstract of the United States 2010: Table 1335; Food and Agriculture Organization of the United Nations, January 27, 2012; p.454: Fig14-05: Source: Based on "The World of the Child 6 Billion" 2000; Haub, Carl, and Toshiko Kaneda. "World Population Data Sheet 2012." Washington, D.C.: Population Reference Bureau, 2012; p.454: Source: Mamdani, Mahmood. "The Myth of Population Control: Family, Caste, and Class in an Urban Village." New York: Monthly Review Press, 1973; p.455: Fig14-06: Source: Based on U.N. Fund for Population Activities; p.456: Fig14-07: Source: Population Today, 26, September 9, 1998: 4, 5; p.457: TBL14-01: Source: Based on Haub and Kaneda 2015; p.458: TBL14-02: Source: By the author. Based on Statistical Abstract of the United States 2014: Table 53; p.458: Fig14-08: Source: Statistical Abstract of the United States 2013: Table 45; p.458: Source: Vladimir Zhirinovsky, Russian politician, January 2010; p.460: Source: Based on Jordan, Miriam. "Among Poor Villagers, Female Infanticide Still Flourishes in India." Wall Street Journal, May 9, 2000: A1, A12; Dugger, Celia W. "Abortion in India Is Tipping Scales Sharply against Girls." New York Times, April 22, 2001; Riley, Nancy E. "China's Population: New Trends and Challenges." Population Bulletin, 59, 2, June 2004: 3–36; Yardley, Jim. "As Wealth and Literacy Rise in India, Report Says, So Do Sex-Selective Abortions." New York Times, May 24, 2011; Yardley, Jim. "Faces of Abortion in China: A Young, Single Woman." New York Times, May 13, 2007; Sharma, Amol, Biman Mukherji, and Rupa Subramanya. "On India's Streets, Women Run Gauntlet of Harassment." Wall Street Journal, February 28, 2013; Nelson 2014; p.461: Fig14-09: Source: By the author. Based on Day, Jennifer Chesseman. "Population Profile of the United States: National Population Projections." Washington, D.C.: U.S. Census Bureau, 2010; p.463: Fig14-10: Source: By the author. Based on Chandler, Tertius, and Gerald Fox. 3000 Years of Urban Growth. New York: Academic Press, 1974; Brockerhoff, Martin P. "An Urbanizing World." Population Bulletin, 55, 3, September 2000: 1–44; United Nations 2008. World Population Prospects 2012; p.463: Fig14-11: Source: By the author. Based on United Nations. "World Urbanizing Prospects: The 2009 Revision." U.N. Department of Economic and Social Affairs, Population Division, 2010; p.467: Fig14-12: Source: By the author. Based on projected 2015 populations by United Nations; p.6467: Fig14-13: Source: By the author. Based on Statistical Abstract of the United States 2013: Table 29; p.468: TBL14-03: Source: By the author. Based on Statistical Abstract of the United States 2014: Table 21; p.469: Source: Based on Leland, John. "A New Harlem Gentry in Search of Its Latte." New York Times, August 7, 2003; Hyra, Derek S. "Racial Uplift? Intra-Racial Class Conflict and the Economic Revitalization of Harlem and Bronzeville." City and Community, 5, 1, March 2006: 71–92; Williams, Timothy. "Old Sound in Harlem Draws New Neighbors' Ire." New York Times, July 6, 2008; Gayles 2014; Kravitz 2014; p.471: Fig14-14: Source: Based on Cousins, Albert N., and Hans Nagpaul. Urban Man and Society: A Reader in Urban Sociology. New York: McGraw-Hill, 1970; Harris, Chauncey D. "The Nature of Cities and Urban Geography in the Last Half Century." Urban Geography, 18, 1997; p.472: Source: McDowell, Bart. "Mexico City: An Alarming Giant." National Geographic, 166, 1984: 139–174. p.172; p.474: Source: Gans, Herbert J. The Urban Villagers. New York: Free Press, 1962; p.475: Source: Karp, David A., Gregory P. Stone, and William C. Yoels. Being Urban: A Sociology of City Life, 2nd ed. New York: Praeger, 1991; p.478: Source: Flanagan, William G. Urban Sociology: Images and Structure. Boston: Allyn and Bacon, 1990.

Chapter 15: pp.481-482: Source: Based on Chase, Arlen F., Diane Z. Chase, and John F. Weishampel. "Lasers in the Jungle." Archeology, 63, 4, July/August 2010; Handwerk, Brian. "Maya City in 3-D." National Geographic Daily News, May 20, 2010; Wilford, John Noble. "Mapping Ancient Civilization, in a Matter of Days." New York Times, May 10, 2010; p.484: TBL15-01: Source: By the author; p.487: Fig15-01: Source: By the author; p.488: TBL15-02: Source: By the author; p.493: Source: Brilliant, Ashleigh E. Social Effects of the Automobile in Southern California during the 1920s. Unpublished doctoral disertation, University of California at Berkeley, 1964; p.493: Source: Flink, James J., The Automobile Age. Cambridge, Mass.: MIT Press, 1990; p.495: Source: Sanger, David E. "Obama Order Sped Up Waves of Cyberattacks against Iran." New York Times, June 1, 2012; p.497: Source: Weiner, Tim. "Air Force Seeks Bush's Approval for Space Weapons Programs." New York Times, May 18, 2005; pp.497-498: Source: Boudreaux, Richard. "Putin Move Stirs Russian Environmentalist Row." New York Times, January 20, 2010; p.499: Fig15-02: Source: By the author. Based on Environmental Protection Agency. "Final National Priorities List." Washington, D.C.: Environmental Protection Agency, March 29, 2013; p.500: Fig15-03: Source: By the author; p.500: Source: Dickey, Christopher, and Adam Rogers "Smoke and Mirrors." Newsweek, February 25, 2002; p.502: Source: Based o[illegible] Durning, Alan. "Cradles of Life." In Social Problems 90/91, LeRoy W. Barn[illegible] ed. Guilford, Conn.: Dushkin, 1990: 231–241; Gorman, Peter. "A People at Ri[illegible] Vanishing Tribes of South America." The World & I, December 1991: 678–[illegible] Linden, Eugene. "Lost Tribes, Lost Knowledge." Time, September 23, 1991[illegible] 48, 50, 52, 54, 56; Stipp, David. "Himalayan Tree Could Serve as Source o[illegible]ti-Cancer Drug Taxol, Team Says." Wall Street Journal, April 20, 1992: B4; [illegible]han, Gary Paul. Cultures in Habitat: On Nature, Culture, and Story. New [illegible] Counterpoint, 1998; Simons, Marlise. "Social Change and Amazon India[illegible] Exploring Social Life: Readings to Accompany Essentials of Sociology: A [illegible]to-Earth Approach, Sixth Edition, 2nd edition, James M. Henslin, ed. Bo[illegible]lyn and Bacon, 2006: 157–165; Okpiliya 2014; pp.503-504: Source: Based [illegible] Klaus. "The Rise of Counter-Culture Movements against Modernity: [illegible] a New Field of Class Struggle." Theory, Culture & Society, 7, 1990: 21–[illegible] Jennifer. "Trying to Take Back the Planet." Newsweek, 115, 6, Februa[illegible] 24–25; Parfit, Michael, "Earth First!ers Wield a Mean Monkey Wren[illegible]sonian, 21, 1, April 1990: 184–204; Reed, Susan, and Lorenzo Benet. [illegible] Dave Foreman Will Do Whatever It Takes in His Fight to Save M[illegible] People Weekly, 33, 15, April 16, 1990: 113–116; Knickerbocker, Brad[illegible] of 'Ecoterrorism' Set Sights on Urban Sprawl." Christian Science [illegible] gust 6, 2003; Gunther, Marc. "The Mosquito in the Tent." Fortun[illegible] 31, 2004: 158; Fattig, Paul. "Good Intentions Gone Bad." Ma[illegible] 6, 2007; Grigoriadis, Vanessa. "The Rise and Fall of the Ec[illegible]ground." Rolling Stone, June 21, 2011; Oxalis 2014.

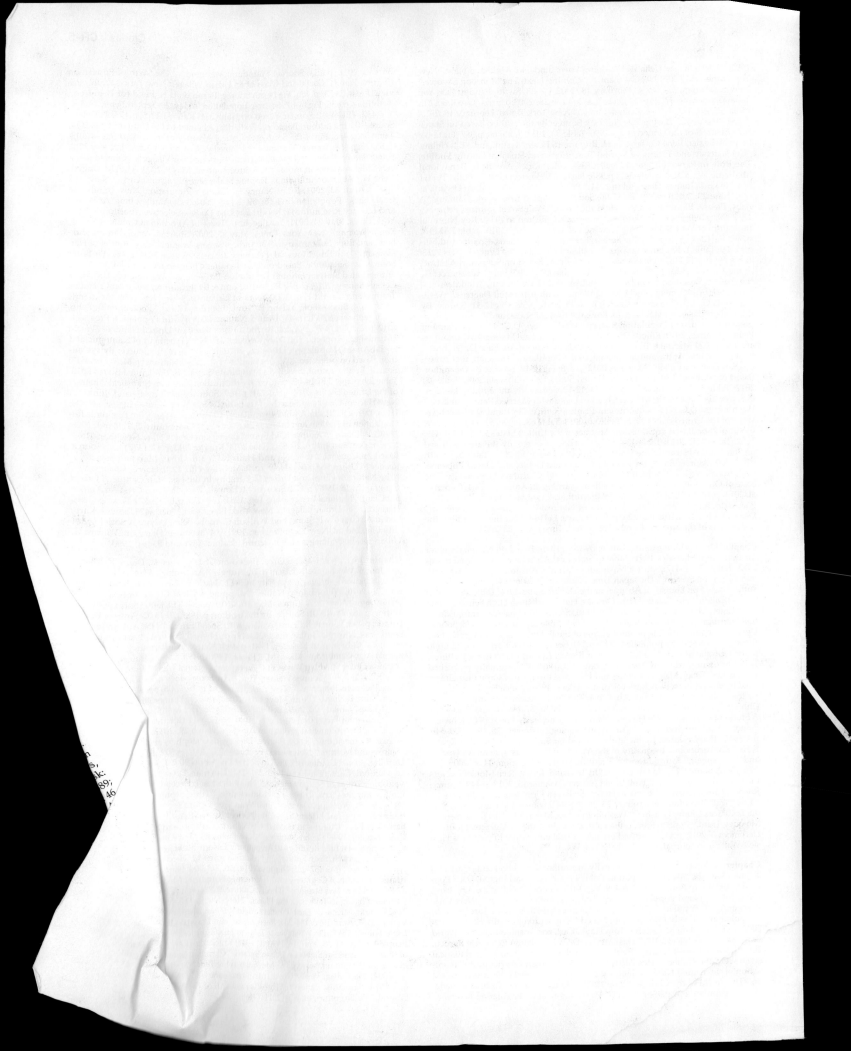